International Human Rights Institutions and Enforcement
Volume II

Human Rights Law

Series Editor: Sarah Joseph
Director, Castan Centre for Human Rights Law
Monash University, Australia

Future titles will include:

Wherever possible, the articles in these volumes have been reproduced as originally published using facsimile reproduction, inclusive of footnotes and pagination to facilitate ease of reference.

For a list of all Edward Elgar published titles visit our website at
www.e-elgar.com

International Human Rights Institutions and Enforcement Volume II

Edited by

Fausto Pocar

Professor Emeritus of International Law
University of Milan, Italy
and Judge at the ICTY, ICTR and ICJ

HUMAN RIGHTS LAW

An Elgar Research Collection
Cheltenham, UK • Northampton, MA, USA

Published by
Edward Elgar Publishing Limited
The Lypiatts
15 Lansdown Road
Cheltenham
Glos GL50 2JA
UK

Edward Elgar Publishing, Inc.
William Pratt House
9 Dewey Court
Northampton
Massachusetts 01060
USA

A catalogue record for this book
is available from the British Library

Library of Congress Control Number: 2018960586

ISBN 978 1 78195 180 4 (2 volume set)

Printed and bound in Great Britain by
TJ International Ltd, Padstow, Cornwall

Contents

**PART IV   A UNIVERSAL JUDICIAL ENFORCEMENT OF HUMAN
RIGHTS?**

Acknowledgements

The editor and publishers wish to thank the authors and the following publishers who have kindly given permission for the use of copyright material.

American Society of International Law via the Copyright Clearance Center's RightsLink service for article: Karen J. Alter, Laurence R. Helfer and Jacqueline R. McAllister (2013), 'A New International Human Rights Court for West Africa: The ECOWAS Community Court of Justice', *American Journal of International Law*, **107** (4), October, 737–79.

American University Washington College of Law for article: Luzius Wildhaber (2007), 'The European Court of Human Rights: The Past, the Present, the Future', *American University International Law Review*, **22** (4), 521–38.

Cambridge University Press for articles: Markus G. Schmidt (1992), 'Individual Human Rights Complaints Procedures Based on United Nations Treaties and the Need for Reform', *International and Comparative Law Quarterly*, **41** (3), July, 645–59; Philip Alston (2014), 'Against a World Court for Human Rights', *Ethics and International Affairs*, **28** (2), Summer, 197–212.

Duncker & Humblot GmbH for article: Tilmann Laubner (2004), 'Relieving the Court of Its Success? – Protocol No. 14 to the European Convention on Human Rights', *German Yearbook of International Law*, **47**, 691–721.

Markus Fyrnys and the *German Law Journal* for article: Markus Fyrnys (2011), 'Expanding Competences by Judicial Lawmaking: The Pilot Judgment Procedure of the European Court of Human Rights', *German Law Journal, Special Issue: Beyond Dispute: International Judicial Institutions as Lawmakers*, **12** (5), 1231–59.

George Washington International Law Review for article: Carolyn Scanlon Martorana (2008), 'The New African Union: Will it Promote Enforcement of the Decisions of the African Court of Human and Peoples' Rights?', **40** (2), 583–610.

Alexandra R. Harrington for her own work: (2012), 'Don't Mind the Gap: The Rise of Individual Complaint Mechanisms within International Human Rights Treaties', *Duke Journal of Comparative and International Law*, **22** (2), Winter, 153–82.

Intersentia for articles: Laurence Burgorgue-Larsen (2009), 'Interim Measures in the European Convention System of Protection of Human Rights', *Inter-American and European Human Rights Journal*, **2** (1–2), 99–118; Laurence Burgorgue-Larsen (2012), 'Interpreting the

European Convention: What Can the African Human Rights System Learn from the Case Law of the European Court of Human Rights on the Interpretation of the European Convention?', *Inter-American and European Human Rights Journal*, **5** (1), 90–123; Jan Schneider (2012), 'Implementation of Judgments: Should Supervision be Unlinked from the General Assembly of the Organization of American States?', *Inter-American and European Human Rights Journal*, **5** (1), 197–215.

Johns Hopkins University Press for articles: Cecilia Medina (1990), 'The Inter-American Commission on Human Rights and the Inter-American Court of Human Rights: Reflections on a Joint Venture', *Human Rights Quarterly*, **12** (4), November, 439–64; Makau Mutua (1999), 'The African Human Rights Court: A Two-Legged Stool?', *Human Rights Quarterly*, **21** (2), May, 342–63; Rachel Murray and Elizabeth Mottershaw (2014), 'Mechanisms for the Implementation of Decisions of the African Commission on Human and Peoples' Rights', *Human Rights Quarterly*, **36** (2), May, 349–72.

Koninklijke Brill N. V. for articles: Marjorie Beulay (2013), 'The Action of Legal Persons in the European System of Human Rights Protection – Collective or Individual Interest?', *Law and Practice of International Courts and Tribunals*, **12** (3), 321–41; Suzanne Egan (2014), 'The New Complaints Mechanism for the Convention on the Rights of the Child: A Mini Step Forward for Children?', *International Journal of Children's Rights*, **22** (1), 205–25.

Max Planck Institute for Comparative Public Law and International Law for articles: Helen Keller and Cedric Marti (2013), 'Interim Relief Compared: Use of Interim Measures by the UN Human Rights Committee and the European Court of Human Rights', *Zeitschrift für ausländisches öffentliches Recht und Völkerrecht*, **73**, 325–72; Diane A. Desierto and Colin E. Gillespie (2013), 'Evolutive Interpretation and Subsequent Practice: Interpretive Communities and Processes in the Optional Protocol to the ICESCR', *Zeitschrift für ausländisches öffentliches Recht und Völkerrecht*, **73**, 549–89.

Lucyline Nkatha Murungi, Jacqui Gallinetti and *Sur – International Journal on Human Rights* for article: Lucyline Nkatha Murungi and Jacqui Gallinetti (2010), 'The Role of Sub-Regional Courts in the African Human Rights System', *Sur – International Journal on Human Rights*, **7** (13), December, 119–42.

N. P. Engel Verlag for article: Paul Mahoney (2003), 'Separation of Powers in the Council of Europe: The Status of the European Court of Human Rights vis-à-vis the Authorities of the Council of Europe', *Human Rights Law Journal*, **24** (5–8), November, 152–61.

Michael O'Boyle and the *German Law Journal* for article: Michael O'Boyle (2011), 'The Future of the European Court of Human Rights', *German Law Journal*, **12** (10), 1862–77.

Oxford University Press via the Copyright Clearance Center's RightsLink service for articles: P.R. Ghandhi (1987), 'The Human Rights Committee and the Right of Individual Communication', *British Year Book of International Law*, **57**, 201–51; Robin R. Churchill and Urfan Khaliq (2004), 'The Collective Complaints System of the European Social Charter: An

Effective Mechanism for Ensuring Compliance with Economic and Social Rights?', *European Journal of International Law*, **15** (3), June, 417–56; Manfred Nowak (2007), 'The Need for a World Court of Human Rights', *Human Rights Law Review, Special Issue: Reform of the UN Human Rights Machinery*, **7** (1), 251–9.

Quebec Journal of International Law for article: Ariel Dulitzky (2011), 'The Inter-American Human Rights System Fifty Years Later: Time for Changes', September, 127–64.

SAGE Publications, Ltd for article: Clara Burbano Herrera and Yves Haeck (2010), 'Letting States off the Hook? The Paradox of the Legal Consequences Following State Non-Compliance with Provisional Measures in the Inter-American and European Human Rights Systems', *Netherlands Quarterly of Human Rights*, **28** (3), September, 332–60.

Martin Scheinin for his own work: (2009), 'Towards a World Court of Human Rights', *Research Report within the Framework of the Swiss Initiative to Commemorate the 60th Anniversary of the Universal Declaration of Human Rights*, June, i, 1–62.

Springer via the Copyright Clearance Center's RightsLink service for article: Christian Tomuschat (2009), 'The European Court of Human Rights Overwhelmed by Applications: Problems and Possible Solutions', in Rüdiger Wolfrum and Ulrike Deutsch (eds), *The European Court of Human Rights Overwhelmed by Applications: Problems and Possible Solutions*, Chapter 1, 1–18.

Nsongurua Udombana and the *Brooklyn Journal of International Law* for article: Nsongurua J. Udombana (2003), 'An African Human Rights Court and an African Union Court: A Needful Duality or a Needless Duplication?', *Brooklyn Journal of International Law*, **28** (3), 811–70.

Victoria University of Wellington Law Review for article: Felipe González (2009), 'The Experience of the Inter-American Human Rights System', *Victoria University of Wellington Law Review*, **40** (1), 103–25.

Every effort has been made to trace all the copyright holders but if any have been inadvertently overlooked the publishers will be pleased to make the necessary arrangement at the first opportunity.

In addition the publishers wish to thank the Library of Indiana University at Bloomington, USA for their assistance in obtaining these articles.

Part I
The Increasing Movement Towards Establishing Treaty Bodies' Quasi-Judicial Procedures

[1]

THE HUMAN RIGHTS COMMITTEE AND THE RIGHT OF INDIVIDUAL COMMUNICATION*

By P. R. GHANDHI[1]

I. INTRODUCTION

THE International Covenant on Civil and Political Rights and the Optional Protocol thereto, adopted by the General Assembly of the United Nations in Resolution 2200A (XXI)[2] of 16 December 1966, entered into force on 23 March 1976 in accordance with Articles 49 of the Covenant and 9 of the Protocol respectively. As at 25 July 1986, there were eighty-three States parties to the Covenant and thirty-seven States parties to the Protocol.

The Covenant established the Human Rights Committee as the principal international organ of its implementation. This body consists of eighteen individuals serving in their personal capacity.[3] The members of the Human Rights Committee are elected by secret ballot by the States parties to the Covenant. Each State may nominate not more than two persons who must be nationals of the nominating State.[4] In the election of the Committee, consideration must be given to equitable geographical distribution of membership and to the representation of the different forms of civilization and of the principal legal systems.[5] As to qualification (other than nationality), the Covenant provides that members of the Committee 'shall be persons of high moral character and recognized competence in the field of human rights, consideration being given to the usefulness of the participation of some persons having legal experience'.[6]

A member of the Human Rights Committee is not the representative of the State of which he is a national and which has nominated him. The Covenant provides, in Article 35, that members of the Human Rights Committee shall receive emoluments from UN resources. This is a factor which strengthens the *de facto* independence of a Committee member. This principle is further emphasized in Article 38 which states: 'Every member of the Committee shall, before taking up his duties, make a solemn declaration in open committee that he will perform his functions impartially and conscientiously'.

---

[1] MA (Oxon.), LL M (Lond.), Solicitor of the Supreme Court; Lecturer in Law, University of Reading.

[2] UN Doc. A/6316.   [3] Article 28.

[4] Article 29. Professor Rosalyn Higgins, QC, is the current UK member and the only woman serving on the Committee at present.

[5] Article 31 (2). At the very first election, this principle resulted in the election of 5 members from Western Europe, 4 from Eastern Europe, 2 from Asia, 3 from Africa, 1 from North America and 3 from Latin America.   [6] Article 28 (2).

In accordance with Articles 28–32 of the Covenant, the States parties, at their first meeting held on 20 September 1976 at UN Headquarters,[7] elected by secret ballot the eighteen members of the Human Rights Committee from a list of persons nominated by the States parties. The States parties decided that the term of office of the members of the Committee should begin on 1 January 1977. The regular term of office of the members of the Committee is four years. However, in accordance with Article 32 (1) of the Covenant, the Chairman of the first meeting of the States parties chose by lot the names of nine members of the Committee whose terms were to expire at the end of two years, in order to avoid a complete change of membership at any one time.

The Covenant, plus the Optional Protocol to it, provides for three distinct procedures as measures of implementation.[8] In each of these procedures the Committee plays a pivotal role. First, the Committee's function is to study reports submitted by the States parties, in accordance with Article 40 (1), and to transmit *its* reports, and such general comments as it may consider appropriate, to the States parties. It may also transmit these general comments to the Economic and Social Council of the UN, along with the copies of the reports it has received from the States parties.[9] It is significant that this is the only activity of the Committee

---

[7] For decisions adopted at the first meeting, see the *Official Records of the First Meeting of States Parties to the International Covenant on Civil and Political Rights* (CCPR/SP.7).

[8] A mass of literature exists on the measures of implementation contained in the Covenant. The following are particularly useful: Robertson, 'The Implementation System: International Measures', in Henkin (ed.), *The International Bill of Rights—The Covenant on Civil and Political Rights* (Columbia University Press, New York, 1981); Pathak, 'The Protection of Human Rights', *Indian Journal of International Law*, 18 (1978), p. 265; Robertson, *Human Rights in the World* (Manchester University Press, 1982); Capotorti, 'The International Measures of Implementation included in the Covenants on Human Rights', in Eide and Schou (eds.), *Proceedings of the Nobel Symposium on the International Protection of Human Rights* (Stockholm, 1967); Mower, 'Organising to Implement the UN Civil/Political Rights Covenant: First Steps by the Committee', *Human Rights Review*, 3 (1978), p. 122; id., 'Implementing United Nations Covenants', in Said (ed.), *Human Rights and World Order* (Transaction Books, 1978); id., 'The Implementation of the U.N. Covenant on Civil and Political Rights', *Human Rights Journal*, 10 (1977), p. 271; Ramcharan, 'Implementing the International Covenants on Human Rights', in Ramcharan (ed.), *Human Rights Thirty Years after the Universal Declaration* (Martinus Nijhoff, 1979); Das, 'Institutions et procédures issues des conventions relatives aux droits de l'homme . . .', in Vasak (ed.), *Les Dimensions internationals des droits de l'homme* (UNESCO Manual, 1978); Schwelb, 'The United Kingdom signs the Covenants on Human Rights', *International and Comparative Law Quarterly*, 18 (1969), p. 457; id., 'The U.K. and the International Covenants on Civil and Political and Economic, Social and Cultural Rights', *Human Rights Review*, 2 (1977), p. 89; id., 'Civil and Political Rights: The International Measures of Implementation', *American Journal of International Law*, 62 (1968), p. 827; Shelton, 'The Optional Protocol to the International Covenant on Civil and Political Rights', in Hannum (ed.), *Guide to International Human Rights Practice* (Macmillan Press, London, 1984). See also 'U.N. Human Rights Covenants become Law: so what?', *Proceedings of the American Society of International Law*, 1976, p. 97.

[9] Article 40 (4). See in particular, on the operation of the reporting system, Fischer, 'Reporting under the Covenant on Civil and Political Rights: The First Five Years of the Human Rights Committee', *American Journal of International Law*, 76 (1982), p. 142; Jhabvala, 'The Practice of the Covenant's Human Rights Committee, 1976–82: Review of the State Party Reports', *Human Rights Quarterly*, 6 (1984), p. 81. See also the Annual Reports of the Human Rights Committee since 1977 for the lists of reports by State parties and their contents. See also the Report issued in March 1985 by Justice commenting on the UK's second Periodic Report to the Human Rights Committee under the

THE RIGHT OF INDIVIDUAL COMMUNICATION   203

to which States are *automatically* subject on becoming parties to the Covenant.

Secondly, the Committee is competent to consider communications from a State party which considers that another State party is not giving effect to the provisions of the Covenant. In such a case, it must make available its good offices to the States parties concerned with a view to a friendly solution of the matter. This capacity can be exercised by the Committee only if *both* States concerned have declared that they recognize its competence to receive and consider such communications from States parties. The operative principle is thus one of reciprocity. Furthermore, this procedure only became applicable when ten States parties accepted this competence of the Committee. As at 25 July 1986, eighteen such declarations of acceptance had been lodged with the Secretary-General of the UN. Other functions in regard to these inter-State allegations are performed by an *ad hoc* conciliation commission. The whole optional inter-State communication procedure is regulated in detail by Articles 41 and 42 of the Covenant.[10]

Generally, one can say that the proceedings are complex, delicate and long-winded. They are based on the goodwill of States. They can be terminated by either State party to the dispute before the *ad hoc* conciliation commission has been appointed. If an *ad hoc* conciliation commission is agreed upon by both States, the respondent State is still entirely free to accept or reject the contents of the report of the *ad hoc* conciliation commission. Commenting generally on inter-State proceedings in international human rights law, Professor John P. Humphrey was provoked to say:

> To give a state the right to complain that another state is violating human rights is one of the weakest techniques for enforcing human rights law. . . . The individual whose rights have been violated has no guarantee that any state will in fact sponsor his case. Indeed, it is unlikely that, unless there is some political motivation for doing so, states will interfere with what is happening in other countries, particularly if their relations with them are friendly.[11]

Thirdly, in regard to States parties to the Optional Protocol, the Committee is competent to receive and consider communications from *individuals* who claim to be victims of a violation by a State which is a party *both* to the Covenant and to the Protocol of any of the rights set forth in the Covenant. When dealing with communications from individuals the Committee's task is not to offer its good offices, but to 'forward its views

International Covenant on Civil and Political Rights. The UK's second Periodic Report may be found in *General Assembly Official Records* (hereinafter *GAOR*), 40th Session, Supplement 40, Report of the Human Rights Committee, p. 97.

[10] On the theoretical operation of this system, see in particular the literature referred to at p. 202 n. 8, above.

[11] 'The International Law of Human Rights in the Middle Twentieth Century', in Bos (ed.), *The Present State of International Law and Other Essays* (Deventer, 1973), p. 75 at p. 86.

to the State party concerned and to the individual'.[12] It is *this* procedure of international individual communication, in which the Committee plays a crucial role, that is to be the subject of detailed scrutiny in this paper.[13]

It is quite a major step forward to give one State *locus standi* to complain about the treatment by another State of its own nationals. Nevertheless, the inter-State communication procedure under the Covenant has yet to be invoked. This is, of course, in stark contrast to the experience of the Strasbourg institutions under the European Convention on Human Rights, 1950, which has produced eighteen inter-State cases, seventeen of which have been declared admissible by the European Commission.[14] But it must be pointed out that this *only* represents about $3\frac{1}{2}$ per cent of the 492 cases in total declared admissible by the Commission as of 1 January 1987. Accordingly, even under the European Convention, the great preponderance of admitted cases ($96\frac{1}{2}$ per cent) have been individual applications.

Why then has the Covenant inter-State procedure not been invoked at all, whereas the Strasbourg institutions have some significant experience of such invocation? The answer seems to lie in the fact that, generally, the procedure for inter-State complaints under the European Convention system is substantially the same as in the case of an individual application. It is true that there are one or two differences. In particular, not all the grounds of inadmissibility which apply to an individual application apply to an inter-State case. For example, the grounds in Article 27 (1) and (2) do not apply to States. Also, at an operational level, it is far more likely that an inter-State complaint, assuming it is declared admissible by the Com-

---

[12] Article 5 (4) of the Optional Protocol.

[13] It is interesting to note that the Covenant does not require that members of the Committee be nationals of a State which is also a party to the Optional Protocol. Therefore, nationals of States which have not accepted this optional arrangement *will* participate in the Committee's procedures under the Protocol.

[14] These eighteen cases can be considered as six complexes:

(1) Two brought by Greece in 1956/7 against the UK concerning the situation in Cyprus: *Yearbook of the European Convention on Human Rights*, 2 (1958–9), pp. 182 and 186.

(2) One by Austria against Italy in 1960: ibid. 6 (1963), pp. 742 and 796.

(3) Three identical applications lodged in 1967 against Greece by Denmark, Norway and Sweden and one substantially the same by The Netherlands; in 1970 a further application against Greece was lodged jointly by Denmark, Norway and Sweden: ibid. 11 (1968), pp. 690 and 737; ibid. 12 (1969), p. 108; ibid. 13 (1970), p. 122; and *Decisions and Reports of the European Commission of Human Rights*, vol. 6, p. 5.

(4) Two lodged by Ireland against the UK in December 1971 and March 1972: *Yearbook of the European Convention on Human Rights*, 15 (1972), pp. 92 and 255, *European Court of Human Rights*, Series B, vol. 23-I, and Series A, No. 25. The second application by Ireland submitted under Article 7 of the Convention was withdrawn following an undertaking by the UK Government that there would be no prosecution of offences under the Northern Ireland Act 1972 for acts or omissions which occurred prior to the enactment of that Act.

(5) Two lodged by Cyprus against Turkey in September 1974 and March 1975. In 1977 a further application was lodged by Cyprus against Turkey: see *Decisions and Reports of the European Commission of Human Rights*, vol. 2, p. 125, and ibid., vol. 13, p. 85.

(6) Five lodged by Denmark, France, The Netherlands, Norway and Sweden against Turkey in July 1982 (case nos. 9940–44/82), declared admissible by the Commission on 6 December 1983. These cases have now been settled.

THE RIGHT OF INDIVIDUAL COMMUNICATION   205

mission, will ultimately be pronounced upon by the Committee of Ministers under Article 32 of the Convention. To date, only one inter-State complaint, *Ireland* v. *UK*, has reached the European Court of Human Rights. By contrast, the inter-State procedure under the Covenant is completely different from, more complex and far weaker than the individual communication procedure under the Optional Protocol. Under the Optional Protocol, the Committee is entitled to state, and always has stated, whether or not particular breaches of the Covenant are revealed when making known its views under Article 5 (4) of that document. However, under the inter-State procedure the *ad hoc* conciliation commission (assuming the complaint gets this far) can only, when it draws up its report, 'embody its findings on all questions of fact relevant to the issues between the States Parties concerned, and its views on the possibilities of an amicable solution of the matter' (Article 42 (7) (c) of the Covenant). The States concerned are then completely free to accept or reject the terms of such a report.

Ultimately, given the likely continued non-invocation of the Covenant's inter-State dispute settlement procedure, the success of the international measures of protection will be gauged by whether or not the individual communication procedure, in which the Committee plays the fundamental role, will provide an effective international remedy to an individual whose rights under the Covenant have been violated. While it is not appropriate at this stage of the paper to offer any detailed evaluation of the work of the Committee in its task of seeing that the rights of the individual are not breached, it may be suggested tentatively that the impartial, conscientious and quasi-judicial attitude adopted by the Committee has won it respect from both States and individuals alike.

II. The First Steps in the Implementation Process

As constituted, the Human Rights Committee held two sessions in 1977. The first was held at UN Headquarters from 21 March to 1 April 1977. The second session was held at the UN Office at Geneva from 11 to 31 August 1977. Several decisions of a fundamental nature, in relation to the right of individual communication, were taken by the Committee at these sessions. First, the Committee adopted its own provisional rules of procedure, in accordance with the terms of Article 39 (2) of the Covenant. Secondly, the Committee discussed its method of work in relation to consideration of individual communications. Thirdly, the Committee established, in accordance with rule 89 of its provisional rules of procedure, a Working Group of five of its members to meet at Geneva from 9 to 13 January 1978, with a view to making recommendations to the Committee regarding the fulfilment of the conditions of admissibility laid down in Articles 1, 2, 3 and 5 (2) of the Protocol.[15]

---

[15] *GAOR*, 32nd Session, Supplement 44, Report of the Human Rights Committee, pp. 4–5.

THE HUMAN RIGHTS COMMITTEE AND

(a) *Establishment of Provisional Rules of Procedure*[16]

In order to facilitate the task of the Committee, the Secretary-General of the UN had prepared draft provisional rules.[17] These draft rules were considered by the Committee at both sessions. At its first session, the Committee adopted those provisional rules of procedure comprising 'General Rules' (rules 1 to 65) and 'Reports from States parties under Article 40 of the Covenant' (rules 66 to 71). Importantly for the purposes of this paper, it also adopted a number of rules concerning 'Consideration of Communications received under the Optional Protocol' (rules 78 to 86 and 88).

Some of these latter rules relate to the question of the *transmission* of communications to the Committee. It is interesting to observe that these rules confer on the Secretary-General important powers on receipt of communications which are, or seem to be, submitted for consideration by the Committee under Article 1 of the Protocol. From a political point of view, it is vital that the Human Rights Committee be seen to be part of the *whole* apparatus of the UN machinery for the international protection of human rights and not merely as an organ of the Covenant. From a practical point of view, the Secretary-General is in the unique position of being the original recipient of the communications and is thus best placed to conduct certain preliminary tasks and so facilitate the subsequent work of the Committee. Nevertheless, he ought not to trespass on the province of the Committee. Accordingly, although his actions are primarily of an administrative and technical nature and should not involve decisions concerning the admissibility of communications, he may solicit clarifications from authors, both where it is unclear whether an author intends his communication to be submitted to the Committee or not, and where the information furnished by an author appears to be insufficient (rules 78 and 80).

In addition to preparing regularly lists of communications containing brief summaries of their contents (rule 79), the Secretary-General must circulate to members of the Committee a summary of the relevant information obtained by him during his preliminary enquiries (rule 81). In this way, the Committee should have before it a working document, including comprehensive fact sheets, concerning each communication submitted for consideration.

It is significant to note that, after some discussion, the Committee also adopted rule 86, which provides that the Committee may inform a State party of its views on whether interim measures may be desirable to avoid irreparable damage to a victim of an alleged violation. In arrogating to itself the right to make such an interlocutory order, the Committee gave

---

[16] These are set out in full in ibid., pp. 48–66, as Annex II. See also Bossuyt, 'Le Règlement interieur du comité des droits de l'homme', *Revue belge de droit international*, 14 (1978–9), p. 104.

[17] CCPR/C/L.2 and Add. 1 and 2.

THE RIGHT OF INDIVIDUAL COMMUNICATION   207

itself an immensely valuable tool which, in theory at least, could prove a formidable weapon in the task of deterring a State from taking further punitive measures, once an applicant has already lodged a communication and is thus in a particularly vulnerable position. One can only speculate on whether the Committee will eventually be able to make effective use of this rule (which some members felt went beyond the power conferred on the Committee under the Optional Protocol).[18]

In practice, the issue of interim measures has most often arisen in relation to the health of the alleged victim. In *Altesor* v. *Uruguay*[19] the authors, who had submitted an application on behalf of their detained father, alleged that in view of their father's very poor state of health, interim measures should be taken (in order to avoid irreparable damage to their father's health and life). The Committee responded by asking the Government concerned for information concerning the state of health of the alleged victim, when requesting its views on admissibility. When the Government objected to admissibility, it made no reference to the alleged victim's state of health. The Committee deplored this lack of information and urged Uruguay to arrange an urgent medical examination by a competent authority and to furnish a copy of the medical report so obtained. Some three months later, Uruguay reported on the general medical condition of Mr Alberto Altesor. A further six months later a medical report was received by the Committee who forwarded a copy to the authors. Again, at the merits stage, the Committee asked for further up-to-date medical information on Mr Altesor. Ten months later, Uruguay provided a further medical bulletin and declared it was willing to carry out any subsequent medical examinations and treatment which might be necessary. Ultimately, in adopting its final views under Article 5 (4) of the Protocol, the Committee urged Uruguay to ensure that Mr Altesor received all necessary medical care.

A similar situation arose in *Sendic* v. *Uruguay*.[20] However, in this instance, Uruguay completely ignored the Committee's repeated requests for information concerning Mr Sendic's state of health and the medical treatment given him. In formulating its final views, the Committee added the rider that Uruguay must also ensure that the alleged victim received all necessary medical care promptly.

Accordingly, it seems that the experience to date does not reveal any great degree of success where interim measures have been indicated. However, the defect would seem to lie not in the substance of the rule, but in the attitude of States towards compliance with the requests of the Committee. It seems probable that as the Committee gains the confidence of States, so the degree of compliance will increase.

At its second session, the Committee discussed and adopted further

[18] See below, under heading (b) 'The Method of Work . . .', in section II, for a discussion as to *when* such interim measures of protection may be stipulated.

[19] Comm. no. R.2/10.   [20] Comm. no. R.14/63.

provisional rules relating to the *admissibility* of communications. One important question which arose for discussion was whether a petitioner should be obliged to submit a communication within a stipulated period after the exhaustion of domestic remedies (prescribed in Article 5 (2) (b) of the Protocol).[21] It was decided that for the present at least, no time limits would be imposed. This was indeed a wise decision. It is hardly conceivable that the rules of procedure are likely to be known to the public at large in various countries. The imposition of a time limit in these circumstances would be an intolerable burden on the petitioner. By way of comparison, it is interesting to note that Article 26 of the European Convention on Human Rights imposes a time-limit of six months in this respect.

Furthermore, assuming that someone other than the alleged victim should be entitled to lodge a communication, which all members agreed upon, the question arose of formulating in a rule who that person could be and under what circumstances such a communication could be admissible. It was decided that, normally, the communication should be submitted by the individual himself or by his representative. However, a communication submitted on behalf of an alleged victim by *others* might be considered when it appeared that he was unable to submit the communication himself (rule 90 (1) (b)).[22] This decision is to be welcomed. It gives a wide and generous ambit of interpretation to the provisions of Article 1 of the Protocol.[23] Equally, it deals adequately with the problem of providing an effective right of communication to detainees who might otherwise be prevented by their governmental authorities from lodging a communication. It had been argued previously by some members of the Committee that a person submitting a communication on behalf of an alleged victim had to be *authorized* to do so. This was rightly rejected as being too restrictive, since it eliminated entirely the possibility of submitting a communication on behalf of an alleged victim who was unable, for reasons beyond his control, to submit it himself or to authorize another person to act on his behalf.

A dispute arose within the Committee as to whether it could consider a communication where the application of the remedies, not only on the national level but also on the *international* level, was unreasonably prolonged. The origins of this dispute lay in the drafting of Article 5 (2) of the Protocol. This reads as follows:

[21] '2. The Committee shall not consider any communication from an individual unless it has ascertained that:

. . .

(b) The individual has exhausted all available domestic remedies . . .'

[22] See below, under heading (a) 'Who can be the Author of a Communication?', in section III, for the requisite criteria applicable in such a case.

[23] 'A State Party to the Covenant that becomes a party to the present Protocol recognizes the competence of the Committee to receive and consider communications from individuals subject to its jurisdiction who claim to be victims of a violation by that State Party of any of the rights set forth in the Covenant.'

THE RIGHT OF INDIVIDUAL COMMUNICATION   209

2. The Committee shall not consider any communication from an individual unless it has ascertained that:

   (a) The same matter is not being examined under another procedure of international investigation or settlement;

   (b) The individual has exhausted all available domestic remedies. This shall not be the rule where the application of the remedies is unreasonably prolonged.

The conflict of opinion within the Committee arose out of a difference of interpretation of the last sentence of Article 5 (2). Should it be read in conjunction with the *whole* of the preceding sentence, which combined both sub-paragraphs (a) and (b)? The Legal Counsel of the UN stated that in his view the last sentence ought to be construed as applying to *both* sub-paragraphs (a) and (b). Ultimately, members of the Committee agreed with this analysis and rule 90 (2), as adopted, coincides with this interpretation. Accordingly, the Committee will have jurisdiction to admit a communication whenever the procedures of *international investigation or settlement* (as well as domestic remedies) have proved to be unreasonably prolonged. Here again, the Committee is to be applauded for adopting the wider rather than the narrower construction, which had been urged by some.

The Committee also had to consider its attitude to pre-admissibility observations from the State party alleged to be in violation of the norms of the Covenant. It agreed that, although it was under no obligation to transmit the text of the communication to the State party concerned at the initial stage of the procedure, nevertheless no communication ought to be declared admissible unless the State party concerned had received the text of the communication and had been given an opportunity to furnish information or observations relevant to the question of admissibility (rule 91 (2)).

However, there was a difference of opinion as to whether to provide in the *rules* for time-limits for the receipt of the additional information or observations on admissibility and if so, what time-limits. Here the Committee had to face the delicate issue of reconciling two conflicting demands. On the one hand, there was the need for the Committee to act as expeditiously as possible, and on the other, the need to offer the State concerned enough time to prepare considered replies (rather than simply proffer blanket denials). Allied to this problem was the need to involve the Secretariat in the role of obtaining the observations on admissibility, particularly in view of the possible delays which these procedural requirements would entail, because of the long intervals between Committee sessions. Rule 91 (1), as finally adopted, reflected the consensus that for the sake of flexibility the Committee ought not to stipulate for precise time-limits in the rules themselves, but ought instead only to indicate a time-limit within which such further information or observations on admissibility should be delivered to avoid unnecessary delay. Furthermore, the rule also empowers the Secretary-General to obtain these observations, etc., on behalf of the Committee, whenever requested to do so by the Committee itself, or by an appropriately constituted working party.[24]

The last major bone of contention, in formulating rules on admissibility, lay in a difference of opinion about the circumstances in which the Committee might *re*consider a previously taken decision to declare a communication inadmissible. Some members of the Committee took a wide view and considered that the Committee ought to have the power to review any decision in favour of inadmissibility taken on any ground, including the grounds outlined in Article 3 of the Protocol, viz. anonymity, abuse of the right of submission or incompatibility with the provisions of the Covenant. However, a more restrictive view finally prevailed. Rule 92 (2), as drafted, only authorized the Committee to *re*consider its decision in favour of inadmissibility if requested to do so in writing by the applicant, and only if the reasons for inadmissibility under Article 5 (2) of the Protocol no longer applied, viz. that the same matter was no longer being examined by another international body or that domestic remedies had, since the original decision on admissibility, been exhausted. It is a pity that the Committee did not see fit to adopt the wider formulation since this would have given it greater flexibility, and it is desirable that the Committee should have the power to reconsider a case where an author has failed to plead a breach of a right contained in the Covenant, but could easily have done so if properly advised.

The Committee also discussed rules governing *consideration* of communications at its second session. Several points need to be stressed here. The Committee agreed that there should be no hard and fast time-limit, imposed by the rules of procedure, within which an author could comment on the post-admissibility statements made by the State party against which a claim had been lodged. This time-limit was left entirely to the discretion of the Committee (rule 93 (3)). Such flexibility is certainly desirable, since the circumstances in which a petitioner may find himself are infinitely variable.

Whether or not members of the Committee should be at liberty to append their individual or dissenting opinions to the view of the majority of the Committee, under Article 5 (4) of the Protocol, caused considerable diversity of opinion.[25] Ultimately, the Committee decided that an individual member could request that a *summary* of his individual opinion be attached to the views of the Committee when they are communicated to

---

[24] See below, under heading (c) 'Commencement of Consideration . . .', in section II, for the decision of the Committee that, normally, a time-limit of six weeks ought to apply to pre-admissibility observations. This limit has since been extended to eight weeks: see *GAOR*, 40th Session, Supplement 40, Report of the Human Rights Committee, p. 7.

[25] 'The Committee shall forward its views to the State Party concerned and to the individual.'

THE RIGHT OF INDIVIDUAL COMMUNICATION   211

the individual and to the State party concerned (rule 94 (3)).[26] Some protests were voiced that the publication of dissent would weaken the authority of the Committee. However, it is suggested that, far from weakening the opinion of the majority, the ability to publish dissent will strengthen the quasi-judicial nature of the Committee, particularly so, perhaps, where an individual member holds that particular breaches of the Covenants are disclosed, contrary to the beliefs of the majority.[27]

The Committee also considered what its position should be if the author of a communication subsequently wished to withdraw it. Was the Committee in duty bound to consider the communication despite the purported withdrawal, with a discretion to continue or discontinue consideration in the light of all information received? Or did the wish of the author to withdraw override the competence of the Committee to consider the communication? The decision that finally emerged was that no specific rule was needed. The Committee could reconsider the issue later, after it had gained more experience. It is interesting to observe, by way of comparison, that under the procedures of the European Convention on Human Rights, 1950, the applicant in *Tyrer* v. *UK*[28] was *refused* leave to withdraw an admitted application by the European Commission on Human Rights. Accordingly, the European Court of Human Rights then proceeded to pronounce on the conformity of judicial corporal punishment with Article 3 of the Convention, which outlaws 'torture or . . . inhuman or degrading treatment or punishment'. The real difficulty here is in determining whether a communication has been *voluntarily* withdrawn or withdrawn under pressure. In view of the inherent risk of State pressure of various kinds to withdraw, the Committee would perhaps have strengthened the right of individual communication by adopting the bolder and more protectionist attitude displayed by the European Commission in the *Tyrer* case.

An examination of the provisional rules as a whole calls for several concluding comments. Generally, the Committee has seen fit to draft rules that are both generous to the applicant and fair to the State against which a communication has been lodged. The Committee had to tread carefully in a matter which went to the heart of what was, formerly, exclusively within a State's own domestic jurisdiction. It has done so. It has displayed the essential even-handedness of approach which was crucial to foster both the confidence of the applicant that his claim would be dealt with impartially and expeditiously, and that of the State that it would receive a fair hearing. The draft rules successfully tread this fine line and the Committee is to be warmly congratulated. Whether this delicate balance is

[26] This privilege has been resorted to fairly regularly. See, e.g., the cases of: *Santullo, Grille Motta, Celiberti de Casariego, Lovelace, Lopez Burgos, Hertzberg, A.M.* and *A.D.*, all discussed later in the paper at various stages, and *Muteba.*

[27] e.g. as in the cases of *Santullo* and *Lovelace*, discussed below.

[28] ECHR, Series A, No. 26 (1978). See comments by Bonner, *Modern Law Review*, 42 (1979), p. 580, and Zellick, *International and Comparative Law Quarterly*, 27 (1978), p. 665.

maintained in the developing jurisprudence of the Committee will be examined later in this paper. It is also important to stress that the rules drafted are only *provisional* rules. They are, thus, capable of amendment in the light of the future experience of the Committee. This was a far-sighted precaution.

(b) *The Method of Work in relation to the Handling of Individual Communications*

At its second session, Committee members discussed, in public session, a number of questions mainly (but not exclusively) relating to the *handling* of communications at the *admissibility* stage. Some important matters were considered. Committee members felt that, although the principle of confidentiality should govern their deliberations when dealing with communications, a minimum of information about cases of admissibility *under consideration* should be made available in the report of the Committee without disclosing the contents of the communications, the nature of the allegations, the identity of the author or the name of the allegedly infracting State party. Only such limited and basic information as was commensurate with the legitimate interest of the public at large in knowing the main trends of the decisional process of the Committee should be made available at *this* stage. Of course, the Committee must 'hold closed meetings when examining communications under the . . . Protocol' (Article 5 (3) of the Protocol). Confidentiality *during* deliberation is thus mandatory by the terms of the Optional Protocol.

Committee members also took pains to point out that the Secretary-General ought to adopt a liberal interpretation in deciding which communications should be forwarded to the Committee under the Optional Protocol for its consideration, since this was an entirely new procedure which would need a number of years for the public to become fully acquainted with it. Indeed, the Secretariat was pressed to take the initiative when appropriate, and advise an author as to the propriety of addressing his communication to the Committee. Furthermore, if there was any doubt, Committee members felt that the Secretariat should seek further information from the author in accordance with rule 80. In addition, the Secretary-General should, it was agreed, under rule 80, notify authors, where appropriate, that the Committee could only consider violations of the Covenant occurring *on* or *after* the entry into force of the Covenant and the Protocol for the State party concerned *unless* the alleged violations, although occurring before that date, continued to have effects which themselves constituted a violation after that date. This instruction was issued in the light of experience arising from the Committee's being asked to consider, at its second session, a number of communications which concerned violations which allegedly occurred *only before* entry into force of the requisite instruments for the State party concerned.

THE RIGHT OF INDIVIDUAL COMMUNICATION   213

Committee members also agreed that (although the provisional rules did not deal with the subject) authors should be free to lodge communications in the language of their choice and that the Secretariat should, within ten to twenty days, respond with a formal acknowledgement of receipt to authors in the *same* language as the initial communication. If a communication was received in a language other than a working language of the Committee, a full translation should be made of it. Clearly these developments are matters of fundamental importance from the point of view of the author and thus are to be welcomed.

An important point of procedure in the application of interim measures of protection under rule 86 was clarified by the Committee. It decided that, in the interests of speed, the possibility of the imposition of interim measures in respect of any particular communication should not be dependent on the prior inclusion of that communication on the lists of communications drawn up under rule 79 by the Secretary-General, and submitted to the Committee for its attention under rule 78. This was a particularly important decision from the petitioner's point of view, since it will enable the Committee, where appropriate, to adopt protective measures at a very early stage in the proceedings.

Finally, the Committee agreed to publish its final decisions made under Article 5 (4) of the Protocol. However, some members warned that the Committee should proceed with caution in this respect and avoid any action which might discourage member States from ratifying the Covenant or becoming parties to the Protocol. The Committee has also decided that it will normally make public also all final decisions declaring a communication *inadmissible*, substituting initials for the names of the alleged victim(s) and the author(s). This decision to publish its final decisions under Article 5 (4) of the Protocol was of crucial importance, since it is only through publicity given to the developing case law that an individual can properly vindicate his rights in international human rights law. Furthermore, publication of final decisions on admissibility is also of great significance because it is only through such decisions that a petitioner will know whether or not his communication will be admissible. This is obviously of fundamental importance. Equally, the comments and criticisms by international lawyers, inspired by the open law-reporting of the decisions, which develop both the substantive rights and procedural provisions in the Covenant and Protocol, can only enhance the prestige of the Committee and engender confidence in its procedures from the point of view of both individuals and States alike. It is only in this way that the implied pledge of impartial objectivity by the Committee can be redeemed.

In sum, these further decisions on the handling of petitions taken by the Committee show a balanced and careful appraisal of its role in the international adjudication process on human rights violations.

(c) *Commencement of Consideration of Individual Communications*

The advent of its second session heralded the fulfilment of one of the Committee's principal roles in implementing the Covenant. First, it began to consider individual communications received in accordance with the provisions of the Protocol. Of course, at such an early stage, the Committee was only competent to begin to consider the admissibility issue in a number of cases, advised as appropriate by the Working Group's recommendations.

Secondly, in its discretion, the Committee decided that normally a six weeks' time-limit for the submission of information and observations relevant to the question of admissibility under rule 91 (1) would apply. This limit has since been extended to eight weeks. A further four weeks' time-limit was set for the submission by either party of comments on the information or observations obtained. Bearing in mind the usual dilatoriness with which governments tend to deal with human rights issues and the fact that many petitioners may be detainees (and their mail subject to scrutiny or stoppage), these time-limits still seem to be quite severe. However, they do ensure that the wheels of the Protocol machinery keep turning, especially in cases where time is of the essence. It seems, therefore, that the right balance has been struck.

In general, these decisions indicate a promising start to the individual communication procedure. Whether these trends have been consolidated and further developed in the emerging jurisprudence of the Committee will be considered next.

III. Some Aspects of the Jurisprudence of the Committee under the Optional Protocol

The general trend of the emerging case law[29] of the Committee is most promising. This is not, of course, to say that various criticisms cannot be made in some areas. The Committee has displayed a determined desire to be seen to be acting in, at least, a quasi-judicial manner. Its impartiality is beyond doubt. It has been scrupulously fair to both petitioners and States parties. Within the confines of this impartiality, it has generally displayed a willingness to veer toward a liberal interpretation of the Covenant and the Protocol in favour of the alleged victim, whenever more than one inter-

---

[29] There is, as yet, far less literature on the concrete case law of the Committee than there is on the theoretical aspects of the measures of implementation. On the former, see, in particular, Nowak, 'The Effectiveness of the International Covenant on Civil and Political Rights—Stocktaking after the first eleven sessions of the U.N. Human Rights Committee', *Human Rights Law Journal*, 1 (1980), p. 136; Tomuschat, 'Evolving Procedural Rules: The U.N. Human Rights Committee's First Two Years of Dealing with Individual Communications', ibid., p. 249; Nowak, 'UN Human Rights Committee: Survey of Decisions given up till July 1981', ibid., 2 (1981), p. 168; id., 'UN Human Rights Committee: Survey of Decisions given up till October 1982', ibid., 3 (1982), p. 207; id., 'UN Human Rights Committee: Survey of Decisions given up till July 1984', ibid., 5 (1984), p. 199; id., 'UN Human Rights Committee: Survey of Decisions given up till July 1986', ibid., 7 (1986), p. 287; Graefrath, 'Trends Emerging in the Practice of the Human Rights Committee', *Bulletin of the GDR Committee for Human Rights*, no. 1/80 (1980), p. 3.

pretation has been possible. Such an attitude is welcomed and can only enhance the prestige of the UN organs generally in their efforts to ensure an even greater measue of protection to individuals in public international law. The ensuing analysis will illustrate the nature and breadth of the Committee's decisions on communications lodged by individuals. However, for reasons of space, this analysis will concentrate on the extraction of some of the more important pronouncements of *principle* by the Committee.[30]

(a) *Who can be the Author of a Communication?*

Article 1 of the Protocol states that the Committee can receive communications from individuals who claim to be victims of violations of rights set forth in the Covenant. This does not mean that the individual must sign the communication himself in every case. He may also act through a duly appointed representative. However, there may be other cases in which the author of the communication may be accepted as having the necessary authority to act on behalf of the alleged victim. Accordingly, the normal position is that 'the communication should be submitted by the individual himself or by his representatives' (e.g. the alleged victim's lawyers). Exceptionally, 'the Committee may . . . accept to consider a communication submitted on behalf of an alleged victim when it appears that he is unable to submit the communication himself',[31] as where he has been detained.

The case law of the Committee illustrates its approach to this question. It regards a close family connection to be a link which justifies an author in acting on behalf of an alleged victim. As a corollary of this, it will not consider communications where the author fails to demonstrate any genuine link between himself and the alleged victim. In *Massera* v. *Uruguay*,[32] the author petitioned on behalf of herself, her husband, her mother and her stepfather, José Luis Massera (an internationally renowned mathematician). The Committee decided that the 'author of the communication was justified by reason of close family connexion in acting on behalf of the other alleged victims'.[33] The cases are replete with examples of communications submitted by close relatives and others being admissible.[34]

---

[30] The reader should consult the variously cited Reports of the Human Rights Committee for full details of factual situations and arguments, etc., giving rise to the issues of principle.

[31] Rule 90 (1) (b).

[32] Comm. no. R.1/5.

[33] *GAOR*, 34th Session, Supplement 40, Report of the Human Rights Committee, p. 126.

[34] It is interesting to note that J. L. Massera, who was arrested by the Uruguayan authorities in October 1975 on the grounds of 'subversive association', was finally released in March 1984. His plight was highlighted in a letter to *The Times* on 30 November 1982 by a group of eminent British mathematicians. However, the case of *Gomez de Voituret* v. *Uruguay* (Comm. no. 109/1981) is also particularly interesting because it was the first case in which a close relative of a person detained in *Uruguay* submitted a communication from *inside* the country.

THE HUMAN RIGHTS COMMITTEE AND

In other cases, the Committee has found that the author of the communication lacked sufficient *locus standi* to submit a petition on behalf of others.[35] In *Grille Motta* v. *Uruguay*,[36] the author submitted a communication on his own behalf and on behalf of other persons who allegedly were not in a position to submit a communication on their own. The Committee decided to request the author to furnish further information on 'the grounds and circumstances justifying his acting on behalf of the other alleged victims mentioned in the communication'.[37] The author failed to respond to this request and therefore the Committee had no alternative but to declare the communication inadmissible in so far as it related to *other* alleged victims, because of the lack of relevant additional information from the author. This decision shows that the Committee requires some clear proof that an author is acting on behalf of others.

In the case of *U.R.* v. *Uruguay*,[38] the author was a member of a non-governmental organization (Amnesty International) and had taken an interest in the alleged victim's situation. He said he had been working on the case for two and a half years, without avail, and claimed to have the authority to act on behalf of U.R. because he believed 'that every prisoner treated unjustly would appreciate further investigation of his case by the Human Rights Committee'.[39] The Committee recalled its previous case law and declared the application inadmissible. It stated that it had 'established through a number of decisions on admissibility that a communication submitted by a third party on behalf of an alleged victim can *only* be considered if the author justifies his authority to submit the communication'.[40]

The onus is thus clearly placed on the author.[41] In *Mbenge* v. *Zaire*,[42] the Committee held that the author had no authority to act on behalf of one particular alleged victim. In *A.D.* v. *Canada*[43] the Committee rejected the *locus standi* of the author to act on behalf of the alleged victim in the following way:

The Human Rights Committee observes that the author has not proved that he is authorized to act as a representative on behalf of the Mikmaq tribal society. In

[35] See *Hartikainen* v. *Finland*, Comm. no. R.9/40, and *D.F.* v. *Sweden*, Comm. no. 183/1984.
[36] Comm. no. R.2/11.
[37] *GAOR*, 35th Session, Supplement 40, Report of the Human Rights Committee, p. 133.
[38] Comm. no. 128/82. The present position is that communications are numbered consecutively, indicating also the year of registration. The numbering system was changed at the 18th Session of the Committee. Formerly, the reference number of each case consisted of the serial number of the case in the register, preceded by the number of the list of communications in which it was summarized and the letter 'R' indicating 'restricted' (e.g. R.18/73).
[39] *GAOR*, 38th Session, Supplement 40, Report of the Human Rights Committee, p. 239.
[40] Ibid. at p. 239.
[41] See also *S.G.F.* v. *Uruguay* (Comm. no. 136/1983) and *J.F.* v. *Uruguay* (Comm. no. 137/1983).
[42] Comm. no. 16/1977.
[43] Comm. no. 78/1980.

addition, the author has failed to advance any pertinent facts supporting his claim that he is personally a victim of a violation of any rights contained in the Covenant.[44]

Thus the Committee has made it abundantly clear that, where the author himself is not the alleged victim, he must indicate the grounds and circumstances justifying his acting on behalf of the alleged victim. He must also include his reasons for believing that the alleged victim would approve the author's acting on his behalf and the author's reasons for believing that the alleged victim is unable to act on his own behalf. These criteria for adjudicating upon authorship, where the author is not the alleged victim, seem to strike the right balance between flexibility and the need to prevent the Protocol system from being overburdened by a mass of unauthorized communications.

Furthermore, the Committee has declared that an organization as such cannot submit a communication. In the case of *A Group of Associations for the Defence of the Rights of Disabled and Handicapped Persons in Italy etc.* v. *Italy*,[45] the authors of the communication were a non-governmental organization (Coordinamento) and the representatives of those associations, who claimed that they were themselves disabled or handicapped or that they were parents of such persons. Although the representatives were primarily acting for Coordinamento, they also claimed to act on their own behalf. The Committee declared:

> According to Article 1 of the Optional Protocol, only individuals have the right to submit a communication. To the extent, therefore, that the communication originates from the 'Coordinamento', it has to be declared inadmissible because of lack of personal standing.[46]

Similarly, in *J.R.T. and the W.G. Party* v. *Canada*,[47] the Committee stated that the W.G. Party (which was in fact an unincorporated political party under the leadership of J.R.T.) was 'an association and not an individual, and as such cannot submit a communication to the Committee under the Optional Protocol'.[48] Accordingly, the communication was inadmissible under Article 1 of the Optional Protocol in so far as it concerned the W.G. Party.

These cases seem to strike the right balance between allowing the maximum possible scope for petitioners who, for one reason or another, are unable to act on their own initiative and, on the other hand, allowing the Optional Protocol procedure to be swamped by a deluge of unauthorized communications. This is done by placing the onus of proving that he is acting for an alleged victim on the author. This seems fair. Particularly where the victim may wish to lodge a petition in one forum and the petitioner in fact lodges it in another, it seems appropriate

[44] *GAOR*, 39th Session, Supplement 40, Report of the Human Rights Committee, p. 202. The individual opinion of Mr Errera in this case raised further interesting questions. For details, see the report of the case.   [45] Comm. no. 163/1984.

[46] *GAOR*, 39th Session, Supplement 40, Report of the Human Rights Committee, p. 198.

[47] Comm. no. 164/1981.

[48] *GAOR*, 38th Session, Supplement 40, Report of the Human Rights Committee, p. 263.

that the victim should not be bound by the actions of an unrelated third party. However, the scope of legitimate authority under this procedure is far narrower than, for example, under the ECOSOC Resolution 1503 (XLVIII) procedure, which allows petitions from an author with only second-hand knowledge of violations provided he accompanies it with clear evidence and also allows petitions from non-governmental organizations in certain circumstances.

(b) *The Notion of the Victim*

Article 1 of the Protocol insists that potential petitioners must claim to be *victims* of a violation of the rights set forth in the Covenant. The Committee has declared that a person is not to be considered a victim unless he has been affected *personally* by a violation of the protected rights.[49] Accordingly, in the case of *Aumeeruddy-Cziffra and Nineteen Other Mauritian Women* v. *Mauritius*[50] (in which it was alleged that certain domestic legislation constituted, *inter alia*, discrimination based on sex against Mauritian women and was thus a breach of the Covenant), the Committee declared that:

> A person can only claim to be a victim in the sense of Article 1 of the Optional Protocol if he or she is *actually*[51] affected. It is a matter of degree how concretely this requirement should be taken. However, no individual can in the abstract, by way of an *actio popularis*, challenge a law or practice claimed to be contrary to the Covenant. If the law or practice has not already been concretely applied to the detriment of that individual, it must in any event be applicable in such a way that the alleged victim's risk of being affected is more than a theoretical possibility.[52]

Referring to the *Mauritian Women* case, the Committee endorsed its jurisprudence in *Hertzberg and others* v. *Finland*,[53] wherein it stated that it wished

> to stress that it has only been entrusted with the mandate of examining whether an individual has suffered an actual violation of his rights. It cannot review in the abstract whether national legislation contravenes the Covenant, although such legislation may, in particular circumstances, produce adverse effects which directly affect the individual, making him thus a victim in the sense contemplated by Articles 1 and 2 of the Optional Protocol.[54]

In the case of *A Group of Associations for the Defence of the Rights of Disabled and Handicapped Persons in Italy etc.* v. *Italy*,[55] the Committee expressed itself thus:

> ... the author of a communication must himself claim, *in a substantiated manner*,[56] to be the victim of a violation by the State party concerned. It is not the task of the

---

[49] See, e.g., *D.F.* v. *Sweden* (Comm. no. 183/1984).
[50] Comm. no. R.9/35.   [51] Emphasis added.
[52] *GAOR*, 36th Session, Supplement 40, Report of the Human Rights Committee, p. 139.
[53] Comm. no. R.14/61.
[54] *GAOR*, 37th Session, Supplement 40, Report of the Human Rights Committee, p. 164.
[55] Comm. no. 163/1984.   [56] Emphasis added.

THE RIGHT OF INDIVIDUAL COMMUNICATION   219

Human Rights Committee, acting under the Optional Protocol, to review *in abstracto* national legislation as to its compliance with obligations imposed by the Covenant. It is true that, in some circumstances, a domestic law may by its mere existence directly violate the rights of individuals under the Covenant.[57]

The Committee has thus gone out of its way to stress that it cannot examine abstract or potential breaches of the Covenant. A person must actually be a victim. This interpretation is necessitated by the strict terms of the Optional Protocol, which is in accord with other international instruments having the same purpose, e.g. the European Convention on Human Rights, 1950.[58] Furthermore, it would seem that any other interpretation would severely prejudice the successful operation of this particular method of implemention by attracting the criticism of States parties. Equally, such an interpretation will act as a potential filter and thus ensure that the task of the Committee is kept within reasonable bounds. Of course, under the inter-State procedure, States parties are given the role of *policing* the Covenant. They need not allege that their nationals are victims of a violation. It is enough to allege that the infractor State is violating the rights of its own inhabitants.

(c) *Operative Time of the Alleged Breaches*

In the very first case in which it formulated views under Article 5 (4),[59] the Committee rejected the communication as inadmissible in so far as it related to the author 'since it concerned events which allegedly took place prior to the entry into force of the Covenant and the Optional Protocol in respect of Uruguay'.[60] Accordingly, the Committee has often stated that it can only consider an alleged violation of human rights occurring *on or after* the date of entry into force of the Covenant and the Protocol for the State party concerned *unless* it is an alleged violation which, although occurring before that date, continues or has effects which themselves constitute a violation after that date.[61] According to this case law, many communications (or parts of them) have been declared inadmissible *ratione temporis* because the alleged violations occurred prior to the entry into force of the Covenant and the Optional Protocol for the State party concerned.[62] Inadmissibility *ratione temporis* is a feature common to other systems of international adjudication. For example, the case law of the European Commission is replete with decisions of inadmissibility on this ground. It also accords with the general rule of international law that a treaty does not create binding obligations for its participants until ratification or

---

[57] *GAOR*, 39th Session, Supplement 40, Report of the Human Rights Committee, p. 198. See the pronouncement in almost identical terms in *J.H.* v. *Canada* (Comm. no. 187/1985).

[58] See Article 25 of European Convention on Human Rights.

[59] *Massera* v. *Uruguay* (Comm. no. R.1/5).

[60] *GAOR*, 34th Session, Supplement 40, Report of the Human Rights Committee, p. 126.

[61] Many cases have involved a continuing element. See, e.g., *Weinberger Weisz* v. *Uruguay* (Comm. no. R.7/28) and *Lovelace* v. *Canada* (Comm. no. R.6/24) for a complex example of continuing effect.   [62] e.g. *M.A.* v. *Italy* (Comm. no. 117/1981).

accession, apart from those provisions which are declaratory of existing customary international law.

Generally, this issue is disposed of at the admissibility stage. However, this does not, of course, preclude the Committee from indicating in its final views under Article 5 (4) that 'the facts as found by the Committee, in so far as they continued or occurred after [the date on which the Covenant and the Optional Protocol entered into force for the State party concerned] disclose violations of various articles of the Covenant'.[63]

(d) *The Concept of the Individual as Subject to a State Party's Jurisdiction*

According to Article 1 of the Optional Protocol, the Committee is only competent to consider a communication from an individual against a State party if he is 'subject to its jurisdiction'. On several occasions, the Committee has had to consider the meaning of this phrase. In *Viana Acosta* v. *Uruguay*,[64] the applicant, a Uruguayan national who at the time of filing his communication was living in Sweden, complained *inter alia* of his arbitrary arrest and detention by the authorities during the last few years of his residence in Uruguay. In its observations on admissibility, Uruguay submitted that in view of the above terms of Article 1 of the Protocol, it considered that the communication in question was in-admissible. In particular, Uruguay stressed that after he had been unconditionally released he went to live abroad and was therefore *not* subject to the jurisdiction. When discussing the question of admissibility, the Committee observed that the events complained of allegedly occurred in Uruguay while the author was subject to the jurisdiction of Uruguay. It recalled that by virtue of Article 2 (1) of the Covenant, each State party undertakes to respect and to ensure to 'all individuals within its territory and subject to its jurisdiction' the rights recognized in the Covenant: 'Article 1 of the Optional Protocol was clearly intended to apply to individuals subject to the jurisdiction of the State party concerned *at the time of the alleged violation of the Covenant*.[65] This was manifestly the object and purpose of Article 1.'[66] Hence, the Committee was able to dismiss this alleged ground of inadmissibility.

Similarly, in *Amendola Massiotti and Baritussio* v. *Uruguay*,[67] both the applicants were Uruguayan nationals, residing in the Netherlands and Sweden respectively, at the time their applications were lodged with the Committee. Both alleged massive violations of the Covenant, including arbitrary arrest and detention, committed by the governmental authorities in Uruguay against themselves. In its submissions under Article 4 (2) of

[63] *Lluberas* v. *Uruguay* (Comm. no. 123/1982), *GAOR*, 39th Session, Supplement 40, Report of the Human Rights Committee, p. 180.
[64] Comm. no. 110/1981.   [65] Emphasis added.
[66] *GAOR*, 39th Session, Supplement 40, Report of the Human Rights Committee, p. 171.
[67] Comm. no. R.6/25.

THE RIGHT OF INDIVIDUAL COMMUNICATION   221

the Protocol,[68] Uruguay contended that there was no justification for the continued consideration of the case. It said:

> The alleged victims were not under the jurisdiction of the State accused. To consider the communication further would therefore be incompatible with the purpose for which the Covenant and its Protocol were established, namely, to ensure the effective protection of human rights and to bring to an end any situation in which these rights were violated.

Uruguay concluded that 'in this case no *de facto* situation existed to warrant findings by the Committee, and that consequently, by intervening, the Committee would not only be exceeding its competence but would also be departing from normally established legal procedures'.[69] The Committee categorically rejected such an argument as being entirely misconceived. It stated:

> With respect to the State party's submission under Article 4 (2) of the Optional Protocol that consideration of the communication should be discontinued, the Committee notes that the victims were under the jurisdiction of Uruguay while the alleged violations took place. The Committee therefore rejects the contention of the State party that further consideration of the case would be beyond its competence or contrary to the purposes of the International Covenant on Civil and Political Rights and the Optional Protocol thereto.[69]

Such a robust view appears to be amply justified by the terms of the Optional Protocol. There can be little doubt that where a violation occurs towards an individual who was at *that* time residing in his country and subject to the jurisdiction of the State party concerned, he ought to be entitled to lodge a valid communication, notwithstanding that he is residing elsewhere at the time of lodgement. However, it must be stressed that all the cases just discussed have concerned persons who were still *nationals* of the State *in which* the violations actually took place at the time of the lodgement of the communications, although they were by then residing elsewhere. Thus there was no doubt that, at the time of the violations, they were both within the territory and subject to the jurisdiction of the State party concerned. The reports do not indicate whether these persons were *permanently* resident elsewhere at the time of lodgement. Given the interpretation of the Committee that the operative moment is *at the time when the alleged violation of the Covenant took place*, it follows inexorably that the Committee would still be competent to deal with the matter even if such persons had since taken up residence permanently elsewhere. This conclusion is in harmony with the position under the European Convention on Human Rights, under which as a

---

[68] 'Within six months, the receiving State shall submit to the Committee written explanations or statements clarifying the matter and the remedy, if any, that may have been taken by that State.'

[69] *GAOR*, 37th Session, Supplement 40, Report of the Human Rights Committee, p. 190.

general rule the Convention is applicable *ratione loci* if the event or act which is the subject of the complaint has *taken place within the national boundaries* of a Contracting State.

What, however, is the position when the alleged violation of rights of a national of a State party occurs when that person is *not* residing in his country at the time of the alleged violation? Is a communication involving such a situation admissible? This question arose for consideration by the Committee in *Vidal Martins* v. *Uruguay*.[70] The applicant was a Uruguayan national who worked as a journalist residing in Mexico at the time of her communication. After several previous failed attempts to have her passport renewed by the Uruguayan consulate in both Paris and Mexico, the applicant requested a new passport from the consulate in Mexico in October 1978. This request was refused and caused her considerable practical difficulty. She complained, *inter alia*, of a violation of Article 12 (2) of the Covenant which reads: 'Everyone shall be free to leave any country, including his own.' The Human Rights Committee, on its own initiative, examined the question whether the fact that the petitioner resided abroad affected the competence of the Committee to receive and consider the communication under Article 1 of the Optional Protocol, taking into account the provisions of Article 2 (1) of the Covenant. Whereas Article 1 of the Optional Protocol (a procedural provision) declares that 'A State Party to the Covenant that becomes a party to the present Protocol recognizes the competence of the Committee to receive and consider communications from individuals *subject to its jurisdiction*[71] who claim to be victims of a violation . . .', Article 2 (1) of the Covenant (a substantive provision) by contrast imposes an *additional* requirement. It states that 'Each State party to the present Covenant undertakes to respect and to ensure to all individuals *within its territory*[71] and subject to its jurisdiction the rights recognized in the present Covenant . . .'.

In an obscure passage, the Committee declared:

Article 1 of the Optional Protocol applies to individuals subject to the jurisdiction of the State concerned who claim to be victims of a violation by that State of any of the Covenant rights. The issue of a passport to a Uruguayan citizen is clearly a matter within the jurisdiction of the Uruguayan authorities and he is 'subject to the jurisdiction' of Uruguay for that purpose. Moreover, a passport is a means of enabling him 'to leave any country, including his own', as required by Article 12 (2) of the Covenant. It therefore follows from the very nature of the right that, in the case of a citizen resident abroad, it imposes obligations both on the state of residence and on the state of nationality. Consequently, Article 2 (1) of

---

[70] Comm. no. R.13/57. This issue had also arisen previously in the *Waksman* case (the facts being essentially the same as in *Vidal Martins*) but the Committee did not give the matter detailed consideration, preferring instead to make a peremptory declaration of admissibility. In any event, Uruguay informed the Committee in its observations under Article 4 (2) of the Protocol that a renewed passport had been delivered to the applicant (Comm. no. R.7/31).

[71] Emphasis added.

THE RIGHT OF INDIVIDUAL COMMUNICATION   223

the Covenant cannot be interpreted as limiting the obligations of Uruguay under Article 12 (2) to citizens within its own territory.[72]

Although the motivation behind such a liberal interpretation of the Covenant and Protocol in favour of the applicant is laudable, its legal justification appears more dubious. Also, the reasoning of the Committee in arriving at such a solution is far from clear. However, it seems that the Committee was confining the conclusion that the wider procedural protection of the Protocol ('subject to its jurisdiction' *only*) overrode the narrow substantive scope of the Covenant ('*within its territory* and subject to its jurisdiction') to the case of refusal to grant a passport. Normally it would seem that, *logically*, the scope of the procedural protection *cannot* be greater than the scope of the substantive protection.

In *Angel Estrella* v. *Uruguay*,[73] the question arose whether a foreigner (an Argentinian national) resident in the territory of a State party in which alleged breaches of the Covenant had occurred in respect of him could be said to be 'subject to the jurisdiction' of that State. The Committee ruled in favour of the applicant, stating:

Article 1 of the Optional Protocol was clearly intended to apply to individuals subject to the jurisdiction of the State party concerned at the time of the alleged violation of the Covenant, irrespective of their nationality. This was manifestly the object and purpose of Article 1.[74]

In *Lopez Burgos* v. *Uruguay*,[75] the question arose whether the phrase 'subject to its jurisdiction' included the acts of a State party's agents committed *abroad*. The author claimed that her husband, a Uruguayan national, had been kidnapped in Argentina by members of the Uruguayan security and intelligence forces and had been secretly detained there, before being clandestinely transported to Uruguay, where he had been arbitrarily detained in prison. In formulating its final views under Article 5 (4) of the Protocol the Committee observed:

. . . although the arrest and initial detention and mistreatment of Lopez Burgos allegedly took place on foreign territory, the Committee is not barred either by virtue of Article 1 of the Optional Protocol . . . or by virtue of Article 2 (1) of the Covenant . . . from considering these allegations together with the claim of subsequent abduction into Uruguayan territory, inasmuch as these acts were perpetrated by Uruguayan agents acting on foreign soil. The reference in Article 1

---

[72] *GAOR*, 37th Session, Supplement 40, Report of the Human Rights Committee, p. 160. See also for confirmatory jurisprudence on this point the cases of *Lichtenszteyn* v. *Uruguay* (Comm. no. 77/1980), *Pereira Montero* v. *Uruguay* (Comm. no. 106/1981) and *Varela Nunez* v. *Uruguay* (Comm. no. 108/1981). The Committee expressed a similar view at its 21st Session when it declared communication no. 125/1982 admissible. It stated: 'The question of the issue of a passport by [the State party] to a national of [the State party] wherever he may be, is clearly a matter within the jurisdiction of [the State party's] authorities and he is "subject to jurisdiction" of [the State party] for that purpose.'

[73] Comm. no. 74/1980.

[74] *GAOR*, 38th Session, Supplement 40, Report of the Human Rights Committee, p. 156.

[75] Comm. no. R.12/52.

of the Optional Protocol to 'individuals subject to its jurisdiction' does not affect the above conclusion because the reference in that article is not to the place where the violation occurred, but rather to the relationship between the individual and the state in relation to a violation of any of the rights set forth in the Covenant, wherever they occurred.[76]

Accordingly, the kidnapping of Lopez Burgos had to be treated as an assertion of jurisdiction by Uruguay. The Committee added:

... Article 2 (1) of the Covenant places an obligation upon a State party to respect and to ensure rights 'to all individuals within its territory and subject to its jurisdiction', but it does not imply that the State party concerned cannot be held accountable for violations of rights under the Covenant which its agents commit upon the territory of another state, whether with the acquiescence of the Government of that state or in opposition to it. ... In line with [Article 5 (1) of the Covenant[77]], it would be unconscionable to so interpret the responsibility under Article 2 of the Covenant as to permit a State party to perpetrate violations of the Covenant on the territory of another state, which violations it could not perpetrate on its own territory.[78]

It is interesting to observe that Mr Tomuschat attached an individual concurring opinion to that of the Committee. He declared that 'in principle, the scope of application of the Covenant is not susceptible to being extended by reference to Article 5 . . .'.[79] This was contrary to the view taken by the Committee as a whole. However, he added that

. . . to construe the words 'within its territory' pursuant to their strict literal meaning as excluding any responsibility for conduct occurring beyond the national boundaries would, however, lead to utterly absurd results. The formula was intended to take care of objective difficulties which might impede the implementation of the Covenant in specific situations. ... Never was it envisaged, however, to grant States parties unfettered discretionary power to carry out wilful and deliberate attacks against the freedom and personal integrity [of] their citizens living abroad.[80]

It is illuminating to compare the jurisprudence of the Committee on territorial jurisdiction with that of the European Convention institutions. Here too, it seems that an individual who alleges that he is a victim need not in fact be within the territory of the State alleged to be in breach of its

---

[76] *GAOR*, 36th Session, Supplement 40, Report of the Human Rights Committee, p. 182.

[77] 'Nothing in the present Covenant may be interpreted as implying for any State, group or person any right to engage in any activity or perform any act aimed at the destruction of any of the rights and freedoms recognized herein or at their limitation to a greater extent than is provided for in the present Covenant.'

[78] *GAOR*, 36th Session, Supplement 40, Report of the Human Rights Committee, p. 183.

[79] For his reasoning and interpretation of Article 5 of the Covenant see his individual opinion, ibid. at p. 184.

[80] Ibid. at p. 184. Precisely the same question arose in the case of *Celiberti de Casariego* v. *Uruguay* (Comm. no. R.13/56). On this point the Committee and Mr Tomuschat, respectively, adopted exactly similar reasoning.

Conventional obligations. In *X* v. *Austria*,[81] a case which concerned the lawfulness of the arrest of the applicant carried out by Austrian authorities in Italy, the competence *ratione loci* of the Commission was not disputed, the application being dismissed for non-exhaustion of domestic remedies. In *Cyprus* v. *Turkey*,[82] the Turkish Government argued that the applications ought to be declared inadmissible *ratione loci* since they related to alleged violations on Cyprus, because the Commission was only competent to examine acts committed in the *national* territory of the State concerned. Furthermore, Turkey had not extended her jurisdiction to Cyprus or any part of it. In dealing with this issue, the Commission interpreted the phrase 'within their jurisdiction' occurring in Article 1 of the Convention. The Commission held that this phrase was not limited to the *national* territory of the Contracting States. On the contrary, taking into account the phraseology of Article 1 and the purpose of the Convention as a whole, the rights enshrined in it had to be afforded to all persons under their *actual* authority and responsibility, whether that authority was exercised within their own territory or abroad. Furthermore, the Commission stressed that authorized agents of a State party, e.g. diplomatic and consular agents and armed forces, to the extent that they exercise authority abroad, do in fact bring persons or property within the jurisdiction of that State party. Accordingly, since Turkish armed forces had landed on Cyprus and operated there under the direction of the Turkish Government, they were authorized agents of Turkey and brought any other persons or property in Cyprus within the jurisdiction of Turkey to the extent that they exercised control over such persons or property.

(e) *Inadmissibility under Article 5 (2) (a) of the Optional Protocol*

Article 5 (2) states: 'The Committee shall not consider any communication from an individual unless it has ascertained that: (a) the same matter is not being examined under another procedure of international investigation or settlement.' Accordingly, the Committee cannot 'consider' any communication which is being examined simultaneously under any other international procedures of investigation or settlement, for example, under the Inter-American Commission on Human Rights (IACHR) or the European Commission of Human Rights.[83] In such cases, the Secretariat, on the instruction of the Committee, will notify the author

---

[81] For the decision of February 1966, see *Yearbook of the European Convention on Human Rights*, 9 (1966), p. 458; for the decision of July 1966, see ibid., p. 464, and *Collection of Decisions of the European Commission of Human Rights*, vol. 20, p. 79.

[82] See *Yearbook of the European Convention on Human Rights*, 18 (1975), p. 82, and *Decisions and Reports of the European Commission of Human Rights*, vol. 2, p. 125.

[83] On overlapping generally, see Tardu, 'The Protocol to the United Nations Covenant on Civil and Political Rights and the Inter-American System: A Study of Co-existing Petition Procedures', *American Journal of International Law*, 70 (1976), p. 778, and Eissen, 'The European Convention on Human Rights and the United Nations Covenant on Civil and Political Rights—Problems of Co-existence', *Buffalo Law Review*, 22 (1972), p. 181.

that the Committee has no competence to examine the matter. Most cases of overlapping jurisdiction have concerned the IACHR. The experience of the Committee in these cases is that the author has preferred to have the Committee examine his case and has accordingly withdrawn his petition from consideration by the IACHR. However, in one instance the author chose to withdraw his communication from the Committee in order that it could be considered by the European Commission of Human Rights.

Many difficult issues of interpretation in the terminology of Article 5 (2) (a) have had to be resolved by the Committee. For example, is the Committee prevented from considering a communication received by it when an unrelated third party has simultaneously lodged an application in respect of the same victim with another organ of international settlement? The Committee had to consider this question in *Altesor* v. *Uruguay*.[84] In this case, the authors (who were Uruguayan nationals living in Mexico) submitted an application on behalf of their father, Alberto Altesor, also a Uruguayan citizen, alleging *inter alia* that he had been arbitrarily detained by governmental authorities, to the IACHR in October 1976. They then submitted their father's case to the Committee on 10 March 1977. In March 1979, an unrelated third party lodged a complaint with the IACHR in respect of the treatment of Alberto Altesor. Subsequently, by letter dated 6 May 1980, the son and daughter withdrew their application on behalf of their father from the IACHR. There remained the outstanding petition to the IACHR by an unrelated third party. Did this constitute a bar to consideration by the Committee? The Committee concluded that 'it was not prevented from considering the communication submitted to it by the authors on 10 March 1977 by reason of the subsequent complaint made by an unrelated third party under the procedures of the IACHR'.[85]

In the case of *Angel Estrella* v. *Uruguay*,[86] the Committee observed that the provisions of Article 5 (2) (a) of the Optional Protocol 'cannot be so interpreted as to imply that an unrelated third party, acting without the knowledge and consent of the alleged victim, can preclude the latter from having access to the Human Rights Committee'.[87] It therefore concluded that

. . . it was not prevented from considering the communication submitted to it by the alleged victim himself, by reason of a submission by an unrelated third party to the IACHR. Such a submission did not constitute the 'same matter', within the meaning of Article 5 (2) (a).[88]

What constitutes 'the same matter' within the meaning of Article 5 (2) (a) has been the subject of several pronouncements by the Committee. In

---

[84] Comm. no. R.2/10.
[85] *GAOR*, 37th Session, Supplement 40, Report of the Human Rights Committee, p. 125.
[86] Comm. no. 74/1980.
[87] *GAOR*, 38th Session, Supplement 40, Report of the Human Rights Committee, p. 156.
[88] Ibid. See also *Celiberti de Casariego* v. *Uruguay* (Comm. no. R.13/56) for confirmatory jurisprudence on this point.

THE RIGHT OF INDIVIDUAL COMMUNICATION   227

Millan Sequeira v. *Uruguay*,[89] the Committee held that 'the two-line reference to [the applicant] in [a case] before the Inter-American Commission on Human Rights—which case lists in a similar manner the names of hundreds of other persons allegedly detained in Uruguay—did not constitute the same matter as that described in detail by the author in his communication to the Human Rights Committee'.[90] In *Fanali* v. *Italy*,[91] the Italian Government contended that the 'same matter' had been brought before the European Commission of Human Rights, since *other* individuals had brought their *own* cases before that body concerning claims which seemed to arise from the same incident (the so-called 'Lockheed Affair'). The Committee categorically rejected such an interpretation. It held that the concept of 'the same matter' within the meaning of Article 5 (2) (a) of the Optional Protocol had to be understood as 'including the *same*[92] claim concerning the *same*[92] individual, submitted by him or someone else who has the standing to act on his behalf before the other international body'.[93] Accordingly, since Italy itself recognized that the author of the communication before the Committee had not submitted his specific case to the European Commission of Human Rights, the Committee considered that the communication was not inadmissible.

The Committee has also decided that an examination of situations which 'appear to reveal a consistent pattern of gross and reliably attested violations of human rights and fundamental freedoms' in a particular country under ECOSOC Resolution 1503 (XLVIII)[94] does *not* constitute an examination of the 'same matter' as a claim by an individual submitted to the Committee under the Optional Protocol, within the meaning of Article 5 (2) (a) of the Protocol. Accordingly, the invocation of the ECOSOC resolution does not constitute a bar to the consideration of an *individual* case. This decision of the Committee is amply justified. In

---

[89] Comm. no. R.1/6.

[90] *GAOR*, 35th Session, Supplement 40, Report of the Human Rights Committee, p. 129.

[91] Comm. no. 75/1980.   [92] Emphasis added.

[93] *GAOR*, 38th Session, Supplement 40, Report of the Human Rights Committee, p. 163.

[94] On the Resolution 1503 procedure generally, see in particular: Moller, 'Petitioning the United Nations', *Universal Human Rights*, 1 (1979), p. 57; Humphrey, 'The Right of Petition in the UN', *Human Rights Journal*, 4 (1971), p. 463; Zuijdwijk, *Petitioning the United Nations* (St Martins Press, New York, 1982). On admissibility under the procedure, see Cassesse, 'The Admissibility of Communications to the U.N. on Human Rights Violations', *Human Rights Journal*, 5 (1972), p. 275. On the procedure in particular, see Cassesse, 'The New UN Procedure for Handling Gross Violations of Human Rights', *Comunità Internazionale*, 30 (1925), p. 49; Ermacora, 'Procedure to Deal with Human Rights Violations: A Hopeful Start in the UN?', *Human Rights Journal*, 7 (1974), p. 670; Guggenheim, 'Key Provisions of the UN Rules dealing with Human Rights Petitions', *New York University Journal of International Law and Politics*, 6 (1973), p. 427; Newman, 'The New United Nations Procedures for Human Rights Complaints: Reform, Status Quo, or Chambers of Horror?', *Annales de Droit*, 34 (1974), p. 129; Tardu, 'United Nations Response to Gross Violations of Human Rights: The 1503 Procedure', *Santa Clara Law Review*, 20 (1979), p. 559; Prasad, 'The Role of Non-governmental Organisations in the New United Nations Procedures for Human Rights Complaints', *Denver Journal of International Law and Policy*, 5 (1976), p. 441; Rodley, 'Monitoring Human Rights by the UN System and Non-governmental Organisations', in Kommers and Loescher (eds.), *Human Rights and American Foreign Policy* (University of Notre Dame Press, 1979); Wiseberg and Scoble, 'Monitoring Human Rights Violations: The Role of Non-governmental Organisations', ibid.

essence, there is no duplication or overlapping between the procedure regulated by the Council resolution and the Optional Protocol procedure, since the former does *not* aim to redress violations of the rights of any particular *individual*. Rather, the Resolution 1503 procedure, which is generally controlled by the Sub-Commission on the Prevention of Discrimination and Protection of Minorities and its parent body the Human Rights Commission, is concerned with gross violations of the rights of wide *groups* of people as in the case of the policy of *apartheid* in South Africa. No immediate remedy is afforded to *individuals*, as such, under the Resolution 1503 procedure. Hence it can be seen that the Committee is perfectly justified in refusing to consider the Council resolution as amounting to the 'same matter'.

In *Baboeram et al.* v. *Suriname*,[95] when declaring admissible a number of similar cases involving the utmost brutality, the Committee remarked that

. . . a study by an intergovernmental organization either of a human rights situation in a given country (such as that by the IACHR in respect of Suriname) or a study of the trade union rights situation in a given country (such as the issues examined by the Committee on Freedom of Association of the ILO in respect of Suriname), or of a human rights problem of a more global character (such as that of the Special Rapporteur of the Commission on Human Rights on summary or arbitrary executions), although such studies might refer to or draw on information concerning individuals, cannot be seen as being the same matter as the examination of individual cases within the meaning of Article 5, paragraph (2) (a) of the Optional Protocol. Secondly, a procedure established by non-governmental organizations (such as Amnesty International, the International Commission of Jurists or the International Committee of the Red Cross, irrespective of the latter's standing in international law) does not constitute a procedure of international investigation or settlement within the meaning of Article 5, paragraph (2) (a) of the Optional Protocol.[96]

Finally, the question arises as to what the appropriate point in time is for adjudging if the 'same matter' is not being investigated under other international procedures. In *Torres Ramirez* v. *Uruguay*,[97] the Committee concluded that 'Article 5 (2) (a) of the Protocol did not preclude it from declaring the communication admissible, although the same matter had been submitted to another procedure of international investigation or settlement, if the matter had been withdrawn from and was no longer under active consideration in the other body at the time of the Committee's decision on admissibility'.[98] Thus the appropriate point in time is the moment when the Committee makes its decision on admissibility.

In general, the jurisprudence of the Committee under Article 5 (2) (a) of the Protocol narrowly confines the operation of the grounds of inadmissi-

[95] *GAOR*, 40th Session, Supplement 40, Report of the Human Rights Committee, p. 187.
[96] Ibid. at pp. 191–2.   [97] Comm. no. R.1/4.
[98] *GAOR*, 35th Session, Supplement 40, Report of the Human Rights Committee, p. 123.

bility stated in that article to situations where an appropriate *analogous* body (such as the IACHR or ECHR) is actively considering the 'same matter' at the time of the Committee's decision on admissibility.[99] This strict interpretation is in harmony with the terms of the Protocol itself and gives individuals the widest possible scope of access to the Committee. This is obviously desirable if the whole procedure is not to be thwarted or protection rendered illusory at the slightest semblance of *any other* international body being involved in the general situation in relation to which a particular breach or breaches of the Covenant are alleged by an *individual* with respect to *himself*.

(f) *The Operation of Reservations to Article 5 (2) (a) of the Protocol*

The competence of the Committee to consider petitions when the 'same matter' is not *being* examined under another procedure of international investigation is further narrowed in some cases by reservations entered to Article 5 (2) (a) of the Protocol by some States parties. In particular, Denmark, Iceland, Italy, Norway, France, Luxembourg, Spain and Sweden have made reservations which further preclude examination by the Committee of individual communications where the 'same matter' *has* already been examined in another procedure of international investigation. These reservations more fully circumscribe the competence of the Committee, since the formal terms of Article 5 (2) (a) only prevent the Committee from an examination of a communication *while* another process of international investigation is *being* conducted. These reservations mean that the Committee cannot consider *at all* any communication where the 'same matter' has already been examined in another international forum (the principle of *non bis in idem*). The obvious intent of the above mentioned States which have made such reservations is to prevent any possibility of appeal from any decisions of the Strasbourg institutions under the European Convention on Human Rights to the Human Rights Committee.[100]

In the case of *A.M.* v. *Denmark*,[101] the author had already submitted a communication concerning the 'same matter' to the European Commission of Human Rights, which had found it inadmissible as 'manifestly ill-founded' under Article 27 (2) of the European Convention.[102] Thus, although there was technically nothing in Article 5 (2) (a) of the Protocol to prevent the Committee from considering the case, the effect of the Danish reservation (as delineated above) was to render the Committee

---

[99] See, e.g., the inadmissibility decision in *D.F.* v. *Sweden* (Comm. no. 183/1984).

[100] For the effects of the various international human rights instruments providing a mechanism for individual communications on the machinery of protection established under the European Convention on Human Rights, see the Secretariat Memorandum prepared by the Directorate of Human Rights (Doc. no. H(85)3).   [101] Comm. no. R.26/121.

[102] App. no. 9490/81, decision of 1 March 1982.

incompetent to deal with the matter. The Committee put its ruling on inadmissibility in this way:

> In the light of the . . . reservation and observing that the same matter has already been considered by the European Commission of Human Rights and therefore by another procedure of international investigation within the meaning of Article 5 (2) (a) of the Optional Protocol to the International Covenant on Civil and Political Rights, the Committee concludes that it is not competent to consider the present communication.[103]

In *O.F.* v. *Norway*,[104] the author had approached the European Commission of Human Rights with a view to lodging an application but had been informed that he was out of time since he had not submitted his application within six months of the date of exhaustion of domestic remedies in accordance with Article 26 of the European Convention. Subsequently, the State party itself informed the Committee that it would not object to the admissibility of the communication on the basis of its reservation, since it was unarguable that the case had not in fact been examined in Strasbourg at all for there had not even been a declaration of inadmissibility there. The case had not even been registered by the European Commission. The Committee agreed with this analysis since there was no room for any doubt.

Of course, States parties are free to enter such a reservation to Article 5 (2) (a), but it cannot be denied that such action does further delimit the competence of the Committee. Nevertheless, it is understandable that States parties which have also ratified the European Convention should not wish the final decisions of the Strasbourg bodies to be the subject of further scrutiny in New York or Geneva. Such further examination would, it seems, tend to weaken the authority of the European Commission or Court, as appropriate, especially if the Committee disagreed with the European institutions and came to the conclusion that a breach or breaches of rights covered in both instruments had occurred. Such a finding could be very embarrassing for the European organs. Furthermore, such reservations are generally in harmony with the terms of Article 27 (1) (b) of the European Convention which bars the Commission from handling applications which deal with matters that are substantially the same as those already submitted to another procedure of international investigation, e.g. the Human Rights Committee, unless it contains 'relevant new information'. Thus, in effect, appeals from any decision of, for example, the Human Rights Committee will *not* be entertained in Strasbourg unless new and relevant information, which was not before the Committee, is adduced.

However, it is suggested that in one respect the Committee took a very timid view in *A.M.* v. *Denmark*.[105] In this connection, it is worth studying

---

[103] *GAOR*, 37th Session, Supplement 40, Report of the Human Rights Committee, p. 213.
[104] Comm. no. 158/1983.   [105] Comm. no. R.26/121.

THE RIGHT OF INDIVIDUAL COMMUNICATION   231

the dissenting view of Mr Bernhard Graefrath. He refused to share the view of the Committee as a whole that it was barred from considering the application because of the Danish reservation. He explained that the reservation referred only to matters which had already been *considered* under other procedures of international investigation. It did *not, in particular* refer to matters, the *consideration* of which had been *denied* under any other procedure by a decision of inadmissibility. The reason was that

[i]f the Committee interprets the reservation in such a way that it would be excluded from considering a communication when a complaint referring to the same facts has been declared inadmissible under the procedure of the European Convention, the effect would be that any complaint that has been declared inadmissible under that procedure could later on not be considered by the Human Rights Committee, despite the fact that the conditions for admissibility of communications are set out in a separate international instrument and are different from those under the Optional Protocol. . . . A decision on non-admissibility of the European Commission, therefore, has no impact on a matter before the Human Rights Committee and cannot hinder the Human Rights Committee from reviewing the facts of a communication on its own legal basis and under its own procedure and from ascertaining whether they are compatible with the provisions of the Covenant. This might lead to a similar result as under the European Convention, but not necessarily so.[106]

Mr Graefrath's opinion is to be preferred to the view of the Committee as a whole, both because it is clear that the word 'considered' cannot include situations where the case has *not* been considered on the merits because of a ground of inadmissibility in another forum which might not be applicable under the Optional Protocol, and because there cannot be any fear of weakening the authority of the Strasbourg institutions where no final decision has been taken under the European Convention.

More recently, another spirited attempt to outflank the Norwegian reservation to Article 5, paragraph (2) (a), of the Protocol was made in *V.O.* v. *Norway*.[107] The Committee thus had a further opportunity to pronounce upon the meaning of the phrase 'the same matter'. It said: 'This phrase in the view of the Committee refers, with regard to identical parties, to the complaints advanced and facts adduced in support of them.'[108] The Committee thus found that the matter which was before the Committee now was in fact the same matter that was examined by the European Commission of Human Rights and hence inadmissible.

In essence, the applicant claimed that, with regard to the custody of his infant daughter by marriage, one-sided and biased decisions in divorce proceedings conducted before Norwegian courts had resulted in a *de facto* separation between himself and his child. Accordingly, he alleged that he

---

[106] *GAOR*, 37th Session, Supplement 40, Report of the Human Rights Committee, pp. 214-15.

[107] Comm. no. 168/1984; *GAOR*, 40th Session, Supplement 40, Report of the Human Rights Committee, p. 232.

[108] Ibid. at p. 235.

was a victim of violations of various provisions of the Covenant. An earlier application to the European Commission had been dismissed by that body as being manifestly ill-founded.

By concentrating on the general nature of the *complaints* advanced and *facts* adduced in support of them (in its analysis of 'the same matter') the Committee was able to ignore the arguments of the author that, first, the provisions of the European Convention pleaded before the European Commission differed in several respects from those of the Covenant invoked in the instant communication to the Committee; secondly, that breaches of certain additional Covenant rights other than those involved in the application to Strasbourg were involved, and thirdly, that his communication to the Committee in no sense amounted to an appeal against the European Commission's decision. Instead, the Committee preferred to adopt the argument of the government that the communication amounted to 'the same matter' since it referred to 'the same facts, no new events being submitted to the Committee, and because the legal arguments in the two proceedings [were] the same'.[109]

Such reasoning, while having the advantage of simplicity, scarcely does justice to the main thrust of the petitioner's argument that where different rights, which were not alleged to have been violated before the European Commission, are pleaded under the Covenant or where the nature of the substantive rights in the Covenant differs from the formulation under the European Convention, the examination of the communication by the Committee cannot amount to the consideration of 'the same matter' already adjudicated upon by the European Commission. Whereas it is easy to criticize the decision of the Committee, not least because of the somewhat Delphic nature of its pronouncement, it is obvious that the Committee intended to demonstrate to States parties to both the European Convention and the Covenant, which had entered a reservation to Article 5, paragraph (2) (a), of the Protocol, that it would adopt a wider rather than a narrower interpretation of such a reservation in order to give it the maximum possible scope. No doubt the Committee wished both to assure States parties that their reservations would be respected and also to encourage those States such as the United Kingdom which have accepted the Article 25 individual application procedure under the European Convention but have not yet ratified or acceded to the Optional Protocol, 1966, to do so speedily, without fear that the decisions of the Strasbourg organs could in effect be appealed against in Geneva or New York.

(g) *Inadmissibility under Article 5 (2) (b) of the Optional Protocol*

Article 5 (2) of the Protocol states that '[t]he Committee shall not consider any communication from an individual unless it has ascertained that: . . . (b) the individual has exhausted all available domestic remedies'.

---

[109] Ibid. at p. 234.

THE RIGHT OF INDIVIDUAL COMMUNICATION   233

Many cases have been declared inadmissible on this ground.[110] In other cases, the Committee have considered the essential pre-conditions to the invocation of this ground of inadmissibility.

In the case of *Torres Ramirez* v. *Uruguay*,[111] the government objected to admissibility with the bald statement that 'the alleged victim had not exhausted all available domestic remedies'.[112] The Committee brushed aside such an unqualified assertion and informed the State party that

... in the absence of more specific information concerning the domestic remedies said to be available to the author of [the] communication, and the effectiveness of those remedies as enforced by the competent authorities in Uruguay, the Committee was unable to accept that he had failed to exhaust such remedies and the communication would therefore not be considered inadmissible in so far as exhaustion of domestic remedies was concerned, unless the State party gave details of the remedies which it submitted had been available to the author in the circumstances of his case, together with evidence that there would be a reasonable prospect that such remedies would be effective.[113]

Despite such a clear indication as to what was required, Uruguay responded with a general description of domestic remedies available but failed to specify which remedies were available to the author in the *particular* circumstances of *his* case. Accordingly, the Committee concluded:

. . . Article 5 (2) (b) of the Protocol did not preclude it from considering a communication received under the Protocol where the allegations themselves raise issues concerning the availability or effectiveness of domestic remedies and the State party, when expressly requested to do so by the Committee, did not provide details on the availability and effectiveness of domestic remedies in the particular case under consideration.[114]

Hence the Committee was able to consider the case on the merits. This jurisprudence was confirmed in *Millan Sequeira* v. *Uruguay*.[115]

Similarly, in *Grille Motta* v. *Uruguay*,[116] the Committee decided to declare a communication admissible, since it was unable to conclude on the basis of the information before it that, with regard to the exhaustion of domestic remedies, there were any remedies which the alleged victim should or could have pursued. However, in this case the Committee warned that it was reserving the right to review its decision on admissibility 'in the light of any further explanations which the State party may submit giving details of any domestic remedies which it claims to have been available to the author in the circumstances of his case, together with

[110] See, e.g., *J.S.* v. *Canada* (Comm. no. 130/1982) and *N.B.* v. *Sweden* (Comm. no. 175/1984). See also the article by Cançado Trindade, 'Exhaustion of Local Remedies under the UN Covenant on Civil and Political Rights and its Optional Protocol', *International and Comparative Law Quarterly*, 28 (1979), p. 734.   [111] Comm. no. R.1/4.

[112] *GAOR*, 35th Session, Supplement 40, Report of the Human Rights Committee, p. 122.

[113] Ibid. at pp. 122 and 123.   [114] Ibid. at p. 123.

[115] Comm. no. R.1/6. See also later cases such as *Dermit Barbato* v. *Uruguay* (Comm. no. 84/1981), *Marais* v. *Madagascar* (Comm. no. 49/1979), *Oxandabarat Scarrone* v. *Uruguay* (Comm. no. 103/1981) and *Gomez de Voituret* v. *Uruguay* (Comm. no. 109/1981).   [116] Comm. no. R.2/11.

evidence that there would be a reasonable prospect that such remedies would be effective'.[117] This decision again reflects the desire of the Committee to be seen to be acting impartially and to be offering the State party every opportunity to submit evidence on the application of domestic remedies. Furthermore, it is firmly based on the text of rule 93 (4) of the provisional rules which states: 'The Committee may review its decision that a communication is admissible in the light of any explanation or statements submitted by the State Party pursuant to this rule.' This rule was invoked for the first time in the case of *C.F. et al.* v. *Canada*,[118] wherein the Committee reversed its previous decision in the light of new evidence and made a declaration of inadmissibility.

In *Weinberger Weisz* v. *Uruguay*,[119] the Committee made a declaration of admissibility on the basis that, on the information before it at that stage, there were no further domestic remedies which the alleged victim could have pursued.[120] Uruguay pressed non-exhaustion of domestic remedies when asked for written explanations on the merits under Article 4 (2) of the Optional Protocol. However, the Committee decided that since more than four and a half years had passed since the arrest of the applicant and still no final judgment on the legality of his detention had been delivered by the appropriate organ, it was not barred from considering the case on the merits since 'the application of the remedy [was] unreasonably prolonged'.[121] In making this decision, the Committee was able to invoke the last sentence of Article 5 (2) (b) which states, *inter alia*, that this bar to admissibility 'shall not be the rule where the application of the remedies is unreasonably prolonged'.

In the case of *Baboeram et al.* v. *Suriname*,[122] all the petitioners openly admitted that they had not exhausted domestic remedies because it was clear that, in the political situation then existing there, there were *no* effective legal remedies, and they submitted some evidence in support. The State party did not challenge the authors' contention that there were no effective legal remedies to exhaust. The Committee recalled that 'it had already established in numerous other cases that exhaustion of domestic remedies could be required only to the extent that these remedies were effective and available within the meaning of Article 5, paragraph 2 (b), of the Optional Protocol'.[123] Accordingly, the Committee was not barred

[117] *GAOR*, 35th Session, Supplement 40, Report of the Human Rights Committee, p. 134. In *Martinez Machado* v. *Uruguay* (Comm. no. 83/1981), the Committee found no reason to review its decision on admissibility since no further details had been provided by the State party under Article 4 (2) of the Protocol of the remedies available and the prospects of their effectiveness.

[118] Comm. no. 113/1981; *GAOR*, 40th Session, Supplement 40, Report of the Human Rights Committee, p. 217. See also *J.H.* v. *Jamaica* (Comm. no. 165/1984).   [119] Comm. no. R.7/28.

[120] See also, among others, *Buffo Carballal* v. *Uruguay* (Comm. no. R.8/33) on this point.

[121] *GAOR*, 36th Session, Supplement 40, Report of the Human Rights Committee, p. 118. See also *Solorzano* v. *Venezuela* (Comm. no. 156/1983).

[122] *GAOR*, 40th Session, Supplement 40, Report of the Human Rights Committee, p. 187.

[123] Ibid. at p. 192. The requirement that domestic remedies must be effective and available entails that procedural guarantees of a 'fair and public hearing by a competent, independent and impartial tribunal' must be scrupulously observed: see *Gilboa* v. *Uruguay* (Comm. no. 147/1983).

from making a declaration of admissibility. That domestic remedies must, in principle, be available and effective before exhaustion is required is commensurate with the generally recognized rules of international law.

In *Pietroroia* v. *Uruguay*,[124] the Committee stated that to require resort to remedies of an 'exceptional nature' would unreasonably prolong the exhaustion of domestic remedies, and it doubted their applicability. This case laid the foundations for the view that extraordinary remedies are not required to be exhausted. In *Cubas Simones* v. *Uruguay*,[125] the Government objected to admissibility because it claimed that, although the ordinary appeals procedure had been completed by the applicant who alleged, *inter alia*, arbitrary detention, there still remained certain 'extraordinary' remedies[126] which had not been exhausted. However, this objection was disregarded by the Committee because the Government had failed to show why these extraordinary remedies should be pursued and they had not been invoked by the officially appointed defence counsel. Accordingly, they could not be regarded as being 'available' within the meaning of Article 5 (2) (b) of the Protocol.[127] The Government further pursued its arguments on non-exhaustion when giving explanations on the merits under Article 4 (2) of the Protocol. It suggested that the applicant had applied for 'conditional release' and no decision had yet been reached by the Court. The Committee said that this procedure did not amount to a 'remedy' within the meaning of Article 5 (2) (b) of the Protocol. Although extraordinary remedies, because of their limited scope, are not in general required to be exhausted before a declaration of admissibility can be made, especially where the petitioner has been led to believe that there were no further remedies, the case of *Muhonen* v. *Finland*[128] is authority for the proposition that there can be a declaration of inadmissibility for failure to exhaust extraordinary remedies if the State party can show that there were grounds for believing that such a remedy could be or could have been effective in the particular circumstances of the case.

Finally, it is interesting to note that in *C.F. et al.* v. *Canada*,[129] the Committee left open the question of whether a domestic remedy which was established *after* the submission of a communication to the Committee needs to be resorted to in order to comply with the terms of Article 5 (2) (b) of the Protocol.

The case law of the Committee on exhaustion of local remedies is forthright, confirmatory and aims to grant to the author every reasonable possibility that his communication will be examined on the merits. The State party is, at least, required to point to remedies in its domestic law that both are applicable and afford to the author a reasonable prospect of success before a declaration of inadmissibility can be made. It is then up to

---

[124] Comm. no. R.10/44.
[125] Comm. no. R.17/70.   [126] Those of 'annulment' and 'review'.
[127] See also *Teti Izquierdo* v. *Uruguay* (Comm. no. R.18/73) and *Campora Schweizer* v. *Uruguay* (Comm. no. 66/1980) for confirmation of this jurisprudence.
[128] Comm. no. 89/1981.   [129] Comm. no. 113/1981.

the petitioner to prove exhaustion, or that exhaustion is not required because, for example, there are no effective remedies to be exhausted, or that he is relieved from the duty to exhaust because, for example, the application of the remedies is unreasonably prolonged. If the Committee is in any doubt about the exhaustion of local remedies through lack of information from the State party concerned, it has the power to review its decision when dealing with the merits of the communication. This gives to States every opportunity to furnish information relevant to admissibility even at a very late stage.

On the issue of burden of proof in exhaustion of domestic remedies, it is interesting to examine the position of the European Human Rights Convention institutions by way of comparison.[130] In the original rule 41 (2) of the rules of procedure of the European Commission of Human Rights adopted on 2 April 1955, the issue of burden of proof in exhausting domestic remedies under Article 26 of the Convention was put in this way: 'In pursuance of Article 26 of the Convention a party shall provide evidence to show that all domestic remedies have been exhausted.' In a series of decisions from 1955 until 1959, the Commission followed the principle that it was for the applicant to prove that he had exhausted all domestic remedies. Accordingly, it held that substantial evidence of compliance with the rule must be adduced.[131] This interpretation was criticized as being too onerous and at variance with the position in general international law which imposes the burden of proof on the particular party alleging a fact. In other words, there is a division of the burden of proof—whichever party makes an assertion is under an obligation to prove it.[132] Furthermore, the Commission itself had taken a more liberal approach in inter-State cases.[133]

In 1960, the rule of procedure regarding burden of proof was revised. The amended rule 41 (2) stated: 'The applicant shall provide information enabling it to be shown that the conditions laid down in Article 26 of the Convention have been satisfied.' No longer has the applicant to provide substantive evidence of exhaustion. All that is required is prima-facie evidence. According to Trindade, the new rule

lends support to the shifting or division of the burden of proof between the contending parties before the Commission. Thus with regard to Article 26 of the Convention, it lays upon the respondent party the initial burden of proving the existence of local remedies to be exhausted; the burden then shifts to the applicant

---

[130] The leading monograph on exhaustion of domestic remedies generally in international law (including under the European Convention and other human rights instruments) is Cançado Trindade, *The Application of the Rule of Exhaustion of Local Remedies in International Law* (Cambridge University Press, 1983).

[131] See application nos. 188/56, *Yearbook of the European Convention on Human Rights*, 1 (1956–7), p. 178; 232/56, ibid., p. 144; and 222/56, ibid., 2 (1958–9), p. 351.

[132] Cançado Trindade, op. cit. above (n. 130), pp. 145–53.

[133] See, e.g., the second *Cyprus* case, application no. 299/57, *Yearbook of the European Convention on Human Rights*, 2 (1958–9), p. 186.

THE RIGHT OF INDIVIDUAL COMMUNICATION   237

to prove either that local remedies have been exhausted, or that they are not adequate and effective for redress, or else that there are special circumstances relieving him from the duty to exhaust local remedies.[134]

Later, he describes the position reached by the jurisprudence of the Commission as follows:

> Thus, the individual applicant has the duty to prove that he has exhausted local remedies, or else that he has not exhausted them because he was relieved by special circumstances from doing so, or because remedies did not exist, or were ineffective, as much as the respondent government is bound to prove that local remedies existed and had not been exhausted, and that they were adequate and effective.[135]

Accordingly, the position reached by the European Commission is virtually similar to that reached by the Human Rights Committee in the matter of burden of proof. However, the European institutions at Strasbourg have gone further in one respect. In the case of *Fifty-seven Inhabitants of Louvain and Environs* v. *Belgium*,[136] the Commission expressly declared that the burden of proof did *not* fall on the individual applicant if the respondent Government had manifestly failed to plead non-exhaustion of domestic remedies when invited to express its opinion on the admissibility of an application.

(h) *Other Grounds of Inadmissibility*

Other grounds of inadmissibility are stated in Article 3 of the Protocol which reads: 'The Committee shall consider inadmissible any communication under the present Protocol which is anonymous, or which it considers to be an abuse of the right of submission of such communications or to be incompatible with the provisions of the Covenant.' Furthermore, the Committee can only consider communications from individuals who claim that 'any of their rights enumerated in the Covenant have been violated . . .' (Article 2 of the Protocol). Accordingly, communications which relate to violations of rights not included in the Protocol must be declared inadmissible *ratione materiae*. For example, the Committee declared communication no. 53/1979 inadmissible because 'the right to dispose of property, as such, is not protected by any provision of the

---

[134] Op. cit. above (p. 236 n. 130), pp. 145–6.

[135] Ibid., pp. 149–50. Compare also the position under the Inter-American Commission on Human Rights, for which see Cançado Trindade, 'Exhaustion of Local Remedies in the Inter-American System', *Indian Journal of International Law*, 18 (1978), p. 345. See further, for the position under the International Convention on the Elimination of All Forms of Racial Discrimination, 1965, id., 'Exhaustion of Local Remedies under the United Nations International Convention on the Elimination of All Forms of Racial Discrimination', *German Yearbook of International Law*, 22 (1979), p. 374. On burden of proof under the ECOSOC Resolution 1503 (XLVIII) procedure, see id., op. cit. above (p. 236 n. 130), at pp. 163–8.

[136] Application no. 1994/63. See *Yearbook of the European Convention on Human Rights*, 3 (1960), p. 252.

International Covenant on Civil and Political Rights'.[137] Similarly, one of the reasons why *I.M.* v. *Norway*[138] was declared inadmissible was because 'the assessment of taxable income and allocation of houses are not in themselves matters to which the Covenant applies'.[139]

An interesting question involving Article 2 of the Protocol arose for consideration in *J.K.* v. *Canada.*[140] The author of the communication alleged that he had been unjustly convicted of a criminal offence and sentenced to a term of imprisonment. An appeal before the Court of Appeals of Vancouver was rejected and a petition to the Supreme Court of Canada for leave to appeal was denied. The author alleged that he was innocent of the charge and, *inter alia*, that the Court of Appeal erred in not considering, or not properly evaluating, the new evidence submitted on appeal. Although all the events took place *prior* to the entry into force of the International Covenant on Civil and Political Rights and the Optional Protocol for Canada, the author pleaded that the stigma of the allegedly unjust conviction and the social and legal consequences thereof, including the general prejudice in society against convicted persons, made him a victim today of a number of articles of the Covenant. The author requested the Committee to invite the State party to ensure an annulment of the conviction and pay him an equitable indemnity for the injuries suffered as a consequence of his conviction.

The Committee noted that in so far as the communication related to events that occurred prior to 19 August 1976 (the date when the Covenant and the Optional Protocol entered into force for Canada) the communication was inadmissible *ratione temporis*. Furthermore, it was beyond the competence of the Committee to review findings of fact made by national tribunals or to determine whether national tribunals had properly evaluated new evidence submitted on appeal. Accordingly, in *these* circumstances, the Committee held that the author's contention that the continuing consequences of his conviction made him a victim today of violations of the Covenant 'do not themselves raise issues under the International Covenant on Civil and Political Rights in his case'.[141] The Committee thus concluded that 'the author has no claim under Article 2 of the Optional Protocol'.[142]

In effect, what the Committee was arguing here was that where the allegedly unjust conviction was unchallengeable *in itself*, both because it was delivered prior to entry into force of the relevant instruments for Canada and because, in any event, the finding of fact that the author had committed the crime was unreviewable by the Committee, then the effects

---

[137] *GAOR*, 39th Session, Supplement 40, Report of the Human Rights Committee, p. 118.

[138] Comm. no. 129/1982.

[139] *GAOR*, 38th Session, Supplement 40, Report of the Human Rights Committee, p. 242. See also *M.A.* v. *Italy* (Comm. no. 117/1981) and *L.T.K.* v. *Finland* (Comm. no. 185/1984). See further *J.B. et al.* v. *Canada* (Comm. no. 118/1982).

[140] *GAOR*, 40th Session, Supplement 40, Report of the Human Rights Committee, p. 215.

[141] Ibid. at p. 216.   [142] Ibid. at p. 216. See also *M.F.* v. *Netherlands* (Comm. no. 173/1984).

THE RIGHT OF INDIVIDUAL COMMUNICATION   239

of the conviction (which itself was not a violation of the Covenant) could not of themselves amount to a violation. The Committee had no alternative but to declare the communication inadmissible because, as it pointed out, it had no authority to investigate findings of fact made by domestic tribunals. Any such investigation would be an unwarrantable extension of the terms of the Covenant and unacceptable to States parties. As such, any such intrusion into a matter beyond doubt within the domestic jurisdiction would be bound to attract severe criticism and seriously weaken the growing prestige and authority of the Committee.

Although an author need not prove his case at the admissibility stage, he must produce sufficient evidence to substantiate a prima-facie case. This approximates somewhat to the 'manifestly ill-founded' ground of inadmissibility under the European Convention. Accordingly, the Committee has declared a number of communications inadmissible on the grounds of non-substantiation. For example, in *I.M.* v. *Norway*,[143] the Committee rejected the author's claim that he was a victim of racial discrimination for lack of evidence in substantiation. In *J.S.* v. *Canada*,[144] the Committee rejected the applicant's claim, *inter alia*, on the ground of non-substantiation of allegations. Similarly, in *J.D.B.* v. *Netherlands*,[145] the Committee reached a similar conclusion because no facts had been submitted in substantiation of the author's claim that he was a victim of a violation of any of the rights guaranteed by the Covenant.[146]

When is a communication 'incompatible' with the provisions of the Covenant in accordance with the terms of Article 3 of the Protocol? Generally it seems that communications are inadmissible if their authors complain of restrictions or limitations on particular substantive rights, which are actually justified by the need to ensure that those rights are not abused. Accordingly, in *M.A.* v. *Italy*,[147] where the author had been convicted of reorganizing the dissolved Fascist party, the Committee declared that these acts

were of a kind which are removed from the protection of the Covenant by Article 5[148] thereof and which were in any event justifiably prohibited by Italian law having regard to the limitations and restrictions applicable to the rights in question under the provisions of Articles 18 (3), 22 (2) and 25 of the Covenant . . . [T]herefore, the communication is inadmissible under Article 3 of the Optional Protocol, as incompatible with the provisions of the Covenant, *ratione materiae*.[149]

The limitations invoked by the Committee in this case were those on freedom to manifest one's religion or beliefs (Article 18 (3)), freedom of expression (Article 19 (3)), freedom of association (Article 22 (2)) and freedom to take part in the conduct of public affairs, etc. (Article 25).

---

[143] Comm. no. 129/1982.   [144] Comm. no. 130/1982.   [145] Comm. no. 178/1984.
[146] See also *O.F.* v. *Norway* (Comm. no. 158/1983) and *E.H.* v. *Finland* (Comm. no. 170/1984).
[147] Comm. no. 117/1981.   [148] See p. 224 n. 77 above.
[149] *GAOR*, 39th Session, Supplement 40, Report of the Human Rights Committee, p. 196.

Similarly in *J.R.T. and the W.G. Party* v. *Canada*,[150] the applicants' contention that their right to freedom of expression under Article 19 (2) of the Covenant was being violated by Canada was rejected as being incompatible with the provisions of the Covenant in these terms:

> ... not only is the author's 'right' to communicate racist ideas not protected by the Covenant, it is in fact incompatible with its provisions ... [T]he opinions which [the applicant] seeks to disseminate through the telephone system clearly constitute the advocacy of racial or religious hatred which Canada has an obligation under Article 20 (2) of the Covenant to prohibit.[151]

These decisions on other grounds of inadmissibility by the Committee really go no further than the strict terms of the Protocol require. By comparison with the European Convention, there is no concept precisely similar to the 'manifestly ill-founded' ground of inadmissibility contained in Article 27 (2) of that Convention. However, the Committee does insist on some substantiation of a prima-facie case at the admissibility stage. By September 1986, 211 communications had been received for placement before the Committee. Out of these, one hundred and six had been discontinued, suspended, withdrawn, or been declared inadmissible. Since the Committee has only published forty-six of these decisions, it is only possible to say that much less than 50 per cent of communications received have been declared inadmissible. By contrast, under the procedure established by the Strasbourg institutions, by 1 January 1987, out of a total of 11,659 decisions on admissibility taken by the European Commission, only 492 had been declared admissible. Accordingly, almost 96 per cent of applications to Strasbourg have been declared inadmissible!

IV. SOME PROBLEMS OF PROCEDURAL METHOD

The Human Rights Committee has unequivocally held that the right of an individual under the Protocol to communicate with it regarding violations of rights contained in the Covenant must be effective and not rendered illusory by the State party. Nowhere is this more forcefully stated than in the case of *Sendic* v. *Uruguay*.[152] In an interim decision taken on 24 October 1980, the Committee decided (principally because of the failure of the State party concerned to respond to repeated requests to provide it with full details about Mr Sendic's medical condition) that Mr Sendic 'should be given the opportunity himself to communicate directly with the Committee'.[153]

Uruguay alleged that this decision exceeded the authority of the

[150] Comm. no. 104/1981.

[151] *GAOR*, 38th Session, Supplement 40, Report of the Human Rights Committee, pp. 234 and 236.

[152] Comm. no. R.14/63 submitted by the alleged victim's wife claiming that he had been arbitrarily detained and subjected to torture.

[153] *GAOR*, 37th Session, Supplement 40, Report of the Human Rights Committee, p. 118. Such a request has been repeated in other cases such as *Larrosa Bequio* v. *Uruguay* (Comm. no. 88/1981).

THE RIGHT OF INDIVIDUAL COMMUNICATION   241

Committee. The Committee categorically refuted such a suggestion in the following unequivocal terms:

> The Human Rights Committee cannot accept the State party's contention that it exceeded its mandate when in its decision of 24 October 1980, it requested the State party to afford to [the alleged victim] the opportunity to communicate directly with the Committee. The Committee rejects the State party's argument that a victim's right to contact the Committee directly is invalid in the case of persons imprisoned in Uruguay. If governments had the right to erect obstacles to contacts between victims and the Committee, the procedure established by the Optional Protocol would, in many instances, be rendered meaningless. It is a prerequisite for the effective application of the Optional Protocol that detainees should be able to communicate directly with the Committee. The contention that the International Covenant and the Protocol apply only to states, as subjects of international law, and that, in consequence, these instruments are not directly applicable to individuals is devoid of legal foundation in cases where a state has recognized the competence of the Committee to receive and consider communications from individuals under the Optional Protocol. That being so, denying individuals who are victims of an alleged violation their rights to bring the matter before the Committee is tantamount to denying the mandatory nature of the Optional Protocol.[154]

The Committee was obviously right to conduct such a bold defence of the victim's right to uninterrupted access to, and communication with, the Committee, otherwise the right of individual petition is rendered nugatory. It is interesting to note by way of comparison that Article 25 of the European Convention on Human Rights, which enshrines the right of individual application to the Strasbourg institutions, also extracts from those High Contracting Parties who recognize the right an undertaking 'not to hinder in any way the effective exercise of this right'. This is buttressed by the European Agreement of 6 May 1969 relating to Persons Participating in Proceedings of the European Commission and Court of Human Rights, especially Article 3. This article imposes on States a duty to respect the rights of persons who take part in proceedings before the Commission to correspond freely with the Commission. As far as persons under detention are concerned the exercise of the right implies that if their correspondence is examined by the competent authorities, its dispatch and delivery shall nevertheless take place without undue delay and without alterations. Thus *at most* passive censorship is lawful. The European Commission has developed an impressive jurisprudence on the *effective exercise* of the individual right of petition. Problems have arisen especially in relation to prisoners' access in the European experience. There seems little doubt, therefore, that by analogy, the Committee should also ensure the effective exercise of the right of individual communication by the insertion of a suitable further rule in the provisional rules of procedure.[155]

[154] Ibid. at p. 120.
[155] See Mikaelson, *European Protection of Human Rights* (Sijthoff & Noordhoff, 1980) for a full discussion of the European case law.

Equally, the Committee has gone out of its way to afford to a State party the opportunity to deliver a full refutation of allegations. In the case of *Bleier* v. *Uruguay*,[156] one of the principal issues was what had happened to Eduardo Bleier. The authors (the victim's wife and daughter) alleged and produced information that he had been arrested, detained and tortured by the governmental authorities. The Government had only responded by stating that a warrant had been issued for his arrest but that his whereabouts was unknown. In its interim decision, the Committee decided:

. . . the failure of the State party to address in substance the serious allegations brought against it and corroborated by unrefuted information, cannot but lead to the conclusion that Eduardo Bleier is either still detained, incommunicado, by the Uruguayan authorities or has died while in custody at the hands of the Uruguayan authorities.[157]

The Government replied alleging that the Committee had displayed not only an ignorance of legal rules relating to presumption of guilt, but a lack of ethics in carrying out its tasks. Again, the Committee categorically rejected such a criticism. It stated:

The Human Rights Committee cannot accept the State party's criticism that it has displayed an ignorance of legal rules and a lack of ethics in carrying out the tasks entrusted to it or the insinuation that it has failed to carry out its task under the rule of law. On the contrary, in accordance with its mandate under Article 5 (1) of the Optional Protocol, the Committee has considered the communication in the light of the information made available to it by the authors of the communication and by the State party concerned. In this connexion the Committee has adhered strictly to the principle *audiatur et altera pars* and has given the State party every opportunity to furnish information to refute the evidence presented by the authors.[158]

It is perfectly clear from the case law that the Committee has gone out of its way to afford to a State party every chance to furnish evidence in defence of the allegations. Indeed, the cases are replete with examples of the Committee allowing Uruguay (in particular) repeated extensions of the time-limits for submissions, in an effort to afford *every* opportunity to refute allegations. The concessions on the time-limits, stipulated in Article 4 (2) of the Protocol, afforded to State parties are probably justified on the grounds of flexibility, despite the fact that they may result in an undue and sometimes intolerable delay for the author, since in principle decisions will be better informed and the views of the Committee will carry greater weight if seen to be balanced with appropriate submissions in defence. Thus it seems that late submissions should be and are taken into account by the Committee. Furthermore, being as generous as is possible

[156] Comm. no. R.7/30.
[157] *GAOR*, 37th Session, Supplement 40, Report of the Human Rights Committee, pp. 134–5.
[158] Ibid., p. 135.

THE RIGHT OF INDIVIDUAL COMMUNICATION   243

to States, commensurate with the rights of a petitioner, can only encourage States to believe that they will get an impartial hearing from the Committee. This will encourage confidence in the system.

Nevertheless, there comes a point beyond which the Committee is not prepared to wait in the interests of justice to the author. In its very first final decision in *Massera* v. *Uruguay*,[159] where no detailed reply to the substance of the allegations was received by July 1979, when the formal time-limit had expired in August 1978, the Committee decided to proceed to deliver its final views in August 1979. The Committee made what was in effect a default judgment. It accepted the facts alleged by the author as proved in the absence of any controverting evidence. This decision was necessary because otherwise the whole optional procedure could be brought to a halt by the recalcitrance of States.[160] Such an approach would seem to place due weight on the Committee's responsibility to petitioners and, therefore, ultimately on the success of the whole procedure. As such, its justification is secure.

However, the overall principle guiding the Committee when considering communications under Article 5 (1) of the Protocol remains one of offering the maximum possible opportunity to the State to furnish evidence. It was summarized by the Committee in the following way in *Quinteros* v. *Uruguay*:[161]

> In accordance with its mandate under Article 5 (1) of the Optional Protocol, the Committee has considered the communication in the light of the information made available to it by the author of the communication and by the State party concerned. In this connection, the Committee has adhered strictly to the principle *audiatur et altera pars* and has given the State party every opportunity to furnish information to refute the evidence presented by the author.[162]

The Committee's response to the many occasions when it has been faced with an outright refusal or an inadequate attempt by a State party to provide it with the written information required by Article 4 (2) of the Protocol once again shows up the strength of the Committee's commitment to the protection of human rights. The general principles underlying the Committee's approach were clearly stated in the *Quinteros* case.[163] It said:

> The State party appears to have ignored the Committee's request for a thorough inquiry into the author's allegations. The Committee reiterates that it is implicit in Article 4 (2) of the Optional Protocol that the State party has the duty to investigate in good faith all allegations of violation of the Covenant made against it and its authorities, especially when such allegations are corroborated by evidence

---

[159] Comm. no. R.1/5.
[160] Similar problems have arisen in other cases and have been dealt with similarly by the Committee. See, e.g., *Millan Sequeira* v. *Uruguay* (Comm. no. R.1/6).
[161] Comm. no. 107/1981.
[162] *GAOR*, 38th Session, Supplement 40, Report of the Human Rights Committee, p. 223.
[163] Loc. cit. above (n. 161).

submitted by the author of the communication, and to furnish to the Committee the information available to it. In cases where the author has submitted to the Committee allegations supported by substantial witness testimony . . . and where further clarification of the case depends on information exclusively in the hands of the State party, the Committee may consider such allegations as substantiated in the absence of satisfactory evidence and explanations to the contrary submitted by the State party.[164]

This approach was emphatically endorsed and carried one stage further in *Bleier* v. *Uruguay*.[165] Here, the Committee declared: 'With regard to the burden of proof, this cannot rest alone on the author of the communication, especially considering that the author and the State party do not always have equal access to the evidence and that frequently the State party alone has access to relevant information.'[166] This view represents the constant jurisprudence of the Committee and was, for example, fully endorsed in *Larrosa Bequio* v. *Uruguay*,[167] *Marais* v. *Madagascar*[168] and *Conteris* v. *Uruguay*.[169]

There can be little doubt that such a courageous approach, while not reversing the normal burden of proof completely, goes some considerable distance in outflanking deliberately obstructive tactics by a State party, the sole objective of which is simply to deny the petitioner access to information by which he may establish a prima-facie case. By stipulating an equivalent burden of proof on the State concerned, it is hoped that the Committee may prevent a State from shielding its violations behind a veil of impenetrability. Such a positive stance from the Committee can only be welcomed, especially in the experience of the recalcitrance of some States, notably Uruguay.

As well as dealing with this issue on the general level, the Committee laid down concrete guide-lines in some of the early cases in which it delivered final views. These definite indications of what is required from a State party under Article 4 (2) of the Protocol represent its established jurisprudence. As mentioned above, in the *Massera* case,[170] where no information had been provided, the Committee did not find any difficulty in proceeding to formulate its final views. In *Santullo* v. *Uruguay*,[171] the Committee found Uruguay's response under Article 4 (2) of the Protocol to be totally inadequate. It contained no explanations concerning the merits of the *specific* case. The Committee declared that a refutation of the allegations raised in general terms was totally insufficient. The allegations themselves should have been investigated.

[164] *GAOR*, 38th Session, Supplement 40, Report of the Human Rights Committee, p. 223. See also *Jaona* v. *Madagascar* (Comm. no. 132/1982) for a briefer endorsement of this principle, and *Baboeram et al.* v. *Suriname* (Comm. nos. 146/1983 and 148 to 154/1983) for an almost identical enunciation.

[165] Loc. cit. above (p. 242 n. 156). See also *Romero* v. *Uruguay* (Comm. no. 85/1981).

[166] *GAOR*, 37th Session, Supplement 40, Report of the Human Rights Committee, p. 135.

[167] Comm. no. 88/1981.

[168] Comm. no. 49/1979. The facts of this case were very similar to those in the case of *Wight* v. *Madagascar* (Comm. no. 115/1982).

[169] Comm. no. 139/1983.   [170] Loc. cit. above (p. 243 n. 159).   [171] Comm. no. R.2/9.

THE RIGHT OF INDIVIDUAL COMMUNICATION   245

In *Lanza* v. *Uruguay*,[172] the Committee confirmed its jurisprudence in *Santullo* that denials of a general character are totally insufficient to rebut specific allegations of violations. What were required were *specific* responses and *pertinent* evidence. A similar view was taken by the Committee in *Torres Ramirez* v. *Uruguay*.[173] In *Millan Sequeira* v. *Uruguay*,[174] the Committee informed Uruguay that when it made its submissions under Article 4 (2) of the Protocol, they must relate to the substance of the matter under consideration, and in particular the *specific* violations alleged to have occurred. It also requested copies of any court orders or decisions of any relevance. In *Grille Motta* v. *Uruguay*,[175] the Committee declared:

> A refutation of [the] allegations in general terms is not sufficient. The State party should have investigated the allegations in accordance with its laws and its obligations under the Covenant and the Optional Protocol and brought to justice those found to be responsible.[176]

This case law has been constantly reaffirmed by the Committee. The cases display a systematic and coherent approach to building up a logical and complete case law on particular issues. However, the Committee has on occasion been driven to launch an unveiled attack on a State party's failure to co-operate. Whether or not such an aggressive step is desirable, it occurred in the case of *Oxandabarat Scarrone* v. *Uruguay*.[177] In this case (as in many others) the Committee had repeatedly asked Uruguay to enclose copies of any relevant court decisions taken in respect of Mr Oxandabarat Scarrone. No documents were disclosed in spite of these requests. The Committee protested:

> In these circumstances and considering that the State party has never offered any explanation as to why the documents in question have not been made available to [the Committee], the failure to produce these documents inevitably raises serious doubts concerning them. If reasoned decisions exist, it is not understandable why such pertinent information is withheld. The lack of precise information seriously hampers the discharge of the functions of the Committee under the Optional Protocol.[178]

The achievements of the Committee may also be gauged against the effect of its final views under Article 5 (4) of the Optional Protocol. The first success achieved by the Committee was in *Waksman* v. *Uruguay*,[179] in which after its decision on admissibility the Committee was informed by Uruguay that it had instructed its appropriate consulate abroad to issue the author with a new Uruguayan passport. The Committee was thus able

---

[172] Comm. no. R.2/8.
[173] Comm. no. R.1/4.
[174] Comm. no. R.1/6.   [175] Comm. no. R.2/11.
[176] *GAOR*, 35th Session, Supplement 40, Report of the Human Rights Committee, p. 136.
[177] Comm. no. 103/1981.
[178] *GAOR*, 39th Session, Supplement 40, Report of the Human Rights Committee, p. 157.
[179] Comm. no. R.7/31.

to discontinue consideration of the communication. By notes dated 31 May and 10 July 1984 the Government of Uruguay furnished the Secretary-General of the UN with lists of persons released from imprisonment with the request that these lists be brought to the attention of the Committee. The lists included the names of two persons whose cases had been considered and concluded by final views of the Committee—Alberto Altesor and Ismael Weinberger Weisz. From other sources, the Committee heard of the relese of José Luis Massera, Lillian Celiberti, Rosario Pietraroia and Rita Ibarburu by Uruguay, all of whose cases had been considered by the Committee. The Committee was also informed in 1984 of the release of Dave Marais by the Malagasy authorities and his subsequent departure from Madagascar following the completion of his sentence.

Furthermore, when forwarding its views to a State party, the Committee invites the State party to inform it of any action taken pursuant to its views. Canada informed the Committee on 6 June 1983,[180] with regard to the *Lovelace* case, of its commitment to remove from its Indian Act any provisions which discriminate on the basis of sex. Mauritius informed the Committee on 15 June 1983[181] with regard to the *Mauritian Women* case, that the allegedly discriminatory legislation on grounds of sex had been amended by the Immigration and Deportation Amendment Acts of 1983. Finland informed the Committee on 20 June 1983[182] of special measures it had taken in response to the Committee's views in the *Hartikainen* case. It is also interesting to observe that, by a note delivered to the Committee by a representative of the Malagasy Government on 19 July 1985, the Government apologized for being unco-operative in the case of *Jaona* v. *Madagascar*,[183] and promised to co-operate more fully with the Committee in the future. Thus, although the Committee has no executive powers to enable it to enforce its views, in this way the Committee is able to monitor the implementation of its decisions.

It is also interesting to note that at the twenty-fourth session of the Committee held in New York from 25 March to 12 April 1985, a representative of the Government of Uruguay conveyed a message to the Committee from the Minister for Foreign Affairs of that country. Referring to the solemn announcement of the Government of Uruguay regarding its intention to observe faithfully the provisions of the Universal Declaration of Human Rights, 1948, and of *all* international human rights instruments, the message listed a variety of measures that had already been taken to that end. The message also stressed the appreciation of the people of Uruguay for the close attention the Committee had given to communications from Uruguay. In reply the Committee indicated that it

[180] *GAOR*, 38th Session, Supplement 40, Report of the Human Rights Committee, pp. 249–53.
[181] Ibid., p. 254.
[182] Ibid., pp. 255–6.
[183] Comm. no. 132/1982.

hoped this message showed that Uruguay had embarked on a new path towards full compliance with the Covenant.[184]

Has the Committee any power under the Optional Protocol to take any further action in cases which have already been concluded by the adoption of *final* views or declared inadmissible? The problem has arisen because, in a number of cases, authors have requested the Committee to take additional steps to persuade the allegedly delinquent State to act in conformity with the views expressed by the Committee. In other cases which have been concluded by a declaration of inadmissibility, authors have asked for a review. This question was discussed by the Committee at its seventeenth session. After much discussion, the view of the Committee was that, in general, its role in the examination of a case comes to an end either when final views are adopted or when a final declaration of inadmissibility is made. In wholly exceptional cases the Committee may agree to reconsider its final decision. It was agreed that this could only occur when the Committee is satisfied that new facts have been put before it by a party claiming that these facts were not available to it at the time of the consideration of the case and that these facts would have materially altered the final decision of the Committee.[185]

It is suggested that this conclusion represents a fair balance between the need to prevent the Optional Protocol machinery from degenerating into an 'exercise of futility'[186] and, on the other hand, the need to reassure States that there is no danger that the Committee will add additional obligations and procedures to the Optional Protocol, beyond that formally contained therein, which would make States 'think twice before ratifying the Optional Protocol'.[186] Furthermore, it reinforces the conclusion that the Committee is anxious to be seen to be confirming its judicial character, since most tribunals limit revision in a similar way to situations where material new facts have emerged.

One of the most disturbing difficulties faced by the Committee is the problem of delay. Since the Committee, which meets three times a year, must allow both the author and the State party enough time to prepare their submissions, a decision on admissibility can only be taken between six months and one year after the initial submission. Views under Article 5 (4) of the Protocol may follow one year later. The Committee, keen to act as expeditiously as possible, aims to complete the procedure within two or three years. The Committee is helped in its task by Working Groups on Communications (consisting of not more than five of its members) which submit recommendations to the Committee on the action to be taken at various stages in the consideration of each case. In a number of cases, the Committee has also designated individual members to act as Special

---

[184] See also the plaudits awarded to the new Government of Uruguay in *Conteris* v. *Uruguay* (Comm. no. 139/1983).

[185] *GAOR*, 38th Session, Supplement 40, Report of the Human Rights Committee, pp. 93–4.

[186] Ibid. at p. 93.

Rapporteurs, who place their recommendations before the Committee for consideration. Nevertheless, unconscionable delays may occur. In the case of *Drescher Caldas* v. *Uruguay*,[187] the final views of the Committee were expressed some four years after its decision on admissibility. A delay of three and a half years before a decision on the merits is not uncommon. Such delays cannot but damage the prestige of the Committee in the eyes of the petitioner. However, the appropriate solution to this difficulty is far from clear.

The problem of delay is inextricably bound up with a very heavy and rapidly increasing workload that is being thrust upon the Committee. The Committee is certainly aware of these difficulties. Some members believe that the present workload has reached saturation point. How the Committee (and the Secretariat) will cope in future with the unremitting flow of cases to it will have to be seen. Of course, if the Committee were somehow to admit *oral* evidence, these problems would only become more acute. At present, under the terms of the Optional Protocol, the Committee is confined to an evaluation in the light of all written information. In 1979 the Committee discussed whether it would be possible to hear witnesses or to inspect any relevant object with the consent of the State party concerned.[188] Mr Tomuschat, commenting on this discussion, has observed:

> To enlarge thus the circle of means of proof would entail a multitude of problems. Above all: can the stage of taking evidence take place differently according to the greater or lesser degree of preparedness of the State party concerned to allow for additional methods of proof? And how could the Human Rights Committee itself, being a body composed of experts in the service of the U.N. on a part-time basis only, cope with such a burden of work? In any event, these questions will become more urgent as proceedings progressively attain a higher degree of complexity.[189]

V. Evaluation

John P. Humphrey wrote in 1973 that 'the conclusion must be . . . that while a really independent, courageous and imaginative Human Rights Committee may be able to build on the highly circumscribed base provided by the Covenant and Protocol, the enforcement procedures which they contemplate are weak'.[190] The Human Rights Committee has been bold and imaginative. Generally, whenever the Protocol has been silent on a particular point, the Committee has sought to fill the legal vacuum. Whenever the terminology in the Protocol has been capable of

---

[187] Comm. no. 43/1979.

[188] UN Doc. CCPR/C/SR.138, paras. 105–21.

[189] 'Evolving Procedural Rules: The UN Human Rights Committee's First Two Years of Dealing with Individual Communications', *Human Rights Law Journal*, 1 (1980), p. 249 at pp. 254–5.

[190] 'The International Law of Human Rights in the Middle Twentieth Century', in Bos (ed.), *The Present State of International Law and Other Essays* (Deventer, 1973), p. 75 at p. 88.

THE RIGHT OF INDIVIDUAL COMMUNICATION   249

differing interpretations, the Committee has invariably opted for that offering the greater measure of protection to the human rights of individuals in international law. The Committee has used the limited base of the Covenant and Protocol to etch for itself a significant place in the hierarchy of international organs active in the field of protection of human rights. Its prestige and authority are now very well established.

Some years ago Professor Humphrey declared: 'what is needed, and what does not yet exist, is some effective and orderly machinery whereby the actual victims whose rights have been violated can bring their complaints before some United Nations body on their own initiative for objective consideration in an atmosphere of judicial impartiality'.[191] Although, of course, in no sense a court of law, the Committee has striven to be seen to be acting in a way as nearly as possible similar to that in which a court of law acts. As Christian Tomuschat has aptly remarked:

> The Human Rights Committee has managed to make 'views' under Article 5 (4) of the Optional Protocol an efficient tool of its evaluation. None of the decisions hitherto handed down reads like a communiqué. Obviously, they have all been drafted on the pattern of a judicial decision. After an accurate description of the facts of the case and of the proceedings before the Human Rights Committee, legal reasons are set out. In a final operative part a precise enunciation of the violations having occurred is given, coupled with the invitation to the Government concerned to take immediate steps in favour of the victims.[192]

He concludes:

> Legally, the views formulated by the Human Rights Committee are not binding on the State party concerned which remains free to criticize them. Nonetheless, any State party will find it hard to reject such findings in so far as they are based on orderly proceedings during which the defendant party had ample opportunity to present its submissions. The views of the Human Rights Committee gain their authority from their inner qualities of impartiality, objectiveness and soberness. If such requirements are met, the view of the Human Rights Committee can have a far-reaching impact, at least *vis-à-vis* such governments which have not outrightly broken with the international community and ceased to care any more for concern expressed by international bodies. If such a situation arose, however, even a legally binding decision would not be likely to be respected.[192]

Sean McBride has made the criticism that UN Committees are not ideal bodies to be charged with implementation because they are subject to political and ideological idiosyncrasies.[193] As far as the Human Rights Committee is concerned, such fears have in large measure proved

    [191] 'The Revolution in the International Law of Human Rights', *Human Rights*, 4 (1975), p. 205 at p. 213.
    [192] Loc. cit. above (p. 248 n. 190), at p. 255.
    [193] 'The Strengthening of International Machinery for the Protection of Human Rights', in Eide and Schou (eds.), *Proceedings of the Nobel Symposium on the International Protection of Human Rights* (Stockholm, 1967).

250   THE HUMAN RIGHTS COMMITTEE AND

groundless. Manfred Nowak has summarized the Human Rights Committee's experience in this regard thus:

> In contrast to political U.N. bodies . . . and also to other committees of experts, the Human Rights Committee has succeeded surprisingly in avoiding political confrontations. It strives for *consensus* in all questions, and up to now no decision has been reached by a majority vote . . . The amicable, co-operative and restful atmosphere does not seem to be directed exclusively towards the outside . . . Despite the above mentioned tendency to avoid political confrontations, one can readily identify different theoretical and ideological approaches to the question of international measures of implementation. Those differences have almost exclusively emerged between East and West as concerns the issue of the Committee's power regarding the examination of state reports—and much less between North and South *or with respect to other functions such as the consideration of communications from individuals.*[194] The latter fact is a cause for particular surprise in view of the negative attitude of many states towards international procedures for dealing with individual complaints.[195]

Many writers have called for the creation of an International or Universal Court of Human Rights. The origins of a *positive* suggestion in favour may perhaps be traced to a proposal first advanced by Australia at the Paris Peace Conference in 1946 and to the suggestion of the Australian representative, Colonel Hodgson, at the Human Rights Commission in 1947. It was never discussed in detail. In 1950 the Commission on Human Rights failed to refer a proposal regarding implementation by international jurisdiction to the International Law Commission. In 1961 the Colombian representative to the Sixth Committee of the General Assembly proposed that the question of the establishment of an International Tribunal for the protection of human rights be put on the agenda for the 1962 session of the General Assembly. In 1968 the issue of an International Court of Human Rights was discussed by Judge Elias of the International Court of Justice, in a paper delivered to the International Conference on Human Rights.[196] Furthermore, in October 1970 President Kaunda of Zambia, speaking to the General Assembly of the UN, said: 'the creation of an international tribunal to deal with complaints against violations of human rights must be given serious consideration'.[197] However, no one put the suggestion more eloquently than Sir Hersch Lauterpacht. Rejecting the conclusion he himself had reached earlier, that such a court would be unsound and impracticable, in 1950 he boldly declared:

> In the matter of the fundamental rights of man the remedy is not complete—it is defective—unless in the last resort a judicial remedy is available . . . This means

---

[194] Emphasis added.
[195] 'The Effectiveness of the International Covenant on Civil and Political Rights—Stocktaking after the first eleven sessions of the UN Human Rights Committee', *Human Rights Law Journal*, 1 (1980), p. 136 at pp. 163–5.
[196] A/CONF.32/L.3.   [197] *GAOR*, 25th Session, Plenary Meetings, 1872nd meeting.

THE RIGHT OF INDIVIDUAL COMMUNICATION   251

that in the long run an International Court of Human Rights must be regarded as an essential part of the Bill of Rights.[198]

The creation of such a court would need to solve a host of intractable problems, beyond the scope of this paper. However, detailed suggestions have been made by some, such as MacBride[199] and Das.[200] In essence, it has been suggested that the jurisdiction of such a court could be twofold. It could have ordinary or first instance jurisdiction and an appellate jurisdiction over regional courts of human rights, such as the Inter-American Court of Human Rights or the European Court of Human Rights. In essence, the claim for such a court is founded on the twin necessities of the independence and objectivity of any tribunal called upon to decide issues relating to the international protection of the rights of individuals.

Whatever the merits or demerits of the suggestion for the creation of such a court, it is tolerably clear that the UN is still not ready for it. Furthermore, it does not necessarily follow that the regional Court of Human Rights, which has been so successful in Europe, could be imitated at the international level. Equally, it is arguable that the experience of the Human Rights Committee shows that the creation of such a court is not necessarily the *sine qua non* of the effective protection of human rights at the international level. The Committee has shown itself more than capable of defending the rights of the individual in the international forum. Its success may raise issues about the necessity to establish such a court. Even if, in the last resort, such an institution is both a desirable and an achievable objective, the Human Rights Committee can 'hold the fort' in the meantime. To date, it has emerged with flying colours. It is hoped that these colours will never be lowered.

[198] *International Law and Human Rights* (F. A. Praeger, New York, 1950), pp. 194 and 382.
[199] Loc. cit. above, p. 249 n. 194.
[200] 'Some Reflections on Implementing Human Rights', in Ramcharan (ed.), *Human Rights Thirty Years after the Universal Declaration* (Martinus Nijhoff, 1979).

[2]

INDIVIDUAL HUMAN RIGHTS COMPLAINTS PROCEDURES BASED ON UNITED NATIONS TREATIES AND THE NEED FOR REFORM

A.   Introduction

The right of individuals to complain about alleged violations of their human rights to expert bodies established under United Nations human rights instruments is one of the major achievements of UN efforts aimed at the protection and promotion of human rights. Three such expert committees currently implement treaty-based individual complaints procedures: the Human Rights Committee under the Optional Protocol to the International Covenant on Civil and Political Rights (since 1977); the Committee on the Elimination of Racial Discrimination (CERD) pursuant to Article 14 of the International Convention on the Elimination of All Forms of Racial Discrimination (since 1982); and the Committee against Torture under Article 22 of the Convention against Torture and Other Forms of Cruel, Inhuman and Degrading Treatment (since 1988). Article 77 of the Convention on the Rights of Migrant Workers and Their Families, which will enter into force three months after the 20th ratification of the Convention, adds another procedure to this panoply.

Of these procedures, that under Article 14 of the Convention on the Elimination of All Forms of Racial Discrimination has seldom been resorted to since 1982; few communications have thus far been considered and disposed of by CERD.[1] While only 14 States have recognised CERD's competence to consider complaints under Article 14 of the Convention, one may nonetheless wonder why the procedure has been used so sparingly; CERD intends to investigate ways and means to encourage the submission of individual complaints.[2]

The procedure under Article 22 of the Convention against Torture became operative in the spring of 1988, and several cases have since been considered by the Committee against Torture,[3] which continues, in that particular aspect of its activities, to explore new terrain.

With some degree of simplification, individual complaints registered under one of the above procedures are considered in three stages.

---

* Senior Lecturer in Law, University of Dundee.

1. See Case No.1/1984 (*Yilmaz-Dogan* v. *The Netherlands*), opinion of 10 Aug. 1988; and No.2/1989 (*D.T. Diop* v. *France*), opinion of 18 Mar. 1991.

2. See CERD/C/SR.934 (23 Aug. 1991), p.14.

3. See e.g. communications 1 to 3/1988 (*O.R., M.M. and M.S.* v. *Argentina*), decision of 23 Nov. 1989; 5/1990 (*W.J.* v. *Austria*), decision of 20 Nov. 1990; 4/1990 (*E.G.* v. *Turkey*), decision of 29 Apr. 1991.

(1) Pre-admissibility: this involves the preliminary screening of every complaint by the Communications Section of the UN Centre for Human Rights, based in Geneva, whose staff routinely ascertains whether the complaints received raise issues under any of the relevant instruments. If a *prima facie* case is deemed to have been made by the applicant, his complaint will be transmitted to the State party, which will be given a specific time limit for the submission of its observations and comments on the admissibility of the communication.

(2) Adoption of a decision on admissibility or inadmissibility, as the case may be. At this stage, it must be determined whether the applicant has exhausted all available domestic remedies; whether the claim is not being examined by another instance of international investigation or settlement (such as the European Commission of Human Rights or the Inter-American Commission on Human Rights); whether the claims are sufficiently substantiated; and whether they are compatible with any of the rights protected by the relevant instrument.

(3) Consideration of the substance of cases previously declared admissible.

Undoubtedly, the procedure under the Optional Protocol to the International Covenant on Civil and Political Rights has developed into the most visible and most effective of all the complaints procedures administered by human rights treaty bodies. Since the entry into force of the Optional Protocol on 23 March 1976, some 500 cases have been registered under the procedure; consideration of 134 communications has been concluded by the adoption of meritorious decisions (so-called "Final Views" under Article 5, paragraph 4, of the Optional Protocol); 140 cases have been declared inadmissible; 73 have been discontinued; and about 150 communications are currently pending.[4]

The 25th anniversary of the adoption of the Covenants and the Optional Protocol (16 December 1966) is an appropriate opportunity to take stock of the effectiveness of the treaty bodies' implementation of individual complaints procedures and to formulate a number of recommendations for the future. Furthermore, it is likely that the forthcoming World Conference on Human Rights, to be convened in 1993, will devote an appreciable amount of its discussions to the issue of enhanced implementation of human rights instruments by treaty bodies; this is laid down in paragraph 1(c) of General Assembly Resolution 45/155 of 18 December 1991,[5] and was reiterated by several delegations to the first meeting of the Preparatory Committee for the World Conference in September 1991.[6]

Proposals for a more effective implementation of UN human rights instruments abound. By Resolution 1989/47, the UN Commission on Human Rights requested the Secretary-General to "entrust an independent expert with the task of preparing a study ... on possible long-term approaches to enhancing the effective operation of existing and prospective bodies established under United

---

4. Statistical survey as of 29 Apr. 1992.

5. Pursuant to this para., one of the Conference aims is to "examine ways and means to improve implementation of existing human rights standards and instruments".

6. See Statement of the Delegation of the Netherlands, on behalf of the European Community, 10 Sept. 1991 (mimeo); Statement of the Delegation of Norway, on behalf of the Nordic States, 10 Sept. 1991 (mimeo).

Nations human rights instruments".[7] The independent expert, Professor Philip Alston, presented his report in November 1989, formulating a number of recommendations concerning reporting obligations by States parties, monitoring of compliance with obligations assumed under the various instruments, and more effective standard-setting procedures.[8] Significantly, the study devotes little attention to possibilities of improving the functioning of existing complaints procedures.

At the regional and especially the European level, procedural reform of complaints procedures has received considerable attention for several years. Thus, Protocol No.8 to the European Convention for the Protection of Human Rights and Fundamental Freedoms, adopted in March 1985, was designed to improve and in particular expedite the procedure of the European Commission of Human Rights. Under it, the Commission may set up chambers, each composed of seven members; these may examine petitions submitted under Article 25 of the Convention "which can be dealt with on the basis of established case law or which raise no serious question affecting the interpretation or application of the Convention". Similarly, the Commission may set up committees, each composed of at least three members, who may declare inadmissible by unanimous vote cases manifestly devoid of substance.[9] Furthermore, the right of individuals to seise the European Court of Human Rights under narrowly circumscribed circumstances has been accepted. Finally, the Steering Committee for Human Rights has been actively considering a draft Protocol No.10 to the Convention, which would amend Article 32 of the Convention, by replacing the qualified two-thirds majority for decisions in the Committee of Ministers by a simple majority requirement.

Undoubtedly, procedural reforms are equally possible for existing UN human rights treaty bodies. They deserve increased attention, as treaty-based complaints procedures move towards universal acceptance, and an ever increasing number of complaints is channelled year after year into the appropriate procedures. Implementation of UN human rights conventions and resolutions through processing of complaints has been among the high visibility activities of the organisation's human rights programme, and treaty bodies must anticipate future developments and prepare procedurally and structurally to cope with vastly increased workloads, resulting from the much-fought-for and soon-to-be-achieved universality of their respective procedures.

The work of the Human Rights Committee under the Optional Protocol to the Covenant on Civil and Political Rights is a case in point. As of 6 May 1992, 65 States had ratified the Protocol, most recently Australia, Russia (formerly the Soviet Union), Estonia, Poland, Lithuania, Angola, Bulgaria, Cyprus, Benin and the Seychelles; others have expressed their intention of doing so in the foreseeable future or are studying the possibility of ratification.[10] Since 1987 the number of complaints has not only grown exponentially, the cases themselves have also

---

7. Res. 1989/47 (6 Mar. 1989), para.5, in Doc.E/1989/20, pp.119–121.
8. See Doc.A/44/668 (8 Nov. 1989).
9. European Convention on Human Rights, *Collected Texts—1987* (1987), pp.58–62.
10. These States include Belgium, the Republic of Belarus (formerly Byelorussian Soviet Socialist Republic) and Romania.

tended to become more legally complex. While many of the Committee's decisions adopted during the early years of operation concerned human rights violations which were relatively easy to pinpoint from a legal point of view, such as ill-treatment of political prisoners or arbitrary detention, the Committee has since been called upon to examine, for instance, discriminatory aspects of social security legislation in certain countries, or the economic aspects of the enjoyment of minority rights.[11] Procedural flexibility and innovation are called for if the Committee is not to become a victim of its own success.

B. *Procedural Amendments Introduced by the Human Rights Committee*

The Committee has endeavoured to meet this challenge through a series of procedural amendments. These are designed primarily to enable it to consider more cases in the course of its three annual sessions and, secondarily, to address situations of particular urgency.

In the autumn of 1987 the Committee nominated a Special Rapporteur for Cases involving Capital Punishment, with the power to take action on behalf of the Committee, even between sessions and at extremely short notice, in urgent cases involving the death penalty. Similarly, the institution, in the spring of 1989, of the mandate of a Special Rapporteur for New Communications was designed to enable quick action on new communications, which are screened by the Special Rapporteur in consultation with the Committee's secretariat and, wherever appropriate, sent to the State party for observations on admissibility. If the Special Rapporteur considers a communication manifestly inadmissible, he may directly refer his recommendation to the Committee plenary. Finally, the Committee's Working Group on Communications may, since the summer of 1989, declare a communication admissible if all five members of the Working Group so agree.[12] In the summer of 1989, the Committee amended its rules of procedure to reflect these procedural changes.[13]

All these measures enable the Committee to devote more time to the consideration of final decisions, i.e. decisions of inadmissibility and decisions on the merits. Notwithstanding, recent statistics show that these changes are insufficient, and a growing backlog in the considerations of pending cases has opened the Committee to charges of "justice delayed is justice denied". Thus, in previous years, an average of two years passed between receipt of a communication and a final decision; today, consideration of a communication frequently averages four to five years. This means that the advantage of "speedy disposal" of complaints, in comparison to other regional complaints procedures, in particular at the European level, is slowly disappearing.

---

11. See e.g. Views on communication No.182/1984 (*Zwaan-de Vries* v. *Netherlands*), adopted on 9 Apr. 1987, in *Selected Decisions of the Human Rights Committee under the Optional Protocol*, Vol.II, pp.209–214; Views on communication No.197/1985 (*Kitok* v. *Sweden*), Doc.CCPR/C/33/D/197/1985.

12. Rule 87, para.2, of the Committee's amended rules of procedure reads: "A Working Group established under rule 89, paragraph 1, may also declare a communication admissible when it is composed of five members and all the members so decide."

13. For details see Schmidt (1989) 4 Interights Bull. 27–30.

C.   *Joinder of Admissibility and Merits*

One means of shortening the time of consideration presents itself in cases in which the parties have already, at the admissibility stage, made such substantial submissions as to allow the Committee to adopt a decision on the merits. The Committee's current rules of procedure do not allow for the simultaneous consideration of admissibility and merits: accordingly, the Committee has suggested to the parties that it disposes of all the necessary information and that it will adopt a final decision at its next session if no further information is received. If the parties accept, the time gains may be considerable; as they retain the right to furnish further information, however, the number of decisions adopted under this "accelerated procedure" has been limited indeed,[14] since States parties seldom waive their right to submit additional observations on the merits of a complaint.

The Committee, and other treaty bodies implementing comparable procedures, should therefore consider the following suggestion for streamlining the procedure: whenever a complaint meets all the admissibility criteria but clearly would be dismissed on the merits, the body seised should be in a position to dispose of the case by joining considerations of admissibility and merits. This could be done through simple amendment to the rules of procedure of the relevant body.[15] It is worth noting that this possibility is expressly provided for at the European level, in Article 27, paragraph 2, of the European Convention for the Protection of Human Rights and Fundamental Freedoms: the European Commission annually disposes of a large percentage of complaints received by declaring them inadmissible as "manifestly ill-founded". Time has come to endow UN treaty bodies with similar powers.

Similar considerations apply to situations where the treaty body was furnished by the parties concerned with all the necessary information to enable it to dispose of the substance: in the absence of objections from the parties, it should be empowered to address considerations of admissibility and of substance simultaneously. This solution is an equitable one; moreover, it would free both Secretariat resources and valuable Committee time, thereby expediting the examination of other complaints.

D.   *Follow-Up Mechanisms*

One of the principal lacunae of the implementation machinery established for UN human rights instruments remains the lack of appropriate enforcement or follow-up mechanisms. Decisions adopted by treaty bodies under the various procedures lack legal enforceability, such as the judgments of the European Court of Human Rights. Treaty bodies are frequently kept in the dark as to what the

---

14. The first communication thus decided was No.198/1985 (*Stalla Costa* v. *Uruguay*), paras.7.4 and 8, views adopted on 9 July 1987: see *Selected Decisions, op. cit. supra* n.11, at pp.221–223.

15. Rule 91 of the rules of procedure of the Human Rights Committee could be amended by addition of the following para.: "5. The Committee may decide to discontinue consideration of a communication which, although meeting the criteria for admissibility, reveals no facts or issues which warrant further consideration on the merits. A decision to discontinue consideration of a communication in such circumstances shall be taken by the Committee in plenary."

650   *International and Comparative Law Quarterly*   [VOL. 41

addressee of a decision or recommendation has done to implement them. Admittedly, the Human Rights Committee has been informed by a number of States parties that they did amend national legislation in response to the Committee's views, or awarded compensation to victims of violations of rights protected by the Covenant on Civil and Political Rights,[16] but the record of compliance remains remarkably incomplete. During the early years of its existence, the Committee seldom enquired of States parties as to the measures taken to implement its Views.

Creating new and strengthening existing follow-up mechanisms are necessities if governments and public opinion are to keep faith in the effectiveness of the treaty bodies' implementation machinery. The issue of "follow-up" should therefore be put squarely on the agenda of the forthcoming World Conference on Human Rights: with the emergence of what may be termed a more "human rights-orientated" conscience, the legitimacy for States to deny treaty bodies the conduct of follow-up activities in instances where they have found human rights violations is being further eroded.

An effective and flexible system of follow-up on human rights violations would be one step towards the recognition of legally binding decisions adopted by UN human rights bodies. The treaty bodies and in particular the Human Rights Committee consider that it is time to look for appropriate mechanisms to make their decisions legally binding and thus enforceable. So as to strengthen any follow-up mandate, one might envisage amendments to the respective treaty-based instruments. In the case of the Human Rights Committee, for instance, Article 5 of the Optional Protocol could be amended by insertion of an additional paragraph 5: "States parties to the present Protocol undertake to comply with the Committee's final Views."[17]

1.   *Human Rights Committee*

The first treaty body to institute a formal follow-up mechanism has indeed been the Human Rights Committee. At its 39th session in July 1990, it instituted the mandate of a Special Rapporteur for the Follow-Up on Views, i.e. decisions on the merits adopted under the Optional Protocol.[18] The first responses from States parties to requests for follow-up information from the Special Rapporteur have been encouraging; yet, at the same time, they display a certain reticence on the part of States parties to accept the Committee's decisions as legally binding—

16. See e.g. *Selected Decisions, op. cit. supra* n.11, at pp.224–226; *Annual Report of the Human Rights Committee, 1990* (A/45/40), Vol.II, Annex XII, pp.207–211.

17. This proposal was made by Ms Christine Chanet, member of the Human Rights Committee, in a background paper for the preparation of the World Conference on Human Rights, and taken up in a background paper of the Committee's Working Group on Art.40 of the Covenant, prepared during the Committee's 42nd session in July 1991.

18. The first Special Rapporteur on Follow-Up of Views is Dr Janos Fodor of Hungary. See *Annual Report, op. cit. supra* n.16, Vol.I, at pp.144–145, Vol.II, at App.XI; CCPR/C/SR.1063/Add.1 (16 Apr. 1991), paras.6–15; *Law Society's Gazette* (London), 28 Nov. 1990, pp.11–12.

compensatory payments to victims of human rights violations, it was emphasised in some of the government replies, were made *ex gratia*.

2. Fact-finding powers

Committee members have emphasised the necessity of endowing the Special Rapporteur with all the necessary powers to perform his mandate effectively. At this point in time, it is too early to draw conclusions from his experience. In the future, it would be desirable to strengthen the Special Rapporteur's powers by, for example, granting him fact-finding capabilities, in particular wherever States parties refuse to implement a final decision or simply ignore repeated requests for follow-up information. Furthermore, other treaty bodies such as the Committee against Torture or the Committee on the Elimination of Racial Discrimination would be well advised to emulate the example of the Human Rights Committee.

If such "fact-finding powers" would be a procedural novelty, they are still compatible with the mandate entrusted to the Committee under the Optional Protocol ("implied powers"). The preamble to the Optional Protocol declares that the Committee receives and considers communications "in order to achieve the purposes of the Covenant and the implementation of its provisions". It does not bar the Committee from engaging in exchanges, by whatever means, with States parties about their reaction to the Committee's Views. The International Court of Justice has held that even in the absence of specific enabling powers, an international body may act in ways not specifically forbidden, so as to ensure the attainment of its purposes and objectives.[19] Further, the word "consider" need not be taken as meaning consideration only until the moment of adoption of final Views, but consideration in the sense of engaging in those tasks deemed necessary to ensure implementation of the Covenant's provisions.

3. Publication of annual follow-up reports

Finally, so as to increase the visibility of the follow-up activities described above, they should be included in the annual reports of the treaty bodies concerned; the Human Rights Committee, for instance, has decided to include a summary on its follow-up activities under the Optional Protocol in its future annual reports.[20] Such publicity would be further enhanced by the publication of an annual report on follow-up activities under treaty-based complaints procedures, which would summarise and analyse *all* the follow-up activities conducted under UN auspices.

E. Delays Caused by Written Proceedings and Possible Remedies

Individual complaints procedures implemented by UN human rights treaty bodies are currently written procedures: no provision is made for oral hearings or independent fact-finding. This, it must be admitted, has caused considerable delays in the consideration of many factually or legally complex communications, since the treaty body concerned was forced to engage in time-consuming

---

19. See *Case of Certain Expenses* I.C.J. Rep. 1962.
20. See CCPR/C/SR.1063/Add.1 (16 Apr. 1991), para.15.

exchanges of correspondence with either of the parties before disposing of the necessary information enabling it to adopt a decision.[21] More seriously, the unavailability of relevant information may have resulted in decisions which were, either in law or in fact, incomplete or misleading.

Two solutions are conceivable to remedy this unsatisfactory situation: first, the institution of a system of Special Rapporteurs for particularly complex or contentious cases or categories of cases, and, second, provision—however carefully circumscribed—for oral hearings.

1. *Special Rapporteurs*

The nomination of Special Rapporteurs for individual cases is not unknown in the practice of the regional human rights bodies: it is, for instance, a general practice in the European Commission of Human Rights and used for particularly complex cases in the Inter-American Commission on Human Rights. The Human Rights Committee has, in the past, appointed Special Rapporteurs for particularly contentious cases or certain categories of cases. It should be acknowledged, however, that its practice in this respect has been experimental and *ad hoc*; moreover, it was resorted to only when the Committee's debates were threatened with deadlock, and when it was clear that no consensus was emerging on the proposed solution. Notwithstanding, it enabled the Committee to dispose of the complaints in question in a timely and satisfactory manner, and its experience provides useful lessons for the future.

It is suggested that treaty bodies should institutionalise the system of Special Rapporteurs for legally or factually complex communications or categories of cases. The Special Rapporteurs should be assisted by the Secretariat as appropriate and be able to research complaints properly, pinpoint legal issues and investigate the factual situation. Where necessary, a Special Rapporteur should be entitled to investigate the facts *in situ*, as well as to initiate direct contacts with the parties for purposes of information gathering. It is arguable whether this form of fact-finding would not require an amendment to Article 5, paragraph 1, of the Optional Protocol, which provides that the Committee shall consider communications "in the light of all *written* information made available to it by the individual and by the State party concerned". It may, however, be assumed that, in practice, the Special Rapporteur would succeed in obtaining rapid *written* clarifications in reply to his requests for information.

Upon conclusion of his investigations, the Special Rapporteur would, again with Secretariat assistance, prepare a draft decision for consideration by the Committee. This procedure would have a twofold advantage: first, it would economise valuable plenary meeting time, as the Committee could focus exclusively on the legal issues involved in any given case. Second, it would obviate the need for the body concerned to request additional written information from either of the parties. If the Special Rapporteur system does not altogether

---

21. A much-cited example is communication No.167/1984 (*B. Ominayak and the Lubicon Lake Band* v. *Canada*), submitted to the Human Rights Committee on 14 Feb. 1984, and concluded on the merits on 26 Mar. 1990; the final decision was adopted on the basis of a total of 78 documents, fact sheets and conference room papers submitted by the parties or prepared by the Secretariat, as well as decisions adopted by the Committee.

eliminate the potential of factually or legally questionable decisions, it certainly reduces the danger of such decisions being adopted.

2. *Oral hearings*

The provision for oral hearings presents more serious problems. In the past, treaty bodies rejected this possibility because it was feared that such a practice would open the proverbial "Pandora's box", as it would have to be extended to each and every case, thus creating logistical problems and "agenda crunches" that only a standing body could be expected to cope with. More important, in the case of the Human Rights Committee, provision for oral hearings would *prima facie* appear to be incompatible with Article 5, paragraph 1, of the Optional Protocol; if one considers, however, that oral hearings would in practice serve primarily to clarify the significance of written information already made available to the Committee by the parties concerned, it is possible to argue, as in the case of the follow-up competence of treaty bodies, that the doctrine of implied powers justifies the resort to oral hearings. In fact, several States parties and authors have in the past offered to present oral clarifications in the Committee plenary, from which it may be deduced that oral hearings would not be challenged as an *excès de pouvoir*.

In the case of the other treaty bodies, the question does not arise with the same acuity: Article 14, paragraph 7(a), of the Convention on the Elimination of All Forms of Racial Discrimination, and Article 22, paragraph 4, of the Convention against Torture merely stipulate that the Committee shall consider communications "in the light of all information made available to it" by the parties.

It is beyond question that the consideration of many communications would benefit from the parties' oral testimony or clarifications. The "judicial economy" of the procedure would benefit through considerable shortening of the time frame in which a complaint may be adjudicated; so would the "legal cogency" of decisions, as the presence of the parties during consideration of the merits of a complaint could serve to dispel doubts or misunderstandings, on the part of the treaty body concerned, about the operation of the legislation, the regulations or the State practice that is being challenged. Many States parties may not, however, be prepared to accept the resort to oral hearings by human rights treaty bodies at this point in time. This consideration undoubtedly carries weight and makes it necessary to circumscribe carefully the provision for oral hearings by these bodies. This could be done, for example, by stipulating that a treaty body must decide unanimously on the appropriateness of oral hearings.

F.   *Duplication of Complaints to Treaty Bodies*

Another issue which deserves increased attention concerns possible conflicts of competence between two or more treaty bodies, for example between the Human Rights Committee and the Committee on the Elimination of Racial Discrimination or the Committee against Torture. Many complaints in fact simply contain a request for UN intercession, without specifying the body to be seised of the matter. To take an extreme example, which body should consider the complaint, received by the Secretariat, of a migrant worker alleging ill-treatment, on account of national origin, of his children: the Human Rights Committee, the Committee on the Elimination of Racial Discrimination, the Committee against Torture, or the (future) Committee on Migrant Workers and Their Families?

No guidelines for the handling of complaints falling within the competence of two or more treaty bodies are presently available. The Secretariat generally informs applicants about possible options, and if they opt for a specific forum, the matter is settled in this way. Where the complainant's intentions cannot be ascertained, the Secretariat normally channels the communication into the procedure which appears to offer the most appropriate avenue of redress. The situation is simple if the case concerns a State which is party to only one of the existing complaints procedures: the competent treaty body will then be seised of the matter. A decision is more difficult if the State is party to two or more instruments which may be relevant. The latter scenario has been put before the chairmen of the treaty bodies on the occasion of their recent meetings in Geneva.[22] It is in the framework of these consultations that solutions to potential conflicts of competence should be sought and stricter guidelines formulated.

G.   Criteria to Determine the Competent Body

As a rule of thumb, a communication potentially addressing the competence of two treaty bodies should be considered in the light of the "proximity" of the claim to their respective mandates. This requires a *prima facie* legal evaluation of the complaint by the UN Secretariat: a complaint primarily raising issues of torture or ill-treatment should be registered under Article 22 of the Convention against Torture; a complaint essentially raising issues of discrimination based on national origin should be considered by the Committee on the Elimination of Racial Discrimination; and other complaints by the Human Rights Committee. For purposes of the determination of the most appropriate forum, the Secretariat could submit appropriate cases to a co-ordinating group composed of, say, one member of each treaty body: this group would determine the competent body.

If the previous suggestions may be criticised as an overly academic exercise based on hypothetical considerations, they help solve the question about the possibility of sequential consideration of a complaint by two treaty bodies. It has indeed been suggested that the prohibition of cumulative consideration of complaints (see, for instance, Article 5, paragraph 2(a), of the Optional Protocol to the International Covenant on Civil and Political Rights) does not apply to procedures of international investigation or settlement for complaints of human rights violations.[23] Where the substantive law applicable to the claim differs, one could in fact conceive that the complainant might successively seise different treaty bodies of the same claim.

On the basis of the above suggestions, however, this possibility would be excluded: if the appropriate forum has been determined by a co-ordinating group composed of experts from the treaty bodies, a final decision of the body considering the claim is dispositive of the matter. Any treaty body subsequently seised of the claim may invoke the principle of *res judicata*.

---

22. See Doc.A/44/98 (3 Feb. 1989); Doc.A/45/636 (30 Oct. 1990).

23. This solution appears to be advocated by M. Nowak, *UNO-Pakt über bürgerliche und politische Rechte und Fakultativprotokoll (CCPR-Kommentar)* (1989), commentary on Art.5 of the Optional Protocol, No.9, p.783.

H. Advisory Opinions

It is conceivable that the courts of States parties to UN human rights instruments are requested, in the course of criminal, civil or administrative proceedings, to decide on the applicability of selected provisions of these instruments. Treaty bodies do not currently have the power of handing down what might be called advisory opinions or interpretative rulings on the application of UN human rights instruments. The question is in fact an old one: a report submitted to the Commission on Human Rights in 1950 addressed the issue of whether the future Human Rights Committee should be entitled to request advisory opinions on its own initiative. The Secretary-General, at the time, concluded that the Committee would not be competent to do so, but that it could instruct an organ properly authorised to request advisory opinions, such as the General Assembly or the UN Secretariat, to take into account its recommendations and suggestions.[24]

As human rights instruments move towards universal acceptance and as the place of international human rights standards in domestic legal and constitutional systems is increasingly recognised, it is both desirable and possible to provide for such a competence. In this context, Article 177 of the Treaty of Rome could provide some guidance for UN treaty bodies;[25] the jurisprudence of the Court of Justice of the European Communities under this provision is an eloquent testimony to the power of such interpretative rulings.

There are, of course, differences between advisory opinions within the meaning of Article 65 of the Statute of the International Court and interpretative decisions handed down by the European Court under Article 177 of the Treaty. The former are designed to assist the political organs of the UN in settling disputes and to give authoritative (but non-binding) guidance on questions of law that may arise in the context of the functioning of UN organs and specialised agencies. They require the consent of the parties involved, and while the International Court has taken a broad view of Article 65 of its Statute, objections to the Court's power to deal with political questions have been numerous.[26]

On the other hand, the Article 177 procedure may be initiated by any court of a EC member State; it is designed to induce national courts to apply the law in a way compatible with the European Court's *interpretation* of the Treaty of Rome and of secondary legislation. While the Court has emphasised that it may rule on the interpretation of the Treaty, it cannot apply the law to a given case, and cannot decide on the compatibility of domestic law with EC law. Article 177 rulings are thus binding in respect of the hypothetical application of EC law *in the circumstances* specified by national courts.[27]

---

24. Cited by Schwebel in J. Makarczyk (Ed.), *Essays in International Law in Honour of Judge Manfred Lachs* (1984), pp.519–529, at p.520.

25. In its relevant section, Art.177 of the EEC Treaty reads: "Where [a question of interpretation of the Treaty] is raised before any court or tribunal of a Member State, that court or tribunal may, if it considers that a decision on the question is necessary to enable it to give judgment, request the Court of Justice to give a ruling thereon."

26. Brownlie, *Principles of Public International Law* (3rd edn, 1979), pp.728–730.

27. Judgment in *Costa* v. *ENEL* [1964] E.C.R. 585, 593; see Wyatt and Dashwood, *The Substantive Law of the EEC* (1980), pp.56–71.

656   *International and Comparative Law Quarterly*   [VOL. 41

In the context of human rights complaints procedures, consideration should be given to affording domestic courts harbouring doubts about the applicability of a human rights treaty provision to a given case the ability to suspend their proceedings and refer the matter to the competent human rights treaty body, for formulation of an advisory opinion or an interpretative ruling.

It is clear that such a solution would require an amendment to the relevant instrument, or an additional Optional Protocol. Notwithstanding, the benefits would be manifold. Treaty bodies would be enabled to give authoritative interpretations on the provisions of the instrument whose implementation they supervise. The prospect of "direct applicability" of UN human rights standards would be enhanced; and the courts of States parties would be placed in a position where they can provide effective judicial redress in disputes which hitherto required the complainant to seise an international instance of investigation or settlement of his or her claim. Where the issue referred to a UN human rights treaty body concerns the interpretation of substantive rights falling within the competence of two or several bodies (e.g. prohibition of discrimination; torture or other forms of cruel, inhuman and degrading treatment), the treaty bodies concerned could envisage the possibility of handing down joint advisory opinions or interpretative rulings.

I.   *Alternative Decision-Making Mechanisms*

All the human rights bodies implementing individual complaints procedures operate on the basis of consensus; decisions under the various procedures are taken by consensus.[28] The increasing resort to consensual procedures in the negotiation of UN instruments and in the adoption of decisions and resolutions in UN forums may be traced to the mid-1960s.[29] Indeed, in the law-making process, proceeding by consensus has its undoubted merits, as majority voting conjures up the danger of calling into play what Barry Buzan has termed "powerful alienated minorities". One may ponder, however, whether in the context of human rights implementation mechanisms and the consideration of individual human rights complaints by expert bodies, consensus remains the most appropriate form of decision-making.

The rules of procedure of the treaty bodies do not prescribe consensus as the *modus operandi* for the consideration of complaints. In practice, treaty bodies have opted for a consensual procedure because they have considered it the most opportune way of avoiding deadlock attributable to unspoken but nonetheless existing political alignments in the plenary. One may hypothesise about the reasons for such alignments, and the former East–West confrontation that long bedevilled the work of UN human rights bodies provides no doubt part of the explanation.

The operation of consensus in such instances has sometimes contributed to the gradual watering down of the legal context of decisions: as it is sufficient for one expert to oppose strongly a draft text otherwise acceptable to all the others, the search for consensus not only necessitates protracted consultations about a com-

---

28. Art.161, para.8(e), of the UN Convention on the Law of the Sea defines consensus as "the absence of formal objection".

29. For an interesting analysis of the development of consensual procedures in UN forums, see Buzan (1981) 75 A.J.I.L. 324–348.

promise text, it has also occasionally resulted in final decisions in which the close observer will find it difficult to follow the thread, or the logic, of the legal argument.[30]

J.   Individual Opinions

As political alignments in treaty-based human rights forums are becomingly increasingly rare and as East–West confrontation appears to be relegated to the drawers of history, it is appropriate to consider alternative decision-making mechanisms. In this context, the recent practice of the Human Rights Committee may provide some guidelines: over the past three years, its members, rather than formally insisting upon the adoption of decisions by consensus, have increasingly resorted to the formulation of individual opinions which are appended to the Committee's decisions. Thus, out of 34 final decisions adopted between the 37th and 39th sessions (October 1989 to July 1990), ten had a total of 14 individual opinions appended to them.[31]

This development should be seen as a positive one, and it has not diminished the authority of the Committee's decisions; it merely reflects the fact that in complex factual and legal situations, concerning for example the issue of enjoyment of minority rights or alleged discrimination in social security matters, deciding by consensus has become a mere fiction. One close observer of the Committee's practice has even contended that the increased use of individual opinions reinforces the quasi-judicial character of the procedure.[32]

Notwithstanding, the search for consensus still applies to the consideration of the majority of cases, thus frequently necessitating protracted debates and at times causing a loss of cogency of the legal argument.

K.   Resort to Majority Voting

Under individual complaints procedures, the treaty bodies should therefore consider the bold step of abandoning the practice of consensus and adopt their decisions on the basis of majority voting instead. Majority decisions would generally improve the quality of decisions and, far from eroding their authority, contribute to the enhancement of their standing. No one would, for instance, question the authority of judgments handed down by a narrow majority of the US Supreme Court, the German Constitutional Court or the European Court of Human Rights, and UN human rights treaty bodies need not be afraid to emulate the practice of these bodies. The provision for individual opinions still enables those experts who disagree with the majority to formulate and publicise their dissenting views. In the final analysis, majority voting may help treaty bodies to

---

30. One example is the decision in communication No.204/1986 (*A.P.* v. *Italy*), adopted on 2 Nov. 1987, para.7.3, in *Selected Decisions, op. cit. supra* n.11, at pp.67–68; similarly, the decision of the Human Rights Committee in *Lubicon Lake Band, supra* n.21, has been criticised as having fallen victim of the search for consensus.

31. See *Annual Report, op. cit. supra* n.16, Vol.II, Table of Contents, at pp.vii–ix; no less than four individual opinions were appended to the inadmissibility decision on Communication 354/1989 (*L.G.* v. *Mauritius*), adopted on 31 Oct. 1990; see *Annual Report of the Human Rights Committee, 1991* (A/46/40), Annex XII.K.

32. See Cohen-Jonathan, in *Mélanges René-Jean Dupuy* (1991), pp.83–97, at p.92.

658   *International and Comparative Law Quarterly*   [VOL. 41

rid themselves of the slight opprobrium of implementing merely "quasi-judicial procedures", and constitute one step towards the recognition of their decisions as legally binding.

L.   *Permanent Court or Standing Body?*

Lastly, it would also be appropriate to evaluate whether the time has not come to reflect on the institution of standing bodies, or one standing UN "superbody", to consider and adjudicate individual complaints under the existing procedures. Under the Optional Protocol, for instance, the number of communications will soon assume such unmanageable proportions that only a standing body would be able to dispose of them in a timely manner. In the long run, an expert body meeting, on the average, three times a year for a total of nine weeks cannot be expected to perform this task satisfactorily.

At present, few governments would endorse the creation of a standing body with the power to adjudicate complaints. Indeed, this could well become a deterrent for the ratification of, or accession to, a number of human rights instruments by States investigating this possibility. While a standing body without the power to adopt *binding* decisions might conceivably be a justifiable step in a time of increased efforts for the international protection of human rights, the political implications of accepting a powerful UN human rights judiciary remain too daunting for many governments seriously to envisage steps in this direction now.

Finally, the composition of standing bodies or *one* superbody poses difficult problems: should the terms of office be modelled on those of the International Court of Justice, or should there be shorter elective terms? A survey of the current membership of treaty bodies reveals that most experts carry heavy professional responsibilities, be it in academia, in diplomatic or in government service, that would appear to be difficult to reconcile with their participation in a panel of eminent jurists sitting permanently.[33] Such problems must be addressed and solved if, as would be desirable, a future standing body is to be composed of individuals with the highest qualifications. In this context, it would be necessary to create a number of established but elective posts at an appropriately senior level for the prospective members of a standing body,[34] similar to those of the judges of the International Court of Justice.

The World Conference on Human Rights provides a timely opportunity to examine the arguments for and against the institution, in the UN framework, of a standing human rights body or international court of human rights, as well as the scope of its powers. It is to be hoped that it will also address, in the context of debates on improvements of treaty-based procedures, some of the other issues

---

33. The apparent irreconcilability with professional obligations currently seems to be a major argument of experts against their participation in a standing body. In the alternative, they would appear to favour shorter elective terms of one to two years.

34. The judges of the ICJ are nominated at the level of Under-Secretary-General.

examined in this article—if it does, it will be a considerable step towards making UN human rights complaints procedures more effective and preparing for the challenges of the next century.

MARKUS G. SCHMIDT*

[3]

Evolutive Interpretation and Subsequent Practice
Interpretive Communities and Processes in the Optional Protocol to the ICESCR

Diane A. Desierto*/Colin E. Gillespie**

Abstract

The entry into force on 5.5.2013 of the Optional Protocol to the International Covenant on Economic, Social and Cultural Rights (ICESCR) augurs significant developments for the principle of "evolutionary interpretation" in relation to subsequent practice in the application of a treaty under Article 31(3)(b) of the Vienna Convention on the Law of Treaties. The ICESCR, by treaty design and expressed intent of the States Parties, is one such treaty that purposely embraces an evolving meaning and content (see fundamental obligations under Article 2(1) ICESCR) that treaty interpreters are tasked to continually and contemporaneously assess when determining State compliance with obligations to respect, fulfill, and protect economic, social, and cultural rights. The passage and entry into force of the Optional Protocol to the ICESCR establishes three key procedures – an individual/group communications procedure, an extensive and far-reaching inquiry procedure, and a unique inter-State communications procedure not found in the treaty

---

* Assistant Professor University of Hawaii, William S. Richardson School of Law, Honolulu, United States of America. J.S.D., LL.M. (Yale Law School); J.D. (BSc Economic, University of the Philippines).

** C.V. Starr Lecturer-in-Law, Peking University School of Transnational Law, China; incoming Law Clerk, U.S. Court of Appeals 2nd Cir. N.Y. ; J.D. (New York University School of Law); B.A. (Eng., Northwestern University).

procedures under the International Covenant on Civil and Political Rights (ICCPR).

We theorize that these new procedures in the Protocol meaningfully situate the principle of evolutionary interpretation in this treaty regime in three concrete ways. First, the Protocol purposely accepts the inherent dynamism of ICESCR norms in the process of determining State responsibility, and accordingly embraces States' "margin of discretion" over the "reasonableness" of means adopted to comply with the ICESCR obligations, similar to the interpretive positions already extant from regional and national jurisprudential practices. Second, the Protocol deliberately expands the epistemic, forensic, and law-applying communities that may bear upon the interpretive process for determining State responsibility over ICESCR violations. Finally, the Protocol's new inter-State procedure rejects the hard adversarial paradigm prevalent in inter-State dispute settlement processes, in favor of an inclusive and cooperative process focused on realigning or changing State policy to reach conformity with the ICESCR, rather than the standard forms of reparation under the general law of State responsibility. The horizontal design of the Protocol's inter-State procedure thus appears to incentivize, rather than coerce, compliance with the ICESCR.

I. Introduction: From Authentic Elements of Interpretation to "Evolution"

> *"Should the events of yesterday ever have the law of to-day applied to them? ... 'generic clauses' and human rights provisions are not really random exceptions to a general rule. They are an application of a wider principle – intention of the parties, reflected by reference to the objects and purpose – that guides the law of treaties."*
>
> Dame Rosalyn Higgins[1]

> *"The practice of evolutionary interpretation is another expression of the art of judging, which is constantly balanced between providing for stability based on respect for the principle of autonomy of the will of the parties, and a quest for the necessary flexibility to keep a treaty afloat by meeting the objectives it was designed to address."*
>
> Prof. Pierre-Marie Dupuy[2]

> *"The importance of [...] subsequent practice in the application of the treaty, as an element of interpretation, is obvious; for it constitutes evidence of the understanding of the parties as to the meaning of the treaty."*
>
> International Law Commission[3]

Interpretation inimitably involves a process of decoding the authoritative exegesis for any given text. Scholars of semiotics refer to the task of interpretation as an inevitable struggle for control over meaning, while avoiding the dangers of "overinterpretation" of texts.[4] Similarly concerned about the

---

[1] *R. Higgins*, Time and the Law: International Perspectives on an Old Problem, ICLQ 46 (1997), 501 et seq., at 507 and 519.

[2] *P.-M. Dupuy*, Evolutionary Interpretation of Treaties: Between Memory and Prophecy, 124 et seq., at 137, in: E. Cannizzaro (ed.), The Law of Treaties Beyond the Vienna Convention, 2011.

[3] International Law Commission, Commentaries to the Draft Articles on the Law of Treaties (1966), Yearbook of the International Law Commission, 1966, Vol. II (hereafter, ILC Commentaries on the VCLT), 219, paras. 6, 15, 221.

[4] See *U. Eco*, Interpretation and Overinterpretation, 1992, 40 ["... there are somewhere criteria for limiting interpretation. Otherwise we risk facing a merely linguistic paradox ..."];

hazards of limitless interpretation within the international legal canon, the International Law Commission (ILC) codified the integral rule of treaty interpretation under Article 31 of the Vienna Convention on the Law of Treaties (VCLT) to set the boundaries of permissible interpretation of treaty texts.[5] The customary nature of Article 31 VCLT has since become a well-established and generally accepted rule in international jurisprudence.[6]

However, the codification of Article 31 VCLT did not reduce treaty interpretation into a formulaic procedure. Even within the terms of Article 31 VCLT as a "single, closely integrated rule",[7] the ILC nevertheless created specific gateways for treaty interpreters to consider external rules and juridical phenomena arising subsequent to the conclusion of a treaty, deemed to be "authentic elements of interpretation".[8] Article 31(3) VCLT thus enumerates three such rules and phenomena that treaty interpreters may take into account together with context: 1) "any *subsequent agreement* between the parties regarding the interpretation of the treaty or the application of its provisions";[9] 2) "any *subsequent practice* in the application of the treaty which establishes the agreement of the parties regarding its interpretation";[10] and 3) "any *relevant rules of international law* applicable in the relations between the parties".[11] By including these provisions in Article 31 VCLT, the ILC rejected any static or hermetic interpretation of treaties, but also omitted providing detail on the operational parameters governing such

---

52 ["…we can accept a sort of Popperian principle according to which if there are no rules to help to ascertain which interpretations are the 'best' ones, there is at least a rule for ascertaining which ones are 'bad'."]; 63 et seq. ["The classical debate aimed at finding in a text either what its author intended to say, or what the text said independently of the intentions of its author. Only after accepting the second horn of the dilemma can one ask if what is found is what the text says *by virtue of its textual coherence* and of an original underlying signification system, or what the addressees found in it by virtue of their own systems of expectation." (Italics added)].

[5] For a succinct summary of the historical developments of the rule of interpretation under VCLT, Art. 31 and the supplementary rule of interpretation under VCLT, Art. 32, see *J. R. Weeramantry*, Treaty Interpretation in Investment Arbitration, 18 et seq.

[6] *Arbitral Award of 31 July 1989*, Judgment, I.C.J. Reports 1991, 53, at 70, para. 48; *Territorial Dispute (Libyan Arab Jamahiriya v. Chad)*, Judgment, I.C.J. Reports 1994, 6, para. 41; *Maritime Delimitation and Territorial Questions between Qatar and Bahrain*, Jurisdiction and Admissibility, Judgment, I.C.J. Reports 1995, 6, at 18, para. 33; *Oil Platforms (Islamic Republic of Iran v. United States of America)*, Preliminary Objections, Judgment, I.C.J. Reports 1996, 812, para. 23; *Kasikili v. Sedudu Island (Botswana v. Namibia)*, Judgment, I.C.J. Reports 1999, 1045, at 1059, para. 18.

[7] ILC Commentaries on the VCLT, 220, para. 8.

[8] ILC Commentaries on the VCLT, 221 et seq., paras. 14-16.

[9] Vienna Convention on the Law of Treaties, UN Doc. A/Conf.39/27; 1155 UNTS 331 (hereafter, VCLT), Art. 31(3)(a).

[10] VCLT, Art. 31(3)(b).

[11] VCLT, Art. 31(3)(c).

"authentic elements of interpretation" in Article 31(3) VCLT. Not unexpectedly, therefore, the main challenge for treaty interpreters and law-appliers applying Article 31(3) VCLT remains one of ascertaining *which* external rules and subsequent juridical phenomena could fall within the permissible outer limits of treaty interpretation. The cognitive complexity of this question strengthens the ILC's view of treaty interpretation as, ultimately, a process involving "to some extent an art, not an exact science".[12]

Beyond brief descriptions in its 1966 commentaries to the draft articles of the VCLT,[13] the ILC has not yet elaborated criteria to aid treaty interpreters in determining an acceptably legitimate degree of "dynamic" or "evolutionary" interpretation arising from the "authentic elements of interpretation" enumerated in Article 31(3) VCLT. In 2006, the ILC Study Group on the Fragmentation of International Law issued several conclusions on Article 31(3)(c) VCLT (on "relevant rules of international law applicable in the relations between the parties") as a principle of "systemic integration",[14] but the breadth of these conclusions has since been criticized and remains much-disputed within the international legal community.[15] On the other hand, the ILC Working Group on "Treaties over Time/Subsequent Agreements and subsequent practice in relation to interpretation of treaties" has not yet issued any definitive report on Article 31(3)(a) VCLT and Article 31(3)(b) VCLT, although it has considered several oral reports of then "Treaties over

---

[12] ILC Commentaries to the VCLT, 218, para. 4.

[13] ILC Commentaries to the VCLT, 221, paras. 14-16.

[14] See Conclusions of the work of the Study Group on the Fragmentation of International Law: Difficulties arising from the Diversification and Expansion of International Law (2006), Yearbook of the International Law Commission, 2006, Vol. II, Part Two, paras. 17-42.

[15] For the defence of the "principle", see *C. Mclachlan*, The Principle of Systemic Integration and 31(3)(c) of the Vienna Convention, ICLQ 54 (2005), 279 et seq. For critical views of the "principle", see among others *R. Higgins*, A Babel of Judicial Voices? Ruminations from the Bench, 55 ICLQ 4 (2006), 791 et seq., at 796, 803 et seq.; *A. Orakhelashvili*, The Interpretation of Acts and Rules in Public International Law, 2008, 367 ("... 'the principle of systemic integration goes further than merely restate the applicability of general international law in the operation of particular treaties. It points to a need to take into account the normative environment more widely.' But the use of this notion does not by itself clarify the essence of the process, in terms of what is integrated, how and on what conditions. More importantly, integration relates to a result, while interpretation methods definitionally relate to methods and means. From the perspective of the law of interpretation, reference to the relevant rules of international law will in some cases produce the result of integration while in other cases it will not. The positive or negative outcome in each case will in its turn be produced by circumstances more specific to the relevant interpretative method and context than is the general notion of 'systemic integration'. All these factors require some degree of caution in advancing such a far-reaching notion. Although the integration of extraneous rules into a treaty can be an interpretative outcome in some cases, it is certainly not a principle, still less a principle that applies across the board.")

Time" Working Group Chairman *Georg Nolte*[16] and adopted several preliminary conclusions in 2011 and 2012.[17] Following the reconstitution of the
Treaties over Time Working Group into the "Subsequent Agreements and
Subsequent Practice on the Interpretation of Treaties" Working Group, as
of this writing the reconstituted ILC Working Group is considering the
19.3.2013 First Report by Special Rapporteur *Georg Nolte*.[18]

Based on his analytical survey of international jurisprudence in his First
Report, the Special Rapporteur issued four draft conclusions on treaty interpretation and subsequent practice. These conclusions are significant, in
that they are the first recent indications from the ILC on the contemporary
functions of subsequent practice as an authentic element of treaty interpretation. First, the Rapporteur proposed that there could be a "different emphasis on the various means of interpretation contained in Articles 31 and
32 of the Vienna Convention",[19] such as a shift from a primarily textual to
more purposive or teleological interpretation when the treaty authorizes it,
a prominent example of which is the European Convention on Human
Rights.[20] Second, he contended that authentic elements of interpretation

---

[16] International Law Commission, Report of the Sixty-first session (2009), A/64/10,
Chapter XII, (Treaties over Time), paras. 217-226; International Law Commission, Report of
the Sixty-second session (2010), A/65/10, Chapter X, (Treaties over Time), paras. 344-354;
International Law Commission, Report of the Sixty-third session (2011), A/6610, Chapter
XI, (Treaties over Time), paras. 333-344; International Law Commission, Report of the Sixty-
fourth session (2012), A/67/10, Chapter X, (Treaties over Time), paras. 222-240.

[17] International Law Commission, Report of the Sixty-third session (2011), A/6610,
Chapter XI, (Treaties over Time), para. 344, (enumerating nine preliminary conclusions on: 1)
the general rule on treaty interpretation; 2) approaches to interpretation; 3) interpretation of
treaties on human rights and international criminal law; 4) recognition in principle of subsequent agreements and subsequent practice as means of interpretation; 5) concept of subsequent practice as a means of interpretation; 6) identification of the role of a subsequent
agreement; 7) evolutionary interpretation and subsequent practice; 8) rare invocation of subsequent agreements; and 9) possible authors of relevant subsequent practice); International
Law Commission, Report of the Sixty-fourth session (2012), A/67/10, Chapter X, (Treaties
over Time), para. 240, (enumerating six additional preliminary conclusions on: 1) subsequent
practice as reflecting a position regarding the interpretation of a treaty; 2) specificity of subsequent practice; 3) the degree of active participation in a practice and silence; 4) effects of contradictory subsequent practice; 5) subsequent agreement or practice and formal amendment or
interpretation procedures; and 6) subsequent practice and possible modification of a treaty).

[18] G. *Nolte*, Special Rapporteur, First Report on Subsequent Agreements and Subsequent
Practice in Relation to Treaty Interpretation, A/CN.4/660, 19.3.2013, International Law
Commission Sixty-fifth session (2013) (hereafter, Nolte First Report 2013).

[19] Nolte First Report 2013 (note 18), para. 28.

[20] See *J. Christoffersen*, Impact on General Principles of Treaty In)terpretation, Chapter 3,
38 et seq., in: M. T. Kaminga/M. Scheinin (eds.), The Impact of Human Rights Law on General International Law, 2009, (arguing that the method of interpretation of the European
Court of Human Rights, in reality, is "firmly rooted within the traditional canons of interpretation of general international law").

Evolutive Interpretation and Subsequent Practice   555

(such as subsequent practice) "may guide the evolutive interpretation of a treaty",[21] in light of the dispositive reasoning of the International Court of Justice in its 2009 Judgment in *Dispute regarding Navigational and Related Rights (Costa Rica v. Nicaragua)*, which recognized evolutive interpretation as an acceptable method of treaty interpretation within Article 31 VCLT.[22] With respect to the evidentiary threshold for subsequent practice, the Special Rapporteur's third and fourth draft conclusions declared, respectively, that subsequent practice could be evidenced by "conduct, including pronouncements, by one or more parties to the treaty after its conclusion regarding its interpretation or application",[23] and such conduct could be located from "all State organs" as well as "non-State actors ... as far as it is reflected in or adopted by subsequent State practice".[24]

The ILC Special Rapporteur's 2013 draft conclusions on subsequent practice suggest some watershed developments arising from modern treaty-making practices and current trends in the interpretive methods of modern international courts and specialized treaty-based tribunals. They affirm that States might "contract out" of applying the primarily text-based integral rule of interpretation under Article 31 VCLT,[25] through a treaty clause or provision reordering the relative weights of the elements of treaty interpretation in Article 31 VCLT. They also convey the ILC's possible acceptance of conceptual linkages existing between subsequent practice and the method of evolutive interpretation, despite the key distinction that subsequent practice entails the interpretation of a treaty "on the basis of something about the later behavior of the parties", while evolutive interpretation involves "developmental interpretation ... based on some evidence of the original

---

[21] Nolte First Report 2013 (note 18), para. 64.

[22] *Dispute regarding Navigational and Related Rights (Costa Rica v. Nicaragua)*, Judgment, I.C.J. Reports 2009, 213, paras. 63-66, (declaring in particular in para. 66 that "where the parties have used generic terms in a treaty, the parties necessarily having been aware that the meaning of the terms was likely to evolve over time, and where the treaty has been entered into for a very long period or is 'of continuing duration', the parties must be presumed, as a general rule, to have intended those terms to have an evolving meaning").

[23] Nolte First Report 2013 (note 18), para. 118.

[24] Nolte First Report 2013 (note 18), para. 144.

[25] *J. Pauwelyn* maintains that, "by concluding a treaty, states can contract out of or deviate from general international law (other than *jus cogens*). States do so regularly, for example, in the final provisions of treaties on how to amend the treaty (thus contracting out of rules of general international law of treaties) ... The treaty must exclude the rules of general international law that the parties do not want to apply with respect to the treaty, not the reverse (i. e. the treaty does not have to list all such rules that are to apply to it) ... the text of the Vienna Convention does not have to be attached to the new treaty for general international law rules on the law of treaties to be applicable to it ..." *J. Pauwelyn*, The Role of Public International Law in the WTO: How Far Can We Go?, AJIL 95 (2001), 535, at 537.

intention of the parties that the treaty be capable of evolution".[26] Finally, contrary to the traditional view that subsequent practice as an authentic element of treaty interpretation implies a high evidentiary threshold,[27] the 2013 draft conclusions suggest some loosening of this standard in order to enable law-appliers to fully utilize subsequent practice within the interpretive process.[28]

The International Court of Justice's express acceptance of evolutive interpretation in its 2009 Judgment in *Costa Rica v. Nicaragua*, taken together with the abovementioned studies of the ILC Working Group, clearly presage the increasing normative importance of subsequent practice as an authentic element of treaty interpretation. This Article aims to contribute further analysis on evolutive interpretation and subsequent practice by situating both in a distinct treaty regime, namely the International Covenant on Economic, Social and Cultural Rights (hereafter, the Covenant),[29] and its singularly innovative Optional Protocol (hereafter OP-ICESCR) that entered into force on 5.5.2013.[30] In pursuing this project some conceptual clarity might be useful in order to distinguish between the emphasis which a treaty interpreter might give to subsequent practice or the technique of evolutive interpretation as compared to other sources of treaty interpretation laid out in Article 31 VCLT (or what might, given the recent interest in evolutive interpretation, be called "normal" operations of treaty interpretation),

---

[26] *J. Arato*, Subsequent Practice and Evolutive Interpretation: Techniques of Treaty Interpretation over Time and Their Diverse Consequences, The Law and Practice of International Courts and Tribunals 9 (2010), 443 et seq., at 445.

[27] *A. Orakhelashvili* (note 15), 362, ("… subsequent practice under the Vienna Convention has a similar nature and requirements to international law-making in general, whether through agreements, custom, acquiescence or unilateral acts: it has to involve concordance of actions and attitudes. Therefore, it is not surprising that the burden of proof in the case of establishing subsequent practice is as high as in the case of establishing other law-making processes. In the end, it is the treaty which is interpreted and in which the parties place confidence; the proof of any deviation therefrom must meet a high threshold of evidence."); *M. E. Villiger*, Commentary on the 1969 Vienna Convention on the Law of Treaties, 2009, 431 et seq. ("… The active practice should be consistent rather than haphazard and it should have occurred with a certain frequency. However, the subsequent practice must establish the agreement of the parties regarding its interpretation. Thus, it will have been acquiesced in by the other parties, and no other party will have raised an objection.").

[28] See also 8.8.2011 Statement of the Study Group Chairman, Report of the International Law Commission, Sixty-fourth session, A/67/10, paras. 222-240.

[29] International Covenant on Economic, Social, and Cultural Rights, G.A. Res. 2200A (XXI), 21 UN GAOR Supp. (No. 16), 49, UN Doc. A/6316 (1966), (hereafter, ICESCR).

[30] See Statement by Mr. *Ivan Simonovic*, Assistant Secretary-General, Deposit of the 10th Instrument of Ratification of the Optional Protocol to the International Covenant on Economic, Social and Cultural Rights, (hereafter, OP-ICESCR), New York, 5.2.2013, available at <http://www2.ohchr.org>.

and the distinctions developing between an interpretive heuristic which takes for its starting point the evolutive nature of treaty norms as compared to the subsequent practice of states with respect to those norms.

With respect to the first distinction, between evolutive interpretation or subsequent practice and the other modes of interpretation laid out in the general rule of Article 31 VCLT, we would endorse the notion that the rule laid down in the VCLT "must not 'be taken as laying down a hierarchical order' of different means of interpretation contained therein, but that these are to be applied by way of a 'single combined operation'".[31] This single combined operation, in addition, must include consideration of "the terms of the treaty in their *context*, and in light of its object and purpose".[32] The particular notion of context, as an element in the operation of treaty interpretation, has been analyzed in a number of different manners. In one sense it is a question of the place of a treaty term in relation to other terms in the treaty as a matter of textual interpretation, that is to say, a question of how different treaty terms combine to produce meaning. In another sense, in the case of contested meanings, the need to pay attention to context has been read as a requirement to look beyond the text to the "force that makes the treaty – the will behind the text".[33] Accepting those definitions of context, we will advance the view that the importance of context in the instance of the ICESCR is its ability to harmonize particular treaty obligations with the dynamic obligation to "progressively ensure" Covenant rights.

The second distinction that needs to be elucidated in this case is that between techniques of interpretation in the manner of their operation, an interpreter might emphasize the question of the subsequent practice of the parties to a treaty, following Article 31(3)(b) VCLT, or evolutive interpretation, which derives its place in the operation of treaty interpretation from the necessity that treaties be interpreted in light of their "object and purpose", and from a further supposition in a given case that parties to the treaty intended that a treaty term "be capable of evolution".[34] The distinction between the two operations is illustrated by the differences between the majority opinion in *Costa Rica v. Nicaragua*, and the concurring opinion of Judge *Skotnikov*.

The dispute concerned the definition of the term "*comercio*", which appeared in an 1858 treaty that delimited a maritime boundary between the

---

[31] Nolte First Report 2013 (note 18), para. 9.

[32] VCLT, Art. 31(1).

[33] *I. Venzke*, The Role of International Courts as Interpreters and Developers of the Law: Working Out the Jurisgenerative Practice of Interpretation, Loy. L.A. Int'l & Comp. L. Rev. 34 (2011), 99, 111 et seq.

[34] *J. Arato* (note 26), 445.

two states, and which granted Nicaragua sovereignty over the San Juan River, but allowed Costa Rica rights of navigation for commercial purposes.[35] The issue was whether the use of the river for purposes of tourism by Costa Rica fell under the definition of "*comercio*". The majority concluded that it did, basing its decision on the fact that "*comercio*" was a generic term "incorporated into a treaty intended to remain in force in perpetuity".[36] Judge *Skotnikov*, in contrast, concluded that the subsequent practice of Nicaragua, in particular not objecting to Costa Rica's use of the river for purposes of tourism for ten years, indicated that the term had come to include Costa Rica's right to use the river for the purposes of services as well.[37] These differing interpretive frames – evolutive interpretation in light of the object and purpose of parties at the time of drafting and interpretation of treaties in light of the subsequent practice of parties – yield different results in different cases.[38]

The OP-ICESCR offers the opportunity to explore some of the nuances of the operations of treaty interpretation in one specific iteration. The new-found applicability of the individual communications, fact-finding inquiry, and inter-State procedures in the OP-ICESCR,[39] in our view, arguably *institutionalizes* subsequent practice for an inherently *evolutive* treaty such as the Covenant. Beyond the consequentialist arguments that have been articulated thus far in favour of ratifying the OP-ICESCR,[40] we submit that what is more revolutionary from the OP-ICESCR's entry into force is how the new OP-ICESCR procedures before the Committee on Economic, Social, and Cultural Rights, coupled with the well-settled Articles 16 and 17 reportage State process to the Committee, establishes a more distinguishable, centralized, coherent, and publicly available index of relevant subsequent practice of States on the interpretation and application of the Covenant. It is

---

[35] *J. Arato* (note 26), 447. The debate is also summarized in the ILC report. See Nolte First Report 2013 (note 18), paras. 58-61.

[36] *J. Arato* (note 26), 447.

[37] *J. Arato* (note 26), 448.

[38] *J. Arato* (note 26), 448.

[39] OP-ICESCR, G.A. Res. A/RES63/117, 10.12.2008. Full text available at <http://www2.ohchr.org>.

[40] *Beth Simmons* observed in 2009 that OP-ICESCR ratification would provide legal clarity as to the nature of ICESCR obligations, improve treaty implementation and compliance, and open further opportunities for domestic mobilization vindicating economic, social, and cultural rights. See *B. A. Simmons*, Should States Ratify the Protocol? Process and Consequences of the Optional Protocol of the ICESCR, Norwegian Journal of Human Rights 27 (2009), 64 et seq. See also *C. Mahon*, Progress at the Front: The Draft Optional Protocol to the International Covenant on Economic, Social and Cultural Rights, HRLR 8 (2008), 617 et seq.

a distinctly novel situation where subsequent practice concretely features in the purposely-evolutive interpretation of a treaty.[41]

These developments lead us to anticipate that law-appliers will be better equipped to manage and resolve the complex interpretive and evidentiary issues arising from normative uncertainties created by the dynamic nature of the Covenant, which have besieged this treaty regime particularly from the earliest drafting debates.[42] We expect that by cyclically and publicly revealing the crystallizing subsequent practices of States in the implementation and application of the Covenant, the new procedures under the OP-ICESCR could also help defuse continuing criticisms on the supposed manipulability of Covenant obligations.[43] This would eventually lend a fairly more predictable and increasingly participatory dimension for States and non-State actors in the interpretation and application of the Covenant through better-centralized Committee procedures.[44] Finally, we contend that subsequent practice gleaned from the fact-finding and softly adjudicative Committee procedures institutionalized under the OP-ICESCR will

---

[41] See Nolte First Report 2013 (note 18), para. 54, ("The possible legal significance of subsequent agreements and subsequent practice as means of interpretation also depends on the so-called intertemporal law. This concerns the question whether a treaty must be interpreted in the light of the circumstances at the time of its conclusion ['contemporaneous interpretation'], or rather in the light of the circumstances at the time of its application ['evolutive interpretation'] ...").

[42] On the drafting history and conceptual debates surrounding the meaning, content, and implementation of ICESCR obligations, see *M. A. Baderin/R. McCorquodale*, The International Covenant on Economic, Social and Cultural Rights: Forty Years of Development, in: M. A. Baderin/R. McCorquodale, Economic, Social, and Cultural Rights in Action, 2007, 3 et seq. On the evolving conceptual content of the famous triage of State obligations under the ICESCR (the "obligation to respect, to protect, and to fulfill"), see *A. Eide*, Economic, Social and Cultural Rights as Human Rights, Chapter 2, in: A. Eide/C. Krause/A. Rosas (eds.), Economic, Social and Cultural Rights, 2001, 9 et seq., at 30. For observations on the difficulties behind empirical measurement of ICESCR compliance, see *R. E. Robertson*, Measuring State Compliance with the Obligation to Devote the Maximum Available Resources to Realizing Economic, Social, and Cultural Rights, HRQ 16 (1994), 693.

[43] *K. G. Young*, The Minimum Core of Economic and Social Rights: A Concept in Search of Content, Yale J. Int'l L. 33 (2008), 113, at 116, (arguing that absent clear interpretation, the concept of minimum core obligations under the ICESCR "cannot supply a predetermined content to economic and social rights, rank the value of particular claims, or offset the level and criteria of state justification required for a permissible infringement ... it is unlikely that the concept will ever offer the relative determinacy required for these three states"). For similar criticisms in constitutional discourses on the interpretation and application of socio-economic rights, *E. Rosevear/R. Hirschl*, Constitutional Law Meets Comparative Politics: Socio-economic Rights and Political Realities, in: T. Campbell/K. D. Ewing/A. Tomkins (eds.), The Legal Protection of Human Rights: Sceptical Essays, 2011.

[44] See *P. Alston*, Out of the Abyss: The Challenges Confronting the New U.N. Committee on Economic, Social and Cultural Rights, HRQ 9 (1987), 332, (on the early structural challenges identified at the inception of the Committee).

not just "guide", but ultimately, shape the evolutive interpretation of the Covenant and control against its unjustified and limitless "overinterpretation".

We show in Part II (The Covenant and Inherently Evolutive Interpretation) that the Covenant, by treaty design and expressed intent of the States Parties, is one such treaty that purposely embraces an evolving meaning and content (see fundamental obligations under Article 2 [1] ICESCR) that treaty interpreters are tasked to continually and contemporaneously assess when determining State compliance with obligations to respect, fulfil, and protect economic, social, and cultural rights. The passage and entry into force of the OP-ICESCR establishes three key procedures – an individual/group communications procedure, an extensive and far-reaching inquiry procedure, and a unique inter-State communications procedure not found in the treaty procedures under the ICCPR – which, we theorize, concretely situates the principle of evolutionary interpretation in this treaty regime. The OP-ICESCR purposely accepts the inherent dynamism of Covenant norms in the process of determining State responsibility, and accordingly embraces States' "margin of discretion" over the "reasonableness" of means adopted to comply with Covenant obligations, similar to the interpretive position articulated in the Limburg Principles, and subsequently adopted in the jurisprudence of the European Court of Human Rights and the African Commission on Human and Peoples' Rights "Principles and Guidelines on the Implementation of Economic, Social and Cultural Rights in the African Charter on Human and Peoples' Rights".

In Part III (Evolutive Interpretation and Individual Complaints in the Optional Protocol of the Covenant on Economic, Social and Cultural Rights), we further illustrate how the OP-ICESCR deliberately expands the epistemic, forensic, and law-applying communities that may bear upon the interpretive process for determining State responsibility over Covenant violations. To this end, the Committee on Economic, Social and Cultural Rights is authorized to designate and outsource part of its fact-finding and interpretive functions to Working Groups and Rapporteurs, as well as to accept information and reports from a vast range of governmental and intergovernmental sources (e. g. UN specialized agencies, non-governmental organizations, national governments, among others).[45] The Committee is

---

45 On recent developments in the UN High Commissioner's endorsement of indicators to empirically monitor ICESCR compliance, see Article on Indicators for Monitoring Compliance with International Human Rights Instruments, HRI/MC/2006/7, 11.5.2006, available at <http://hrbaportal.org>; United Nations Office of the High Commissioner for Human Rights, Human Rights Indicators: A Guide to Measurement and Implementation, United Nations 2012, available at <http://www.ohchr.org>. See also *B. Simma/D. A. Desierto*, Bridg-

also vested with significant *proprio motu* evidence-gathering and fact-finding powers well outside the traditional model of the State reportage process in Articles 16 and 17 of the Covenant. The plural sources of information and empirical data now open through the Committee procedures both under the Covenant as well as the OP-ICESCR, in our view, respond well to democratic deficit and legitimacy issues currently afflicting the international human rights fact-finding process.[46]

We conclude in Part IV (Evolutive Interpretation and Inter-State Dispute Resolution in the Optional Protocol of the Covenant on Economic, Social and Cultural Rights), that the OP-ICESCR's new inter-State procedure rejects the hard adversarial paradigm prevalent in inter-State dispute settlement processes, in favour of an inclusive and cooperative process focused on realigning or changing State policy to reach conformity with the Covenant. Rather than adjudicating individual claims for reparations under the general law of State responsibility, this new inter-State procedure seeks to incentivize, rather than coerce, treaty compliance. While the findings elicited from these procedures will certainly not preclude future or parallel resort to individual reparations claims in national courts or other international tribunals, we are also of the view that the reasoned elaboration of decisions involving State responsibility for Covenant violations[47] would henceforth require some recalibration. The interpretive results available in the future from OP-ICESCR procedures would fulfil a gap-filling function for law-appliers, most crucially in regard to the process for determining *legitimate* changes in regard to "evolving" terms within the Covenant.

II. The Covenant and Inherently Evolutive Interpretation

From the earliest treaty drafting debates up to its present implementation,[48] the Covenant has not lacked in perennial challenges against, and

---

ing the Public Interest Divide: Committee Assistance for Investor-Host State Compliance with the ICESCR, in: Essays in Honour of Eibe Riedel, 2012, 1 et seq. reprinted in: Transnational Dispute Management 1 (2013); *J. V. Welling*, International Indicators and Economic, Social, and Cultural Rights, HRQ 30 (2008), 933 et seq.

[46] On these issues, see *P. Alston/C. Gillespie*, Global Human Rights Monitoring, New Technologies, and the Politics of Information, EJIL 23 (2012), 1089.

[47] We observe that the International Court of Justice was quite laconic in its analysis of state responsibility for ICESCR violations, as seen in the *Advisory Wall* opinion. See *Legal Consequences of the Construction of a Wall in the Occupied Palestinian Territory*, Advisory Opinion, ICJ Reports 2004, 136, at paras. 133-134.

[48] See *M. Craven*, The International Covenant on Economic, Social and Cultural Rights: A Perspective on Its Development, 1995; *P. Alston/G. Quinn*, The Nature and Scope of States

scrutiny of, its legal enforceability.[49] While the International Court of Justice has recognized the Covenant as a binding source of international legal obligation in its *Wall* advisory opinion,[50] and States Parties have regularly participated for around four decades in the Committee reportage process required by the Covenant,[51] the programmatic nature of this treaty nevertheless continues to invite some scepticism of the precise determinability of obligations contained therein.[52] For a multilateral treaty almost five decades into existence and global implementation, however, Covenant obligations have, at the very least, arguably gained their place within the *opinio juris* lexicon of its States Parties.[53]

Among the major international human rights treaties, the normative design of Covenant obligations stands out for being purposely evolutive and dynamic. Article 2(1) best capsulizes the evolutive nature of the Covenant, through its cornerstone obligation requiring States Parties to "take steps ... to the maximum of its available resources, with a view to achieving progressively the full realization of the rights recognized in the present Covenant by all appropriate means, including particularly the adoption of legislative measures".[54] As the Committee on Economic, Social and Cultural Rights (hereafter, Committee) emphasized, "while the Covenant provides for pro-

---

Parties' Obligations under the International Covenant on Economic, Social and Cultural Rights, HRQ 9 (1987), 156 et seq.

[49] See among others *M. J. Dennis/D. P. Stewart*, Justiciability of Economic, Social, and Cultural Rights: Should There be an International Complaints Mechanism to Adjudicate the Rights to Food, Water, Housing, and Health?, AJIL 98 (2004), 462 et seq.; *A. Ely Yamin*, The Future in the Mirror: Incorporating Strategies for the Defense and Promotion of Economic, Social and Cultural Rights into the Mainstream Human Rights Agenda, HRQ 27 (2005), 1200 et seq.; *P. O'Connell*, The Death of Socio-Economic Rights, The Modern Law Review 74 (2011), 532 et seq.

[50] Legal Consequences of the Construction of a Wall in the Occupied Palestinian Territory, Advisory Opinion, ICJ Reports 2004, 136, at paras. 133-134.

[51] See *C. Puta-Chekwe/N. Flood*, From Division to Integration: Economic, Social, and Cultural Rights as Human Rights, in: I. Merali/V. Oosterveld (eds.), Giving Meaning to Economic, Social and Cultural Rights, 2001, 39 et seq.

[52] *M. Dowell-Jones*, Contextualising the International Covenant on Economic, Social and Cultural Rights: Assessing the Economic Deficit, 2004, 23.

[53] See *M. A. Baderin/R. McCorquodale* (note 42), 14, ("... there have been considerable debates about the nature and scope of the obligations of ESC rights, both during the forty years of the existence of the ICESCR and beforehand. The essence of the arguments that doubted the nature, the justiciability, and the scope of obligations of ESC rights have, in our view, now all been comprehensively rebutted in the literature and jurisprudence, both through strong conceptual analysis and clear applications of ESC rights."). On recent issues in the implementation of the ICESCR, see Committee on Economic, Social and Cultural Rights, Report on the forty-sixth and forty-seventh sessions, E/2012/22, E/C.12/2011/3, Supplement No. 2 (2012), 439 et seq.

[54] ICESCR, Art. 2(1).

gressive realization and acknowledges the constraints due to the limits of available resources, it also imposes various obligations which are of immediate effect".[55] The principle of non-discrimination in Article 2(2) and the right to equal pay for equal work in Article 7 are examples of Covenant obligations deemed immediately effective upon State Parties from the time of accession to the Covenant.[56]

A State Party's obligation "to take steps" is one that should be "deliberate, concrete, and targeted as clearly as possible towards meeting the obligations recognized in the Covenant,"[57] with the means to be used to fulfil the obligation to take steps being "all appropriate means, including particularly the adoption of legislative measures",[58] which may also include, and are not limited to, "administrative, financial, educational and social measures".[59] This obligation of "result" through progressive realization[60] concedes programmatic flexibility in the State's implementation of Covenant obligations, but does not eliminate the State's duty to "move as expeditiously and effectively as possible" towards realizing Covenant rights, with a further duty to justify any measures that appear "deliberately retrogressive" as compared with the State's previous modes of implementation of, and compliance with, its Covenant commitments.[61] The United Nations High Commissioner for Human Rights operationally regards the principle of non-retrogression to mean that "no right can be permitted deliberately to suffer an absolute decline in its level of realization, unless the relevant duty-bearer(s) can justify this by referring to the totality of the rights in force in the given situation and fully uses the maximum available resources. So when allocating more resources to the rights that have been accorded priority at any given time, the other rights must be maintained at least at their initial level of realization."[62]

---

[55] Committee on Economic, Social and Cultural Rights, General Comment 3 (The nature of States parties obligations [Art. 2, para. 1]), 14.12.1990, para. 1, available at <http://www.unhchr.ch>.

[56] See *U. Khaliq/R. Churchill*, The Protection of Economic and Social Rights: A Particular Challenge?, in: H. Keller/G. Ulfstein (eds.), UN Human Rights Treaty Bodies: Law and Legitimacy, 2012, 199 et seq., at 210.

[57] CESCR General Comment 3 (note 55), para. 2.

[58] CESCR General Comment 3 (note 55), para. 3.

[59] CESCR General Comment 3 (note 55), at para. 7.

[60] CESCR General Comment 3 (note 55), at para. 9.

[61] CESCR General Comment 3 (note 55). Underscoring in the original.

[62] United Nations, Office of the High Commissioner for Human Rights, Frequently Asked Questions on a Human Rights Based Approach to Development Cooperation, 2006, 12.

The classic tripartite typology of State duties to "respect", "protect", and "fulfil" Covenant rights[63] encapsulates both the principles of progressive realization with non-retrogression.[64] The obligation to respect the Covenant "requires States to abstain from performing, sponsoring or tolerating any practice, policy, or legal measure violating the integrity of individuals or infringing upon their freedom to use those material or other resources available to them in ways they find most appropriate to satisfy economic, social and cultural rights".[65] The obligation to protect Covenant rights "requires the State and its agents to prevent the violation of any individual's rights by any other individual or non-State actor",[66] while the obligation to fulfil Covenant rights "requires positive measures by the State when other measures have not succeeded in ensuring the full realization of these rights, [such as] public expenditure, governmental regulation of the economy, the provision of basic public services and infrastructure, taxation and other redistributive economic measures".[67] These three obligations capture the broad spectrum of State Party actions and measures necessary to comply with the Covenant.[68]

Apart from the tripartite typology and the principles of progressive realization and non-retrogression under Article 2(1), a further crucial aspect of the Covenant is its mandatory minimum social protection baseline. As explained by the Committee, States must observe, regardless of resource or material constraints, a "minimum core obligation to ensure the satisfaction of, at the very least, minimum essential levels of each of the rights".[69] A State Party can only justify its failure to meet this minimum core content

---

[63] See "The Right to Adequate Food as a Human Right", Final Report prepared by Special Rapporteur *A. Eide*, E/CN.4/Sub.2/1987/23 (where the tripartite typology was first proposed in the context of the Covenant).

[64] For other key studies that apply the principles of non-retrogression and progressive realization under Art. 2(1) of the Covenant to specific rights, see among others "Realization of Economic, Social and Cultural Rights", Preliminary Report by Special Rapporteur *D. Turk*, E/CN/4/Sub.2/1989/19; Progress Report by Special Rapporteur *D. Turk*, E/CN.4/Sub.2/1990/19; Second Report by Special Rapporteur *D. Turk*, E/CN.4.Sub.2/1991/17; Third Report by Special Rapporteur *D. Turk*, E/CN.4/Sub.2/1992/16; "The Human Right to Adequate Housing", Final Report by Special Rapporteur *R. Sachar*, E/CN.4/Sub.2/1995/12.

[65] See United Nations High Commissioner for Human Rights, Economic, Social and Cultural Rights: Handbook for National Human Rights Institutions, 2005, 15.

[66] United Nations High Commissioner for Human Rights, Economic, Social and Cultural Rights: Handbook for National Human Rights Institutions, 2005, 17.

[67] United Nations High Commissioner for Human Rights, Economic, Social and Cultural Rights: Handbook for National Human Rights Institutions, 2005, 18.

[68] See *A. Eide* Economic, Social and Cultural Rights as Human Rights, in: A. Eide/C. Krause/A. Rosas (eds.), Economic, Social and Cultural Rights: A Textbook, 2001, 9 et seq., at 30 et seq.

[69] CESCR General Comment 3 (note 55), para. 10.

---

due to a lack of available resources if it shows that "every effort has been made to use all resources that are at its disposition in an effort to satisfy, as a matter of priority, those minimum obligations".[70] The Committee was explicit in requiring continued observance of Covenant's minimum core obligations even in times of "economic recession", where "the vulnerable members of society can and indeed must be protected by the adoption of relatively low-cost targeted programmes".[71]

The "minimum core" content of Covenant obligations for each State Party is determined contextually by the State Party with the Committee, from the time of the State Party's accession to the Covenant and the submission of the initial report required under Articles 16 and 17 of the Covenant. The Committee's initial assessment of the particular "minimum core" content or baseline applicable to a given State Party takes into consideration the State's resource capacities, population needs, scientific and technological advancement, among others.[72] The assessment is a broad-based information-gathering process, one that is intended to elicit the essential levels of a Covenant right, "without which a right loses its substantive significance as a human right".[73] *Manisuli Ssenyonjo* describes the minimum core obligation as an "absolute international minimum", applicable "whatever the State's level of development and resources" since the minimum core obligation entails "the basic level of sustenance necessary to live in dignity ... the baseline below which all States must not fall, and should endeavor to rise above".[74]

The process of identifying a State Party's minimum core obligations under the Covenant is quite similar to proportionality analysis common in judicial reasoning.[75] To this end, the Committee has defined criteria for de-

---

[70] CESCR General Comment 3 (note 55), para. 10.

[71] CESCR General Comment 3 (note 55), para. 12.

[72] See *P. Alston* (note 44), 332 et seq., (discussing at 351-353 how the Committee's mandate includes identification of the minimum core content of Covenant obligations). This process of identification, as evidenced by the Committee's varying practices across State reporting processes, has not been immune from criticism. See *M. Langford/J. A. King*, Committee on Economic, Social and Cultural Rights, in: M. Langford (ed.), Social Rights Jurisprudence: Emerging Trends in International and Comparative Law, 2008, 477 et seq., at 492 et seq.

[73] *F. Coomans*, Identifying the Key Elements of the Right to Education: A Focus on its Core Content, 2, unpublished paper available at <http://www.crin.org>.

[74] *M. Ssenyonjo*, Economic, Social and Cultural Rights in International Law, 2009, 66 et seq.

[75] See *A. Barak*, Proportionality: Constitutional Rights and Their Limitations, 2012, 202 et seq., (on proportionality and international and national human rights law); 422 et seq., (on proportionality and positive constitutional rights).

termining the minimum core content of the right to food,[76] the right to health,[77] the right to social security,[78] the right to water,[79] among others. The minimum core content of Covenant rights is meant to "establish [...] a minimum quantitative and qualitative threshold enjoyment of each [ESC] right that should be guaranteed to everyone in all circumstance as a matter of top priority ... [it] is linked to vital interests of individuals that are often connected to their survival".[80] Additionally, academic literature is replete with quantitative and empirical proposals to measure this minimum core content of Covenant rights for particular States, factoring in resource constraints, governmental capabilities, and population needs of each State on a case-by-case basis.[81]

The Committee's methodology of setting "minimum core obligations" (and from which progressive realization of Covenant rights would then be ascertained) also finds support in parallel or subsequent national and international practices demonstrating the acceptance of some notion of a binding

---

[76] CESCR General Comment 12, (The right to adequate food [Art. 11]), 1999, para. 17. See also *R. Künnemann*, The Right to Adequate Food: Violations Related to Its Minimum Core Content, in: A. Chapman/S. Russell (eds.), Core Obligations: Building a Framework for Economic, Social and Cultural Rights, 2002, 161 et seq.

[77] CESCR General Comment 14, (The right to the highest attainable standard of health [Art. 12 of the International Covenant on Economic, Social and Cultural Rights]), para. 43. See also *A. R. Chapman*, Core Obligations Related to the Right to Health, in: A. Chapman/S. Russell (note 76), 185 et seq.

[78] CESCR General Comment 19, (The right to social security [Art. 9]), 2007, para. 59. See also *L. Lamarche*, The Right to Social Security in the International Covenant on Economic, Social and Cultural Rights, in: A. Chapman/S. Russell (note 76), 87 et seq.

[79] CESCR General Comment No. 15, (The right to water [Arts. 11 and 12 of the International Covenant on Economic, Social and Cultural Rights]), 2002, para. 37.

[80] *A. Müller*, The Relationship Between Economic, Social and Cultural Rights and International Humanitarian Law: An Analysis of Health-Related Issues in Non-International Armed Conflicts, 2013, 75.

[81] See *G. S. McGraw*, Defining and Defending the Right to Water and Its Minimum Core: Legal Construction and the Role of National Jurisprudence, Loyola University Chicago International Law Review 8 (2011), 127; *S. Kalantry/J. E. Getgen/S. Arrigg Koh*, Enhancing Enforcement of Economic, Social, and Cultural Rights Using Indicators: A Focus on the Right to Education in the ICESCR, Cornell Law Faculty Working Papers 63, available at <http://scholarship.law.cornell.edu>; *E. Anderson*, Using Quantitative Methods to Monitor Government Obligations in Terms of the Rights to Health and Education, Center for Economic and Social Rights Working Paper, November 2008, available at <http://www.cesr.org>; *E. Felner*, A New Frontier in Economic and Social Rights Advocacy? Turning Quantitative Data into a Tool for Human Rights Accountability, Sur International Journal on Human Rights 9 (2008), 109 et seq., available at <http://www.surjournal.org>. On auditing national government policies in light of the ICESCR, see methodology developed in *R. Balakrishnan/D. Elson*, Auditing Economic Policy in the Light of Obligations on Economic and Social Rights, Essex Human Rights Review 5 (2008), 1 et seq., available at <http://www.cwgl.rutgers.edu>.

essential minimum of economic, social, and cultural rights. Albeit with some variances between them, constitutional courts of Colombia, India, and South Africa have also referred to "minimum" requirements or minimum essential levels of compliance with economic, social and cultural rights.[82] The same concept of a minimum core has also been argued to be well within the penumbra of fundamental obligations of the American Convention on Human Rights[83] and the European Social Charter.[84] Notably, the African Commission on Human and People's Rights made the most explicit incorporation of the "minimum core" methodology in 2010, specifying a minimum in regard to substantive rights enumerated in the Principles and Guidelines on the Implementation of Economic, Social and Cultural Rights in the African Charter of Human and People's Rights.[85]

After the Committee and the State Party jointly determine the applicable minimum baseline, the State Party is then obligated to move progressively towards the full realization of Covenant rights. For obligations to take action, this would mean that the Committee's periodic review would examine whether a State Party's claimed implementation of the Covenant through certain measures "is reasonable or proportionate with respect to the attainment of the relevant rights", "complies with human rights and democratic

---

[82] *J. Chowdhury*, Judicial Adherence to a Minimum Core Approach to Socio-Economic Rights – A Comparative Perspective, Cornell Law School Graduate Paper 27 (2009), citing CC decision, C-251, 1997; CC decision, SU-225, 1998; *Paschim Banga Khet Mazdoor Samity v. State of West Bengal*, (1996) AIR SC 2426; *Government of Republic of South Africa v. Irene Grootboom and Petitioners*, 2001 (1) SA 46 (CC) (S. Afr.); *Minister of Health v. Treatment Action Campaign (No. 2)*, 2002(5) SA 721 (CC) (S. Afr.). On the reasonableness review and minimum core approach of the South African Constitutional Court, see *S. Liebenberg*, Socio-Economic Rights: Revisiting the Reasonableness Review/Minimum Core Debate, available at <http://justiciabilityconference.wikispaces.com>.

[83] *T. Melish*, Protecting Economic, Social and Cultural Rights in the Inter-American Human Rights System: A Manual on Presenting Claims, (Orville H. Schell Jr. Center for International Human Rights, Yale Law School), 170 et seq.

[84] See *F. Coomans*, Economic, Social and Cultural Rights, 26 et seq., paper available at <http://www.uu.nl>; *O. de Schutter*, The Protection of Social Rights by the European Court of Human Rights, in: P. van der Auweraert/T. de Pelsmaeker/J. Sarkin/J. Vande Lanotte (eds.), Social, Economic and Cultural Rights: An Appraisal of Current European and International Developments, 2002, 207 et seq. See also *R. R. Churchill/U. Khaliq*, The Collective Complaints System of the European Social Charter: An Effective Mechanism for Ensuring Compliance with Economic and Social Rights?, EJIL 15 (2004), 417 et seq., (acknowledging determinability problems with the substantive obligations in the Charter in the process of adjudicating collective complaints).

[85] Principles and Guidelines on the Implementation of Economic, Social and Cultural Rights in the African Charter on Human and People's Rights, Nairobi, Kenya, 2010, full text available at <http://www.escr-net.org>. See also *A. Chidi Odinkalu*, Analysis of Paralysis or Paralysis by Analysis? Implementing Economic, Social and Cultural Rights under the African Charter on Human and Peoples' Rights, HRQ 23 (2001), 327 et seq.

principles", and "is subject to an adequate framework of monitoring and accountability".[86] The review process entails considerable detailed factual data, where the Committee can, at any point, amplify its requests for information from a State Party on its domestic implementation of Covenant obligations.[87] While the Committee's processes are structurally designed to be cooperative, dialogic, and solution-oriented, the Committee is not at all precluded from publicly declaring, at any relevant or appropriate juncture, that a State Party has failed to comply with Covenant obligations.[88] In practice, however, the Committee has done this quite sparingly, declaring, for example, that certain mass expulsion policies of the Dominican Republic in 1990 had violated the right to housing, and likewise with regard to Panama's implementation of forcible evictions and demolitions of certain community areas in early 1990.[89] Rather, the Committee has tended to function instead in a broad-based consultative manner with States Parties, non-governmental organizations, and related international organizations and specialized agencies of the United Nations to urge States Parties to adopt new legislation to implement the Covenant, urge the repeal of non-conforming domestic legislation, appeal to the implementation of pre-existing legislation, and recommend preventive action to avoid or forestall Covenant violations.[90] Lacking procedural standardization, the Committee has drawn criticism of its ability to effectively discharge the mandate delegated to it by the United Nations Economic and Social Council (ECOSOC).[91]

In performing those core functions that have been delegated to it in response to the needs of an intrinsically evolutive set of Covenant obligations, the question arises as to the extent to which the Committee might be said to be exercising international public authority. The concept of international public authority has been developed "in order to better identify those international activities that determine other legal subjects, curtail their freedom in a way that requires legitimacy and therefore a public law framework",

---

[86] *J. M. Diller*, Securing Dignity and Freedom Through Human Rights: Article 22 of the Universal Declaration of Human Rights, 2011, 138.

[87] *D. P. Forsythe* (ed.), Encyclopedia of Human Rights, 2009, 93.

[88] See "The Limburg Principles on the Implementation of the International Covenant on Economic, Social and Cultural Rights", Note verbale dated 5.12.1986 from the Permanent Mission of the Netherlands to the United Nations Office at Geneva addressed to the Centre for Human Rights, E/CN.4/1987/17, 8.1.1987 (hereafter, Limburg Principles), para. 12.

[89] *S. Leckie*, The Committee on Economic, Social and Cultural Rights: Catalyst for Change in a System Needing Reform, in: P. Alston/J. Crawford (eds.), The Future of UN Human Rights Treaty Monitoring, 2000, 129.

[90] *S. Leckie* (note 89), 129 et seq.

[91] See *B. Lyon*, Discourse in Development: A Postcolonial Agenda for the United Nations Committee on Economic, Social, and Cultural Rights through the Postcolonial Lens, American University Journal on Gender Society Policy and Law 10 (2002), 535.

with the public law framework in turn defined as a framework in which authoritative actions must be "based on public law (constitutive function)", that authority is also controlled and limited by the substantive and procedural standards provided by public law (limiting function).[92] To round out this conceptual framework, authority is defined as "the legal capacity to determine others and reduce their freedom", a conceptual innovation which includes not only the ability to modify a legal situation but also to condition it.[93]

The institution of the Committee, as an evolutive interpreter of Covenant obligations, is bound in the exercise of the international public authority by the remaining constituent elements of this definition which identifies those institutions exercising "international" and "public" authority as institutions which exercise authority to further a goal defined to be "in the public interest" on the basis of "authority attributed to them by political collectives on the basis of binding or non-binding international acts".[94] Given this definition of international public authority, we would be likely to accept the observation that the function of the Committee with respect to evolving norms under the Covenant is an instance of the exercise of international public authority. At the level of two constituent elements necessary to classify an act as an exercise in international public authority, the Committee, as an international body, is constituted as by law by States Parties to the Covenant. In a more sophisticated manner, the interpretations of the Covenant promulgated by the Committee, either in the context of general comments or in the individual state reporting process are designed to condition, in certain respects, the Parties to the Covenant, either as a matter of individual State evaluation, or as an interpretation of treaty norms which might influence or bind all States Parties to the Covenant.[95]

While the nature of Covenant obligations necessitates their continuous evolutive interpretation,[96] such repeated interpretation has been narrowly

---

[92] A. von Bogandy/P. Dann/M. Goldman, Developing the Publicness of Public Law: Towards a Legal Framework for Global Governance Activities, GLJ 9 (2010), 1375, 1380.

[93] A. von Bogandy/P. Dann/M. Goldman (note 92), 1381 et seq.

[94] A. von Bogandy/P. Dann/M. Goldman (note 92), 1383.

[95] We have focused, in this intervention, on the institutional and conditioning aspects of the exercise of international public authority, which seem to interface most directly with the work of evolutive interpretation with respect to the Committee's work on the Covenant. We would wish to reserve judgment, however, on the question of whether each act of interpretation which has a manner of operation that emphasizes the intention of the parties that a treaty term evolve over time might also be an instance of the exercise of public authority, as opposed to an act of interpretation. Such a question would require a different, and more substantive, line of inquiry than that pursued here.

[96] J. M. Diller (note 86), 141, ("The changing scope and substance of the entitlement and the corresponding core obligations reflect the principle of evolving interpretation of rights

facilitated in the regular State reportage process originally built into the Committee's treaty monitoring mandate. As we show in the following Part III, however, the recent entry into force of the OP-ICESCR effectively entrenched the Committee's competence to determine and verify a State Party's compliance or lack of compliance with the Covenant in specific fact-situations. Determining a Covenant violation may not necessarily be just a matter of selective discretion and prudence for the Committee, as it has hitherto shown throughout its thin practice in publicizing findings of State violations of the Covenant.[97] Following the entry into force of the OP-ICESCR, however, we expect that future Committee determinations of state responsibility for Covenant violations could conceivably be more a matter of institutionalized practice and legal obligation arising from its new mandate. In addition, because the acts of the Committee may be said to condition State behaviour in the matter described, we discuss in detail the procedures which are laid out in the Optional Protocol which we believe address legitimacy concerns stemming from exercises of public authority vested in the Committee by States Parties to the Protocol.

III. Evolutive Interpretation and Individual Complaints in the Optional Protocol of the Covenant on Economic, Social and Cultural Rights

Having established the inherently evolutive nature of Covenant obligations, and the degree to which State Parties have expressly consented to this normative evolution, we now turn to the OP-ICESCR to examine in detail how a robust individual complaints mechanism would enrich the interpretive landscape for economic, social, and cultural rights. Our thesis in the section that follows is that the individual complaints mechanism provides a forum for the articulation of inherently evolving treaty norms in a manner that crystallizes the interpretive inquiry for finding state consent to evolving treaty norms. We further theorize that, given the inherently evolutive nature

---

and are a natural outgrowth of the change over time in the notion and context for realization of the rights. Exactly what constitutes the minimum essential level of each right which States parties must meet as their minimum core obligation is subject of evolving international interpretation.").

[97] We note the concerns expressed nearly two decades ago that effective monitoring of the Covenant could not be genuinely conducted unless the Committee was willing to publicly and regularly articulate its analysis of State Party violations of the Covenant. See *A. R. Chapman*, A "Violations" Approach for Monitoring the International Covenant on Economic, Social and Cultural Rights, HRQ 18 (1996), 23 et seq., at 29 et seq.

of Covenant norms, if the Committee is interpreted as exercising international public authority in the assessment of individual complaints the various procedural mechanisms in these procedures adequately address risks that Committee findings might be accused of illegitimacy.

To make such a point we first explore the current state of the reporting process under the Covenant, and second, explain the two ways in which the OP-ICESCR builds on this reporting process (both by the incorporation of an individual complaints mechanism, as well as by granting certain powers of investigation to the Committee which it may exercise independent of an individual complaint). We conclude that the OP-ICESCR provides a model of institutionalized continuing practices on evolutive interpretation, by authorizing the Committee to draw on the work of a wide range of actors when it first evaluates the individual complaints. Additionally, the Committee is now well-positioned to establish a State Party's fulfilment of its obligations to avoid taking deliberately retrogressive measures with respect to core Covenant rights. Finally, in its role as an evaluator of the "reasonableness",[98] of the steps taken by a State Party with respect to particular Covenant rights, the Committee is in a position to do powerful work that could serve to rebut the proposition that economic, social, and cultural rights are non-justiciable.

Before the entry into force of the OP-ICESCR, the Committee's work of evaluating compliance with state obligations under the Covenant was primarily governed by the periodic state reporting process laid out in Articles 16 and 17 of the Covenant. Article 16 obligates States to "submit ... reports on the measures which they have adopted and the progress made in achieving the observance of the rights recognized herein".[99] Article 17 mandates that these reports be submitted "in accordance with a program" established by the Committee,[100] and that such reports "may indicate factors and difficulties affecting the degree of fulfilment of obligations under the present Covenant".[101] The current model for this schedule of reporting allows the Committee to consider, on average, between ten to fifteen state reports yearly, spread over two sessions. In addition to information from states, the

---

[98] OP-ICESCR, Art. 8(4).

[99] CESCR, Art. 16(1).

[100] CESCR, Art. 17(1). In point of fact the original obligation for monitoring State compliance with the Covenant fell on the Economic and Social Council, whose functions have since been transferred to the Committee. See *P. Alston* (note 44).

[101] CESCR, Art. 17(2).

Committee will entertain reports submitted by Non-Governmental Organizations bearing on state behaviour as well.[102]

Two aspects of this model are important to tease out. First, given the number of State Parties to the Covenant, and the limited amount of time given the Committee in the course of its working sessions, there will be often many years between executing obligations and the submission of an assessment of compliance with the Covenant. Second, and more importantly, the Committee's concluding obligations, in addition to focusing on substantive compliance with the Covenant, often include either calls for additional information, or request that states monitor the fulfilment of economic, social, and cultural rights in the case of ongoing social welfare projects. The Committee's concluding remarks in its periodic evaluation of Azerbaijan, completed in May 2013, are not atypical:

> "The Committee recommends that the State party ensures that the State Program on Development of Official Statistics in 2013-2017 includes all the data necessary to monitor the enjoyment of economic, social and cultural rights under the Covenant disaggregated by sex, disability, ethnicity, urban and rural area and other relevant criteria."[103]

The significance of this data monitoring, and the disaggregation of this data, to state responsibility under the Covenant is a subject to which we will soon return.

In keeping with the work of the Committee with respect to periodic reporting, the OP-ICESCR envisions a number of sorts of engagement in the case of a fact-finding procedure prompted by communications from within a State Party to the Covenant. The modalities of this engagement are laid out primarily in two sets of articles under the OP-ICESCR. After clarifying the rules regarding the competence of the Committee to receive individual communications from those "under the jurisdiction of a State Party" to the OP-ICESCR,[104] as well as the rules regarding admissibility (which mainly speak to the necessity of the exhaustion of local remedies),[105] and finally various other sets of procedural rules,[106] the OP-ICESCR lays out the modalities the Committee may make use of in examining communications that it receives. These passages deserve quoting at length.

---

[102] On recent developments regarding the Committee's use of indicators to monitor State Party compliance with the Covenant, see *O. de Schutter*, International Human Rights Law, 2010, 492 et seq.

[103] Committee on Economic, Social, and Cultural Rights, Concluding Observations on the Third Periodic Report of Azerbaijan, UN Doc. E/C.12/AZE/CO/3 (19.5.2013).

[104] OP-ICESCR, Art. 1.

[105] OP-ICESCR, Art. 2.

[106] OP-ICESCR, Arts. 3-7.

"3. When examining a communication under the present Protocol, the Committee may consult, as appropriate, relevant documentation emanating from other United Nations bodies, specialized agencies, funds, programmes and mechanisms, and other international organizations, including from regional human rights systems, and any observations or comments by the State Party concerned.

4. When examining communications under the present Protocol, the Committee shall consider the reasonableness of the steps taken by the State Party ... In doing so, the Committee shall bear in mind that the State Party may adopt a range of possible policy measures ..."[107]

As a descriptive matter, one can say that one paradigmatic conceptual principle governing modalities of information-gathering available to the Committee in considering individual complaints is that of integration. This integration operates both at the institutional level of the United Nations human rights architecture, that is, vertically, and within the institution, and explicitly across the multiplicity of what the Protocol calls "human rights systems",[108] that is, horizontally, across various potential treaty regimes. Both have a bearing on the strength of the Committee, exercising its powers under the OP-ICESCR, and might play as a crystallization of an evolutive approach to treaty interpretation.

In the first place, as a matter of vertical integration, the range of information available to the Committee from relevant UN bodies is expansive. The Committee, as well, is on the plain language of the Article given the leeway to establish its own interpretation of relevance. This range of information at the very least draws on the work of the numerous Special Rapporteurs working in thematic areas directly related to those rights protected under the ICESCR, which might include for example housing,[109] water,[110]

---

[107] OP-ICESCR, Art. 8(2)-(3). A fruitful comparison might be drawn with the analogous provisions of the First Optional Protocol to the International Covenant on Civil and Political Rights at this point, see Optional Protocol to the International Covenant on Civil and Political Rights, G.A. Res. A/6316, 23.3.1976 (hereafter OP-ICCPR). Those articles entitle the corresponding Human Rights Committee to consider communications "in light of all written information made available to it by the individual and the State Party." (OP-ICESCR, Art. 5[1]). The "evolution" in the scope of the reach of these paradigmatic treaty bodies is one sort of evolution that, we would submit, has a bearing on, and also reflects, developments in treaty interpretation theory of the sort that are discussed here. For present purposes however, the focus is on the OP-ICESCR.

[108] OP-ICESCR, Art. 8(2).

[109] Commission on Human Rights, Resolution 2000/9, 17.4.2000, (establishing for an office of Special Rapporteur in this area).

[110] Human Rights Council, Resolution 7/22, 28.3.2008, (establishing for an office of a Special Rapporteur on the right to water).

and health.[111] These mandates themselves work to increase the range of authoritative sources identified as relevant in the context of making determinations on subsequent practice under evolutive interpretation of international legal obligations, as the work of the Special Rapporteurs, often also synthesize state practices as regards treaty obligations.[112]

The horizontal work of integration envisioned in this model of resolving individual complaints also has various implications for crystallizing some aspects of the evolutive approach to treaty interpretation. In particular, the explicit reference to regional human rights systems augurs an opening for documentation collected in conjunction with regional human rights treaties, that is, in the terminology of Article 31(3)(c) VCLT, "relevant rules of international law".[113] In his first report, *Nolte* noted in particular that the European Court of Human Rights has seen fit, for various reasons, to embrace the model of interpretation laid out in the VCLT.[114] The directions of influence, in the fact-finding model of the Committee provided for, run in two ways. They flow both from the global to the regional (via the use of the VCLT in interpreting regional human rights instruments) and from the regional to the global (via the adjudication of individual complaints by the Committee in the context of documentation by regional human rights institutions).

In addition to the model of fact-finding envisioned by Article 8 of the OP-ICESCR, Article 11 also provides for additional evaluation of the compliance of a State Party with its obligations under the Covenant. It is not sufficient to call the procedure in Article 11 an individual complaint mechanism. Rather, it is an evaluative procedure that states may recognize after ratifying the Protocol that serves at least as an early warning system in the case of serious deprivations of rights. It provides as follows.

"2. If the Committee receives reliable information indicating grave or systematic violations by a State Party of any of the economic, social and cultural rights set forth in the Covenant, the Committee shall invite that State Party to cooperate in the examination of the information and to this end to submit observations with regard to the information concerned.

3. Taking into account any observations that may have been submitted by the State Party concerned as well as any other reliable information available to it, the Committee may designate one or more of its members to conduct an inquiry and

---

[111] Human Rights Council, Resolution 15/22, 30.9.2010, (establishing the Special Rapporteur on the right to the highest attainable standard of health).

[112] See, e. g., Report of the Special Rapporteur on the Right to Food *O. de Schutter*, Agribusiness and the Right to Food, U.N. Doc. A/HRC/13/33 (22.12.2009).

[113] VCLT, Art. 31(3)(c).

[114] Nolte First Report 2013 (note 18), paras. 15-21.

to report urgently to the Committee. Where warranted and with the consent of the State Party, the inquiry may include a visit to its territory."[115]

We do not wish to place an undue emphasis on this provision of the OP-ICESCR, which has the ability to serve as independent adjudicatory mechanism within the Committee. It is, first of all, a mechanism that parties must opt-in to in order for the Committee to exercise its authority.[116] In the second place, it is a procedure that is limited only to those violations of Covenant rights that are either "grave or systematic".[117]

Nevertheless, the evidence-gathering functions attributed to the Committee by the Article are quite powerful. The Committee itself, as with questions regarding what might constitute "relevant" information, is likewise under its Article 11 powers within its competence to evaluate the meaning of "grave or systematic" violations of rights protected under the Covenant. Coming to an independent evaluation of the quality of the information available to it in order to prompt further evaluation of State behaviour in keeping with its powers under the Article is also within the discretion of the Committee. In particular Article 11 burdens the Committee with the task of evaluating, in the first instance, the "reliability" of the information submitted, without reference to a source for that information which is, as in Article 8, "under the jurisdiction" of the State Party to the Protocol.[118] After satisfying itself as to reliability, and to the standard of "grave or systematic" abuses, the Committee may, then, *proprio motu*, both conduct internal investigations on the territory of a State Party, with the consent of the respective State Party to take other investigatory measures.

We will draw three conclusions from this expansion of the interpretive communities now involved in the evaluation of complaints under the OP-ICESCR. The first conclusion is that these communities have expanded beyond merely those individuals "under the jurisdiction" of a State Party to the OP-ICESCR engaged in the complaint making process. At least under Article 8, at the forensic level, they involve a wide swath of the United Nations architecture engaged in the protection of economic, social, and cultur-

---

[115] OP-ICESCR, Art. 11(2)-(3).

[116] OP-ICESCR, Art. 11(1), ("A State Party to the present Protocol may at any time declare that it recognizes the competence of the Committee provided for under the present article."); see also OP-ICESCR, Art. 11(8), ("A State Party ... may, at any time, withdraw this declaration by notification ..."). Two ratifying states have thus far deposited instruments that recognize the power of the Committee under this article – El Salvador and Portugal.

[117] OP-ICESCR, Art. 11(2).

[118] OP-ICESCR, Art. 1.

al rights.[119] In conjunction with Article 11, the forensic community involved in the evaluation of State performance of obligations under the ICESCR includes two sets of parties that previously would not have had access to reporting procedures. Those communities are, in the first instance, human rights actors that are in a position to bring "reliable information" to the attention of the Committee. In the second instance, the forensic community has been expanded to include Committee members themselves. As a matter of expanding the legal community tasked with articulating the meaning of a given economic, social, and cultural right, the individual complaints mechanism of Article 8, standing alone, invites the Committee to actively give content to these rights by relying on the expertise of regional human rights systems, as well as by relying on the expertise of individual U.N. mandate holders that have developed right-specific expertise in these areas.[120]

Second, this process of fact-finding and complaint evaluation has a direct bearing on the ongoing interpretation of the nature of State obligations under the Covenant. Setting aside the frequent critique of imprecision concerning the "minimum core" of State compliance with Covenant obligations,[121] it is axiomatic that the core obligation under the Covenant is to "progressively ensure" the enjoyment of basic economic, social, and cultural rights. What this has meant, for the last twenty-five years, is that at the very least, States have an obligation not to take "deliberately retrogressive" measures with respect to these rights.[122] The difficulty in this sort of evaluation, if there has been one, has been in establishing the baseline against which deliberately retrogressive measures might be evaluated. The OP-ICESCR, by expanding the range of sources against which state performance might be measured, resolves the difficulties in this baseline. At this point, states have to a large extent been subject to an evaluation of their performance of treaty obligations under the mandatory reporting procedures discussed above.[123] And it is clearly within the prerogative of the Commit-

---

[119] We note that the Committee has long followed this practice of institutional cooperation and fact-finding with other specialized agencies of the United Nations. See for example Concluding Observations adopted in 1996 by the Committee on Economic, Social, and Cultural Rights, 415 et seq., at 448, in: A. von Bogdandy/R. Wolfrum (eds.), Max Planck UNYB, Vol. 1 (1997).

[120] See *M. Langford/J. A. King*, Committee on Economic, Social and Cultural Rights, in: M. Langford (ed.), Social Rights Jurisprudence: Emerging Trends in International and Comparative Law, 2008, 477 et seq., at 504 et seq., (illustrating this practice in regard to the right to social security and the role of the International Labour Organization/ILO in the assessment of compliance with this right).

[121] *K. G. Young* (note 43).

[122] CESCR General Comment 3 (note 55), para. 9.

[123] See text accompanying notes 99-104. Similar observations on the wealth of information already institutionally available to the Committee has been previously made and dis-

tee, in evaluating complaints, to rely on previous reports submitted to it in conjunction with these mandatory reports.[124] As a matter of evolutive interpretation of treaty norms, any perceived difficulty with establishing prior state practice, or the clear and convincing evidence of state understanding of a norm, would asymptotically diminish. State reports, if they are anything after all, are definitive statements of the State's own interpretation of the meaning of its obligation under the treaty, and provide one concrete starting point against which later state performance can be judged.[125]

Finally, and as a matter intrinsic to elaboration of Covenant norms, the requirement that the Committee undertake its evaluation with a view towards the "reasonableness" of the steps taken by the State offers an opportunity to rebut the notion that economic, social, and cultural rights are non-justiciable.[126] The reasonability heuristic can be grounded both in traditional models, on the one hand of proportionality analysis, and on the other of the behaviour of a common law model of a reasonable actor. In either event, it offers the opportunity for the Committee to expand on its original articulation of "deliberately retrogressive measures", which the Committee has reasoned, are measures that would "need to be fully justified by reference to the totality of the rights provided for in the Covenant and in the context of the full use of the maximum available resources".[127] Reasonableness performs this analytical work by providing an offensive frame in which to evaluate state behaviour, as opposed to the merely defensive posture at stake when a state is obligated to justify retrogressive measures. It thus offers a rich ground to observe the development of evolving interpretations of an international norm.

The question remains, however, as to the extent to which such interpretive acts, in conjunction with individual complaints and Committee actions, suffer from allegations of illegitimacy, that is, whether such evaluations are capable of addressing criticisms of democratic deficits in acts of international legal interpretation taken as a whole. The argument has been formulated in conjunction with respect to international courts and tribunals,[128] and thus

---

cussed in *B. Simma/D. Desierto* (note 45), special issue on Aligning Investment Protection and Human Rights.

[124] OP-ICESCR, Art. 8(2).

[125] See *M. Kjærum*, State Reports, in: G. Alfredsson/J. Grimheden/B. G. Ramcharan/A. de Zayas (eds.), International Human Rights Monitoring Mechanisms: Essays in Honour of Jakob Th. Möller, 2nd revised ed. 2009, 17 et seq.

[126] *H. J. Steiner/P. Alston/R. Goodman*, International Human Rights in Context: Law, Politics, Morals, 2007, 312 et seq., (laying out the debates).

[127] CESCR General Comment 3 (note 55), para. 9.

[128] *A. von Bogandy/I. Venzke*, In Whose Name? An Investigation of International Courts' Public Authority and Its Democratic Justification, EJIL 23 (2012), 7.

might justifiably be directed at the work of the Committee in the context of individual complaints. We consider the most important aspects of this question to have two aspects. The first might perhaps be said to exist at the macro-level, and pertains to the notion that legitimacy is strained in the context of international legal disputes because international treaty obligations, among others, are products bound in time, and that "[o]nce an international agreement is in place, it is largely withdrawn from the grasp of its individual makers".[129] A second set of particularized objections to the work of the Committee with respect to individual complaints would focus on the procedures in place in these mechanisms, and attempt to determine what safeguards remain in place to ensure that state consent remains the basis of the work of the Committee.

With respect to the first objection, we would again refer to the inherently progressive nature of state obligations in the Covenant. If the objections to legitimacy are based on the notion that there is no responsive mechanism in place to address treaty obligations, the response is that the ICESCR has been uniquely calibrated to accommodate individual state policy-makers on contested questions.[130] Progressive realization is best conceived of as the responsibility of the state not to retreat from its commitments absent compelling circumstances.[131] Policymakers in States Parties are, in a sense, the "responsive"[132] community here, taking steps with respect to the rights enshrined by the Covenant, and constantly evaluating those steps both as a matter of state policy and, if they are acting in conformity with international obligations, in keeping with the protection of rights enumerated under the Covenant. The design of the Covenant pre-commits states to fulfil Covenant obligations but provides flexibility for them to do so.

With respect to the second set of objections, specific to the assessment of individual complaints, it is our view that the expansion of interpretive communities enhances the legitimacy of Committee determinations that have the weight of interpretation. The procedures governing Committee determination of complaints are structured in such a way as to decrease the risks of illegitimacy. First, as *von Bogandy* and *Venzke* have argued, processes of politicization in international bodies might reduce the risks of illegitimacy. One way in which they assert this is done is by international bodies "refraining adding to the substance of disputed norm" but rather including procedural rights of participation by affected actors in certain decisions,

---

129 *A. von Bogandy/I. Venzke* (note 128), 21.
130 See text and footnotes in Part II of this Article.
131 See text and footnotes in Part II of this Article.
132 *A. von Bogandy/I. Venzke* (note 128), 19.

a practice that they recognize occurring in WTO decisions as well as in determinations of rights under the United Nations Convention on the Law of the Sea.[133] Such participatory process-based rights form an important element of the meaning of rights under the Covenant as well.[134] Second, the expanded forensic community involved in the determination of an individual complaint does not include any group whose competence to participate in such a proceeding is not based on prior state consent. To the extent that this forensic community includes prior reporting to the Committee in the state reportage process of periodic reporting by national stakeholders, such participation is an established matter of practice. With respect to reporting across U.N. bodies, such information must be public.[135] It is regrettable that such determinations, perhaps, will not be openly contested,[136] but the bases on which decisions of the committee are made are public.

IV. Evolutive Interpretation and Inter-State Dispute Resolution in the Optional Protocol of the Covenant on Economic, Social and Cultural Rights

The final manner in which we anticipate the OP-ICESCR would enrich the jurisprudence on evolutive interpretation of international legal treaty obligations arises from the establishment of an inter-State communication procedure and dispute resolution procedure in Article 10 of the Protocol. We fully acknowledge that similar inter-State procedures already exist with respect to the Convention against Torture, the Convention on the Rights of the Child, the Convention on the Elimination of Racial Discrimination, the Convention on the Elimination of All Forms of Discrimination against Women, the International Convention on Enforced Disappearances, and the Convention on the Protection of the Rights of All Migrant Workers and

---

[133] *A. von Bogandy/I. Venzke* (note 128), 31.

[134] See, e. g., Committee on Economic, Social and Cultural Rights, General Comment No. 15, The Right to Water, para. 37 (f), E/C.12/2002/11, ("The state must immediately take steps [t]o adopt and implement a national water strategy and plan of action addressing the whole population; the strategy and plan of action should be devised, and periodically reviewed, on the basis of a participatory and transparent process; it should include methods, such as right to water indicators and benchmarks, by which progress can be closely monitored; the process by which the strategy and plan of action are devised, as well as their content, shall give particular attention to all disadvantaged or marginalized groups.") The procedural right involved exists at a different level of participation, but the principle is intact.

[135] *A. von Bogandy/I. Venzke* (note 128), 27 et seq., (setting out various procedural rules that might enhance openness in international adjudication).

[136] OP-ICESCR, Art. 8(2).

Members of their Families, and that these procedures remain, as yet, dormant and unutilized.[137] While several explanations have been made for States' reluctance to use any of these inter-State procedures to date (such as States' preferences for less adversarial enforcement, avoidance of litigation costs, prevention of retaliatory counter-complaints, or the fact that a State may simply not regard itself as having a sufficient interest in another State's implementation of human rights obligations when the latter does not have transboundary effects reaching into its territory),[138] we believe, however, that there may be two particular incentives specific to the Covenant as a treaty regime which could encourage States to opt in and use the Article 10 OP-ICESCR inter-State procedure in the future.

First, unlike the other aforementioned human rights treaties whose inter-State complaints procedures have either not yet entered into force (as with the Migrant Workers' Convention or the Optional Protocol to the Convention on the Rights of the Child) or which contemplate readily identifiable or discrete State conduct amounting to treaty violations at a static point in time (such as under the Convention against Torture or the Convention on the Elimination of Racial Discrimination),[139] States could well anticipate that the programmatic and inherently evolutive nature of Covenant obligations makes it more advantageous for them to undertake regular clarification with the Committee in regard to specific programs, governmental policies or measures that could bear upon the fulfilment of economic, social, and cultural rights. The inter-State procedure in Article 10 OP-ICESCR provides a nonpartisan venue to clarify and test Covenant obligations as they apply to concrete State policy situations or governmental measures, without incurring punitive consequences or damaging inter-State political sensitivities as is the case with a hard adversarial paradigm typical to international adjudi-

---

[137] See Art. 21 of the Convention Against Torture; Art. 74 of the Convention on the Protection of the Rights of All Migrant Workers and Members of their Families; Art. 32 of the International Convention on Enforced Disappearances; Art. 12 of the Optional Protocol to the Convention on the Rights of the Child; Arts. 11-13 of the Convention on the Elimination of Racial Discrimination; Arts. 41-43 of the International Covenant on Civil and Political Rights.

[138] *S. Leckie*, The Inter-State Complaint Procedure in International Human Rights Law: Hopeful Prospects or Wishful Thinking?, HRQ 10 (1988), 249 et seq.; *A. L. Paulus*, Dispute Resolution, in: G. Ulfstein/T. Marauhn/A. Zimmermann (eds.), Making Treaties Work: Human Rights, Environment, and Arms Control, 2007, 351 et seq., at 356.

[139] Certainly, none of the other fundamental human rights treaties carry a comparable or identical "progressive realization" obligation in Art. 2(1) of the Covenant. Unlike, say, the specific obligations of States to prevent and punish torture under the Convention Against Torture, verifying State compliance with the Covenant first requires the State to accept that the normative obligations contained therein are ultimately "moving targets" throughout the life of this particular treaty regime.

cation.[140] As we show in this Part IV, the Article 10 OP-ICESCR procedure mainly seeks to cooperatively encourage non-conforming States to design policy realignments or adjustments towards Covenant compliance. States Parties to the Covenant thus have a pragmatic, as well as principled, stake in actively shaping its evolutive interpretation.

Second, increasing concerns about the potential extraterritorial application of the Covenant[141] particularly in regard to how a State is bound by the tripartite typology of the duties to "respect", "protect", and "fulfil" obligations under the Covenant for "territories over which a State party has sovereignty and to those over which that State exercises territorial jurisdiction"[142] could also make Article 10 of the OP-ICESCR attractive to States as a less confrontational and more expeditious inter-State dispute resolution option. On the one hand, States could resort to this inter-State procedure where particular consequences are felt within their respective territories resulting from another State Party's actions or omissions in regard to the Covenant. The affected State could thus invite the non-complying State

---

[140] See *C. Menkel-Meadow*, The Trouble with the Adversary System in a Postmodern, Multicultural World, William and Mary Law Review 38 (1996), (on the general polarizing consequences of the adversarial system in law); *G. A. Raymond*, International Adjudication and Conflict Management, in: H. M. Hensel (ed.), Sovereignty and the Global Community: The Quest for Order in the International System, 2004, 221 et seq., at 221, ("To be sure, there are drawbacks to [international] adjudication. Because the process is adversarial, relations between the litigants may deteriorate during the course of the proceedings. Plaintiffs may feel constrained by rules of procedure that limit what can be introduced as evidence of wrongdoing, and defendants may believe these same rules circumscribe their ability to mount a stout defense. Even after a verdict is reached, resentment may continue as the losing side harbors grievances over remedies imposed by the court.").

[141] See *M. Langford/F. Coomans/F. Gomez Isa*, Extraterritorial Duties in International Law, in: M. Langford/M. Vandenhole/M. Scheinin/W. van Genugten (eds.), Global Justice, State Duties: The Extraterritorial Scope of Economic, Social and Cultural Rights in International Law, 2013, 51 et seq., at 61, (citing the Maastricht Guidelines' perspective on State jurisdiction to respect, protect, and fulfil Covenant obligations in "situations over which it exercises authority or effective control, whether or not such control is exercised in accordance with international law; situations over which State acts or omissions bring about foreseeable effects on the enjoyment of economic, social and cultural rights, whether within or outside its territory; situations in which the State, acting separately or jointly, whether through its executive, legislative or judicial branches, is in a position to exercise decisive influence or to take measures to realize economic, social and cultural rights extraterritorially, in accordance with international law").

[142] Wall Advisory Opinion, para. 112, at 180, ("The International Covenant on Economic, Social and Cultural Rights contains no provision on its scope of application. This may be explicable by the fact that this Covenant guarantees rights which are essentially territorial. However, it is not to be excluded that it applies both to territories over which a State party has sovereignty and to those over which that State exercises territorial jurisdiction ...").

Party to recalibrate its measures first through this mostly confidential[143] procedure before the Committee, rather than immediately moving towards initiating a contentious case where a full-blown decision would yield a finding of international responsibility, such as those found in decisions issued by the International Court of Justice. On the other hand, bringing an inter-State communication on the issue of the Covenant's extraterritoriality also affords the Committee the distinct opportunity to fully clarify and explicate the operational parameters of what it holds to be the actual extraterritorial scope of States Parties' Covenant obligations.[144] A case of first impression, such as the complex question of whether a State Party has the duty to control the conduct of transnational corporations and ensure that the latter does not cause that State Party to breach its Covenant obligations,[145] could be one example of an interpretive issue that could be cautiously brought for Committee clarification and early dialogue between States Parties under the OP-ICESCR inter-State procedure, without ripening into a contentious case leading to a finding of international responsibility (and the corollary reparations consequences), to which States might be more loathe to give consent.

With the foregoing incentive considerations in mind, and anticipating that the inter-State complaints mechanism in Article 10 of the OP-ICESCR would likely be more strategically used in the future by States Parties to the Covenant opting in to this mechanism, we then turn to discuss the procedures therein, their unique place in the Covenant given its inclusion of important obligations with respect to international cooperation, and the gap-filling role that state-state resolution of complaints under the mechanism

---

[143] OP-ICESCR, Art. 10(1)(e), ("The Committee shall hold closed meetings when examining communications under the present article.").

[144] See *F. Coomans*, The Extraterritorial Scope of the International Covenant on Economic, Social, and Cultural Rights in the Work of the United Nations Committee on Economic, Social and Cultural Rights, HRLR 11(2011), 1 et seq.

[145] Academic literature on the Covenant remains tentative and undertheorized on the subject of State Parties' duties as members of international financial institutions that issue decisions with development consequences for other states, as well as for State Parties' duties as "home States" of transnational corporations whose conduct may injure economic, social, or cultural rights in other jurisdictions. For an interesting set of recent proposals, however, see *S. Narula*, International Financial Institutions, Transnational Corporations and Duties of States, in: M. Langford/W. Vandenhole/M. Scheinin/W. van Genugten (note 141), 114 et seq., (arguing that IFIs and TNCs can be held indirectly accountable for Covenant violations in three ways – by requiring Member States in IFIs to take the Covenant into account when participating in IFI decision-making processes; applying a "decisive influence" and "due diligence" standard to the relationship between the home State and the TNC as would make the home State accountable for TNC violations of the Covenant; and by requiring the home States of TNCs to enact domestic legislation applying the Covenant with extraterritorial reach).

will have on the articulation of norms under the CESCR with respect to reasoned elaborations of State Responsibility under the Covenant.

The inter-State communication mechanism provided for in Article 10 codifies, as a procedural matter, the ways in which a State might lodge a complaint both with another State, as well as with the Committee, alleging non-compliance with obligations provided for in the Covenant. Like Article 11, the inquiry procedure is an opt-in provision – States may declare that they recognize the competence of the Committee to entertain such communications.[146] Three crucial procedural steps of this inter-State dispute mechanism provide stages at which the various actors involved in the procedure – the transmitting State, the receiving State, and the Committee – are required to establish the steps taken (or allegedly not taken) with respect to the particular norm at issue, and in so doing, to elaborate the content of a norm that must be progressively achieved. In the first instance, this burden of norm-elaboration falls on the complaining state. "If a State Party to the present Protocol considers that another State Party is not fulfilling its obligations under the Covenant it may, by written communication, bring the matter to the attention of that State Party."[147] In the second instance, the burden of norm elaboration falls on the receiving State, which is obligated to "afford the State that sent the communication an explanation … clarifying the matter" within three months of receiving the communication.[148]

At the final stage of the norm elaboration process, the Committee is involved in the process if, within six months of the communication, "the matter is not settled to the satisfaction of both State Parties concerned".[149] Either the transmitting state or the receiving State has the right to refer the matter to the Committee. At this stage, a quasi-judicial proceeding is envisioned, at which the Committee, in closed meetings, will consider "relevant information" pertaining to the communications,[150] and at which the States Parties "shall have the right to be represented when the matter is being considered by the Committee and to make submissions orally and/or in writing".[151] The Committee's own responsibilities with respect to norm elaboration take the form of its ultimate evaluation of the communications, as it is obligated to report, in the event that a settlement is not reached between the parties, on the nature and factual issues involved in the dispute.[152] In the

---

146 OP-ICESCR, Art. 10(1).
147 OP-ICESCR, Art. 10(1)(a).
148 OP-ICESCR, Art. 10(1)(a).
149 OP-ICESCR, Art. 10(1)(b).
150 OP-ICESCR, Art. 10(1)(f).
151 OP-ICESCR, Art. 10(1)(g).
152 OP-ICESCR, Art. 10(1)(h)(ii).

event that a settlement is reached, this report will not necessarily include the communications that gave rise to the dispute.[153]

This inter-State communications procedure is, in our view, calibrated to the particular needs of the economic, social, and cultural law-making communities, and also appears as a method of dispute resolution in the context of human rights regimes. The Optional Protocol to the ICCPR, by contrast, has no comparable mechanism, and limits its procedures to individual communications from those subject to the jurisdiction of a State Party.[154] Similar regional bodies are likewise limited in the scope of applications that they might be able to consider.[155]

However, the unique nature of State obligations with respect to cooperation in achieving the enjoyment of rights in the CESCR arguably requires this sort of inter-State procedure. The operative obligation in the Covenant, Article 2, invokes not only the obligation to "progressively ensure" rights, but does not do so without first requiring that States take these steps "individually and through international assistance and co-operation, especially economic and technical".[156] No comparable reference to international engagement exists, for example, in the ICCPR, which restricts obligations by focusing in great detail on the rights of individuals in the jurisdiction of a State Party.[157] This vision of international cooperation under the Covenant, at the very least, belies a strictly territorial conception of this particular human rights treaty, as would seek to restrict its scope merely to the relationship between the State and those individuals in its jurisdiction. Rather, the Covenant is explicit. It envisages a cooperative and engaged State, an actor both domestically and in the international community.[158] For those States pursuing technical or economic assistance in conjunction with another State Party to the Covenant there is also a question, to our knowledge undertheorized at this point,[159] as to the nature of the obligation of a State in a

---

[153] OP-ICESCR, Art. 10(1)(h)(i).

[154] OP-ICCPR, Art. 1.

[155] See, e. g., European Convention on Human Rights, Art. 34, (limiting the adjudicative mechanism to persons, non-governmental organizations, or groups).

[156] ICESCR, Art. 2(1).

[157] ICCPR, Art. 2(1).

[158] On States Parties' control of extraterritorial conduct by private actors in relation to the States' duties to provide access or not to impede access or not to tolerate private actors' conduct that impedes access, see General Comment No. 15, (on the right to water), paras. 23-24; General Comment No. 18, (on the right to work), para. 25; General Comment No. 19, (on the right to social security), paras. 45 and 54.

[159] We note that General Comment No. 2, (on international technical assistance matters) bypasses this question altogether.

position to provide this assistance.[160] In a progressive reading of its mandate under the OP-ICESCR, we would at the very least expect that the Committee, entitled as it is to request "relevant information" from parties involved in the procedure, to deem that relevant information should include steps taken by a complaining party with respect to actions it has taken to fulfil its obligations of cooperation.[161]

State-state resolution of disputes under this procedure has the potential not simply to build out this cooperative aspect of the Covenant, but to elaborate the meaning of the Covenant's substantive norms as well. The starting point for this contention is the discussion of state responsibility for violations of economic, social, and cultural rights found in the ICJ's *Wall Advisory Opinion*.[162] Ultimately, the Court reached the conclusion that the construction of the wall "impeded the exercise by the persons concerned of the right to work, to health, to education and to an adequate standard of living as proclaimed in the International Covenant on Economic, Social and Cultural Rights …".[163] In reaching this conclusion the Court relied on region-specific United Nations Rapporteurs, as well as the Rapporteur on the Right to Food, who had both reported that the proposed construction of the wall would cut off Palestinians from educational institutions, for example, as well as from agricultural land and other means of transport, thus im-

---

[160] Although we note the Committee's recently increasing practice of issuing statements on topical applications of the Covenant in States' economic policy-making. See Committee on Economic, Social and Cultural Rights, Statement on the obligations of States Parties regarding the corporate sector and economic, social and cultural rights, E/C.12/2011/1, 20.5.2011, holding, among others, that "Respecting rights requires States Parties to guarantee conformity of their laws and policies regarding corporate activities with economic, social and cultural rights set forth in the Covenant … States Parties shall ensure that companies demonstrate due diligence to make certain they do not impede the enjoyment of Covenant rights by those who depend on or are negatively affected by their activities" (para. 4); "Protecting rights means that States Parties effectively safeguard rights holders against infringements of their economic, social and cultural rights involving corporate actors, by establishing appropriate laws, regulations, as well as monitoring, investigation, and accountability procedures to set and enforce standards for the performance of corporations" (para. 5); "Fulfilling rights entails that States Parties undertake to obtain the corporate sector's support to the realization of economic, social and cultural rights" (para. 6); 16.5.2012, Letter of the Chairperson of the Committee on Economic, Social and Cultural Rights in relation to the protection of Covenant rights in the context of economic and financial crisis.

[161] CESCR General Comment 3 (note 55), para. 9 (where a similar point has been argued in regard to the meta-obligation of international cooperation built into the Covenant).

[162] See Legal Consequences of the Construction of a Wall in the Occupied Palestinian Territory, Advisory Opinion, ICJ Reports 2004, 136, at paras. 133-134.

[163] Legal Consequences of the Construction of a Wall in the Occupied Palestinian Territory (note 162), at para. 134.

plicating the rights which the Court discussed.[164] This brief discussion, while useful in its insistence that rights protected under the Covenant are obligatory, rather than hortatory, as a matter of international law, arguably left open the discussion of how one can attribute wrongfulness to a state which is failing in its obligation to progressively ensure these rights, rather than an attribution of wrongfulness to a state engaged in a program with retrogressive effects, such as the construction of the wall.

It is our view that the OP-ICESCR inter-State procedure could help towards framing a coherent, consistent, and authoritative response in the future to the issues of causation and attribution peculiar to the Covenant and its inherently evolutive interpretation. The Court's silence on these issues in the *Wall Advisory Opinion* could certainly be read as a policy favouring judicial parsimony, where the Court instead chose to refrain from further explication since it was unnecessary to the assessment of the international legal consequences of the construction of the wall.[165] But it may not be as easy for the Court to remain silent on these questions in the future, should an actual contentious case be brought requiring it to assess international legal responsibility for Covenant violations. This is where we particularly find the OP-ICESCR inter-State procedure to be relevant to filling these gaps in the assessment of international responsibility for Covenant violations. At each level of the interstate procedure, the burden is placed on the State Party to articulate the legal content that it ascribes to a Covenant norm. This process of norm-elaboration establishes evidence of state practice with respect to these norms. If the procedures laid out in Article 8 and 11, and discussed in Part III, operate against a backdrop of extensive technical data supplied in the context of State reporting procedures, and investigations into individual complaints or systemic abuses, in order to adjudicate a particular complaint, the procedure laid out in Article 10 helps to establish a legal baseline against which state behaviour will both be judged in the course of the dispute, and which can serve as a benchmark for later attributions of state responsibility. The twin sets of procedures – one dependent on a rich factual matrix, one on a rich legal matrix – are not, of course, invitations to law-making, but rather to clarification, and will give predictability

---

[164] Legal Consequences of the Construction of a Wall in the Occupied Palestinian Territory (note 162), at para. 133.

[165] On the Court's sometimes-restrictive posture in regard to its law-making function as part of its judicial function, see *S. Wittich*, The Judicial Functions of the International Court of Justice, in: I. Buffard/J. Crawford/A. Pellet/S. Wittich (eds.), International Law between Universalism and Fragmentation: Festschrift in Honour of Gerhard Hafner, 2008, 981 et seq., at 994, ("… the International Court has always taken a restrictive approach towards the idea of expressly contributing to the development of international law [let alone international law-making] …").

and guidance to states in how they must fulfil their obligations under the Covenant.

While we agree that the entry into force of the OP-ICESCR would indeed give rise to "individual entitlements at the level of public international law, [where] the individual himself or herself would be in a position to claim respect for his or her rights within an international procedural arrangement",[166] in our view, what has been rather more striking from the new procedures established under the OP-ICESCR are their long-term impacts on the democratic (and ultimately more legitimate) assessment of international responsibility for Covenant violations. On one end, the Committee's expanded mandate under the OP-ICESCR to interpret and normatively evolve the content of Covenant obligations in the discrete cases or situations giving rise to the individual or inter-State communications procedures, in our view, ultimately strengthens the evidentiary weight of the Committee's future factual findings and interpretive pronouncements upon other international courts, regional tribunals, or local courts adjudicating claims of a State's alleged violation of the Covenant.[167] This is the case, we would assert, because such assessments will be based on an index of state practices generated by states themselves. This index, moreover, is generated in light of state consent to committee authority to pronounce on determinations of state action under the Covenant.

On the other hand, the coordinated and participatory role for States Parties in the new procedures of the OP-ICESCR also provides both the necessary interpretive controls and index of authoritative subsequent State practice. The full involvement of all States Parties, the Committee, and other sources of information (whether from international organizations, private entities, individuals or other non-state actors) now welcomed within the new framework of procedures in the OP-ICESCR, creates enduring interpretive communities that will crystallize subsequent practices relevant to the present and future evolutive interpretation of the Covenant.

---

[166] *T. Marauhn*, Social Rights Beyond the Traditional Welfare State: International Instruments and the Concept of Individual Entitlements, in: E. Benvenisti/G. Nolte/D. Baraq-Erez (eds.), The Welfare State, Globalization, and International Law, 2004, 275 et seq., at 288.

[167] On the complexity and lack of standardization of fact-finding and evidentiary treatment in the International Court of Justice, see *S. Rosenne*, Essays on International Law and Practice, 2007, Ch. 14, ("Fact-finding before the International Court of Justice"), 235 et seq. While the Court may request information from international organizations (including specialized agencies within the United Nations), it is not clear what probative weight is assigned to information submitted by such organizations, if at all. See Art. 34(2) Statute of the International Court of Justice; Art. 69(1), Rules of Court of the International Court of Justice.

V. Conclusion

"Protean" international law is a paradox for one's conception of the rule of law,[168] but in the case of the Covenant, States Parties have uniquely pre-committed themselves to adaptation and change in the performance of obligations to respect, protect, and fulfil economic, social, and cultural rights. Perhaps more than any other treaty regime, the Covenant is unquestionably of an evolutive character. How does one then determine the path of its normative and interpretive evolution, and yet assure both individual and State stakeholders in economic, social, and cultural rights, that international legality and decision-making legitimacy will be attained in the process of implementing the Covenant?

We conclude that the entry into force of the OP-ICESCR completes the system of broad-based monitoring and contextual assessment that was uniquely established in the Covenant. The expansion of the Committee's mandate to include institutional oversight and soft quasi-adjudicative interpretation within the OP-ICESCR's cooperative framework of inter-State and individual communications procedures, administratively complements the reportage and information-gathering functions earlier established in the Covenant's periodic reporting system. Nearly five decades into the binding effect of the Covenant, one could readily expect a vast repository of documented information on State practice towards progressive realization of Covenant obligations. The establishment of the individual and inter-State communications procedures and the fact-finding inquiry procedure of the Committee stands to further amplify such information, but also to streamline and systematize its use in the assessment of international responsibility for Covenant violations.

Most importantly, institutionally intertwining and entrenching subsequent practice (combining the information sources, legal and factual output from both the OP-ICESCR's new procedures with the Covenant's reportage procedures) with the continuing evolutive interpretation of the Covenant, is a remarkable decision that seeks to avoid the classic problems of lacunae in international law. A State's economic planning and decision-making, by nature, depends crucially on designing public programs, measures, and policies far into the future to achieve desired social welfare outcomes. The adaptation and adjustment of State fiscal and public programs, measures, and policies to ensure consistency with State duties to re-

---

[168] The pejorative metaphor is more closely associated with *jus ad bellum* interpretive debates. See *S. D. Murphy*, Protean Jus Ad Bellum, Berkeley J. of Int'l L. 27 (2009), 22.

spect, protect, and fulfil economic, social, and cultural rights is the critical normative challenge for all States Parties to the Covenant. The quiet revolution behind the entry into force of the OP-ICESCR lies with how it could institutionalize and integrate discourses within and across the constituencies that comprise the interpretive communities driving economic, social and cultural rights today – from States Parties, the Committee, individuals and groups enjoying their new entitlements to remedies, and all other non-State actors. When the subsequent practices of these communities collectively inform and guide the evolutive interpretation of the Covenant, our global project of building a postmodern culture of compliance with economic, social, and cultural rights would appear less of a Manichean exercise.

[4]

BRILL
NIJHOFF

INTERNATIONAL JOURNAL OF CHILDREN'S RIGHTS
22 (2014) 205-225

THE INTERNATIONAL
JOURNAL OF
CHILDREN'S RIGHTS

brill.com/chil

The New Complaints Mechanism for the Convention on the Rights of the Child

A Mini Step Forward for Children?

Suzanne Egan
School of Law, University College Dublin, Ireland
Visiting Fellow, Human Rights Program, Harvard Law School (2011–2012)
suzanne.egan@ucd.ie

Abstract

The UN General Assembly has recently adopted a third Optional Protocol to the CRC, providing for an individual complaint mechanism for children. The product of a sustained campaign on the part of NGOs and children's rights advocates, the Protocol achieves a certain parity of esteem for children vis-à-vis complainants under other core UN human rights instruments by enabling them to make complaints specifically with respect to rights guaranteed by the Convention and its two substantive protocols. This article examines the terms of this new procedure in the light of its drafting history and explains why the resulting text has in many respects disappointed in terms of delivering a much-hoped for "child-friendly" complaint mechanism for children.

Keywords

Optional Protocol to the UN Convention on the rights of the Child – complaints procedure – right of individual petition

Introduction

In recent years, the absence of an individual complaint mechanism in the Convention on the Rights of the Child (CRC) has been a mounting source of concern for children's rights advocates. At the time that the Convention was drafted, the idea of such a mechanism was not seriously entertained at any stage of the negotiations, with attention focused exclusively in implementation

© KONINKLIJKE BRILL NV, LEIDEN, 2014 | DOI 10.1163/15718182-55680014 terms on the standard periodic reporting procedure. However, the fact that complaint mechanisms have subsequently been established in respect of all of the core UN human rights treaties meant that the momentum to establish one in respect of the CRC began to gather pace rapidly. A coordinated campaign on the issue by NGOs worldwide, supported by the Committee on the Rights of the Child (CRC Committee), undoubtedly contributed to the decision of the Human Rights Council in 2009 to establish an open-ended working group to explore the possibility of elaborating a complaints procedure in a Protocol to the Convention.[1] After several rounds of negotiations, the working group produced a draft text for a Protocol which was ultimately adopted by the General Assembly of the United Nations without a vote on 19 December 2011.[2] This article examines the complaints procedure provided for in the Protocol in the light of its drafting history and explains why the resulting text has in many respects disappointed in terms of delivering a much-hoped for 'child-friendly' complaint mechanism for children.

Background

At its first session in December 2009, the working group began its deliberations by considering the need for an individual complaint mechanism for children.[3] The majority of delegations expressed the view that a communications procedure would constitute an additional tool to make further progress in the implementation of children's rights at national level. If established, it would be part of a 'continuum of accountability mechanisms', beginning at the community level and comprising national and regional mechanisms. Further reasons cited in favour of the proposal included the fact that the CRC was now the only major human rights treaty which did not have such a procedure. While children could make complaints under the other UN treaties, not all of the rights

---

1   Resolution No 11/1 of 17 June 2009, UN Doc A/HRC/11/L 3.

2   Resolution adopted by the UN General Assembly, 19 December 2011, UN. Doc. A/RES/66/138. The text of the Protocol is annexed to the Resolution.

3   For a full account of the deliberations, see the Report of the first session of the open-ended working group to explore the possibility of elaborating an optional protocol to the Convention on the Rights of the Child to provide a communications procedure: UN Doc A/HRC/13/43 (21 January 2010), (First Report of the working group). Some 37 delegations participated in the debate. Two NGOs, one of which represented a coalition of 11 organisations, and UNICEF also made statements. The contributions of various experts and NGOs are also available at: http://www2.ohchr.org/english/bodies/hrcouncil/OEWG/1stsession.htm (last visited, September 2012).

INTERNATIONAL JOURNAL OF CHILDREN'S RIGHTS 22 (2014) 205-225

in the CRC were covered by those treaties. In any case, it was pointed out that claims regarding children's rights should be assessed by the Committee on the Rights of the Child since it was the treaty body with the appropriate, multi-disciplinary expertise to deal with them. A complaints procedure would assist in the development of the interpretation of the CRC's provisions, which in itself would be of assistance to national mechanisms and bodies operating in the field. No arguments appear to have been raised against the elaboration of a new complaints procedure in principle, save for the caveat entered by some delegations that one should not be elaborated '…simply to replicate the procedures established under other treaties, but only after careful examination of its added value'.[4] Given the specific characteristics of the CRC, it was pointed out that 'new and differentiated' approaches must be considered and that existing procedures could not simply be reproduced.[5]

Amongst the key issues identified during the session that would need to be addressed in any such instrument included the legal capacity of children; representation of children in a complaints procedure and the exercise of the child's right to be heard; how to ensure that complaints filed on behalf of children would be in the best interests of the child; the scope of an optional protocol (including the question of whether it should include an inquiry procedure); the possibility of submitting collective complaints; the implications of the procedure for the workload of the CRC Committee; as well as the resource constraints affecting the treaty body system generally. In regard to the latter issues, the CRC Committee itself indicated that methods of work could be devised to examine communications (taking into account the experience gained by the other treaty bodies) but that the budgetary implications of implementing such a procedure would need to be tabled to ensure additional resources necessary to allow the Committee to deal with complaints.

Having taken note of the working group's report of its first session, the Human Rights Council (HRC) decided in March 2010 to extend its mandate and requested the working group '…to elaborate an optional protocol to provide a communications procedure…'.[6] It further requested the chairperson of the working group to prepare a proposal for a draft optional protocol, based on the earlier debate, which should take into account the views of the CRC Committee, the UN special procedures and other experts.[7] Having engaged in informal consultations with States, as well as consultations with UN and civil

---

4   First Report of the working group, para. 20.

5   *Ibid.*

6   Resolution No 13/3: UN Doc A/HRC/13/L 5, paras. 1–3.

7   *Ibid*, para. 3.

INTERNATIONAL JOURNAL OF CHILDREN'S RIGHTS 22 (2014) 205-225

society experts and members of the Committee, the chairperson prepared a proposal for a draft Optional Protocol together with a detailed explanatory memorandum on the text.[8] While clearly based on the agreed terms of previous complaints mechanisms so as to ensure consistency and coherence, the proposal also incorporated specific child-sensitive elements based on the discussions that had taken place at the first session. These included, *inter alia*, the specific reaffirmation of the 'best interests of the child' principle in the body of the draft Protocol,[9] inclusion of a collective complaints provision[10] and reduced time limits to ensure speedy consideration of complaints.[11] As envisaged by the HRC's resolution, this proposal served as the basis for the negotiations of the working group at its second session which took place over the course of two meetings in December 2010 and February 2011.[12] The final text of the draft Protocol that emerged from those meetings was adopted by consensus by the working group in February 2011.[13] It is the text that was ultimately adopted by the Human Rights Council in June 2011[14] and by the General Assembly in December 2011. As will be seen, some of the more progressive elements envisaged in the chairperson's original draft text were ultimately jettisoned in favour of a text which makes few concessions to the specific needs of children.

Framework of the Protocol

General Provisions
The first section of the Protocol sets forth a series of general provisions regarding the operation of the complaints procedure. Of particular interest here are

---

8   Proposal for a draft optional protocol prepared by Chairperson-Rapporteur of the Open-ended Working Group on an optional protocol to the Convention on the Rights of the Child to provide a communications procedure: UN Doc A/HRC/WG7/2/2 (1 September 2010) (hereinafter referred to as Chairperson's Draft Protocol).

9   Article 1(2), Chairperson's Draft Protocol.

10 Article 3, Chairperson's Draft Protocol.

11 Article 6(3) and Article 9(1), Chairperson's Draft Protocol.

12 Following the first meeting of the second session of the working group, the chairperson produced a 'Revised Draft Protocol' which served as a basis for the discussion at the second meeting of the second session in February 2011.

13 Report of the Open-ended Working Group on an optional protocol to the Convention on the Rights of the Child to provide a communications procedure: UN Doc A/HRC/17/36, Annex, p. 24 (hereinafter referred to as Second Report of the Working Group).

14 UN Doc. A/HRC/17/L8 (9 June 2011).

the terms of Article 2, which include a requirement on the CRC Committee, in exercising the functions conferred on it by the Protocol, to be guided by:

> ...the best interests of the child. It shall also have regard to the rights and views of the child, the views of the child being given due weight in accordance with the age and maturity of the child.[15]

The chairperson's draft Protocol had initially made reference to the 'best interests' principle, by providing that the CRC Committee should exercise its functions in a manner that '... respects the rights of the child and ensures that the best interests of the child are a primary consideration in all actions concerning the child'.[16] The inclusion of the 'best interests' principle was intended to reflect the emphasis placed during the first session of the working group on the importance of reflecting the special status of the child and the rights of children in the text.[17] While this explicit reference to the principle was welcomed at the second session, concern was expressed by numerous State representatives, NGOs and the CRC Committee that the chairperson's original draft had not gone far enough in reflecting the child's right to be heard in line with Article 12(1) of the CRC itself. This concern was accommodated in the final text by the insertion of a reference to the 'views of the child' in the body of Article 2. Article 3 of the Protocol goes on to provide specifically that in adopting rules of procedure, the CRC Committee shall have regard, in particular, to Article 2 '...in order to guarantee child-sensitive procedures'.[18]

Anticipating possible negative consequences for complainants and others who participate in the procedure, Article 4(1) of the Protocol requires each State party to take all appropriate steps to ensure that such individuals are '... not subjected to any human rights violation, ill-treatment or intimidation as a consequence of communications or cooperation with the Committee pursuant to the present Protocol'. The reference to 'any human rights violation' expands on the scope of protective measures stipulated in the recently drafted *Optional Protocol to the International Covenant on Economic, Social and Cultural Rights* (OP-ICESCR) and was inserted having regard to the heightened vulnerability of child complainants.[19] Article 4(2) provides further that the identity

---

15 Protocol, Article 2.

16 Chairperson's Draft Protocol, Article 1(2).

17 See 'explanatory memorandum', Chairperson's Draft Protocol, Pt II, para. 4.

18 Protocol, Article 3(1).

19 This issue had been highlighted by the NGO group for the CRC in its joint submission to the working group in advance of the second session in which it stressed the need for the

of any individual or group of individuals concerned shall not be revealed publicly without their express consent. This provision represents a compromise from the chairperson's original proposal that the author's identity not be revealed to the State party without his or her consent.[20] In the light of practical concerns on the part of States about their ability to respond effectively to complaints without knowing the alleged victim's identity, it was agreed that confidentiality could still be maintained by not disclosing the victim's identity (or that of his or her representative where relevant) to the public without their consent.[21]

Complainants

As regards eligibility to make a complaint, Article 5(1) of the Protocol provides for the possibility of communications being submitted by individuals or groups of individuals, within the jurisdiction of a State party, claiming to be victims of a violation by that State of any of the rights in the Convention or its two Protocols (i.e., the *Optional Protocol to the Convention on the Sale of Children, Child Prostitution and Child Pornography* (OPSC) and *the Optional Protocol to the Convention on the Involvement of Children in Armed Conflict* (OPAC)).[22] Where a communication is submitted on behalf of an individual or group of individuals, this is to be with their consent, unless the author can justify acting on their behalf without such consent.[23] The issue of submission of complaints 'on behalf of children' proved to be particularly contentious during the second session of the working group's deliberations. As was pointed out during the debate, the need to make provision for indirect submission is particularly acute in the case of children since it is highly unlikely that they could submit

---

instrument to be '...particularly attentive to the vulnerability of children as complainants'. In its view, the requirement only to prevent ill-treatment or intimidation (as was provided for in the original draft as well as in Article 13 of OP-ICESCR) did not reflect the full range of negative measures to which child complainants could be subjected as a result of making a complaint under the Protocol. Accordingly, it recommended that the scope of protection measures be extended to prevent *any* retaliatory measures (para. 11).

20   Chairperson's Draft Protocol, Article 6(2).

21   Note that the wording refers to all individuals 'concerned' so as to include representatives of children who have submitted a complaint on their behalf.

22   Protocol, Article 5(1).

23   Protocol, Article 5(2). The reference to 'individuals' as opposed to 'children' in Article 5(1) was deliberately chosen for being more inclusive and so as to facilitate the making of complaints by victims who were children at the time of the violation(s) in question, but who had not exhausted domestic remedies before they reached the age of majority.

complaints in most cases on their own.[24] While some delegations wished to restrict the categories of persons who could bring complaints on children's behalf, for example, to parents, legal guardians or relevant third parties, others warned against such a restrictive approach on the basis that it would not cover the case of children who did not have a legal guardian or situations where the parents themselves might be violating their children's rights. In the end, the final wording agreed upon is sufficiently wide to embrace the submission of complaints by persons other than parents or legal guardians.[25] It was decided to insert a further safeguard against the risk of manipulation into the text of Article 3(2) whereby the CRC Committee may decline to examine any communication which it considers not to be in the best interests of the child.

Consideration was also given during the drafting process to the possibility of including an explicit provision for 'collective complaints' in the body of the Protocol. Collective complaints may be differentiated from individual complaints insofar as they may be launched by representative organisations without the usual requirements to demonstrate victim status, the exhaustion of domestic remedies or indeed any particular time limit.[26] Attempts to make provision for such complaints in analogous UN treaty procedures have thus far foundered, notably in respect of the *Optional Protocol to the Convention on the Rights of Persons with Disabilities* (OP-CRPD) and the OP-ICESCR, and the experience under the CRC proved to be no different. Following discussions on the issue during the first session of the working group, the chairperson's original draft had provided for the possibility of such complaints. In general terms, he proposed that National Human Rights Institutions (NHRIs), ombuds-institutions and NGOs in consultative status with ECOSOC should be entitled to make complaints in respect of 'grave or systematic violations' of any of the rights in the Convention and its two substantive Protocols.[27] During

---

24 See the comments made by independent expert, Peter Newell: CRIN Daily Summary on Articles 1 and 2.

25 The final wording would allow for third parties (such as social workers) to bring complaints in situations where a conflict of interest between parent(s) and the child existed. The latter point was made by the NGO group for the CRC during the debate in a Joint Statement on Articles 1 and 2 of the draft optional protocol.

26 Collective complaints but not individual ones are currently possible under the Council of Europe's, *European Social Charter*: Additional Protocol to the European Social Charter Providing for a System of Collective Complaints (1995): http://conventions.coe.int/treaty/en/treaties/html/158.htm.

27 See Article 3(1) of the Chairperson's Draft Protocol. A further requirement under Article 3(1) was that the institutions in question should have particular competence in the rights

the initial debate on this in the second session of the working group, a number of States voiced their concerns about the provision for collective complaints on a variety of grounds.[28] These included specific concerns that the submission of such abstract complaints might mislead the CRC Committee or 'sap' its limited resources[29] and undermine the integrity of the individual complaints procedure.[30] It was also argued that such complaints could be time-consuming without adding value;[31] and that they would, in any event, overlap with the inquiry procedure envisaged elsewhere in the draft Protocol.[32] Other States,[33] independent experts[34] (including the CRC Committee)[35] and civil society[36] spoke in favour of including collective complaints to cater for cases in which individual complaints would be impossible or impractical, for example, where the victims are unable to lodge complaints or cannot be identified.[37] Somewhat predictably, however, the momentum to maintain a provision for collective complaints (even on an optional basis) did not survive the final drafting stages, with 'numerous delegations' at this

---

covered by the CRC and its Protocols and have been approved by the CRC Committee for that purpose.

28   Denmark, Greece and the Russian Federation each sought deletion of draft Article 3 at this stage of the negotiations.

29   Statement of the United Kingdom: CRIN Daily Summary on Article 3 and 12.

30   United States, Australia and Mexico: CRIN Daily Summary on Articles 3 and 12.

31   New Zealand: CRIN Daily Summary on Articles 3 and 12.

32   Switzerland, Japan and Belgium: CRIN Daily Summary on Articles 3 and 12. This point was made also by Brazil during discussions on the proposed inquiry procedure provided for in Articles 10 and 11 of the draft Protocol.

33   Notably Liechtenstein, Uruguay, Slovenia, Brazil, Argentina: CRIN Daily Summary on Articles 3 and 12.

34   See the comments of independent expert Peter Newell: CRIN Daily Summary on Articles 3 and 12.

35   See the comments of the vice-chair of the CRC, Jean Zermatten during the debate: CRIN Daily Summary on Article 3 and 12; and the CRC Committee's Comments, paras. 13–15.

36   See the Preliminary Joint NGO submission on the Revised Draft Protocol in February 2011, pp. 2, 3.

37   The European Network of Ombudspersons for Children (ENOC) further submitted that such complaints add a 'valuable preventive element: the process does not have to wait until violations have occurred and victims have been identified and come forward...it could also avoid the need for the Committee to consider multiple similar communications on behalf of individual victims'.

stage reiterating the concerns raised earlier.[38] At the initiation of the chair-person, it was agreed to delete the article in its entirety as part of a final compromise text.

Scope of the Complaints Mechanism

Another contentious issue that provoked considerable debate during the drafting of the Protocol was the question of the scope of complaints that could be made under it. In this respect, the chairperson's initial draft Protocol extended the competence of the CRC Committee to complaints against a State party in respect of any of the rights in the Convention and its substantive Protocols.[39] However, the original proposal allowed States to 'opt-out' at the time of ratification/accession to the possibility of complaints in respect of either of the two Protocols.[40] This formulation would have enabled States that were not party to the OPSC and the OPAC to ratify the Protocol on communications and opt-out of the procedure in respect of instruments which they had not actually ratified. A consequence of this approach, however, was that the 'opt-out' provision could also be invoked by States which had ratified one or both of the substantive Protocols. Not surprisingly, this formulation proved to be unpopular with the CRC Committee and with NGOs because of its potential to lead to a differentiation in rights protection by States in respect of obligations already assumed by them in respect of children.[41] One means of resolving this dilemma suggested by NGOs would be to delete the opt-out clause entirely and insert a provision to the effect that a complaint may not be made against a State in respect of rights set forth in an instrument to which that State is not a party.[42] The issue remained contentious until the final drafting session, at which it was ultimately decided not to maintain the 'opt-out' provision. Thus, the combination of Article 5(1) and Article 1(2) of the final Protocol (which expressly excludes the competence of the CRC Committee in respect of violations of rights set forth in an instrument to which the State is not party) means that a State which ratifies the Protocol will necessarily be accepting the competence

---

38   The provision for collective complaints was retained in Article 7 of the Revised Draft Protocol after the first meeting of the second session (Revised Draft Protocol) but it was dropped from the Final Draft Protocol after the second meeting in February.

39   Articles 2(1) and 3(1) respectively of the Chairperson's Draft Protocol.

40   Articles 2(3) and 3(2) respectively provided for the possibility of States withdrawing such a declaration at a later date: Chairperson's Draft Protocol.

41   See Joint NGO Submission, para. 3 and CRC Committee's Comments, para. 10.

42   Joint NGO Submission, para. 3.

of the CRC Committee to receive communications in respect of the CRC itself and either of the two Protocols to which it may be party.

Admissibility

As regards the admissibility criteria for making individual complaints, Article 7 of the Protocol provides that the CRC Committee may deem an application to be inadmissible when:

(a)   The communication is anonymous;

(b)   The communication is not in writing.

(c)   The communication constitutes an abuse of the right of submission or is incompatible with the provisions of the Convention and/or the Optional Protocols thereto;

(d)   The same matter has already been examined by the CRC Committee or has been or is being examined under another procedure of international investigation or settlement;

(e)   All available domestic remedies have not been exhausted. This shall not be the rule where the application of the remedies is unreasonably prolonged or unlikely to bring effective relief;

(f)   The communication is manifestly ill-founded or not sufficiently substantiated;

(g)   The facts that are the subject of the communication occurred prior to the entry into force of the Protocol for the State party concerned, unless those facts continued after that date.

(h)   The communication is not submitted within one year after the exhaustion of domestic remedies, except in cases where the author can demonstrate that it had not been possible to submit the communication within that time limit.

The ultimate failure of the working group to make concessions to the special position of children is perhaps most stark in the realm of admissibility. The chairperson's original draft was largely modelled on the agreed terms of the OP-CRPD, but it did incorporate a specific provision in respect of the domestic remedies rule which would have required the CRC Committee to apply the rule in a child-sensitive way.[43] However, during the debate on his proposal in the

---

43   See Article 4(d) of the Chairperson's Draft Protocol. The added wording would have required the CRC Committee to take into account the standpoint of the child when considering whether to waive the application of the domestic remedies rule on the commonly accepted ground of delay, by requiring it to '... interpret the application of the

second session of the working group, States decided to delete this provision on the basis that it departed from the wording used in other instruments. Moreover, the working group went on to insert further restrictive criteria into the body of the final Protocol, derived largely from the additional criteria incorporated into the OP-ICESCR. These include the requirement in para. (b) that the complaint be in writing; and the imposition of a time limit in para. (h) that the complaint must normally have been submitted within one year of the exhaustion of domestic remedies. Despite vigorous opposition from NGOs and the CRC Committee that such requirements would particularly disadvantage children, each was ultimately included in the text.[44] Serious consideration was also given to the possibility of adding a further criterion, ruling out communications where the author had not suffered a '... clear disadvantage, unless the Committee considers that the complaint raises a serious issue of general importance'.[45] While the latter proposal was eventually dropped, it is hard to reconcile the restrictive menu of admissibility criteria ultimately adopted in the final Protocol with the hortatory goals announced in the first session of making the procedure as 'child-friendly' as possible.

Interim Measures

Article 6 of the Protocol makes explicit provision for the CRC Committee, at any time after the receipt of a complaint, to request that a State party take such interim measures as may be necessary to avoid irreparable damage to the victim(s) of alleged violations. While this power has long since been regarded as implicit in the operation of early complaint procedures, and made explicit in later ones, it has increasingly become a source of tension vis-à-vis the United Nations treaty bodies and the contracting States. The tension is evident in the strident stance adopted on the matter by the Human Rights Committee (CCPR)

---

remedies in a manner sensitive to the impact that delays may cause to a child's well-being and development'.

44   A proposal to supplement the requirement that complaints must be in writing by making allowance for the submission of further non-written materials was also deleted at a late stage in the drafting: See Article 9(b) of the Revised Draft Protocol. However, it would seem open to the CRC Committee to receive such material as evidence in any case having regard to Article 10(1) of the final text of the Protocol which provides that the Committee shall consider communications received under the Protocol in the light of all 'documentation' submitted to it.

45   This criterion was included in square brackets in Article 10 of the Revised Draft Protocol which emerged from the negotiations at the first meeting of the second session. A similar criterion has recently been added to the framework of admissibility provided for in the ECHR and for the first time included in UN treaties in OP-ICESCR, Article 4.

in holding that a State which deliberately flouts a request for interim measures commits 'grave breaches' of its obligations under the *First Optional Protocol to the International Covenant on Civil and Political Rights* (OP-ICCPR)[46] and that a failure by a State to implement such interim measures as are indicated by the CCPR in a particular case is incompatible with the obligation to respect the procedure of individual petition established under that Protocol.[47] In its annual report in 2011, the Committee against Torture (CAT) acknowledged that complaints had been made by a number of States parties to *United Nations Convention Against Torture and Other Cruel, Inhuman and Degrading Treatment or Punishment* (UNCAT) about the high volume of requests for interim measures being made by the CAT in respect of complaints alleging violations of the principle of non-refoulement in Article 3 of the latter Convention.[48]

In this context, it is hardly surprising, therefore, that the NGO lobby and the CRC Committee[49] each advocated explicit recognition in the text of the mandatory nature of such measures.[50] This position was supported by Liechtenstein during the debate in the working group. Its delegate proposed that additional language be inserted, requiring States parties to take all appropriate steps to comply with such requests, leaving a certain 'margin of appreciation for acceptable responses'.[51] Mexico pressed further that interim measures should be taken by States parties as soon as complaints are received.[52] These suggestions were, however, given very short shrift by the majority of delegations. The United States, for example, advocated the very opposite approach, arguing that language should be added to the text to make it explicit that interim measures 'are not considered binding'.[53] Sweden suggested that the power to request interim measures should be removed entirely, or at least be limited only to situations where a complainant's life was at risk, while New Zealand believed that such measures should only be requested in 'exceptional circumstances'.[54]

---

46 *Piandiong et al v. The Philippines*, Communication No 869/1999 (2000), para. 5.2.

47 CCPR General Comment No 33, UN Doc CCPR/C/GC/33, para. 19.

48 Annual Report of the United Nations Committee against Torture (2009–2010): UN Doc A/65/44, para. 97.

49 See CRC Committee's Comments, para. 17.

50 Joint NGO Submission, para. 7.

51 See CRIN Daily Summary on Articles 4, 5 and 6.

52 See CRIN Daily Summary on Articles 4, 5 and 6.

53 A similar position was adopted by China, Singapore and Australia though the latter did not see the need for adding additional language to the text in this respect: see CRIN Daily Summary on Articles 4, 5 and 6.

54 See CRIN Daily Summary on Articles 4, 5 and 6. This is the formulation adopted in OP-ICESCR, Article 5(1).

Accordingly, the suggestion for tougher wording was not taken up and it is likely that at some stage in the future, the CRC Committee will find itself (like some of its counterparts) in a 'stand-off' situation with non-compliant respondent States in the matter of interim measures.

Procedure

Transmission of the Communication

As regards the processing of complaints, Article 8 of the Protocol provides that unless the CRC Committee considers a complaint inadmissible without reference to the State party concerned, it shall bring the complaint confidentially to the attention of the State party. The State party is then required to submit written explanations or statements, clarifying the matter and the remedy, if any, that may have been provided. In this regard, the State party must '...submit its response as soon as possible and within six months'.[55] Originally, the chairperson's draft protocol had proposed a time-line of three months[56] for States to revert to the CRC Committee, taking into account the emphasis that had been placed on ensuring speedy processing of complaints concerning children at the working group's first session.[57] When this proposal was initially discussed, objections[58] raised to such a tight time frame resulted in a considerable relaxation of the text to a requirement that States should merely 'endeavour' to submit their responses as soon as possible within six months.[59] On review of the latter text, a compromise formula which now requires State parties to revert to the CRC Committee as soon as possible and within six months was eventually agreed to in the final text. Thus, notwithstanding the special context of

---

55   Protocol, Article 8(2).

56   The only other complaints procedure which provides for a three-month time limit in this respect is ICERD, Article 14(6)(b).

57   Chairperson's Draft Protocol, Article 6(3) and see para. 21 of explanatory memorandum. This position was welcomed by civil society groups and the CRC Committee and also by certain States (notably the United Kingdom and Argentina) during the debate at the second session of the working group: See CRIN Daily Summary on Articles 4, 5 and 6.

58   Canada and the United States argued that a six-month limit would be more appropriate as a three-month limit would be very difficult to comply with for federal states in which the gathering of necessary facts and information can be more time-consuming. Thailand, the Czech Republic, Germany, Singapore, Belgium, Brazil, Egypt, New Zealand also supported extending the time limit to six months: See CRIN Daily Summary on Articles 4, 5 and 6.

59   Revised Draft Protocol, Article 11(2).

INTERNATIONAL JOURNAL OF CHILDREN'S RIGHTS 22 (2014) 205-225

children, the formula arrived at is essentially the same as that which is provided for in the other complaint procedures, and is even broader than the
three-month time limit provided for in *International Convention on the
Elimination of All Forms of Racial Discrimination* (ICERD).[60]

Friendly Settlement

Following the lead taken by the drafters of the OP-ICESCR, Article 9 of the
Protocol makes provision for the CRC Committee to make available its offices
to the parties concerned with a view to reaching a 'friendly settlement' of the
matter on the basis of respect for the obligations set forth in the Convention
and/or its substantive Protocols.[61] It may be expected that the CRC Committee
will develop rules regarding the approval of such settlements in its Rules of
Procedure, and in this respect, the overarching obligation on the Committee,
stipulated in Article 2, to be guided by the best interests of the child and to
have regard to the rights and views of the child, will also have to be taken into
account.

As with Article 7(2) of the OP-ICESCR, the chairperson had proposed in his
original draft Protocol that an agreement on a friendly settlement would
close consideration of a complaint under the Protocol.[62] However, the CRC
Committee and the NGO group for the CRC had urged the inclusion of further
safeguards in the text whereby the implementation of any settlement reached
could be monitored by the Committee and the case re-opened or re-submitted
in the event of non-implementation or unsatisfactory implementation of the
settlement.[63] The value of a post-settlement monitoring mechanism was
acknowledged by several States during the debate in the first meeting of the
second session.[64] As a result, an extra sentence was added to the text on
friendly settlements which specifically provided for the CRC Committee to
follow-up on the implementation of any friendly settlement within 12 months
of such settlement being reached.[65] While this was undoubtedly a progression
in terms of the development of the friendly settlement procedure, it stopped

---

60   ICERD, Article 14(6)(b). This point was made by NGOs at the working group's second
      meeting, who '...recalled that a three month limit exists in the ICERD and saw no reason
      not to follow this precedent'.
61   Final Draft Protocol, Article 9(1).
62   Chairperson's Draft Protocol, Article 7(2).
63   CRC Committee's Comments, para. 19 and Joint NGO Submission, para. 9.
64   Positive views in this respect were expressed by France, Brazil, Slovenia, Sweden and
      Spain. CRIN daily Summary of the working group's discussion on Articles 7, 8, 9 and 13 of
      the draft Protocol.
65   Revised Draft Protocol, Article 12(2).

short of explicitly empowering the Committee to re-open a case in the event of the settlement not being properly implemented.[66] Efforts to persuade the majority of States to agree to the re-opening of a settlement failed again at the final drafting session. Instead, it was decided to revert to the original formula employed by the chairperson, whereby agreement on a settlement 'closes consideration of the case',[67] with the caveat that the CRC Committee may follow-up on the question of implementation in the context of the relevant reporting procedure.[68]

Consideration of the Communication

As with the other treaty body complaint procedures, consideration of communications under the Protocol will be entirely confidential. In this respect, Article 10(2) of the Protocol provides that the CRC Committee shall hold 'closed meetings' when examining communications under the Protocol. In making its assessment, the Committee is required to consider communications 'as quickly as possible', in the light of documentation submitted to it, provided that this documentation is transmitted to the parties concerned.[69] The Protocol also includes a provision requiring the Committee to expedite its consideration of communications with respect to which it has requested interim measures.[70]

It may be noted that in directing the CRC Committee to consider complaints 'in light of all the documentation submitted to it', the text says nothing about the possibility of oral hearings. However, the Committee itself has stressed the need for it to be able to hear the views of any children when it examines

---

66   In this respect, note that an analogous provision in the ECHR, Article 37 and 39 provides that a case may be struck from the list of the European Court of Human Rights following a friendly settlement of the matter. Article 39(4) mandates the Committee of Ministers of the Council of Europe to 'supervise the execution of the terms of the friendly settlement as set out in the decision of the Court', while Article 37 empowers the court to restore any application to the list that has been previously struck off 'if it considers that the circumstances justify such a course'.

67   Protocol, Article 9(2).

68   Protocol, Article 11(2).

69   Protocol, Article 10(2). In this respect, it may be noted that a provision that had appeared during the drafting stage, specifying possible sources of other information was dropped from the text of the Revised Draft Protocol, Article 13(3). However, it would seem that Article 10(2) is thus widely drawn to include not only the parties' submissions but also any other documentation that may have been submitted to it by other bodies which appears to the CRC Committee to be relevant to the case.

70   Protocol, Article 10(3).

complaints submitted on their behalf. In its submissions to the working group, it urged that the draft text should indicate that '...when appropriate, the Committee will seek and invite the child or children to express their views (orally or in writing) in a manner compatible with the necessary celerity of the procedure and the spirit of the Convention'.[71] While the issue does not appear to have been pressed during the debate, Slovenia and Brazil did make the positive suggestion that the CRC Committee should incorporate child-sensitive and child-friendly provisions into its Rules of Procedure '...including a means to hear from children where appropriate'.[72] This suggestion is in line with the prevailing view that the failure to allude specifically to oral hearings in the texts of any of the UN treaty complaint procedures does not necessarily rule them out in principle. Accordingly, it should be open to the CRC Committee to make provision for oral hearings, especially in view of the stipulation in Article 12(2) of the CRC of the child's right to be heard in any judicial or administrative proceedings affecting him or her. For resource reasons, however, the implementation of any such practice seems unlikely.

A further blow to the hopes of achieving a child-centred Protocol was dealt in the final drafting session when assessment criteria for consideration of complaints regarding economic, social and cultural rights were incorporated into the text of Article 10(4). Inspired, obviously, by the successful inclusion of such criteria in the terms of the OP-ICESR,[73] the United Kingdom argued that similar criteria should be introduced which would require the CRC Committee to consider the 'reasonableness of State actions and the variety of possible alternatives' where economic, social and cultural rights were at issue.[74] This suggestion was supported by New Zealand, Switzerland and Canada, with the United States and Algeria actually proposing that the 'reasonableness' standard of review should be incorporated as regards all complaints brought under the Protocol.[75] NGOs and the CRC Committee had vigorously opposed this move on the basis that it would be difficult, impractical and unworkable to treat economic, social and cultural rights differently from civil and political rights as they appear in the CRC.[76] While the chair had apparently resisted the

---

71　CRC Committee's Comments, para. 20.

72　CRIN Daily Summary on Articles 7, 8, 9 and 13.

73　OP-ICESCR, Article 8(4).

74　CRIN Daily Summary on Articles 7, 8, 9 and 13.

75　CRIN Daily Summary on Articles 7, 8, 9 and 13.

76　See the arguments made by the NGO Coalition for a CRC Complaints Mechanism, the ICJ, the vice-chair of the CRC Committee (Jean Zermatten) and Peter Newell (independent expert): CRIN Daily Summary on Articles 7, 8, 9 and 13.

inclusion of such criteria in earlier drafts, the groundswell of support for such a provision during the final meeting resulted in its ultimate adoption in the text. There can be little doubt that its inclusion highlights the 'Pandora's box' that was arguably opened by the inclusion of such criteria in the text of the OP-ICESCR.

Once the Committee has reached a decision on the communication, its only formal obligation under the Protocol is that it must, without delay, 'transmit its views' to the State party concerned and to the complainant.[77] It is likely that the CRC Committee will follow the practice of the other treaty bodies in reaching its 'views' on communications, i.e., by means of consensus, with the proviso that members are free to append to any views their individual opinions (either concurring or dissenting). While the CRC Committee will be constrained by the Protocol to conduct its proceedings in 'closed meetings', the text actively requires the contracting States to 'make widely known' both the Protocol and the views and recommendations of the Committee, particularly in regard to matters involving the State party itself. This must be done by 'appropriate and active means and in accessible formats to adults and children, including those with disabilities'.[78]

Like the *Optional Protocol to the Convention on the Elimination of All Forms of Discrimination Against Women* (OP-CEDAW) and the OP-ICESCR, Article 11 of the third Protocol to the CRC provides specifically for a 'follow-up' procedure. As initially drafted, this procedure required the State party to give due consideration to the views of the CRC Committee, together with its recommendations, and submit a written response within three months.[79] Once again, in spite of vigorous objections from civil society and the CRC Committee itself regarding the importance of timely follow-up action in regard to children,[80] a suggestion to extend the time limit to six months for State responses was endorsed by the majority of States at the second session.[81] It should be noted in this context, however, that the Committee is empowered to invite the State to submit further information about any measures it has taken in response to its views or recommendations, including, as deemed appropriate, in periodic

---

77 Protocol, Article 10(5).

78 Protocol, Article 17.

79 Chairperson's Draft Protocol, Article 9(1).

80 CRIN Daily Summary on Articles 7, 8, 9 and 13.

81 Article 11(1) specifically provides that the State party shall submit its response '...as soon as possible and within six months'. An even weaker formulation that merely obliged States to 'endeavour' to submit its response 'as soon as possible within six months' was at one stage on the table, though this formulation (incorporated temporarily in Article 14(1) of the Revised Draft Protocol) was strongly resisted by NGOs and experts.

INTERNATIONAL JOURNAL OF CHILDREN'S RIGHTS 22 (2014) 205-225

reports to the Committee under the relevant provisions of the CRC (Article 44), OPSC (Article 12) and OPAC (Article 8).[82]

Article 15(1) of the Protocol enables the CRC Committee to transmit to the UN specialised agencies, funds and programmes and other competent bodies, with a State's consent, its views or recommendations concerning communications and inquiries that indicate a need for technical advice or assistance. By virtue of Article 15(2), the Committee may also bring to the attention of such bodies any matter arising from the communications which may assist them in deciding on the advisability of international measures likely to help States in implementing the rights in the CRC and/or the Optional Protocols thereto. These provisions are derived entirely from Article 14(1) and (2) of the OP-ICESCR. As such, the latter instrument was the first complaints procedure to introduce a formal means by which a treaty body's views and recommendations could be used to alert other relevant UN bodies and agencies of the need for technical advice and assistance in particular States. The insertion of such a measure in the OP-ICESCR, however, was deemed necessary because of the ambiguous reference in Article 2(1) of the parent instrument to the obligation on each State party to the ICESCR to take steps '... individually and through international assistance and cooperation, especially economic and technical, to the maximum of its available resources ...' with a view to achieving progressively the rights in the Covenant. To give further expression to this obligation, the drafters of the OP-ICESCR also agreed to the establishment of a trust fund with a view to providing expert and technical assistance to States that are experiencing difficulties in implementing the rights in the ICESCR on account of resource constraints.[83] Although the idea of establishing a similar trust fund in the context of the CRC was discussed at the second session, it did not receive significant support.

Conclusion

The elaboration of the complaints procedure for the CRC and its substantive Protocols certainly completes the jigsaw in terms of enabling individual complaints to be made under each of the core UN human rights treaties. While this was not the only motivation driving the campaign for such an instrument, it was clearly a dominant theme for those organisations that had lobbied intensively on the matter. As outlined at the outset, positive reasons for drafting the

---

82   Protocol, Article 11(2).

83   OP-ICESCR, Article 14(3).

Protocol appear to have been thoroughly endorsed by the States which took part in the opening session of the working group in 2009. Delegates at that session stressed the importance of ensuring that any such procedure should be 'child-friendly' and tailor-made in respect of the particular context at hand. Limited concessions to these goals have been made in the final text that emerged from the negotiations of the working group. These include the addition of the 'best interests' principle as a guiding one for the CRC Committee in exercising its functions under the Protocol; and the expansion of the range of 'protective measures' that should be taken by States in respect of child-complainants. On the other hand, there are no meaningful allowances made for children in respect of the time limits provided for in the Protocol for responding to complaints or indeed in respect of the follow-up procedure; the admissibility criteria are in some respects more rigorous than other complaint mechanisms; and provision has been made to constrain the CRC Committee's assessment of communications where violations of economic, social and cultural rights are alleged. On top of all this, the compelling arguments made to introduce a system for collective complaints in the case of children were ultimately rejected by the drafters. In the result, the bare text that has emerged demonstrates very little context-specific, innovation from that of other UN treaty individual complaints procedures. Indeed, this point was poignantly made by the chairperson of the CRC Committee in her closing contribution to the proceedings when she said: 'I am afraid that we have affirmed that children are mini-humans with mini-rights and the current draft fits this idea of children'.[84] It may be expected, however, that the CRC Committee itself will do its very best through its Rules of Procedure to develop the operation of the Protocol in a manner calculated to serve the best interests of children.

References

Egan S., *The UN Human Rights Treaty System: Law and Procedure* (Bloomsbury, 2011) 433–450. This article is a substantial extract from this work.

Child Rights Information Network, http://www.crin.org/law/CRC_complaints/ (last visited, September 2012).

---

84   CRIN Daily Summary: Complaints Mechanism: Chair's proposal largely accepted (16 February 2011), http://www.crin.org/resources/infodetail.asp?id=24181. The reference to 'mini-humans with mini-rights' is a quotation from a speech made by Maud de Boer Buquicchio, Deputy Secretary General of the Council of Europe: http://www.coe.int/t/dc/press/news/20061216_disc_sga_EN.asp (last accessed January 2012).

Child Rights Information Network, Daily Summaries of the Second Meeting of the Working Group on an optional protocol to the Convention on the Rights of the Child to provide a communications procedure that took place in Geneva from December 6 to December 10, 2010, available at http://www.crin.org/resources/ infodetail.asp?id=23489 (CRIN Daily Summaries, last visited, January 2012).

Churchill R. & KhaliqU., 'The collective complaints system of the European social charter: An effective mechanism for ensuring compliance with economic and social rights?', *European Journal of International Law*15 (2004): 417–456.

Comments by the Committee on the Rights of the Child on the proposal for a draft optional protocol prepared by the Chairperson-Rapporteur of the Open-ended Working Group on an optional protocol to the Convention on the Rights of the Child to provide a communications procedure, UN Doc A/HRC/WG.7/2/3 (October 2010), available at http://www2.ohchr.org/english/bodies/hrcouncil/OEWG/2nd session.htm (CRC Comments, last visited, September 2012).

Comments by ENOC on the proposal for a Draft Optional Protocol to the Convention on the Rights of the Child to provide a communications procedure (para. 7): http:// www2.ohchr.org/english/bodies/hrcouncil/OEWG/docs/ENOC_Comments_2nd Session.pdf (last visited, September 2012).

Joint NGO Submission to the Open-ended Working Group on an Optional Protocol to the Convention on the Rights of the Child to provide a communications procedure, submitted in advance of the second session in October 2010, p. 3: http://www2.ohchr .org/english/bodies/hrcouncil/OEWG/2ndsession.htm (Joint NGO Submission, last accessed January 2012).

Mahon C., 'Progress at the front: The draft optional protocol to the international covenant on economic, social and cultural rights', HRL Rev617 (2008): 636–637.

NGO Group for the CRC, http://www.crin.org/NGOGroup/childrightsissues/ ComplaintsMechanism (last visited, September 2012).

NGO Group for the CRC, Joint Statement on Articles 1 and 2 of the draft optional protocol: http://www.crin.org/resources/infoDetail.asp?ID=23683&flag=news (last visited, September 2012).

Optional Protocol to the Convention on the Rights of the Child on a Communications Procedure: Resolution of the General Assembly, UN. Doc. A/RES/66/138.

Preliminary Joint submission by the NGO group for the CRC on the Revised Draft Protocol (February 2012): http://www.crin.org/docs/Joint_NGO_Submission_OP _CRC_OEWG_Feb2011.pdf (last visited, September 2012).

Porter B., 'The reasonableness of Article 8(4) – Adjudicating claims from the margins', *Nordic Journal of Human Rights*27 (2009): 48–50.

Proposal for a draft optional protocol prepared by Chairperson-Rapporteur of the Open-ended Working Group on an optional protocol to the Convention on the Rights of the Child to provide a communications procedure: UN Doc A/HRC/ WG7/2/2 (1 September 2010) (Chairperson's Draft Protocol).

Report of the First Session of the open-ended working group to explore the possibility of elaborating an optional protocol to the Convention on the Rights of the Child to provide a communications procedure': UN Doc A/HRC/13/43 (21 January 2010), available at http://www2.ohchr.org/english/bodies/hrcouncil/OEWG/1stsession .htm (last visited, September 2012).

Report of the Second Session of the open-ended Working Group on an optional protocol to the Convention on the Rights of the Child to provide a communications procedure: UN Doc A/HRC/17/36 (16 May 2011), available at http://www2.ohchr.org/ english/bodies/hrcouncil/OEWG/2ndsession.htm (last visited, September 2012).

Revised Proposal for a draft optional protocol prepared by the Chairperson-Rapporteur of the Open-ended Working Group on an optional protocol to the Convention on the Rights of the Child to provide a communications procedure: UN Doc A/HRC/ WG7/2/4 (13 January 2011) (Revised Draft Protocol).

Statement by Yanghee Lee, chairperson of the CRC Committee to the 63rd session of the General Assembly, Third Committee, Item 60 (15 October 2008): www2.ohchr .org/english/bodies/crc/docs/Oral_statement_GA_63.doc (last accessed January 2012).

Vandenbogaerde A. & Vandenhole W., 'The optional protocol to the international covenant on economic, social and cultural rights: An Ex Ante assessment of its effectiveness in light of the drafting process', HRL Rev207 (2010): 223–226.

[5]

DON'T MIND THE GAP: THE RISE OF INDIVIDUAL COMPLAINT MECHANISMS WITHIN INTERNATIONAL HUMAN RIGHTS TREATIES

ALEXANDRA R. HARRINGTON*

INTRODUCTION

An iconic message of the London subway system is its warning to passengers to "mind the gap," or, in other words, to be careful of the space between the platform and the subway train.[1] This simple warning is applicable in many contexts. It has been particularly applicable to individuals in the international human rights law context. Traditionally, there has been a large gap between the human rights afforded to individuals as a matter of international law and the state-based ability to enforce these rights. However, the rise in the creation and use of individual complaint mechanisms as a part of international human rights treaties has created a significant challenge to the maintenance of this gap.

As this article will explain, the increase in the creation of these procedures for specific groups through specific conventions indicates an attempt to close the gap into which individuals with a human rights-based grievance usually have fallen, despite the essential nature of the rights guaranteed in such foundational documents as the Universal Declaration of Human Rights. This rise also indicates that individuals per se are being provided with a greater ability to close the gap by accessing the international human rights law system that has for so long regarded them as only peripheral actors to be given rights rather than as actors having the agency to claim these rights at the international level. In sum, the result is a steady penetration of the international system by individuals. Still, this access is designed by traditional international actors and therefore has

---

* Visiting Assistant Professor of Law, Albany Law School of Union University; Doctor of Civil Law Candidate, McGill University Faculty of Law. An earlier draft of this paper was presented at the 2009 McGill Law Faculty Graduate Students' Association Conference in Montreal, Canada. The author wishes to thank her family for their comments on this article. She also wishes to thank Kate Hunter, Jenna Feistritzer, and the staff of the Duke Journal of Comparative & International Law for their assistance with this article.

1. Signs informing passengers to "Mind the Gap" can be seen throughout the London subway system and have spawned an artistic movement centered on their content.

structural limitations. While some gap might indeed remain, increased access has demonstrated that individual complaint mechanisms, and those persons willing to utilize them to claim their international human rights, are closing the gap.

Part I of this article provides a brief discussion of the international human rights system generally and presents the concept of providing for an individual complaint mechanism within an international human rights treaty. Part II then discusses the individual complaint mechanisms that exist—or will exist—within key international human rights law treaties, specifically the International Covenant on Civil and Political Rights (ICCPR), the International Covenant on Economic, Social and Cultural Rights (ICESCR), the International Convention on the Elimination of All Forms of Racial Discrimination (CERD), the Convention on the Elimination of All Forms of Discrimination Against Women (CEDAW), the Convention against Torture and Other Cruel, Inhuman or Degrading Treatment or Punishment (CAT), the International Convention on the Protection of the Rights of All Migrant Workers and Members of Their Families (CMW), and the Convention on the Rights of Persons with Disabilities (CRPD).

Part III of this article compares the status, rights, and abilities of individuals under each of the human rights treaties. This Part argues that there is a discernible trend in the increase of asserted rights and claimed abilities of individuals through the expansion of individual complaint mechanisms. With the necessary background and a comparison of individual complaint mechanisms established, Part IV then examines individual access to the international human rights system and discusses the implications of this trend for the individuals themselves and the international human rights law system as a whole.

Although the state-centric nature of the international legal system necessarily results in a state-centric structure for individual complaint systems, Part IV argues that the increasing prominence of the individual in international human rights law is a discernible trend which stands to alter the current understanding of the international system. This prominence is based on a sense of individual empowerment which is greater than any one articulation of individual rights in the traditional sources of international human rights law. This Part goes on to argue that the increase in individual prominence is certainly laudable but that, by attaching this increased individual penetration of the international human rights law system to an ever-increasing series of specialized conventions, there is a significant risk of fragmenting the concept of the international human rights law system.

This Part suggests that a better alternative would be for individuals, as the foundation of international human rights law, to be able to access the system based on their identity as the holder of human rights and human dignity, rather than due to some specialized avenue of redress. This is especially so because these concepts of essential human rights and human dignity are at the core of the entire international human rights law system. This recommendation stresses both the internal status of people as holders of human rights and human dignity while also doing away with the need to create new quasi-judicial structures that are themselves potentially limiting depending on the ways in which they are drafted and function. Whether the appropriate body to handle such a concept is the Human Rights Committee or another body is not the overall concern of this article; rather, this article highlights an important trend in international human rights law and discusses the potential impacts of this trend on the international law system. Underlying this discussion is the overall question of how the ability of an individual to assert his human rights in an international legal context impacts the international community, the idea of state-centricity, and the understanding of international human rights law. At the individual level, the underlying question is whether individual identity, which is reinforced through access to the international human rights law system, is threatened by the fragmentation often related to asserting individual human rights violations.

Finally, the Conclusion summarizes the previous Parts and asserts that the international human rights law system has created a system wherein the individual has been empowered to the point of having a voice. The individual can now use that voice in order to claim a place—however limited—within the realm of international human rights law in a way that is at once quite important structurally and yet can also fragment individual identity when not understood holistically within the international human rights law system.

I. THE INTERNATIONAL HUMAN RIGHTS SYSTEM

The modern international human rights system is generally regarded as the product of World War II and the immediate post-war era,[2] although the antecedents of this system can be traced to the League of Nations.[3] In the Charter of the United Nations (UN Charter), the foundational document for the United Nations, the concept of human rights, including the

---

    2. Kitty Arambulo, *Drafting an Optional Protocol to the International Covenant on Economic, Social and Cultural Rights: Can an Ideal Become Reality?*, 2 U.C. DAVIS J. INT'L L. & POL'Y 111, 112-13 (1996).

    3. *See* League of Nations Covenant art. 23.

recognition of human dignity, is prevalent,[4] and this recognition has filtered through to the current organization and operation of the United Nations.[5]

Several years after the adoption of the UN Charter, the world community endorsed the Universal Declaration of Human Rights (UDHR), a sweeping statement recognizing and valuing the essential human rights and human dignities that are inherent in all persons.[6] The rights recognized in the UDHR include civil, political, economic, social, and cultural rights.[7] Although it is, as a matter of law, a non-binding instrument, the UDHR is regarded as an instrument of customary law and thus is binding on the international community as a whole.[8]

In the years following the adoption of the UDHR, the international community began to enshrine human rights in a series of treaties, most seminally the International Covenant on Civil and Political Rights and the International Covenant on Economic, Social and Cultural Rights.[9] A variety of theories exist as to the political and legal motivations for splitting human rights into these two categories for the purposes of legalization,[10] and a full discussion of these theories is outside the scope of this article. What is important to note is that these treaties were wide-ranging individually and also when ratified collectively. The international human rights treaties discussed below state that the principles and essential human rights guarantees made under the two Covenants, as well as the UDHR and the UN Charter, form the backbone of their content.[11]

Each of the international human rights treaties that contains an individual complaint mechanism is overseen in its implementation by a committee that is vested with the ability to decide on individual complaints.[12] A note should be made here that, as with all international treaties and agreements, international human rights treaties are only binding on those states that have consented to be bound by them.[13] Further,

---

4. *See generally* U.N. Charter.

5. *See, e.g., Human Rights,* UNITED NATIONS, http://www.un.org/en/rights/ (last visited July 23, 2011) (providing information on the involvement of the United Nations and its subsidiary agencies in human rights development and protection).

6. *See* Universal Declaration of Human Rights, G.A. Res. 217 (III) A, U.N. Doc. A/RES/217(III) (Dec. 10, 1948).

7. *See id.; see also* Arambulo, *supra* note 2, at 112-13 (describing the rights guaranteed by the Universal Declaration of Human Rights).

8. Arambulo, *supra* note 2, at 113.

9. *See Arambulo, supra note 2,* at 113-14.

10. *See* Arambulo, *supra* note 2, at 114-22.

11. *See infra* Part II.

12. *See infra* Part II.

13. *See* Vienna Convention on the Law of Treaties, art. 11, *opened for signature* May 23, 1969, 1155 U.N.T.S. 331 (entered into force Jan. 27, 1980).

when an individual complaint mechanism is contained within the text of a treaty rather than adopted as an optional protocol, States Parties do not become bound by the individual complaint mechanism provisions unless they specifically express that they intend to be bound upon ratification or afterward.[14]

As a general rule, the purpose of an individual complaint mechanism within a human rights treaty is to allow an individual, or the individual's representative, or, in some circumstances, a group of individuals to complain to the treaty committee regarding alleged violations of the human rights contained within the terms of the treaty.[15] The ability of an individual to bring such a complaint hinges first and foremost on whether the state alleged to have committed the violation is a State Party to the individual complaint mechanism.[16] Once this hurdle has been cleared, the individual then must satisfy the standing and justiciability requirements contained in the text of the instrument creating the individual complaint mechanism.[17] The treaty committee may dismiss the complaint on grounds of inadmissibility, or it may decide to hear the complaint in full, after which it can still dismiss the case on inadmissibility or can decide the case on the merits.[18] There is no appeals process once the treaty committee has made a decision on a complaint, rendering the decision of the treaty committee final.[19]

---

14. The terms of each human rights treaty provide the exact methods by which a State Party may agree to be bound under the individual complaint mechanism established in the overall treaty.

15. *See infra* Part II.

16. *See infra* Part II.

17. *See infra* Part II.

18. *See infra* Parts II, III.

19. *See generally* Optional Protocol to the International Covenant on Civil and Political Rights, *opened for signature* Dec. 19, 1966, 999 U.N.T.S. 171 (entered into force Mar. 23, 1976) [hereinafter Optional Protocol to ICCPR]; Optional Protocol to the International Covenant on Economic, Social and Cultural Rights, G.A. Res. 63/117, Annex, U.N. Doc. A/RES/63/117 (Dec. 10, 2008) [hereinafter Optional Protocol to ICESCR]; International Convention on the Elimination of All Forms of Racial Discrimination, *adopted and opened for signature* Dec. 21, 1965, 660 U.N.T.S. 195 (entered into force Jan. 16, 1969) [hereinafter CERD]; Optional Protocol to the Convention on the Elimination of All Forms of Discrimination Against Women, *adopted* Oct. 6, 1999, 2131 U.N.T.S. 83 (entered into force Dec. 22, 2000) [hereinafter Optional Protocol to CEDAW]; Convention Against Torture and Other Cruel, Inhuman or Degrading Treatment or Punishment, *adopted and opened for signature* Dec. 10, 1984, 1465 U.N.T.S. 85 (entered into force June 26, 1987) [hereinafter CAT]; International Convention on the Protection of the Rights of All Migrant Workers and Members of Their Families, *adopted* Dec. 18, 1990, 2220 U.N.T.S. 3 (entered into force July 1, 2003) [hereinafter CMW]; Optional Protocol to the Convention on the Rights of Persons with Disabilities, G.A. Res. 39/46, Annex, U.N. Doc. A/RES/39/46 (Dec. 10, 1984) [hereinafter Optional Protocol to CRPD].

In the event that a treaty committee decides in favor of the claimant, it has far less enforcement power than a domestic court.[20] The treaty committee may publicly pronounce that there has been a violation[21] and, depending on the depth of the violation, has issued language condemning the state practice that gave rise to it.[22] The treaty committee may also require that the errant State Party follow up within a stipulated period of time and provide the treaty committee with information on the measures taken to address the violation.[23] A further tool is to declare that the complainant is entitled to financial compensation for the wrongs done,[24] although an exact amount of compensation is not typically stated and such a finding is not enforceable in a domestic or international court.[25] While the individual complaint mechanism exists under the rubric of international law, much of its direct impact on States Parties depends upon the attitude of the States Parties themselves, as some have been far more amenable to bringing the findings of treaty committees into the realm of domestic legal influence.[26]

---

20. *See generally* Optional Protocol to ICCPR, *supra* note 19; Optional Protocol to ICESCR, *supra* note 19; CERD, *supra* note 19; Optional Protocol to CEDAW, *supra* note 19; CAT, *supra* note 19; CMW, *supra* note 19; Optional Protocol to CRPD, *supra* note 19; *see also* Human Rights Committee, General Comment No. 33: The Obligations of State Parties Under the Optional Protocol to the International Covenant on Civil and Political Rights, U.N. Doc. CCPR/C/GC/33 (Nov. 5, 2008), at http://www2.ohchr.org/english/bodies/hrc/comments.htm [hereinafter Human Rights Committee, General Comment No. 33].

21. *See* Human Rights Committee, General Comment No. 33, *supra* note 20, para. 12; Wade M. Cole, *When All Else Fails: International Adjudication of Human Rights Abuse Claims, 1976-1999*, 84 SOCIAL FORCES 1909, 1911-12 (2006) (discussing the prevalence of public shaming through the finding of a violation as a meaningful method of ensuring State Party compliance with a finding of the Human Rights Committee).

22. *See* Judge v. Canada, Views, Human Rights Comm. 78th Sess., July 14-Aug. 8, 2003, U.N. Doc. CCPR/C/78/D/829/1998 (Oct. 20, 2003) (regarding the deportation of an individual to a state in which he would face the death penalty); Johnson v. Jamaica, Views, Human Rights Comm. 56th Sess., Mar. 18-Apr. 4, 1996, U.N. Doc. CCPR/C/56/D/588/1994 (Aug. 5, 1996) (noting the Committee's disapproval of the imposition of the death penalty where the ICCPR's provisions are not respected during the trial).

23. *See* Human Rights Committee, General Comment No. 33, *supra* note 20, para. 14.

24. *See, e.g.,* Wilson v. Philippines, Views, Human Rights Comm. 79th Sess., Oct. 20-Nov. 7, 2003, U.N. Doc. CCPR/C/79/D/868/1999 (Nov. 11, 2003).

25. *See, e.g., id.*

26. *See* Shotaro Hamamoto, *An Undemocratic Guardian of Democracy – International Human Rights Complaint Procedures*, 38 VICTORIA U. WELLINGTON L. REV. 199, 200 (2007).

II. INTERNATIONAL HUMAN RIGHTS TREATIES CONTAINING INDIVIDUAL COMPLAINT MECHANISMS

A. International Covenant on Civil and Political Rights

The International Covenant on Civil and Political Rights (ICCPR) was adopted in 1966 and became effective in 1976.[27] Although the provisions of the ICCPR are themselves comprehensive and manifest the collective understanding by the international community regarding the civil and political rights enjoyed by individuals,[28] particularly as linked to the statements in the UDHR,[29] the individual complaint mechanism established for the ICCPR is not contained in its main body.[30] Rather, the individual complaint mechanism is located in the First Optional Protocol to the International Covenant on Civil and Political Rights (ICCPR Protocol).[31]

The ICCPR Protocol was also adopted in 1966 and became effective in 1976.[32] As of the writing of this article, there are 167 States Parties to the ICCPR[33] and 114 States Parties to the ICCPR Protocol,[34] establishing both the ICCPR and the ICCPR Protocol as two of the most universally ratified conventions within the modern international law system. Under the terms of the ICCPR Protocol, jurisdiction to hear complaints from individuals who assert that they have been victims of violations of human rights guaranteed under the ICCPR is vested in the Human Rights Committee.[35] In order to assert such a complaint against a State Party, an individual must be subject to the jurisdiction of the State Party,[36] the meaning of which has caused no small level of controversy throughout the life of the ICCPR Protocol.[37]

---

27. International Covenant on Civil and Political Rights, *adopted* Dec. 16, 1966, 999 U.N.T.S. 171 (entered into force Mar. 23, 1976).

28. *See generally id.*

29. *See id.* at pmbl.

30. *See generally id.*

31. *See* Optional Protocol to ICCPR, *supra* note 19, arts. 1 to 5.

32. *See* Optional Protocol to ICCPR, *supra* note 19; *see also Optional Protocol to the International Covenant on Civil and Political Rights*, UNITED NATIONS TREATY COLLECTION, http://treaties.un.org/Pages/ViewDetails.aspx?chapter=4&lang=en&mtdsg_no=IV-5&src=TREATY (last visited Nov. 8, 2011) [hereinafter Optional Protocol to ICCPR Summary].

33. *International Covenant on Civil and Political Rights*, UNITED NATIONS TREATY COLLECTION, http://treaties.un.org/pages/ViewDetails.aspx?src=TREATY&mtdsg_no=IV-4&chapter=4&lang=en (last visited July 23, 2011).

34. Optional Protocol to ICCPR Summary, *supra* note 32.

35. Optional Protocol to ICCPR, *supra* note 19, at pmbl., art. 1.

36. Optional Protocol to ICCPR, *supra* note 19, art. 1.

37. For a discussion of these issues, see Orna Ben-Naftali, *The Extraterritorial Application of Human Rights to Occupied Territories*, 100 PROC. OF THE ANN. MEETING (AM. SOC. OF INT'L L.) 90 (2006).

Once a complaint is filed with the Human Rights Committee, the Committee reviews it for admissibility. In order to have standing to bring a complaint under the ICCPR, an individual must have exhausted all domestic remedies that are available to them in the context of the matter giving rise to the complaint.[38] Furthermore, the complaint cannot be submitted by an individual anonymously,[39] cannot fall into either category of "an abuse of the right of submission" or "incompatible with the provisions of the [ICCPR]" as determined by the Human Rights Committee,[40] and cannot be pending before another international body or be the subject of a settlement as determined by an international body.[41] There is an exception to the domestic remedy exhaustion requirement: where the Human Rights Committee decides that there is an unreasonable delay in allowing the complainant to proceed with the requisite domestic remedies, the Committee may waive that prong of standing.[42]

In recent years, there has been another admissibility hurdle where the individual bringing the claim is not the individual whom the State Party is alleged to have harmed.[43] In this regard, the Human Rights Committee has been largely willing to grant standing to immediate family members of the alleged victim—particularly in cases of disappearance,[44] alleged unlawful detention and torture,[45] and extrajudicial killings[46]—but has been far more

---

38. Optional Protocol to ICCPR, *supra* note 19, art. 2.; *see also* Mireille G.E. Bijnsdorp, *The Strength of the Optional Protocol to the United Nations Women's Convention*, 18 NETH. Q. HUM. RTS. 329, 331 (2000) (discussing the tie between resources available to potential claimants and their actual tendency to both follow the requisite domestic procedures and file international claims).

39. Optional Protocol to ICCPR, *supra* note 19, art. 3.

40. Optional Protocol to ICCPR, *supra* note 19, art. 3.

41. Optional Protocol to ICCPR, *supra* note 19, art. 5.

42. Optional Protocol to ICCPR, *supra* note 19, art. 5.

43. *See infra* notes 44-48.

44. *See, e.g.*, Grioua, née Atamna v. Algeria, Views, Human Rights Comm. 90th Sess., July 9-27, 2007, U.N. Doc. CCPR/C/90/D/1327/2004 (July 10, 2007); Kimouche, née Cheraitia v. Algeria, Views, Human Rights Comm. 90th Sess., July 9-27, 2007, U.N. Doc. CCPR/C/90/D/1328/2004 (July 10, 2007); Bousroual v. Algeria, Views, Human Rights Comm. 86th Sess., Mar. 13-31, 2006, U.N. Doc. CCPR/C/86/992/2001 (Mar. 15, 2006); Bautista v. Colombia, Views, Human Rights Comm. 55th Sess., U.N. Doc. CCPR/C/55/D/563/1993 (Oct. 27, 1995); Izquiero v. Uruguay, Views, Human Rights Comm. 15th Sess., U.N. Doc. CCPR/C/15/D/73/1981 (Apr. 1, 1982).

45. *See, e.g.*, Bondonga v. Democratic Republic of the Congo, Views, Human Rights Comm. 96th Sess., July 13-31, 2009, U.N. Doc. CCPR/C/96/D/1483/2006 (July 30, 2009); Khuseynova & Butaeva v. Tajikistan, Views, Human Rights Comm. 94th Sess., Oct. 13-31, 2008, U.N. Doc. CCPR/C/94/D/1263-1264/2004 (Oct. 20, 2008); Izquiero v. Uruguay, *supra* note 44; Khudayberganova v. Uzbekistan, Views, Human Rights Comm. 90th Sess., July 9-27, 2007, U.N. Doc. CCPR/C/90/D/1140/2002 (Aug. 7, 2007); Aber v. Algeria, Views, Human Rights Comm. 90th Sess., July 9-27, 2007, U.N. Doc. CCPR/C/90/D/1439/2005 (Aug. 16, 2007).

46. *See, e.g.*, Bazarov v. Uzbekistan, Views, Human Rights Comm. 87th Sess., July 10-28, U.N. Doc. CCPR/C/87/D/959/2000 (Aug. 8, 2006); Bautista v. Colombia, *supra* note 44; Camargo v.

reticent to grant standing to those claiming to speak for a particular community or even where a physician or lawyer has lodged a claim on behalf of a patient[47] or client.[48] In these cases, the Human Rights Committee typically has been unable to substantiate that those other than immediate family members have the appropriate agency to speak for the alleged victim.[49] What this practice highlights is that the ICCPR Protocol and the Human Rights Committee are focused on the individual and those directly affected by violations, rather than outside persons or groups.

If a complaint survives the initial admissibility decision, it then goes before the Human Rights Committee for a decision on the merits. These decisions focus on the strength of the allegations made and, in light of the additional evidence that is provided at that point, frequently return to the issue of admissibility.[50] In particularly dire situations, the Human Rights Committee has interpreted its mandate under the ICCPR Protocol to include the ability to request that the accused State Party take interim measures to guarantee the protection of the claimant.[51] These requests have been prevalent in complaints involving the imposition of the death penalty.[52]

The ICCPR Protocol permits a state to renounce its status as a party to the Protocol provided that it follows a specific procedure.[53] The renunciation is not legally effective until three months after notification and

---

Colombia, Views, Human Rights Comm. 15th Sess., U.N. Doc. CCPR/C/15/D/45/1979 (Mar. 31, 1982).

47. *See, e.g.*, L.A. & U.R. v. Uruguay, Views, Human Rights Comm. 18th Sess., U.N. Doc. CCPR/C/18/D/128/1982 (Apr. 6, 1983).

48. *See, e.g.*, Palma v. Panama, Decisions, Human Rights Comm. 51st Sess., U.N. Doc. CCPR/C/51/D/436/1990 (July 26, 1994); Thompson v. Panama, Decisions, Human Rights Comm. 52nd Sess., U.N. Doc. CCPR/C/52/D/438/1990 (Oct. 21, 1994); Simons v. Panama, Decisions, Human Rights Comm. 52nd Sess., U.N. Doc. CCPR/C/52/D/460/1991 (Oct. 25, 1994); Leach v. Jamaica, Views, Human Rights Comm. 57th Sess., July 8-26, 1996, U.N. Doc. CCPR/C/57/D/546/1993 (Aug. 1, 1996); Y. v. Australia, Decisions, Human Rights Comm. 69th Sess., July 10-28, 2000, U.N. Doc. CCPR/C/69/D/772/1997 (Aug. 8, 2000); Padilla v. Philippines, Views, Human Rights Comm. 70th Sess., Oct. 16-Nov. 3, 2000, U.N. Doc. CCPR/C/70/D/869/1999 (Oct. 19, 2000).

49. *See* L.A. v. Uruguay, *supra* note 47; Palma v. Panama, *supra* note 48; Thompson v. Panama, *supra* note 48; Leach v. Jamaica, *supra* note 48; Y. v. Australia, *supra* note 48; Padilla v. Philippines, *supra* note 48.

50. *See, e.g.*, K.L. v. Denmark, Views, Human Rights Comm. 10th Sess., July 14-Aug. 1, 1980, U.N. Doc. CCPR/C/10/D/72/1980 (July 31, 1980).

51. Bijnsdorp, *supra* note 38.

52. For a discussion of this trend in regards to complaints brought against Jamaica,Trinidad and Tobago in particular, and the resulting actions taken by these states to avoid agreement with the Human Rights Committee's decisions, *see* Laurence R. Helfer, *Overlegalizing Human Rights: International Relations Theory and the Commonwealth Caribbean Backlash Against Human Rights Regimes*, 102 COLUM. L. REV. 1832 (2002).

53. Optional Protocol to ICCPR, *supra* note 19, art. 12.

does not void the applicability of the Human Rights Committee's jurisdiction over cases already pending against the State Party.[54]

B. International Covenant on Economic, Social & Cultural Rights

The International Covenant on Economic, Social & Cultural Rights (ICESCR) was adopted in 1966 and became effective in 1976.[55] At the time of writing, there are 160 States Parties to the ICESCR.[56] While there are many points at which the ICESCR mirrors the ICCPR, it is widely held that the terms of the ICCPR are quantifiable and thus subject to quasi-judicial oversight,[57] while the rights guaranteed under the ICESCR are more fluid and essentially aspirational, making them inappropriate for quasi-judicial oversight.[58] At the time they were adopted, there were also concerns that the rights contained in the ICESCR were new, or at least largely uncodified, at the national level, whereas the rights guaranteed under the ICCPR were typically found in the national laws of UN member states.[59] As a result, unlike the ICCPR, the ICESCR did not contain direct provisions or a protocol creating an individual complaint mechanism.[60]

Throughout the history of the ICESCR, and particularly over the past few decades, a mounting chorus of civil society actors, the Committee on Economic, Social and Cultural Rights (ICESCR Committee), and some governments began to pressure the international community to create an individual complaint mechanism within the ICESCR context.[61] In particular, the ICESCR Committee asserted that an individual complaint mechanism was necessary in order to develop an understanding of the terms contained in the ICESCR, to establish how these terms should be implemented, and to create an effective method for and forum in which

---

54. Optional Protocol to ICCPR, *supra* note 19, art. 12.

55. *International Covenant on Economic, Social and Cultural Rights*, UNITED NATIONS TREATY COLLECTION, http://treaties.un.org/Pages/ViewDetails.aspx?src=TREATY&mtdsg_no=IV-3&chapter=4&lang=en (last visited July 23, 2011).

56. *Id.*

57. *See* Tara J. Melish, *Introductory Note to the Optional Protocol to the International Covenant on Economic, Social and Cultural Rights*, 48 INT'L L. MATERIALS 256, 256-57 (2009); Michael J. Dennis & David P. Stewart, *Justiciability of Economic, Social, and Cultural Rights: Should There Be an International Complaints Mechanism to Adjudicate the Rights to Food, Water, Housing, and Health?*, 98 AM. J. INT'L L. 462, 464-67 (2004); Wouter Vandenhole, *Completing the UN Complaint Mechanisms for Human Rights Violations Step by Step: Towards a Complaints Procedure Complementing the International Covenant on Economic, Social and Cultural Rights*, 21 NETH. Q. HUM. RTS. 423, 431 (2003).

58. *See* Melish, *supra* note 57, at 256-57; Dennis & Stewart, *supra* note 57, at 464-67.

59. Arambulo, *supra* note 2, at 116.

60. *See* Melish, *supra* note 57, at 256-57; Arambulo, *supra* note 2, at 113-17.

61. *See* Melish, *supra* note 57, at 256; Vandenhole, *supra* note 57, at 425.

individuals could voice alleged violations of their rights.[62] Others argued that the ICESCR would be unable to give effect and credence to the rights it created without an individual complaint mechanism.[63]

Many of the issues associated with acceptance of an individual complaint mechanism focus on the collective or community-based nature of the rights provided for under the ICESCR.[64] There is still a good deal of debate as to whether this will be detrimental to the implementation of a respected and well-functioning individual complaint mechanism under the ICESCR or whether the individual complaint mechanism will serve as a means to clarify that the rights and guarantees under the ICESCR are in fact primarily and essentially individual in nature.[65]

During the drafting process that led to the creation of the ICESCR Protocol text, prominent human rights scholars attempted to draw distinct categories within each right under the ICESCR, such that there would be an obligatory element that could be made the subject of an individual complaint.[66] These scholars asserted that the system would establish a softer set of elements and recommended state practices that would be beneficial to the implementation of each particular right but which would not create an obligation that would be sufficient to use as the basis for a complaint.[67] Other arguments centered on the idea of establishing minimum levels of rights protections based on the importance of certain rights within the ICESCR.[68] The ICESCR Protocol negotiation proceedings generated several other similar formulas regarding the levels of immediate and future state obligations for the purposes of justiciability.[69] At heart, they all establish that there is such a dichotomy and that the ICESCR Protocol is intended to allow for an individual complaint mechanism that at the very

---

62. *See* Melish, *supra* note 57, at 257.

63. Dennis & Stewart, *supra* note 57, at 462; *but see id.* at 466 (stating the author's views that the rights contained in the ICESCR are not in fact better off in a judicial setting and that empowering the ICESCR Committee to render judgments on the extent of obligations under the ICESCR is potentially dangerous as a practice).

64. *See* Melish, *supra* note 57, at 259.

65. Melish, *supra* note 57, at 259.

66. *See* Arambulo, *supra* note 2, at 130-31.

67. Arambulo, *supra* note 2, at 131. It should be noted that, despite the deeply held differences in state opinion regarding the justiciability of the rights guaranteed under the ICESCR, the international community and the states that comprise it do, with near unanimity, agree that the rights created under the ICESCR itself are essential human rights. *See* Vandenhole, *supra* note 57, at 430.

68. Vandenhole, *supra* note 57, at 437-438.

69. Vandenhole, *supra* note 57, at 443 (discussing several forms of obligation dichotomies, particularly the idea of the obligations to respect, to protect, and to fulfill); Cees Flinterman, *Appendix II: The Maastricht Guidelines on Violations of Economic, Social and Cultural Rights*, 15 NETH. Q. HUM. RTS. 244, 247 (1997).

least holds States Parties accountable under the minimum obligation standards.[70]

The preamble to the ICESCR Protocol depends heavily on the terms and guarantees of the UDHR and the ICCPR, as well as the ICESCR, emphasizing the individual and the rights guaranteed to him as a result of his essential human dignity.[71] All States Parties agree to and recognize that "[c]ommunications may be submitted by or on behalf of individuals or groups of individuals, under the jurisdiction of a State Party, claiming to be victims of a violation of any of the economic, social and cultural rights set forth in the Covenant by that State Party."[72] Those drafting the ICESCR Protocol specifically chose the term "victim" to ensure that the individual complaint mechanism would not be read narrowly in terms of standing, and to guarantee that the mechanism would have a broad construction into the future.[73] In terms of standing, the ICESCR Protocol provides that an agent is only allowed to submit a complaint on behalf of another person with that person's consent or, in the event that consent cannot be established, that the complainant provide a justification as to why consent is unavailable.[74] Jurisdiction over individual complaints brought under the ICESCR Protocol is vested in the ICESCR Committee.[75]

Under the ICESCR Protocol, an individual complaint is not admissible if: all appropriate domestic remedies have not been exhausted (unless "the application of such remedies is unreasonably prolonged");[76] the complaint was submitted more than a year after the final exhaustion of appropriate domestic remedies (unless the complainant was demonstrably unable to comply with this limitation);[77] the facts upon which the complaint is based occurred before the relevant State Party became legally bound by the terms of the ICESCR Protocol (unless the acts continued after the State Party became bound by the ICESCR Protocol);[78] the subject of the complaint is pending before another international body or there was an examination of the subject of the complaint by another international body;[79] the terms of the complaint are "incompatible with the provisions of the Covenant;"[80]

---

70. Vandenhole, *supra* note 57, at 443.
71. Optional Protocol to ICESCR, *supra* note 19, at pmbl.
72. Optional Protocol to ICESCR, *supra* note 19, art. 2.
73. Arambulo, *supra* note 2, at 132.
74. Optional Protocol to ICESCR, *supra* note 19, art. 2.
75. *See* Optional Protocol to ICESCR, *supra* note 19, art. 1; Melish, *supra* note 57, at 257.
76. Optional Protocol to ICESCR, *supra* note 19, art. 3(1).
77. Optional Protocol to ICESCR, *supra* note 19, art. 3(2)(a).
78. Optional Protocol to ICESCR, *supra* note 19, art. 3(2)(b).
79. Optional Protocol to ICESCR, *supra* note 19, art. 3(2)(c).
80. Optional Protocol to ICESCR, *supra* note 19, art. 3(2)(d).

there is insufficient evidence presented to substantiate the complaint or the complaint is "exclusively based on reports disseminated by mass media;"[81] "[i]t is an abuse of the right to submit a communication;"[82] or, the complaint is submitted anonymously or not in writing.[83] The Protocol requires that a complaint allege a particular, individual harm, however there are certain limited circumstances in which this requirement can be softened to allow for admissibility where the ICESCR Committee decides that the complaint alleges "a serious issue of general importance."[84]

The ICESCR Protocol vests the ICESCR Committee with the ability to request that the State Party involved in a complaint take steps necessary to protect the life, integrity, and security of the complainant until there is a final decision on the complaint.[85] Further, the Protocol explicitly requires that States Parties "take all appropriate measures to ensure that individuals under its jurisdiction are not subjected to any form of ill-treatment or intimidation as a consequence of communicating with the Committee."[86]

The ICESCR Protocol provides that States Parties are able to renounce their status as a party to the ICESCR Protocol and to withdraw from the ICESCR Protocol with the limitation that the renunciation does not become effective for six months.[87] During that six-month time period, the ICESCR Committee may consider existing complaints against the renouncing State Party.[88]

Due to the nature of the rights contained in the ICESCR, the ICESCR Protocol allows the ICESCR Committee to use a reasonableness standard when addressing whether a particular State Party is fulfilling its obligations.[89] Additionally, the Protocol vests the ICESCR Committee with the ability to consult UN and other relevant bodies to receive information appropriate to its determinations.[90]

---

81. Optional Protocol to ICESCR, *supra* note 19, art. 3(2)(e).
82. Optional Protocol to ICESCR, *supra* note 19, art. 3(2)(f).
83. Optional Protocol to ICESCR, *supra* note 19, art. 3(2)(g).
84. Optional Protocol to ICESCR, *supra* note 19, art. 4.
85. Optional Protocol to ICESCR, *supra* note 19, art. 5(1).
86. Optional Protocol to ICESCR, *supra* note 19, art. 13.
87. Optional Protocol to ICESCR, *supra* note 19, art. 20(1).
88. Optional Protocol to ICESCR, *supra* note 19, art. 20(2).
89. Optional Protocol to ICESCR, *supra* note 19, art. 8(4).
90. Optional Protocol to ICESCR, *supra* note 19, art. 8(3).

C. International Convention on the Elimination of All Forms of Racial Discrimination

The International Convention on the Elimination of All Forms of Racial Discrimination (CERD) was adopted in 1965 and entered into force in 1969.[91] Although the CERD has been widely ratified by the global community,[92] the individual complaint mechanism established under it has not been as successful in attracting States Parties.[93] Indeed, the CERD individual complaint mechanism only became effective in 1982, when it received the requisite number of States Parties.[94]

As with the ICESCR Protocol, states are concerned with the potentially broad and difficult to define (as well as limit) jurisdiction of an individual complaint mechanism established to hear alleged violations of the CERD, which has been drawn in a fluid manner to allow for a high amount of flexibility in its overall application.[95] Interestingly, the opening paragraph of the CERD preamble contains a broad statement regarding the essential human rights and dignities of individuals and their place in non-discrimination laws and protections, which itself can be seen as a vehicle to support the expansion of the role of the individual in the international system where violations of the CERD's provisions occur.[96]

The individual complaint mechanism is set out in Article 14 of the CERD.[97] Under the terms of this mechanism, both individuals and groups of individuals have standing to bring complaints against States Parties to the CERD Committee, provided that the offense occurred within the jurisdiction of the relevant State Party and pertains to an alleged violation of the rights contained in the CERD.[98] Unlike other international human rights treaties with individual complaint mechanisms, the CERD requires that a State Party indicate a domestic body that will be charged with examining the complaint first.[99] In the event that there is no satisfaction

---

91. *International Convention on the Elimination of All Forms of Racial Discrimination*, UNITED NATIONS TREATY COLLECTION, http://treaties.un.org/Pages/ViewDetails.aspx?src=TREATY&mtdsg_no=IV-2&chapter=4&lang=en (last visited July 23, 2011) [hereinafter CERD Summary].

92. To date, there are 175 States Parties to the CERD. *See* CERD Summary, *supra* note 91.

93. *See id.* (providing the statements of States Parties that have become part of the individual complaint mechanism); *see also* William F. Felice, *The UN Committee on the Elimination of All Forms of Racial Discrimination: Race, and Economic and Social Human Rights*, 24 HUM. RTS. Q. 205, 213 (2002).

94. Rüdiger Wolfrum, *The Committee on the Elimination of Racial Discrimination*, 3 MAX PLANCK Y.B. U.N. L. 489, 511-13 (1999).

95. Felice, *supra* note 93, at 213.

96. *See* CERD, *supra* note 19, at pmbl.

97. CERD, *supra* note 19, art. 14.

98. CERD, *supra* note 19, art. 14(1).

99. CERD, *supra* note 19, art. 14(2).

from this body, the CERD Committee may then exercise jurisdiction over the matter.[100] Some States Parties elected to bypass this step and declare that the CERD Committee has jurisdiction without having to go through a domestic body first—a step which is allowable under the CERD and arguably promotes individual access to the international system since it results in an international body having jurisdiction.[101]

The only justiciability requirement is that a complainant must have exhausted all applicable domestic remedies prior to bringing the complaint to the CERD Committee.[102] This requirement can be waived when "the application of the remedies is unreasonably prolonged."[103]

States Parties are allowed to withdraw their assent to the CERD Committee's jurisdiction over individual complaints without the usual waiting period for effectiveness,[104] although the CERD ensures that a withdrawal may not impact any of the complaints pending before the CERD Committee prior to withdrawal.[105]

D. Convention on the Elimination of All Forms of Discrimination Against Women

The Convention on the Elimination of All Forms of Discrimination against Women (CEDAW) entered into force in 1981 without any provisions relating to an individual complaint mechanism.[106] In subsequent years, the idea of creating an individual complaint mechanism for CEDAW began to gain popularity, resulting in several high-level international workshops and meetings which sought to frame a potential optional protocol that would establish an individual complaint mechanism.[107]

---

100.   CERD, *supra* note 19, art. 14(5).

101.   CERD Summary, *supra* note91.

102.   CERD, *supra* note 19, art. 14(7)(a).

103.   CERD, *supra* note 19, art. 14(7)(a).

104.   CERD, *supra* note 19, art. 14(3).

105.   CERD, *supra* note 19, art. 14(3).

106.   Convention on the Elimination of All Forms of Discrimination Against Women, *opened for signature* Mar. 1, 1980, 1249 U.N.T.S. 13 (entered into force Sept. 3, 1981) [hereinafter CEDAW]; *see also Convention on the Elimination of All Forms of Discrimination Against Women*, UNITED NATIONS TREATY COLLECTION, http://treaties.un.org/Pages/ViewDetails.aspx?src=TREATY&mtdsg_no=IV-8&chapter=4&lang=en (last visited July 23, 2011) [hereinafter CEDAW Summary].

107.   Kwong-Leung Tang, *The Leadership Role of International Law in Enforcing Women's Rights: The Optional Protocol to the Women's Convention*, 8 GENDER & DEV. 65, 67-69 (2000); Bijnsdorp, *supra* note 38, at 330; *see also* Felipe Gomez Isa, *The Optional Protocol for the Convention on the Elimination of All Forms of Discrimination Against Women: Strengthening the Protection Mechanisms of Women's Human Rights*, 20 ARIZ. J. INT'L & COMP. L. 291, 305 (2003) (discussing the generally accepted idea among the international community that it would be easier to craft an optional protocol for CEDAW to implement an individual complaint mechanism than to amend CEDAW itself).

Interestingly, the many official justifications for the proposed optional protocol tended to focus on benefits that would accrue to society and women's rights as a whole, while largely overlooking the effects of bringing the individual herself into the realm of international human rights.[108] Ultimately, these efforts bore fruit, and in 1999 an optional protocol providing for an individual complaint mechanism as part of CEDAW (CEDAW Protocol) was adopted.[109] The CEDAW Protocol subsequently went into effect in 2000[110] and currently has 102 States Parties.[111]

The preamble to the CEDAW Protocol places heavy emphasis on the role of CEDAW and other key international human rights documents (particularly the UN Convention, the UDHR and the combination of the ICCPR and ICESCR) in crafting the system of international law under which the individual complaint mechanism for CEDAW could be created.[112]

The CEDAW Protocol begins by establishing that States Parties recognize the CEDAW Committee as having the ability to receive complaints and also to make decisions regarding these complaints.[113] Specifically, the CEDAW Protocol provides that complaints "may be submitted by or on behalf of individuals or groups of individuals, under the jurisdiction of a State Party, claiming to be victims of a violation of any of the rights set forth in the Convention by that State Party."[114] The CEDAW Protocol requires that complainants acting on behalf of another individual or group establish that they have received the consent of the person or group on whose behalf they claim to be acting. Nevertheless, a complainant is permitted to proceed if he is able to provide a sufficient explanation as to why he is acting without the appropriate consent.[115]

The justiciability requirements for those seeking to bring complaints under the CEDAW Protocol are similar to those contained in other instruments establishing individual complaint mechanisms. All appropriate domestic remedies regarding the subject matter of the complaint must have been exhausted prior to bringing a claim under the CEDAW Protocol

---

108. Tang, *supra* note 107, at 69.

109. Optional Protocol to CEDAW, *supra* note 19.

110. CEDAW Summary, *supra* note 106.

111. CEDAW Summary, *supra* note 106.

112. Optional Protocol to CEDAW, *supra* note 19, at pmbl.; *see also* Tang, *supra* note 107, at 67 (discussing the gender violence protections attributed to other international human rights instruments but not to CEDAW).

113. Optional Protocol to CEDAW, *supra* note 19, art. 1.

114. Optional Protocol to CEDAW, *supra* note 19, art. 2.

115. Optional Protocol to CEDAW, *supra* note 19.

"unless the application of such remedies is unreasonably prolonged or unlikely to bring effective relief."[116] In addition, the same issue cannot have been brought before another international body, nor can it be pending before another international body at the time the complainant brings the CEDAW Protocol-based complaint.[117] Furthermore, the complaint cannot be "incompatible with the provisions of the Convention;"[118] it cannot be "manifestly ill-founded or not sufficiently substantiated;"[119] it cannot be "an abuse of the right to submit a communication;"[120] and the facts upon which the complaint is based cannot have occurred before the State Party was legally bound under the CEDAW Protocol, except in instances where the complained-of facts continued to occur after the State Party became legally bound under the CEDAW Protocol.[121]

The CEDAW Protocol allows the CEDAW Committee to request that the State Party at issue take interim measures to protect the complainant(s) from harm until the outcome of the complaint.[122] In a further step, the CEDAW Protocol explicitly requires that "[a] State Party shall take all appropriate steps to ensure that individuals under its jurisdiction are not subjected to ill treatment or intimidation as a consequence of communicating with the Committee pursuant to the present Protocol."[123] Additionally, the CEDAW Protocol requires States Parties to provide their citizens with information on the Protocol, its terms, and the results of complaints brought before the CEDAW Committee that involve the State Party,[124] thus empowering individuals through the dissemination of information.

The CEDAW Protocol requires States Parties to give six months notice prior to renouncing and withdrawing from the Protocol.[125] During that six-month period, complaints submitted to the CEDAW Committee prior to the notification date may still be decided.[126]

---

116. Optional Protocol to CEDAW, *supra* note 19, art. 4(1).
117. Optional Protocol to CEDAW, *supra* note 19, art. 4(2)(a).
118. Optional Protocol to CEDAW, *supra* note 19, art. 4(2)(b).
119. Optional Protocol to CEDAW, *supra* note 19, art. 4(2)(c).
120. Optional Protocol to CEDAW, *supra* note 19, art. 4(2)(d).
121. Optional Protocol to CEDAW, *supra* note 19, art. 4(2)(e).
122. Optional Protocol to CEDAW, *supra* note 19, art. 5.
123. Optional Protocol to CEDAW, *supra* note 19, art. 11.
124. Optional Protocol to CEDAW, *supra* note 19, art. 13.
125. Optional Protocol to CEDAW, *supra* note 19, art. 19(1).
126. Optional Protocol to CEDAW, *supra* note 19, art. 19(2).

170   DUKE JOURNAL OF COMPARATIVE & INTERNATIONAL LAW   [Vol 22:153

E. Convention Against Torture and Other Cruel, Inhuman or Degrading Treatment or Punishment

The Convention Against Torture and Other Cruel, Inhuman or Degrading Treatment or Punishment (CAT) was adopted in 1984 and entered into effect in 1987.[127] Currently, there are 149 States Parties to the CAT, and sixty-five of these have also agreed to be bound by its individual complaint mechanism.[128] The CAT itself provides for an individual complaint mechanism under Article 22.[129] In line with the general trend, the preamble to the CAT reinforces the universality of human rights and dignities, especially those set forth in earlier international human rights law tenets.[130]

States Parties to the CAT recognize the ability of the CAT Committee to consider complaints from individuals, or made on behalf of individuals, who are subject to the jurisdiction of the state and who allege that they are victims of a violation of the CAT by the State Party.[131] In terms of justiciability, the CAT Committee cannot hear complaints that are made anonymously;[132] complaints which it finds "to be an abuse of the right of submission . . . or incompatible with the provisions of [the CAT];"[133] complaints where the complainant has not exhausted all relevant domestic remedies, unless "the application of the remedies is unreasonably prolonged or is unlikely to bring effective relief to the person who is the victim of the violation;"[134] or where the subject matter of the complaint has been or is being heard by another international body.[135]

States Parties to the CAT are able to withdraw from the individual complaint mechanism at any time, although withdrawal does not prevent the CAT Committee from considering complaints that had been lodged at the time of the withdrawal.[136] Found in a separate section of the CAT, Article 13 requires that States Parties against whom an individual makes a complaint of torture or related activities provide protection for that

---

127. *Convention Against Torture and Other Cruel, Inhuman or Degrading Treatment or Punishment*, UNITED NATIONS TREATY COLLECTION, http://treaties.un.org/Pages/ViewDetails.aspx?src=TREATY&mtdsg_no=IV-9&chapter=4&lang=en (last visited July 23, 2011) [hereinafter CAT Summary].

128. CAT Summary, *supra* note 127.

129. *See* CAT, *supra* note 19, art. 22.

130. CAT, *supra* note 19, at pmbl.

131. CAT, *supra* note 19, art. 22(1).

132. CAT, *supra* note 19, art. 22(2).

133. CAT, *supra* note 19.

134. CAT, *supra* note 19, art. 22(4)(b).

135. CAT, *supra* note 19, art. 22(4)(a).

136. CAT, *supra* note 19, art. 22(8).

individual "against all ill-treatment or intimidation."[137] These protections are also extended to witnesses in such claims.[138]

F. International Convention on the Protection of the Rights of All Migrant Workers and Members of Their Families

The International Convention on the Protection of the Rights of All Migrant Workers and Members of Their Families (CMW) was adopted in 1990 and entered into force in 2003.[139] An individual complaint mechanism was created under its core terms.[140]

States Parties to the CMW individual complaint mechanism agree to allow the CMW Committee to hear complaints from or on behalf of individuals who are within the State Party's jurisdiction and assert that they have been the victim of a CMW right-based violation by the State Party.[141] In order to be justiciable, a complaint brought before the CMW cannot be brought anonymously.[142] The complaint cannot, in the view of the CMW Committee, be "an abuse of the right of submission . . . or [] be incompatible with the provisions of the [CMW]."[143] Further grounds for non-justiciability include where the same subject matter has been brought or is before another international body,[144] and where all relevant domestic remedies have not been exhausted (although this requirement can be waived where the CMW Committee finds that "the application of the remedies is unreasonably prolonged or is unlikely to bring effective relief to that individual").[145]

The CMW provides that a State Party to the individual complaint mechanism can withdraw from it at any time, although a withdrawal will not terminate complaints pending against the State Party at the time of the withdrawal.[146]

---

137. CAT, *supra* note 19, art. 13.

138. CAT, *supra* note 19, art. 13.

139. *International Convention on the Protection of the Rights of All Migrant Workers and Members of Their Families,* UNITED NATIONS TREATY COLLECTION, http://treaties.un.org/Pages/ViewDetails.aspx?src=TREATY&mtdsg_no=IV-13&chapter=4&lang=en (last visited July 23, 2011).

140. CMW, *supra* note 19, art. 77.

141. CMW, *supra* note 19, art. 77(1).

142. CMW, *supra* note 19, art. 77(2).

143. CMW, *supra* note 19, art. 77(2).

144. CMW, *supra* note 19, art. 77(3)(a).

145. CMW, *supra* note 19, art. 77(3)(b).

146. CMW, *supra* note 19, art. 77(8).

G. Convention on the Rights of Persons with Disabilities

The Convention on the Rights of Persons with Disabilities (CRPD) was adopted in 2006 and entered into effect in 2008.[147] The CRPD itself does not contemplate an individual complaint mechanism;[148] instead, the Optional Protocol to the Convention on the Rights of Persons with Disabilities (CRPD Protocol) was adopted as a separate instrument and also entered into effect in 2008.[149] Of the 106 States Parties to the CRPD,[150] 64 are currently parties to the individual complaint mechanism.[151]

There was widespread international questioning as to the need for the CRPD since essentially it addresses rights that have already been enshrined as human rights.[152] However, proponents successfully argued that these already existing rights were too broad to provide full protections to those with disabilities in particular.[153] It should be noted that even proponents of the CRPD assert that the terms of the CRPD are impossible for most States Parties to implement immediately given that its terms run the gamut of civil, political, economic, cultural, and social rights.[154] Thus, there is arguably a level of uncertainty regarding whether rights are best decided in a quasi-judicial setting that is similar to that of the ICESCR Protocol. Regardless of the stance one takes on this issue, however, it is difficult to deny that the CRPD and the CRPD Protocol represent a large step in advancing the individual within the sphere of international human rights law by allowing the individual to penetrate the international human rights law system in a meaningful way.[155]

States Parties to the CRPD Protocol agree to recognize the jurisdiction of the CRPD Committee to hear complaints brought against them by either individuals or groups of individuals who are within the State Party's

---

147. *Convention on the Rights of Persons with Disabilities*, UNITED NATIONS TREATY COLLECTION, http://treaties.un.org/Pages/ViewDetails.aspx?src=TREATY&mtdsg_no=IV15&chapter=4&lang=en (last visited Nov. 8, 2011) [hereinafter CRPD Summary].

148. *See generally* Convention on the Rights of Persons with Disabilities, *adopted* Dec. 13, 2006, 2515 U.N.T.S. 3 (entered into force May 3, 2008).

149. Optional Protocol to CRPD, *supra* note 19; *see also Optional Protocol to the Convention on the Rights of Persons with Disabilities*, UNITED NATIONS TREATY COLLECTION, http://treaties.un.org/Pages/ViewDetails.aspx?src=TREATY&mtdsg_no=IV-15-a&chapter=4&lang=en (last visited Nov. 8, 2011) [hereinafter Optional Protocol to CRPD Summary].

150. CRPD Summary, *supra* note 147.

151. Optional Protocol to CRPD Summary, *supra* note 149.

152. Don MacKay, *The United Nations Convention on the Rights of Persons with Disabilities*, 34 SYRACUSE J. INT'L L. & COM. 323, 323 (2007).

153. *Id.* at 326-28.

154. *Id.* at 330.

155. *See generally id.*

jurisdiction and who allege a violation of the CRPD.[156] The requirements for justiciability of a complaint are that the complaint not be made anonymously;[157] that the complaint is not "an abuse of the right of submission" and is not "incompatible" with the CRPD;[158] that the complaint has not been examined or is not under present examination by another international body;[159] that all domestic remedies have been exhausted unless the exhaustion of these remedies is unreasonable or not likely to bring about meaningful relief to the complainant;[160] that the complaint is not "manifestly ill-founded or not sufficiently substantiated;"[161] and that the events involved in the complaint happened after the date on which the State Party became bound by the CRPD Protocol, unless the events complained of continued to occur after the date on which the State Party became bound by the CRPD Protocol.[162]

Following the trend in individual complaint mechanism creation, the CRPD Protocol allows the CRPD Committee to request that a State Party implement interim measures for the protection of the complainant prior to the CRPD's final decision in a complaint.[163] States Parties to the CRPD Protocol are able to denounce the CRPD Protocol and withdraw from it, although the renunciation will not become effective for a year.[164]

III. CONVENTION COMPARISIONS

It is evident from Part II that there are many procedural similarities among the international human rights law treaties that contain individual complaint mechanisms. Indeed, there are telling similarities for the individual beyond the fact that the individual has the ability to bring a complaint before the relevant committee.

Generally, the same standing requirements apply across the international human rights treaties, namely that the individual must be under the jurisdiction of a State Party to bring a complaint and that the violation alleged must be of a right contained in the appropriate treaty.[165] This requirement places limits on the individual's ability to complain and

---

156. Optional Protocol to CRPD, *supra* note19, art. 1.
157. Optional Protocol to CRPD, *supra* note 19, art. 2(a).
158. Optional Protocol to CRPD, *supra* note 19, art. 2(b).
159. Optional Protocol to CRPD, *supra* note 19, art. 2(c).
160. Optional Protocol to CRPD, *supra* note 19, art. 2(d).
161. Optional Protocol to CRPD, *supra* note 19, art. 2(e).
162. Optional Protocol to CRPD, *supra* note 19, art. 2(f).
163. Optional Protocol to CRPD, *supra* note 19, art. 4.
164. Optional Protocol to CRPD, *supra* note 19, art. 16.
165. *See supra* Part II.A-G.

requires that the State Party itself demarcate who constitutes a person within its jurisdiction. Indeed, this issue has caused much debate at the international level in those situations where an individual, by asserting a violation, has triggered a massive juridical and theoretical undertaking to determine what it means to be within a state's jurisdiction.[166]

There is a split in the international human rights law treaties between those that only allow individuals to bring complaints,[167] those that allow third parties to complain on behalf of individuals provided that certain circumstances are met,[168] and those that allow individuals, groups of individuals, or groups acting on behalf of groups or individuals to bring complaints.[169] In part, this procedural break could be a result of differences in the rights protected by each treaty: some human rights violations are essentially individual in nature, whereas others, such as racial discrimination, can be perpetrated against a group as well as against one individual. Regardless of these procedural differences, individual complaint mechanisms serve to reinforce the agency of the individual and the extent to which the individual, whether as a single claimant or as part of a group of individual claimants, has accessed international legal remedies. Additionally, those conventions which do require consent for agency representation reiterate the importance of the individual by seeking to ensure that complaints are not brought in a manner that could be regarded as frivolous or otherwise detracting from the seriousness of the allegations raised.

Much the same can be said for the justiciability requirements that are standard across most of the international human rights law treaties discussed above.[170] In several instances, international human rights law treaties contain fewer bars to justiciability,[171] which increases the ability of individuals to assert their rights. Across the instruments, the justiciability provisions which allow the exhaustion of relevant domestic remedies requirement to be waived where a strict application of the requirement would in essence bar the individual from bringing a complaint are protective measures for the complainant.[172] These provisions are crucial to

---

166. *See* Ben-Naftali, *supra* note 37.

167. *See supra* Part II.A (explaining that the general standing requirement under the ICCPR is centered on an individual); *supra* Part II.F.

168. *See supra* Part II.A (explaining a recent spike in third parties given standing to assert claims when the injured party has been proven to be unavailable through no fault of his own); *supra* Part II.B, II.E.

169. *See supra* Part II.C-D, II.G.

170. *See supra* Part II.

171. *See supra* Part II.C, II.F.

172. *See supra* Part II.

enabling the individual to assert his rights at the international level when that individual's ability to assert his rights domestically is thwarted by the State Party itself.

At the same time, the common treaty provisions which bar an individual from bringing his claim before more than one international rights body at a time serve a dual purpose.[173] As a purely practical matter, these provisions ensure that multiple cases will not be filed with multiple bodies, thus resulting in an uneven or confused outcome. The second consideration is discussed at greater length in Part IV below. By allowing an individual to bring his claim before only one international body, the combined international human rights treaties require the individual to select a single facet of his harm or identity under which to raise his claim, rather than allowing him to bring a holistic complaint that recognizes the entirety of his identity and the harms that he has suffered.

Several international human rights law treaties contain provisions which either require States Parties to protect complainants and witnesses when they make assertions of wrongdoing at the international level,[174] or allow the appropriate treaty committee to request that the State Party take interim measures to protect the complainant until the complaint is fully decided by that treaty committee.[175] Perhaps the importance of these provisions to the individual is obvious. At the same time, these provisions are essential to the overall availability of the international human rights law system to individuals because they recognize the unique status of individuals as potential targets of state or state-sponsored retaliation or repression, whereas the same is not true in state-to-state complaints in other legal arenas. By allowing for these protections, the international human rights law treaties attempt to ensure some level of equality between states and individuals in terms of potential harms as a result of a treaty-based complaint.[176]

The common provisions of the international human rights treaties that relate to the ability of a State Party to renounce and withdraw from the

---

173. *See supra* Part II.

174. *See supra* Part II.B, II.D, II.G.

175. *See supra* Part II.A-B, II.D-E.

176. Of course, to think that these provisions would automatically provide protection to those individuals who come forward with complaints would be naïve, especially in situations where the state is accused of gross human rights violations such as extra-judicial killings or disappearances. However, as a matter of drafting, these provisions do give an important window into the place of the individual as protected within the international human rights law system. These provisions also demonstrate the importance of the individual's ability to assert his rights and to penetrate the international human rights law system.

individual complaint mechanism,[177] and the effect that this has on pending individual complaints,[178] is perhaps less obviously related to the penetration of the individual into the international human rights law system. Clearly, the terms of these provisions reflect the continued primacy of states in international law. They also reflect the importance attached to the international obligations undertaken by states in the international human rights realm in that they do not allow State Parties to suddenly withdraw from the jurisdiction of the relevant committee and also do not allow State Parties to use withdrawal as a way to stop the investigation of a complaint that has already been filed. In addition, they reflect the importance of the relevant treaty committee's ability to consider individual complaints even where the State Party seeks to shield itself from such considerations.

The more recent human rights treaties establishing individual complaint mechanisms tend to allow their respective committees to examine information from UN agencies and entities deemed relevant, as well as from other human rights organizations and even regional entities.[179] This further contributes to the fragmentation of the individual discussed in Part IV because it focuses the treaty committee's attention on a particular facet of an individual's identity and leads the committee to disregard other facets that may be relevant to the human rights violation.

All of the international human rights law treaties that have individual complaint mechanisms share a common weakness in that the decisions of their respective committees cannot reliably be enforced at the domestic level.[180] As such, it is widely acknowledged that the punitive and coercive abilities of these treaty committees are limited to shaming States Parties by announcing their culpability for human rights violations.[181] Some states do have strong track records of implementing at least a good portion of treaty committee findings at the domestic level, while others are generally apathetic to the incorporation of these findings at the state level, often citing issues of sovereignty.[182] Dismissing the punitive weaknesses of the individual complaint mechanism structure disregards the importance of the structure to the place of the individual within the international system. The individual's ability to penetrate the international system lies not in his ability to receive compensation—monetary or non-monetary—from the State Party at the treaty committee's request, but rather in the ability of the

---

177. *See supra* Part II.
178. *See supra* Part II.
179. *See, e.g., supra* Part II.B.
180. *See supra* Part II.
181. *See supra* Part II.
182. *See* Helfer, *supra* note 52, at 1894.

individual to bring a state to account for its violations before an international body and an international audience. In this sense, the ability of the individual to complain against a state and to receive a finding from a treaty committee that is critical of the state and that acknowledges to the world the violations committed by the state is in itself a unique remedy.

On a more theoretical level, it has been argued that the rise of international human rights law treaties which target certain issues or groups creates a "pluralization" within international human rights law, whereby the particular requirements of a group defined by a certain trait or standing within the community—for example those with disabilities—are given special protections beyond the existing human rights conventions.[183] Under this model, there is an essential clash between human rights per se, which are defined as centering on "sameness and unity,"[184] and more specific, group-oriented conventions with human rights law, which can be viewed as centering on the "difference and pluralism" of the groups being protected.[185] From this supposition, it is then surmised that human rights themselves may also be used as instruments to examine the concept of identity as well as dignity within groups rather than within humanity itself.[186] This is important to the comparison of the international human rights law treaties with individual complaint mechanisms because it applies as much to them and to the jurisprudence which they produce as to the overall international human rights treaty system.

IV. ANALYSIS OF INDIVIDUAL PENETRATION OF INTERNATIONAL HUMAN RIGHTS LAW

The idea of individual human rights, particularly as an outgrowth of the human rights violations that savaged the world during World War II, has become an anchor of the international legal system.[187] As a field, international human rights law is centered on asserting the rights of all mankind and, subsequently, on ensuring that states guarantee and respect these rights.[188] A primary way in which the system holds states accountable has been to grant individuals stature within the international community to

---

183. Frédéric Mégret, *The Disabilities Convention: Human Rights of Persons with Disabilities or Disability Rights?*, 30 HUM. RTS. Q. 494, 495 (2008).

184. *Id.* at 496.

185. *Id.*

186. *Id.*

187. Cole, *supra* note 21, at 1912 ("Postwar world culture endows individuals with tremendous amounts of moral worth and agency . . . . It also invests them with universal human rights, admonishes states to respect and protect those rights, and, when necessary, authorizes individuals to defend their rights against state infringement.").

188. *See* Helfer, *supra* note 52, at 1842.

charge their governments with human rights violations. Thus, unlike other regimes of international law, there is an automatic place for the individual within the international human rights law system.[189]

At least theoretically, the individual complaint mechanisms used in international human rights law allow individuals to bring their claims to a body that is regarded as less biased than domestic courts.[190] These bodies also allow individuals whose voices are frequently not given attention or value at the domestic level to have greater power and influence in asserting their rights and claiming personal agency over the acts committed against them.[191] The growth of the individual complaint mechanism within well-accepted international human rights law treaties has resulted in the placement of the individual in a different sphere than has been traditionally accepted as part of the international system;[192] and, consequently, has empowered a new set of international actors to gain a place of primacy.

As an international actor in the human rights system, the individual is able to express his voice directly without the need to seek representation from a state or non-governmental organization. Specifically in this context, the individual has done more than equal traditional international actors; he has gained a place of primacy. Indeed, by definition, the individual is at the center of the individual complaint mechanism. Accordingly, a determination of the violations done to the individual takes precedence over other considerations which often characterize international legal adjudications, such as the wishes of the states involved.

Some authors have studied the international human rights law system and argued that it is becoming "overlegalized," creating a situation in which States Parties are under pressure to sign treaties but have difficulty fulfilling the legal responsibilities therein.[193] This is particularly true where the treaty has been operative for a number of years and has been subject to interpretation by an oversight body.[194] Although this argument has great merit in some respects, it tends to ignore, or at least undervalue, the place of the individual in the international human rights law system. It does this by placing the onus on the applicable oversight body as the instrument of change and treaty construction over time, and neglecting the impact of

---

189. *Id.* (describing the right of individuals under human rights law to enforce international legal commitments through recourse to international courts and quasi-judicial bodies).

190. *See supra* Part I.

191. *See* Bijnsdorp, *supra* note 38, at 337.

192. *See* Tang, *supra* note 107, at 67-68.

193. *See generally* Helfer, *supra* note 52; *id.* at 1854-55.

194. *Id.* at 1854-55.

individuals on both the relevant State Party and the international system as a whole.

Some have asserted that the creation of new international human rights law treaties, and associated individual complaint mechanisms, works to reinforce the rights granted to individuals by fostering a series of interlocking understandings of international human rights law.[195] In the same vein, it has been asserted that these systems work together and indeed must do so given the nature of the rights that are protected.[196] However, this argument, while attractive, tends to undermine the idea of the universality of individual human rights and norms that is associated with such seminal documents as the ICCPR.[197] Rather than creating a system in which the individual, though given a prominent role within the human rights system, is potentially subject to the jurisdiction of multiple treaties and their oversight bodies, perhaps the international community ought to amend the foundational documents of international human rights law, such as the ICCPR or the ICESCR, so that they cover a wider—or at least more in-depth—spectrum of individual rights and protections.

As has been noted, scholars have criticized the pluralization of international human rights law by treaties which create various communities or violations.[198] This is an important observation and leads one to question the point at which the inviolable rights germane to all of mankind as envisioned by original human rights treaties ceases to be uniform and begins to fragment into sub-classifications of various human rights-based identities.[199]

The rise of the individual as more than simply a passive subject and holder of rights, but rather as an entity that is able to assert—and thereby make a claim to—these rights demonstrates an evolution in the dynamics of the actors involved in the international rights law system. However, this evolution has been carefully tailored by the international human rights law system, as is evidenced by the justiciability and standing requirements which are nearly universal to the individual complaint mechanisms discussed above. A careful tailor can craft something that is as deceptive from the outside as it is from the inside. Similarly, a careful crafter of any

---

195. *See, e.g.,* Bijnsdorp, *supra* note 38, at 332 (describing the positive, stimulating influence which bodies dealing with the same issue of discrimination against women have on one another).

196. Bijnsdorp, *supra* note 38, at 330-31.

197. For an argument specifically discussing the overlaps in individual complaint mechanism bodies, see Dennis & Stewart, *supra* note 57, at 501-04.

198. *See* Mégret, *supra* note 183 (analyzing the pluralization of human rights under the CRPD).

199. *Id.*

180   DUKE JOURNAL OF COMPARATIVE & INTERNATIONAL LAW   [Vol 22:153

international instrument can create a document that is at once expansive at first glance yet restrictive in terms of its actual implementation procedure.

To the outside, individual complaint mechanisms are a state-centered way to ensure that States Parties are accountable for the obligations that they undertook as part of the international human rights law system. On the inside, however, the mechanism is a powerful tool for the individual— whether directly or through representatives where necessary—to actively assert and claim his human rights. It cannot be denied that the punitive aspects of individual complaint mechanisms in the international human rights law context are weak and most often rely on the power of shame and international condemnation. This does not, however, defeat the importance of the ability of the individual to bring these cases in the first place and to at least generate some form of discussion on these topics. The importance of this individual role is perhaps best evidenced by the fact that, regardless of the treaty, states are unwilling to bring human rights law based complaints against other states.[200] Thus, without the individual complaint mechanism, the horrors of state enforced disappearances and extra-judicial killings that have occurred under a variety of dictatorships would not be as well known to the world. It is only through this knowledge that the international community is forced to see many of the unpleasant truths that occur within it and to understand the impacts of these human rights violations on a very personal and intimate level that state-to-state dialogue does not generate.

At the same time that individual infiltration of the international human rights law system is beneficial, it creates a danger of fragmentation. Here, the threat lies in the plethora of international human rights law treaty committees to which an individual might complain. Much as pluralization in the group context has a dangerous element to it, fragmentation of essential human rights and dignities into many international human rights law treaties with many venues for individuals to complain does not create a greater unity of understanding or guarantee of human rights. Nor does it allow the individual to fully assert and claim all of the human rights and dignities to which he is entitled.

For example, a woman might also be disabled, be part of a national minority group that is barred from voting, and be tortured by the state in which she lives. Many of her essential human rights have been violated, but how is she to know which individual complaint mechanism to use? She qualifies under several different international human rights treaties and

---

200. Laboni Amena Hoq, *The Women's Convention and Its Optional Protocol: Empowering Women to Claim Their Internationally Protected Rights*, 32 COLUM. HUM. RTS. L. REV. 677, 685 (2001).

identifying her by only one of her traits or allowing her to assert one set of her rights denies her both individual identity and agency over the human rights that the international community recognizes are vested in her. By asking her to choose which aspects of her identity she wishes to express and which of her human rights she wishes to assert, the international human rights law system is in fact denying her the active ability to assert herself, her full identity and her human rights, and is, in effect, reducing the benefits that it has created through the establishment of individual complaint mechanisms as accepted tools of international human rights law.

Essentially, this example demonstrates that the more specific international human rights treaties perpetuate the very harm they claim to remedy: the broad human rights treaties' failure to recognize the full identity of the individual. The flaw here, however, is in a fragmentation of identity rather than an overly broad or non-specific notion of rights protection. Ultimately, this diminishes the gains made by individuals in achieving access to the international human rights system by preventing them from enforcing the totality of the rights granted them by that system.

CONCLUSION

Human rights are at once a concern of all mankind and intensely personal rights that touch the core of individuality. They are in need of protection from violation by states and yet also are intangible entities that are individual in nature. This sense of duality permeates the key international human rights law treaties, which provide or will provide a place for the individual to assert and claim his human rights on the international stage.

This article established the fundamental background of international human rights law, discussed the provisions of various individual complaint mechanisms contained in key international human rights law treaties, and then compared these mechanisms in order to highlight their importance. This discussion demonstrated the many points at which individuals are able to access international human rights law through individual complaints mechanisms.

Next, this article argued that, while the prominence of the individual is crucial to assert and claim human rights, the plethora of international human rights law treaties threatens to fragment individual identity. In the process, several arguments and theories regarding the place of the individual in international human rights law were evaluated, with the benefits and pitfalls of these arguments analyzed.

Rather than allow an ever more specialized international human rights treaty system to force the fragmentation of individual identity, this article suggests that it is better to attend to the full array of individual identities that could be protected and asserted through already existing international human rights treaties. In this way, the international human rights law system could stave off the threat of a fragmented relationship to individuals by acknowledging all elements of the individual's identity.

[6]

....

The Collective Complaints System of the European Social Charter: An Effective Mechanism for Ensuring Compliance with Economic and Social Rights?

Robin R. Churchill and Urfan Khaliq*

Abstract

In 1995 the Council of Europe, as part of the revitalization process of the European Social Charter, adopted a Protocol providing for a system of collective complaints. The Protocol came into force in 1998. So far 23 complaints have been lodged under it. The aim of this article is to critically examine the practical operation of this collective complaints system during its first five years. After placing the system in a general human rights context by giving an overview of mechanisms for ensuring compliance with other treaties concerned with economic and social rights, the article then analyses the system for making collective complaints and its functioning in practice to date. The latter part of the article considers the likely utility and effectiveness of the system and concludes that without a major change in the practice hitherto of the Committee of Ministers, the system is unlikely to achieve its objectives.

* Professor of Law and Lecturer respectively, Cardiff Law School, UK. Earlier versions of this paper were given by Robin Churchill at a workshop on 'European Integration and Legal Changes', Prague, April 2002 and the German Academic Exchange Service Conference for Law Lektors, Cumberland Lodge, Windsor, June 2002. We are grateful for comments made by participants at those two meetings. We would also like to thank members of the Secretariat of the European Social Charter for providing us with information and documentation. The usual disclaimer applies.

....

418 *EJIL* 15 (2004), 417–456

1 Introduction

The European Social Charter (ESC)[1] is the counterpart, in the field of economic and social rights, of the Council of Europe's much better known European Convention on Human Rights (ECHR).[2] Originally the only machinery that the Charter provided for seeking to ensure that its parties[3] complied with their obligations was a system of reporting. Under this system states parties report every two years on their implementation of the Charter. Such reports are first examined by the European Committee on Social Rights (ECSR), a 13-member body of independent experts in international social questions (formerly known as the Committee of Independent Experts (CIE)). Thereafter reports and the ECSR's views on them are considered by the Governmental Committee (a body of national senior civil servants) and the Committee of Ministers. The latter may make recommendations to states parties that are not fully complying with the Charter.[4]

In the early 1990s the Council of Europe embarked on a process of revitalizing the Charter. As part of this process (which also included overhauling the reporting system and drawing up the Revised Charter), the Council in 1995 adopted a Protocol to the Charter that provides an additional compliance mechanism in the form of a system of collective complaints.[5] This Protocol came into force in July 1998, the first complaint under the new system was made in October 1998, and by February 2004 a further 22 complaints had been made. Of these complaints, 12 have now been disposed of. After more than five years of operation, it seems an appropriate time to examine how the collective complaints system has so far worked in practice and to attempt an initial stocktaking.[6]

To place the Collective Complaints Protocol (CCP) in a general human rights context, this article begins by discussing the question of the justiciability of economic and social rights and then goes on to give an overview of mechanisms for seeking to ensure compliance by states with their obligations under other treaties concerned with such rights. The article then describes the system for making collective

---

[1] The Charter was originally adopted in 1961. A Protocol adding further rights was adopted in 1988, while a revised version of the Charter, which updates and extends the rights protected, was adopted in 1996. The texts of these three instruments can be found at ETS Nos. 35, 128 and 163; and I. Brownlie and G. Goodwin-Gill, *Basic Documents on Human Rights* (4th ed., 2002) (hereinafter *Basic Documents*), at 423, 439 and 455. References to the 'Charter' in this article refer to all three instruments unless otherwise indicated.

[2] ETS No. 5; and *Basic Documents*, at 398.

[3] 10 members of the Council of Europe are parties to the Charter only in its 1961 version. Eight states are parties to the 1961 Charter as supplemented by the 1988 Additional Protocol, while a further 16 states are parties to the Revised Charter.

[4] For further discussion of the reporting system, see Harris, 'Lessons from the Reporting System of the European Social Charter', in P. Alston and J. Crawford (eds), *The Future of UN Human Rights Treaty Monitoring*, (2000) 347, and D. Harris and J. Darcy, *The European Social Charter*, (2nd ed., 2001), at 293–354.

[5] Additional Protocol to the European Social Charter Providing for a System of Collective Complaints, ETS No. 158; 34 *ILM* (1995) 1453; and *Basic Documents*, at 451.

[6] Particularly as most of the existing literature on the collective complaints system predates the lodging of the first complaint.

complaints introduced by the 1995 Protocol and examines its practical operation in the light of the complaints so far lodged. The article ends with some remarks about the likely utility and effectiveness of the system.

2 The Question of Justiciability and Mechanisms to Protect Economic and Social Rights

A *The Justiciability of Economic and Social Rights*

Although the international community puts increasing emphasis on the indivisibility between economic, social and cultural rights on the one hand and civil and political rights on the other,[7] this is in contrast to many of the assumptions underlying the mechanisms for their enforcement. Economic and social rights have traditionally been considered as lacking justiciability, a quality which civil and political rights are deemed to possess.[8] The reason usually given is that economic and social rights are often progressive in nature and that many such rights are couched in language that is too imprecise to be judicially enforceable. Thus a traditional view has been that only bodies that are charged with the enforcement of civil and political rights treaties should be able to provide remedies, of some sort, for their violation and be given powers to that effect.[9]

Although there is a degree of merit in these arguments, they do not always hold true. As is well known, the mechanisms adopted for the enforcement of the International Covenant on Civil and Political Rights (ICCPR) and the International Covenant on Economic, Social and Cultural Rights (ICESCR) were the results of political compromise and the categorization of rights was hardly an exact science.[10]

---

[7]   Emphasis on this relationship has existed since the Universal Declaration of Human Rights (UDHR) 1948, UN Doc. A/811; *Basic Documents*, at 18. Also see, the Vienna Declaration and Programme of Action–World Conference on Human Rights, Vienna, 14–25 June 1993, UN Doc. A/CONF.157/23.

[8]   For detailed discussion of the issue of justiciability, see Addo, 'Justiciability Re-Examined', in D. Hill and R. Beddard (eds), *Economic, Social and Cultural Rights*, (1991) 93; Craven 'The Justiciability of Economic, Social and Cultural Rights', in R. Burchill, D. Harris and A. Owers (eds), *Economic, Social and Cultural Rights: Their Implementation in UK Law* (1999) 1; Craven, *The International Covenant on Economic, Social and Cultural Rights: A Perspective on its Development* (1995), at 106 *et seq*; Eide, 'Economic, Social and Cultural Rights as Human Rights', in A. Eide, C. Krause and A. Rosas (eds), *Economic, Social and Cultural Rights: A Textbook*, (2nd ed., 2001) 9; Scheinin, 'Economic and Social Rights as Legal Rights', in *ibid.*, at 29; *Report of the Expert's Roundtable Concerning Issues Central to the Proposed Optional Protocol to the International Covenant on Economic, Social and Cultural Rights* (2002); and H. Steiner and P. Alston, *International Human Rights in Context: Law, Politics, Morals* (2nd ed., 2001) 275.

[9]   See the discussion in Eide, *supra* note 8, at 10 and Novitz, 'Are Social Rights Necessarily Collective Rights? A Critical Analysis of the Collective Complaints Protocol to the European Social Charter', *EHRLR* (2002) 50, esp. at 57–65.

[10]   International Covenant on Civil and Political Rights 1966, 999 UNTS 171; *Basic Documents*, at 182 and International Covenant on Economic, Social and Cultural Rights 1966, 993 UNTS 3; *Basic Documents*, at 172. For a discussion of the debates at the time and on the splitting up of the rights and perceptions of the protagonists see Craven, 'The UN Committee on Economic, Social and Cultural Rights', in Eide *et al.*, *supra* note 8, 455 at 456 *et seq*.

420   *EJIL* 15 (2004), 417–456

To consider that all of the rights that are found in treaties which promote and protect economic and social rights are incapable of being judicially determined is an oversimplification. Some such rights (for example, the right to equal pay) are sufficiently precisely drafted to be judicially enforceable; and for some rights (such as equal pay or consultation rights in the workplace) a judicial remedy may be suitable. While not all economic and social rights are immediately justiciable, it is clear that some can become so over time, as states parties take measures to give them effect.[11] There are, of course, some methodological problems in determining whether a state is complying with its obligations,[12] but these are far from being insurmountable. There is now ample jurisprudence on these issues to illustrate that they can be overcome.[13] Furthermore, some national courts have adopted decisions as to the obligations imposed by provisions of national constitutions, many of which are couched in terms similar to those found in treaties protecting economic and social rights, in which they have not only defined the obligation but also the remedy.[14] It is important to note, therefore, that there is nothing inherent in economic and social rights that prevents judicial determination of their content.[15]

---

[11]   See, for example, the Limburg Principles on the Implementation of the International Covenant on Economic, Social and Cultural Rights, UN Doc. E/CN.4/1987/17, Annex, Part I, reproduced in 9 *HRQ* (1987) 122 and General Comment 9 of the Committee on Economic, Social and Cultural Rights (hereinafter CESCR) UN Doc. E/1999/22 Annex IV. It is also worth noting that the Convention on the Rights of the Child, 1577 UNTS 3; *Basic Documents*, at 241, which includes some economic and social rights, does not, unlike the ICESCR, require their 'progressive' realization, but does make allowances for the means available to a state.

[12]   For a discussion of this issue, see Leckie, 'Another Step towards Indivisibility: Identifying the Key Features of Violations of Economic, Social and Cultural Rights', 20 *HRQ* (1998) 81; Craven, *supra* note 8, at 106–150; Alston and Quinn, 'The Nature and Scope of States Parties' Obligations under the International Covenant on Economic, Social and Cultural Rights' 9 *HRQ* (1987) 156 ; Van Hoof, 'The Legal Nature of Economic, Social and Cultural Rights: A Rebuttal of Some Traditional Views', in P. Alston and K. Tomaševski (eds), *The Right to Food*, (1984) 97; Vierdag, 'The Legal Nature of the Rights Granted by the International Covenant on Economic, Social and Cultural Rights', 7 *NYIL* (1978) 69, esp. at 83 *et seq*; and General Comment 3 of the Committee on Economic, Social and Cultural Rights (CESCR), UN Doc. E/1991/23 Annex III.

[13]   In General Comment 9, *supra* note 11, the CESCR considered the domestic application of the Covenant and clearly envisaged the use of judicially determined remedies for violations of it. See also on this issue Craven, 'The Domestic Application of the International Covenant on Economic, Social and Cultural Rights', 40 *NILR* (1993) 367.

[14]   See, in particular, the jurisprudence of the Indian Supreme Court and the South African Constitutional Court. For an excellent discussion of this issue, see Liebenberg, 'The Protection of Economic and Social Rights in Domestic Legal Systems', in Eide *et al.*, *supra* note 8, at 55, and Steiner and Alston, *supra* note 8, at 283–302. In the context of South Africa see de Vos, 'Pious Wishes or Directly Enforceable Human Rights? Social and Economic Rights in South Africa's 1996 Constitution', 13 *South African Journal of Human Rights* (1997) 67.

[15]   General Comment 3 of the CESCR, *supra* note 12, expressly recognizes this in para. 5. Also see General Comment 9, *supra* note 11, which recognizes that judicial remedies will not always be necessary but will be where administrative remedies are not adequate.

B *Mechanisms for the Enforcement of Economic and Social Rights*

At the international level, there are various mechanisms for ensuring compliance with treaties containing economic and social rights, some of which illustrate the justiciability of such rights. In the case of treaties which primarily or only contain economic and social rights, the normal mechanism is a system of reporting. This is the case with the ICESCR. It is also largely the case with the San Salvador Protocol of 1988 to the American Convention on Human Rights,[16] although there is a right to individual petition with regard to the right to education and the right to organize.[17]

There are also treaties which contain both civil and political rights as well as economic and social rights.[18] Right-specific treaties, such as the Convention on the Rights of the Child, the International Convention on the Elimination of All Forms of Racial Discrimination[19] and the Convention on the Elimination of All Forms of Discrimination against Women,[20] cover a broad spectrum of different rights. While reporting is the principal mechanism in all these treaties, the now functioning Optional Protocol to the Women's Convention provides a petition system that can be utilized by individuals, for all of the rights protected.[21] Similarly, Article 14 of the Race Convention, which establishes the right to individual petition, does not distinguish for enforcement purposes between the different types of rights protected by Article 5 of that treaty. In addition, the African Charter on Human and Peoples' Rights[22] also contains a mixture of rights. The experience of the African Commission illustrates that individual complaints that seek to ensure the protection of economic and social rights are certainly possible, even if they have not yet been utilized to their full potential.[23]

The ILO system, in particular the eight core ILO Conventions,[24] protects many rights that are found in economic and social rights treaties. The main compliance mechanism is a reporting system. However, there are also other mechanisms. Of

---

[16] Additional Protocol to the American Convention on Human Rights in the Area of Economic, Social and Cultural Rights, 1988, OAS Treaty Series 69 (1988); *Basic Documents*, at 693.

[17] Art. 19(6). However, claims with regard to all other protected economic and social rights may be brought under the American Declaration of the Rights and Duties of Man 1948, OAS Resolution XXX; *Basic Documents*, at 665. For discussion see Craven, 'The Protection of Economic, Social and Cultural Rights Under the Inter-American System of Human Rights', in D. Harris and S. Livingstone (eds), *The Inter-American System of Human Rights* (1998) 289.

[18] Furthermore, some civil and political rights have been deemed to have an economic or social rights aspect to them. In practice this has primarily been limited to inhuman treatment and health conditions in prisons under Article 3 of the ECHR and Articles 7 and 10 of the ICCPR, although see the HRC's General Comment 6 on the Right to Life of 30 April 1982.

[19] International Convention on the Elimination of All Forms of Racial Discrimination, 660 UNTS 195; *Basic Documents*, at 160.

[20] Convention on the Elimination of All Forms of Discrimination against Women, 1249 UNTS 13; *Basic Documents*, at 212.

[21] UN Doc. A/54/49 (Vol. I); *Basic Documents*, at 224.

[22] 21 ILM (1982) 58; *Basic Documents*, at 728.

[23] See Odinkalu, 'Implementing Economic, Social and Cultural Rights under the African Charter on Human and Peoples' Rights', in M. Evans and R. Murray (eds), *The African Charter on Human and Peoples' Rights: The System in Practice, 1986–2000* (2002) 178.

[24] Convention Nos 29, 87, 98, 100, 105, 111, 138 and 182. Although these Conventions are defined as core, many of the ILO's other Conventions also protect aspects of economic and social rights.

particular importance, in our context, is the procedure under Article 24 of the ILO Constitution which provides for examination, in certain circumstances, of representations by employers' or workers' organizations concerning an ILO Member State's alleged failure to apply the ILO Conventions on Freedom of Association.[25] The Collective Complaints Protocol of the European Social Charter was consciously modelled on this system.

Outside the human rights context, in the strict sense, other international mechanisms exist that judicially protect and enforce economic and social rights. The European Court of Justice, for example, is competent to adjudicate on the compliance of Member States with obligations imposed by Community law dealing with issues such as health and safety at work, equal pay and treatment, and conditions of employment, among others.

The preceding discussion highlights a number of issues. First, many economic and social rights and the obligations they impose upon states are capable of judicial determination. The fundamental issues are the manner in which the provision in question is drafted and the extent of the obligation it contains. Secondly, while the right to individual and/or collective petition exists in a number of international and domestic fora, there is no generally accepted approach as to who has *locus standi* to bring claims nor with regard to which particular economic and social rights.

3 The Collective Complaints System

A *Genesis of the Collective Complaints System*[26]

As mentioned earlier, the collective complaints system was introduced as part of the revitalization process of the Charter. This process began in December 1990 with the establishment by the Committee of Ministers of a Committee on the European Social Charter (generally known as the Charte-Rel Committee) to draw up proposals to reform the Charter. At its second meeting in May 1991, the Committee decided to set up a working party to draw up proposals for a collective complaints system. On the basis of proposals produced by this working party, the Charte-Rel Committee adopted draft articles for an additional Protocol in September 1991. These draft articles were discussed at the Ministerial Conference held in Turin in October 1991 to mark the

---

[25] The ILO Committee on Freedom of Association has now examined over 2000 complaints. For detailed discussion of this procedure and the ILO's human rights work, see Leary, 'Lessons from the Experience of the International Labour Organisation', in P. Alston (ed.), *The United Nations and Human Rights — A Critical Appraisal* (1992) 580; Rosas and Scheinin, 'Implementation Mechanisms and Remedies', in Eide *et al.*, *supra* note 8, 425; and Samson and Shindler, 'The Standard-Setting and Supervisory System of the International Labour Organisation', in R. Hanski and M. Suski (eds.), *An Introduction to the International Protection of Human Rights: A Textbook*, (1999) 185. The ILO Committee on Freedom of Association's web page also contains details of the procedure at http://www.ilo.org/ilolex/english/index.htm and the cases brought before it at http://ilolex.ilo.ch:1567/english/.

[26] This section draws heavily on Council of Europe, *Explanatory Report on the Collective Complaints Protocol* (1995), paras 1–8, http://conventions.coe.int/treaty/en/Reports/HTML/158.htm.

30th anniversary of the signing of the Charter, but no agreement could be reached on them.[27]

The Charte-Rel Committee resumed its examination of the draft Protocol and succeeded in finalizing the text of a draft Protocol in May 1992, which it transmitted to the Committee of Ministers. The latter, after consulting the CIE and the Parliamentary Assembly, adopted the text of the Protocol in June 1995 and opened it for signature on 9 November 1995. Under Article 14(1) the Protocol requires five ratifications for its entry into force. This condition was met in May 1998 and the Protocol accordingly entered into force on 1 July 1998. In brief outline, the Protocol allows certain types of organization to make complaints to the ECSR of non-compliance with the Charter by a state party. The ECSR first decides whether the complaint is admissible, and, if it is, it then draws up a report with its conclusions on the merits of the case. On the basis of this report the Committee of Ministers takes the final decision as to whether the complaint is upheld.

According to the Explanatory Report on the Protocol,[28] the introduction of a system of collective complaints is 'designed to increase the efficiency of supervisory machinery based solely on the submission of governmental reports. In particular, this system should increase participation by management and labour and non-governmental organizations ... The way in which the machinery as a whole functions can only be enhanced by the greater interest that these bodies may be expected to show in the Charter.' These views are reflected in the preamble to the Protocol, which speaks of the resolve of the signatories to the Protocol to 'take new measures to improve the effective enforcement of the social rights guaranteed by the Charter', an aim which 'could be achieved in particular by the establishment of a collective complaints procedure, which, *inter alia*, would strengthen the participation of management and labour and of non-governmental organizations'.

Unlike the reporting system, which applies to all states parties to the Charter, acceptance to be bound by the collective complaints system is optional. The first way in which a state may manifest such acceptance is by ratifying the 1995 Protocol. So far 11 states have done so — Belgium, Croatia, Cyprus, Finland, France, Greece, Ireland, Italy, Norway, Portugal and Sweden. The second way is for a state which is a party to the Revised Charter (but which is not a party to the Protocol) to make a declaration under Article D2 of the Revised Charter that it accepts to be bound by the collective complaints system. So far two states — Bulgaria and Slovenia — have made such a declaration. Thus, of the 34 states parties to the Charter, only 13 are currently bound by the system.

Discussion of the collective complaints system will begin by considering who is eligible to make a complaint and then go on to examine the procedure by which

---

[27]   Harris, 'A Fresh Impetus for the European Social Charter', 41 *ICLQ* (1992) 659, at 673 says that the reason for the failure to agree was not so much the opposition from certain governments as the fact that representatives of the ILO and international employers' associations and trade unions did not think that the system proposed at that time would be of much interest to employers' associations and trade unions.

[28]   *Supra* note 26, at 2.

424 *EJIL* 15 (2004), 417–456

complaints are made and dealt with. The practical operation of the system so far will be reviewed in the following two sections.

B *Who May Complain?*

It is important to note at the outset that the system is one of collective, not individual, complaints. At the time the Protocol was being negotiated, the members of the Council of Europe were not prepared to accept a right to individual petition. Nor was there any suggestion of having an inter-state complaints procedure, probably because of the failure of such procedures in other human rights treaties to be widely utilized. This means that complaints may only be made by some kind of organization, not by one or a number of individuals or a state. There are four types of organizations that are eligible to make complaints under the system.[29] The first comprises international organizations of employers and trade unions that are observers at meetings of the Governmental Committee under the reporting system. There are three such organizations — the European Trade Union Confederation, the Union of the Confederation of Industry and Employers of Europe, and the International Organization of Employers.[30] The second type of organization entitled to make a complaint are other international non-governmental organizations (NGOs) that have consultative status with the Council of Europe and have been placed on a list drawn up by the Governmental Committee for the purpose of making complaints. To be put on this list, an NGO must show that it has 'access to authoritative sources of information and is able to carry out the necessary verifications, to obtain appropriate legal opinions etc. in order to draw up complaint files that meet the basic requirements of reliability'.[31] Organizations are put on the list for renewable four-year periods.[32] There are currently 58 NGOs on this list.[33] Harris and Darcy comment that this number is surprisingly small, given that several hundred NGOs have consultative status with the Council of Europe. They criticize the restriction of international NGOs that may make complaints to those on the list, and argue that if the intention was by this means to exclude badly prepared or propagandistic complaints, this would be better done through admissibility criteria rather than a list of approved NGOs.[34] Organizations in

---

[29] Arts. 1 and 2, 1995 Protocol.

[30] It has been argued that the International Confederation of Free Trade Unions should be included in this category of complainant, even though it does not currently take part in meetings of the Governmental Committee: see K. Löchner, 'The Social Partners' Opinion', in Council of Europe, *The Social Charter of the 21st Century. Colloquy Organized by the Secretariat of the Council of Europe* (1997) 130, at 133.

[31] Committee of Ministers Decision of 22 June 1995, as summarized by the Explanatory Report, *supra* note 26, at para. 20. This paragraph also summarizes that part of the Committee of Ministers decision setting out the procedure by which the list is drawn up.

[32] See the *Explanatory Report, supra* note 26, at para. 20.

[33] For this list, see http://www.coe.int. Harris and Darcy, *supra* note 4, at 357, state that the process of dealing with applications to be put on the list has operated without controversy and that nearly all applications have been accepted.

[34] Harris and Darcy, *supra* note 4, at 357.

this second category are only entitled to submit complaints in respect of those matters in which they have been recognized as having 'particular competence'.[35]

The third type of organization entitled to make complaints comprises 'representative national organizations of employers and trade unions within the jurisdiction of the Contracting Party against which they have lodged a complaint'.[36] It is up to the ECSR when dealing with the admissibility of a complaint to determine whether a national employers' association or trade union is a 'representative' one. The ECSR has taken the view that the representativeness of a trade union is 'an autonomous concept, beyond the ambit of national considerations as well [as] the domestic collective relations context'.[37] In the first two cases (Complaint Nos. 6/1999 and 9/2000) brought by complainants in this third category (both complainants were French trade unions), the ECSR, after making the observation just referred to concerning the autonomous nature of the concept of representativeness, simply noted that having made an overall assessment of the documents in the file, its conclusion was that the trade union concerned was a representative one. In the next two complaints brought by this type of complainant, the ECSR made a rather more thorough examination of the representativeness of the complainant. This was despite the fact that, as with the first two cases, the representativeness of the organization concerned had not been challenged by the defendant state. In Complaint No. 10/2000 the ECSR noted that the complainant Finnish trade union represented the great majority of employees in the sector concerned (health care) and participated in the collective bargaining process in that sector. It thus held that the complainant was a representative trade union.[38] In Complaint No. 12/2002, brought by a Swedish employers' association, the ECSR noted that the association was the largest body of its kind in Sweden, representing 47,000 companies with about 1.45 million employees; that it had concluded several central-level collective agreements in the private sector; and that it sought to promote general understanding of the needs of enterprise and its contribution to society. The ECSR therefore concluded that the complainant was a representative employers' organization.[39] In Complaint No. 23/2003, the French Government challenged the representativeness of a regional trade union in the education sector, pointing out that the union was not considered a representative one under French law. The ECSR, in rejecting this challenge, again stated that the representativeness of a trade union is 'an autonomous concept'. More importantly,

---

[35]   Art. 3, 1995 Protocol.

[36]   Art. 1(c), 1995 Protocol.

[37]   Complaint No. 6/1999, *Syndicat National des Professions du Tourisme v France*, Decision on Admissibility, para. 6. This view has been repeated in later complaints: see, for example, Complaint No. 9/2000, *Confédération Française de l'Encadrement — CGC v. France*, Decision on Admissibility, para. 6; and Complaint No. 10/2000, *Tehy ry and STTK ry v. Finland*, Decision on Admissibility, para. 6. The texts of the ECSR's decisions on both admissibility and the merits of collective complaints can be found on the Council of Europe's webpage. Some of the decisions on the merits are also reproduced in *IHRR*, and these references will also be given where they exist. After their initial reference, complaints, both in the text and in the footnotes, will be cited by number only.

[38]   Complaint No. 10/2000.

[39]   Complaint No. 12/2002, *Confederation of Swedish Enterprise v. Sweden*, Decision on Admissibility, para. 5.

426   *EJIL* 15 (2004), 417–456

however, it considered the Union to be representative on the basis that it represented a considerable number of employees in the education sector in the geographic region in which it was based and was completely independent of employers.[40] On the basis of this admittedly limited practice, it would seem that the main tests of whether a trade union or an employers' association is a 'representative' organization will be its size (in terms of the number of its members) relative to the sector or region in which it operates and the degree to which it has participated in collective bargaining in the sector concerned.[41]

The final category of complainant organizations comprises 'other representative national' NGOs with 'particular competence in the matters governed by the Charter'.[42] Again it will be up to the ECSR in its decisions on admissibility to determine whether such an organization is 'representative' and has the 'particular competence' referred to. While the latter qualification may not be so difficult to assess, the former is not so straightforward, certainly not as straightforward as with a trade union or employers' association. Presumably the kinds of factors the ECSR will look for when it comes to making an assessment about representativeness (which it has not yet had to do) are likely to be the number of members (although an organization could have a lot of members but nevertheless such members could still be a small proportion of the total potential membership, e.g. a pensioners organization); the size of an organization in terms of its income/turnover and number of staff; the degree to which it is recognized/consulted by public authorities; and the relationship of all these qualities to other national NGOs working in the same field.[43] A national NGO falling into this fourth category of complainant may only make complaints if the state in which it is located has made a declaration allowing it to do so.[44] Finland is the only state so far to have made such a declaration. According to the Explanatory Report on the Protocol, a state that has made such a declaration may not draw up a list of national NGOs permitted to make complaints, nor may it restrict such organizations to making complaints in respect of only certain provisions of the Charter.[45] Cullen has suggested that the fact that states may not draw up a list of approved organizations may discourage them from making the necessary declaration since the number of groups which could make complaints is open-ended, unlike the international NGOs in the

---

[40] Complaint No. 23/2003, *Syndicat occitan de l'éducation v. France*, Decision on Admissibility, paras 3–5.

[41] These factors are in fact suggested by the Explanatory Report on the 1995 Protocol as being the relevant ones: *supra* note 26, para. 23.

[42] Art. 2(1), 1995 Protocol.

[43] For a fuller discussion of this issue and a somewhat similar viewpoint, see Birk, 'The Collective Complaint: A New Procedure in the European Social Charter', in C. Engels and M. Weiss (eds), *Labour Law and Industrial Relations at the Turn of the Century* (1998) 261, at 266–268. See also Prouvez, 'Opinion of the Non-Governmental Organizations', in Council of Europe, *supra* note 30, 140 at 144–145.

[44] Art. 2(1), 1995 Protocol.

[45] Explanatory Report, *supra* note 26, at para. 28.

second category of complainant.[46] Where a state has not made a declaration, it may be possible for a national NGO to act through an international NGO, if there is an appropriate body on the list.[47]

Organizations of the second and fourth types may make complaints 'only in respect of those matters in which they have been recognised as having particular competence'.[48] Again, it will be up to the ECSR, when considering the admissibility of a complaint, to decide if a complainant in one of these categories has brought a complaint in relation to a matter in which it has such competence. In practice, the ECSR, when considering this question *proprio motu* in admissibility proceedings, does not carry out a very rigorous assessment. For example, in Complaints Nos. 7/2000 and 14/2003 the International Federation of Human Rights Leagues (IFHR) brought complaints against Greece[49] and France[50] concerning the unsatisfactory application of Article 1(2) of the Charter (prohibiting forced labour) and the unsatisfactory application of Articles 13 and 17 and E of the Revised Charter (the right of persons with disabilities and children to protection, and discrimination), respectively. In neither of these complaints did the French or Greek Governments contest the admissibility of the applications. The ECSR, in the admissibility phase, nevertheless considered whether the IFHR had 'particular competence' in relation to the subject matter of the complaints. The IFHR's goal is to 'promote the implementation of the Universal Declaration of Human Rights and other international instruments of human rights protection ... and to contribute to the enforcement of the rights guaranteed by these instruments'.[51] This was considered by the ECSR, in both complaints, to satisfy the stipulation that the organization had 'particular competence' in relation to the subject matter of those complaints. While it is undeniable that the IFHR, as a major international human rights NGO, has some competence with regard to the specific issues raised in both complaints, it is worth noting that the ECSR did not examine the scope of the IFHR's activities nor where its 'particular competence' stemmed from.[52] In the only cases so far in which a challenge was made by the defendant state that a complainant did not comply with Article 3, the ECSR seems to have adopted a relaxed reading of the provision. In Complaint No. 8/2000,

---

[46] Cullen, 'The Collective Complaints Mechanism of the European Social Charter', 25 *ELRev HR*/18 (2000) at HR/22. She probably goes too far when she suggests that a national NGO could be formed purely for the purpose of bringing a complaint, because it is necessary under Article 2 both that it is 'representative' and that it has 'particular competence' in a matter governed by the Charter.

[47] Harris, 'The Collective Complaints Procedure', in Council of Europe, *supra* note 30, 103 at 115; and Harris and Darcy, *supra* note 4, at 359.

[48] Art. 3, 1995 Protocol. The relevant part of the equally authentic French text reads 'dans les domains pour lesquels elles [i.e. organizations] ont été reconnues particulièrement qualifiées'.

[49] Complaint No. 7/2000, *International Federation of Human Rights Leagues v. Greece.*

[50] Complaint No. 14/2003, *International Federation of Human Rights Leagues v. France.*

[51] See FIDH, home page http://www.fidh.org and Complaint No. 14/2003, Decision on Admissibility, para. 5.

[52] For further examples of the ECSR's approach, see its decisions on admissibility in Complaint No. 1/1998, *International Commission of Jurists v. Portugal*, 6 *IHRR* 1142 (1999); Complaint No. 2/1999, *European Federation of Employees in Public Services v. France*; and Complaint No. 15/2003, *European Roma Rights Centre v. Greece.*

the Quaker Council for European Affairs brought a complaint that Greece was not in compliance with the Charter in respect of the way its legislation dealt with the conditions of conscientious objectors performing civilian service as an alternative to military service. The Greek Government challenged the competence of the Council to make such a complaint. The ECSR rejected this challenge. It pointed out that the Council's objective, according to its Statute, was to promote the traditions of the Quakers and, to this end, its task was to bring to the attention of the European institutions the concerns of Quakers, which relate to peace, human rights and economic justice. The Committee, therefore, concluded that the Council had made a complaint in a field in which it had 'particular competence' within the meaning of Article 3.[53] Secondly, in Complaint No. 17/2003, the World Organization against Torture alleged that Greek law was not in compliance with the Charter because it did not prohibit the corporal punishment or other forms of degrading punishment or treatment of children. The Greek Government challenged the competence of the Organization to make such a complaint because it was 'not particularly qualified in the field of degrading treatment of children'. The ECSR rejected this challenge, simply pointing out that the Organization was a body 'whose aim is to contribute to the struggle against torture, summary executions, disappearances, arbitrary detention, psychiatric internment for political reasons, and other cruel, inhuman and degrading treatment, regardless of the age of the persons against whom such treatments are directed' and therefore was 'particularly qualified' in relation to the subject matter of the complaint.[54] On the whole, therefore, it would seem that in practice the test is one of 'some competence' with regard to the issue raised by the complaint rather than 'particular competence' in the matters governed by the Charter.

Of the four categories of complainant, the first and the third are concerned with employment issues (broadly, economic rights), while the second and fourth categories may cover such issues but will predominantly be concerned with other aspects of the Charter (broadly, social rights). The fact that the second and fourth categories of complainant are more restricted than the first and third (in that they must be included on a list or operate in a state which has made a declaration accepting their competence to make complaints) illustrates the historic bias of the Charter in favour of employers' organizations and trade unions.[55] All of the first three categories of complainant have links with the reporting system — the first category comprises the organizations that participate in meetings of the Governmental Committee; the second consists of those bodies that are to be sent copies of national reports and may be consulted by the Governmental Committee;[56] while the third category comprises

---

[53] Complaint No. 8/2000, *Quaker Council for European Affairs v. Greece*, Decision on Admissibility, para. 9.

[54] Complaint No. 17/2003, *World Organization Against Torture v. Greece*, Decision on Admissibility, paras 2 and 6.

[55] Harris, *supra* note 47, at 126.

[56] Arts. 23(2) and 27(2), European Social Charter, as amended.

organizations that are to be sent national reports on which they may comment.[57] The fact that the fourth category does not feature in the reporting system may help to explain why it is optional under the complaints system. In linking the categories of complainant to the reporting system, the collective complaints system helps to achieve one of its aims, which (as noted above) is to 'strengthen the participation of management and labour and of non-governmental organizations' in the operation of the Charter.

C *The Complaints Procedure*

1 *Initiating a Complaint*

The procedure begins by a qualified complainant making a complaint in writing to the secretary of the ECSR[58] alleging that a state party 'has not ensured the satisfactory application' of one or more of the provisions of the Charter by which it is bound.[59] Complaints made by the first two categories of complainant (i.e. international organizations) must be in one of the official languages of the Council of Europe: complaints by national employers' associations, trade unions and NGOs may be submitted in another language.[60]

The terminology of a failure to ensure 'the satisfactory application' (or, as it is put more bluntly in Article 1 of the Protocol, the 'unsatisfactory application' (*'application non satisfaisante'*)) of the Charter is a somewhat unusual one. Birk, along with a number of other commentators, points out that the term 'satisfactory application' is not a legal one: it may be equated with 'compliance', which is the term used in the Charter in connection with the role of the ECSR in the reporting system.[61] The reason for the change in terminology is not apparent, and the Explanatory Report frequently uses the term 'compliance' instead of 'satisfactory application' (e.g. in paras 11 and 31).[62] The terminology of unsatisfactory application may also be contrasted with that of most civil and political rights treaties, where an individual applicant must claim to be the 'victim of a violation' of one of the recognized rights.[63] It may be that the

---

[57] Art. 23(1), European Social Charter, as amended. In practice not many national employers' organizations or trade unions show much interest in the reporting system: see Novitz, 'Remedies for Violation of Social Rights within the Council of Europe: The Significant Absence of a Court', in C. Kilpatrick, T. Novitz and P. Skidmore (eds), *The Future of Remedies in Europe* (2002) 231, at 243.

[58] Rule 20 of the ECSR's Rule of Procedure (1999). This explains that the secretary of the ECSR acts on behalf of the Secretary General of the Council of Europe, who is specified as the addressee of complaints in Art. 5 of the 1995 Protocol.

[59] Art. 4, 1995 Protocol. The French text reads: *'n'aurait pas assuré d'une manière satisfaisante l'application. . .'*. Note that a state party is not required to accept all the rights contained in the Charter, only a certain minimum.

[60] Rule 21 of the ECSR's Rules of Procedure.

[61] Art. 24 Charter, as amended.

[62] Birk, *supra* note 43, at 270.

[63] For example, Art. 34, ECHR; Art. 14, CERD; and Art. 1, Optional Protocol to the International Covenant on Civil and Political Rights, 1966, 999 UNTS 171; *Basic Documents*, at 199.

terminology of unsatisfactory application which, according to Sudre,[64] is broadly inspired by Article 24 of the Constitution of the ILO, is used rather than 'violation' because some (but certainly not all) of the provisions of the Charter are sufficiently vague and general and/or programmatic that they do not lend themselves to a straightforward determination that there has been a 'violation'. Novitz, one of the themes of whose writings on the Charter is that economic and social rights are unjustifiably much more weakly protected by the Council of Europe than civil and political rights, argues that the difference in terminology between the ECHR and the Charter indicates the 'inferior status of social rights' protected under the Charter because a 'violation' is implicitly a 'much more serious matter' than 'unsatisfactory application'.[65]

The terminology generally utilized in practice by the ECSR and the Committee of Ministers when referring to defendant states considered not to be ensuring the 'satisfactory application' of the Charter is being 'not in conformity' with the Charter, although occasionally the terms 'breach' or 'violation' have also been used.[66] The use of such language was challenged, on one occasion, in the dissenting opinion of Alfredo Bruto da Costa in Complaint No. 1/1998. Mr da Costa considered that the approach of the ECSR, which he felt focused on the situation in the defendant state (rather than on its performance), was not in conformity with the idea of 'satisfactory application'. There is a degree of merit in this argument, as the idea of 'satisfactory application' can be deemed to be concerned with the overall approach of the state party to the issue in question and not necessarily with assessing 'violations' of Charter provisions out of the context of overall policy and approach to the protected right(s) in question. Although the choice of terminology in the Charter is probably not a case of semantics, the language utilized by the ECSR in practice is noteworthy. In particular, the use of 'violation' and 'breach' lends further weight to the idea of the justiciability of economic and social rights.

A complainant, when bringing a complaint, must 'indicate in what respect' there has been unsatisfactory application of the Charter.[67] This means that a complainant must provide some evidence to support its allegation of unsatisfactory application. It seems that such evidence need not be extensive or comprehensive. In Complaint No. 5/1999 Portugal argued that the complainant had not indicated in what respect it had failed to ensure satisfactory application of the provisions of the Charter dealing with the rights to organize and bargain collectively as far as members of the armed forces were concerned, and therefore should be rejected as inadmissible. The ECSR rejected this challenge to admissibility. It pointed out that the complainant had referred to provisions of the Portuguese Constitution and legislation which were alleged to contravene the Charter. 'The reasons given in the complaint, although

---

[64]   Sudre, 'Le protocole additionel à la Charte Sociale Européenne prévoyant un système de réclammations collectives', 100 *RGDIP* 715 (1996) 724–725.

[65]   Novitz, *supra* note 9, at 53.

[66]   See, e.g., Complaints Nos. 7/2000, 8/2000 and 10/2000.

[67]   Art. 4, 1995 Protocol.

succinct, are sufficiently indicative of the extent to which the Portuguese Government is alleged not to have ensured the satisfactory application of the provisions concerned.'[68] On the other hand, in Complaint No. 2/1999 (which dealt with a similar issue in France) the ECSR found at the merits stage that the complainant had produced no evidence to rebut the defendant government's claim that French armed forces enjoyed certain rights of consultation and thus that the requirements of Article 6 were satisfied. The complaint was therefore dismissed.[69] The ECSR will also take account of evidence supplied by those other than the complainant. Thus, for example, in Complaint No. 1/1998, which concerned child labour in Portugal, the ECSR took account of information supplied by the Portuguese Government itself to conclude that in fact there had been an unsatisfactory application of the Charter in that case. Where a complaint relates to legislation that is alleged to be incompatible with the Charter, this is normally sufficient by way of evidence to support an allegation of unsatisfactory application: the ECSR does not normally require the complainant to provide examples of the practical application of the legislation to support a claim of unsatisfactory application of the Charter.[70] On the other hand, where legislation on its face is compatible with the Charter, the ECSR obviously requires evidence that the application of the legislation in practice is contrary to the Charter in order for a complaint to be upheld. This was successfully shown in the case of Complaint No. 1/1998 (child labour in Portugal), but not in respect of certain aspects of Complaint No. 9/2000 (the right to bargain effectively in France).

A somewhat related issue is the question of the level of generality at which a complaint must be made. The Explanatory Report on the 1995 Protocol notes that it was agreed during the negotiation of the Protocol that because of their collective nature, complaints could only raise questions concerning non-compliance of a state's law or practice with one of the provisions of the Charter: individual situations could not be submitted.[71] Clearly, if a complaint alleges that legislation as such is incompatible with the Charter, this is a general (or collective) complaint and therefore permissible. On the other hand, a complaint that there has been a breach of, say, Article 4(3) (on equal pay) because Ms X has been paid less than her male colleagues performing work of equal value, would be an individual complaint and, therefore, impermissible. However, there may be a grey area in between these two extremes where complaints may be made that the practical application of legislation or an administrative practice, as shown in its application to particular individuals, is contrary to the Charter. It would seem that as long as there are a reasonably significant number of groups of individuals involved demonstrating a generality of practice, complaints of this nature will be admissible. Thus, in Complaint No. 6/1999

---

[68] Complaint No. 5/1999, *European Federation of Employees in Public Services v. Portugal*, Decision on Admissibility, para. 10.

[69] Complaint No. 2/1999, Decision on the Merits, 8 *IHRR* 564 (2001) para. 32.

[70] See, for example, Complaints Nos. 7/2000 and 8/2000 on forced labour in Greece; and Complaint No. 9/2000, *Confédération Française de l'Encadrement — CGC v. France* on the length of working hours in France.

[71] *Supra* note 26, at para. 31.

the ECSR accepted as admissible a complaint which concerned the treatment of guides at general categories of historical and cultural sites in France and which also referred specifically to the position at the Louvre. Likewise, in Complaint No. 10/2000 the ECSR accepted as admissible a complaint that concerned workers in general in the Finnish health service exposed to radiation. Although, as mentioned, individual complaints as such may not be made, there seems no reason why an individual who believes his/her rights under the Charter have been violated should not contact an organization entitled to make complaints to request it to make a complaint about that individual's situation. That organization should then be entitled to make a complaint, provided that the situation concerned can be generalized, by showing that the alleged violation of the individual's rights is an example of a general pattern of non-compliance applying in the same way to others in the same position as the individual concerned.[72] A final point is that issues that are abstract in nature will not be dealt with by the ECSR in the collective complaints procedure. Thus, in Complaint No. 2/1999 the complainant sought to argue that as a general principle the right to collective bargaining under Article 6 of the Revised Charter could be exercised only through trade unions. The ECSR considered that this was an issue that in the context of a collective complaint could not be assessed in the abstract, but needed to be assessed on a concrete case-by-case basis.[73]

2 Admissibility

Once it has received a complaint, the ECSR must first decide whether the complaint is admissible. Unlike many human rights treaties, the CCP does not contain an explicit or comprehensive list of conditions that must be met before a complaint will be considered admissible. A number of conditions are, nevertheless, referred to in the Protocol and applied in practice by the ECSR. The complainant must be a qualified organization; the complaint must be in writing, against a state party to the Charter, and relate to a provision or provisions of the Charter that has/have been accepted by that state; and the complaint must state in what respect that state has not ensured the satisfactory application of the provision(s) concerned.[74] The Explanatory Report to the 1995 Protocol says that the ECSR may stipulate the conditions governing admissibility in its Rules of Procedure.[75] In fact, the ECSR has not (yet) done so, except in one minor respect. Rule 20 of the Rules of Procedure provides that the complaint must be signed by a person authorized to represent the complainant organization. In practice, in its decisions on admissibility, the ECSR considers whether this condition has been satisfied.[76]

---

[72] If the complaint is successful, it should lead to the offending legislation or practice being amended, but the individual who initiated the complaint will not, of course, obtain a remedy herself/himself. In practice, this is also often the situation where human rights treaties permit individual complaints.

[73] Complaint No. 2/1999, Decision on the Merits, at paras 30–31.

[74] Art. 4, 1995 Protocol.

[75] *Explanatory Report, supra* note 26, para. 31.

[76] For unsuccessful attempts by a defendant state to argue that Rule 20 had not been complied with, see, for examples, Complaints No. 6/2000, No. 15/2003 and No. 17/2003.

The Explanatory Report then goes on to say that should the ECSR decide to include conditions for admissibility in its Rules of Procedure, it must take account of the fact that the following points were agreed in the course of negotiating the Protocol. First, a complaint may be declared admissible 'even if a similar case has already been submitted to another national or international body', such as the ILO.[77] This differs from the ECHR, for example, which takes the opposite position.[78] An interesting question, not raised in the Explanatory Report, is whether a second complaint may be raised in relation to the same issue. For example, suppose a complaint is made and found to be well-founded and the defendant state fails to take corrective action, may a second complaint be made? Common sense suggests that as long as the defendant state has been given a reasonable period of time within which to take corrective action, a second complaint may be made. If it were not so, the effectiveness of the collective complaints system would be significantly impaired. On the other hand, where a complaint has been found not to be substantiated, it would seem impermissible to bring a new complaint relating to the same issue unless there were new material that might alter the view of a state's compliance with the Charter. This seems to be the implication of the ECSR's decision on admissibility in Complaint No. 16/2003. Here the ECSR noted that the complaint was not identical to Complaint No. 9/2000 (in which the Committee of Ministers had found France to be in compliance with the Charter) because it involved new legislation that had been enacted since the earlier complaint. The complaint was therefore admissible.[79]

A second point that the Explanatory Report says that the ECSR must take account of is the fact that the substance of a complaint that has been examined as part of the normal governmental reporting procedure 'does not in itself constitute an impediment to the complaint's admissibility. It has been agreed to give the ECSR a sufficient margin of appreciation in this area.'[80] The relationship between the collective complaints system and the reporting system is explored in more detail in section 5D below.

Compared with an individual application under the ECHR, for example, the conditions for the admissibility of a collective complaint differ quite considerably: in particular, a number of conditions for the admissibility of an individual application under the ECHR have no counterpart under the collective complaints procedure. First, there is no time limit for bringing a complaint. This is presumably because as the complaint relates to non-compliance of a law or practice with the Charter, the

---

[77] Sudre, *supra* note 64, at 731 questions whether this should be so, and says the point is a difficult one. It has also been questioned whether a 'similar' case also includes the same case: see Jaeger, 'The Additional Protocol to the European Social Charter providing for a System of Collective Complaints', 10 *LJIL* (1997) 69, at 74.

[78] See Art. 35(2)(b).

[79] Complaint No. 16/2003, *Confédération française de l'Encadrement CFE-CGC v France*, Decision on Admissibility, para. 8.

[80] Para. 31.

434 *EJIL* 15 (2004), 417–456

non-compliance is a continuing one.[81] A second difference is that there is no requirement to exhaust domestic remedies. The reason for this is presumably that in many (if not most) cases there will be no domestic remedy available because many of the provisions of the Charter are not part of domestic law and/or are not self-executing,[82] and even if they were, it is unlikely that a potential complainant would have *locus standi* to challenge the national legislation or practice alleged to be contrary to the Charter.[83] A third difference with the ECHR is that a complaint may not be declared inadmissible because it is manifestly ill-founded. Arguments by defendant governments that a complaint should be rejected as inadmissible because it is manifestly ill-founded have been consistently rejected by the ECSR, which has held that this issue is a matter for the merits stage.[84] Presumably the reason why there is no threshold of *prima facie* non-compliance is because it is anticipated that complainant organizations will not bring frivolous claims, but will bring only complaints with a considerable degree of plausibility. If this is the assumption, then it has certainly been borne out in practice so far. Finally, unlike the ECHR, there is no requirement that a complaint must not be an abuse of the right of petition. An attempt by the Portuguese Government to invoke such a requirement in Complaint No. 11/2001 was unsuccessful. The Government's argument that the complainant (the European Council of Police Trade Unions) was motivated by political considerations was rejected by the ECSR as being 'invalid, not being one which may be relied on to establish the inadmissibility or ill-foundedness of a complaint'.[85]

As far as procedure in admissibility proceedings is concerned, once the ECSR is seized of a complaint, a rapporteur for the complaint is appointed.[86] The ECSR 'may' request the defendant state and the complainant to submit written information and observations on the admissibility of the complaint within such time limit as it shall prescribe.[87] In practice the defendant state has been asked to submit observations in

---

[81]   In fact under the ECHR the six-month rule for bringing an application does not apply to continuing violations of the Convention: see *De Becker v. Belgium*, 2 *Yearbook of the European Convention on Human Rights* (1958) 214, at 230–234.

[82]   However, it should be noted that for many rights the ECSR has read in a remedy: see Harris and Darcy, *supra* note 4, at 30.

[83]   But both Birk, *supra* note 43, at 271, and Harris, *supra* note 47, at 106, argue that if there were a domestic remedy, it should be exhausted before a collective complaint is made. This point has not yet arisen in practice before the ECSR.

[84]   See, for example, Complaint No. 4/1999, *European Federation of Employees in Public Services v. Italy*, Decision on Admissibility, para. 12; Complaint No. 8/2000, Decision on Admissibility, para. 10; Complaint No. 11/2001, *European Council of Police Trade Unions v. Portugal*, Decision on Admissibility, paras 7 and 8; and Complaint No. 18/2003, *World Organization against Torture v. Ireland*, Decision on Admissibility, para. 7. Similarly, arguments by a defendant state that it has taken or is taking the necessary measures to amend the legislation/practice alleged to contravene the Charter have also been rejected as irrelevant to admissibility and considered to be a matter for the merits stage: see, for example, Complaint No. 1/1998, Decision on Admissibility, para. 14; Complaint No. 7/2000, Decision on Admissibility, para. 9.

[85]   Complaint No. 11/2001, Decision on Admissibility, para. 8.

[86]   Rule 24(1) of the ECSR's Rules of Procedure.

[87]   Art. 6, 1995 Protocol and Rule 26 of the ECSR's Rules of Procedure.

every case so far, except Complaint No. 3/1999 where it was obvious that the complaint was inadmissible because the defendant state, Greece, had not accepted to be bound by the provisions of the Charter which were the subject of the complaint.[88] According to the Explanatory Report, a case may only be declared admissible if the defendant state has been asked to submit its observations.[89] Only in one case (Complaint No. 1/1998) does it appear that the complainant was asked for its views on the defendant state's observations. Otherwise, the complaint and the documentation attached to it appear to have been regarded as sufficient to give the complainant's viewpoint on the question of admissibility. The written submissions of the parties are all the material that the ECSR has in order to determine the admissibility of a complaint: unlike the merits stage (as will be seen) there is no provision for oral hearings. On the basis of the written submissions, the rapporteur then drafts a decision on admissibility, which is considered by the ECSR in private session.[90] At these meetings, as with the ECSR's meetings to examine the reports of states parties to the Charter, a representative of the ILO is invited to be present.[91] According to the published decisions on admissibility, an ILO representative has participated in only four of the 23 complaints on which a decision on admissibility has been taken.[92] Once the ECSR has deliberated, it takes a decision on admissibility, which must be reasoned. The decision is then communicated to the parties to the complaint and to the states parties to the Charter, and made public.[93] Even if there has been no challenge to the admissibility of a complaint, which has been the position in almost half of the complaints so far,[94] the ECSR nevertheless goes through the conditions of admissibility outlined above[95] to satisfy itself that they have been fulfilled. Where a challenge has been made to the admissibility of a complaint, the ECSR first satisfies itself that the unchallenged conditions of admissibility have been met before considering the challenge(s) to admissibility put forward by the defendant state.

Overall, the ECSR has taken a rather relaxed attitude to admissibility so far. Cullen has suggested that if complaints become more numerous, the ECSR may need to be

---

[88] Complaint No. 3/1999, *European Federation of Employees in Public Services v. Greece*, Decision on Admissibility. Cf. para. 35 of the *Explanatory Report, supra* note 26, which notes that there is no obligation on the ECSR to 'request information from the defendant state, in order to permit it to reject a complaint that is manifestly inadmissible of its own volition'.

[89] *Supra* note 26, at para. 35.

[90] Rules 24(3) and 27(1) of the ECSR's Rules of Procedure.

[91] Rule 10 of the ECSR's Rules of Procedure; *Explanatory Report, supra* note 26, at para. 34.

[92] Complaints Nos. 1/1998, 7/2000, 8/2000 and 10/2000.

[93] Rule 27(2)(3)(4) of the ECSR's Rules of Procedure.

[94] Complaints Nos. 2/1999, 9/2000, 10/2000, 12/2002, 13/2002, 14/2003, 19/2003, *World Organization Against Torture v. Italy*, 20/2003, *World Organization Against Torture v Portugal* and Complaint No. 22/2003, CGT (*Confédération générale du travail*) *v. France*.

[95] Viz. that the complaint is in writing; made by a qualified organization; signed by an authorized person; relates to a provision of the Charter accepted by the defendant state; and sets out the grounds for the allegation of unsatisfactory application of the provision concerned.

436   *EJIL* 15 (2004), 417–456

more restrictive in its approach.[96] As things stand at present, however, there seems to be little likelihood of this situation occurring in the immediate future.

3 The Merits Stage

If the ECSR decides that a complaint is admissible, it then asks the complainant and the defendant state to submit their views on the merits of the complaint in writing within a specified time limit.[97] Other states parties to the Protocol and organizations belonging to the first category of complainant referred to above (i.e. international organizations of employers and trade unions) are also invited to submit their views on the complaint.[98] In practice so far no state party to the Protocol has yet submitted observations on a complaint not involving itself.[99] Of international organizations of employers and trade unions, the European Trade Union Confederation has submitted observations in in all the cases that have been disposed of so far. The International Organization of Employers has submitted its observations on one occasion, in Complaint No. 12/2002, the first complaint to have been brought by an employers' association. Following the receipt of all the written material referred to, each of the parties to the complaint may submit any additional information or observations it wishes within such time limit as the ECSR may prescribe.[100] The ECSR may then, if it considers it desirable, either on its own initiative or at the request of one of the parties, organize a hearing with the representatives of the parties.[101] Of the 11 complaints that have so far been dealt with on the merits, a hearing has been held in five cases.[102] Harris has argued that hearings should generally be held in order both to give the ECSR 'a better sense of the issues and arguments' and to promote the familiarity of complainant organizations with the system.[103]

On the basis of the written materials, the hearing (if held) and a draft report prepared by the rapporteur,[104] the ECSR deliberates in private[105] on the merits of the complaint and draws up its report. In this it is required to describe the steps it has

---

[96]   Cullen, *supra* note 46, HR/22.

[97]   Art. 7(1), 1995 Protocol; Rule 28(1) and (2) of the ECSR's Rules of Procedure. Time limits are usually quite short: e.g. the defendant state is normally given around two months from the date of the decision on admissibility to submit its views.

[98]   Art. 7(1) and (2), 1995 Protocol; Rule 28(3) and (4) of the ECSR's Rules of Procedure.

[99]   Cf. practice before the European Court of Human Rights, where states have from time to time submitted observations in cases brought against other states because they had a particular interest in the subject matter of the case.

[100] Art. 7(3), 1995 Protocol.

[101] Art. 7(4), 1995 Protocol and Rule 29 of the ECSR's Rules of Procedure. As well as the parties, states and organizations that have submitted observations shall be invited to attend.

[102] Complaints Nos. 2/1999, 4/1999 and 5/1999 (a joint hearing for the three cases which were concerned with the same matter), Complaint No. 9/2000, 10 *IHRR* 559 (2003) and Complaint No. 12/2003. A sixth hearing was held on 29 September 2003 in Complaint No. 13/2002. The decision on the merits, at the time of writing, had not been given.

[103] Harris, *supra* note 47, at 106.

[104] Rule 24(3) of the ECSR's Rules of Procedure.

[105] Again, as with admissibility proceedings, an ILO representative may take part, and has in fact done so in five complaints so far — Complaints Nos. 1/1998, 2/1999, 4/1999, 5/1999 and Complaint No. 6/1999, 8 *IHRR* 554 (2001).

taken to examine the complaint and to give, with reasons, its conclusions as to whether or not the defendant state has 'ensured the satisfactory application' of the provision(s) of the Charter referred to in the complaint.[106] In this latter respect the ECSR's role is essentially a quasi-judicial one, applying law to the facts to reach a considered conclusion.[107] This conclusion is not final and binding, however, as the ECSR's report is then transmitted to the Committee of Ministers for a definitive disposal of the complaint. At the same time the report is also sent to the complainant and the states parties to the Charter.[108] Subsequently, the report is also transmitted to the Parliamentary Assembly and made public, either at the same time as the resolution of the Committee of Ministers concluding proceedings for the complaint concerned or four months after the report has been sent to the Committee of Ministers, whichever is the earlier.[109]

In its report the ECSR is limited to expressing a view as to whether the defendant state has complied with the Charter or not. It seems that it is not entitled to award or suggest compensation if it finds the defendant state in non-compliance. A request in Complaint No. 9/2000 for it to do so, for the sum of FF78 billion, was summarily dismissed without any discussion of the issue.[110] While it may be possible that the Committee did not entertain the request due to the size of the claim, a power to award compensation is not in accordance with the nature and purpose of the Protocol.[111] Likewise, it seems that the ECSR has no power to award costs to a successful complainant. In Complaint No. 1/1998 the complainant, the International Commission of Jurists, requested that the defendant state, Portugal, pay it the sum of FF50,000 in respect of its costs in preparing and submitting the complaint. The ECSR decided to leave this matter for the Committee of Ministers to determine.[112] The matter was not, however, referred to in the resolution of the Committee of Ministers concluding the complaint.[113] The question of costs was raised again in Complaint No. 16/2003, where the complainant sought costs of 9,000 Euros. In its decision on admissibility, the ECSR decided to deal with this issue at the merits stage (which at the time of writing had not yet taken place).[114] It remains to be seen, therefore, whether the ECSR will decide that it does have the power to make an award as to costs. It seems clear, however, that the ECSR does not have the power to promote a friendly

---

[106] Art. 8(1), 1995 Protocol. The requirement of reasons is found in Rule 30(1) of the ECSR's Rules of Procedure.

[107] In so doing the ECSR frequently refers to and follows the 'case law' as to the meaning and scope of Charter rights that it has developed in the reporting procedure.

[108] Art. 8(2), 1995 Protocol.

[109] Art. 8(2), 1995 Protocol; Rule 30(2)-(4) of the ECSR's Rules of Procedure.

[110] Complaint No. 9/2000, para. 58.

[111] Harris and Darcy, however, argue that it would be open to the Committee of Ministers, when making a recommendation to a defendant state found to be in non-compliance with the Charter, to make a recommendation suggesting that appropriate reparation be made to anyone particularly affected by such non-compliance: Harris and Darcy, *supra* note 4, at 367.

[112] Complaint No. 1/1998, Report to the Committee of Ministers, para. 5.

[113] Res. ChS (99) 4.

[114] Complaint No. 16/2003, Decision on Admissibility, para. 9.

438 *EJIL* 15 (2004), 417–456

settlement or order provisional measures, something that Harris has argued is regrettable.[115]

As mentioned above, it is up to the Committee of Ministers to make a definitive disposal of the complaint. Its role in so doing is described in Article 9(1) of the 1995 Protocol as follows:

> On the basis of the report of the Committee of Independent Experts [now the ECSR], the Committee of Ministers shall adopt a resolution by a majority of those voting. If the Committee of Independent Experts finds that the Charter has not been applied in a satisfactory manner, the Committee of Ministers shall adopt, by a majority of two-thirds of those voting, a recommendation addressed to the Contracting Party concerned. In both cases, entitlement to voting shall be limited to the Contracting Parties to the Charter.

Of this provision the Explanatory Report says:

> The duties of the Committee of Ministers are similar to those it carries out as a supervisory body in the procedure instituted by the Charter [i.e. the reporting procedure].
>
> On the basis of the report of the Committee of Independent Experts, the Committee of Ministers adopts a resolution by a majority of those voting. However, if the conclusions of the Committee of Independent Experts are negative, the Committee of Ministers must adopt a recommendation addressed to the State concerned. ... The Committee of Ministers cannot reverse the legal assessment made by the Committee of Independent Experts. However, its decision (resolution or recommendation) may be based on social and economic policy considerations.[116]

These somewhat opaque texts, which are equally unclear in their French versions, have given rise to differing views among commentators. It is generally agreed that if the ECSR reaches the conclusion that the defendant state has ensured the satisfactory application of the Charter, the Committee of Ministers shall do no more than adopt a resolution, by a simple majority of those voting,[117] concurring with the finding of the ECSR. This is indeed what has happened in practice.[118] Where the views of commentators diverge widely is over what the position should be where the ECSR reaches the conclusion that the defendant state has not ensured the satisfactory application of the Charter. Harris, relying on the use of the mandatory term 'shall' in Article 9(1), is of the view that the Committee of Ministers may not make its own findings of compliance but must endorse the findings of the ECSR and address a recommendation to the defendant state. He regards the reference in the Explanatory Report to account being taken by the Committee of Ministers of economic and social considerations as confusing (even though admittedly this happens in the reporting procedure) and contrary to the clear wording of Article 9(1), and notes that the Explanatory Report is not an authoritative source of interpretation.[119] Trechsel has

---

[115] Harris, *supra* note 47, at 120. See also Harris and Darcy, *supra* note 4, at 365.

[116] *Explanatory Report*, *supra* note 26, para. 46.

[117] It is arguably anomalous that all parties to the Charter are permitted to vote, and not simply those bound by the collective complaints system.

[118] See Res ChS (2001)2, 8 *IHRR* 570 (2001); (2001)3; (2001)4; and (2002)5 relating to Complaints Nos 2/1999, 4/1999, 5/1999 and 11/2001 respectively. In these Resolutions the Committee of Ministers simply 'takes note' of the ECSR's report.

[119] Harris, *supra* note 47, at 107 and 121. See also Harris and Darcy, *supra* note 4, at 365–367.

queried Harris' view on the basis that if the Committee of Ministers was bound to follow the ECSR's conclusion, what would be the point of giving the Committee of Ministers the power to consult the Governmental Committee in certain circumstances (a point dealt with below) or requiring a two-thirds majority, which implies that states have a discretion to vote against the ECSR's findings.[120] To this Harris and Darcy have responded that 'although there is a vote on the adoption of the recommendation, the vote concerns the content of the recommendation and not whether any recommendation should be addressed to the contracting party concerned at all.'[121] They also respond to the point in the Explanatory Report about account being taken of 'social and economic policy considerations' that this relates to the content of the resolution and/or recommendation, not to whether a recommendation should be adopted at all.[122] Although discussing the issue only briefly, Brillat appears to share the views of Harris.[123]

Sudre and Cullen take a very different position, however. Sudre, placing considerable reliance on the passage of the Explanatory Report quoted above, concludes that while the Committee of Ministers may not question the ECSR's findings on compliance, it may reach a decision contrary to that implied by the legal position and take account of non-legal considerations, so that in essence the Committee of Ministers, while legally bound by the opinion of the ECSR, politically is free to disregard that opinion.[124] Similarly, but more precisely, Cullen concludes that 'the Committee of Ministers may decide, on the basis of economic and social factors, not to make a recommendation to the defendant state to redress the area of non-compliance found by the ECSR in its conclusions, but it may not reject the legal basis of the conclusions.'[125] All commentators are agreed, however, that any recommendations or resolutions adopted by the Committee of Ministers are not legally binding.

The practice of the Committee of Ministers so far is much closer to the position of Sudre and Cullen than that of Harris (and Harris and Darcy). Of the seven complaints for which the ECSR reached the conclusion that the defendant state had not ensured the satisfactory application of the Charter (and where, therefore, in Harris' view the Committee of Ministers should have addressed a recommendation to the defendant state), only in one case (Complaint No. 6/1999) did the Committee of Ministers in fact address a recommendation to the defendant state (in which it endorsed the ECSR's findings).[126] In the other six cases the Committee of Ministers merely adopted a resolution concluding the proceedings. These resolutions are examined in detail in the next section of this article. The broader issues raised by the role of the Committee of Ministers are examined later.

---

[120] Trechsel, 'Conclusion', in *Council of Europe, supra* note 30, at 185.
[121] Harris and Darcy, *supra* note 4, at 366.
[122] *Ibid.*
[123] Brillat, 'A New Protocol to the European Social Charter Providing for Collective Complaints', 1 *EHRLR* (1996) 52 at 61.
[124] Sudre, *supra* note 64, at 737.
[125] Cullen, *supra* note 46, at HR/27.
[126] Res. ChS (2000)1.

440   *EJIL* 15 (2004), 417–456

As mentioned earlier, the Governmental Committee plays a role in the reporting procedure. One of the most contentious issues in negotiating the 1995 Protocol was what kind of role (if any) the Governmental Committee should play in the collective complaints procedure. Initially the Charte-Rel Committee proposed that the Governmental Committee should have a role similar to the one that it has in the reporting procedure, but this was opposed by the social partners and some governments, which did not wish the Governmental Committee to have any role at all because of its composition (national civil servants) and the delay that its involvement might entail.[127] The Charte-Rel Committee, therefore, amended its draft Protocol accordingly, and in that form (with no role for the Governmental Committee) the draft was sent to the Committee of Ministers.[128] The draft was not acceptable to a majority of the Committee of Ministers and, as a compromise, the draft was amended to give a modest role for the Governmental Committee in what is now Article 9(2). This provides that, at the request of the defendant state, the Committee of Ministers may decide, where the report of the ECSR raises 'new issues', by a two-thirds majority of the parties to the Charter, to consult the Governmental Committee. It is not altogether clear what is meant by 'new issues'. Commentators have suggested that the term refers to a new point of interpretation or application of the Charter.[129] The 1995 Protocol is silent on the procedure to be followed where the Governmental Committee is consulted and as to the significance of any opinion that it might give. In practice, the Committee of Ministers has not yet consulted the Governmental Committee in relation to a complaint.[130]

If the Committee of Ministers endorses the findings of non-compliance by the ECSR and addresses a recommendation to the defendant state, the latter is to 'provide information on the measures it has taken to give effect' to the recommendation of the Committee of Ministers in the 'next report' that it submits under the reporting procedure.[131] If that report shows the defendant state to have complied with the recommendation of the Committee of Ministers, all well and good. If not, the Committee of Ministers could presumably address a further recommendation to the defendant state urging it to comply. Given that recommendations of the Committee of Ministers are not legally binding, it is unrealistic to expect the collective complaints system to have any stronger sanction against recalcitrant states. In the one recommendation addressed by the Committee of Ministers to a defendant state so far,

---

[127] D. Gomien, D. Harris and L. Zwaak, *Law and Practice of the European Convention on Human Rights and the European Social Charter* (1996), at 428.

[128] Brillat, *supra* note 123, at 61. See also Harris, *supra* note 47, at 108 and 122.

[129] Harris, *supra* note 47, at 122; Harris and Darcy, *supra* note 4, at 367–368; and Sudre, *supra* note 64, at 735. Less convincingly perhaps, Sudre suggests that the term could also concern the essential interests of the defendant state.

[130] The writers assume this to be the case, as none of the resolutions or recommendations so far made by the Committee of Ministers refer to it having consulted the Governmental Committee.

[131] Art. 10, 1995 Protocol. It should be noted that the term 'next report' means literally that. Thus, if the provision of the Charter with which the defendant State has failed to comply is a non-core right, and the next report due covers only core rights, the response to the recommendation of the Committee of Ministers must nevertheless be contained in that report: see *Explanatory Report*, *supra* note 28, para. 50.

the state concerned (France) reported on various steps that it had taken. The ECSR was only partially satisfied with these measures, and asked the French Government both to take further measures and to supply it with more detailed information.[132]

Having now examined at considerable length how the collective complaints system operates in general terms, it is time to consider how it has worked in practice and to see what the outcome of the first lot of complaints has been before making a critical assessment of the system.

4 An Overview of the Operation of the Collective Complaints System So Far

By February 2004, five and a half years after the entry into force of the CCP, 23 complaints had been made. These complaints have been made against eight of the 13 states that are bound by the system (eight complaints against France; five against Greece; four against Portugal; two against Italy and one each against Belgium, Finland, Ireland and Sweden). The complainants have all come from the second or third categories of those organizations entitled to make complaints.[133] Harris' prediction that the first category of complaint (international employers' organizations and trade unions) would want to make complaints[134] has not yet been borne out.

The complaints to date concern: child labour in Portugal;[135] the capacity of members of the armed forces to form trade unions and bargain collectively in France, Greece, Italy and Portugal,[136] and of the police to do the same in Portugal;[137] discrimination against certain tourist guides in France;[138] certain forms of forced labour in Greece;[139] the working conditions of managers in France;[140] the working conditions of health care workers in Finland exposed to radiation;[141] the closed shop in Sweden;[142] educational provision for autistic children in France;[143] discrimination in the provision of social and medical assistance in France;[144] discrimination against the

---

[132] ECSR, *European Social Charter (Revised): Conclusions 2002 (France)*, at 14.

[133] 16 from the second category and seven from the third category (six of which are national trade unions and the other an employers' association).

[134] Harris, *supra* note 47, at 111.

[135] Complaint No. 1/1998. For comment, see Cullen, *supra* note 46.

[136] Complaint Nos. 2/1999, 3/1999, 4/1999 and 5/1999.

[137] Complaint No. 11/2001, 10 *IHRR* 572 (2003).

[138] Complaint No. 6/1999.

[139] Complaint No. 7/2000, 8 *IHRR* 1153 (2001) and Complaint No. 8/2000 (8) *IHRR* 1158 (2001). For comments on these complaints, see Darcy, 'Forced Labour in Greece', 27 *ELRev.*, (2002) 218.

[140] Complaints Nos. 9/2000 and 16/2003.

[141] Complaint No. 10/2000, 10 *IHRR* 554 (2003).

[142] Complaint No. 12/2002.

[143] Complaint No. 13/2002.

[144] Complaint No. 14/2003.

442 *EJIL* 15 (2004), 417–456

Roma in the field of housing in Greece;[145] and the absence of effective prohibition against corporal punishment of children in Belgium, Greece, Ireland, Italy and Portugal;[146] working conditions in general in France;[147] and the prohibition on non-representative professional organizations from presenting candidates in professional elections in France.[148]

Of the 23 complaints, all but one have been declared admissible.[149] Of the 22 admissible complaints, the ECSR has upheld the complaint in seven cases,[150] rejected the complaint in four cases[151] and in eleven cases has not yet concluded its consideration of the merits.[152] In the four cases where the ECSR rejected the complaint, the Committee of Ministers adopted a resolution concurring with the conclusions of the ECSR.[153] Of the seven complaints where the ECSR found non-compliance with the Charter by the defendant state, only in one case did the Committee of Ministers address a recommendation to the defendant state, as Article 9(1) appears to suggest it should. This was Complaint No. 6/1999, which concerned a complaint of discriminatory treatment by the French Government against certain kinds of tourist guides. Here the Committee of Ministers addressed a number of quite specific recommendations to the French Government to take certain action to put an end to the discriminatory treatment.[154] Compared with recommendations addressed to states parties at the end of the reporting procedure, this recommendation is unusual because of its detail and specificity. In the recommendations adopted in the reporting procedure, the Committee of Ministers usually does no more than recommend that the state concerned 'takes account, in an appropriate manner, of the negative conclusion' of the ECSR.[155]

In the other six cases where the ECSR found non-compliance by the defendant state, the Committee of Ministers failed to endorse the ECSR's finding and address a recommendation to that state. In Complaint No. 1/1998 the International Commission of Jurists alleged that Portugal was not complying with Article 7(1) of the Charter, which prohibits the employment of children below the age of 15, in that, although there was legislation that laid down such a prohibition, that legislation was not being fully enforced in practice. The ECSR, while recognizing that the Portuguese Government had taken steps that had significantly improved the situation in recent years, nevertheless found that Portugal was still not fully in conformity with Article 7(1) and therefore upheld the complaint. The Committee of Ministers, however,

---

145 Complaint No. 15/2003.
146 Complaints Nos. 17/2003, 18/2003, 19/2003, 20/2003 and 21/2003.
147 Complaint No. 22/2003.
148 Complaint No. 23/2003.
149 Complaint No. 3/1999. That such a high proportion of complaints has been found admissible is scarcely surprising, given the nature of those entitled to make the complaints and the limited admissibility criteria.
150 Complaints Nos. 1/1998, 6/1999, 7/2000, 8/2000, 9/2000, 10/2000 and 12/2002.
151 Complaints Nos. 2/1999, 4/1999, 5/1999 and 11/2001.
152 Complaints Nos. 13–23.
153 See *supra* note 118.
154 Rec. ChS (2001)1.
155 See, for example, Rec. ChS (2001)3 (addressed to Malta).

rather than addressing a recommendation to Portugal, adopted a resolution[156] in which it 'takes note' of the ECSR's findings and, after pointing out that it had adopted a recommendation to Portugal on the same issue the previous year,[157] 'recalls that the Government of Portugal will present, in its next report on the application of the European Social Charter, the measures taken in application of the said recommendation'. This action by the Committee of Ministers has been criticized as being 'a very weak response' and as taking insufficient account of the differences between the collective complaints system and the reporting procedure.[158] More could have been achieved if the Committee of Ministers' second recommendation had called on Portugal to improve the enforcement of its child labour legislation, a recommendation on which Portugal would subsequently have had to report. Although Portugal has now taken some action to rectify the situation,[159] the ECSR in its conclusions on Portugal's report for the period 1996–1998 still did not consider that Portugal was fully in compliance with Article 7.[160]

In the case of Complaint No. 7/2000 the ECSR found Greece in non-compliance with the Charter's provisions prohibiting forced labour in respect of three particular pieces of legislation. These instances of non-compliance had been pointed out by the ECSR under the reporting system and had been the subject of a series of recommendations by the Committee of Ministers dating back to 1993. When the Committee of Ministers came to consider the first piece of legislation at issue in Complaint No. 7/2000, it took note of the fact that the Greek Government had advanced additional considerations not relied on during the examination of the merits of the complaint by the ECSR, namely a law of 1995, and the Committee went on to note that the Greek Government 'will give a full account of these' in its next report due under the reporting system.[161] That the Greek Government should be allowed to raise arguments before the Committee of Ministers which it did not raise (but presumably could have raised) before the ECSR, seems questionable. And even more surprising is the fact that these arguments related to a piece of legislation of 1995 which presumably the Greek Government could have advanced when its failure to comply with the Charter was being revealed in the 1995, 1997 and 1999 reporting cycles. In relation to the second and third pieces of legislation at issue in this complaint, the Committee of Ministers 'takes note that . . . the Greek Government undertakes to bring the situation into conformity with the Charter in good time'.[162] Given that the reporting system had revealed failures of compliance of the relevant legislation with the Charter going back nearly 10 years, it seems feeble in the extreme that the Committee should simply wait for the Greek Government to take action in its own

---

[156] Res. ChS (1999) 4.
[157] Res. ChS (1998) 5.
[158] Harris and Darcy, *supra* note 4, at 367. Cf. Cullen, *supra* note 46, at HR/26, who describes the Committee of Ministers' actions as 'minimalist'.
[159] See Governmental Committee of the European Social Charter, *15th Report (II)* (2001) at 11.
[160] ECSR, *European Social Charter: Conclusions XV-2 (Portugal)* (2001) at 4.
[161] Res. ChS (2001) 6.
[162] *Ibid.*

444   *EJIL* 15 (2004), 417–456

good time. Complaint No. 8/2000 also concerned alleged forced labour in Greece, this time in respect of conscientious objectors performing civilian service as an alternative to military service. The ECSR, by a majority of 6–3, found that the greater length of civilian service compared with military service, while not as such forced labour, was nevertheless a disproportionate restriction on the freedom to earn one's living in an occupation freely entered upon and thus was contrary to Article 1(2) of the Charter. The fact that the ECSR was quite deeply divided as to the scope of Article 1(2) may help to explain why the Committee of Ministers did not address a recommendation to Greece but instead adopted a resolution.[163] In this resolution the Committee of Ministers noted that the ECSR's report had been 'circulated to the competent authorities' and was being translated into Greek; noted recent developments in Greece, including a decrease in the length of military service; and finally 'takes note that the Greek Government undertakes to take the matter into consideration with a view to bring the situation into conformity with the Charter in good time'. This final part of the resolution constitutes the same feeble response as was seen in Complaint No. 7/2000, a feebleness which is compounded by the fact that the earlier part of the resolution noted a decrease in the length of military service, thus if anything making the disproportionate length of civilian service worse.

The fourth case of failure by the Committee of Ministers to address a recommendation to a non-complying defendant state concerns Complaint No. 9/2000. Here the ECSR (admittedly by a 5–3 majority) found two breaches of the Charter by France in respect of the length of the working hours of managers. The Committee of Ministers, however, did not endorse this finding. Instead, it noted a number of factors, which collectively appear to amount to a view as to the meaning and application of the relevant provisions of the Charter quite different from that of the majority of the ECSR (but close to the views expressed in a dissenting opinion by two members of the minority), and therefore implicitly finding no breach by France.[164] Here the Committee of Ministers has effectively substituted its own view of the law for that of the ECSR — something which, as noted earlier, all commentators are agreed that the Committee of Ministers is not supposed to do.

The Committee of Ministers did not adopt a recommendation to a non-complying defendant state in Complaint No. 10/2000 either. Here the ECSR found that the exposure of health workers to ionizing radiation was dangerous and unhealthy work within the meaning of Article 2(4) of the Charter and that therefore the failure of the Finnish Government to ensure that such workers were entitled to additional paid holidays or reduced working hours (as Article 2(4) requires) amounted to non-compliance with that article. The Committee of Ministers in its resolution[165] began by noting that the primary concern of the Finnish Government was to eliminate risks created by working with ionizing radiation and that workers in the health sector in Finland were exposed to doses of radiation well below the maximum limits required by

[163] Res. ChS (2002) 3, 10 *IHRR* 583 (2003).
[164] Res. ChS (2002) 4, 10 *IHRR* 571 (2003).
[165] Res. ChS (2002) 2.

international standards. The Committee of Ministers then went on to take note of the impending ratification by Finland of the Revised Social Charter, including the revised Article 2, paragraph 4, which puts the emphasis on elimination of risks rather than on additional paid holidays or reduced working hours. The Committee of Ministers' resolution is again open to criticism. The complaint and the ECSR's report are couched purely in terms of the original Charter. It was, therefore, at best premature, at worst irrelevant, for the Committee of Ministers to consider the issue in terms of the Revised Charter (which Finland did in fact ratify six months after the resolution was adopted). The resolution can be read as suggesting that once Finland ratified the Revised Charter, it would be in compliance with it. This would mean that the Committee of Ministers had formed a view about the standard of protection required by Article 2(4). This is really a matter for the ECSR.

The final case, to date, where the ECSR found a state in violation of the Charter but the Committee of Ministers did not address a recommendation to that state, is Complaint No. 12/2002. Sweden's representative to the Committee of Ministers had declared Sweden's intent to comply with the Charter through renegotiating collective agreements (of which 4,388 required renegotiation as of August 2003).[166] The Committee of Ministers, in the operative part of its resolution,[167] simply stated that it 'looks forward to Sweden reporting that the problem has been solved at the time of the submission of the next report' on Article 5 of the Revised Social Charter. The Committee of Ministers seems unduly complacent here as there is no guarantee that such a large number of agreements will be renegotiated within the timeframe envisaged. Furthermore, the ECSR had called on Sweden to use legislative, regulatory or judicial means in order to bring about conformity with the Charter.[168]

5 Some Comments on the Collective Complaints System

A *The Degree of Use of the Complaints System*

Since the CCP entered into force, 23 complaints have been lodged, which works out at about four complaints a year on average. Whether the number of complaints that has so far been made is more or less than might have been expected is an impossible question to answer, and one that is perhaps not even worth asking. Instead, it is more fruitful to consider the factors that are likely to influence the degree of use that has been made and probably will be made of the complaints system. These factors include the following. The first is the number of states that have accepted the system. Obviously the more states that have accepted the system, the more complaints it is likely that there will be (although it should be noted that just over a third of the states that have so far accepted the system have not yet had a complaint made against

---

[166] Appendix to Res ChS (2003) 1.
[167] Res. ChS (2003) 1.
[168] Complaint No. 12/2002, Decision on the Merits, para. 28.

them). Currently the number of states that have accepted the system is disappointingly low — only just over one third of parties to the Charter. A second factor is the degree of knowledge of the system by potential complainants. Obviously the more well known the system is, the greater the likelihood of complaints. Complainants coming into the first two categories of complainant will by definition know about the system. The third category of complainant, national organizations of employers and trade unions, will know about the Charter generally from their involvement in the reporting system, but they may not be very familiar with the collective complaints system. This is likely especially to be the case in states that have been parties to the Charter for a relatively short period of time. The Council of Europe is trying to promote awareness and knowledge of the collective complaints system among potential complainants by holding occasional conferences on the system. A third factor influencing the degree of use of the collective complaints system is the general perceived level of compliance with the Charter (as revealed, at least in part, by the reporting system). The more instances of non-compliance that are revealed, the more likely it is that complaints will be made. Fourthly, the number of complaints will to some degree be influenced by the suitability of provisions of the Charter to be subject to complaints. Not all provisions are so suitable, being too general in nature. A fifth factor is the willingness of potential complainants to bear the costs and effort of making a complaint. Sixth, the speed of the system will be a factor. The quicker that complaints are processed, the more attractive the collective complaints system is likely to be perceived. Finally, the degree of use that will be made of the collective complaints system is heavily dependent on the perceived effectiveness of the system by potential complainants. Such perceptions will depend, in part, on the outcome of the complaints already made under the system. As has been seen, the picture so far is fairly discouraging.

B *Speed of the System*

It is a common feature of human rights compliance systems that they are not particularly speedy. However, the collective complaints system has so far functioned relatively speedily. The period of time taken to reach a decision on admissibility is about four months on average, while the complete disposal of a complaint takes about 18 months. Of course, the fact that the complaints have been dealt with quite quickly is at least, in part, a consequence of there being relatively few complaints so far. It must be remembered that the bodies that deal with complaints, the ECSR and the Committee of Ministers, are part-time and also exercise a considerable role under the reporting system. Thus, should the number of complaints significantly increase, it is to be expected that it will take longer to deal with them.

C *The Role of the Committee of Ministers*

As has been seen, the Committee of Ministers has been reluctant to endorse findings of non-compliance by the ECSR, having only done so once out of seven possible occasions. This hardly seems in accordance with the spirit of the CCP and arguably is not consistent with the letter of Article 9(1). This situation appears symptomatic of a fundamental problem with the role of the Committee of Ministers, which is that it is in principle undesirable that a political body should be involved in what ought to be an independent, quasi-judicial process.[169] Even if one accepts that there is a role for the Committee of Ministers, there are a number of features about the way in which the Committee functions that are unsatisfactory. The defendant state, unlike the complainant, takes part in the Committee's proceedings and may vote; the decisions of the Committee are unreasoned; and a finding of non-compliance requires a two-thirds majority, whereas the ECSR decides by a simple majority.[170] It is possible that for political reasons the Committee may delay in dealing with a complaint. In Complaint No. 8/2000, for example, the Committee took far longer to deal with this complaint (over a year) than it has done with any of the other complaints referred to it. Whether this was because of political factors is impossible to know. Many of the same criticisms were made about the role that the Committee of Ministers originally had under the ECHR, when it ruled on the merits of cases that were not referred to the European Court of Human Rights.[171] This role was removed by Protocol 11 to the ECHR. It is unfortunate that the Council of Europe persisted with a determinative role for the Committee of Ministers in the CCP, even though the latter was adopted a year after Protocol 11. This means that the collective complaints system is now the only international human rights mechanism where a governmental body has a decisive say in the outcome of the proceedings.

The efficacy of the CCP is to a considerable degree dependent upon the Committee of Ministers showing the necessary political will and playing a full role by making detailed recommendations to state parties if they are found by the ECSR to be in breach of the Charter, rather than implicitly questioning the assessment of the ECSR. If the Committee of Ministers continues to take the approach that it often has done so far, there is a real danger that this approach will undermine the credibility of the system and dissuade potential complainants from utilizing it.

D *The Relationship between the Collective Complaints and Reporting Systems*

One of the issues concerning the Protocol, which in practice seems to have been largely already settled, is the relationship between it and the pre-existing reporting mechanism. The existence of more than one compliance mechanism in a human rights treaty is nothing new. However, the fact that the same body engages in both

---

[169] The same comment can be made about the possible involvement of the Governmental Committee in the collective complaints system under Art. 9(2) of the CCP, given that the Committee consists of national officials. So far such criticism is purely theoretical, as up to now this Committee has not in practice been involved in a complaint.

[170] See further Sudre, *supra* note 64, at 733–737.

[171] See further Leuprecht, 'The Protection of Human Rights by Political Bodies — The Example of the Committee of Ministers of the Council of Europe', in M. Nowak and D. Steurer (eds), *Progress in the Spirit of Human Rights* (1988); and Tomkins, 'The Committee of Ministers: Its Roles under the European Convention on Human Rights' 1 *EHRLRev.* (1995) 49.

constructive dialogue through the reporting procedure with state representatives and also sits in judgment upon a state's compliance with its obligations under the same treaty is not without problems. The first is a concern for the workload of the individuals involved. If the system is more extensively used in the future, the burden that this will impose on the part-time ECSR members, in addition to their duties under the reporting system, will become more difficult to manage.

A more fundamental problem, however, may be the potential incompatibility of the two functions the ECSR has. The Independent Expert on the Draft Optional Protocol to the ICESCR has noted '[i]t is a hard assignment for one body, first to engage a State party in constructive, fruitful dialogue ... on the steps it has taken ... a non-confrontational, consultative exercise — and then to behave as a quasi-judicial investigative and settlement body. It should opt for one or the other.'[172] He observes that as a consequence a state may become reluctant to engage in frank constructive dialogue of its problems in the reporting phase, if it is likely to have to face that same committee in a quasi-judicial context.[173] The establishment of a complaints system under the Social Charter may thus have some adverse consequences for the reporting system.

The preamble to the Collective Complaints Protocol refers only to the fact that it is designed to improve the effective enforcement of the social rights guaranteed by the Charter. It does not elaborate on the relationship between the complaints and reporting mechanisms. The Explanatory Report to the Protocol does state that the reporting system is to remain the 'basic mechanism' for enforcement, with the CCP designed to 'increase the efficiency' of the existing machinery[174] and is to be seen as a 'complement' to the pre-existing system. The exact details of how the two interrelate is for the ECSR to work out.

The relationship between the two procedures was examined by the ECSR in its very first decision on admissibility in Complaint No. 1/1998, which concerned the existence of child labour in Portugal. The Portuguese Government argued that the complaint should be rejected as inadmissible because the matter had already been the subject of a recommendation by the Committee of Ministers to Portugal in an earlier reporting cycle. The ECSR rejected Portugal's argument. It considered that the object of the system of collective complaints, 'which is different in nature from the procedure of examining national reports, is to allow the Committee to make a legal assessment of the situation of a State in the light of the information supplied by the complaint and the adversarial procedure to which it gives rise.'[175] The fact that the Committee had already examined the situation relating to the object of the complaint within the framework of the reporting system, and would do so again, did not in itself imply the

---

[172]　*Report of the Independent Expert on the Question of a Draft Optional Protocol to the International Covenant on Economic, Social and Cultural Rights*, U.N. Doc. E/CN.4/2002/57, at 10. The view of the Independent Expert has been challenged by the participants to the ICJ organized roundtable on the Draft Optional Protocol to the ICESCR, *supra note* 8, at 10.

[173]　*Report of the Independent Expert, supra* note 172, at 10.

[174]　*Explanatory Report, supra* note 26, at paras 1–2.

[175]　Complaint No. 1/1998, Decision on Admissibility, para. 10.

inadmissibility of a collective complaint. Furthermore, Portugal's compliance with Article 7 of the Charter (the article at issue) was examined only once every four years, and so the situation would not be assessed again for a further two years. Also the recommendation of the Committee of Ministers related to the period 1994–1995, whereas the complaint referred to legislation and factual circumstances subsequent to that period. The complaints procedure therefore allowed Portugal to furnish information and evidence relating to the actions it had taken since the reporting period concerned.

Portugal also argued that for the ECSR to declare the complaint admissible and subsequently adjudicate on it, would contravene the principles of *res judicata* and *non bis in idem*.[176] If the ECSR had accepted this line of reasoning, the CCP would have become largely redundant as it would, in practice, have prohibited examination of a complaint if the matter had been addressed by the ECSR, possibly even in passing, in the reporting procedure. The ECSR firmly rejected Portugal's argument, declaring that:

> [n]either the fact that the Committee has already examined this situation in the framework of the reporting system, nor the fact that it will examine it again during subsequent supervision cycles do not in themselves imply the inadmissibility of a collective complaint concerning the same provision of the Charter and the same Contracting Party.[177]

The ECSR went on to note that these principles, i.e., *res judicata* and *non bis in idem*, 'do not apply to the relation between the two supervisory procedures'.[178]

If the Protocol is to be effective, the ECSR's approach is essential as it will allow detailed legal analysis and determination of the extent to which a state party is complying with its obligations. Criticism of the duplication of effort can be rebutted on the basis that as the same body will be involved in both compliance mechanisms, it can utilize its own work for both procedures. In declaring Portugal's application admissible, the ECSR also noted that one of the CCP's objectives was to consolidate the participation of the social partners and non-governmental organizations.[179] This in itself is quite interesting as one of the distinguishing features of the CCP is the increased involvement of such organizations compared with the reporting mechanism. Thus to declare an application inadmissible, due to the fact that the issue with which it is concerned may already have been addressed in the reporting procedure, would effectively deprive such organizations of their enhanced status and role.[180] It is worthy of note that in subsequent complaints no state has objected to admissibility on the grounds raised by Portugal in Complaint No. 1/1998. It is worth questioning,

---

[176] See para. 4.

[177] See para. 10. However, the fact that the ECSR found the complaint admissible was to some extent undermined by the decision of the Committee of Ministers not to issue a recommendation to Portugal on the ground that a recommendation had already been issued under the reporting procedure. See text at *supra* note 156.

[178] *Ibid.*, at para. 13.

[179] *Ibid.*

[180] The CCP is, as far as is known, the first time NGOs other than workers' and employers' organizations have been specifically recognized in an international instrument as having standing to bring a complaint.

however, whether the ECSR will or should maintain its current approach if or when its workload increases significantly. This point can be seen in relation to Complaint No. 7/2000. Unlike Complaint No. 1/1998, the provision at issue in Complaint No. 7/2000 was a core right and thus was examined every two years. It is therefore questionable whether the finding under the CCP of a violation really added anything to the earlier finding of non-compliance under the reporting procedure, as the complainant did not refer to any developments subsequent to the most recent report. Darcy has questioned whether complaints that have nothing new to add to the reporting procedure, such as Complaint No. 7/2000, should be declared admissible.[181]

Although the ECSR did not reject Complaint No. 7/2000 as inadmissible, the fact that according to the Explanatory Report the ECSR has a 'margin of appreciation' in this matter means that it may in future, if it so wishes, follow the point of view advocated by Darcy and Sudre, especially if it becomes over-burdened by complaints. However, to do so would be to overlook the advantages of a mechanism like the CCP. First, because it is based on comprehensive written proceedings presented by both complainants and governments, it will allow the ECSR to analyse the legislation and the situation in practice, in a manner that is unlikely to happen under the reporting procedure. It will thus highlight in more detail the extent of the non-compliance and will allow the ECSR to provide the state party with greater guidance as to the measures that need to be taken to ensure compliance.[182] This should ensure that national provisions are brought fully into compliance with the Charter. Secondly, complaints under the CCP should not only lead to a consolidation of standards but also allow their progressive development. In numerous complaints to date the ECSR has referred to its conclusions from the reporting cycles to define the standards and the basic requirements of the Charter provisions in question. That much is to be expected. The collective complaints system importantly, however, provides an opportunity for non-governmental bodies to try to persuade the ECSR towards the progressive development of standards. Complaint No. 2/1999 is an instance in question. Here the allegation was that France did not comply with Articles 5 and 6 of the Charter in so far as members of the armed forces did not enjoy the right to organize and there was no right to bargain collectively.[183] One of the fundamental questions for the ECSR was not only the scope of the obligation but also the construction of the exception clause in the final sentence of Article 5 as regards military personnel.[184] The Committee had elaborated over the years in the reporting procedure what this actually meant, but it is clear from the submissions made that one of the express purposes of the complaint was

---

[181] Darcy, *supra* note 139, at 218. A similar point has also been made by Sudre, *supra* note 64, at 731.
[182] See, for example, Complaint No. 6/1999.
[183] Substantively, Complaints Nos. 3/1999, 4/1999 and 5/1999 are identical.
[184] See para. 26.

to push for a more restrictive interpretation of the exception[185] and for the interpretation of the Charter as a 'living instrument'.[186] However, on this matter the complainant was not successful.[187]

In terms of substance, a complaint can involve a variety of situations *vis-à-vis* the reporting system and offer a number of strategies to supplement it. These situations include the following:

1. The complaint concerns a matter where in the reporting system the ECSR found non-compliance and the Committee of Ministers addressed a recommendation to the defaulting state with which the latter has not complied. Here a complaint can be used to put pressure on the recalcitrant state to comply. Complaints No. 1/1998 and 7/2000 are examples of this.

2. The complaint concerns a matter where in the reporting system the ECSR found non-compliance, but the Committee of Ministers failed to address a recommendation to the state concerned. Here a complaint can be used to try to persuade the Committee of Ministers to issue a recommendation.

3. The complaint concerns a matter where in the reporting system the ECSR found the state concerned to be complying with the Charter. Here the purpose of the complaint will be to persuade the ECSR to reverse its earlier finding.

4. The complaint concerns a matter that does not appear (yet) to have been addressed under the reporting system or that has arisen since the previous report. Here the complaint is essentially designed to raise an issue under the Charter *de novo*. Many of the complaints appear to be of this nature.

Although the collective complaints and reporting systems are different procedures operating in different ways, they do have a number of similarities. The same bodies (the ECSR and the Committee of Ministers) are involved in both procedures, although the ECSR acts in a more quasi-judicial way in the complaints procedure, especially at the admissibility stage, than in the reporting system.[188] Secondly, each procedure involves an examination of the law and practice of the state concerned in general terms, rather than their application to specific individuals. Finally and most importantly, the outcome in cases of non-compliance is the same in each system — the issuing of a non-binding recommendation to the state concerned, to which the latter is then required to give its response in the next cycle of the reporting procedure.

E *The Desirability/Feasibility of Bringing More States into the Collective Complaints System*

It is obviously disappointing that only 13 out of 34 parties to the Charter have so far become bound by the collective complaints system. Such a low level of participation

---

[185] See para. 27.
[186] See para. 14.
[187] See para. 29.
[188] Cullen, *supra* note 46, HR 27–28.

reduces the utility of the system, and to some extent undermines its legitimacy and credibility. It would clearly be desirable to have more states bound by the system. This would make the system a standard part of the Charter machinery, rather than an optional minority extra as at present; would increase awareness and knowledge of the Charter; and would make the Charter more effective as more instances of non-compliance were identified and hopefully rectified. Once the collective complaints system was working regularly and frequently, and probably as a result states gained more confidence in it, it might make it easier to amend the CCP to remove some of its more obvious defects, notably the current role of the Committee of Ministers.

It is not clear why more states have not ratified the CCP (or made the necessary declaration under the Revised Charter). There are a number of possible reasons (which are not mutually exclusive). In some cases it may be bureaucratic inertia or inability/unwillingness by governments to find the necessary Parliamentary time in those states where Parliamentary approval is necessary for ratification. In other cases states may be waiting to see how the collective complaints system operates in practice before taking a decision whether to ratify.[189] In the case of Central and East European states (where only three out of 14 such states parties to the Charter have so far accepted the collective complaints system), it may well be that their relative inexperience with the Charter system (all have ratified the Charter since 1997 and most have yet to go for the first time through a full cycle of reporting) has led most of them to decide to obtain more experience with the Charter generally (not least to see how far they are considered to be complying with it as revealed by the reporting system) before deciding whether to take the further step of becoming bound by the collective complaints system. Then there are a small number of older members of the Council of Europe that seem to have limited interest and enthusiasm for the Charter as evidenced by the fact that they have ratified only the Charter in its original form and not any additional or amending protocols or the Revised Charter. Such states include Germany, Iceland, Luxembourg and the United Kingdom. States (such as Turkey) that have been shown by the reporting system to have a poor compliance record with the Charter are obviously less likely to accept the collective complaints system, although it is in such states that the system is potentially most useful.[190] Finally, it may be that there are states that are opposed to the collective complaints system for reasons of principle or that simply have a poor record of accepting optional petition systems in other human rights treaties.

What can be done to persuade states to accept the collective complaints system?

---

[189] For an example of such a 'wait and see' approach (but in relation to the Revised Charter rather than the CCP) see the answer by Mr. Macshane, the UK Minister of State for Foreign and Commonwealth Affairs, to a Parliamentary question dealing with these issues. WA 14 May 2003 Col. 289 W. It has been suggested that some states may fear that the collective complaints system will be abused, will lead to the unrestrained development of social rights, and disturb the way the Charter has operated up until now. See comment by Vandamme in Council of Europe, *supra* note 30, 181 at 183–184.

[190] Nevertheless, four states with indifferent records of compliance (i.e. having been found to comply with less than half the Charter provisions they have accepted) — Belgium, Greece, Ireland and Italy — have accepted the collective complaints system.

Five states (Austria, Czech Republic, Denmark, the Netherlands and Slovakia) have so far signed the CCP but have not yet ratified it. Such signature indicates that these states are seriously considering ratification, and it may, therefore, be only a matter of time before they ratify. In the case of other states, the Council of Europe, particularly through the Parliamentary Assembly and the Committee of Ministers, should encourage participation in the collective complaints system. More effective will probably be domestic political pressure from potential complainants, notably employers' organizations and trade unions. Where such bodies already play an active role in the reporting procedure, pressure to ratify will be greatest. Unfortunately, however, in too many states parties to the Charter such organizations do not get actively involved in the reporting procedure and therefore are unlikely to campaign for their state to participate in the collective complaints system.

While encouraging increased participation in the CCP is in principle desirable, such participation may be of limited benefit in the case of states parties only to the original Charter. Many of the rights contained in the latter are outdated and lag behind the national laws of states parties and EU law (where applicable), so that the bringing of collective complaints is likely to be of limited use. The collective complaints system is likely to be of greatest utility in those states parties to the Revised Charter where the level of protection afforded by the rights of that instrument is higher and less likely to be met by the national laws of its parties. In practice, 10 of the 13 states that are so far bound by the collective complaints system are parties to the Revised Charter, and these 10 states represent two-thirds of the 16 parties to the Revised Charter.

As well as increasing participation in the collective complaints system generally, it would also be desirable to increase the number of acceptances of the optional fourth category of complainant, national NGOs, from its current pitiful total of one (Finland). Allowing such organizations to make complaints would generate more complaints about social rights and increase the level of domestic awareness of the Charter, and also move the Charter away from its historic bias towards employment rights. It is not clear why more parties to the system have not made the necessary declaration under Article 2 of the CCP to accept national NGOs as complainants. It may be that some states have been put off by the rather open-ended nature of this category of complainant.

Finally, it needs to be borne in mind that a substantial number of new accessions to the CCP or widespread acceptance of national NGOs as complainants may not be entirely desirable or deliver some of the expected benefits without some further reform of the overall supervisory system. The increased workload of the ECSR in carrying out its functions should not be underestimated, nor should the repercussions that this could potentially have on both the quality of its work and the length of time taken to reach its conclusions.

454 *EJIL* 15 (2004), 417–456

F *The Relationship between the Collective Complaints System and Other Economic and Social Treaty Provisions*

One of the consequences of the existence of the CCP is that it will bring into sharper focus the issue of the difference in standards and the obligations imposed upon states by different treaties in relation to certain economic and social rights and the mechanisms available for their enforcement. As regards the latter, a decision by potential complainants whether to use the CCP or whether to try an alternative mechanism will always be strategic in attempting to achieve a certain objective, but will also depend on their standing to bring a complaint. As an *actio popularis*, the CCP cannot and is not designed to provide individual remedies and thus is of limited utility to provide redress for individual grievances, even if an organization with standing can be convinced to lodge a complaint. Any action taken by the defendant state seeking to rectify the situation will almost certainly not be retrospective in effect and will seek only to ensure that the Charter is not breached in future, no matter the degree of detriment already suffered by individuals. The same is also true of ILO procedures. By contrast, there is the possibility of an individual remedy under, for example, the ECHR and EU law. The choice of remedy may depend on a comparison of Charter rights with any comparable rights under the ECHR and EU law. The content of a right under one instrument may be superior to that under another. Thus complainants may have to choose between a higher level of protection under the Charter but with limited likelihood of its enforcement, and lesser protection under the ECHR or EU law but with a greater prospect of compliance by the Member States.

6 Conclusions

Although the collective complaints system has been in force for over five years, there is still relatively little experience with its practical operation. Nevertheless, there is enough to reveal a number of serious concerns. First, as an alternative to the reporting system as a method of trying to secure the compliance of states parties with the Charter, the collective complaints system is still very much a minority option. Only about one-third of the states parties to the Charter have accepted the system. The reasons behind the lack of acceptances are not entirely clear. Nevertheless, it is desirable, in principle, that the collective complaints system should become generally accepted and used as a compliance mechanism: this will strengthen its legitimacy and probably result in more complaints, thereby helping to increase knowledge of the Charter. The Council of Europe and NGOs (both national and international) ought therefore to lobby governments that have not yet done so, to accept the collective complaints system. Likewise the fact that only Finland, so far, has exercised the option of permitting national NGOs other than trade unions and employers' associations (the fourth category of complainant) to make complaints is another worrying factor. Again, governments need to be encouraged and pressured into accepting this category of complainant.

Once a complaint has been made, the role of the ECSR in dealing with the admissibility of the complaint and giving an opinion on the merits has worked well. The ECSR has acted speedily, has not been unnecessarily restrictive on issues of admissibility, and has generally given well-reasoned opinions on the merits. Unfortunately, however, it is not possible to be anything like as positive about the role of the Committee of Ministers. While it has generally acted speedily, its handling of those complaints where the ECSR has found non-compliance with the Charter by the defendant state has been quite unsatisfactory. Only in one of the seven complaints has it endorsed the findings of the ECSR and addressed a recommendation to the defendant state. In the other cases it has either effectively decided not to pursue the matter further or improperly adopted an interpretation of the Charter quite different from that of the ECSR. If this trend continues, it will serve only to discredit the system and discourage complaints because complainants will feel that there is little point in utilizing the system if a finding of non-compliance by the ECSR will not be endorsed and a recommendation addressed to the defendant state by the Committee of Ministers. More fundamentally, it is undesirable that the Committee of Ministers, a political body, should have any role to play in what is, or at least ought to be, a quasi-judicial process. Before 1998 the Committee of Ministers was an alternative to the European Court of Human Rights as a body for determining breaches of the ECHR, and both the principle of this and its exercise in practice were rightly criticized.[191] The states members of the Council of Europe decided in Protocol 11 to the ECHR to abolish this role. In view of the fact that the CCP was adopted one year after Protocol 11, it is unfortunate, to say the least, that those same states decided that it was nevertheless appropriate for the Committee of Ministers to have a determinative role in the collective complaints system.

A more fundamental issue than any of the above concerns is whether the CCP actually serves a useful purpose. While the complaints system has a number of advantages over the reporting procedure, the real test is whether complaints will actually induce any changes in behaviour on the part of defendant states. It is too early to say yet whether states will amend their behaviour if they are found in violation of the Charter under the CCP, because in nearly all cases the state concerned has not yet reported under the following reporting cycle on the issues that were the subject of the complaint; and, in any case, only one complaint so far has resulted in a recommendation from the Committee of Ministers to the defendant state to take corrective action. The one partial exception to this is Complaint No. 12/2002, where Sweden had already begun making reforms to try to bring it in to conformity with the Revised Social Charter, as interpreted by the ECSR, prior to the adoption of a recommendation by the Committee of Ministers. The action (or lack of it) taken by defendant states in response to other successful complaints is a matter that will deserve close attention in the future. If it turns out that states do not take action, then various approaches could be adopted. First, the CCP could be amended so that decisions of the ECSR became legally binding, with the Committee of Ministers having the same role of supervising the execution of decisions as it has under the ECHR. If the

---

[191] See the literature referred to in note 171.

CCP is to achieve its objectives, it is imperative that the Council of Europe learns from the experiences of the ILO mechanisms upon which it is modelled. States, such as the UK in the *GCHQ* case for example, have for many years simply ignored findings of violations by the Freedom of Association Committee primarily because its decisions are not legally binding.[192] It is unlikely that the UK would have taken the same approach if the then functioning European Commission of Human Rights had found the application concerning the same issues admissible and the European Court had subsequently found it in violation.[193] But strengthening the CCP in this way is an approach that some Council of Europe States are unlikely to agree to in the foreseeable future. Even less likely are they to support proposals made by some for a right to individual petition to a new European Social Rights Court or a specialized chamber of the European Court of Human Rights.[194]

Secondly, the ECSR should try to ensure compatibility between the standards it defines for the Charter, not only under the CCP but also under the reporting procedure, and other relevant treaties. Ensuring such compatibility is more likely to mean that its findings will not be ignored because similar breaches under other treaties are more likely to be enforceable, especially in the case of EU law. In taking this approach, however, there is a risk that the ECSR may need to water down its approach to the obligations imposed by certain Charter provisions, thus to some extent defeating the object of the exercise.

The omens for the CCP, in its current form, are not positive. There is a palpable danger that without some reform the practical long-term impact of the CCP will not be significant in increasing the utility of the rights protected by the Charter.

---

[192] Although as Novitz has noted, the current Labour Government in the UK has now given effect to the ILO finding in the *GCHQ case*, whereas the previous Conservative Government, whose policy it was to abolish unions at GCHQ, ignored it. See Novitz, 'International Promises and Domestic Pragmatism: To What Extent Will the Employment Relations Act 1999 Implement International Labour Standards Relating to Freedom of Association?', 63 *MLR* (2000) 379.

[193] Application No. 11603/85. It is worth noting that the UK was not found in breach of the European Social Charter, CIE, *European Social Charter: Conclusions XI–1 (United Kingdom)* at 80.

[194] See, for example, Parliamentary Assembly Rec. 1354 (1998); Harris and Darcy, *supra* note 4 at 373–374; Novitz, *supra* note 57.

[7]

HUMAN RIGHTS QUARTERLY

Mechanisms for the Implementation of Decisions of the African Commission on Human and Peoples' Rights

Rachel Murray* & Elizabeth Mottershaw**

ABSTRACT

The African Commission on Human and Peoples' rights issued its first decision on an individual communication in 1994. It is self-evident, however,
that the potential for improvement in human rights protection held by such
judgments and decisions can only be realized with implementation. Yet,
there is very little written either in academic literature or policy documents
and little available information at national or regional levels about what
happens to decisions of the African Commission or other regional human
rights organs once they have been published. These challenges provide the
backdrop against which this article examines the potential for strengthening
implementation mechanisms at both national and regional levels.

* *Rachel Murray* is Professor of International Human Rights Law and Director of the Human
Rights Implementation Centre at the University of Bristol. She works on the African human
rights system, the Optional Protocol to the UN Convention Against Torture, and mechanisms
for implementing human rights law.
** *Elizabeth Mottershaw* is an independent human rights consultant. She works with NGOs
and universities carrying out research and providing advice on human rights policy and
law. Her work focuses on poverty, conflict, and the practical impact of law. She works with
Amnesty International UK in a voluntary capacity advising on international human rights
and governance. From 1998–2008 she worked at the International Secretariat of Amnesty
International.
    This article draws upon research initially carried out under an Arts and Humanities
Research Council grant, and subsequently followed up with further analysis of documentary sources, insights from interviews with a variety of human rights actors, discussions at
a seminar we held in Addis Ababa, and case studies of particular decisions of the African
Commission on Human and Peoples' Rights.

Human Rights Quarterly 36 (2014) 349–372 © 2014 by The Johns Hopkins University Press

I.   INTRODUCTION

The African Commission on Human and Peoples' Rights (African Commission) issued its first decision on an individual communication in 1994.[1] In 2009, the African Court on Human and Peoples' Rights (African Court) issued its first judgment.[2] Two years later, in 2011, the African Committee of Experts on the Rights and Welfare of the Child (ACERWC) issued its first decision— a preliminary finding that Kenya was in violation of its obligations under the African Charter on the Rights and Welfare of the Child (ACRWC).[3] The various decisions emanating from these institutions have been welcomed as having considerable potential to offer redress to victims of human rights violations, to prevent future violations in Africa, and to contribute to a better understanding of the content of the rights and obligations in question. Such decisions co-exist with pronouncements from international—UN-level— mechanisms, for the protection of human rights. It is self-evident, however, that the potential for improvement in human rights protection held by such judgments and decisions can only be realized with implementation.

Yet, there is little written either in academic literature or policy documents and little available information at national or regional levels about what happens to decisions of the African Commission or other regional human rights organs once they have been published.[4] Beyond some key pieces of research that attempted to track implementation of decisions,[5] the literature is mostly general in its approach, citing the poor human rights records of African states, lack of political will, illiteracy and lack of human rights education, and other political and social factors that play a role in the success or failure of implementation.[6] This article begins by discussing

---

1.   *See* Seventh Activity Report of the African Commission on Human and Peoples' Rights, 1993–1994, Annex VI.
2.   Michelot Yogogombaye v. Republic of Senegal, App. No. 001/2008, Judgment 15 Dec. 2009, *available at* http://www.jstor.org/stable/pdfplus/10.5305/amerjintelaw.104.4.0620.pdf?acceptTC=true&acceptTC=true&jpdConfirm=true.
3.   Institute for Human Rights and Development in Africa (IHRDA) and Open Society Justice Initiative (on behalf of children of Nubian Descent in Kenya) v. Kenya, 002/09, Decision March 2011.
4.   *See*, however, the excellent recent report by the Open Society Justice Initiative (OSJI), From Rights to Remedies: Structures and Strategies for Implementing International Human Rights Decisions (2013).
5.   Frans Viljoen & Lirette Louw, *The Status of the Findings of the African Commission: From Moral Persuasion to Legal Obligation*, 48 J. Afr. L. 1 (2004) 1–22; Open Society Justice Initiative (OSJI), From Judgment to Justice: Implementing International and Regional Human Rights Decisions (2010); George Mukundi Wachira & Abiola Ayinla, *Twenty Years of Elusive Enforcement of the Recommendations of the African Commission on Human and Peoples' Rights: A Possible Remedy*, 6 Afr. Hum. Rts. L. J. 465 (2006); Chidi Anselm Odinkalu, *Implementing Economic, Social and Cultural Rights under the African Charter on Human and Peoples' Rights*, *in* The African Charter on Human and Peoples' Rights: The System in Practice 1986–2000, at 178 (Malcolm D. Evans & Rachel Murray eds., 2002).
6.   Christof Heyns & Frans Viljoen, *The Impact of the United Nations Human Rights Treaties on the Domestic Level*, 23 Hum. Rts. Q. 483 (2001).

the challenges that have led to the failure of states to implement decisions of the African Commission. These include the fact that the decisions are not viewed as legally binding, are perceived as unacceptable interferences with state sovereignty, that the African Charter on Human and Peoples' Rights (African Charter) not been incorporated into national law, that implementation is difficult, and that the process of implementation is adversarial in nature.

These challenges provide the backdrop against which this article examines the potential for strengthening implementation mechanisms at both national and regional levels. There is a burgeoning body of literature on implementation and compliance that attempts to identify why and how states comply or do not comply with human rights law.[7] Treaty bodies have established follow up mechanisms with varying degrees of sophistication to verify compliance with their own findings. Within these discussions there is an apparent trend to look less at the international mechanisms and more at national mechanisms.[8] This focus on the national mechanisms does two things.

First, it reasserts the obligation on the state to implement. In practice, it is the executive arm of the state through which this responsibility must be exercised. Component parts of the state—the legislature and the judiciary, as well as national human rights institutions (NHRIs) and nonstate, civil society organizations, all contribute to monitoring that implementation, but a meaningful and practical translation of state obligations requires that the responsibility for ensuring implementation falls to the executive.

Second, the focus underscores the need for a coherent system to respond to treaty body findings. The obligations of states to establish National Preventive Mechanisms (NPMs) under the Optional Protocol to the Convention Against Torture (OPCAT)[9] and independent frameworks to monitor, promote, and protect implementation of the rights in the Convention on the Rights of Persons with Disabilities reflect a move toward meeting this need.[10] This is

---

7.　*See, e.g.,* Frans Viljoen, *Exploring the Theory And Practice of the Relationship Between International Human Rights Law and Domestic Actors,* 22 Leiden J. Int'l L. 177 (2009); Todd Landman, *Measuring Human Rights: Principle, Practice, and Policy,* 26 Hum. Rts. Q. 906 (2004);Ted Piccone, *The Contribution of the UN's Special Procedures to National Level Implementation of Human Rights Norms,* 15 Int'l J. Hum. Rts. 206 (2011). *See also* Alice Donald & Elizabeth Mottershaw, *Evaluating the Impact of Human Rights Litigation on Policy and Practice: A Case Study of the UK,* 1 J. Hum. Rts. Prac. 339 (2009). Courtney Hillebrecht, *Rethinking Compliance: The Challenges and Prospects of Measuring Compliance with International Human Rights Tribunals,* 1 J. Hum. Rts. Prac 362 (2009).

8.　Courtney Hillebrecht, *Rethinking Compliance: The Challenges and Prospects of Measuring Compliance with International Human Rights Tribunals,* 1 J. HUM. RTS. PRAC 362 (2009); OSJI, *supra* note 4.

9.　*See* Rachel Murray, et al., The Optional Protocol to the UN Convention Against Torture (2011).

10.　Convention on the Rights of Persons with Disabilities, *adopted* 13 Dec. 2006 GA Res. U.N. Doc. A/RES/61/106, art. 33(2) [hereinafter CRPD].

consolidated further in the 2012 Report of the High Commissioner on Human Rights regarding treaty body strengthening, which recommends that states each establish a standing National Reporting and Coordinating Committee to follow up on state reporting and communications.[11]

Based on research, this article looks first at the plausibility and utility of strengthening the ways in which states respond to findings of the African Commission. It aims to dissect what happens at the national level once the African Commission issues its decision on a particular communication.

However, the article will go further. In the African context, national mechanisms cannot be the only approach to follow up and implementation. Research has found that one of the factors impacting state compliance in the African context is the failings of the African Commission itself: weak powers of investigation, the ability of states to argue that recommendations are nonbinding,[12] and the inability of the African Commission, African Court, or African Union to operate follow up and enforcement mechanisms.[13] Our research also found that there is a perception that by failing to implement a coherent follow up procedure, the African Commission is not taking itself seriously and therefore neither are others.[14] Accordingly, although attention on national level mechanisms is important, it is crucial in this region that implementation is carried out in combination with an effective regional follow up system. There must be an integrated regional system that utilizes legal and political tools and that is able to pressure African states to comply with the findings of the African Commission. The combination of actors, the interaction between them, and the resulting pressure may prove to be decisive: "While the Commission may fairly and necessarily be upbraided when it fails to make its views known to the state parties, it cannot take responsibility for the failure of states to implement its recommendations, decisions or views."[15] Further, as Harold Koh, a professor of international law at Yale, has argued, "If transnational actors obey international law as a result of repeated *interaction* with other actors in the transnational legal process, a first step is to empower more actors to participate."[16] This article will address both the mechanisms at the national level as well as the follow up procedures at the regional level. It will argue that effective implementa-

---

11. OHCHR, *Strengthening the United Nations Human Rights Treaty Body System: A Report by the United Nations High Commissioner for Human Rights, Navanethem Pillay* (2012), 85–88.
12. *See, e.g.,* Wachira & Ayinla, *supra* note 5, at 471.
13. *Id.*
14. Interview, anonymous, on file with authors.
15. Chidi Anselm Odinkalu, *The Role of Case and Complaints Procedures in the Reform of the African Regional Human Rights System*, 1 Afr. Hum. Rts. L. J. 228 (2001).
16. Harold Hongju Koh, *Why do Nations Obey International Law?*, 106 Yale L.J. 2599, 2656 (1997).

tion requires complementary changes at both levels. Such changes have the potential to reinforce one another and strengthen implementation.

II. CHALLENGES IN ENCOURAGING AFRICAN STATES TO ESTABLISH NATIONAL MECHANISMS

There are various challenges in convincing states of the need to establish national mechanisms or, indeed, systematic responses to African Commission findings on individual communications. First, there is a question mark over the legal status of the decisions of the African Commission.[17] Some argue that the decisions of the African Commission are not binding. Indeed, such an argument was raised as a key element in the need for the African Court.[18] The 2010 *Good v. Botswana* case illustrates this difference of opinion on legal status.[19] This case concerned the expulsion of a professor from Botswana after he had written a criticism of that country's presidential system. The African Commission found a number of violations of the African Charter, including violations of Articles 1, 2, 7(1)(a), 9, 12(4), 18(1) and 18(2), and recommended that the government pay the victim compensation and ensure that its immigration legislation complied with international human rights obligations. In response, the government stated, "We are not going to follow on the recommendation made by the commission; it does not give orders, and it is not a court. We are not going to listen to them. We will not compensate Mr. Good."[20] This is not an unusual approach:

> [T]he attitude of state parties, since the Commission's inception two decades ago, by and large has been generally to ignore these recommendations, with no attendant consequences victims of human rights violations often find themselves without any remedy, even after resorting to the African Commission, which erodes and undermines its credibility and authority as an effective protector of the rights enshrined in the African Charter.[21]

The view of the African Commission is that whilst its decisions are not binding prior to the adoption by the Assembly of Heads of State of the African Union of the Annual Report containing them, they are binding once this report has been adopted.[22] This is also in line with Article 14 of the Vienna

---

17. See, e.g., OSJI, *supra* note 5, at 77; Wachira & Ayinla, *supra* note 5.
18. Viljoen & Louw, *supra* note 5, at 12.
19. Communication 313/05, Good v. Botswana 28th Activity Report of the African Commission on Human and Peoples' Rights (2010).
20. *Botswana will not Honour African Union Ruling on Prof Good*, SUNDAY STANDARD, 2 Aug. 2010, *available at* http://www.sundaystandard.info/article.php?NewsID=8415&GroupID=1. *See also* Franny Rabkin, *Botswana: Country Reprimanded for Denying Critic Access to Court*, ALL AFRICA, 12 Aug. 2010, *available at* http://allafrica.com/stories/201008120009.html.
21. Wachira & Ayinla, *supra* note 5, at 466–67.
22. OSJI, *supra* note 5, at 96.

Convention on the Law of Treaties: "By signing and ratifying the Charter, states signify their intention to be bound by and to adhere to the obligations arising from it even if they do not enact domestic legislation to effect domestic incorporation."[23] Commentators agree.[24] Ratification of the African Charter implies an undertaking by states parties that they will abide by its decisions in accordance with Article 1 of the Charter:[25]

> State Parties in ratifying without any reservation, the African Charter on Human and Peoples' Rights have thus agreed to accept the authority and the essential role of the Commission in the promotion and protection of Human and Peoples' Rights throughout Africa.

Accordingly, the African Commission "Calls upon all state parties to the African Charter on Human and Peoples' Rights to respect without delay the recommendations of the Commission."[26]

How states view the decisions of the African Commission will depend in part on the relationship between international and national law within each African state, as set out in the state's constitution or otherwise.[27] There are a few instances of African states adopting legislation that implements the decisions of treaty bodies.[28] However, in the majority of states where such legislation does not exist, the position with respect to the implementation of African Commission decisions and their subsequent jurisprudential value is unclear. This is particularly true in cases where remedial measures are required, which, it could be argued, national courts should decide. Within some states, the decisions of the African Commission and other bodies are considered to be foreign judgments that are not formally recognized by the national courts.[29] In others, however, there may be simply a lack of

---

23. Sabelo Gumedze, *Bringing Communications before the African Commission on Human and Peoples' Rights*, 3 Afr. Hum. Rts. L. J. 143 (2003). *See also* Wachira & Ayinla, *supra* note 5, at 468.

24. Viljoen & Louw, *supra* note 5, at 4.

25. Communication 227/99, *Democratic Republic of Congo v. Burundi, Rwanda, Uganda*, 20th Annual Activity Report of the African Commission on Human and Peoples' Rights, ¶ 53.

26. Resolution on the Importance of Implementing the Recommendations of the African Commission on Human and Peoples' Rights by States Parties, ACHPR/Res.97(XXXX) 06, *adopted* 40th Ordinary Session in Banjul, the Gambia, from 15–29 Nov. 2006.

27. *See* Michael Kirby, *Domestic Implementation of International Human Rights Norms*, 5 Australian J. Hum. Rts. 121–24 (1999); Sanzhuan Guo, *Implementation of Human Rights Treaties by Chinese Courts: Problems and Prospects*, 8 Chinese J. Int'l L. 161 (2009); Osai Ojigho, *Evaluating the Application, Implementation and Enforcement of International Human Rights Instruments and Norms in Nigeria*, 31 Commonwealth L. Bull. 103–16 (2005).

28. *See, e.g.*, Burundi, where the Supreme Court can enforce decisions of treaty bodies, Loi No.1/07, Regissant la Cour Supreme, 25 Feb. 2005, *see* OSJI, *supra* note 5, at 81, 59–61.

29. Osai Ojigho, *Evaluating the Application, Implementation and Enforcement of International Human Rights Instruments and Norms in Nigeria*, 31 Commonwealth L. Bull. 103

confidence to use or lack of awareness of international human rights law by national judges.[30]

Furthermore, it is debatable whether on every occasion the African Commission's findings and recommendations in its decisions are implementable. The language the African Commission uses in its findings does not always assist the state in identifying what it should practically do to implement the decision, even if the state were willing to do so. The African Commission, for example, does not have a consistent approach to remedies in its individual communications:[31] "The commission has issued a wide variety of rulings, ranging from no recommendations at all to a wide array of individual and general measures."[32] The reasons given are not always clear:

> The elaboration of reasons may also be a factor that influences government, not just the explicit orders (and) the general measures but the way in which the Committee or Commission gets there, which was very dubious in the (post election violence) case.[33]

The strong desire for civil society organizations and others to accord these decisions binding status is premised on a belief or assumption that states would be more likely to implement binding decisions or the pressure to implement would be greater. However, there are examples from elsewhere, including decisions of the European Court of Human Rights and the Inter-American Court of Human Rights, of a poor record of implementation of findings that are unequivocally binding on a state.[34] Conversely, there are also other instances in which states have taken action on nonbinding decisions and recommendations: states are more actively involved in follow up activities on the Concluding Observations of the African Commission on state party reports submitted in accordance with Article 62 of the African Charter and in responding to Universal Periodic Review (UPR) recommendations,[35] even though these could be considered nonbinding. Political rather than legal factors are therefore often more determinative of compliance.[36]

(2005). However, see Campbell v. Zimbabwe where there was an initially unsuccessful attempt to enforce a SADC Tribunal decision in the Zimbabwe courts but a subsequently successful attempt to do so in the South Africa High Court: Gramara Ltd. v. Zimbabwe, HC33/09, 2010; Case No.47954/10, respectively, see OSJI, *supra* note 5, at 84–85.

30.   *See, e.g.,* Thomas Trier Hansen, *Implementation of International Human Rights Standards Through the National Courts in Malawi,* 46 J. Afr. L. 31 (2002).

31.   OSJI, *supra* note 5, at 24.

32.   *Id.* Viljoen & Louw, *supra* note 5, at 16.

33.   Interview with Frans Viljoen, Professor, Centre for Human Rights, University of Pretoria, (Oct. 2011), referring to the *Association of Victims of Post Electoral Violence and Interights v. Cameroon* (2009) case.

34.   Frans Viljoen & Lirette Louw, *State Compliance with the Recommendations of the African Commission on Human and Peoples' Rights, 1994–2004,* 101 Am. J. Int'l L. 1, 33 (2007). *See also Increasing the Impact of Human Rights Litigation: Implementation of Judgments and Decisions,* 16 Interights Bul. (2010).

35.   *See, e.g.,* Jarvis Matiya, *Repositioning the International Human Rights Protection System: The UN Human Rights Council,* 36 Commonwealth L. Bull. 313, 320 (2010).

36.   Viljoen & Louw, *State Compliance, supra* note 34, at 32.

Although the arguments the African Commission and eminent scholars propound that the decisions of the African Commission are binding, the response of the government to the *Good* decision illustrates that this "weary debate"[37] as to the binding nature of the decisions of the African Commission will "continue to be a source of contention and act as an impediment to implementation."[38]

The existing body of research indicates that the binding nature of the findings of the African Commission is secondary to other factors in influencing whether states implement the findings.[39] Among these factors is the perception that the decisions, the decision process, and the follow up are purely adversarial. The legal nature of the process means that certain aspects will always be adversarial. However, it is possible to promote a shift away from confrontation and toward constructive dialogue through better communication between the involved actors and a more integrated approach to decision making and follow up. This has the potential to assist in implementation. Cases and subsequent decisions could be regarded as an entry point for engaging with a government on a particular issue and as an opportunity for the various stakeholders, at both national and regional levels, to work together with the government in a positive and constructive manner in order to rectify the problem at issue. This discussion should take place while the case is pending before the African Commission. Such a shift would also mean that debates as to whether a decision was binding upon a state would be less significant.

The establishment of a system at the national level, over which the state has ownership, to implement treaty body findings could contribute to a dialogue-led, more holistic approach.

III. NATIONAL FOLLOW UP PROCEDURES

Once the African Commission has declared a case admissible, the state typically receives a *note verbale* informing it that the African Commission has declared the case admissible. This is sent along with a copy of the decision on admissibility, the complaint from the individual, and supporting documents.[40] The state concerned is informed that the next stage will be the

---

37. *Id.* at 467.
38. OSJI, *supra* note 5, at 96.
39. Human Rights Implementation Centre, *Summary and Recommendations From an Expert Seminar on Identifying National Mechanisms to Follow up and Implement Decisions of the African Commission on Human and Peoples' Rights, 21–22 November 2011* (Dec. 2011), *available at* http://www.bristol.ac.uk/law/research/centres-themes/hric [hereinafter Expert Seminar].
40. Rules of Procedure of the African Commission on Human and Peoples' Rights, Rule 107 (2011) [hereinafter Rules of Procedure].

decision on the merits of the case. The state is invited to submit arguments on the merits to the African Commission.[41]

At the conclusion of the merits stage of the process the state is informed of the decision. If the African Commission has decided that the state has violated any provisions of the African Charter, a copy of the decision and recommendations to be implemented are forwarded to the state. This happens only after the Assembly of the African Union has authorized it through the adoption of the annual activity report of the African Commission.[42] Commonly, either the Ministry of External Relations or Foreign Affairs first receive notification of the adoption of a decision on a communication by the African Commission.[43]

A. Governmental Mechanisms

Some states, albeit few, have set up specific units within ministries to liaise with other national bodies and with the African Commission and UN treaty bodies on individual communications and other matters.[44] These units are commonly situated in either the Ministry of Justice or Ministry of Foreign Affairs. The activities of these bodies vary from state to state, but typically include helping to prepare the defense of the state before human rights bodies, advising the government on matters related to human rights, liaising with human rights treaty bodies, and disseminating decisions on communications received from treaty bodies.[45]

For example, in 2005 the government of Cameroon established a Department of Human Rights and International Cooperation, within its Ministry of Justice. This department issues an annual report on human rights, which includes details of legal and institutional steps taken to implement Cameroon's human rights obligations.[46] The 2009 Report includes a chapter, not previously included, on cooperation with international human rights mechanisms. For example, with regard to two judgments issued in 2009,[47] the Ministry of Justice Report stated that: "The conditions for the implementation of the

---

41. *Id.* Rule 108.
42. African Charter on Human and Peoples' Rights, *adopted* 27 June 1981, art. 59, O.A.U. Doc. CAB/LEG/67/3 Rev. 5, 1520 U.N.T.S. 217 (*entered into force* 21 Oct. 1986).
43. *See* Expert Seminar, *supra* note 39.
44. OSJI, *supra* note 5, ch. 2.
45. *Id.*
46. REPUBLIC OF CAMEROON, REPORT BY THE MINISTRY OF JUSTICE ON HUMAN RIGHTS IN CAMEROON IN 2009, at 7 (2010), *available at* http://www.spm.gov.cm/uploads/media/Rapport_Minjustice_Ang_2009.pdf.
47. Communication 266/2003, Kevin Ngwang Gumne v. the State of Cameroon, African Commission on Human and Peoples' Rights, 2009; Communication 1397/2005, Pierre Désiré Engo v. the State of Cameroon, before the Human Rights Committee, 22 July 2009, CCPR-10-1.

recommendations of the African Commission and the Human Rights Committee relating to the two communications are under study."[48]

The process for collating information and writing the 2009 Report involved collaboration with fourteen ministries and three "independent administrative structures," including the National Commission on Human Rights and Freedoms, and also incorporated contributions from four civil society organizations (CSOs).[49] The Report also notes that the process involved "dialogue, consultation and consolidation of partnership between government and the civil society in the human rights domain."[50] In 2011, Cameroon subsequently adopted a ministerial decree that set up an inter-ministerial committee that now monitors implementation of decisions.[51]

The human rights units of some states, such as that of Lesotho, include only members of the executive branch. However, other states have set up units that have a wider membership and include representatives from the national human rights institutions and CSOs.[52] These bodies have a broad mandate that can include advising the government on human rights issues, receiving complaints of human rights violations, and conducting human rights training to various stakeholders. Where these bodies exist, they also have a role to play in examining decisions and encouraging follow up on decisions on communications and the implementation of any recommendations contained within decisions.[53]

Beyond these specific examples, information about whether a process or mechanism at the national level exists within African states and if it does, what it entails, is not easily obtainable. CSOs and lawyers litigating before the African Commission are unsure about the mechanisms by which states engage with cases and respond to judgments. NGOs seeking to engage with various governments across the continent about implementation of specific decisions have commented: "we don't know who to talk to."[54]

As one litigator said, "[t]he greatest single challenge is simply not knowing who the government interlocutor should be. . . . It's impossible to know."[55] Practically, attending the African Commission sessions and seeking out the relevant government representative may be the only way of identifying someone responsible for a case. In addition, the varied nature of the state's

---

48. Report by the Ministry of Justice on Human Rights in Cameroon in 2009, ¶ 67 (on file with authors).
49. *Id.* ¶ 16.
50. *Id.*
51. Order No.081/CAB/PM, 15 Apr. 2011, copy reproduced in OSJI, *supra* note 5, at 148–50.
52. *Id.* ch. 2.
53. *Id.*
54. Interview with litigant, anonymous (Oct. 2011).
55. Interview with Julia Harrington, Open Society Justice Initiative, Gambia (Oct. 2011).

response appears to indicate a lack of permanent, consistent coordination, or possibly that coordination is difficult to discern.

It appears that state activities are not expressly coordinated across different departments, unless the case is particularly controversial and the government has a strong desire to defend itself—then it may draw from different departments. Changes within a government compound the difficulty of knowing where responsibility lies, particularly when a government does not respond to the African Commission, making it more difficult to find out who is working on the case:

> Follow-up becomes difficult . . . you get into a black hole of who should and who should not have been involved, who to talk to and how to talk to them . . . it's important to know who was involved in the response . . . that makes follow-up easier.[56]

There may be no government official or lawyer specifically tasked with managing human rights decisions and implementation. Government legal advisers are often expected to cover a wide range of issues across the spectrum of international law with outside experts. Expertise may therefore be lacking. In addition, there is often a lack of a legal framework to facilitate this implementation and only rarely does national legislation deal with international decisions specifically.[57]

It is perhaps not surprising that African states have failed to establish any national processes to respond to African Commission decisions. The mechanisms set up in the European system are seen as significant and advanced, but this system is, of course, much older and generates a far greater number of judgments.[58] In the African context there may be no incentive for states to establish more easily operable national mechanisms for interacting with the African Commission and for implementation as the decisions from the African Commission are few and far between and the African Commission has itself not taken follow up seriously.[59]

---

56. Interview with Sheila Keetharuth, former Executive Director, Institute for Human Rights and Development in Africa, Gambia (Oct. 2011).

57. *E.g.* in Burundi.

58. See for example Dia Anagnostou, *Does European Human Rights Law Matter? Implementation and Domestic Impact of Strasbourg Court Judgments on Minority-Related Policies*, 14 INT'L J. HUM. RTS. 721 (2012). Dia Anagnostou & Alina Mungiu-Pippidi, Why Do States Implement Differently the European Court of Human Rights Judgments? The Case Law on Civil Liberties and the Rights of Minorities (work in progress) (Juristras Project, Apr. 2009); Andrew Drzemczewski & James Gaughan, *Implementing Strasbourg Court Judgments: the Parliamentary Dimension, in* EUR. Y.B. HUM. RTS. 2010, VOL. II, at 236 (W. Benedek, W. Karl & A. Mihr eds., n.d.); E. LAMBERT ABDELGAWAD, THE EXECUTION OF JUDGMENTS OF THE EUROPEAN COURT OF HUMAN RIGHTS (2d ed., 2008).

59. The government of Cameroon, for example, has faced eleven cases before the Commission in twenty-two years. Of these violations were found in just four. Over a similar period of time—twenty-three years—there have been five cases concerning Zambia

B. Monitoring Implementation Outside Government

To what extent does monitoring and follow up take place at the national level outside of government? There are a number of factors that have a role to play here. First, the potential role NHRIs can play in following up and monitoring treaty body decisions and findings has been highlighted on numerous occasions,[60] but there are challenges in making this an effective means of monitoring compliance in the African continent. Where such institutions exist, they are often insufficiently independent to properly follow up on government decisions or lack the capacity to follow up. They may simply be unaware of the existence of the African Commission and its decisions. The number of NHRIs that engage directly with the African Commission, despite the formal mechanism of affiliated status, is limited.[61,62] The International Coordinating Committee of NHRIs has accredited only eighteen with A status, which is a measure of their independence.[63] There is also some evidence that given a paucity of resources, the NHRIs would prefer to spend their energies in Geneva rather than in Banjul, in the belief that this is likely to have more impact and be more visible, because UN bodies will be taken more seriously by government.[64]

However, the ability of NHRIs to follow up on decisions of the African Commission is considerable.[65] They could coordinate follow up, as has been done in other regions,[66] and they could potentially use their own powers,

---

before the Commission. Violations were found in three. Botswana has faced fewer cases in total—just three—and these are more recent, with the first case being heard in 2000. Violations were found in all three cases.

60. Conclusions of the International Roundtable of the Role of NHRIs and Treaty Bodies, held in Berlin in December 2006, stated that "NHRIs should follow up to treaty bodies assessment of complaints to monitor State Party action undertaken in relation to it" and "NHRIs should follow up on interim orders of Treaty Bodies given to States Parties in relation to complaints where irreparable harm is envisaged." *See also* Belgrade Principles on the Relationship between National Human Rights Institutions and Parliaments (Belgrade, 22–23 Feb. 2012), A/HRC/20/9, 1 May 2012, Annex. *See generally* Human Rights, State Compliance, and Social Change: Assessing National Human Rights Institutions (Ryan Goodman & Thomas Pegram eds., 2012). *See also* OSJI, *supra* note 5, ch. 5.

61. *See* African Commission on Human and Peoples' Rights, *Resolution on the Granting of Observer Status to National Human Right Institutions* (1998), *available at* http://www.achpr.org/sessions/24th/resolutions/31/.

62. Few NHRIs regularly attend the African Commission sessions.

63. Chart of the Status of National Human Rights Institutions, as of May 2012, *available at* http://nhri.ohchr.org/EN/Documents/Chart%20of%20the%20Status%20of%20NIs%20%2830%20May%202012%29.pdf.

64. *See* Human Rights Implementation Centre, *Report of Workshop for East African National Human Rights Institutions on the Implementation of Torture Prevention Standards, Held between 18 and 19 October 2010 Nairobi, Kenya, available at* http://www.bristol.ac.uk/law/research/centres-themes/hric/.

65. *See* OSJI, *supra* note 5, ch. 5.

66. *See* Amrei Müller, Frauke Seidensticker, German Institute for Human Rights, The Role of National Human Rights Institutions in the United Nations Treaty Body Process (2007).

such as ordering the release of detainees, if a decision of the African Commission recommended such.[67] However, in order for the NHRI to follow up on decisions of the African Commission, the latter must inform national institutions in the relevant countries of its decision as a matter of course. This does not always happen.[68]

Similarly, whereas political bodies, such as the Committee of Ministers of the Council of Europe, and parliamentary committees, such as the Joint Committee on Human Rights[69] in the United Kingdom, have seen a role for parliaments in following up on decisions of treaty bodies,[70] in Africa this has been limited. In the African continent the extent to which there is formal engagement by parliamentarians on these issues and on the African Commission decisions is extremely limited. Individuals who had undertaken litigation before the African Commission noted in interviews that in some instances there was very little awareness among parliamentarians on the matter.[71] There are few examples of parliamentarians forming groups to engage in issues around implementation of decisions.[72]

Thus far, our research has found that monitoring and follow up of decisions of the African Commission often rely principally on the creativity and commitment of national CSOs and the litigators themselves. The impact and effectiveness of such is increased further where buy-in on the ground exists:

> [T]he prospects for compliance seem to be enhanced when communications are framed as communal rather than individualized claims, and when they are invoked as part of a broader social movement rather than an insular interest. By availing themselves of the "usual means of lobbying and public opinion campaigns" at their disposal, NGOs contribute significantly to contextualising complaints in this way, increasing the prospects for compliance.[73]

---

67. The Ugandan Human Rights Commission for example can review the case of a person detained and may order their release, Const. of the Republic of Uganda 1995, § 48. It has a general function in *id.* § 52(h) to "monitor the government's compliance with international treaty and convention obligations on human rights." *Id.* § 53 (2) notes that "the commission may, if satisfied that there has been an infringement of a human right or freedom, order—(a) the release of a detained or restricted person; or (b) payment of compensation; or (c) any other legal remedy or redress."

68. See, for example, the follow up to the McCallum case before the UN Human Rights Committee by the South African Human Rights Commission, *see* OSJI, *supra* note 5, at 101–02.

69. *See* Murray Hunt, Haley Hooper, Paul Yowell, Arts and Humanities Research Council, Parliaments and Human Rights: Redressing the Democratic Deficit (2012).

70. *See, e.g.,* Carolyn Evans & Simon Evans, *Evaluating the Human Rights Performance of Legislatures*, 6 Hum. Rts.L. Rev. 545 (2006); OSJI, *supra* note 5, ch. 3.

71. *See, e.g.,* S. Kateule, D.R.M. Katundu, A.S. Sife, *Parliamentarians Access to Information: A Case of Dodoma Parliamentary Library in Tanzania*, 6 Univ. Dar es Salaam Lib. J. 44 (2004). Evans & Evans, *supra* note 70.

72. *Id.*; OSJI, *supra* note 5, ch. 3.

73. Viljoen & Louw, *State Compliance, supra* note 34, at 28–29.

Where CSOs have involved victims directly in the case and litigation from the start, beyond having victims simply appear as witnesses before the African Commission hearings, this has had an impact on the decision's ultimate effect: "It's important to keep the community involved at all levels of the case . . . it's really for them . . . it's a victim-centered approach."[74] Nor is it limited to contact with victims: "It pays to be seen working together not only with the victims themselves . . . but making it an agenda item for other groups, including civil society organisations working on human rights and social justice issues."[75]

On a few occasions, the applicant has come back to the African Commission to notify it of non-compliance, successfully exploiting Article 1 of the Charter which provides that states parties "shall recognise the rights, duties and freedoms enshrined in the Charter and shall undertake to adopt legislative or other measures to give effect to them."[76] Whilst innovative and important in terms of contributing to jurisprudence, such an approach is time consuming and does not provide the immediacy required—victims may already have been waiting many years for the decision on the initial case. More recently, some litigants have initiated implementation dossiers and implementation hearings to follow up on communications. For example, in relation to Communications 54/91-61/91, 98/93-164/97, 196/97-210/98, *Malawi Africa Association and others v. Mauritania*, a number of organizations brought together information on the extent of compliance with the decision of the African Commission.[77] It contains an impressive list of supporting documents, including legislation, NGO reports, and interviews with key individuals and organizations, and provides updated information on the situation in the state with respect to each of recommendations in its decision. It details specific additional requests for the African Commission to clarify with the state and further action it should take to ensure state implementation of the findings.

The current use, therefore, of national mechanisms, is limited. Given resource constraints and the small number of cases emanating from the African Commission, it is perhaps inevitable that governments and national actors will respond on a a case by case basis, rather than developing processes and mechanisms to facilitate consistent responses to multiple cases. However, small improvements, including better communication, could build a more coherent approach to implementation. In turn, the further develop-

---

74. Interview with Sheila Keetharuth, former Executive Director, Institute for Human Rights and Development in Africa, Gambia (Oct. 2011).
75. *Id.*
76. Communications 137/94, 139/94, 154/96 and 161/97, *International Pen, Constitutional Rights Project, Civil Liberties Organisation and Interights on behalf of Ken Saro-Wiwa v. Nigeria* (1998).
77. *Implementation Dossier* (Oct. 2011), on file with author.

ment of its follow up procedure by the African Commission would increase the pressure to create a more coherent response to decisions. This is crucial to how seriously others perceive the African Commission and how seriously others perceive it to take itself.

IV. THE AFRICAN UNION, THE AFRICAN COMMISSION, AND THE AFRICAN COURT

It is only recently, with the amendments to its Rules of Procedure, that a follow up procedure by the African Commission on its own decisions has been explicitly developed. Until then, the approach was rather ad hoc and relied on a number of weaker avenues, such as sending reminders to states, "calling upon them to honour their obligations,"[78] and following up on recommendations when visiting state parties.[79] These approaches have clear limitations, lack creativity and proactivity, and tended to suggest a "return to domestic remedies, already exhausted without success (which) can only awaken disinterest in the regional system for protecting human rights in Africa."[80]

The state party reporting procedure under Article 62 has been regarded as another form of follow up where states, the African Commission, CSOs, and other stakeholders can use the opportunity to raise questions or submit information regarding the status of implementation of a decision.[81] However, the nature of the process, in which questions are asked first and answers provided separately, enables states to evade detail and responses to particular questions that they may not wish to answer in a public forum. Because the African Commission has rarely published states' written responses to its questions subsequent to the oral presentation and given that the Concluding Observations often lack detail, the effectiveness of the state reporting procedure as a method of follow up is problematic.

Given the challenges litigants face in finding out exactly what has happened to their cases at the national level, there is a clear need for an authoritative, external actor to obtain this information. Indeed, the lack of information can be related to the absence of follow up on the part of the African Commission, leaving a gap in formal provision of information on

---

78. ACHPR Information Sheet No. 3: Communication Procedure, *available at* http://www. achpr.org/english/_info/communications_procedure_en.html.
79. Wachira & Ayinla, *supra* note 5, at 468.
80. J. Didier Boukongou, *The Appeal of the African System for Protecting Human Rights*, 6 Afr. Hum. Rts. L. J. 271, 291–92 (2006).
81. Article 62 provides: "Each State Party shall undertake to submit every two years, from the date the present Charter comes into force, a report on the legislative or other measures taken, with a view to giving effect to the rights and freedoms recognised and guaranteed by the present Charter."

implementation. Professor Jean Didier Boukongou notes that: "in the vast majority of cases, the absence of a follow up procedure makes it impossible to ascertain any improvement to the initial situation."[82]

There is a need for the African Commission to bolster national systems and for the African Union to have an increasingly clear and coordinated system for following up on the former's decisions.

A. The Credibility of the Commission and the Issue of Political Will

Implementation of any decision of a human rights body, binding or otherwise, depends on the will of the state in question—a fact that the African Commission itself has recognized: "The major problem . . . is that of enforcement. There is no mechanism that can compel States to abide by these recommendations. Much remains on the good will of the States."[83] Whether this political will exists depends upon a range of factors, including the respect accorded to the institution issuing the decision:

> Every human rights institution has its Achilles heel. For the African Commission, it lies in the reality that African leaders always exhibit a spirit of furious indifference to the Commission's findings and recommendations. There is nothing more damaging to the cause of human rights than an ineffective complaint procedure. In particular, the right to a fair trial is meaningless where there is no effective remedy.[84]

It is therefore crucial for its own integrity and legitimacy that the African Commission make its follow up procedure operational in order to be taken seriously. Rule 112 of the amended Rules of Procedure for the African Commission sets out the follow up procedure on recommendations. It is worth stating this in full:

Rule 112 Follow-up on the recommendations of the Commission

1. After the consideration of the Commission's Activity Report by the Assembly, the Secretary shall notify the parties within thirty (30) days that they may disseminate the decision.

2. In the event of a decision against a State Party, the parties shall inform the Commission in writing, within one hundred and eighty (180) days of being informed of the decision in accordance with paragraph one, of all measures, if any, taken or being taken by the State Party to implement the decision of the Commission.

---

82. *Id.* at 288.
83. African Commission Information Sheet No.3, *supra* note 78.
84. Nsongurua J. Udombana, *The African Commission on Human and People's Rights and the Development of Fair Trial Norms in Africa*, 6 Afr. Hum. Rts. L. J. 299, 330–31 (2006).

3. Within ninety (90) days of receipt of the State's written response, the Commission may invite the State concerned to submit further information on the measures it has taken in response to its decision.

4. If no response is received from the State, the Commission may send a reminder to the State Party concerned to submit its information within ninety (90) days from the date of the reminder.

5. The Rapporteur for the Communication, or any other member of the Commission designated for this purpose, shall monitor the measures taken by the State Party to give effect to the Commission's recommendations on each Communication.

6. The Rapporteur may make such contacts and take such action as may be appropriate to fulfill his/her assignment including recommendations for further action by the Commission as may be necessary.

7. At each Ordinary Session, the Rapporteur shall present the report during the Public Session on the implementation of the Commission's recommendations.

8. The Commission shall draw the attention of the Sub-Committee of the Permanent Representatives Committee and the Executive Council on the Implementation of the Decisions of the African Union, to any situations of non-compliance with the Commission's decisions.

9. The Commission shall include information on any follow-up activities in its Activity Report.[85]

Indeed, the African Commission has started the process of following up on earlier cases by sending out letters to litigants and asking them for information regarding implementation of decisions in which they have been involved.[86] It is not clear if the African Commission has sent out similar requests for information to states, although Rule 112 provides for this. Exactly what the African Commission will do with this information is not entirely clear, but it has been suggested that this is part of a broader process of considering its relationship with the African Court and which cases it should submit to the African Court, on the basis of Rule 118(1) of the Rules of Procedure.[87] In addition, in line with Rule 112(9), the Activity Reports of the African Commission now contain some information on implementation of decisions.[88] Further, for the first time, at its fifty-fourth session in October 2013

---

85. Rules of Procedure, *supra* note 40.
86. One presumes this is under *id.* Rule 112(6).
87. *Id.* Rule 118(1) provides:

> If the Commission has taken a decision with respect to a communication submitted under Articles 48, 49 or 55 of the Charter and considers that the State has not complied or is unwilling to comply with its recommendations in respect of the communication within the period stated in Rule 112(2), it may submit the communication to the Court pursuant to Article 5 (1) (a) of the Protocol and inform the parties accordingly.

88. *See, e.g.*, Combined 32nd, 33rd Activity Reports Of The African Commission on Human And Peoples' Rights, EX.CL/782 (XXII) Rev. 2, (Jan. 2013), ¶ 24.

the African Commission adopted a resolution on implementation after an oral hearing, attended by the government and the complainants, was held at its previous session.[89]

There are a number of challenges with the implementation of Rule 112. First, the African Commission is significantly under-resourced and lacks the full capacity to carry out follow up activities effectively. In some instances it appears that the African Commission finds it difficult to get information from complainants once a decision has been adopted, perhaps due to the combination of the length of time taken to obtain a decision, a lack of transparency within the decision making process that is so severe that parties are unaware that a decision has been adopted, a lack of funds for follow up, and a lack of interest from the government.

In addition, it is debatable whether the time limit of 180 days for the parties to inform the African Commission of all measures taken to implement the decision is too short and fails to acknowledge the fact that decisions may require the involvement and consultation of many government departments and that national legislation may need to be changed or drafted in order to implement the decision fully.

Furthermore, the African Commission has set up a Working Group on Communications and has recently extended its mandate to coordinate follow up to decisions and collect information on the status of implementation.[90] CSOs have expressed disappointment and concern at the communications and follow up process, noting a recent suggestion by the African Union that annual reports of the African Commission be restricted to ten pages, and questioning how this will impact on the inclusion of decisions in the annual reports.[91] Furthermore, they have noted: "The Commission's lack of emphasis on the implementation of its own decisions disappoints victims of human rights violations from across the continent."[92]

Finally, there is a crucial flaw with Rule 110 of the Rules of Procedure. Rule 110(3) states that the decision of the African Commission shall remain confidential and shall not be transmitted to the parties until the Assembly of Heads of State of the African Union authorizes its publication. In practice, the Assembly has delegated this responsibility to the Executive Council, which in recent years has led to more substantial debate on the activity reports.

---

89. Resolution Calling on the Republic of Kenya to Implement the Endorois Decision, ACHPR/ Res.257 (LIV) 2013.

90. African Commission on Human and Peoples' Rights [ACHPH], *Resolution on the Expansion of the Mandate of the Working Group on Communications and Modifying Its Composition*, Res. #255 (52d Ordinary Sess., 9-22 Oct. 2012).

91. Interights, Statement to the African Commission on Human and Peoples' Rights regarding protective measures, Apr. 2012, 51st ordinary session, *available at* http://www.interights.org/document/213/index.html [hereinafter Statement to Afr. Comm. Apr. 2012]

92. *Id.*

Where the Executive Council defers the authorization of the activity report, as was the case with the twenty-ninth Activity Report,[93] there can be significant delay in the dissemination of a decision to the parties concerned. The time for informing the parties involved in a communication of a decision is unnecessarily long and the parties are often unaware of when a decision has been adopted by the African Commission. While the timetable for response is short, the timing of dissemination is long and unwieldy—an indication that the approach is far from coordinated. These considerable challenges have led many to start looking at the role of the African Court.[94]

B. Use of the African Court

Rule 118(1) of the African Commission's Rules of Procedure:

> If the Commission has taken a decision with respect to a Communication submitted under Articles 48, 49 or 55 of the Charter and the Commission considers that the State has not complied or is unwilling to comply with its recommendations in respect of the Communication within the period stated in Rule 112(2), the Commission may submit the Case to the Court pursuant to Article 5 (1) (a) of the Protocol and inform the parties accordingly.

So far the African Commission has not exploited this Rule. It has only referred three cases to the African Court—two against Libya and one against Kenya[95]—and none of these are with respect to follow up, although it has made a passing reference to the potential to do so in a later case.[96] To what

---

93.   See Decision of the African Union Executive Council, EX.CL/Dec.666(XIX), *available at* http://www.au.int/en/sites/default/files/EX%20CL%20Dec%20644-667%20(XIX)%20_E.pdf.
94.   "We call on the Working Group to seriously consider various ways of improving their work on implementation, including the use of the protective mandate of the African Court where applicable." Statement to Afr. Comm. Apr. 2012, *supra* note 91.
95.   African Commission on Human and Peoples' Rights v. Libya, App. No.002/2013; African Commission on Human and Peoples' Rights v. the Republic of Kenya, 006/2012; In the Matter of the African Commission on Human and Peoples' Rights v. Great Socialist Peoples' Libyan Arab Jamahiriya Order for Provisional Measures, App. No. 004/2011. *See* Rachel Murray, *The African Court on Human and Peoples' Rights Order for Provisional Measures Against Libya: Greater Promise for Implementation of Human Rights in Africa?*, 4 Eur. Hum. Rts. L. Rev. 465 (2011). Conversely, the African Court has decided to refer several cases to the Commission, where it has lacked jurisdiction, see Daniel Amare and Mulugeta Amare v. Republic of Mozambique and Mozambique Airlines, App. No.005/2011, Decision; Association Juristes d'Afrique Pour La Bonne Gouvernance v. Republique de Cote d'Ivoire, Requete No.006/2011, Decision; Ekollo Moundi Alexandre v. République de Cameroun et République Fédérale du Nigéria, Requete No.008/2011. With respect to the latter, Judge Fatsah Ouguergouz provides a dissenting opinion urging greater thought regarding when cases should be submitted to the African Commission if the Court does not have jurisdiction.
96.   In its Resolution calling on Kenya to implement the Endorois Decision, the African Commission notes Rule 118(1) although does not say further whether this will be used. Rules of Procedure, *supra* note 40, Rule 118(1).

extent should the African Court play a greater role in following up on decisions of the African Commission? On the one hand, it is inappropriate for the African Court to be involved. In terms of the Protocol on the African Court and its own Rules of Procedure, the African Court cannot follow up on its own judgments; this role is mandated to the Executive Council of the African Union.[97] On the other hand, however, when states do not comply with decisions of the African Commission, the African Court could play an enforcement role. This would depend on a number of factors. First, Rule 118(1) of its own Rules requires that the African Commission initiate such a process. This requires that the African Commission have accurate records of state compliance, necessitating a clear follow up procedure. It cannot therefore delegate all responsibility for follow up to the African Court. Second, what is the role of the African Commission once it submits a case to the Court? Is it then a party to the case, and does this not jeopardize its independence? How will the African Commission obtain evidence on implementation? Will it need to rely on the evidence provided by the parties? Third, if the African Commission has taken the trouble to obtain this information, why would it hand over to the Court at this stage? Would this not imply a failure on its part? At the very least, the Commission needs to develop a clear strategy for when it should do so. The African Court would also need to develop its own opinion on any communication referred to it by the African Commission, and this could entail looking at the facts and merits again. This could negatively impact the credibility and legitimacy of the Commission.

The African Court and African Commission would need to collaborate and discuss how to send cases to each other in a way that reinforces and strengthens each body, their decisions and their implementation. The rules of procedure stipulate that they must meet once a year and this provides an opportunity to consider ways to establish a constructive relationship.[98]

Despite these difficulties, there is potential for the African Court to "complement the protective mandate of the Commission," as reiterated in Article 2 of the Protocol establishing it. In order to do so, the African Court must be seen as part of a coordinated strategy to follow up on decisions of the African Commission, rather than as something that undermines the latter's legitimacy.

C. Political Bodies

One of the reasons for states' greater awareness of and willingness to respond to the judgments of the European Court of Human Rights is that

---

97. Protocol to the African Charter on Human and Peoples' Rights on the Establishment of an African Court on Human and Peoples' Rights, art. 29(2), *adopted* 10 June 1998 (*entered into force* 25 Jan. 2004).

98. Rules of Procedure, *supra* note 40, Rule 115(1).

there is political engagement through the Committee of Ministers, which is responsible for follow up. To a certain extent this political involvement already takes place: the African Commission is required under Article 59 to submit its annual report, containing the decisions on communications, to the Executive Council and Assembly of Heads of State before it can be made public. The Rules of Procedure of the African Commission note that the role of the African Union is to consider the report and that the role of the Assembly is to authorize it.[99] Rule 125(2) notes that: "The Commission shall bring all its recommendations to the attention of the Sub-Committee on the Implementation of the Decisions of the African Union of the Permanent Representatives Committee."[100]

This engagement with the political organs of the African Union is crucial and perhaps, in the African context, one of the most important part of the process of follow up. If there were proper engagement by the Executive Council and Assembly in follow up and implementation of the decisions of the African Commission, this could add the much-needed political pressure for states to respond. However, it would appear that the opportunities for meaningful engagement at this level are limited. The communications are contained in an annex to the annual report. Given that the annual report has been restricted to ten or twelve pages, the Permanent Representatives Committee, the Executive Council, and the Assembly rarely see the annex.[101] Despite concerns that states may therefore influence the content of the findings of the African Commission, of more concern is the fact that there appears to be no awareness of their content at all.

Yet the African Union is not short of organs which could also play a role in follow up and therefore maintaining the momentum and pressure on states to respond to decisions of the African Commission. The Peace and Security Council (PSC), for example, is responsible for the promotion of peace, security and stability in Africa, preventive diplomacy, the maintenance of peace, and the management of catastrophes and humanitarian actions.[102] Its powers include: "follow-up, within the framework of its conflict prevention responsibilities, the progress towards the promotion of democratic practices, good governance, the rule of law, protection of human rights and fundamental freedoms, respect for the sanctity of human life and international humanitarian law by Member States."[103] Composed of fifteen member states of the

---

99.   *Id.* Rule 59(3), Rule 110(3).
100. *Id.* Rule 125(2).
101. *See* University of Bristol, Office of the High Commissioner for Human Rights, High Level Seminar on the Role of AU Bodies in Follow up to the Decisions of the African Commission on Human And Peoples' Rights, Addis Ababa (Sept. 2012), *available at* http://www.bristol.ac.uk/law/research/centres-themes/hric/softlawrigproject/.
102. Protocol Relating to the Establishment of the Peace and Security Council (PSC) of the African Union, *entered into force* 26 Dec. 2003, art. 3(f).
103. *Id.* art. 7(1)(m).

African Union, it consults CSOs and other stakeholders within its mandate on conflict prevention.[104] Article 19 of the Protocol specifically requires it to:

> seek close cooperation with the African Commission on Human and Peoples' Rights in all matters relevant to its objectives and mandate. The Commission on Human and Peoples' Rights shall bring to the attention of the Peace and Security Council any information relevant to the objectives and mandate of the Peace and Security Council.[105]

Arguably, in this context the PSC could examine decisions of the African Commission as indicators under their early warning system.

In 2003 the African Union established the African Peer Review Mechanism (APRM)[106] in the framework of the implementation of the New Partnership for Africa's Development (NEPAD).[107] The APRM, a process of state peer review, is used by member states as a means to share experiences and to self-monitor all aspects of governance and socioeconomic development. As the APRM already looks at findings relating to human rights as part of its mandate,[108] this could provide a useful process for following up on decisions of the African Commission and for considering the steps required to implement a decision at the national level. The APRM has seen some positive results in establishing a constructive dialogue among states,[109] and synergies could be made between the African Commission and the APRM. CSOs and NHRIs could consider using the APRM within their implementation strategy on a decision.

The Pan-African Parliament (PAP) is the legislative body of the African Union and as part of its mandate holds public hearings that can be viewed live. The PAP can put a range of issues on its agenda for debate. These debates provide opportunities for CSOs, NHRIs, and other stakeholders to raise questions about the decisions of the African Commission and to encourage a constructive dialogue on the steps required to implement a decision and to apply pressure on states to comply with a decision.

If the procedures at the regional level focused less on the mandate of individual organs and more on ensuring a coordinated and integrated response to the decisions of the African Commission, there would be greater potential to tackle state implementation from a variety of different pressure

---

104. *Id.* art. 20.
105. *Id.* art. 19.
106. Base Document, NEPAD/HSGIC/03-2003/APRM/MOU/Annex II, *adopted* 6th summit of the NEPAD Heads of States and Government Implementation Committee, 9 Mar. 2003, Abuja, Nigeria.
107. The New Partnership for Africa's Development, The NEPAD Framework Document, *available at* http://www.nepad.
108. *See, e.g.,* Declaration on Democracy, Political, Economic and Corporate Governance, AHG/235 (XXXVIII).
109. *See, e.g.,* Magnus Killander, *The African Peer Review Mechanism and Human Rights: The First Reviews and the Way Forward,* 30 Hum. Rts. Q. 41 (2008). *See also* Bronwen Manby, *The African Union, NEPAD and Human Rights: The Missing Agenda,* 26 Hum. Rts. Q. 983 (2004).

points.[110] At the moment, however, few of these bodies have shown an interest in looking at decisions of the African Commission or following up on them. Overall, there is little strategic coordination,[111] consistency, or reference to existing standards within the AU system. As the AU Human Rights Strategy for Africa recognizes, the challenges on the continent include "inadequate coordination and collaboration among AU and RECs organs and institutions" and "insufficient implementation and enforcement of human rights norms and decisions."[112] However, this strategy is part of a "broader process to establish greater coordination amongst AU organs and institutions."[113] There needs to be not only coherence with respect to the mandate of the various institutions and how they can interact most effectively to ensure greater implementation, but also with respect to the standards being developed. A proper reporting mechanism to follow up on decisions of the African Commission could assist here: "Linkages and partnerships between continental and national mechanisms would, therefore, facilitate accurate and effective reporting as well as harmonise such reporting."[114]

V. CONCLUSIONS

The treaty body reform processes at the United Nations, reinforced by the High Commissioner's 2012 Report, advocate for national mechanisms to follow up on decisions of treaty bodies. The same issues could equally apply to the African system. The African Commission, when ruling on a particular case, could require a state to put in place a mechanism or system that can be employed in the future and to identify the relevant government departments or ministries responsible for its implementation. It is unrealistic to expect too much given the lack of cases and the lack of resources at the state level. However, this need not be a complicated mechanism. Perhaps even a simple template would suffice for existing officials to foster discussion at the national level about what procedure should be adopted when the African Commission issues a decision.

Second, states could consider the procedure or template to have a mandate beyond responding to decisions of the African Commission. It could extend to coordinating state reporting under the African Commission as well

---

110. OSJI, *supra* note 5, at 108.
111. Bience Gawanas, *The African Union: Concepts and Implementation Mechanisms Relating to Human Rights* 156 (nd), *available at* http://www.kas.de/upload/auslandshomepages/namibia/Human_Rights_in_Africa/6_Gawanas.pdf.
112. Department of Political Affairs, African Union Commission, Human Rights Strategy for Africa, ¶ 23 (nd), *available at* http://pa.au.int/en/sites/default/files/HRSA-Final-table%20(EN)[3].pdf.
113. *Id.* at 4.
114. Gawanas, *supra* note 111, at 159. *See also* OSJI, *supra* note 5, at 111.

as state reporting and responses to UN treaty bodies and the UPR.[115] This would enable greater coordination across regional and international treaties. Institutionalized focal points within governments could also facilitate implementation and monitoring and act as communication points for civil society to interaction. The current lack of access points or known interlocutors is clearly felt among CSOs.

National actors, including NHRIs and CSOs, need to perform an independent monitoring role. The most effective way of ensuring impact is by identifying and working with local community actors as well as engaging with government and relevant authorities at every stage of the litigation process, not just once a decision has been reached.

National activities need to be complemented by the development of regional mechanisms. With an increasing sense of frustration among litigants and others about the integrity and reputation of the African Commission, the latter needs to look seriously at how it can improve its public perception. A proper, coherent, transparent and operational follow up mechanism, which is already provided for by its Rules of Procedure, could go some way. But, given this context, other AU organs also have a role to play: the African Court should consider carefully how it interprets any enforcement role with respect to decisions of the African Commission and how it draws lessons from the African Commission with respect to follow up of its own decisions. The political organs of the African Union need to exploit the provisions in the Rules of Procedure of both the African Commission and the African Court to develop their role. Although the will may be there, in practice there is limited awareness—and therefore limited discussion—of decisions of the African Commission within the political organs of the African Union. The African Commission needs to take the initiative and find further ways to engage with these key political organs. One way is to ensure, as required by Rule 112(9), that information on follow up is included in the annual report of the African Commission. Although the African Commission has started to do this, the detail is limited. It also needs to go further than this and find alternative fora outside the summit in which to discuss its findings. This may require it to adopt a more strategic, focused, and nuanced approach to its presentation of findings to the specific organs. Only then will it be possible for redress to be accorded in practice to victims of human rights violations.

---

115. UNGA, Implementation of Human Rights Instruments: Note by the Secretary-General, U.N. Doc. A/67/28442 (July 2012). This recent report noted ideas for collaboration between the African regional bodies and UN treaty bodies, including exchange of information, "enhanced use by the UN treaty bodies of the regional instruments, policies and actions and their impact when reviewing the reports of states parties from the region" (*Id.* ¶ 12), and "strengthened cooperation between the two systems to ensure mutual follow-up on the implementation of country-based recommendations, including through the sharing of good practices and the organization of joint workshops on follow-up. (*Id.* ¶ 13). With respect to individual communications it also notes cooperation between the UN bodies and the African bodies on "matters related to the individual complaint mechanisms, including issues related to jurisprudence, procedure, methods of work and implementation of their respective decisions" (*Id.* ¶ 14), the establishment of "permanent channels of communication." (*Id.* ¶ 15).

Part II
The Judicial Enforcement of Human Rights at the Regional Level

A
Europe

[8]

SEPARATION OF POWERS IN THE COUNCIL OF EUROPE: THE STATUS OF THE EUROPEAN COURT OF HUMAN RIGHTS VIS-À-VIS THE AUTHORITIES OF THE COUNCIL OF EUROPE*

by **Paul Mahoney,** Strasbourg

I. Foreword

In a preparatory report on a preliminary draft of the European Convention on Human Rights written towards the end of 1949, the Secretariat General of the Council of Europe had included in the list of questions to be examined the relations between the administrative services of the Court and the Secretariat General.[1] This advice would not appear to have been acted on before the Convention was opened for signature in November 1950. The following discussion will take up examination of the question of the status of the Registry of the Court in the light of subsequent developments, with a view to assessing its implications for the wider issue of the independence of the permanent, single Court set up as from November 1998 under Protocol No. 11 to the Convention. The delimiting of the respective prerogatives of the Secretary General and the Committee of Ministers, on the one hand, and the Court itself, on the other, over the Registry of the Court and its functioning is of interest not only for the three institutional actors and staff concerned but also for the individuals who address themselves to the Court in Strasbourg seeking justice against their own governments.

The former Court, under the pre-Protocol No. 11 system, was ever alert in defending its independence, not only independence in adjudicating on the cases brought under the Convention but also independence from interference by the authorities of the Council of Europe in the way it managed its judicial business and the staff placed at its disposal. Although jealous of this dual independence, the former Court always recognised that it operated within the institutional framework of the Council of Europe. During the life of the former Court, "separation of powers" was on the whole an uncontroversial issue in practice, only giving rise to isolated incidents. It was by no means an evident feat, however, to maintain the act of comfortably balancing judicial independence and integration within the structures of an international intergovernmental organisation in the absence of any "constitutional" delimitation of respective powers. That achievement was in no mean part attributable to the diplomatic skills of the successive Presidents of the Court and Secretaries General of the Council of Europe.

The conclusion of this article is that, with the full judicialisation of the international system of human rights protection under the Convention as a result of Protocol No. 11, the time for amateur balancing acts, however skilful they may be, has passed and that the democratic principle of the separation of powers should be formally recognised through a text regulating the relations between the Court and the (political and executive) authorities of the Council of Europe. The fuzziness attaching to the status of the Registry of the Court is symptomatic of a more general legal vacuum. No other comparable international court, whether created before or after Protocol No. 11, has the lack of status – or, to put it in another way, the apparent status of dependency on the umbrella organisation – of the European Court of Human Rights. Other comparable international courts, the International Criminal Court being the latest example, are recognised, in the status accorded to them, as occupying a special position vis-à-vis the umbrella organisation by reason of their judicial independence. It is paradoxical that the Council of Europe, with its idealistic mission of promoting political democracy, the rule of law and human rights, should be alone of all international organisations in not formally recognising the separation of powers in relation to its court.

II. The setting up of the old Court

A. The text of the Convention in 1950

The text of the Convention adopted in 1950, and in particular Section IV which concerned the Court, did not contain any express provision on the Registry. The institution of a Registry was laid down, and its organisation defined, by the Court itself, when it was set up in 1959, in the exercise of the rule-making power conferred by Article 55 of the Convention, which read: "The Court shall draw up its own rules and shall determine its own procedure." In so doing, the Court took the Rules and the Registry of the International Court of

---

* A revised version of an article published in Paul Mahoney / Franz Matscher / Herbert Petzold and Luzius Wildhaber, eds., *Protecting Human Rights: The European Perspective – Studies in Memory of Rolv Ryssdal,* pp. 845-861 (2000).

Paul Mahoney, Registrar of the European Court of Human Rights. Any views expressed are personal. I am grateful for the comments on this text offered by Roderick Liddell, Head of the Private Office of the President of the Court, although he is not responsible for the end result.

[1] Preparatory report by the Secretariat General concerning a preliminary draft convention to provide a collective guarantee of human rights, Document B22, *Collected Edition of the Travaux Préparatoires of the European Convention on Human Rights,* vol. III, pp. 34-35.

Justice as a model. A preparatory working paper drafted by the Council of Europe's Directorate of Human Rights in 1959 at the time of the setting up of the Court analysed the meaning and scope of Article 55 as follows: "Article 55 appears to confer upon the Court a *competence of its own*, which it may exercise in complete freedom, provided that the Convention is adhered to."[2] Article 58 of the Convention provided that "the expenses of ... the Court shall be borne by the Council of Europe", and Article 61 specified that " nothing in this Convention shall prejudice the powers conferred on the Committee of Ministers by the Statute of the Council of Europe". Hence, since the budget of the Council of Europe is adopted by the Committee of Ministers under the terms of Statute (see Articles 20 (d) and 38 (c)), the Court was – and still is, former Articles 58 and 61 having been re-enacted by Protocol No. 11 as Articles 50 and 54 in the amended Convention – dependent on the Committee of Ministers in the matter of finances.

Quite a different approach on the staffing issue was taken in Section III of the 1950 Convention as regards the European Commission of Human Rights. Firstly, the Commission's rule-making competence was limited to "draw[ing] up its own rules of procedure" (Article 36). Former Article 37 then expressly stated that "the secretariat of the Commission shall be provided by the Secretary General". The intention of the drafters was to "attach the Commission, from the administrative point of view, to the Council of Europe",[3] whereas they said nothing of the kind in relation to the Court.

In addition to former Article 37, further Articles of the Convention can be seen as confirming the Secretary General's involvement in the functioning of the Commission by making him the channel or addressee of applications, the convenor of the Commission's meetings and the addressee responsible for publication of the Commission's friendly settlement reports (see former Articles 24, 25, 30 and 35); in stark contrast, the few provisions in Section IV mentioning the Secretary General had nothing to do with the functioning of the Court (see former Articles 40 §§ 2 and 4, and 46 § 3).

In sum, former Article 37 and its companion Articles spell out the non-judicial, or rather quasi-judicial, character of the Commission as compared with the fully judicial character of the Court and, *a contrario*, reinforce the status of independence both adjudicative and functional of the Court vis-à-vis the authorities of the Council of Europe.

B. Analysis made by the Council of Europe Secretariat General prior to the setting up of the Court

The status of the Registry of the European Court of Human Rights was discussed within the Secretariat of the Council of Europe even before the Court was created. As early as 1953, the distinctive features of the future Registry were adverted to in a document submitted to the Committee of Ministers:

"The Commission and the Court have been set up, to quote Article 19 of the Convention, 'to ensure the observance of the engagements undertaken by the High Contracting Parties in the present Convention'... . The Court will naturally have the services of *a Clerk's office answerable only to the Court* and the duties of which will be governed by the Rules of Procedure established by the Court (Article 55)."[4] (Emphasis supplied)

In 1958, shortly before the Court was set up, in a document prepared by the Directorate of Human Rights and communicated to the Committee of Ministers in the name of the Secretary General, the Registry of the Court was foreseen in the following terms:

"B. Office of the Court

23. The Convention contains no provision concerning the Clerk of the Court. Study of the preparatory work discloses that the omission was not due to any oversight, for Article 20 (b) of the 'draft Statute of the European Court of Human Rights', annexed to the draft Convention submitted to the Council of Europe by the European Movement in July 1949, provided that 'the Court shall appoint its Registrar (i.e. Clerk) and may provide for the appointment of such other officers as may be necessary' (Doc. INF/5/E/R, p. 23) ... . This Article was obviously founded on Article 21 of the Statute of the International Court of Justice ... . The Secretariat-General, in its Preparatory Report on a preliminary draft Convention of collective guarantee of Human Rights written towards the end of 1949 for the Committee of Experts on Human Rights, had included in the list of questions to be examined the nature of the relations between the administrative services (Clerk) of the Court and the Commission, on the one hand, and the Secretariat General of the Council of Europe, on the other (Doc. B 22, Section 12).

24. Thus the problem did not pass unnoticed. Moreover, the Convention settled it explicitly for the European Commission of Human Rights in Article 37, which lays down that 'the Secretariat of the Commission shall be provided' by the Secretary-General of the Council of Europe' ... . Its silence regarding the Clerk of the Court must be due to the fact that *its authors wished*:

– *to leave the Court free to organise its own administrative services;*

– to avoid committing themselves in advance, in view of the lack of precise particulars of the volume of work to be dealt with and having regard to the necessity of providing for a full-time Clerk.

25. It will be for the Court itself, when it draws up its rules and determines its procedure (Article 55 of the Convention), to decide on the duties of its Clerk and the organisation of his office. It may, nevertheless, appear expedient for the Court, before deciding, to consult the Committee of Ministers and the Secretary General in order that a solution may be found which will safeguard the independence of the Court and assure its satisfactory operation, while avoiding dissipation of energy, duplication of work and unnecessary expense."[5] (Emphasis supplied)

There is no reason why the Secretariat General's analysis of 1953 and 1958, recognising the operational as well as adjudicative independence of the Court, with Registry staff answerable only to the Court, should not be equally valid today, especially since there is now a full-time Court with professional judges operating under a system the judicial character of which has been strengthened in comparison with that of the original 1950 model.

C. The attitude of the Court when adopting its Rules in 1959

The Court, agreeing with the earlier view of the Secretariat of the Council of Europe, deduced from the

---

[2] Doc. CDH (59)1, "Rules and procedure of the Court (Article 55 of the Convention): Preparatory working paper drafted by the Directorate of Human Rights", para. 1, p. 3 (emphasis in the original text).

[3] Preliminary draft report and report by the Committee of Experts to the Committee of Ministers, *Collected Edition of the Travaux Préparatoires*, vol. III, p. 270, and vol. IV, p. 36.

[4] Doc. CM (53) 135, "Memorandum concerning the Secretariat of the European Commission of Human Rights", p. 2.

[5] Doc. CM (58) 114, "European Court of Human Rights Constitution Problems", paras. 23-25.

relevant provisions of the Convention that, subject to the budgetary competence of the Committee of Ministers (former Article 58 of the Convention), it was itself responsible for determining the organisation of the Registry, including the appointment of its Registrar and other staff. A preparatory paper on the Rules prepared for the Court by the Council of Europe's Directorate of Human Rights reiterated as the starting point of principle that "the fact that Section IV of the Convention makes no mention of this matter justifies the belief that it was intended to leave the Court free, as an independent body having power of decision [under Article 55 of the Convention], to organise its own administrative services"; and then went on to state that three choices were available to the Court, namely to have the Registry

– remain entirely separate from the Council of Europe Secretariat,
– simply form part of the Secretariat, or
– be associated with the Secretariat to an extent to be determined by the Court.[6]

The third and intermediate solution was preferred. The Court opted for a largely autonomous Registry under its control but with close administrative links with the Secretariat of the Council of Europe.

The original Rules of Court laid down that the Court would itself elect its Registrar and Deputy Registrar, after the President had consulted the Secretary General (Rules 11 and 12); the President would direct the administration of the Court (Rule 8), sanction general instructions relating to the working of the Registry (Rule 14 § 4 – subsequently Rule 14 § 5) and request the Secretary General to provide the Court with the necessary personnel, equipment and facilities (Rule 13). Under the original Rules, the manner in which the Secretary General was to "provide" the necessary personnel requested, including permanent staff, was not specified. Scope was left for various possibilities: secondment of Council of Europe Secretariat staff to the Court, creation of specific posts attached to the Registry, etc. In point of fact, in the beginning the Secretary General "lent" the Court staff on a part-time basis from the Directorate of Human Rights.

It should be noticed that from the very outset the Secretary General's involvement in the "provision" of the Court's personnel, and the wide discretion then accorded to him in that respect, derived not from the Statute of the Council of Europe but from a delegation expressly made by the Court in its Rules of Court. As such that power was subject to amendment by the Court and indeed it was so amended subsequently (see below).

The reasons for the Court's "self-limitation" in 1959 are not difficult to deduce. When the Court was set up, it could not be foreseen whether the future workload would even warrant a full-time Registry. The Court judged it wise to exploit to the maximum the resources that were in fact available, namely the Secretariat General of the Council of Europe, whilst providing for a Registry that would be largely autonomous in operational terms. The essential point of principle that the Registry should come under the sole authority of the Court was safeguarded and the material considerations left subject to future developments.

III. Subsequent developments in the old Court

A. Early history of the Registry

During the first years of the Court's existence, the Registry shared staff with the Directorate of Human Rights, Mr Polys Modinos being at one and the same time Director of Human Rights and Registrar of the Court.

The Committee of Ministers, when it had the occasion, drew a clear distinction between the status of these two functions of Mr Modinos. Thus, the Committee of Ministers noted in 1961 that the Registrar, appointed by the Court, "is not within the hierarchy of Council of Europe officials; he is therefore outside the Secretariat establishment".[7] This analysis the Committee of Ministers formally reiterated in the general considerations stated in its Resolution (61) 10 (assimilating the rank of Mr Modinos, "in his personal capacity", to that of a Deputy Secretary General):

"Whereas ... the Court has elected Mr Polys Modinos ... as Registrar,
Whereas in his capacity as Registrar of the ... Court ..., Mr Modinos is outside the Secretariat establishment ..."[8]

These are considerations that must be valid for all Registrars – and Deputy Registrars – of the Court who are likewise elected by the Court.

As from 1963, with the election of Mr Heribert Golsong as Registrar and the disappearance of somewhat personal tie which had existed at the beginning between the Directorate of Human Rights and the Registry, the Registry became established as an administrative unit separate from that of the Directorate. Following the reference to the Court in June 1965 of the "Belgian Linguistic" case, the staff of the Registry was increased, from a stated total of two lawyers in 1965 (the Registrar and Deputy Registrar) to one of three lawyers and four assistants in 1968.[9]

The Secretary General in office in 1960 (Mr Benvenuti) went on record, in a memorandum addressed to the Committee of Ministers, to explain that the Registrar and the Registry fell outside his sphere of authority:

"*The Registry of the Court* comes directly under the Court itself, which, as a judicial body, appoints its own Registrar and Deputy Registrar (Rules 11 and 12 of the Rules of Court). The duties of the Registrar are laid down mainly in Rules 14, 19 and 45.
While the Secretary of the Commission exercises powers delegated by the Secretary General, the Registrar of the Court acts by virtue of the powers conferred on him by his election."[10]

In late 1961 the Secretary General introduced Regulation No. 324 on the functioning of the Directorate of Human Rights. In the preamble to this Regulation, the Secretary General, whilst asserting his power to "define the duties and organisation of the Directorate of Human Rights and of the Secretariat of the Commission of Human Rights", restricted himself to "taking into account the functions of the Registry of the Court". Article 2, after

---

[6] *Loc. cit., supra* note 2.

[7] CM/Del/Concl (61) 95, item IX (relevant extract reproduced as doc. CM (61) 29).

[8] The expression "outside the Secretariat establishment" is rendered in the French text as "*hors du cadre*", which should not be confused with "*agent hors cadre*" ("a specially appointed official", such as the Secretary General, the Deputy Secretary General and the Clerk of the Assembly). The language of Resolution (61) 10 covers a functional notion deriving from the legal character of the post, not a hierarchical notion of rank or grade.

[9] In 1965 the Registry was described in the Yearbook on the Convention ("YB") as consisting of a Registrar assisted by a Deputy Registry (8 YB 49 (1965)). By 1968 the list given in the YB included an additional legal officer, an archivist and three secretarial assistants (11 YB 67 (1968)).

[10] Doc. CM (60) 10, "Reorganisation of the Human Rights Directorate", p. 3, para. 7.

listing the staff in the Directorate, provided that, "by agreement with the Court, the Director of Human Rights may place some of these officials at the disposal of the Registry of the Court".

The early recognition in Regulation No. 324, that in matters relating to Registry staff the agreement of the Court was a necessary pre-condition for the exercise of any administrative authority by the Secretary General or his subordinates, was followed seven years later by Regulation No. 394 of December 1968 and Office Circular No. 451 of June 1969. The preamble to Regulation No. 394, after reciting the intention of the Secretary General (Mr Smithers) "to redefine the respective responsibilities, powers and functions of the Directorate of Human Rights and the Secretariat of the Commission of Human Rights", in contrast simply acknowledged that "the responsibilities, powers and tasks of the Registry of the Court are laid down by the Rules of Court and the instructions of its President". Mr Smithers appended to the implementing circular when issued a statement noting that "by a general instruction ... signed in accordance with Rule 14 § 4, the President of the Court has made this text applicable to the Registry of the Court". Mr Smithers' action in appending this statement may be seen as a particular application by a Secretary General of the general principle that any amendment of the status or responsibilities of the Registry requires a decision by the Court. And thirty-five years later, under a strengthened, more judicialised system of international human rights protection, the dividing line between the spheres of authority of the Court and the Secretary General, as explicitly recognised by Mr Smithers, cannot surely have shifted away from the Court and towards administrative subordination of the Registry to the Secretary General.

B. *The 1969 amendment to Rule 13 of the Rules of Court*

In 1969 the Court, prompted by the appointment of an official to the Registry which had been made by the Secretary General against the wishes of the Court, felt that the time had come to review the manner of appointment of Registry staff in the light of the previous ten years' experience. It added to Rule 13 a second paragraph reading as follows:

> "The officials of the Registry, other than the Registrar and the Deputy Registrar, shall be appointed by the Secretary General, with the agreement of the President or the Registrar."

The Court of its own motion thus reduced the hitherto unrestricted power of appointment delegated to the Secretary General under Rule 13. The amendment was officially notified to the Secretary General (Mr Toncic-Sorinj) in person by the President of the Court (Mr Rolin) and no objection of any kind was raised by the Secretary General.

On the other hand, nothing was introduced into Rule 13 on the other aspects of the Registry's status, such as transfers, disciplinary sanctions, etc. Again, this can be seen as being not an oversight but a deliberate omission, in view of the small size of the Registry and it being thought inconceivable that a Secretary General would proceed other than by analogy with the provision regarding appointments.

Interestingly the Commission subsequently chose to follow the example of the Court by arrogating a similar power for itself in relation to appointment of staff to its Secretariat: as from 1992 Rule 12 of the Commission's Rules of Procedure provided that such appointments were to be made by the Secretary General, but "on the proposal of the Commission" as far as the Secretary and Deputy Secretary were concerned (paragraph 2) and only "with the agreement of the President of the Commission or the Secretary acting on the President's instructions" for other officials (paragraph 3). The Commission evidently felt it expedient to adopt such a provision in order to protect its independence, notwithstanding the wording of Article 37 of the Convention and the understanding both of the drafters of the Convention and previous Secretaries General that the Commission's Secretariat was attached "from the administrative point of view" to the Council of Europe and under the direct hierarchical authority of the Secretary General. Rule 12 §§ 2 and 3 of the Commission's Rules of Procedure was never mirrored by a corresponding clause in the Council of Europe's Regulations on Appointments (as to which, see below).

C. *General Instructions*

A number of General Instructions to the Registrar were issued by the President of the Court from 1969 onwards. As recounted above, the first made the Secretary General's administrative Regulation No. 394 and its implementing circular on the organisation of the various human rights departments within the Council of Europe applicable to the Registry. The considerations figuring in the preamble to these Instructions are instructive in that they enunciate what the Court took to be governing principles as regards the status of its Registry, namely that

– "the responsibilities, competence and duties of the Registry ... are defined in the Rules of Court and in the general instructions provided for in Rule 14 § 4";[11]

– "it is the especial duty of the Registry to assist the Court and the Judges in the exercise of their judicial functions";

– "the Registry is subject in the exercise of its functions to the sole authority of the Court".[12]

The preamble to General Instruction No. 3 (1973) also spoke of "the bond of allegiance... linking the Registry to the Court" which "finds expression in the oath or solemn declaration which [Registry staff] make". These governing principles, and their evident implications as regards the relationship between the Registry and the "political" authorities of the Council of Europe, were not invented by the Court: as noted above, they had already been identified and enunciated by the Council of Europe Secretariat in preparatory documents prior to the setting up of the Court. As also noted above, they must be equally valid today for the single Court.

D. *Amendment and revision of Council of Europe staff regulations in 1977 and 1981*

In 1977 and 1981 the Committee of Ministers adopted and then revised "Regulations on Appointments" setting out "the conditions under which permanent posts are filled by transfer, recruitment or promotion". Whilst the Regulations included clauses regarding appointment of the staff of the Registry of the Court, the relevant clauses simply reproduced in substance certain of the already existing provisions in the Rules of Court, to which express reference was made in a footnote, and therefore did not prompt any fundamental objections on the part of the Court.

---

[11] Rule 17 § 4 under the present Rules (see below at p. 282).

[12] See, e.g., General Instructions Nos. 2 and 3 of 27 September 1969 and 10 August 1973 respectively. I am grateful to the Court for agreeing to the declassification of these texts.

IV. Conclusion as regards the old Court

Perhaps the most authentic statement of the status of the Registry under the 1950 Convention is that given by the old Court itself in 1973 in its comments submitted to the Committee of Ministers in connection with a management-survey report of the Council of Europe:

"4. The Convention lays down that 'the Court shall draw up its own rules and shall determine its own procedure' (Article 55); and whereas the Convention prescribes that the Secretariat of the Commission is to be provided by the Secretary General (Article 37), it leaves the organisation of the Registry to the Court. The position of the Registry is in this respect similar to that of the Registry of the International Court of Justice, the organisation of which is the responsibility of the International Court, not of the Secretariat of the United Nations. Indeed, it is simply an expression of the judicial character of the Court and of the principles of the independence of the judiciary.

5. When the Court was established in 1959, the Court considered whether it should create a Registry entirely separate from the General Secretariat of the Council of Europe or a Registry which, while separate and independent, would be linked to the Secretariat. The Court for practical reasons decided upon the latter solution, as is apparent from Rules 8, 11, 12 and 13 of its Rules of [Court] ... . Thus, although for budgetary and similar purposes the Registry is treated as an administrative unit of the Council of Europe, it remains at all times under the sole authority of the Court; and it is this which makes the arrangement compatible with the Court's judicial character. The special status of the Registry is recognised in Resolution (62) 10 of the Committee of Ministers in which it is underlined that the Registrar is 'outside the Secretariat establishment' ...

6. The Registrar and the Registry thus operate under the authority and control of the Court and it is for the Court itself to determine the functions and responsibilities of its Registry. Accordingly, as was stated in Regulation No. 394 promulgated by the Secretary General on 7 December 1968, 'the responsibilities, powers and tasks of the Registry of the Court are laid down by the Rules of Court and the instructions of its President' ... . The functions and responsibilities entrusted to the Registry ... are those normally discharged by the Registry of an international tribunal and are no more than are necessary to safeguard the judicial character and independence of the Court."[13]

In view of the fact that the drafters of the Convention, the Secretariat General of the Council of Europe prior to the setting up of the Court and then the Court once it was set up explicitly intended the position of the Strasbourg Registry to be similar to that of the Registry of the International Court of Justice, it is instructive to cite Professor Shabtai Rosenne, a leading authority who has written extensively on the latter Court:

"[T]he most important of [the Registrar's] duties are those which relate to the preparation of cases for trial, and the fact that all judgments, advisory opinions and orders are signed by him, and that all correspondence passes through his hands, emphasize the judicial element in this post. Regulations such as these require the co-operation of the Registrar in the judicial activities of the Court, and prevent his relegation solely to the administrative aspects of its work. Through the Registrar the other officers of the Court's staff likewise play their role in the performance of the Court's duties.
...
The fact that the Court is empowered to appoint its own staff, and is in this respect not directly bound by the provisions of the Charter, is one of the elements which

sharply distinguishes the Court from the other principal organs. ... From an administrative point of view these differences have become more marked in the light of the amplifications given by the Court, in the Rules of Court and in other instructions, to the skeleton provisions of the Statute ... [B]efore taking up his duties, each official has to make a declaration before the President, the Registrar being present, to the effect that he will perform the duties incumbent upon him as an official of the International Court of Justice in all loyalty, discretion and good conscience. The interesting feature of this declaration is not that it has to be made (a similar declaration is required from officials of the United Nations under Article 1.9 of the Staff Regulations), but that no reference to the United Nations appears in it. This fundamental differentiation, and the distance which it creates between the Registry staff and the members of the Secretariat, has many advantages. It helps to preserve the necessary degree of detachment between the Court and the remainder of the Organization ... . Indeed, the maintenance of this system is probably essential if anything like an independent judiciary is to exist in the international sphere.

The differentiation of the Registry staff from the Secretariat staff is thus seen to be a question of principle, which was wisely left alone in the new arrangements of 1945. Once that differentiation is accepted as a fundamental, and desirable, postulate, then the assimilation of the two as a matter of administrative practice is to be commended. The condition for this, however, is that the ultimate control over the staff should remain with the Court, and should not be resigned to the Secretary-General of the United Nations ... .

...

... The creation of a post such as [that of Registrar] in independence of the similar post of Secretary-General is one of the guarantees for the independence of the Court. The formal provisions of the Statute and other instruments are enhanced by the dignity with which the office has been invested. ... All these aspects, which have their influence also on the Registry staff, are considered absolutely essential for the proper performance of the functions of the Court."[14]

Professor Rosenne's analysis both of the underlying principle (ultimate control over the Registry staff to remain with the Court and not the Secretary General, as a fundamental and essential pre-requisite for the existence of an independent judiciary in the international sphere) and of the practical considerations (the greatest degree of assimilation of Registry staff and UN Secretariat staff being desirable as a matter of administrative practice) does not depend upon the particular wording of the ICJ Statute and Rules or the particular situation of the ICJ, but upon quite general factors.

Indeed the independence and judicial character of international courts constitute a generally recognised principle in the international sphere. As evidenced by the practice and legal provisions governing other comparable international courts,[15] that generally recognised principle

---

[13] Doc. CDH (73) 17. Again I am grateful to the Court for agreeing to the declassification of this material.
[14] Shabtai Rosenne, *The Law and Practice of the International Court*, vol. 1, pp. 251-259 (1965).
[15] Such as the International Court of Justice, the Inter-American Court of Human Rights and the Court of Justice of the European Communities. See also, more recently, the relevant provisions concerning the International Tribunal for the Law of the Sea and the International Criminal Court.

has as one of its concrete consequences that the competence to decide both on the appointment and duties of the court's staff and on the court's internal organisation properly belongs to the court itself and not to some outside authority such as the secretary general or the governing political organ of the umbrella organisation. Financial provisions allocating a power of decision over the court's budget to an outside, even political, authority do not in themselves detract from that generally recognised principle. Any exception, for example as to nomination or provision of staff, requires an express and unambiguous provision in the treaty instrument. Significantly, one rare example of the Secretary General of the umbrella organisation being empowered in the treaty to "appoint" court staff, found in Article 59 of the American Convention on Human Rights, has been superseded by a relationship agreement whereby the Inter-American Court's officials are selected and hired by the Registrar, the Secretary General merely making the formal appointment in consequence.[16] The agreement furthermore specifies that the staff are exclusively officials of the Court and not members of the Secretariat General of the umbrella organisation, the Organisation of American States.

The inferences as to the status of the Registry of the European Court of Human Rights made by the drafters of the Convention, by the Council of Europe Secretariat prior to the setting up of the Court and then by the Court itself thus do no more than reflect what are generally accepted principle and practice in the international sphere. That principle and that practice have most recently been confirmed in the arrangements provided by the Contracting States for the operation of the International Tribunal of the Law of the Sea and the International Criminal Court. Confirmation of a comparable approach at national level is to be found in the Beijing Statement of Principles of the Independence of the Judiciary, dating from 1995 and signed (as at 1997) by the Chief Justices and other judges of 32 countries in the Asia-Pacific region,[17] which provides in principle 36, under the head of "Judicial Administration": "The principal responsibility for court administration, including appointment, supervision and disciplinary control of administrative personnel and support staff must vest in the Judiciary, or in a body in which the Judiciary is represented and has an effective role." It is difficult to conceive that lower standards apply in the European region.

V. The situation subsequent to Protocol No. 11

A. Text of the Convention

As amended by Protocol No. 11, the Convention now makes explicit provision in Article 25 for a Registry to be placed at the disposal of the Court:

"Registry and legal secretaries

The Court shall have a Registry, the functions and organisation of which shall be laid down in the rules of the Court. The Court shall be assisted by legal secretaries."

Article 26 (e) further provides that the plenary Court shall elect the Registrar and one or more Deputy Registrars.

The Explanatory Report to Protocol No. 11 explains (at paragraph 65) that the first sentence of Article 25 is derived from the former Rules of Court. The Explanatory Report also states (at paragraph 66): "The Court's Registry is provided by the Secretary General of the Council of Europe." This is evidently a reference back to the principle embodied in former Article 37 of the Convention in relation to the Secretariat of the

Commission, which was originally intended, unlike the Registry of the Court, to be an integral part of the Secretariat General of the Council of Europe (see above). No such statement appears in the new Article 25 or elsewhere in the Convention.

B. The Rules of Court

One difference between the Rules of the new Court and the former Rules as regards staff appointments is that the new Rules do not contain any requirement for the opinion of the Secretary General of the Council of Europe to be sought before the Court elects its Registrar and Deputy Registrars (Rules 15 § 1 and 16 § 1 as compared with former Rules 11 § 1 and 12 § 1). The consequence is that the relevant article on "special appointments procedures" in the Council of Europe's Regulations on Appointments (article 26 § 1), which was inserted to take account of the Court's Rules, no longer reflects those Rules, in that it continues to specify a procedural requirement (of prior consultation) which the Court has suppressed of its own motion. In short, the legal basis for the provision in the Regulations no longer exists. Further, it would appear that the three initial appointments (of the Registrar and the two Deputy Registrars) made in November 1998 were made without this procedural condition in the Regulations having been fulfilled, although consultation of the Secretary General did take place for subsequent appointments as a matter of courtesy on the part of the Court.

VI. Looking ahead

Is it possible to bring together these various strands so as to identify what the new Court should be aiming to establish as the status of its Registry, now that it has had the time to settle its judicial procedures and working methods?

A. General principles and legal framework

Doubtless the principle of the separation of powers cannot be transposed in all its aspects from the national context to the international, intergovernmental context of the Council of Europe. It may also be said that the principle, and the separation it imposes, are not absolute, with for example some blending of powers being a characteristic of some systems of government. But the insulation of the judiciary from encroachment by the political organs of government is taken to remain a constant, whatever the context. Put in another way, the operational (or functional) independence of a judicial body is a fundamental requirement of the rule of law, for all systems of law.

---

[16] See below at p. 301: Agreement between the General Secretariat of the Organization of American States and the Inter-American Court of Human Rights on the Administrative Operation of the Court's Secretariat (signed by the President of the Court on 12 November 1997 and the Secretary General of the OAS on 1 January 1998), Article III. Article 59 of the Inter-American Convention further provides that the San José Court "shall establish its Secretariat, which shall function under the direction of the Secretary of the Court, in accordance with the administrative standards of the General Secretariat of the Organization in all respect not incompatible with the independence of the Court".

[17] The signatories include Chief Justices and other judges from Australia, India, Japan, New Caledonia, New Zealand, Pakistan, the Philippines and the Russian Federation. The principles in the Statement "represent the minimum standards necessary to be observed in order to maintain the independence and effective functioning of the Judiciary".

The ultimate hierarchical superior of officials of the Secretariat General of the Council of Europe is the Secretary General; and the Secretary General, by virtue of the Statute of the Council of Europe, "is responsible to the Committee of Ministers for the work of the Secretariat" (Article 37 (b)). It is surely indisputable that the staff of the Registry should be answerable only to the Court and not to the Secretary General or, ultimately through the Secretary General, to the Committee of Ministers, both of which are political entities. The Committee of Ministers in particular is composed of the representatives of the Governments, which are potential respondents before the Court. In this respect, by analogy with national systems, the Committee of Ministers represents the political organs of government and cannot therefore interfere, or be seen to interfere, with the Court's judicial business or the way in which that business is managed. The judicial independence of the Court requires that the ultimate hierarchical superior of the staff who assist it in its judicial work be the President of the Court. This has, moreover, been explicitly recognised by previous Secretaries General. As Professor Rosenne put it, "the maintenance of this system" – namely the fundamental differentiation as to hierarchical authority between the Registry staff and the members of the Secretariat General of the Organisation – "is probably essential if anything like an independent judiciary is to exist in the international sphere".

The answerability of the Secretary General to the Committee of Ministers for the work of the Secretariat General in itself necessarily excludes that the Registry staff can be treated as members of the Secretariat General within the meaning, or for the purposes, of the Statute of the Council of Europe and, consequently, any staff regulations made thereunder – unless the Court has given its consent thereto. As a matter of principle, if any delegation to the Secretary General of managerial power over the Registry staff were to be conceivable, this could only be on the basis of the Secretary General being answerable to the President of the Court, not the Committee of Ministers.

If it is not the Statute of the Council of Europe, what then is the legal source for the exercise of authority over Registry staff? The answer, given as early as 1953 and 1959 by the Council of Europe Secretariat itself, is that it is the Convention, an international treaty postdating the Statute, which defines the powers of the Court and therefore provides the legal framework for the status of its Registry. The first branch of this equation was expressed in similar terms in 1963 by Heribert Golsong, one of the first writers to address the issue of the Court's legal status vis-à-vis the Council of Europe: "The creation, powers and functions of the European ... Court are ... not regulated by the Statute of the Council of Europe but by a specific treaty, the European Convention on Human Rights."[18] The Secretariat's early assumption as to the legal position has been reinforced by the wording of Article 25 of the Convention as amended by Protocol No. 11, which explicitly confers on the new single Court a rule-making power covering the functions and organisation of its Registry.

The relationship between the Statute of the Council of Europe and the Convention, and between the various functions conferred by these two instruments, has been analysed in a consistent fashion over the years by a number of leading commentators on the Convention. Thus, Golsong in his early study in 1963 wrote: "Between the Convention and the Statute there is no situation of subordination or control. The two instruments are

international treaties and are equally valid as sources of obligations and rights." A distinction is to be drawn between the functions exercised under the terms of the Statute and those deriving from the Convention. When, for example, the Committee of Ministers is exercising functions by virtue of the Convention, Golsong concluded, its activities are governed solely by the provisions of the Convention instead of by the Statute of the Council of Europe.[19] Almost forty years later Hans Christian Krüger (writing with Jörg Polakiewicz) was saying more or less the same thing: "Like other Council of Europe treaties, the Convention is not an act of the Council itself, but an independent international treaty which may contain special regulations going beyond the Statute's provisions."[20] Article 25 of the Convention, embodying the Court's power to lay down the functions and organisation of its Registry, is just one such special regulation. As Andrew Drzemczewski has put it in another context,

"...[T]reaties elaborated within the framework of the Council of Europe ... are not strictly speaking acts of the Organisation as such. The adoption of the text of a convention and its opening for signature give the treaty an independent life. *Only those links with the Council of Europe which are explicitly foreseen by the treaty itself maintain it in the sphere of the Organisation.* Instead, these matters are primarily governed by general principles of international law and/or by specific provisions contained in the treaties themselves. ..."[21] (Emphasis supplied)

The fact that the Committee of Ministers and the Secretary General have rule-making and hierarchical or managerial powers under the Statute of the Council of Europe over staff members of the Secretariat General of the Council of Europe does not detract from the powers vested in the Court "by general principles of international law and/or by specific provisions contained in the [Convention]" (to quote Drzemczewski) in relation to the Registry. In a broad sense both categories of staff are Council of Europe staff but there is a "separation of powers" that exists in relation to them to the extent that they cannot answer to the same hierarchical authority. In the words of Golsong, "the Registry, though technically attached to the Secretariat General of the Council of Europe, is in the exercise of its functions not subject to control by the Secretary General. The Registrar, as head of the Registry, is responsible only to the Court".[22]

---

[18] Heribert Golsong, "Implementation of International Protection of Human Rights", *Académie de Droit international, Recueil des Cours*, 1963-III, tome 110, para. 12. Golsong was the second Registrar of the Court and subsequently Director of Legal Affairs, and then Director of Human Rights, of the Council of Europe.

[19] *Loc. cit.*, note 18, paras. 12-30.

[20] Hans Christian Krüger and Jörg Polakiewicz, "Proposals for a Coherent Human Rights Protection System in Europe/The European Convention on Human Rights and the European Charter of Fundamental Rights", 22 HRLJ 1 at p. 12 (2001). Krüger was for 20 years Secretary to the European Commission of Human Rights before being elected Deputy Secretary General of the Council of Europe.

[21] Andrew Drzemczewski, "The Prevention of Human Rights Violations: Monitoring Mechanisms of the Council of Europe", in L.-A. Sicilianos (ed.), *The Prevention of Human Rights Violations*, pp. 139-177 (2001).

[22] *Supra* note 18, para. 24.

In sum, the judicial character of the Court requires its operational independence from the political entities that are the Secretary General and the Committee of Ministers, and the text of the Convention provides the legal basis for the practical implementation of this principle. As to how that practical implementation should be envisaged, again one can do no better than to repeat Professor Rosenne's analysis:

> "The differentiation of the Registry staff from the Secretariat staff is thus seen to be a question of principle, which was wisely left alone in the new arrangements of 1945. Once that differentiation is accepted as a fundamental, and desirable, postulate, then the assimilation of the two as a matter of administrative practice is to be commended."

B. Historical background

This rather clear legal picture has been somewhat muddied by the various practical expedients that have been adopted over the years. In the early days it made no sense for the Court to have its own Registry until it had sufficient work for it to do. As the volume of business increased, so there was a greater need for staff and thus for the Court to assume more administrative responsibility. However, the Registry remained a fairly small administrative unit and the Court still sat on a part-time basis. It was therefore for practical reasons convenient and indeed necessary for the Court to avail itself of the administrative facilities offered by the Council of Europe. One can say that throughout this period the Court chose to delegate its administrative authority to the Secretary General.

Although the old Court never questioned that the budgetary competence of the Committee of Ministers (former Article 58 of the Convention) prevented it from, for example, deciding on the creation or upgrading of posts, its consistent position, willingly recognised by several Secretaries General, was that the Registry was solely dependent on the Court's authority, which is what made the system compatible with the Court's judicial character. In particular, it made it clear that such appointment powers as the Secretary General had over Registry staff were ones delegated by the Court itself in the exercise of its rule-making competence under the Convention and not ones derived from the earlier Statute of the Council of Europe or the administrative regulations made thereunder. The amendment made to the Rules of Court in 1969, whereby the Court of its own motion henceforth made appointments by the Secretary General subject to the agreement of the President or the Registrar, is an illustration of the operation in practice of these principles. What is more, although the position of the Commission was different both in terms of its judicial character and the legal basis under the Convention, the Commission likewise amended its Rules of its own motion so as to limit in the same way the Secretary General's power to appoint staff to its Secretariat. Evidently, in the Commission's opinion its quasi-judicial independence carried with it the same authority over the appointment of its staff and the same rule-making competence.

C. Changes resulting from Protocol No. 11

On a general level, the reform introduced by Protocol No. 11 has reinforced the judicial character of the enforcement system under the Convention, in particular by making the Court's jurisdiction to receive both individual and inter-State petitions compulsory and by abolishing the adjudicative role of the Committee of Ministers. More particularly, the amended Convention text has made it explicit that the Court itself is to be responsible for the functions and organisation of its Registry, thereby providing a clear legal basis for the hierarchical and administrative authority of the Court over the Registry. Further, on a practical level, the Court has become a permanent body with a substantial staff at its disposal.[23] Thus, the practical considerations that had dictated the administrative arrangements in place hitherto, both for the Commission and the old Court, no longer exist. If nothing else, this major change in the practical landscape would seem to call for the Court to retrieve some of the administrative responsibility for regulating "the functions and organisation of the Registry" – to use the terminology of the amended Article 25 of the Convention – hitherto delegated to the Secretary General.

It is hardly conceivable that the new single Court would accept less administrative autonomy, in principle or in practice, than its two predecessors whose functions it has inherited. It would indeed be strange if the new Court decided either (i) that it had a more limited rule-making competence under the clearer wording of Article 25 of the Convention as amended by Protocol No. 11 than its predecessor had under former Article 55 or (ii) to exercise its rule-making competence so as to give itself, as a permanent institution, a lesser degree of functional independence from the political and executive authorities of the Council of Europe than its semi-permanent predecessor or even the Commission, which was originally conceived of under former Article 37 as having a secretariat functionally integrated within the Secretariat General of the Council of Europe.

D. Implementation of any retrieval of administrative responsibility

In the present writer's view, in order to avoid any misunderstanding in the future and to announce clearly to the outside world the functional independence of the Court, it would be preferable for the principle that Registry staff are hierarchically accountable to the Court rather than to the Secretary General and the Committee of Ministers of the Council of Europe to be explicitly recognised in the relevant administrative texts of the Council of Europe.

The resultant functional independence of the Court – that is, the principle of no interference by the Council of Europe authorities in the exercise of the Court's hierarchical and organisational prerogatives over its staff – applies to all the members of the Registry, be they lawyers, translators, administrative assistants or secretaries. Since they all assist the Court in carrying out its judicial business, they must answer solely to the Court and the Court must alone be in a position to issue instructions to them and ultimately, if necessary, impose disciplinary sanctions. The Court must also retain authority as to the allocation of work and more generally the assignment of different officials to different tasks. The final arbiter of what is in the interests of the service must be the Court itself. Since appointment of the "right person in the right place" is by definition a matter going directly to the interest of the service, it is difficult to see how this can be achieved without investing the Court with at least some responsibility for appointment, promotion and disciplinary procedures. These are organisational not

---

[23] As at 1 May 2003, there were 229 permanent officials and 149 temporary officials in the Registry.

budgetary questions, and as such are covered by the authority conferred on the Court under Article 25 of the Convention.

The fact that the President of the Court and not the Secretary General is recognised as being the ultimate hierarchical superior of Registry staff does not and should not necessarily involve a split in the unicity of Council of Europe staff as far as career development and employment conditions are concerned: the same – or similar – appointment procedures, disciplinary procedures, salary and pension scales, holiday entitlements, etc., could be maintained, as well as full mobility from one Council of Europe post to another. Indeed Registry staff have a legitimate concern that any variation of the previously existing procedures under Council of Europe staff regulations should not be to their detriment. The Council of Europe procedures have been devised to ensure proper career development and adequate legal protection for staff vis-à-vis their employer. Those social *acquis* should be maintained in the context of any changes made to accommodate the Court's "functional" independence. Mobility of staff to and from the Court, for example, is a benefit for all concerned: the Court, the other sectors of the Council of Europe and all the staff. The guarantees of objective consideration of job applications and of an independent disputes mechanism should not be diluted either.

Not only do staff, both within and without the Registry, have legitimate concerns as to the emergence of this new institutional animal, the permanent, single Court, but the Secretary General and the Council of Europe administration may well have some misgivings. The Court could be perceived as something of a cuckoo in the nest, a small even insignificant dot on the Council of Europe's institutional map in 1969 whose pretentions to "functional" independence could then be willingly accepted with a smile, but which is now viewed as a fully grown competitor for scarce governmental funds and institutional influence. It would indeed be regrettable if the (albeit unintended) consequence of the arrival on the scene of the new Court were to be a weakening of the authority of the Secretary General and a cutback in the other activities of the Council of Europe. The Secretary General has traditionally been a friend and ally of the Convention institutions throughout the years of their steady growth since 1953. Furthermore, economies of scale dictate that many areas of administrative responsibility would best remain with the Council of Europe administration.

In the latter connection European taxpayers, who at the end of the day fund the Court as well as being its clients, also have a legitimate concern as to the efficient use of their money. The Court, like any public body, has a duty of prudent stewardship, and also of accountability, as regards the spending of public funds put at its disposal. Its being subject to external financial control or audit is thus not in itself at odds with the principle of functional independence. Likewise, when it comes to deciding how the Council of Europe is to bear the costs of the Court in accordance with Article 50 of the Convention, the Committee of Ministers, as the governmental budgetary authority of the Council of Europe, represents the interests of the taxpayers in ensuring that public money is being well spent.

In sum, the main parameters for suitable retrieval of administrative authority over the Registry should be

– first and foremost, ensuring the necessary operational as well as adjudicative independence of the Court;

– facilitating the efficient and cost-effective functioning of the Court, within the framework of budgetary arrangements designed to avoid unnecessary duplication of expenditure as between the Court and the Council of Europe administration;

– taking due account both of the institutional role of the Secretary General and of the interests of staff (in the Registry and elsewhere in the Council of Europe).

Other international organisations have acted on the advice mentioned at the beginning of this paper, by settling a regulatory framework determining the modalities of the relationship between themselves and their courts. The basic implications of the separation of legislative, executive and judicial powers usually figure in primary treaty provisions or an accompanying statute. The Inter-American Court of Human Rights and the International Tribunal for the Law of the Sea have negotiated formal agreements going into detail on administrative matters.[24] This latter kind of arrangement is what the Strasbourg Court should be aiming at as a minimum: a "relationship agreement" with the Secretary General of the Council of Europe covering the administrative relations between the Registry and the Secretary General's sphere of authority and, where appropriate, being reflected in the text of Council of Europe staff regulations. The old Court set up two joint working parties with the Secretary General, in 1982 and then in 1990, in an endeavour to arrive at such a working agreement. Although *ad hoc* solutions to specific problems were found, no formal document or general regulatory framework resulted.

E. From the status of the Registry to the separation of powers

The status of the Registry is one facet, albeit the most evident, of the functional independence of the Court. Other facets include the legal capacity of the Court,[25] the status of the judges[26] and the organisation of the financial arrangements between the Court and the Council of Europe for the implementation of the obligation placed by Article 50 of the Convention on the Council of Europe as an organisation (rather than on the collectivity of

---

[24] See the Agreement on Co-operation and the Relationship between the United Nations and the International Tribunal for the Law of the Sea (approved by the Tribunal on 12 March 1998 and by the General Assembly of the United Nations on 8 September 1998 in Resolution 52/521); and the Agreement between the General Secretariat of the Organization of American States and the Inter-American Court of Human Rights on the administrative functioning of the Court's Secretariat, *supra* note 16. The Rome Statute of the International Criminal Court also provides (in Article 2) that: "The Court shall be brought into relationship with the United Nations through an agreement to be approved by the Assembly of States Parties ... and thereafter concluded by the President of the Court on its behalf."

[25] See, e.g. Article 4 § 1 of the Statute of the International Criminal Court: "The Court shall have international legal personality. It shall also have such legal capacity as may be necessary for the exercise of its functions and the fulfilment of its purposes."

[26] The Committee of Ministers' Resolution (97)9 (infra p. 213) on the Status and Conditions of Service of Judges of the European Court of Human Rights declares in its Article 1 that "elected members of the Court ... shall enjoy the special status of 'judges of the European Court of Human Rights'", but it offers no further specification as to what this "special status" entails or consists of.

Contracting States, as is the case for some other international courts) to bear the expenses of the Court.[27] In these areas the same lack of legal recognition reigns.

The Court does clearly operate within, and not outside, the Council of Europe; it is one component, it is the judicial arm, of a wider Council of Europe system for the protection and promotion of human rights. The view of Golsong in 1963 was that, taking what he called the Court's "independent legal status with regard to the Council of Europe" together with its nonetheless numerous links with the Council, the Court had in some respects a position at least equivalent to that of an organ of the Council.[28]

Yet the status to be accorded to the Court as an independent international judicial institution has not been adequately settled in the legal texts of the Organisation, in particular in the Council of Europe's constitutional instrument, the Statute (which dates from 1949). The Court has over the years progressively grown to maturity from very small beginnings, when some doubted whether it had a future,[29] but the legal order of the Council of Europe has not been formally adapted so as to recognise the changed institutional and constitutional reality: unlike other international organisations, the Council of Europe has not accommodated the existence of an independent judicial institution in its constitutional structure. Now, with the permanentisation and consolidation of the Court, there is no longer any excuse for a state of affairs to persist in which the status of the Court and its relationship with the Council of Europe (dependence or independence) is left in legal limbo.[30]

There is on the horizon the perspective of reform of the Convention machinery in order to introduce adaptations that would allow it to remain effective in the face of the ever-mounting flood of applications being lodged in Strasbourg.[31] Should any process for amendment of the Convention be set in motion, this would be an ideal opportunity for the principle of the separation of powers to be formally written into the Council of Europe system of judicial protection of human rights and for the status of the Court as an independent international judicial institution vis-à-vis the political and executive authorities of the Council of Europe to be spelt out.

[27] See e.g., principle 37 of the Beijing Statement of Principles of the Independence of the Judiciary: "The budget of the courts should be prepared by the courts or a competent authority in collaboration with the courts having regard to the needs of the independence of the Judiciary and its administration. The amount allotted should be sufficient to enable each court to function without an excessive workload." See also Roderick Liddell, "Art. 50: Spese di funzionamento della Corte", in Sergio Bartole, Benedetto Conforti and Guido Raimondi (eds.), *Commentario alla Convenzione Europea per la Tutela dei Diritti dell'Uomo e delle Libertà Fondamentali* (2001).

[28] Golsong, *supra* note 18, para. 12, citing other authors who went even further and asserted, wrongly in his opinion given the state of the statutory texts of the Council of Europe, that the Court could indeed be considered as an autonomous organ of the Council in the full legal sense, in the same way that the International Court of Justice is an autonomous organ of the United Nations under Article 92 of the United Nations Charter.

[29] Henri Rolin, "Has the European Court of Human Rights a Future?", Howard Law Journal (Washington, D.C.) 442 (1965). Rolin was one of the early Presidents of the Court. For Professor Hersch Lauterpacht in 1951 it had even been a matter of speculation when and in what manner the then optional provisions in the Convention concerning the Court would be accepted by Governments: Hersch Lauterpacht, *International Law and Human Rights*, chapter 18 at p. 436 (1951). The Court was in fact set up in 1959 – six years later than the Commission – after eight Contracting States had made declarations accepting its jurisdiction.

[30] It is significant to compare the legal status accorded to the permanent International Criminal Court with the arrangements provided for its ad hoc precursor, the International Criminal Tribunal for the Former Yugoslavia, which formally speaking has a large degree of administrative dependence on the Secretariat General of the United Nations. Even in this context however, in practice the full authority to appoint staff of the ad hoc Tribunal has been relinquished by the Secretary General of the United Nations to the Registrar of the Tribunal.

[31] For one view on the reform issue, see Luzius Wildhaber, "A Constitutional Future for the European Court of Human Rights?" 23 HRLJ 161 (2002). Wildhaber is currently President of the Strasbourg Court. See also the French and German versions of this article: "Un avenir constitutionnel pour la Cour européenne des Droits de l'Homme?", 14 Revue universelle des droits de l'homme 1 (2002); "Eine verfassungsrechtliche Zukunft für den Europäischen Gerichtshof für Menschenrechte?" 29 Europäische Grundrechte-Zeitschrift 569 (2002).

[9]

ESSAY

THE EUROPEAN COURT OF HUMAN RIGHTS: THE PAST, THE PRESENT, THE FUTURE*

LUZIUS WILDHABER**

INTRODUCTION

Today, I wish to introduce you to the European Court of Human Rights. I shall first offer some remarks about the history of the Court, the changing perceptions, the underlying theories, and the way the Court has shaped European reality. Then I shall discuss a few recent cases as specific illustrations of the Court's work. Towards the end, I shall add a few remarks about the difficult relationship between terrorism and human rights.

I. PAST

We began the 20th century with an international law that viewed only sovereign States as actors, unbridled and uncontrolled, entitled to go to war, and also entitled to treat citizens and foreigners alike as

---

* This piece is based on remarks given by President Wildhaber at the American University Washington College of Law on April 21, 2006.
** Mr. Luzius Wildhaber, President of the European Court of Human Rights 1997–2007, Doctor of Law, Basel, 1961; LL.M. Yale, 1965; J.S.D., Yale, 1968; Dres.h.c., LL.D.h.c.

objects, whose legal status and whose human rights were defined solely by national law. We end the 20th and begin the 21st century with individuals who have become subjects of international law and a European Court of Human Rights which is the most spectacular illustration of this change in paradigms.[1] In the same vein, modern sovereignty should be understood as requiring respect for, rather than the breach of human rights, minority rights, democracy, and the rule of law.

One of the founding fathers of the European Convention on Human Rights, the Frenchman Pierre-Henri Teitgen, explained this in 1949 in moving words. He spoke about the time when he was in the Gestapo prisons while one of his brothers was at Dachau and one of his brothers-in-law was dying at Mauthausen.[2] He said: "I think we can now . . . confront 'reasons of State' with the only sovereignty worth dying for, worthy in all circumstances of being defended, respected and safeguarded—the sovereignty of justice and of law."[3]

Let us look even farther back into history. Already in ancient and medieval times, European political theories endeavoured to moderate the power of the rulers and to realise justice. Bracton demanded in 1250 the rule of law and the restriction of the unbridled State and the King. Even the King, he said, was subject to God and the law, because only the law made him King (*quia lex facit regem*). For there was no King, where arbitrariness and not the law ruled.[4]

Let me now bring you back to the year of 1950 and the signing ceremony of the European Convention on Human Rights in Rome.[5] A small group of far-sighted, idealistic lawyers, determined to

---

1. *See* Luzius Wildhaber, *Sovereignty and International Law, in* THE STRUCTURE AND PROCESS OF INTERNATIONAL LAW: ESSAYS IN LEGAL PHILOSOPHY DOCTRINE AND THEORY 425, 438 (R. St. J. Macdonald & Douglas M. Johnston eds., 1983) (describing the evolution of international law from that dealing with relations between states to law relating to a wide range of issues, including human rights).

2. 1 COLLECTED EDITION OF THE "TRAVAUX PRÉPARATOIRES" 48–50 (1975).

3. *Id.* at 50.

4. *See* 2 BRACTON (HENRY OF BRATTON), DE LEGIBUS ET CONSUETUDINIBUS ANGLIAE 33 (G.E. Woodbine & S.E. Thorne eds., Cambridge/Massachusetts 1968), *cited by* LUZIUS WILDHABER, MENSCHEN- UND MINDERHEITENRECHTE IN DER MODERNEN DEMOKRATIE 4 (1992).

5. COLLECTED EDITION OF THE "TRAVAUX PRÉPARATOIRES," *supra* note 2, at XXII.

prevent the recurrence of the devastation of war and the attendant horrendous crimes, argued that the best way to achieve that end was to guarantee respect for democracy and the rule of law at the national level. They believed that only by the collective enforcement of fundamental rights was it possible to secure the common minimum standards that form the basis of democratic society. It was Churchill himself who had referred first to a "European Court before which the violation of [human] rights . . . might be brought to the judgment of the civilised world."[6] Lord Layton, a member of the British delegation, saw the Convention as "a means of strengthening the resistance in all our countries against insidious attempts to undermine our democratic way of life, and thus to give to Western Europe as a whole a greater political stability."[7] For the first time individuals could challenge the actions of Governments before an international mechanism under a procedure leading to a binding judicial decision. The mandate which the founders of the Convention intended to entrust to the Court was eminently, even surprisingly, political.[8] The Court was to constitute a collective insurance policy against the relapse of democracies into dictatorships. What is nowadays identified as the hallmark of the Court, i.e. a generalised right of individual application for all sorts of possible victims, does not figure prominently in the original discussions on the Convention.

II. PRESENT

Now we move fifty years ahead, to 1998, when the Convention system underwent a major reform.[9] The original institutions, the European Court and the Commission of Human Rights, were replaced by a single Court functioning on a full-time basis.[10] The optional elements of the earlier system, the right to individual petition and the acceptance of the Court's jurisdiction, were

---

6. *Id.* at 34.

7. *Id.* at 30.

8. *See id.* (describing the Convention's goal of upholding democracy by preventing the destruction of democracy by dictatorships).

9. *See* EUROPEAN COURT OF HUMAN RIGHTS, HISTORICAL BACKGROUND, http://www.echr.coe.int/ECHR/EN/Header/The+Court/The+Court/History+of+the +Court/ (last visited Jan. 20, 2007).

10. *See id.*

eliminated; so was the Committee of Ministers' adjudicative role.[11] The Convention process, directly accessible to individuals, became fully judicial in character. The two initial bodies, the Commission from 1954 and the Court from 1959, gave life to the Convention, through their pioneering case-law.[12] Their purposive, autonomous, and at times creative interpretation of the Convention enhanced the rights protected to ensure that they had practical effect. Just to take one example, the right of access to a court, a right that lies at the heart of the Convention and a key element of the rule of law, was not expressly mentioned in the due process provision, Article 6, Section 1.[13] The Court's observation was of beautiful simplicity: "[t]he fair, public and expeditious characteristics of judicial proceedings are of no value at all if there are no judicial proceedings."[14] To this the Court later added that the right of access "would be illusory if a Contracting State's domestic legal system allowed a final, binding judicial decision to remain inoperative to the detriment of one party."[15] On the basis of such case-law, the Court established the principle that the Convention is to be interpreted as a living instrument, to be construed in the light of present day conditions.

Let me add a few personal remarks on the doctrine of the Convention as a living instrument. Our Court has of course followed precedent, except where cogent reasons impelled it to adjust the interpretation of the Convention to changes in societal values or in present-day conditions. And it has followed precedent not only with respect to judgments against a respondent State, but it recognises that the same European minimal standards should be observed in all member States. It is indeed in the interests of legal certainty, of a coherent development of the Convention case-law, of equality before

---

11. *See id.*

12. *See id.* (explaining the respective roles of the Commission, which made initial determinations on the admissibility of applications, and the Court, which could issue binding judgments).

13. European Convention for the Protection of Human Rights and Fundamental Freedoms art. 6, Nov. 4, 1950, Europ. T.S. No. 5 [hereinafter European Convention on Human Rights] (establishing the right to a "fair and public hearing").

14. Golder v. United Kingdom, 18 Eur. Ct. H.R. (ser. A) 1, 17–18 (1975).

15. Hornsby v. Greece, 1997-II Eur. Ct. H.R. 495, 510.

the law, of the rule of law, and of the separation of powers for the Court to follow in principle a moderated doctrine of precedent.[16]

Obviously in describing the Court's tasks in this way, I espouse a certain image of what the role of a European quasi-constitutional Judge should be. Our Court is to a certain extent a law-making body. How could it be otherwise? How is it possible to give shape to Convention guarantees such as the prohibition of torture, equality of arms, freedom of expression or private and family life, if—like Montesquieu—you see in the judge only the mouthpiece of the law? Such guarantees are programmatic formulations, open to the future, to be unfolded and developed in the light of changing conditions. My personal philosophy of the task of judges is that they should find their way gradually, in a way experimentally, inspired by the facts of the cases that reach a court. As you will realise, I do not believe in closed theoretical systems that are presented as sacrosanct on the basis of speculative hypotheses or ideologies. Such mono-causal explanations ignore the complex and often contradictory manner in which societies and international relations (and incidentally also individual human beings) evolve. Conversely, it has to be acknowledged that in developing the law it is difficult to avoid value judgments, whether on domestic or on international law. This applies especially to human rights, which, anchored as they are in the concepts of constitutionalism, democracy and the rule of law, are value judgments *par excellence.*

I might emphasise that I do not plead for a "Gouvernement des Juges."[17] Giving broad answers which are in no way called for by the facts of a case is to confuse a judicial mandate with that of the legislature or of the executive, and cannot and should not be the role of courts. In the famous "Federalist" Papers, Alexander Hamilton, the great theoretician of the American Constitution, wrote that the

---

16. *See* Luzius Wildhaber, *Precedent in the European Court of Human Rights,* *in* PROTECTING HUMAN RIGHTS: THE EUROPEAN PERSPECTIVE 1529 (Paul Mahoney, Franz Matscher, Herbert Petzold, Luzius Wildhaber eds., 2000).

17. *See* Un gouvernement des juges est-il à craindre?, http://www.oboulo.com/expose/gouvernment-juges-est-il-craindre.html (last visited Jan. 26, 2007) (describing that "Gouvernment des Juges" is a shift of power to the judiciary to make arbitrary decisions at the expense of the balance of powers found in modern day democratic governments; namely the Executive and Legislative branches of government).

526 *AM. U. INT'L L. REV.* [22:521

government holds the sword, the legislature holds the money box, and the only thing the courts hold for themselves is their independence.[18] It is that independence which places us in a position to watch over fairness and justice within governments.

Let me also add that whereas international human rights judges should do what is fair and fear no one, as the puritans would have put it, they should at the same time have regard for the context in which they live and for the aims they are serving. Human rights are our common responsibility. First and foremost they must be respected by the national parliaments, governments, courts and civil society at large. Only if they fail does our Court come in. The subsidiary aspect I describe and advocate here is more than pragmatic realism; it is also a way of paying respect to democratic processes (always provided they are indeed democratic); and I am firmly convinced that it is the best means of translating the "human rights-law-in-the-books" not only into a "human rights-law-in-the-court", but into a "human rights-law-in-action" and—hopefully—in reality in all of our member States.

The full-time European Court of Human Rights which was set up in 1998 under Protocol No. 11 to the European Convention on Human Rights is the biggest international Court that has ever existed.[19] It is composed of a number of judges equal to that of the Contracting States.[20] With the sole exception of Belarus, all European States are today members of the Council of Europe and have ratified the European Convention on Human Rights, whose protection now stretches from Iceland to Turkey, from Lisbon to Wladúwostok, from Riga to Malta, but also from Chechnya to the

---

18. THE FEDERALIST No. 78, at 378 (Alexander Hamilton) (Terence Ball ed., 2003) (asserting that of the three branches, the judiciary poses the least threat to individual liberties).

19. *See* Protocol 11 to the European Convention for the Protection of Human Rights and Fundamental Freedoms, Nov. 4, 1950, Europ. T.S. No. 5 [hereinafter Protocol 11]; *see also* European Court of Human Rights – Description, http://www.worldlii.org/int/other/PICTRes/2003/10.html (last visited Jan. 27, 2007) (recounting that over the years the ECHR has grown into the largest international bench and into one of the biggest and most respected international judicial bodies).

20. *See* Protocol 11, *supra* note 19, art. 20.

Basque region, from Northern Ireland to Cyprus and Nagorno-Karabach.[21]

Whereas the official languages of the Court are English and French, applications may be drafted in any one of the official languages of the Contracting States, and there are at present 41 official languages in these States.

The Court receives around 900 letters per day and some 250 international telephone calls a day. Its internet site was visited by 57 million hits in 2005. From 1998 to 2003, the number of applications has increased by about 15% in comparison with each preceding year.[22] In 2005, there was only an increase of 2%.[23] We now have some 81,000 pending applications before us.[24] In the past two years, we received some 45,000 applications.[25] The highest number of cases have come from Russia, Poland, Turkey and Romania (the so-called "big four"), which account for some 50% of all applications that reach our Court.[26] Some 63% of all cases have in recent years come from the 21 new member states of Central and Eastern Europe (at present about 18% come from Russia), some 11% from Turkey and only some 26% from the traditional Western European States.[27] Future historians might well argue that one of the biggest achievements of the Convention system was to be present and active when the Iron Curtain fell in 1989, so that the new member states had a whole body of case-law of which they could avail themselves.

---

21. *See generally* The Council of Europe's Member States, http://www.coe.int/T/E/Com/About_Coe/Member_states/default.asp (last visited Jan. 21, 2007).

22. *See* EUROPEAN COURT OF HUMAN RIGHTS, SURVEY OF ACTIVITIES 2005, at 33 *available at* http://www.echr.coe.int/NR/rdonlyres/4753F3E8-3AD0-42C5-B294-0F2A68507FC0/0/2005_SURVEY__COURT_.pdf [hereinafter SURVEY OF ACTIVITIES 2005].

23. *See* EUROPEAN COURT OF HUMAN RIGHTS, STATISTICS 2005, *available at* http://www.echr.coe.int/NR/rdonlyres/5211CDBA-8208-47DE-A9CA-AE8B8FD13872/0/stats2005.pdf (noting that 45,000 applications were filed in 2005, compared to 44,100 in 2004) [hereinafter STATISTICS 2005].

24. *See id.* (reporting a 4% increase in pending applications from Jan. 1 through Dec. 31, 2005).

25. *See id.*

26. *See* SURVEY OF ACTIVITIES 2005, *supra* note 22, at 35.

27. *See id.*

All sorts of cases reach our Court. Issues of the Communist nationalizations of property in Czechoslovakia, Slovakia and Eastern Germany and the question of whether the Czech Republic after the fall of the Iron Curtain could restrict the restitution of nationalized goods to Czech nationals only were declared inadmissible.[28] Two applicants elected to the parliament of San Marino refused to take the required oath on the Holy Gospels and were disqualified from sitting in the parliament, which our Court qualified as a violation of the freedom of religion in the *Buscarini* case.[29] A French-Moroccan drug trafficker held in custody was beaten up so severely by the police that medical certificates listed about 40 visible injuries all over his body, for which no plausible explanation was given, so our Court had to decide in the *Selmouni* case that he had been tortured.[30] The Swiss Animal Protection Society wanted to run an ad on TV, showing piglets and encouraging people to "eat less meat"; the TV refused saying this was "political" speech, whereas, if people had been invited to "eat more meat", this would have been "commercial" speech and therefore permissible; our Court saw in this a violation of the freedom of expression in the case of *Vereinigung gegen Tierfabriken*.[31] An imaginative applicant complained that the right to marriage of Article 12 must mean that the State was under an obligation to provide him with a suitable wife; unfortunately for him, the applicant was turned down.[32]

Functionally speaking, the European Court of Human Rights is becoming a European quasi-Constitutional Court. It is less handling the exceptional cases which captivated the attention of the founders of the Convention, but is becoming more and more a broad-based, "normal" institution, although a very symbolic one. Let me now discuss a few recent cases as illustrations.

---

28. *See generally* Malhous v. Czech Republic, 2000-XII Eur. Ct. H.R. 533; Gratzinger & Gratzingerova v. Czech Republic, 2002-VII Eur. Ct. H.R. 399; Kopecký v. Slovakia, 2004-IX Eur. Ct. H.R. 131.

29. Buscarini v. San Marino, 1999-I Eur. Ct. H.R. 605, 616.

30. Selmouni v. France, 1999-V Eur. Ct. H.R. 149, 183.

31. VgT Verein gegen Tierfabriken v. Switzerland, 2001-VI Eur. Ct. H.R. 243, 266.

32. European Convention on Human Rights, *supra* note 13, art. 12.

III. RECENT CASELAW

In a series of important judgments over the past few years, the Court has sought to explain the implications the Convention has for the political systems of the Contracting States and, in particular, the notion that pluralist democracy is the only political system that is compatible with the Convention. In an earlier judgment in 1998, in the *Turkish Communist Party* case the Court had found that democracy appeared to be the sole political model contemplated by the Convention and, consequently, the only one that was compatible with it.[33] But this raised the question of what that concept meant.

It is here that the Court has a role to play in identifying the constituent elements of democracy and in reminding us of the minimum essential requirements of a political system where human rights are respected. In the *Refah Partisi (Welfare Party) v. Turkey* judgment,[34] it carried out a thorough examination of the relationship between the Convention, democracy, political parties, and religion. The case concerned the dissolution, by the Turkish Constitutional Court, of a political party, the Welfare Party, on the grounds that it wanted to introduce sharia law and a theocratic regime.[35] A Grand Chamber of the Court found unanimously that there had been no violation of Article 11 of the Convention, which protects freedom of association.[36] The judgment provides some elements of an answer to the question which we have raised today concerning the dimensions of the New Europe.

The Court first noted that freedom of thought, religion, expression, and association as guaranteed by the Convention could not deprive the authorities of a State in which an association jeopardized that State's institutions, of the right to protect those institutions.[37] It necessarily followed that a political party whose leaders incited to violence, or put forward a policy which failed to respect democracy, or which was aimed at the destruction of democracy and the flouting

---

33. United Communist Party of Turkey v. Turkey, 1998-I Eur. Ct. H.R. 1, 22.

34. Refah Partisi v. Turkey, 2003-II Eur. Ct. H.R. 267, 300–03.

35. See *id.* at 269–70.

36. *See id.* at 316 (reasoning that Refah's dissolution, restricting the freedom of assembly and association guaranteed in Article 11, was necessary to protect the rights and freedoms of others).

37. *Id.* at 303.

of the rights and freedoms recognised in a democracy, could not invoke the protection of the Convention.[38] Penalties imposed on those grounds could even, where there was a "sufficiently established and imminent" danger for democracy, take the form of preventive intervention.[39]

The Court noted that the leaders of the Welfare Party had pledged to set up a regime based on sharia law.[40] It found that sharia, as defined by the leaders of the Welfare Party, was incompatible with the fundamental principles of democracy as set forth in the Convention.[41] It considered that "sharia, which faithfully reflects the dogmas and divine rules laid down by religion, is stable and invariable.[42] Principles such as pluralism in the political sphere or the constant evolution of public freedoms have no place in it."[43] According to the Court, it was difficult to declare one's respect for democracy and human rights, while at the same time supporting a regime based on such a sharia.[44] Such a regime clearly diverged from Convention values, particularly with regard to its criminal law and criminal procedure, its rules on the legal status of women, and the way it intervened in all spheres of private and public life in accordance with religious precepts.[45]

Next, let me describe the case of *Ilaşcu, Ivanţoc, Leşco and Petrov-Popa v. Moldova and Russia* which concerned events that occurred in the "Moldavian Republic of Transdniestria" ("MRT"), the region of Moldova to the East of the river Dniester known as Transdniestria.[46] This region declared its independence in 1991, which in turn led to a civil war and to the self-proclamation of a breakaway regime. This regime is not recognized by the international community. The case concerned the unlawful detention of the four applicants, following their arrest in 1992 and their subsequent trial

---

38. *Id.* at 303–04.

39. *See id.* at 305 (recognizing the possibility of a preventative intervention where "the national courts, after detailed scrutiny subjected to rigorous European supervision," identify an imminent danger).

40. *Id.* at 310–11.

41. *Id.* at 312.

42. *Id.*

43. *Id.*

44. *Id.*

45. *Id.*

46. *See* Ilaşcu v. Moldova & Russia, 2004-VII Eur. Ct. H.R. 179.

by the so-called "Supreme Court of the MRT" and the ill-treatment, inhuman prison conditions and torture inflicted on them during their detention, as well as the death penalty imposed on Mr. Ilaşcu and the mock executions to which he was subjected.[47]

The European Court of Human Rights established the responsibility of both respondent States (that of Moldova for the period after 2001) and found a violation of Articles 3, 5 and 34 of the Convention.[48] The Court ordered the immediate release of the applicants still in detention.[49] It emphasised the urgency of this measure in the following terms: "any continuation of the unlawful and arbitrary detention of the . . . applicants would necessarily entail a serious prolongation of the violation of Article 5 found by the Court and a breach of the respondent States' obligation under Article 46 § 1 of the Convention to abide by the Court's judgment."[50]

Only two of the four applicants have been released to date. Mr. Ilaşcu was released in May 2001 and Mr. Leşco at the expiry of the sentence imposed on him by the "Supreme Court of the MRT" in June 2004.[51] The other two applicants, Mr. Ivanţoc and Mr. Petrov-Popa, are still in custody.[52]

States have to report to the Committee of Ministers of the Council of Europe on the execution of judgments.[53] During the first examination of the case before the Committee of Ministers, the Moldovan authorities considered that, for the time being, their influence on the separatists was minimal or even non-existent.[54] As regards just satisfaction, the Ministry of Finance had ordered its

---

47. *See generally id.* at 232–45 (discussing in depth the arrest, detention, and conviction of the applicants as well as the events occurring after their convictions including actions taken to secure their release).

48. *Id.* at 303–05.

49. *Id.* at 302.

50. *Id.*

51. Press Release, European Court of Human Rights, Forthcoming Judgments (June 25, 2004).

52. *Ilaşcu*, 2004-VII Eur. Ct. H.R. at 302.

53. *See* European Convention on Human Rights, *supra* note 32, art. 46(2) (granting the Committee of Ministers the power to supervise the execution of final judgments of the Court).

54. Meeting of the Comm. of Ministers, 896th Sess., Notes on the Agenda ¶ 9 (2004).

payment.[55] The Representative of the Russian Federation in the Committee of Ministers emphasised the Russian authorities' disagreement with the judgment on both the legal and political levels and their view that since the applicants' lives were not in danger, the Convention was not pertinent.[56] Concerning possible execution measures or measures already taken, the Russian authorities considered that they were not in a position to execute the judgment, since the use of force to release the applicants was out of the question.[57] Furthermore, the Representative informed the Committee that he had been instructed not to participate in its examination of the case until directed otherwise.[58] He said that the Court's judgment was "inconsistent, controversial, subjective, politically and legally wrong and based on double standards."[59] It should therefore be noted that the Court's judgment in the *Ilaşcu* case has yet to be fully complied with.[60] In the meantime, Russia has paid the just satisfaction sums awarded by the Court.[61]

Next I wish to describe the case of *Broniowski v. Poland.*[62] The *Broniowski* case concerned the Polish State's continued failure to implement the applicant's "right to credit" under Polish legislation. This "right to credit" furnished compensation with respect to property abandoned by his family at the end of the Second World War in the territories "beyond the Bug River", as a result of the change of boundary between the former USSR and Poland.[63] The *Broniowski* application was chosen as a "pilot case" since at that time many similar applications were already pending before the

---

55. *See id.* ¶ 10.
56. *See id.* ¶ 15.
57. *See id.*
58. *See id.*
59. Press Release, European Court of Human Rights, Grand Chamber Judgement in the Case of Ilascu and Others v. Moldova and Russia (Jul. 8, 2004) http://cmiskp.echr.coe.int/tkp197/view.asp?action=html&documentId=800708&portal=hbkm&source=externalbydocnumber&table=F69A27FD8FB86142BF01C116 6DEA398649.
60. Council of Europe Adopts New Resolution in Ilascu Case (March 3, 2006), http://politicom.moldova.org/stiri/eng/10221/.
61. See *id.* (noting that the new resolution was an attempt to achieve progress in releasing the prisoners and thereby adhere to the Court's ruling).
62. Broniowski v. Poland, 2004-V Eur. Ct. H.R. 1.
63. *Id.* ¶¶ 11–12.

Court.[64] The Section relinquished jurisdiction in favour of the Grand Chamber and adjourned the remaining applications pending the outcome of the leading case.[65]

By adopting both the 1985 and 1997 Land Administration Acts, the Polish State reaffirmed its obligation to compensate the "Bug River claimants" and to incorporate into domestic law obligations it had taken upon itself by virtue of international treaties concluded in 1944.[66] However, the Polish authorities, by imposing successive limitations on the exercise of the applicant's right to compensation, and by resorting to practices which made it unenforceable in concrete terms, rendered that right illusory, and destroyed its very essence.[67] Moreover, the right was extinguished by legislation of December 2003 under which claimants in the applicant's position who had been awarded partial compensation (2% of the value of the property, in the applicant's case) lost their entitlement to additional compensation, whereas those who had never received any compensation were awarded an amount representing 15% of their entitlement.[68] This obviously raised an issue of discrimination.[69] In the light of these considerations, the European Court concluded that the applicant "had to bear a disproportionate and excessive burden which cannot be justified in terms of the legitimate general community interest pursued by the authorities."[70]

The Court was informed that there were roughly 80,000 potential applicants with analogous claims.[71] It concluded in the operative provisions of the judgment that the violation found had

> originated in a systemic problem connected with the malfunctioning of domestic legislation and practice caused by the failure to set up an effective mechanism to implement the "right to credit" of Bug River claimants; . . . the respondent State must, through appropriate legal measures and administrative practices, secure the implementation of the

---

64. *Id.* ¶ 5.
65. *Id.*
66. *Id.* ¶ 162.
67. *Id.* ¶ 173.
68. *Id.* ¶ 186.
69. *Id.* ¶ 110.
70. *Id.* ¶ 187.
71. *Id.* ¶ 193.

534   *AM. U. INT'L L. REV.*   [22:521

property right in question in respect of the remaining Bug River claimants or provide them with equivalent redress in lieu, in accordance with the principles of protection of property rights under Article 1 of Protocol No. 1.[72]

The Court reiterated that the violation of Article 1 of Protocol No.1 had originated in a widespread problem which resulted from deficiencies in the domestic legal order which affected a large number of people, and which might give rise in future to numerous, subsequent well-founded applications.[73] It decided to indicate the measures that the Polish State should take, under the supervision of the Committee of Ministers, and in accordance with the subsidiary character of the Convention, so as to avoid a large number of additional cases being referred to it.[74] It also decided that all similar applications—including future applications—should be adjourned pending the outcome of the leading case and the adoption of measures at the national level.[75] This is the first time that the Court has ruled in the operative provisions of a judgment on the general measures that a respondent State should take to remedy a systemic defect at the origin of the violation found.[76]

IV. HUMAN RIGHTS AND TERRORISM

Allow me now to briefly address the topical question of human rights and terrorism. Let me say first of all that I hope that it will have been obvious from what I have said that human rights law does not operate in a vacuum, but in a given context. It is an integral part of democratic society and a threat to that society will impact the way in which it is applied. The majority of the rights set out in the Convention are not absolute in that they may be curtailed in the wider interest of the community, to the extent strictly necessary and provided that this does not impose an excessive and disproportionate burden on individuals or a sector of the population. This could be formulated the other way round, that is that the individual exercising his civil liberties cannot be allowed to impose a disproportionate burden on the

---

72. *Id.* ¶ 200.
73. *Id.* ¶ 189.
74. *Id.* ¶190.
75. *Id.* ¶ 5.
76. *Id.* ¶ 193.

community. So essentially the Convention guarantees are applied in a context defined by the democratic society in which they function. This is just common sense. Human rights cannot be and should not be divorced from the practical day-to-day functioning of society.

The Strasbourg Court has consistently recognised the particular difficulties which combating terrorism creates for democratic societies.[77] It has accepted that the use of confidential information is essential in combating terrorist violence and the threat that organised terrorism poses to the lives of citizens and democratic society.[78] This does not mean however that the investigating authorities should be given *carte blanche* under Article 5 of the Convention to arrest suspects for questioning free from effective control by the domestic courts or by the Convention supervisory mechanism.[79] Again, in the context of Article 5 of the Convention, "the Contracting States cannot be asked to establish the reasonableness of the suspicion grounding the arrest of a suspected terrorist by disclosing the confidential sources of supporting information or even facts which would be susceptible of indicating such sources or their identity".[80] But the exigencies of the situation cannot justify stretching the notion of reasonableness to the point where the essence of the safeguard secured by Article 5, Section 1 (c) (requiring among other things "reasonable suspicion" of having committed an offence) is impaired.[81]

Democratic society acting in full conformity with the Convention is therefore not defenceless in the face of terrorism. It would run counter to the fundamental object and purpose of the Convention, for national authorities to be prevented from making a proportionate response to such threats in the interests of the safety of the community as a whole.

In saying this, one should never forget that the insidious undermining of fundamental rights is one of the dangers of terrorism. Limitations which may be possible within the margin of appreciation granted under the Convention must not be so broad as to impair the

---

77. Chadhal v. United Kingdom, 1996-V Eur. Ct. H.R. ¶ 79.
78. *Id.* ¶ 131.
79. *See id.*; *see also* Murray v. United Kingdom, 300 Eur. Ct. H.R. (ser. A) 1, 27 (1996).
80. Fox, Campbell & Hartley v. United Kingdom, 182 Eur. Ct. H.R. (ser. A) 1, 17 (1990).
81. *See id.* at 16–18.

very essence of the right in question; they must, in Strasbourg terms, also pursue a legitimate aim and bear a reasonable relationship of proportionality between the means employed and the aims sought to be achieved.[82] One question that needs to be asked in connection with exceptional measures taken to combat terrorism is whether there are techniques that can be employed which both accommodate legitimate security concerns and yet accord the individual a substantial measure of procedural justice.[83] Nor should it be possible for the national authorities to free themselves from effective control by the domestic courts, or ultimately international jurisdiction, simply by asserting that national security and terrorism are involved. At the same time "the Convention should not be applied in such a manner as to put disproportionate difficulties in the way of the police authorities of the Contracting States in taking effective measures to counter organised terrorism."[84]

There are moreover Convention rights which are absolute in nature and in respect of which no derogation is possible under Article 15 of the Convention.[85] Thus Article 3 prohibiting torture and inhuman or degrading treatment enshrines one of the most fundamental values of democratic society.[86] While the Strasbourg Court is well aware of the immense difficulties faced by States in protecting their communities from terrorist violence, even in these circumstances the Convention prohibits torture or inhuman or degrading treatment or punishment. Where substantial grounds have been shown for believing that an individual would face a real risk of being subjected to treatment contrary to Article 3 if removed to a particular receiving State, the responsibility of the Contracting State to safeguard him or her against such treatment may be engaged in the event of expulsion.

Let me turn to two other courts for a moment. In rendering his court's decision of September 1999 that physical interrogation

---

82. *See generally* Chadhal v. United Kingdom, 1996-V Eur. Ct. H.R. ¶¶ 135, 136.

83. *See, e.g., id.* ¶ 131 (illustrating that there are ways to both accommodate concerns about the security of intelligence information and give the individual procedural justice).

84. *Fox, Campbell & Hartley*, 182 Eur. Ct. H.R. (ser A.) at 17.

85. European Convention on Human Rights, *supra* note 13, art. 15.

86. *Id.* art. 3.

techniques were unlawful even in ticking-bomb situations, Justice Aharon Barak, the President of the Israeli Supreme Court, said this:

> We are aware that this decision does not ease dealing with [the harsh] reality. This is the destiny of democracy, as not all means are acceptable to it, and not all practices are open to it. Although a democracy must often fight with one hand tied behind its back, it nonetheless has the upper hand. Preserving the rule of law and recognition of an individual's liberty constitutes an important component in its understanding of security. At the end of the day they strengthen its spirit and strength and allow it to overcome its difficulties.[87]

Given the particular context existing in Israel, at the time and unfortunately still today, his words carry special weight.

In the same vein, Judge Anand, former Chief Justice of the Supreme Court of India, when confronted with the deaths and torture of alleged terrorists in police custody, had this to say:

> [The] challenge of terrorism must be met with innovative ideas and approach. State terrorism is no answer to combat terrorism. State terrorism would only provide legitimacy to 'terrorism'. That would be bad for the State, the community and above all for the rule of law. The State must, therefore, ensure that various agencies deployed by it for combating terrorism act within the bounds of law and not become law unto themselves.[88]

CONCLUSION

So my conclusion is that human rights are not anti-democratic; terrorism is anti-democratic; arbitrary interference with individual rights and freedoms is anti-democratic; democracy without the rule of law is anti-democratic as is, self-evidently, the rule of law without democracy. In their wisdom the authors of the European Convention on Human Rights over fifty-five years ago constructed a framework for the effective operation of democracy and the rule of law based on minimum standards that are now in principle shared throughout

---

87. HCJ 5100/94 Public Committee Against Torture v. Israel [1999] IsrSC 37, http://www.hamoked.org.il/items/260_eng.pdf.

88. Shri D.K. Basu v. State of West Bengal (1997) 1 S.C.C. 416, 418.

538   *AM. U. INT'L L. REV.*   [22:521

forty-six European States. That framework, evolving as it has done through the Strasbourg case-law, remains as relevant today as it was then. It still represents a more long-term but ultimately more effective means of protecting democracy than short-term, disproportionately repressive measures which may purport to do the same, but which in the end court the risk of undermining the foundations of democratic society. In the *Klass* case in 1978, the Court warned against the danger of undermining or even destroying democracy on the ground of defending it.[89] That is a warning that we would all do well to keep in sight, if we wish to preserve a living democracy, one which is neither under-protected nor over-protected.

---

89. Klass v. Germany, 28 Eur. Ct. H.R. (ser. A) 1, 23 (1978).

[10]

Relieving the Court of Its Success? – Protocol No. 14 to the European Convention on Human Rights

By Tilmann Laubner

On 13 May 2004, the Council of Ministers (CM) of the Council of Europe (CoE) adopted Protocol No. 14[1] to the Convention for the Protection of Human Rights and Fundamental Freedoms[2] and opened it for signature by Member States of the CoE which are parties to the Convention.[3] This article provides an overview and an initial evaluation of the Protocol's main provisions.

A. Introduction

I. Background

Not long after the entry into force of Protocol No. 11 to the Convention on 1 November 1998,[4] first "distress calls" could be heard from amidst the Euro-

---

[1] Protocol No. 14 to the Convention for the Protection of Human Rights and Fundamental Freedoms amending the Control System of the Convention, 13 May 2004, ETS No. 194 (Protocol No. 14).

[2] Convention for the Protection of Human Rights and Fundamental Freedoms, 4 November 1950, ETS No. 5 (Convention) as amended by Protocol No. 11, 1 November 1998, ETS No. 155 (Protocol No. 11). For an unofficial consolidated version of the Convention as amended by Protocol No. 14 see CoE (Directorate General of Human Rights), Applying and Supervising the ECHR, Guaranteeing the Effectiveness of the European Convention on Human Rights: Collected Texts, 2004, Appendix I, 85.

[3] Protocol No. 14 (note 1), Art. 18.

[4] See *Rudolf Bernhardt,* Reform of the Control Machinery under the European Convention on Human Rights, American Journal of International Law, vol. 89, 1995, 145; *Iain Cameron,* Protocol 11 to the European Convention on Human Rights: The European Court of Human Rights as a Constitutional Court?, Yearbook of European Law, vol. 15, 1995, 219; *Andrew Drzemczewski,* The European Human Rights Convention: Protocol No. 11 – Entry into Force and First Year of Application, Human Rights Law Journal (HRLJ), vol. 21, 2000, 1.

pean Court of Human Rights (Court).[5] Measured by its caseload, the Strasbourg Court, newly set up as a single, full-time institution, already seemed to be on the way to falling victim to its own success.[6] More than half of today's 45 State Parties have acceded to the Convention since 1988 (19 of them between 1989 and November 1998), raising the number of potential applicants before the Court to more than 800 million. Between 1990 and 2000, the number of individual applications brought before the European Commission of Human Rights and the Court had risen by over 500 %.[7] In 2003, approximately 38,500 new applications were lodged, more than 60 % of them coming from Eastern and Central European States,[8] raising the number of applications pending to approximately 65,000 at the end of that year.[9] Clearly, this development had not been anticipated by Protocol No. 11, which originated in proposals first submitted in the 1980s and had been opened for signature in 1994.[10] However, it threatens to

---

[5] *Cf.* President *Luzius Wildhaber,* A Constitutional Future for the European Court of Human Rights?, HRLJ, vol. 23, 2002, 161, 163. Also see European Court of Human Rights (ECtHR), *Broniowski v. Poland,* Judgment of 22 June 2004, para. 193, available at: http://hudoc.echr.coe.int/hudoc/; and *Herbert Petzold,* Epilogue: la réforme continue, in: *Paul Mahoney/Franz Matscher/Herbert Petzold/Luzius Wildhaber* (eds.), Protecting Human Rights: The European Perspective – Studies in Memory of Rolv Ryssdal, 2000, 1571, 1573.

[6] *Cf. Céline Husson/Nicolas Riou,* Statistiques et projections – L'évolution du nombre de requêtes présentées à Strasbourg: la Cour européenne des droits de l'homme, victime de son succès?, Revue Universelle des Droits de l'Homme (RUDH), vol. 14, 2002, 259; *Christian Tomuschat,* Quo Vadis Argentatorum? The Success Story of the ECHR – And a Few Dark Stains, HRLJ, vol. 13, 1992, 401.

[7] *Cf.* ECtHR, Survey of Activities 2003, 34, available at: http://echr.coe.int/Eng/EDocs/2003surveycourt.pdf (Survey). In comparison to these figures, inter-State applications under Art. 33 of the Convention do not contribute significantly to the Court's workload.

[8] *Id.,* 34 *et seq.*

[9] CoE, Explanatory Report to Protocol No. 14 to the Convention for the Protection of Human Rights and Fundamental Freedoms, amending the Control System of the Convention, para. 7, available at: http://conventions.coe.int/Treaty/EN/Reports/Html/194.htm (Explanatory Report).

[10] *Cf.* Statement of President *Luzius Wildhaber,* quoted in: *Ingrid Siess-Scherz,* Bestandsaufnahme: Der EGMR nach der Erweiterung des Europarates, Europäische Grundrechte-Zeitschrift (EuGRZ), vol. 30, 2003, 100, 103; *Norbert Paul Engel,* Status, Ausstattung und Personalhoheit des Inter-Amerikanischen und des Europäischen Gerichtshofs für Menschenrechte, EuGRZ, vol. 30, 2003, 122, 127 *et seq.*

put the Court in a situation where it will no longer be able to meet the standards it set up itself with respect to the length of proceedings before national courts.[11]

II. Main Challenges to the Court

Two main factors deserve to be singled out in analyzing the reasons[12] for the Court's excessive caseload.[13] First to be named is the huge number of 'unmeritorious' applications, *i.e.* individual applications which do not reach the stage of proceedings on the merits. In 2003, 96 % of all applications dealt with by the Court have either been rejected as inadmissible (93 %) or struck off the Court's list of cases under Articles 35 and 37 of the Convention.[14] Of the applications found to be admissible and decided by judgment of the Court in 2003, some 60 %[15] pertained to so-called repetitive or 'clone' cases, making this the second most prominent factor for the situation the Court currently faces. The issues raised by such cases are identical or very similar to ones already decided by the Court as they are rooted in specific structural deficits within certain Contracting States.[16] Repetitive or 'clone' cases may thus be defined as "cases in which the

---

[11] *Cf. Patricia Egli,* Zur Reform des Rechtsschutzsystems der Europäischen Menschenrechtskonvention, Zeitschrift für ausländisches öffentliches Recht und Völkerrecht, vol. 64, 2004, 759, 760. On length of proceedings before the Court see Evaluation Group, Report of the Evaluation Group to the Committee of Ministers on the European Court of Human Rights, 27 September 2001, CoE Doc. EG Court(2001)1, para. 31.

[12] For an in-depth analysis, see *id.,* paras. 22 *et seq.*

[13] *Cf.* Reflection Group on the Reinforcement of the Human Rights Protection Mechanism (CDDH-GDR), Activity Report, 15 June 2001, CoE Doc. CDDH-GDR (2001)010, 4.

[14] In absolute numbers: 17,272, as opposed to 753 applications declared admissible, see Survey (note 7), 33–34.

[15] Explanatory Report (note 9), para. 7.

[16] In this regard see also Resolution (2004)3 of the Committee of Ministers on Judgments Revealing an Underlying Systemic Problem, 12 May 2004, in which the CM invited the Court "to identify in its judgments [...] what it considers to be an underlying systemic problem and the source of that problem, in particular when it is likely to give rise to numerous applications, so as to assist States in finding the appropriate solution and the Committee of Ministers in supervising the execution of judgments." As to the implementation of this resolution see *Broniowski v. Poland* (note 5), paras. 190 *et seq.;* and ECtHR, *Sejdovic v. Italy,* Judgment of 10 November 2004, para. 46 and para. 2 of the *dispositif,* available at: http://hudoc.echr.coe.int/hudoc/. On the former judgment see *Marten Breuer,* Urteilsfolgen bei strukturellen Problemen – Das erste "Piloturteil" des EGMR, EuGRZ, vol. 31, 2004, 445.

same shortcoming of the domestic situation resulted in further violations of the Convention."[17]

III. Process Leading to the Adoption of Protocol No. 14

Alarmed by the Court's increasing workload, the European Ministerial Conference on Human Rights, held in Rome on 3–4 November 2000 on the occasion of the 50th anniversary of the adoption of the Convention, called on the CM to explore possibilities and options "with a view to ensuring the effectiveness of the Court in the light of this new situation."[18] As a follow up, the Ministers' Deputies, in February 2001, assigned a prominent "Evaluation Group"[19] in order to develop proposals on guaranteeing continued effectiveness of the Court. The Evaluation Group received additional input from a "Reflection Group" set up by the CoE's Steering Committee on Human Rights (CDDH)[20] and submitted its report to the CM in November 2001.[21] Subsequently, the CDDH was instructed to further pursue the matter on the basis of the recommendations made by the Evaluation Group and to propose specific measures involving amendment of the Convention.

---

[17] CoE Doc. CDDH-GDR (2003)001, 4, quoted in: *Siess-Scherz* (note 10), 101, fn. 13; *cf.* Reflection Group (note 13), Appendix II, para. 16; Evaluation Group (note 11), para. 60(c); CDDH, Interim Report of the CDDH to the Committee of Ministers, Guaranteeing the Long-Term Effectiveness of the European Court of Human Rights, 18 October 2002, CoE Doc. CM(2002)146, paras. 67 *et seq.* (CDDH Interim Report 2002). Other terms used in this regard are "straightforward" (*id.*, para. 74) or "manifestly well-founded" cases (CDDH, Guaranteeing the Long-Term Effectiveness of the European Court of Human Rights, Final Report Containing Proposals of the CDDH, 4 April 2003, CoE Doc. CM(2003)55, Proposal B.1 (CDDH Final Report 2003)). Cases regarding the length of civil proceedings in Italy may be named as a classic example for cases of this category. Further see *Wildhaber* (note 5), 164.

[18] Declaration of the Ministerial Conference, quoted in: CDDH, Guaranteeing the Long-Term Effectiveness of the European Court of Human Rights, Final Activity Report, 13 April 2004, CoE Doc. CDDH(2004)004 Final, para. 2.

[19] The Group was composed of *Justin Harman*, Permanent Representative of Ireland to the CoE, Chairman of the Ministers' Deputies Liaison Committee with the Court (in the Chair), *Luzius Wildhaber*, President of the Court, and *Hans Christian Krüger*, Deputy Secretary General of the CoE.

[20] Reflection Group (note 13).

[21] Evaluation Group (note 11).

The CM set the frame for subsequent reform efforts by defining the following priorities: first, "preventing violations at [the] national level and improving domestic remedies," second, "optimizing the effectiveness of the filtering and subsequent processing of applications," and third, "improving and accelerating execution of judgments of the Court."[22] However, it was clear that the substantive rights guaranteed by the Convention and its Protocols should remain untouched. Likewise, the right of individual application, embodied in Article 34 of the Convention, was to be preserved "in its essence" as it lay "at the heart of the Strasbourg machinery."[23]

The priorities identified by the CM required reform efforts to be implemented in various fields. Thus, the CDDH's work, which had been accompanied by various actors in- and outside the CoE institutional framework, not only resulted in the adoption of Protocol No. 14.

The CM also adopted a set of non-binding instruments requesting the CoE Member States to take measures at the national level in order to prevent and redress human rights violations by bringing national legislation and administration in conformity with Convention standards as well as by making findings as to violations and, ultimately, remedying those.[24] By doing so, the CM took account of the principle of subsidiarity enshrined in Articles 1 and 19 of the

---

[22] CM, Declaration on "The Court of Human Rights for Europe", 7 November 2002, available at: https://wcm.coe.int/ViewDoc.jsp?id=320197&Lang=en, para. 14.

[23] Evaluation Group (note 11), para. 41; *cf.* CM, Declaration on the Protection of Human Rights in Europe, "Guaranteeing the Long-Term Effectiveness of the European Court of Human Rights", 8 November 2001, CoE Doc. CM(2001)164, para. 5.

[24] CM, Recommendation (2004)4 on the European Convention on Human Rights in University Education and Professional Training, 12 May 2004; Recommendation (2004)5 on the Verification of the Compatibility of Draft Laws, Existing Laws and Administrative Practice with the Standards Laid Down by the European Convention on Human Rights, 12 May 2004; Recommendation (2004)6 on the Improvement of Domestic Remedies, 12 May 2004; Resolution (2004)3 (note 16). See also Recommendation (2000) 2 on the Re-Examination or Reopening of Certain Cases at Domestic Level Following Judgments of the European Court of Human Rights, 19 January 2000; as well as Recommendation (2002)13 on the Publication and Dissemination in the Member States of the Text of the European Convention on Human Rights and of the Case-Law of the European Court of Human Rights, 18 December 2002; Resolution (2002)58 on the Publication and Dissemination of the Case-Law of the European Court of Human Rights, 18 December 2002; and Resolution (2002)59 Concerning the Practice in Respect of Friendly Settlements, 18 December 2002.

Convention, which allots responsibility for the protection of human rights first and foremost to the State Parties.[25]

Furthermore, the Court itself, already in November 2003, had taken steps on the procedural level by amending its Rules of Court based on the recommendations submitted by an internal working party established in 1999.[26] *Inter alia,* it abolished the so called "warning letters" to those whose applications are likely to be rejected as inadmissible.[27] Moreover, it substituted formal decisions on the inadmissibility of applications taken by a three-judge-committee under Article 28 of the Convention by a mere informal letter lacking any further reasoning.[28]

Finally, the CM for its part increased the Court's budget for the years 2003 to 2005.[29]

However, the present article will focus on the measures requiring amendment of the Convention, as these lie at the core of this round of reform.

B. Amendments to the Convention

"Considering the urgent need to amend certain provisions of the Convention in order to maintain and improve the efficiency of the control system for the

---

[25] Generally, see *Herbert Petzold,* The Convention and the Principle of Subsidiarity, in: *Ronald St. J. Macdonald/Franz Matscher/Herbert Petzold* (eds.), The European System for the Protection of Human Rights, 1993, 63.

[26] CoE, Three Years' Work for the Future: Final Report of the Working Party on Working Methods of the European Court of Human Rights, 2002 (Working Party Final Report); Rules of Court, as of November 2003, available at: http://echr.coe.int/Eng/BasicTexts.htm.

[27] Critical in this regard *Christoph Grabenwarter,* Zur Zukunft des Europäischen Gerichtshofs für Menschenrechte, EuGRZ, vol. 30, 2003, 174, 175 *et seq.* Also see *Siess-Scherz* (note 10), 104.

[28] Rules of Court (note 27), Art. 53 para. 2. As to the wording of such a letter see Working Party Final Report (note 26), 85 *et seq.,* reprinted also in: EuGRZ, vol. 30, 2003, 180. It seems difficult, however, to reconcile such practice with Art. 45 para. 1 of the Convention. Critically in this regard and further on the measures taken by the Court, see *Siess-Scherz* (note 10), 103 *et seq.;* and *Brigitte L. Ohms,* Bewertung des Diskussionsstands über die Entlastung des Europäischen Gerichtshofes für Menschenrechte, EuGRZ, vol. 30, 2003, 141, 145 *et seq.*

[29] See *Jeroen Schokkenbroek,* Überblick über die Arbeit des Europarates betreffend die Reform des Gerichtshofes, EuGRZ, vol. 30, 2003, 134, 135 *et seq.*

long term,"[30] Protocol No. 14 contains a number of changes pertaining to the individual application procedure before the Court as well as to the stage of the execution of judgments. It lies in the very nature of a drafting process that not all proposals that were made have found their way into the final text. Nonetheless, having a glance at some of the suggestions that have not been sustained may provide useful guidance in analyzing those that were more successful.

Among the proposals of a more general character that were rejected at an early stage was the idea of 'regional courts of first instance.'[31] It was feared that their establishment would bear the risk of diverging standards and case-law along with associated high costs.[32] The same fate ultimately awaited the proposition to introduce a procedure of preliminary rulings at the request of national courts comparable to that before the European Court of Justice under Article 234 of the EC Treaty.[33] At least in the short term, this proposal was deemed to result in additional rather than less work for the Court as was also believed for an expansion of the Court's competence to give advisory opinions under Articles 47 to 49 of the Convention.[34]

I. Filtering of Applications

"Optimizing the effectiveness of the filtering [...] of applications," was one of the priorities identified by the CM. Currently, an application upon receipt will be preprocessed by the Registry before the President of one of the four Sec-

---

[30] Protocol No. 14 (note 1), preambular para. 5.

[31] For a more detailed discussion on this subject, see *Jiry Malenovsky,* Faut-il révolutionner le système actuel? Pour et contre l'institution de cours régionales, RUDH, vol. 14, 2002, 303.

[32] Explanatory Report (note 9), para. 34; Evaluation Group (note 11), para. 83; Reflection Group (note 13), para. 39; *cf.* CDDH Interim Report 2002 (note 17), para. 21.

[33] On this matter see *Dominique Ritleng,* La réforme de la CJCE, modèle pour une réforme de la Cour européenne des droits de l'homme?, RUDH, vol. 14, 2002, 288, 292 *et seq.; Florence Benoît-Rohmer,* Les perspectives de réformes à long terme de la Cour européenne des droits de l'homme: certiorari versus renvoi préjudiciel, RUDH, vol. 14, 2002, 313. Consolidated Version of the Treaty Establishing the European Community, 24 December 2002, O.J. C 325/33 (EC Treaty).

[34] Explanatory Report (note 9), para. 34; *cf.* Evaluation Group (note 11), para. 84; CDDH Interim Report 2002 (note 17), para. 14; Amnesty International *et al.,* Joint Response to Proposals to Ensure the Future Effectiveness of the European Court of Human Rights, AI Index IOR 61/008/2003, para. 14.

tions of the Court will nominate a member of the Section to function as judge-rapporteur. The latter will examine and prepare the case and will then – depending on the complexity of the case – seize one of the Court's committees of three judges or one of the Chambers consisting of seven judges. To this panel, he or she will submit a proposal as to the further proceedings.

When faced with the task of reducing a court's workload and increasing its capacities to filter out 'unmeritorious' applications, the natural reaction would be to increase the personnel involved. And indeed, Draft Protocol No. 14 as adopted by the CDDH in April 2004 authorized the CM to modify the number of judges upon request of the plenary Court.[35] This option was eliminated from the final text only upon last minute intervention by the CoE's Parliamentary Assembly (PA), which was concerned about inequalities between the State Parties if additional judges were to be appointed in respect of only some of them.[36]

1. Single-Judge Formation

However, Protocol No. 14 as finally adopted nevertheless increases the number of units involved in filtering out 'unmeritorious' applications. This is done mainly by reducing the number of actors working on a single case during the admissibility stage: Article 26 as revised by Protocol No. 14 will allow the Court to not only sit in committees of three, Chambers of seven and a Grand Chamber of seventeen judges, but also in single-judge formation.[37] The competence of single judges will largely equate that of three-judge-committees under the current Article 28 of the Convention. Thus, according to revised Article 27, he or she may – by means of a final decision – declare inadmissible or strike out of the Court's list an application "where such a decision can be taken without

---

[35] Draft Protocol No. 14 to the Convention for the Protection of Human Rights and Fundamental Freedoms, adopted by the CDDH, 5–8 April 2004, Art. 1, CoE Doc. CDDH(2004)004 Final, Addendum I. Under this the Court was supposed to indicate both the number of additional judges as well as the State Parties in respect of which they were to be elected.

[36] PA, Opinion No. 251 on Draft Protocol No. 14 to the Convention for the Protection of Human Rights and Fundamental Freedoms, Amending the Control System of the Convention, 18 April 2004, para. 7 (PA Opinion No. 251). Also see *Grabenwarter* (note 27), 175. As to proposals for stand-by judges see Evaluation Group (note 11), para. 87; CDDH Interim Report 2002 (note 17), 8, para. 19.

[37] Protocol No. 14 (note 1), Art. 6.

further examination,"[38] *i.e.* in, as the official Explanatory Report puts it, "clear-cut cases," where the application's inadmissibility is "manifest from the outset."[39] Applications not fulfilling these prerequisites shall be referred to either a committee or a Chamber. However, judges may not sit as single judge in cases to which their State party is the respondent party.

The single-judge arrangement has been subject to critique especially by several NGOs.[40] Indeed, the final character of any such inadmissibility decision – which previously could only be effected by unanimous decision of three judges – combined with the vagueness of the supposedly restricting criterion and that of the new admissibility provision introduced by Protocol No. 14,[41] warrant special scrutiny as regards the Court's future practice. The filtering capacities released by introducing the single-judge formation will have to make up for the loss of confidence applicants so far could have in collegial decisions derived from different judicial and national perspectives. Whether this will be the case remains to be seen, given the fact that most of the work in filtering applications currently is done by the registry rather than the judges.[42]

2. 'Rapporteurs'

In addition to the single-judge formation, Protocol No. 14 seeks to enhance the Court's filtering capabilities by introducing a new category of personnel called 'rapporteurs.'[43] They will replace the legal secretaries introduced by Protocol No. 11 under current Article 25 of the Convention. The purpose of the rapporteurs will be to assist the single judges. As their designation suggests, they will not only do the preparatory "pre-judicial" work of registry case-lawyers but will also relieve the judges sitting as single judges of their

---

[38] Protocol No. 14 (note 1), Art. 7.

[39] Explanatory Report (note 9), para. 67.

[40] Amnesty International *et al.* (note 34), para. 7; Amnesty International, Comments on the Interim Activity Report: Guaranteeing the Long-Term Effectiveness of the European Court of Human Rights, AI Index IOR 61/005/2004, para. 44.

[41] See, *infra,* Sect. B. III.

[42] CDDH Interim Report 2002 (note 17), paras. 25, 27. Also see ECtHR, Response of the European Court of Human Rights to the CDDH Interim Activity Report Prepared Following the 46th Plenary Administrative Session, 2 February 2004, CoE Doc. CDDH-GDR(2004)001, para. 5, note 2 (ECtHR Response).

[43] Art. 24 para. 2 of the Convention as revised by Protocol No. 14 (note 1), Art. 4.

rapporteur functions. These currently form the most labor-intensive part of the judges' filtering work. Thus, rapporteurs will provide a first legal analysis of the case-file and draft a rapporteur's note which will be submitted directly to the single judge for decision.[44] Ideally, judges should be assisted by rapporteurs with knowledge of the language and legal system of the respective respondent party.

The institution of 'rapporteurs' is a remnant of the protracted debate on the question whether a special filtering unit should be established in Strasbourg. While a return to a two-tier system as had existed before Protocol No. 11 entered into force was not only considered too expensive but, above all, politically unacceptable,[45] the Court itself throughout the drafting process strongly advocated the creation of a separate filtering body within the structure of the Court.[46] Such division was thought to be composed of "assessors" forming a second category of personnel vested with judicial powers, apart from the elected judges.[47] However, such a proposal was viewed very critically from the beginning by the CDDH as well as by external observers – and rightly so: It would have posed serious questions as to the legitimacy of (in-)admissibility decisions and, furthermore, would have run counter to the objective of Protocol No. 11 to render the Convention's control system in general and the individual application procedure in particular fully judicial and to have decisions taken by a single body composed of elected judges.[48]

Furnishing non-judicial personnel with rapporteur functions might be questionable enough, bearing in mind the influence rapporteur's notes currently have on actual admissibility decisions of the Court and viewed against the background provided by the new single-judge formation. In this regard it shall only be noted here that the rapporteurs will "function under the authority of the President of the Court" but at the same time will "form part of the Court's registry."[49]

---

[44] Explanatory Report (note 9), paras. 58, 62; ECtHR Response (note 42), para. 9.

[45] *Cf.* Reflection Group (note 13), para. 40; CDDH Interim Report 2002 (note 17), 2.

[46] ECtHR Response (note 42), para. 7; *cf.* Evaluation Group (note 11), para. 98.

[47] Evaluation Group (note 11), para. 98; *cf.* ECtHR Response (note 42), para. 7. On further variants see *Ohms* (note 28), 146.

[48] *Cf.* CDDH Interim Report 2002 (note 17), paras. 23 *et seq.;* Amnesty International *et al.* (note 34), para. 7.

[49] Art. 24 para. 2 of the Convention as revised by Protocol No. 14 (note 1), Art. 4.

The latter is "provided by the Secretary General of the CoE,"[50] a fact which has occasionally given rise to critical observations.[51]

II. Subsequent Processing of Applications

1. The Exception Becomes the Rule: Joint Decisions on the Admissibility and Merits of Individual Applications

Current Article 29 para. 3 of the Convention generally requires decisions on the admissibility of an individual application to be taken separately from the judgment on the merits. Only in exceptional cases may the Court decide otherwise.[52] Under Article 29 para. 1 of the Convention as revised by Article 9 of Protocol No. 14, the current exception will become the rule: In Chamber proceedings on individual applications, "[t]he decision on admissibility may be taken separately."[53] However, this amendment will (merely) "legalize" and adapt the Convention to an actual practice that recently has developed in the Court under Rule 54A (1) of the Rules of Court, particularly with regard to cases on length of proceedings and other subjects of established case-law of the Court.[54] Bearing in mind that according to Article 45 of the Convention, admis-

---

[50] CoE, Explanatory Report on Protocol No. 11 to the Convention for the Protection of Human Rights and Fundamental Freedoms, Restructuring the Control Machinery Established thereby, para. 66, available at: http://conventions.coe.int/Treaty/en/Reports/Html/155.htm (Explanatory Report on Protocol No. 11).

[51] *Engel* (note 10), 132 *et seq.; Grabenwarter* (note 27), 175. *Engel* has been countered by Deputy Secretary General of the CoE *Maud de Boer-Buquicchio,* Klarstellung zum Status des Europäischen Gerichtshofs für Menschenrechte und seiner Beziehungen zum Europarat, EuGRZ, vol. 30, 2003, 561 *et seq.* On the whole issue see *Paul Mahoney,* Separation of Powers in the Council of Europe: The Status of the European Court of Human Rights vis-à-vis the Authorities of the Council of Europe, HRLJ, vol. 24, 2003, 152.

[52] According to the Explanatory Report on Protocol No. 11 (note 50), para. 78, "[t]he separate decision on admissibility is important for the parties when considering whether they should start friendly settlement negotiations." On amendments to the friendly settlement procedure see, *infra,* Sect. B. II. 3.

[53] As to proceedings before committees of the Court see, *infra,* Sect. B. II. 2. The principle of the taking of separate decisions by Chambers will be upheld with respect to the admissibility and merits of inter-State applications, see Art. 29 para. 2 of the Convention as revised by Protocol No. 14 (note 1), Art. 9.

[54] *Cf.* Explanatory Report (note 9), para. 73; *Siess-Scherz* (note 10), 105. Also see, *infra,* Sect. B. II. 2.

sibility decisions must be reasoned, omitting the stage of separate admissibility decisions appears useful in order to expedite and streamline the individual applications procedure considerably.[55]

2. Simplified Procedure for "Manifestly Well-Founded Applications"

In order to gain control in particular over the large number of repetitive or 'clone' cases, Protocol No. 14 will "supplement existing procedures for manifestly ill-founded applications with a simplified procedure for manifestly well-founded applications."[56] To this end, amended Article 28 para. 1 lit. b of the Convention will empower committees of the Court to

> declare [an individual application] admissible and render at the same time a judgment on the merits, if the underlying question in the case concerning the interpretation or the application of the Convention or the Protocols thereto is already the subject of well-established case-law of the Court.[57]

Consequently, the competence to deliver decisions on the merits will no longer be reserved to the Court's Chambers consisting of seven judges, but will be extended to its committees of three judges. Under current Article 28 of the Convention, committees are confined to inadmissibility decisions in clear-cut cases. A further integral part of the new simplified procedure is the principle of joint decisions on the admissibility and merits of individual applications, which has already been referred to above.

These amendments promise to reduce both the time and the judicial capacity invested in a single repetitive or 'clone' case.[58] Joining a number of similar cases for decision might even add further to these positive effects.[59]

The Court's competence to resort to the new simplified procedure will depend on whether the questions underlying the case are "subject of well-

---

[55] *Cf. Egli* (note 11), 782; *Grabenwarter* (note 27), 177.

[56] CDDH Final Report 2003 (note 17), Proposal B.1.

[57] Art. 28 para. 1 lit. b of the Convention as amended by Protocol No. 14 (note 1), Art. 8. As to the parallels with proceedings before the German Constitutional Court under Sect. 93 lit. c of the German Law on the Federal Constitutional Court (*Bundesverfassungsgerichtsgesetz*), see *Klaus Stoltenberg,* Neuere Vorschläge zur Reform des EGMR aus dem Kreis der Mitgliedstaaten, EuGRZ, vol. 30, 2003, 139, 140.

[58] Also see CDDH Final Report 2003 (note 17), Proposal B.1.

[59] *Ohms* (note 28), 147.

established case-law."[60] According to the official Explanatory Report, this will normally refer to case-law which has consistently been applied by a Chamber but in exceptional cases may also relate to a single decision on a question of principle, particularly if rendered by the Grand Chamber.[61]

Committee decisions under new Article 28 para. 1 lit. b of the Convention must be taken by unanimous vote[62] and will be final. Due to the nature of the cases, they would not qualify for referral to the Grand Chamber under Article 43 of the Convention anyhow.

Two aspects are worth mentioning with regard to the position of the respondent State under the new procedure. Firstly, the respondent State may well challenge the applicability of the new procedure, but may not veto it.[63] Secondly, the new procedure, as a "by-product" of entrusting decisions on the merits to committees, will deviate from the principle of mandatory participation in all decisions on the merits by the judge elected with respect to the respondent State. This principle will continue to apply only to Chamber and Grand Chamber proceedings.[64] Instead, new Article 28 para. 3 of the Convention will provide the committees with the possibility to invite the 'national' judge of the respondent State, if not a regular member of the committee already, to replace one of its members at any stage of the proceedings "having regard to all relevant factors, including whether that Party has contested the application of the [summary] procedure."[65]

As has already been stated, the new simplified procedure promises to release time as well as capacities and thus to significantly reduce the workload of the judges of the Court. The registry of the Court has estimated that it could affect

---

[60] *Cf., supra*, Sect. B. II. 1.

[61] Explanatory Report (note 9), para. 68.

[62] Unanimity will be required on each aspect of the decision. Otherwise the Chamber procedure under Art. 29 of the Convention will apply; see *id.*, para. 69.

[63] *Id.*

[64] Current Art. 27 para. 2 in combination with Arts. 29 *et seq.* of the Convention.

[65] This latter provision has raised some concerns of being both detrimental to the Court's outside appearance of independence, and unnecessary considering the special nature of the cases concerned, see Amnesty International (note 40), paras. 22 *et seq.; cf.* PA, Committee on Legal Affairs and Human Rights, Report on Draft Protocol No. 14 to the Convention for the Protection of Human Rights and Fundamental Freedoms, Amending the Control System of the Convention, Explanatory Memorandum, 23 April 2004, CoE Doc. 10147, para. 36, which voiced concerns about the State Party being given "too prominent a place."

more than 50 % of the cases currently dealt with by a Chamber.[66] However, it remains to be hoped that the State Parties will not thwart this potential by unreasonably challenging the procedure's applicability.

In the context of releasing judicial capacities, note should also be taken of the CM's authority under new Article 26 para. 2 of the Convention to reduce by unanimous decision and for a fixed period the number of judges of the Chambers from seven to five if so requested by the plenary Court.[67]

3. Friendly Settlements

The benefit of the friendly settlement procedure under the Convention is not undoubted.[68] However, during the drafting process leading to the adoption of Protocol No. 14, a recently increasing practice was noted of resolving cases before the Court by means of friendly settlement between the individual complainant and the respondent State, particularly in the context of repetitive cases and other cases where questions of principle or changes in domestic law are not involved.[69]

Protocol No. 14 thus seeks to facilitate the conclusion of friendly settlements in several ways. In a first step, the relevant procedure will be merged into a single consolidated provision (new Article 39 of the Convention). Second, the Court's obligation to place itself at the disposal of the parties as a mediator will no longer be restricted to the post-admissibility stage but will extend to any stage of the proceedings. Such adaptation will become necessary as the imple-

---

[66] However, for the sake of completeness, it has also projected that the procedure would not significantly alleviate the workload currently weighing on the registry, see CDDH Final Report 2003 (note 17), Proposal B.1.

[67] See Protocol No. 14 (note 1), Art. 6; and Explanatory Report (note 9), para. 63.

[68] *E.g., Vincent Berger,* Le règlement amiable devant la Cour européenne des Droits de l'Homme, in: *Franz Matscher/Herbert Petzold* (eds.), Protecting Human Rights: The European Dimension – Studies in Honour of Gérard J. Wiarda, 1988, 55, 59.

[69] Explanatory Report (note 9), para. 93; CM, Resolution (2002)59 Concerning the Practice in Respect of Friendly Settlements, 18 December 2002; *cf.* Evaluation Group (note 11), para. 62. Also see Explanatory Report on Protocol No. 11 (note 50), para. 94; and *Ohms* (note 28), 147.

mentation of new Articles 28 and 29 of the Convention most likely will lead to far fewer separate admissibility decisions which currently trigger the friendly settlement procedure.[70] Third, future Article 39 para. 4 of the Convention will expressly subject friendly settlement agreements to the supervision of the CM. Recently, the Court had adopted a practice of endorsing friendly settlements through judgments instead of decisions in order to render Article 46 para. 2 of the Convention applicable. This practice not only runs counter the current wording of Article 39, but has also been recognized as hampering friendly settlements due to the negative connotations a formal judgment of the Court often has for respondent States.[71] While it is to be hoped that a strengthened friendly settlement procedure will reduce the Court's workload, it must of course also be ensured that it does not work to the applicant's disadvantage.[72]

III. Introduction of a New Admissibility Criterion

Throughout the drafting process, no other issue has generated as much debate as has the new admissibility criterion to be inserted into new Article 35 para. 3 lit. b of the Convention.[73] It received opposition from almost all sides including members of the CDDH itself,[74] the Court,[75] the PA,[76] State Parties[77] and NGOs.[78]

---

[70] CDDH Final Report 2003 (note 17), Proposal B. 3; Explanatory Report (note 9), para. 92.

[71] Explanatory Report (note 9), para. 94; *cf. Ohms* (note 28), 147.

[72] *Cf.* Committee on Legal Affairs and Human Rights (note 65), para. 52.

[73] See Protocol No. 14 (note 1), Art. 12.

[74] *Cf.* CDDH Final Report 2003 (note 17), Proposal B. 4, fn. 2.

[75] ECtHR Response (note 42), para. 24, note 5.

[76] PA Opinion No. 251 (note 36), para. 11; *cf.* CDDH, Guaranteeing the Long-Term Effectiveness of the European Court of Human Rights, Interim Activity Report, 26 November 2003, CoE Doc. CDDH(2003)026 Addendum I Final, para. 26 (CDDH Interim Activity Report 2003).

[77] *Cf.* CDDH Interim Activity Report 2003 (note 76), para. 33.

[78] Amnesty International *et al.* (note 34), paras. 8 *et seq.;* Amnesty International (note 40), paras. 33 *et seq.; cf.* CDDH Final Report 2003 (note 17), Proposal B. 4, fn. 2.

706   *Tilmann Laubner*

According to the provision finally adopted, the Court shall declare inadmissible an individual application if it considers that

> the applicant has not suffered a significant disadvantage, unless respect for human rights as defined in the Convention and the Protocols thereto requires an examination of the application on the merits and provided that no case may be rejected on this ground which has not been duly considered by a domestic tribunal.

"[T]he Court's 'productivity' cannot be increased *ad infinitum* if the quality of its judgments is to be maintained."[79] Based on this assessment the Evaluation Group concluded that the Court's workload should be reduced "by modulating the treatment afforded to applications and reserving full judicial treatment for applications that *warrant* it."[80] In order to exclude cases of "minor or secondary importance," the panel proposed to raise the admissibility threshold for individual applications by inserting in the Convention a provision "that would, in essence, empower the Court to decline to examine in detail applications which raise *no substantial issue under the Convention*."[81]

This proposal of the Evaluation Group points to the "fundamental dichotomy"[82] underlying the Convention's human rights system. By giving paramount priority to the objective relevance of an application, *i.e.* its importance beyond the individual case, the Evaluation Group appears to have adopted the view which primarily assigns to the Court functions of "quasi-constitutional justice." Individual applications, according to this view, mainly if not solely, serve as a means of disclosing and remedying grievances at the national level. Individual applications, thus, merely give reason to answer overarching legal questions of fundamental character and so, ultimately, raise the general standard of human

---

[79] Evaluation Group (note 11), para. 90.

[80] *Id.* (emphasis added). In this context, the Evaluation Group aptly considered that granting the Court unfettered discretion as to which applications are accepted for examination comparable to that enjoyed by the US Supreme Court under the *writ of certiorari* procedure (see *Elisabeth Zoller,* Avantages et inconvénients du système américain du writ of certiorari, RUDH, vol. 14, 2002, 278 *et seq.*) would be inappropriate for the Strasbourg system as the Court does not stand at the top of a homogenous judicial hierarchy and would be exposed to charges of non-transparency and inconsistency, Evaluation Group (note 11), para. 91. Also see Reflection Group (note 13), Appendix II, paras. 9 *et seq.;* and *Christian Tomuschat,* Individueller Rechtsschutz: Das Herzstück des "ordre public européen" nach der Europäischen Menschenrechtskonvention, EuGRZ, vol. 30, 2003, 95, 99.

[81] Evaluation Group (note 11), para. 93 (emphasis added).

[82] *Cf. Wildhaber* (note 5), 162.

rights protection in Europe and establish an European *"ordre public."*[83] The opposite view gives priority to "individual justice," *i.e.* providing legal protection and subjective relief to the individual applicant in order to enforce his or her human rights guaranteed under international law by means of a judicial procedure outside and 'above' his or her State.[84]

The CDDH, for its part, did not take sides in this dispute, but considered both functions as legitimate functions of the Court, none of which excluded the other.[85] Accordingly, while in principle retaining the idea of raising the admissibility threshold for individual applications, the committee rejected the formula developed by the Evaluation Group as going too far.[86] An additional competence of the Court to decline applications as inadmissible should be based on objective criteria taking into account both the general interests, *i.e.* the objective "value" of an application, such as its importance for the interpretation and application of the Convention, as well as the perspective of the individual applicant.[87] Decisive impetus for the provision finally adopted came from a proposal submitted by Switzerland and Germany.[88]

In fact, future Article 35 para. 3 lit. b of the Convention will comprise a combination of subjective and objective criteria.[89] As had been proposed by the Evaluation Group, the principle of *de minimis non curat praetor* will be introduced. Contrary to the ideas of that panel, however, it will not apply to the ob-

---

[83] *Cf., e.g., id.,* 162 *et seq.* Further on the 'constitutional issue' see *Evert Albert Alkema,* The European Convention as a Constitution and its Court as a Constitutional Court, in: *Mahoney/Matscher/Petzold/Wildhaber* (note 5), 41.

[84] *Cf., e.g., Tomuschat* (note 80), 97 *et seq.*

[85] CDDH Final Report 2003 (note 17), para. 11.

[86] It also rejected the Evaluation Group's proposal ((note 11), para. 96) to compensate for any restriction on the right of individual application through a system whereby cases rejected by the Court would be referred back to the courts and authorities of the respondent State for new decision, see CDDH Interim Report 2002 (note 17), para. 17; CDDH Final Report 2003 (note 17), para. 14.

[87] CDDH Final Report 2003 (note 17), para. 15.

[88] According to this proposal, an application ought to be inadmissible "if the applicant has not suffered a significant disadvantage and if the case raises neither a serious question affecting the interpretation or application of the Convention or the protocols thereto, nor a serious issue of general importance," *cf. id.,* Proposal B. 4. For more on the proposal, see *Stoltenberg* (note 57), 140 *et seq.*

[89] On comparisons with Sect. 93a para. 2 German Law on the Federal Constitutional Court, see *Stoltenberg* (note 57), 140 *et seq.; Grabenwarter* (note 27), 176.

jective importance of an individual application but to the subjective *gravamen* sustained by the applicant ("significant disadvantage") which consequently will be the starting point for the Court in examining the admissibility of an application under the new provision. The "objective value" of an application circumscribed by a formula taken from current Article 37 para. 1 of the Convention will serve as the first of two restrictions imposed on the Court's competence of rejecting applications where the applicant has not suffered a "significant disadvantage." The second safeguard clause shall prevent the Court from declining such applications if they have not been duly considered by a domestic tribunal.

However, there are, as a matter of fact, some issues arising with regard to the new admissibility criterion that need to be addressed by the future practice of the Court at the latest.

First is the considerable vagueness of the requirement of a "significant disadvantage" on the part of the applicant. In order to prevent decisions applying the new criterion from degrading into pure value judgments, it is imperative that objective and plausible criteria be evolved, a need that has been recognized.[90] Hence, the Court will face the challenge of carefully developing criteria which are equally applicable to cases from all 45 State Parties to the Convention featuring fundamentally different, *e.g.* economic, circumstances.[91] This task will require increased efforts as regards reasoning on the admissibility of applications.[92] At least in the short-term perspective, this appears difficult to reconcile with the Protocol's overall objective of reducing the Court's workload.[93]

---

[90] Explanatory Report (note 9), para. 80. It should be noted that according to Protocol No. 14 (note 1), Art. 20 para. 2, single-judge formations and committees will be prevented from applying the new criterion during a period of two years following the entry into force of Protocol No. 14.

[91] *E.g.* civil proceedings involving an equivalent of € 500 will affect applicants from Albania much differently than applicants from Germany. Putting a premium on financial disadvantages *per se* might even have the effect – albeit unintended – of discriminating against female applicants, a concern voiced by PA Opinion No. 251 (note 36), para. 11. Also see *Alkema* (note 83), 58.

[92] This of course would require reintroduction of reasoned (in-)admissibility decisions where they have been abolished. Hereto see, *supra*, note 28.

[93] According to the Explanatory Report (note 9), para. 79, however, it is expected that the new criterion "will be easier for the Court to apply" than some other (narrower!) admissibility criteria. Whether this, if accepted, would qualify as a value by itself is yet another question.

Secondly, the relationship between the requirement of a "significant disadvantage" and Article 34 of the Convention requiring the applicant to be the "victim" of a violation needs to be clarified. The Court traditionally has interpreted the latter requirement rather favorably for the applicant, not demanding any damage on his or her part.[94] It has plausibly been suggested that if the Court had seen a need for a *de minimis*-criterion as regards the applicant's *gravamen* in the past, Article 34 would have offered an opportunity to consider this aspect.[95] Thus, the new provision's necessity may be called into question.

Questions also arise as to the second safeguard clause, requiring that cases to be rejected on the grounds of the applicant not having suffered a "significant disadvantage" must have been "duly considered by a domestic tribunal." Emphasizing the principle of subsidiarity, this condition has been included in order to avoid the new admissibility criterion from misconception by State Parties as allowing them to disregard certain minor violations of the Convention.[96] However, from a systematic point of view, again the relationship to existing admissibility criteria – here (effective) domestic remedies under Article 35 para. 1 of the Convention – appears somewhat unclear. But more importantly, the question once more arises whether such provision will not be likely to thwart the overall objective of Protocol No. 14 by adding to the Court's workload instead of reducing it. For any finding as to whether a case in fact has been "duly considered by a domestic tribunal" would require the Court to examine in detail the proceedings on the national level and thus might call for a decision on aspects belonging to the merits at the admissibility stage.[97]

On the whole, raising the admissibility threshold will render applications inadmissible which under the current state of the law would not only be admissible but also well-founded on the merits. It will thus in essence curtail the right of individual application under Article 34 of the Convention. The question arises whether such curtailment of the right which "lies at the heart of the Stras-

---

[94] *Cf. Jochen A. Frowein/Wolfgang Peukert*, Europäische Menschenrechtskonvention, 2nd ed. 1996, Art. 25, mn. 20; *Ohms* (note 28), 148.

[95] *Ohms* (note 28), 148.

[96] CDDH Interim Activity Report 2003 (note 76), paras. 34 *et seq.; cf.* ECtHR Response (note 42), para. 18.

[97] *Cf.* Amnesty International (note 40), para. 37.

bourg system"[98] is compensated by an adequate gain elsewhere, *i.e.* whether it is proportionate.

It could be argued that the curtailment effected by the new admissibility criterion will not question the right of individual application as such as it is projected to affect only some 5 % of currently admissible cases.[99]

However, it appears that such figures point rather in another direction. Less than 10 % of all applications being lodged with the Court reach the admissibility stage. A reduction of these cases by 5 % certainly would not qualify as a significant effect on the Court's workload. Moreover, the new admissibility provision will not address at all the two categories of cases that have been identified as the main challenges to the Court. It will neither affect the vast number of cases that already now are inadmissible nor will it specifically affect repetitive or 'clone cases.' Like any other case, the Court would only be able to reject one of these "manifestly well-founded" applications if the applicant has not suffered a "significant disadvantage."[100] Considering, furthermore, the new provision's inherent potential to create new work for the Court, it at least seems highly questionable whether it is suitable at all to serve the overall purpose of Protocol No. 14. Questions as to whether the new criterion is necessary have been dealt with above.

Finally, even if one were to accept that the immediate curtailment of the right of individual application will not be dramatic as regards numbers of current cases, these figures do not necessarily reveal the whole impact of the new admissibility criterion on the human rights situation in Europe. Rather, any curtailment of the right of individual application must be presumed to send a signal that despite all safe-guard clauses might be misconceived by some State Parties to the Convention[101] – probably even willingly so. This might ultimately even lead to a further increase in the number of individual applications lodged with the Court.

---

[98] See, *supra,* note 23.

[99] CDDH Final Report 2003 (note 17), para. 17, Proposal B. 4. According to estimates of the PA, 1.6 % of "all existing cases" or of "all cases dealt with by the Court" will be affected, see PA Opinion No. 251 (note 36), para. 11 and Committee on Legal Affairs and Human Rights (note 65), para. 44; it is somewhat unclear exactly which numbers of cases these figures refer to. Also *cf.* ECtHR Response (note 42), para. 23.

[100] *Cf. Stoltenberg* (note 57), 141.

[101] *Cf. Françoise Tulkens,* Les réformes à droit constant, RUDH, vol. 14, 2002, 265, 273.

IV. Supervision of Execution of Judgments

According to Article 46 para. 1 of the Convention, State Parties are obliged to abide by judgments of the Court,[102] which shall be supervised by the CM under Article 46 para. 2 of the Convention.[103] As regards the instruments placed at its disposal to fulfil this task, the CM's choice currently is limited to either *interim* resolutions which may "express concern and/or [...] make relevant suggestions with respect to the execution"[104] or what has been labelled by the Court as the "nuclear options,"[105] *i.e.* measures provided for by Article 8 of the CoE's Statute ranging from suspension of rights of representation to expulsion from the organization.[106] The lack of intermediate measures is evident and considerably weakens the Convention's supervisory system,[107] as is illustrated

---

[102] Generally see *Jörg Polakiewicz,* The Execution of Judgments of the European Court of Human Rights, in: *Robert Blackburn/Jörg Polakiewicz* (eds.), Fundamental Rights in Europe: The European Convention on Human Rights and its Member States, 1950–2000, 2001, 55.

[103] As to the supervisory procedure applied by the CM, see Rules Adopted by the Committee of Ministers for the Application of Art. 46, Paragraph 2, of the European Convention on Human Rights (CM Rules), available at: http://cm.coe.int/intro/e-rules 46.htm. Also see *Ronald St. J. Macdonald,* The Supervision of the Execution of Judgments of the European Court of Human Rights, in: *Sienho Yee/Wang Tieya* (eds.), International Law in the Post-Cold War World: Essays in Memory of Li Haopei, 2001, 409; *Yvonne S. Klerk,* Supervision of the Execution of the Judgments of the European Court of Human Rights: The Committee of Minister's Role under Art. 54 of the European Convention on Human Rights, Netherlands International Law Review, vol. 45, 1998, 65.

[104] CM Rules (note 103), Rule 7.

[105] ECtHR Response (note 42), para. 28.

[106] *Cf. Rolv Ryssdal,* The Enforcement System Set up under the European Convention on Human Rights, in: *Mielle K. Bulterman/Martin Kuijer* (eds.), Compliance with Judgments of International Courts, 1996, 64 *et seq.;* European Commission for Democracy through Law (Venice Commission), Opinion on the Implementation of the Judgments of the European Court of Human Rights (Opinion No. 209/2002), CoE Doc. CDL-AD (2002) 34, para. 44.

[107] *E.g.* in ECtHR, *Loizidou v. Turkey,* Judgment of 28 July 1998, Reports of Judgments and Decisions 1998-IV, 1807 (*Loizidou* Case) it took more than five years and four *interim* resolutions before Turkey in December 2003 payed the applicant a sum for damages as well as costs and expenses that had been imposed on it by the Court. For a detailed analysis, see Venice Commission (note 106), paras. 17 *et seq.*

712   *Tilmann Laubner*

by the high number of repetitive cases before the Court.[108] Protocol No. 14 seeks to address some of the existing *lacunae*.[109]

1. Interpretation Proceedings

Firstly, future Article 46 para. 3 of the Convention will provide that "[i]f the Committee of Ministers considers that the supervision of the execution of a final judgment is hindered by a problem of interpretation of the judgment, it may refer the matter to the Court for a ruling on the question of interpretation."[110] In order to ensure sparing use of this possibility and avoid (further) overburdening of the Court,[111] any such referral decision will require a majority vote of two thirds of the representatives entitled to sit on the CM.

It is to be expected that under normal circumstances the formation of the Court which has rendered the original judgment will also decide on questions of its interpretation; other procedural aspects as well as the form of such interpretative rulings will be for the Court to decide upon.[112] However, while interpretation proceedings under future Article 46 para. 3 are intended to overcome obstacles

---

[108] Reflection Group (note 13), 4. Also see *Wolf Ókresek,* Die Umsetzung der EGMR-Urteile und ihre Überwachung – Probleme der Vollstreckung und der Behandlung von Wiederholungsfällen, EuGRZ, vol. 30, 2003, 168. The Court itself had advocated a 'pilot judgment' procedure to handle repetitive cases. This would have included an accelerated execution process, including an obligation for the respondent State to create retroactive domestic remedies for repetitive cases, which would have allowed the Court to decline to examine these: Reflection Group (note 13), para. 24; *cf.* CDDH Interim Activity Report 2003 (note 76), paras. 20 *et seq.;* Evaluation Group (note 11), para. 51. The CDDH, while acknowledging the usefulness of special (retro-active) domestic remedies for repetitive cases, such as the *Pinto* legislation in Italy, took the view that from a legal perspective this issue was more appropriately addressed through a recommendation of the CM to the COE Member States, see CDDH Interim Activity Report 2003 (note 76), para. 20. This view resulted in Recommendation (2004)6 (note 24).

[109] See Protocol No. 14 (note 1), Art. 16.

[110] Introduction of such competence had been recommended by the PA, Execution of Judgments of the European Court of Human Rights, Recommendation 1477 (2000), 28 September 2000 and Resolution 1226 (2000), 28 September 2000, para. 11 A.i. Currently, a party to a case may request the interpretation of a judgment within a period of one year following the delivery of that judgment under Art. 79 para. 1 of the Rules of Court (note 27).

[111] Explanatory Report (note 9), para. 96.

[112] *Id.,* para. 97.

standing in the way of prompt execution based on differences regarding the interpretation of judgments,[113] the official Explanatory Report stresses that they did
not aim at enabling the Court "to pronounce on the measures taken by a High
Contracting Party to comply with that judgment."[114] This reading appears strictly
consistent with the traditional view adopted by the Court itself on various occasions, according to which a judgment of the Court "is essentially declaratory in
nature and leaves to the State the choice of the means to be utilised in its domestic legal system for performance of its obligations under Article [46 para. 1]."[115]
However, it is difficult to foresee *in abstracto* how in practice the Court will be
able to meet the dual demand of interpreting a judgment with a view to its implementation on the one hand while being silent on the measures (to be) taken on
the other. Furthermore, it also seems difficult to reconcile with more recent practice of the Court itself to indicate – in the context of Article 41 of the Convention
relating to the award of "just satisfaction" to applicants – measures that would
constitute *restitutio in integrum*,[116] a development that so far has culminated in
the prescription of concrete remedial measures in the *dispositif* of the *Assanidze*
judgment.[117] In any event, the new interpretation proceedings will at least in the
short-term perspective bring additional work for the Court.

2. Infringement Proceedings

Beyond the interpretation procedure, Protocol No. 14 will supplement the
Convention by empowering the CM to institute infringement proceedings

---

[113] *Cf.* Venice Commission (note 106), para. 76.

[114] *Id.,* para. 97.

[115] ECtHR, *Marckx v. Belgium,* Judgment of 13 June 1979, Series A, No. 31,
para. 58; also see ECtHR, *Scozzari and Giunta v. Italy,* Judgment of 13 July 2000, Re-
ports of Judgments and Decisions 2000-VIII, 471, para. 249. *Cf.* CM Rules (note 103),
Rule 3 lit. b; *J.G. Merrills/A.H. Robertson,* Human Rights in Europe, 4th ed. 2001, 319;
Georg Ress, Wirkung und Beachtung der Urteile und Entscheidungen der Straßburger
Konventionsorgane, EuGRZ, vol. 23, 1996, 350, 351.

[116] See *e.g.* ECtHR, *Görgülü v. Germany,* Judgment of 26 February 2004, para. 64,
available at: http://hudoc.echr.coe.int/hudoc/ (on the repercussions of this judgment in
Germany, see *Rainer Hofmann,* The German Federal Constitutional Court and Public
International Law: New Decisions, New Directions?, German Yearbook of International
Law (GYIL), vol. 47, 2004, 9; and *Sejdovic v. Italy* (note 16), para. 46.

[117] ECtHR, *Assanidze v. Georgia,* Judgment of 8 April 2004, paras. 203 *et seq.,*
para. 14 lit. a of the *dispositif,* available at: http://hudoc.echr.coe.int/hudoc/.

against State Parties to the Convention. According to future Article 46 paras. 4 and 5 of the Convention, the CM, if it considers that a Party to the Convention "refuses to abide by a final judgment in a case to which it is a party," may refer to the Court the question "whether that Party has failed to fulfil its obligations under [Article 46] paragraph 1." Any such referral will require formal notice to the Party affected as well as, again, a majority vote of two thirds of the representatives entitled to sit in the CM.[118] The Court will sit as a Grand Chamber[119] and its decision is envisaged to take the form of a judgment.[120]

While resemblances of this new procedure to that provided for by Article 228 para. 2 of the EC Treaty are evident, so are the differences between the two systems. Unlike the EC Treaty, future Article 46 para. 5 of the Convention is silent on the legal consequences resulting from a finding by the Court of a violation of the obligation to abide by its judgments. A proposal to introduce a system of *"astreintes," i.e.* financial penalties to be imposed on defaulting State Parties, which had been forcefully advocated by the PA,[121] has finally been discarded by the CDDH.[122] Instead, if it finds a violation of Article 46 para. 1 of the Convention, the Court shall refer the case to the CM "for consideration of the measures to be taken" (new Article 46 para. 5). Otherwise, if no violation is found, the CM shall close its examination of the case.

Consequently, the Convention system, also in the future, will have to rely on its capability to exert political ("peer") as well as moral pressure on its Member States to ensure execution of the Court's judgments. A (public) finding by the Court to the effect that a Member State has failed to fulfil its obligations under Article 46 para. 1 of the Convention should carry some weight in this regard.[123] However, the two-thirds majority requirement raises doubts as to the infringe-

---

[118] The applicant to a case however, is not accorded the right to lodge infringement proceedings.

[119] Art. 31 lit. b of the Convention as amended by Protocol No. 14 (note 1).

[120] Explanatory Report (note 9), para. 100.

[121] PA Opinion No. 251 (note 36), paras. 5, 14 (ix); Recommendation 1477 (2000) (note 110). For an evaluation of this proposal see Venice Commission (note 106), paras. 78–85.

[122] CDDH Interim Activity Report 2003 (note 76), para. 44.

[123] *Cf. id.*

ment proceedings' feasibility in practice.[124] Moreover, the procedure raises a variety of issues that yet need to be resolved. For instance, any finding by the Court as to whether a Contracting Party has fulfilled its obligations arising from Article 46 para. 1 of the Convention would presuppose that the scope of these obligations is clear. And again, any assessment of the implementation of judgments appears hard to imagine if it was to exclude any pronouncement on the measures (to be) taken by the respondent State. Furthermore, the prerequisites for the Court to make a finding on an infringement of the obligations under Article 46 para. 1 of the Convention still appear somewhat unclear. Would it for example require the Contracting Party to have violated its obligations intentionally or would any failure of fulfilment suffice, *e.g.* undue delays in legislation?[125] Would such failure have to qualify as "persistent?"[126] Questions also arise as to the procedural rights and the role of the respondent State as well as that of the applicant. The Court itself obviously felt uneasy with unresolved issues like those mentioned above; furthermore, it expressed concerns about the distinction between the political/executive branch of the CoE and its judicial branch being blurred if the Court was to be involved in the execution of judgments.[127] It therefore ultimately rejected infringement proceedings in the form provided for by Protocol No. 14.[128]

Nevertheless, it appears that despite the questions referred to above, the arrangement laid down in future Article 46 paras. 4 and 5 of the Convention may, after all, be characterized as "a step in the right direction."[129]

---

[124] *Cf.* ECtHR Response (note 42), para. 30.

[125] The former is suggested by the words "refuses to abide," the latter by the phrase "whether a Party has failed to fulfil its obligation." Apart from questions of evidence, the latter would appear more plausible given the fact that cases of outright refusal to comply have been very rare so far. On the cases of Greece (Eur. Commission H.R., *Denmark v. Greece, Norway v. Greece, Sweden v. Greece, The Netherlands v. Greece,* Yearbook of the European Convention on Human Rights, vol. 11, 1968, 690) and Turkey (*Loizidou* Case (note 107)), see *Macdonald* (note 103), 417 *et seq.*

[126] *Cf.* CDDH Interim Activity Report 2003 (note 76), para. 43; CDDH Final Report 2003 (note 17), Proposal C. 4 (ii).

[127] Also see Evaluation Group (note 11), para. 49.

[128] ECtHR Response (note 42), para. 29.

[129] Committee on Legal Affairs and Human Rights (note 65), para. 54.

V. Miscellaneous Provisions

1. Judges: Terms of Office and Selection of Judges Ad Hoc

As has been mentioned already, Protocol No. 14 as finally adopted leaves untouched the principle laid down in Article 20 of the Convention according to which the number of judges is equal to that of the Contracting Parties. However, it seeks to redress critique as to the independence and impartiality of the judges of the Court.

Firstly, taking up a recommendation by the Evaluation Group which had referred to the standards set up under the Court's own case-law[130] and in order to guarantee both the appearance and reality of independence from the Contracting Parties' governments,[131] the judges' terms of office will be increased from six to nine years.[132] At the same time, the possibility of re-election will be excluded.[133]

Secondly, the procedure of appointing *ad hoc* judges will be revised. If no judge is available who has been elected for the respondent party to a case, the latter will no longer be allowed to appoint a person to sit as judge "on its behalf" after the beginning of proceedings (current Article 27 para. 2 of the Convention). Instead it will be for the President of the Court to select such person from a list submitted in advance by the relevant party.[134] While not furnishing the judges *ad hoc* with the same legitimacy as provided to regular judges

---

[130] Evaluation Group (note 11), para. 89, Conclusion 20 (b). Also see PA, Recommendation 1649 (2004), 30 January 2004, paras. 13, 21; *cf.* PA Opinion No. 251 (note 36), para. 8.

[131] *Cf.* ECtHR Response (note 42), para. 32.

[132] The Court itself, however, stressing the need to "ensure a sufficient nucleus of experienced Judges," preferred a term of twelve years, ECtHR Response (note 42), para. 34. Also see CDDH Interim Report 2002 (note 17), paras. 46 *et seq.*

[133] Art. 20 para. 1 of the Convention as amended by Protocol No. 14 (note 1), Art. 2. More detailed on the new arrangement Explanatory Report (note 9), paras. 50 *et seq.* As to the transitional provision, see Protocol No. 14 (note 1), Art. 21. Efforts of the PA (see Opinion No. 251 (note 36), para. 14 (ii) and Committee on Legal Affairs and Human Rights (note 65), paras. 14 *et seq.*) to insert into Art. 22 of the Convention relating to the election of judges a clause prescribing the candidature of at least one person of each gender for every vacancy on the bench ultimately failed, see Explanatory Report (note 9), para. 49.

[134] Art. 26 para. 4 of the Convention as amended by Protocol No. 14 (note 1), Art. 6. Also see Explanatory Report (note 9), para. 64.

through the process of election by the PA under Article 22 of the Convention,[135] this amendment will certainly serve the interests of independence and impartiality of the Court.

2. Council of Europe Commissioner for Human Rights

Currently the CoE Commissioner for Human Rights, whose post was established by the CM in 1999,[136] is not expressly assigned a role in the Convention system. Like any natural or legal person, he may be invited by the President of the Court to function as *amicus curiae* under current Article 36 para. 2 of the Convention. Protocol No. 14 upon entry into force will upgrade the Commissioner's position. Under future Article 36 para. 3 he or she will expressly be permitted to intervene on his or her own initiative in all cases before a Chamber or the Grand Chamber as a third party and thus to submit written comments and take part in hearings. However, the Protocol will not go so far as to allow the Commissioner to lodge applications with the Court against one or more State Parties. Such competence had been requested by the PA and the Commissioner himself, in particular with respect to cases raising serious issues of a general nature or cases of mass violations of human rights.[137] The PA in this regard had envisaged introduction of an *actio popularis* procedure along with appointing a "public prosecutor" at the Court, and to entrust this task to the Commissioner.[138] Ultimately, however, the view seems to have prevailed within the CDDH that contrary to the Commissioner's and the PA's assessment, such competence would be incompatible with the Commissioner's current rather consul-

---

[135] *Cf.* Committee on Legal Affairs and Human Rights (note 65), paras. 29 *et seq.*

[136] CM, Resolution 99 (50), 7 May 1999.

[137] As to the Commissioner's request see CoE Commissioner for Human Rights, 3rd Annual Report 2002, CoE Doc. CommDH(2003)7, 7; and 4th Annual Report 2003, CoE Doc. CommDH(2004)10, 6, 17.

[138] PA Opinion No. 251 (note 36), paras. 4, 13; Recommendation 1640 (2004), 26 January 2004, para. 7 (a), (b); Recommendation 1606 (2003), 23 June 2003, para. 10 (ii), (iii); Committee on Legal Affairs and Human Rights (note 65); PA, Rapporteur *Rudolf Bindig,* Committee on Legal Affairs and Human Rights, Report on the 3rd Annual Report on the Activities of the Council of Europe Commissioner for Human Rights 2002, 18 December 2003, Doc. 10024, paras. 42 *et seq.*

tative role[139] and would damage his or her relationship with the governments of the State Parties.[140]

3. Accession of the European Union to the Convention

Obviously, accession of the European Union (EU) to the Convention is a matter outside the general scope of Protocol No. 14 as it neither relates directly to the control system of the Convention as such nor will it contribute to a reduction of the Court's workload.[141] Rather it will achieve the opposite. However, in the light of the developments within the European Union that led to the adoption of the Treaty establishing a Constitution for Europe, which makes provision for the Union's accession to the Convention,[142] it was decided to lay a first cornerstone for such possibility also on the CoE's side. Consequently, Article 17 of Protocol No. 14 will insert a new paragraph 2 into Article 59 of the Convention providing that "[t]he European Union may accede to this Convention."[143] Further modifications to the Convention which will become necessary in order to make such accession possible from a legal and technical point of view, as well as other issues that will or might require prior negotiation with the EU, have been left for regulation by a separate instrument.[144] Upon instruction by the CM, these aspects have been examined by the CDDH in an additional

---

[139] *Cf.* the Commissioner's terms of reference contained in CM Resolution 99 (50) (note 136).

[140] *Cf.* CDDH Interim Activity Report 2003 (note 76), para. 24.

[141] For an overview of the subject see *Hans Christian Krüger/Jörg Polakiewicz,* Proposals for a Coherent Human Rights Protection System in Europe: The Convention on Human Rights and the EU Charter of Fundamental Rights, HRLJ, vol. 22, 2001, 1.

[142] Treaty establishing a Constitution for Europe, 29 October 2004, O.J. 2004 C 310/1, Arts. I-9 para. 2 and III-325 para. 6 lit. a (ii). For more on the Treaty, the relationship between the EC/EU and the Convention as well as the issue of accession from the EC/EU perspective see *Ronald Steiling/Alexander Schultz,* Changes and Challenges to the EU Judicial System after the Constitutional Treaty – An Overview, GYIL, vol. 47, 2004, 666, 683 *et seq.* Also see *Claus Dieter Classen,* The Draft Treaty Establishing a Constitution for Europe: A Contribution to the Improvement of Transparancy, Proximity, and Efficiency of the European Union, GYIL, vol. 46, 2003, 323, 332 *et seq.*

[143] Additionally, in those provisions amended by Protocol No. 14 the term "State Party" will be replaced by "High Contracting Party," see *e.g.* future Art. 26 para. 4 of the Convention.

[144] Explanatory Report (note 9), para. 101.

study.[145] As regards the form of such instrument, the CDDH expressed preference for an accession "in one go,"[146] *i.e.* through an accession treaty between the EU and the State Parties to the Convention, as opposed to the "classic" method consisting of another amending protocol which, after its entry into force, would be followed by the EU's accession to the revised Convention.[147]

C. Concluding Observations

The CM has urged the Member States of the CoE to ensure entry into force of the Protocol within two years from its opening for signature on 12 May 2004.[148] So far, seven States have followed this appeal by ratifying the Protocol.[149] In this regard it is worth mentioning that the CDDH had discussed the idea of transferring certain "matters of procedure" now dealt with in the Convention to a separate instrument (such as a "Statute" of the Court) capable of amendment by a simpler procedure. Such matters could have included the number of judges, the number of members of a Chamber or issues that are currently

---

[145] CDDH, Study of Technical and Legal Issues of a Possible EC/EU Accession to the European Convention on Human Rights, 28 June 2002, CoE Doc. DG-II(2002)006 [CDDH(2002)010 Addendum 2] (Study on Accession). Such issues, which cannot be discussed further in the present context, would include *e.g.* the question of representation of the EU in the CM when supervising the execution of judgments under Art. 46 para. 2 and its contribution to the expenditure of the Convention's supervisory system. For an overview see *Pierre-Henri Imbert* (Director General of Human Rights, CoE), Speech given on the occasion of "The Council of Europe's European Convention on Human Rights and the European Union's Charter of Fundamental Rights: Judges' Symposium," 16 September 2002, available at: http://www.coe.int/T/e/com/files/events/2002-09-Symposium-Judges/Imbert.asp. Also see *Krüger/Polakiewicz* (note 141), 10 *et seq.*

[146] *Imbert* (note 145), Sect. I.

[147] Study on Accession (note 145), paras. 12, 20.

[148] CM, Declaration of the Committee of Ministers Ensuring the Effectiveness of the Implementation of the European Convention on Human Rights at National and European Levels, 12 May 2004, available at: http://www.coe.int/T/E/Human_rights/execution/02_Documents/CMdec12052004.asp.

[149] As of 14 February 2005, these States are Armenia, Denmark, Georgia, Ireland, Malta, Norway, and the United Kingdom. A further 31 States have signed the Protocol, which will enter into force, according to its Arts. 18 and 19, three months after all Parties to the Convention have expressed their consent to be bound. The status of signatures and ratifications is available at: http://conventions.coe.int/Treaty/Commun/ChercheSig.asp?NT=194&CM=1&DF=14/02/05&CL=ENG.

regulated in the Rules of Court.[150] However, ultimately this idea was not re-tained although the CM's possibility to temporarily reduce the number of judges in a Chamber upon request of the Court appears as a remnant thereof.[151]

An overall evaluation of Protocol No. 14 appears difficult due to the variety of issues provided for therein. Bearing in mind its overall objective to "maintain and improve" the efficiency of the control system under the Convention, Proto-col No. 14 certainly contains a number of amendments which, in the short-term will release both court time as well as judicial capacities in the treatment of indi-vidual applications and thus increase the effectiveness of the Court. To be named here are the introduction of the single-judge formation, the simplified procedure, particularly affecting repetitive cases, as well as the farewell to a general rule of separate decisions on the admissibility and merits of individual applications. Most of the issues that have remained unclear or questionable in this regard should be capable of being resolved in practice. However, this does not seem to be the case with respect to the new admissibility criterion envisaged in Protocol No. 14. It raises far more questions and concerns than the potential to enable the Court to successfully encounter the challenges it faces. And these challenges will increase in scale with, Armenia and Finland having deposited their instruments of ratification in December 2004, Protocol No. 12 to the Con-vention[152] on a general prohibition of discrimination coming into force on 1 April 2005, and with accession of the EU to the Convention at least appearing foreseeable.

Coming back to this article's somewhat heretical title, Protocol No. 14 will neither relieve nor deprive the Court of its success. It will not relieve it of its success if measured by the number of individual applications lodged with the Court as it will not reduce their number but only facilitate and expedite the Court's handling of them. Neither will it (yet) deprive the Court of its success in terms of credit and confidence vested in it by (potential) applicants through-out Europe, despite all doubts on the new admissibility provision. However, it has been aptly noted that taking into account the steps undertaken by the Court

---

[150] CDDH Interim Report 2002 (note 17), paras. 54–56; CDDH Final Report 2003 (note 17), Proposal B. 8. The starting point for this discussion was a proposal of the Evaluation Group (note 11), para. 88, Conclusion 20 (c).

[151] See, *supra,* Sect. B. II. 2. *in fine.*

[152] Protocol No. 12 to the Convention for the Protection of Human Rights and Funda-mental Freedoms, 4 November 2000, ETS No. 177.

itself, the wind on the faces of individual applicants has become chillier.[153] If the right of individual application was to be restricted in order to preserve its essence, this ought to be accompanied by more tangible pressure on the State Parties to comply with their obligations under the Convention.

---

[153] *Siess-Scherz* (note 10), 107.

[11]

The European Court of Human Rights Overwhelmed by Applications: Problems and Possible Solutions

Christian Tomuschat

I. Introduction

Is it not an almost unbelievable success story? Currently, the jurisdiction of the European Court of Human Rights (ECtHR) extends to 47 States with more than 800 million inhabitants. Accordingly, international judges review the activities of 47 governments as to their compatibility with the European Convention on Human Rights (ECHR). No injusticiable areas or groups of acts exist. The ECtHR has abstained from evolving a doctrine of act of State or *acte de gouvernement*.[1] Everyone who feels aggrieved by a decision or some factual conduct of public authorities can bring the relevant dispute before the Strasbourg judges after having exhausted domestic remedies. Invariably, the case will be heard.[2] The Strasbourg Court has no discretion to accept or reject a case *a limine*. In 2006, it handed down no less than 1.560 full judgments. Thus, paradise in full blossom seems to have been ushered

---

[1] But see the Grand Chamber decision in *Markovic v. Italy*, application 1398/03, 14 December 2006, where the ECtHR had to assess a doctrine of *acte de gouvernement* evolved in Italy.

[2] This is the excruciating strength and weakness of the system of the ECHR, see Paul Mahoney, "Thinking a Small Unthinkable: Repatriating Reparation from the European Court of Human Rights to the National Legal Order", in Lucius Caflisch *et al.* (eds.), Liber Amicorum *Luzius Wildhaber: Human Rights – Strasbourg Views*, Kehl 2007, p. 263, at 267.

R. Wolfrum and U. Deutsch (eds.), *The European Court of Human Rights Overwhelmed by Applications: The Problems and Possible Solutions,* DOI: 10.1007/978-3-540-93960-3_1, © Springer-Verlag Berlin Heidelberg 2009

in. Can we therefore assume that the rule of law, as encapsulated in human rights, has found its definitive consecration in Europe?

II. The Growth of the Strasbourg System

Indeed, who would have thought, when the journey to the peak we have reached by now began in the late forties of the last century, that human rights in Europe would ever be based on such strong foundations? There is no need to dwell at length on the political and historical origins of the ECHR. I shall confine myself to mentioning some basic facts. After the horrors of the Nazi regime in Germany, the world community was generally agreed that any recurrence of a murderous dictatorship should be forestalled by all conceivable means. For that reason, the UN Charter defined the promotion and the encouragement of respect for human rights and fundamental freedoms as one of the primary purposes of the World Organization (Article 1 (3)). A few years later, on 10 December 1948, with a view to particularizing this general formula, the Universal Declaration of Human Rights was proclaimed. This Declaration served as a source of inspiration for the newly founded Council of Europe (the Statute of the Council of Europe entered into force on 3 August 1949). Taking the work which had already been performed by the UN Commission on Human Rights for a world covenant on human rights as the basis for its own drafting efforts, the Council of Europe succeeded in finalizing the draft text of the ECHR in the autumn of the next year. On 4 November 1950 the ECHR could be signed during a solemn ceremony in Rome. After having received the first ten ratifications, it entered into force on 3 September 1953. The UK had been the first State to accept the new instrument, but Germany was also among the pilot group of ten States who had the courage to bind themselves under the terms of an international regime the effects of which were unforeseeable at that time.

The first years saw a slow, but progressive enlargement of the circle of States parties. Especially the bigger States hesitated initially to follow the adventurers who had paved the way. While Turkey joined the group in May 1954, Italy took the decision not earlier than in October 1955. But it was France which adjourned its ratification for more than two decades. Although the ECtHR took its seat in Strasbourg, and although *René Cassin* was one of the first Presidents of the ECtHR (1965–1968), the French government waited until May 1974 before finally joining the

The European Court of Human Rights Overwhelmed by Applications   3

States that had manifested their confidence in the operation of the new regime by submitting to it. Apparently, France felt that as the country where the Déclaration des droits de l'homme et du citoyen had been proclaimed in 1789, in other words, as "la patrie des droits de l'homme", it had no ground to submit to international control its governmental conduct. In a country which had "invented" human rights, everything was fine by definition.

Until the great change in Europe, the number of parties to the ECHR remained at the level of 22 States. The demise of socialism as a political doctrine brought about by the political occurrences in 1989/90 entailed dramatic results and led eventually to a tremendous increase in membership to more than the double of the figures reached until then. The first State to become a member of the Council of Europe and thereafter to ratify the ECHR was Finland (10 May 1990), which during the reign of socialism in Eastern Europe had not dared to embark on the way to Strasbourg, out of fear to antagonize its great neighbour to the east, the Soviet Union. With some slight delay, taking a lot of precautions, the former satellites of the Soviet Union followed suit: the Czech Republic on 3 March 1992, Hungary on 5 November 1992, and Poland on 19 December 1993. Currently, all the Eastern European States have joined the family of nations grouped around the ECHR, with the sole exception of Belarus which, because of open disregard for the rule of law, being under the tight grip of a dictatorship, is currently still unfit for membership in the Council of Europe. It was a dramatic event when the former superpower itself, now under the name of Russia, was admitted to membership in the Council of Europe in February 1996 and thereafter ratified the ECHR in May 1998. It is not absolutely clear what objectives were pursued by Russia when it made that move to the west of the continent. One may presume that in 1996/98 Russia felt that in order to demonstrate its definitive rupture with its Stalinist past it should accept international obligations to respect and observe human rights. It must have felt politically weak, seeking to rehabilitate itself morally by cooperating with the other States of the continent on a level of parity, without enjoying any prerogatives. Indeed, within the Council of Europe, contrary to the configuration obtaining at the United Nations, the larger States have not been granted any special status, which, in principle, is acceptable even for more powerful countries since the Council of Europe has no true decision-making power.

However, such powers do exist under the regime of the ECHR. From the very outset, it was the particularity of the ECHR that it established not only a certain number of substantive guarantees but that it sought at the same time to make those guarantees truly effective by providing for enforcement machinery. It was an exceptionally bold decision to introduce an inter-State application by virtue of which every State party is entitled – and politically even called upon – to act as guardian of legality in instances where another State party is seen as breaching the provisions of the ECHR (formerly Article 24, now Article 33). This was a principled departure from the rule of consent which normally governs international dispute settlement: under general international law, reflected in Article 33 (1) of the UN Charter, States have the right of free choice regarding the way in which they wish to lay to rest any international disputes that they may have with another State. Here, by contrast, they accepted to be made accountable before the European Commission for any violation of the obligations incumbent upon them under the ECHR. The relevant provision can be seen as the precursor of what the ICJ, many years later, in its famous *Barcelona Traction* judgment, called 'obligations *erga omnes*'. The provision giving leave to challenge another State must be viewed as the expression of the idea that the ECHR as a whole protects common goods, the preservation of which lies in the public interest of the community of States assembled under the roof of the ECHR.

As everyone here knows, little use was made of the inter-State application. A couple of years ago, the Parliamentary Assembly invited the States parties to bring an application against Russia on account of the tragic occurrences in Chechnya,[3] but no government took up that challenge. Notwithstanding that reluctance to put into motion a procedure specifically designed for such occurrences,[4] one should not lose sight of the fundamental importance which the inter-State application holds as a matter of principle. The existence of this remedy underlines the position of the community of States parties as guarantors of the rights set forth by the ECHR. In practice, though, it has been more or less supplanted by the individual application which permits the victim of a violation directly to bring his/her case to the Strasbourg system, without having to prevail upon his/her home state to initiate a process of diplomatic protection.

Originally the individual application depended on a special declaration which every State party was free to make or not to make (Article 25). A

---

[3]   Recommendation 1456 (2000), 6 April 2000, *HRLJ* 21 (2000) 286.

[4]   On 27 March 2007, an application was filed by Georgia against Russia. It is still pending.

The European Court of Human Rights Overwhelmed by Applications 5

government could choose just to be bound by the substantive provisions of the ECHR without assuming at the same time the remedy of individual application. In this regard, progress was slow. The Scandinavian States Sweden, Denmark and Iceland, together with Ireland, took the lead. The acceptance of the individual application by both Belgium and Germany in July 1955 brought the procedure into force (Article 24 (4) required six declarations before it could be applied). Again, many of the bigger States had enormous difficulties in taking this second step which moved the ECHR to the top of all mechanisms of human rights protection world-wide. The United Kingdom waited for more than ten years before making its declaration under Article 25 on 14 January 1966. Italy came several years later, it followed suit in July 1973. Again, France was the last one of the big European nations to submit to the control mechanism of individual application. Only in October 1981, more than 30 years after the signature of the ECHR, did it take the step which Germany had taken a quarter of a century earlier.[5] Was it fear, was it arrogance, was it the mindset of sovereignty which prevented the French government from accepting the principle of international monitoring of its activities? In any event, it was a hard decision for it to take. Obviously, France needed a lot of time in order to get accustomed to the idea that the last word in a dispute was not spoken in Paris but in Strasbourg, and by an international body.

After France had eventually overcome its hesitations, the conviction spread that the split between accepting the ECHR as an instrument embodying substantive guarantees and rejecting its jurisdictional clauses had become outdated and could not be accepted any longer. Whoever takes a commitment to respect and observe human rights seriously must also be prepared to submit to international monitoring.[6] Eventually, only three States remained outside the jurisdiction of the ECtHR, namely Malta, Turkey and Cyprus. Pressure was increased on these three States. Bowing to that pressure, they made the requisite declarations. Turkey's declaration under Article 25 of 28 January 1987 was accompanied by far-reaching reservations through which Turkey sought to evade any accountability for the activities of its armed forces

---

[5] See Christian Autexier, "Frankreich und die EMRK nach der Unterwerfungserklärung (Art. 25) vom 2. Oktober 1981", *ZaöRV* 42 (1982) 327.

[6] See Luzius Wildhaber, "The European Convention on Human Rights and International Law", *ICLQ* 56 (2007) 217, at 222.

in Cyprus.[7] In 1989/90, at the time when the Berlin wall fell and thereby the artificial division of Europe into east and west, all of the then 22 States parties had finally made the declarations permitting individuals to file complaints and recognizing the jurisdiction of the Court at a second level after the Commission.

It was even more difficult to get the control machinery rolling. After the individual application had become applicable for six States in 1955, one might have expected that lawyers from those countries would not wait for a second to make use of the new legal opportunity offered to them. But that was not the case. In 1955, just 138 applications were registered, and this number decreased over the next years: in 1956 only 104 applications were filed, 101 in 1957, and 1958 reached a low point with no more than 96 applications. It was not so much ignorance on the part of lawyers which explains this drop. On the contrary, the legal profession noted with great attention that the European Commission conceived of its role as being that of a defender of governmental interests, to put it drastically. With stubborn rigidity, initially it rejected all incoming applications as being inadmissible, basing itself largely on the criterion of "manifestly ill-founded". The Strasbourg system appeared to be just an artificial construction, not really caring for the common man. Since the Commission swept any complaints away, there was not even any need for the Court that was to commence its activity after eight States would have recognized its jurisdiction. Only in 1959 did the Court come into being, and it could hand down its first judgment on 14 November 1960 in the case of *Lawless*. After having rejected the preliminary objections raised by the respondent, the government of Ireland, it pronounced its first judgment on the merits of that case on 1 July 1961.

But this was by no means the great breakthrough which the elected judges had hoped for. In the second case, a case against Belgium (*De Becker*), the Court could only note that the case had become moot as a consequence of a number of measures taken by the Belgian authorities with a view to rehabilitating the complainant who had been sanctioned for collaboration with the German occupation forces during World War

---

[7]   For a comment see Christian Tomuschat, "Turkey's Declaration under Article 25 of the European Convention on Human Rights", in *Progress in the Spirit of Human Rights. Festschrift für Felix Ermacora*, Kehl *et al.* 1988, p. 119. In its judgment of 23 March 1995 in *Loizidou v. Turkey (Preliminary Objections)*, A 310, p. 34, the Court declared Turkey's restrictions to its declarations under Articles 25 and 46 of the Convention to be invalid.

II (judgment of 27 March 1962). Then there was again a long interval for many years. In 1967 and 1968, the Court delivered its judgments on admissibility and merits in its third case, the *Belgian Linguistic* cases, where it came to the conclusion that Belgium had breached the principle of non-discrimination in regard to the right to education by not allowing certain children, on the basis of the residence of their parents, to have access to the French-language schools existing in six communes on the periphery of Brussels. By the end of the sixties, the Court had pronounced judgment in four other cases (*Wemhoff, Neumeister, Stögmüller, Matznetter*). On the whole, this harvest for an entire decade was disappointingly low.

Obviously, a new approach was necessary. The Commission had to understand that it was not tasked with fending off as many applications as possible, but to provide a forum for persons who could plausibly contend that their rights had been breached by their national authorities. Furthermore, it also had to understand that its mandate was essentially to pre-screen the registered applications but that defining determinations on the construction of the ECHR should be left to the Court. It was unacceptable that the Commission, by making wide use of its power to reject applications as being manifestly ill-founded, assumed the role of the pivotal body that decides on the great orientations to be followed in interpreting the ECHR. In the seventies, while *Jochen Frowein* was a member of the Commission, this new spirit progressively gained ground in that body. More applications were declared admissible, and more applications were eventually sent to the Court. Thus, the number of judgments rose steadily. In the last year before the fundamental reform of the system came into force (1997), involving the abolition of the Commission and the inclusion of the individual application in the regular treaty obligations which need no special acceptance and to which no reservation can be made, the Commission received 14.166 applications, 703 of which were declared admissible, and the Court handed down 106 judgments. That was really a maximum of what could be achieved with a Court composed of part-time judges who received no regular salary from the Council of Europe, but only a *per diem* for the days of their presence in Strasbourg.

It stands to reason that the new arrivals from Eastern Europe changed the picture profoundly. Although in all the former communist States new constitutions were enacted, their traditions and the mental structures of many of the leading politicians had been shaped by 45 years of the dictatorship of a political party. Therefore, to embrace the rule of law as the decisive yardstick in handling public affairs amounted to a political and also intellectual revolution. In order not to fall back into the unfortunate situation of split acceptance of the ECHR as to its substantive and procedural parts, a political agreement was concluded with all the candidates wishing to join the Council of Europe: after a short period they would have to ratify the ECHR, making at the same time the declarations under Articles 25 and 64. This strategy proved indeed successful. Only in the case of Russia there was a longer interval of more than two years between accession to the Council of Europe (28 February 1996) and its ratification of the ECHR (5 May 1998). With the advent of the 11th Protocol (1 November 1998), the option to shun the individual communication disappeared even formally. The alternative was clear. One could either become a State party to the ECHR, or one could remain aloof from it. The middle-ground was abandoned. No compromises were tolerated any longer. The alternative was: either yes or no.

III. The Control Machinery of the ECHR – Through its Successes on the Brink of Failure

To unite all the States of Europe under the roof of the Council of Europe was a great achievement. Today, this seems almost natural. But it was not. It is true that Eastern Europe lay in intellectual ruins. There were no firm national constitutional traditions that could have guided the countries liberated from the yoke of socialist dictatorship into the uncertain future. The value system that was embodied in the ECHR and had been further strengthened over the years by the work of the two monitoring institutions, the Commission and the Court, seemed to constitute the only constitutional philosophy that could be relied upon in building democratic institutions in consonance with the wishes of the peoples. Indeed, the logic of the ECHR can be described as aiming at the creation of a common constitutional space deeply permeated by the rights and freedoms enunciated by it.

In this regard, the control machinery provided for by the ECHR, which by now comprises only two organs, the Court and the Committee of Ministers, constitutes an indispensable element. Just the jurisprudence evolved by the Court evinces the necessity of a supervisory mechanism. National judges do assist in enforcing the rights under the ECHR. In recent times, the Court has even insisted on the necessity of preventive procedures at national level. The Court does not stick with the customary principle according to which the implementation of international commitments falls within national jurisdiction. Rightly, the Court emphasizes Article 13, which enjoins States to put at the disposal of everyone whose rights may have been violated, an "effective remedy", which means in fact that essentially defects should, to the extent possible, be ironed out at national level so that seizure of the Court becomes unnecessary. But it is unrealistic to assume that the highest national courts could make supervision by the Court redundant. International judges have a different outlook. They are not imprisoned in the thinking habits of a particular national school of reasoning. In particular, they are able to compare the practices of different countries in order to ascertain what is not only legal, but also practicable.

On the other hand, it is trivial to note that the European control machinery functions best if little is to be corrected, if the requisite review processes are activated at national level. Without being a chauvinist, one can say that Germany is particularly successful with the institutional arrangement it has put into place. On the one hand, the ECHR is part and parcel of the law applicable in Germany. On the other hand, the special remedy of constitutional complaint (*Verfassungsbeschwerde*) is well suited to address complaints against governmental conduct. It need not be explained here that the rights under the ECHR and the fundamental rights under the German Basic Law run largely parallel to one another. Consequently, if a person alleges that basic rights have been infringed such allegation implies mostly also the allegation that the corresponding guarantee of the ECHR has been breached. Since the political philosophy of the German Constitutional Court is not different from the general political approach of the ECtHR to the cases brought before it, the Constitutional Court will normally be able to sort out any major inconsistencies between the law and the practice governed by it. Concrete figures show that indeed the balance sheet of Germany is quite a favourable one. At first glance, this does not emerge very clearly. As of 31 December 2006, there were no less than 3.950 pending cases against Germany, and 2.217 new cases were lodged during 2006. But only eight cases were declared admissible, and the number of convictions, where a violation was found, was even lower: just six cases. The conclusion to be drawn is obvious: many people see Strasbourg as a kind of *ultima ratio* which they will in any event resort to after their efforts to vindicate the rights which they believe to hold have proved of no avail before German courts. Most of the time, criticism of the Court with regard to Germany concerns inability to comply with the rule that proceedings should be brought to a speedy end.

With regard to Switzerland, the ratio between cases handled and final pronouncements by the Court is slightly less favourable. In 2006, remaining also within the last year of reference for which specific data is available, saw 335 applications lodged. Five applications were declared admissible, and in nine cases the Court found a violation. A perusal of those cases leads to the conclusion that no structural deficiencies have emerged. Here and there problems came to light, even problems related to freedom of expression. But on the whole Switzerland has again confirmed its fine reputation of a country that remains firmly attached to the rule of law.

The diagnosis is more dramatic mainly with regard to the new States parties from Eastern Europe. The number of new applications is almost frightening. Again in 2006, Russia topped the list with 12.241 applications, followed by Romania with 4.878, and Poland which has added 4.646 new cases to the roll of the Court. At the end of last year, Russia had 19.300 pending cases, Poland 5.100, and Romania 10.850. But there are also 9.000 cases from Turkey waiting to be adjudicated, 4.300 from France and 3.400 from Italy. These figures show that it is not only the "new" States that face serious problems, but also those which since decades have been associated with the work of the Court. Nonetheless, the conclusion seems to be warranted that the centre of gravity of the ECHR has shifted towards Eastern Europe. As indicated by the figures just mentioned, much remains to be done to put the house in order, to achieve more than only semantic congruence with the requirements of the ECHR.

The weight of this workload is tremendous. One should congratulate the judges currently in office for having accepted their mandates and working hard to address the mass of human misery that has been placed before them, without losing courage. It is clear that without the effective assistance of the Court's staff[8] their battle would be lost from the very outset. But notwithstanding that valuable support, the mountain seems to grow in a way which nobody really knows how to manage

---

[8] On the legal configuration of the staff see Norbert Engel, "Status, Ausstattung und Personalhoheit des Inter-Amerikanischen und des Europäischen Gerichtshofs für Menschenrechte. Facetten und Wirkungen des institutionellen Rahmens", *EuGRZ* 30 (2003) 122 *et seq.*; Erik Fribergh, "The Authority over the Court's Registry within the Council of Europe", in Liber Amicorum *Luzius Wildhaber* (above n. 2), p. 145; Paul Mahoney, "Separation of powers in the Council of Europe. The status of the European Court of Human Rights vis-à-vis the authorities of the Council of Europe", *HRLJ* 24 (2003) 152 *et seq.*

The European Court of Human Rights Overwhelmed by Applications   11

any longer, despite all the efforts deployed by the judges and their staff. While, as I told a few minutes ago, in the early days the Court was happy to see a case generously attributed to it by the Commission, it handed down 107 judgments before the great reform in 1997. Numbers jumped quickly up to 889 judgments in 2001, 1.105 judgments in 2005 and 1.560 full judgments in 2006. Counting 300 workdays per year, this means that on average 5.2 judgments were pronounced per day. And the provisional statistics for 2007, which bring the data up to 30 November 2007, inform the reader that until that date 1.649 judgments had already been handed down. Thus, quite a significant additional number can be expected before the end of the year – the result of a work discipline which can hardly be surpassed. In sober mathematical figures this amounts to an increase of roughly 20 per cent from one year to the next.

One should not expect that this acceleration can be continued *ad infinitum*. Gross rates of 20 per cent cannot easily be repeated. And even more: such increases in productivity are not even desirable. Each case requires sufficient attention. In particular, the specificities of a particular set of facts should not be disregarded. It may well be that by standardizing the legal reasons given by the Court things could be dealt with even faster. But the danger is that then the actual case at hand gets out of sight, that essential details are overlooked. The Court is of course well-advised to rely on the assistance which is provided by its staff. Eventually, however, the personal responsibility of the judges must remain the key element of the adjudicatory process. It would be unacceptable – and even immoral – to transfer the assessment to be carried out almost in its entirety to the staff people in the service of the Court. Judges must have the time to familiarize themselves with the cases placed before them. It would be unacceptable to see their role confined to signing a product ready-made by their support services. The judges are elected by the Parliamentary Assembly. They are the people in whom trust resides, not the bureaucrats in the Registry, no matter how able and zealous they are.

But the situation as it obtains today is indeed alarming. While at the end of 2006, just one year ago, the number of pending cases had risen to nearly 90.000, the data made public for the first eleven months of the current year show that the symbolic borderline of 100.000 cases has now been crossed. On 30 November, less than three weeks ago, the number of pending cases had risen to 103.950.

This figure invites the reader to proceed to a few fairly simple calculations. In 2006, the record-breaking year, the number of full judgments, which addressed the complaints of the applicant extensively, either on admissibility, or on the merits, or on both, stood at 1.560, as already mentioned. Additionally, 28.160 cases were disposed of by judicial decision, i.e. by decisions declaring an application inadmissible or striking it out of the list. Lastly, 12.251 cases were dealt with administratively by the Registry in cases, above all, where the applicant either did not submit the necessary basic information or where the case was not actively pursued. Adding these figures, one obtains a sum of roughly 42.000 cases, which, under the current circumstances, may be regarded as the maximum that can be reached. This means that the Court, in spite of increasing its output, has a structural backlog of 2 ½ years to tackle. The average case will inevitably sit in the archives for 30 months before it can be touched.

This is a deplorable situation. The English adage: justice delayed is justice denied, is well-known. It is not just a light, ephemeral proposition, having no real significance. It plays a major role in the Court's work. Its agenda is packed with tens of thousands of cases in which judges did not comply with their duties or were overburdened because of neglect on the part of the authorities responsible for the provision of logistics and manpower.[9] Should the Court itself become unable to live up to the standard it requires to comply with from the domestic courts under its supervision, it would soon lose its well-deserved reputation. In fact, for people in quite a number of countries, and principally in countries of Eastern Europe, the Court has become a symbol of hope. Justice they could not get from their own courts because of systemic disturbances within the judicial system of their home country they hope to get from Strasbourg. And in fact, Strasbourg has not disillusioned them. As far as my personal knowledge goes, the European judges have never bowed before governmental authority, putting the *raison d'Etat* ahead of the defence of human rights. Many writers have attacked the *Bankovic* decision as such a departure from the correct path of the law. But in that case the Court did not yield to the pressure of NATO and/or its European members. It made clear that jurisdiction is something else than factual contact; this is the solid consideration upon which the *Bankovic* decision rests.[10] And future cases will show, I have no doubt about that,

---

[9]   See Andrea Gattini, "Mass Claims at the European Court of Human Rights", in Liber amicorum *Luzius Wildhaber* (above n. 2), p. 271, at 274.

[10]   See also Lucius Caflisch and Antonio A. Cançado Trindade, "Les conventions américaine et européenne des droits de l'homme et le droit international général', *RGDIP* 108 (2004) 5, at 36; Wildhaber (above n. 6), p. 223.

that *Bankovic* has a limited scope only. One example in particular comes easily to mind: once a person is in the custody of the armed forces of anyone State party, and therefore committed to its care, wherever that may be, inside or outside the territory of the 47 States parties, the Court will unequivocally affirm the responsibility of that State. Mistreatment during custody, in particular, will never escape the censure of the Court.

IV. Improving the Control Machinery

We are assembled here to reflect on possible remedies. The Court itself, first under President *Wildhaber*, now under President *Costa*, has done whatever is feasible. The judges cannot be blamed, on the contrary, they deserve praise. It is now incumbent on politicians to evolve a new strategy. But they need advice from the scholarly community, notwithstanding their intimate knowledge of the inner workings of the Council of Europe where ministerial delegates are involved, in particular, in supervising the execution of the judgments rendered – which can be a struggle almost as challenging as the assessment of an application.

1) One of the most obvious remedies is the ratification of Protocol No. 14, which would allow the adjudication of the merits of so-called "repetitive cases" where a "well-established case law of the Court exists". This particular procedure could bring an enormous gain of time, if handled intelligently, without harming the individual applicant. Furthermore, Protocol No. 14 would permit the entry onto the European stage of the single Judge, a figure which is known from domestic legal systems mostly from the lowest level. *Le juge de paix – voilà* the resemblance. The single Judge formation, as the text says, does have its problematic side. Of course, the single Judge will be confined to declaring an application inadmissible or striking it off the list of cases if this is possible without any further examination. In that regard, recommendations will be made by rapporteurs functioning under the authority of the President of the Court. Other than *Monsieur le juge de paix*, the single Judge will thus not be alone. He will be advised. I therefore take it that no such unfortunate developments will ever take place as they were reported from the working group of the UN-Subcommission on the Promotion and Protection of Human Rights tasked with pre-screening complaints under ECOSOC-Resolution 1503 (XLVIII). In that body, composed of five persons from the five regions acknowledged in the

World Organization, decisions were generally taken according to a la-ger mentality. Anything that could have political overtones was simply declared inadmissible by a majority of three members. However, it should simply be recalled that the system envisioned in Protocol No. 14 would be workable only as long as the single Judge acts in full impartiality, not being led by considerations of enmity or friendship. Currently, this would certainly be the case. Thus, no serious obstacles stand in the way of the single Judge – except for the fact that Russia stubbornly refuses to ratify the Protocol. There seems to be no real possibility to overcome its reluctance. Hence, realistically, one cannot reckon with the coming into force of the Protocol as long as the current tensions between the Russian government and the other governments of the States parties persist.

2) Could or should we increase the number of judges by just doubling them? The result would be 94 European judges – as compared to the nine judges of the US Supreme Court, for instance. This would look fairly odd – although it would not be that odd, after all. It is true that most national supreme courts are fairly lean bodies. But most of them are protected from becoming over flooded by rigid provisions on leave to appeal. Within domestic legal systems, not everyone has access to the highest judicial body. Some lower court must have granted a specific authorization – or it is the Supreme Court itself which selects the cases deserving to be reviewed at the highest level. Such procedures do not exist in Strasbourg. Professor *Bernhardt* will talk about the intrinsic worth of a *certiorari* procedure as it exists in the United States. In any event, the open gates of the ECtHR have entailed a workload which no other comparable institution has to shoulder. Comparisons with the US Supreme Court are therefore quite inappropriate. For a legal community of more than 800 million people, from which tens of thousands of applications will be received each year on a regular basis, 94 judges would certainly not be disproportionate. Still, the idea of having 94 judges creates a certain malaise. Above all, it would become extremely difficult to ensure the unity of the case law. In the long run, however, it may become inevitable to provide for such a tremendous increase in numbers, which, objectively, is not excessive either if compared with the number of judges operating at the highest level of just one country. In Germany, for instance, the Constitutional Court comprises 16 judges. Additionally, Germany has five more specialized supreme courts, each one with several chambers. Two German judges at the highest level, the European level, would therefore not be a luxury, and the additional expenditure would be minimal.

3) Limiting access to the ECtHR and confining its role to rendering judgments on key issues with far-reaching consequences[11] cannot be the ideal solution either. First of all, the Strasbourg judgments do not exist in the national languages of all of the 47 States parties to the ECHR. This makes them inaccessible to many of the domestic European judges, in spite of the saying that English has become the common language of our societies. One simply has to acknowledge the fact that many national judges are unable to read a legal document in the English (or the French) language. This is not only a technical problem, but affects very badly the authority of the judgments, which in the eyes of the *juge de paix* in Albania or Azerbaijan, or even in the German province, seem to pertain to a different world, a world far removed from their daily experiences.[12]

More generally, there are other structural grounds as well implying that the Strasbourg Court cannot have the same authority as a supreme court within a national system. In France or in Germany, for instance, one may safely assume that a decision rendered by such a court will not only become known to all of the lower tribunals, but that it will also be heeded in the future. Notwithstanding their judicial independence, lower judges will normally follow the jurisprudence of the superior echelons of the judicial hierarchy, mainly out of fear to see their decisions reversed in case they pursue a different line. The ECtHR is much more remote from the national judges. Their reluctance to adopt the propositions evolved by the Court may even receive some support from national governments. Therefore, if the Court is really meant to help the victims of injustices, it must necessarily address the factual substance of individual cases. Its general guidelines alone do not have the necessary impact.[13] No judgment from Strasbourg will really penetrate the wide plains of Siberia – to put it somewhat polemically. But it

---

[11]   As suggested by Luzius Wildhaber, "A Constitutional Future for the European Court of Human Rights?", *HRLJ* 23 (2002) 161, at 164. The Group of Wise Persons, entrusted with making reform proposals, withdrew its suggestion to render "judgments of principle", made in its Interim Report, 3 May 2003, *HRLJ* 27 (2006), 274, at 278, paras. 50-51, in its Final Report, 15 November 2006, *HRLJ* 27 (2006), 279, at 284, paras. 69-69.

[12]   Highlighted also in the Final Report of the Group of Wise Persons (above n. 11), 284, para. 71.

[13]   Christian Tomuschat, "Individueller Rechtsschutz: das Herzstück des 'Ordre public européen' nach der Europäischen Menschenrechtskonvention", *EuGRZ* 30 (2003) 95 *et seq.*

is certainly true that the calculation of full reparation for injury suffered could be left to national judicial systems – which would save an enormous amount of time.[14]

4) Could one re-delegate a great part of the bulk currently being handled by Strasbourg to the supreme courts of the States parties? It is certainly worthwhile testing this modality, which would be in line with the tendency of the Court to render pilot judgments.[15] An appeal to the highest court(s) should be opened to everyone claiming that his/her rights under the ECHR have been violated.[16] In Germany, the controversial decision of the Constitutional Court in the *Görgülü* case acknowledges, notwithstanding its somewhat strange insistence on German sovereignty, that disregard of the guarantees of the ECHR could amount to a violation of the fundamental rights under the Basic Law.[17] If made the guardians of the ECHR, the highest national courts would follow the jurisprudence of the Strasbourg Court with the greatest attention. They would become valuable interlocutors who could enter into a constructive dialogue with their partner from the Council of Europe. But it is clear that the way to the highest national courts should not bar the way to Strasbourg, *inter alia* because to file an application there is cost-free and does not require the services of a lawyer. It is evident that careful coordination with domestic legal procedures would be necessary.

V. Concluding Observations

It is our personal view that governments in Western Europe have not yet become sufficiently aware of the inappreciable contribution of the

---

[14]   See Mahoney (above n. 2), 279 *et seq.*

[15]   The first pilot judgment was rendered in *Broniowski v. Poland*, application 31443/96, 22 June 2004, *HRLJ* 25 (2004), 23. For a comment see Lech Garlicki, "Broniowski and After: On the Dual Nature of 'Pilot Judgments'", in Liber Amicorum *Luzius Wildhaber* (above n. 2), 177; Vladimiro Zagrebelsky, "Questions autour de Broniowski", ibid. 521; Gattini (above n. 9), *passim*.

[16]   The Group of Wise Persons (above n. 11) focused mainly on remedies lying in case of excessive length of proceedings, but eventually made a comprehensive recommendation to that effect (p. 288, para. 136).

[17]   111 *Entscheidungen des Bundesverfassungsgerichts* 307, at 323; English translation: *HRLJ* 25 (2004) 99, at 105-6.

ECtHR to the establishment and strengthening of a common European culture of democracy, human rights and the rule of law. Many see the work carried out in Strasbourg as just one of the facets within the vast array of international expert bodies as they have sprung up in recent years. Such lack of attention, which eventually translates into insufficient funding, is a big mistake. Undeniably, the ECHR together with its enforcement machinery has grown up in the climate of the liberal State of the Western constitutional civilization. The former socialist States of Eastern Europe are today full members of that constitutional network, on a level of parity and without any discrimination. Their status as equals is reflected, in particular, by their right to participate in the development of the Strasbourg system through judges of their nationality. Every State party has the right to nominate one lawyer for the discharge of that important task. And yet, it can be said that the groundwork had already been laid when the former socialist nations acceded to the ECHR. The principles and concepts which determine the jurisprudence of the Court were defined in the formative years of the seventies, eighties and nineties of the last century. As far as my knowledge goes, there was never any explicit talk of the "*acquis de Strasbourg*" while the European Communities branded the banner of "*acquis communautaire*" continually while they were engaged in negotiations on further enlargement. In the accession treaties, acceptance of the "*acquis communautaire*" was made a formal condition of accession. In fact, however, with regard to the ECHR exactly the same occurred. The new States could not seriously hope to escape the influence of the established case law. Today, the new judges all have the right to introduce their specific ideas and concepts into the process of construction of the ECHR. But the main structures of that edifice were already in existence when they joined the ECHR.

This seems to be particularly important with regard to Russia. The domestic constitution of Russia is a wonderful instrument, which satisfies all the needs of a hasty reader. Human rights, division of powers, constitutional court – everything is on display. But it is mostly just on display. Some of it works in practice. Yet, whenever strong political elements come into play, the system operates in consonance with the factual strength of the actors involved. The ECHR, on the other hand, cannot be marginalized as easily. No one of the States parties to it can unilaterally determine their scope and contents. Through its decisions on individual cases, the ECtHR has a strong impact on developments in Russia. That impact, unfortunately, does not seem to go beyond the individual case that has been adjudicated. Although the Court has made it clear that States have to take general measures in case it has emerged that some systemic deficiency exists, that effect of Articles 41 and 46 has not yet materialized as it should do. In any event, however, through its work, the Court is involved in a continual process of raising the level of constitutional culture in Russia and also in the other Eastern European States that currently have to struggle with hard problems, as reflected in the statistics with which I have confronted you. This is a far smoother process than the "dialogue" between politicians which more often than not falls on deaf ears.

The Western nations have a tremendous interest in seeing this process continue, inasmuch as it has no patronizing elements and permits Russian actors to participate actively in remedying any inconsistencies found. Just for this reason, they should shed their reluctance to provide substantial financing to the Strasbourg system. No investment may be as profitable in the long run. It is precisely the experience of European integration that peace and understanding can best be promoted by together conceiving and carrying out a common project. To make the rights under the ECHR a living reality is such a common project. Any effort should be made to ensure that the journey that was commenced together can be continued together.

[12]

Beyond Dispute:
International Judicial Institutions as Lawmakers

Expanding Competences by Judicial Lawmaking: The Pilot Judgment Procedure of the European Court of Human Rights

By Markus Fyrnys[*]

A. Introduction

The institutional design of the Strasbourg system that has evolved over the last decades is an expression of contemporary debates surrounding the system's very nature and purpose. The current debate primarily bears on the range of choices that the Council of Europe faces in adapting to the changes in Europe, which largely have been caused by its expansion to cover nearly all post-Communist States of Central and Eastern Europe since the 1990s. This expansion, and with it the extension of the scope of the European Convention on Human Rights (the Convention) to now more than 800 million people in forty seven countries, has confronted the European Court of Human Rights (the Court) with a far broader range of human rights problems than had previously existed.[1] By 2010, the number of pending cases had risen to 139,650 but the Court's adjudicative capacity remains limited.[2]

Against the background of an overwhelming number of applications,[3] the current debate regarding its core functions raises the question of whether the Court should engage in

[*] Research fellow at the Chair of Public Law and Philosophy of Law at the University of Mannheim. The author wishes to thank Armin von Bogdandy, Hans-Joachim Cremer, Isabel Feichtner, Ingo Venzke and the *Dienstagsrunde* at the Max Planck Institute for Comparative Public Law and International Law in Heidelberg for their helpful comments and discussion. Comments are welcome at markus.fyrnys@web.de

[1] Robert Harmsen, *The European Court of Human Rights as a 'Constitutional Court': Definitial Debates and the Dynamics of Reform*, in: JUDGES, TRANSITION, AND HUMAN RIGHTS, 33 (John Morison, Kieran McEvoy & Gordon Anthony eds, 2007).

[2] On the latest data, *see* Eur. Court H.R., *Analysis of Statistics 2010, 7*. On the Court's adjudicative capacity, *see* Steering Committee for Human Rights (CDDH), *Explanatory Report to Protocol No. 14 to the Convention for the Protection of Human Rights and Fundamental Freedoms amending the control system of the Convention*, Document CM(2004)65 Addendum, 7 April 2004, para. 7, also published in 26 HUMAN RIGHTS LAW JOURNAL 90, 91 (2005).

[3] *See* THE EUROPEAN COURT OF HUMAN RIGHTS OVERWHELMED BY APPLICATIONS: PROBLEMS AND POSSIBLE SOLUTIONS, (Rüdiger Wolfrum & Ulrike Deutsch eds, 2009).

"constitutional," in contrast to "individual," adjudication. The "constitutional"[4] concept highlights the Court's function in a pan-European standard setting. In this respect, individual cases are the material from which legal arguments about what the concrete provisions of the Convention mean are extrapolated[5] and the general content of the legal order provided by the Convention is developed.[6] According to this conception, it is the lawmaking role—the generation and stabilization of normative expectations beyond an individual case by providing legal arguments for later disputes[7]—that should be seen as the Court's main *raison d'être.*[8] In contrast, the "individual" concept emphasizes the Court's core function of individual human rights adjudication that is geared towards ensuring, on a case-by-case basis, that every genuine victim of a violation receives a judgment from the Court.[9]

It is worth noting that approximately two-thirds of the admissible complaints[10] are repetitive cases that concern systemic human rights violations within the domestic legal order. Against this backdrop, the Court's judicial elaboration of the so-called "pilot judgment procedure" is an innovative response to the problem of repetitive cases and rests on the idea of the Court's constitutional function. Besides finding an individual violation of Convention rights, a "full" pilot judgment[11] consists of the following steps: first, identifying a systematic malfunctioning of domestic legislation or administrative practice; second, concluding that this systematic problem may give rise to numerous subsequent well-founded applications; third, recognizing that general measures are called for and suggesting the form such general measures may take in order to remedy the systematic defect; and fourth, adjourning all other pending individual applications deriving

---

[4] STEVEN GREER, THE EUROPEAN CONVENTION ON HUMAN RIGHTS: ACHIEVEMENTS, PROBLEMS AND PROSPECTS 7 (2006), stating that the Court "is already 'the Constitutional Court for Europe', in the sense that it is the final authoritative judicial tribunal in the only pan-European system." *See also* Luzius Wildhaber, *A Constitutional Future for the European Court of Human Rights?*, 23 HUMAN RIGHTS LAW JOURNAL 161, 162 (2002). On the constitutional role of the Inter-American Court of Human Rights, *see* Christina Binder, *The Prohibition of Amnesties by the Inter-American Court of Human Rights*, 12 GERMAN LAW JOURNAL 1203 (2011).

[5] Harmsen (note 1), 36.

[6] Wildhaber (note 4), 162.

[7] On the lawmaking role of judicial decisions, *see* Armin von Bogdandy & Ingo Venzke, *Beyond Dispute? International Judicial Institutions as Lawmakers*, 12 GERMAN LAW JOURNAL 979, 986 (2011).

[8] Harmsen (note 1), 36.

[9] Christian Tomuschat, *Individueller Rechtsschutz: das Herzstück des „ordre public européen" nach der Europäischen Menschenrechtskonvention*, 30 EUROPÄISCHE GRUNDRECHTE ZEITSCHRIFT 95, 96 (2003).

[10] Around 90 % of all individual applications are inadmissible.

[11] On a systematic analysis of different types of pilot judgments, *see* PHILIP LEACH, HELEN HARDMAN, SVETLANA STEPHENSON & BRAD K. BLITZ, RESPONDING TO SYSTEMATIC HUMAN RIGHTS VIOLATIONS 13 (2010).

from the same systematic defect. Finally, the Court uses the operative part of the judgment to reinforce the obligation to take general measures.[12]

The very fact that pilot judgments are focused on the identification of systematic malfunctioning of the domestic legal order and on the indication of appropriate general remedial measures normatively extends the binding effect of the Court's judgments and changes their legal nature, accentuating the Court's constitutional function. The pilot judgments' legal nature reveals features combining individual and general effect in the domestic legal order by extending an individual complaint procedure through elements of judicial review of legislation. The paper argues that a pilot judgment is an innovative strategy of imposing the Court's judicature on the domestic legislative process. The Court generalizes the legal arguments of its judgment beyond the individual case by issuing a programmed lawmaking obligation to the domestic legislature. The Court uses the generality of domestic legislative acts to solve its docket problem of repetitive cases. This judicial lawmaking by requesting domestic legislation is a remarkable judicial strategy of compliance or internalization, which is able to substitute the lack, in doctrinal terms, of direct effect of the Convention and the lack of *erga omnes* effect of the Court's judgments in the domestic legal system.

The judicial elaboration of the pilot judgment procedure with its extension of the effect of the Court's judgments has an impact on the distribution of competences in the multi-leveled Convention system, particularly between the Court and the state parties in a vertical dimension, but also between the Court and the Committee of Ministers in a horizontal dimension. This judicialization of politics on different levels of the Convention system is a particularly interesting example in the broader perspective of this project on "International Judicial Institutions as Lawmakers." In order to elucidate and explore repercussions in the distribution of competences, this paper first highlights the judicial elaboration of the pilot judgment procedure in *Broniowski v. Poland* (B.). Second, the paper explores the judicial elaboration of the pilot judgment as procedural and substantial lawmaking by the Court and analyses the vertical and horizontal impact on the Convention's system of competences (C.). Third, the paper addresses the issue whether such lawmaking by an international adjudicative authority can be justified particularly in terms of procedural and democratic legitimacy and in respect of the consequences for the individual in the Convention system (D.), followed by a concluding outlook (E.).

---

[12] Luzius Wildhaber, *Pilot Judgments in Cases of Structural or Systematic Problems on the National Level*, in: THE EUROPEAN COURT OF HUMAN RIGHTS OVERWHELMED BY APPLICATIONS: PROBLEMS AND POSSIBLE SOLUTIONS, 69, 71 (Rüdiger Wolfrum & Ulrike Deutsch eds, 2009).

1234   German Law Journal   [Vol. 12 No. 05

B. Judicial Elaboration of the Pilot Judgment Procedure

The Court's judicial elaboration of the pilot judgment procedure extends, *inter alia*, the binding effect of its judgment beyond the decisive case, with a vertical and horizontal impact on the multileveled Convention system's distribution of competences.   It is therefore of critical importance to first outline the prevalent understanding of the effect of the Court's judgments, to show how they are executed by state parties and to discuss the supervisory authority of the Committee of Ministers (B.I.).   After recapitulating the unsuccessful initiative of installing the pilot judgment with Protocol No. 14 (B.II.), the section highlights the judicial elaboration of the pilot judgment procedure in *Broniowski v. Poland* (B.III.).

I. Effect, Execution, and Supervision of the Court's Judgments

From the perspective of the Convention, the substantive binding effect of the operative part of the Court's judgment is limited *ratione personae, ratione temporis,* and *ratione materiae.*

According to effects *ratione personae,* the judgment of the Court has a binding effect *inter partes*—on the individual applicant and on the state party against which an individual application is directed. Article 46 of the Convention clarifies this by providing: "The High Contracting Parties undertake to abide by the final judgment of the Court in any case to which they are parties." Basically, no other state party is legally bound by the judgment in the sense of the doctrine res judicata. [13] At the same time, in accordance with Article 1 of the Convention, [14] the state parties are, however, obliged to respect the rights and freedoms defined in Section I of the Convention, [15] and the Court's judicature substantially concretizes the rights and freedoms' substance. [16] Thus, even if the Court's case law may only be considered to have the normative effect of orienting [17] and guiding others, as opposed to creating legal obligations in the sense conveyed by the doctrine of res judicata,

---

[13] Eckart Klein, *Should the Binding Effect of the Judgments of the European Court of Human Rights be Extended?*, in: Protecting Human Rights: The European Perspective – Studies in Memory of Rolv Ryssdal, 705, 706 (Paul Mahony, Franz Matcher, Herbert Petzold & Luzius Wildhaber eds, 2000).

[14] Art. 1 of the Convention reads: "The High Contracting Parties shall secure to everyone within their jurisdiction the rights and freedoms defined in Section I of this Convention."

[15] Peter Leuprecht, *The Execution of Judgments and Decisions*, in: The European System for the Protection of Human Rights, 801, 812 (Ronald St. J. Macdonald, Franz Matscher & Herbert Petzold eds, 1993).

[16] Klein (note 13), 706.

[17] Georg Ress, *The Effect of Decisions and Judgments of the European Court of Human Rights in the Domestic Legal Order*, 40 Texas International Law Journal 359, 374 (2005).

many domestic authorities (legislative, executive, and judicial) recognize the Court's case law and act accordingly.[18]

With regard to *ratione temporis*, the binding effect of judgments of the Court is retrospectively limited to the matter in dispute. There is no direct prospective effect apart from the normative effect of orientation mentioned above.

Finally, under *ratione materiae*, the binding effect is generally limited to the facts of the individual case. Taking into account the fact that the state parties have accepted the jurisdiction of the Court in certain cases as final, the term of Article 46 (1) of the Convention "to abide by the judgment" primarily means that the responsible state party has to accept that, with regard to a certain case, a violation of the Convention has, or has not, occurred.[19]

Despite the limitations of the effect of its judgments, the Court has never hesitated in identifying the legislative origin of an individual violation.[20] As the Court has observed in several judgments, "in ratifying the Convention the Contracting States undertake to ensure that their domestic legislation is compatible with it."[21] Right from the beginning of its case law, the Court has stipulated that a judgment might create the obligation for a state party to amend its legislation if a violation of the individual applicant's right caused by legislation would otherwise continue.[22] Even if the violation is caused by an individual judgment by a domestic judicial authority, or by an administrative act of a domestic authority, the responsible state party is obligated to investigate whether an abstract provision of law predetermines the individual violation of the applicant's right. If this is the case, it must amend its legislation in order to avoid repeating the violation of the same individual, as established by the Court's judgment,[23] or foreseeable violations in parallel cases.[24]

---

[18] *Id.*, 706. Parliamentarians across Europe sometimes consult the Courts case law when drafting and revising statutes and administrative regulations, *see* Tom Barkhuysen & Michel L. van Emmerik, *A Comparative View on the Execution of Judgements of the European Court of Human Rights*, in: European Court of Human Rights: Remedies and Execution of Judgments, 1, 15 (Theodora A. Christou & Juan Pablo Raymond eds, 2005). On the differences of the effect of the judgments of the Inter-American Court of Human Rights, *see* Binder (note 4), 1218.

[19] Jörg Polakiewicz, Die Verpflichtungen der Staaten aus den Urteilen des Europäischen Gerichtshofs für Menschenrechte 251 (1993).

[20] Eur. Court H.R., *Marckx v. Belgium*, Judgment of 13 June 1979, Series A, No. 31, paras 25-68.

[21] Eur. Court H.R., *Maestri v. Italy*, Judgment of 17 February 2004, Reports of Judgments and Decisions 2004-I, para. 47.

[22] Jochen Abr. Frowein, *The Binding Force of ECHR Judgments and its Limits*, in: Human Rights, Democracy and the Rule of Law – Liber amicorum Luzius Wildhaber, 261, 262 (Stephan Breitenmoser, Bernhard Ehrenzeller, Marco Sassòli, Walter Stoffel & Beatrice Wagner Pfeifer eds, 2007).

[23] In order to adapt its legislation to the requirements of the Convention for cases, which are merely parallel as they are normatively not pre-determined by law at the national level, the State Party is obligated to do legal

1236   German Law Journal   [Vol. 12 No. 05

Even where violations stem from discretionary acts of national courts or authorities, that is the legislation has not strictly programmed the violation, or where other cases are only similar without being connected to the same legal provision, it is quite plausible to consider the responsible state party to be bound to avoid similar infringements in parallel cases.[25] This obligation, however, does not extend the binding effect of the Court's judgment in the sense of the doctrine res judicata, but rather derives from the normative effect of the concrete Convention provision concerned[26] and/or from the general obligation of the state parties to respect the Convention in accordance with Article 1 of the Convention.

Consequently, the legislative origin of an individual violation has not affected the mode in which the operative part of the judgment used to be drafted.[27] The malfunctioning of domestic legislation was only sometimes discussed in the reasoning followed by suggestions for prospective amendments.[28]

The *travaux préparatoires* suggest that the Court was for a moment intended to be empowered to nullify internal administrative and judicial decisions or legislation, but the state parties eventually rejected this constitutional or supranational approach.[29] Although it is not written anywhere in the Convention, it follows from its structure, its preparatory

---

"comparisons" because cases have to be tested whether they are truly in parallel to the case decided by the Court or whether they can for some reason be distinguished, HANS-JOACHIM CREMER, HUMAN RIGHTS AND THE PROTECTION OF PRIVACY IN TORT LAW 12 (2010).

[24] JOCHEN ABR. FROWEIN & WOLFGANG PEUKERT, EUROPÄISCHE MENSCHENRECHTSKONVENTION KOMMENTAR 604 (2009). The non-application of the legal provision violating the Convention is insufficient. The existence of the legal provision presents a steady and imminent danger to the Convention guarantees. In democracies governed by the rule of law the law-applying national authorities will have difficulties avoiding the application of a norm that has not been nullified. Therefore legislative action is necessary, *see* Klein (note 13), 707.

[25] CREMER (note 23), 11.

[26] *Id.*, 12.

[27] Lech Garlicki, *Broniowski and After*, in: LIBER AMICORUM LUZIUS WILDHABER – HUMAN RIGHTS – STRASBOURG VIEWS, 177, 183 (Lucius Caflisch, Johan Callewaert, Roderick Lidell, Paul Mahoney & Mark Villiger eds, 2007).

[28] Eur. Court H.R., *Scozzari and Giunta v. Italy*, Judgment of 13 July 2000, Reports of Judgments and Decisions 2000-VIII, para. 249; Eur. Court H.R., *Kudla v. Poland*, Judgment of 26 October 2000, Reports of Judgments and Decisions 2000-XI, para. 150-160; Eur. Court H.R., *Assanidze v. Georgia*, Judgment of 8 April 2006, Reports of Judgments and Decisions 2004-II, para. 198.

[29] COUNCIL OF EUROPE, COLLECTED EDITION OF THE „TRAVAUX PRÉPARATOIRE" OF THE EUROPEAN CONVENTION ON HUMAN RIGHTS 45 (1975). On nullifying effects of the judgments of the Inter-American Court of Human Rights, *see* Binder (note 4), 1212.

work and the wording of Article 41 of the Convention,[30] that there is no positive legal basis empowering the Court as an appellate or cassation body.[31]

Created to provide subsidiary human rights protection in relation to the state parties,[32] the Court is limited to issuing declaratory judgments.[33]   By virtue of Article 1 of the Convention, the primary competence for securing compliance with the Convention's provisions is placed on the authorities of the state parties.[34]   The state party, which is found to violate the Convention, has the discretion to decide on the "means to be utilized in its domestic legal system for performance of its obligation."[35]   The state party enjoys certain discretion that can be conceptualized as a concretization of the principle of subsidiarity.[36]   Only "if the internal law of the High Contracting Party concerned allows only partial reparation to be made,"[37] does the Court have the authority to demand a just satisfaction (*restitutio in integrum*) in accordance with Article 41 of the Convention. In all other respects, the Convention entrusts the choice regarding the execution of a judgment to the domestic authorities under the supervision of the Committee of Ministers.

In accordance to Article 46 (2) of the Convention, the judgments "shall be transmitted to the Committee of Ministers, which shall supervise its execution." The Committee of Ministers consists of one representative from each state party of the Council of Europe and is considered to be the Council of Europe's policy-making and executive organ.[38]   In

---

[30] Art. 41 of the Convention reads: "If the Court finds that there has been a violation of the Convention or the protocols thereto, and if the internal law of the High Contracting Party concerned allows only partial reparation to be made, the Court shall, if necessary, afford just satisfaction to the injured party."

[31] Frowein (note 22), 261; FROWEIN & PEUKERT (note 24), 603.

[32] Eur. Court H.R., *Handyside v. United Kingdom*, Judgment of 18 January 1978, Series A, No. 24, para. 48; Eur. Court H.R., *Sadik v. Greece*, Judgment of 15 November 1996, Reports of Judgments and Decisions 1996-V, para. 30.

[33] FROWEIN & PEUKERT (note 24), 602; POLAKIEWCZ (note 19), 217; Helmut Steinberger, *Reference to the Case Law of the Organs of the European Convention on Human Rights before National Courts*, 6 HUMAN RIGHTS LAW JOURNAL 402, 407 (1985).

[34] Paul Mahony, *Judicial Activism and Judicial Self-restraint in the European Court of Human Rights: Two Sides of the Same Coin*, 11 HUMAN RIGHTS LAW JOURNAL 57, 78 (1990).

[35] Eur. Court H.R., *Marckx v. Belgium* (note 20), para. 58.

[36] Mark E. Villiger, *The Principle of Subsidiarity in the European Convention on Human Rights*, in: PROMOTING JUSTICE, HUMAN RIGHTS AND CONFLICT RESOLUTION THROUGH INTERNATIONAL LAW – LIBER AMICORUM LUCIUS CAFLISCH, 623, 632 (Marcelo G. Kohen ed., 2007).

[37] *Id.*, para. 58.

[38] *See* Leo Zwaak, *The Supervisory Task of the Committee of Ministers,* in: THEORY AND PRACTICE OF THE EUROPEAN CONVENTION ON HUMAN RIGHTS, 291, 291 (Pieter van Dijk, Fried van Hoof, Arjen van Rijn & Leo Zwaak eds, 2006).

1238 German Law Journal [Vol. 12 No. 05

accordance with Rule 16 of the Rules of the Committee of Ministers,[39] "the Committee of Ministers may adopt interim resolutions, notably in order to provide information on the state of progress of the execution or, where appropriate, to express concern and/or to make the suggestion with respect to the execution."[40] Aside from these political and diplomatic injunctions, expulsion of a responsible state party is the *ultima ratio* sanction in accordance with Article 8 of the Statute of the Council of Europe.[41] Expulsion, however, would be counterproductive since the violating state party would no longer be under the control of the Strasbourg system.[42] Therefore, the Committee of Ministers regularly refrains from applying this sanction; instead, it usually provides a monitoring system of compliance and functions as a political forum for constructive dialogue assisting state parties in amending domestic legislation. Briefly, the Convention system attributes the power to supervise the execution of judgments to the Council of Europe's political body.

Despite the lack of a mechanism of direct coercion with respect to the implementation of judgments, the Court generally enjoys a high rate of compliance with its judgments.[43] Nonetheless, there have been several instances of slow and reluctant reactions by domestic governments and legislators and, in effect, repetitive cases kept accumulating before the Court,[44] derived from the same structural cause as an earlier application that had lead to a judgment finding a breach of the Convention.[45] The situation of repetitive cases appeared dangerous for both the authority of the Court as well as the effectiveness of the Strasbourg system as a whole.[46]

---

[39] Adopted by the Committee on Ministers on the basis of Art. 46(2) of the Convention.

[40] Interim resolutions take various forms, *see* ELIZABETH LAMBERT-ABDELGAWAD, THE EXECUTION OF JUDGMENT OF THE EUROPEAN COURT OF HUMAN RIGHTS 40 (2002).

[41] *Id.*, 40.

[42] *See* Steering Committee for Human Rights, Explanatory Report to Protocol No. 14 (note 2), 100; Helen Eaton & Jeroen Schokkenbroek, *Reforming the Human Rights Protection System Established by the European Convention on Human Rights: A New Protocol No. 14 to the Convention and Other Measures to Guarantee the Long Term Effectiveness of the Convention System*, 26 HUMAN RIGHTS LAW JOURNAL 1 (2005).

[43] Laurence Helfer & Anne-Marie Slaughter, *Towards a Theory of Effective Supranational Adjudication*, 107 YALE LAW JOURNAL 273, 296 (1997); DAVIS HARRIS, MICHAEL O'BOYLE & COLLIN WARBRICK, LAW OF THE EUROPEAN CONVENTION 878 (2009).

[44] Garlicki (note 27), 183.

[45] Steering Committee for Human Rights, Explanatory Report to Protocol No. 14 (note 2), 91.

[46] Garlicki (note 27), 183.

II. Protocol No. 14 as a Failure

The judicial elaboration of the pilot judgment procedure as a legal framework to deal with repetitive cases is no *deus ex machina*.[47] The innovation has to be seen in the context of the broader reform discussion regarding Protocol No. 14. The Court itself initially demanded an explicit jurisdiction to issue pilot judgments in its September 2003 Position Paper, submitted as part of the drafting process for Protocol No. 14.[48] According to this proposal, a pilot judgment would be delivered where the Court deemed that a systematic malfunctioning of domestic legislation or practice of the respondent state party causes a violation in an individual case. Such finding of systematic malfunctioning would be communicated to both the Committee of Ministers and the state party concerned, triggering an accelerated execution process. The respondent state party would be obliged by a pilot judgment to introduce a general remedy, by regularly amending domestic legislation. Furthermore the pilot judgment would have the effect of suspending applications of other individuals against the state party before the Court concerning the same matter. Once the Court has assured that the domestic legal order had been amended appropriately, the remaining applications issued on the same matter could be struck off the docket and referred back to the appropriate domestic authorities.[49] The intention of the Court was to provide for a procedure dealing more effectively with systematic human rights violations causing repetitive cases by obliging the responsible state party to adopt general remedial measures rather than dealing with each repetitive complaint individually case-by-case.[50]

The Steering Committee for Human Rights[51] was sympathetic to the Court's proposal and recognized the usefulness of such a solution,[52] but it was against amending the Convention due to political resistance that had been expressed within Council of Europe governmental circles against the introduction of a Convention-based pilot judgment procedure that

---

[47] Elizabeth Lambert-Abdelgawad, *La Cour européenne au secours du Comité des Ministres pour une meilleure execution des ârrets "pilot,"* 61 REVUE TRIMESTRIELLE DES DROITS DE L'HOMME 203, 213 (2005); Stefanie Schmahl, *Piloturteile des EGMR als Mittel der Verfahrensbeschleunigung,* 35 EUROPÄISCHE GRUNDRECHTE ZEITSCHRIFT 369, 371 (2008).

[48] *See* EUR. COURT H.R., DOCUMENT CDDH-GDR (2003) 024, POSITION PAPER OF THE EUROPEAN COURT OF HUMAN RIGHTS, 12 September 2003, paras 12-13; Harmsen (note 1), 45.

[49] Harmsen (note 1), 45, 46.

[50] *Id.*, 46.

[51] The Steering Committee for Human Rights (usually known by its French acronym, CDDH) is the expert, intergovernmental body within the Council of Europe charged with overseeing the functioning and development of the organization's human rights activities. As such, it plays a proactive role in the process of amending the Convention.

[52] Steering Committee for Human Rights, Explanatory Report to Protocol No. 14 (note 2), 92.

would create formal obligations for the respondent state parties to adopt general measures.[53]

Therefore, the Court's proposal has not found its way into the new wording of Article 46 of the Convention as amended by Protocol No. 14.[54] However, the Committee of Ministers adopted a resolution in which it invited the Court:

> to identify . . . what it considers to be an underlying systemic problem and the source of this problem, in particular when it is likely to give rise to numerous applications, so as to assist states in finding the appropriate solution and the Committee of Ministers in supervising the execution of judgments.[55]

The Committee of Ministers concurrently recommended[56] the improvement of domestic remedies, emphasizing that, in addition to the obligation under Article 13 of the Convention to provide an individual who has an arguable claim with an effective domestic remedy, state parties have a general obligation to solve the problems underlying the violations found.[57] Mindful that the improvement of remedies at the domestic level, particularly in relation to repetitive cases, should also contribute to reducing the workload of the Court, the Committee of Ministers advised the state parties, executing the judgments that point out domestic structural deficiencies, to review and "[to] set up

---

[53] Harmsen (note 1), 46.

[54] Art. 46 of the Convention reads: "(1) The High Contracting Parties undertake to abide by the final judgment of the Court in any case to which they are parties. (2) The final judgment of the Court shall be transmitted to the Committee of Ministers, which shall supervise its execution. (3) If the Committee of Ministers considers that the supervision of the execution of a final judgment is hindered by a problem of interpretation of the judgment, it may refer the matter to the Court for a ruling on the question of interpretation. A referral decision shall require a majority vote of two thirds of the representatives entitled to sit on the Committee. (4) If the Committee of Ministers considers that a High Contracting Party refuses to abide by a final judgment in a case to which it is a party, it may, after serving formal notice on that Party and by decision adopted by a majority vote of two thirds of the representatives entitled to sit on the Committee, refer to the Court the question whether that Party has failed to fulfil its obligation under paragraph 1. (5) If the Court finds a violation of paragraph 1, it shall refer the case to the Committee of Ministers for consideration of the measures to be taken. If the Court finds no violation of paragraph 1, it shall refer the case to the Committee of Ministers, which shall close its examination of the case."

[55] Committee of Ministers of the Council of Europe, Resolution Res(2004)3 on Judgments Revealing an Underlying Systemic Problem, 12 May 2004, 26 HUMAN RIGHTS LAW JOURNAL 119 (2005).

[56] Committee of Ministers of the Council of Europe, Recommandation Rec(2004)6 on the Improvement of Domestic Remedies, 12 May 2004, 26 HUMAN RIGHTS LAW JOURNAL 116 (2005).

[57] Garlicki (note 27), 184. Art. 13 of the Convention reads: "Everyone whose rights and freedoms as set forth in this Convention are violated shall have an effective remedy before a national authority notwithstanding that the violation has been committed by persons acting in an official capacity."

effective remedies, in order to avoid repetitive cases being brought before the Court."[58] In spite of the state parties' resistance to the Court's initiative in the reform process of Protocol No. 14, in its executive documents the Committee expressed the political will[59] to handle the problem of repetitive cases and invited the Court to do so.

III. Broniowski v. Poland

The Court immediately acted on those political suggestions when it delivered its precedent pilot judgment in the case of *Broniowski v. Poland*[60] in June 2004.[61] The case concerned a compensation claim for the loss of property that is located in an area known as the "territories beyond the Bug River," which comprises pre-World War II eastern provinces of Poland. As a consequence of the changes of Poland's borders, more than one million people had to leave this territory that became incorporated into the Soviet Union. While many of the repatriates received some land in the new Western territories of Poland, a group of nearly 80,000 people remained uncompensated, although Polish legislation has recognized since 1946 that the repatriates were entitled to receive the value of their surrendered property. Over the next fifty years, several legislative acts of compensation appeared ineffective. These ineffective entitlements were dubbed as "right to credit," by Polish legislation (the Land Administration Act 1985) and by the Polish Constitutional Court, which held that the "right to credit" has a special nature as an independent constitutionally guaranteed property right, allowing repatriates to bid for state assets. Due to the unwillingness of the Polish authorities to take effective and necessary action, in practice, however, only few "Bug River claims" could be satisfied by the system of "right to credit."

In 1996, the first applications of the "Bug River claims" were brought to the Court. In 2002, it declared the application by *Broniowski* admissible.[62] The applicant claimed that the

---

[58] Committee of Ministers of the Council of Europe, Recommandation Rec(2004)6 (note 56), 117; Garlicki (note 27), 184.

[59] Art.15.b of the Statute of the Committee of Ministers, provides for the Committee of Ministers to make recommendations to member states on matters for which the Committee has agreed "a common policy."

[60] Eur. Court H.R., *Broniowski v. Poland (GC)*, Judgment of 22 June 2004, Reports of Judgments and Decisions 2004-V. Since *Broniowski v. Poland* in 2004 the Court had issued several judgments that are expressly identified as pilot judgments by the Court itself: Eur. Court H.R., *Hutten-Czapska v. Poland*, Judgment of 19 June 2006, Reports of Judgments and Decisions 2006-VIII; Eur. Court H.R., *Burdov v. Russia (No. 2)*, Judgment of 15 January 2009; Eur. Court H.R., *Olaru and others v. Moldova*, Judgment of 28 July 2009; Eur. Court H.R., *Yuri Nikolayevich Ivanov v. Ukraine*, Judgment of 15 October 2009; Eur. Court H.R., *Suljagic v. Bosnia and Herzegovina*, Judgment of 3 November 2009; Eur. Court H.R., *Rumpf v. Germany*, Judgment of 2 September 2010; see LEACH, HARDMAN, STEPHENSON & BLITZ (note 11), 13.

[61] Garlicki (note 27), 184; Harmsen (note 1), 52.

[62] Eur. Court H.R., *Broniowski v. Poland (GC)*, Decision on Admissibility of 19 December 2002, Reports of Judgments and Decisions 2002-X, see Garlicki (note 27), 178.

compensation, which he had received for the loss of his mother's property in the former Polish territory, was inadequate under the terms of Article 1 of Protocol No. 1 to the Convention.[63] In particular, the application contended that the system of "right to credit" had proven to be of little or no value as the relevant assets had largely been withdrawn from the bidding process.

In 2004, the Court issued the judgment[64] that a claimant's entitlement to compensation, which represented only 2% of the original value of the lost property, was in violation of Article 1 of Protocol No. 1 to the Convention[65] and reserved the question of the application of Article 41 of the Convention for a future decision.

In the operative part of the 2004 judgment, the Court found that the violation of *Broniowski's* right provided by Article 1 of Protocol No. 1 to the Convention "has originated in a systemic problem connected with the malfunctioning of domestic legislation and practice caused by the failure to set up an effective mechanism to implement the 'right to credit' of Bug River claimants."[66] Therefore, the Court stated:

> [t]he respondent State must secure, through appropriate legal measures and administrative practices, the implementation of the property right in question in respect of the remaining Bug River claimants or provide them with equivalent redress in lieu, in accordance with the principles of protection of property rights under Article 1 of Protocol No. 1.[67]

---

[63] Art. 1 of Protocol No. 1 to the Convention reads: "(1) Every natural or legal person is entitled to the peaceful enjoyment of his possessions. No one shall be deprived of his possessions except in the public interest and subject to the conditions provided for by law and by the general principles of international law. (2) The preceding provisions shall not, however, in any way impair the right of a State to enforce such laws as it deems necessary to control the use of property in accordance with the general interest or to secure the payment of taxes or other contributions or penalties." *See* Garlicki (note 27), 178.

[64] Eur. Court H.R., *Broniowski v. Poland (GC)* (note 60).

[65] The relocation that took place at the end of the 1940s remains – *rationae temporis* – outside the jurisdiction of the Convention and the Court. The situation is different when a State Party enacts new legislation or maintains old legislation providing compensation for loss property confiscated under a previous regime. Once such a entitlement has been provided for by legislation post-dating the ratification of the Convention and of its Protocol No. 1, the compensation claim for the loss of property enjoy full protection under the Convention, Garlicki (note 27), 179, 181. *See* Eur. Court H.R., *Broniowski v. Poland (GC)* (note 60), para. 125.

[66] *Id.*, operative part, para. 3.

[67] *Id.*, operative part, para. 4.

In the reasoning of the judgment, the Court firstly cited the Committee of Minister's resolution,[68] which invited the Court to identify in its judgments an underlying systemic problem and to assist state parties in finding the appropriate solution. The Court secondly cited the Committee of Minister's recommendation[69] reminding the state parties of their obligation to set up effective remedies, in order to avoid repetitive cases being brought before the Court.[70] According to the Court's estimation, 167 further applications were already on its docket concerning the same subject matter, while the settlement of the Bug River claims more generally concerns nearly 80,000 people.[71] The Court thus recognized the "threat to the future effectiveness of the Convention machinery."[72]

The Court argued that:

> a judgment in which the Court finds a breach imposes on the respondent State a legal obligation . . . also to select, subject to supervision by the Committee of Ministers, the general and/or, if appropriate, individual measures to be adopted in their domestic legal order to put an end to the violation found by the Court and to redress so far as possible the effects.

The Court also noted that:

> [a]lthough it is in principle not for the Court to determine what remedial measures may be appropriate to satisfy the respondent State's obligations under Article 46 of the Convention, in view of the systemic situation which it has identified, the Court would observe that general measures at national level are undoubtedly called for in execution of the present judgment, measures which must take into account the many people affected.[73]

Once Poland adopted new legislation providing for adequate compensation, the Court

---

[68] Committee of Ministers of the Council of Europe, Resolution Res(2004)3 (note 55), 119.

[69] Committee of Ministers of the Council of Europe, Recommandation Rec(2004)6 (note 56), 116.

[70] Eur. Court H.R., *Broniowski v. Poland (GC)* (note 60), para. 190.

[71] *Id.*, para. 193.

[72] *Id.*, para. 193.

[73] *Id.*, paras 192, 193. *See* Garlicki (note 27), 185.

confirmed a friendly settlement concluded by the parties in 2005.[74]

C. Judicial Lawmaking and Its Impact on the Distribution of Competencies Within the Convention System

This part first briefly analyses the judicial elaboration of the pilot judgment procedure in the case of *Broniowski v. Poland* as procedural but also as substantive lawmaking by the Court (C.I.). It then examines the impact of such judicial lawmaking on the institutional design of the Strasbourg system particularly in regard with the state parties' competence to amend the Convention (C.II.), the state parties' competence to implement the Convention (C.III.), and the Committee of Ministers' competence to supervise the implementation by state parties (C.IV.).

I. Pilot Judgment as Judicial Lawmaking

In its precedent pilot judgment the Court evolved a new procedural regime by extending the operative part of the final judgment far beyond the individual case identifying a structural problem, and requested the respondent state party to adopt specific general and/or individual measures.

Next to this procedural lawmaking the request may be understood as a substantively programmed lawmaking obligation, which demands the domestic authorities of the respondent state party to amend specific legislation to remedy the systemic defect of its domestic legal order. In post-*Broniowski* pilot judgments the Court further stated, "measures must also be taken in respect of other persons in the applicant's position."[75] By issuing such a programmed lawmaking obligation, which demands national authorities to amend legalization in respect of other individuals, the Court uses the generality of domestic legislative acts to generalize the legal argument of its judgment beyond the concrete individual complaint to solve its docket problem of repetitive cases. By generating domestic legislation the Court stabilizes normative expectations, which are enshrined in the Convention and are concretized by the Court, in the domestic legal order for numerous cases. This judicially decreed cooperation of an international court with domestic legislation is an innovative judicial strategy of imposing the Court's legal arguments on domestic legal and political systems.

---

[74] Eur. Court H.R., *Broniowski v. Poland (GC)*, Judgment of 28 September 2005 (friendly settlement and just satisfaction), Reports of Judgments and Decisions 2005-IX.

[75] Eur. Court H.R., *Olaru and Others v. Moldavia (GC)*, Judgment of 28 July 2009, para. 49; citing Eur. Court H.R., *Scozzari and Giunta v. Italy* (GC), Judgment of 13 July 2000, Reports of Judgments and Decisions 2000-VIII, para. 249; Eur. Court H.R., *Christine Goodwin v. the United Kingdom (GC)*, Judgment of 11 July 2002, Reports of Judgments and Decisions 2002-VI, para. 120; Eur. Court H.R., *Lukenda v. Slovenia*, Judgment of 6 October 2005, Reports of Judgments and Decisions 2005-X, para. 94; Eur. Court H.R., *S. and Marper v. the United Kingdom (GC)*, Judgment of 4 December 2008, para. 134.

As mentioned above, the Court has no appellate jurisdiction, nor is there an *erga omnes* effect of the Court's judgments or any mechanism of preliminary reference to the Court for domestic judges. Thus, internalization by cooperation between the Court and domestic courts or executive authorities seems to be ineffective in contrast to the judicial system within the European Union. The judicial lawmaking in cooperation with domestic legislation can be ascribed as a Court's strategy to secure compliance against the backdrop of the lack of doctrines of direct effect and supremacy of the Convention and the lack of *erga omnes* effect of the Court's judgments in the domestic legal order.

In the follow-up friendly settlement the Court reviewed Poland's domestic legislation in regard of the individual applicant but also in a general perspective in regard of all other repetitive cases. The very fact that pilot judgments are focused on the identification of a systematic problem and on the indication of appropriate general remedial measures has an impact on their binding effect and their legal nature, accentuating the Court's lawmaking function in terms of the constitutional concept. The pilot judgments' legal nature reveals features combining individual and general effect in the domestic sphere by extending an individual complaint procedure by elements of judicial review of legislation[76] in regard of the concrete application but also in general.

The idea of judicial discretion and agency in lawmaking that exceed the lines between discourses of norm application and discourses of norm generation[77] challenges the principle of democracy as well as the understanding of the rule of law. In any domestic democratic legal order with a constitutional guarantee of fundamental rights and the rule of law, it is necessary to develop a theory of law and a theory of democracy combined in a theory of judicial review, that is a theory of separation of powers, to define the proper role of the judiciary in relation to the legislative.[78] This need of theoretical reflection nonetheless exists in regard to the multileveled Convention system.

The primary function of the Court is the settlement of legal disputes. In the exercise of this function, however, the Court quite inevitably concretizes and develops the provisions of the Convention, thus portraying an important lawmaking dimension. It was the Court that answered the question as to its function by interpreting the Convention not as an asset of

---

[76] Garlicki (note 27), 186.

[77] Jürgen Habermas, Between Facts and Norms 192-193 (1997); Armin von Bogdandy & Ingo Venzke, *Zur Herrschaft internationaler Gerichte: Eine Untersuchung internationaler öffentlicher Gewalt und ihrer demokratischen Rechtfertigung*, 70 Zeitschrift für ausländisches öffentliches Recht und Völkerrecht 1, 14 (2010); von Bogdandy & Venzke (note 7), 988, 989.

[78] Habermas (note 77), 238 *et seq.*; Mahony (note 34), 58; Christoph Möllers, Gewaltengliederung – Legitimation und Dogmatik im nationalen und internationalen Rechtsvergleich (2005).

reciprocal rights and duties among the state parties, but, far more momentously,[79] as a "constitutional instrument of European public order."[80] The term "constitutional" is ambiguous and has appeared in several judicial forms. The Court maintains the "European public order" by balancing its lawmaking function and the legislative power of the state parties.

The Court is prone to an evolutionary interpretation of the Convention, with results that could hardly be foreseen at the Convention's ratification. By virtue of the Convention, the Court is empowered by the state parties to exercise public authority by issuing final judgments, which determine the legal or factual situation of domestic authorities, of the judgment supervisory machinery within the Strasbourg system and of individuals.[81] Due to the combination of the wide-reaching substantive scope, the compulsory character—in law, in fact or both—and the lawmaking function the Court exercises functions may interfere with the domestic legislative, executive, and judicative in a vertical dimension but also in a horizontal one with the supervisory machinery within the Convention system.[82]

This paper cannot provide the elaboration on a comprehensive theory of judicial review in the multileveled Convention system. With an interest in highlighting the political repercussions of the Court's pilot judgment procedure, it may suffice to offer an analysis of the impacts on the distribution of competences between the Court, the state parties and the Committee of Ministers within the Convention system.

II. Judicial Lawmaking and the State Parties' Competence to Amend the Convention

By elaborating the pilot judgment procedure the Court has extended the binding effect *ratione personae*, and *ratione materiae* beyond the wording and the prevalent understanding of Article 46 of the Convention. According to Article 35 of the Convention,[83] the Court's competence is to interpret and to apply, not to amend, the

---

[79] Laurence R. Helfer, *Redesigning the European Court of Human Rights: Embeddedness as a Deep Structural Principle of the European Human Rights Regime*, 19 EJIL 125, 138 (2008).

[80] Eur. Court H.R., *Loizidou v. Turkey*, Judgment of 23 March 1995, Series A, No. 310, para. 75.

[81] For the concept of international public authority, *see* Armin von Bogdandy, Philipp Dann & Matthias Goldmann, *Developing the Publicness of Public International Law: Towards a Legal Framework for Global Governance Activities*, 9 GERMAN LAW JOURNAL 1375, 1381 (2008). *See* for judicial decisions von Bogdandy & Venzke (note 7), 989.

[82] Compare von Bogdandy & Venzke (note 7), 990. More generally on the international judiciary in a constitutionalist reading, Geir Ulfstein, *The International Judiciary*, in: THE CONSTITUTIONALIZATION OF INTERNATIONAL LAW, 126, 127 (Jan Klabbers, Anne Peters & Geir Ulfstein eds, 2009).

[83] Art. 35 of the Convention reads: "(1) The jurisdiction of the Court shall extend to all matters concerning the interpretation and application of the Convention and the protocols thereto which are referred to it as provided in Articles 33, 34 and 47. (2)In the event of dispute as to whether the Court has jurisdiction, the Court shall decide."

Convention. The competence of amendment as such rests with the state parties of the Council of Europe. Thus, the elaboration of the pilot judgment procedure causes the judicialization of politics[84] at the Convention's amending level.

III. Judicial Lawmaking and the State Parties' Competence to Implement the Convention

The distinction between the Court's competence of judicial review by interpretation, on the one hand, and the state parties' competence to amend the Convention, on the other, is not the only distribution of competences operated by the Convention. [85] By virtue of Article 1 of the Convention, the primary competence for securing compliance with the Convention provisions is placed on the domestic authorities (legislative, executive and judicial) under the supervisory authority of the Committee of Ministers in accordance with Article 46 (2) of the Convention. [86]

As mentioned above, the Court interprets the Convention as a "constitutional instrument of European public order."[87] The Court maintains the "European public order" by calibrating the balance between judicial review and deference to domestic law-makers.[88] In accordance with Article 1 and Article 46 of the Convention the Court concretized the principle of subsidiarity in relation to the implementation of judgments of the Court[89] in terms of judicial self-restraint to recognize the horizontal and vertical distribution of competences between the Court and domestic authorities of the state parties with consequences for the supervisory function of the Committee of Ministers. Deriving from the principle of subsidiary and linked with the principle of democracy,[90] the state parties enjoy a certain margin of appreciation that gives them the discretion to decide "the choice of means to be utilized in its domestic legal system for performance of its obligation"[91] because "[t]he national authorities have direct democratic legitimation and are . . . in

---

[84] Torbjörn Vallinder, *When the Courts go Marching in*, in: THE GLOBAL EXPANSION OF JUDICIAL POWER, 13 (C. Neal Tate & Torbjörn Vallinder eds, 1995).

[85] Mahony (note 34), 78.

[86] Art. 1 of the Convention reads: "The High Contracting Parties shall secure to everyone within their jurisdiction the rights and freedoms defined in Section I of this Convention." *See* Mahony (note 34), 78.

[87] Eur. Court H.R., *Loizidou v. Turkey* (note 80), para. 75.

[88] Laurence R. Helfer, *Redesigning the European Court of Human Rights: Embeddedness as a Deep Structural Principle of the European Human Rights Regime*, 19 EJIL 125, 131 (2008).

[89] Eur. Court H.R., *Norris v. Ireland*, Judgment 26 October 1988, Series A , No. 142, para. 50; Eur. Court H.R., *Clooth v. Belgium*, Judgment of 5 March 1998, Reports of Judgments and Decisions 1998-I, para. 14.

[90] Dinah Shelton, *Subsidiarity and Human Rights Law*, 27 HUMAN RIGHTS LAW JOURNAL 4, 9 (2006); Villiger (note 36), 632.

[91] Eur. Court H.R., *Marckx v. Belgium* (note 20), para. 58.

principle better placed than an international court to evaluate local needs and conditions."[92]   Furthermore, state parties have different written and unwritten constitutional systems and traditions and are exposed to different challenges when implementing international decisions.[93] For instance, the relations between national and international law differ or federal state parties encounter the particular problem of a separation of powers on different levels.[94] In such varying pluralistic democracies there is a spectrum of measures to the domestic authorities for fulfilling their obligation of implementation.   Any choice within this spectrum is within their discretion and not contrary to the Convention.[95]

The Convention system, like a domestic constitution protecting fundamental rights and freedoms, reflects the function to restrict democratic discretion to a certain extent.[96] Nonetheless, not all discretion is removed since the state parties have preserved the competence for implementing the execution of judgments. The Court's judicial review forms part of a vertical system of checks and balances. A degree of judicial self-restraint can be required for an appropriate balance between judicial review and deference to domestic law-makers. On the one hand, the Court stresses the subsidiary nature of the Strasbourg system in relation to domestic human rights protection systems.[97] On the other hand, the Court, however, proactively reviews domestic legislation, administrative acts and judicial rulings using distinctive methods of interpretation and an evolving understanding of Convention rights and freedoms.[98] Over time, the Court has employed the judicial methodological instruments to generate a slow but constant change of the sphere of autonomy of the state parties.[99]

This is the case in a pilot judgment. Although Poland was technically given a choice of how to comply, the *Broniowski* judgment did not exemplify the same discretion usually given to the respondent state party. Instead, Poland had only two choices left: Firstly, to amend domestic legislation to provide the realization of the property rights, or secondly, to

---

[92] *Id.*, para. 48.

[93] Villiger (note 36), 632.

[94] *Id.*, 632.

[95] Mahony (note 34), 78.

[96] *Id.*, 81.

[97] Eur. Court H.R., *Handyside v. United Kingdom* (note 32), para. 48; Eur. Court H.R., *Sadik v. Greece* (note 32), para. 30, *see* Helfer (note 79), 138.

[98] Id., 138.

[99] Id., 138; Ress (note 17), 374.

compensate the claimants with equivalent redress. Another pilot judgment, the *Hutten-Czapska* judgment,[100] illustrates that this discretion can be further narrowed.

Similar to the *Broniowski,* the *Hutten-Czapska* case concerned the violation of Article 1 of Protocol No. 1. Here the applicant was one of around 100,000 landlords in Poland affected by a restrictive system of rent control. The Court held that the violation has originated in a systemic problem connected with the malfunctioning of domestic legislation imposing restrictions on landlords' rights, including defective provisions on the determination of rent and not providing for any procedure or mechanism enabling landlords to recover losses incurred in connection with property maintenance. The Court commanded that Poland had to, through appropriate legal and/or other measures, secure in its domestic legal order a mechanism to maintain a fair balance between the interests of landlords and the general interest of the community, in accordance with the standards of protection of property rights under the Convention.

This case illustrates that it:

> is not simply a question of instituting a compensation procedure which . . . applies to a series of clearly defined individual cases. On the contrary, the solution to the problem in the present case involves a total overhaul of the legal system governing owners' rights vis-à-vis tenants, taking into account all the known difficulties, options and alternatives in such matters and the need to adopt a gradual approach in such a sensitive area—what is more, during the transition from a communist to a free-market regime.[101]

By issuing such a programmed lawmaking obligation in the operative part of the judgment, the judicial review in the follow-up procedure of a friendly settlement in accordance to Article 38 of the Convention innovatively moves "beyond the sole interests of the individual applicant and requires the Court to examine the case also from the point view of 'relevant general measures.'"[102] The Court, in accepting the terms of the settlement in respect of both individual and general measures, attached particular weight to the general measures already taken and to be taken by the state party. These measures include legislation that had been passed between the initial judgment and the friendly settlement judgment, which was intended to remedy the structural problem.

---

[100] Eur. Court H.R., *Hutten-Czapska v. Poland,* Judgment of 19 June 2006, Reports of Judgments and Decisions 2006-VIII.

[101] *Id.,* Partly Dissenting Opinion of Judge Zagrebelsky.

[102] Eur. Court H.R., *Broniowski v. Poland (GC)* (note 74), paras 5-10.

1250 German Law Journal [Vol. 12 No. 05

The legal nature of friendly settlements after pilot judgments reveals different features, combining individual and general effects by extending an individual complaint procedure with elements of judicial review of legislation in regard to plaintiffs of parallel cases. It is questionable whether the Court is at all competent and has the necessary knowledge to express a view in abstract and in advance on the consequences of legislative reforms already introduced by a state party and to give a vague positive assessment of a legislative development whose practical application might subsequently be challenged by new applicants. [103]

IV. Judicial Lawmaking and the Committee of Minister's Competence to Supervise the Implementation

The distinction between the Court's competence of judicial review and the state parties' primary competence for securing compliance with the Convention provisions is not the only distribution of competence operated by the Convention. According to Article 46 (2) of the Convention, once the Court's final judgment has been transmitted to the Committee of Ministers, the latter invites the respondent state party to inform it of individual and general measures taken to abide by the judgment and of steps taken to pay any amounts awarded by the Court in respect of just satisfaction.

The Court's competence to examine the judgments' execution in regard of the vertical relation to the state parties is related to the Court's competence in regard to the supervisory function of the Committee of Ministers in a horizontal relation.

An ordinary judgment of the Court does not expressly order the respondent state party to a specific measure to rectify the applicant's situation and prevent further violations. According to the principle of subsidiarity the state parties have discretion to choose the means by which they will implement individual or general measures under the supervision of the Committee of Ministers. This political body provides a forum of constructive dialogue and political review of individual and general measures. The supervision of execution is treated as a co-operative political task and not an inquisitorial one[104] with the lawful/unlawful concluding binary decision. By issuing a substantively programmed lawmaking obligation pilot judgments impose the legal arguments on the political process at the supervisory level. This form of judicialization of the political mechanism of supervision[105] restricts the Committee of Ministers' competence to supervise the

---

[103] Eur. Court H.R., *Hutten-Czapska v. Poland*, Judgment of 28 April 2008 (friendly settlement), Separate Opinion of Judge Zagrebelsky joined by Judge Jaeger.

[104] Committee of Ministers of the Council of Europe, CM/Inf(2008)8 final, Committee of Ministers on Human Rights Working Methods – Improved Effectiveness of the Committee of Minister's Supervision of Execution of Judgments, 7 April 2004, para 13.

implementation of judgments.

D. Justification of Judicialization of Politics within the Convention System

The pilot judgment causes the judicialization of politics[106] at the Convention's amending level, at the domestic legislative level as well as at the Convention's supervisory level. This section addresses the issue of how such lawmaking by the Court can be justified particularly in terms of procedural and democratic legitimacy.

I. Justification of Judicial Lawmaking at the Convention's Amending Level

The Court has extended the binding effect *ratione personae*, and *ratione materiae* beyond the wording and the prevalent understanding of Article 46 of the Convention. Thus the question arises, whether the judicial elaboration of the pilot judgments procedure is an *ultra vires* act. The extensive interpretation of Article 46 of the Convention as an act of judicial lawmaking in relation to the amendment competence of the state parties affects the tension between international judicialization and democratic control. This tension should influence the Court in exercising its power in terms of an appropriate balance between activism and restraint. The application of an expansive or more restrictive approach is primarily determined on the basis of the mandate of the Court.[107]

According to Article 35 of the Convention the Court's mandate is to interpret and to apply Article 46 of the Convention, not to amend. The Court has opted for an approach of developing the meaning of indeterminate concepts by employing the method of evolutionary interpretation.[108] In its case law, the Court affirmed, "the Convention is a living instrument which . . . must be interpreted in the light of present-day conditions."[109] The Convention's Preamble explicitly states that the purpose of the Convention is both the "maintenance" and the "further realization of human rights and fundamental freedoms." Therefore, the Court concluded that its "judgments in fact serve not only to decide those cases brought before the Court but, more generally, to elucidate, safeguard, and develop the rules instituted by the Convention."[110] The interpretation of human-rights treaties falls

---

[105] Helfer (note 79), 149.

[106] Vallinder (note 84).

[107] Ulfstein (note 82), 150.

[108] Rudolf Bernhardt, *Evolutive Treaty Interpretation, Especially of the European Convention on Human Rights*, 42 GERMAN YEARBOOK FOR INTERNATIONAL LAW 11, 17 (1999); Mahony (note 34), 61.

[109] Eur. Court H.R., *Tyrer v. United Kingdom*, Judgment of 25 April 1978, Series A, No. 26, para. 31, *see* Mahony (note 34), 61.

[110] Eur. Court H.R., *Ireland v. United Kingdom*, Judgment of 18 January 1978, Series A, No. 25, para. 154.

into a special category, since the quite distinct object and purpose of a human-rights treaty take on a special importance.[111] The distinctive nature of the Convention as a human-rights treaty compels a flexible and evolutionary teleological interpretation of its open-textured terms if the Convention is not to become progressively ineffective with time.[112]

The overwhelming number of applications often concerning repetitive cases threatens "the future effectiveness of the Convention machinery."[113] However, questions arise whether the approach of evolutionary interpretation only allows the development and concretization of material provisions of fundamental rights and freedoms that are already spelled out in the Convention.   In this respect the Court's practice in developing procedures of judicial review, which are not spelled out in the Convention, would no longer correspond to the essence of the evolutionary method.

Furthermore, the preparatory works of the Convention speak against the extension of res judicata of the Court's judgments. As emerges from the *travaux préparatoires,* it was at some point proposed that the Court's judgments should have *erga omnes* effect on national jurisdictions, but the state parties rejected this approach.[114] In addition, Protocol No. 14 has not formally introduced the pilot judgment procedure.[115]

Next to formal mandating by the Convention, the Court's mandate in terms of Article 46 of the Convention can also be extensively interpreted in the light of consensual subsequent practice of the state parties in accordance with Article 31 (3) lit. b of the Vienna Convention on the Law of Treaties. The application of the pilot judgment procedure is broadly considered to have been successful, because many post-*Borniowski* pilot judgments have led to legislative changes in the domestic legal orders.[116] Thus, the state parties accepted the new procedure. Furthermore, the resolution of the Committee of Ministers[117] inviting the Court to identify in its judgments finding an underlying systemic problem and to assist state parties in finding the appropriate solution allows for an assumption of consensual subsequent practice of the state parties. Thus, the judicial elaboration of the pilot judgment procedure is based on the political will of the state

---

[111] Rudolf Bernhardt, *Thoughts on the Interpretation of Human Rights Treaties,* in: PROTECTING HUMAN RIGHTS: THE EUROPEAN DIMENSION – STUDIES IN HONOUR OF GERARD WIARDA, 65 (Franz Matscher & Herbert Petzold eds, 1988).

[112] Mahony (note 34), 65.

[113] Eur. Court H.R., *Broniowski v. Poland (GC)* (note 60), para. 193.

[114] *Id.*, Partly Dissenting Opinion of Judge Zupančič.

[115] Eur. Court H.R., *Hutten-Czapska v. Poland,* Judgment of 19 June 2006, Reports of Judgments and Decisions 2006-VIII, Partly Dissenting Opinion of Judge Zagrebelsky.

[116] LEACH, HARDMAN , STEPHENSON & BLITZ (note 11), 178.

[117] Committee of Ministers of the Council of Europe, Resolution Res(2004)3 (note 55), 119.

parties. Nonetheless, the judicial lawmaking relies on the consensual or majoritarian[118] will of the executives of the state parties represented in the Committee of Minister; it does not rest on the will of the legislator in the Strasbourg system, which is the consensual will of the state parties' legislatives, who regularly amend the Convention in a formal process of democratic delegation. Otherwise domestic parliaments tend to be deferential to the executive in treaty negotiations.[119] Thus, the autonomy of governmental-administrative elites in amending the Convention is relatively great.[120]

II. Justification of Judicial Lawmaking at the Domestic Legislative Level

In a concurring opinion to the *Hutten-Czapska* friendly settlement Judge Ziemele wrote: "As to the scope of the Court's competence, the fact that the Court has the jurisdiction to develop procedures, especially where States have invited it to do so, does not answer the question about the scope and the limits of the exercise of such a power."[121] In relation to the domestic legislative the pilot judgment moves towards a constitutional court-type jurisdiction reviewing domestic legislation and issuing a programmed lawmaking obligation in its operative part. One could use the constitutional argument conferring legitimacy by a higher order of norms that guides and channels the parliamentary legislative process.[122] The presence of such norms within the framework of an international organization could promote its legitimacy by virtue of the norm's status, which could impose a legal duty to comply even against the will of the parliamentary majority. This "constitutional" argument is often made in respect to international human rights treaties. The provisions of the Convention as mutually defined by the state parties, but beyond the reach of domestic legislation, may justify restrictions on the national legislator[123] to protect human rights within an international constitutional framework.[124]

---

[118] Under Art. 20 of the Statute the Committee of Ministers, adoption of a recommendation requires an unanimous vote of all representatives present or a majority of those entitled to vote. However, at their 519 bis meeting in November 1994 the Ministers' Deputies decided to make their voting procedure more flexible and made a "Gentleman's agreement" not to apply the unanimity rule to recommendations.

[119] von Bogdandy & Venzke (note 7), 994.

[120] *Id.*

[121] Eur. Court H.R, *Hutten-Czapska v. Poland* (note 103), Concurring opinion of Judge Ziemele; citing *Nuclear Tests Case* (Australia v. France), ICJ Reports 1974, para. 23, Joint Dissenting Opinion of Judges Onyeama, Dillard, Jimenez de Arechaga and Sir Humphrey Waldock.

[122] von Bogdandy & Venzke (note 77), 22-25; Joshua L. Jackson, *Broniowski v. Poland: A Recipe for Increased Legitimacy of The European Court of Human Rights as a Supranational Constitutional Court*, 39 CONNECTICUT LAW REVIEW 759, 799 (2006).

[123] Ulfstein (note 82), 151.

[124] GREER (note 4), 7; Wildhaber (note 4), 162.

The purpose of the Court is, according to its own understanding, "to elucidate, safeguard, and develop the rules instituted by the Convention"[125] as a "constitutional instrument of European public order."[126] One could view the Court as "the Constitutional Court for Europe,"[127] in the sense that it is the final authoritative adjudicative body in the pan-European constitutional system,[128] performs its adjudicatory role within the limits of the Convention system.[129]

Nonetheless, such interpretation in terms of the liberal paradigm of judicial constitutional review[130] camouflages the vertical relation between the Court and domestic legislator in regard of the pilot judgment procedure. Pilot judgments do not restrict the domestic legislator to regulating a matter concerning human rights provisions of the Convention. In contrast, by its programmed lawmaking obligation the Court mobilizes the democratic legislator to amend in a self-regulatory manner domestic legislation in a Convention provision-related matter. As mentioned above, the Court wants to use the generality of domestic legislative acts to internalize and generalize the legal argument of its judgment in the domestic legal order. Pilot judgments are a form of judicially decreed cooperation between the Court and national parliaments. Thus, pilot judgments have a catalyzing effect on the domestic democratic legislative process, especially in the ongoing democratic transition in the new state parties of the Central and Eastern Europe.

As mentioned above, the state parties' discretion secures the vertical distribution of competences between the Court and the domestic legislator, that is the relation between the co-original individual autonomy protected by fundamental rights and freedoms and the autonomy of the domestic democratic sovereign. The Court has to respect this flexible principle in programming its lawmaking obligation. The scope of discretion should differ according to the type of Convention provisions of the alleged violation. In the context of the right to property, the state parties should enjoy wide discretion, particularly in redistributing private property, being a domain where differences of opinion may vary largely in pluralistic democracies.[131] The Court should exercise judicial self-restraint in programming the lawmaking obligation in pilot judgments related to economic and social rights. In the context of procedural and participatory rights, providing procedural and

---

[125] Eur. Court H.R., *Ireland v. United Kingdom* (note 110), para. 154.

[126] Eur. Court H.R., *Loizidou v. Turkey* (note 80), para. 75.

[127] STEVEN GREER, THE EUROPEAN CONVENTION ON HUMAN RIGHTS: ACHIEVEMENTS, PROBLEMS AND PROSPECTS 7 (2006).

[128] *Id.*, 7.

[129] Jackson (note 122), 799.

[130] HABERMAS (note 77), 240-253.

[131] Mahony (note 34), 79.

democratic participation and effective legal protection, the discretion should be reduced.[132]

III. Justification of Judicial Lawmaking at the Supervisory Level

By issuing a substantively programmed lawmaking obligation, a pilot judgment imposes its legal arguments on the political process at the supervisory level. The question arises whether such judicial lawmaking at the supervisory level would be an *ultra vires* act. Indeed, the judicial lawmaking at the supervisory level can be justified by a resolution[133] and a recommendation[134] of the Committee of Ministers itself.[135] Nonetheless, the concern of the Court's competence in regard to the supervisory authority of the Committee of Ministers is not only formal. Reminiscent of the *Hutten-Czapska* case, the structural problem was a large-scale one and required the adoption and carrying out of complex measures of a legislative and administrative character with an economic and social content.

On the one hand, it has been argued that such cases would pose legal and practical difficulties that the Committee of Ministers would be much better equipped to monitor than the Court, especially as to the implementation of complex, long-term measures.[136] The Committee of Ministers could take prospective examination into consideration in its initial interim resolutions. By contrast, the Court would regularly be the inadequate institution for the prospective examination of domestic legislative amendment because it might have to exercise caution in relation to future applications or it might have to examine impartially in adversarial proceedings.

On the other hand, the judicial lawmaking at the supervisory level is in accordance with the political reform process of Protocol No. 14. The question of the Court's relationship to the Committee of Ministers can be linked with the reform process leading to Protocol No. 14. The amended Article 46 of the Convention extends the judicial role in the supervisory

---

[132] *Compare* Shelton (note 90), 10, stating: „the Court has applied a reduced margin of appreciation ... where the government has interfered with democratic institutions, such as dissolving political parties or restricting freedom of information on issues of public interest." *See* Eur. Court H.R., *Refah Partisi (The Welfare Party) and Others v. Turkey (GC)*, Judgment of 13 February 2003, Reports of Judgments and Decisions 2003-II; Eur. Court H.R., *Scharsach and News Verlagsgesellschaft mbH v. Austria*, Judgment of 13 November 2003, Reports of Judgments and Decisions 2003-XI. Nonetheless, it should grant wide margin of appreciation for matters concerning elections, noting that there are numerous ways of organising and running electoral systems and a wealth of differences in historical development, cultural diversity and political thought within Europe, *see* Shelton (note 90), 10.

[133] Committee of Ministers of the Council of Europe, Resolution Res(2004)3 (note 55), 119.

[134] Committee of Ministers of the Council of Europe, Recommandation Rec(2004)6 (note 56), 116.

[135] Schmahl (note 47), 379.

[136] Eur. Court H.R, *Hutten-Czapska v. Poland* (note 103), Concurring Opinion of Judge Ziemele.

German Law Journal [Vol. 12 No. 05

mechanism by introducing two new mechanisms enabling the Committee of Ministers to bring supervision matters before the Court. First, the Protocol establishes a form of infringement proceedings, modeled on that existing in European Union Law.[137] This provision permits the Committee, by a two-thirds majority vote, to make a reference to the Court seeking to determine whether a state party has fulfilled its obligation regarding the execution of a previous judgment.[138] Second, the Protocol institutes a form of clarification ruling.[139] Under this provision, the Committee of Ministers, again by a two-thirds majority vote, may request a ruling on a question of interpretation where the Committee of Ministers has found that its supervision of execution of a judgment has been hindered by the existence of problems surrounding the interpretation of that judgment.[140]

Both amendments clarify the nature of the Convention as an interlocking horizontal set of institutions in which both the judicial and the political organs have distinctive and necessary functions.[141] Nonetheless, Protocol No. 14 particularly strengthens the judicial role in the supervisory mechanism. In combination with a pilot judgment requesting the respondent state party in the operative part to adopt general measures in terms of a substantively programmed lawmaking obligation, an infringement proceeding will generate a "judicial review of legislative action" in general as well as a friendly settlement past to a pilot judgment.

Furthermore, much criticism has been levied at the effectiveness of, the lack of access to, the transparency of, and the publicness of the supervisory mechanism of the Committee of Ministers.[142] In practice, the Committee only meets twice a year.[143] In the meantime its tasks are discharged by the so-called "Committee of the Ministers Deputies," consisting of high officials who are generally the permanent representatives of their governments to the Council of Europe.[144] The sessions of the Committee of Ministers are not public, unless the Committee decides otherwise.[145]

---

[137] Harmsen (note 1), 52.

[138] *Id.*, 52.

[139] *Id.*, 52.

[140] *Id.*, 52.

[141] *Id.*, 52.

[142] Philip Leach, *On Reform of he European Court of Human Rights*, 14 EUROPEAN HUMAN RIGHTS LAW REVIEW 725, 732 (2009).

[143] *See* Art. 21(c) of the Statute of the Council of Europe.

[144] Zwaak (note 38), 45.

[145] *See* Art. 21(a) of the Statute of the Council of Europe.

In this respect, the Court's procedural legitimacy is much more developed. Under Article 40 of the Convention, all the Court's hearings are public absent exceptional circumstances, and all documents are open to the public unless the President of the Court decides otherwise. In accordance with Article 36 of the Convention,[146] third parties have the right to submit written comments and to take part in hearings. According to Article 45[147] of the Convention, all judgments have to be reasoned. With regard to democratic legitimacy, the Court' judges are elected by the Parliamentary Assembly in accordance with Article 22 of the Convention.[148]   In order to improve independence and impartiality of the judges, Protocol 14 extends the terms of office period to nine years while abolishing the re-election of judges.

IV. The Individual?

From the perspective of the individual applicant, the whole complicacy of the pilot judgment procedure becomes particularly apparent. The adjournment of similar, pending cases is the central element of a pilot judgment to solve the Court's docket problem.[149] Coevally, the adjournment weakens the individual's right of access to the Court in accordance with Article 34 of the Convention.[150]   Once the respondent state party has introduced a remedy in compliance with the pilot judgment these adjourned cases can subsequently be referred back. If the state response is insufficient, the adjourned cases could be re-opened by the Court. There is no guarantee that the application of the pilot judgment exactly reflects all the facts and legal issues related to numerous violations.[151]

---

[146] Art. 36 of the Convention reads: "(1) In all cases before a Chamber or the Grand Chamber, a High Contracting Party one of whose nationals is an applicant shall have the right to submit written comments and to take part in hearings. (2) The President of the Court may, in the interest of the proper administration of justice, invite any High Contracting Party which is not a party to the proceedings or any person concerned who is not the applicant to submit written comments or take part in hearings."

[147] Art. 45 of the Convention reads: "(1) Reasons shall be given for judgments as well as for decisions declaring applications admissible or inadmissible. (2) If a judgment does not represent, in whole or in part, the unanimous opinion of the judges, any judge shall be entitled to deliver a separate opinion."

[148] Art. 22 of the Convention reads: "(1) The judges shall be elected by the Parliamentary Assembly with respect to each High Contracting Party by a majority of votes cast from a list of three candidates nominated by the High Contracting Party. (2) The same procedure shall be followed to complete the Court in the event of the accession of new High Contracting Parties and in filling casual vacancies."

[149] However, similar pending cases will not always be adjourned. This is a matter of discretion for the Court depending on all relevant circumstances, see LEACH, HARDMAN, STEPHENSON & BLITZ (note 11), 176.

[150] Art. 34 of the Convention reads: "The Court may receive applications from any person, non-governmental organisation or group of individuals claiming to be the victim of a violation by one of the High Contracting Parties of the rights set forth in the Convention or the protocols thereto. The High Contracting Parties undertake not to hinder in any way the effective exercise of this right."

[151] Helfer (note 79), 154.

Furthermore, the applicant of the pilot judgment is privileged in relation to the others. Whilst reviewing the application of the pilot judgment, the others remain in stasis.[152] Justice delayed is justice denied. The possibility that the applicant of the pilot judgment will negotiate a friendly settlement that favors an individual damages award over systematic non-monetary remedies is even more worrying for subordinated applicants.[153] If the state party's response is insufficient, the adjourned cases could be re-opened by the Court, of course. However, the re-opening of similar, pending cases is a discretionary act by the Court[154] that could leave the remaining applicants in an uncertain position[155] and extend considerably the length of such proceedings.[156] The Court has to pay attention to the procedure's legitimacy if the pilot judgment is to serve as an effective tool for improving compliance with the Convention.[157] The elaboration of procedural safeguards to ensure the adjudication on class-wide relief applications appropriate to the systematic human rights issues could improve the procedural situation. In this respect the establishment of Rule 61 of the Rules of the Court in February 2011 is a substantial progress. However, the term of "class action" and "collective applications"[158] has not yet been defined and further research needs to be conducted into their potential efficacy at the international level.[159]

E. Outlook

Referring to this paper's title and the question whether the pilot judgment is a form of judicial expansion of competences without politics, it has been shown that the procedural lawmaking by elaborating the pilot judgment procedure was carried by the political will of

---

[152] *Id.*, 154; citing Registrar of the European Court of Human Rights, *"Pinto" cases adjourned pending decision on test case*, Press Release 014, 18 January 2005, stating that the Court had adjourned over 800 Italian length-of-proceedings cases, pending its decision in a test case concerning the application of Italy's "Pinto Law."

[153] Helfer (note 79), 154; citing Andreas von Staden, *Assessing the Impact of the Judgment of the European Court of Human Rights on Domestic Human Rights Policies*, paper prepared for delivery at the Annual Meeting of the American Political Science Association, noting that a "state may prefer to simply pay just satisfaction without taking substantive steps to remedy the situation and fully remove the consequences of the violation and suggesting that many governments enter into friendly settlements for that reason." Helfer points out that the Court "may not approve a friendly settlement unless it manifests a "respect for human rights as defined in the Convention and the Protocols thereto" in accordance to Art. 37 of the Convention."

[154] LEACH, HARDMAN, STEPHENSON & BLITZ (note 11), 176.

[155] *Id.*, 30.

[156] *Id.*, 31.

[157] Helfer (note 79), 154.

[158] Eur. Court H.R., Memorandum of the President of the European Court of Human Rights to the States with a View to Preparing the Interlaken Conference, 3 July 2009, 8.

[159] Leach (note 142), 731.

the state parties' executives convened in the Committee of Ministers. Even though the international legislator had not solved the docket problem by Protocol No. 14 the political body of the Convention system invited the Court to react to the crisis. In the absence of a functional legislator, lawmaking by an international adjudicative body tried to solve a functional crisis in an international legal regime by realigning the competences in the Convention system. The state parties in post-*Broniowski* pilot judgments have accepted this shift of competences.[160] Furthermore, pilot judgments are a form of judicially decreed cooperation between the Court and national parliaments and have a catalyzing effect on the domestic democratic legislative process. Thus, the pilot judgment is a form of judicial lawmaking including domestic legislatives at the expense of the individual. That might be the cause for the Court's reasoning not invoking the effectiveness of the concrete Convention provision applied by the individual but the "effectiveness of the Convention machinery"[161] as a whole.

---

[160] LEACH, HARDMAN, STEPHENSON & BLITZ (note 11), 178.

[161] Eur. Court H.R., *Broniowski v. Poland (GC)* (note 60), para. 193.

[13]

Articles

The Future of the European Court of Human Rights

By Michael O'Boyle[*]

A. Introduction

It is a pleasure to be back in Dublin and to have this opportunity to speak to you about the Court and its future. Reading the outpourings of denigration in the newspapers recently you can be forgiven for believing that the Court is about to be towed into the middle of the Rhine and scuppered by a coalition of unhappy State Parties. So where does the future of the Court lie and how should one respond to such media buffetings?

The Court has never, in its 50-year history, been subject to such a barrage of hostile criticism as that which occurred in the United Kingdom in February 2011. In the past it was not infrequent that particular judgments were criticized and called into question. The *McCann v. the United Kingdom* case concerning the Gibraltar killings and the *Lautsi v. Italy* judgment concerning the presence of crucifix in schools are good examples of this.[1] Over the years certain governments have discovered that it is electorally popular to criticize international courts such as the Strasbourg court: they are easy targets, particularly because they tend, like all courts, not to answer back.

On this occasion, the case that became the focus of national opprobrium was a judgment of the Grand Chamber that had been handed down more than five years ago and that had not yet been implemented by the United Kingdom authorities. It had been held in *Hirst (no. 2) v. the United Kingdom* that a blanket ban on the exercise of voting rights by prisoners was incompatible with the right to free elections guaranteed by Article 3 of Protocol No. 1. In essence, the Court was saying that not all prisoners should be put into the same basket and that legislation should be adopted by the United Kingdom that sought to make distinctions between different categories of prisoners.[2] An important feature of

---

[*] Deputy Registrar of the European Court of Human Rights. All views are personal. This address was given at University College, Dublin, on 1 April 2011 on the occasion of the launch of the new Masters Degree program in UCD run jointly by the School of Law and the UCD Department of Politics and International Relations. The event was hosted by the UCD Human Rights Network that is composed of academic staff and researchers at UCD who are working in the field of human rights. Email: Michael.Oboyle@echr.coe.int.

[1] McCann v. the United Kingdom, 324 Eur. Ct. H.R. (ser. A, 1995). Lautsi v. Italy, Eur. Ct. H. R., judgment of 18 March 2011, available at: http://www.echr.coe.int/echr/resources/hudoc/lautsi_and_others_v__italy.pdf (last accessed: 27 September 2011).

[2] Hirst v. the United Kingdom (no. 2), 2005-IX Eur. Ct. H.R.

the case was that there had been no substantive parliamentary debate on the issue of prisoners voting since the 19th century. Coincidentally a similar analysis based on the blanket nature of the law had been made in *S and Marper v. the United Kingdom* concerning the retention of the DNA of all persons who had been acquitted of offenses as well as those who had been convicted of offenses. But that judgment was rather popular and received good press.[3]

The issue of prisoners' voting rights was transformed into a national interrogation in the United Kingdom about the legitimacy of the European Court of Human Rights. The Daily Mail led the charge. On 5 February 2011, five days before a free vote on the issue of prisoners' voting rights in the House of Commons, the Daily Mail carried an article with the following heading *"The European Human Rights judges [are] wrecking British law."*

> For the third time in a week, Strasbourg's unelected European Court of Human Rights is under the spotlight. First, Tory MPs made it clear they have no intention of bowing to the court's demand to grant the vote to tens of thousands of prisoners. Next Lord Carlisle, the government's reviewer of anti-terror laws, said its rulings against deportation had turned Britain into a 'safe haven' for those who wish the country harm. Now Damien Green, the immigration minister, has said its rulings have turned human rights into a 'boo phrase'. He said the court's judgments – and our own judiciary's liberal interpretation of them – meant the public immediately expected bad news when the phrase 'human rights' was uttered. 'Clearly something is wrong when you get to that stage,' Mr Green said. His remarks will fuel the anger of MPs towards the European Court. In 2005, 17 judges ruled in favor of John Hirst, who argued prisoners should be able to vote. He had been in jail for killing his 69-year-old landlady with an ax, after which he had calmly made a cup of coffee. Under pressure from the court, the British government announced last year that it would comply with the ruling. Hirst celebrated by drinking champagne and smoking cannabis – and put a video of it all on YouTube.[4]

Warming to its theme, the Daily Mail on 7 February 2011 carried the headline *"European Court of Human Rights Court is out of control – we must pull out."*

---

[3] S. and Marper v. the United Kingdom, 48 E.H.R.R.50 (2009).

[4] James Slack, *Named and Shamed: The European Human Rights Judges Wrecking British Law*, DAILY MAIL, 5 Feb. 2011, available at: http://www.dailymail.co.uk/news/article-1353860/Named-shamed-The-European-human-rights-judges-wreckingo-British-law.html#ixzz1QNTg8Uz2 (last accessed: 27 September 2011).

One of Britain's most senior judges called last night for Britain to pull out of the European Court of Human Rights following its controversial ruling that prisoners should be given the vote. Lord Hoffman, who served as a Law Lord for 14 years until last year, said the court had gone beyond its remit in a way that would have 'astonished' its founding fathers. The prominent human rights campaigner said that in recent years 'human rights have become, like health and safety, a byword for foolish decisions by courts and administrators.' He said the 60-year-old principles of the European Convention on Human Rights were 'in general terms admirable'. But he said the Strasbourg Court had got out of control, handing itself 'an extraordinary power to micromanage the legal systems (of member states). He said the court was 'in practice answerable to no one.'[5]

It was significant that this recent spate of attacks on the Court involved not only the tabloid press in the United Kingdom but also senior members of parliament known for their attachment to human rights (Jack Straw and David Davis), as well as distinguished judicial figures such as Lord Hoffman.

Lord Hoffman had previously launched a frontal attack on the constitutional legitimacy of the Court in his farewell lecture to the Judicial Studies Board in 2009.[6] For him there was something fundamentally wrong with an international court seeking to impose common solutions on national legal systems. How could it ever have been thought appropriate that an international court of human rights deal with the concrete application of rights in different countries? This was surely a basic flaw in the arrangements. After taking to task various court judgments in cases against the United Kingdom he concluded "unlike the Supreme Court of the United States or the supreme courts of other countries performing a similar role, the European Court of Human Rights lacks constitutional legitimacy."[7] He was clearly irritated by the fact that there was virtually no aspect of "our legal system, from land law to social security, to torts to consumer contracts, which is not touched by some point by human rights. But we have not surrendered our sovereignty over all these matters."[8]

---

[5] Jason Groves, *'Europe's human rights court is out of control... we must pull out': Call by top British judge after ruling that prisoners should get the vote*, DAILY MAIL, 7 Feb. 2011, available at: http://www.dailymail.co.uk/news/article-1354362/Europes-human-rights-court-control--pull-Call-British-judge-ruling-prisoners-vote.html#ixzz1QNV45SLd (last accessed: 27 September 2011).

[6] Lord Leonard Hoffmann, *The Universality of Human Rights,* 125 Law Quarterly Review 416 (2009).

[7] *Id.* at 430.

[8] *Id.* at 431.

If one is allergic to foreign judges meddling in national law, the "constitutional legitimacy" argument is a potent antidote since it contains the implicit suggestion that no right-thinking people or government should give credence to its pronouncements since it enjoys no legitimacy to make them. One immediate reaction to this criticism of the Court is to ask why it has taken 50 years to challenge such a fundamental flaw. It is very strange to wake up to this reality about the Convention so late in its 50-year history. Lord Hoffman provided the answer himself. The Convention has a relevance to every area of law. This means that the Court is being called on to adjudicate many of the most difficult human rights issues of our time and that no area of law escapes its scrutiny. Not only the sheer number, but the sensitivity of cases being brought to Strasbourg against many different countries underlines this fact.

B. The Tasks – and Challenges – of the Court

Look at the Court's recent docket. The jury system in Belgium,[9] the prohibition of abortion in Ireland,[10] the presence of the crucifix in Italian schools,[11] the applicability of the Convention in the war theater of Iraq[12] two inter-state cases brought by *Georgia against Russia*[13] - are a few of the cases pending before or recently decided by the Grand Chamber of the Court. However there is nothing new in this. It is inherent in the right of individual petition that the Court can be seized of such issues when all domestic remedies have been exhausted. The difference is that today there are many more such cases being brought against a greater number of states. In the 1980's and 1990's, the Court examined cases against the United Kingdom concerning telephone-tapping,[14] marital rape,[15] freedom from

---

[9] Taxquet v. Belgium, Eur. Ct. H. R., judgment of 16 November 2010, available at: http://www.menschenrechte.ac.at/orig/10_6/Taxquet (last accessed: 27 September 2011).

[10] A, B and C v. Ireland, 2032 Eur. Ct. H. R. (2010), available at: http://cmiskp.echr.coe.int/tkp197/view.asp?item=1&portal=hbkm&action=html&highlight=A%2C%20|%20B% 20|%20C%20|%20v.%20|%20Ireland&sessionid=78694016&skin=hudoc-en (last accessed: 27 September 2011).

[11] *Lautsi, supra* note 1.

[12] *See* the cases Alo Skeini and Others v. United Kingdom (GC), Eur. Ct. H. R, judgment of 7 July 2011, available at: http://www.bailii.org/eu/cases/ECHR/2010/2032.html (last accessed: 19 September 2011) and Alo Jedda v. United Kingdom (GC), Eur. Ct. H. R., judgment of 7 July 2011, available at: http://www.bailii.org/eu/cases/ECHR/2011/1092.html (last accessed: 27 September 2011).

[13] Georgia v. Russia – pending before the Grand Chamber, available at: http://cmiskp.echr.coe.int/tkp197/search.asp?sessionid=72691944&skin=hudoc-cc-en (last accessed: 27 September 2011).

[14] Malone v. United Kingdom, 82 Eur. Ct. H.R. (ser. A, 1984).

[15] S.W. v. United Kingdom, 335-B Eur. Ct. H.R. (ser. A, 1995) and C.R. v United Kingdom, 335-C Eur. Ct. H.R. (ser. A, 1995).

1866   German Law Journal   [Vol. 12 No. 10

self-incrimination,[16] blasphemy[17,] and the closed shop[18] – all highly sensitive issues. But crucially, such human rights issues could not be examined by the national courts since the Convention had not been incorporated into national law and the judges had set their face against giving even limited effect to Strasbourg case law. So one can understand that following the introduction of the Human Rights Act in 2002 when the domestic courts were empowered to apply the Convention directly, questions would inevitably arise as to the necessity or the utility of having a European Human Rights Court. Questions such as – "why do we need these foreign judges telling us how to interpret fundamental rights?"

But what answers can one give to the claim that the Court is constitutionally illegitimate?[19] In my view, this cannot be a debate about the legitimacy of the system in any real sense. One only has to look at the record. The system has been operating for years without being called into question by the High Contracting Parties. They ratified the Convention freely, presumably because they believed in what it stood for, and it is open to them at any stage to denounce it if they so desire. Far from seeking to escape from their Convention obligations, the States are keen to observe and build upon the Convention *acquis* and to reform the system so that it can perform its tasks in a more efficient manner.

The jurisprudence that the Court has established over the last 50 years is generally accepted to constitute the major achievement of the European system of human rights protection. This law is applicable by national superior courts throughout Europe and there is no sign on the horizon that the States desire to dismantle the Court out of a suddenly acquired conviction that its activities are constitutionally questionable or disreputable. Rather the contrary is true. They are seeking to devise a long-term blueprint for the Court that will enable it to come to terms with the large mass of cases before it and confront the challenges of its own success. The impact of the Convention *acquis* to contributing to the reform of the legal systems in Eastern and Central European countries following the fall of the Berlin wall has boosted the political appreciation of the Court as a source of fundamental values that bind European Countries together and give concrete expression to what it is to be European. It is undoubtedly for this reason that the States have laid the basis for a crucial future development of the Convention system by providing in the Lisbon Treaty that the European Union should accede to the Convention.

---

[16] Saunders v. United Kingdom, Eur. Ct. H. R., judgment of 17 December 1996, available at: http://www.unhcr.org/refworld/topic,4565c22520,4565c25f263,3ae6b68010,0.html (last accessed: 27 September 2011).

[17] Wingrove v. United Kingdom, 1996o V Eur. Ct. H. R., judgment of 25 November 1996, available at: http://cmiskp.echr.coe.int/tkp197/view.asp?item=1&portal=hbkm&action=html&highlight=Wingrove%20|%20v%20|%20United%20|%20Kingdom&sessionid=78694016&skin=hudoc-en (last accessed: 27 September 2011).
[18] Young, James and Webster v. United Kingdom, 44 Eur. Ct. H.R. (ser. A, 1981).

[19] *See also* Michael O'Boyle *The legitimacy of Strasbourg Review: Time for a reality check, in* Mélanges en L'Honneur de Jean-Paul Costa, La Conscience Des Droits (2011).

Against this broad background of support and acclaim - the argument of "constitutional legitimacy" lacks substance. In reality the claim that the Court is not constitutionally legitimate has nothing to do with constitutionalism or flawed legal theories. It reposes on a basic dislike, even rejection, of the fact that the Court is called upon to review the decisions of superior national courts in sensitive cases concerning human rights. It is also a critical reaction to what is perceived by national judges as impermissible judicial activism. Some national judges no longer accept that Strasbourg law should take precedence over national law.

However, the strongest rebuttal of this criticism is that many of the Court's critics have lost sight of the origins of the Convention as a system of collective guarantee of human rights. This concept is the cornerstone of the Convention system. Without it the treaty would have little sense. The idea of the collective guarantee of rights is essentially a reciprocal agreement by the Contracting Parties embodied in the Convention and its machinery of supervision, that each of them and their peoples has an enduring interest in how fundamental rights are being protected in other State Parties. In short, it was legitimate for States to be concerned with how human rights were being protected in other European States.[20] However, in return, each Party would itself be exposed to the same possibility of scrutiny through the operation of the right of individual petition or a case brought against it by another State. The close connection between the effective protection of human rights and peace, as highlighted in the Preamble to the Convention, provides the underlying rationale of the concept.

The notion that a community of like-minded States has a treaty right to question the behavior of other States, provided it accepts the *quid pro quo* that I have just outlined, is one of the milestones of civilized legal development of the last century. The entire edifice of the system has been constructed on this simple but powerful premise and it lies at the source of the extraordinary development of the Court over the last 50 years. The legitimacy polemic has failed to take it into account and, for that reason alone, cannot be sustained since what is at stake − regional political stability, prosperity and peace - is simply more vital than purely national concerns.

---

[20] For an interesting discussion on the duty to have regard to human rights outside national boundaries, *see* Christopher McCrudden's blog, *Duties beyond borders: the external effects of our constitutional debate*, UK Constitutional Law Group, available at: http://ukconstitutionallaw.org/2011/05/30/christopher-mccrudden-duties-beyond-borders-the-external-effects-of-our-constitutional-debates/ (last accessed: 27 September 2011).

1868   German Law Journal   [Vol. 12 No. 10

C. The Future of the Court

So far I have been addressing the question of whether the Court has any future at all or whether it should be seen as an interesting experiment in international law, which should be brought to an end. My answer is unreservedly positive.

In the first place the achievements of the system speak for themselves. The European Court of Human Rights has developed an unparalleled corpus of law in the area of human rights. It has set common standards which permeate the legal orders of the Contracting States, standards which influence and shape domestic law and practice in areas such as criminal law, the administration of justice in civil and administrative matters, family law, refugee and immigration law, media law and property law. It has also become deeply entrenched in the legal and moral fabrics of the societies of the older Council of Europe states and this same process is well underway in newer state parties. The system has also become a symbol of the protection of human rights through law and a shining example to those parts of the world where human rights protection by any court, national or international, is purely aspirational.

In the second place, notwithstanding the criticisms directed at the Court, the 47 Contracting Parties - to judge by their actions - are concerned to ensure the survival of the Court and to seek to place it on a proper footing. This is the goal of the Interlaken Declaration and the Izmir Conference on 26-27 April 2011. The States are aware of the contribution that a functioning human rights system makes to the maintenance of peace in Europe. As Sir David Maxwell-Fyfe pointed out in August 1949 to those who were concerned at the financial implications of setting up an international court "there will never be a lower insurance rate this side of paradise."[21] Paradoxically, it is a measure of the strength and political appeal of the European system that it will ultimately be defended and enhanced even by its fiercest detractors, partly because of the degree of popular support that it receives but also because of its dispute resolution potential and its attested civilizing influence in Europe. The States also recognize that the ECHR has created a corpus of European values that radiate a powerful effect on the standards underlying their own conceptions of democracy.

Of course, there are many problems to be resolved and these criticisms by national judges cannot be taken lightly and deserve a response. The Court today more than 140,000 cases pending before it, 90-95% of which will eventually be rejected as inadmissible. More than 60% of the cases are brought against 5 States – Russia, Ukraine, Poland, Romania and Italy and 80% against ten. Many of these complaints fall into the category of repetitive or clone applications that considerably clog the Court's docket.

---

[21] CORDULA DRÖGE, POSITIVE VERPFLICHTUNGEN DER STAATEN IN DER EUROPÄISCHEN MENSCHENRECHTSKONVENTION 238 (2003).

Recently a new and serious problem has emerged in the area of immigration law. For many immigration lawyers the Court has become the forum of last resort in deportation and extradition cases. The number of requests for interim measures has rocketed by more than 4,000% between 2006-2010 with literally thousands of applications being brought relating to deportations to Iraq or Afghanistan (4,786 in 2010 compared with 112 in 2006). The President of the Court has taken the unprecedented step of issuing a formal Statement addressed to both the High Contracting Parties and applicants' lawyers, pointing out that the Court is not an Immigration Appeal Tribunal, that "where immigration and asylum procedures carry out their own proper assessment of risk and are seen to operate fairly and with respect for human rights, the Court should only be required to intervene in truly exceptional cases" and that "the States must ensure that there exist adequate national remedies with suspensive effect which operate effectively and fairly, in accordance with the Court's case law and that provide a proper and timely examination of the issue of risk."[22] Thus we have a triangular confrontation between States seeking to control immigration, immigration lawyers bombarding the Court with cases (many of which are unsubstantiated) and the Court seeking to define and make visible its limited responsibilities in this area.

Important developments have taken place over the last year. Protocol 14 finally came into force in June 2010 after its ratification by the Russian Federation. This Protocol, amongst other important changes, created single judge formations empowered to reject obviously inadmissible cases, 3 judge committees that could adopt judgments in cases where the case law is well established. In addition the States gathered at Interlaken in February 2010 and adopted a Declaration and Action Plan.[23] In particular, the Declaration reaffirmed the States' attachment to the Convention and recognized "the extraordinary contribution of the Court through its protection of human rights in Europe."[24] The Declaration also made important statements concerning the right of individual petition, the implementation of the Convention at national level, the filtering of applications, the handling of repetitive cases, the supervision of the execution of judgments of the Court by the Committee of Ministers and the introduction of a statute facilitating a simplified amendment of the Convention.

It is not my intention to dwell on the details of the Interlaken Declaration except to highlight it as a watershed in the future of the Court's development. It stands both as a

---

[22] *See* Statement By the President of the European Court of Human Rights, *Requests For Interim Measures (Rule 39 of the Rules of Court)*, (11 Feb. 2011), available at: http://www.echr.coe.int/NR/rdonlyres/ B76DC4F5-5A09-472B-802C-07B4150BF36D/0/20110211_ART_39_Statement_EN.pdf (last accessed: 27 September 2011).

[23] *See* the Interlaken Declaration of 19 February 2010, available at: http://www.eda.admin.ch/etc/medialib/downloads/edazen/topics/europa/euroc.Par.0133.File.tmp/final_en.pdf (last accessed: 27 September 2011).

[24] *Id.*

1870   German Law Journal   [Vol. 12 No. 10

milestone pointing toward the short and long-term development of the Convention system and as an institutional obstacle to those states who are seeking to weaken and diminish the Court for political reasons. I seek rather to focus on what are the key areas that are central to the success and long-term stability of the Court's mission. So, how should the Court go about fulfilling its mission?

The dominant consideration in the reform process must be to place the Court in a position where it can concentrate its resources on what it does best, namely the adjudication of the mainstream human rights problems facing European societies and to do so within a reasonable time frame. It is this role, carried out mainly by the Grand Chamber and in leading Chamber judgments, that has the strongest and most significant impact throughout Europe with many of the Court's leading pronouncement assuming *de facto* the character of judgments *erga omnes* (owed towards all). The Court is hampered today in fulfilling this role satisfactorily because of the crippling docket of individual complaints and repetitive applications, as well as a failure of the States to give proper affect to their Convention obligations. The future of the Court lies in removing these impediments successfully.

The following five areas occupy a central place in the short and long-term development of the Court: the effective filtering of applications by the Court; the national implementation of the Convention; pilot judgments; improving dialogue with national courts and accession of the EU to the Convention. Let me say a word about each.

I. Filtering

The number of cases brought to the Court increases by around 10 to 12% each year. If this trend continues it will not be long before the Court has a backlog of 200,000 complaints. The single judge procedure, although only in force since June 2010, has already demonstrated its potential to dispose of large numbers of obviously inadmissible cases. However, a routine disposal of such cases takes time and resources whereas the Court should be concentrating its resources in cases that do raise serious human rights problems.

There are two possible solutions to this conundrum neither of which is mutually exclusive. The first is to introduce measures that seek to staunch the flow of hopeless cases. The second is to improve the Court's filtering capacity. Both are controversial. One idea, which was discussed at the Izmir conference in April 2011, is that of imposing a modest fee on applicants to require them to think twice before complaining to Strasbourg, bearing in mind that 90% of all applications are rejected as inadmissible. Such a scheme could be introduced in a way that protects the substance of the right of individual petition if appropriate exemptions are made between different categories of applicants (e.g. those in custody, the indigent, mentally ill persons) and the level of fee is pegged to the standard of living of the relevant country and is not excessive.

While the idea of such a deterrent is attractive, it has not been greeted with favor within the Court both for reasons of principle - the risk of those with well-founded applications not being able to pay the fee - and for practical reasons concerning the administrative difficulties of implementing such a fee system in respect of applications from 47 countries and policing the exemptions. The Contracting States are also seriously divided on the matter.[25] Another alternative, more in keeping with the principle of subsidiarity, is that of compulsory legal representation for applicants with national lawyers acting as a form of national filter. However, for such a system to operate some form of legal aid would have to be made available to those without the necessary resources. This is unlikely to be the subject of agreement between the States because of its budgetary implications.

It is clear, however, that the system simply cannot continue to function with a 10% increase in applications every year and that some fairly radical steps will have to be taken to reduce the sheer mass of unfounded cases.

The second possible solution is to substantially improve the Court's filtering capacity, either by empowering members of the Court's registry to act as assistant judges or by creating a judicial filtering body to be set up as an additional section of the Court composed of a core of more "junior" judges assisted by the registry. It would function as an adjunct to the existing Court. They would be selected by the Court itself on the recommendation of the States and would work at the Court for several years only. It seems clear from the sheer number of cases being brought to Strasbourg that it is only through a combination of both of these unpopular ideas or the introduction of even more radical changes that the Court can free itself up to examine more serious applications. [26]

II. National Measures

The Interlaken Declaration has emphasized the importance of the States' responsibility for national implementation of the Convention. As the President of the Court, Jean Paul Costa, has pointed out the founding fathers of the Convention never intended to shift

---

[25] There was no consensus reached on this issue during the Izmir Conference. *See* the Izmir Declaration of 26-27 April 2011, and the various speeches made by State representatives during the meeting. Available at http://www.coe.int/t/dghl/standardsetting/conferenceizmir/Declaration%20Izmir%20E.pdf (last accessed:27 September 2011).

[26] As has been recently stated by the UK Bill of Rights Commission in its Interim Advice to the Government, the Court should not be the first port of call for aggrieved applicants, and it should not be examining cases in the tens of thousands but in the hundreds. *See Reform of the European Court of Human Rights – Our Interim Advice to Government*, available at: http://www.justice.gov.uk/downloads/about/cbr/cbr-court-reform-interim-advice.pdf (last accessed: 27 September 2011).

1872   German Law Journal   [Vol. 12 No. 10

responsibility exclusively or even predominantly to the Court.[27] On the contrary, the Convention emphasizes the obligations of States: for example, an obligation to secure Convention rights to everyone within their jurisdiction; a duty to provide effective remedies before domestic courts and in particular to set up judicial systems that are independent, impartial, transparent, fair and reasonably quick; an undertaking to comply with the Court's judgments at least in those disputes to which the state is a party and increasingly where judgments identify similar shortcomings in other states.[28]

The future of the system is thus bound up with the direct application of the Convention by national courts and other bodies. This presupposes that the Court's essential case-law is translated into the official language of the contracting party and that national judges are provided with training in how this law is applied in practice and that they seek to do so in cases before them. In short, if the Court is to function effectively it is paramount that the 47 states that have ratified the Convention take seriously their obligation to integrate it effectively into national law and practice or as the Council of Europe Commissioner for Human Rights, Thomas Hammarberg, has put it "to adopt a strategic and holistic strategy for giving effect to human rights treaty obligations and, in particular, Convention obligations and case law."[29]

A note of realism is nevertheless necessary in this context. The importance of modernizing and reinforcing the concept of subsidiarity in this way has been repeatedly stressed throughout the life of the Convention - yet the numbers of cases have continued to rise. More recently, similar strongly worded exhortations can be found in the Explanatory Report to Protocol no. 11,[30] in the Evaluation Report,[31] the Woolf Report,[32] and in The Wise

---

[27] Jean-Paul Costa, *Speech at the Solemn Hearing on the Occasion of the Opening of the Judicial Year, in* DIALOGUE BETWEEN JUDGE: THE CONVENTION IS YOURS 30, 35. Available at: http://www.echr.coe.int/NR/ rdonlyres/3F410EB0-4980-4562-98F1-B30641C337A5/0/DIALOGUE_2010_EN.pdf (last accessed: 27 September 2011).

[28] *See inter alia*, Council of Europe, *President Costa's speech at the Interlaken Conference* (Febr. 18-19 2010). Available in French at: http://www.eda.admin.ch/etc/medialib/downloads/edazen/topics/europa/euroc/ouvert.Par.0005.File.tmp/cour. pdf (last accessed: 27 September 2011).

[29] *Id.*

[30] Council of Europe, *Explanatory Report to the Protocol No. 11 to the Convention for the Protection of Human Rights and Fundamental Freedoms, restructuring the control machinery established thereby* (1994). Available at: http://conventions.coe.int/treaty/en/reports/html/155.htm (last accessed: 27 September 2011).

[31] Council of Europe, Committee of Ministers, *Report of the Evaluation Group to the Committee of Ministers on the European Court of Human Rights* (2001), available at: https://wcd.coe.int/wcd/ViewDoc.jsp?id=226195&Lang=fr#P364_39957 (last accessed: 27 September 2011).

[32] The Right Honorable Lord Woolf *et. al., Review of the Working Methods of the European Court of Human Rights* (2005). Available at: http://www.echr.coe.int/NR/rdonlyres/40C335A9- F951-401F-9FC2-241CDB8A9D9A/0/LORDWOOLFREVIEWONWORKINGMETHODS.pdf (last accessed: 27 September 2011).

Persons' Report.[33] Is there good reason to expect that the message will be acted on more purposefully post-Interlaken? It seems clear that the real benefits to the Court's docket will only be perceptible in the long-term. However, the basic message is crystal clear for the future development of the system. The States must, in accordance with the principle of subsidiarity, make provision for more effective national implementation of Convention principles.

III. Pilot Judgments

The pilot judgment procedure that has been endorsed by the States in the Interlaken Declaration offers substantial promise in dealing with the phenomenon of repetitive complaints that account for up to 70% of the Court's judgments. It cannot be right that the Court is required to act as a Compensation Claims Commission awarding damages in large numbers of judgments applying well-established case law. It seems clear that the Court has taken a wrong turning in pursuing this policy. The focus today is on the identification of the systemic or structural causes that give rise to these problems and to use the pilot procedure as a method of obliging the state to introduce national remedies capable of providing effective redress. This is the only appropriate role for an international court to play. Once it is established that the law or practice in question violates the Convention it must be the duty of the state to provide appropriate redress for all those similarly affected. The pilot procedure offers the best hope of doing this in a manner that will lead to national reform.

The Court was requested in the Interlaken Declaration to "develop, clear and predictable standards for the pilot judgment procedure as regards selection of applications, the procedure to be followed and the treatment of adjourned cases."[34] This has resulted in Rule 61 of the Rules of Court which came into force on 31 March 2011 and which provides (1) that the Court will consult the parties before starting the procedure; (2) that the Court shall identify in the judgment the remedial measures the State is required to take and may impose a time-limit on the adoption of such measures; (3) that any friendly settlement must also cover general measures and redress for other /potential applicants and (4) where a State fails to abide by a pilot judgment, the Court will normally resume examination of the adjourned cases.[35]

---

[33] Council of Europe, Committee of Ministers, *Report of the Group of Wise Persons to the Committee of Ministers* (2006). Available at: https://wcd.coe.int/wcd/ViewDoc.jsp?id=1063779&Site=CM

(last accessed: 27 September 2011).

[34] Interlaken Declaration, *supra* note 23.

[35] *See* Rule 61 of Rules of Court. 1 April 2011. Available at: http://www.echr.coe.int/NR/rdonlyres/6AC1A02E-9A3C-4E06-94EF-E0BD377731DA/0/RulesOfCourt_April2011.pdf (last accessed: 27 September 2011).

1874   German Law Journal   [Vol. 12 No. 10

IV. Advisory Opinions

Increasing the dialogue with national courts is an obvious way of improving the relationship between national courts and the Court in Strasbourg. But surely the time has come in the development of the Convention system to create a more formal structure for this dialogue to take place. This could take the form of an advisory opinion procedure. It was recently revived by the Wise Persons in their report as a method of fostering dialogue with national courts and of enhancing the Court's constitutional role.[36] The Wise Persons envisaged that States could join the procedure if they so desired as third parties as they do from time to time in contentious cases of great interest, most recently in the *Lautsi v. Italy* case.[37]

Regrettably the proposal was not taken up in the Interlaken Declaration and is not yet part of the Interlaken follow up.[38] Yet there are clear advantages to this idea in terms of strengthening links with the national judiciary and persuading national judges to play their legitimate and designated role in applying the Court's case law. Under the UK Human Rights Act, for example, the courts are bound to have regard to Strasbourg case law but it occurs occasionally that they are not prepared to follow certain judgments either because it is considered that they are not correctly decided or are inconsistent with other judgments. Such a situation is clearly unsatisfactory since the clash of opinion between the two systems is not resolved and another harmful disagreement is recorded - compounded perhaps by a later Strasbourg judgment finding the State to be in violation of the Convention. Had the issue concerned a question of EU law the courts could avail of the preliminary ruling procedure under Article 267 of the TFEU to raise their concerns. By enabling national judges to request an advisory opinion where the case law is controversial or unclear the procedure would no longer be as confrontational as it is today. Moreover experience from EU law has shown that the preliminary ruling system, *mutatis mutandis*, has proved to be a useful instrument for laying down fundamental principles of interpretation.

---

[36] Report of the Group of Wise Persons to the Committee of Ministers, *supra* note 33 at paras. 76-86.

[37] *See Lautsi, supra* note 1.

[38] *See* the Izmir Declaration, *supra* note 25. The Advisory Opinion proposal was eventually endorsed at point D of the Izmir Declaration of 26-27 April 2011 as follows. "The Conference:

1. Bearing in mind the need for adequate national measures to contribute actively to diminishing the number of applications, invites the Committee of Ministers to reflect on the advisability of introducing a procedure allowing the highest national courts to request advisory opinions from the Court concerning the interpretation and application of the Convention that would help clarify the provisions of the Convention and the Court's case-law, thus providing further guidance in order to assist States Parties in avoiding future violations;

2. Invites the Court to assist the Committee of Ministers in its consideration of the issue of advisory opinions."

There are other advantages. Such a procedure has the potential to be even more influential and authoritative than a judgment in a contentious case in that it provides an opportunity to develop the underlying principles of law in a manner that is less confined by the facts of the case and more tilted to the legal systems of a wider number of Contracting Parties. In short it is an idea that has come of age.

Of course there are also disadvantages. Some obvious questions may be asked. Would there not be a tendency for some supreme courts to send too many requests once ECHR issues arose in cases before them leading to an increase of the Court's burden? What model would be best for the Court – the Inter-American Court model or the EU preliminary reference model? Is there a risk that such a system would operate to the detriment of the right of individual petition if the Court's opinion were to prejudge an issue already pending before the Court?

V. Accession of the EU to the ECHR

The future of the Court is also linked to accession of the EU to the Convention. The fact that the EU is not a Party today creates an imbalance and uncertainty as to who can be held legally responsible for breaches of Convention rights when matters of EU law are involved as we saw in *Bosphorus* and (to a lesser extent) *MSS v. Greece and Belgium*.[39] Accession of the EU has now become a reality with the entry into force of the Lisbon Treaty that imposes an obligation on the EU to adhere to the Convention. Accession is much more that the EU demonstrating its commitment to human rights. It will mean that individuals will be able to complain directly to the Court about acts or omissions of the EU in the same way that they can complain today about State action. It will thus result in all European legal systems being subject to the same supervision in relation to the protection of human rights. It will also ensure that the development of human rights law in Europe is harmonious although, as with the superior courts of all Contracting Parties, nothing will prevent the ECJ from interpreting either the Charter of Fundamental Rights and Freedoms or the Convention as imposing higher human rights requirements than the minimum standards contained in the Convention. Negotiations began in July 2010 and a draft agreement ought to be ready by July of this year. The agreement will provide for a co-respondent mechanism, which will enable the EU to join the case as a co-respondent when the complaint involves a substantial link with EU law. Had accession been in force at the time of the *Bosphorus* case where Ireland had no option but to give effect to an EU regulation (requiring the impounding of a Turkish airplane) the EU would have become a co-respondent and afforded the opportunity to argue the compatibility of the provisions of

---

[39] Bosphorus Hava Yolları Turizm ve Ticaret Anonim Şirketi v. Ireland, 2005-VI Eur. Ct. H. R. (2005) and M.S.S. v Belgium and Greece, 53 E.H.R.R. 2 (2011).

1876   G e r m a n L a w J o u r n a l   [Vol. 12 No. 10

the regulation with principles of Convention law. One of the most difficult questions to be resolved by the negotiators – that relating to the prior involvement of the ECJ in cases where it has not had an opportunity to examine the complaint from the standpoint of EU law – has been tentatively resolved on the lines set out in a joint statement by the respective Presidents of both courts proposing that the proceedings in a case against both a State and the EU be organized in such a way as to provide for the possibility of a speedy internal examination of the complaint by the ECJ prior to its examination in by the Court in Strasbourg.

However, there are many obstacles ahead. The agreement must reflect the unique position of the EU as a High Contracting Party where the implementation of EU law is divided between the EU and its member states. In addition the ratification process foreseen in the Lisbon Treaty is complex and requires the agreement of two-thirds of the European Parliament, a unanimous Council and all of the EU States in accordance with their respective constitutional positions. It will also require agreement by the 20 non-EU States of the Council of Europe who will insist that the EU is placed on an equal footing with all the other High Contracting Parties and not given preferential treatment.

The political and legal importance of the docking of the EU into the Convention on Human Rights should not be underestimated either for its impact on policy making in the EU but also as a stabilizing factor for the Court itself which will of undoubtedly be strengthened by accession. Its implications for the development of the Council of Europe will also be of great significance in the future.

D. Conclusion

I began this lecture by looking at the so-called legitimacy debate and the storm of protest against the Court that was unleashed in February. I have nothing against criticism of international courts and their decisions. In my opinion and, without a doubt, that of the Court itself - it is rather essential. All courts need a certain dose of criticism and international courts are not "cloistered virtues". But we should be aware that politically motivated campaigns of criticism can be destructive and can threaten a court's independence. It is worth bearing this in mind.

But two other developments, going in the opposite direction, also occurred at around the same time. They both fell under the radar.

The first was a letter to the Financial Times from a group of senior political figures in the UK headed by Peter Mandelson calling on the MENA countries (Middle East and North African region) to incorporate into their law the principles of the ECHR and for the EU to support this process.[40] The letter was based on a reflection on the lessons learned from the last mass pro-democracy movement that occurred following the fall of the Berlin Wall and the need to "embed a new judicial and political culture" in MENA countries. The letter hits the nail on the head. But what an extraordinary contrast with the prevailing mood!

The second was a talk given in Strasbourg by Robert Badinter – a very eminent French lawyer. In his first week as French Justice Minister in 1981, after the election of President Francois Mitterand, he abolished the death penalty in France and accepted the right of individual petition to the then European Commission of Human Rights. He has the reputation in France of being a brilliant orator and a *sage*. In his talk, which can be seen on the Court's Internet site, he points to the Convention principles as representing the strongest expression of a community of European values. He makes the point forcefully that Europe should not allow these values to be nationalized by the States since history shows that they will inevitably be weakened and diminished. It is only by being internationalized that the essence of these values can be maintained. He also affirmed that without the European Court of Human Rights - European civilization would not be as it is today and Europe would not be eyed enviously by other continents as a beacon of human rights protection. He thanked the Court for the contribution it has made as Europe's conscience over the last 50 years.[41]

I could not think of a more appropriate testimony on which to bring these reflections to a close.

---

[40] Lord Mandelson, Lord Kinnock, Lord Ashdown and others, *"EU must make a wider offer – with conditions,"* FINANCIAL TIMES (Mar. 12, 2011), available at: http://www.ft.com/cms/
s/0/1bd19b2a-4c47-11e0-82df-00144feab49a.html#axzz1QOT9c9dG (last accessed: 27 September 2011). Letter to the Financial Times dated 11 March 2011 from Lord Mandelson, Lord Kinnock, Lord Ashdown and others. The text reads: "As European politicians start to formulate a 'response to the changes' in the Middle East and North Africa region (MENA) they should reflect on the lessons from the last mass proo democracy movement which occurred as the Berlin Wall fell more than 20 years ago. The support that Western Europe offered the east at that time has strengthened the whole of the region both politically and economically in the subsequent two decades. If the European Union wants to influence its southern neighbors, with whom it shares so much common history, it must make a wider offer in terms of aid, markets and mobility. That means more generous and better targeted development packages, removing the last barriers to the import of fruit and vegetables from the region, and adopting more flexible visa regimes. The customs union between the EU and Turkey could be extended to North African countries. But the generous offer must be coupled with strict conditionality to raise standards of governance and improve human rights. As a first step towards this, MENA countries should begin the process of incorporating into their law the principles of the European Convention on Human Rights, of which Turkey is a signatory. The EU should give technical and moral support to this process, which would remain a sovereign decision but one that would help to embed a new judicial and political culture in these countries."
[41] Robert Badinter, *France and the European Convention on Human Rights as seen by a privileged witness*, COUNCIL OF EUROPE WEBTV (Mar. 16, 2011). Available at mms://coenews.coe.int/vod/20110316_02_w.wmv (last accessed: 27 September 2011).

[14]

MARTINUS
NIJHOFF
PUBLISHERS

The Law and Practice of
International Courts and Tribunals 12 (2013) 321–341

brill.com/lape

The Action of Legal Persons in the European System of Human Rights Protection – Collective or Individual Interest?

Marjorie Beulay*
Ph.D. student at the University of Nanterre Paris Ouest la Défense –
Centre of International Law of Nanterre (CEDIN)

Abstract

Human Rights are accustomed to being linked to individual interests, i.e. to defend the rights of individuals. But the development of their international protection has led to emphasizing new realities. With the globalization of law, the globalization of the subjects of international law has also appeared. If States gradually act collectively thanks to international organizations, individuals seem to follow the same path in forming collective entities named legal persons, which are entitled to rights. The main problem of this situation is defending these rights in front of international courts and, in particular, in front of the European Court of Human Rights. Representing a community leads to defending a collective interest, however, it is not easy to distinguish between the rights of the legal person itself and the rights of the collectivity the legal person is representing. Despite the fiction of the legal person, these entities seem to be collective claimants and consequently to defend a collective interest. Can we conclude that the actions of legal persons before European bodies of Human Rights protection are actions with a collective aim? Indeed this situation implies needing to define which entity retains cited rights and which interest is being defended, that of the individual or that of a collectivity of individuals? This article looks for some answers in the case law of the European Court, which can be considered unequivocal in the light of the case law of other jurisdictions.

Keywords

legal persons; human rights; collective interest; individual interest; collective actions; collective claimants; European Court of Human Rights; international protection of human rights; comparative analysis

---

*⟩ This article is the updated version of a contribution prepared for the Colloquium "Actors, Collective Strategies and the European Field of Human Rights" held at the University of Strasbourg on 21–22 June 2010. I would like to thank Ms Nili CYTRYNOWICZ for her helpful and insightful comments during the preparation of this article.

"[...] [O]ne day, legal persons like individuals will have their existence and rights protected by a norm of international law".[1] Like a prediction, Prof. DE VISSCHER expressed this opinion in 1961 during his lesson at The Hague Academy of International Law. Nowadays the international protection of Human Rights has become a more tangible reality than it was. Because of its function – which is to regulate the relationship between individuals and the State[2] – it must adapt itself to the social realities of the world in which it exists.[3]

Among these realities we find the situation of legal persons which are entitled to rights. Whereas this affirmative sentence might have called for criticism a few years ago, today the legal situation has changed.[4] Individuals, first possessors of rights, are forming collective entities all of the time. In reality, the right of association[5] is the most effective way for individuals to realize common goals.[6] Therefore, associations, unions, companies, or non-governmental organizations increasingly appear as frequent partners.[7] The terminology of "legal person" includes a large plurality of potential possessors of rights without any final inventory or determined list. The European Convention of Human Rights and Fundamental Freedoms (ECHRFF),

---

[1] P. DE VISSCHER, "La protection diplomatique des personnes morales", *Collected Courses of The Hague Academy of International Law*, 1961, p. 408. Author's translation of "*[...] [U]n jour viendra où les personnes morales, au même titre que les personnes physiques, verront leur existence et leurs droits fondamentaux garantis par une norme de droit international général*".

[2] H. GOLSONG, "La Convention européenne des Droits de l'Homme et les Personnes Morales", *in* U.C.L., *Les droits de l'Homme et les personnes morales*, Bruxelles, Bruylant, 1970, pp. 15–16.

[3] See X. DUPRÉ DE BOULOIS, "Les droits fondamentaux de la personne morale – 1e partie: Pourquoi"?, *R.D.L.F.*, 2011, Chronique n°15, pp. 2–3.

[4] See J.-F. FLAUSS, "Les organisations non gouvernementales devant les juridictions internationales compétentes dans le domaine de la protection des droits de l'Homme", *in* G. COHEN-JONATHAN & J.-F. FLAUSS (ed.), *International Human Rights Law and Non-Governmental Organizations*, Bruxelles, Bruylant, Publication de l'I.I.D.H., 2005, p. 71.

[5] For a complete analysis of the right of association linked with this topic, see J. MCBRIDE, "NGO Rights and their Protection under International Human Rights Law", *in* G. COHEN-JONATHAN & J.-F. FLAUSS (ed.), *International Human Rights Law and Non-Governmental Organizations, op. cit.*, pp. 157–232.

[6] P. WACHSMANN, "Droits fondamentaux et personnes morales", *in* J.-C. BARBATO & J.-D. MOUTON, *Vers la reconnaissance de droits fondamentaux aux Etats membres de l'Union Européenne? – Réflexions à partir des notions d'identité et de solidarité*, Bruxelles, Bruylant, 2010, p. 230.

[7] Since the end of the 19th century, legal persons have had to deal with a *"démographie pullulante"* (*"pullulating demography"*) as said by G. CORNU *in Droit civil – Introduction, les personnes, les biens*, Paris, Montchrestien, Précis Domat, 2001, 10th edition, n°732.

Beulay /
The Law and Practice of International Courts and Tribunals 12 (2013) 321–341   323

in one of its early drafts,[8] excluded the term, "individual" to replace it by "person".[9] In this way it extended the access to the Court to the larger category of legal persons, and the system of social rights protection reinforces this approach. But the *stricto sensu* expression "legal person" is only used in the First Protocol to the ECHRFF. In such a situation there is a place for discussion and interpretation by a judge regarding the protection of legal persons.

The place of legal persons in the European system of Human Rights takes into account their plurality.[10] In actual fact, the terminology used in Article 34 of the ECHRFF or in Article 1 of the Protocol to the European Social Charter includes a large number of these entities. The jurisprudence of the Court and the decisions of the Social Committee confirm this analysis. Therefore, we are required to accept a large definition of the notion of legal person, and nowadays their right to act in legal proceedings is no longer questioned. However, it is very difficult to substantiate their claims because of their competition with the individual right of petition. This point is highly debated.

The link between legal persons and the notion of collective strategies is obvious. Many of the people we mentioned represent a community, like an association or a union for example. Nonetheless, it is difficult to translate the terminology which refers to their action. In fact, the vocabulary is very extended: multi-party actions, group action, class action, collective interests actions, class suits or representative actions... and the list is not exhaustive. Like C. Hodges has emphasized, *"[a] multi-party action has sometimes been known in the UK as a group action and elsewhere as a class action. Although the terms are sometimes used interchangeably, there are technical differences between these terms when applied in the context of a specific jurisdiction [...]"*.[11] It is even more ambiguous when the concept is unknown or almost unknown in the court system of a particular country, like in France. It is necessary to explain what is understood when we talk

---

[8] K. VASAK, *La Convention européenne des droits de l'homme*, Paris, L.G.D.J., Bibliothèque Constitutionnelle et de Science Politique, Tome X, 1964, p. 77, §145.

[9] See C. SCHWAIGHOFER, "Legal Persons, Organisations, Shareholders as Applicant (Article 25 of the Convention)", *in* M. DE SALVIA & M. E. VILLIGER (eds.), *The Birth of European Human Rights Law – Liber Amicorum Carl Aage Nørgaard*, Baden-Baden, Nomos Verlagsgesellschaft, 1998, p. 321.

[10] *Ibid.*, pp. 323–331.

[11] C. HODGES, *Multi-party actions*, Oxford, Oxford University Press, 2001, p. 3.

Beulay /
324   *The Law and Practice of International Courts and Tribunals 12 (2013) 321–341*

about "group action" in the present contribution. It refers to an "*action of a group with the legal personality (company, association, unions), so a legal person, initiated in the name of the group to defend its own rights or to protect the interests of a community*".[12] This definition is not that of the class action. However, both of these actions are almost similar as to the notion of interest, whether it is collective or shared.

In this contribution we refer to a "group action" as an effective petition of legal persons representing a community and not only as a simple right of intervention, such as in the practice of *amicus curiae*. In this way, the legal person seems to be able to initiate a single legal action with a collective aim according to the previous definition. This means that one legal person could initiate an action to protect the right of a community, for example, an action initiated by a trade union or a group of trade unions against a company in order to protect workers' rights, like in the *Viking Case* in 2007.[13] In actual fact, this kind of proceeding is one of the main ways in which trade unions protect the interests of their members,[14] and this means that it is focused on a shared interest of its members. In the field of Human Rights this question is important because most systems of protection do not expect these entities to have a specific function. When the Court of the European Union mentions the fundamental right to initiate a collective action,[15] can we conclude that the actions of legal persons before European bodies of Human Rights are actions with a collective aim?

This question raises two issues. On one hand, we have to consider the collective dimension of the claimant – the legal person (I). On the other hand, we have to appreciate the collective character of the legal person's claim in order to know if it can lead to a collective interest action (II).

---

[12] Cf. G. CORNU, *Vocabulaire juridique*, Paris, PUF – Quadrige, 2007, 8th edition, p. 22: Author's translation of "*[a]ction d'un groupement doté de la personnalité juridique (société, association, syndicat [c'est à dire une personne morale]) intenté en son nom [...] pour faire valoir des droits qui lui appartiennent en propre ou pour défendre les intérêts de la collectivité*".

[13] See C.E.U., *Case of International Transport Worker's Federation & Finnish Seamen's Union v. Viking Line ABP & OÜ Viking Line Esti*, C-438/05, 11th December 2007, *Report* I-10779.

[14] See E.C.H.R., *Case of Syndicat national de la police belge v. Belgium*, 27th October 1975, Applications n°4464/70, and E.C.H.R., *Case of National Union of Journalists and Others v. United Kingdom*, 2nd July 2002, Applications n°30668/96, 30671/96 and 30678/96.

[15] See C.E.U., *Case of International Transport Worker's Federation & Finnish Seamen's Union v. Viking Line ABP & OÜ Viking Line Esti*, C-438/05, 11th December 2007, *Report* I-10779, §44 and C.E.U., *Case of Laval un Partneri Ltd v. Svenska Byggnadsarbetareförbundet e.a.*, C-341/05, 18th December 2007, *Report* I-11767, §91.

Beulay /
The Law and Practice of International Courts and Tribunals 12 (2013) 321–341 325

I. The Legal Person as a Collective Claimant before European Bodies of Human Rights Protection

It is interesting to start with an analysis of the claimant's essence because of the plurality principle implied by the notion of group action. We need to go back to the origins of the notion of a legal person (A) to understand the specificity of the concept in European law (B).

A. *Thoughts about a Legal "Fiction"*

The first elements to analyze are the characteristics of the concept of legal person, which are the basis of the legal personality. A fictional person is *"[a]n entity, such as a corporation, created by law and given certain legal rights and duties of a human being"*,[16] in the French system *"a group with more or less complete legal personality under conditions"*.[17] In the French definition the collective aspect of the concept is more obvious than it is in the English definition, but the reality is the same. The legal person has a double face like Janus: collective and individual at the same time. However, this fact leads to problems in the protection of Human Rights where the notion of victim is very important. Concretely, the essence of the legal person seems uncertain.[18] A sociological or economic analysis shows that the legal person leads to the satisfaction of similar interests for a large majority of people in a more efficient way than a sole physical claimant.[19] Fictional persons strive to share a common aim between all of their members, but present themselves as the sole possessors of rights. With that idea in mind, is there a risk of those interests intermingling? For example, the interests of a company are not the same as those of its shareholders and workers' interests are different from those of unions. Furthermore, this analysis is not in contradiction with the classical analysis according to which the organization has to serve the interest of its members,[20] because it was created

---

[16] B. A. GARNER (ed.), *Black's Law Dictionary*, Saint Paul, West, 2009, 9th edition, p. 1258.

[17] Author's translation of a *"groupement doté sous certaines conditions de la personnalité juridique plus ou moins complète"*, in G. CORNU, *Vocabulaire juridique, op. cit.*, p. 680.

[18] J.-F. RENUCCI, *Traité de droit européen des droits de l'Homme*, Paris, L.G.D.J., 2007, p. 52.

[19] M. OLSON, *Logique de l'action collective*, Paris, PUF, Collection Sociologie, 1987, 2nd edition, pp. 27–28.

[20] *Ibid.*, p. 27.

Beulay /
326　　　*The Law and Practice of International Courts and Tribunals 12 (2013) 321–341*

for this sole purpose.[21] In fact, if members share a common interest, each of those members has a personal interest as well, and both are not necessarily in harmony.

The second element of the analysis derives from the first element. This has occurred through the interpretation of this phenomenon by legal writing and the different legal theories which have been elaborated on this topic. As for any legal concept, it is crucial to analyse its full details to separate the entity's legal personality from its members' individual legal personalities. First, it was grasped as a screen or a "veil"[22] that follows the will of its members.[23] Currently, it is understood like a basic legal technique. The explanation does not come from the creators' wish any longer, however, it is built on tangible criteria: the reality of a collective interest and the capacity to defend it.[24] So this new way of thinking analyses this phenomenon as the first gathering action designed to bring out a proper will and capacity on their own. However, the limits of this theory are highlighted by several examples of *"non-collective legal persons"*, *"personnes morales non-collectives"*, like foundations or corporations with only one member.[25] But we will keep this frame of reference because it reinforces the collective aspect of the artificial person and, at the same time, emphasizes the unique character of the legal personality.

So the legal person is a legal instrument with a shared interest that it can defend. At least that is the analysis that prevails in French private law. This very theoretical analysis may seem unnecessary in the sense that this vocabulary *"exist[s] only in contemplation of law"*.[26] Yet the quality of the

---

[21]　M. OFFERLÉ, *Sociologie des groupes d'intérêt*, Paris, Montchrestien, Collection Clefs politiques, 1998, 2ᵉ édition, p. 57.

[22]　P. H. VAN KEMPEN, "The recognition of Legal Persons in International Human Rights Instruments: Protection Against and Through Criminal Justice?", *in* M. PIETH & R. IVORY (eds.), *Corporate Criminal Liability – Emergence, Convergence and Risk*, New York, Springer, Collection Ius Gentium: Comparative Perspectives on Law and Justice n°9, 2011, p. 365. See also M. EMBERLAND, "The Corporate Veil in the Jurisprudence of the Human Rights Committee and the Inter-American Court and Commission of Human Rights", *Human Rights Law Review*, 2004, n°4, pp. 257–275.

[23]　N. BARUCHEL, *La personnalité morale en droit privé – Eléments pour une théorie*, Paris, L.G.D.J., 2004, pp. 22 *et seq.*

[24]　L. MICHOUD, *La théorie de la personnalité morale et son application en droit français*, Paris, L.G.D.J., 1906, Tome 1, n°21.

[25]　R. MORTIER, "L'instrumentalisation de la personne morale", *in* ASSOCIATION H. CAPITANT, *La personnalité morale*, Dalloz, Collection Thèmes et Commentaires, 2010, p. 34.

[26]　U.S. Supreme Court, *Dartmouth College v. Woodward*, 17 U.S. 518 (1819).

Beulay /
The Law and Practice of International Courts and Tribunals 12 (2013) 321–341   327

applicant before an international court is fundamental to establish the competence of such court. This point explains the importance of the autonomous concept analysis by the European organs of Human Rights protection.

B. *The Autonomous Nature of the Concept in European Human Rights Law*

The European Court of Human Rights, having the authority of *kompetenz-kompetenz*,[27] acts in order to protect Human Rights in a continually expanding way. Keeping this goal in mind, courts and other bodies have developed their own analysis of the concept.[28] The notion of legal personality is not an exception to this general trend.[29] Indeed, the definition in national law *"only has a relative normative value and only is a starting point"*.[30] Therefore, the Commission and the Court have analyzed texts establishing their jurisdiction in order to bring out a specific and particular interpretation.

The concept of legal person is not used *per se*, or only rarely, in European texts. Larger concepts are used, such as "all non-governmental organizations" or "all groups of individuals". The latter refers to a notion with a more restrictive and casual temporality.[31] The notion of a group of individuals implies the reality of a shared interest between the members, but without any legal existence for the group itself.[32] Whereas it is not the topic of this analysis, it is interesting to note that the constitution of such a group is an efficient way to defend a selective shared interest without having the problem of demonstrating the quality of victim.[33] In any event, such terminology resonates by its indistinctive aspect and raises a certain amount of ambiguity. The European perspective is necessarily larger than that of nations: European judges are not as interested in legal capacity as are their

---

[27] See, in particular, B. DELZANGLES, *Activisme et Autolimitation de la Cour européenne des droits de l'homme*, Clermont Ferrand, L.G.D.J., Fondation Varenne, 2009, pp. 44 *et seq.*

[28] See, in particular, E.C.H.R., *Case of Airey v. United Kingdom*, 9th October 1979, Application n°6289/73, §24.

[29] E.C.H.R., *Case of Chassagnou and others v. France*, 29th April 1999, Applications n°25088/94, 28331/95 and 28443/95, §100.

[30] Author's translation of *"n'a qu'une valeur normative relative et ne constitue qu'un simple point de départ"*, *ibid.*, §100.

[31] Th. DOURAKI, "Les associations devant la Commission et la Cour européennes des Droits de l'Homme", *The Hague Yearbook of International Law*, 1989, vol. 2, p. 141.

[32] P. H. VAN KEMPEN, "The recognition of Legal Persons in International Human Rights Instruments: Protection Against and Through Criminal Justice?", *op. cit.*, pp. 359–360.

[33] E.C.H.R., *Case of Di Sarno and others v. Italia*, 10th January 2012, Application n°30765/08.

national counterparts, but rather in the right of the prospective claimant to act in legal proceedings.[34] This right to act in legal proceedings is easily recognized to "all non-governmental organizations",[35] with a sufficient autonomy[36] and apart from legal persons of public law's legal persons.[37] In reality, a lot of distinct entities are included in this concept: associations,[38] companies,[39] trade unions,[40] political parties[41] or religious organizations.[42] The European Court looks into the question of the right to act in legal proceedings with a focus on the notion of victim. The admissibility of the request is examined *in concreto*. The analysis tries to uncover whether the legal person has suffered violations of its *own (proper)* rights. This point explains why "all groups of individuals"[43] have the possibility to act in legal proceedings before the Court even though they lack the legal personality

---

[34] O. DE SCHUTTER & L. E. PETTITI, "Le rôle des associations dans le cadre de la C.E.D.H.", *Journal des Tribunaux – Droit européen*, vol. 4, 1996, p. 146, §3.

[35] E.C.H.R., *Case of Open Door and Dublin Well Woman v. Ireland*, 29th October 1992, Applications n°14234/88 and 14235/88, Series A, n°246.

[36] E.C.H.R., *Case of The Holy Monasteries v. Greece*, 9th December 1994, Applications n°13092/87 and 13984/88, Series A, n°301-A.

[37] E.C.H.R., *Case of Section de la Commune d'Antilly c. France*, 23th November 1999, Application n°45129/98. About the notion of fundamental rights and public legal persons in French public law, see R. DRAGO, "Droits fondamentaux et personnes publiques", *A.J.D.A.*, special number, 1998, pp. 130–135.

[38] For a recent example, see E.C.H.R., *Case of L'Erablière A.S.B.L. v. Belgium*, 24th February 2009, Application n°49230/07 or E.C.H.R., *Case of Animal Defender International v. United Kingdom*, 22nd April 2013, Application n°48876/08.

[39] E.C.H.R., *Case of Autronic A.G. v. Switzerland*, 22nd May 1990, Application n° 12726/87, Series 1, n°178; E.C.H.R., *Case of Société Colas Est and Others v. France*, 16th April 2002, Application n°37971/97; E.C.H.R., *Case of Bernh Larsen Holding AS and Others v. Norway*, 14th March 2013, Application n°24117/08.

[40] E.C.H.R., *Case of National Union of Belgian Police v. Belgium*, 27th October 1975, Application n°4464/70, Series A, n°19; E.C.H.R., *Schmidt & Dahlström v. Sweden*, 6th February 1976, Application n°5589/72, Series A, n°21; E.C.H.R., *Sindicatul Pastorul Cel Bun v. Romania*, 31st January 2012, Application n°2330/09; E.C.H.R., *Case of Trade Union of the Police in the Slovak Republic and Others v. Slovakia*, 25th September 2012, Application n°11828/08.

[41] E.C.H.R., *Case of the United Communist Party of Turkey and Others v. Turkey*, 30th January 1998, Application n°19392/92.; E.C.H.R., *Case of Christian Democratic People's Party v. Moldova*, 2nd February 2010, Application 25196/04.

[42] E.C.H.R., *Case of Association les Témoins de Jéhovah c. France*, 30th June 2011, Application 8916/05; E.C.H.R., *Case of Catholic Archdiocese of Alba Iulia v. Romania*, 29th September 2012, Application n°33003/03.

[43] E.C.H.R., *Case of Athanassoglou and others v. Switzerland*, 6th April 2000, Application n°27644/95: petition of 12 neighbours worried about the renewal of the exploitation's authorization for a nuclear station in their neighbourhood.

Beulay /
The Law and Practice of International Courts and Tribunals 12 (2013) 321–341   329

at the national level. The same analysis can be applied to non-governmental organizations, which have a different status in every Member State of the European Council. The Court places individuals and legal persons in the same category, that of victims. Therefore, it does not consider artificial persons as collective claimants. *"This automatic assimilation of legal persons to individuals finally is a return to origins. Etymologically the word* persona *referred to the mask that Roman actors used to wear to hide their face and to concentrate the public's attention on the character whom they represented. It is the same on the legal scene. The game is played by 'persons' that are not men or women, rich or poor, young or old, but the owners of rights and obligations. The law reduces the diversity to the essential level: a will which can express itself in the same way whether its author has a physical existence or not".*[44] The only way to confront a community is under the notion of a group of individuals, however, it cannot be interpreted as meaning to substitute one applicant for a multitude of applicants, as, for example, an association.

The European Committee of Social Rights (E.C.S.R.) operates according to a different logic. Individual petitions are not allowed: only collective ones can be presented by legal persons.[45] The Committee keeps the same definition of these entities as the Court but potential claimants are first listed. Here, the criterion is not the victim's condition but the notion of *"representativeness"*.[46] It is an interesting notion but a dangerous one also. Indeed, in a sociological approach, this concept can lead to at least two realities: a social one and a legal one. Both are not really similar. The first one is more global than the second one and the second one can be less

---

[44] Author's translation of *"Cette assimilation de principe des personnes morales aux personnes physiques n'est finalement qu'un retour aux sources. Etymologiquement le mot* persona *désignait le masque que portaient les acteurs romains afin de dissimuler leur visage et de concentrer l'attention des spectateurs sur le personnage qu'ils représentaient. Il en va de même sur la scène juridique. Le jeu est joué par des 'personnes', qui ne sont pas des hommes ou des femmes, des riches ou des pauvres, des jeunes ou des vieux mais des titulaires de droits et d'obligations. Le droit réduit ces diversités à l'essentiel, une volonté qui peut s'exprimer de la même manière que son auteur ait ou non une existence corporelle"* (Y. GUYON, "Droits fondamentaux de la personne morale", *AJDA*, 1998, special number, p. 139).

[45] See, for example, S. EVJU, "The Rights to Collective Action Under the European Social Charter", *European Labour Law Journal*, vol. 2, issue 3, pp. 196–224.

[46] E.C.S.R., *Syndicat national des professions de tourisme v. France*, 10th February 2001, Complaint n°6/1999; E.C.S.R., *C.E.S., C.G.S.L.B., C.S.C. & F.G.T.B. v. Belgium*, 8th December 2009, Complaint n°59/2009; E.C.S.R., *Fellesforbundet for Sjøfolk (FFFS) v. Norway*, 23rd May 2012, Complaint n°74/2011.

Beulay /

330   *The Law and Practice of International Courts and Tribunals 12 (2013) 321–341*

representative than the other.[47] The E.C.S.R., like the European Court, refers to the autonomous nature of the notion.[48] In any event, we can observe a variation in the approaches of the concept of legal person. For the E.C.S.R., the legal person must be a collective entity representing a vast number of people and acting in their interest. We can analyze this point of view as a social interpretation of the notion. It is necessary to add that only NGOs that are accredited by States can make a claim before the Committee, which leads to a restricted scope of the procedure.[49]

Before other bodies of Human Rights protection, the interpretation of this concept can be analyzed in various ways. Before the Inter-American Commission and Court, the place of the legal person is clear: the American Convention does not protect its rights. Legal persons are excluded from the benefit of the protection;[50] the American Convention insures rights of "persons" which means "every human being".[51] Therefore, the Commission will reject the claim on the ground of its lack of *ratione personae* jurisdiction.[52] In order for such a claim to be potentially accepted, it must be presented in the name of the firm's shareholders. The Commission's decisions are not very clear on this point.[53] It makes a distinction between the claim of the shareholders and the claim of the legal person, but without really taking into account the rights of the shareholders,[54] and it refers to the national law to determine if an entity has the requisite legal personality.[55] This last

---

[47] M. OFFERLÉ, *Sociologie des groupes d'intérêt, op. cit.,* p. 73.

[48] E.C.S.R., *Syndicat national des professions de tourisme v. France, op. cit.,* §6.

[49] See J.-M. BELORGEY, "La Charte sociale du Conseil de l'Europe et son organe de régulation (1961–2011) le Comité européen des droits sociaux : esquisse d'un bilan", *R.T.D.H.,* 2011/4, vol. 88, pp. 800–802.

[50] But legal persons can involve a violation of the American Declaration against a non-party State to the Convention (see Inter-American Commission, *Case 9250 (ABC Color c. Paraguay),* 17th May 1984, Report 6/84, *Annual Report* 1983–1984).

[51] Inter-American Commission, *Case of Cantos v. Argentina,* 7th September 2001, Series C, n°97, §§22 et seq.; Inter-American Court, *Case of Perozo and others v. Venezuela,* 28th January 2009, Series C, n°195, §§74 and 399.

[52] See Inter-American Commission, *Case of Mevopal S.A. v. Argentina,* 11th March 1999, Report n°39/99, Annual Report 1998, §§16–20.

[53] See, in particular, L. HENNEBEL, *La Convention américaine des droits de l'Homme – Mécanismes de protection et étendue des libertés,* Bruxelles, Bruylant, 2007, pp. 133–134.

[54] See, for example, Inter-American Commission, *Case 10.169 (Banco de Lima v. Peru),* 22nd February 1991, Admissibility, Report 10/91, *Annual Report* 1990/1991.

[55] See Inter-American Commission, *Case of Carlos Alberto Lopez Urquía v. Honduras,* 24th October 2005, Admissibility, Report n°83/05, *Annual Report* 2005.

Beulay /
The Law and Practice of International Courts and Tribunals 12 (2013) 321–341   331

point clearly underlines the difference from the analysis of the European Court. The position of the Court is more qualified. It refers to international law to distinguish between the shareholders' rights and the company's rights[56] but it easily accepts the claim of shareholders by making the legal fiction of legal personality disappear,[57] thus extending its competence. Before the Human Rights Committee, legal persons are not allowed to act in legal proceedings because legal persons do not qualify as beneficiaries of the rights recognized in the Covenant[58] and the Optional Protocol.[59] However, the right of the legal person may be involved in an individual claim if the legal person's rights and the individual's rights are similar.[60] In conclusion, a legal fiction does not have any right to act in legal proceedings in the UN system. In the African system, the individual procedure is largely open to non-governmental entities,[61] which act in legal proceedings on behalf of a community.[62] Unlike the European and UN legal proceedings, applicants do not have to be the victim also.[63] The numerous NGO cases already settled by the African Commission demonstrate the importance of this opportunity. Before the new African Court of Justice and Human Rights Committee, NGOs must be accredited; thus, the African Union chose a more restrictive rule.[64] Obviously, the question of the right of associations to act in legal proceedings is not only a regional or international problem

---

[56] In the *Case of Ivcher Bronstein v. Peru* (6th February 2001, Series C, n°74, §127), the Court quotes the ICJ decision in the *Case of Barcelona Traction, Light and Power Company Limited* (*ICJ Reports 1970*, p. 36, §47).

[57] Inter-American Court, *Case of Cantos v. Argentina*, 7th September 2001, Admissibility, Series C, n°85, §25.

[58] Human Rights Committee, *The Nature of the General Legal Obligation Imposed on States Parties to the Covenant*, General Comment n°31, 29th March 2004, §9.

[59] Human Rights Committee, *J.R.T. & the W.G. Party v. Canada*, 1983, Complaint n°104/1981, §8(a).

[60] Human Rights Committee, *Case of Allan Singer v. Canada*, 1994, Complaint n°455/1991, §11.2.

[61] Article 56 of the African Charter on Human and Peoples' Rights (ACHPR). For a commentary, see F. OUGUERGOUZ, "Article 56" *in* M. KAMTO, *La Charte africaine des droits de l'Homme et des Peuples et le Protocole y relative portant création de la Cour africaine des droits de l'Homme*, Bruxelles, Bruylant, 2011, pp. 1025–1050.

[62] P. H. VAN KEMPEN, "The recognition of Legal Persons in International Human Rights Instruments: Protection Against and Through Criminal Justice?", *op. cit.*, pp. 361–364.

[63] African Commission on Human and Peoples' Rights, *Case of Art. 19 v. The State of Eritrea*, 30th May 2007, Communication n°275/2003.

[64] See M. A. NAMOUNTOUGOU, "La saisine du juge international africain des droits de l'Homme", *R.T.D.H*, 2011, n°86, pp. 261–294, in particular p. 281.

Beulay /
332   *The Law and Practice of International Courts and Tribunals 12 (2013) 321–341*

but can also be found in national systems like that of the U.S.[65] The problems involved therein show the particular link between legal persons and collective interests.

The aim defended by both the ECHRFF and the European Social Charter is not the same and the function of legal persons before respective bodies of protection is analyzed in different ways. But the analysis of the other systems can lead to the conclusion that it is not only the category of the defended rights which influences the place and the conceptualization of legal personality, but the notion of the defended interest as well.

This distinction about the qualification of the legal person as collective claimants before European bodies of Human Rights protection leads necessarily to a distinction in the appreciation of the claim as a collective interests action.

II. The Claim of Legal Persons as Collective Interests Actions before European Bodies of Human Rights Protection

When we talk about "collective interests actions", we immediately think about the famous U.S. class action,[66] which means *"[a] law suit in which the court authorizes a single person or small group of people to represent the interest of a larger group"*.[67] However, as we can see, the notion of legal personality is not taken into account in this definition, unlike in the subject matter at hand. Nevertheless, this procedure may be helpful to understand the logic of the action. Therefore, after studying the right of legal persons to act in legal proceedings, the topic is necessarily the legal persons' interest[68] to act in legal proceedings. This concept refers to *"the importance of the*

---

[65] U.S. Supreme Court, *Case of Lujan v. Defenders of Wildlife*, 504 U.S. 555 (1992).

[66] *Rule 23 of Federal Rules of Civil Procedure.*

[67] Or specifically *"a law suit in which the convenience either of the public or of the interested parties requires that the case be settled through litigation by or against only a part of the group of similarly situated persons and in which a person whose interests are or may be affected does not have an opportunity to protect his or her interests by appearing personally or through a person specially appointed to act as trustee or guardian"*. Cf. B. A. GARDNER, *Black's Law Dictionary*, op. cit., p. 284.

[68] For an analysis of the notion of interest in International Law, see A. DE HOOGH, *Obligations Erga Omnes and International Crimes: A Theoretical Inquiry into the Implementation and Enforcement of the International Responsibility of States*, Leiden, Martinus Nijhoff Publishers, 1996, pp. 10–17.

legal action for the claimant, that is at the basis of his ability to act in legal proceedings and without which the claimant does not have any right to act in legal proceedings".[69] The central term of the expression "collective interests action" is the word *"interests"*. To understand the logic of the action, we need to study the subject of the action (A), before looking at the recent evolutions and perspectives in the European system for the opening of a collective interests action to legal persons (B).

A. *The Subject of the Collective Interests Action*

From a sociological point of view, *"interest"* is a complex notion and that is even more so the case when this interest is common to many people. Indeed, how can we conceptualize the result of a mechanism that is made of the gathering of many different people around one or more common goals of action? This phenomenon cannot be objectively appreciated. Many factors enter into account, factors that are sociological, professional, human, symbolic, moral or material.[70] In this way, the legal concept of interest can represent many realities and becomes difficult to really appreciate. This point may explain the position of European Human Rights protection bodies.

As previously mentioned, the European system is founded on the notion of victim, another autonomous concept.[71] The establishment of the right to individual petition, and its progressive binding nature, leads to extending the right to an open individual petition only to victims of violations.[72] Even if this condition has been largely accepted, first by the Commission and later by the Court, this procedural specificity hampers an eventual opening to a collective interests claim. A legal person only has an interest to act in legal

---

[69] Author's translation of *"importance qui s'attachant pour le demandeur à ce qu'il demande, le rend recevable à le demander en justice [...] et à défaut de laquelle le demandeur est sans droit pour agir"* from G. CORNU, *Vocabulaire juridique, op. cit.,* p. 506.

[70] M. OFFERLÉ, *Sociologie des groupes d'intérêt, op. cit.,* pp. 44–45.

[71] European Commission of Human Rights, *Case of N. Narvii Tauira v. France,* 4th December 1995, Application n°28.204/95, *D.R.* 83-A, p. 130: *"the concept of 'victim' must be interpreted independently of concepts of domestic law concerning such matters as interest or capacity to take legal proceeding. In order for an applicant to claim to be a victim of violation of the Convention, there must be a sufficiently direct link between the applicant and the loss which he considers he has suffered as a result of the alleged violation (n°9939/82, Dec. 4.7.83, D.R. 34, p. 213)."*

[72] Article 34 of the European Convention of Human Rights and Fundamental Freedoms.

Beulay /
334   *The Law and Practice of International Courts and Tribunals 12 (2013) 321–341*

proceedings in the case of a direct violation of its own rights.[73] Therefore, all claims concerning the violation of its social purpose[74] or in case of massive Human Rights' violations at a national or regional level are prohibited. From the opposite spectrum, *actio popularis* cases will increase even though this objective procedure is reserved to member States.[75] However, in some cases the European Commission or the Court recognizes the existence of a shared interest between the organization and its members, for example as regards the freedom of religion.[76] A recent decision in the *Stitching Mothers of Srebrenica and others v. the Netherlands Case*[77] also proved the limit of the notion of "shared interest" in rejecting the application of a non-governmental association which promoted the interests of surviving relatives of the Srebrenica massacre concerning the right to a fair trial. This decision strengthened the traditional position of the European Court and Commission to reject applications of associations which aim to vindicate the rights of alleged victims[78] or whose purpose is "only" to defend Human Rights.[79]

Once again, the European Committee of Social Rights adopts different reasoning.[80] As the notion of victim is totally unknown, the Committee's logic is completely opposite that of the Court. The claimant must

---

[73] E.C.H.R., *Case of Collectif National d'Information et d'Opposition à l'Usine Melox - Collectif Stop Melox et Mox v. France,* 28th March 2007, Application n°75219/01.

[74] E.C.H.R., *Case of Conka and others and Ligue des droits de l'Homme v. Belgium,* 5th February 2002, Application n° 51564/99. For a recent illustration, see E.C.H.R., *Youth Initiative For Human Rights v. Serbia,* 25th June 2013, Application n°48135/06.

[75] Article 33 of the European Convention of Human Rights and Fundamental Freedoms. *A contrario,* the victim notion is sometimes interpreted in a very large way, not very far from the *actio popularis:* E.C.H.R., *Case of Miscallef v. Malta,* 15th October 2009, Application n°17056/06.

[76] See, for example, European Commission, *Kustannus Oy Vappa Ajattelija AB & a. v. Finland,* 15th April 1996, DR n°85-B, p. 29.

[77] E.C.H.R., Case of *Stitching Mothers of Srebrenica and others v. The Netherlands,* 11th June 2013, Application n°65542/12, §§ 114–117.

[78] E.C.H.R., *Smits, Kleyn, Mettler Toledo B.V. and others, Raymakers, Vereniging Landelijk Overleg Betuweroute and Van Helden v. the Netherlands,* 3 May 2001, Applications n° 39032/97, 39343/98, 39651/98, 43147/98, 46664/99, 61707/00.

[79] E.C.H.R., *Van Melle and others v. the Netherlands,* 29 September 2009, Application n°19221/08.

[80] For an analysis of potential links between the E.C.H.R. and E.C.S.R., see J.-F. AKANDJI-KOMBÉ, "Charte sociale européenne et Convention européenne des droits de l'Homme: quelles perspectives pour les dix prochaines années?" *in* O. DE SCHUTTER (ed.), *The European Social Charter: a Social Constitution for Europe,* Bruxelles, Bruylant, 2010, pp. 147–165.

not defend his own interest[81] or the interests of a set group of individuals.[82] The subject of the claim has to be a collective one. This admissibility element has consequences on the other conditions such as, for example, the absence of the obligation to have exhausted all domestic remedies.[83] This situation allows legal persons to compose their claims as an *"element of a general campaign seeking to put legislation and practices of the larger number of States in compliance with the European Social Charter"*.[84] As an illustration we can observe the current strategy of the Association for the Protection of All Children (APPROACH) Ltd. who registered complaints against seven different States concerning the same subject – the prohibition of corporal and cruel punishment of children.[85] In another way, this action in collective interests can also lead to reopen a debate or a discussion about a sensitive political question.[86] To illustrate this, we can make reference to *Cases of A.T.D.-Quart Monde v. France*[87] and *F.E.A.N.T.S.A. v. France*[88] in 2007, regarding the right to housing. In those cases, associations used their right to act in legal proceedings before the European Committee in order to open discussions with public authorities about a stagnating situation. The choice of the State was likewise not a coincidence. France is not

---

[81] E.C.S.R., *Case of SAIGI – Syndicat des Hauts Fonctionnaires (SHF) v. France*, 14th June 2005, Complaint n°29/2005 and E.C.S.R., *Case of F.C.S.A.P. v. Portugal*, 5th December 2006, Complaint n°36/2006.

[82] E.C.S.R., *Case of SAIGI – Syndicat des Hauts Fonctionnaires (SHF) v. France*, 14th June 2005, Complaint n°29/2005.

[83] Classical condition before the European Court (Article 35 E.C.H.R.) rejected before the E.C.S.R.: E.C.S.R., *European Roma Rights Center (EERC) v. Bulgaria*, 10th October 2005, Complaint n°31/2005.

[84] Author's translation of: *"élément d'une campagne générale, recherchant la mise en conformité à la Charte sociale des législations et des pratiques du plus grand nombre d'Etats possibles"*. J.-F. Akandji Kombe, "Chronique des décisions du Comité européen des droits sociaux sur les réclamations collectives (May 2005–December 2007)", *R.T.D.H.*, 2008, n°74, p. 508.

[85] E.C.S.R., *Pending Cases of APPROACH Ltd. v. France, Ireland, Italy, Slovenia, Czech Republic, Cyprus and Belgium*, registered on 4th February 2013, Complaints n°92/2013, 93/2013, 94/2013, 95/2013, 96/2013, 97/2013 and 98/2013.

[86] See, for the same idea, M. Bell, "Promoting Equality through Social Inclusion: Case Studies from the European Social Charter", *in* T. Novitz & D. Mangan, *The Role of Labour Standards in Development: from Theory to Sustainable Practice?*, Oxford, O.U.P., 2011, pp. 76–94.

[87] E.C.S.R., *Case of A.T.D.-Quart Monde v. France*, 5th December 2007, Complaint n°33/2006. See N. Bernard, "Le droit au logement dans la Charte sociale révisée: à propos de la condamnation de la France par le Comité européen des droits sociaux", *R.T.D.H.*, 2009, pp. 1061 *et seq.*

[88] E.C.S.R., *Case of Fédération européenne des associations nationales de travail avec les sans-abris (F.E.A.N.T.S.A.) v. France*, 5th December 2007, Complaint n°39/2006.

considered to be a poor State without any effective social policies and leg-islation protecting the right to housing. In choosing this State, A.T.D.-Quart Monde and F.E.A.N.T.S.A. wanted to set an example in order to obtain a higher level and more efficient protection of such right. The decisions of the European Committee of Social Rights provided them with a great opportunity to achieve such protection, in addition to some strong argu-ments for future discussions.[89] Thus, unlike the European Court, we note here that this consisted of a real will of collective interests action in which the claimant represented for the first time a collective interest shared by many people. This feeling was confirmed by the admissibility condition, which implies that the claim was linked to the activities of the concerned associations.

This distinction between these two procedures seems to find an expla-nation in the difference between the categories of protected rights. The Court essentially protects individual rights and the European Convention was founded on an individualistic concept of Human Rights,[90] whereas the Committee generally protects the rights of people belonging to a particular category, like workers or minorities. This review remains effective even if all members of these categories gain advantages from the collective action. Indeed, with a comparative analysis of distinct international Human Rights bodies, we can conclude that there is a lack of consensus between the sys-tems. Nonetheless, the position of the European Court seems to reach a good compromise. On one hand, the Human Rights Committee declares itself incompetent to look into communications exclusively founded on the violation of the rights of the legal person[91] and rejects communications of non-individual claimants.[92] In these circumstances, potential collective interests actions presented by a legal person or protecting legal person's rights are not allowed before the Human Rights Committee.[93] On the other

---

[89] See N. BERNARD, "Le droit au logement dans la Charte sociale révisée: à propos de la condamnation de la France par le Comité européen des droits sociaux", *R.T.D.H.*, 2009, n°80, pp. 1061–1089.

[90] J.-M. LARRALDE, "La Convention européenne des droits de l'Homme et la protection de groupes particuliers", *R.T.D.H.*, 2003/4, vol. 56, p. 1248.

[91] H.R.C., *Case of Wallman and others v. Austria*, 2004, n°1002/2001.

[92] See H.R.C., *Disabled and handicapped persons in Italy v. Italy*, 1984, n°163/1984, but *a con-trario* H.R.C., *Case of Jouni Länsman and the Muotkatunturi Herdmen's Committee v. Finland*, 2005, n°1023/2001, §1.1.

[93] H.R.C., *Case of Allan Singer v. Canada*, 1994, n°455/1991, §11.2.

Beulay /
The Law and Practice of International Courts and Tribunals 12 (2013) 321–341   337

hand, the Inter-American Court and Commission of Human Rights have some leeway thanks to the American Convention, which allows a kind of *actio popularis*[94] for legal persons, in particular for associations and non-governmental organizations.[95] The Inter-American system adopts a larger vision of potential claimants. We can observe that this system accepts the notion of group action because of the open possibility for NGOs[96] to act in legal proceedings in place of individual victims and, also, without the consent of potential victims.[97] *"The American Convention considers the individual in a comprehensive way, which can mean alone, in a group or organized in an institutional structure representing civil society"*.[98] The Inter-American system can be described as a *"pro victima"* system[99] because it makes a difference between the notion of petitioner and the notion of victim.[100] This situation results in opening litigation to potential victims who cannot or do not want to go to the Commission.[101] In this way, some types of collective interests actions are allowed for non-governmental legal persons or groups of persons,[102] unlike in the European system. But in this collective petition the real victims of violations must be identified. For Judge A. A. CANÇADO TRINDADE it is the expression of the collective guarantee enclosed in the

---

[94] See L. HENNEBEL, *La Convention américaine des droits de l'Homme – Mécanismes de protection et étendue des libertés, op. cit.*, 2007, p. 141, §154.

[95] Article 44 of the American Convention of Human Rights and Resolution n°59/81 of the Inter-American Commission.

[96] *A contrario* in the Inter-American system all legal persons have the right to sue as in the European system. If a firm wants to sue, the Commission will get rid of the legal personality and will accept the petition in the name of its members.

[97] Article 43 of Inter-American Commission's Regulations. See Inter-American Court, *Acevedo Jaramillo y otros v. Peru*, 7th February 2006, n°144, §142.

[98] Author's translation of: *"L'individu est envisagé par la Convention américaine de façon compréhensive, i.e. pris individuellement, en groupe ou encore institutionnellement, organisé au travers d'une structure représentant la société civile"*. L. BURGORGUE-LARSEN & A. UBEDA DE TORRES, *Les grandes décisions de la Cour interaméricaine des droits de l'Homme*, Bruxelles, Bruylant, 2008, p. 128.

[99] *Ibid.*, p. 129.

[100] See Inter-American Commission, *Case 1954*, 16th October 1981, Resolution 59/81, Annual Report 1981–1982; Inter-American Commission, *Case 10.970, (Raquel Martin de Mejía v. Peru)*, 1st March 1996, Resolution 5/96, Annual Report 1995; and Inter-American Court, *Yatama v. Nicaragua*, 23rd June 2005, n°127, §82.

[101] See Inter-American Court, *Castillo Petruzzi v. Peru*, 4th September 1998, Preliminary exceptions, n°41, §77.

[102] This is a wide interpretation of the notion of "group". The legal personality is not necessary and the group need only be non-governmental (Inter-American Court, *Castillo Petruzzi v. Peru*, *op. cit.*, §77).

Beulay /
338   *The Law and Practice of International Courts and Tribunals 12 (2013) 321–341*

American Convention of Human Rights.[103] The interpretation of the condition of representation by the Inter-American Court translates this wide acceptance of the petitioner's quality;[104] however, it can be analyzed as a disadvantage if the objective petition is an obstacle for the victim's action in legal proceedings.

In the African system, in contrast to the European system, the existence of an objective right to act in legal proceedings allows one to observe a real *actio popularis* without any victim condition and a larger petitioner function than in the Inter-American system. Indeed, by reading Article 56 of the ACHPR, we can observe that applicants only have to prove the existence of violations which "are not based exclusively on news disseminated through the mass media". They do not have to prove any violation of their own interest or to fulfil any condition of "representativeness" as in the European system. Furthermore, they do not have to include the name of the victims of the real violation, as the petitioner is required to do before the Inter-American Commission.[105] In this case, we can notice a new degree in the opening of the right to act in legal proceedings before a Human Rights protection body. We can explain this large difference between regional systems by the distinct social and political regional backgrounds which influence the structure of the regional bodies of Human Rights protection.

The large number of potential proceedings and the current trend for the cross fertilization between regional systems may help the European system to progress towards allowing collective interests actions of legal persons. If there is no real solution yet for a group action of legal persons without the ability to act in legal proceedings, we can draw on potential elements to open litigation before the European Court.

B. *Ideas to Introduce a Collective Interests Action before the European Court*

As previously stated, the system of the European Committee of Social Rights is an important innovation in the field of collective petition, although it is

---

[103] A. A. Cançado Trindade, Concurring Opinion, in Annex of the *Case Castillo Petruzzi v. Peru, op. cit.*, §32.

[104] It is only a formal element that does not enter into account for analyzing a petition's admissibility (Inter-American Court, *Castillo Petruzzi v. Peru, op. cit.*, §78).

[105] See, for example, African Commission, *Case of Sudan Human Rights Organisation & Centre on Housing Rights and Evictions (COHRE) v. Sudan*, 27th May 2009, Joint applications n°279/03 & 296/05, 28th Report.

not a restrictive one. However, the European Court took a softer approach regarding some legal persons in cases of violations of rights other than the rights of legal persons. Currently, joint actions of legal persons and their members are allowed under certain conditions. The first condition seems to be the protection of a shared interest between an association and its members. In this way, collective rights are the first targets because individuals cannot use them as efficiently as a legal person in which all powers are concentrated.[106] In other words, the legal person has to be their representative.[107] The notion of representation is understood as a pooling of interests, but it cannot lead to accept an *actio popularis* based only on the purpose of an association. The case, *Gorraiz Lizarraga v. Spain* illustrates this phenomenon.[108] The Court used an extensive interpretation of the notion of victim to allow associations to represent aggrieved individuals, but only if they could prove that they were entitled to the involved rights.[109] Such "representativeness" is used before the European Committee of Social Rights within the framework of collective actions.[110]

The second conceivable condition may be the subsidiarity of the collective interests action. It will be used, for example, in the case of a victim's failure. The case, *Agrotexim and others v. Greece* supports *a contrario* this theory. Indeed the claimants, who were shareholders of a company in liquidation, were not able to act in legal proceedings because the company itself was not able to act.[111] Some observers expressed reservations about the ambit of this decision. It limits the potential evolution because the legal person is not an association but a firm that involves another kind of

---

[106] O. DE SCHUTTER, "L'accès des personnes morales à la Cour européenne des droits de l'homme", *in Mélanges offerts à Silvio Marcus Helmons*, Bruxelles, Bruylant, 2003, pp. 100–101.

[107] O. DE SCHUTTER, "Sur l'émergence de la société civile en droit international: le rôle des associations devant la Cour européenne des droits de l'Homme", *European Journal of International Law*, 1996, n°3, p. 373.

[108] E.C.H.R., *Case of Gorraiz Lizarraga and others v. Spain*, 27th April 2004, Application n°62543/00, §38.

[109] *Ibid.*, §45.

[110] See Article 1.c of the Additional Protocol to the European Social Charter Providing for a System of Collective Complaints.

[111] E.C.H.R, *Case of Agrotexim and others v. Greece*, 24th October 1995, Application n°14807/89, Series A, n°330. See E.C.H.R., *Case of Vides Aizsardzibas Klubs (VAK) v. Latvia*, 27th May 2004, Application n°57829/00; E.C.H.R., *Case of Steel & Morris v. United Kingdom*, 15th February 2005, Application n°68416/01; E.C.H.R., *Case of L'Erablière A.S.B.L. v. Belgium*, 24th February 2009, Application n°49230/07.

relation between the artificial person and its members. It is necessary to add here that the purpose of a firm and that of an association are not similar, which can explain why it is easier to find the collective interest behind the former than it is to find it before the latter. Nevertheless, the articulation of the three criteria – representativeness, collective rights and the principle of collective action subsidiarity – can explain the admissibility of religious communities' claims instead of those of their members,[112] and the claims of environmental protection associations.[113] We cannot analyze this as a collective interests action but as an enlargement of the right to file a joint petition in the interest of legal persons.

To summarize the result of this analysis, what are the means of action for legal persons in the European system? Whereas they are fewer than in the Inter-American system but largely more important than in other systems, this is due to the large opening of European bodies to non-governmental legal persons. With what result? There are encouraging results in view of the large number of claims.[114]

But if the collective interests actions of legal persons can be interpreted as an improvement in the protection of Human Rights, they can also be viewed as a threat. Indeed, legal persons are not the *alter ego* of individual persons "on a large scale", and being too protective towards legal persons' rights can lead to a lesser protection of individuals' rights,[115] because of the

---

[112] European Commission of Human Rights, *Church of Scientology of Paris v. France*, 9th January 1995, Application n°19509/92; European Commission, *Pasteur X & Church of Scientology v. Sweden*, 5th May 1979, Application n°7805/77, *D.R.* 16, p. 68; E.C.H.R., *Supreme Holy Council of the Muslim Community v. Bulgaria*, 16th December 2004, Application n°39023/97; E.C.H.R., *Church of Scientology Moscow v. Russia*, 5th April 2007, Application n°18147/02; E.C.H.R., *Case of Religionsgemeinschaft der Zeugen Jehovas and others v. Austria*, 31st July 2008, Application n°40825/98. For a recent application about the satisfaction, see E.C.H.R., *Case of Holy Synod of the Bulgarian Orthodox Church (Metropolitan Inokentiy) and others v. Bulgaria*, 16th September 2010 (just satisfaction), Joint applications n°412/03 & 35677/04.

[113] See E.C.H.R., *Case of Vides Aizsardzibas Klubs (VAK) v. Latvia*, 27th May 2004, Application n°57829/00; E.C.H.R., *Case of Steel & Morris v. United Kingdom*, 15th February 2005, Application n°68416/01.

[114] A study of recent cases of the European Committee of Social Rights shows the important place of this procedure in the European protection of Human Rights. See, in particular, J.-F. AKANDJI-KOMBÉ, "Chronique des décisions du Comité européen des droits sociaux sur les réclamations collectives (2008–2011)", *R.T.D.H.*, 2012, n°91, pp. 547–590.

[115] J.-F. RENUCCI, *Traité de droit européen des droits de l'Homme, op. cit.*, p. 52.

complexity of the notion of "representativeness".[116] The system of the European Committee of Social Rights can represent an effective alternative to this potential problem: introducing a right to act in legal proceedings in the general interest for the protection of the community and its components at the same time, but with a selection of collective petitioners. Another alternative would be an action in substitution along the lines of the distinction between petitioner and victim operated by the Inter-American system. It leads to federating numerous cases of Human Rights violations in which the victims are probably not able to present individual claims. This solution guarantees those victims the means to bring an effective action.[117]

While the European system is changing with the aim of reducing the overload of litigation, it does not seem that the grounds to seize the Court will be broadened any time shortly. In fact, paragraph 20 of the recent Declaration of Brighton[118] proposes to enlarge the pilot judgment procedure, without opening the right to seize the Court in a collective interest in case of structural problems. This problem is only analyzed from the angle of the processing of the application and not from that of the application itself. It seems to be a trend which needs to be reversed. In reality, the creation of a federative claim, with conditions, as a substitute for many claims and for a more important prejudice – because it reveals repetitive violations – would be able to give a new impetus to the European system of Human Rights protection, for a better justiciability of rights, the first *leitmotif* of the European system, and not only for the sole interest of the smooth functioning of the Court.

---

[116] G. COURTY, *Les groupes d'intérêt*, Paris, La Découverte, Collection Repères, 2006, pp. 58 *et seq.*

[117] O. DE SCHUTTER, "Sur l'émergence de la société civile [...]", *op. cit.*, pp. 406–407.

[118] See, in particular, §20d): "*Building on the pilot judgment procedure invites the Committee of Ministers to consider the advisability and modalities of a procedure by which the Court could register and determine a small number of representative applications from a group of applications that allege the same violation against the same respondent State Party, such determination being applicable to the whole group*".

B
Americas

[15]

The Inter-American Commission on Human Rights and the Inter-American Court of Human Rights: Reflections on a Joint Venture

Cecilia Medina

I. INTRODUCTION

With the entry into force of the American Convention on Human Rights,[1] the inter-American system for the promotion and protection of human rights became a two-prong system. The first prong is formed by the mechanisms developed under the Charter of the Organization of American States (OAS), which authorizes the Inter-American Commission on Human Rights to supervise human rights in the territories of OAS member states. The second prong is composed of the mechanisms set forth in the Convention, which authorizes the Commission and the Inter-American Court of Human Rights to handle complaints of human rights violations allegedly committed by any state party to the Convention, and further provides for the Court to exercise advisory jurisdiction.

The purpose of this article is to analyze the manner in which these second, Convention-based mechanisms have started to operate. In Part I, I briefly examine the way the Commission operated before the Convention entered into force and then describe the changes that the Convention brought. This section concludes with a discussion of limitations that may impede the

---

1. *See* American Convention on Human Rights, *adopted* 22 Nov. 1969, *entered into force*, 18 July 1978, *reprinted in* Org. Am. States, *Basic Documents Pertaining to Human Rights in the Inter-American System*, OEA/Ser.L/V/II.71, Doc. 6 Rev. 1, 25–53 (1987). As of March 1988, twenty states have ratified the Convention: Argentina, Barbados, Bolivia, Colombia, Costa Rica, Dominican Republic, Ecuador, El Salvador, Grenada, Guatemala, Haiti, Honduras, Jamaica, Mexico, Nicaragua, Panama, Peru, Surinam, Uruguay, and Venezuela. *Id.* at 55.

Human Rights Quarterly 12 (1990) 439–464 © 1990 by The Johns Hopkins University Press

440   **HUMAN RIGHTS QUARTERLY**   **Vol. 12**

system. In Part II, I analyze the relationship between the Commission and the Court in the context of several recent cases. The article concludes with a look to the future and some suggestions for improving the system.

II. THE DEVELOPMENT OF THE INTER-AMERICAN SYSTEM

The Inter-American Commission on Human Rights was established as an autonomous entity of the OAS by a resolution of the Fifth Meeting of Consultation of Ministers of Foreign Affairs in 1959.[2] The Commission was originally conceived as a study group concerned with abstract investigations in the field of human rights.[3] However, the creators of the Commission did not foresee the appeal this organ would have for the individual victims of human rights violations. As soon as it was known that the Commission had been created, individuals began to send complaints about human rights problems in their countries.[4] Prompted by these complaints, the Commission started its activities with the conviction that in order to promote human rights it had to protect them.

A significant part of the Commission's work was addressing the problem of countries with gross, systematic violations of human rights, characterized by an absence or a lack of effective national mechanisms for the protection of human rights and a lack of cooperation on the part of the governments concerned.[5] The main objective of the Commission was not to investigate

---

2. Org. Am. States, Resolution VIII, 5th Meeting of Consultation of Ministers of Foreign Affairs, *reprinted in* Org. Am. States, *Basic Documents*, OEA/Ser.L/V/1.4, 35–36 (1960). *See also* Schreiber, *The Inter-American Commission on Human Rights* (1970); and Leblanc, *The Promotion and Protection of Human Rights* (1977).

3. For the debates on Resolution VIII, see Org. Am. States, *Quinta Reunion de Consulta de Ministros de Relaciones Exteriores, Actas y Documentos*, OIEA/Ser.F/III.5. For the text of the 1960 Statute, see Org. Am. States, *Basic Documents* (1960), *supra* note 2, at 9–13. Article 9 allows the Commission to study the condition of human rights in member states and make recommendations to the governments of those states. According to Article 1, the rights to be supervised were those of the American Declaration of the Rights of Man, adopted 2 May 1948. *See* American Declaration of the Rights of Man, *reprinted in* Org. Am. States, *Basic Documents, supra* note 1, at 18–24.

4. Forty-five communications concerning violations of human rights in Cuba and several others against the Dominican Republic and Paraguay had reached the Commission by its Second Session. *See generally* Inter-Am. Comm'n H.R., *Report on the Work Accomplished during its First Session, 3–28 October 1960*, OEA/Ser.L/V/II,1, Doc. 32 (1961); Inter-Am. Comm'n H.R., *Report of the Work Accomplished during its Second Session, 10–26 April 1961*, OEA/Ser.L/V/II.2, Doc. 24 (1961).

5. "Gross, systematic violations of human rights" I understand to be "those violations, instrumental to the achievement of governmental policies, perpetrated in such a quantity and in such a manner as to create a situation in which the rights to life, to personal integrity or to personal liberty of the population as a whole or one or more sectors of the population of a country are continuously infringed or threatened." *See* Medina, *The Battle of Human Rights; Gross, Systematic Violations of Human Rights and the Inter-American System* ch. II (1988) (particularly at 16).

isolated violations but to document the existence of these gross, systematic violations and to exercise pressure to improve the general condition of human rights in the country concerned. For this purpose, and by means of its regulatory powers, the Commission created a procedure to "take cognizance" of individual complaints and use them as a source of information about gross, systematic violations of human rights in the territories of the OAS member states.[6]

The Commission's competence to handle individual communications was formalized in 1965, after the OAS reviewed and was satisfied with the Commission's work.[7] The OAS passed Resolution XXII, which allowed the Commission to "examine" isolated human rights violations, with a particular focus on certain rights.[8] This procedure, however, provided many obstacles for the Commission. Complaints could be handled only if domestic remedies had been exhausted, a requirement that prevented swift reactions to violations. Also, the procedure made the Commission more dependent on the governments for information. This resulted in the governments' either not answering the Commission's requests for information or answering with a blanket denial that did not contribute to a satisfactory solution of the problem.

Furthermore, once the Commission had given its opinion on the case, there was nothing else to be done; the Commission would declare that a government had violated the American Declaration of the Rights and Duties of Man and recommend the government take certain measures, knowing that this was unlikely to resolve the situation. The fact that some of the Commission's opinions could reach the political bodies of the OAS did not solve the problem, because the Commission's opinions on individual cases were never discussed at that level. Consequently, in order not to lose the flexibility it had, the Commission interpreted Resolution XXII as granting the Commission power to "examine" communications concerning individual

---

6. The original procedure was set forth in Articles 25 through 29 of the 1960 regulations. The text of these regulations is reprinted in Org. Am. States, *Basic Documents* (1960), *supra* note 2. This procedure allowed the Commission to request information from the government and the complaining party and investigate the facts in the communication. The Commission used this information to negotiate the fate of certain victims or to attempt improving the general situation of human rights in the country. The Commission also published the information for the purpose of "mobilizing shame."

7. The Commission had been particularly successful in its handling of the situation in the Dominican Republic in the early 1960s. *See* Schreiber, *The Inter-American Commission on Human Rights in the Dominican Crisis*, XXII International Organization, 508–28 (1968). *See also,* Thomas & Thomas, *Human Rights and the OAS: International Law in the Western Hemisphere* 137–95 (1974).

8. *See* Org. Am. States, Resolution XXII of the Second Special Inter-American Conference, OEA/Ser.E/XIII.l Doc. 150 Rev. (1965). The human rights given particular attention were those in Articles 1 (right to life, liberty, and personal security), 2 (right to equality before the law), 3 (right to religious freedom and worship), 4 (right to freedom of investigation, opinion, expression, and dissemination of information), 18 (right to a fair trial), 25 (right of protection from arbitrary arrest), and 26 (right to due process of law).

442 **HUMAN RIGHTS QUARTERLY** **Vol. 12**

violations of certain rights specified in the resolution without diminishing its power to "take cognizance" of communications concerning the rest of the human rights protected by the American Declaration. The Commission preserved this broader power for the purposes of identifying gross, systematic human rights violations.[9]

The procedure to "take cognizance" of communications evolved and became the general case procedure and was later used in examining the general human rights situation in a country. This procedure, maturing with the Commission's practice, had several positive characteristics in view of the Commission's purposes. First, it could be started without checking whether the communications met any admissibility requirements or even in the absence of any communication. All that was necessary was for news to reach the Commission that serious violations were taking place in the territory of an OAS member state.[10] Second, the Commission assumed a very active role by requesting and gathering information by telegram and telephone from witnesses, newspapers, and experts, and also requesting consent to visit the country at the Commission's convenience. Third, the Commission could publicize its findings in order to put pressure upon the governments. Finally, the report resulting from the investigation could be sent to the political bodies of the OAS, thereby allowing for a political discussion of the problem which, at least theoretically, could be followed by political measures against the governments involved.

Since financial and human resources were limited, the Commission concentrated all its efforts on the examination of the general situation of human rights in each country. The examination of individual cases clearly took a secondary place. The Commission appeared to process them only because it had a duty to do so and not because of a conviction that its intervention would be helpful. After all, the special procedure for individual cases did not improve the victims' possibilities for redress, and the Commission could attempt to solve the cases through an examination of the general human rights situation in the country.

In short, the Commission was the sole guarantor of human rights in a continent plagued with gross, systematic violations, and the Commission was part of an international organization for which human rights were definitely not the first priority, and these facts made an imprint on the way the

---

9. *See* Inter-Am. Comm'n H.R., 1970 Regulations, *reprinted in* OEA/Ser.L/V/II.23 Doc. 21, español, (1970). Article 37 regulated the "taking of cognizance" of communications and Article 53 the examination of communications. The advantage of "examining" communications instead of "taking cognizance" of them was that the Commission could write its opinion at the end of the procedure.

10. The Commission stated its power to start a procedure by its own motion in Article 23(2) of the 1980 Regulations. *See* Inter-Am. Comm'n H.R., *Handbook of Existing Rules Pertaining to Human Rights*, OEA/Ser.L/V/II.50 Doc. 6, 126 (1980).

Commission looked upon its task. Apparently, the Commission viewed itself more as an international organ with a highly political task to perform than as a technical body whose main task was to participate in the first phase of a quasi-judicial supervision of the observance of human rights. The Commission's past made it ill-prepared to efficiently utilize the additional powers the Convention subsequently granted it.

A. The System Under the American Convention on Human Rights

The Convention vested the authority to supervise its observance in two organs: the Inter-American Commission, which pre-existed the Convention, and Inter-American Court of Human Rights, which was created by the Convention.

The Inter-American Commission is composed of seven members elected in a nongovernmental capacity by the OAS General Assembly and represents all the OAS member states.[11] The entry into force of the Convention in 1978 invested the Commission with a dual role. It has retained its status as an organ of the OAS, thereby maintaining its powers to promote and protect human rights in the territories of all OAS member states. In addition, it is now an organ of the Convention, and in that capacity it supervises human rights in the territories of the states parties to the Convention.

The Commission's functions include: (1) promoting human rights in all OAS member states; (2) assisting in the drafting of human rights documents;[12] (3) advising member states of the OAS; (4) preparing country reports, which usually include visits to the territories of these states; (5) mediating disputes over serious human rights problems;[13] (6) handling individual complaints and initiating individual cases on its own motion, both with regard to states parties and states not parties to the Convention; and (7) participating in the handling of cases and advisory opinions before the Court.[14]

---

11. American Convention on Human Rights, arts. 34–36, *reprinted in* Org. Am. States, *Basic Documents, supra* note 1, at 25–53.
12. The Commission played a major role in drafting the American Convention on Human Rights, the Inter-American Convention to Prevent and Punish Torture, and the Additional Protocol to the American Convention on Economic, Social and Cultural Rights.
13. The Commission played such a role when guerrillas seized the Embassy of the Dominican Republic in Colombia. *See* Uribe, *La Comisión Inter-americana de Derechos Humanos y la toma de la Embajada Dominicana en Bogotá,* in *Human Rights in the Americas: Homage to the Memory of Carlos A. Dunshee de Abranches* 330–38 (1984); do Nascimento e Silva, *O papel da Comissào Interamericana de Direitos Humanos no Sequestro de Diplomatas em Bogotá,* in *id.* 319–29.
14. American Convention on Human Rights, arts. 48, 57, *reprinted in* Org. Am. States, *Basic Documents, supra* note 1, at 25–53; Rules of Procedure of the Court, art. 52, *reprinted in* Org. Am. States, *Basic Documents, supra* note 1, at 117–37; Commission's Statute, arts. 18, 20, *reprinted in* Org. Am. States, *Basic Documents, supra* note 1, at 65–73.

444   **HUMAN RIGHTS QUARTERLY**   **Vol. 12**

The Inter-American Court consists of seven judges irrespective of the number of states that have recognized the jurisdiction of the Court.[15] Although the Court is formally an organ of the Convention and not of the OAS,[16] its judges may be nationals of any member state of the OAS whether or not they are parties to the Convention.[17]

The Court has contentious and advisory jurisdiction.[18] In exercising its contentious jurisdiction, the Court settles controversies about the interpretation and application of the provisions of the American Convention through a special procedure designed to handle individual or state complaints against states parties to the Convention. Under its advisory jurisdiction, the Court may interpret not only the Convention but also any other treaty concerning the protection of human rights in the American states. The Court may also give its opinion regarding the compatibility of the domestic laws of any OAS member state with the requirements of the Convention or any human rights treaties to which the Convention refers.[19] In addition, the Court is not prevented from giving its opinion regarding any question relating to the content or scope of the rights defined in the Convention or any question that might have to be considered by the Court in the exercise of its contentious jurisdiction or by the Commission's supervision of human rights. The advisory jurisdiction of the Court may be set in motion by any OAS member state, whether or not it is a party to the Convention, or by any OAS organ listed in Chapter X of the OAS Charter, which includes the Commission.[20]

---

15. The first election of judges for the Court took place in May 1979 and the Court was installed on 3 September 1979 in its seat in San Jose de Costa Rica. The Statute of the Court was approved by the OAS General Assembly at its Ninth Regular Session, 22–31 Oct. 1979 by Resolution 448. For the text of the Statute, see Org. Am. States, *Basic Documents, supra* note 1, at 105–15. The Rules of Procedure of the Court were adopted at its Third Regular Session in 1980. For the text of the Rules, see Org. Am. States, *Basic Documents, supra* note 1, at 117–37.

16. Efforts were made to include the Court in the OAS Charter when it was amended by the Protocol of Cartagena de Indias. According to the Court, the efforts were unsuccessful due to an apparent misunderstanding. *See* Inter-Am. Ct. H.R., *Annual Report*, OEA/Ser.L/ V/III.15 Doc. 13, 8–9 (1986).

17. American Convention on Human Rights, art. 52, *reprinted in* Org. Am. States, *Basic Documents, supra* note 1, at 25–53.

18. For a more detailed study of the Court, see Medina, *The Battle of Human Rights, supra* note 5, ch. VII. *See also* Buergenthal, *The Inter-American Court of Human Rights*, 76 Am. J. Int'l L., 231–45 (1982); Cerna, *La Cour Interamericaine des Droits de l'homme. Ses premiere affaires*, XXIX Annuaire Francaise de Droit International (A.F.D.I.), 300–12, (1983); Cerna, *La Cour Interamericaine des Droits de l'Homme. Les Affaires Recentes*, XXXIII A.F.D.I., 351–69 (1987).

19. *See* Inter-Am. Ct. H.R., *The effect of reservations on the entry into force of the American Convention (arts. 74 and 75)*, Advisory Opinion OC-2/82, Series A No. 2, para. 16 (1982).

20. American Convention on Human Rights, art. 64, *reprinted in* Org. Am. States, *Basic Documents, supra* note 1, at 25–53. For the interpretation of the expression "other treaties," see Inter-Am. Ct. H.R., *Other Treaties Subject to the Advisory Jurisdiction of the Court (art. 64 American Convention on Human Rights)*, Advisory Opinion OC-1/82, Series A (1982). For the power to interpret the American Declaration of the Rights and Duties of

The procedure for handling individual or state complaints begins before the Commission.[21] The procedure resembles those set forth in the European Convention and in the Additional Protocol to the International Covenant on Civil and Political Rights.[22] It is a quasi-judicial mechanism which may be started by any person, group of persons, or nongovernmental entity legally recognized in one or more of the OAS member states, regardless of whether the complainant is the victim of a human rights violation. This right of individual petition is a mandatory provision in the Convention, binding on all states parties. Inter-state communications, however, are dependent upon an explicit recognition of the competence of the Commission to receive and examine them.[23] In addition, the Commission may begin processing a case on its own motion.[24]

After receiving the communication, the Commission determines the admissibility of the complaint. The Commission will judge any communication admissible if all the following requirements are met: (1) the communication alleges a violation of a right or rights protected by the Convention; (2) a communication on the same subject is not pending or has not previously been studied by the Commission or any other international organization; (3) the remedies under the state's domestic laws have been exhausted or the state does not respect the due process of law for the alleged violation; and (4) the communication is brought in a timely manner.[25]

The Commission has powers to request information from the government concerned and, with the consent of the government, to investigate the facts in the complaint at the location of the alleged violation. If the government does not cooperate in the proceedings by providing the requested information

---

Man, which is not a treaty, see Inter-Am. Ct. H.R., *Interpretation of the American Declaration of the Rights and Duties of Man Within the Framework of Article 64 of the American Convention on Human Rights,* Advisory Opinion OC-10/89 (1989).

21. American Convention on Human Rights, arts. 44–51, *reprinted in* Org. Am. States, *Basic Documents, supra* note 1, at 25–53. *See also* Inter-Am. Comm'n H.R. Regulations, arts. 31–50, *reprinted in* Org. Am. States, *Basic Documents, supra* note 1, at 75–103.

22. For a succinct description of the procedure, see Medina, *Procedures in the Inter-American System for the Promotion and Protection of Human Rights,* 6 Netherlands Q. Hum. Rts. 83–102 (1988). For the procedure followed in the European Convention, see Zwaak, *The Protection of Human Rights and Fundamental Freedoms within the Council of Europe,* id. at 43–68. For a more detailed study, see Van Dijk & Van Hoof, *Theory and Practice of the European Convention on Human Rights* (1982). For the Covenant's additional protocol, see de Zayas, Moller, & Opsahl, *Application of the International Covenant on Civil and Political Rights under the Optional Protocol by the Human Rights Committee,* 28 German Y.B. of Int'l L. 9–64 (1985).

23. American Convention on Human Rights, arts. 44 and 45, *reprinted in* Org. Am. States, *Basic Documents, supra* note 1, at 25–53.

24. *Id.;* Inter-Am. Comm'n H.R. Regulations, art. 26(2), *reprinted in* Org. Am. States, *Basic Documents, supra* note 1, at 75–103.

25. American Convention on Human Rights, arts. 46 and 47, *reprinted in* Org. Am. States, *Basic Documents, supra* note 1, at 25–53.

within the time limit set by the Commission, Article 42 of the Commission's Regulations allows the Commission to presume that the facts in the petition are true, "as long as other evidence does not lead to a different conclusion."[26] Following this, the Commission need investigate the case no further.

Before ending its consideration of a case, the Commission "shall place itself at the disposal of the parties with a view to reaching a friendly settlement of the matter on the basis of respect for the human rights recognized in the Convention."[27] In following the regulations, the Commission attempts a friendly settlement only when (1) both parties to the dispute expressly agree to cooperate in this effort; (2) the positions and allegations of the parties are sufficiently precise; and (3) in the judgment of the Commission, the dispute is susceptible to this settlement procedure.[28]

If no friendly settlement is reached, Article 50 of the Convention directs the Commission to draw up a draft report setting forth the facts and stating the Commission's conclusions. This first report is not published but is transmitted only to the state concerned so the state's officials may respond. When the Commission transmits the report, it may also make proposals or recommendations to the state.[29] Under Article 51 of the Convention, the Commission may write a second report if, within the period prescribed in that article, the matter has not been submitted to the Court by the Commission or by the state concerned, or it has not been settled by other means. This second report will contain the Commission's opinion and conclusions regarding the case, the measures the Commission recommends, and a time limit for the state to comply with these measures. When the time limit has expired, the Commission decides whether the state has responded with adequate measures and whether to publish the report.[30]

The Court may consider a case that is brought either by the Commission or by a state party to the Convention.[31] For the Commission to refer a case to the Court, the case must have been admitted for investigation and the

---

26. Inter-Am. Comm'n H.R. Regulations, art. 42, *reprinted in* Org. Am. States, *Basic Documents, supra* note 1, at 75–103.
27. American Convention on Human Rights, art. 48, *reprinted in* Org. Am. States, *Basic Documents, supra* note 1, at 25–53.
28. Inter-Am. Comm'n H.R. Regulations, art. 45, *reprinted in* Org. Am. States, *Basic Documents, supra* note 1, at 75–103. The Commission has repeatedly stated that the friendly settlement procedure is not effective in cases of disappearances or illegal executions. *See, e.g.,* Resolutions 7/86, 9/86, and 10/86 against Nicaragua, *reprinted in* Inter-Am. Comm'n H.R., *Annual Report* (1985–1986), OEA/Ser.L/V/II.68 Doc. 8 Rev. 1, 105–12 (1986); and Resolutions 17/87, 18/87, and 19/87 against Peru, *reprinted in* Inter-Am. Comm'n H.R., *Annual Report,* OEA/Ser.L/V/II.71 Doc. 9 Rev. 1, 114–27 (1987).
29. American Convention on Human Rights, art. 50, *reprinted in* Org. Am. States, *Basic Documents, supra* note 1, at 25–53. *See also* Inter-Am. Comm'n H.R. Statute, art. 23(2), *reprinted in Basic Documents, supra* note 1, at 65.
30. American Convention on Human Rights, art. 51, *reprinted in* Org. Am. States, *Basic Documents, supra* note 1, at 25–53.
31. *Id.* at art. 61(1).

Commission's draft report sent to the state party.[32] In addition, the state must recognize the Court's general contentious jurisdiction or a limited jurisdiction specified by a time period or case.[33] For a state party to be able to place a case before the Court, the only requirement is that both states must have recognized the Court's contentious jurisdiction.[34]

During the proceedings, the Court has powers to investigate the facts as it deems necessary.[35] The Court ordinarily concludes its consideration of a case by issuing a judgment. If the Court finds that there has been a violation of a right or freedom protected by the Convention, it shall rule "that the injured party be ensured the enjoyment of his right or freedom that was violated."[36] If appropriate, it may also rule that "the consequences of the measure or situation that constituted the breach of such a right or freedom be remedied and that fair compensation be paid to the injured party."[37] States are under the international obligation to comply with the judgment of the Court in any case to which they are parties. The part of the judgment that stipulates compensatory damages has executory force in the state concerned.[38]

If a state does not comply with the decision of the Court, the Court may inform and make recommendations to the OAS General Assembly.[39] There is no reference in the Convention to any action that the General Assembly might take; the assembly, being a political body, may take any political action it deems necessary to persuade the state to comply with its international obligations.[40]

As may be apparent, a petition to the Court by the Commission or state party to the Convention is meant to handle isolated violations of human rights committed by a state which otherwise respects the rule of law. This procedure functions efficiently when the states concerned act in goodwill and cooperate with the human rights supervisory organs. In the reality of the inter-American system, unfortunately, goodwill and cooperation on the

---

32. Inter-Am. Comm'n H.R. Regulations, art. 50, *reprinted in* Org. Am. States, *Basic Documents, supra* note 1, at 75–103.
33. *Id.*
34. American Convention on Human Rights, art. 62, *reprinted in* Org. Am. States, *Basic Documents, supra* note 1, at 25–53. By 1981, two years after the Court had been established, only four states (Costa Rica, Peru, Honduras, and Venezuela) had recognized the Court's contentious jurisdiction. In 1984, Ecuador and Argentina joined in, and in 1985 Colombia and Uruguay. Guatemala and Surinam made the pertinent declaration in 1987, and Panama in 1989.
35. Inter-Am. Ct. H.R. Rules of Procedure, art. 34, *reprinted in* Org. Am. States, *Basic Documents, supra* note 1, at 117–35.
36. American Convention on Human Rights, art. 63(1), *reprinted in* Org. Am. States, *Basic Documents, supra* note 1, at 25–53.
37. *Id.*
38. *Id.* at art. 68(2).
39. *Id.* at art. 65.
40. *See* Medina, *The Battle of Human Rights, supra* note 5, 173–74.

448   **HUMAN RIGHTS QUARTERLY**   **Vol. 12**

part of the states are seldom seen. This being the case, the procedure is bound to be inadequate.[41]

In addition to the problems posed by the Commission's status as part of a political organization and by the lack of cooperation among the states, financial limitations are also potentially troublesome. The OAS does not provide the Commission with the necessary means to carry out all its various activities. The Commission usually receives about 500 complaints a year, with each complaint frequently involving more than one victim. At times the number is much higher; in 1980, when members of the Commission visited Argentina, 5,000 complaints were received. Furthermore, in any one year, the Commission carries out two or three observations on location and monitors the general situation of human rights in at least six or seven countries. To perform all these functions the Commission holds, in principle, two ten-day sessions a year. To support these activities the Commission currently has only seven lawyers, including the Executive Secretary, four secretaries and one administrative official, and its budget is less than 2 percent of the OAS budget. Under these circumstances, the Commission inevitably makes a choice as to what it can accomplish and places a priority on tasks it perceives as most likely to increase the general respect for human rights. In this ordering, the handling of individual complaints does not rank very high.

The Court fares somewhat better, but this is only because until recently it had not been able to carry out a normal amount of activities. As will be seen when the Velásquez case is examined, the Court did not carry out investigatory work by itself. Had the Court wished to do so, it would have probably been limited by a lack of funds.

III. THE RELATIONSHIP BETWEEN THE COMMISSION AND THE COURT

The Court was constituted in 1979, a year after the Convention entered into force, and depended on the organs of the OAS or the states parties to the Convention to initiate its work. With regard to its contentious jurisdiction in particular, the Court needed some collaboration on the part of the Commission. Although states and the Commission could present a case before the Court, states were reluctant to do so, for political reasons.[42] This left the Commission as the most important provider of work for the Court. The

---

41. *See id.* at ch. II.
42. This procedure exists in several international treaties, but until now only the European system has handled inter-state communications and only in very small numbers. Since 1953, when the European Convention entered into force, eighteen inter-state complaints have been lodged in Strasbourg, compared to an annual average of 300 to 400 individual applications.

Commission, however, did not resort to the Court's contentious jurisdiction until 1986. As for the Court's advisory jurisdiction, the Commission waited three years before requesting an opinion from the Court.

A. The First Stage: Noncooperation

On 15 July 1981, the government of Costa Rica brought the Court its first contentious case, asking the Court to investigate an alleged violation by Costa Rican authorities of human rights guaranteed by the Convention. This was a peculiar request in several regards. The first oddity of the case of Viviana Gallardo, et al.,[43] was that a state initiated procedures against itself. International supervision of human rights is designed to be subsidiary to that of the state. It seems strange that a government seriously concerned with human rights, as the government of Costa Rica appeared to be, would ask an international organ to investigate an alleged human rights violation instead of undertaking an internal investigation and attempting to settle the case domestically.[44]

A second peculiarity was that the government asked the Court to investigate whether there had been a violation of a human right protected by the Convention, a task that comes under the mandate of the Commission. The government stated that it would waive its right to have the case investigated by the Commission, because the only advantage of such an investigation was that Commission procedures allow for a friendly settlement, while the government was only interested in the Court's decision on whether the facts of the case showed that a violation had occurred.[45] This left the Commission in a difficult position because according to the system, the investigation of alleged human rights violations is one of the Commission's primary tasks.

In its final decision, the Court did not admit the application of the government of Costa Rica, finding that the state could not waive the Commission's admissibility, investigation, and report procedures, because these were instituted to benefit not only the states but also individuals.[46] Having

---

43. Viviana Gallardo was a suspected terrorist who had allegedly been murdered while in prison. The two other victims in the case were Alejandra M. Bonilla and Magaly Salazar, who had been wounded on the same occasion. Inter-Am. Ct. H.R., *In the Matter of Viviana Gallardo et al.*, No. G 101/81. Series A (1984) and Series B (1986).
44. Domestic legal remedies were in progress when the government presented the case to the Court, and the government formally waived the requirement of the prior exhaustion of these remedies in order to be able to resort to the Court.
45. *Gallardo*, Series B, *supra* note 43, at 13.
46. The Court concluded that the procedures before the Commission could not be waived by the state, since they had not been created for the sole benefit of the states, but also to allow for the exercise of important individual rights. The Court gave two reasons for

rejected the main petition, the Court proceeded to grant the government's alternative plea to refer the case to the Commission. However, this was not the end of the matter, as the Court also decided to retain the application on its docket pending the Commission's proceedings.[47] The Court thus retained jurisdiction over the case, which would have allowed it to pronounce on the merits once the procedural objections had been cleared.

However, after a two-year investigation, the Commission declared the case inadmissible under Article 48(1)(c) of the Convention on the basis of information or evidence subsequently received. The Commission's principal reason was that the system established by the Convention was meant to operate in lieu of the domestic legal system, and the information received from the government of Costa Rica made it clear that government had "acted in conformity with current legal provisions and punished with the full force of the law the person responsible for the acts charged."[48]

The question that immediately arises is why the Commission decided to declare the complaint inadmissible after an investigation that lasted for almost two years. On the same grounds it declared the case inadmissible, the Commission could have decided the merits of the case. By declaring the application inadmissible, the Commission barred the Court from considering the substantive issues in the case, since it is a prerequisite for the Court to exercise its contentious jurisdiction that the Commission examine and report its findings regarding these issues.[49]

The Commission's decision could be perceived as aimed at preventing the Court from exercising its powers, and in fact, as a result of this decision, the Court struck the case from its list.[50] Judge Piza dissented and made a reference to the "error [of the Commission] of ending [the procedures] by declaring the case inadmissible when in fact what it did was to resolve it by dismissing it for being inadmissible."[51] The Costa Rican government's handling of its application could also be perceived as a sign of distrust in

---

this conclusion: first, the Commission was "the channel through which the Convention gives the individual qua individual the possibility to activate the international system for the protection of human rights," since individuals were not empowered to submit cases to the Court; second, only the Commission had the power to discharge the important function of promoting friendly settlements within a broad conciliatory framework. *Id.* at paras. 23, 24, and 25.

47. *Id.,* Decision of 13 Nov. 1981, at para. 1.
48. While the procedure before the Court was being carried out, Costa Rica continued with its domestic procedures. Sentences were finally handed down against Jose Manuel Bolanos for the crimes of qualified homicide, aggravated assault, and simple assault of Viviana Gallardo, Alejandra Bonilla, and Magaly Salazar. *See id.,* Decision of 8 Sept. 1983, at para. 3.
49. American Convention on Human Rights, art. 61(2), *reprinted in* Org. Am. States, *Basic Documents, supra* note 1, at 25–53.
50. *See Gallardo, supra* note 43, Decision of 8 Sept. 1983.
51. *Id.* at para. 26 (Piza, J., dissenting).

the Commission's work. The request of Costa Rica does not seem to have helped the system to a good start.

B. The Second Stage: The Commission Requests Advisory Opinions

The Commission resorted to the Court for the first time on 28 June 1982 when it requested an advisory opinion concerning the interpretation of Articles 74 and 75 of the Convention which concern the ratification and reservation process for the Convention.[52] In answering the Commission's request,[53] the Court took the opportunity to stress that "given the broad powers relating to the promotion and observance of human rights which Article 112 of the OAS Charter confers on the Commission," the Commission, unlike other OAS organs, enjoyed "as a practical matter, an absolute right to request advisory opinions within the framework of Article 64(1) of the Convention."[54]

The second time that the Commission consulted the Court was by far more important and more relevant toward addressing the problem of the protection of human rights. On 18 September 1982, the Commission began actively seeking to have the government of Guatemala suspend the death sentences handed down by special courts that were created outside the regular judicial apparatus and operated without due process of law.[55] Moreover, these courts imposed the death sentences for offenses not previously punishable by death. The Commission's previous efforts had been unsuccessful and several individuals had been executed. The legal basis for the Commission's request was the Convention's provision on due process and the provision of Article 4(2) of the Convention that prohibits extending the death penalty to crimes to which it did not apply when the Convention entered into force. The Guatemalan government counterargued that it had made a reservation regarding Article 4(4) and therefore was allowed to apply the death penalty to new crimes.[56]

---

52. The Commission asked the Court for an interpretation of the reservation provision of the Convention that appeared to conflict with the reservation provision in the Vienna Convention on the Law of Treaties.
53. The Court stated, "[T]he Convention enters into force for a State which ratifies or adheres to it with or without reservation on the date of the deposit of its instrument of ratification or adherence." Inter-Am. Ct. H.R., *The effect of reservations, supra* note 19, at 19.
54. *Id.* at para. 16, 9. Article 64(1) allows consultation on the interpretation of the American Convention or other human rights treaties in force for American states.
55. The case of Guatemala and the death penalty has been analyzed in Moyer & Padilla, *Executions in Guatemala as decreed by the Courts of Special Jurisdiction in 1982–83,* in *Human Rights in the Americas, supra* note 13, at 280–89.
56. *See* Inter-Am. Comm'n H.R., *Informe sobre la Situacion de los Derechos Humanos en Guatemala,* OEA/Ser.L/V/II.61 Doc. 47, 47–65 (1983).

452   **HUMAN RIGHTS QUARTERLY**   **Vol. 12**

The Commission decided to ask the Court to determine the scope of Guatemala's reservation and issue an advisory opinion. Guatemala was a party to the Convention but had not recognized the contentious jurisdiction of the Court, and therefore, in principle, the case was barred from reaching the Court. Despite Guatemala's objection that the Commission's request was a ruse to have the Court pronounce on a matter, the Court accepted the request. The Court stated that the Convention,

> [b]y permitting Member States and OAS organs to seek advisory opinions, creates a parallel system to that provided for under Article 62 and offers an alternate judicial method of a consultative nature, which is designed to assist states and organs to comply with and to apply human rights treaties without subjecting them to the formalism and the sanctions associated with the contentious judicial process.[57]

The Commission's decision to resort to the Court and the Court's acceptance of the request despite Guatemala's objection were not only productive for the case,[58] but also for the system. A door was opened to joint efforts between the Commission and the Court to protect human rights, particularly in situations of gross, systematic violations, because such states often are not parties to the Convention, or if they are, have not recognized the competence of the Court.

This positive development was undermined, however, by the later handling of the case submitted by Stephen Schmidt. Mr. Schmidt, an American residing in Costa Rica, had been sentenced to three months in prison because he was working as a journalist without having a license issued by the Association of Journalists, in violation of Costa Rican law. According to Mr. Schmidt's complaint, the license law violated Article 13 of the Convention, which protects the freedom to seek, receive, and impart information and ideas.

After an attempt at a friendly settlement failed, the Commission decided in favor of the Costa Rican government. The Commission found that the license law did not restrict the freedoms guaranteed by the Convention, but was only a way of monitoring and controlling the exercise of a profession.[59]

At this point, the Commission could take one of two actions: it could either end the case, or it could send the case to the Court in order to seek

---

57. Inter-Am. Ct. H.R., *Restrictions to the Death Penalty (arts. 4(2) and 4(4) American Convention on Human Rights)*, Advisory Opinion OC-3/83, Series B No. 3, para. 43, 72–73 (1983).
58. The Court's advisory opinion was contrary to Guatemala's interpretation of its reservation, but even before it was given, the government of Guatemala cabled the Commission to announce that it had decided to reexamine and suspend, for the time being, the carrying out of death sentences handed down by the courts of special jurisdiction. *Id.* at 221–24.
59. Inter-Am. Comm'n H.R., *Annual Report 1984–1985*, Resolution 17/84, OEA/Ser.L/V/II.66 Doc. 10 Rev. 1, 51–77 (1985).

an authoritative judicial interpretation of Article 13. There were a number of reasons to refer the case to the Court: (1) the Commission had not reached a unanimous decision,[60] (2) several member states of the OAS had legislation similar to that of Costa Rica and therefore the problem affected many people, and (3) freedom of expression is an important human right often violated by governments. In spite of these considerations, the Commission chose not to send the case to the Court.

The government of Costa Rica, however, in fulfillment of a commitment it had made to the Inter-American Press Association, decided to request that the Court issue an advisory opinion on the matter.[61] The Court then ruled that Costa Rica's legislation did violate the Convention and went on to comment on the Commission's failure to submit the case to the contentious jurisdiction of the Court:

> Considering that individuals do not have standing to take their case to the Court and that a Government that has won a proceeding in the Commission would have no incentive to do so, in these circumstances the Commission alone is in a position, by referring the case to the Court, to ensure the effective functioning of the protective system established by the Convention. In such a context, the Commission has a special duty to consider the advisability of coming to the Court.[62]

By not sending the case to the Court, the Commission lost an opportunity to have an authoritative interpretation of an important human right in the Convention and created the awkward situation of having two contradictory opinions, the Commission's report and the Court's advisory opinion, on the same subject. Regardless of the resulting decision on the merits of the case, it would have been preferable to have the Commission's view changed by a binding decision of the Court.

C. The Third Stage: The Commission Seizes the Court

In 1986, the Commission submitted three contentious cases to the Court.[63] In addition to the historical significance of this step, the cases were also of

---

60. The resolution had been approved by a vote of five to one.
61. *See* Inter-Am. Ct. H.R., *Compulsory Membership in an Association Prescribed by Law for the Practice of Journalism (arts. 13 and 29 American Convention on Human Rights),* Advisory Opinion OC-5/85, Series A No. 5, 86 (1985).
62. Judge Cisneros was still more outspoken and expressed that "the love that we have put into our work has not been sufficient to avoid the sense of frustration that I feel in leaving the Court before it has had the opportunity to hear a single case of a violation of human rights, in spite of the sad reality of our America in this field." *Id.* at 145 (Declaration of Judge Maximo Cisneros).
63. The three cases were the *Velásquez Rodríguez Case,* the *Godinez Cruz Case,* and the *Fairen Garbi and Solis Corrales Case.* This article will only examine the first case.

great significance because of their subject matter. All of the cases, including the Velásquez case[64] discussed below, concerned individuals who disappeared in Honduras at a time when the general situation of human rights in that country was extremely serious. Actually, the disappearances were instances of gross, systematic violations of human rights and were to test whether a judicial mechanism could contribute to solving or alleviating a problem that, in its roots, escaped a legal solution. Moreover, the cases offered the possibility for the relatives of the victims and the inter-American community to see justice done. The Court's involvement also opened the possibility for the relatives of the victims to be given compensation for the human rights violations committed by the government.

Angel Manfredo Velásquez Rodríguez, a student, was allegedly detained and tortured by the armed forces of Honduras.[65] The government denied that he was being held.[66] At the time of the disappearance of Mr. Velásquez, the Commission was processing several communications concerning the disappearances of individuals. The Velásquez case was just one instance of more than a hundred disappearances in Honduras.[67]

The Commission received the complaint in October 1981. In October 1983, after several unsuccessful attempts at obtaining information on the case from the government of Honduras, the Commission decided to apply Article 42 and presume the facts of the complaint to be true. A friendly settlement was not attempted.[68]

The Commission issued a first report, Resolution 30/83, as provided in Article 50 of the Convention.[69] The Commission concluded that Honduras had seriously violated Articles 4 and 7 of the Convention, which protect the rights to life and personal liberty. The Commission recommended that the government: (1) order a thorough and impartial investigation to determine who was responsible for the acts denounced; (2) punish those responsible in accordance with Honduran law; and (3) inform the Commission within sixty days about the measures taken to carry out the recommendations set forth in the Resolution.[70]

---

64. *See* Inter-Am. Comm'n H.R., *Annual Report 1985–1986*, OEA/Ser.L/V/II.68 Doc. 8 Rev. 1, 40–47 (1986) for a text of Resolution No. 22/86, case 7920.
65. Inter-Am. Ct. H.R., *Velásquez Rodríguez Case*, Judgment of 28 July 1988, Series C, No. 4, para. 3.
66. *Id.*
67. Since Honduras was party to the American Convention, the Velásquez case was handled as an individual case according to the procedure set forth beginning at Article 44 of the American Convention and Article 31 of the Commission's regulations.
68. *See supra* note 28.
69. The resolution was not published in the Commission's Annual Report. Its text can be found under document OEA/Ser.L/V/II.62 Doc. 44.
70. Inter-Am. Ct. H.R., *Velásquez Rodríguez Case*, Preliminary Objections, Judgment of 26 June 1987, Series C, No. 1, para. 19.

On 18 November 1983, within the sixty-day period, the government submitted a petition for reconsideration on the grounds that domestic legal remedies had not been exhausted, because a writ of habeas corpus before the Supreme Court of Justice of Honduras was still pending and the government had not ceased making efforts to establish the whereabouts of Mr. Velasquez. The Convention does not provide for reconsideration of a resolution in cases against states parties,[71] and the grounds for requesting reconsideration in this case were highly questionable from a legal standpoint, since Honduras had not objected to the Commission's involvement at the first opportunity.[72] The Commission nevertheless agreed to reconsider the case. The Commission received additional information from the complaining party and sent it to the government. Despite the requests of the Commission, the government did not provide any additional information.

On 4 April 1986, the government of Honduras sent a cablegram to the Commission informing it that proceedings had been instituted against several individuals for the crimes of murder, torture, abuse of authority, and disobedience, and that all charges had been dismissed except for the proceedings against General Gustavo Alvarez Martínez, "whose testimony was not taken because he was outside the country."[73]

With this information, the Commission decided to close the case and approve Resolution 22/86, confirming Resolution 30/83 and referring the case to the Court. From a procedural standpoint, Resolution 22/86 was confusing. The Commission may send a case to the Court after it has written the first report mentioned in Article 50 of the Convention. That report was Resolution 30/83, in which the Commission issued recommendations and set a time limit for the government to take certain measures. By confirming Resolution 30/83, the Commission appeared to renew its previous recommendations, including the sixty-day time period it had granted Honduras. On 24 April 1986, before this second sixty-day period ended, the Commission submitted the case to the Court.

The Commission asked the Court to determine whether Honduras had violated Articles 4 and 7, as well as Article 5, which guarantees the right to humane treatment. The Commission also asked the Court to order, if there was a violation, that "the consequences of the situation that constituted the breach of such right or freedom be remedied and that fair compensation be

---

71. Article 54 of the Commission's Regulations allows a request for reconsideration in cases against states that are not parties to the Convention, probably because this procedure ends with a report that may be immediately published. The procedure against states parties contemplates a first report with eventual recommendations and then a second report. The first report is confidential. See *supra* notes 29–30 and accompanying text.
72. Non-exhaustion of domestic remedies must be alleged at the earliest opportunity possible, or the government is deemed to have waived the requirement.
73. Resolution 22/86 of the Commission, *supra* note 64, para. 19.

456   **HUMAN RIGHTS QUARTERLY**   **Vol. 12**

paid to the injured party or parties."[74] The following discussion will focus on some procedural aspects of the case that are important for the future work of the Commission and the Court.

1. Procedural Challenges to the Commission's Handling of the Case

The government of Honduras posed several preliminary objections before the Court against the Commission's procedures. The Commission then questioned whether the Court had jurisdiction to consider the government's procedural objections. The Commission contended that the Court was not an appellate tribunal and therefore had limited jurisdiction. This would prevent the Court from reviewing certain procedural aspects of the case, including those raised by the Honduran government. The Court rejected this argument, stating that it was competent to decide all matters relating to the interpretation or application of the Convention according to Article 62(1), including the procedural objections raised.[75]

The first objection made by Honduras was that the Commission had not formally declared the complaint admissible. On this point, the Court concluded that, although a declaration of inadmissibility was essential, a formal declaration of admissibility was not.[76] The Court's rationale was that "failure to observe certain formalities is not necessarily relevant when dealing on the international plane." The Court found it essential that "the conditions necessary for the preservation of the procedural rights of the parties not be diminished or unbalanced, and that the objectives of the different procedures be met."[77]

A second objection of the government was that the Commission had improperly applied Articles 50 and 51 of the Convention concerning the procedures of the draft and final reports when no friendly settlements have been reached. The government of Honduras argued that the confirmation of Resolution 30/83 by Resolution 22/86 "should have reinstated the sixty-day period granted therein for the Government to adopt the Commission's recommendations."[78] Furthermore, the government argued, Resolution 22/86 had "allowed the Court and the Commission to consider the matter simultaneously," inasmuch as within the sixty-day period Honduras still had an opportunity to reply to the Commission's recommendations.[79]

The Court answered the government argument by stating that the purpose

---

74. *Velásquez*, Preliminary obj., *supra* note 65, para. 2.
75. *Id.* at paras. 28–30.
76. *Id.* at paras. 39–41.
77. *Id.* at para. 33.
78. *Id.* at para. 72.
79. *Id.* at para. 75.

of the procedure is to allow a reasonable period of time for the government to resolve the matter before coming to the Court. Because the Commission reconsidered the case, the government actually had been afforded a much longer period of time to adopt the recommendations.[80] Similarly, the Court stated that the government's second objection was invalid because the Commission's application to the Court unequivocally showed that it had concluded its proceedings and submitted the matter for judicial settlement.[81] The Court stated that once the Commission has sent a case to the Court, its powers to continue handling the case cease, because the filing of the second report mentioned in Article 51 is conditional on the failure to file a case with the Court.[82] The Court concluded that "although the requirements of Article 50 and 51 have not been fully complied with, this has in no way impaired the rights of the government and the case should therefore not be ruled inadmissible on those grounds."[83]

The Court noted that the Commission's decision to reconsider Resolution 30/83 had "negative effects on the complaining party's right to obtain the international protection offered by the Convention within the legally established time frames."[84] The Court did not dismiss the possibility of a reconsideration, although the Commission's regulations explicitly provide for reconsideration only of cases against non-parties to the Convention. The procedure might be appropriate for states parties, the Court observed, when the government shows an intention to resolve the case through domestic channels within a reasonable time.[85] This shows that to some extent, the Court shares the Commission's loose approach and is willing to give more weight to the general aim of the procedures than to the formal written rules.

A third objection of Honduras was that the Commission had not attempted a friendly settlement. The Commission's decision was based on the regulation developed from Article 48(f) of the Convention, which provided that the Commission should be in a position to facilitate a friendly settlement.[86] Article 45 of the Commission's regulations outlines the procedures for establishing a friendly settlement. In addition, Article 45 permits the Commission not to initiate negotiations if the Commission determines that a case is not amenable to friendly settlement. The government maintained that an attempt at a friendly settlement was obligatory since the rule in the Commission's regulations contradicted the requirements of the Convention

---

80. *Id.* at para. 70.
81. *Id.* at para. 75.
82. *Id.* at paras. 75–76.
83. *Id.* at paras. 77, 80.
84. *Id.* at para. 69.
85. *Id.*
86. American Convention on Human Rights, art. 48(f), *reprinted in* Org. Am. States, *Basic Documents, supra* note 1, at 25–53.

and the latter should prevail. The Court interpreted the phrase in Article 48(f) within the context of the Convention and concluded, "[I]t is clear that the Commission should attempt such friendly settlement only when the circumstances of the controversy make that option suitable or necessary, at the Commission's sole discretion."[87] The Court found no grounds to challenge the Commission's handling of the issue.[88]

It should be noted that the statement of the Court does not imply the approval of the practice that the Commission is developing that certain matters are beforehand not susceptible to a friendly settlement.[89] The Commission should be free to decide on a case-by-case basis whether or not to attempt this procedure, which could provide a means by which the Commission could resolve some individual petitions. In the case of Honduras, for example, where the Commission is handling many cases of disappearances similar to the Velásquez case, a number of court decisions condemning the government might lead it to consider the possibility of settling the rest of the cases, paying compensation to the victims and agreeing to seriously investigate the disappearances still pending.

A fourth objection raised by the government of Honduras was the non-exhaustion of domestic legal remedies. Although this objection was joined to the merits of the case, it should be noted that the manner in which the Commission handled this problem made the decision of the Court more difficult. Since the government had not invoked the non-exhaustion argument at the earliest opportunity, it would have been simple for the Court to conclude that the government had waived the objection. This could not be done, however, because the Commission agreed to reconsider the case after the government alleged that domestic remedies had not been exhausted. The issue was thus preserved and could be raised later.

Furthermore, the Commission could have maintained from the inception of the case that the exhaustion of domestic remedies was not required because there were no effective judicial remedies in the period in which the events occurred. The absence of effective judicial remedies was an element of the violation, and the Commission intended to prove that the government's policies supported disappearances during this period. However, this argument was belatedly used by the Commission, emerging only before the Court.[90]

As can be seen, three of the four objections could have been avoided had the Commission closely followed the procedural rules. However, the Commission seems to have been trying to obtain an overall picture of the

---

87. *Gallardo, supra* note 50, para. 44.
88. *Id.* at para. 46.
89. *See supra* note 28.
90. *Velásquez,* Preliminary obj., *supra* note 70, paras. 82, 90. *See also* American Convention on Human Rights, art. 46(2), *reprinted in* Org. Am. States, *Basic Documents, supra* note 1, at 25–53.

human rights situation in Honduras and attempting to document the existence of a systematic practice of disappearances in that country. In taking the broader view, the procedural details of this particular case were lost.

2. Procedural Issues in the Court's Consideration of the Case

The principal procedural issue in the Court's proceedings was the proper role of the Commission before the Court. Article 57 of the Convention states that "[t]he Commission shall appear in all cases before the Court." This provision is placed in Chapter VII, titled "Inter-American Court of Human Rights," Section 1, under the heading "Organization." This strongly suggests that the Commission is identified more as an organ of the system than as a party before the Court.

The functions of the Commission are specified in: (1) Article 61(1) of the Convention, and Article 51(1), which state that the Commission or a state party may submit a case to the Court; (2) Article 63(2), which states that the Commission may ask the Court to adopt provisional measures in cases of extreme gravity and urgency that have not yet been submitted to the Court; and (3) Article 64(1), which provides that the Commission, in its capacity as an OAS organ and within its sphere of competence, may consult the Court regarding the interpretation of the Convention or other human rights treaties. None of these references suggests that the Commission is meant to play the role of a "party" in cases before the Court. Likewise, many of the provisions in the Rules of Procedure of the Court clearly distinguish the Commission from the parties to the case.[91] It seems evident that neither the Convention nor the Rules of Procedure of the Court put the Commission in the role of a party. Yet, the Court did assign the Commission this role in the Velásquez case.

The Commission may have been given this role due to the manner in which the proceedings are regulated in the Court's Rules of Procedure. The rules set forth that there will be a written part of the procedure consisting of a memorial, which states the complaint, and a counter-memorial, which presents the opposing party's answer. These are followed by a reply and a rejoinder. All four presentations are meant to bring out the issues that divide the parties.[92] This procedure reflects the assumption that there will be two parties to the case, two states, each arguing for its version of the facts and of the law.[93] Since there was only one state involved in the Velásquez case,

---

91. *See* Inter-Am. Ct. H.R. Rules of Procedure, arts. 27(4), 32, 33, 34(1), 38(1)–(2), *reprinted in* Org. Am. States, *Basic Documents, supra* note 1, at 117–35.
92. *Id.* at art. 30.
93. However, this is almost never the case. The alleged victim of the violation is legally nonexistent in the case, since the Convention does not accord it *locus standi* and the rules of the Court do not allow for independent participation of the victim or its repre-

the Court put the Commission in the role of the missing party. The Commission's presentation was considered the memorial, and the Commission was asked to produce evidence to support its opinion that the government of Honduras has violated certain provisions in the Convention.[94] This arrangement would raise considerable problems if two states were before the Court. It is difficult to imagine how two states and the Commission would file memorials, counter-memorials, replies, and rejoinders.

In essence, the Court placed the Commission in the position of representative for the complaining party. The Commission worked closely with the lawyers of Mr. Velásquez' relatives to gather the evidence needed and to see to it that the case was "won." This solution is not only legally mistaken but is also inappropriate for the future status of the Commission vis-à-vis the states it has to supervise. The Commission's task is to search for the truth, and for this it has to enjoy the trust of both the victims and the states. The Commission should not represent the interests of the victim. Not only impartiality in fact but also the appearance of impartiality is essential for the Commission. It must be remembered that the Commission's participation in contentious cases before the Court is only a small part of its activities in the field of human rights. All the Commission's activities may be affected if it loses its status as "organ" of the Convention and of the OAS and becomes a "party" to cases before the court.

A better solution would have been to follow the example of the European Court and use the Rules of Procedure to grant the victim or his representatives the status lacking under the Convention to bring their individual case to the Court.[95] In this sense, the Court should follow the reasoning of Judge Piza in his separate opinions in the matter of Viviana Gallardo[96] and in his dissenting opinion in the Velásquez case.[97] Judge Piza argued that the parties before the court are the state and the party entitled to the remedies provided by the judgment. The relatives of Mr. Velásquez are the beneficiaries of the remedy awarded and should negotiate any agreement reached with Honduras; the Commission should not take this role.[98]

---

sentatives in the case. The only potential party is thus another state interested in the observance of human rights in the state where the alleged violation occurred. Such a situation is highly unlikely to occur. It is most probable that the case will be submitted to the Court by the Commission and that the only legal party present will be the state against which the complaint has been lodged.

94. Inter-Am. Ct. H.R., *Velásquez Rodríguez Case,* Judgment of 28 July 1988, Series C, No. 4, para. 18.

95. *See* Eur. Ct. H.R., Revised Rules of the Court, rules 30, 37, 38, 39 & 40, *reprinted in* Council of Europe, *European Convention on Human Rights, Collected Texts* (1987).

96. *See Gallardo,* Series A, *supra* note 43, Decision of 13 Nov. 1981, at 93–100 (Explanation of Vote by Judge Piza); Decision of 8 Sept. 1983, *supra* note 43, 107–33 (Dissenting Opinion of Judge Piza).

97. *Velásquez, supra* note 94, at 165–71 (Dissenting Opinion of Judge Piza).

98. *Id.*

Another procedural issue in the Court's consideration of the case concerns its request for the presentation of extensive evidence. Since the Commission's investigation ended when it applied Article 42 of its regulations and assumed the facts of the complaint to be true, it appears that the only way the Court could obtain additional information was by reopening the investigation. This delayed the case and added significant expenses. The investigation of a case by the Commission and at the proper time would be more convenient and less expensive and time-consuming.

In spite of these procedural problems, the Velásquez case ended with a decision of the Court declaring that Honduras had violated Articles 1(1), 4, 5, and 7 of the Convention and that fair compensation had to be paid to the relatives of Mr. Velásquez.[99] On 21 July 1989, the Court determined appropriate compensation to be 750.000 lempiras (approximately US $375,000).[100] Prompted by a request of the Commission and of the victim's relatives, the Court also clarified its decision by stating that Honduras was obliged to prevent the practice of disappearances in the future, to investigate the disappearance of Mr. Velásquez, and to punish those found responsible for his disappearance.[101]

IV. RECOMMENDATIONS FOR THE FUTURE

The system for handling individual and state complaints set forth in the Convention has finally begun to operate. Many adjustments remain to be made, but this is understandable and should not be discouraging. The development of efficient human rights protections requires time and, above all, practice.

In particular, procedural mechanisms to deal with individual cases are essential. In the inter-American human rights system, the Court is a welcome and necessary addition. The importance of legally binding decisions against states needs no emphasis. Not only do binding decisions provide authoritative interpretations of the rights in the Convention, but the Court's decisions may have an enormous political importance as well, making it more difficult for governments to persistently disregard human rights. The Velásquez case shows how important it is for the system to receive and rule on individual cases.

The usefulness of these procedures will be increasingly visible as individuals learn about this option. The Commission is already receiving complaints from individuals alleging isolated human rights violations in states

---

99. *Velásquez, supra* note 94, para. 194.
100. Inter-Am. Ct. H.R., *Velásquez Rodríguez Case,* Judgment of 21 July 1989, Series C.
101. *Id.*

462   **HUMAN RIGHTS QUARTERLY**   **Vol. 12**

where the rule of law generally prevails. Individuals are likely to resort to the OAS human rights supervisory organs with far greater frequency. The political situation in many of the countries in the region has changed for the better, and this undoubtedly facilitates the process.[102] Furthermore, to this date eleven states have recognized the contentious jurisdiction of the Court, and this means that there are now real possibilities that the Court will begin to do its share in the supervision of human rights violations.

Moreover, states may consult the Court on a variety of legal matters, thus fostering uniform standards throughout the region. Although advisory opinions are not binding, the authority that usually emanates from a court gives them a significant weight. In the case of the Inter-American Court, this possibility is further enhanced by the broad powers of the Court in this respect. The advisory opinion on the death penalty in Guatemala shows the positive impact an advisory opinion can have on serious human rights violations.

Certain changes would allow the system to operate more effectively. The Commission should follow its procedural rules more carefully. The Commission should prepare its case from a procedural point of view, beginning with a careful assessment of the admissibility requirements. Also, a clear distinction should be made between cases against states parties to the Convention and those against states not parties to the Convention.

The Commission should also review its policy concerning application of Article 42 of its Regulations, which up to now has been interpreted as releasing the Commission from the responsibility for investigating a case in certain circumstances. The Commission should consider the financial implications a complete trial before the Court would have on the complainant. When the complainant has limited resources, the Commission should undertake an in-depth investigation of the case, Article 42 notwithstanding.

The Commission should also maintain some flexibility in its use of friendly settlements. A strict application of Article 45 ruling out friendly settlements would not always serve the interests that the mechanism is designed to protect, namely, those of the state, those of the victim, and the general interests of human rights on the continent.

---

102. Argentina and Uruguay have now elected governments and have ratified the American Convention and recognized the contentious jurisdiction of the Court. Brazil has an elected government as well, and although it has not ratified the Convention, its attitude towards human rights seems to be improving with the recently enacted Constitution in which human rights have a prominent place. As of the elections held on 14 December 1989, when Mr. Patricio Aylwin was chosen as President of Chile and a new Congress was elected, Chile has returned to democratic rule. Even before elections took place, all human rights treaties to which Chile is a party were incorporated into Article 5 of the amended 1980 Constitution. Furthermore, the new government has pledged to ratify the American Convention on Human Rights in the shortest time possible.

The Court generally has shown the flexibility appropriate in a court of law. Perhaps this has been partly inspired by the context in which the cases were brought before the Court and partly by the practice of the Commission, which has demonstrated how far an organization can go when it is seriously determined to carry out its functions as effectively as possible. Specifically, the Court should review the participation of the Commission in its proceedings and abandon the idea that the Commission is a party to cases.

The cases handled by the Court thus far do not indicate whether a great deal of evidence will generally be needed in future cases. A thorough investigation by the Commission will eliminate the need for extensive evidence-gathering at a later stage. Frequent application of Article 42 of the Commission's Regulations is bound to make the Court a sort of second-instance court, to the detriment of the individuals who hope to obtain prompt redress.

All these changes presuppose that the Commission either will give more attention to individual complaints and thus be diverted from its other activities or that its financial resources will be substantially increased to allow it to carry out these functions efficiently. A substantial increase in the resources of the Commission and the Court is not likely, however, due to financial constraints on the OAS and its members. Furthermore, even a substantial increase would not help the Commission put an end to gross, systematic violations of human rights.

A better solution might be to examine the system in light of the general human rights situation on the continent. A division of functions between the Commission and the Court may be useful. The Commission could concentrate on the problem of gross, systematic violations of human rights, work that the Commission has proved it can carry out very well, and the Court could handle individual and state complaints in a judicial fashion.[103] This would reduce the Commission's workload and would dramatically decrease the amount of time and money needed to move complaints concerning isolated violations through the system. It would therefore result in a more efficient and effective mechanism for dealing with these problems. The Commission could develop a procedure to handle gross, systematic violations, including a procedure to allow the Commission to consider individual violations that took place in this context. This procedure should have a first phase in the Commission and a second before the political bodies of the

---

103. The European system seems also to be arriving at this same conclusion. *See Merger of the European Commission and European Court of Human Rights, Second Seminar on International Law and European Law at the University of Neuchatel, 14–15 March 1986,* 8 Hum. Rts. L.J. 1–216 (1987).

OAS.[104] Changes would also be necessary to devise a single-organ procedure to ensure that the Court has a manageable amount of work and also cases that merit review.

The advancement of democracy on the continent hopefully will increase concern for human rights. This concern should be reflected in changes in the inter-American human rights system. Whether these changes preserve the system or radically alter it, they should be directed toward the effective and efficient protection of human rights in the region.

---

104. For a proposal for handling gross, systematic violations, see Medina, *The Battle of Human Rights, supra* note 5, ch. XI.

[16]

THE EXPERIENCE OF THE INTER-AMERICAN HUMAN RIGHTS SYSTEM

*Felipe González**

This article is one of four which provide a useful comparative paradigm to any discussion of a Pacific human rights charter or regional mechanism. The article describes the Inter-American system of human rights protection, which stretches across the Americas. After an historical introduction, the article analyses the advances that took place after 1990. The discussion focuses mainly on the roles of the Inter-American Commission on Human Rights and the Inter-American Court of Human Rights. The article concludes that the system is able to influence state behaviour and has made significant contributions to the protection of human rights in the region.

I   INTRODUCTION

This article reviews the main features of the evolution of the Inter-American System of Human Rights ("the System"), which belongs to the Organization of American States (OAS). All independent countries of the Americas are members of the OAS, although Cuba has been suspended from it since 1962.

The article begins by presenting the main aspects of the evolution of the Inter-American System of Human Rights until 1990, as a means to have some basis for a comparison with later developments. This is followed by an analysis of the advances that took place after 1990, and of the obstacles that have prevented further changes. For these purposes, the article focuses primarily on the role of the two human rights bodies of the System, namely the Inter-American Commission on Human Rights ("the Commission" or IACHR) and the Inter-American Court of Human Rights ("the Court"), but it also makes references to some initiatives of the political organs of the OAS and the non-governmental organisations (NGOs). The study does not include a comprehensive analysis of the jurisprudence of the System, focusing instead on some landmark cases that have produced an impact on the OAS policies or on the institutional development of OAS organs. Through these

* Felipe González is a Commissioner at the Inter-American Human Rights Commission. He is also a Professor of International Law and Constitutional Law at Diego Portales University, Santiago de Chile. Currently he is a Visiting Professor at the University Carlos III of Madrid. The views expressed in this article are the author's own.

means, I will discuss whether significant transformations have taken place at the OAS regarding human rights since civilian government became the rule at this organisation.

II THE EVOLUTION OF THE INTER-AMERICAN HUMAN RIGHTS SYSTEM UNTIL THE ARRIVAL OF CIVILIAN GOVERNMENTS

Along with the creation of the OAS, the state parties to this organisation adopted in October 1948 a human rights instrument: the American Declaration of the Rights and Duties of Man ("the American Declaration").[1] This was almost simultaneous with the adoption of the Universal Declaration of Human Rights[2] by the United Nations.

From then on, however, the UN and the OAS followed different routes in the human rights field. While the UN, albeit slowly, started to establish organs and mechanisms to protect these rights, the OAS took no further action in this respect for more than a decade. At the moment of the adoption of the American Declaration, the states party to the OAS ("the states") had also approved a resolution recognising the need for a judicial organ in charge of the protection of human rights in the Americas, and requested the Inter-American Juridical Committee to prepare a draft statute for an Inter-American Court.

This Committee, nevertheless, considered it premature to work on such a statute, pointing out that this should be preceded by the adoption by the OAS of a general human rights treaty. This would only be achieved in the late 1960s. While it is true that during the 1950s two treaties concerning the political rights of women were subscribed to, the absence of organs and mechanisms of protection made it, strictly speaking, inappropriate to refer to an "Inter-American Human Rights System" at that stage.

In addition, during these first years, the Inter-American Commission of Women became an OAS body. It was not, however, an organ specifically conceived for rights protection, but rather for the study and preparation of international instruments, such as those referred to above as well as for some promotional initiatives.[3]

It was only in 1959, primarily as a reaction to the Cuban Revolution and to the dictatorship of Rafael Trujillo in the Dominican Republic, that the OAS created the Inter-American Commission on Human Rights. The Commission started work in 1960. According to the Statute of the Commission ("the Statute"), which was approved by the OAS, this human rights body obtained a mandate to protect and promote human rights in the states, through the preparation of studies and reports that it

---

1   American Declaration of the Rights and Duties of Man (2 May 1948) OAS Res XXX OAS Doc. OEA/Ser. L/V/I. 4 Rev.XX.

2   Universal Declaration on Human Rights (10 December 1948) UN Doc GA/Res/217A (III).

3   The Inter-American Commission of Women continues to date to be an OAS organ. It was originally established in 1928 by the Sixth American International Conference.

may deem necessary, recommendations to the states on this matter, human rights education, and other means. According to the Statute, the American Declaration would serve as the parameter to evaluate the behaviour of the states. Additionally, the Statute authorised the Commission to make *in loco* visits (that is, visits in terrain) to the countries of the Americas, provided that the state concerned gave its permission for this purpose. Over the years, this power would become crucial for the visibility of the Commission throughout the American continent, as the population of the countries most affected by grave violations would become aware of the Commission's existence and roles, enhancing, in the end, the impact of the work being done by this body.

From the very beginning, a key element for the development of the Commission was the fact that its members were elected in their individual capacities, and not as state representatives. This characteristic has proved to be a significant factor for the work of the Commission, especially considering the adverse political environment in the Americas that existed for a long time.

For almost 20 years, the IACHR was the sole body in charge of the protection of human rights within the OAS. During that period, it had to confront many dictatorships in the Americas. Under these circumstances, and considering the fact that these regimes committed massive, systematic violations of rights, the Commission used as its principal tool the preparation and publication of country reports. These reports provided a whole description of the human rights conditions in a specific country, with a special focus on attacks on the right to life, the extended practice of torture, and arbitrary detention and imprisonment. During its first years of work, the Commission issued reports on Cuba, the Dominican Republic, Guatemala and Haiti.

In the mid-1960s, the Commission started to open and decide specific cases of human rights abuses. Initially, the IACHR did not have an explicit mandate for this purpose, and when it received complaints it usually integrated the information gathered into a country report (provided that a report on the country denounced was in preparation, which was not always the case). Then, the Commission obtained the power to open cases through a reform of its Statute.

Nevertheless, during the years between 1960 and 1990, the publication of country reports remained the main mechanism used by the Inter-American Commission. This happened for two basic reasons. First, many of the states against which specific cases were opened did not participate at all in the litigation; they did not respond to the complaint, nor did they present any sort of evidence to deny the charges. Many of the states at most would respond in a merely ritual, formalistic manner. Given this context, the Commission adopted a provision in its Rules of Procedure, according to which the allegations presented by the complainants would be considered to reflect reality so long as they had not been disputed by the state or rebutted by other sources. During the period in analysis, the IACHR decided a high percentage of the cases based on this assumption of responsibility.[4]

A second reason for the Commission to keep the publication of country reports as its main focus was the fact that in many states the violations committed were of a systematic nature and practised on a massive scale. When hundreds and even thousands of violations had to be confronted by the Commission within a short period of time, the decision of individual cases would barely address the situation in an effective way. A decision on a few paradigmatic cases may have been important, but most of the cases had to be addressed through the country report method.

From the very beginning, the Commission made an extensive use of *in loco* visits to prepare its country reports. This contributed to raising the public profile of the Commission, as it called the attention of the press during the visits, giving also visibility and legitimacy to the victims and their relatives. Not only did the Commission gather in these visits further information about denunciations already lodged, but it also received many additional ones from victims who had been afraid to do so before or had not been able to send their complaints to the Commission (at a time when international communications were much more expensive and difficult than today). Even in situations when a state banned a visit by the IACHR, this would call public attention and would expose the state at an international level.

The original OAS goal of enacting a general treaty on human rights was finally achieved in 1969, with the adoption of the American Convention on Human Rights ("the Convention").[5] In this way, the OAS followed the same path as the UN, which three years before (and also after two decades of promises) had passed the International Covenant on Civil and Political Rights (ICCPR)[6] and the International Covenant on Economic, Social and Cultural Rights (ICESR).[7]

Looking back after almost 40 years since the adoption of the Convention, it seems surprising that such an instrument was enacted by the OAS at a time when many states were living under authoritarian rule. This is especially surprising if one considers that today, in a context of civilian governments, not a few feel uncomfortable under the parameters of this Convention. So one keeps asking, how did the states decide to adopt the Convention in 1969?

In this respect, two tentative answers could be provided. The first is that a significant number of states may not have had the intention to ratify the Convention, and their consent to adopt it was only

---

4   This provision has remained throughout the different Rules of Procedure enacted by the Commission over the years. It is currently established by the Rules of Procedure of the Inter-American Commission of Human Rights, Art 39 that entered into force in 2001.

5   American Convention on Human Rights (22 November 1969) 1144 UNTS 123 [the Convention].

6   International Covenant on Civil and Political Rights (16 December 1966) 999 UNTS 171 [ICCPR].

7   International Covenant on Economic, Social and Cultural Rights (16 December 1966) 993 UNTS 3.

a rhetorical gesture. In fact, it took nine more years for the Convention to enter into force, and this occurred as a result of the decision of civilian governments that replaced the dictatorships in some countries.

A second answer is that many states conceived the Convention's provisions in the same way that they have historically understood the Bills of Rights contained in their constitutions since they gained independence in the 19th century: as non-operative clauses. If tribunals at the domestic level had failed to enforce these rights, why should states care about a potential enforcement by distant, international bodies? For other groups of states, perhaps the Convention was envisioned more as a direction to follow in the long run rather than as an instrument establishing legally binding rules. This may also explain why, according to the Convention, the newly established Court would require an additional declaration on the part of a state to have contentious jurisdiction for cases concerning that country.

While the Convention regulates in detail the guarantees concerning civil and political rights, it does not do the same regarding economic, social and cultural rights. As for the first type of rights, the Convention gives more protection than the ICCPR. This conclusion can be reached by comparing the provisions of both treaties concerning due process of law, judicial guarantees, freedom of expression and other rights. This is barely a surprise, because the broad spectrum of regimes within the UN states led to a series of agreements that were not always very protective for human rights. However, it is surprising that the Convention also provides more protection for some rights than the European Convention on Human Rights,[8] for instance freedom of expression.[9]

The Convention has only minor reference to economic, social and cultural rights. They are mentioned in just two provisions[10] and for several decades these were interpreted as preventing the presentation of individual claims. Even at the level of country reports, the issue of economic, social and cultural rights began to be addressed from the late 1970s. An additional Protocol on these rights was later adopted (see below).

The adoption of the Convention in 1969 and its entering into force in 1978 strengthened the System, since then there would be two bodies in charge of supervising states' behaviour on these

---

8   European Convention for the Protection of Human Rights and Fundamental Freedoms (4 November 1950) 213 UNTS 221 [ECHR].

9   It cannot be overlooked that the European Convention was adopted in 1950, that is, 19 years before its American counterpart. Therefore, the progressive development of international human rights law partially explains this situation. It is only a partial explanation, because it is indisputable that democracy and enforcement of rights prevailed in 1950 in the countries that adopted the ECHR to a much larger extent than in the countries which adopted the Convention in 1969. Therefore, the states of the Americas set for themselves higher goals, despite the fact they were more distant from enforcing those standards than the Western European states had been in 1950.

10   The Convention, above n 5, Arts 26 and 42.

matters: the Commission and the Court. As provided in the Convention, their mandate would not be restricted to deal with gross, systematic violations committed by dictatorships, but it would encompass the states' behaviour regarding a wide range of rights, in order to enhance rule of law throughout the Americas and to ensure that democratic systems with independent judiciaries would effectively enforce human rights. It is important to emphasise this point, because in the 1990s a number of civilian governments, feeling uncomfortable with the Commission's supervision, would argue that this organ's function was to deal with the abuses committed by dictatorial regimes.

Despite these advances in the legal framework of the System, an overwhelming part of the Commission's work until the late 1980s was still devoted to confronting systematic violations. The scale of the abuses (as shown by the practice of forced disappearances in Guatemala since the 1960s until the 1990s, in Argentina and Chile in the 1970s and in Peru in the 1980s and early 1990s), unprecedented in Latin America in the 20th century, required such a dedication on the part of the IACHR.

Given this context, the Commission continued to make permanent use of country reports, which remained its main task throughout the 1980s. A paradigm case in this regard was the IACHR's visit to Argentina in 1979 and the subsequent report published in 1980. This report and the facts that surrounded its preparation not only produced a significant impact in the OAS, but also at the UN, representing a key factor to end the thousands of forced disappearances that had taken place in that country over the previous years.

The Commission spent 17 days in Argentina, a fact that was by itself significant, as this was much longer than its usual *in loco* visits. During the visit, the IACHR obtained information that several dozens of people were being held in clandestine detention in an isolated area of an otherwise public prison. It also obtained the names of some of those detained. When the Commission went to the prison, it asked the authorities for a list of the people jailed there, which was then provided. The clandestine detainees were not on the list. Without making the prison authorities aware of the information it had already obtained about these prisoners, the Commission then asked to look at all the prison's areas. The authorities were at first reluctant, but they finally had to concede, in the hope that they would still manage to prevent the Commission from having contact with the clandestine prisoners. At some time the members of the IACHR heard people screaming from behind a wall "we are here, we are here!" ("¡Estamos aquí, estamos aquí!"). Confronted by this evidence, it became inevitable for the prison's authorities to allow the Commission to meet with about 30 clandestine prisoners, who would have otherwise swelled the list of the disappeared.[11]

---

11   For a detailed description of the discovery of these prisoners, see Buergenthal, Norris and Shelton "Discovering Disappeared Persons: A Staff Member Notes" in *Protecting Human Rights in the Americas* (International Institute of Human Rights, Strasbourg, 1990) 299-301.

Until this visit, the dictatorship in Argentina had systematically denied that it was practising the clandestine detention of persons as well as its responsibility in the massive forced disappearances that had taken place. When the Commission informed the OAS General Assembly about its findings, this produced a tremendous debate, to the point that the delegation from Argentina threatened to withdraw from the OAS if the General Assembly issued a resolution condemning it for this situation. Finally, the Assembly adopted a general resolution[12] condemning the practice of this crime but without mentioning Argentina, but the Argentinean Government had already been exposed internationally as a result of the Commission's findings. This visit produced a similar impact at the UN, which had not previously confronted Argentina on this matter, leading to the creation of a Working Group on Forced Disappearances, whose main initial task was to investigate the situation in this country. Overall, the Commission's visit and the subsequent report saved many lives, including those of the clandestine prisoners and many other potential victims, as this crime ceased almost immediately.[13]

Another country report which had a significant impact was that published on Nicaragua in the late 1970s, during the Somoza dictatorship. Anastasio Somoza himself pointed out in a book written in his exile after leaving power that this report was a trigger factor for his defeat.[14]

Notwithstanding this principal focus on the country reports, the Commission continued working on specific cases. Due to the nature of the violations denounced through this mechanism, the Commission designed some methodologies of work that fitted well to them. However, while these methodologies proved to be instrumental in such context, later they would make it more complex for the Commission to adapt to new circumstances, when civilian governments became the rule in the OAS. For instance, well beyond the entering into force of the Convention, the IACHR still made wide use of the assumption of responsibility in cases where the state did not litigate in a serious manner.

Another example is the friendly settlement of cases. This is a mechanism established by the Convention, by which a case can be closed by an agreement between complainants and the state. The agreement could consist of pecuniary compensation, public recognition of the abuses and other

---

12 Presentation at the OAS General Assembly by Carlos Washington Pastor, Minister of Foreign Affairs of Argentina, cited at *Convicción* (21 November 1980) 12-13.

13 Forced disappearances in Argentina stopped abruptly in October 1979, that is, one month after the Commission's visit. From then on, the IACHR did not receive further complaints about disappearances in this country. About the visit's impact, see David Weissbrodt and Maria Luisa Bartolomei "The Effectiveness of International Human Rights Pressures: The Case of Argentina, 1976-1983" (1991) 75 Minn L Rev 1009; Iain Guest *Behind the Disappearances: Argentina's Dirty War against Human Rights and the United Nations* (University of Pennsylvania Press, Philadelphia, 1990); Tom Farer (President of the Commission at the time of the visit) "The OAS at the Crossroads: Human Rights" (1987) 72 Iowa L Rev 401.

14 Anastasio Somoza (as told to Jack Cox) *Nicaragua Betrayed* (Western Islands, 1980) cited by Farer, above n 13, 402.

forms of symbolic reparation, as well as the creation of internal mechanisms to conduct a full investigation or to prevent similar situations and trigger legislative reform.[15] Because many states did not actually engage in the litigation of individual cases at the Commission, this organ often had no way to seek a friendly settlement. Even in those cases in which a state did litigate, given the context of massive, systematic violations, it was often inconclusive for the Commission to seek such a settlement, as the violation was part of a general, deliberate trend, and a state willingness to reach a settlement may not have been more than a token gesture.

The Court ratified the policy of the IACHR not to seek friendly settlement in the 1980s case of *Velásquez Rodríguez*,[16] when Honduras argued that the Commission had violated the Convention by not seeking a friendly settlement between the parties. In interpreting the Convention, the Court stated that it was not mandatory for the IACHR to seek such settlement in all cases, allowing it some discretion (but not arbitrariness).[17] The problem was that the Commission was slow to react to the new circumstances, and it did not resort to the option of seeking a friendly settlement almost at all for a number of years, regardless of whether the abuse denounced was part of a systematic policy of a state.[18]

Other practices by the Commission during this period included development in its discretion, such as regarding the time to formally open a case after a claim was lodged, and, generally speaking, about the timing of the litigation;[19] its lack of standard procedures to determine whether to call for public audiences during litigation; and the usual practice of postponing the decision on admissibility until a final decision on the case was made. These practices had been developed at a time when most states did not play an active role in litigation and many complainants had no way to effectively follow up their claims. The problem was that the IACHR continued with these practices well into the 1980s regarding states that did engage in litigation, and even into the 1990s when the context was very different.

---

15 Patricia Standaert "The Friendly Settlement of Human Rights Abuses in the Americas" (1999) 9 Duke Journal of Comparative and International Law 519, 519 -542.

16 *Velasquez Rodriguez Case* Inter-American Court of Human Rights, Preliminary Objectives (26 June 1987).

17 Ibid, 19-20. See Standaert, above n 15.

18 Among the few exceptions was the *Miskitos* case against Nicaragua: the Commission did try to reach a friendly settlement in this case from the early 1980s, but it did not succeed in the end. See Hurst Hannum "The Protection of Indigenous Rights in the Inter-American System" in David Harris and Stephen Livingstone (eds) *The Inter-American System of Human Rights* (Oxford University Press, New York, 1998) 323, 329.

19 See Ariel Dulitzky "La Duración del Procedimiento: Responsabilidades Compartidas" in Juan Méndez and Francisco Cox (eds) *El Futuro del Sistema Interamericano de Protección de los Derechos Humanos* (Inter-American Institute of Human Rights, San José, Costa Rica, 1998) 363.

Another aspect that shows the difficulty for the Commission to adapt to the emerging new circumstances in the 1980s was the relationship with the Court. In fact, it took seven years for the IACHR to send the first cases to the Court.[20] The Commission's initiative in this matter was, and still is, decisive, as states (who are also allowed by the Convention to present cases before the Court) are reluctant to do so.[21]

These first cases also showed some inconsistencies within the System's procedural framework that have not yet been completely solved. Honduras, the state denounced before the Court, had hardly participated in the litigation of the cases before the Commission, so most of the arguments presented to the Court to rebut the evidence had not been previously raised during the procedure at the Commission. Because the Convention provides only a few general rules about evidence, the Court had to construe some rules. The Court rejected the Commission's petition to accept the evidence already accepted at the Commission's procedure when it had not been controverted by the state at that stage. The problem was that the Court started developing its jurisprudence on this key matter (with an impact that continues today) in a somehow abnormal situation from the point of view of the Convention (a state that did not engage in the procedure at the Commission). One can wonder whether the Court would have reached a different conclusion had the context of these first cases been different, with active state participation.

Further obstacles for a normal development of the System arose in this first group of contentious cases before the Court, due to the fact that Honduras lacked at that time a judicial system effective in dealing with grave human rights violations, especially when they had been committed in the context of a deliberate systematic state policy. Although by the time the cases against Honduras were at the Court a policy of disappearances no longer existed in that country, an environment of impunity for grave crimes still persisted, and open hostility occurred against the witnesses who took

---

20   They were the *Velasquez Rodriguez*, *Fairen Garbi* and *Solis Corrales* and *Godinez Cruz* cases, all presented by the Commission against Honduras denouncing the forced disappearances of these persons. For an analysis of these cases, see Juan Méndez and José Miguel Vivanco "Disappearances and the Inter-American Court: Reflections on a Litigation Experience" (1990) 13 Hamline L Rev 507; see also Claudio Grossman "Disappearances in Honduras: the Need for Direct Victim Representation in Human Rights Litigation" (1992) 15 Hastings Int'l & Comp L Rev 363.

21   The single exception has been Costa Rica, which lodged a case in 1981; however, the Court declined jurisdiction due to the lack of a prior decision by the Commission on the merits of the case (according to the Convention, a case has to go through the Commission's individual system procedure before being presented to the Court). *In the Matter of Viviana Gallardo and Others* Inter-American Court of Human Rights (15 July 1981) G101/81. The second case arrived at the System 25 years later, when, in 2006, Nicaragua lodged a complaint against Costa Rica at the Commission. This body, however, declared the case inadmissible in 2007, thus it never reached the Court. The inadmissibility was due to lack of prima facie grounds for a violation, as the Commission considered that the complaint described in very generic terms the alleged discrimination of Nicaraguan nationals living in Costa Rica by this state. See *Nicaragua v Costa Rica* Inter-American Commission on Human Rights Report (8 March 2007) Nº11/07, Interstate Case 01/06.

the stand to testify against the state. This would lead to the assassination of two of the witnesses: Miguel Angel Pavón and José Isaías Vilorio.[22]

On the positive side, it is interesting to observe how the Court made use of its advisory function to contribute to stopping grave violations in the 1980s.[23] In principle, the Court's function is conceived of as a means to interpret law, but as the tribunal issued some Advisory Opinions at very crucial moments, their impact was in effect much more immediate and wide. For instance, in the early 1980s Guatemala was executing a significant number of people for crimes which had lighter penalties at the time that the country ratified the Convention. The Convention, in the same manner as the ICCPR, somehow "freezes" the application of the death penalty, by providing that a state cannot extend its application to crimes with lighter penalties at the time of the ratification. In an Advisory Opinion, the Inter-American Court declared that a reservation to the treaty such as the one that Guatemala was invoking did not allow the extension of the death penalty.[24] As a result, the state stopped the executions and modified its legislation.[25] In the same years, something analogous occurred regarding Nicaragua, after the Court interpreted the Convention in an Advisory Opinion as banning the suspension of habeas corpus in states of emergency.[26] It has to be noted that none of these Opinions were explicitly directed to any country (they cannot, according to the Convention), but even so Guatemala and Nicaragua modified legislation and practices.

During the 1980s the Court also worked on several other issues in the context of its advisory role, including the mandatory affiliation of journalists and its impact on freedom of expression, the naturalisation of persons, and the use of treaties from other human rights systems by Inter-American organs. By the end of the 1980s, an additional Protocol to the Convention was adopted.[27] This Protocol refers to economic, social and cultural rights. It contains a long list of such rights, although it established that only a few of them could be the basis for lodging complaints before the Commission. This Protocol entered into force in 1999.

It must be noted that at the time the OAS political organs were comprised both by civilian governments and dictatorships, strong debates on human rights issues usually took place, especially

---

22   See Méndez and Vivanco, above n 20, 557-558.

23   The Court has two basic functions: to decide on contentious cases, and to issue Advisory Opinions.

24   Inter-American Court of Human Rights, Restrictions to the Death Penalty (American Convention on Human Rights, Arts 4(2) and 4(4)) Advisory Opinion 3 (8 September 1983).

25   See Charles Moyer and David Padilla "Executions in Guatemala as Decreed by the Courts of Special Jurisdiction in 1982-1983: A Case Study" (1984) 6 Hum Rts Q 507.

26   Inter-American Court of Human Rights, Habeas Corpus in Emergency Situations Advisory Opinion 8 (30 January 1987).

27   Additional Protocol to the American Convention on Human Rights in the area of Economic, Social and Cultural Rights (17 November 1988) OEA/Ser.L.V/II.82 doc 6 rev 1, 67.

on occasion of the Commission's country reports. Not only the reports themselves were discussed at the General Assembly, but also the actual human rights conditions in the countries reported. It was also a practice for the General Assembly to issue a specific resolution about a country reported.

In fact, there was a sort of dichotomy between the military and the civilian regimes represented at the OAS during this period and this had consequences on the level of attention given to these two types of states. This was because, compared with the systematic violations to the right to life and other basic rights committed by many of the military regimes, abuses by civilian governments did not seem so significant; the latter were not actually under close scrutiny.

A turning point seems to have been a report on several consolidated cases published by the IACHR in 1990.[28] The report stated that the electoral system of Mexico was in contravention of the Convention. This produced a tremendous reaction from that country against the Commission. Since the Commission's inception, Mexico had been on the side of the civilian governments, supporting the IACHR, and denouncing the violations of human rights by a number of dictatorships.[29] However, as of 1990, the context had changed and this affected Mexico. Almost all dictatorships had ended (Paraguay in 1989, Chile in early 1990); the civil war in Nicaragua had come to a conclusion and with it the end of the Sandinista Regime; the armed conflicts in El Salvador and Guatemala seemed to be about to end; and only in Colombia and Peru did the situation look worse than in the past. The Berlin Wall had fallen the previous year and had contributed to diminishing some of the tensions and polarisations in Latin America. Also as a result of the end of the Cold War, Canada decided to join the OAS.[30] For the first time, all the OAS active members were states governed by civilian governments.[31] A country like Mexico, which had not been closely supervised in the past, became a subject for analysis. The same would start to happen to other countries. This would have a significant impact in the relationship between the OAS political organs and human rights organs from then on.[32]

---

28   *IACHR Annual Report 1989-1990* Report on Cases N°s 9768, 9780 and 9828 (Mexico) 101.

29   Farer, above n 13, 405, notes that, along with Venezuela, Mexico was the state that gave the strongest support to the Commission in the late 1970s and early 1980s.

30   See Andrew Cooper and Thomas Legler *Intervention Without Intervening? The OAS Defense and Promotion of Democracy in the Americas* (Palgrave McMillan, New York, 2006) 9 and 36-37.

31   I am not considering Cuba here, as it is not an active OAS member, since it was suspended from the organisation in 1962.

32   For a comprehensive study about the System until the late 1980s, see Cecilia Medina *The Battle of Human Rights: Gross, Systematic Violations and the Inter-American System* (Martinus Nijholf, Dordrecht, 1988).

III   TRANSITIONS TO DEMOCRACY AND THE EVOLUTION OF THE SYSTEM

A   Background

In the early 1990s, new circumstances at the OAS changed the expectations of NGOs that did litigation or other work at the System. To some extent, there was optimism about a potential strengthening of the System, based on the overwhelming presence of civilian governments. A more diverse docket of cases at the Commission and Court was expected, and an increasing number of cases were thought to be handled by the latter. It was envisioned that the use of friendly settlements would become more frequent, and that the same would happen regarding cautionary and provisional measures.

An enhancement of participation of civil society at the System and, more generally, at the OAS was expected; in particular, there was hope that victims would soon achieve full autonomy through the Court's contentious proceedings, and that a kind of consultative status at the OAS could be granted for NGOs. There were different levels of optimism about a potential strengthening of the judiciaries throughout the continent and about an increased reception of international human rights standards in domestic legislation.

Generally speaking, it was envisioned that states would have a more active role in litigation at the System, and that the enforcement of the System's decisions would be enhanced.[33]   In conclusion, at the beginning of the 1990s there were some prospects for change. Below, I will analyse whether substantial changes have actually taken place.

B   Developments at the Inter-American Human Rights Commission

The transitions to democracy in the Americas brought about a series of changes in the work of the Commission. As a result of them and of the decline of systematic violations to the right to life in many countries of the region, the functioning of this organ has experienced significant changes. In fact, over the last 15 years or so, the handling of cases has become the main task of the Commission, with country reports losing the centrality they used to have, notwithstanding the fact that they maintain their importance for a number of states where serious conditions persist. Furthermore, the Commission established in the 1990s thematic rapporteurships as a new function.

---

33   Several of these ideas were presented, for instance, at a roundtable about the System at the Latin American Studies Association Conference (Los Angeles, 1992). Participants included representatives from NGOs active in the System, such as the Centro para la Acción Legal en Derechos Humanos, the Center for Justice and International Law, the Colombian Section of the Andean Commission of Jurists (currently the Colombian Commission of Jurists), Human Rights Watch, and the International Human Rights Law Group (currently Global Rights).

1   Case system

During the period in which authoritarian regimes prevailed in the Americas, states rarely participated in litigation at the Commission, or did so to a limited extent. In addition, as most of the violations confronted at that time by the Commission were massive and systematic, the mechanism of cases usually was not effective.

However, with the transition to democracy the context changed, as did the role of the majority of states in litigation, which became active, and the nature of the violations, which became more feasible for confrontation through the case system. These changes, in turn, had the effect of producing a series of procedural transformations at the Commission. Because the Convention provides only generic rules of procedure, the Commission had to develop a series of reforms.

As a general trend, in the new context the litigation at the Commission has become more formal, as opposed to the loose rules and practices that used to govern it. This more formal approach does not mean that the proceedings are now as formal as those at a court, as it continues to be semi-judicial. Over time, this has been reflected, for instance, in the establishment of a series of terms for the proceedings, set by the Rules of Procedure of the Commission, which have been amended to an important extent during the last two decades. However, so far this has not fast-tracked proceedings, as the complexity of the Commission's caseload has increased.

One important step toward a more formal approach has been the distinction of two stages during the proceedings: a stage of admissibility and another on the merits. Although the Convention makes reference to admissibility and merits, it does not explicitly provide that they have to be treated separately. The practice of the Commission until the mid-1990s consisted of issuing a single decision covering both aspects. However, from 1996 the opposite became the rule, as today the Commission issues first a decision on admissibility and then another on the merits. This is also set out in the new Rules of Procedure.[34] The Commission left open the possibility of deciding both aspects in a single resolution, especially but not limited to cases of forced disappearances and others of an urgent nature.

The adoption of this two-stage approach has not been immune from criticism. Some critics argue that, while contributing to the formality of the proceedings, the distinction between admissibility and merits has a flaw, consisting of the delay of justice. The proceedings have become adversarial, with states taking part in litigation in virtually all cases and victims represented by NGOs or attorneys. This has an effect on the evidence presented before the Commission: the amount and complexity of the proof submitted has increased exponentially.

The new context has also facilitated in making friendly settlements operative. Although established by the Convention, this mechanism was virtually impossible to apply when states

---

34   Rules of Procedure of the Inter-American Commission on Human Rights, Arts 30-37.

violated human rights as a deliberate policy on a grand scale and did not engage actively in the litigation. With these features changing, the chance for friendly settlement has increased. In any event, the will to reach these agreements presents wide variations depending on the states involved and even the changes of government in a state.

In the new context, the Commission has increased in a significant manner the number of cases that it submits to the Court. While the 1990s saw a development in this regard, real change occurred as a result of the new Rules of Procedure, which entered into force in 2001, which provide that when a state does not comply with a decision on the merits, as a general rule, the Commission will send the case to the Court.[35] The Rules of Procedure also establish a list of aspects to be considered in reaching a decision to submit a case, namely, the position of the petitioners, the nature and seriousness of the violation, the need to develop or clarify the jurisprudence of the System, the potential impact at the domestic level, and the evidence available at the case.[36]

The effectiveness of the decisions by the Commission has been strengthened since transitions to democracy began in the Americas. However, this does not mean that a high rate of compliance has been achieved. This rate varies significantly from one state to another. The fact that the Commission is now sending cases on a regular basis to the Court has contributed to an increase of the rate of compliance of its own resolutions to some extent, as states try to avoid being subject to a complaint at the tribunal. This is applicable only to those states which have recognised the Court's jurisdiction (approximately two-thirds), and even they fail to follow the Commission's decisions quite frequently.

For the benefit of the Commission, it has to be noted that its decisions become at times enforced through indirect mechanisms, especially when domestic courts apply the Commission's jurisprudence, a process that began in the 1990s and has been growing since then.

2   Country reports

While not as important as in the past, the preparation, publication and follow-up of country reports continues to be a key tool for the Commission. This is because despite the process of democratisation in the region, some authoritarian regimes persist, the rule of law is weak in a number of states, and widespread human rights violations continue to occur.

The Commission prepares and publishes country reports in two ways. The first, through a report dealing exclusively with one country, may be very extensive (ranging from 150 to 300 pages) and is usually preceded by a visit to the respective state, unless that state does not authorise the IACHR to enter, in which case the Commission will prepare a report anyway if it decides to do so. The second consists of a brief report, usually around 20 to 30 pages, that is included in the Commission's

---

35   Ibid, Art 44.

36   Ibid.

Annual Report. Generally, these shorter reports serve to follow up on reports devoted exclusively to a single country. They may or may not be preceded by a visit of the Commission or some of its members.

In the 1990s, the Commission's function of producing country reports was challenged by a number of governments, which asserted that that was a tool appropriate for the Commission to deal with dictatorships but not with democratic regimes.[37] The IAHCR, though, maintained that this function was important, regardless of the kind of political regime of the states member to the OAS, considering that the key issue was the nature and extent of the abuses. Additionally, the Commission made explicit for the first time the criteria according to which it would decide what states would be subject to reports, which are:[38]

a)   States ruled by governments that have not come to power through free, genuine and periodic popular elections by secret ballot, according to internationally accepted norms;

b)   States where the free exercise of the rights enshrined in the Convention or the American Declaration have been in effect suspended, totally or partially, by the imposition of exceptional measures such as a state of emergency, state of siege, prompt security measures and others;

c)   When there is reliable evidence that a state commits gross and massive abuses of human rights as guaranteed in the Convention, American Declaration or other applicable human rights instruments. Violations of rights that may not be suspended, such as extra-judicial executions, torture and forced disappearances, are of special concern in these cases;

d)   States that are in a process of transition from any of the three above-mentioned situations;

e)   When there are interim or structural situations that grossly and seriously affect human rights, including grave situations of violence, serious institutional crises, institutional reform processes with a serious negative impact on human rights, or grave omissions in the adoption of measures necessary to make human rights effective.

Furthermore, the Commission adopted a practice of sending a copy of the complete draft report to the state that is the subject of that report. In this way, the state may make the observations it considers relevant. The Commission later prepares a final version, dealing with the observations of the state according to its judgment.

---

37   Felipe González "La OEA y los derechos humanos después del advenimiento de los gobiernos civiles: expectativas (in)satisfechas" in Felipe González (ed) *Derechos Humanos e Interés Público* (Universidad Diego Portales, Santiago, 2001) 147.

38   The first four of these criteria were first issued by the Commission in its 1997 Annual Report. The fifth was added in its 1998 Annual Report.

The substantial component of the country reports has continued the process of widening the scope of interest, addressing different types of rights, including civil, political, economic, social and cultural rights, and emphasising the monitoring of the situations of persons and groups that may be vulnerable, such as women, indigenous peoples, afrodescendants, migrants, those living with disabilities and children.

The preparation of country reports by the Commission continues to make sense in certain situations. As such, this role has been reaffirmed by the IACHR. The reports fulfil needs that are not satisfied by the processing of individual cases alone, particularly when it is necessary to examine the general human rights situation in a country, to verify progress or setbacks, to monitor certain rights, or to make suggestions to state authorities (who on occasion request these reports themselves).

It has to be observed that the country reports of the Commission and those prepared by UN bodies are complementary, and it is generally suitable for civil society to attempt both routes. Unlike the case system, where duplication is not allowed (for the benefit of a consolidated jurisprudence), no such incompatibility exists between reports from different inter-governmental human rights organs concerning the same country; quite the contrary, they reinforce each other.

3 Thematic rapporteurships

Since the 1990s the Commission has also developed thematic rapporteurships. Currently there are seven such mechanisms, which refer to freedom of expression, women's rights, children's rights, indigenous rights, the rights of persons deprived of liberty, the rights of migrant workers and their families, and the rights of afrodescendants.

These rapporteurships, however, cannot be compared to those of human rights organs at the UN, which are stronger. This is because with the exception of that of freedom of expression, the rapporteurships at the Commission are part-time only, each one led by a Commissioner, who serve on a part-time basis at the Commission and have many roles to play. The Special Rapporteurship on Freedom of Expression is different because it has a full-time professional in charge and its own staff (this rapporteurship, however, relies entirely on funds external to the OAS).

So far, the usual tasks of the rapporteurships at the Commission have consisted in issuing some thematic reports from time to time (usually every several years), doing some promotional work, and conducting some follow-up on the most relevant cases on the respective matter pending. At the Commission, thematic rapporteurships currently have a limited impact. This is the result of deliberate priorities on the part the Commission, which keeps the investigation and decision of cases and the preparation of country reports as the mechanisms of special concern. It does not seem likely that thematic rapporteurships will be significantly enhanced in the absence of specific, additional funding for them.

4 The Commission's other functions

In addition to the previously described functions, the IACHR undertakes initiatives of promotion of human rights, as well as other tasks.

(a)   Promotion of human rights

This work, which the IACHR engages in through seminars, publications, internships and other means, has basically been developed in three broad areas: the dissemination of human rights in general, the promotion of the System, and education on the necessity of incorporating human rights into domestic law.

The first of the aforementioned areas refers to the work carried out by the Commission regarding the need for citizens of the Americas to become aware of their own rights. This is an effort aimed at emphasising human dignity, the essence of human rights. This path intends human rights not to merely remain a legal/normative institution, but rather to become a reality within the culture of the societies of the Americas. This is closely connected to the effectiveness of these rights, given that if the victims of violations are not fully aware of them, impunity is likely to prevail. It is also tied into support for genuinely democratic systems; in effect, the awareness of rights is a galvanising factor in citizen participation, as well as in citizen control of public administration.

The second area refers to the work that the Commission has undertaken in making the region's inhabitants aware of the existence of the System, as well as of the basic steps that must be taken to file complaints with the Commission. Given that the Commission lacks the means to carry out investigations motu proprio, it depends upon civil society to find out about human rights violations. A large part of the IACHR's promotional work has concentrated on this aspect, due to the Commission's direct interest in ensuring that civil society is well informed and knows what to do in cases of human rights abuses.

The third area consists of raising the awareness about the need for incorporating human rights into domestic legal systems. The international bodies play subsidiary roles in the understanding that, under normal conditions, domestic institutions are in a position to resolve situations of rights violations most quickly and efficiently. This is an aspect that the Commission has also placed emphasis on, given that it is the party most interested in ensuring that the System is used only in cases of real necessity.

Nonetheless, these activities cannot be understood as anything but a complement to the central tasks of the Commission: the tasks of protection of human rights. There are numerous academic, non-governmental and state bodies that carry out human rights promotional and educational work, and for that reason, the role of the IACHR in this respect is not unique. In contrast, as a body for the protection of such rights, the Commission's role is irreplaceable, since no other entity (not even the Inter-American Court of Human Rights, which does not possess the same functions as the

120 (2009) 40 VUWLR

Commission) has the same role as the IACHR. Thus, in spite of the fact that at some points in its history the Commission has been pressured by some states to concentrate on promotional activities, it has continued to maintain the work of protection at the crux of its action, making advocacy a complement.

(b)   Other activities of the IACHR

The Commission has a very broad mandate, for which it is authorised to carry out a diverse range of initiatives. Standing out among them are its participation in the preparation of human rights treaties and declarations in the OAS and the exercise of an advisory function.

In relation to the first of these aspects, the Commission participates along with the political bodies of the OAS in the preparation of Inter-American human rights instruments. In the case of some treaties and declarations, the IACHR has played a very important part; at other times, the political bodies of the OAS have not followed closely the proposals of the Commission.

As for the second aspect, the Commission is authorised to receive inquiries from the OAS political bodies and states on issues relating to human rights. Recently the Commission has been giving greater attention to this function, having rendered opinions on the issue of quotas for women to guarantee their representation in political systems, and engaging in the study of affirmative action for African-descendant populations.

C   *Developments at the Inter-American Court of Human Rights*

The Court has experienced significant transformations during the process of democratisation in states that belong to the System.

1   *Role of the victims at the Court*

In 1996, through an amendment of its Rules of Procedure, the Court recognised the victims' autonomy during the phase of reparations.[39] This meant that, while continuing to be "attached" to the Commission as advisors throughout the litigation of a case at the final stage, that of reparations, the victims' and their representatives would be able to act by themselves, without having to resort to the Commission for such purpose. This was an important step forward, as potential disagreements between the Commission and the victims regarding the nature, extent and enforcement of the reparations would no longer exist. In fact, from then on, the Commission would basically leave room for the victims and their lawyers to take the initiative.

In 2000, the Court moved further when it enacted new Rules of Procedure that allowed the victims autonomy from the beginning through to the end of litigation.[40] Once the Commission has

---

39   Rules of Procedure of the Inter-American Court of Human Rights, Art 23 adopted in September 1996.

40   Rules of Procedure of the Inter-American Court of Human Rights (25 November 2000).

presented its complaint before the Court, the victims and their lawyers will participate by themselves at each phase of the process. The victims are notified of each written presentation submitted by the Commission and the state, have the right to present their own points of view in writing, and can intervene in an autonomous way at the hearings, submitting the evidence that they consider appropriate.

2 A trust for the victims?

The reform described above, that significantly enhanced the role of the victims, created, nonetheless, new challenges. Among the most important is the matter of funding for the litigation, as victims cannot rely on the Commission for such purposes. The Court itself has established that a person who does not have access to justice guaranteed at the domestic level is exempt from the obligation to exhaust internal remedies.[41] Applying the same rationale, it would be a contradiction of terms if victims could not pursue their case at the Inter-American Court due to lack of funds.

However, seven years have passed and so far no mechanism has been created to deal with this matter. It has been suggested that a trust could serve to accomplish such an objective. Establishing a trust of this nature would go well beyond the competence – not to speak the finances – of the Court, and it is a matter for the political organs of the OAS. Despite this, it seems unlikely that in the foreseeable future a trust will be created, so victims will have to continue relying on donations.

3 Speeding up the judicial proceedings

As the Court began to deal with many more cases than in the past (as a result of the reform of its Rules of Procedure), it has envisioned new ways to avoid delaying justice. An important step has consisted in an increasing flexibility on the part of the Court concerning the stages of the proceedings. In particular, the Court no longer makes a clear-cut distinction between admissibility and merits. As a result, in a number of cases (especially for those at which there is no dispute about the facts but only on matters of law), the Court has held audiences at which both the admissibility of a complaint and its merits are been discussed, issuing a decision on both aspects.

Additionally, the Court has moved towards deciding by itself the issue of reparations rather than open a period for negotiations between the parties (as it did in some cases in the past). This is notwithstanding the possibility that the parties by themselves may reach such agreement during the judicial proceedings. One further aspect concerns the issue of evidence. The new Rules of Procedure provide room for validating the proof submitted at the proceedings in the Commission (provided that some requisites are met), as a way to save time and costs.[42] However, so far this rule has scarcely been applied, probably due to a longstanding tradition of not doing this validation.

---

41 Inter-American Court of Human Rights, Exceptions to the Exhaustion of Domestic Remedies (American Convention on Human Rights, Arts 46(1), 46(2)(a) and 46(2)(b)) Advisory Opinion 11 (10 August 1990).

42 Rules of Procedure of the Inter-American Court of Human Rights, Art 44(2).

4   The scope of the human rights matters the Court deals with

Since the late 1990s and especially early in the current decade, the Court has diversified its docket of cases. This is not a result of a decision on the part of Court (which cannot select the cases that it will decide), but of the Commission, that sends the cases. As a consequence, the Court has moved from a docket of cases consisting almost exclusively of systematic violations to the right to life and to the right not to be tortured, to a much more diverse one. In the last few years, the Court has decided a number of landmark cases concerning indigenous rights, due process, freedom of expression and children's rights. It has also decided cases on economic and social rights, although with less impact, as its jurisdiction is more limited in this regard.[43]

Concerning indigenous rights (a matter of utmost importance for states of the Pacific region), the Court has developed an extensive *corpus iuris*, especially regarding the scope of the right to property, and the way it should be interpreted under international law, which should go well beyond the individual component of this right. The Court has construed this right as including collective aspects, particularly in cases in which indigenous rights are at stake.[44] In addition, in this type of case the Court has addressed the issue of cultural rights, highlighting the duties of the states to safeguard traditional cultures of indigenous peoples.[45]

This more diversified docket does not imply that the Court does not decide cases on systematic violations anymore. In fact, over the last few years the Court has strengthened its jurisprudence, emphasising the obligation of democratic regimes to confront abuses of that nature committed by prior Governments and the incompatibility of international law with amnesty laws for those crimes.[46]

---

43   The Court has been criticised on this matter, because many authors consider it has shown a restrictive interpretation of its powers concerning economic and social rights. See Christian Courtis "La protección de los derechos económicos, sociales y culturales a través del artículo 26 de la Convención Americana sobre Derechos Humanos" in Christian Courtis, Denise Hauser and Gabriela Rodríguez (eds) *Protección Internacional de Derechos Humanos: Nuevos Desafíos* (Editorial Porrúa/ITAM, Mexico City, 2005) 56; Julieta Rossi and Víctor Abramovich "La tutela de los derechos económicos, sociales y culturales en el artículo 26 de la Convención Americana sobre Derechos Humanos" in Claudia Martin, Diego Rodríguez-Pinzón and José A Guevara B (eds) *Derecho Internacional de los Derechos Humanos* (Universidad Iberoamericana Mexico City, American University Washington College of Law and Distribuciones Fontamara, Ciudad de México, 2004) 457-478; Viviana Krsticevic "La protección de los derechos económicos, sociales y culturales en el sistema interamericano" in *Construyendo una Agenda para la Justiciabilidad de los Derechos Sociales* (CEJIL, San José, Costa Rica, 2004) 145.

44   *Mayagna (Sumo) Awas Tingni Community v Nicaragua* Inter-American Court of Human Rights Merits, Reparations and Costs (31 August 2001).

45   Ibid.

46   *Barrios Altos v Peru* Inter-American Court of Human Rights Interpretation of the Judgment on the Merits (3 September 2001); *Almonacid-Arellano et al v Chile* Inter-American Court of Human Rights Preliminary Objections, Merits, Reparations and Costs (26 September 2006).

5 The enforcement of the decisions of the Court

Generally speaking, there is a better record of compliance with Court decisions than with Commission resolutions. However, the balance regarding the Court is mixed. On the positive side, it is usual that states that are condemned by judgments of the tribunal do pay the monetary compensation established. However, it is not uncommon that this payment takes several years to become effective. On the negative side, states are typically reluctant or extremely slow to accomplish other reparatory components that a judgment of the Court may have. This may include, for instance, a full domestic investigation and sanction of the perpetrators of the violation; constitutional or legislative reforms and the creation of internal mechanisms to deal with certain type of violations.

In more extreme situations, states openly confronted the Court. In the late 1990s, as a result of a series of confrontations with the Commission and the Court over the issue of the death penalty, Trinidad and Tobago denounced the American Convention, thus the tribunal no longer has jurisdiction there. Also, Perú, during the Fujimori Government, stated that from then on it would not recognise the Court's jurisdiction. However, as Perú did not denounce the Convention, the Court, in interpreting this instrument, established that statements such as Perú's were not in accord with the Convention and decided that it maintained its competence. After the Fujimori Administration came to an end, the new democratic regime re-established the relationship with the Court on good terms.

6 Advisory Opinions

Due to the expanded work of the Court on contentious cases, its advisory role has lost centrality. Despite this, its Advisory Opinions have continued to provide understanding of the Inter-American instruments on human rights and treaties from other international human rights systems applicable in the Americas. Therefore, during the 1990s and the current decade, the Court has issued Advisory Opinions on a series of topics, ranging from children's rights to immigrant rights and freedom of expression. In addition, through this function, the tribunal has addressed some matters relating to procedural aspects of the System. [47]

D Urgent Measures at the Commission and Court

Both organs of the System have mechanisms to deal with urgent situations. They are called "cautionary measures" at the Commission and "provisional measures" at the Court. In parallel with the competence of these organs regarding specific cases, concerning these measures the Commission has jurisdiction over all states while the Court has jurisdiction only over those states which have made an explicit declaration of recognition of its jurisdiction for contentious cases.

---

47 For a comprehensive study on the litigation and functioning of the Commission and the Court, see Héctor Faúndez Ledesma *El Sistema Interamericano de Protección de los Derechos Humanos: Aspectos Institucionales y Procesales* (3 ed, IIDH, San José, Costa Rica, 2004); see also Felipe González, above n 37.

Also, while any person or organisation based in a state member of the OAS can request a cautionary measure at the Commission, only the Commission can ask for a provisional measure at the Court.

The scope of the Commission's measures is larger than that of most international human rights organs, as it is not necessary that a case is pending before the Commission may have standing to request a measure. This practice was the result of the widespread forced disappearances and extra-judicial executions in the region (although forced disappearances are currently not as extended as in the past, they continued to occur regularly in some countries of the OAS).

Provisional measures can be requested by the Commission to the Court regardless of their connection with a case pending. In fact, the majority of requests by the Commission are a last resort when the Commission finds that a state is reluctant to enforce a cautionary measure. Unlike the situation of enforcement of decisions in specific cases, states' record of compliance with the Commission's cautionary measures is very high, particularly regarding the protection of life. As for the provisional measures adopted by the Court, only in a handful of decisions have the states not obeyed them.[48]

E   Budget of the Commission and Court

Both human rights organs have a chronic lack of enough funding from the OAS. Despite public appreciation of the OAS political bodies and many of its states' contribution to the Commission and the Court, their budgets have scarcely increased over the past fifteen years. The budget of the Commission represents 4 per cent of that of the OAS as a whole,[49] and that of the Court even less.

As a result, both human rights organs do make permanent efforts to obtain funding from other sources such as states and private foundations, doubling their current budgets. Among the problems of this practice, of course, is the difficulty in making mid- and long-term plans on the basis of these contingent external donations and the fact that they usually require the human rights bodies to accomplish tasks additional to those they are already bound to undertake according to their statutes and to other instruments.

VI   CONCLUSIONS

Despite an adverse context, in which many authoritarian regimes existed in the Americas for a long time, the Inter-American Human Rights System has been able to make significant contributions to the protection of such rights. Among the relevant factors in this regard are that the members of the human rights bodies of the System operate in their individual capacities (not as state representatives), support from some states, and that from civil society.

---

48   See Juan Méndez and Ariel Dulitzky "Medidas Cautelares y Provisionales" in Courtis, Hauser and Rodríguez, above n 43, 67-93.

49   Comisión Interamericana de Devechos Humanos www.cidh.org/ (accessed 12 January 2009).

Later on, transitions to democracy took place in almost all countries of the region. In this context the System has also made valuable contributions, although it has had to undergo reform so as to adapt to the new situation. Emphasis has been placed on states to amend their legislation, jurisprudence and practices to make them compatible with international standards on a wide range of matters, as the System is no longer paying attention exclusively (as at the time of the dictatorships) to massive violations to the right to life and other basic rights, but to other kinds of abuses.

It has to be underlined that the Commission and Court complement each other. This ensures that the System enjoys several tools to address violations of rights in the Americas. Notwithstanding these advances, problems persist. In particular, there is a chronic lack of financing and there are insufficiencies in states' implementing the decisions made by the human rights bodies, especially by the Commission. However, the System is able, to some extent, to influence state behaviour, by promoting the application of its standards by domestic judges. To be sure, a regional human rights system cannot by itself produce a complete transformation of state practices, and, in the case of the Americas, many serious abuses persist. Co-operation of states is indispensable in this regard, as is strong participation from civil society.

[17]

IMPLEMENTATION OF JUDGMENTS: SHOULD SUPERVISION BE UNLINKED FROM THE GENERAL ASSEMBLY OF THE ORGANIZATION OF AMERICAN STATES?

Jan Schneider*

Abstract

Implementation of judgments of the Inter-American Court of Human Rights remains the weakest point of the Inter-American human rights protection system. At the end of 2011, out of 136 cases decided by the Court, 124 were still open for supervision. This evidences that purely judicial supervision, as is currently applied by the Court, is not sufficient. Complementary political action is inevitable.

After serious conflicts between the Court and the General Assembly on exhortation of recalcitrant states at the beginning of the 2000s, the Court had completely left the Assembly out of the process for years, developing its own supervision procedure. Nevertheless, in view of several cases pending without progress for years, the question of application of Article 65 ACHR has recently been discussed again among the Judges of the Court.

This paper will briefly present the background of the Court's dismay with the General Assembly, recount former reform proposals, critically assess the Judges' arguments for and against submission of cases to the Assembly, and finally make a proper proposal of how a more efficient political supervision mechanism might be conceived.

*   Magister iuris; Ph.D Researcher, Johannes-Gutenberg-Universität Mainz, Germany; Research Assistant, German National Agency for the Prevention of Torture; <duesseljan@gmail.com>. The views and opinions expressed in this article are those of the author only and do not in any way represent the views of any of the aforementioned institutions or their members.

Jan Schneider

Resumen

La implementación de las decisiones de la Corte Interamericana de Derechos Humanos sigue siendo el punto más débil del Sistema Interamericano de protección de derechos humanos. A finales del 2011, de 136 casos decididos por la Corte, 124 estaban todavía abiertos en la etapa de supervisión de cumplimiento. Eso demuestra que un monitoreo puramente judicial, tal como lo aplica la Corte en la actualidad, es insuficiente, y que acciones políticas complementarias son inevitables.

Después de serios conflictos entre la Corte y la Asamblea General sobre la exhortación a los estados recalcitrantes a inicios de los años 2000, la Corte dejó a la Asamblea completamente por fuera del proceso durante años, y desarrolló su propio procedimiento de monitoreo. No obstante, visto varios casos donde no hubo ningún progreso durante años, la cuestión de volver a aplicar el artículo 65 de la CADH ha sido discutida nuevamente entre los Jueces de la Corte.

Este artículo va a presentar brevemente el trasfondo del desaliento de la Corte respecto a la Asamblea General; revisar las anteriores propuestas de reforma; evaluar críticamente los argumentos de los Jueces a favor y en contra de la remisión de casos a la Asamblea, y finalmente elaborar una propuesta propia de cómo se podría concebir un mecanismo político de monitoreo más eficaz.

1. INTRODUCTION

The Inter-American Court of Human Rights (or the Court) is internationally recognized for its detailed reparations practice. Unlike the European Court of Human Rights, it hardly leaves any margin of appreciation to the states on how to implement its decisions. This should make supervision easier, as the supervising organ does not have to evaluate the appropriateness of the measures taken because this was already done by the Court in its decision on reparations.[1] Nonetheless, compliance with decisions remains one of the most fundamental issues the Court is confronting. At the end of 2011, 124 out of the 136 contentious cases decided by the Court up to then were not or only partially complied with.[2] Moreover, the supervision and the adoption of provisional measures ties up almost half of the working capacity of the Court's

---

[1]   A typical reparations order by the Inter-American Court of Human Rights may comprise more than ten specific orders on cessation, restitution, compensation, satisfaction and guarantees of non-repetition. The decision of IACtHR (Judgment) 26 May 2010, *Manuel Cepeda-Vargas* v. *Colombia*, gives a good exemplary overview of a typical set of measures.
       The decisions of the Inter-American Court of Human Rights are available from <www.corteidh.or.cr/casos.cfm>.

[2]   IACtHR, *Informe Anual de la Corte Interamericana de Derechos Humanos 2011*, <www.corteidh.or.cr>, p. 13 and data from <www.corteidh.or.cr/casos.cfm>.

registry, according to estimations made by lawyers there.[3] Proposals for improvements of compliance mainly concentrate on the Court's judgments and national mechanisms, while inter-American cooperation remains largely unconsidered as an option.[4] We assume that, in addition to modifications on other levels, an inter-American approach is necessary to deal with recalcitrant states. This paper therefore concentrates on the inter-American organs' role in the process of monitoring and implementing judgments of the Court.

After having been disappointed twice by the General Assembly, which is endowed with reacting to cases of non-compliance, the Court has taken supervision into its own hands, and developed a complex process of written reports and private and public hearings (2). Today, though, it is again facing situations of persistent non-compliance which had the issue of reporting cases of non-compliance to the General Assembly be discussed again among the Judges (3). Nevertheless, it has to be asked whether the procedure under Article 65 of the American Convention on Human Rights (ACHR or the Convention) is appropriate to confront the phenomenon of non-compliance (4).

2. A SHORT HISTORY OF MONITORING COMPLIANCE

The American States, when adopting the human rights protection system, took inspiration from the European Convention on Human Rights (ECHR), but conceived the monitoring system differently. The fact that they have not adopted the European monitoring mechanism but have shared the burden of supervision between the Court and the General Assembly can be explained by the different structure of the Organization of American States, which does not provide an organ similar to the Committee of Ministers.[5]

The corresponding Article 65 ACHR reads:

> "To each regular session of the General Assembly of the Organization of American States the Court shall submit, for the Assembly's consideration, a report on its work during the previous year. It shall specify, in particular, the cases in which a state has not complied with its judgments, making any pertinent recommendations."

---

[3]   Estimation made by a Senior Lawyer at the Registry of the Inter-American Court of Human Rights in an interview conducted in September 2010.

[4]   Cf.: Asociación por los Derechos Civiles, *La Efectividad del Sistema Interamericano de Protección de Derechos Humanos*, 2011, <www.adc.or.ar>, p. 29 ff.; A. Huneeus, "Courts Resisting Courts", 44 *Cornell International Law Journal* 3 (2011), pp. 101–155.

[5]   Details on the discussions about Article 65 ACHR in the *travaux préparatoires* can be found at M.E. Ventura Robles, *La supervisión del cumplimiento de sentencias en el sistema interamericano de protección de los Derechos Humanos*, Presentation at the XXIV Congreso del Instituto Hispano-Luso-Americano de Derecho Internacional, 11–16 September 2006, <www.corteidh.or.cr/tablas/25340.pdf>.

Jan Schneider

The Court has to monitor how the responding state complies with the judgments and, in case it does not comply, has to report this to the General Assembly together with the pertinent recommendations.

The Court had assumed the power to monitor compliance with its judgments already in the first cases that it closed with a sentence on reparations.[6] Although the monitoring procedure was not established in the Court's rules, a process emerged from practice, based principally on the submission of reports by all parties on compliance of the measures ordered. Upon reception of the reports, the Court evaluates them and issues, when the situation is fitting, orders on compliance, pointing out advances and demanding further steps to be taken in case of non-compliance.[7] The Court usually orders the state to submit every six months a report on measures taken to comply with the judgment.[8]

Only in moments of manifest crises did the Court submit cases to the General Assembly. The first such situations occurred at the end of the 1990s, in Trinidad and Tobago. On 22 May 1998, the Inter-American Commission on Human Rights had requested the Court to order provisional measures in the cases of several persons who had been sentenced to death in proceedings that were considered to violate several Convention guarantees.[9] As a consequence, Trinidad denounced the Convention on 26 May 1998, the denunciation becoming effective one year later according to Article 78(1) ACHR.[10] On 27 May 1998, the President of the Court ordered provisional measures in the case of *James et al.* v. *Trinidad and Tobago*, extending them in the following months to several other persons in similar circumstances. When the Court summoned the Inter-American Commission on Human Rights and Trinidad for an audience on the measures, the state declared that it would not respect the Court's orders and would not refer to the Court on this as well as any other case.[11] Thereupon the Court informed the General Assembly in its Annual Report for 1998 under Article 65 ACHR of Trinidad's attitude and expressed its serious concerns about the repercussions of the denunciation for the protection of human rights, and called the Assembly to exert influence on Trinidad to reconsider its decision.[12] Despite the clear advice from the Court, the Committee on Judicial and Political Affairs did not include any reference to the Trinidad issue in its resolution on the Annual Report of the Court. The Court consequently sent notes to the Secretary of the Permanent Council and, as

---

[6]   IACtHR (Judgment) 21 July 1989, *Velásquez Rodríguez* v. *Honduras*.

[7]   General: IACtHR (Judgment) 28 November 2003, *Baena-Ricardo et al.* v. *Panama*, para. 105 and in practice: IACtHR (Order) 17 November 1999, Compliance with *Loayza Tamayo* v. *Peru*.

[8]   E.g. IACtHR (Judgment) 31 August 2001, *Mayagna (Sumo) Awas Tingni Community* v. *Nicaragua*, operative para. 8.

[9]   IACtHR, *Informe Anual de la Corte Interamericana de Derechos Humanos 1998*, <www.corteidh.or.cr>, p. 39 ff.

[10]   Hereon: IACtHR (Judgment) 1 September 2001, *Hilaire* v. *Trinidad and Tobago*, para. 28.

[11]   IACtHR, *supra* n. 9, p. 40.

[12]   Ibid., p. 41.

he neither showed any willingness to include the issue in the proposal resolution for the General Assembly, also urged the Secretary General of the Organization of American States to refer the issue to the General Assembly, but to no avail. In the summer of 1999, in flagrant disrespect of the provisional measures ordered by the Court to protect the life of the presumed victims, Trinidad executed two of them without causing any reaction in the other American States.[13]

In the same year, the Court found severe violations in several cases related to the times of internal conflict between the Government of Peru and the guerrilla group called Movimiento Revolucionario Tupac Amaru and, in particular, had declared the trials of civilians before military tribunals a violation of the Convention, and required Peru to annul the decisions.[14] Peru's reaction – probably influenced by the Organization of American States's absolute silence on Trinidad's denunciation – was to withdraw its recognition of the Court's contentious jurisdiction with immediate effect on 9 July 1999 for all cases in which Peru had not yet replied to the application.[15] The Court, performing a thorough interpretation of the Convention, resolved that the denunciation of the recognition of competence was not possible, and that a state could only denounce the Convention as a whole under the terms of Article 78, giving one year prior notice and thus decided to remain seized of the case.[16] Again, it reported these incidents under Article 65 ACHR to the General Assembly.[17]

The General Assembly, with respect to both situations, did not take any serious decision to urge either state to comply with their obligations under the Convention. The only reference in the resolution on the Annual Report by the Court to its session in 2000 was the reiteration that the Court's judgments were final and not subject to appeal, and the call upon the states that had denounced the Convention to reconsider their decisions.[18]

After the destitution of the Fujimori government, Peru reassumed the Court's jurisdiction in 2001.[19] While that year's General Assembly recognized Peru's return to the inter-American human rights system, it had apparently considered Trinidad a lost

---

13   Ibid., p. 47.

14   IACtHR (Judgment) 17 September 1997, *Loayza Tamayo v. Peru* and subsequently IACtHR (Judgment) 27 November 1998, *Loayza Tamayo v. Peru* and IACtHR (Judgment) 30 May 1999, *Castillo-Petruzzi et al. v. Peru*.

15   IACtHR (Judgment) 24 November 1999, *Constitutional Court v. Peru*, para. 23; the denunciation would also affect the case of IACtHR (Judgment) 6 February 2001, *Ivcher Bronstein v. Peru*. On the reasons for the withdrawal: D. Cassel, "El Perú se retira de la Corte: ¿Afrontará el reto el Sistema Interamericano de Derechos Humanos?", *29 Revista IIDH* (1999), p. 73 ff.

16   IACtHR (Judgment) 24 November 1999, *Constitutional Court v. Peru*, paras. 38 ff. and 54.

17   IACtHR, *supra* 9, p. 49 ff.

18   Nos. 3 and 4 of the *Resolution on the Annual Report of the IACtHR 1999*, reprinted in IACtHR, *Informe Anual de la Corte Interamericana de Derechos Humanos 2000*, <www.corteidh.or.cr>, pp. 55 ff.

19   IACtHR, *Informe Anual de la Corte Interamericana de Derechos Humanos 2001*, <www.corteidh.or.cr>, p. 69.

Jan Schneider

state and did not refer to the issue ever after.[20] Nevertheless, in a resolution on the perfection and strengthening of the inter-American system, it invited the Court to continue to include information on compliance within its annual reports which would be analysed by the General Assembly.[21] Thereupon, the Court once again brought cases to the General Assembly's knowledge, and asked it to exhort the responding states to comply with their obligations.[22] Again, despite the general reiteration "that the judgments of the Inter-American Court of Human Rights are final and may not be appealed and that the States Parties to the Convention undertake to comply with the rulings of the Court in all cases to which they are party", no specific reference to the cases was included in the General Assembly's resolution.[23]

In view of the outcome of the process before the General Assembly, the Court made two concrete proposals in 2002 and 2005 to modify the system of implementation of judgments.[24] Despite this, the Organization of American States did not make any modification whatsoever to its organs or their functioning with respect to the Court's reports. The Court thus finally gave in and began to find solutions within its own margin of powers. Its hitherto last act concerning the repartition of powers during the monitoring phase was a resolution adopted in 2005, wherein it decided – and to this end informed the General Assembly and the Secretary General of the Organization of American States – to relinquish its monitoring activities for cases that had been submitted to the General Assembly under Article 65 ACHR. In the future it would only receive notifications of compliance from the state and, in the opposite case, continue to include the case in each annual report.[25] Thus, the Court drew a clear line between its monitoring competence, which is limited to the preparation of reports to the General Assembly, and the transfer to the General Assembly as an *"ultima ratio"* in cases of recalcitrant states. It has never again submitted cases under Article 65 ACHR to the General Assembly since.

Despite the very general text of Article 65 ACHR and apart from the aforementioned situations, states generally participate in the monitoring process established by the Court. Only once was this process directly challenged by a state. After having submitted several reports on compliance and having participated in meetings with the victims' representatives at the seat of the Court, Panama alleged in the *Baena-Ricardo* case "that the stage of monitoring compliance with judgment is a 'post-judgment' stage that 'is not included in the norms that regulate the jurisdiction and

---

20   *Resolution on the Annual Report of the IACtHR 2000*, reprinted in IACtHR, *supra* n. 19, p. 80.

21   No. 5(a) of Resolution AG/RES. 1828 (XXXI-O/01).

22   IACtHR, *Informe Anual de la Corte Interamericana de Derechos Humanos 2003*, <www.corteidh.or.cr>, pp. 44f.

23   No. 3 of Resolution AG/RES 2043 (XXXIV-O/04).

24   *Infra.*

25   IACtHR, *Resolución de la Corte Interamericana de Derechos Humanos de 29 de junio de 2005, Supervisión de cumplimiento de sentencias*, <www.corteidh.or.cr>.

the procedure of the Court'."[26] It argued that monitoring execution was not a judicial but a political task and, as such, exclusive to the General Assembly, a fact that would be confirmed by Article 65 ACHR. The Court could not extend its competence assuming that it had a *compétence de compétence*. Panama made reference to the situation under the Charter of the United Nations, which assigned monitoring of execution of judgments of the International Court of Justice to the United Nations Security Council. The European Court of Human Rights had no monitoring competence either; only the Council of Ministers did. Furthermore, the 14-years old practice of the Court could not be considered jurisprudential practice. Any submission by the states would hence be made on a voluntary basis. Finally, it accused the Court of having exceeded its powers also because it had interpreted its judgment outside of the official interpretation procedure.

This challenged the Court to adopt a fundamental decision on its monitoring competence by proceeding to a rigorous interpretation of the Convention and showing that its competence rooted therein. Its reasoning principally relied on the question of effectivity of its decisions. It held that monitoring compliance was part of its judicial functions because otherwise its decisions would not be effective but merely of a declaratory nature.[27] This would not coincide with the right to a fair trial and that of an effective remedy stipulated in Articles 8 and 25 ACHR. Both the Inter-American and the European Court of Human Rights had decided in several cases that an effective remedy presupposed that judicial decisions be effectively implemented by the state.[28] The Court elaborated the specific role and function of the European Committee of Ministers and pointed out that the member states of the Organization of American States had not set up a similar organ, stating that it is clear that, when regulating monitoring compliance with the judgments of the Inter-American Court, it was not envisaged that the OAS General Assembly or the OAS Permanent Council would carry out a similar function to the Committee of Ministers in the European system.[29]

Then, it interpreted the *travaux préparatoires* of the Convention, finding that the states, not only by establishing in Article 65 ACHR that the Court should submit a report to the General Assembly, but also by introducing the concept that it must indicate the cases of non-compliance and make pertinent recommendations, intended to endow it with a veritable monitoring competence.[30] Without monitoring compliance, it could not know in which cases states did not comply and thus select these cases to present them to the General Assembly and make the pertinent recommendations.[31] The same resulted from Article 62(1) ACHR which extends the

---

[26]   IACtHR (Judgment) 28 November 2003, *Baena-Ricardo et al. v. Panama*, para. 26.

[27]   Ibid., para. 72.

[28]   Ibid., paras. 77–82.

[29]   Ibid., para. 88.

[30]   Ibid., paras. 89 ff.

[31]   Ibid., para. 134.

Jan Schneider

Court's jurisdiction to "all matters relating to the interpretation or application of the Convention." Also, Article 29(a) ACHR provided that the Convention should not be interpreted in such a way that the rights and freedoms could be "restricted to a greater extent than is provided for therein." Should none of the bodies of the Organization of American States be enabled to monitor compliance with the Court's judgments, this principle would remain void.[32] Finally, the Court made reference to the tacit agreement of the states which had accepted the Court's monitoring in all previous cases, revealing an *opinio juris communis*.[33] It repealed Panama's argument that such an opinion could only be assumed after a lapse of time of more than 14 years. Lastly it made reference to the General Assembly's attitude towards the monitoring practice, stating that the Assembly was informed about the Court's monitoring practice since the first cases it had decided, and that it had never objected to it. On the contrary, on several occasions the General Assembly requested states to submit the information required by the Court on the monitoring stage.[34] It finally rejected Panama's claim, pointing out that the state had initially complied with the orders of the Court. Its opposition to the procedure would therefore amount to an estoppel, although the Court does not call it by this name.[35]

This fundamental decision by the Court received support from the General Assembly, which nowadays expressly welcomes in its resolutions on the Court's annual reports the progress made in its monitoring procedure, thus expressing the states' agreement with it.

In the same year, the Court announced another fundamental change to its monitoring procedure: the introduction of hearings on compliance.[36] These announcements coincided with the disappointing outcome of the Article 65 proceeding before the General Assembly. The first private hearings on compliance were conducted in 2007 in order to obtain the information required to assess whether the state had complied with its obligations.[37]

In 2009, the Court went one step further and convened the first public hearing on compliance. This measure was preceded by a modification of the Rules of Procedure in the same year, which implemented a new Article 63 on the process of monitoring compliance.[38] According to this new article, monitoring principally relies on the submission of written reports by the state and observations by the victims and their

---

[32] Ibid., para. 95.

[33] Ibid., para. 102.

[34] Ibid., paras. 110 ff.

[35] Ibid., para. 126.

[36] IACtHR (Order) 20 November 2000, Compliance with *El Amparo* v. *Venezuela*, considerando para. 1.

[37] IACtHR (Order) 27 November 2007, Compliance with *Garrido and Baigorria* v. *Argentina*, para. 11 and IACtHR, *Annual Report of the Inter-American Court of Human Rights 2007*, <www.corteidh.or.cr>, p. 23.

[38] Today Article 69 of the Rules of Procedure of the Inter-American Court of Human Rights.

legal representatives. The Inter-American Commission on Human Rights may make observations on both documents. Furthermore, the Court may require information from any other source of information, including expert witnesses and reports. The written procedure may be accompanied by hearings on monitoring compliance. There is no restriction as to the type of hearing so that private as well as public hearings may be convened. There is no escalation either, i.e. a public hearing does not necessarily have to be preceded by a private one, although this is generally the case.

The first public hearing in *Sawhoyamaxa Indigenous Community* v. *Paraguay* on 20 May 2009 had been preceded by a private hearing. Despite this hearing, the state had not progressed on several crucial issues of a case about an indigenous community that was living in conditions that affected the lives of its members due to an eviction from their traditional lands. The Court had ordered the state to title determinate areas for the community. As several members of the community had died due to the failing support by the state and education for children was not possible, the Court decided to summon the parties to a public hearing in which the state should inform of the measures it planned to adopt.[39]

Nowadays the Court has further developed the system of hearings by grouping cases from one country that suffer from the same problem of compliance, e.g. cases concerning medical and psychological assistance to massacre victims in several Colombian cases.[40]

The developments in supervision coincide with a generally elevated activity and presence by the Court since 2005. This was enabled mainly by agreements with the European Union in 2004 on USD 800,000 and in 2006 with Norway on USD 3,319,390.25. These additional financial resources permitted the employment of more lawyers in the Court's registry and an increase in sessions. The Court could thus begin to hold sessions away from its seat, a practice it maintains since 2005.[41] In 2007, the agreement with Norway was expanded by an additional USD 120,000.[42] The increased number of lawyers working in the Court's registry and the higher frequency of sessions allowed the Court to dedicate more time to the treatment of cases and finally permitted the introduction of monitoring audiences in 2007. The Court began with the most ancient cases that had not shown any progress.

The Court has recently summed up its function on the monitoring stage as going beyond the strict supervision of compliance but defines its aim as "that the reparations ordered by the Court in the specific case are implemented effectively and complied with."[43] It gathers information on compliance from all parties to the case, evaluates

---

[39]   IACtHR (Order) 20 May 2009, Compliance with *Sawhoyamaxa Indigenous Community* v. *Paraguay*.

[40]   IACtHR, *Informe Anual de la Corte Interamericana de Derechos Humanos 2010*, <www.corteidh.or.cr>, p. 10.

[41]   IACtHR, *Informe Anual de la Corte Interamericana de Derechos Humanos 2005*, <www.corteidh.or.cr>, p. 12 ff. The itinerant sessions in 2007 and 2008 were financed with funds provided by Spain: IACtHR, *supra* n. 37, p. 58.

[42]   Ibid., p. 57.

[43]   IACtHR, *supra* n. 2, p. 13 (our translation).

Jan Schneider

the situation of compliance and takes the pertinent recommendations. Consistent with the observation that implementation fails in many cases due to internal obstacles such as missing legal prerequisites to reopen cases, political conflicts between different interest groups or funding issues, the Court, after a public hearing, may give to the state "very clear and detailed" directions on how compliance may be obtained, driven by an "intention to support the states to effectuate compliance".[44] Hearings play a special role according to this understanding. The oral presentation, in particular the contradictory nature of the hearing, allows the Court to get a better idea of the obstacles to implementation than a written procedure would allow. Thus, it underlines its conciliatory approach in these sessions which is not limited to merely taking note of the information presented by the parties, but suggests alternative solutions, draws the attention to marked noncompliance for failing desire, fosters the adoption of timetables for compliance by all parties and even puts the Court's installations at the disposition of the parties to hold conversations that in many cases are not easy to realize in the responding state.[45]

Again, the Court interprets its competences widely. It does not limit itself to merely collecting information on the status of execution and eventually other facts it requires to make pertinent recommendations to the General Assembly. The states in the General Assembly have nonetheless welcomed this development in their 2009 resolution on the Court's Annual Report.[46] Although their intentions are not made evident, it is well imaginable that the states, who have never shown big interest in the Court's issues, consider the monitoring practice a good way to achieve better execution results without having to look at the cases themselves. The parties and the Court also recognized hearings as a good way to evaluate the state's willingness to comply with the Court's orders.[47]

Another, more controversial modification to the Court's supervision process was the partial closure of cases according to the state of compliance. Instead of recognizing merely in the deliberative part of the judgment what measures had been complied with, it now expressly maintains cases open for supervision only for the parts that have not been complied with.[48] It stresses in its annual reports that, despite the huge number of cases under supervision of compliance, in most of them, the majority of measures had been complied with.[49] This differentiation makes sense given the variety of measures ordered by the Court. Thus, payment of reparations or symbolic measures and restitution usually are easier to be achieved than complicated investigations into the whereabouts of massacre victims, legislative changes or large-scale modernization

---

[44] IACtHR, *supra* n. 40, p. 4 (our translation).

[45] Ibid., p. 5 (our translation).

[46] No. 5(d) of Resolution AG/RES. 2652 (XLI-O/11), <www.oas.org/consejo/sp/AG/resoluciones-declaraciones.asp>.

[47] IACtHR (Order) 27 November 2007, Compliance with *Blake* v. *Guatemala*, para. 12.

[48] See e.g. IACtHR (Order) 18 November 2010, Compliance with *Almonacid-Arellano et al.* v. *Chile*, operative paras.; Ventura Robles, "Conference: Advocacy before Regional Human Rights Bodies: A Cross-Regional Agenda", 59 *American University International Law Review* (2009), p. 192.

[49] IACtHR, *supra* n. 2, p. 13.

measures of parts of public administration.[50] Nonetheless, partial closure of cases met objection from former President of the Court, Cançado Trindade, who argues that partial closure is misleading as it covers the fact that there are parts of the judgment that remain unfulfilled.[51] In recent orders on compliance, the Court mentions as well the parts of the judgment that have been fulfilled as the parts in which monitoring remains open, thus preventing to give a false picture of the situation in the case.[52]

The states in general participate in the new monitoring proceedings, so that in the past few years several cases could finally be closed.[53]

Despite these advances, the Court's authority has recently been under fire again, this time from Venezuela. The Court had handed down several judgments concerning the domestic political order, in particular the independence of justice and the prison condition of a convicted terrorist.[54] The first case affected judges of an administrative tribunal who were alleged to be members of the political opposition planning a coup d'état against President Chávez. After a constitutional reform at the beginning of the 2000s, most Venezuelan judges were appointed temporally and could be removed easily. This had happened to the affected judges who had been appointed to the tribunal competent to judge most political decisions by the government. After the Court had handed down its decision ordering Venezuela to reinstate the judges, the Venezuelan Supreme Court, adopting an extremely dualist position, held that the sentence could not be executed as this would result in the violation of the Venezuelan constitution, and called the government to denounce the Convention.[55] Although the government did not react immediately to this request, the *Usón-Ramírez* v. *Venezuela* decision, in which the Court found that a terrorist had been detained in inhuman

---

50 See also ibid., p. 13 and EFE, "Sólo el 12% de las sentencias de la Corte Interamericana se ha cumplido", *El Mundo*, 3 April 2009 <www.elmundo.es>.

51 L. Tanner, "Interview with Judge Antônio A. Cançado Trindade, Inter-American Court of Human Rights", *4 Human Rights Quarterly 31* (2009), p. 994.

52 See e.g. IACtHR (Order) 18 November 2010, Compliance with *Almonacid-Arellano et al.* v. *Chile*.

53 E.g. IACtHR (Order) 24 November 2008, Compliance with *Claude Reyes* v. *Chile*; IACtHR (Order) 22 November 2010, Compliance with *Herrera Ulloa* v. *Costa Rica*; IACtHR (Order) 1 September 2010, Compliance with *Tristan Donoso* v. *Panama*: In none of these cases, though, were "complicated" measures such as investigations required. A study on compliance with pecuniary measures conducted by the Court in 2008 showed that 81% of orders to reimburse costs and expenses were totally or partially complied with, while 83% of indemnifications were totally or partially complied with (IACtHR, *Annual Report of the Inter-American Court of Human Rights 2009*, <www.corteidh.or.cr>, p. 12). A grimmer picture was drawn by the President of the Court in 2008, who said that only 12% the of cases decided by the Court had been complied with completely, the most difficult measures to comply with being the investigation, process and eventually sentencing of human rights violators (EFE, *supra* n. 50). Another statistic demonstrates that, from the cases decided between June 2001 and June 2006, 64% were totally or partially not complied with by June 2009: Asociación por los Derechos Civiles, *supra* n. 4, p. 13.

54 IACtHR (Judgment) 5 August 2008, *Apitz-Barbera et al.* v. *Venezuela* and IACtHR (Judgment) 20 November 2009, *Usón-Ramírez* v. *Venezuela*.

55 Tribunal Supremo de Justicia [Sala Constitucional], 18 December 2008, *Expediente No. 08–1572*, <www.tsj.gov.ve>, punto resolutivo 2.

Jan Schneider

conditions, gave President Chávez the reason to announce Venezuela's retreat from the Convention.[56] Again, it will be up to the General Assembly to react to this decision and hopefully take a stronger stand than in the Peruvian and Trinidadian cases. In the meantime, the Court's possibilities are limited to maintaining supervision of the judgments open and eventually submitting the cases to the General Assembly in application of Article 65 ACHR.

This renewed episode of objection by a state to politically inconvenient decisions, but also the still very high number of not fully complied with cases, gives a clear example of the politically sensitive environment among the Latin-American states and evidences the need to continue to critically evaluate the process of implementing judgments.

3. RECENT DISCUSSIONS AROUND ARTICLE 65 ACHR

Although its proactive jurisprudence of broad interpretation of the Convention rights has brought huge advances in the field of human rights protection in the affected countries and has influenced international courts, the Court must be aware of the unstable support it receives from several states, and that missing support from influential domestic actors may render implementation of its judgments almost impossible. Only close respect of the limitations set by the Convention can prevent too easy rejection of its judgments by the states in case of politically inconvenient decisions. This includes the submission of cases to the General Assembly in accordance to Article 65 ACHR, although the outlook there may appear grim. But, as former President of the Court, Judge Cançado Trindade, said accordingly: "I think that protection is a matter of principle and there is no room under the American Convention for pragmatism."[57] Insofar it is good to see that the inter-American judges are apparently considering the possibility to submit cases to the General Assembly again:

In *Blanco-Romero et al.* v. *Venezuela*, a forced disappearance case, the Court had ordered in 2005 a set of measures to be adopted by the state.[58] Nevertheless, even after a private hearing on compliance in 2009 in which the state and the victims had agreed to adopt a schedule for the implementation of measures, again the state had taken hardly any steps to comply with its obligations, including simple ones such as publication of the judgment or payment of compensation remaining unfulfilled six years after the original judgment. Despite this apparent unwillingness by the state, the Court, on 22 November 2011, adopted another order on compliance in which it stressed the state's obligation to comply with the reparation orders.[59] However,

---

[56]   OAS, *Press Release E-307/12*, 10 September 2012, <www.oas.org>.

[57]   L. Tanner, *supra* n. 51, p. 995.

[58]   IACtHR (Judgment), 28 November 2005, *Blanco-Romero v. Venezuela*.

[59]   IACtHR (Order) 22 November 2011, Compliance with *Blanco Romero et al. v. Venezuela*.

concurring opinions of Judges García Sayán and Vio Grossi on this and two other cases which were decided at the same session, evidence the lines of discussion about Article 65 ACHR among the judges.[60]

García Sayán's opinion deals with the important question of when a case has to be submitted to the General Assembly by the Court. He repeats the Court's constant jurisprudence that its monitoring competence followed from the fact that it first had to identify the cases in which states were persistently not complying in order to then report these cases. He concludes that the Court had to single out "exceptional cases in which a real reticence or refusal of the state concerned to comply with the provisions of the judgment has been verified." Reticence had to amount to the state "expressly indicat[ing] that it will not comply totally or partially with the decisions, added to the failure of all possible monitoring measures."[61] According to him, none of the cases to which he had added his opinion had amounted to this level yet.

Vio Grossi, for his part, underlines that Article 65 ACHR would not create an option but an obligation for the Court to submit cases to the General Assembly. Merely enumerating decisions on compliance in its annual report would not be sufficient, because it was not for the Assembly to pick cases from this list, but for the Court to specify them. The Court could not adopt its own monitoring competence, arguing that the General Assembly would not be complying with its tasks under the Convention. He recognizes that the Court could not extend monitoring procedures into an uncertain future without setting the state specific deadlines for complying with its obligations. Otherwise, the Court would end up in a situation of having to apply political pressure to induce the state to comply. He also opposes the argument that if the Court submitted one case to the Assembly, it would subsequently have to submit many more cases which would amount to the recognition of inefficiency of the inter-American human rights system. Vio Grossi explicitly rules out that the respect for human rights or the *"pro homine"* principle could justify the Court to deviate from its legal basis and autonomously create procedures outside of the Convention. He opines that the best protection for human rights could be provided if the Court kept closely to the rules, in particular the Convention. Nonetheless, he underlines that his intention was not to undermine the monitoring practice of the Court, but to make clear that the execution of this function should not eliminate the application of Article 65 ACHR. The Court's role on this stage of the proceedings would be limited to supervision and would not entail imparting new obligations to the states. If a state did not show progress in compliance, it corresponded to the General Assembly to draw the pertinent conclusions from this behaviour.[62]

---

[60] IACtHR (Order) 22 November 2011, Compliance with *Servellón García v. Honduras* and IACtHR (Order) 23 November 2011, *Saramaka People v. Suriname*, all with the same wording.

[61] IACtHR (Order) 22 November 2011, Compliance with *Blanco Romero et al. v. Venezuela*, separate opinion of Judge García Sayán, para. 8.

[62] IACtHR (Order) 22 November 2011, Compliance with *Blanco Romero et al. v. Venezuela*, Concurring opinion of Judge Vio Grossi.

Jan Schneider

Besides its purely judicial role when deciding cases, the Court also has a political role to play when supervising execution. Nonetheless, its possibilities in this area are limited. Apart from offering a forum to the parties to discuss their opinions, make proposals and bring cases back to public awareness by organizing public or private hearings, it cannot exert any type of pressure. Therefore, the rigid *ultima ratio* approach taken by Garcia Sayán is too narrow. The Court has to accept its limitations and the General Assembly's primordial political role. Thus, it would be better if the Court did not select cases to submit to the Assembly according to formalist criteria, but rather made these decisions on a case-to-case basis, taking into account the specific political circumstances of each case. Insofar Vio Grossi is right when he points out the Assembly's role under the Convention. It is not correct to completely exclude the Assembly from supervision despite its apparent shortcomings, given the Court's limited possibilities to effectively press the states. The question of whether it would be good for the development of the inter-American human rights system to make its failure on the political level evident, is, however, a critical one to ask. The Peru and Trinidad and Tobago cases have shown a tendency towards the contrary, leaving no apparent effect on the Organization of American States and putting a strain on the human rights protection system. The selection of cases to be relinquished by the Court must therefore be done with good political sense.

Vio Grossi's criticism alluding that the Court had created its monitoring competence outside of the Convention does, however, not meet the point. The Court's competences in this area derive from Article 65 ACHR as described in *Baena-Ricardo et al. v. Panama*. The wide interpretation of the Convention has, apart from this case, never been attacked by any state as being *ultra vires*, but was explicitly accepted by the General Assembly which even invited the Court to continue this practice. States have followed the Court summonses and some have even solicited hearings on compliance themselves, evidencing support of these measures. Vio Grossi's implicit criticism of the *pro homine* principle is also not justified. It is specifically the interpretation of the Convention following this principle that has, in large parts, allowed the Court to be the success story it is. The Court is an eminently progressive element in the inter-American human rights system and has to maintain this attitude given the states' flawy compromise. Vio Grossi is correct, though, when he concludes that the Court must not relinquish the General Assembly from its obligations. The political assessment of cases as mentioned above, is therefore essential as long as the monitoring system continues to function as it currently does.

This renewed discussion of the application of Article 65 ACHR, after having evaded it's application since 2003, is necessary. The Court has had undeniable successes with its own monitoring procedure of combining a written procedure with private and public hearings, and lately the combination of cases in one country in which similar measures are pending. A major disadvantage of an exhaustive monitoring procedure is, though, that it binds a significant part of the already sparse funds of the Court. Although there are no statistics on the workload of the Court's registry, lawyers there estimate that about half of their working time is dedicated to monitoring compliance and adoption of provisional measures.[63] In each session, the Court has to monitor compliance in 15 to 20 cases, holding five to six sessions thereon, while only two to three sessions are dedicated to the (more extensive) deliberations on the merits. The Court's dilemma is that it has to choose whether to ensure, as good as possible, compliance with its decisions, thus limiting the throughput of cases and probably placing situations that would merit judgment by the Court out of its reach, or to limit its monitoring activity, thus running the risk that its decisions will not be effectively complied with and that it will become a "toothless tiger". This dilemma cannot be resolved by the Court itself, but requires the dedication of the member states who will have to act correspondingly to their obligations under the Convention and consistently within the General Assembly when discussing the Court's report. This, however, also requires the Court to stop evading the Assembly and respect the shared responsibilities established by the Convention.

4. REFORMING THE MONITORING PROCEDURE

Taking into account this repartition of responsibilities, the monitoring and implementation procedure offers margin for improvement. Despite the different organizational setting, the inter-American procedure could be inspired by the pilot-judgment proceeding that was only recently introduced in the European system: Just as is the case there, Court and Commission have an advantage of information concerning the situation in the states with respect to the General Assembly.[64] The Court is aware of the situation in the respective states through the situations that were submitted to it and that may have been caused by similar structural reasons – it actually specifically replied to the issue of systemic problems by grouping cases suffering from similar problems in the same state –, and through the reports submitted by the parties to the case under its monitoring. It is therefore in a better position to identify the obstacles to execution than the General Assembly is. The quality of the Court's reports could even be further improved by closer co-operation with the Inter-American Commission. Unlike in Europe, the Court does not receive complaints itself but through the Inter-American Commission. Despite having better knowledge than the General Assembly, the Court only knows of a limited number of cases in a state and is therefore not in an ideal position to identify underlying systemic problems of execution. The Inter-American Commission, which is the first filter in the process of the inter-American human rights system and as such receives all complaints,[65]

---

[63] Estimation made by a Senior Lawyer at the Registry of the Inter-American Court of Human Rights in an interview conducted in September 2010.

[64] Cfr. A. Szklanna, "The impact of the pilot judgment procedure of the European Court of Human Rights on the execution of its judgments", in *European Yearbook on Human Rights* (2010), p. 226.

[65] Article 61(2) ACHR.

Jan Schneider

should therefore complete the picture by providing the Court with information on other cases concerning similar situations in the same state, to enable the Court to really identify the problems underlying a case and to make the pertinent recommendations to the General Assembly. Court and Commission should hence provide the Assembly with more detailed information on the aforementioned points in order to effectively deal with cases of persistent objection to compliance. When future cases will be reported to the Assembly, the Court should therefore consider to modify its reports, and put more emphasis on the reasons of non-compliance by the states.

Additionally, the more general question of whether the General Assembly is an appropriate organ to deal with issues of non-compliance should be considered. This may be doubted for several reasons. Firstly, the powers of the General Assembly regarding recalcitrant states are not clearly defined in the Convention. It must therefore be assumed that, being the supreme political body of the Organization of American States, its political appreciation of the case is wide and, under its power to authoritatively interpret the OAS Charter, it may take whatever decision it deems appropriate in the specific case. Thus, suspension similar to the Cuban case, or even rejection of the state could be envisaged, taking into account that law and good faith are a basic principle of the relations of the American States (Article 3 of the OAS Charter) and that each state shall respect the individual rights of the person (Article 17 of the OAS Charter). However, whatever decision the General Assembly takes, a stain will remain on the state's face as it will be publicly marked not only a human rights violator, but also a recalcitrant objector to assume its responsibilities for the violations occurred and will put the political integrity of the Organization of American States at risk. Hopes should therefore not be raised too high on substantial actions by the Assembly.

Secondly, and presumably more important, the Assembly convenes only once a year during three days. In these sessions, it adopts about 60 resolutions on all subjects of concern to the Organization of American States. Naturally, extensive discussions on individual issues such as the Court's Annual Report cannot take place. For this reason, the Assembly adopts a resolution prepared by the Committee on Judicial and Political Affairs of the Permanent Council of the Organization and to which the President of the Court has presented the annual report some three months before the Assembly's session. Unlike what is stipulated in Article 57(b) of the Rules and Procedures of the Permanent Council,[66] according to which decisions in committees are adopted by simple majority, decisions on the report in the Committee on Judicial and Political Affairs are, in practice, adopted unanimously, i.e. including the vote of the affected state.[67] Furthermore, none of the organs that are involved with the Court's

---

[66] Rules and Procedures of the Permanent Council, adopted on 1 October 1980, last amendment on 26 June 2003, OEA/Ser.G, CP/doc.1112/80 rev. 4 corr. 1.

[67] IACtHR (Judgment) 11 March 2005, *Caesar* v. *Trinidad and Tobago*, separate opinion of Judge Manuel E. Ventura Robles, para. 26.

report votes or even deliberates on measures for specific cases; they only vote on the entire annual report.[68] It is evident that this constellation makes the adoption of any measure against a state that is not complying with its obligations from Court judgments highly unlikely.

The Court, under the presidency of Judge Cançado Trindade in 2002, in view of the negative effects that the failing political support by the member states in the General Assembly had caused in the early 2000s, had developed a proposal for an amendment of the Convention in order to ensure better supervision of compliance. The proposal centred on the introduction of a permanent political monitoring body, namely a working group within the Committee on Judicial and Political Affairs.[69]

To this end, a new sentence should be added to Article 65 ACHR, stating:

> "La Asamblea General [...] remitirá [los casos donde un Estado no ha cumplido con sus obligaciones] al Consejo Permanente, para estudiar la materia y rendir un informe, para que la Asamblea General delibere al respecto."[70]

The OAS though did not adopt this solution but maintained the way it dealt with the Court's reports as it was.

Given the improbability that the states would decide a modification of the Convention, Judge Ventura Robles made another proposal in his separate opinion to the case of *Caesar* v. *Trinidad and Tobago* in 2005. In his view, immediate improvement could be obtained by establishing a permanent working group within the Committee on Judicial and Political Affairs, to properly discuss the reports on non-execution without amending the Convention, rather than having the states file their observations and propose a resolution that is then passed on to the General Assembly.[71] Again, this proposal did not cause remarkable responses neither among academics nor politicians.

It can be concluded that modifications to the political organs of the Organization of American States as a whole to improve the implementation of Court judgments are very unlikely to succeed. Particularly nowadays, with the Organization being marked by political disruptions, which became manifest in particular through the

---

[68] IACtHR (Judgment) 11 March 2005, *Caesar* v. *Trinidad and Tobago*, separate opinion of Judge Manuel E. Ventura Robles, para. 30.

[69] A.A. Cançado Trindade, "Hacia la consolidación de la capacidad jurídica internacional de los peticionarios en el sistema interamericano de protección de los derechos humanos", in A.A. Cançado Trindade (ed.), *Memoria del seminario "El sistema interamericano de protección de los derechos humanos en el umbral del siglo XXI", vol. 2* (San José, CorteIDH 2003), p. 795.

[70] "The General Assembly [...] shall refer [the cases in which a State has not complied with its obligations] to the Permanent Council, to study the matter and issue a report, in order for the General Assembly shall discuss it." (our translation). A.A. Cançado Trindade, "Informe: Bases para un Proyecto de Protocolo a la Convención Americana sobre Derechos Humanos, para Fortalecer su Mecanismo de Protección", in A.A. Cançado Trindade, *supra* n., p. 369 ff.; a complete recount of the development of these proposals can be found in IACtHR (Judgment) 11 March 2005, *Caesar* v. *Trinidad and Tobago*, separate opinion of Judge Manuel E. Ventura Robles, para. 19.

[71] Ibid., Separate opinion of Judge Manuel E. Ventura Robles, paras. 32ff.

Jan Schneider

establishment of several other regional organisations such as UNASUR or ALBA and the opposition by some states to the Organization,[72] it must be assumed that the General Assembly is not going to adopt politically risky decisions that might widen the already existing gap by pointing out particular states as recalcitrant human rights violators.

This problem, though, may be tackled. The political debility of the General Assembly not only rests in the above mentioned particularities of its decision making, but also in the fact that all member states of the Organization of American States decide on the measures against the recalcitrant state, be they subject to the Court's jurisdiction themselves or not.[73] Even Trinidad and Tobago maintains its voting right on issues concerning the Court after its denunciation of the Convention. But also states like the United States of America who, despite having signed the Convention, have never ratified it, may judge the human rights record of other American States who have taken a much more serious commitment. Therefore, political monitoring of compliance would be more credible and decisions could be adopted more easily if it were in the hands of a body conformed only by those states that are subject to the jurisdiction of the Court. Thus, no state would be in the situation where its acts are judged by others who are not even subject to the same strict regime of international responsibility for human rights violations, but by a group of like-minded states. Under these circumstances, a process of peer review as it was originally thought for the European Council of Ministers could be applied. Such a body should hold regular meetings several times a year to discuss cases of non-compliance and have a permanent secretariat to constantly monitor cases and procure assessment to the states. Court and Commission would have to maintain this body informed about situations under their investigation, so that it can identify systemic problems and take corresponding action.

Such a body could be imagined in several forms. It could either be conceived as an independent body under the Convention, consisting for example of the ambassadors to Costa Rica, who already maintain relations between the states and the Court. Its treaty base could be a protocol to the Convention. Ideally, signature would be made obligatory for all states parties having recognized the Court's jurisdiction. States that only recognize the Court's jurisdiction on a case-to-case basis according to Article 62(2) ACHR should be admitted to sessions on cases that concern them.[74]

To the same effect there could also be working groups of the states subject to the Court's jurisdiction within the organs of the Organization of American States. The concept of fragmentation is not unknown to the Convention. Thus, the seat of the

---

72   Cf. OAS, *supra* n. 56.

73   From the 35 member states of the OAS, 25 ratified the ACHR; Trinidad and Tobago denounced it. From these, 21 recognized the jurisdiction of the IACtHR.

74   An amendment to the ACHR to introduce a permanent observation mechanism had already been proposed in 2007 by Uruguay: cf. Corasantini, "Implementación de las sentencias y resoluciones de la Corte Interamericana de Derechos Humanos: un debate necesario", 49 *Revista IIDH* (2009), p. 16.

Implementation of Judgments

Court is to be determined within the General Assembly only by the States Parties to the Convention according to Article 58(1) ACHR. Similarly, permanent working groups of the states subject to the Court's jurisdiction could be established in all organs currently concerned with the Court's annual reports. These working groups would, similar to Cançado Trindade's and Ventura Roble's proposals, constantly monitor compliance by the states. This solution however has the disadvantage of keeping supervision within the organs of the Organization of American States in Washington, D.C., which have already shown to be unwilling to modify their procedures. At least the establishment of these working groups would require the vote of all member states to the Organization. Nevertheless, it would not require the adoption of a protocol, thus making a prolonged time of political discussions on the inter-state level unnecessary.

In whichever way such a new body would be implemented, the old problem remains: As long as there is no real political will of the governments to take their responsibilities towards the inhabitants of the Americas seriously, no improvement whatsoever will be reached. Hence the ball remains in the states' court.

[18]

THE INTER-AMERICAN HUMAN RIGHTS SYSTEM FIFTY YEARS LATER: TIME FOR CHANGES

ARIEL DULITZKY[*]

This article analyzes the latest reforms of rules and regulations of the Inter-American Commission on Human Rights (IACHR) and the Inter-American Court of Human Rights and the overall functioning of the Inter-American human rights system. Particularly the article focuses on the strengths and weaknesses of the *judicialization* of the Inter-American *amparo*. The paper identifies the measures necessary to allow the Inter-American system to play a more prominent role in the promotion and protection of human rights. Specific measures include mainstreaming the work of the OAS around human rights issues, including in the Inter-American Democratic Charter a stronger link between democracy and the protection of human rights, and balancing the work on individual complaints with other tools available to the IACHR. It proposes a fundamental change in the IACHR's profile through the modification of its participation in the individual petition system. The Commission should only act as an organ of admissibility and facilitator of friendly solutions, and the Court as a tribunal that carries out findings of fact and makes legal determinations on the merits of complaints. The IACHR needs to concentrate more heavily on political and promotional activities that complement its limited participation in the processing of individual cases.

Cet article examine les dernières réformes des lois et réglementations de la Commission Interaméricaine des Droits de l'Homme (CIDH) et de la Cour interaméricaine des droits de l'homme, ainsi que le fonctionnement général du système des droits de l'homme interaméricain. Plus particulièrement, cet article s'intéresse aux atouts et aux inconvénients de la « judiciarisation » de l'amparo interaméricain. Ce document introduit les mesures nécessaires afin de promouvoir le rôle décisif du système interaméricain en matière de protection des droits de l'homme. Parmi ces mesures, certaines consistent à recentrer le travail de l'OEA autour de questions de droits de l'homme, à instaurer dans la Charte interaméricaine des droits de l'homme un lien plus substantiel entre la démocratie et la protection des droits de l'homme, et à compenser le travail portant sur les plaintes individuelles par d'autres outils dont dispose la CIDH. Ces propositions visent à modifier fondamentalement le mode de participation de la CIDH au système de pétition individuel. La Commission ne devrait agir qu'en tant qu'organe de recevabilité et dans le but de faciliter les solutions à l'amiable, tandis que la Cour ne devrait agir qu'en tant que tribunal, poursuivant la découverte de faits nouveaux et jugeant du mérite légal des plaintes. La CIDH doit se concentrer de manière plus appuyée sur les activités politiques et promotionnelles qui contrebalancent sa participation restreinte au traitement de dossiers individuels.

---

[*] Clinical Professor of Law and Director, Human Rights Clinic and Director, Latin America Initiative, Austin, TX, USA. Abogado (JD) Facultad de Derecho de la Universidad de Buenos Aires; LLM, Harvard Law School. I would like to thank Robert Goldman, Pedro Nikken, José Zalaquett, Víctor Abramovich, Paolo Carroza, Elizabeth Abi-Mershed, Christina Cerna, Daniel Brinks, Eduardo Bertoni, Carmen Herrera, Carolina de Campos Melo, Mariela Puga, Lucie Lamarche, Bernard Duhaime, Carlos Quesada, Diego Camaño, and Andrés Ramírez; the participants of the 34th Annual Wolfgang Friedmann Conference, "Reform and Challenges Confronting Regional Human Rights Regimes," at the Columbia University School of Law on April 8, 2008 in New York, NY, USA; the participants of the Seminar "Commemoration of the Sixtieth Anniversary of the American Declaration of the Rights and Duties of Man," on May 28, 2008, in Bogotá, Colombia; and the participants of a dialogue that took place at the Center for Legal and Social Studies on July 8, 2008, in Buenos Aires for their commentary, reflections, and critiques of the original ideas and preliminary versions of this article. Special recognition to Emily Spangenberg and Celina van Dembroucke for their assistance with research for part of this article. I would like to give special thanks to Denise Gilman, permanent source of inspiration, for many of the ideas developed here. Of course, all errors are my exclusive responsibility. Different and partial versions of this article, written prior to the reforms of 2009, have been published in Spanish under the following titles: Ariel Dulitzky, "50 Años del Sistema Interamericano de Derechos Humanos: Una Propuesta Reflexión sobre Cambios Estratégicos Necesarios" in Gonzalo Aguilar Cavallo, ed., *60 Años Después: Enseñanzas Pasadas y Desafíos Futuros* (Santiago: Libротecnia, 2007) 491; Ariel Dulitzky, "La OEA y los Derechos Humanos: nuevos perfiles para el Sistema Interamericano" (2008) 4 Diálogo Político 69; Ariel Dulitzky, "Reflexiones sobre la judicialización interamericana y propuesta de nuevos perfiles para el amparo interamericano," in Samuel B. Abad Yuparqui & Pablo Pérez Tremps, eds., *La Reforma del Proceso de Amparo: La Experiencia Comparada* (Lima: Palestra, 2009) 327.

In 2009, the Inter-American Commission on Human Rights (Commission or IACHR) and the Inter-American Court of Human Rights (Court) substantially reformed their rules and regulations, making important changes to the procedures for the processing of petitions and contentious cases.[1] These modifications were made in the year of the 50th anniversary of the establishment of the IACHR, the 40th anniversary of the adoption of the *American Convention on Human Rights*,[2] and the 30th anniversary of the installation of the Court. The year 2008 marked the 60th anniversary of the creation of the Organization of American States (OAS) and the adoption of the *American Declaration of the Rights and Duties of Man*,[3] as well as the 30th anniversary of the *Convention* coming into effect. These procedural reforms and important historical landmarks offer opportunities for reflection on goals that have been met and current challenges facing the Inter-American system. In other words, it is an ideal time to analyze the current situation of the Inter-American human rights system and to think about how to prepare for the next fifty years.[4]

The OAS has developed a complex mechanism designed to protect and promote human rights over the past fifty years. The Inter-American human rights system has brought attention to the OAS, making it well-known throughout the Americas and worldwide.[5] Throughout the dark times of military dictatorship and

---

[1]   See *Rules of Procedures of the Inter-American Court of Human Rights*, 28 November 2009, LXXXII Ordinary Sess. in Exposición de motivos de la Reforma Reglamentaria, online: Court <http://www.corteidh.or.cr/regla_esp.pdf> and Inter-American Commission on Human Rights, Press Release, No. 84/09, "CIDH Publishes Its New Rules of Procedure" (9 December 2009), online: IACHR <http://www.cidh.oas.org/Comunicados/English/2009/84-09eng.htm>.

[2]   *American Convention on Human Rights*, 22 November 1969, O.A.S.T.S. No. 36 (entered into force 27 August 1978) [*Convention*].

[3]   OAS, General Assembly, 3rd Sess., *American Declaration of the Rights and Duties of Man*, OR OEA/AG/RES.1591 (XXVIII-O/98) (1998) [*Declaration*].

[4]   In reality, when speaking of the Inter-American human rights system, one should think more broadly than the Commission and Court. States take primary responsibility for and are the intended recipients of the decisions handed down by the Commission and Court. But States should be considered multifaceted entities, not monolithic, with multiple actors with distinct agendas, responsibilities, and perspectives, from foreign relations ministers to judicial and legislative powers, offices of the Ombudsman, public prosecutors and defenders, as well as the multiple authorities at the national, provincial, and municipal levels, that have different responsibilities in the area of human rights. Additionally, the OAS and its organs, particularly the General Assembly, the Permanent Council, and the Committee on Political and Juridical Affairs, play very important roles within the system, such as electing members of the Commission and Court, the discussion of these organs' annual reports, the approval of their budgets, and the adoption of new human rights instruments. The Secretary General of the OAS is also very important within the system, as he or she can influence the agenda of the regional organization, has the final word in the naming of Commission officials, and can interact politically with States as well as the human rights organs of the system. Civil society organizations–broadly conceived, not only those which specialize in human rights–are a fundamental part of the interrelations of the Inter-American system, as they are the principle users and present complaints, provide information to the human rights organs and to society, advise victims, and train local actors. Finally, and perhaps most importantly, is civil society, particularly abuse victims who come to the system looking for the justice that they have not been able to find in their home countries. Victims have influenced the work of the Commission and of the Court, including pro-victim normative interpretations. The protection of their rights is the ultimate goal of the Inter-American system.

[5]   As the Dominican Republic's ex-Ambassador to the OAS said, "*En casi cada ocasión en que un representante ante la OEA hace mención del sistema interamericano de derechos humanos, utilice adjetivos descriptivos superlativos, tal como 'la joya de la corona de nuestra Organización'.* (Almost

The Inter-American Human Rights System Fifty Years Later 129

civil wars of the past, and during the current era of persistent structural human rights violations within democratic systems, the Commission and Court have been and continue to act as the conscience of the hemisphere, supporting States–when the conditions allow–and their inhabitants through the effective protection of human rights. The strengths of the Inter-American system, which lie in the resolution of individual cases, on-site visits, thematic and country reports, the Court's judgments, and the adoption of precautionary or provisional measures, play a fundamental role in denouncing and providing an early warning of situations that could compromise the consolidation of democracy and rule of law, while at the same time protecting individual rights when they are not guaranteed at the domestic level. The Commission and Court have saved (and continue to save) lives, permitted the opening of democratic spaces in the past and contributed to the ongoing consolidation of democracy, combated impunity and helped establish the truth, and provided justice and reparations to victims of human rights violations.

All of these achievements have been attained when the system, particularly the IACHR, has strategically combined different available tools. Of all the available human rights mechanisms, the processing of individual cases – which various authors have dubbed the Inter-American *amparo*[6] – has become the Commission's tool *par excellence*. The Inter-American *amparo* consists of the right to petition to appear before the Commission to complain about human rights violations carried out by the action, omission, or tolerance of State agents or entities of any of the OAS member States. Under certain circumstances, the Inter-American *amparo* can be decided through a judicial decision handed down by the Court.

One characteristic that distinguishes the Inter-American system from other human rights systems has been its capacity to adapt to hemispheric conditions within the last fifty years to respond the demands of specific historical moments.[7] The most successful tools of the system, namely the individual complaints mechanism, on-site visits, preparation and publication of reports, adoption of precautionary and provisional measures, friendly solutions, thematic reports, and jurisprudence on reparations, arose or were strengthened or redefined in specific historical contexts in

---

every time an OAS representative mentions the Inter-American human rights system, he or she uses superlative descriptive adjectives, such as ' the crown jewel of our Organization. '") [translated by author]. See Roberto Álvarez Gil, "Desafíos y retos en el uso del sistema interamericano" (2007) 46 Revista Instituto Interamericano de Derechos Humanos 19 at 21.

6 See generally Carlos Ayala Corao, *Del amparo constitucional al amparo interamericano como institutos para la protección de los derechos humanos* (San Jose, Costa Rica: Editorial Jurídica Venezolana, 1998); Eduardo Ferrer Mac-Gregor, "Breves notas sobre el amparo Iberoamericano" (2006) 15 Díkaion: revista de actualidad jurídica 173; Sergio García Ramírez, "La protección de derechos y libertades en el sistema jurisdiccional interamericano. El amparo interamericano" in Hector Fix-Zamudio & Eduardo Ferrer Mac-Gregor, eds., *El Derecho de amparo en el mundo* (Mexico City: Konrad-Adenauer-Stiftung, 2006), 985; Nestor Sagüés, "Tomo 3: Acción de Amparo" in *Derecho procesal constitucional: 5° Edición actualizada y ampliada* (Buenos Aires, Editorial Astrea, 2007); Humberto Nogueira Alcalá, "El Recurso de Protección en el Contexto del Amparo de los Derechos Fundamentales Latinoamericano e Interamericano" (2007) 13 no. 1 Revista Ius et Praxis 75.

7 For a historical evolution of the system and the different mechanisms it uses, see Robert K. Goldman, "History and Action: The Inter-American Human Rights System and the Role of the Inter-American Commission on Human Rights" (2009) 31 no. 4 Hum. Rts. Q. 856.

130   2011 *Quebec Journal of International Law* (Special Edition)

response to the demands of the times. For this reason, it is not possible to think about the Inter-American system either outside the political, economic, and social context in which it operates or without taking into account the current human rights situation in the Americas.

This article analyzes the latest reforms of rules and regulations and commemorates the recent anniversaries of the OAS through a reflection on the overall functioning of the Inter-American human rights system, particularly the strengths and weaknesses of the judicialization of the Inter-American *amparo*. I identify the measures necessary to allow the Inter-American system to play a more prominent role in the promotion and protection of human rights in the region. I seek to reinforce mechanisms that work efficiently and that enjoy broad support; strengthen the successful areas of the work of the Commission and the Court; identify those situations or groups that are not adequately attended to; and, finally, to eliminate, modify, or improve those aspects that do not effectively advance the goal of protecting human rights.

The objective of this article is not to identify substantive tasks or jurisprudential guidelines to strengthen democracy in the region.[8] This is a more limited proposal, since it concentrates on certain issues that would fundamentally change the IACHR's profile through the modification of its participation in the individual petition system. I propose that the Commission only act as an organ of admissibility that negotiates friendly solutions, and that the Court act as a tribunal that carries out findings of fact and makes juridical decisions on the merits of complaints. I also propose that the IACHR concentrate more heavily on political and promotional activities that complement its limited participation in the processing of individual cases. This article only outlines crucial changes in other aspects of the system, so it should be understood as the first step in a much more ambitious project–a systematic and structural analysis of the treatment of human rights within the OAS.

I.   Brief critical analysis of certain aspects of the Inter-American *amparo*

Considering the framework and context in which it operates, which at first glance may seem discouraging, the Inter-American *amparo*, remarkably,

> has led to developments, including, among other things, the establishment of internal laws in the countries of the hemisphere based on international human rights standards in such areas as forced disappearance, the death penalty, and terrorism; the repeal of amnesty laws because of their incompatibility with the *Convention*; the repeal of the so-called "desacato laws" because of their incompatibility with freedom of expression; the adoption of laws to protect

---

[8]   For critiques on certain aspects of the Inter-American system case law, see Ariel Dulitzky, "El Principio de Igualdad y no Discriminación. Claroscuros de la Jurisprudencia Interamericana" (2007) 3 Anuario de Derechos Humanos 15, and Ariel Dulitzky, "Cuando los Afrodescendientes se transformaron en 'Pueblos Tribales': El Sistema Interamericano de Derechos Humanos y las Comunidades Rurales Negras" (2010) 41 El Otro Derecho 13.

women who are victims of domestic violence; the implementation of public policy to promote racial equality; the adoption of legislative and administrative measures for creating effective mechanisms for the delimitation, demarcation, and titling of properties of indigenous communities; the progressive adjustment of conditions in prison systems to international standards for the protection of human rights; and the development of judicial mechanisms for combating impunity for human rights violations.[9]

The processing of individual complaints has many other benefits that go beyond specific cases and produce a ripple effect in both the domestic sphere as well as in the international system. As indicated by a former President of the Commission:

> The processing of cases has very valuable effects. In the first place, it allows for justice in situations in which there has been no domestic resolution of a dispute. Second, the system enriches the regional and national juridical tradition through its interpretation of human rights norms, creating a shared hemispheric vision of the basis of freely-ratified treaties. [...] [C]ases [...]offer solid, well-founded interpretations on [different] rights [...] From a procedural point of view, the group cases [...] offer valuable insight on different admissibility criteria [...] [T]he constant and growing judicial complexity on the cases that the Commission resolves [...] brings simultaneously growing demands that require expansive judicial knowledge, as much on the content of the rights themselves as on compliance with procedures already established within the system. The judicial processing of these cases contributes to the "depolitization" of human rights, strengthening the system and its legitimacy.[10]

In this context, it is possible to offer a critical view of the Inter-American system because its strengths and success outweigh fears that such criticism may weaken or discredit the system.

A.   An Unequal Protection System

There are currently three different models that the *amparo* can follow, depending on the rights it can protect and on the body and type of protection–judicial or quasi-judicial–that it offers. First, there is the "judicial" *amparo*, which applies to States that have ratified the *Convention*[11] and recognized the competence of the Court. This *amparo* protects the rights recognized by the *Convention* through a judicial mechanism with final decisions adopted by the Court after the case passes through the

---

[9]   According to the Commission's own description. See OAS, Inter-American Commission on Human Rights, *Annual Report of the Inter-American Commission on Human Rights: 2007*, OR OEA/Ser.L/V/II.130/Doc. 22, rev. 1 (2007) at c.1, para. 7 [*IACHR 2007 Annual Report*].

[10]   OAS, Committee on Juridical and Political Affairs, *Dean Claudio Grossman, President of the Inter-American Commission on Human Rights, Presenting the 2000 Annual Report of the IACHR to the Committee on Juridical and Political Affairs of the OAS Permanent Council*, OEA/Ser.G/CP/CAJP-1798/01 (2001).

[11]   Argentina, Barbados, Bolivia, Brazil, Colombia, Costa Rica, Chile, the Dominican Republic, Ecuador, El Salvador, Guatemala, Haiti, Honduras, Mexico, Nicaragua, Panama, Paraguay, Peru, Suriname, Uruguay and Venezuela. Trinidad and Tobago, despite having ratified the Convention and accepting the jurisdiction of the Court, denounced the Convention in 1999.

132   2011 *Quebec Journal of International Law* (Special Edition)

IACHR. The "quasi-judicial" *amparo* has two facets: the conventional one applicable to those States which have ratified the *Convention* but do not recognize the jurisdiction of the Court.[12] This "conventional quasi-judicial" version of the *amparo* also protects the rights guaranteed in the *Convention*, but only through decisions handed down by the Commission. The "declarative quasi-judicial" *amparo* protects the rights included in the *Declaration* through the actions of the IACHR. It applies to member States of the OAS that have not yet ratified the *Convention*.[13]

This is clearly a situation of unequal protection in the Americas, in a substantive as well as procedural sense, which is neither ideal nor satisfactory for the protection of human rights.[14] The following graph demonstrates the disadvantage the OAS faces in relation to other regional human rights systems:

---

[12] Dominica, Grenada, and Jamaica.

[13] Antigua and Barbuda, the Bahamas, Belize, Canada, Cuba, Guyana, St. Lucia, St. Kitts and Nevis, St. Vincent and the Grenadines, Trinidad and Tobago, and the United States. The Commission has power over these States, by virtue of being a principal organ of the OAS and for the attributes given to it through Article 20 of its Statute; OAS, General Assembly, 9th Sess., *Statute of the Inter-American Commission on Human Rights*, OR OEA/Ser. P/IIX.0.2 (1979) [*Statute of the Commision*]. See *Interpretation of the American Declaration of Rights and Duties of Man Within the Framework of Article 64 of the American Convention on Human Rights* (1989), Advisory Opinion OC-10/89, Inter-Am. Ct. H.R. (Ser. A) No. 10, at paras. 35-45; *James Terry Roach and Jay Pinkerton v. United States of America* (1987), Inter-Am. Comm. H.R. No.3/87, at paras. 46-49, *Annual Report of the Inter-American Commission on Human Rights: 1986-87*, OR OEA/Ser.L/V/II.71/doc. 9, rev. 1; *Rafael Ferrer-Mazorra and Others v United States of America* (2001), Inter-Am. Comm. H.R. No.51/01, *Annual Report of the Inter-American Commission on Human Rights: 2000*, OR OEA/Ser./L/V/II.111/doc.20, rev.

[14] Additionally, it should be noted that the Commission and Court have jurisdiction to receive and process an *amparo* in relation to petitions that reference other international human rights treaties, see e.g. *Inter-American Convention on the Prevention, Punishment, and Eradication of Violence Against Women "Convention of Belém do Pará"*, 9 June 1994, O.A.S.T.S. 1994 A-61 (entered into force 5 March 1995), art. 12 [*Convention of Belém do Pará*]; *Inter-American Convention on Forced Disappearance of Persons*, 9 June 1994, O.A.S.T.S. 1994 A-60 (entered into force 28 March 1996), art. 13 [*Convention on Forced Disappearances*]; *Inter-American Convention to Prevent and Punish Torture*, 12 September 1985, O.A.S.T.S. 1985 No. 67 A-51 (entered into force 28 February 1987), arts. 8, 16; *Additional Protocol to the American Convention on Human Rights in the Area of Economic, Social, and Cultural Rights "Protocol of San Salvador"*, 17 November 1988, O.A.S.T.S. 1988 No. 69 A-52 (entered into force 16 November 1999), arts. 19, s. 6.

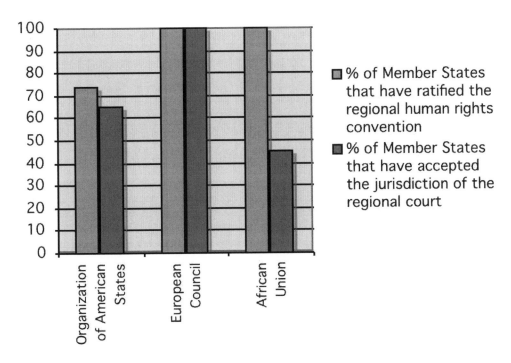

□ % of Member States that have ratified the regional human rights convention

■ % of Member States that have accepted the jurisdiction of the regional court

Although in this system all OAS member States fell under the Commission's jurisdiction, the type of protection and supervisory mechanisms vary according to category of member State. Some individuals in the Americas benefit from the more specific legally-binding provisions of the *Convention*, while others can only depend on the *Declaration*. In a similar vein, some individual's rights are guaranteed through an Inter-American mechanism which ends with a contentious judicial procedure before the Inter-American Court, while others can only seek reparation through a more limited quasi-judicial *amparo* before the Commission.

B.   An Underfinanced System

One would hope that the OAS would be able to finance its activities adequately, particularly in the realm of human rights protection. In reality, however, the total budget of the Commission and the Court that is meant to finance all of these organs' activities, including the processing of the *amparo*, is less than 10 % of the total budget of the OAS. This has forced the Commission and the Court to rely on voluntary financial contributions from some member States and from various countries outside the region to finance their activities. For example, the Commission depends on the European Union to be able to attend its backlog of thousands of petitions that have been delayed due to the fact that the OAS cannot provide sufficient personnel to process them. The Court depends on external support to be able to hold hearings outside of its headquarters, as a way of bringing the system closer to societies in the region.[15]

The following chart compares the Inter-American system to other international tribunals and commissions:

International Court/Commission	Budget (US $)
Inter-American Commission on Human Rights	$3,845,100.00
Inter-American Court of Human Rights	$1,656,300.00
International Court of Justice[16]	$36,785,000.00
International Criminal Court	$120,015,000.00
European Court of Human Rights[17]	$72,171,000.00
Central American Court of Justice	$1,560,000.00[18]
Andean Tribunal of Justice	$1,137,600.00
African Commission on Human and Peoples Rights[19]	$1,199,557.80 (fiscal year 2007)

C.   Increase in Complaints Received and Diminishing Capacity to Resolve Cases

In the last decade or so there has been an exponential increase in the number of petitions received by the Commission. This increase and the stagnation and reduction of the budget in real terms have caused a serious delay in the processing of the individual complaints. Between 1997 and 2002, the Commission received 4,048 complaints, and in the period 2003-2008, it received 7,803—an increase of 92.76 %. Nevertheless, the IACHR initiated the processing of 718 petitions in the period 1997-2002 and 816 between the years 2003-2008, an increase of only 14.44 %.[20] This

---

[15]   This could be a topic for further investigation, on which States, foundations, inter-governmental agencies or regional organizations make monetary contributions to the Commission and Court, and which activities these contributions are intended to finance. Undoubtedly, this has a significant impact on the Commission and Court's capacities to effectively set priorities and work agendas, and it could generate profound imbalances in the dispersion of resources between each organ's respective areas of work.

[16]   Budget for the two-year period 2006/2007.

[17]   Budget for fiscal year 2008.

[18]   "Mercosur y sistema de solución de controversias. El presupuesto más reducido de la región" (10 July 2008), online: Mercosurabc <http://www.mercosurabc.com.ar/nota.asp?IdNota=1601&IdSeccion=14>.

[19]   Budget increased significantly for 2008 fiscal year to $6,003,856.86 to decrease reliance on external funds and contributions by States Parties.

[20]   OAS, Inter-American Commission on Human Rights, *Annual Report of the Inter-American Commission on Human Rights: 2008*, OR OEA/Ser.L/V/II.134/Doc. 5, rev. 1 (2008) at c. III [*2008 Annual Report*]. This increase also shows a greater emphasis on the part of those who come before the system to use the individual petitions mechanism over other available tools. Generally this increase is explained in light of the fact that democratic governments allow the possibility of presenting a complaint without fear of retaliation by authoritarian governments. However, it should be made clear that in moments of military dictatorship or authoritarian governments, the Commission received many complaints. During its on-site visit to Argentina in 1979, during a time of military dictatorship, the IACHR received 4,153 complaints. In November of 1998, when visiting Peru under the authoritarian

shows that either the delay in the preliminary analysis of petitions has increased exponentially in the last five years, or that the Commission has heightened the level of *in limine* rejection of complaints filed, making accessibility to the system more difficult. If the latter explanation is correct, it could be viewed as an indication of the "judicialization" of the system for its greater strictness in the application of requirements for processing cases. Given the lack of public statistical and qualitative information,[21] I can only speculate that the most plausible explanation is a combination of the two.

In the same period, the Commission's capacity to adopt final decisions on the merits of petitions has fallen. The three ways in which the processing of a petition before the IACHR ends with some decision on the merits are as follows:[22] through reports that approve friendly settlements,[23] the publication of final reports on the merits of the complaint,[24] or the filing remission of the case to the Court for a final decision.[25] If the number of these three types of decisions is added up, the number of final decisions on petitions adopted by the Commission decreased 12.71 % between the years 2002-2008 in relation to the period 1997-2002, falling from 173 decisions to 151.[26]

D.   A Slow System

The duration of processing an individual petition by the Commission is troubling, especially if one presumes that the processing of the *amparo*, even when done at the international level, should be simple and speedy.

For example, using data from the 747 reports that have been published by the IACHR between 1996 and 2007, there are two main phases or stages in the Commission's procedure: admissibility and merits. The admissibility phase had an average duration of 3.10 years, with a median of 2.62. The fastest decision on admissibility was adopted in 0.47 years, and the longest was handed down in 15.12 years. The duration until the Commission's publication of final decisions on the merits of the petition[27] was an average of 6.16 years, a median of 5.95. The case

---

regime of Alberto Fujimori, the Commission received approximately 600 complaints. This demonstrates the importance, as outlined in this text, of the presence of the Commission in the countries of the region, as it facilitates victims' access to the Inter-American system.

[21]   For instance, the Commission does not provide information on the reasons for not processing petitions.

[22]   Excluding the possibilities for withdrawal or archiving. If one takes into account the amount of cases decided by the IACHR, the data are equally revealing. In the period 1997/2002, 216 cases were archived, as were 93 in the last six-year period, without a single case being archived in the year 2008.

[23]   *Convention, supra* note 2, art. 49.

[24]   *Ibid.*, art. 51.

[25]   *Ibid.*, arts. 51, 61.

[26]   Data taken from Chapter III of the *2008 Annual Report, supra* note 20. Distribution is as follows: 1997/20022003/2008Friendly Settlements3041Final Reports Published11636Cases Remitted to the Court2774Total173151

[27]   Duration from admissibility to final decision was computed if there were two separate decisions or from the processing of the petition until the final decision if the admissibility and the final decision were presented in a single report.

whose decision was reached most quickly was processed in 0.48 years, and the longest duration was 14.46 years. The decisions on friendly settlements do not perform better. Just to give one example of an extreme situation of delays, the IACHR approved a friendly solution report after over 20 years of processing.[28]

	Duration for admissibility (years)	**Duration for inadmissibility (years)**	**Duration for Friendly Settlement (years)**	**Duration for Substantive Decision (years)**
Average	3.10	4.03	5.79	6.16
Median	2.62	10.22	5.27	5.95
Max	15.12[29]	12.34[30]	20.28[31]	14.46[32]
Min	0.47[33]	0.30[34]	0.97[35]	0.48[36]
Number of decisions	420	111	68	148

In contrast, the duration of processing before the Inter-American Court has diminished considerably in the last few years. This is remarkable, given that the Court reduced its timeframe at the same time that the number of cases filed with the tribunal has multiplied. According to official information, under the rules of 1980, the duration of processing of claims was 39 months; under the rules of 1991, 38 months; under the rules of 1996, 40.5 months; and under the current rules of 2000, it has been 19 months.[37]

---

[28]   *Jorge Alberto Rosal Paz v. Guatemala* (2004), Inter-Am. Comm. H.R. No. 29/04, at 710, *Annual Report of the Inter-American Commission on Human Rights: 2004*, OEA/Ser.L/V/II.122/doc.5, rev. 1 [*Jorge Alberto v. Guatemala*].

[29]   *El Mozote Massacre v. El Salvador* (2006), Inter-Am. Comm. H.R. No. 24/06, *Annual Report of the Inter-American Commission on Human Rights: 2006*, OEA/Ser.L/V/II.124/doc.5.

[30]   *Pedro Velázquez Ibarra v. Argentina* (2007), Inter-Am. Comm. H.R. No. 40/06, *Annual Report of the Inter-American Commission on Human Rights: 2007*, OEA/Ser.L/V/II.127/doc.4, rev. 1.

[31]   *Jorge Alberto v. Guatemala, supra* note 28 at 710.

[32]   *Parque São Lucas v. Brasil* (2003), Inter-Am. Comm. H.R No. 40/03, at 677, *Annual Report of the Inter-American Commission on Human Rights: 2003*, OEA/Ser./L/V/II.114/doc.70, rev. 2 .

[33]   *Yvonne Neptune v. Haiti* (2005), Inter-Am. Comm. H.R No. 64/05, *Annual Report of the Inter-American Commission on Human Rights: 2005*, OEA/Ser.L/V/II.124/doc.5.

[34]   *Christián Scheib Campos v. Chile* (2001), Inter-Am. Comm. H.R. No. 69/01, at 379, *Annual Report of the Inter-American Commission on Human Rights: 2001*, OEA/Ser./L/V/II.114/doc.5, rev. (2001).

[35]   *Víctor Hugo Arce Chávez v. Bolivia* (2007), Inter-Am. Comm. H.R. No. 70/07, *Annual Report of the Inter-American Commission on Human Rights: 2007,*, OEA/Ser.L/V/II.130/doc.22, rev. 1.

[36]   *Alejandra Marcela Matus Acuña et al. v. Chile* (2005), Inter-Am. Comm. H.R. No. 90/05, *Annual Report of the Inter-American Commission on Human Rights: 2005*, OEA/Ser.L/V/II.124/doc.5.

[37]   *2008 Annual Report, supra* note 20 at 67.

E.   A System that Duplicates Processes

There are two areas in which the Inter-American system's processing of individual petitions seems to be duplicative. The first is related to questions of admissibility, which the Commission decides and which could be and sometimes is re-examined by the Court as preliminary exceptions. Even when the *Convention* clearly indicates that the Commission has the power to declare a petition admissible or inadmissible,[38] the Court uses Article 62, Section 3, which indicates that it has jurisdiction over "all cases concerning the interpretation and application of the provisions of [the] *Convention* that are submitted to it", as the basis for reviewing everything that has been decided by the Commission, including its determination on admissibility.[39] If, for example, after two or three years of processing, the Commission determines that a case is admissible, years later the Court can go back and deliberate the exact same issue with the exact same arguments and facts if the State requests that it be done. Worse, this possibility of appealing the determinations on admissibility at the request of States does not exist for individuals whose petitions were declared inadmissible by the Commission, because they cannot appear before the Court to challenge the inadmissibility decision.

A dysfunctional duplication of efforts is the presentation of evidence and finding of facts. The IACHR should receive, debate, and analyze all questions relating to the determination of fact as well as the examination of documents and testimony. Then, once the case is in front of the Court, all the evidence should be produced anew and reevaluated by the Tribunal. Article 57, paragraph 1 of the new *Rules* of the Court (*New Rules*), which literally replicates Article 44, paragraph b of the previous *Rules*,[40] stipulates that "[i]tems of evidence tendered before the Commission will be incorporated into the case file as long as they have been received in adversarial proceedings, unless the Court considers it indispensable to duplicate them."[41] The Court has never explicitly invoked this stipulation since it was included in the rules of 2001 nine years ago. The situation is so dysfunctional that the Court has made full factual determinations even when the State has accepted the version of the facts presented by the Commission.[42]

---

[38]   See *Convention*, supra note 2, arts. 46, s. 1 ("Admission by the Commission of a petition or communication [...] shall be subject to the following requirements"), 47 ("The Commission shall consider inadmissible any petition or communication"), 48, s. 1, para. a ("When the Commission receives a petition or communication [...] it shall proceed as follows: a. If it considers the petition or communication admissible").

[39]   See generally *Constantine and others Case (Trinidad and Tobago)* (2001), Inter-Am. Ct. H.R. (Ser. C) No.82, at para. 71, *Annual Report of the Inter-American Court of Human Rights: 2001*, OEA/Ser.L/V/III.54/doc.4 (2000) 29.

[40]   *Rules of Procedures of the Inter-American Court of Human Rights*, 4 December 2003, LXI Ordinary Sess.

[41]   *Rules of Procedures of the Inter-American Court of Human Rights*, 28 November 2009, LXXXII Ordinary Sess., art. 57, at para. b [*New Rules* or *Rules*].

[42]   For example, in the cases *Goiburu* and *Vargas Areco v. Paraguay* the government accepted the facts presented by the Commission. The Court established that the dispute over these facts had ended. However, it required the parties to produce testimonial, witness, and documentary evidence about the undisputed facts that had already been determined by the Commission and recognized by the State. *Vargas Areco v. Paraguay (2006)*, Inter-Am Ct. H.R. (Ser.C) No. 155, *Annual Report of the Inter-American Court of Human Rights: 2006*, at 14 online: Inter-Am. Ct. H.R.

138   2011 *Quebec Journal of International Law* (Special Edition)

This duplication of procedures on the part of the Court generates unnecessary financial, human, and time expenditures in a system that already lacks resources for all three. This problem, which has been reproduced since the Court processed its first contentious case over 20 years ago, has been aggravated since 2001, given the increase of cases that go before the Court, the autonomous representations of the victims, and the greater emphasis that has been placed by the Court on the factual determinations. With the *New Rules*, which substantially limit the Commission's participation, it remains to be seen if the tribunal can strike a balance between the non-repetition of production of evidence and establishing a clear judicial record.

F.   A System with a Low Level of Compliance with its Decisions

Once the Commission renders a decision on petitions finding human rights violations, it makes recommendations to the State to resolve the situation. Said recommendations may be contained within the agreements reached in friendly settlement procedures or in merits final reports.[43] The level of compliance with these recommendations is far from ideal. Almost 60 % of the IACHR's recommendations contained in merits reports are never carried out. Just under 40 % are partially complied with. In contrast, there has not been a total failure to comply with any agreement reached through friendly settlement. In fact, approximately 85 % of these agreements have had to be partially complied with.[44]

The situation is similar with the Court. The tribunal reports that 81 % of compensatory aspects of its sentences are totally or at least partially complied with.[45] However, the ex-President of the Court has said that only 11.57 % of the cases resolved have met total compliance, allowing the Court to close these cases.[46]

In any case, these data should not be used to judge the effectiveness of the system of petitions or individual cases. The degree of compliance with recommendations or decisions is one element to take into consideration. It is more important to analyze the total impact of the system to advance its objectives of protecting and promoting human rights.[47]

<http://www.corteidh.or.cr/docs/informes/20063.pdf>; *Goiburú and others vs. Paraguay (2006)*, Inter-Am. Ct. H.R. (Ser. C) No. 153, *Annual Report of the Inter-American Court of Human Rights: 2006*, at 30, online: Inter-Am. Ct. H.R. <http://www.corteidh.or.cr/docs/informes/20063.pdf>.

[43]   See *Convention, supra* note 2, arts. 49, 51.

[44]   OAS, Inter-American Commission on Human Rights, *Annual Report of the Inter-American Commission on Human Rights: 2006*, OR OEA/Ser.L/V/II.127/Doc.4, rev. 1 (2007), c. 3.

[45]   OAS, Inter-American Court of Human Rights, *Annual Report of the Inter-American Court of Human Rights: 2008*, at 75, online: Inter-Am. Ct. H.R. <http://www.corteidh.or.cr/docs/informes/eng2008.pdf>.

[46]   See the Summary of Paolo Carroza, *Presentation of the 2007 Annual Report of the Inter-American Commission on Human Rights to the Committee on Juridical and Political Affairs of the Permanent Council of the Organization of American States* (Washington, D. C., 2008), online: Inter-American Commission on Human Rights <http://www.cidh.oas.org/discursos.eng.htm>; and EFE, "Sólo el 12% de las sentencias de la Corte Interamericana han sido cumplidas por los Estados" online: Soitu.es <http://www.soitu.es/soitu/2009/03/30/info/1238450213_900885.html>.

The Inter-American Human Rights System Fifty Years Later   139

G.   Increase in the Number of Cases Filed with the Court

In the last decade the number of cases that the IACHR has remitted to the Court has increased by 190 %, from 20 cases in the period 1997/2001 to 58 between the years 2002-2007. Recently, the IACHR has indicated that "in the past two decades, the Commission has submitted a total of 114 cases to the Court, more than half of these cases (65) submitted from the year 2003 to the present."[48] Obviously, these figures need to be contextualized, since the percentage of complaints that are presented to the Commission and eventually end with a Court sentence has remained at a constant figure of hardly 1 %.[49]

In conclusion, speaking of individual petitions or of the Inter-American *amparo* is really a discussion on a system with at least three different levels of protection, with a tendency toward an increase in the number of petitions, with a slow timeline for processing them, with a low level of compliance with recommendations from the Commission, and with a tendency toward judicialization.

II.   The Regional Human Rights Situation as a Point of Departure

Discussions on the evaluation, reform, and perfecting or strengthening of the Inter-American system cannot take place without considering the historical context and human rights needs and challenges that arise within each time period. Although many times the terms "evaluation," "reform," "perfecting," and "strengthening" are used interchangeably,[50] they have very different meanings and serve different purposes, coming from different positions on the current and future value of the Inter-American human rights system. To speak of evaluation and reform generally implies that the Inter-American system is not carrying out its functions adequately, presupposing either that the system continues operating under the logic of dealing mostly with States under dictatorship or that the system does not adequately guarantee the "rights" of States that appear before the Commission and Court. For this reason, the "evaluation" and "reform" of the system generally are proposed to limit in one way or another the power of the Inter-American Commission. On the contrary, "improving" and "strengthening" are generally used to convey that the system is largely perceived as legitimate and effective, and that it would be possible to adopt measures to make States comply with the decisions of the organs of the Inter-American system, to incorporate Inter-American norms within the domestic arena, to

---

[47]   See Ariel Dulitzky, "The Inter-American Commission On Human Rights" in Katya Salazar & Thomas Antkowiak, eds., *Victims Unsilenced: The Inter-American Human Rights System And Transitional Justice In Latin America* (Washington, DC: Due Process of Law Foundation, 2007) 129.

[48]   *IACHR 2007 Annual Report, supra* note 9 at c.1.

[49]   See Víctor Abramovich, "De las violaciones masivas a los patrones estructurales: nuevos enfoques y clásicas tensiones en el Sistema Interamericano de Derechos Humanos" (2009) 63 Revista Derecho PUC 37 [Abramovich].

[50]   For an example of the indiscriminate use of these terms, see OAS, General Assembly, 7th Sess., *Evaluation and Improvement of Workings of the Inter-American System for the Promotion and Protection of Human Rights*, OR OEA/AG/RES.1488 (XXVII-O/97) (1997).

facilitate broader access and participation for victims, to increase its budget, and, of particular interest to this piece, to further "judicialize" the system. Yet, almost dogmatically, the "improvement" and "strengthening" positions are opposed in any initiative to reform the *Convention*.[51]

One constant throughout the last 20 years has been that State proposals regarding changes to the system have been volatile and contingent on a number of factors. Generally speaking, these proposals reflect individual reactions of State representatives, rather than coherently-articulated State policies. Many have tended to arise in response to an IACHR decision or report, or, more recently, from a Court's sentence.[52] There have been few instances in which State proposals for reform have been based on a detailed analysis of human rights realities and needs.

In fact, discussions on the system tend to limit themselves to proposing reforms of the rules of the Commission or Court, or to procedures on admissibility, merits, precautionary measures, the role of the Commission before the Court, etc. In other words, they tend to focus on the procedures rather than on ways to improve the human rights situation in member States or in the region as a whole. In fact, there have been very few if any profound reflections on whether the individual petition system is the best response to meet the human rights needs of the region.[53] These

---

[51] It is usually argued that, if States are not willing to comply with the Commission's decisions or to provide the Inter-American organs with a sufficient budget, they also will not be willing to pass reforms to the Convention that would strengthen protective mechanisms. For these reasons, they maintain that now is not the proper time to discuss changes to the *Convention*. It is interesting to note that this position has been maintained throughout the last 10 or 15 years. If it is indeed difficult to empirically demonstrate that there is room for progressive reform at the international level, it would at least signal that Latin America and the Caribbean have been at the forefront of promoting the adoption of the most important and progressive norms during the last decade that contain important mechanisms for international prosecution, such as the *Rome Statute of the International Criminal Court*, United Nations Diplomatic Conference of Plenipotentiaries on the Establishment of an International Criminal Court, July 17, 1998, Annex II, U.N.Doc A/CONF. 183/9 (1998) the adoption of the new *Convention on Forced Disappearances*, *supra* note 14 or the *Convention on the Rights of Persons with Disabilities (CRPD)*, adopted December 13, 2006 G.A. Res. 61/106, Annex I, U.N. GAOR, 61st Sess., Supp. No. 49, at 65, U.N. Doc. A/61/49 (2006), entered into force May 3, 2008, U.N. Doc. A/61/611.

[52] Felipe Gonzalez, "La OEA y los derechos humanos después del advenimiento de los gobiernos civiles: expectativas (in)satisfechas" in Felipe Gonzalez, ed., *Cuaderno de Análisis Jurídicos Serie Publicaciones Especiales: Derechos Humanos e Interés Público No. 11* (Santiago: Universidad Diego Portales, 2001) 147.

[53] The most recent example of the "procedural" position is the proposal that a group of States offered as a dialogue on the functioning of the Inter-American human rights system. The document is divided into three parts: A. Proposals to the Commission on modification of the current rules and regulations, which lists the following: 1. Necessity of establishing time limits in the IACHR; 2. Filing of petitions; 3. Obligation to individualize and name the alleged victims to effect admissibility of petitions before the IACHR and of complaints before the Court; 4. Establishment of admissibility and background; 5. Precautionary measures; 6. Thematic hearings; and 7. Hearings on petitions or cases. B. Proposals to the Court on: 1. The need to guarantee procedural equality; 2. Obligation to individualize and name the alleged victims, to effect admissibility of petitions before the IACHR and complaints before the Court; and 3. Reparations; and, finally, C. General proposals that do not suggest normative modification, including: 1. The necessity of contextualizing the IACHR's recommendations; 2. Improving accessibility to the system: Judicial assistance for Victims; 3. Strengthening of the advisory capacity of the Court; 4. Hearings with the participation of experts and witnesses; 5. Processing friendly settlements; 6. Functioning and financing of the system; 7. Principle of subsidiarity in relation to an action aimed at obtaining reparation; and 8. Diffusion of the system. Only in the last section are there

debates on the Inter-American system usually also mention, but do not find a solution to, the triad of problems that face the system: budget shortfalls, lack of compliance with Commission and Court decisions, and a lack of universal ratification of Inter-American human rights treaties.

Periodically, in its Annual Report, the Commission evaluates the human rights situation in the Americas. This situation should be the guide to discuss the Inter-American system. Consistently, the Commission indicates that citizen security, social inequality, access to justice, and democratic consolidation are areas which require ongoing attention for their relation to human rights. It highlights the structural weaknesses of democratic institutions, as well as the gaps and contrasts present within the most socio-economically unequal region. It mentions the fragility of the judiciary in the region; the attacks on its independence and impartiality; and problems of unequal access, slow trials, and impunity in cases of serious violations of fundamental rights and of due process. According to the Commission, marginalization and social exclusion continue to characterize the region. It also mentions that intolerable prison conditions, arbitrary detentions, police brutality, and the inequality that affects women, as well as other groups that have traditionally been discriminated against–such as indigenous peoples, Afro-descendants and homosexuals–has also not changed.[54]

If this diagnostic, along with others that may put more or less emphasis on some of the same factors, is correct,[55] it is worth inquiring what type of Inter-

---

any brief references to the States' specific needs, such as strengthening the governability or fomenting dialogue between the Commission and national entities. See the note of the delegations of Panama, El Salvador, Brazil, Chile, Peru, Colombia, and Mexico, remitting a document for dialogue between the member States and the members of the Inter-American Commission on Human Rights and the Inter-American Court of Human Rights in OAS, Committee on Political and Juridical Affairs, *Results of the Process of Reflection on the Inter-American System for the Promotion and Protection of Human Rights (2008-2009)*, OR OEA/Ser.G/CP/CAJP-2584/08 rev. 8 (2009).

[54] See e.g. OAS, Inter-American Commission of Human Rights, *Annual Report of the Inter-American Commission of Human Rights: 2009*, OR OEA/Ser.L/V/II/Doc.51, corr.1 (2009), c. 1.

[55] For example, in its Annual Report of 2008, Amnesty International indicated that institutional weaknesses continued to perpetuate problems of impunity, denial of equal protection before the law, and police brutality in many Latin American countries, particularly in Central America; *Amnesty International Report 2008: State of the World's Human Rights. Regional Overviews: America*, online: Amnesty International <http://archive.amnesty.org/air2008/eng/regions/americas.html>. Human Rights Watch discussed the situation of 10 Latin American countries in its World Report of 2008 (Argentina, Brazil, Chile, Colombia, Cuba, Guatemala, Haiti, Mexico, Peru, and Venezuela). Some of the patterns common to these ten countries are: deplorable prison conditions, weakening of the freedom of expression, corruption, problems associated with lack of judicial independence and violence associated with problems to access of land, elections, narcotrafficking or with the presence of paramilitaries and guerrillas; *World Report 2008*, online: Human Rights Watch <www.hrw.org/legacy/wr2k8/introduction/index.htm>. The Political Terror Scale (PTS) gave Latin America a score of 2.4 in 2007, on a scale of 1 to 5. This puts the region approximately halfway between levels 2 and 3. Level 2 is assigned to States which have a limited number of detentions for nonviolent political activities, and where torture and beatings, as well as political assassinations, are rare. Category 3 is made up of States that have extensive political detentions or a recent history with these detentions, where political executions and brutality are common, and arbitrary detention is accepted. PTS includes Brazil, Colombia and Guatemala among the 31 worst States with regard to protection of physical integrity; *Political Terror Scale Data*, online: Political Terror Scale <http://www.politicalterrorscale.org/ptsdata.php>. Transparency International indicated in its Annual

American system is required to overcome these challenges. In other words, a reflection on the system should not be made exclusively from a *procedural* perspective, which focuses on the rules and regulations or how the Commission or the Court processes individual petitions, but from a *substantive* perspective that is attuned to the human rights demands of the region and how to approach them from within the regional system. This requires an analysis of the role of the Inter-American system in a regional political scenario with democratically-elected governments but with grave problems of social exclusion and institutional degradation.

From this perspective, it is necessary to strengthen the ability of the Inter-American system to influence the general orientation, formulation, implementation, evaluation, and supervision of public policies that overcome the weaknesses and structural problems of the region. To achieve this goal, it is necessary to rethink the thematic and jurisprudential agenda of the Inter-American system as well as its institutional design, the coordination and balance between its political and judicial tools, its insertion within the OAS, and its working relationship with the States.[56] To put it briefly, the reflection should transcend the simple analysis of procedural questions in the processing of individual complaints.

III.   A Brief Interlude one the Legalization and *Judicialization* of the Inter-American System

As previously noted, in the last two decades, there has been a strong emphasis placed on the process of the "judicialization" of the system, or in other words, on the central focus placed on the Inter-American *amparo* as an instrument *par excellence* of the system.

In fact, judicialization is part of a wider process that has been dubbed "legalization" in international relations. Legalization, in international relations, is understood as a form of institutionalization along three dimensions.[57] *Obligations*, in the sense that States are juridically related through international rules, and to this end are subject to the rules and procedures of international law, such as those present in the *Convention*. *Precision* in the sense that the rules are clear, defining behavior that is required, authorized, or prohibited. Obligations and precision could explain the preference of a system built around the *Convention* rather than the *Declaration*. Finally, legalization is understood through *delegation* that grants authority to institutions–created by but distinct from States–to implement, interpret, and apply rules, as well as to resolve disputes and, in certain cases, adopt new juridical norms. This dimension could be applied to the Commission, and, more particularly, the

---

Report of 2007 that the level of perceived transparency in Latin America is 3.8 on a scale of 0 to 10, where 0 represents the highest level of corruption and 10 the highest level of transparency; *Transparency International's Global Corruption Report 2007*, online: Transparency International <http://www.transparency.org/regional_pages/americas/publicaciones>.

[56]   Abramovich, *supra* note 49.

[57]   See Kenneth W. Abbott *et al.*, "The Concept of Legalization" (2000) 54 International Organization 401.

Court, as the institutions created to interpret and apply the *Convention*.

Judicialization could be defined as the manifestation of this latter aspect, when dispute resolutions are assigned to a judicial organ. Some have limited the use of the term "judicialization" to the process by which an administrative entity monitors member States through means that resemble legal procedures. This type of institution functions with a judicialized instrumentation of a formal tribunal, as happens when formal legal opinions are handed down, through the development of "jurisprudence", the presence of judicial criteria to evaluate evidence or criteria of active or passive procedural standing.[58] This could be the case with the Commission that increasingly adopts a judicial approach to the individual complaints despite the fact that the IACHR is not a judicial body.

The system's approach to "legalization"/"judicialization" can be analyzed from definitions that are not offered in international relations theory, but from political science. For example, Brinks and Gauri maintain that "legalization" of a particular policy area requires that (i) the case successfully becomes a legal case (legal mobilization), (ii) the case reaches a decision, (iii) the guarantee of its compliance, and, in many cases (iv) some type of post-litigation follow-up. Legalization of politics or of a specific policy occurs once the courts and lawyers are considered important actors and legal categories and legal discourse are prominent in the design and implementation of public policies.[59] This is precisely what is happening, at least in part, within the Inter-American system, where debates on human rights are increasingly rising out of the processing of individual cases in lieu of other mechanisms and, are being shaped in the domain of lawyers who specialize in litigation (representatives of victims, State's legal bureaucracies, staff of the Secretariats of the Court and the Commission, and judges and commissioners). For instance, in the last 10 years only one Commissioner, Susana Villarán, was not a lawyer.

In the case of the Inter-American system, I apply the term "judicialization" to understand three parallel and complementary processes: (i) an increased emphasis in the processing of cases over other tools within the system such as on-site visits or technical assistance; (ii) a belief that the judicial Inter-American *amparo* is better than the quasi-judicial *amparo* and (iii) an increased understanding that the individual petitions should be handled as a judicial process (particularly by the Commission, a quasi-judicial).[60]

---

[58]   See Edgard Weisban, "Verdictive discourses, shame and judicialization in pursuit of freedom of association rights" in Mecklend-García & Çali Başak, eds., *The Legalization of Human Rights* (New York: Routledge, 2006) 134.

[59]   Varun Gauri & Daniel Brinks, "Introduction: The Elements of Legalization and the Triangular Shape of Social and Economic Rights" in Varun Gauri & Daniel Brinks, eds., *Courting Social Justice: Judicial Enforcement of Social and Economic Rights in the Developing World* (New York: Cambridge University Press, 2008) 1.

[60]   For example, in the IACHR's Report, OAS, Inter-American Commission on Human Rights, *Access to Justice as a Guarantee of Economic, Social, and Cultural rights. A Review of the Standards Adopted by the Inter-American System of Human Rights*, OR OEA/Ser.L/V/II.129/Doc.4 (2007), the Commission indicates that it "elaborated this study with the goal of revising and systematizing *the jurisprudence of the Inter-American System of Human Rights, as much the IACHR as the Court* [...] on

144   2011 *Quebec Journal of International Law* (Special Edition)

The type of judicialization of most concern is the concentration of the IACHR's resources and time in the processing and resolution of individual cases.[61] Faced with non-full-time commissioners who only meet three or four times per year, the concentration on cases leaves the Commission and its Secretariat with very limited time for the development of its political and promotional functions. Additionally, these cases become one of the Commission's main, if not only, sources of information on the human rights situation. This is especially problematic because individual cases do not necessarily address structural problems. Many collective demands cannot be litigated given the general lack of action such as class action cases or collective *amparos*. The cases also only reflect the interests of the organizations that come before the Inter-American system and that know how to deal with another aspect of "judicialization" (the strictest application of procedural and judicial criteria). Finally, many times the focus on the processing of cases limits the possibility or is invoked to facilitate the limitation of the Commission's involvement in current events or in general debates or public policies, since it could mean a pre-judgment on a case that could eventually reach the IACHR.[62]

IV.   The Need to Centralize Human Rights Within the OAS

The Inter-American human rights system is a mechanism that operates within a regional intergovernmental organization. For this reason, the member States collectively and the OAS as an institution should integrate a human rights perspective in a more systemic, coherent, and prominent way.[63] The Secretary-General of the

---

four central themes that it has prioritized with respect to judicial protection" [emphasis added] [translated by author].

[61] Some have called attention to the risks that *legalization* and *judicialization* may pose, especially through the phenomenon of *overlegalization* that occurs when substantive rules of a treaty or the processes inherent to international monitoring of obligations outlined in human rights instruments are too invasive to States' sovereignty, which leads governments to fail to comply with international supervisory organs, or they may go as far as withdrawing from or denouncing the treaty at hand. In other words, expensive interpretations by international organs that expand the reach of treaties could demand profound changes in domestic practices and legislation. This could provoke internal opposition to compliance with such interpretations and even pressure to modify or denounce the treaty. Two examples that illustrate this phenomenon within the Inter-American system are: 1) the withdrawal of the contentious jurisdiction of the Court by the government of Peru under Alberto Fujimori, after the Court had resolved a few cases on terrorism and that the Commission had remitted to the Court the complaints on the situation of the television channel belonging to regime opponent Baruch Ivcher and the removal of independent judges from the Peruvian Constitutional Tribunal, and 2) the denouncing of the Convention on the part of Trinidad and Tobago upon seeing itself judicially complained against before the Court for its way of regulating and applying the death penalty. See Laurence R. Helfer, "Overlegalizing Human Rights: International Relations Theory and the Commonwealth Caribbean Backlash Against Human Rights Regimes" (2002) 102 Colum. L. Rev. 1832. I agree with the conclusions on the risks inherent to excessively legalizing the mechanism for protection of rights, although not with the examples used to illustrate this point, and neither with the idea that a stronger concern should be placed on the dangers of being too invasive to State's sovereignty.

[62] See Abramovich, *supra* note 49. See also *infra*, note 101 and accompanying text.

[63] I will leave for another opportunity a reflection on if, within the next fifty years, the OAS and the Inter-American human rights system will continue to be the regional forum *par excellence* with regard to human rights. It is worth briefly mentioning a few initiatives that could be indicative of either new regional trends alternative to the role of the OAS with regard to human rights or, on the contrary,

OAS has noted that "[a]s far as the Secretary General is concerned, in line with the mandates of the Presidential Summits and the OAS General Assemblies, I have included the area of human rights as one of the four programmatic themes of the hemispheric agenda, which will orient its work during the remainder of the term."[64] However, this and other similar manifestations do not translate in the daily operation or in the strategic short-, medium-, or long-term work agenda of the different Inter-American organs, nor in the collective OAS actions.

Normatively, Article 2 of the *Charter of the Organization of American States* does not include the defense or promotion of human rights as part of the Organization's "essential purposes."[65] If the effective promotion and protection of

---

expressions of subregional complementarity to regional Inter-American mechanisms. For example, the Andean Presidential Council adopted the *Andean Charter for the Promotion and Protection of Human Rights*, Bolivia, Columbia, Ecuador, Peru and Venezuela, 26 July 2002, online: UNHCR <http://www.unhcr.org/refworld/docid/3de4f94a4.html>. The *Charter* declares that it "is the first comprehensive manifestation of the Andean Community on the subject of human rights in the Community sphere, and that it complements national, international, and universal regulations thereon" (Article 63) and States indicate that "[t]hey shall cooperate actively with the United Nations and Inter-American systems for the protection and promotion of human rights, and foster cooperation between both systems" (Article 82). However, it leaves the door open, since "[t]hey agree to promote the principles and objectives of the *Andean Charter for the Promotion and Protection of Human Rights* through the mechanisms mentioned in this section, without prejudice to the future incorporation of other follow-up ways and means through the pertinent Community channels" (Article 86). The XI Reunion of the High-Level Authorities in Human Rights of MERCOSUR and Associated States approved a proposal for the creation of a Human Rights Public Policy Institute for MERCOSUR. This project has been brought to the Common Market Council for its final consideration. The Institute, according to the adopted proposal, will arrange the design of and compliance with public policies related to the subject matter. It would be designed to provide technical assistance to the States. The institution's activities should "be complementary to the efforts of the various actors operating within the region" (Preamble). See "MERCOSUR Human Rights Public Policy Institute" *INTAL Monthly Newsletter* (June 2008), online: INTAL <http://www.iadb.org/intal/articulo_carta.asp?tid=5&idioma=eng&aid=448&cid=234&carta_id=759>. In 1997, the Heads of State of the Carribean Community (CARICOM) approved a *Charter of Civil Society* that enumerated a series of rights and established a system of reporting to CARICOM on the implementation of the *Charter* in every country. The Caribbean Court of Justice, also created under CARICOM, has jurisdiction of appeal over the majority of the Caribbean countries and the mandate to unify the interpretation of the advisory norms of CARICOM; *Charter of Civil Society for the Carribean Community*, online: <http://actrav.itcilo.org/actrav-english/telearn/global/ilo/blokit/caricha.htm>. The President of the Supreme Court of Venezuela, Magistrate Luisa Estella Morales Lamuño, in the IV Summit of Presidents of Judicial Powers of the Union of South American Nations (Unasur), which took place in Cartagena de Indias, Colombia, from August 26-29 of 2009, proposed the creation of a Tribunal to promote, protect, and enforce human rights in the region. See "Presidenta del TSJ expresó necesidad de crear Tribunal Regional de Derechos Humanos" online: Supreme Court of Venezuela, <http://www.tsj.gov.ve/informacion/notasdeprensa.asp?codigo=7119>. Many have analyzed the recently-concluded Summit of Unity, which took place in Rivera Maya, Mexico, as the embryo for the birth of a new regional organization. See e.g., Alberto Najar, "Cumbre de Cancún: ¿Adiós a la OEA?" (22 February 2010), online: BBC Mundo <http://www.bbc.co.uk/mundo/america_latina/2010/02/ 100222_0950_mexico_cumbre_rio_sao.shtml>.

[64] José Miguel Insulza, Address (Secretary General of the Organization of American States in the Inaugural Session of the 127th Period of Sessions of the Inter-American Commission on Human Rights, 26 Februrary, 2007) online: OAS <http://www.oas.org/en/media_center/videos.asp?sCodigo=07-0032> [translated by author].

[65] These essential purposes are: a) to strengthen the peace and security of the continent; b) to promote and consolidate representative democracy, with due respect for the principle of nonintervention; c) to

146   2011 *Quebec Journal of International Law* (Special Edition)

these rights is effectively among the priorities of the region, the text of the *OAS Charter* should be modified to include this promotion and protection of human rights as one of the central goals of the Organization. In fact, the normative lacuna is indicative that the OAS was not created to be and does not act as a regional organization to protect or promote human rights. Also, this explains why, in many aspects, the Commission and the Court are so marginalized within the OAS. In the same sense, given that the central organs of the system are the Court and Commission, the *OAS Charter* should include the Court to fill the gap, as the *OAS Charter* currently only recognizes the Commission.[66] This would mean that the Court is an integral part of the OAS and it is a collective duty of all OAS member States to enforce its judgments but not that the Court has full jurisdiction over all member States of the OAS.

The principal source of effectiveness, legitimacy, and credibility of the Inter-American system is the independence and autonomy of the Commission, the Court, and its respective Secretariats. The process of judicialization requires that the organs that handle individual petitions act with independence and impartiality. Obviously, independence and autonomy are also essential for the development of the political/promotional activities of the Commission. Impartiality, independence, autonomy, and technical expertise are important elements in the development of its activities in the matters of cooperation, technical assistance, promotion, and supervision with relevant political and social actors of the different countries. For this reason, the OAS should guarantee the independence and impartiality of the IACHR and Court as well as the financial and administrative autonomy of their Secretariats. At the same time, the OAS should adopt a more transparent process for the selection of commissioners and judges that assures that members that arrive at the Commission and Court are the most capable and qualified.[67]

---

prevent possible causes of difficulties and to ensure the pacific settlement of disputes that may arise among the member States; d) to provide for common action on the part of those States in the event of aggression; e) to seek the solution of political, juridical, and economic problems that may arise among them; f) to promote, by cooperative action, their economic, social, and cultural development; g) to eradicate extreme poverty, which constitutes an obstacle to the full democratic development of the peoples of the hemisphere; and h) to achieve an effective limitation of conventional weapons that will make it possible to devote the largest amount of resources to the economic and social development of the member States. *Charter of the Organization of American States*, 30 April 1948, O.A.S.T.S. Nos. 1-C & 61, 119 U.N.T.S. No. 1609 (entered into force 13 December 1951), art. 2 [*OAS Charter*].

[66]   Articles 53 and particularly 106 of the *OAS Charter*, *ibid.*, only refer to the Inter-American Commission on Human Rights. There is no explicit reference to the Court in the *OAS Charter*.

[67]   The actual system for naming judges and commissioners is as follows: nomination of up to three candidates by the States (members of the OAS for the Commission and parties to the Convention for the Court), followed by election by the General Assembly (with votes from all member States in the case of the Commission and only States parties to the Convention for the Court). Both nomination and election lack transparency and control. At the domestic level, States enjoy complete and absolute discretion with respect to the system of nomination that they adopt. The *OAS Charter*, the *Convention*, and the *Statutes* of the Commission and the Court do not say anything about the domestic nomination process; *Statute of the Commission*, *supra* note 13; OAS, General Assembly, 9th Sess., *Statute of the Inter-American Court of Human Rights*, OR OEA/Ser. P/IIX.0.2 (1979). The OAS has not established any criteria on the nomination procedures at the domestic level, nor does it require States to indicate which mechanism they have used. At the moment of election, at the international level, the OAS only utilizes the perfunctory Resolutions AG/RES.2120 XXXV-O/05 that invites "to consider the possibility

More than just a normative change, it is required that the OAS itself centralize its work on human rights. If the budget reflects the political priorities of the OAS, then the promotion and protection of human rights is only 5 % of those political priorities. If what the Secretary General has indicated is true, that human rights make up one of the four central themes in the programmatic agenda of the hemisphere, then 25 % of the Organization's budget should go toward the Inter-American human rights system. Likewise, the external fundraising efforts of the OAS should also reflect this centrality. By providing limited financial resources, the OAS conditions the functioning of the human rights system in a highly political way. It is not only that the OAS does not provide enough resources to hire more lawyers or have more sessions; it also affects the work the system is able to carry out. The processing of the individual petitions is less costly than the permanent or frequent presence of the Commission in the OAS countries, or the development of stable and sustainable technical assistance programs. At the same time, this lack of resources creates tensions in decisions on how to use the few resources that the IACHR and Court have. If the Commission is not able to hold more sessions, should it grant more hearings to hear arguments on individual cases or on general human rights situations? Should the IACHR hire more lawyers to deal with the backlog and problems of procedural delay indicated above, or more personnel to make economic, social, political, or anthropological analyses that would allow it, in turn, to make better, more precise diagnostics on domestic and regional human rights realities? The latter would also allow the Commission to design proposals for the elaboration, adoption, implementation, evaluation, and investigation of public policies from the Inter-American human rights perspective.

Placing the human rights agenda at the center of the activities of the OAS would require more cooperation between the IACHR and the key areas functioning within or under the auspices of the OAS, such as the Inter-American Committee

---

of organizing consultations with civil society organizations in order to help propose the best candidacies for positions with the Inter-American Commission and the Inter-American Court of Human Rights" and asks the Secretary General to "publish the corresponding candidate's curriculum vitae on the OAS website."; OAS, General Assembly, 4th Sess., *Presentation of Candidates for Membership of the Inter-American Commission on Human Rights and the Inter-American Court of Human Rights*, OR OEA/AG/RES.2120 (XXXV-O/05) (2005). However, there is no space that allows for the questioning of the suitability of the candidates for each position, for them to be able to make public presentations on their positions and qualifications in the area of human rights, for them to be questioned by the States, nor for States to express which criteria have been used to evaluate and support candidates. International mechanisms for judge selection generally suffer from the same problems, but there are incipient advances in mechanisms provided for the selection of judges for the International Criminal Court and the European Court of Human Rights. These mechanisms are meant to increase transparency and ensure the quality of those who are part of the international judiciary. See Neil Falzon, Matthias Goldmann & Ketevan Khutsishvili, eds., *Nomination and Election of Judges to International Courts: A Comparative Study* (Brussels: The European Law Students' Association Legal Research Group, 2002); Jutta Limbach *et al.*, *Judicial Independence: Law and Practice of Appointments to the European Court of Human Rights* (London: Interights, 2003); Ruth Mackenzie & Phillipe Sands QC, "Judicial Selection for International Courts: Towards Common Principles and Practices," in Kate Malleson & Peter Russell, eds., *Appointing Judges in an Age of Judicial Power: Critical Perspectives from Around the World* (Toronto: University of Toronto Press, 2006) 21. In fact, the mechanism that has been established by the IACHR for the election of Special Rapporteurs, Resolution 04/06, could be a model for consideration by the OAS.

against Terrorism, the Executive Secretary for Integral Development, the *Mechanism for Follow-Up on Implementation of the Inter-American Convention Against Corruption*,[68] Meeting of Ministers of Justice, and Attorneys General of the Americas (REMJA), to name a few. Although these institutions or meetings include human rights issues in their mandates, rarely do they interact with the IACHR, and neither do they take the case law developed by the Court seriously.

For example, one of the means of monitoring the *Convention of Belém do Pará* on violence against women is through the *Mechanism for Follow-Up on Implementation of the Inter-American Convention on the Prevention, Punishment, and Eradication of Violence Against Women (MESECVI)*. This Mechanism's statute establishes that the Secretariat should be made up of the Permanent Secretariat of the Inter-American Women's Commission and "with the assistance, when necessary, of the Inter-American Commission of Human Rights (IACHR)".[69] However, the *Method for Evaluation of and Follow-Up on the Implementation of the Provisions of the Convention of Belém do Pará*, approved by States parties, does not foresee any formal role for the IACHR as a source of information, as a technical assistant for evaluation, or for monitoring the implementation of the recommendations.[70] Normatively, it is assumed that there would be a relationship between the States and the IACHR, but in practice, the OAS and its member States do not implement the central role that the IACHR should have in putting the human rights perspective in practice.

The same can be said for the Inter-American Council for Integral Development (CIDI). According to its *Statute*, "it is an organ of the Organization of American States (OAS) that directly answers to the General Assembly, with decisive powers in the subject of solidarity and cooperation for integral development. It also constitutes a forum for Inter-American dialogue on matters of interest in the hemisphere in this area." It has "as an end goal to promote solidarity and cooperation among member States to support integral development, and in particular to contribute to the elimination of poverty" and "it carries out its objectives through the *Strategic Plan for Partnership for Integral Development and Solidarity*." However, the *Strategic Plan for Partnership for Integral Development and Solidarity 2006-2009 (Plan)* only mentions human rights in the following point: "To contribute to member States' efforts to develop educational materials on the matters of democracy and human rights, including women's human rights." This approach highlights the fact that the OAS has still not developed a human rights perspective on integral development.[71] Additionally, the Executive Secretary of Integral Development, who coordinates activities of cooperation among the different departments and other

---

[68]   OAS, General Assembly, 3rd Sess., *Mechanism for Follow-Up on Implementation of the Inter-American Convention Against Corruption*, OR OEA/AG/RES.1784 (XXXI-O/01) (2001).

[69]   OAS, General Assembly, 4ᵗʰ Sess., *Mechanism for Follow-Up on Implementation of the Inter-American Convention on the Prevention, Punishment, and Eradication of Violence Against Women, "Convention of Belém do Pará"*, OR OEA/AG/RES.2371 (XXXVIII-O/08) (2008), art. 5.4.

[70]   OAS, Committee of Experts on Violence, *Method for Evaluation of and Follow-Up on the Implementation of the Provisions of the Convention of Belém do Pará*, OR OEA/Ser.L/II.7.10/MESECVI/CEVI/Doc.7/05 rev.1 (2005).

[71]   Of course, it is important to keep in mind that development and respect for human rights, though they may be interrelated, are not the same.

dependencies of the General Secretary who deal with this *Plan*, has never developed activities in conjunction with the IACHR, nor has it sought the Commission's advice. It has also never invited the Commission to any of its meetings.

REMJA also serves as an example of the lack of strategic vision of the Inter-American organs. At a meeting of the Attorneys General and Ministries of Justice there is no doubt that human rights issues should and are on their agendas. However, there is no evidence that REMJA has ever included the Inter-American Commission in a discussion on the administration of justice, judicial issues, or related matters.

Finally, the seriousness and credibility of the OAS as a whole and of each member State depends on the integration and full participation of all member States in the human rights system. The OAS should encourage, and ideally require, its member States to be parties to the *Convention* and accept the jurisdiction of the Court. In other words, the Inter-American *amparo* should be a recognized right of all residents of the OAS member States. This would require the creation of sufficient incentives so that, within a reasonable time frame, all member States would become parties to the *Convention* and would be under the jurisdiction of the Court.[72] For example, the year 2019–almost eight years from now and fifty years after the adoption of the *Convention*–could be an appropriate time for general ratification of the Convention and acceptance of the jurisdiction of the Court. To achieve this ambitious goal, the Commission and General Secretary should design a strategic plan, together with the States, to support them and provide them with incentives throughout this process. Perhaps at the end of this suggested time frame for full participation in the human rights system, the OAS should consider whether those States that have not adhered to the central human rights treaty should still be part of the Organization,[73] or if they can enjoy the same rights as the States that do fully participate in the Inter-American system.[74]

The States that have still not ratified the Convention nor accepted the jurisdiction of the Court could be required to periodically inform the Permanent Council, the Secretary General, and the Commission of the status of legislation and practice of rights protected through the *Convention*, indicating in what ways they either have implemented or propose to implement any of the provisions of the *Convention*. They should also indicate the steps they have taken toward ratification of the *Convention*, as well as the difficulties that impede or delay ratification and

---

[72]   This is the system that is used within the European Council, where full acceptance of the European Convention on Human Rights, including acceptance of the jurisdiction of the European Court of Human Rights, is a condition for the admission of new States to the European Council. See Peter Leuprecht, "Innovations in the European System of Human Rights Protection: Is Enlargement Compatible with Reinforcement?" (1998) 8 Transnat'l L. & Contemp. Probs. 327.

[73]   The exclusion from the OAS of important countries due to the non-ratification of the *Convention* is not only a political impossibility in current conditions, but it could also be harmful for protection of human rights and put the existence of the OAS itself in risk. Precisely for this reason, all possible mechanisms and incentives should be used to fully integrate said States in the regional human rights system.

[74]   For example, this could stop said States from nominating members to the IACHR or to participate in elections for commissioners or judges – in a case in which the State has ratified the *Convention* but has not accepted the Court's jurisdiction.

150   2011 *Quebec Journal of International Law* (Special Edition)

measures that have been adopted to overcome these obstacles.[75] The Commission should then elaborate a working plan, including technical assistance, to facilitate the process of ratification and acceptance of the jurisdiction of the Court.

V.   Links Between the Protection of Democracy and the Defense of Human Rights

The *Inter-American Democratic Charter* clearly points to the inter-relationship between democracy and human rights.[76] In practice, however, the OAS has limited itself to the application of mechanisms to defend democracy outlined in the *OAS Charter* and in the *Democratic Charter* on the exercise of the right to vote (origins of the democratic system), but not on the overall quality of democracy. This is dangerous for two clear reasons. On the one hand, it gives international legitimacy to governments with hints of authoritarianism that comply with basic democratic requirements, but only in a formal way. On the other hand, it prohibits the democratic clause from being understood and interpreted as the fundamental axis around which governments should act to protect and guarantee all the rights espoused in the Inter-American system.[77]

It is of fundamental importance to link the reactionary mechanisms of the Organization before the crisis of democratic governability with the full guarantee of human rights. Particularly, grave and systematic violation of human rights and consistent, repeated failure to comply with the decisions of the Inter-American human rights system should be recognized as disparaging elements of the mechanisms for protection of democracy that are included in the *Democratic Charter*. At the same time, in order to avoid worsening a crisis that often unfolds with institutional degradation or generates political violence, the *Democratic Charter* should establish a preventive mechanism to react to the calls to attention and early warnings that the Commission issues.

Lastly, it is essential to give the IACHR the capacity to activate the mechanisms of institutional protection of democracy as outlined in the *Democratic Charter* (Articles 18 and 20). This would not only grant more credibility and

---

[75]   This proposed system is similar to the mechanism outlined in Article 19 of the *Constitution of the International Labor Organization with respect to international labor conventions*. International Labour Organization, *Constitution of the International Labour Organisation*, art. 19, 1 April 1919, online: UNHCR <http://www.unhcr.org/refworld/docid/3ddb5391a.html>.

[76]   OAS, General Assembly, 4ᵗʰ Session, *Inter-American Democratic Charter*, OR OEA/AG/RES.1838 (XXXI-O/01) (2001) [*Democratic Charter*]. Article 3 of the *Democratic Charter* establishes that essential elements of representative democracy, among others, are the respect of human rights and fundamental liberties. Article 7 says that democracy is indispensable to the effective exercise of fundamental liberties and human rights, through its universal, indivisible, and interdependent character, written in the States' respective constitutions and in Inter-American and international human rights instruments.

[77]   Even before the adoption of the *Democratic Charter*, the limitation of the IACHR's role and the governability crisis were criticized. See Juan Méndez & Gastón Chillier, "La Cláusula Democrática y el Derecho Interamericano", online: Universidad Diego Portales <http://www.udp.cl/derecho/publicaciones/clausula_demo.pdf>.

independence to this mechanism; it would also introduce a means by which to analyze the democratic quality of our countries, through a human rights perspective.[78]

VI.   New Roles for the Commission and Court

The reform of the rules and regulations of the Commission and Court in the year 2001[79] affected the various areas of the system. To name a few: a larger number of cases were sent to the Court; there was greater autonomous participation of victims before the Court; there was an exponential increase in the area of Inter-American jurisprudence; a larger number of decisions on admissibility from the Commission, and a decrease in number of published final reports by the Commission. There has been an overall decrease in the total number of cases that reach final decision in the system. In sum, "judicialization" has not brought a rise in productivity in the processing of the Inter-American *amparo*.[80] The reforms to the rules and regulations of the year 2009 have fundamentally changed the role that the Commission plays in contentious cases before the Court, but not the nature of its work or the focus on individual cases.

Aside from the many virtues that can be attributed to the process of "judicialization," it has not been able to give an adequate response to the demands of wide sectors of the population, as the human rights situation in the region shows. Nor has it taken advantage of all the spaces that democratic societies have offered.

A.   The Proposal for Reform

To fix the dysfunctional aspects, but fundamentally to make the Inter-American system more effective, efficient, and to have more presence in domestic political processes, there is a need to free time and necessary resources of the Commission to allow it to be able to focus more heavily on its political and promotional activities. In order to accomplish this goal, the procedural aspects of the *Convention* must be reformed. The reformed *Convention* should more clearly establish the division of duties between the Commission and Court in the matter of the processing of individual complaints.

In this new conventional model, the Commission would be exclusively an organ of admissibility and friendly settlements, and the Court would be in charge of

---

[78]   States rejected the proposal to include the Commission as one of the bodies that would oversee the implementation of the *Democratic Charter* and implement its protective mechanisms. See Andrew F. Cooper & Thomas Legler, *Intervention without Intervening? The OAS Defense and Promotion of Democracy in the Americas* (New York: Palgrave MacMillan, 2006) at 152.

[79]   The reforms in rules and regulations for the Commission and Court came into force in the year 2001. For all of them, see Veronica Gomez, **"Inter-American Commission on Human Rights and the Inter-American Court of Human Rights: New Rules and Recent Cases"**, (2001).1 Human Rights Law Review 111

[80]   By this, I do not mean to imply that productivity should be the parameter *par excellence* by which to measure the effectiveness of the system.

gathering and receiving evidence and deciding on factual and legal matters. The Commission, in addition to its tasks outside of the case system, would be limited to approving reports on admissibility and to opening a stage of friendly settlements.[81] The production of evidence before the IACHR would be strictly limited to aspects of admissibility. Its decision on the admissibility of a petition would be final and unable to be appealed before the Court, and the Court would not have jurisdiction to review them.

The conciliatory phase, or that of friendly settlement, should have a pre-determined time frame, of six months, for example, which could be extended only by agreement between the petitioners and the respective State.[82] If the matter is resolved, the Commission would publish a report, as it currently does. If the friendly settlement fails, the case would automatically go to the Court without the Commission preparing a complaint or becoming a complainant. Most importantly, the Commission would send the case to the Court without making any determination of fact or law on the matter. Once the case reached the Court, the dispute would be between the alleged victim and the respective State. The Commission would not play the role of litigant, but only as the principal organ of the Organization that represents States and as an assistant in the search for justice. In this regard, the Commission should have the right to question the parties (States and victims). In this way, it could help the Court rule on the essential points in the dispute and contextualize the structural dimensions of a case. It should also be possible for the IACHR to be able to interrogate witnesses and experts. Given that the Court only decides on alleged and proven facts, and that these are essential for the determination of the amount, form, and mode of reparations, the Commission should be able to question those who inform the Court on these aspects. Later the IACHR should be able to present its views, legal opinion, and proposed solution for the Court's consideration.[83]

The *New Rules* of the Court partially and inconsistently adopt certain proposals, outlined here. On one hand, they establish that the Commission is no longer required to present a complaint. It is only required to file its Article 50 report. The *New Rules* also do not require the Commission to represent victims who do not have a legal representative. The *New Rules* created the Inter-American Public

---

[81]   Other articles of this special edition discuss specific procedures in detail.

[82]   In fact, the *Statute of the Commission*, in Article 23, point b, states that: "If the friendly settlement referred to in Articles 44-51 of the *Convention* is not reached, the Commission shall draft, within 180 days, the report required by Article 50 of the Convention." I am not aware of any case in which the Commission has applied this article. *Statute of the Commission, supra* note 13.

[83]   This proposal would be similar to that of the Advocate-General of the Court of Justice of the European Communities. First, the IACHR would not act as a party. The Advocate-General is considered integral to the European Court of Justice. In our proposal, the Commission would be considered a conventional organ distinct from the intervening parties. Second, it would not be the responsibility of the Commission – as it is not the responsibility of the Advocate-General – to prove facts or produce witnesses, experts, or documentary evidence. Third, the Commission would act impartially and independently as an organ of the OAS – like the Advocate-General – but not as a complainant. Fourth, the Commission would be able to question parties on facts and law. Finally, in a way similar to that of the Advocate-General, it would present its conclusions for the Court's consideration. See generally, Noreen Burrows & Rosa Greaves, *The Advocate General and EC Law* (Oxford: Oxford University Press, 2007) at 19-30.

Defender to assist victims who lack legal representation to appear before the Court.[84] The *New Rules* also limit the Commission's ability to present and interrogate witnesses, since it can only question experts about prior authorization from the Court and only if it is relevant to the Inter-American public order.

The Court's *New Rules* reaffirm the role of the Commission as a body of the system rather than as a litigant. Article 51 of the *New Rules* establishes that the oral hearing will be open by the IACHR[85] and it will also conclude with the Commission's presentation. The *New Rules* indicate that, upon submitting a case, the Commission should give its reasons for bringing the case to the Court (Article 35.1.c),

---

[84]   The *New Rules* of the Court neither explain nor develop any standard on the Inter-American Public Defender. They do not explain who would be able to fill this position, who would cover its costs, to which professional ethics norms it would be subject, nor the pertinent disciplinary mechanism. Nor do they determine when the Inter-American Public Defender would be elected, what would happen if, during the two-month period given to present its statement, the Defender has not yet been chosen, or if it has not had sufficient time to digest the case. In September of 2009, the Court made an agreement with the Inter-American Association of Public Defenders (Asociación Interamericana de Defensorías Públicas or AIDEF), with the objective of "providing free legal assistance to alleged victims who lack economic resources or legal representation to appear before the Inter-American Court of Human Rights." [translated by author]. The agreement specifically develops a mechanism for the naming of an Inter-American Public Defender as a representative of victims who lack legal representation. In fact, it was recently reported that 35 of the public defenders who belong to AIDEF would be trained by the Inter-American Court of Human Rights in "techniques for litigation before the Court" in a series of seminars that would take place at the tribunal. See "Propician actividades académicas en la Defensa Pública" *El pais* (28 February 2010), online: <http://www.elpais.cr/articulos.php?id=20035>. Aside from the potential conflicts of interest, roles, and appearance of lack of impartiality that could arise out of the fact that the tribunal would be training public officials to litigate against the States, agreements and this training program seem to indicate that that the States' public defenders would be the ones to fill the position of the Inter-American Public Defender. If this were so, many questions would arise immediately. How can a State official, which the Inter-American Public Defender is, represent a victim before an international tribunal against the State? What would happen if an act that triggered the international responsibility of the State was an action or omission of a Inter-American Public Defender? Would there be conflicting responsibilities? Do Inter-American Public Defenders have legal authorization to appear before international tribunals? Do they have the technical knowledge to do so? If Inter-American Public Defenders generally concentrate on criminal cases within domestic legal systems, why would they have the training to assist victims in non-criminal cases, for example in cases that deal with access to and protection of land (as in the *Sawhoyamaxa Indigenous Community Case (Paraguay)* (2006) Inter-Am. Ct. H.R. (Ser. C) No. 146, *Annual Report of the Inter-American Court of Human Rights: 2006*, at 13, online: Inter-Am. Ct. H.R. <http://www.corteidh.or.cr/docs/informes / 20063.pdf> [*Sawhoyamaxa Case*], cases dealing with social security (as in the case *Carlos Torres Benvenuto, Javier Mujica Ruiz-Huidobro, Guillermo Alvarez Fernández, Reymer Bartra Vásquez & Maximiliano Gamarra Ferreyra v. Peru* (1999), Inter-Am. Comm. H.R. No.89/99, *Annual Report of the Inter-American Commission on Human Rights: 1999*, OEA/Ser.L/V/II.106/doc.6, rev. c.3.), cases on labor rights (as in the *Baena-Ricardo Case (Panama)* (2003), Inter-Am. Ct. H.R. (Ser. C) No. 104, OAS, Inter-American Court of Human Rights, *Annual Report of the Inter-American Court of Human Rights: 2003*, OEA/Ser.L/V/III.61/doc.1 (2004) 36.), or on access to information (*Claude Reyes Case (Chile)* (2006), Inter-Am. Ct. H.R. (Ser. C) No. 151, *Annual Report of the Inter-American Court of Human Rights: 2006*, at 46, online: Inter-Am. Ct. H.R. <http://www.corteidh.or.cr/docs/informes / 20063.pdf> [*Claudio Reyes Case*].)? Is the Court equating the Inter-American Public Defenders' representation in a domestic criminal trial of a person charged with a crime with the representation of a victim of human rights abuse in an international tribunal? What would happen to the independence and impartiality of the Inter-American Public Defender? How would they be guaranteed? Do they have sufficient economic resources? In the signed agreement, it says that reasonable costs will be covered through a victim assistance fund. However, the *Rules of Procedure of the Fund* state that if a person

demonstrating that the IACHR is an impartial representative of the Inter-American public interest. The Court then authorizes the Commission to propose and question experts "when it legitimately affects the Inter-American public order of human rights" (Article 35.1.g and 52.3). Nevertheless there are some shortcomings in the *New Rules*. They still maintain certain aspects of the Commission in its role as an active litigant and closer to the victims rather than as an impartial entity. For example, the *New Rules* require that the IACHR give the "names, address, telephone number, email address, and fax number of the representatives of the alleged victims" (Article 35.1.b) when it is not necessary in the Commission's process to present due and formal accreditation, neither is it the Commission's responsibility to obtain this information. The *New Rules* also require the Commission to establish the "claims, including those related to reparations," as if the IACHR should have plans for reparations before knowing the reparations requested by the victims or offered by the State. It is unclear why the *New Rules* do not limit the participation of the Commission in this area to request only those reparations necessary for maintaining the "Inter-American public order" (as it is referred to in various articles of the *New Rules*) or those that have a structural character.[86]

---

lacks economic resources, he or she can say so in the statement of application, argument, and evidence (ESAP: Escrito de Solicitudes, Argumentos y Pruebas); OAS, Permanent Concil, *Rules of Procedure for the Operation of the Legal Assistance Fund of the Inter-American Human Rights System*, OR OEA/Ser.G/CP/RES.963 (1728/09) (2009) art. 2 [*Rules of Procedure of the Fund*]. According to Article 40.2.b of the *New Rules*, *supra* note 41, alleged victims should present all documentary evidence and offer expert and witness evidence in the ESAP. In this crucial stage of the proceedings, neither the alleged victim nor the public defender (now transformed into the Inter-American Public Defender) can count on having economic resources from the assistance fund. Will they be relieved of their domestic duties while they exercise their international representation? What would happen to the people they represent in the domestic arena? Would Inter-American Public Defenders litigate in cases from their own countries or from third countries? In the case of third countries, how would knowledge of language, facts, and domestic legal systems of that country be guaranteed? Who would finance travel to the country in question? How would continual communication with the represented victim be ensured? Countries that are neither members of the OAS nor independent States participate in AIDEF – like Puerto Rico. It is also made up of States who have not ratified the Convention nor accepted the jurisdiction of the Court, such as Antigua and Barbuda or the United States, or who have not accepted the jurisdiction of the Court, like Jamaica. What are the consequences of this? Could an Inter-American Public Defender from a country that is not a member of AIDEF, such as Canada or Dominica, be named as an Inter-American Public Defender? If that is not possible, it would seem that it is not the quality of the Inter-American Public Defender, but membership to a civil association like AIDEF, that would qualify someone to be a potential Inter-American Public Defender. Why does the Court grant this monopoly to a civil organization? Finally, why could other non-State entities not exercise this representation and fill the role of inter-American defender, such as for example, law schools, non-governmental organizations, or legal clinics within universities? Why could other State institutions, such as offices of the Ombudsman or State human rights commissions, or even prosecutors, not fill this role? For now, we have nothing but questions and it would be important for the Court to clarify publicly the role of this innovative mechanism, which is meant to fill the essential role of representing victims before the Court.

[85] To present "the report provided for in Article 50 of the *Convention*. The Commission's application shall be accompanied by certified copies of the items in the file that the Commission or its delegate considers pertinent" [translated by author].

[86] *New Rules*, *supra* note 41.

The Inter-American Human Rights System Fifty Years Later   155

B.   Some benefits of the proposal

The Commission, upon being relieved of its duties to make factual and legal determinations on the merits of a complaint, can count on having more time and resources to make more detailed and precise decisions on admissibility, with better and more juridical analyses. Additionally, upon no longer having to eventually become a decision-making and at the same time a litigation organ, can play a more active and impartial role in the friendly settlement process. The possibility that the case would automatically go before the Court within an established time frame if a friendly settlement was not reached would be an incentive for the State to use all of its efforts to reach a solution before it would be judicially mandated.

The Court, for its part, would continue to be a judicial tribunal that should conduct the hearing as well as the finding of fact. The Court should not admit preliminary exceptions related to the admissibility of the petition, as it should go directly to the presentation of evidence. This would reduce the topics and points to be proven, debated, and resolved. The only difference with the current system is that it would rely neither on the body of evidence produced in the IACHR, nor on the factual determinations that the Commission carries out. Given that the Court grants little or no weight to the evidence produced before the Commission, this should not overburden the Court.

The implementation of this proposal would require precise management of the victim assistance fund, given the differentiated role that it would grant the IACHR.[87] Since full ratification of the Convention and acceptance of the jurisdiction of the Court has not yet been reached, the IACHR should keep its current authority with relation to States that have not ratified the *Convention* or accepted the Court's jurisdiction.

This proposal, aside from reducing instances of duplication of procedures, would leave intact the two decisions of the organs of the Inter-American system with a higher degree of compliance: friendly settlements at the Commission and judgments of the Court. It also eliminates the existing tension between the Commission's role as an impartial decision-maker in the petitions that are brought before it, and its later role as plaintiff before the Court. Additionally, it would resolve the apparent disadvantage that States have before the Court, as they have to respond simultaneously to the arguments of the Commission and of the victim.[88] Finally, this proposal would

---

[87]   The General Assembly of the OAS decided to create this fund. See OAS, General Assembly, 4th Sess., *Establishment of the Legal Assistance Fund of the Inter-American Human Rights System*, OR OEA/AG/RES.2426 (XXXVIII-O/08) (2008). It was also regulated through Resolution of the Permanent Council CP/RES 963, *Rules of Procedure of the Fund, supra* note 84. The Court has just outlined the rules for the fund for the phase of litigation in front of the tribunal: *Rules of Procedure of the Inter-American Court of Human Rights on the Functioning of the Legal Assistance Fund*, 4 February, 2010. The Court has just announced that the government of Norway has made a donation to this fund.

[88]   I do not believe that there is a situation of inequality of arms. The State is guaranteed full procedural opportunities to respond to the victims' and the Commission's claims, as well as procedural equality. In all procedural systems, there could potentially be multiple complainants. Even in criminal procedure, the majority of modern procedural codes predict that the accused should defend him- or

significantly reduce the Commission's workload, and ideally the total duration of processing cases within the system, allowing the IACHR to carry out its political/promotional functions, as well as provide technical assistance. Fundamentally, this increase in the Commission's available time would allow it to focus its financial, human, and time resources to more–and more profound–activities of promotion, cooperation, assistance, and impact.

VII.   New Profiles for the Commission and the Court

The change in procedures and division of labor in the processing of individual petitions is not sufficient, however. Nor is it merely a thematic expansion of cases that are processed. On the contrary, given the human rights situation in the Americas, it is necessary to reform the methodology of the Commission's work and its profile. The proposed new assignment of responsibilities within the individual petition system would ostensibly grant the Commission more freedom with its human and financial resources to carry out more tasks related to the promotion of human rights, giving advice, general monitoring, and interacting with governments and civil society, as well as reacting expeditiously to humanitarian crises.

The structural problems limiting the effective guarantee of rights and political spaces for democratic governance call for the strengthening of the political tools of the IACHR to balance out the judicialization process of the Inter-American system. The Commission should play a more important role in the processes associated with the adoption of public policies, making use of the opportunities that democratically-elected governments offer, and where important government sectors are genuinely interested in improving the overall human rights situation.

To carry out this role, the Commission should reinforce its technical cooperation with the governments of the region and create and develop better strategic alliances with different relevant actors in each one of the member States. For example, in countries where they exist and function efficiently, national human rights institutions could become strategic allies of fundamental importance.[89] Supreme or constitutional courts could also become allies of the Commission, given their central institutional position.[90] However, the Commission currently focuses very little or not at all on these sectors.

The Commission should draw up a thematic agenda based on an evaluation and contributions from governmental and civil society actors in the region, identifying priority areas for work in each State and in the region as a whole. This would allow

---

herself against the accusations of the prosecutor, joint plaintiff, amicus curiae, civil complainant, or similar entities.

[89]   See e.g. Emilio Álvarez Icaza Longoria, "El papel de los organismos públicos de derechos humanos en el fortalecimiento y promoción del sistema interamericano. La experiencia suscitada desde la Comisión de DDHH del DF" (2003) 1 Revista CEJIL No. 2 147.

[90]   See e.g. Diego Garcia Sayán, "Una Viva Interacción: Corte Interamericana y Tribunales Internos," in *La Corte Interamericana de Derechos Humanos: Un Cuarto de Siglo: 1979-2004* (San Jose, Costa Rica: Organization of American States, 2005) 323.

The Inter-American Human Rights System Fifty Years Later   157

the Commission to better focus its efforts.

One example of a sustained effort to influence public policy that is just beginning to unfold is that of the IACHR's following of the demobilization process in Colombia, and in particular the discussion on integral reparations in the country. In the past few years, the Commission's work in Colombia has shown how the use of its multiple tools can effect change in the adoption of concrete, far-reaching public policies.[91]

This change in profile would also imply a reorganization of the IACHR's activities. To this end, the tools that allow for clearest diagnosis of the human rights situations and needs in the countries of the region—on-site visits, thematic hearings, the preparation and elaboration of general reports[92]—should be reinforced. This would also imply an internal reorganization of the Secretariat of the Commission, which is essentially made up of lawyers who are experts in the processing of cases and petitions. Very few, if any, of the professionals within the Secretariat of the Commission have any training in relevant disciplines such as economics, political science, or sociology, nor do they have experience in the design, implementation, or evaluation of public policy or legislative techniques.

Changes in its work profile and of its methodology, a more permanent

---

[91] See for example the IACHR reports: OAS, Inter-American Commission on Human Rights, *Principle Guidelines for a Comprehensive Reparations Policy*, OR OEA/Ser.L/V/II.131/Doc.1 (2008); OAS, Inter-American Commission on Human Rights, *Statement by the Inter-American Commission on Human Rights on the Application and Scope of the Justice and Peace Law in Colombia*, OR OEA/Ser.L/V/II.126/Doc.16 (2006); OAS, Inter-American Commission on Human Rights, *Report on the Implementation of the Justice and Peace Law: Initial Stages in the Demobilization of the AUC and First Judicial Proceedings*, OR OEA/Ser.L/V/II/Doc.3 (2007); OAS, Inter-American Commission on Human Rights, *Violence and Discrimination Against Women in the Armed Conflict in Colombia*, OR OEA/Ser.L/V/II/Doc.67 (2006); OAS, Inter-American Commission on Human Rights, *Report on the Demobilization Process in Colombia*, OR OEA/Ser.L/V/II.120/Doc.60 (2004). See also the Commission's arguments on reparations in various Colombian cases before the Court, like, for example, *Rochela Massacre Case (Columbia)* (2007), Inter-Am. Ct. H.R. (Ser.C) No.163, *Annual Report of the Inter-American Court of Human Rights: 2007*, at 9 online: Inter-Am. Ct. H.R <http://www.corteidh.or.cr/docs/informes/Inf%20anua%202007%20ING.pdf>. However, it should not be forgotten that these results, which particularly influence the discussion and adoption of a global plan for reparations, have been handed down in a context of continual armed conflict. Violence against vulnerable sectors of society continues, the problem of displacement has not been solved, impunity continues to be a serious problem, and paramilitary groups are re-forming and resurging. This would require a more profound investigation on how to evaluate the effectiveness and efficiency of the Inter-American human rights system. It would also require contextual consideration on the situation in each country. For example, what are the factors that contribute to Colombia's dialogue with the IACHR, in a country with a judicial system that is highly sophisticated in many areas, but that still has a high level of violence and absence of the State in many regions of the country? In this context, how would one measure the effectiveness of the IACHR? This is a crucial, central question that goes beyond the scope of this article, but that is part of its broader agenda.

[92] On the importance of country reports, see especially Tom Farer, "The future of the Inter-American Commission on Human Rights: Promotion versus Exposure" in Juan Méndez & Francisco Cox, eds., *El Futuro del Sistema Interamericano de Protección de los Derechos Humanos* (San Jose, Costa Rica: Instituto Interamericano de Derchos Humanos, 1998) 515; Felipe Gonzalez, "Informes sobre Países, Promoción y Protección" in Juan Méndez & Francisco Cox, eds., *El Futuro del Sistema Interamericano de Protección de los Derechos Humanos* (San Jose, Costa Rica: Instituto Interamericano de Derechos Humanos, 1998) 493 [Gonzalez, "Informes"].

presence in the field, and increased interaction with relevant social and governmental actors would also improve the analytical capacity of the Commission, and, to paraphrase the Court, would permit the IACHR to comprehend more clearly "the difficulties implicit to the planning and adoption of public policies and the choices of operative character that should be taken in light of priorities and resources" as well as the need to prevent the interpretation of positive State obligations as measures that would "impose an impossible or disproportionate task upon the authorities."[93]

The Commissioner's rapporteurs would play a fundamental role. They already carry out important tasks in the selection of priority areas for the Commission's work, as well as in advocacy for legislative reform and for the adoption of certain public policies. For example, the Special Rapporteur on Indigenous Peoples has focused heavily on the protection of collective rights to indigenous territories. It has done this through friendly settlements,[94] resolution of cases,[95] strategic litigation of cases before the Court,[96] the inclusion of chapters on the situation of indigenous rights in various country reports,[97] and providing technical advice to the Working Group discussing the American Declaration on the Rights of Indigenous Peoples.[98] It is also worth mentioning the sustained work of the Commission and its Rapporteur for Freedom of Expression on the subject of

---

[93]   See *Sawhoyamaxa Case, supra* note 84 at para. 155.

[94]   *Comunidades Indígenas Enxet-Lamenxay y Kaleyphapopyet-Riachito v. Paraguay* (1999), Inter-Am. Comm. H.R. No. 90/99, Annual Report of the *Inter-American Commission on Human Rights: 1999*, OEA/Ser.L/V/II.106/doc.6 rev. (1999) 350.

[95]   *Mary and Carrie Dann v. United States* (2002), Inter-Am. Comm. H.R. No. 75/02, *Annual Report of the* Inter-American Commission on Human Rights,OEA/Ser.L/V/II/doc.106, rev. (2002) 860.

[96]   *Mayagna (Sumo) Awas Tingni Community Case (Nicaragua)* (2001), inter-Am Ct. H.R. (Ser.C) No. 79, *Annual Report of the Inter-American Court of Human Rights: 2001*, OEA/Ser.L/V/III.54/doc.4 (2000) 29; *Indígena Yakye Axa Community Case (Paraguay)* (2005), Inter-Am. Ct. H.R. (Ser.C) No. 125, *Annual Report of the Inter-American Court of Human Rights: 2005*, at 8 online: Inter-Am. Ct. H.R. < http://www.corteidh.or.cr/docs/informes/Inf%20anua%202005%20diag%20ingles.indd.pdf>; *Sawhoyamaxa Case, supra* note 84.

[97]   See generally OAS, Inter-American Commission on Human Rights, *Justicia e Inclusión Social: Los Desafíos de la Democracia en Guatemala*, OR OEA/Ser.L/V/II.118/Doc.5, rev. 1 (2003), c. IV; OAS, Inter-American Commission on Human Rights, *Tercer Informe Sobre La Situación De Los Derechos Humanos En Paraguay*, OR OEA/Ser./L/VII.110/Doc.52 (2001), c. IX; OAS, Inter-American Commission on Human Rights, *Segundo Informe Sobre La Situación De Los Derechos Humanos En El Perú*, OR OEA/Ser.L/V/II.106/Doc.59 (2000), c. X; OAS, Inter-American Commission on Human Rights, *Tercer Informe Sobre La Situación De Los Derechos Humanos En Colombia*, OR OEA/Ser.L/V/II.102/Doc.9 rev. 1 (1999), c. X; OAS, Inter-American Commission on Human Rights, *Informe Sobre La Situación De Los Derechos Humanos En México*, OR OEA/Ser.L/V/II.100/Doc.7, rev. 1 (1998), c. VII; OAS, Inter-American Commission on Human Rights, *Informe Sobre La Situación De Los Derechos Humanos En Brasil*, OR OEA/Ser.L/V/II.97/Doc.29, rev. 1 (1997), c. VI; OAS, Inter-American Commission on Human Rights, *Informe Sobre La Situación De Los Derechos Humanos En Ecuador*, OR OEA/Ser.L/V/II.96/Doc.10, rev. 1 (1997), c. IX.

[98]   See "Proyecto de Declaración Americana sobre los Derechos de los Pueblos Indígenas", online : Inter-Am. Comm. H.R. <http://www.cidh.org/Indigenas/ProyectoDeclaracion.htm>.

The Inter-American Human Rights System Fifty Years Later   159

decriminalization of criticism of public officials[99] and on access to public information.[100]

In order to assure and increase visibility, credibility, and legitimacy of the Commission and its rapporteurs, the IACHR should analyze their work holistically and establish a few common parameters to guide the various rapporteurs' work. For example, various rapporteurs have conducted important visits to document some of the central themes of their work, creating the expectation that they would produce reports on these areas and offer concrete recommendations to the States. However, several years after these visits, these reports were not published, and the Commission lost its opportunity to influence public discussions and brought disillusionment and frustrations among State officials and members of civil society who collaborated with the rapporteurs during their visits, and who were genuinely interested in the IACHR's positions on these matters.[101] The Commission should also adopt clearer parameters

---

[99] See e.g. *Verbitsky v. Argentina* (1994), Inter-Am. Comm. H.R. No. 22/94, *Annual Report of the Inter-American Commission on Humans Rights: 1994*, OEA/Ser.L/V.88/Doc.9, rev. 1 (1995) 40; OAS, Inter-American Commission on Human Rights, *Report of the Compatibility of* Desacato *Laws and the American Convention on Human Rights*, OR OEA/Ser. L/V/II.88/Doc.9,, rev. (1995) at 206; and the cases litigated before the Court, *Herrera Ulloa Case (Costa Rica)* (2004), Inter-Am. Ct. H.R. (Ser.C) No. 107, *Annual Report of the Inter-American Court of Human Rights: 2004*, OEA/Ser.L/V/III.65/doc.1 (2004) 8; *Ricardo Canese Case (Paraguay)* (2004), Inter-Am. Ct. H.R. (Ser.C) No. 111, *Annual Report of the Inter-American Court of Human Rights: 2004*, OEA/Ser.L/V/III.65/doc.1 (2004) 14; *Palamara-Iribarne Case (Chile)* (2005), Inter-Am. Ct. H.R. (Ser.C) No. 135, *Annual Report of the Inter-American Court of Human Rights: 2005*, at 12 online: Inter-Am. Ct. H.R. < http://www.corteidh.or.cr/docs/informes/Inf%20anua%202005%20diag %20ingles.indd.pdf>; *Kimel Case (Argentina)* (2008), Inter-Am. Ct. H.R. (Ser.C) No. 177, *Annual Report of the Inter-American Court of Human Rights: 2008*, at 14 online: <http://www.corteidh.or.cr/docs/informes/eng2008.pdf>.

[100] See e.g. *Annual Report of the Special Rapporteur for Freedom of Expression 2003*, vol. III, c. IV "Special Study on the Right of Access to Information" online: OAS <http://www.cidh.org/relatoria/showarticle.asp?artID=139&lID=1>; *Claudio Reyes Case*, *supra* note 84.

[101] The following can be mentioned as examples of rapporteur visits to countries that do not produce reports, despite the fact that it could be so: Rapporteur for the Rights of Children, together with UNICEF, to analyze the situation of children and adolescents linked to gangs in El Salvador, Guatemala and Honduras in December of 2004; of the Rapporteur for the Rights of Women to Guatemala in September of 2004; and finally the visits of the Rapporteur on Rights of People Deprived of Liberty in the Americas, between 2004 and 2007 to Argentina, Bolivia, Brazil, Colombia, the Dominican Republic, Guatemala, Haiti, and Honduras. See generally Inter-American Commission on Human Rights and UNICEF, Press Release, No. 26/04, "Inter-American Commission on Human Rights and UNICEF Express Concern over Situation of Boys, Girls and Adolescents Involved with Gangs in el Salvador, Guatemala, and Honduras" (4 December 2004), online: Inter-Am. Comm. H.R. <http://www.cidh.org/Comunicados/English/2004/26.04.htm>; Special Rapporteur for the Rights of Women, Press Release, No. 20/04, "IACHR Special Rapporteur evaluates the effectiveness of the right of women in Guatemala to live free from violence and discrimination" (18 September 2004), online: Inter-Am. Comm. H.R. <http://www.cidh.oas.org/women/Press20.04.htm>; Rapporteur on the Rights of Persons, Press Release, No. 38/05, "The Rapporteurship on the rights of persons deprived of freedom of the IACHR and the Office of the United Nations High Commissioner for Human Rights to pay a visit to Colombia" (8 November 2005), online: Inter-Am. Comm. H.R. <http://www.cidh.org/Comunicados/English/2005/38.05eng.htm>; Rapporteur for Bolivia and Rapporteur on the Rights of Persons Deprived of Liberty in the Americas, Press Release, No. 48/06, "IACHR checks situation of persons deprived of liberty in some jails en the Republic of Bolivia" (30 November 2006), online: Inter-Am. Comm. H.R. <http://iachr.org/Comunicados/English/2006/48.06 eng.htm>; Rapporteur on the Rights of Persons Deprived of Liberty, Press Release, No. 29/06,

on the motives for using a Special Rapporteur for Freedom of Expression who is not a member of the Commission and has not been elected by the General Assembly, and who, unlike other thematic rapporteurs, works full-time for the Commission and can manage a budget and staff autonomously from the rest of the budget and staff of the IACHR. This creates perceptions of disparities between the different thematic rapporteurs, which, in turn, affects the work of the Commission as a whole.

Special recognition should also be given to country reports, which allow for more holistic diagnoses and recommendations. The Commission has begun to take steps to assure that these reports are written and published in the quickest manner possible.[102] At the same time, it should also work toward more sustained and timely follow-up on the recommendations offered in these reports, ensure their widest possible diffusion, especially that they are sent to relevant domestic and international actors, and ensure that they are presented publicly in the countries on which they focus.

The diffusion of the Commission's work is an essential element to any strategy for greater political advocacy. One positive measure that the IACHR has taken recently is the creation of a press office that is designed to ensure the heightened presence of the Commission in the Inter-American public opinion.

Of course, this political and promotional role, along with technical assistance, should not affect or diminish the autonomy, independence, and impartiality of the Commission, which constitutes its greatest strength. Nor should this role imply the abandonment of the role of processing the *individual petitions*. The Commission should find a balance between the pressing need to cooperate with the national governments of the region and its capacity for critical independent analysis of the human rights situation in different States, which it is able to do through its various mechanisms, including the processing of petitions and cases.

The proposed new role for the Commission in the processing of the individual petitions would permit it to complement its role as a technical assistant. With a deeper involvement in the process of reaching friendly settlements, the Commission could advocate for the adoption of policies that attempt to resolve not only the specific case at hand, but also the structural problems that brought it into being. Additionally, by playing the role of neither complainant nor litigant before the Court, and given its auxiliary capacity, it should be able to play a more active role in the facilitation of compliance with the judicial decisions of the Court and the carrying out of the recommendations that it itself has made, thereby influencing the adoption

---

"IACHR Rapporteur on the Rights of Persons Deprived of Liberty visists the Dominican Republic" (8 August 2006), online: Inter-Am. Ct. H.R. <http://iachr.org/Comunicados/English/2006/29.06eng.htm>; Rapporteur on the Rights of Persons Deprived of Liberty, Press Release, No. 32/07, "Rapporteur on the Rights of Persons Deprived of Liberty concludes visit to the Republic of Haiti" (21 June 2007), online: Inter-Am. Ct. H.R. <http://www.iachr.org/Comunicados/English/2007/32.07eng.htm>; *Visitas*, online : Inter-Am. Comm. H.R. <http://www.cidh.org/PRIVADAS/visitas.htm>.

[102] See e.g. OAS, Inter-American Commission on Human Rights, *Informe Acceso A La Justicia E Inclusión Social: El Camino Hacia El Fortalecimiento De La Democracia En Bolivia*, OR OEA/Ser.L/V/II/Doc.34 (2007), prepared in less than six months.

The Inter-American Human Rights System Fifty Years Later   161

and/or modification of public policy.

The synergy that is produced between the political and promotional activities of the IACHR and the processing of individual petitions should also not be forgotten. As noted, and as the work in various countries and of some rapporteurs exemplifies, the Commission can develop fundamental standards for the implementation of its thematic agendas through paradigmatic cases. Judgments or reports that carry orders or recommendations for structural changes can open spaces for the political and promotional work of the Commission. Decisions in individual cases also legitimize social actors that could have been questioned by States.[103] They also open spaces for negotiation and dialogue between governments and social actors through friendly settlement procedures and orders to implement precautionary or provisional measures, and through processes of negotiating reparations through consultations and coordination between governments and civil society. All of these processes facilitate and reinforce the political/promotional work of the IACHR.

Some have rejected proposals such as those outlined here because a significant strengthening of these initiatives for technical assistance would imply a reduction in financial and human resources for other areas and would also require that the Commission evaluate and make an early judgment on issues that might later come to it through the case system.[104] This proposal would overcome this criticism because it proposes that the IACHR reduce its participation in these cases, as it would no longer need to decide on their merits, nor would it appear before the Court as a litigant. This would free up human and financial resources to be able to focus on other areas. Additionally, technical advice or political/promotional activities do not constitute prejudgment. Even now the IACHR has this dual role as it is called in individual cases to consider a specific situation in a concrete case, while it speaks to general situations–not specific, concrete cases–in its political/promotional activities. If there were a problem with prejudgment, it would also exist in the case of thematic or country reports,[105] which even the critics of the proposals outlined here maintain are fundamental to the IACHR's duties,[106] an idea that we share with them.

The reconfiguration of the functions of the IACHR cannot leave out those of the Court. As a judicial tribunal, it lacks the political/promotional role of the Commission, but this does not mean that its functioning, procedures, and jurisprudence do not have a political impact, nor that they can be conceived of as mere technical questions of juridical interpretation. It is particularly important for the Court to be conscious of the fact that simple orders contained in its sentences are not

---

[103] Thomas M. Antkowiak, "Remedial Approaches to Human Rights Violations: The Inter-American Court of Human Rights and Beyond" (2008) 46 Colum. J. Transnat'l L. 351 at 360.

[104] As expressed by the President of the IACHR in Felipe Gonzalez, "La Comisión Interamericana de Derechos Humanos: antecedentes, funciones y otros aspectos" (2009) 5 Anuario de Derechos Humanos 35 at 55.

[105] The Commission has maintained that its statements on specific situations in general reports do not constitute prejudgment nor do they prevent the Commission from studying, processing, and resolving individual petitions on the same issues. See *Díaz et al. v. Colombia* (1997), Inter-Am. Comm. H.R. No. 5/97, *Annual Report of Inter-American Commission on Human Rights: 1996*, OEA/Ser.L/V/II.95/doc.7, rev., c. III.

[106] See Gonzalez, "Informes", *supra* note 92 at 39, 55.

162   2011 *Quebec Journal of International Law* (Special Edition)

necessarily sufficient to promote permanent or structural changes. These changes are brought about through a confluence of social actors who are dedicated to them, such as social movements, human rights defenders, mass media, governmental officials, and other allies. In this sense, the Court's efficiency would depend on the extent to which its procedures as well as its jurisprudence are relevant to short, medium, and long-term goals of the social actors dedicated to defending human rights.[107]

From this perspective, the organization of the Court's procedures is an important consideration, as it constitutes a space for development of lobbying and promotional activities, diffusion of information, public debate, and accountability. This means that if the number of the Court's public hearings were reduced, if the number of witnesses were to diminish, and if hearings on compliance with judgments were to be private rather than public, the public visibility of the Court's actions and of the governments' positions would diminish, and there would therefore be no generation of domestic public mobilization. This would also mean that juridical and factual findings of the Court should pay particular attention to the structural factors that give rise to human rights violations, as well as those that would promote greater respect for human rights. In other words, it should be understood that human rights violations and implementation of reparations are not produced in a vacuum, but in specific social and political contexts that require consideration in finding of fact, in the application of the law, in orders for reparation, and in supervision of compliance with Court sentences.[108] The legitimacy and credibility of the tribunal does not depend exclusively upon the supposed progressive jurisprudential developments, if these same developments do not translate into systematic domestic changes. At the same time, notions of jurisprudence that import ideas from other systems, or that go beyond the regional consensus might also affect the credibility of the tribunal.[109] This does not mean that the Court should limit itself to reflecting the existing consensus on judicial interpretation in its decisions, especially given the problems confronting the judicial systems of the region. It should just be conscious of the consensus, of existing regional trends, and of jurisprudential developments that have been carried out in certain national tribunals, and of the factors that have brought about said developments.

Finally, a new form of supervision and implementation of the decisions of the organs of the Inter-American system is essential. In order to facilitate compliance with the decisions and following recommendations, each State should establish a domestic mechanism to coordinate and implement the decisions of the Inter-American system.[110] This mechanism would need the participation of the most relevant

---

[107] James Cavallaro & Stephanie Brewer, "Reevaluating Regional Human Rights Litigation in the Twenty-First Century: the Case of the Inter-American Court" (2008) 102 A.J.I.L. 768.

[108] On the implementation of reparations and the context in which they occur, see especially Carlos Beristain, *Diálogos sobre la reparación: experiencias en el sistema interamericano de derechos humanos* (San Jose, Costa Rica: Instituto Interamericano de Derechos Humanos, 2008).

[109] Gerald L. Neuman, "Import, Export, and Regional Consent in the Inter-American Court of Human Rights" (2008) 19 E.J.I.L. 101.

[110] Conventions that demand the establishment of a domestic mechanism for the implementation of treaties already exist. For example, Article 3 of the Optional Protocol of the Convention against Torture relative to the periodic visits to places where there are persons deprived of liberty, stipulates

institutions and ministries, such as those in the areas of justice, foreign and internal relations, defense, economy, the Attorney General, Inter-American Public Defender, and the Ombudsman or similar institution.[111] The Commission should be a permanent member of this institutional body and periodically participate in its meetings, giving technical advice and highlighting best practices from its regional and historical experience. This domestic mechanism and the Commission should offer reports twice a year on its work to the OAS. Victims should be invited to participate in this mechanism's meetings when their cases are being analyzed.

All of the proposals outlined here are interdependent. Since they intend to rethink the Inter-American system in its entirety, each should be understood as part of the whole system of the OAS and should not be considered in isolation.

***

The perspective outlined in this article posits that the Inter-American system has worked against States during periods of dictatorship, and often in spite of States during periods of democratic transition. Now, it is essential for the system to work with States when possible. New examples of collaboration between the States and the IACHR are developing, showing that it is possible for the Inter-American system to be an ally in increasing the effective protection of fundamental rights and liberties, as well as finding justice in numerous individual cases. With this in mind, the role of the Commission should be modified and strengthened in the upcoming years to include the cooperation with and counsel for member countries on how to tackle the many structural problems that predominate in the region.

The proposal to rethink the Inter-American system maintains that the individual petition system should continue playing an important role. However, it should neither be the sole focus nor use the majority of the Commission's time and resources. The processing of individual petitions should be reconfigured to respond to human rights needs in the region in the most efficient manner possible.

---

that "[e]ach State Party shall set up, designate or maintain at the domestic level one or several visiting bodies for the prevention of torture and other cruel, inhuman or degrading treatment (hereafter referred to as the national preventive mechanism)." *Optional Protocol to the Convention against Torture and other Cruel, Inhuman or Degrading Treatment or Punishment*, 18 December 2002, 2375 U.N.T.S. 237, art. 3, GA Res. A/RES/57/199 (entered into force 22 June 2006).

[111] An interesting model is the Inter-institutional Commission that Paraguay created to comply with decisions handed down by the Commission and Court. Said Commission is made up of the Ministries of the Interior, Foreign Relations, Housing, Public Health and Social Welfare, Justice and Labor, Education, and Culture, the Attorney General of the Republic and the Secretary General of the Presidency of the Republic. As an advisory board, it is made up of 16 State entities and, in a "guest" capacity, a representative of the petitioner who appeared before the system. Decree number 1595, approved on February 26, 2009 in Paraguay, created the "Interinstitutional Commission responsible for the Implementation of Actions Needed for Compliance with International Statements issued by the Inter-American Court of Human Rights and the recommendations of the Inter-American Commission on Human Rights." See Paraguay's Ministry of the Interior online: <www.cej.org.py/files/decreto1595_ComisionInterinstitucionalCumplimientoSentenciasInternacionales.pdf>.

164   2011 *Quebec Journal of International Law* (Special Edition)

The emphasis on the Inter-American individual petition system at the expense of other available tools presumes that structural human rights problems in the region can be resolved through legal and judicial responses. I believe that this is an erroneous view.

C
Africa

[19]

INTERPRETING THE EUROPEAN CONVENTION:
WHAT CAN THE AFRICAN HUMAN RIGHTS SYSTEM LEARN FROM THE CASE LAW OF THE EUROPEAN COURT OF HUMAN RIGHTS ON THE INTERPRETATION OF THE EUROPEAN CONVENTION?

Laurence Burgorgue-Larsen*

Abstract

The methods of interpretation under the European Convention on Human Rights range from multifaceted judicial activism to judicial restraint aimed notably at avoiding needless antagonisation of the States. On the one hand, the Court's judicial activism developed through the use of several different types of interpretations. Alongside the 'cosmopolitical' method of interpretation, a very bold approach that ensured that the European Convention on Human Rights was always on the cutting edge and never ossified or became outdated, there were also several more targeted interpretive techniques that served the same end, i.e. to broaden the Convention's purview. On the other hand, the Court disposes of an array of tools allowing it to exercise strategic self-restraint to avoid arousing the ire of States intent on making sovereign decisions about their own societal choices. These include the national margin of appreciation, whose handling has not gone without criticism.

* Professor of Public Law at the Sorbonne Law School (Paris I), Research institute for international and European law at the Sorbonne (IREDIES); <Laurence.Burgorgue-Larsen@univ-paris1.fr>. This article is a rewritten version of a presentation at the 25th Anniversary of the African Commission on Human and Peoples' Rights, Yamoussoukro, Côte d'Ivoire, October 2012.

Resumen

Los métodos de interpretación del Convenio europeo oscilan entre un activismo judicial de múltiples facetas y una reserva judicial empleada particularmente para no atraer desmesuradamente la cólera de los Estados. Equilibrio precario que todos los sistemas regionales de protección de derechos humanos conocen. El activismo judicial del Tribunal Europeo de Derechos Humanos se desarrolla gracias a la movilización de varios tipos de interpretación. Junto al método "universalista" de interpretación que permite, de manera extremamente audaz, hacer que el Convenio Europeo de Derechos humanos esté siempre actualizado, jamás obsoleto ni esclerótico, existen varias técnicas interpretativas más precisas que tienen in fine la misma finalidad, acrecentar el alcance del control convencional, ampliando el ámbito de aplicación del Convenio como el contenido de los derechos protegidos. En cuanto al judicial self restraint – que es estratégico, para no atraer la ira de los Estados que prefieren decidir soberanamente su tipo de sociedad – el Tribunal Europeo de Derechos Humanos utiliza la famosa teoría del margen nacional de apreciación, cuyo manejo no está exento de críticas. Si permite por un lado que el principio de subsidiariedad sea vivo, por otro lado, su manejo demuestra lo difícil que es mantener una coherencia jurisprudencial interna.

1. INTRODUCTION

International protection of human rights arose from the ashes of the Second World War. Although, on the heels of the founding of the United Nations Organisation – intended as a political bulwark against a recurrence of such atrocities – the States parties made a universal commitment in favour of a solemn declaration of rights,[1] we owe to the European, American and African continents the establishment and development of jurisdictionalised human rights protection. The European conventional system established by the adoption of the Convention for the Protection of Human Rights and Fundamental Freedoms (hereinafter, the 'Convention' or the 'European Convention'), on 4 November 1950, is emblematic of the vital need, in the wake of the war, to protect the rights of persons against State interference by any means necessary. Tersely put, the establishment of an international system to legally protect human rights on the heels of World War II could be summed up as 'Human dignity versus State prerogatives'.

After innumerable political difficulties, the American and African continents followed suit in the twofold process of internationalising and jurisdictionalising human rights protection in the framework of the activities of the Organization of

---

[1] By adopting The Universal Declaration of Human Rights on 10 December 1948.

Laurence Burgorgue-Larsen

American States (OAS) and the Organisation of African Unity (OAU), which later
became the African Union (AU). A complex procedure had to be completed before the
African Court could set up headquarters in Arusha, Tanzania. The Court[2] could not
be created until after the Protocol to the African Charter on Human and Peoples'
Rights on the Establishment of the African Court on Human and Peoples' Rights[3] was
adopted in Nairobi in 1981. The Ouagadougou Protocol, which was signed in 1998 and
entered into force in 2004, was the legal instrument that allowed the continent to join
in the wide-ranging process of jurisdictionalisation. However, in its first decision on
15 December 2009,[4] the African Court declined competence. To date, it has yet to rule
on the merits of a case in light of the rules governing case referral.[5] Let us hope that
this will soon change so that the African Court can effectively fulfil its mission of
upholding human rights and increase its visibility and influence. Meanwhile, the
'jurisprudence' of the African Commission on Human and Peoples' Rights continues
to be an important benchmark in Africa, where it has been active for the past 25 years.
It pioneered the interpretation of the African Charter; naturally, it did not hesitate to
refer to the precedents set by the European Court.[6] At this stage in the evolution of the
African system, which is undergoing a clear acceleration,[7] it can be useful to take

---

[2]   There is a very abundant body of literature, including: S. Belassen, *La Cour africaine des droits de
      l'homme et des peuples: vers la Cour africaine de justice et des droits de l'homme: guide pratique*
      (Paris, FIDH 2010), 218 p.; H. Boukrif, "La Cour africaine des droits de l'homme et des peuples: un
      organe judiciaire au service des droits de l'homme et des peuples en Afrique", 10 *Revue Africaine de
      Droit international et Comparé* (1998), p. 60–87; N. Chouachi, "La Cour africaine des droits de
      l'homme et des peuples", in R. Ben Achour and S. Laghmani (eds.), *Justice et Juridictions
      internationales* (Paris, Pedone 2000), p. 271–290; M. Mubiala, "La Cour africaine des droits de
      l'homme et des peuples: mimétisme institutionnel ou avancée judiciaire?", *Revue Générale de Droit
      international public* (1998–3), p. 765–780; M. Mutua, "The African Human Rights Court: a two
      Legged Stool?", 21 *Human Rights Quarterly* (1999), p. 342–363; F. Ouguergouz, "La Cour africaine
      des droits de l'homme et des peuples. Gros plan sur le premier organe judiciaire africain à vocation
      continentale", *Annuaire français de droit international* (2006), p. 231–240; L. San Martin Sanchez
      De Muniaian, "Comentarios acerca de la creación de un Tribunal africano de derechos humanos y
      de los pueblos", *Anuario de Derecho internacional* (1999), p. 505–528.

[3]   M. Mubiala, *Le système régional africain de protection des droits de l'homme* (Brussels, Bruylant
      2005), 53 p.; M. Kamto (ed.), *La Charte africaine des droits de l'homme et des peuples et le protocole
      y relatif portant création de la Cour africaine des droits de l'homme. Commentaire article par article*
      (Brussels, Bruylant 2011), 1628 p.; F. Viljoen, *International Human Rights Law in Africa* (Oxford,
      Oxford University Press 2012, 2nd ed.), 672 p.

[4]   AfrCtHPR (Decision) 15 December 2009, *Michelot Yogogombaye v. Senegal*. See A-D. Olinga,
      "Regards sur le premier arrêt de la Cour africaine des droits de l'homme et des peuples", 83 *Revue
      trimestrielle des droits de l'homme* (2010), p. 749 et seq.

[5]   See its website: <www.african-court.org/en/>.

[6]   E. Lambert-Abdelgawad, "Le rayonnement de la jurisprudence de la Cour européenne à l'égard de
      la Commission africaine des droits de l'homme et des peuples. Analyse empirique des références à
      la Cour européenne dans les communications de la Commission africaine", in *Le rayonnement
      international de la jurisprudence de la Cour européenne des droits de l'homme* (Brussels, Bruylant
      2005), p. 139–184.

[7]   S.T. Ebobrah, "Litigating Human Rights Before sub-regional courts in Africa: prospects and
      challenge", 17 *African Journal of International and Comparative Law* (2009), p. 79–101.

stock of the major trends in the interpretation of the European Convention by the Court in Strasbourg, to determine exactly what precedents the members of the African Court and the African Commission have been in a position to take into consideration.

It is unsurprising to note that the methods of interpretation employed range from multifaceted judicial activism (2) to judicial restraint aimed notably at avoiding needless antagonisation of the States (3). This delicate balance is an art practiced by all regional human rights systems.

2.   PROTEAN JUDICIAL ACTIVISM

The Court's judicial activism developed through the use of several different types of interpretations. Alongside the 'cosmopolitical' method of interpretation, a very bold approach that ensured that the European Convention was always on the cutting edge and never ossified or became outdated (2.1), there were also several more targeted interpretive techniques that served the same end, i.e. to broaden the Convention's purview (2.2).

2.1.   THE "COSMOPOLITICAL" METHOD OF INTERPRETATION

The *Demir and Baykara* judgment,[8] having unleashed a storm of legal scholarship, needs no introduction: the decision crystallised all opposing views and revived the era of the great legal disputatio. In its progressive interpretation of Article 11(1) of the Convention (freedom of association), which included the right for civil servants to bargain collectively, the judgment did not hesitate to call upon an abundance of instruments outside the scope of the Convention *stricto sensu*, specifically including an international treaty – the European Social Charter – that contained clauses that had not been ratified by Turkey, which was the respondent in this case.[9] The Court stressed in paragraph 78 of its judgment that 'in searching for common ground among the norms of international law, it has never distinguished between sources of law according to whether or not they have been signed or ratified by the respondent State'.

Aside from this approach, which radically overturned all of the fundamental principles of international public law – which is consensual law par excellence[10] – experts on the Convention were flabbergasted by the interpretive audacity of the

---

8   ECtHR (Judgment) 12 November 2008, Case No. 34503/97, *Demir and Baykara* v. *Turkey*. The judgment was handed down on referral of a judgment by the Chamber two years previously: ECtHR (Judgment) 21 November 2006, Case No. 34503/97, *Demir and Baykara* v. *Turkey*.

9   The European Social Charter mechanism allows for varying degrees of acceptance of its provisions. Indeed, Turkey did not adhere to Articles 5 (the right to organise) and 6 (the right to collective bargaining) of the European Social Charter and did not ratify them.

10   This was made perfectly clear by Turkey's defence, which considered that 'An interpretation that rendered these provisions binding on an indirect basis was even more problematic where, as in the present case, the absence in the Convention of an express provision guaranteeing the right to enter

Laurence Burgorgue-Larsen

Strasbourg bench. This audacity was carefully thought out, since it was explicitly set forth for the first time in no ambiguous terms,[11] undoubtedly with a view to establishing its legitimacy. The methodological approach was lauded by some[12] and castigated by others,[13] whilst a handful of authors situated it in the timeline of methodological history.[14] Jean-François Flauss stood among the detractors of the approach, which he described as both 'sensationalistic and disturbing'.[15]

The analysis provided in the *Demir and Baykara* judgment is far from innovative in its substance: the open approach that it highlights has in fact been visible for many years. However, this approach, which is marked by the 'decompartmentalisation' of its sources (2.1.1) – used essentially with a view to the interpretation of the Convention[16] – does not do away with the 'European consensus' as such, but rather includes it in what it describes as 'a growing measure of agreement on the subject at international level'.[17] Beyond the legal problems inherent in the method, which have been the

---

into collective agreements was counterbalanced by consideration of other instruments to which the State concerned was not a party'. ECtHR (Judgment) 12 November 2008, Case No. 34503/97, *Demir and Baykara* v. *Turkey*, para. 62.

[11]   The Grand Chamber indeed laid down a third point – following its presentation of the arguments of both parties and the position of the Chamber – which it entitled: 'The practice of interpreting Convention provisions in the light of other international texts and instruments'. This was the first judgment that clearly and explicitly explained the Court's position and its intention to accept full responsibility in that regard.

[12]   J.-P. Marguenaud and C. Mouly, "L'avènement d'une Cour européenne des droits sociaux", *Dalloz, Etudes et commentaires* (2009), p. 739–744.

[13]   J.-F. Flauss, "Actualité de la Convention européenne des droits de l'homme (septembre 2008-février 2009)", *AJDA* (2009), p. 872 et seq. and J.-F. Flauss and G. Cohen-Jonathan, "La Cour européenne des droits de l'homme et le droit international (2008)", *AFDI* (2008), p. 529–546. For criticism formulated following the first judgment by the Chamber, see J.-F. Renucci and C. Birsan, "La Cour européenne des droits de l'homme et la Charte sociale européenne: les liaisons dangereuses", *Dalloz, Etudes et commentaires* (2007), p. 410. p. Wachsmann writes in a similar vein in his critical analysis: "Réflexions sur l'interprétation "globalisante" de la Convention européenne des droits de l'homme", in *La conscience des droits. Mélanges en l'honneur de Jean-Paul Costa* (Paris, Dalloz 2011), p. 667–676.

[14]   F. Sudre, "L'interprétation constructive de la liberté syndicale au sens de l'article 11 de la Convention EDH. Note sous l'arrêt Demir et Baykara", *JCP, Gen.*, N°5, 28 January 2009; S. Van Drooghenbroeck, "Les frontières du droit et le temps juridique: la Cour européenne des droits de l'homme repousse les limites. CEDH, Grande chambre, Demir et Baykara c. Turquie, 12 novembre 2008", 79 *Revue trimestrielle des droits de l'homme* (2009), p. 811–849. For a very thorough analysis founded notably on the first judgment handed down by the Chamber on 21 November 2006, we refer the reader to the work of F. Tulkens and S. Van Drooghenbroeck, "Le soft law des droits de l'homme est-il vraiment si soft? Les développements de la pratique interprétative récente de la Cour européenne des droits de l'homme", in *Liber amicorum Michel Mahieu* (Brussels, Larcier 2008), p. 505–526.

[15]   J.-F. Flauss, "Actualité de la Convention européenne des droits de l'homme (septembre 2008-février 2009)", *AJDA* (2009), p. 872.

[16]   The practice of litigation reveals that this statement can be further refined if we consider that recourse to external sources can have multiple functions. We refer notably to the contribution of J.-F. Flauss at the 7th Congress of the SIPE (Strasbourg, 10–12 June 2010). Dealing more specifically with use of European soft law, Professor Flauss shows that it can help to establish facts, provide grounds for judgments and further the caseload.

[17]   ECtHR (Judgment) 12 November 2008, Case No. 34503/97, *Demir and Baykara* v. *Turkey*, para. 77.

subject of in-depth analyses, it is interesting to show that this approach can tend, *in fine*, to reveal the universalism of the interpreted Convention. Thus, rather than situating his function within the specific context of the European continent, the human rights judge understands it in the universal context represented by the rights protected by the European Convention (2.1.2).

2.1.1. Deliberate decompartmentalisation

For some years now, the Strasbourg Court has entered into an age of decompartmentalisation[18] regarding the sources it uses to interpret the European Convention.[19] A variety of formulas have been used in legal scholarship to refer to this phenomenon. Very early on, Jean-François Flauss and Gérard Cohen-Jonathan referred to the 'methodological option of comparative international human rights law'[20]; Frédéric Sudre spoke of the 'globalisation of sources'[21]; Sandrine Turgis of 'cross-interpretation'[22]; Françoise Tulkens and Sébastien Van Drooghenbroeck, of an 'enrichment process'[23] and, for our part, we have referred to 'normative cosmopolitanism'[24] as revelatory of a 'decompartmentalised' vision of the law and legal systems. Whichever formula the reader prefers, the actual phenomenon described

---

[18]   The phenomenon affects various jurisdictions. At the domestic level, Supreme Courts, which are sometimes also Constitutional Courts depending on the system, experience it in the form of 'judicial dialogue', see S. Sanders "Judicial dialogue in Common law countries" in *Renouveau du droit constitutionnel. Hommage à Louis Favoreu* (Paris, Dalloz 2007), p. 413–428; D. Maus, "Le recours aux précédents étrangers et le dialogue des Cours constitutionnelles", 80 *Revue française de droit constitutionnel* (2009), p. 675–696. However, we should also mention the exception represented by the International Court of Justice, which has remained aloof from the general 'judicial dialogue' movement. For further information on this aspect and for a viewpoint that 'legitimises' this approach, see M. Forteau, "La Cour internationale de justice et les systèmes régionaux. Plaidoyer pour le pluralisme désordonné", in *Les droits fondamentaux: charnières entre ordres et systèmes juridiques*, E. Dubout and S. Touzé (eds.) (Paris, Pedone 2010), p. 39–64.

[19]   Several authors of reviews regularly reassert this position. We refer to the review by J.-F. Flauss and G. Cohen-Jonathan on the "Cour européenne des droits de l'homme et droit international général" in the *Annuaire français de droit international*. The authors noted the trend as far back as 2001 and since then have highlighted it in every review. We also refer to the review in the *Revue du droit public*, focusing on an analysis of comparative European case-law: "Jurisprudence européenne comparée".

[20]   J.-F. Flauss and G. Cohen-Jonathan, "La Cour européenne des droits de l'homme et le droit international (2008)", *AFDI* (2008), p. 530. See also: J.-F. Flauss, "Du droit international comparé des droits de l'homme dans la jurisprudence de la Cour européenne des droits de l'homme" in *Le rôle du droit comparé dans l'avènement du droit européen* (Zürich, Schulthess 2002), p. 159–182.

[21]   F. Sudre, "L'interprétation constructive de la liberté syndicale au sens de l'article 11 de la Convention EDH. Note sous l'arrêt Demir et Bakayra", *JCP, Gen.*, No. 5, 28 January 2009.

[22]   S. Turgis, *Recherches sur l'interaction entre les normes internationales relatives aux droits de la personne* (Paris, Pedone 2012), 642 p. (Preface by Jean Dhommeaux).

[23]   Tulkens and Van Drooghenbroeck, *supra* n. 14, p. 512.

[24]   L. Burgorgue-Larsen, "Le destin judiciaire strasbourgeois de la Charte des droits fondamentaux de l'Union européenne. Vices et vertus du cosmopolitisme normative", in *Chemins d'Europe. Mélanges en l'honneur de Jean-Paul Jacqué* (Paris, Dalloz 2010), p. 145–173.

Laurence Burgorgue-Larsen

is one and the same: the propensity of the Strasbourg Court to use a variety of sources from outside the scope of the Convention *stricto sensu*, in order to enrich its interpretation of the European Convention. It thereby renews the meaning of the Convention in a way that is consistent with normative and case-law trends at international level. In so doing, it ensures that the European Convention is always on the cutting edge and never outdated, ossified or archaic.

Experienced observers know the phenomenon is hardly new, even though it unquestionably gained momentum following the establishment of the new Court through the reform brought about by Protocol No. 11.[25] The Court has never really opted for a restrictive interpretation of Article 32 of the European Convention on Human Rights, according to which 'The jurisdiction of the Court shall extend to all matters concerning the interpretation and application of the Convention and the Protocols thereto [...]'. Because of its focus on legitimisation, it recalls this rather forcefully in the *Demir and Baykara* judgment: '[...] the Court has never considered the provisions of the Convention as the sole framework of reference for the interpretation of the rights and freedoms enshrined therein. On the contrary, it must also take into account any relevant rules and principles of international law applicable in relations between the Contracting Parties.'[26] This statement of principle is followed by a list, which, although it was not intended to be a 'laundry list', was described by Jean-François Flauss and Gérard Cohen-Jonathan as a haphazard and opportunistic grab bag.[27] The intention of the Court, however, was to be educational, as it listed a series of concrete examples demonstrating that its open approach reflected established practice. It cited 'relevant international treaties that are applicable in the particular sphere',[28] 'general principles of law recognized by civilized nations'[29] and Council of Europe instruments[30]; whether they are hard or soft, and whether the instruments are adopted by States' representatives or experts independent from the Council of Europe,[31] all of these elements contribute to its analytical approach.[32] In this syncretic

---

[25] The same process could be observed in the days of the European Commission of Human Rights.

[26] ECtHR (Judgment) 12 November 2008, Case No. 34503/97, *Demir and Baykara* v. *Turkey*, para. 67.

[27] Indeed, it was the view of G. Cohen-Jonathan and J.-F. Flauss that: 'As set forth by the Grand Chamber, this method of interpreting the Convention was similar to a traditional patchwork quilt. External references and/or indications are piled up somewhat haphazardly, according to the Clerk's research and the perspicacity. The Court establishes no hierarchical relationship between them on the basis of whether or not they are binding, or of whether they are regional or universal in scope.' Flauss and Cohen-Jonathan, *supra* n. 19, p. 533 (our translation).

[28] ECtHR (Judgment) 12 November 2008, Case No. 34503/97, *Demir and Baykara* v. *Turkey*, para. 69.

[29] Ibid., para. 71.

[30] Ibid., paras. 74–75.

[31] The Court refers to the work of the European Commission for Democracy through Law or 'Venice Commission'. Ibid., para. 75.

[32] This 'digest', as it was described by J.-F. Flauss and G. Cohen-Jonathan, was not without its idiosyncrasies... As the authors wrote: 'To illustrate the multidimensional nature of this practice of interpretation in the light of international human rights law, the Court presented a sort of 'digest' of various international instruments and texts that were already used to interpret the

process, the Court insists that the status of the international instruments cited has little import, nor does the fact that they have been accepted by the respondent States: it is not necessary for the respondent State to have ratified the entire collection of instruments that are applicable in respect of the precise subject matter of the case concerned. It will be sufficient for the Court that the relevant international instruments denote a continuous evolution in the norms and principles applied in international law or in the domestic law of the majority of member States of the Council of Europe and show, in a precise realm, that there is common ground in modern societies'.[33] By decoding its policy on case law, we can understand that it is the substance of the standards that is considered important, rather than, *ne varietur*, the source in which they are enshrined. To state it yet another way, the *pro homine* principle[34] becomes a major interpretive guide and, in this context, hard law is not the only valid instrument. The *negotium* incontestably takes precedence over the *instrumentum*. The 'relative normativity' denounced with such brio by Prosper Weil in 1982[35] seems to be losing its lustre as a criticism, at least in the complex reality of the judicial use of legal instruments on behalf of human rights. In this regard, we take note of the European Court's use of the Charter of Fundamental Rights of the European Union[36] – before it received the seal of positivity through the wording of Article 6(1) of the Treaty on the Union as adopted in Lisbon[37] – and the Universal Declaration of Human Rights.[38]

Convention. To that purpose, it cited references to general international law, in which it (curiously) included international treaties.' Flauss and Cohen-Jonathan, *supra* n. 19, p. 531 (our translation).

[33] ECtHR (Judgment) 12 November 2008, Case No. 34503/97, *Demir and Baykara* v. *Turkey*, para. 86.

[34] M. Pinto, "El principio pro homine. Criterios de la hermenéutica y pautas para la regulación de los derechos humanos", in *La aplicación de los tratados sobre derechos humanos por los tribunales locales* (Buenos Aires, Ediciones del Puerto 1997), p. 163–171. Mónica Pinto defines the principle as follows: "El principio pro homine es un criterio hermenéutico que informa todo el derecho de los derechos humanos, en virtud del cual se debe acudir a la norma más amplia, o a la interpretación más extensiva, cuando se trata de reconocer derechos protegidos e, inversamente, a la norma o a la interpretación más restringida cuando se trata de establecer restricciones permanentes al ejercicio de los derechos o su suspensión extraordinaria. Este principio coincide con el rasgo fundamental del derecho de los derechos humanos, esto es, estar siempre a favor del hombre."

[35] P. Weil, "De la normativité relative du droit international public", *RGDIP* (1982), p. 5–47.

[36] L. Burgorgue-Larsen, *supra* n. 24, p. 145–173. For an example that allows the Court to enrich the interpretation of Article 14 using the wording of Article 21 of the Charter of Fundamental Rights: ECtHR (Judgment) 1 December 2009, Case No. 43134/05, *G.N. and Others* v. *Italy*, paras. 52 and 126.

[37] It reads as follows: "The Union recognises the rights, freedoms and principles set out in the Charter of Fundamental Rights of the European Union of 7 December 2000, as adopted in Strasbourg on 12 December 2007, which shall have the same legal value as the Treaties. The provisions of the Charter shall not extend in any way the competences of the Union as defined in the Treaties."

[38] P. Tavernier, "La Déclaration universelle des droits de l'homme dans la jurisprudence de la Cour européenne des droits de l'homme" in *Les droits de l'homme au seuil du troisième millénaire. Mélanges en hommage à Pierre Lambert* (Brussels, Bruylant 2000), p. 859–875.

Laurence Burgorgue-Larsen

The progress this represents is extraordinary in every way. Indeed, this use of soft law[39] – and of simple drafts of international treaties or of international treaties that have yet to be adopted by the States parties to the Convention – undermined the formalistic theory of sources of international law. The violence of the criticisms levelled by legal scholars[40] was due to the fact that many of them perceived it as an outright attack on 'the foundations of the international order built in the aftermath of the Second World War on the legal principle of the sovereign equality of States'.[41] In the end, this interpretive approach is based on an assessment of the state of international law (taken *lato sensu*) relative to a specific issue, not only with a view to handing down informed rulings, but also to staying in line with planetary trends, if not to say universal trends. This approach can be seen as striking a perfect balance between regionalism and universalism where human rights are concerned.

2.1.2. Universalism revisited

When the Court draws on the United Nations Convention on the Rights of the Child[42] and the Hague Convention on the Civil Aspects of International Child Abduction[43]; when it demonstrates regard for the multiple 'doctrines' of Convention Committees[44]; when it does not hesitate to use case law solutions formulated by the

---

[39] G. Abi-Saab points out that in the original English, the term 'soft' lacks the negative connotations it acquires in the French translation. See his article in praise of soft law: G. Abi-Saab, "Éloge du "droit assourdi". Quelques réflexions sur le rôle de la soft law en droit international contemporain", in *Nouveaux itinéraires en droit: hommage à F. Rigaux* (Brussels, Bruylant 1993), p. 59–68.

[40] Although Sébastien Van Drooghenbroeck does not reject the open approach per se, it is his view that: 'in the absence of a convincing explanation for its extreme flexibility, the practice of interpretive enrichment runs the risk, not only of being described as arbitrary, but also of undermining the credibility of the external sources it uses.', in Van Drooghenbroeck, *supra* n. 14, p. 832 (our translation).

[41] This formula was coined by Isabelle Duplessis in an article focusing on soft law: I. Duplessis, "Le vertige et la soft law: réactions doctrinales en droit international", *Revue québécoise de droit international* (2007), p. 246–268 (our translation).

[42] E.g. ECtHR (Judgment) 6 July 2010, Case No. 41615/07, *Neulinger and Shuruk* v. *Switzerland*, paras. 48, 50–51.

[43] C. Pettiti, "La jurisprudence de la Cour européenne des droits de l'homme et la Convention de La Haye sur les enlèvements d'enfants", *A.J. Famille* (2006), p. 185; F. Marchadier, "La contribution de la Cour européenne des droits de l'homme à l'efficacité des conventions de La Haye de coopération judiciaire et administrative", 4 *RGDIP* (2007), p. 677–715.

[44] Such as the United Nations Human Rights Committee, the European Committee for the Prevention of Torture, the European Committee of Social Rights, etc. For a theoretical analysis of the jurisdictional authority of these different bodies, see E. Decaux, "Que manque-t-il aux quasi-juridictions internationales pour dire le droit?" in *Le dialogue des juges. Mélanges en l'honneur du président B. Genevois* (Paris, Dalloz 2009), p. 217–232.

national courts of other States[45], by the International Court of Justice[46] or by its sister institution, the Inter-American Court of Human Rights,[47] etc.; in short, when the European Court integrates its function into the planet-wide movement of globalisation –marked by interconnecting economic and financial markets, movements of populations, ideas, beliefs and last but not least of law – surely it can be considered that its analytical approach reveals the universal purview of the European Convention rights.

While some may think that such normative cosmopolitanism – wherein a distinction is no longer made between 'inside' and 'outside', 'us' and 'them'[48] – is actually driven by opportunistic motives, it is not unreasonable to wonder whether this approach might culminate in the positive consequence of a return to the universalism enshrined in the European Convention as regional protective instrument, as opposed to an increased fragmentation of international law.[49] Because – and this is a fundamental point – the open interpretation process is never based on a single external reference, but instead on a set, often a very large set, of different sources which enables the Court to point to a consensus on the planetary scale or, to repeat the wording used by the Court in *Demir and Baykara*, 'common ground in modern societies'.[50] In other words, the combinatory process is integral to the enrichment process; it is obviously a means of legitimising it as an interpretive methodology. This

---

[45]   E.g. ECtHR (Judgment) 1 June 2010, Case No. 22978/05, *Gäfgen v. Germany*, paras. 73–74, in which the Court mentions case law decisions by the United States Supreme Court and the Supreme Court of Appeal of South Africa. For a general analysis of the use of North American case law in European litigation, see J.-F. Flauss, "La présence de la jurisprudence de la Cour Suprême des Etats-Unis dans le contentieux européen des droits de l'homme", 62 *Revue trimestrielle des droits de l'homme* (2005), p. 313–331.

[46]   E.g. ECtHR (Judgment) 4 February 2005, Case Nos. 46827/99 and 46951/99, *Mamatkulov and Askarov v. Turkey*, para. 117; ECtHR (Judgment) 10 March 2009, Case No. 39806/05, *Paladi v. Moldova*, para. 62.

[47]   E.g. ECtHR (Judgment) 18 September 2009, Case Nos. 16064/90, 16065/90, 16066/90, 16068/90, 16069/90, 16070/90, 16071/90, 16072/90 and 16073/90, *Varnava v. Turkey*, paras. 93–98.

[48]   Sociologist Ulrich Beck demonstrates with brio in his stimulating essay U. Beck, *Qu'est-ce que le cosmopolitisme?* (Alto Aubier, 2006), p. 11, that cosmopolitanism has become a reality. He therefore advocates for the urgent necessity of developing a 'cosmopolitan outlook', meaning that "in a world of global crises and dangers produced by civilisation, the old distinctions between inside and outside, national and international, us and them, lose their validity" (our translation). Carrying this approach over to the judicial world, it can be seen that the Strasbourg Court has opted for a 'cosmopolitan outlook' with regard to the interpretation of the Convention.

[49]   This was the view of G. Cohen-Jonathan and J.-F. Flauss, who wrote that: "A sufficiently rationalised and controlled appeal to external sources of inspiration with a view to enriching convention law can in fact have two unintended consequences. Firstly, the European Court might contribute, despite appearances, to the fragmentation of international human rights law, to the extent that it would 'independently' interpret the external standard. Secondly, and most importantly, the fragmentation of international human rights law (which is unfortunately a reality) could, to the extent that the latter was purely and simply received, undermine the consistency of Convention rights."? Flauss and Cohen-Jonathan, *supra* n. 19, p. 533–534 (our translation).

[50]   ECtHR (Judgment) 12 November 2008, Case No. 34503/97, *Demir and Baykara v. Turkey*, para. 86.

Laurence Burgorgue-Larsen

can be demonstrated through a brief presentation of a case that was a forerunner of the *Demir and Baykara* judgment, to wit, the *Sergey Zolotukhin*[51] case. The core issue here was to review the meaning of the fundamental tenet of criminal law: *non bis in idem*. Recognising that its precedents had thus far engendered 'legal uncertainty incompatible with a fundamental right, namely the right not to be prosecuted twice for the same offence',[52] the Grand Chamber decided to 'provide a harmonised interpretation of the notion of the "same offence" – the "idem" element of the *non bis in idem* principle'. It was in that context that the Court stated that 'Article 4 of Protocol No. 7 must be understood as prohibiting the prosecution or trial of a second "offence" in so far as it arises from identical facts or facts which are substantially the same'.[53] Here, the Court's cosmopolitical approach was made formal, whereas it was absent from the Chamber decision handed down on the same case.[54] The body of international and comparative law used to justify the reversal of the decision based on numerous arguments was impressive: in terms of international law, it ranged from Article 14(7) of the International Covenant to Article 20 of the Statute of the International Criminal Court; as for European law, it included Article 50 of the Charter of Fundamental Rights of the European Union, Article 54 of the Convention implementing the Schengen Agreement and the case law of the Court of Justice; in terms of regional human rights law it evoked Article 8(4) of the American Convention as interpreted by the Inter-American Court and, last but not least, where national law was concerned, it cited precedents set by the American Supreme Court.[55] The open approach does not stop at presenting the nomenclature of various external sources, far from it. It is masterfully integrated into the argumentation of the Court, the only difference being that the case law held up as precedent comes from two very different jurisdictions: the Court of Luxembourg on the one hand and the Court of San José on the other hand.[56]

The 'common ground' that the Court referred to in paragraph 86 of its judgment was unquestionably universal in scope. However, we do agree that the expression immediately following the formula was particularly clumsy: 'common ground in modern societies'. Doubtless it would have been more judicious to use the expression

---

[51] ECtHR (Judgment) 10 February 2009, Case No. 14939/03, *Sergey Zolotukhin* v. *Russia*.

[52] Ibid., para. 78.

[53] ECtHR (Judgment) 10 February 2009, Case No. 14939/03, *Sergey Zolotukhin* v. *Russia*, para. 82.

[54] ECtHR (Judgment) 7 June 2007, Case No. 14939/03, *Sergey Zolotukhin* v. *Russia*, this judgment is available in English only.

[55] ECtHR (Judgment) 10 February 2009, Case No. 14939/03, *Sergey Zolotukhin* v. *Russia*, paras. 31–44 of the 'In Fact' section of the judgment.

[56] The reason is simple, they allow the Grand Chamber to interpret rights 'concretely and effectively', in other words, in ways that are useful to people. In their understanding of the concept of non bis in idem, both Community case law and inter-American precedents have granted primacy to the facts rather than their legal classification.

'democratic societies' as it is interpreted by the Court.[57] After all, what is a 'modern' society? How can one measure modernity? What legal parameters can be used to assess it? Questions abound and apparently remain unanswered... At any rate, it seems clear that – from a material standpoint – the consistency of the interpretations arising from cosmopolitanism leads to the recognition of common ground in the different legal systems: paragraph 85 is particularly meaningful in this sense.[58] It states that 'The Court, in defining the meaning of terms and concepts in the text of the Convention, can and must take into account elements of international law other than the Convention, the interpretation of such elements by competent organs, and the practice of European States reflecting their common values. The consensus emerging from specialised international instruments and from the practice of contracting States may constitute a relevant consideration for the Court when it interprets the provisions of the Convention in specific cases.' Could this not be considered a modern form of universalism? Thanks to this syncretic process, the rights enshrined in the Declaration of 1948 remain topical, as they are revisited in the light of contemporary evolutions. At a time when universalism is facing attacks from all quarters,[59] it makes sense for the Court, without setting European law[60] aside, to interpret it in the light of universal trends. In our view, this approach deals with the need for consistency in the protection of human rights at international level, which is something the Inter-American Court of Human Rights has been doing in its own way for quite some time.

In this context, the 'European consensus' no longer has the same strategic importance in the Court's precedents. Not that it has disappeared entirely – far from it – but it no longer possesses the same analytical impact. Whereas the 'domestic legislation and practices of the member States' of the Council of Europe have long been the interpretive guide par excellence; now they are not relegated to the background, but rather used alongside other international references. Combined references increasingly favour the 'international consensus': in other words, they are a

---

[57]   J. Andriantsimbazovina, "L'Etat et la société démocratique dans la jurisprudence de la Cour européenne des droits de l'homme" in *Mélanges en l'honneur de Cohen-Jonathan* (Brussels, Bruylant 2004), p. 57–78.

[58]   In a way, it makes a systematic principle out of a point brought to light by para. 76 of the *Demir and Baykara* judgment: "The Court recently confirmed, in the Saadi v. the United Kingdom judgment (...), that when it considers the object and purpose of the Convention provisions, it also takes into account the international law background to the legal question before it. Being made up of a set of rules and principles that are accepted by the vast majority of States, the common international or domestic law standards of European States reflect a reality that the Court cannot disregard when it is called upon to clarify the scope of a Convention provision that more conventional means of interpretation have not enabled it to establish with a sufficient degree of certainty."

[59]   We refer you to the useful and stimulating essay by C. Fourest, *La dernière utopie. Menaces sur l'universalisme* (Paris, Grasset 2009), 283 p.

[60]   The Court has, in fact, pointed out that 'looking to European law generally [...] provides useful guidance', ECtHR (Judgment) 19 April 2007, Case No. 63235/00, *Vilho Eskelinen and Others v. Finland*, para. 60 (in casu, it was referring to the law of the European Union).

Laurence Burgorgue-Larsen

practical demonstration of the fact that, *in fine*, external sources are decisive elements in the argumentation of the Court. It remains that the opposite is also true, but undoubtedly to a lesser extent. This is, the law of the Council of Europe (hard and soft) and the law of the European Union can still have strategic importance[61] – particularly in relation to the specific nature of certain cases. The *D.H.* case[62] is a good example of the latter hypothesis. In this case, indirect discrimination, which had been timidly used in previous cases,[63] made a dramatic entrance into Strasbourg in a case that thrust the Court into the spotlight of human rights organisations in general and those focusing on minority rights in particular. The 'vulnerability' that emerges whenever the subject involves detention conditions of prisoners or the status of children, made a noted entrance here since it is applied to 'groups'.[64] The Grand Chamber criticised the solution of the judgment of 7 February 2006.[65] It based its arguments both on sources from within the Council of Europe, the 'relevant instruments of the United Nations Organisation', comparative law sources (notably, precedent from the House of Lords and the United States Supreme Court), but also 'the relevant laws and practices within the community'. It also presented the emblematic Article 13 EC[66] (now Article 19 TEEC), the directives adopted pursuant thereto and, last but not least, the abundant case law of the Court of Justice which, through its dealings with numerous cases, enabled Community legislators to integrate the concept of 'indirect

---

[61] Even though it is quantitatively (with regard to the number of cases dealt with by the Court) less present.

[62] ECtHR (Judgment) 13 November 2007, Case No. 57325/00, *D.H.* v. *Czech Republic*.

[63] ECtHR (Decision) 6 June 2005, Case No. 58641/00, *Hoogendijk* v. *Netherlands*.

[64] Although it had already been highlighted by the Chapman case (ECtHR (Judgment) 18 January 2001, Case No. 27238/95, *Chapman* v. *United Kingdom*, para. 96), the prominence of the *D.H.* case lent particular importance to the dictum according to which "the vulnerable position of Roma/ Gypsies means that special consideration should be given to their needs and their different lifestyle both in the relevant regulatory framework and in reaching decisions in particular cases" (para. 181). This "special consideration" becomes a requirement for "special protection" in the following paragraph (para. 182). Does this imply that the sorts of measures commonly known as "positive discrimination" are integrated into the Convention? Although the term would probably be unwelcome within the sphere of the Convention, its underlying philosophy would undoubtedly prosper through positive obligations. This would be one way of giving practical meaning to the solemn statement by the Court that "diversity [should not be] perceived as a threat but as a source of enrichment" (para. 176). In addition to existentialising the fight against ethnic discrimination which "is a form of racial discrimination" in the light of a "democratic vision of society" and requiring the States to "use all available means to combat racism" (para. 176), the *D.H.* case also made a mark in one of the more technical areas regarding evidentiary matters. The Court allows that where indirect discrimination is concerned, "less strict evidential rules should apply" (para. 186). It also accepts statistics as relevant evidence and allows that the burden of proof should be on the State, contradicting (although it does not say so) the *Nachova* judgment that had closed the door to that possibility where acts motivated by racial prejudice were concerned... (para. 189).

[65] See "Chronique de jurisprudence européenne comparée", 4 *RDP* (2007), p. 1133–1134.

[66] E. Dubout, *L'article 13 TCE. La clause communautaire de lutte contre les discriminations* (Brussels, Bruylant 2005), 845 p.

discrimination' into the body of legislation of the Union (points 81–91).[67] We could cite numerous examples where European law(s) were taken into consideration to extend the scope of protected rights. For instance, we could refer to the judgment handed down in the *Konstantin Markin* case[68] which, contrary to the *Petrovic* precedent, considered that the difference in treatment between men and women with respect to parental leave was not founded on an objective and reasonable justification and told the States in no uncertain terms that they should promote equality between the sexes. In fact, we cannot resist the temptation of quoting the decision: "The Court agrees with the Chamber that gender stereotypes, such as the perception of women as primary child-carers and men as primary breadwinners, cannot, by themselves, be considered to amount to sufficient justification for a difference in treatment, any more than similar stereotypes based on race, origin, colour or sexual orientation."[69]

European law(s) are therefore not excluded from the cosmopolitical vision of the Court; however, they are increasingly combined, allied and intertwined with standards that are also the subject of international consensus. The new interpretation of Article 4 of Protocol No. 4 in the *Hirsi Jamaa* case is a clear testimony to this state of affairs. For the first time in its litigious history, the Court examined the applicability of this provision in a case of removal of foreigners to a third State occurring outside of national territory. The Court was to decide whether the transfer of the applicants – migrants intercepted on the high seas – to Libya constituted a 'collective expulsion of aliens'.[70] In response to the argument of the respondent Government, which submitted that there was a 'logical obstacle'[71] to the applicability of Article 4 of Protocol No. 4 in that the applicants were not on the respondent's territory at the time of their transfer to Libya, the Court countered that 'while the cases thus far examined have concerned individuals who were already, in various forms, on the territory of the country concerned, the wording of Article 4 of Protocol No. 4 does not in itself pose an obstacle to its extra-territorial application.'[72] The progressive interpretation of the Convention implied the applicability of the provision and, while European Union legislation played an important role[73] – indeed, a greater role than the legislation of

---

[67] It is defined as follows in paragraph b of Article 2 of Directive 2000/43 of the European Council, dated 29 June 2000, on implementing the principle of equal treatment between persons irrespective of racial or ethnic origin: "indirect discrimination shall be taken to occur where an apparently neutral provision, criterion or practice would put persons of a racial or ethnic origin at a particular disadvantage compared with other persons, unless that provision, criterion or practice is objectively justified by a legitimate aim and the means of achieving that aim are appropriate and necessary".

[68] ECtHR (Judgment) 22 March 2012, Case No. 30078/06, *Konstantin Markin v. Russia.*

[69] Ibid., para. 143.

[70] ECtHR (Judgment) 23 February 2012, Case No. 27765/09, *Hirsi Jamaa and Others v. Italy.*

[71] Ibid., para. 172.

[72] Ibid., paras. 173 et seq., 180.

[73] Ranging from Article 19 of the Charter of Fundamental Rights to Article 17 of the Schengen Agreement, and naturally including Regulation No. 2007/2004 establishing the FRONTEX border management agency, the regulation governing the movement of persons across borders, as well as a

Laurence Burgorgue-Larsen

the Council of Europe[74] – the role of international law was also substantial.[75] A combination of sources, aimed in this case at recognising the violation of Article 4 of Protocol No. 4 to the extent that the Italian authorities decided to transfer the applicants without the slightest concern for the individual situations of the persons concerned.

The use of universal trends generally leads to enrichment of the Convention in relation to its stated objective and purpose; in other words, interpretive enrichment results in benefits for individuals. Interpretation is systematically *pro homine*, with the exception of one major and particularly objectionable case, the *Saadi* case.[76] It is not without interest at this stage to draw a parallel with the analysis that demonstrated that the 'European consensus' was very often cited by the Court, not to ensure progressive interpretation of rights in the victims' favour, but rather to legitimise the status quo.[77] Decompartmentalisation of sources is far distant from such a static, if not to say conservative, approach. The Convention is, now more than ever, a 'living instrument'. Individual rights are reinforced and universalism is revisited. The Court takes a bold, committed approach to its function. As Françoise Tulkens, who has left an indelible mark on the work of the European Court, and Sébastien Van Drooghenbroeck have written 'the most beautiful pages of European Convention law – those that have made the Convention a 'living instrument' - could only be described as 'borderline', as they are posited on the porousness of the borders and the fuzziness of the lines themselves.[78]

2.2.   TARGETED METHODS OF INTERPRETATION

There are a number of targeted methods of interpretation and each of them aims, not only to broaden the scope of application of protected rights (2.2.1), but also to extend their content (2.2.2).

Council decision of 26 April 2010, *inter alia*. (See paras. 28 to 32 of the decision).

[74]   The Court only cited one Resolution of the Parliamentary Assembly of the Council of Europe (Res. No. 1821 of 27 June 2011) on interception and rescue at sea. However, long and important passages of this text were reproduced, since they demonstrated the body of obligations binding on the States in relation to rescue at sea.

[75]   The decision referred to: the 1951 Geneva Convention relating to the Status of Refugees, the 1982 Montego Bay Convention, the 1979 International Convention on Maritime Search and Rescue ("SAR Convention") (amended in 2004) and the Protocol against the Smuggling of Migrants by Land, Sea and Air ("the Palermo Protocol") (2000).

[76]   ECtHR (Judgment) 29 January 2008, Case No. 13229/03, *Saadi v. United Kingdom*.

[77]   F. Sudre, "A propos du dynamisme interprétatif de la Cour européenne des droits de l'homme", *JCP* (2001-I), 335.

[78]   Tulkens and Van Drooghenbroeck, *supra* n. 14, p. 522 (our translation). The authors recall with interest that, in *Marckx*, Belgium had been out-manoeuvred as was Turkey in *Demir and Baykara*. The Court based its progressive interpretation on two international conventions, respectively dated 1962 and 1975, which Belgium, like the other States parties to the Convention, had yet to ratify at the time, see ECtHR (Judgment) 13 June 1979, Case No. 6833/74, *Marckx v. Belgium*, para. 41.

2.2.1. Broadening the area of application of the rights embodied in the Convention

2.2.1.1. Autonomous concepts

The technique of 'autonomisation' of concepts found in the Convention has mobilised judicial activism in the European Court in recent years. In order to apply the Convention uniformly across staggeringly eclectic legal systems, the European Court engaged very early on in a vast process of uniform interpretation of concepts enshrined in the Convention that – although they existed in the different national legal traditions – did not necessarily have the same meaning. This process has rightfully been the focus of comment in legal doctrine. While Marc-André Eissen, in a study published in the Revue du droit public in 1986,[79] counted no fewer than fifteen concepts that – in his view – had been made autonomous by the Court,[80] other authors counted only seven. The latter notably included Frédéric Sudre, who wrote, in 1998, that the concepts of 'arrest', 'civil rights and obligations', 'criminal', 'witness', 'charge', 'sentence' and 'property'[81] were the only valid 'autonomous concepts'... Such studies demonstrate the difficulty, in legal scholarship, of drawing definite and indisputable lines in a subject matter that is both evolving and complex. What is clear is that the technique exists, that it has been implemented and that is has enabled the Court to establish the applicability of the Convention to a considerable number of different situations. Above all, the theory of autonomous concepts is 'progressing' and, in the time since these general analyses were written, the Court has continued to move ahead. Thus, to the nomenclature of 'autonomous' concepts, we can now add 'residence'[82] and 'expulsion'.[83] The Court has also effected a special interpretation of the concept mentioned in Article 1 upon which its competence depends directly: this is the concept of 'jurisdiction' which, depending on whether it is broadly or narrowly interpreted, either allows or disallows extraterritorial application of the Convention. In this regard, we should not hesitate to recall that the days are long past when the Court, in its famous decision on the inadmissibility of *Bankovic and Others*,[84] enshrined the importance of 'territorialisation' of the jurisdiction of the High Contracting Parties. Indeed, subsequent case law shows that the Court made a sudden

---

79   M.-A. Eissen, "La Cour européenne des droits de l'homme", *RDP* (1986), p. 1539–1598 and 1773–1783.

80   Thus, alongside the very classic 'criminal charge' and 'civil obligation', he also cited concepts such as 'the mentally ill', 'sentence', 'law', 'magistrate', 'injured party', 'victim', 'witness', 'tribunal', 'public interest', 'vagrant', 'detention', 'conviction', and 'application to set aside'.

81   F. Sudre, "Le recours aux notions autonomes", in F. Sudre (ed.), *L'interprétation de la Convention européenne des droits de l'homme* (Brussels, Bruylant 1998), p. 93–131.

82   ECtHR (Judgment) 18 November 2004, Case. No. 58255/00, *Prokopovich v. Russia*.

83   ECtHR (Judgment) 5 October 2006, Case No. 14139/03, *Bolat v. Russia*.

84   ECtHR (Decision) 12 December 2001, Case No. 52207/99, *Bankovic and Others v. Belgium and sixteen other contracting parties*.

Laurence Burgorgue-Larsen

turnaround as to the recognition of the 'regional' nature of the Convention by openly recognising extraterritorial application of the European Convention. In cases ranging from the *Issa* case[85] to the *Al-Saadoon* case[86], not forgetting the recent *Medvedyev* case[87] which was highly publicised in France,[88] the theory of effective oversight based on the existence of 'full and exclusive control' reasserted itself.[89]

To allow the reader to measure the importance of this approach in terms of broadening the applicability of the Convention, we will focus on the example of Article 6(1), which enshrines the right to a hearing. The European Convention limits the justiciability of Article 6(1) to cases where litigation is grounded on specific objections focusing on 'civil rights and obligations' or 'criminal charges'. It is our view that this limitation of the scope of application of the right to a hearing is rather unfortunate, although it was understandable at the time when the Convention was drafted in 1950.[90] However, it is now in complete contradiction with Article 8(1) of the American Convention, Article 7 of the African Charter and, last but not least, with Article 47 of the Charter of Fundamental Rights of the European Union (EUCFR). All case law of the Court, since 1959, has focused on broadening the scope of application of Article 6 to the furthest extent possible by using progressive interpretation to considerably restrict the civil and criminal realms that still benefit from immunity under the Convention. By playing the 'autonomous' concepts card to achieve this, the Court revealed the extent of its control over all phases leading up to court rulings.

Civil matters. Whilst the authors of the Convention were thinking essentially of private litigation when they wrote the formula 'civil rights and obligations' – to wit litigation between private individuals or between private individuals and the State when it acts like a private individual – the Court decided to include – at the cost of an

---

[85]   ECtHR (Judgment) 16 November 2004, Case No. 31821/96, *Issa and Others* v. *Turkey*, see p. Tavernier, *JDI* (2005), p. 477–479.

[86]   ECtHR (Decision) 30 June 2009, 61498/08, *Al Saadoon and Mufdhi* v. *United Kingdom*, J.-F. Flauss, *AJDA* (2009), p. 1936.

[87]   ECtHR (Judgment) 29 March 2010, Case No. 3394/03, *Medvedyev and Others* v. *France*, para. 67: "That being so, the Court considers that, as this was a case of France having exercised full and exclusive control over the Winner and its crew, at least de facto, from the time of its interception, in a continuous and uninterrupted manner until they were tried in France, the applicants were effectively within France's jurisdiction for the purposes of Article 1 of the Convention (contrast Banković, cited above)."

[88]   The case was widely covered in the media. See Le Monde, 30 March 2010, which headlined: "La CEDH contourne la question du statut du parquet" (The ECtHR skirts the issue of the status of the Court").

[89]   This created a paradoxical situation. In certain cases–which could imperil the peacekeeping actions of the United Nations (particularly in the implementation of its peacekeeping missions) – it has set aside the question of effective control to place the focus of its argumentation on the question of its competence ratione personae (*Behrami and Saramati*), whilst in other situations that less directly involved UN activities, it has not hesitated to play the card of the theory of effective control! A true case of variable geometry in the applicability of the Convention and the scope of application of conventional protection.

[90]   The same unfortunate limitation is found in Article 14 of the ICCPR, drafted in 1966.

unbelievable overstepping of the original intent of the authors of the Convention – all litigation where elements of public law were involved. It was necessary to somehow take account of the 'blurring' of the lines of demarcation between private and public law in European societies, which were strongly marked by interventions by the public authorities in many realms. The Court did so by autonomising the term 'civil' so that it was no longer constrained by domestic law classifications[91] – and allowing the applicability of Article 6 even when a public corporation is involved in the litigation.[92]

Thenceforth, the progressive interpretation of the Convention was used to considerably broaden the scope of application of Article 6 to the extent that today, it is quicker and easier to list the realms that remain excluded from the guarantee of a fair trial in civil matters than to do the opposite. There are only four and they involve four types of parties: taxpayers, as fiscal taxes and customs duty matters still form part of the hard core of public-authority prerogatives[93]; aliens, in that procedures for granting political asylum or lifting entry bans are specific to the immigration police[94]; executive public officials, in that they belong to an administrative system that has expressly excluded their access to domestic courts and in which they exercise a portion of State authority (see exceptions below in the *Vilho Eskelinen* case law); and finally voters and elected officials – in that electoral disputes pertain to 'political rights' which are different from 'civil' rights and are therefore disputes of a political nature (the right to vote and to stand for election).[95]

Excepting these material pockets of immunity – which are difficult to accept in the light of both the importance of the right of access to justice for the protection of other rights and the wording of the other international instruments[96] – the Court has placed a large number of realms under its purview – matters of public law (including litigation involving the civil service) as well as financial, disciplinary and social disputes – on the basis of the 'property' criterion. We will focus here on the first realm. Any civil servant who has a dispute with the administration regarding his or her right to a pension[97] or who claims social assistance[98] can refer to Article 6(1). Proceedings involving the prison system have also managed to come under Article 6(1) in that any decision affecting a prisoner has repercussions on the exercise of his or her civil rights.[99] In that

---

[91] ECtHR (Judgment) 16 July 1971, Case No. 2614/65, *Ringeisen v. Austria.*

[92] ECtHR (Judgment) 28 June 1978, Case No. 6232/73, *König v. Germany.*

[93] ECtHR (Judgment) 12 July 2001, Case No. 44759/98, *Ferrazzini v. Italy.*

[94] ECtHR (Judgment) 12 July 2001, Case No. 44759/98, *Ferrazzini v. Italy.*

[95] ECtHR (Decision) 21 October 1997, Case No. 24194/94, *Pierre-Bloch v. France*; ECtHR (Decision) 14 September 1999, Case No. 41944/98, *Louis Masson v. France*; ECtHR (Decision) 26 January 1999, Case No. 31599/96, *Jacques Cheminade v. France.*

[96] Even though we will see below that the scope of criminal matters partially offsets the jurisdictional immunity of the civil scope (see below).

[97] ECtHR (Judgment) 26 November 1992, Case No. 12490/86, *Giancarlo Lombardo v. Italy*; ECtHR (Judgment) 18 July 2000, Case No. 41453/98, *S.M. v. France.*

[98] ECtHR (Judgment) 26 February 1993, Case No. 13023/87, *Salesi v. Italy.*

[99] ECtHR (Judgment) 6 April 2010, Case No. 46194/06, *Stegarescu and Bahrin v. Portugal.*

Laurence Burgorgue-Larsen

context, civil servant disputes have also come under the province of the Court thanks to a meandering and disconnected body of case law. Meandering, because the jurisprudence took many contradictory twists and turns, which undermined legal certainty by establishing judicial uncertainties at the domestic jurisdictions level. The Grand Chamber decision in *Pellegrin* v. *France*[100] was a major turnaround in case law which opted for a so-called 'functional' criterion to determine the applicability of Article 6(1) to civil service disputes (nature of the duties and responsibilities exercised by the public official). The Court seized on the standards established by the European Commission – for the purposes of determining categories of persons excluded from the right of free movement – and transposed them into the context of the Convention. In the *Vilho Eskelinen* case, the Court considered that there was once again a need to change its case law; the functional criterion had proved disappointing and had failed to simplify decisions on applicability.[101] In order to legitimise this new 'change in direction', the Court once again used European Union law, in this case Article 47 of the EUCFR, an important provision that does not materially limit the right to trial. The case law was a bit vague and continued that same trend, since the *Vilho Eskelinen* judgment – which reflected the state of case law at the time in Strasbourg – is not necessarily any easier to implement. The principle is the applicability of Article 6(1) to all civil service litigation, as the Court considered that the right to a hearing for civil servants under domestic law automatically entailed the applicability of the protection embodied in the Convention. However, this presumption of applicability of Article 6(1) was evacuated in the presence of two cumulative conditions: 'the State in its national law must have expressly excluded access to a court for the post or category of staff in question' and, in addition, the State must prove that 'the subject matter of the dispute in issue is related to the exercise of State power or that it has called into question the special bond' of trust and loyalty between the civil servant and the State, as employer.[102] The French Conseil d'Etat, after having suffered from the turnaround on the Court's case-law policy, accepted the *Vilho Eskelinen* precedent by decreeing the applicability of Article 6(1) to proceedings before the Conseil Supérieur de la Magistrature, France's judicial service commission.[103]

Criminal matters. The process of rendering concepts autonomous has enabled the Court to proceed in the criminal realm in the same manner as in the civil realm. It was therefore able to extend the scope of application of Article 6(1) to sanctions that are not, per se, described as 'criminal' by the legal systems of the States parties. The founding

---

[100]   ECtHR (Judgment) 8 December 1999, Case No. 28541/95, *Pellegrin* v. *France*.

[101]   ECtHR (Judgment) 19 April 2007, Case No. 63235/00, *Vilho Eskelinen and Others* v. *Finland*. Paragraph 55 is eloquent in this respect: "The Court can only conclude that the functional criterion, as applied in practice, has not simplified the analysis of the applicability of Article 6 in proceedings to which a civil servant is a party or brought about a greater degree of certainty in this area as intended (see, mutatis mutandis, Perez v. France [GC], no. 47287/99, §55, ECHR 2004 I.)."

[102]   ECtHR (Judgment) 19 April 2007, Case No. 63235/00, *Vilho Eskelinen and Others* v. *Finland*, para. 62.

[103]   CE, 12 December 2007, M.A.

---

decision here is the *Engel* judgment[104] relating to disciplinary measures imposed on Dutch nationals while they were carrying out their compulsory military service. In the judgment, three criteria were presented as defining 'criminal charges': whether the provisions defining the offence are part of criminal law, the nature of the offence itself and the purpose and degree of severity of the penalty incurred, the latter two being fundamental in cases where the national legal system does not describe the offence as being criminal. After being applied to military disciplinary measures and to disciplinary measures against prisoners[105] – leading to a reversal of the precedent of the Conseil d'Etat on the nature of internal measures not subject to appeal[106] – the phenomenon of criminalisation also entered the realm of administrative sanctions[107] as well as the realm of fiscal penalties.[108] Thus, any penalties – such as endorsement of penalty points on one's driving licence[109] – imposed by the administrative authorities fall within the scope of application of Article 6(1). This phenomenon also applies to independent administrative authorities that exercise powers of repression, such as France's financial markets council (Conseil des marchés financiers),[110] its securities and exchange commission, the COB, and even its competition council (Conseil de la concurrence). Regarding fiscal litigation, although it escaped the influence of Article 6(1) from a 'civil' standpoint (see above), it was made subject thereto through the criminal realm, where the criteria outlined in the Engel judgment can be applied without the seriousness of the penalty being of particular importance.[111] Thus, tax surcharges imposed by the tax authorities, non-litigious fiscal proceedings[112] and penalties under customs law[113] fall under the 'criminal' realm.

One of the notable consequences of the continuous broadening of the area of application of Article 6(1) has been the exceptional scope it has given to the Convention's purview.

2.2.1.2. Dilution of concepts

The extension of a concept under the Convention leads to a broadening of the area of application of the rights embodied in the Convention. The *right to respect for private*

---

[104] ECtHR (Judgment) 8 June 1976, Case Nos. 5100/71, 5101/71, 5102/71, 5354/72 and 5370/72, *Engel and Others v. Netherlands*.

[105] ECtHR (Judgment) 28 June 1984, Case No. 7819/77 and 7878/77, *Campbell and Fell v. UK*.

[106] CE, 17 February 1995, *Marie and Hardouin*.

[107] ECtHR (Judgment) 21 February 1984, Case No. 8544/79, *Oztürk v. Germany*.

[108] ECtHR (Judgment) 24 February 1994, Case No. 12547/86, *Bendenoun v. France*; ECtHR (Judgment) 4 March 2004, Case No. 47650/99, *Silvester's Horeca Service v. Belgium*.

[109] ECtHR (Judgment) 23 September 1998, Case No. 27812/95, *Malige v. France*.

[110] ECtHR (Decision) 27 August 2002, Case No. 58188/00, *Didier v. France*.

[111] ECtHR (Judgment) 23 November 2006, Case No. 73053/01, *Jussila v. Finland*.

[112] ECtHR (Judgment) 26 September 1996, Case No. 18978/91, *Miailhe v. France*.

[113] ECtHR (Judgment) 7 October 1988, Case No. 10519/83, *Salabiaku v. France* and ECtHR (Judgment) 25 February 1993, Case No. 10828/84, *Funke v. France*.

Laurence Burgorgue-Larsen

and family life (Article 8) is a particularly striking example which will be used in further below. The broadening or, some would, say the 'dilution' of the concept of 'private and family life' proceeds from a choice made by a judge who wishes to confer a *useful meaning* on the concept. Such extension of the area of application of private life does not call upon common legal principles or the need to interpret the Convention 'in the light of contemporary conditions': the European judge proceeds by simply making an affirmation at his or her own discretion. Article 8 of the Convention continues to yield extended content, shaped by the changing mores of our times. The image of 'concentric circles' can be helpful in describing this transformation, since it enables us to visualise both temporal and material changes in Article 8. While intimacy is part of the first circle – in that it constitutes the 'hard core' of matters relating to private and family life and in that it formed the basis for the founding decisions of the Court – the latter did not hesitate to set in place a process of broadening its applicability, leading to the creation of a second concentric circle focusing on socialisation, then a third focusing on environmental well-being. This process was made possible by the fact that the Court never attempted to define the concepts of 'private life' or 'family life'. This methodological choice allowed it to progressively include a number of possible cases as European societies evolved. These will be presented below.

Intimacy. An individual's relationship with his or her body and sexuality pertains to personal intimacy, but the first circle also includes relationships formed between individuals in their family circles. The hard core of intimacy comprises issues involving sexual identity[114] and individual sexual practices[115] and has even gone so

---

[114] As early as 1976, the European Commission affirmed that the right to respect for private life implied "the right to establish and develop relationships with other human beings, especially in the emotional field for the development and fulfillment of one's own personality" (ECommHR (Decision) 18 May 1976, Case No. 6825/74, *X.* v. *Iceland*). This obviously includes people's sex lives. The work of the Court has helped us eliminate a great number of stereotypes, particularly regarding homosexuals and transsexuals. By clearly stating the right of all human beings to lead the sex lives of their choice in keeping with their own personalities, the Strasbourg Court was the first international jurisdiction that contributed to extirpating the criminalisation of homosexual acts conducted in private between consenting adults from the European legislative landscape, even though 'members of the public who regard homosexuality as immoral may be shocked, offended or disturbed' (ECtHR (Judgment) 22 October 1981, Case No. 7525/76, *Dudgeon* v. *Ireland*; ECtHR (Judgment) 26 October 1988, Case No. 10581/83, *Norris* v. *Ireland*; ECtHR (Judgment) 22 April 1993, Case No. 15070/89, *Modinos* v. *Cyprus*). Importantly, these cases inspired the American Supreme Court (US Supreme Court, 26 June 2003, *Lawrence* v. *Texas*, 539 US). On the basis of this jurisprudential triptych, the Court combatted all forms of discriminations experienced by homosexual persons–on the sole basis of their sexual identity – in the realms of private and family life. Over time, it built up a very rich body of case law, which was successfully imported by the inter-America human rights system.

[115] The *K.A. and A.D.* decision established the jurisprudential policy of the Court regarding sexual practices falling within the scope of the application of Article 8, to wit sadomasochistic practices (ECtHR (Judgment) 17 February 2005, Case No. 42758/98 and 45558/99, *K.A. and A.D.* v. *Belgium*). The issue can be summarised as follows: can individuals, in the name of their freedom to dispose of their bodies as they wish, freely engage in practices that border on inhuman treatment? The answer of the Court was yes, so long as all the parties involved consent to the commission of such acts. The Court also justifies its presentation of the different facets of "personal freedom". Paragraph 83 of the

far as to include reproductive technology[116] to help people have children, a key element in the theme of 'family life'. The case law has included a great many and very disparate situations in the scope of application of the concept of 'family life'. In a famous judgment that obliged France to review its whole inheritance system – since it had established a difference in the treatment of 'legitimate' and 'adulterine' children – the Court stated that: 'the institution of the family is not fixed, be it historically, sociologically or even legally'.[117] Thus, a broad view is taken of the family, including numerous types of relationships.[118]

---

judgment warrants reproduction (our translation): "Article 8 of the Convention protects the right to personal fulfillment, both in the form of personal development (Christine Goodwin v. United Kingdom, 11 July 2002) or under the aspect of personal autonomy, which reflects an important principle underlying the interpretation of the guarantees provided in Article 8 (Pretty v. United Kingdom, 29 April 2002). This right implies the right to establish and develop relationships with other human beings and the outside world [...] including sexual relationships, which are one of the most intimate areas of the private sphere and are accordingly protected by this provision [...]. The right to entertain sexual relationships also includes the right to dispose of one's body, which is an integral part of personal autonomy. This means that 'one's will to live according to one's wishes must extend to the possibility that the person engages in activities perceived as physically or morally damaging or dangerous to their person. In other words, the concept of personal autonomy can be taken to mean the right to make choices regarding one's own body' (Pretty, op. cit., §66)."

[116] The *S.H.* case is both an extension and a refinement of the change that led to the inclusion of issues involving assisted reproductive technology (ART) in the scope of application of Article 8 (ECtHR (Judgment) 3 November 2011, Case No. 57813/00, *S.H. and Others v. Austria*). This evolution was furthered by the Grand Chamber ruling on the *Evans* case, in which the Court allowed that the concept of private life included the right to respect for the decision of whether or not to have a child (ECtHR (Judgment) 10 April 2007, Case No. 6339/05, *Evans v. United Kingdom*) and continued with the *Dickson* judgment (ECtHR (Judgment) 4 December 2007, Case No. 44362/04, *Dickson v. United Kingdom*), which focused on whether one could carry out an artificial insemination using the frozen sperm of the husband in a couple: the right to become genetic parents fell within the scope of application of private and family life (para. 66). In the case of the *S.H.* judgment, it was the right to become parents through medical techniques in the event of infertility that fell under Article 8 (para. 82).

[117] ECtHR (Judgment) 1 *February* 2000, Case No. 34406/97, *Mazurek v. France*, para. 52.

[118] First, there is the circle of relationships where children are involved. Thus, "A child born out of such a relationship is ipso jure part of that 'family' unit from the moment of his birth and by the very fact of it" (ECtHR (Judgment) 26 May 1994, Case No. 28867/03, *Keegan v. UK*, para. 44), whether the child is born outside of marriage (ECtHR (Judgment) 13 June 1979, Case No. 6833/74, *Marckx v. Belgium*) or not. The Court also stressed the special relationship between grandparents and their grandchildren (ECtHR (Judgment) 9 June 1998, Case No. 22430/93, *Bronda v. Italy*), as well as that between adoptive parents and their adopted child, since de facto family ties were deemed to be important (ECtHR (Judgment) 28 October 1998, Case No. 24484/94, *Söderbäck v. Sweden*), while they also granted the States a considerable margin of discretion to establish a maximal age for adopting (ECtHR (Judgment) 10 June 2010, Case No. 25762/07, *Schwizgebel v. Switzerland*). In this context, whereas the Convention offered no legal foundation in relation to children, the Court built up a highly protective body of case law highlighting the principle of 'the child's best interests' founded on the international corpus juris (New York Convention on the Rights of the Child of 1989 and the Hague Convention on the Civil Aspects of International Child Abduction of 1980) as well as European instruments, notably Article 24(2) of the EU Charter of Fundamental Rights which is highlighted in the case law (ECtHR (Judgment) 6 July 2010, Case No. 41615/07, *Neulinger and Shuruk v. Switzerland*). In family matters, time can have disastrous consequences on parent-child relationships, a fact that often leads the Court to condemn the States, based on the theory of positives

Laurence Burgorgue-Larsen

Socialisation. The expression 'socialisation' should be taken here in its comprehensive sense encompassing both relationships between individuals – as man is undoubtedly a 'social animal' – and also professional relationships without which individuals would be unable to socialise as well as the lives of private companies. The *Société Colas Est* judgment allowed the Court to take another step forward in the process of extending private life in the social realm as well as the professional realm.[119] Indeed, in paragraph 41 it affirms that: 'the rights guaranteed by Article 8 of the Convention may be construed as including the right to respect for a company's registered office, branches or other business premises'. Here, the Court completes its evolution in relation to the private lives of business companies, which timidly began in 1989 with the *Chappel* judgment[120] and was continued and amplified in 1992 with the *Niemietz* judgment.[121]

Environmental well-being. Historically, Article 8 has been the vector of environmental protection. The Court began in a detailed manner in 1994 with the *López Ostra* judgment[122] in which it deemed that the nuisance caused by foul-smelling emissions from a tannery effluent treatment plant violated the applicant's right to respect of his residence. It was a dramatic turn of events, even though it was foreshadowed by previous cases.[123] Thus, the Court began by building on the concept of 'residence'. It should however be pointed out that the subsequent case law was chaotic, marked by sizeable turnarounds in position and subsequent steps forward and backward in relation to the scope of indirect protection of the environment through Article 8 – also known as 'protection by ricochet'. It should be noted that the cases submitted to the Court involved colossal economic stakes that led to a rebellion by the States – supported by certain private entities through the *amicus curiae* technique – which fought to make the Court give ground in terms of its environmentalist approach, which was proving far too costly. Focusing originally on the 'residence', the Court subsequently protected the environment through the all-embracing concept, extremely broad to say the least, of 'private and family life' as such, in the *Guerra*

---

obligations, when they fail to make the necessary efforts to reunite a parent with his or her child (e.g. ECtHR (Judgment) 22 May 2012, Case No. 61173/08, *Santos Nunes v. Portugal*: the inaction and lack of diligence on the part of the Portuguese authorities in the execution of the decision granting the applicant custody of his child violated his right to respect for his family life). There is also the circle of relationships established without children being involved. Thus, family life exists even in the case of an exclusively bilateral relationship between two adults, as long as the relationship is real and genuine. A heterosexual couple can have a 'family life as spouses' (ECtHR (Judgment) 26 mars 1992, Case No. 12083/86, *Beldjoudi v. France*), as can transsexual persons (ECtHR (Judgment) 22 April 1997, Case No. 21830/93, *X., Y., Z. v. United Kingdom*) and homosexual couples (ECtHR (Judgment) 24 June 2010, Case No. 30141/04, *Schalk and Kopf v. Austria*).

[119]   ECtHR (Judgment) 16 April 2002, Case No. 37971/97, *Société Colas Est and Others v. France*.

[120]   ECtHR (Judgment) 30 March 1989, Case No. 10461/83, *Chappel v. United Kingdom*.

[121]   ECtHR (Judgment) 16 December 1992, Case No. 13710/88, *Niemietz v. Germany*.

[122]   ECtHR (Judgment) 9 December 1994, Case No. 16798/90, *López Ostra v. Spain*.

[123]   ECtHR (Judgment) 21 February 1990, Case No. 9310/81, *Powell and Rayner v. United Kingdom*.

case[124] and the *Hatton* case involving nuisances caused by night flights in the area surrounding Heathrow Airport.[125] However, the residence once again played a pivotal role in the Court's consolidation of the right to a healthy environment in the *Moreno Gómez* judgment, which was marked by a tighter analytical focus.[126] Although the environmental component of Article 8 was restricted to focus more tightly on the residence, the Court considerably broadened its scope by highlighting the procedural component of protection beginning with the *Taskin* judgment[127]; the case involved the nuisances inherent in the operation of a gold mine using the cyanide process). The Court found a positive procedural obligation – based on Article 8 – including public access to information and ongoing investigations in relation to the hazardous effects of industrial activities. The *Tatar* judgment[128] on cyanide pollution of a water course, followed – but also furthered – this movement in which public access to environmental studies and the principle of precaution were particularly emphasised by the Court, using a formula that opens up numerous perspectives: 'enjoyment of a healthy and protected environment' …

2.2.2. Extending the content of the rights embodied in the Convention

2.2.2.1. The theory of inherence

By using the theory of 'elements necessarily inherent in a right', the European Court has considerably enriched the content of the law whose application it oversees and has determined positive, substantial and procedural obligations for the States. One example is the right to a fair trial (Article 6(1)). It has been 'reconstituted' by the European Court in three parts: a central element involving procedural guarantees, *stricto sensu*, appearing in the text of Article 6(1), was augmented by two 'material' components: the right of access to a court and the right to the enforcement of legal decisions. Thus, in its *Golder* judgment, the Court, having noted that 'one can scarcely conceive of the rule of law without there being a possibility of having access to the courts',[129] deemed that 'the right of access constitutes an element which is inherent in the right stated by Article 6 para. 1'. Through similar reasoning founded on inherence, the European Court ruled in *Hornsby*[130] that 'execution of a judgement given by any court must therefore be regarded as an integral part of the "trial" for the purposes of Article 6'. The idea here is to give the right to a hearing its full effect. This approach

---

124   ECtHR (Judgment) 19 February 1998, Case No. 14967/89, *Guerra* v. *Italy.*

125   ECtHR (Judgment) 10 February 2001, Case No. 36022/97, *Hatton and Others* v. *United Kingdom*; ECtHR (Judgment) 8 July 2003, Case No. 36022/97, *Hatton* v. *United Kingdom.*

126   ECtHR (Judgment) 16 November 2004, Case No. 4143/02, *Moreno Gómez* v. *Spain.*

127   ECtHR (Judgment) 10 November 2004, Case No. 46117/99, *Taskin and Others* v. *Turkey.*

128   ECtHR (Judgment) 27 January 2009, Case No. 67021/01, *Tatar* v. *Romania.*

129   ECtHR (Judgment) 21 February 1975, Case No. 4451/70, *Golder* v. *United Kingdom*, para. 34.

130   ECtHR (Judgment) 19 March 1997, Case No. 18357/91, *Hornsby* v. *Greece*, para. 40.

Laurence Burgorgue-Larsen

also includes updating of implicit free trial guarantees, first among which is the principle of equality of arms, but also the obligation to provide adequate justification for justice decisions and the right to remain silent and not to incriminate oneself. By affirming that a new guarantee is 'inherent' in a protected right, i.e. that it is consubstantial therewith because it is necessary for the right to have effect, the Court seeks to show that it is not engaging in an extensive interpretation of the Convention *'of a nature to impose new obligations on the contracting States',*[131] but rather that is it simply controlling the logical development of a right embodied in the Convention, so as to ensure its practicality.

The theory of inherence is therefore aimed at protecting the Court against potential accusations of a 'government of judges', but it is unable to hide the fact that the detection of 'inherent' elements in the law falls under the sole responsibility of the judges.

2.2.2.2. The theory of positive obligations

The Court has never theoretically defined and/or systematised its theory of positive obligations.[132] However, it can be discerned based on a great many cases in which statements have been made in that regard. According to the European Court of Human Rights, 'the prime characteristic of positive obligations is that they in practice require national authorities to take the necessary measures to safeguard a right or, more specifically, to adopt reasonable and suitable measures to protect the rights of the individual.'[133] These measures may be of any nature, they may be 'legal' and/or 'practical', e.g. the obligation imposed on national authorities to adopt new legislation (in the former case) or to set up a prison system in which suicides can be prevented (in the latter case). Positive obligations can be distinguished from negative obligations by their nature; the former require positive action on the part of the State whereas the latter require the State to abstain from taking action in the form of 'interference'. 'Violation of the Convention will result in the first case from inaction, i.e. passivity, on the part of the national authorities, and in the second case from their preventing or limiting the exercise of the right through positive action.'[134]

The case law has shown that positive obligations arise from the duty to protect persons placed under State jurisdiction. This duty can be fulfilled essentially, if not to say exclusively, by ensuring compliance with the Convention in relations between private individuals. In other words, the theory of positive obligations has been the theoretical foundation used to establish the extension of the Convention to private relations, i.e. the Convention's famed 'horizontal effect'. Thus, the State may be held liable for violations committed between private individuals to the extent that a

---

[131] ECtHR (Judgment) 21 February 1975, Case No. 4451/70, *Golder* v. *United Kingdom*, para. 76.

[132] It appeared for the first time in the Belgian linguistic case in 1968.

[133] J.-F. Akandji-Kombe, *Positive obligations under the European Convention on Human Rights* (Strasbourg, Council of Europe 2006), p. 7.

[134] Ibid., p. 11.

Interpreting the European Convention

shortcoming is observed on the part of the legal system (in the form of misaction or inaction... as is further demonstrated by the fact that 'the dividing line with negative obligations [is] very tenuous').

The other binary movement characterising this theory is the appearance of so-called 'procedural' and 'substantial' obligations. The former call for the organisation of internal procedures aimed at enhancing personal protection, which command the organisation of appropriate remedies to rights violations; to wit, the obligation of thorough investigation but also, more broadly, the duty of the State to equip itself with effective and dissuasive criminal legislation. The latter are obligations calling for the substantive measures required for full enjoyment of the embodied rights. For example, in relation to Article 2 (the right to life), the material obligation to protect individuals' lives applies in a general way to all persons deprived of their freedom and placed under the control of the public authorities, whether they are held in police custody,[135] in administrative custody[136] or in medical facilities (in prisons or hospitals).

Let us cite the (major) example of the right to life (Article 2) which, by definition, prohibits phenomena such as enforced disappearances, targeted killings, etc. Regarding the matter of enforced disappearances, up until 1999, the European Court only viewed this crime as a violation of freedom and personal safety.[137] Everything changed with the *Cakici* judgment.[138] The Court declared that, in cases involving the disappearance of a person following arrest and detainment by police, it found an infringement of Article 2 due to the attitude of the State that had failed to protect the life of the prisoner. It arrived at that conclusion on the basis of inter-American case law, which is amazingly rich and inventive on that theme to the point of establishing the prohibition of enforced disappearances as a *jus cogens* in addition to the corollary duty of investigating and punishing such crimes.[139] Thus, the Court now considers that in the absence of the body of a disappeared person, that person is to be presumed dead and his or her legal successors are not obliged to prove the death.[140] This material obligation is combined with a procedural obligation on the State to conduct an effective, serious and objective investigation on the disappearance, death and/or injury of any persons placed under its custody with a view to launching legal proceedings to be implemented with all due diligence. Therefore, when the Court finds a systematic lack of investigation[141]; when investigations are conducted by persons who are not independent[142] or when they favour the evidence of persons

---

[135]   ECtHR (Judgment) 27 June 2000, Case No. 21986/93, *Salman* v. *Turkey*.

[136]   ECtHR (Judgment) 27 July 2004, Case No. 57671/00, *Slimani* v. *France*.

[137]   ECtHR (Judgment) 25 May 1998, Case No. 24276/94, *Kurt* v. *Turkey*.

[138]   ECtHR (Judgment) 8 July 1999, Case No. 23657/94, *Cakici* v. *Turkey*.

[139]   IACtHR (Judgment) 22 September 2006, *Goiburu* v. *Paraguay*.

[140]   ECtHR (Judgment) 13 June 2000, Case No. 23531/94, *Timurtas* v. *Turkey*; ECtHR (Judgment) 14 November 2000, Case No. 24396/94, *Tas* v. *Turkey*.

[141]   ECtHR (Judgment) 10 May 2001, Case No. 25781/94, *Cyprus* v. *Turkey*.

[142]   ECtHR (Judgment) 1 June 2003, Case No. 29178/95, *Finucane* v. *United Kingdom*.

Laurence Burgorgue-Larsen

engaging in the commission of illegal acts,[143] the Court finds a procedural violation of Article 2. The finding of procedural violations is very common (sometimes in combination with Article 13),[144] since it allows the Court to remedy the difficulty of finding a material violation of Article 2.[145]

By combining material and procedural obligations, the Court has contributed to considerably enlarging the scope of European control, particularly through Articles 2 (right to life) and 8 (right to respect for one's private and family life). This has added new burdens on the States, which continue to take measure of the extremely high level of protection with each passing day.

3.   JUDICIAL RESTRAINT UNDER DEBATE

Although, since the entry into force of Protocol No. 11, the States have all accepted the obligatory jurisdiction of the Court and the fact that they have no means of removing themselves therefrom (unless they denounce the Convention and withdraw from the system), it so happens that the methods of interpretation of the Convention, because they are often bold, can spark a certain amount of defiance on the part of the States. The States are still highly sensitive to their national interests, which reflect their constitutional specificities and, ultimately, their cultural uniqueness. Practical experience shows to what extent it is not a mere theoretical flight of fancy (3.1). The Court is also aware that is must show judicial restraint to avoid antagonising sovereign nations needlessly (3.2).

3.1.   REASONS FOR JUDICIAL RESTRAINT

The sociology of international organisations clearly shows that relations between creators (in this case, the States) and their creation (in this case, the Court) are always marked by phases of turbulence, incomprehension, even rebellion, more particularly when the creators realise that their creation is escaping their grasp. The case law of the European Court regularly sparks the ire of the State authorities, who have a hard time accepting certain mediatised violation findings. However, the Court does not care to handle their sovereign susceptibility with kid gloves; that is not its role. Its duty is to ensure the protection but also the development of human rights; there is no room in its judicial function for diplomatic concessions that belong in a different arena: that of politics.

The first sign of real 'State defiance' appeared when the largest Council of Europe member State, which is both a former super power – from the days when the world was divided into two blocs – and a present-day political and economic giant that is painfully making its way towards the democratic ideal: Russia. For nearly six years, this country,

---

[143]   ECtHR (Judgment) 28 July 1998, Case No. 23818/94, *Ergi v. Turkey*.

[144]   See ECtHR (Judgment) 19 February 1998, Case No. 22729/93, *Kaya v. Turkey*.

[145]   ECtHR (Judgment) 28 May 2002, Case No. 43290/98, *McShane v. United Kingdom*.

through its legislative body, the Duma, blocked the ratification of Protocol No. 14 even though it had become vital in order to avoid paralysing the system. Dissatisfied with certain judgments that had singled out the Russian judicial system for its lack of independence, the country fought back. This policy showed that the States could still 'do damage' by consciously contributing to the extinction of a system that, although it was created and accepted by them, no longer suited their needs. In this case, defiance triumphed over trust in the institution and bad faith over good faith. This was far from the spirit of 1950. All the skills of President Costa were required to convince Russia to finally bow to legal and political necessity and accept the ratification of Protocol No. 14.

When the Russian crisis was resolved, a new crisis cropped up in the UK. The country of Her Majesty Queen Elizabeth II demonstrated that it was also capable of defiance. Despite considerable openness towards the standards of the European Convention as shown by the adoption of the Human Rights Act in 1998, the authorities of the United Kingdom virulently opposed, not only targeted convictions – relating to voting rights for prisoners[146] or the expulsion of terrorists to third party countries[147] – but also structurally opposed the omnipotence of the Court – notably by taking charge of its reform. Very often, part of British legal scholarship stands behind the criticisms formulated by politicians,[148] which hardly contributes to the establishment of a climate of peace. The British government led by David Cameron did nothing to hide its will to orient the proceedings of the Brighton Conference[149] so as to reduce the influence of the Court by drastically curtailing its functions,[150] a tactic that proved unsuccessful, *in fine*.[151]

These two examples of State 'rebellions' (*inter alia*) show that, from a sociological standpoint, acceptance of a system of rights protection is not definitive but must be renewed continuously by all State stakeholders. In this context, the Court is caught between its judicial function and political reality. It must somehow strike a balance

---

[146] ECtHR (Judgment) 6 October 2005, Case No. 74025/01, *Hirst v. United Kingdom (No. 2)*; ECtHR (Judgment) 23 November 2010, Case No. 60041/08 and 60054/08, *Greens and M.T. v. United Kingdom*.

[147] ECtHR (Judgment) 17 January 2012, Case No. 8139/09, *Othman v. United Kingdom*.

[148] For a very precise and nuanced viewpoint on this issue, we refer you to a remarkable report written by three British academics: A. Donald, J. Gordon and Ph. Leach, *The UK and the European Court of Human Rights* (London, Equality and Human Rights Commission Research Report No. 83 2012), 219 p.

[149] Organised in the framework of the United Kingdom's Chairmanship of the Committee of Ministers of the Council of Europe (18–20 April 2012).

[150] E.g. on 10 February 2012, the Chamber of Commons adopted a motion by 234 votes against 22 which affirmed the primacy of British legislative power in terms of the right of prisoners to vote, while on 25 January 2012, Prime Minister David Cameron made an address before the European Court in which he stated that: "The Court should be free to deal with the most serious violations of human rights; [...] it should not undermine its own reputation by going over national decisions where it does not need to". This address is available at: <www.number10.gov.uk/news/european-court-of-human-rights/>.

[151] The Brighton Declaration reassured many specialists on the Convention since it did not entail radical changes in the fundamental principles of protection afforded by the Convention.

Laurence Burgorgue-Larsen

between avoiding exposing itself to State defiance and preserving its ontological purpose. In this dialectic context, it regularly calls on the theory of the national margin of appreciation.

3.2. MANIFESTATIONS OF JUDICIAL RESTRAINT

The current case law of the Court highlights as never before the major challenge facing judges that consists of finding the proper balance between considered judicial self-restraint and controlled judicial activism in techniques used to interpret rights. This delicate balance, or 'pendulum movement' in the words of Jean-Paul Costa,[152] is constantly being (re)adjusted. In any case, it is apparent that national judges and political authorities are sensitive to these movements and that they contribute to their faith in the regional institution for the protection of human rights.[153] It is therefore important for the Court to remain attentive to reactions, both from the judiciary and legal scholars, in order to remain in phase with the legal systems which it is obliged to oversee. It must strive to ensure that its 'cosmopolitical outlook' is not poorly perceived and poorly understood and, *in fine*, rejected. This highlights the importance of an educational approach, but also, more than ever, a rational approach in order to head off objections[154] before they arise. It would seem that the Grand Chamber of the Court[155] is meeting this challenge (3.2.1), at the cost of some effort, i.e. by focusing *ne varietur* on consistency, even though it gives rise to considerable dissidence within the Court itself (3.2.2).

3.2.1. The national margin of appreciation in action

The Court disposes of an array of tools allowing it to exercise strategic self-restraint to avoid arousing the ire of States intent on making sovereign decisions about their own

---

[152] J.-P. Costa, *Current challenges for the European Court of Human Rights. A Raymond and Beverly Sackler Distinguished Lecture in Human Rights* (Leiden Law School, 10 December 2011).

[153] For an analysis of the reception of the Court's case law in Germany, France and the United Kingdom, see E. Bjorge, "National supreme courts and the development of ECHR rights", 9(1) I-Con (2011), p. 5–31.

[154] In the most recent judgments handed down by the Grand Chamber, which have shown tremendous changes in the interpretation of rights, the Court systematically takes care to show that a major international convention marking a step forward has been ratified by the respondent State. To take the example of Italy, in the *Hirsi Jamaa* Case (ECtHR (Judgment) 23 February 2012, Case No. 27765/09, *Hirsi Jamaa and Others* v. *Italy*, para. 22), the conventions included the Geneva Convention Relating to the Status of Refugees (1951) and the Convention on the Elimination of All Forms of Discrimination against Women (1979); where Russia was concerned, in the *Konstantin Markin* case (ECtHR (Judgment) 22 March 2012, Case No. 30078/06, *Konstantin Markin* v. *Russia*, paras. 49 and 55), the Court highlighted Article 27 of the Revised European Social Charter.

[155] L. Wildhaber, "La Grande Chambre de la Cour européenne des droits de l'homme", in *La conscience des droits. Mélanges en l'honneur de Jean-Paul Costa*, supra n. 13, p. 701. Thus it was the Grand Chamber that resolved the difficult dilemma between self-restraint and judicial activism, which Jean-Paul Costa, in a conference delivered at Leiden Law School, described as the "pendulum movement". See Costa, *supra* n. 152.

societal choices. These include the national margin of appreciation, whose handling has not gone without criticism.[156] The literature on the theory of the national margin of appreciation is considerable and highlights an undeniable fact: there is no consensus on a definition[157] either among the experts or among the judges of the European Court[158] themselves. Be that as it may, the common minimum that emerges from the many different interpretations consists of affirming that it is a theory grounded on two foundations: the philosophy of subsidiarity on the one hand and State sovereignty on the other, implying that space must be given to legal pluralism to ensure respect for the legal specificities of the States. In this regard, 'it is the Grand Chamber of the European Court that sets the tone and weighs and chooses between continuity and change in the case law.'[159] This allows it to remain sensitive to the pressures of all kinds caused by certain ambitious judgments by the seven judge's chambers. In short, it 'keeps its finger on the pulse' of the States. Although it may occasionally be 'audacious',[160] it certainly is not systematically so. Indeed, it sometimes rules in favour of the status quo on highly sensitive cultural,[161] social and/or ethical issues.[162] This

---

[156]   For a stimulating essay on the matter, see J. García Roca, *El margen de apreciación nacional en la interpretación del Convenio europeo de Derechos Humanos: soberanía e integración* (Madrid, Thomson-Civitas 2010), 389 p.

[157]   For a stimulating essay on this issue that outlines the many possible approaches, see Garcia Roca, *supra* n. 156. In French, we highly recommend the article by F. Tulkens and L. Donnay, "L'usage de la marge d'appréciation par la Cour européenne des droits de l'homme. Paravent juridique superflu ou mécanisme indispensable par nature", *Revue de Science criminelle et de droit pénal comparé* (2006), No. 1.

[158]   Rozakis speaks out clearly in this regard: C. Rozakis, "Through the Looking Glass: An "Insider" 's view of the Margin of Appreciation", in *La conscience des droits. Mélanges en l'honneur de Jean-Paul Costa*, *supra* n. 13, p. 528: "The margin of appreciation is, as is well known, a judge-made concept that does not appear in the text of the instrument itself, but which, together with other judge-made concepts (such as the 'autonomous notions'), has played a pivotal role in the creation of European human rights law: and it is a concept about which there is still no obvious unanimity among judges of the Court, with regard to the purview of its applicability" (our emphasis).

[159]   L. Wildhaber, *supra* n. 155, p. 701 (our translation).

[160]   ECtHR (Judgment) 7 July 2011, Case No. 23459/03, *Bayatyan v. Armenia*. Based on Article 9, the right to conscientious objection was recognised by the Grand Chamber, and the precedent has since been confirmed without hesitation: ECtHR (Judgment) 12 June 2012, Case No. 42730/05, *Savda v. Turkey*; ECtHR (Judgment) 17 July 2012, Case No. 9078/06, *Tarhan v. Turkey*.

[161]   ECtHR (Judgment) 18 March 2011, Case No. 30814/06, *Lautsi v. Italy*. Whereas the applicant complained about the presence of crosses in the classrooms of public and primary schools, the chamber of seven judges put forward the principle of secularity and agreed with the applicant, whilst the Grand Chamber overturned the decision of the original judges in reaction to protests against the judgment in Italy and to the arguments of amici curiae representing no fewer than 8 Eastern and Southern European countries (Armenia, Bulgaria, Cyprus, the Russian Federation, Greece, Lithuania, Malta and the Republic of San Marino)... Playing on the absence of a European consensus regarding the presence of religious symbols in the classroom, it granted Italy a wide margin of appreciation and found no violation of Article 2 of Protocol No. 1. On grounds of procedural economy, it also found that Article 9 did not raise a different issue.

[162]   Regarding the right to medically assisted procreation, see ECtHR (Judgment) 3 November 2011, Case No. 57813/00, *S.H. and Others v. Austria*.

Laurence Burgorgue-Larsen

backpedalling (in the view of some) or this status quo respectful of the autonomy of the States (in the view of others) goes against the grain of the dissenting judges who do not mince words in expressing their concerns.[163] When the States are spared, institutional consistency suffers. Perfection is not of this world ...

3.2.2. *The national margin of appreciation in question*

Indeed, internal divisions on the implementation of the margin of appreciation have come to light in a number of relatively recent cases in the Grand Chamber. The Vice President of the Court, Belgian judge Françoise Tulkens, has signed – usually jointly with several of her colleagues – a number of highly explicit and sometimes alarmist dissenting opinions on the dangers of irrational use of the doctrine, which she usually combines with an assessment of the status of the much-touted 'European consensus'. Thus, when the Grand Chamber approved the status quo in the cases of prisoners' retirement pensions in the *Stummer* case,[164] medically assisted procreation in the *S.H.* case[165] and discrimination against unmarried couples not in registered civil unions in the *Van Der Heijden* case[166] Françoise Tulkens dissented. As she is Vice-President of the Court, her dissent is highly significant.

Criticism focuses on the 'relative' use of the European consensus to determine the breadth of the margin of appreciation (broad or narrow). In other words, the determination by the Court (or rather, by the departments of the Court) is haphazard in its use of data derived from comparative law when it comes to determining whether or not there is a 'European consensus'. There is temporal relativism involved in the *Stummer* case; it corresponds to the question 'at what point in time should one place oneself in order to assess the existence of a European consensus?' In the *S.H.* judgment, there is conceptual relativism corresponding to the question 'at what stage can we affirm that a trend is a consensus?' Finally, there is structural relativism in the *Van Der Heijden* case, corresponding to the question of 'how can the European consensus be reconciled with the national margin of appreciation?' A closer look at these cases will allow us to form a clearer idea of the different kinds of relativism.

In the *Stummer* case, according to the majority judges, 'the issue of working prisoners' affiliation to the old-age pension system is closely linked to issues of penal policy [.../...] but also to issues of social policy reflected in the social security system as a whole. In short, it raises complex issues and choices of social strategy, which is an

---

[163]   We refer you to the dissenting opinions in the Palomo Sánchez (ECtHR (Judgment) 12 September 2011, Case No. 28955/06 28957/06 28959/06 28964/06, *Palomo Sánchez and Others* v. *Spain*), Stummer (ECtHR (Judgment) 7 July 2011, Case No. 37452/02, *Stummer* v. *Austria*), and S.H. (ECtHR (Judgment) 3 November 2011, Case No. 57813/00, *S.H. and Others* v. *Austria*) decision.

[164]   ECtHR (Judgment) 7 July 2011, Case No. 37452/02, *Stummer* v. *Austria*.

[165]   ECtHR (Judgment) 3 November 2011, Case No. 57813/00, *S.H. and Others* v. *Austria*.

[166]   ECtHR (Judgment) 3 April 2012, Case No. 42857/05, *Van Der Heijden* v. *Netherlands*.

area in which States enjoy a wide margin of appreciation'.[167] One of the key factors in defining the breadth of such a margin of appreciation may be the existence or non-existence of common ground between the laws of the Contracting States.[168] This is where the gap between the majority and the dissenting judges becomes apparent. This is not to say that, given the same international and comparative law data,[169] they take an opposing view of the existence of a 'European consensus'. Indeed, all sides find an 'evolving trend'[170] towards the provision of social security coverage for prisoners or, to repeat the virtually identical terms used by the dissenting judges, 'an evolving trend in the Council of Europe's member States towards the affiliation of working prisoners to national social security systems'.[171] However, their analytical perspective differs radically as to the point in time at which the status of the right should be appreciated. The majority judges do not challenge the Austrian national Courts since they place themselves at the point in time when the latter handed down their rulings, i.e. between the 1960s and the 1990s. The Court stated that it 'attaches weight to the fact that at the material time there was no common ground regarding the affiliation of working prisoners to domestic social security systems'.[172] The analytical perspective of the dissenting judges is completely different, as they present the whole evolution of international human rights law relating to the matter, such as the European Prison Rules of 2006[173] and criticise the fact that the Supreme Court – which handed down its ruling in 2002 – had only referred in passing to its case law established in 1990. Above all, restating an argument put forward by the respondent State and repeated to the Court according to which the applicant was currently not in a dire situation – he received emergency relief payments complemented by social assistance – the dissenting judges declared with conviction that those two elements could not be compared 'to an old-age pension granted on the basis of the number of years worked and contributions paid. The former constitute assistance, whereas the latter is a right. The difference is significant in terms of respect for human dignity. Social security forms an integral part of human dignity'.[174]

In the *S.H.* case, although the Court recognises the right to medically assisted procreation as an 'expression of private and family life' under Article 8,[175] a violation was not found *in casu*. This judgment once again demonstrates a very unusual way of taking account of the 'European consensus'. Paragraph 96 is startling, to say the least:

---

[167]   ECtHR (Judgment) 7 July 2011, Case No. 37452/02, *Stummer v. Austria*, para. 101.

[168]   Ibid., para. 104.

[169]   Ibid., "The Facts" section of the judgment, paras. 47–60.

[170]   Ibid., para. 105.

[171]   Ibid., para. 5 of the joint partly dissenting opinion.

[172]   Ibid., para. 107.

[173]   Recommendation Rec (2006) 2 of the Committee of Ministers, 11 January 2006.

[174]   ECtHR (Judgment) 7 July 2011, Case No. 37452/02, *Stummer v. Austria*, para. 10 of the dissenting opinion.

[175]   ECtHR (Judgment) 3 November 2011, Case No. 57813/00, *S.H. and Others v. Austria*, para. 82.

Laurence Burgorgue-Larsen

'The Court would conclude that there is now a clear trend in the legislation of the Contracting States towards allowing gamete donation for the purpose of in vitro fertilisation, which reflects an emerging European consensus. That emerging consensus is not, however, based on settled and long-standing principles established in the law of the member States but rather reflects a stage of development within a particularly dynamic field of law and does not decisively narrow the margin of appreciation of the State.' The logic of the Court is hard to follow, but the best way I can summarise it would be as follows: since the emerging consensus applies to a dynamic field of law, well, we'd better stay a few steps behind the consensus. The dissenting judges, including Françoise Tulkens, seem to be of the same opinion when they express their 'dissatisfaction' in much greater detail: 'The Court thus takes the unprecedented step of conferring a new dimension on the European consensus and applies a particularly low threshold to it, thus potentially extending the States' margin of appreciation beyond limits. The current climate is probably conducive to such a backward step. The differences in the Court's approach to the determinative value of the European consensus and a somewhat lax approach to the objective indicia used to determine consensus are pushed to their limit here, engendering great legal uncertainty', according to paragraph 8 of the joint dissenting opinion signed by Françoise Tulkens as well as the Finnish (P. Hirvelä), Macedonian (L. Trajkovska) and Georgian (N. Tsotsoria) judges.

The criticism found at the bottom of the *Van Der Heijden* judgment really drives the point home. In this case, the applicant – who had lived as a couple with her partner for eighteen years without having married or registered as a civil union and had borne two children during this 'stable family life' – felt that she had suffered undue interference in her 'family life' when she was compelled, on the basis of The Netherlands Code of Criminal Procedure, to testify against the father of her children or undergo a prison sentence, which she did. In order to examine the necessity of the interference, the Court began by observing in a particularly roundabout manner that, 'Although the lack of common ground is not in itself decisive, it militates in favour of a wide margin of appreciation in this matter'.[176] In reaction, Françoise Tulkens, along with the Croatian (Vajić), Serbian (Popović), Slovene (Zupančič) and Luxembourgian (Spielmann) judges once again highlighted the issue of the influence of the European consensus in determining the breadth of the national margin of appreciation. They showed that in reality – referring notably to another dissenting opinion signed by the Andorran (Casadevall) and Spanish (López Guerra) judges – that a majority of European States would have *de facto* exempted the applicant from testifying under similar circumstances. As they stated clearly and directly in paragraph 5 of the opinion: 'This observation confirms, once again, the relative nature of the Court's approach to the existence of a consensus and, more generally, raises the question whether it should not be "disentangled" from the margin of appreciation in certain

---

[176]   ECtHR (Judgment) 3 April 2012, Case No. 42857/05, *Van Der Heijden* v. *Netherlands*, para. 61.

types of cases'. This is harsh criticism, since it confirms in no uncertain terms that there are major problems affecting the methods of interpretation of the Court. These issues could undermine the legitimacy of the European Court over the short and medium term, while providing an opportunity for recalcitrant States to take the first opportunity to contest the audacities or simply the protective progress of the Court. Thus, the major question facing the bench at this time is as follows: can this refined critical analysis by some of the judges of the Court – and in particular by Françoise Tulkens – convince the majority to settle the uncertainties as quickly as possible?

Can this critical minority vision become that of the majority and will it inform the destiny of future case law in Strasbourg? This question is not as incongruous as it may appear: after all, yesterday's dissidences are often today's solutions.

4. CONCLUSION

Far be it from me to peremptorily impose my views on what the African Commission or the African Court should do in terms of interpreting the Banjul Charter. Having taken cognizance of the evolution in the interpretation of the European Convention, it is up to the Members of the Commission and the judges of the Court to choose the best way forward for the African system. Specificities such as the continental context should not be overlooked; at the same time, it is not without interest to measure how regional systems, despite their differences, work towards the universal ideal that is still and always embodied by the Declaration of 1948.

[20]

The African Human Rights Court: A Two-Legged Stool?

Makau Mutua*

I. INTRODUCTION

The adoption in June 1998 of the Protocol to the African Charter on Human and Peoples' Rights on the Establishment of an African Court on Human and Peoples' Rights (African Human Rights Court)[1] by the Assembly of Heads of State and Government of the Organization of African Unity (OAU) is potentially an important step in the protection of human rights in the African continental system.[2] The African Human Rights Court would complement[3]

---

* *Makau Mutua* is a Visiting Professor, Harvard Law School, Spring 1999 and Associate Professor, SUNY-Buffalo School of Law. He is Director, Human Rights Center, SUNY-Buffalo and Chair of the Kenya Human Rights Commission. The author received his S.J.D. in 1987 from Harvard Law School, an LL.M. in 1985 from Harvard Law School, an LL.M. in 1984 from University of Dar-es-salaam; and his LL.B. in 1983 from University of Dar-es-salaam.

1. *Draft Protocol to the African Charter on Human and Peoples' Rights on the Establishment of an African Court on Human and Peoples' Rights by the Assembly of Heads of State and Government of the Organization of African Unity*, Conference of Ministers/ Attorneys General on the Establishment of an African Court on Human and Peoples' Rights, OAU/LEG/MIN/AFCHPR/PROT.(I)Rev.2 (1997) [hereinafter *Protocol*].
2. *See* Gino J. Naldi & Konstantinos Magliveras, *Reinforcing the African System of Human Rights: The Protocol on the Establishment of a Regional Court of Human and Peoples' Rights*, 16 Neth. Q. Hum. Rts. 431 (1998); 2 U. Oji Umozurike, The African Charter on Human and Peoples' Rights 92–93 (1997); *Pursuit for Peace Remains Major Task of Africa: Salim*, Xinhua News Agency, 8 June 1998, *available in* LEXIS, News Library, CURNWS File; *International Conference on Human Rights Commission Opens in Addis*, Xinhua News Agency, 18 May 1998, *available in* LEXIS, News Library, CURNWS File. As expected, the Draft Protocol was adopted by the 1998 OAU summit in Ouagadougou, Burkina Faso. *See* Ghion Hagos, *Africa at Large; Conference Adopts Protocol on African Human Rights Court*, Afr. News, 13 Dec. 1997, *available in* LEXIS, News Library, CURNWS File; Ghion Hagos, *Africa at Large; Africa Human Rights Court on the Cards*, Afr. News, 11 Dec. 1997, *available in* LEXIS, News Library, CURNWS File.
3. The Protocol is now open for signature following its adoption by the OAU. It shall come into force thirty days after ratification by fifteen OAU member states, a number that should be reached quickly. *See Protocol, supra* note 1, art. 34. The Protocol states in the preamble that the African Human Rights Court shall "complement and reinforce the

Human Rights Quarterly 21 (1999) 342–363 © 1999 by The Johns Hopkins University Press

the African Commission on Human and Peoples' Rights (African Commission), the body that has exercised continental oversight over human rights since 1987.[4] The Protocol suggests that the African Human Rights Court will make the promotion and the protection of human rights within the regional system more effective.[5] However the mere addition of a court, although a significant development, is unlikely by itself to address sufficiently the normative and structural weaknesses that have plagued the African human rights system since its inception.

The modern African state, which in many respects is colonial to its core, has been such an egregious human rights violator that skepticism about its ability to create an effective regional human rights system is appropriate.[6] Although the African Charter makes a significant contribution to the human rights corpus, it creates an ineffectual enforcement system. Its most notable contributions are the codification of the three "generations" of rights, including the innovative concept of peoples' rights,[7] and the imposition of duties on individuals.[8] But many commentators have focused on the

---

functions of the African Commission on Human and Peoples' Rights." *Protocol, supra* note 1, pmbl. The Protocol continues to clarify and emphasize that the African Human Rights Court shall "complement the protective mandate of the African Commission on Human and Peoples' Rights." *Protocol, supra* note 1, art. 2.

4. The African Commission on Human and Peoples' Rights (African Commission) is the supervisory organ for the implementation of the African Charter on Human and Peoples' Rights. African Charter on Human and Peoples' Rights, *adopted* 26 June 1981, O.A.U. Doc. CAB/LEG/67/3/Rev.5 *(entered into force* 21 Oct. 1986), *reprinted in* 21 I.L.M. 58 (1982) [hereinafter African Charter]. The African Charter is also known as the Banjul Charter.

5. *See Protocol, supra* note 1, pmbl.

6. For discussions and analyses of the colonial imprint on the African post-colonial state, see Mahmood Mamdani, Citizen and Subject: Contemporary Africa and the Legacy of Late Colonialism (1996); Crawford Young, *The Heritage of Colonialism, in* Africa in World Politics 19 (John W. Harbeson & Donald Rothschild eds., 1991); Robert H. Jackson, *Juridical Statehood in Sub-Saharan Africa*, 46 J. Int'l Aff. 1 (1992); Ali A. Mazrui, *The African State as a Political Refugee: Institutional Collapse and Human Displacement*, 7 Int'l J. Refugee L. 21 (1995); and Makau wa Mutua, *Why Redraw the Map of Africa: A Moral and Legal Inquiry*, 16 Mich. J. Int'l L. 1113 (1995). Discussing Africa's colonial legacy, one author notes that the "most obvious and powerful expressions of the continued African conceptual reliance on European political forms are the African states themselves. The states are direct and uncritical successors of the colonies." Art Hansen, *African Refugees: Defining and Defending Their Human Rights, in* Human Rights and Governance in Africa 139, 161 (Ronald Cohen et al. eds., 1993).

7. Peoples' rights, along with rights to environment and group rights, are known as third-generation rights. Civil and political rights are considered first-generation rights, and social, economic, and cultural rights are considered second-generation rights.

8. On duties on the individual, see African Charter, *supra* note 4, at arts. 27–29. For a discussion of the concept of duties in human rights discourse and the African Charter, see Makau wa Mutua, *The Banjul Charter and the African Cultural Fingerprint: An Evaluation of the Language of Duties*, 35 Va. J. Int'l L. 339 (1995). *See also* Obinna Okere, *The Protection of Human Rights in Africa and the African Charter on Human and Peoples' Rights: A Comparative Analysis with the European and American Systems*, 6 Hum. Rts. Q. 141 (1984); Josiah A.M. Cobbah, *African Values and the Human Rights Debate: An African Perspective*, 9 Hum. Rts. Q. 309 (1987).

weaknesses in the African system. These include the "clawback" clauses in the African Charter, the potential abuse of the language of duties, and the absence of an effective protection mandate for the African Commission.[9]

Recent changes in the African states, particularly those changes responding to demands for more open political societies, may augur well for the protection of civil and political rights.[10] Emergent democracies such as Namibia, Malawi, Benin, South Africa, Tanzania, and Mali are more inclined than their predecessors to respect human rights at home and to agree to a more viable regional system. In this context, the proposed African Human Rights Court would operate in a less hostile or cynical environment than the environment that determined and sharply limited the powers and effectiveness of the African Commission. In addition, the 1994 Rwandese genocide and the recent atrocities in Nigeria, Liberia, Somalia, Ethiopia, Sudan, Sierra Leone, Burundi, the Republic of the Congo, and the Democratic Republic of the Congo have further illuminated the need for stronger domestic and regional guarantees for human rights. In fact, at no time in recent African history have the conditions for the creation of an effective regional human rights system been more favorable.

This article critically evaluates the proposed African Human Rights Court and assesses its potential impact on the African human rights system. It probes the powers of the Court and asks whether a clear and mutually reinforcing division of labor between it and the African Commission could be developed to more effectively promote and protect human rights on the continent. For example, should the mandate of the African Commission be limited primarily to promotional activities, and the African Human Rights Court exclusively given the protective function? What relationship should the Court have to the African Commission?

In sum, this article explores the effect that the African Human Rights Court is likely to have in three principal areas. First, it examines the role of the African Human Rights Court in the development of the law of the African Charter and other relevant human rights instruments. Second, it addresses ways in which the Court can fill the lacunae left by the African

---

9. For discussions of these problems, see Richard Gittleman, *The African Charter on Human and Peoples' Rights: A Legal Analysis*, 22 Va. J. Int'l L. 667 (1982); Richard Gittleman, *The African Commission on Human and Peoples' Rights: Prospects and Procedures*, in Guide to International Human Rights Practice 153 (Hurst Hannum ed., 1984); Cees Flinterman & Evelyn Ankumah, *The African Charter on Human and Peoples' Rights*, in Guide to International Human Rights Practice 159 (Hurst Hannum ed., 2d ed. 1992).

10. *See* Makau wa Mutua, *African Renaissance*, N.Y. Times, 11 May 1991, at L23 (describing the demands by Africans for political democracy); Human Rights Watch, Human Rights Watch World Report 1993, at 6–9 (1992) (reporting Africa's political upheavals, including those related to demands for political reforms and democracy).

Commission and alleviate some of its weaknesses. Finally, it discusses ways in which the Court can penetrate the legal and political cultures of African states to inspire, encourage, and ensure the internalization of human rights.

II. AMBIGUITY AND ANEMIA: THE STATUS QUO

The African human rights system is anchored in the African Charter, an instrument that is largely promotional with an ambiguous protective function and no credible enforcement mechanism. This is hardly surprising because virtually no African state, with the exceptions of the Gambia, Senegal, and Botswana could even boast of a nominal democracy in 1981, the year that the OAU adopted the African Charter.[11] Hopes by observers of the African Commission that its commissioners would robustly construe the Charter's powers to alleviate its weaknesses have largely gone unrealized. With respect to specific functions, and to its performance in general, the African Commission has been a disappointment. This section discusses the architecture of the African Commission and outlines its basic strengths and weaknesses.

The basic functions of the African Commission are both promotional and protective.[12] The promotional function, which the Charter emphasizes,[13] includes research and dissemination of information through workshops and symposia, the encouragement of national and local human rights institutions, the formulation of principles to address legal problems in human rights, and cooperation with African and international human rights institutions.[14] The Commission is empowered to interpret the Charter at the request of a state party, the OAU, or any organization recognized by the OAU.[15] In contrast, the provision relating to the protective function is quite terse. It provides, without elaborating, only that the Commission shall "[e]nsure the protection of human and peoples' rights" in the Charter.[16]

More concretely, the African Charter charges the Commission with three principal functions: examining state reports,[17] considering communi-

---

11. *See* Makau wa Mutua, *The African Human Rights System in a Comparative Perspective*, African Commission on Human and Peoples' Rights, 3 Rev. Afr. Comm'n on Hum. & Peoples' Rts. 5 (1993).
12. See African Charter, *supra* note 4, art. 45, which sets out the functions of the African Commission.
13. *Id.* (providing largely for promotional, not protective, functions of the Commission).
14. *See id.* art. 45(1).
15. *See id.* art. 45(3). This role, which allows the Commission to interpret the Charter, is potentially one of the areas that the commissioners could seize upon to expound and clarify the Charter.
16. *Id.* art. 45(2).
17. *See id.* art. 62. States parties must submit, every two years, a report on the legislative and other measures taken to give effect to rights in the African Charter. *Id.*

346   **HUMAN RIGHTS QUARTERLY**   Vol. 21

cations alleging violations,[18] and expounding the African Charter.[19] These functions follow the general script of other regional as well as universal human rights bodies.[20] In particular, the Commission seems to have drawn substantially from the procedures and experiences of the UN Human Rights Committee.[21] Its Rules of Procedure,[22] which provide for process before the Commission, and the Reporting Guidelines,[23] which specify the form and content of state reports, mirror the lessons of other human rights bodies. The Guidelines were supplemented by General Directives, an unpublished document that was sent to foreign ministers of state parties in 1990.[24] The Directives are just a precis of the Guidelines.

The Commission's primary protective function, that of considering complaints filed by individual victims as well as nongovernmental organizations (NGOs),[25] has a large potential that thus far has not been realized. For example, the Charter places no restriction as to who may file a communication. This lack of restriction creates an opening that allows any individual, groups, or NGOs, whether or not they are the direct victims of the alleged violation, to lodge a petition.[26] However, communications[27] can only be

---

18.   See *id.* arts. 47, 55. The Charter permits two types of communications: from individuals, NGOs, and groups, on the one hand, and inter-state communications, on the other. The latter has never been invoked and will not concern this article. *Id.*

19.   See *id.* art. 45(3).

20.   See Philip Alston, *Critical Appraisal of the UN Human Rights Regime, in* The United Nations and Human Rights: A Critical Appraisal 1 (Philip Alston ed., 1992). *See generally* Thomas Buergenthal, International Human Rights: In a Nutshell 21–247 (2d. ed. 1995) (describing UN Charter-based and treaty-based human rights instruments and bodies, as well as the African, Inter-American, and European human rights systems).

21.   The Human Rights Committee is the treaty body that oversees the implementation of the International Covenant on Civil and Political Rights (ICCPR). International Covenant on Civil and Political Rights, *adopted* 16 Dec. 1966, G.A. Res. 2200 (XXI), U.N. GAOR, 21st Sess., Supp. No. 16, at 52, U.N. Doc. A/6316 (1966), 999 U.N.T.S. 171 (*entered into force* 23 Mar. 1976).

22.   *Revised Rules of Procedure of the African Commission on Human and Peoples' Rights, adopted* 6 Oct. 1995, *reprinted in* 18 Hum. Rts. L.J. 154 (1997) [hereinafter Rules of Procedure].

23.   *Guidelines for National Periodic Reports, Second Annual Activity Report of the African Commission on Human and Peoples' Rights,* Annex III, AFR/COM/HPR.5(VI)(1989) [hereinafter Reporting Guidelines].

24.   See Astrid Danielsen, The State Reporting Procedure Under the African Charter 51–52 (1994); Evelyn A. Ankumah, The African Commission on Human and Peoples' Rights: Practice and Procedures 82–83 (1996).

25.   The African Charter requires that the Commission "cooperate" with African and international NGOs in its work. African Charter, *supra* note 4, art. 45(1)(a) & (c). Thus the Commission grants human rights NGOs observer status which allows their representatives to participate in the public sessions of the Commission. *See* Rules of Procedure, *supra* note 22, rule 75.

26.   See African Charter, *supra* note 4, art. 55.

27.   "Communication" is usually used as a euphemism for "complaint" by the international human rights bodies.

considered by the Commission if they meet certain conditions, including the requirements that they: indicate their authors, even if anonymity is requested; are not written in a language that is insulting or disparaging to the state or the OAU; are not incompatible with the OAU Charter and the African Charter; are not based exclusively on media reports; are sent after the petitioner exhausts local remedies, unless these are obviously unduly prolonged; are submitted within a reasonable time after local remedies are exhausted; and do not deal with a matter that has already been settled by the states concerned in accordance with international instruments.[28]

Although the Charter does not explicitly require it, communications are considered in private or closed sessions.[29] If the Commission determines that one or more communications "relate to special cases which reveal the existence of a series of serious or massive violations"[30] of human rights, it must draw the attention of the OAU to such a situation and, presumably, conduct an on-site investigation. In the case of an emergency, the Commission must inform the Chair of the OAU and request an in-depth study, which most likely would call for on-site fact-finding.[31] The Commission's power to conduct such investigations is clearly authorized by the Charter, which empowers it to "resort to any appropriate method of investigation."[32] This provision had remained a dead letter until 1995 when the Commission, with the assistance of the OAU Secretary General, secured the agreement of Senegal and Togo for field investigations.[33] Until this point however, the commissioners had been reluctant to claim these powers.[34]

The Commission's formula for considering individual communications closely mirrors that of the UN Human Rights Committee (HRC).[35] In a

---

28. *See* African Charter, *supra* note 4, art. 56.
29. *See* Rules of Procedure, *supra* note 22, rule 106. The Commission, which makes its own rules of procedure, may justify closed sessions for communications under Article 59 of the Charter which provides, in part, that "[a]ll measures taken within the provisions of the present Chapter [sic] shall remain confidential" until the OAU decides otherwise. African Charter, *supra* note 4, art. 59. But this provision is overbroad and vague. A literal interpretation of "all measures" would be absurd. Perhaps the Commission could open at least part, if not all, of the communications processes to the public.
30. African Charter, *supra* note 4, art. 58(1) & (2).
31. *See id.* art. 58(3).
32. *Id.* art. 46.
33. *See Final Communique: 17th Ordinary Session of the African Commission on Human and Peoples' Rights,* 12–22 Mar. 1995, Lome, Togo, *available in* <http://www1.umn.edu/humanrts/africa/achpr17f.html>; Aɴᴋᴜᴍᴀʜ, *supra* note 24, at 42.
34. Because the Commission did not carry out investigations from 1987 until 1995, it seems to have been reluctant to do so.
35. *See* Optional Protocol to the International Covenant on Civil and Political Rights, *adopted* 16 Dec. 1966, G.A. Res. 2200A (XXI), U.N. GAOR, 21st Sess., Supp. No. 16, at 59, U.N. Doc. A/6316 (1966), 999 U.N.T.S. 171 (*entered into force* 23 Mar. 1976), *reprinted in* 6 I.L.M. 383 (1967) (detailing the HRC's formula for considering individual communications).

format similar to that of the HRC, the Commission arranges its decisions into sections dealing with facts, arguments, admissibility of evidence, merits of the case, and the final conclusion. However, each of these sections is scant in both substance and reasoning. For example, in *Constitutional Rights Project v. Nigeria*,[36] a petition challenging a death penalty that was imposed in violation of due process protections, the Commission adopted a scripted presentation, "declared" a violation of the Charter provisions, and "recommended" that Nigeria free the petitioners.[37] Likewise, in another petition, *Civil Liberties Organization v. Nigeria*,[38] the Commission cursorily found that the government enacted laws, in violation of the African Charter, to abridge due process rights and undermine the independence of the judiciary. However, it is fair to say that the communications procedure has come a long way since the early days. A predictable tradition of more fully considering petitions is slowly evolving.

> A comparison of the decisions over the years shows that while room remains for considerable improvement, the quality of the Commission's reasoning and decision making has continued to evolve positively. In the past two years, the decisions of the Commission have been more substantive and elaborate on the issues of law and fact that are raised in and considered by communications.[39]

Nevertheless, despite signs of progress, the decisions referred to here, and others before them, are formulaic. They do not reference jurisprudence from national and international tribunals, nor do they fire the imagination. They are non-binding and attract little, if any, attention from governments and the human rights community. In the past, this lack of publicity could be attributed to the fact that the Commission prohibited the publication of its decisions. However, as explained by two human rights advocates, the African Commission has revised its strict interpretation of Article 59, which was formerly understood to prohibit the publication of communications:

> This changed with the Seventh Activity Report of the Commission, adopted by the Assembly in June 1994. For the first time, this report made available information on the first fifty-two communications decided by the Commission. The information disclosed includes a summary of the parties to the communication, the factual background, and the Commission's summary decision. With

---

36.   Communication 60/91, Afr. Comm'n Hum. Peoples' Rts., AHG/Res. 240 (XXXI)(1995), *reprinted in* 18 Hum. Rts. L.J. 28 (1997).
37.   *See id.*
38.   Communication 129/94, Afr. Comm'n Hum. Peoples' Rts., AHG/Res.250 (XXXII)(1996), *reprinted in* 18 Hum. Rts. L.J. 35, 36 (1997).
39.   Chidi Anselm Odinkalu & Camilla Christensen, *The African Commission on Human and Peoples' Rights: The Development of its Non-State Communication Procedures,* 20 Hum. Rts. Q. 235, 277 (1998) (footnotes omitted).

the adoption of the Commission's Eighth and Ninth Annual Activity Reports, the Commission went a step further and issued full texts of its final decisions.[40]

Now the decisions may be published but the Commission must first obtain permission from the OAU Assembly of Heads of State and Government.[41]

Although the Commission's decision-making procedure appears quasi-judicial, the Commission sees its principal objective as creating a dialogue between the parties, leading to the amicable settlement of the dispute in question.[42] In any case, neither the Charter nor the Commission provides for enforceable remedies or a mechanism for encouraging and tracking state compliance with decisions. Thus, to many victims, the Commission's findings are too remote if not virtually meaningless.[43]

In addition to, and emblematic of, the Charter and the Commission's lack of enforcement mechanisms is the state reporting procedure that is required by the Charter.[44] The Charter tersely provides that every two years, states shall submit a "report on the legislative or other measures taken with a view to giving effect to the rights and freedoms" enumerated in it.[45] However, the Charter does not say to what body the reports are to be submitted, whether, how, and with what goal the reports should be evaluated, and what action should be taken after such evaluation. The Commission, not surprisingly, has filled in these gaps by borrowing heavily from other treaty bodies.[46] Unfortunately, it has mimicked both the good and the bad in those bodies.

The Reporting Guidelines, which are detailed, are supposed to guide states in the preparation of their reports. In particular, the Guidelines specify both the form and content of reports.[47] Thus reports must describe in detail

---

40. *Id.* at 278.
41. The Charter provides that all "measures taken within the provisions of the present Charter shall remain confidential until such a time as the Assembly of Heads of State and Government shall otherwise decide." African Charter, *supra* note 4, art. 59(1).
42. *See* Communications 16/88, 17/88, 18/88 *Comite Culturel pour la Democratie au Benin, Hilaire Badjogoume, El Hadj Boubacare Diawara v. Benin* (merits), Afr. Comm'n Hum. Peoples' Rts., ¶ 35 (1994), *reprinted in* Odinkalu & Christensen, *supra* note 36, at 244 n.51 (noting, *inter alia*, that "[i]t is the primary objective of the Commission in the Communications procedure to initiate a dialogue between the parties which will result in an amicable settlement to the satisfaction of both and which remedies the prejudice complained of").
43. See AFRICAN SOCIETY OF INTERNATIONAL AND COMPARATIVE LAW, REPORT ON THE 16TH SESSION OF THE AFRICAN COMMISSION ON HUMAN AND PEOPLES' RIGHTS 62–83 (1996) for more communications by the Commission. For a very thoughtful analysis of the communications procedure before the African Commission, see Odinkalu & Christensen, *supra* note 36.
44. African Charter, *supra* note 4, art. 62.
45. *Id.*
46. See Felice D. Gaer, *First Fruits: Reporting By States Under the African Charter on Human and Peoples' Rights*, 10 NETH. Q. HUM. RTS. 29 (1992), for an evaluation of the initial state reporting under the African Charter.
47. *Id.*

the legislative regime as well as the actual application and protection of specific human rights.[48] In reality, however, many of the reports submitted thus far have been woefully inadequate on both counts.[49] For example, the initial report of Ghana was only a scant five pages.[50] Similarly, Egypt's report, although a voluminous fifty pages, only described abstractly some legislation without commentary on the state of human rights conditions on the ground.[51]

Once submitted, reports are examined in public. State representatives and the commissioners engage in "constructive dialogue" to assist and encourage states to implement the Charter. After considering a report, the Commission communicates its comments and general observations to the state in question.[52] However, although the Charter came into force in 1987, the majority of state parties have not submitted their reports, and the Commission has been powerless to force compliance.[53] Thus, the reporting process seems to have yielded very little so far, as many of the state representatives have appeared either incompetent or ill-prepared.[54] In addition to the fact that states do not seem to take the reporting process seriously, the comments and observations of the Commission on the few state reports that have been submitted have not had any discernable effect on those states.

However, the African Commission has taken some steps that have the potential to increase its impact on states. For example, one of the Commission's members has been appointed as a Special Rapporteur on Summary and Extra-judicial Executions.[55] This appointment is potentially significant if the office is used to investigate, report, and facilitate dialogue with states.[56] Additionally, the Commission's country-specific and thematic resolutions raise the Commission's visibility and engage states directly. For example, one Commission resolution called on Sudan to allow detainees access to lawyers and doctors and asked the government to support negotiations for the settlement of the conflict with the south.[57] Another

---

48. *See id.*
49. *See generally* ANKUMAH, *supra* note 24, at 79–110.
50. *See id.* at 91–92.
51. *See id.*
52. *See* Rules of Procedure, *supra* note 22, rules 81–87.
53. *See* Mohamed Komeja, *The African System of Human and Peoples' Rights: an Annotated Bibliography*, 3 E. AFR. J. PEACE & HUM. RTS. 262, 274–75 (1996).
54. *See* ANKUMAH, *supra* note 24, at 99.
55. *See* Rachel Murray, *Report on the 1996 Sessions of the African Commission on Human and Peoples' Rights, 19th and 20th Ordinary Sessions, 26 March–4 April, and 21–31 October 1996*, 18 HUM. RTS. L.J. 16, 18 (1997).
56. *See id.*
57. *See* AFRICAN SOCIETY OF INTERNATIONAL AND COMPARATIVE LAW, *supra* note 40, at 89–90.

Commission resolution[58] urged African states to respect the rights of prisoners and to ratify the Convention Against Torture and Other Cruel, Inhuman or Degrading Treatment.[59] However small and tentative, these are steps in the right direction. Perhaps the African Human Rights Court will help clarify the roles and functions of the Commission and thereby embolden it.

III. THE RATIONALE FOR A HUMAN RIGHTS COURT

Both the European and the Inter-American human rights systems give the impression that a human rights court is an essential, if not indispensable, component of an effective regime for the protection of human rights. Norms prescribing state conduct are not meaningful unless they are anchored in functioning and effective institutions. In the case of the African regional system, this truism merits special attention because both the norms in the African Charter and the African Commission itself have been regarded as weak and ineffectual—hence the push for a human rights court, an institution that would correct some of the more glaring failures of the African system.

There are two possible polar views on the creation of an African Human Rights Court. One view holds that a human rights court must be established as soon as possible to salvage the entire system from its near-total irrelevance and obscurity.[60] According to this view, the deficiencies of the African system—both normative and institutional—are so crippling that only an effective human rights court can jump-start the process of its redemption.[61] The Court is here seen as a way to put some teeth and bite into the system in order to restrain states effectively.

The other view is gradualist and sees the work of the African system as primarily promotional and not adjudicative.[62] According to the gradualist view, the major problem in Africa is the lack of awareness by the general populace of its rights and the processes for vindicating those rights.[63] Proponents argue that the regional system must therefore first educate the

---

58. *See id.* at 95.
59. Convention Against Torture and Other Cruel, Inhuman or Degrading Treatment or Punishment, *adopted* 10 Dec. 1984, G.A. Res. 39/46, U.N. GAOR 39th Sess., Supp. No. 51, U.N. Doc. A/39/51 (1985) (*entered into force* 26 June 1987), *reprinted in* 23 I.L.M. 1027 (1984), *substantive changes noted in* 24 I.L.M. 535 (1985).
60. *See* Mutua, *supra* note 10, at 10; Komeja, *supra* note 51, at 277.
61. *See* Mutua, *supra* note 10, at 10.
62. *See* ANKUMAH, *supra* note 24, at 194–95.
63. *See id.*

public by promoting human rights.[64] The task of protection, which would include a human rights court, is seen here as less urgent.[65] Critics argue that a court might be paralyzed by the same problems that have beset the African Commission.[66] They therefore urge that the African Commission be strengthened instead of dissipating scarce resources to create another, possibly impotent institution.[67]

In the past several years, the gradualist view has given way to the proponents of a human rights court. It had become clear by the mid-1990s, even to pro-establishment figures, that the African system was a disappointment, if not an embarrassment for the continent. In 1994, the conservative OAU Assembly of Heads of State and Government asked its Secretary General to call a meeting of government experts to "ponder in conjunction with the African Commission on Human and Peoples' Rights over the means to enhance the efficiency of the Commission in considering particularly the establishment of an African Court on Human and Peoples' Rights."[68]

Events moved speedily in the next several years. In September 1995, a draft document on an African human rights court was produced by a meeting of experts organized in Cape Town, South Africa by the OAU Secretariat in collaboration with the African Commission and the International Commission of Jurists.[69] Later that month, an OAU meeting of governmental legal experts produced the Cape Town Draft of the draft protocol for a human rights court.[70] After several rounds of meetings and more drafts, the Draft Protocol was adopted by the conference of OAU Ministers of Justice/Attorneys General in December 1997. The OAU Council of Ministers adopted the Draft Protocol in February 1998,[71] and the OAU Assembly gave its final blessing in June 1998,[72] opening the Protocol for signature by OAU member states.

The consensus among government officials, NGOs, and academics on the need for a human rights court in the African regional system has steadily

---

64. *See id.*
65. *See id.*
66. *See id.*
67. *See id.* at 195.
68. Report of Government Experts Meeting, AHG/Res 230(xxx), 30th Ordinary Session of the Assembly of Heads of State and Government, Tunis, Tunisia, June 1994, *cited in* Ibrahim Ali Badawi El-Sheikh, *Draft Protocol to the African Charter on Human and Peoples' Rights on the Establishment of an African Court on Human and Peoples' Rights: Introductory Note,* 9 Afr. J. Int'l & Comp. L. 943, 943 n.1 (1997).
69. *See id.* at 944.
70. *See* Report of Government Experts Meeting on the Establishment of an African Court of Human and Peoples' Rights, September 6–12, 1995, Cape Town, South Africa, OAU/LEG/EXP/AFCHPR/RPT(1)Rev.1, *cited in id.* at 944 n.2.
71. *See International Conference on Human Rights Commission Opens in Addis, supra* note 2.
72. *See Pursuit for Peace Remains Major Task of Africa: Salim, supra* note 2.

gained momentum. This realization is indicative of the shortcomings that currently plague the African system. While the push for the Court is not a repudiation of the African Commission, it is an acknowledgment of its general ineffectiveness. The hope appears to be that a court will strengthen the regional system and aid it in realizing its promise. But that will not happen unless the Court avoids the pitfalls that have trapped the African Commission.

The presence of other regional human rights courts in the Americas and Europe has given impetus to the African initiative and advanced the idea within the modern African state that its conduct toward its own citizens is no longer an internal, domestic matter. In turn, the establishment of the African Human Rights Court will help to promote international human rights in other regions of the world. For example, in Asia, where states have been more resistant to the application and internalization of the human rights corpus—and where as of yet there is no regional human rights system—that resistance is bound to come under increasing attack by NGOs due to the establishment of a human rights court in Africa. The regional supervision of a state's internal conduct toward its nationals is quickly becoming a reality. So too is the recognition that human rights are "a basic requirement in any society and a pre-requisite for human progress and development."[73]

The African Human Rights Court is a potentially significant development in the protection of rights on a continent that has been plagued with serious human rights violations since colonial rule. The problems of the African human rights system,[74] including the normative weaknesses in the African Charter and the general impotence of its implementing body, the African Commission, may now be addressed effectively and resolved by the establishment of this new adjudicatory body.

IV. THE ANATOMY OF THE AFRICAN HUMAN RIGHTS COURT

The function of the African Human Rights Court would be protective, and would seek to complement the work of the African Commission, which is

---

73. *Talks Open in Addis on Establishing African Human Rights Court,* Deutsche Presse-Agentur, 12 Dec. 1997, *available in* LEXIS, News Library, CURNWS File (quoting Salim Ahmed Salim, the OAU Secretary General, at the adoption of the Draft Protocol in December 1997).

74. For analyses of some normative and structural problems of the African human rights system, see Gittleman, *supra* note 9; Flinterman & Ankumah, *supra* note 9; Olusola Ojo & Amadu Sessay, *The OAU and Human Rights: Prospects for the 1980s and Beyond,* 8 Hum. Rts. Q. 89 (1986); and Ankumah, *supra* note 24.

basically promotional.[75] Although the African Commission's mandate includes the protective functions of state reporting[76] and the consideration of communications,[77] promotional activities have been the centerpiece of its operations.[78] Commentators agree that the Commission's state reporting and communications procedures have been disappointing, partly due to the lack of power and textual clarity of purpose for those functions.[79] Can the African Human Rights Court cure these problems?

In order to entrench itself as a protector of international human rights, it is important that the Court's jurisdiction not be circumscribed or limited to cases or disputes that arise out of the African Charter.[80] The Protocol provides that actions may be brought before the Court on the basis of any instrument, including international human rights treaties, which has been ratified by the state party in question.[81] Furthermore, according to the Protocol, the Court can apply as sources of law any relevant human rights instrument ratified by the state, in addition to the African Charter.[82] The Court will be empowered to decide if it has jurisdiction in the event of a dispute.[83] The Court may exercise both contentious and conciliatory jurisdiction.[84] It also will have advisory jurisdiction through which it may issue advisory opinions on "any legal matter relating to the Charter or any other relevant human rights instruments."[85] Such an opinion may be requested by a wide variety of entities including a member state of the OAU, the OAU or any of its organs, or even an African NGO, provided it is recognized by the OAU.[86]

---

75. The Protocol realizes this contrast—in essence the weaknesses and the incompleteness of the African Commission—when its states in its preamble that the African Human Rights Court will "complement and reinforce the functions of the African Commission on Human and Peoples' Rights." *Protocol, supra* note 1, pmbl. The Protocol adds that the African Human Rights Court shall "complement the protective mandate of the African Commission." *Id.* art. 2.
76. *See* African Charter, *supra* note 4, art. 62.
77. *See id.* at arts. 55, 56. These include state-to-state and "other" communications, which could come from individuals, groups, and organizations. *Id.*
78. *See id.* art. 45. The principal activities of the African Charter, which are promotional, are to collect documents, undertake studies, organize seminars, disseminate information, encourage national and local institutions concerned with human rights, formulate principles to resolve human rights problems, and interpret the African Charter. *Id.*
79. *See, e.g.,* Mutua, *supra* note 8; HENRY J. STEINER & PHILIP ALSTON, INTERNATIONAL HUMAN RIGHTS IN CONTEXT: LAW, POLITICS, MORALS 700–704 (1996).
80. *See Protocol, supra* note 1, art. 3(1) (extending the Court's jurisdiction to the African Charter "and any other relevant Human Rights instrument . . .").
81. *Id.*
82. *Id.* art. 7.
83. *See id.* art. 3(2).
84. *Id.* art. 9 Article 9 allows the court to attempt the "amicable settlement" of disputes. *Id.*
85. *Id.* art. 4(1).
86. *See id.*

One serious shortcoming of the proposed African Human Rights Court is the limitation of access placed by the Draft Protocol on individuals and NGOs. The Protocol provides for two types of access to the Court: automatic and optional. The African Commission, state parties, and African intergovernmental organizations enjoy unfettered or "automatic" access to the Court once a state ratifies the Draft Protocol.[87] In stark contrast, individuals and NGOs cannot bring a suit against a state unless two conditions are met. First, the Court will have discretion to grant or deny such access.[88] Second, at the time of ratification of the Draft Protocol or thereafter the state must have made a declaration accepting the jurisdiction of the Court to hear such cases.[89]

While limiting the access of NGOs and individuals to the Court may have been necessary to get states on board,[90] it is nevertheless disappointing and a terrible blow to the standing and reputation of the Court in the eyes of most Africans. After all, it is individuals and NGOs, and not the African Commission, regional intergovernmental organizations, or state parties, who will be the primary beneficiaries and users of the Court. The proposed Court is not meant to be an institution for the protection of the rights of states or OAU organs. A human rights court is primarily a forum for protecting citizens against the state and other state agencies. This limitation will render the proposed Court virtually meaningless unless it is interpreted broadly and liberally.

The Court will be technically independent of the African Commission although it may request the Commission's opinion with respect to the admissibility of a case brought by an individual or an NGO.[91] In ruling on the admissibility of a case, the Court will also be required to take into account the requirements that communications must meet under the African Charter before submission to the Commission.[92] Presumably, the Court will not hear cases that do not meet these criteria. The Court may also consider cases or transfer them to the African Commission.[93]

---

87. *See id.* arts. 5(1), 5(2).
88. *See id.* art. 5(3) (providing that the "*[c]ourt may entitle* relevant Non Governmental Organizations (NGOs) with observer status before the [African] Commission, and individuals to institute cases directly before it") (emphasis added).
89. *See id.* arts. 5(3), 34(6).
90. Ambassador Badawi, a member of the African Commission and its former chair, alludes to this when he notes that "[t]he question of allowing NGOs and individuals to submit cases to the Court was one of the most complicated issues during the consideration of the Draft Protocol." Badawi El-Sheikh, *supra* note 68, at 947.
91. *See Protocol, supra* note 1, art. 6(1).
92. *See id.* art. 6(2). See African Charter, *supra* note 4, art. 56, for a list of the requirements that communications before the African Commission must consider it.
93. *See Protocol, supra* note 1, art. 6(3).

While linked to the Commission it is vital that the Court determines its own rules of procedure in order to enhance its independence. The Protocol provides some general rules of procedure.[94] In addition, the Protocol provides that proceedings before the Court generally should be conducted in public and that parties will be entitled to legal representation of their own choice.[95] As well, witnesses or parties to a case "shall enjoy all protection and facilities, in accordance with international law"[96] in connection with their appearance before the Court. This guarantee will shield witnesses from various pressures and intimidation and facilitate their ability to participate more fully and freely in proceedings.

The proposed Court would be composed of eleven judges elected in their individual capacity by the OAU Assembly of Heads of States and Government from among "jurists of high moral character and of recognized practical, judicial or academic competence and experience in the field of human and peoples' rights."[97] Judges would serve for a six-year term and be eligible for re-election only once.[98] It is a shortcoming that all judges, except the President of the Court, would only serve on a part-time basis.[99] Although the judges' independence would be formally guaranteed and they would be protected by diplomatic immunity under international law,[100] the fact that the judges are only in part-time service would undermine the integrity and independence of the Court. A judge may only be removed by the unanimous decision of all the other judges of the Court.[101] A judge who is a national of a state party to a case must be recused to avoid bias.[102] It is an important consideration that the Court appoints its own registrar and registry staff.[103]

The proposed Court is given wide powers in conducting proceedings. It seems to have discretionary jurisdiction and need not take all the cases that come before it.[104] This should allow the Court to avoid overload and to hear only those cases that have the potential to advance human rights protection in a meaningful way. If the Court does decide to hear a case, the Court may hear submissions from all parties, including oral, written, and expert

---

94. *See id.* art. 33.
95. *See id.* art. 10(1),(2). Free legal representation may also be provided where the "interests of justice so require." *Id.* art. 10(2).
96. *Id.* art. 10(3).
97. *Id.* art. 11(1).
98. *See id.* art. 15 (1).
99. *See id.* art. 15(4).
100. *See id.* art. 17.
101. *See id.* art. 19.
102. *See id.* art. 22.
103. *See id.* art. 24.
104. *See Protocol, supra* note 1, art. 3(2).

testimony.[105] States are required to assist the Court and provide facilities for the efficient handling of cases.[106] Once the Court finds a violation, it may order remedies, including "fair compensation or reparation."[107] In cases of "extreme gravity and urgency," the Court may order provisional remedies, such as an injunction, to avoid actual or potential irreparable harm to victims.[108]

The Court's judgments, which will be final and without appeal,[109] will be binding on states.[110] In its annual report to the OAU, the Court is to list specifically those states that have not complied with its judgments.[111] This is a "shaming" tactic that marks the violator. The OAU Council of Ministers is required to monitor the execution of the judgment on behalf of the OAU Assembly.[112] Presumably the OAU Assembly can take additional measures to force compliance, such as passing resolutions urging states to respect the Court's judgments. Alternatively, the OAU Chairman could be empowered to write to delinquent states asking that they honor the Court's judgments.

V. WHAT SHOULD THE HUMAN RIGHTS COURT DO?

Critics and supporters alike have argued that it makes little sense to create an institution that duplicates the weaknesses of the African Commission. In the context of the OAU, an organization with scarce financial resources and limited moral clarity and vision, the establishment of a new body should be approached somberly. A human rights court will only be useful if it genuinely seeks to correct the shortcomings of the African human rights system and provides victims of human rights violations with a real and accessible forum in which to vindicate their basic rights. What the OAU and the African regional system do not need is yet another remote and opaque bureaucracy that promises little and delivers nothing. If the Court is to be such a bureaucracy, then it would make more sense to expend additional resources and energy to address the problems of the African Commission and defer the establishment of a court for another day. Several important

---

105. *See id.* art. 26.
106. *See id.* art. 26(1).
107. *Id.* art. 27(1).
108. *Id.* art. 27(2).
109. *See id.* art. 28(2).
110. *See id.* art. 30 (providing, in part, that states "*undertake to comply with the judgment* in any case in which they are parties within the time stipulated by the Court and *to guarantee its execution*") (emphasis added).
111. *See id.* art. 31.
112. *See id.* art. 29(1).

questions will have to be addressed if the Human Rights Court is to become a significant player in human rights in Africa.

The most pressing issues facing the new Court are normative and institutional. These issues require the Charter's amendment and revision. First, the African Charter, the Court's basic instrument, has deep normative flaws that must be addressed to give the Court a firm legal basis to protect human rights. In particular, "clawback" clauses permeate the African Charter and permit African states to restrict basic human rights to the maximum extent allowed by domestic law.[113] This is especially significant because most domestic laws in Africa date from the colonial period and are therefore highly repressive and draconian. The post-colonial state, like its predecessor, impermissibly restricts most civil and political rights, particularly those pertaining to political participation, free expression, association and assembly, movement, and conscience. Ironically, it is these same rights that the African Charter further erodes.

> 'Clawback' clauses, that is, qualifications or limitations, permeate the provisions [of the African Charter] dealing with fundamental freedoms . . . . These fundamental civil and political rights are severely limited by clauses like 'except for reasons and conditions previously laid down by law,' 'subject to law and order,' 'within the law,' 'abides by the law,' 'in accordance with the provisions of the law,' and other restrictions justified for the 'protection of national security.'[114]

The African Charter also lacks a general derogation clause, which appears to be unnecessary because states are in effect permitted by the "clawback" clauses to suspend, de facto, certain rights by enacting legislation.[115] In any event, nothing in the Charter prevents African states from denying certain rights during national "emergencies."[116] A revision of the Charter should excise the offending "clawback" clauses, insert a provision on nonderogable rights, and another specifying which rights states can derogate from, when, and under what conditions.

Another area of normative controversy concerns women's rights. There is a perception and fear that either the African Charter does not adequately protect, or it could be used to abuse, women's rights.[117] Of particular

---

113. *See* Mutua, *supra* note 10, at 7.
114. *Id.* at 7.
115. *See* Arthur E. Anthony, *Beyond the Paper Tiger: The Challenge of a Human Rights Court in Africa*, 32 Tex. Int'l L.J. 511, 518 (1997).
116. Buergenthal, *supra* note 19, at 233–34.
117. For discussions of the African Charter's view on women, see Claude E. Welch, Jr., *Human Rights and African Women: A Comparison of Protection under Two Major Treaties*, 15 Hum. Rts. Q. 549 (1993); Florence Butegwa, *Using the African Charter on Human and Peoples' Rights to Secure Women's Access to Land in Africa, in* Human

concern are the "family" provisions that have been thought to condone and support repressive and retrogressive structures and practices of social and political ordering.[118] These provisions, which place duties to the family on the state and individuals, have been interpreted as entrenching oppressive family structures that marginalize and exclude women from participation in most spheres outside the home. Others feel that the provisions support the discriminatory treatment of women on the basis of gender ·in marriage, property ownership, and inheritance, and impose on them unconscionable labor and reproductive burdens. But, as this article has argued elsewhere, the Charter can be read differently:

> However, these are not the practices that the Charter condones when it requires states to assist families as the 'custodians of morals and traditional values.' Such an interpretation would be a cynical misreading of the Charter. The reference is to those traditional values which enhanced the dignity of the individual and emphasized the dignity of motherhood and the importance of the female as the central link in the reproductive chain; women were highly valued as equals in the process of the regeneration of life.[119]

The Charter's veneration of African culture could be construed as reinforcing gender oppression.[120] The charge here is that the Charter sees itself as the savior of an African culture that is permanent, static, and unchanging. Viewed this way, the Charter would freeze in time and protect from reform, radical change, or repudiation of those cultural norms, practices, and institutions that are harmful to women. Again, this article argues that the Charter, taken in its totality as a human rights document, does not support such a reading.

> The Charter guarantees, unambiguously and without equivocation, the equal rights of women in its gender and equality provision by requiring states to

---

RIGHTS OF WOMEN: NATIONAL AND INTERNATIONAL PERSPECTIVES 495 (Rebecca Cook ed., 1994); Chaloka Beyani, *Toward a More Effective Guarantee of Women's Rights in the African Human Rights System, in* HUMAN RIGHTS OF WOMEN: NATIONAL AND INTERNATIONAL PERSPECTIVES 285 (Rebecca Cook, ed. 1994; J. Oloka-Onyango, *The Plight of the Larger Half: Human Rights, Gender Violence and the Legal Status of Refugee and Internally Displaced Women in Africa*, 24 DENV. J. INT'L L. & POL'Y 349, 371–74 (1996).

118. *See* African Charter, *supra* note 4, art. 18 (referring to the family as the "natural unit and basis of society" and requiring the state to "assist the family which is the custodian of morals and traditional values recognized by the community"). Elsewhere, the Charter provides that the individual owes "duties towards his family and society." *Id.* art. 27(1). Further, the African Charter states that every individual has the duty to "preserve the harmonious development of the family and to work for the cohesion and respect of the family; to respect his parents at all times, to maintain them in case of need." *Id.* art. 29(1).

119. *See* Mutua, *supra* note 8, at 371–72 (footnote omitted).

120. *See id.* at 371.

"eliminate every discrimination against women" and to protect women's rights in international human rights instruments. Read in conjunction with other provisions, the Charter leaves no room for discriminatory treatment against women.[121]

To allay these fears, however, and to prevent a conservative human rights court from ever giving the Charter a discriminatory interpretation in gender matters, the African Charter should be supplemented by an optional protocol to fully address women's rights issues in all their complexity and multiple dimensions.[122]

Besides the normative set of problems that face the Human Rights Court, there are also institutional problems. These concerns are external to the Court and are compounded by matters internal to it, such as the tenure of judges and its effect on the independence of the Court and the limitation of access to the Court to individuals and NGOs. In addition, it is absolutely critical that the Court be, and be perceived as, separate and independent from the African Commission to avoid burdening it with the severe image problems and the anemia associated with its older sibling. This is possible if there is a clear division of labor between the African Human Rights Court and the African Commission. That is not currently the case. A court was not contemplated by the drafters of the African Charter, and as a result, the African Commission was vested with both promotional and protective functions, such as the individual complaint procedure, which make the Commission "court-like" because of their quasi-judicial character.

To address this institutional concern, the African Charter should be revised. The protective functions of the African Commission should be removed and vested exclusively within the African Human Rights Court. The African Commission should only be charged with promotional functions including the monitoring of state reporting and the facilitating of dialogue with NGOs and government institutions in member states to encourage the incorporation of human rights norms into state policies and

---

121. *See* Mutua, *supra* note 10, at 372 (footnote omitted). The Charter states that the "state shall ensure the elimination of every discrimination against women and also ensure the protection of the rights of the woman and the child as stipulated in international declarations and conventions." African Charter, *supra* note 4, art. 18(3). The Convention on the Elimination of All Forms of Discrimination Against Women (CEDAW) is among the international conventions that would be applicable here. Convention on the Elimination of All Forms of Discrimination Against Women, *adopted* 18 Dec. 1979, G.A. Res. 34/180, U.N. GOAR, 34th Sess., Supp. No. 46, U.N. Doc. A/34/36 (1980) (*entered into force* 3 Sept. 1981), *reprinted in* 19 I.L.M. 33 (1980). Normatively, the CEDAW is perceived as a very progressive and forward-looking document.

122. There already have been calls for a protocol on women's rights. *See* Murray, *supra* note 48, at 16, 19.

domestic legislation.[123] This unambiguous demarcation of areas of competence should alleviate the problem of hierarchy or "competition" between
the two institutions, and may enhance cooperation and mutual reinforcement. Importantly, such a division of labor should prevent tainting one body
with the baggage of the other. Thus the African Commission would clearly
be the "political" body, while the Court would alone be the judicial or
"legal" organ of the African human rights system.

As the sole adjudicatory body in the African legal system, the African
Court must consider the three basic purposes that are associated with
national and international adjudicatory bodies: 1) vindicating the rule of
law by providing justice in an individual case; 2) protecting rights through
deterrence and behavior modification; and 3) expounding legal instruments
and making law through elucidation and interpretation.[124] To fulfill its
promise, the African Human Rights Court will have to reflect carefully on
these roles and decide where it has the potential to make a meaningful
contribution.

While the African Human Rights Court should primarily be a forum for
protecting citizens against the state, it should not be viewed as a forum for
offering individual justice to victims of human rights violations. While such
a goal is certainly noble, it is by all means impossible. The Court can act
neither as a forum of first instance nor as the mandatory court of appeal for
all cases. Cast in this role, the Court would be paralyzed by a torrential
caseload. The most poignant example that warns of this potential paralysis
is the Human Rights Committee (HRC), the body that oversees the
implementation of the International Covenant on Civil and Political Rights.[125]
Under the Optional Protocol to the ICCPR, individuals can petition the HRC
for the vindication of their rights.[126] The HRC's use of a mandatory jurisdiction to consider all admissible cases has created at least three years of
backlog.[127] The possible ratification of the Optional Protocol by states with

---

123. At a recent meeting, NGOs and members of the African Commission started a dialogue
on possible amendments and revisions to the African Charter. These included women's
rights, "clawback" clauses, and derogation of rights. *See id.* at 19.
124. *See* Henry J. Steiner, *Individual Claims in a World of Massive Violations: What Role for
the Human Rights Committee?, in* THE FUTURE OF UN HUMAN RIGHTS TREATY MONITORING
(Philip Alston & James Crawford eds., forthcoming 1999) (see text at the beginning of
section entitled "Purposes of Adjudication").
125. ICCPR, *supra* note 21.
126. Optional Protocol to the International Covenant on Civil and Political Rights, *adopted*
16 Dec. 1966, G.A. Res. 2200A (XXI), U.N. GAOR, 21 Sess., Supp. No. 16, at arts. 1,
2, U.N. Doc. A/6316 (1966), 999 U.N.T.S. 171 (*entered into force* 23 Mar. 1976),
reprinted in 6 I.L.M. 383 (1967).
127. For statistics on the twenty years since the HRC communications procedure became
effective under the Optional Protocol, see *Report of the Human Rights Committee to the
General Assembly: Official Records,* U.N.GAOR, 52nd Sess., Supp. No. 40, section
VII(A), at 74, U.N. Doc A/52/40, Vol.I (1997).

large populations such as China, India, the United States, and Indonesia—together with the growing familiarity by victims with the procedure—can only underscore the complete inability of the HRC to respond to all individual cases.

The African Human Rights Court need not make the mistake of the HRC. It will not survive if it adopts a mandatory jurisdiction because the volume of cases is bound to be enormous. Instead the Court should only hear those cases that have the potential to expound on the African Charter and make law that would guide African states in developing legal and political cultures that respect human rights. In other words, the Court should not be concerned with individual cases where it looks, as it were, backwards, attempting to correct or punish a historical wrong to an individual. Rather, the Court should look forward and create a body of law with precedential value and an interpretation of the substantive law of the African Charter and other key universal human rights documents to guide and direct states. Such forward-looking decisions would deter states from future misconduct by modifying their behavior. Individual justice would be a coincidence in the few cases the Court would hear. Moreover, individual courts in OAU member states should look to the African Human Rights Court for direction in the development and application of human rights law.

Finally, the African Human Rights Court would benefit tremendously from the experiences of the European Court of Human Rights (ECHR) and the Inter-American Court of Human Rights as well as national fora such as the Constitutional Court of South Africa, which have taken the lead in developing human rights jurisprudence. The Court should closely examine the factors that have made these institutions effective. Some authors have identified a checklist of such factors that the African Human Rights Court ought to contemplate.[128] For example, Helfer and Slaughter have organized these factors into three clusters: 1) factors that state parties to the treaty creating the Court control (such as the tribunal's composition, its investigative powers, and the legal status of its decisions); 2) factors that the tribunal itself controls such as quality of legal reasoning and degrees of autonomy from political interests; and 3) factors beyond the control of the tribunal and the state parties such as the cultural identities of states and the nature of abuses monitored by the tribunals.[129] This checklist can be particularly useful if judges are independent and motivated by the drive to make the African Human Rights Court the central institution in the development of a legal culture based on the rule of law.

---

128.   *See generally* Laurence R. Helfer & Anne-Marie Slaughter, *Toward a Theory of Effective Supranational Adjudication,* 107 YALE L.J. 273, 298–337 (1997).
129.   *Id.* at 298–337.

VI. CONCLUSION

Africa has been traumatized by human rights violations over the last five centuries. The recent chapter in that long history of abuses is still being authored under the direction of the post-colonial state. But the peoples of Africa, like peoples elsewhere, have never stopped struggling for better conditions of life, and especially for more enlightened and accountable political societies. The popular repudiation of one-party and undemocratic states over the past decade has once again given hope that the predatory impulses of the post-colonial state can be arrested. Within states, NGOs have multiplied during the last ten years, and governments have been forced to revise policies and laws that are offensive to basic human rights. At the continental level, NGOs and human rights advocates have demanded that the African Commission become part of this movement toward change.

It is in this context that the idea of an African Human Rights Court was hatched. It was felt by many Africans that, while the African Commission was a step in the right direction, it was largely ineffectual. A regional human rights system worth its name needed strong institutions to anchor its norms. The African Human Rights Court is an attempt to fill this void. However, the Court promises to be a disappointment unless state parties revisit the African Charter and strengthen many of its substantive provisions. Moreover, the Court will not meet the expectations of Africans if the OAU does not provide it with material and moral support to allow it to function as the independent and significant institution that it ought to be. Finally, the initial integrity and vitality of the Court will rest with those who will be privileged to serve as its first bench. Unless these conditions are met, the African Human Rights Court is condemned to remain a two-legged stool, a lame institution unable to fulfill its promise as a seat from which human rights can be effectively protected and advanced.

[21]

AN AFRICAN HUMAN RIGHTS COURT AND AN AFRICAN UNION COURT: A NEEDFUL DUALITY OR A NEEDLESS DUPLICATION?

Nsongurua J. Udombana[*]

"Entia non sunt multiplicanda praeter necessitatem"[1]

I. Introduction

In recent years, the international community has witnessed an avalanche of international dispute settlement mechanisms, which Cesare Romano referred to as "the international judiciary."[2] It is the consequence of a "tumultuous amplification of the number and ambit of institutions consecrated to ensure compliance with international legal obligations and settlement of disputes arising therefrom."[3] Some of these mechanisms are permanent in nature while others are ad hoc; some exercise full judicial powers, while others are quasi-judicial and administrative.[4] This state of affairs would have been inconceivable fifty

---

* Senior Lecturer & Ag. Head, Department of Jurisprudence and International Law, University of Lagos, Nigeria; LL.M., LL.B. (Lagos); Member of the Nigerian Bar. E-mail: udombana@hotmail.com. The author divides his interest and time between international law, African legal System, human rights, and the judicial process. He has published in such representative journals as the American Journal of International Law, Boston University International Law Journal, and the Yale Human Rights and Development Law Journal.

1. "Entities should not be multiplied unnecessarily." Cesare P.R. Romano, *The Proliferation of International Judicial Bodies: The Pieces of the Puzzle,* 31 N.Y.U. J. Int'l L. & Pol. 709 (1999) (quoting William of Ockham).

2. *Id.* at 711 n.7 (defining the phrase to mean "those judicial bodies that have been created to administer international justice, without implying the existence of any degree of coordination among them").

3. *Id.* at 710. Romano also argues that the "'international judicial law and organization' can and should be studied as a discipline in its own right, without the need to be subsumed under the general category of 'Peaceful Settlement of International Disputes.'" *Id.* at 711.

4. For the criteria characterizing an international court, tribunal or body, see generally, Christian Tomuschat, *International Courts and Tribunals with Regionally Restricted and/or Specialized Jurisdiction, in* Judicial Settlement of International Disputes: International Court of Justice,

or so years ago — because at that time the "main concern of international law was to convince states of the attractiveness and usefulness of third-party dispute settlement."[5] Although international arbitration had been in existence — long before modern international courts — very few judicial institutions with universal jurisdiction existed at the international level in the 1950s and 60s. Among these were the International Court of Justice ("ICJ"), the European Court of Justice, and the European Court of Human Rights. In the 70s, the Inter-American Court of Human Rights was established.

Today, however, the landscape has changed, with new judicial institutions springing up throughout the world. These new institutions include the International Tribunal for the Law of the Sea, the World Trade Organization ("WTO") Dispute Settlement System, and, most recently, the International Criminal Court ("ICC"). Earlier institutions have also been strengthened and, in some cases, restructured or reformed for optimal performance.

At the first glance, the proliferation of international tribunals seems to give a reason for cheer, because it indicates the success of peaceful settlement of international disputes — a development that the Charter of the United Nations ("UN") particularly encourages.[6] Peaceful settlement of international disputes

---

OTHER COURTS AND TRIBUNALS, ARBITRATION AND CONCILIATION: AN INTERNATIONAL SYMPOSIUM 285 (1974). According to Tomuschat, an international body must meet five criteria. First, it must be permanent, which is to say that its existence must be independent from the vicissitudes of a given case. Second, an international legal instrument must have established it. Third, in deciding the cases submitted to them, they must resort to international law. Fourth, they must decide those cases on the basis of rules of procedure that pre-exist the case and usually cannot be modified by the parties. Lastly, the outcome of the process must be legally binding. *Id.* at 293–312.

5. Karin Oellers-Frahm, *Multiplication of International Courts and Tribunals and Conflicting Jurisdiction — Problems and Possible Solutions, in* 5 MAX PLANCK Y.B. OF UNITED NATIONS LAW 67, 69 (Jochen A. Frowein & Rudiger Wolfrum eds., 2001). *See also generally* Hermann Mosler et al., *Chapter XIV: The International Court of Justice, in* The CHARTER OF THE UNITED NATIONS: A COMMENTARY 973 (Bruno Simma ed., 1994) (for the efforts within the framework of the United Nations ("UN") towards the pacific settlement of international disputes).

6. *See* U.N. CHARTER arts. 2, paras. 3–4, 33. The ICJ has confirmed that Article 2, Paragraph 4 of the UN Charter is a rule of customary law applying to all states: "All Members shall refrain in their international relations from

by judicial recourse helps parties to clarify their positions. Often, they are led "to reduce and transform their sometimes overstated political assertions into factual and legal claims."[7] The judicial route also moderate tensions and lead to a better and fuller understanding of opposing claims and, in some cases, the resumption of political negotiations even before a court renders judgment.[8] Surprisingly, however, the multiplication of international tribunals has generated heated debates in recent years.[9] Some scholars have expressed the fear that the proliferation of tribunals will result in "the fragmentation of the international legal system or, at least, [in] the fragmentation of the interpretation of its norms."[10] Such proliferation also raises the risk of "forum shopping" — the practice of parties competing for courts — with the overlapping of jurisdictions that could jeopardize both the unity of international law and its role in inter-State relations across the world.

Others, however, believe that there is no cause for alarm and that wine can vary with every valley and every vineyard. Indeed, proponents of multiplicity adduce many reasons to justify their belief that the variety of third-party dispute settlement

---

the threat or use of force against the territorial integrity or political independence of any state, or in any other manner inconsistent with the Purposes of the United Nations." *See* Military and Paramilitary Activities (Nicar. v. U.S.), 1986 I.C.J. 14, at 99-101 (June 27) [hereinafter Nicaragua Case].

7. Address by the Honorable Stephen M. Schwebel, Judge to the General Assembly of the United Nations, President of the International Court of Justice (Oct. 27, 1998), *available at* http://www.lawschool.cornell.edu/library/cijwww/icjwww/ipresscom/SPEECHES/iSpeechPresidentGA98.htm [hereinafter Schwebel Address].

8. *See id.*

9. For the debate, see generally *Implications of the Proliferation of International Adjudicatory Bodies for Dispute Resolution: Proceedings of a Forum Co-Sponsored by the American Society of International Law and the Graduate Institute of Int'l Studies*, 9 ASIL BULLETIN (L. Boisson de Chazournes ed., Nov. 1995); Gilbert Guillaume, *The Future of International Judicial Institutions*, 44 INT'L & COMP. L.Q. 848 (1995); Gerhard Hafner, *Should One Fear the Proliferation of Mechanisms for the Peaceful Settlement of Disputes?*, *in* THE PEACEFUL SETTLEMENT OF DISPUTES BETWEEN STATES: UNIVERSAL AND EUROPEAN PERSPECTIVES 25 (Lucius Caflisch ed., 1998).

10. Pierre-Marie Dupuy, *The Danger of Fragmentation or Unification of the International Legal System and the International Court of Justice*, 31 N.Y.U. J. INT'L L. & POL. 791, 792 (1999).

vehicles for states is generally desirable.[11] The justifications include the desire by states and non-state actors for "secrecy, control over the membership of the forum, panels with special expertise or perceived regional sensitivities, preclusion of third state intervention, and forums that can resolve disputes in which non-state entities may appear as parties."[12] According to proponents, the strength of the multiplicity of international tribunals has the benefit of permitting "a degree of experimentation and exploration, which can lead to improvements in international law."[13] Multiplicity of international tribunals also reflects the vitality and complexity of international life and, therefore, should be welcomed — so long as their jurisdictions do not duplicate each other. Ultimately, such tribunals will contribute significantly to the peaceful and just settlement of international disputes.[14]

Recent events in Africa tend to show that African leaders have been greatly impressed by the proliferation of courts and tribunals. They are preparing to set up two supra-national judicial institutions for the continent, in addition to several other sub-regional judicial institutions that have sprung up in recent years. These sub-regional tribunals include a court set up to interpret the Treaty Establishing the Southern African Development Community ("SADC")[15] and the Community Court of

---

11. *See, e.g.,* Hugh Thirlway, *The Proliferation of International Judicial Organs and the Formation of International Law, in* INTERNATIONAL LAW AND THE HAGUE'S 750TH ANNIVERSARY 433 (Wybo P. Heere ed., 1999) (taking an optimistic view on international organs and international law). *See also* Jonathan I. Charney, *The Impact on the International Legal System of the Growth of International Courts and Tribunals,* 31 N.Y.U. J. INT'L L. & POL. 697, 698 (1999) [hereinafter Charney, *Impact of International Courts*] (focusing on the relationship between the International Court of Justice and other permanent and *ad hoc* tribunals that have shared the responsibility of hearing cases turning on aspects of international law). *See also* Jonathan Charney, *Is International Law Threatened by Multiple International Tribunals?,* 271 RECUEIL DES COURS 101 (1998).

12. Charney, *Impact of International Courts, supra* note 11, at 698.

13. *Id.* at 700.

14. *See* Schwebel Address, *supra* note 7.

15. Treaty Establishing the Southern African Development Community, Aug. 17, 1992, 32 I.L.M. 116 (1993) [hereinafter SADC Treaty].

Justice established pursuant to a protocol[16] adopted by member states of the Economic Community of West African States ("ECOWAS").[17] On June 9, 1998, at its Thirty-fourth Ordinary Session held in Ouagadougou, Burkina Faso, the Assembly of Heads of State and Government of the now-defunct Organization of African Unity[18] ("OAU") adopted a Protocol ("Human Rights Protocol" or "Protocol")[19] to the African Charter on Human and Peoples' Rights ("African Charter")[20] on the Establishment of the African Court on Human and Peoples' Rights ("African Human Rights Court" or "Human Rights Court"). This Protocol establishes a Human Rights Court to complement the protective mandate of the African Commission on Human and Peo-

---

16. For the Protocol Establishing the Community Court of Justice, see Treaty Establishing the African Economic Community, arts. 18–20, 30 I.L.M. 1241 (1991).

17. *See* Treaty of the Economic Community of West African States (ECOWAS), May 28, 1975, 14 I.L.M. 1200 (1975) (original ECOWAS Treaty, superceded by 1993 treaty); Economic Community of West African States (ECOWAS): Revised Treaty, July 24, 1993, 35 I.L.M. 660 (1996) [hereinafter Revised ECOWAS Treaty] (striving to accelerate the economic union of West Africa through effective economic cooperation and integration).

18. The OAU ceased to function as a continental international organization on July 9, 2002, when the African Union (*see infra*) was inaugurated in Durban, South Africa. The occasion witnessed, simultaneously, the last (thirty-eighth) ordinary session of the OAU and the first ordinary session of the African Union.

19. *See* Protocol to the African Charter on Human and Peoples' Rights on the Establishment of an African Court on Human and Peoples' Rights, OAU Doc. OAU/LEG/MIN/AFCHPR/PROT (III), *available at* http://www.dfa.gov.za/for-relations/multilateral/treaties/court.htm [hereinafter Human Rights Protocol].

20. African Charter on Human and Peoples' Rights, June 27, 1981, OAU Doc. OAU/CAB/LEG/67/3/Rev.5, *reprinted in* 21 I.L.M. 58 (1982) [hereinafter African Charter]. For literature, see generally, U. O. UMOZURIKE, *The African Charter on Human and Peoples' Rights*, 77 AM. J. INT'L. L. 902 (1997); Makau Mutau, *The African Human Rights System in a Comparative Perspective*, 3 REV. AFR. COMM'N ON HUM. & PEOPLES' RTS. 5 (1993); Obinna Okere, *The Protection of Human Rights in Africa and the African Charter on Human and Peoples' Rights: A Comparative Analysis with the European and American Systems*, 6 HUM. RTS. Q. 141 (1984); U. Oji Umozurike, *The African Charter on Human and Peoples' Rights*, 77 AM. J. INT'L. L. 902 (1983); and Richard Gittleman, *The African Charter on Human and Peoples' Rights: A Legal Analysis*, 22 VA. J. INT'L L. 667 (1982).

ples' Rights[21] and defines the organization, jurisdiction, and functioning of the Court.[22]

In addition, on July 11, 2000, at its Thirty-sixth Ordinary Session held in Lome, Togo, the OAU adopted the Constitutive Act of the African Union ("AU")[23] to replace the Charter of the [OAU][24] and to strengthen the African Economic Community ("AEC") Treaty.[25] The Act, which entered into force on May 26, 2001, provides for an African Court of Justice ("AU Court") among several other organs of the Union.[26] Unlike the Protocol to the African Charter, the AU Act does not define the composition, mandate, and functioning of the AU Court. It merely pro-

---

21. *See* Human Rights Protocol, *supra* note 19, art. 2 (providing that "[t]he Court shall, bearing in mind the provisions of this Protocol, complement the protective mandate of the African Commission on Human and Peoples' Rights . . . conferred upon it by the African Charter on Human and Peoples' Rights").

22. For commentary on the Protocol, see generally Nsongurua J. Udombana, *Toward the African Court on Human and Peoples' Rights: Better Late Than Never*, 3 YALE HUM. RTS. & DEV. L.J. 45 (2000) [hereinafter Udombana, *Better Late Than Never*]; Gino J. Naldi & Konstantinos D. Magliveras, *Reinforcing the African System of Human Rights: The Protocol on the Establishment of a Regional Court of Human and Peoples' Rights*, 16 NETH. Q. HUM. RTS. 431 (1998) (analyzing the Protocol's provisions and drawing comparisons with other regional human rights judicial organs); Andre Stimmet, Comment, *A Future African Court on Human and Peoples' Rights and Domestic Human Rights Norms*, 23 S. AFR. Y.B. INT'L L. 233 (1998); John Mubangizi & Adreas O'Shea, *An African Court on Human and Peoples' Rights*, 24 S. AFR. Y.B. INT'L L. 256 (1999); Makau Mutua, *The African Human Rights Court: A Two-Legged Stool?*, 21 HUM. RTS. Q. 342 (1999).

23. *See* CONSTITUTIVE ACT OF THE AFRICAN UNION, July 11, 2002, *at* http://www.dfa.gov.za/for-relations/multilateral/treaties/auact.htm [hereinafter AU ACT].

24. *Id.* art. 33(1) (stating that the OAU Charter would remain operational for a transitional period).

25. *See* Treaty Establishing the African Economic Community, June 3, 1991, 30 I.L.M. 1241 (entered into force May 11, 1994) [hereinafter AEC Treaty] (providing for the establishment of an African Economic Community, through a gradual process that would be achieved by coordination, harmonization and progressive integration of the activities of existing and future regional economic communities).

26. *See* AU ACT, *supra* note 23, art. 5(1) (listing nine organs of the AU, including the Assembly of the Union, the Executive Council, the Pan-African Parliament, the Court of Justice, the Commission, the Permanent Representatives Council, the Specialised Technical Committees, the Economic, Social and Cultural Council, and the Financial Institutions). The Act, however, gives the Assembly the power to establish any other organ of the Union. *Id.* art. 5(2).

vides that those matters shall be dealt with in a separate, future protocol,[27] which has yet to be adopted.

This Article examines the developments of African international judicial institutions and discusses whether the proposal for two continental courts is a necessary duality or a needless duplication. Can the AU sustain all the institutions it has created, including the courts, or is it trying to run before walking? Put differently, is it really impracticable for a single court to interpret and apply all the relevant instruments adopted by the OAU/AU, including the African Charter and the AU Act? Did the continent's leaders think through the implications of two courts, or were they simply fascinated and carried away by the European experiences? The author disagrees with the current approach taken by the AU leaders and insists that no new international court should be created without first ascertaining if the existing institutions could better perform their duties.

Part II provides the background by looking at the history of international dispute settlements in Africa in a global comparative context. Part III highlights the normative structure of the proposed African Human Rights Court and the African Union Court (AU Court) by analyzing the enabling protocol and related instruments. Part IV examines the arguments for and against having both courts in light of African realities and peculiarities. The European experience will be brought to bear in the debate. Part V concludes by recapitulating the discourse and providing some feasible recommendations.

II. Dispute Settlements In A Collective Africa In A Global Context

A. Attempts, Not Deeds

The creation of permanent international courts for dispute settlement in a collective Africa is a novelty. It is largely a development of the last decade of the twentieth century. Indeed, the first time in AU history that a reference was made to a "court" as a mechanism for dispute settlement in Africa was in

---

27. *Id.* art. 18.

relation to the 1991 AEC Treaty.[28] Traditionally, African leaders have always favored the use of quasi-judicial commissions (two such commissions will be briefly noted below), rather than a court with full judicial powers. The reason for this anti-court approach stems partly from the nature of African customary law[29] and long-time dispute settlement practice. Traditional African dispute settlement places a premium on improving relations between the parties on the basis of equity, good conscience, and fair play, rather than on strict legality. The African system "is one of forgiveness, conciliation and open truth, not legal friction or technicality."[30] African procedures favor consensus and amicable dispute settlement, frowning upon the adversarial and adjudicative procedures common to Western legal systems.[31]

Another reason for the delayed emergence of courts in a collective Africa is that the emerging African states were reluctant to relinquish their hard won independence and sovereignty to any form of supra-national entity. This reluctance also explained why the OAU Charter stresses full respect for state sovereignty.[32] The OAU was in fact born "in a context of nearly

---

28. *See* AEC Treaty, *supra* note 25, arts. 7, 18; Chris M. Peter, *The Proposed African Court of Justice — Jurisprudential, Procedural, Enforcement Problems and Beyond*, 1 E. AFR. J. PEACE & HUM. RTS. 117, 118 (1993).

29. African customary law has been distinguished from African customary practices, beliefs or value systems. The former represents a generic system of rigid rules "embedded in judicial decisions and statutes, which have lost the characteristics of dynamism and adaptability which distinguished African custom." Thandabantu Nhlapo, *Indigenous Law and Gender in South Africa: Taking Human Rights and Cultural Diversity Seriously,* 1994–1995 THIRD WORLD LEGAL STUD. 49, 53. African customary practices, beliefs, or value systems are more susceptible to change and are thus more receptive to institutions which have the promise of fostering societal development. *See* Laurence Juma, *Reconciling African Customary Law and Human Rights in Kenya: Making a Case for Institutional Reformation and Revitalization of Customary Adjudication Processes,* 14 ST. THOMAS L. REV. 459, 462–65 (2002) (assessing the relevance of African Customary Law in a plural legal system seeking to uphold human rights principles).

30. A. L. Ciroma, *Time for Soul-Searching,* DAILY TIMES (Nig.), Aug. 23, 1979, at 3.

31. *See* Udombana, *Better Late Than Never, supra* note 22, at 74. *See also generally* TASLIM OLAWALE ELIAS, THE NATURE OF AFRICAN CUSTOMARY LAW (1962).

32. *See* Charter of the Organization of African Unity, May 25, 1963, art. III(2), 479 U.N.T.S. 69, 74 [hereinafter OAU Charter].

untrammeled state sovereignty, in which heads of states sought sedulously to safeguard the independence so recently won."[33] This sovereignty principle, together with the non-interference principle — the *reserve domain* — became the identity symbol of the organization. The organization, thus, became a personality club in perpetual mutual adoration.

The reluctance towards modern judicial settlement was manifested at the founding conference of the OAU in 1963. The OAU rejected the draft Charter provision that provided for a Court of Mediation, Conciliation and Arbitration to be set up by means of a separate treaty.[34] Instead, African leaders created an ad hoc body, the "Commission of Mediation, Conciliation and Arbitration," as a mechanism for the peaceful dispute settlement[35] among Member States to accomplish the purposes of the Charter.[36] The Commission was described as the *raison d'etre* of the OAU, given that the "peaceful resolution of conflicts, both large and small, within the established framework of the Organization provides the necessary conditions for orderly progress, not only for the individual Member States but also the entire continent of Africa."[37] A protocol adopted in 1964 defined the duties and powers of the Commission.[38] Pursuant to the article 32, this protocol became an integral part of the OAU Charter.[39]

---

33. Claude E. Welch, Jr., *The African Commission on Human Rights and Peoples' Rights: A Five-Year Report and Assessment*, 14 HUM. RTS. Q. 43 (1992) (discussing the birth of the OAU and noting that the founders did not focus on human rights policy in the original OAU Charter).

34. *See* ORGANIZATION OF AFRICAN UNITY, RESOLVING CONFLICTS IN AFRICA: IMPLEMENTATION OPTIONS ¶ 21, at 8 (OAU Information Services Publication, No. 2, 1993).

35. "Disputes" in this context refer not only to justifiable disputes, i.e., matters that raise legal questions and that can be settled by the application of international law, but also to political issues or other extra-legal considerations. *See, e.g.,* Mavrommatis Palestine Concessions (Greece v. U.K.), 1924 P.I.C.J. (ser. A) No. 2, at 11–12 (Aug. 30); East Timor (Port. v. Austl.), 1995 I.C.J. 90, ¶¶ 20–22, at 99–100 (June 30).

36. *See* OAU Charter, *supra* note 32, arts. xix, VII(4).

37. *See* Dr. Taslim Olawale Elias, *The Commission of Mediation, Conciliation and Arbitration of the Organisation of African Unity*, 40 BRIT. Y.B. INT'L L. 336, 348 (1964). *See also* Colin Legum, *The Specialised Commissions of the Organisation of African Unity*, 2 J. MOD. AFR. STUD. 587 (1964).

38. *See* Protocol of the Commission of Mediation, Conciliation and Arbitration, 3 I.L.M. 1116 (1964).

39. There was no provision for a formal adoption of the Protocol. Article 32 of the Protocol merely required the approval of the OAU Assembly for it to

The Commission was not a judicial body, but it provided three modes of settlement: mediation, conciliation and arbitration. This Commission, however, never became operational. Technically, it continued to exist, since its formal abolition required an amendment to the OAU Charter, which was not done. The OAU Secretary-General was, however, mandated to dispense with all the assets of the Commission, and it was subsequently dissolved.[40]

Another opportunity to establish a judicial institution for the settlement of international disputes in Africa beckoned during the adoption of the African Charter in the early 1980s. However, the OAU refused to establish an African Human Rights Court to enforce the rights guaranteed in the African Charter, the same way as it treated the proposal for a Court of Mediation in the 1960s. African leaders disregarded the recommendations of the 1961 Lagos Conference[41] and the repeated proposals and recommendations over the following twenty years, fearing that such a tribunal would threaten their national sovereignty. The OAU instead established an African Human Rights Commission. This Commission was established in 1987, pursuant to article 64(1) of the African Charter[42] "to promote human and peoples' rights and ensure their protection in Africa."[43] It presently remains the only quasi-judicial body at the continental

---

become an integral part of the OAU Charter; and this approval was given in at the first Assembly in July 1964.

40. *See* Council of Ministers, Res. CM/Res.240 (XVI) (on file with author).

41. In 1961, the International Commission of Jurists ("Int'l. C.J") convened scholars from thirty-three countries to discuss enforcement mechanisms for the protection of human rights in the newly independent states of Africa. At the end of the Conference, participants adopted the "Law of Lagos," calling for the establishment of African Convention on human rights and a court to enforce it. Article 4 declared that "in order to give full effect to the Universal Declaration of Human Rights of 1948, this Conference invites the African Governments to study the possibility of adopting an African Convention of Human Rights in such a manner that the *Conclusions* of this Conference will be safeguarded by the creation of a court of appropriate jurisdiction and that recourse thereto be made available for all persons under the jurisdiction of the signatory States." Editorial, *From Delhi to Lagos*, 3 J. INT'L COMM. JURISTS 2, 9 (1961).

42. *See* African Charter, *supra* note 20, art. 64(1) ("After the coming into force of the present Charter, members of the Commission shall be elected in accordance with the relevant Articles of the present Charter.").

43. *Id.* art. 30.

level to implement the rights guaranteed in the African Charter, but no more than those rights. The Commissions' activities include consideration of communications, examination of State reports, on-site missions, inter-session activities of the Commissioners, reports of Special Rapporteurs, conferences, and seminars, etc.[44] More specifically, the Commission receives communications from states[45] or "other communications"[46] from individuals or Non-Governmental Organizations ("NGO"s),[47] which allege any violation of the Charter provisions. Such communications must, however, satisfy certain "conditions laid down by the . . . Charter."[48]

The African Commission has not been able to effectively fulfill its mandate because of certain normative and structural deficiencies.[49] Its decisions and recommendations to African Heads of States and Governments are frequently disregarded. As a report of the African Commission pointed out, "[w]ith the sovereignty of the Assembly of Heads of State and Government and the Charter's non-provision of alternative methods of compensation for victims of Human Rights violations, the said vic-

---

44. *See id.* art. 45. *See generally* Dr. RACHEL MURRAY, THE AFRICAN COMMISSION ON HUMAN AND PEOPLES' RIGHTS AND INTERNATIONAL LAW (2000); EVELYN A. ANKUMAH, THE AFRICAN COMMISSION ON HUMAN AND PEOPLES' RIGHTS (1996); Emmanuel Bello, *The Mandate of the African Commission on Human and Peoples' Rights: Article 45 Mandate of the Commission*, 1 AFR. J. INT'L L. 31 (1988).

45. *See* African Charter, *supra* note 20, arts. 47–49.

46. *Id.* art. 55.

47. Only NGOs with observer status with the Commission have the competence to institute proceedings before it. Any "serious" NGO desiring to have an observer status with the Commission must submit a documented application to the Secretariat of the Commission showing its willingness and capability to work for the realization of the objectives of the African Charter. It must also provide its status, proof of its legal existence, a list of its members, its last financial statement and a statement of its activities. The Commission thereafter designated a rapporteur to study the application and, if all necessary documents have been received, the Commission considers the application during any of its sessions, usually in October and May each year. *See Resolution on the Criteria for Granting and Enjoying Observer Status to Non-Governmental Organizations Working in the Field of Human Rights with the African Commission on Human and Peoples' Rights,* Afr. Comm'n on Hum. & Peoples' Rts., 25th Ord. Sess., OAU Doc. DOC/OS(XXVI)116 (1999).

48. African Charter, *supra* note 20, art. 45(2).

49. *See* Udombana, *Better Late Than Never, supra* note 22, at 66–73 (discussing the structural and normative deficiencies bedeviling the Commission).

tims find themselves without any remedy."[50] Such non-compliance constitutes "one of the major factors of the erosion of the Commission's credibility,"[51] because it undermines the authority of the Commission as an effective institution capable of ensuring the states' implementation of the rights secured in the African Charter.

B. Global Contrasts

The late arrival of permanent supra-national courts in Africa contrasts with other established global and regional tribunals. This part briefly examines the development at the global level. The Permanent Court of International Justice ("PCIJ") or the "World Court," for example, was established under the League of Nations after World War I and began to function in 1922. Its creation was regarded as a decisive path towards the submission of a sovereign state's activity to the international rule of law.[52] The International Court of Justice ("ICJ")[53] succeeded the PCIJ after World War II as "substantially a continuation of the earlier body."[54] It remains the only international court of a universal character with general jurisdiction.[55] It serves "as a fac-

---

50. African Commission, *Non-Compliance of State Parties to Adopted Recommendations of the African Commission: A Legal Approach,* ¶ 6, adopted at the 24th Ord. Sess. of the Commission Banjul, The Gambia, Oct. 1998, OAU DOC/OS/50b (XXIV).

51. *Id.* ¶ 2.

52. Dupuy, *supra* note 10, at 791. *See generally* SIR HERSCH LAUTERPACHT, THE FUNCTION OF LAW IN THE INTERNATIONAL COMMUNITY (1933).

53. Established pursuant to the Statute of the International Court of Justice, June 26, 1945, 59 Stat. 1031, 33 U.N.T.S. 993 [hereinafter ICJ Statute]. *See generally* SHABTAI ROSENNE, THE LAW AND PRACTICE OF THE INTERNATIONAL COURT (1997).

54. IAN BROWNLIE, PRINCIPLES OF PUBIC INTERNATIONAL LAW 548 (1998).

55. The ICJ is fitted both with contentious jurisdiction and advisory jurisdiction. For its contentious jurisdiction, however, States Parties must recognize the compulsory jurisdiction of the Court. *See* ICJ Statute, *supra* note 53, art. 36(2) ("The states parties to the present Statute may at any time declare that they recognize as compulsory *ipso facto* and without special agreement, in relation to any other state accepting the same obligation, the jurisdiction of the Court in all legal disputes . . . .") (emphasis added). Where, for example, both states have limited the jurisdiction that they will recognize, the ICJ only has power to decide a case to the extent that both states have agreed to the same sort of matters. *Cf.* Eastern Carelia (Fin. v. U.S.S.R.), 1923 P.C.I.J. (ser. B) No. 5, at 27 (July 23) ("It is well established in international law that no State can, without its consent, be compelled to submit its disputes with other

tor and actor in the maintenance of international peace and security."[56] That way, the ICJ assists in furthering one of the purposes of the UN, to wit, "to bring about by peaceful means, and in conformity with the principles of justice and international law, adjustment or settlement of international disputes which might lead to a breach of the peace."[57] As of July 2001, 189 States acceded to the ICJ Statute, out of which 63 have recognized its compulsory jurisdiction.[58]

The ICJ has operated concurrently with other ad hoc tribunals, such as the Nuremberg and Tokyo International Military Tribunals[59] and the international criminal tribunals for the Former Yugoslavia[60] and Rwanda.[61] In recent years, however,

---

States either to mediation or to arbitration, or to any other kind of pacific settlement.").

56. *See* Schwebel Address, *supra* note 7.

57. U.N. CHARTER art. 1, para. 1.

58. *See* 2000–2001 I.C.J. ANN. REP. pt. I, at 1, *available at* http://www.icj-cij.org/icjwww/igeneralinformation/igeninf_Annual_Reports/iICJ_Annual_Rep ort_2000-2001.PDF [hereinafter 2000–2001 I.C.J. ANN. REP.] (containing the 2001 Annual Report of activities of the ICJ to the General Assembly of the UN).

59. These two tribunals were established "for the trial of war criminals whose offences have no particular geographical location whether they be accused individually or in their capacity as members of organizations or groups or in both capacities." Agreement Respecting the Prosecution and Punishment of the Major War Criminals of the European Axis, Aug. 8, 1945, art. 1, 59 Stat. 1544, 82 U.N.T.S. 280.

60. The International Criminal Tribunal for the former Yugoslavia (ICTY), sitting at the Hague, was established in 1993, pursuant to a Statute of that name. *See* Establishing an International Tribunal for the Prosecution of Persons Responsible for Serious Violations of International Humanitarian Law in the Territory of the Former Yugoslavia, U.N. SCOR, U.N. Doc. S/RES/827 (1993), *available at* http://www.un.org/icty/legaldoc/lateestleft-e.htm. It is an *ad hoc* tribunal, with a mandate to prosecute persons responsible for serious violations of international humanitarian law committed in the territory of the former Socialist Federal Republic of Yugoslavia since January 1, 1991. Its Statute defines its jurisdiction and powers. Its *ratione materiae* is limited to grave breaches of the Geneva Conventions of August 12, 1949, *id.* art. 2; violations of the laws or customs of war, *id.* art. 3; genocide, *id.* art. 4; and crimes against humanity, *id.* art. 5. *See also* MANUAL ON INTERNATIONAL COURTS AND TRIBUNALS 277 (Philip Sands ed., 1999) [hereinafter MANUAL ON INTERNATIONAL COURTS]; Sean D. Murphy, *Progress and Jurisprudence of the International Criminal Tribunal for the Former Yugoslavia*, 93 AM. J.INT'L L. 57 (1999).

61. The International Criminal Tribunal for Rwanda ("ICTR") was established in 1994 by a UN Security Council resolution under Chapter VII of the

the rate of change from ad hoc to permanent tribunals and courts has increased dramatically. The International Criminal Court ("ICC"), created in Rome on July 17, 1998, is the latest addition.[62] The ICC is a landmark in international judicial co-operation and possibly the greatest step towards a multilateral justice system since the Nuremberg and Tokyo tribunals. As the direct descendant of these tribunals and the more recent tribunals for the Former Yugoslavia and Rwanda, the ICC will prosecute genocide, crimes against humanity, and war crimes,[63] when national justice systems are either unwilling or unable to do so.

UN Charter. *See* Statute of the International Criminal Tribunal for Rwanda, U.N. SCOR 50th Sess., U.N. Doc. S/RES/955 (1994), *as amended* by SC Res. 1165. It has as its mandate the prosecution of persons responsible for geno-cide and other serious violations of international humanitarian law committed in the course of or in relation to the 1994 Rwanda Genocide. In many re-spects, the ICTR was modeled on the ICTY, with which it maintains signifi-cant institutional links. Like its ICTY counterpart, the ICTR Statute defines the jurisdiction and powers of the ICTR. The crimes on which ICTR exercises jurisdiction include genocide, crimes against humanity, violations of the Ge-neva Convention and the fundamental rules of international humanitarian law, the violation of which entails individual criminal responsibility. *See id.* arts. 2–4. For these crimes, the tribunal exercises concurrent jurisdiction with national courts, although the tribunal has primacy over national courts for this purpose. *Id.* arts. 2–4, 8. *See also* MANUAL ON INTERNATIONAL COURTS, *supra* note 60, at 287–300; VIRGINIA MORRIS & MICHAEL P. SCHARF, 1–2 THE INTERNATIONAL CRIMINAL TRIBUNAL FOR RWANDA (1998); Roy S. Lee, *The Rwanda Tribunal*, 9 LEIDEN J. INT'L L. 37 (1996).

62. *See* Rome Statute of the International Criminal Court, U.N. Doc. A/CONF. 183/9 (1998) (entered into force on July 1, 2002) [hereinafter Rome Statute of the I.C.C.]. The Statute was adopted with 120 in favor, 7 against, and 20 abstentions. The U.S. was, sadly, among the states that voted against the Statute, on the ground, *inter alia,* that the Statute is "overreaching" in that it purports to bind non-state parties through the exercise of jurisdiction over their nationals; besides, the U.S. was seeking "an iron-clad veto of juris-diction over U.S. personnel and officials." *See* M. P. Scharf, *Results of the Rome Conference for an International Criminal Court*, ASIL INSIGHTS, ¶¶ 1–2 (Aug. 1998), *available at* http://www.asil.org/insights/insigh23.htm. The alle-gation that the Statute is overreaching has, however, been refuted; indeed, Richard Dicker of Human Rights Watch calls it "a gross mischaracterization." *Id.* The statute permits the I.C.C. to exercise jurisdiction over the nationals of non-States Parties where there is a reasonable basis to believe they have committed the most serious international crimes. *Id.*

63. *See* Rome Statute of the I.C.C., *supra* note 62, arts. 5–8, for the defini-tion and description of the various crimes covered in the Statute.

There are also numerous treaty-based bodies established to implement various UN-inspired human rights treaties. These bodies include the Human Rights Committee ("HRC") charged with the implementation of the International Covenant on Civil and Political Rights,[64] the Committee on the Elimination of Racial Discrimination ("CERD"),[65] the Committee Against Torture ("CAT"),[66] the Committee on the Elimination of All Forms of Discrimination Against Women;[67] and the Committee on the Rights of the Child.[68] Remarkably, these new judicial and quasi-judicial bodies, including those mentioned in the introductory part of this paper, exercise powers and functions that are substantially different from those of the past. For example, most of these bodies grant standing to both state and non-state entities,[69] not only states, as was previously the case. This change is due partly to the expanding concept of the "international community as a whole," which no longer consists exclusively of states but includes non-state entities towards whom obligations may exist.[70] The phrase now covers such bodies as

---

64. *See* International Covenant on Civil and Political Rights, Dec. 19, 1966, pt. IV, 999 U.N.T.S. 171 [hereinafter ICCPR]. *See generally* DOMINIC MCGOLDRICK, THE HUMAN RIGHTS COMMITTEE: ITS ROLE IN THE DEVELOPMENT OF THE INTERNATIONAL COVENANT ON CIVIL AND POLITICAL RIGHTS (1994).

65. Established pursuant to the International Convention on the Elimination of All Forms of Racial Discrimination, Dec. 21, 1965, art. 18, 660 U.N.T.S. 195 (entered into force Jan. 4, 1969).

66. Established pursuant to the Convention Against Torture, and Other Forms of Cruel, Inhuman or Degrading Treatment or Punishment, *opened for signature*, Dec. 10, 1984, art. 17, 1465 U.N.T.S. 85.

67. Established pursuant to the Convention on the Elimination of All Forms of Discrimination Against Women, *opened for signature*, Dec. 18, 1979, art. 17, 1249 U.N.T.S. 13, 21.

68. Established pursuant to the Convention on the Rights of the Child, *opened for signature*, Nov. 20, 1989, art. 43, 1577 U.N.T.S. 3.

69. *See, e.g.,* Optional Protocol to the International Covenant on Civil and Political Rights, Dec. 19, 1966, art. 2, 999 U.N.T.S. 302 (allowing "individuals who claim that any of their rights enumerated in the Covenant have been violated and who have exhausted all available domestic remedies [to] submit a written communication to the Committee for consideration"); Optional Protocol to the Convention on the Elimination of All Forms of Discrimination Against Women, *opened for signature* Mar. 1, 1980, art. 2, 1249 U.N.T.S. 13 (dealing with the competence of the CEDAW Committee to receive and consider complaints from individuals or groups within its jurisdiction).

70. *Cf. Draft Articles on Responsibility of States for Internationally Wrongful Acts,* U.N. GAOR Int'l L. Comm'n, 56th Sess., Supp. No. 10, at 54, U.N.

the UN, the AU, the EU, and the International Committee of the Red Cross. Indeed, presently judicial bodies that grant standing to non-state entities have outnumbered those with traditional jurisdictions limited to disputes between sovereign states.[71]

III. BRIEF OVERVIEW OF THE PROPOSED AFRICAN COURTS

This Part surveys the legal framework for the Human Rights Court and the AU Court. The next Part will discuss whether two supra-national courts are needed in contemporary Africa.

A. The African Human Rights Court

The African Charter originally did not provide for a court. This omission of an international court undermined public confidence in the African human rights system, because without a court it was impossible to compel violating states to conform to international norms and to provide remedies to victims.[72] The lack of a court also presented obstacles to the development of human rights jurisprudence and the necessary publicity.[73] Perceiving these problems, the member states adopted a protocol to the African Charter in 1998 to give teeth and meaning to the rights guaranteed in the Banjul Charter and "any other relevant Human Rights instrument ratified by the States concerned."[74] According to the Preamble of the Human Rights Pro-

---

Doc. A/56/10 (2001) (preferring the phrase "international community as a whole," instead of simply "international community"). The formulation, however, does not imply that the international community is a legal person, a fallacy exposed by Judge Fitzmaurice in his dissenting opinion in the Namibia advisory opinion case. Legal Consequences for States of the Continued Presence of South Africa in Namibia (South West Africa) Notwithstanding Security Council Resolution 276 (1970), 1971 I.C.J. 16, 241 (June 21, 1971) (dissenting opinion of Judge Fitzmaurice); James Crawford et al., *The ILC's Articles on Responsibility of States for Internationally Wrongful Acts: Completion of the Second Reading*, 12 EUR. J. INT'L L. 963, 973 (2001).

71. Oellers-Frahm, *supra* note 5, at 69.

72. *See* Philip Amoah, *The African Charter on Human and Peoples' Rights: An Effective Weapon for Human Rights?*, 4 AFR. J. INT'L & COMP. L. 226, 237–40 (1992).

73. *Id.*

74. Human Rights Protocol, *supra* note 19, art. 3(1). For an in-depth commentary and analysis on the Protocol establishing the Human Rights Court, see Udombana, *Better Late Than Never*, *supra* note 22.

tocol, the member states were "[f]irmly convinced that the attainment of the objectives of the African Charter on Human and Peoples' Rights requires the establishment of an African Court on Human and Peoples' Rights to complement and reinforce the functions of the African Commission on Human and Peoples' Rights."[75]

The Protocol thus provides the anatomy of the Human Rights Court. It allows any aggrieved persons, whether state or non-state, to bring complaints before the African Human Rights Court for violations of the African Charter. Complaint procedures before international human rights tribunals serve important functions:

> First, as a result of considering such a complaint an individual, whose rights have been violated, may have a remedy against the wrong suffered by him, and the violation could be stopped and/or compensation paid, etc; second, consideration of a complaint may result not only in a remedy for the victim of the violation, whose complaint has been considered, but also in changes to internal legislation and practice; and third, an individual complaint (or more often, a series of complaints) may serve as evidence of systematic and/or massive violations of certain rights in a given country.[76]

According to the Protocol, the Human Rights Court shall consist of eleven judges, who must be nationals of the member states of the OAU.[77] These judges shall be "elected in an individual capacity from among jurists of high moral character and of recognized practical, judicial or academic competence and experience in the field of human and peoples' rights."[78] In addition to having appropriate training or qualifications in law, the judges must also be persons of "high moral character." This morality requirement supposedly encompasses such elements as

---

75. Human Rights Protocol, *supra* note 19, 7th preambular para.

76. Rein Mullerson, *The Efficiency of the Individual Complaint Procedures: The Experience of CCPR, CERD, CAT and ECHR*, *in* MONITORING HUMAN RIGHTS IN EUROPE 25, 27 (Arie Bloed et al. eds., 1993).

77. *See* Human Rights Protocol, *supra* note 19, art. 11(1); *cf.* ICJ Statute, *supra* note 53, art. 2 (declaring that the Court shall be composed of "independent judges elected regardless of nationality").

78. Human Rights Protocol, *supra* note 19, art. 11(1).

impartiality, integrity, independence, and competence.[79] Significantly too, the candidates for judges are not to be limited to the holders of judicial appointments; reputable academics or jurisconsults may be appointed. This approach resembles that taken by the Convention for the Protection of Human Rights and Fundamental Freedoms[80] and the ICJ Statute,[81] and is distinguishable from the requirement of the American Convention on Human Rights ("ACHR") that candidates possess qualifications required for appointment to the highest judicial offices.[82]

Similar to the ICJ composition,[83] the judgeship of the African Human Rights Court must provide a balanced representation of the main African regions and of their principal legal traditions.[84] The main regions of the continent include Northern, Eastern, Central, Southern and Western Africa, while the principal legal traditions in Africa encompass traditional or customary law, Islamic law, common law, and civil law. This rule of balanced representation, in practice, will help to ensure a degree of consistency in the allocation of bench seats to nationals of member states. It may also mitigate any foreseeable reluctance on the part of a member state in submitting to the judgments of a court that consisted of uneven representation of legal traditions. Indeed, to function effectively, the Court must ensure the confi-

---

79. *See* NSONGURUA UDOMBANA, THE AFRICAN REGIONAL HUMAN RIGHTS COURT: MODELING ITS RULES OF PROCEDURE 38 (2002).

80. European Convention for the Protection of Human Rights and Fundamental Freedoms, Nov. 4, 1950, art. 39(3), 213 U.N.T.S. 221, [hereinafter ECHR] ("The [judges] shall be of high moral character and must either posses the qualifications required for appointment to high judicial office or be jurisconsults of recognised competence.").

81. *See* ICJ Statute, *supra* note 53, art. 2 (providing that "[t]he Court shall be composed of a body of independent judges, elected regardless of their nationality from among persons of high moral character, who possesses the qualifications required in their respective countries for appointment to the highest offices, or are jurisconsults or recognised competence in international law").

82. *See* American Convention on Human Rights, Nov. 22, 1969, art. 52(1), 1144 U.N.T.S. 144.

83. The ICJ Statute, *supra* note 53, art. 9, provides that the General Assembly and Security Council are to bear in mind, when proceeding to elect the judges of the ICJ, that in the body as a whole, the representation of the main forms of civilization and of the principal legal systems of the world is assured.

84. *See* Human Rights Protocol, *supra* note 19, art. 14(2) ("The Assembly shall ensure that in the Court as a whole there is representation of the main regions of Africa and of their principal legal traditions.").

dence of an eligible party to any action in the court's impartiality. Therefore, such party must be satisfied that at least one of the judges in the Court has the necessary education, training and experience allowing him to fully understand the interests and submissions of the region where he comes from.[85]

Article 5 of the Human Rights Protocol deals with what common lawyers call *locus standi*, that is, who has a right to bring a case before the Court. The article entitles the following five categories of claimants to direct access to the Court:

(a) The Commission;

(b) The State Party which has lodged a complaint to the Commission;

(c) The State Party against which the complaint has been lodged at the Commission;

(d) The State Party whose citizen is a victim of human rights violation;

(e) African Intergovernmental Organisations.[86]

From the above provisions, the Commission, States and African NGOs will have automatic access to the Court upon a state's ratification of the Protocol.[87] In contrast, the Protocol provides for only optional jurisdiction with respect to individuals and NGOs. It provides that "[t]he Court may entitle relevant Non-Governmental Organisations . . . with observer status before the Commission, and individuals to institute cases directly before it, in accordance with Article 34(6) of this Protocol."[88] Notably, the types of NGOs are circumscribed to those "with

---

85. *See generally* Richard Plende, *Rules of Procedure in the International Court and the European Court,* 2 EUR. J. INT'L L. 1 (1991); Judge Manfred Lachs, *A Few Thoughts on the Independence of Judges of the International Court of Justice,* 25 COLUM. J. TRANSNAT'L L. 593 (1987); Edward Gordon, *Observations on the Independence and Impartiality of the Members of the International Court of Justice,* 2 CONN. J. INT'L L. 397 (1987); Shabtai Rosenne, *Election of Five Members of the ICJ in 1981,* 76 AM. J. INT'L L. 364 (1982); Judge Sir Humphrey Waldock, *The International Court of Justice as Seen from Bar and Bench,* 54 BRIT. Y.B. INT'L L. 1 (1983); Leo Gross, *The International Court of Justice: Consideration of Requirements for Enhancing its Role in the International Legal Order,* 65 AM. J. INT'L L. 253 (1971).

86. *See* Human Rights Protocol, *supra* note 19, art. 5(1).

87. *Id.* art. 5(2).

88. *Id.* art. 5(3).

observer status with the Commission." Thus, the discretion to give individuals and NGOs standing lies jointly with the Court and the target State. On the one hand, the Court has discretion to grant or deny an individual and NGO standing at will. The language of the Protocol is: the *Court may entitle[;]* . . . and, in order for a willing Court to hear a case filed by an individual or NGO, the state must have made an express declaration accepting the Court's jurisdiction to hear such cases. As Article 34(6) provides:

> [A]t the time of the ratification of this Protocol or any time thereafter, the State shall make a declaration accepting the competence of the Court to receive cases under article 5(3) of this Protocol. *The Court shall not receive any petition under article 5(3) involving a State Party which has not made such a declaration.*[89]

This provision was a compromise in order to induce more African states to adopt the Human Rights Protocol.[90] The provision was aimed at achieving an acceptable balance between genuine enforcement of fundamental rights set forth thereunder and respect for the sovereignty of potential signatory states.[91] Such a cautious compromise, however, was really unnecessary. The drafters facing a noble enterprise ought to have drafted the Protocol in a way that significantly attacks the problems it meant to address. However, the drafters appeared to have been too timid, like a frightened beast shying at its own shadow.

Article 5(3) in conjunction with Article 34(6) of the Protocol has article 25 of the former European Convention on Human Rights ("ECHR") as its antecedent. Article 25 provides:

---

89. *Id.* art. 34(b) (emphasis added).

90. *See* Udombana, *Better Late Than Never, supra* note 22, at 87; Ibrahim Ali Badawi El-Sheikh, *Draft Protocol to the African Charter on Human and Peoples' Rights on the Establishment of An African Court on Human and Peoples' Rights: Introductory Note,* 9 AFR. J. INT'L & COMP. L. 943, 947 (1997) ("The question of allowing NGOs and individuals to submit cases to the Court was one of the most complicated issues during the consideration of the Draft Protocol.").

91. *See, e.g.,* 4 COUNCIL OF EUROPE, COLLECTED EDITION OF THE "TRAVAUX PREPARATOIRES" OF THE EUROPEAN CONVENTION ON HUMAN RIGHTS 114 (1977).

The Commission may receive petitions . . . from any person, non-governmental organizations[92] or group of individuals claiming to be the victim of a violation by one of the High Contracting Parties of the rights set forth in this Convention, provided that the High Contracting Party against which the complaint has been lodged has declared that it recognises the competence of the Commission to receive such petitions.[93]

Yet, when the ECHR was adopted, the idea that individuals should be able to bring human rights complaints against states before an international legal authority was so radical that no human rights instruments obliged member states to automatically accept such a procedure. Time has changed, however, and

---

92. The European Commission explained its interpretation of a non-governmental organization in *Ayuntamiento de M v. Spain,* App. No. 15090/89, 68 Eur. Comm'n H.R. Dec. & Rep. 209, 215 (1991). The applicant was the M City Council. It complained, *inter alia,* that it had not had a fair trial (in breach of the ECHR, *supra* note 80, arts. 6, 13) when the domestic Spanish courts prevented it from establishing a drug addicts' rehabilitation centre in a specified district of the city. *Id.* at 213. The Council claimed that it was a 'non-governmental organisation', because the system of administrative decentralisation in Spain meant that the council was independent of (central) Government. *Id.* at 215. The Commission rejected that argument, declaring that the Council was not eligible to make an application under Article 25. The Commission:

> [N]otes that local authorities are public law bodies which perform official duties assigned to them by the Constitution and by substantive law. They are therefore quite clearly governmental organisations. . . . In this connection, the Commission reiterates that in international law the expression 'governmental organisation' cannot be held to refer only to the Government or the central organs of the State. Where powers are distributed along decentralised lines, it refers to any national authority which exercises public functions.

Id.

93. ECHR, *supra* note 80, art. 25. *Cf.* ICCPR, *supra* note 64, art. 41(1), providing that:

> A State Party to the present Covenant may at any time declare under this article that it recognizes the competence of the Committee to receive and consider communications to the effect that a State Party claims that another State Party is not fulfilling its obligations under the present Covenant. Communications under this article may be received and considered only if submitted by a State Party which has made a declaration recognizing in regard to itself the competence of the Committee. No communication shall be received by the Committee if it concerns a State Party which has not made such a declaration.

the revised ECHR now gives aggrieved individuals automatic standing.[94] Furthermore, it seems incongruous that individuals have standing to sue their governments before domestic courts but cannot do so before an international tribunal, such as the African Human Right Court.

The African Human Rights Court has both contentious and advisory jurisdictions.[95] Its contentious jurisdiction extends "to all cases and disputes submitted to it concerning the interpretation and application of the Charter, this Protocol and any other relevant Human Rights instrument ratified by the States concerned."[96] Similarly, "[a]t the request of a Member State of the [AU], the [AU], any of its organs, or any African organisation recognised by the [AU], the Court may provide an opinion on any legal matter relating to the Charter or any other relevant human rights instruments, provided that the subject matter of the opinion is not related to any matter being examined by the Commission."[97] It is not clear, however, what is meant by "any African organisation recognised by the OAU". Presumably, it may refer to different sub-regional organizations, such as the ECOWAS.

Notwithstanding the above-discussed shortcomings, the Protocol provides the Human Rights Court with broad advisory jurisdiction, allowing it to engage in a robust and sustained analysis of the meaning of the African Charter and the Human Rights Protocol, as well as the compatibility of domestic legislation and regional initiatives with the human rights norms contained therein. The advisory opinions of the Inter-American Court, for example, have had a significant impact on both pro-

---

94. *See* Protocol No. 11 to the Convention for the Protection of Human Rights, May 11, 1994, arts. 1, 34, Europ. T.S. No. 155, *reprinted in* 33 I.L.M. 943, 943, 962 (1994) [hereinafter Protocol No. 11] (amending Article 24 of the former ECHR).

> The Court may receive applications from any person, nongovernmental organisations or group of individuals claiming to be the victim of a violation by one of the High Contracting Parties of the right set forth in the Convention or the protocols thereto. The High Contracting Parties undertake not to hinder in any way the effective exercise of this right.

Id.

95. *See* Human Rights Protocol, *supra* note 19, arts. 3–4.

96. *Id.* art. 3(1).

97. *Id.* art. 4.

tecting human rights in the Americas and on providing needed guidance to domestic courts.[98] These advisory opinions have also enabled some governments to introduce necessary domestic reforms or to abandon legislation that would have breached the American Convention on Human Rights without being compelled to do so by contentious decisions stigmatizing them as violators of human rights. As Thomas Buergenthal puts it, "[c]ertain governments, in particular those of fragile emerging democracies, will find it easier to give effect to an advisory opinion than to comply with a contentious decision in a case they lost."[99] Additionally, advisory opinions "can provide speedy judicial responses to questions it would take years to determine in contentious proceedings, while avoiding the friction and bitterness judgments in contentious cases are likely to generate in some countries."[100]

The Human Rights Court is empowered to draft its Rules of Procedure in consultation with the African Commission.[101] The Rules "shall lay down the detailed conditions under which the Court shall consider cases brought before it, bearing in mind the complementarity between the Commission and the Court."[102] The Human Rights Protocol provides that the Court shall conduct its proceedings in public, although it may also hold in camera hearings in certain cases specified by the Rules of Procedure.[103] A party shall be entitled to representation of his case by a legal representative of his choice. Free legal representation may be provided where justice so requires.[104] This provision will

---

98. *See, e.g.,* Ekmekdjian v. Sofovich, CSJN 315 Fallos 1492 (1992) (S. Ct. of Argentina) (discussed in Thomas Buergenthal, *International Tribunals and National Courts: The Internationalization of Domestic Adjudication*, in RECHT ZWISCHEN UMBRUCH UND BEWAHRUNG (FESTSCHRIFT FÜR RUDOLF BERNHARDT) 687, 695 (U. Beyerlin et al. eds, 1995).

99. Thomas Buergenthal, *The European and Inter-American Human Rights Courts: Beneficial Interaction*, in PROTECTING HUMAN RIGHTS: THE EUROPEAN PERSPECTIVE 123, 131 (Paul Mahoney et al. eds., 2000) [hereinafter Buergenthal, *Beneficial Interaction*]. *See also generally* Thomas Buergenthal, *The Advisory Practice of the Inter-American Human Rights Court*, 79 AM. J. INT'L L. 1 (1985).

100. Buergenthal, *Beneficial Interaction, supra* note 99, at 131.

101. Human Rights Protocol, *supra* note 19, art. 33. *See also generally* UDOMBANA, *supra* note 79.

102. Human Rights Protocol, *supra* note 19, art. 8.

103. *Id.* art. 10(1).

104. *Id.* art. 10(2).

be particularly necessary in a continent where the majority of the citizens experience humiliating poverty. In Africa, the lack of resources "is not a special circumstance but rather a common occurrence"[105] and the unavailability of legal aid may have affected the accessibility of a remedy. The Commission has, for example, stressed that "the lack of legal aid in Africa precludes the majority of the African population from asserting their human rights."[106]

The decisions of the Human Rights Court will be final and binding on the parties. However, the court will have the power to review its decisions in light of new evidence under conditions to be set out in the Rules of Procedure.[107] Unlike the African Commission, which merely makes recommendations to the Assembly of Heads of States and Government of the continental body,[108] the Human Rights Court will have the power to issue binding decisions and to order compensation or reparations. The, Executive Council (former Council of Ministers) of the AU, will assist in monitoring the implementation of the court's decisions.[109] This approach is in accord with international law and practice. The binding nature of the decisions rendered by international judicial bodies, however, does not equal to effective enforcement of such decisions, which is a function to be carried out by executive bodies. Thus, enforcing court decisions is a political, rather than a judicial duty.[110]

The good news is that, with limited exceptions, states generally comply with international court judgments. State Parties to

---

105. ANKUMAH, *supra* note 44, at 70. *See also* Andrew S. Butler, *Legal Aid Before Human Rights Treaty Monitoring Bodies*, 49 INT'L & COMP. L.Q. 360, 361 (2000).

106. African Commission on Human and Peoples' Rights, *Conclusions and Recommendations of the Seminar on the National Implementation of the African Charter on Human and Peoples' Rights in the Internal Legal Systems in Africa*, *in* 6 ANNUAL ACTIVITY REPORT OF THE AFRICAN COMMISSION ON HUMAN AND PEOPLES' RIGHTS, Annex VIII, ¶ 6(c) (1993) (recommending that "the question of legal aid and recourse procedures should be accorded greater attention in the work of the African Commission and that States and NGOs should take the initiative to promote the establishment of legal aid services").

107. Human Rights Protocol, *supra* note 19, art. 28(2)–(3).

108. *See* African Charter, *supra* note 20, art. 58(2).

109. Human Rights Protocol, *supra* note 19, art. 29(2). Similarly, the Council of Ministers is entrusted with supervision of the execution of decisions of the E.Ct.H.R. *See* ECHR, *supra* note 80, art. 54.

110. *See* Romano, *supra* note 1, at 714 n.25.

the ECHR, for example, have increasingly complied with judgments of the E.Ct.H.R.[111] Most international organizations also make the execution of such judgments possible by providing for some form of sanctions. For example, the UN Charter provides that where a party fails to obey the judgment of the ICJ, the aggrieved party may apply to the Security Council, "which may, if it deems necessary, make recommendations or decide upon measures to be taken to give effect to the judgment."[112] It is hoped that African States, like their European counterparts, will adopt positive attitudes towards the judgment of the African Human Rights Court or, for that matter, any continental court.

B. The African Union Court

1. Establishment and Organization of the Court

As indicated earlier, the AU Act has not defined the structure and mandate of the AU Court. It is, therefore, not yet clear what the Court' anatomy will be, as a separate protocol is expected to provide further and better particulars, to use the language of trial lawyers. Significantly, the Interim Chairperson of the AU Commission, Amara Essy, has initiated the process for the adoption of a protocol on the Court. Two "brainstorming" meetings have already been held, leading to the elaboration of a Draft Protocol.[113] The Draft Protocol shall form the basis for the discussion that follows. The Court is established to "have a determinative role in the progressive development of African jurisprudence through the judicial process and will make a distinctive contribution to the development of international law."[114]

Meanwhile, the AU Act provides that the judges of the AU Court shall be appointed and terminated by the Assembly.[115] Under the Draft Protocol, the Court shall consist of seventeen

---

111. *See generally* Rolv Ryssdall, *Opinion: The Coming of Age of the European Convention on Human Rights,* 1 EUROP. HUM. RTS. L. REV. 18 (1996) (examining the achievements of the E.Ct.H.R. and the challenges it faces).

112. U.N. CHARTER art. 94, para. 2.

113. *See* Draft Protocol Relating to the Statute, Composition and Functions of the Court of Justice of the African Union, CAB/LEG/23.20/45/VOL.II (2003) [hereinafter Draft Protocol].

114. *Id.* at pmbl.

115. *See* AU ACT, *supra* note 23, art. 9(h).

judges, nationals of Member States, provided that no two judges shall be nationals of the same State.[116] This number, arguably, will allow for viability and successful collective functioning of the Court. Like the Human Rights Protocol, the Draft Protocol provides that the appointment of the Judges must reflect the principal legal systems of Africa; and for this purpose, each region of the continent — that is Northern, Eastern, Central, Southern, and Western Africa — "shall be represented by no less than two (2) Judges."[117] Like earlier noted, this broad composition will give State Parties sufficient confidence to resort to the Court.

The Draft Protocol spells out the qualifications for appointment, which is not different from those of similar international tribunals. It provides that "[t]he Court shall be composed of impartial and independent Judges elected from among persons of high moral character, who possesses the qualifications required in their respective countries for appointment to the highest judicial offices, or are jurists of recognized competence in international law."[118] This formula, which is similar to the provision in the ICJ Statute[119] and the Revised ECOWAS Treaty,[120] "takes in professors, professional lawyers, and civil servant appointees."[121] And in other to avoid any conflict of interest, the Draft Protocol provides that a Judge of the Court shall not exercise any political or administrative function, or engage in other occupation of a professional nature.[122]

The Judges shall be elected for a seven-year period, subject to re-election once.[123] The Draft Protocol, like the Human Rights Protocol, staggers their appointment in order "to ensure a

---

116. *See* Draft Protocol, *supra* note 113, art. 3(1).
117. *Id.* art. 3(2).
118. *Id.* art. 3(3).
119. *See* ICJ Statute, *supra* note 53, art. 2 ("The Court shall be composed of a body of independent judges, elected regardless of their nationality from among persons of high moral character, who possess the qualifications required in their respective countries for appointment to the highest offices, or are jurisconsults of recognized competence in international law.").
120. *See* Revised ECOWAS Treaty, *supra* note 17, art. 20.
121. BROWNLIE, *supra* note 54, at 712.
122. Draft Protocol, *supra* note 113, art. 13(1). *Cf.* ICJ Statute, *supra* note 53, art. 16(1).
123. *See id.* art. 6(1).

measure of continuity of membership of the Court."[124] Consequently, "[t]he term of five (5) Judges elected at the first election shall expire at the end of five (5) years and the other Judges shall serve the full term."[125] The Draft Protocol also provides for "adequate gender representation" in the election of the Judges,[126] similar to the provision in Article 14(3) of the Human Rights Protocol. The empowerment of women, which has been a crusade of the human/women rights movements for years, appears to be yielding some dividends in some areas, though much remains to be done in many others.

The Draft Protocol guarantees the independence of the Judges of the Court; such independence "shall be fully ensured in accordance with international law and, in particular, the United Nations Basic Principles on the Independence of the Judges [("Basic Principles")]."[127] The Basic Principles were formulated, *inter alia*, because of the need to consider "the role of the judges in relation to the system of justice and to the importance of their selection, training and conduct."[128] Consequently, it is vitally important that appointments to the AU Court should be carried out with the utmost circumspection because the way in which the judges are selected could make or mar the Court's performance. Indeed, the Basic Principles provide that "[a]ny method of judicial selection shall safeguard against judicial appointments for improper motives."[129] Allied to the provision on the independence of Judges is the condition for their

---

124. UDOMBANA, *supra* note 79, at 40.

125. Draft Protocol, *supra* note 113, art. 6(1). Immediately after the first election, the Chairperson of the AU Assembly is required to draw lots to determine Judges who will cease to function after the expiration of the initial five years. *See id.* art. 6(2). *Cf.* Human Rights Protocol, *supra* note 19, art. 15.

126. Draft Protocol, *supra* note 113, art. 5(2).

127. *Id.* art. 11(1). *Cf.* Human Rights Protocol, *supra* note 19, art. 17(1).

128. Basic Principles on the Independence of the Judiciary, adopted by the Seventh UN Congress on the Prevention of Crime and the Treatment of Offenders held at Milan from Aug. 26 to Sept. 6 1985, pmbl., UN Doc. A/CONF.121/22Rev. 1 at 59 (1985) [hereinafter Basic Principles]. Principle 4 provides, *inter alia*, that "There shall not be any inappropriate or unwarranted interference with the judicial process, nor shall judicial decisions by the courts be subject to revision." *Id.* Principle 4. Similarly, "[i]t is the duty of each Member State to provide adequate resources to enable the judiciary to properly perform its functions." *Id.* Principle 7.

129. *Id.* Principle 10.

removal. Thus, the Draft Protocol provides that "[a] Judge of the Court shall not be suspended or removed from office unless in the unanimous recommendation of the other Judges, he or she no longer fulfils the requisite conditions to be a Judge."[130] Similar provision is made in the Human Rights Protocol.[131] Meanwhile, Judges engaged in the business of the AU Court, like those of the Human Rights Court, are given diplomatic privileges and immunities.[132]

2. Jurisdiction of the Court

The AU Act did not clearly define the jurisdiction of the AU Court, other than the terse provision on jurisdiction *rationae materiae,* to the effect that that the court "shall be seized with matters of interpretation arising from the application or implementation of this Act."[133] The Court shall also interpret the Protocol to the AEC Treaty on establishing the Pan-African Parliament ("PAP"), which was adopted by the OAU Assembly on March 2, 2001, at its Fifth Extraordinary Summit in Sirte, Libya.[134] Pending the Court's establishment, interpretative matters over both the AU Act and the PAP Protocol shall be submitted to the AU Assembly, "which shall decide [these matters] by a two-thirds majority."[135] It is not clear, however, how

---

130. Draft Protocol, *supra* note 113, art. 10(1). *Cf.* ICJ Statute, *supra* note 53, art. 18(1). *See also* Basic Principles, *supra* note 128, Principle 19 (providing that "[a]ll disciplinary, suspension or removal proceedings shall be determined in accordance with established standards of judicial conduct").

131. *See* Human Rights Protocol, *supra* note 19, art. 18.

132. *See* Draft Protocol, *supra* note 113, art. 12. *Cf.* Human Rights Protocol, *supra* note 19, art. 17(3).

133. AU ACT, *supra* note 23, art. 26. *Cf.* TREATY: TREATY ON EUROPEAN UNION, Feb. 7, 1992, 1992 O.J. (C 191) 1, 1 C.M.L.R. 573 (1992), art. 220 (on the ECJ duties) [hereinafter TEU].

134. *See* Protocol to the Treaty Establishing the African Economic Community ("AEC") Relating to the Pan-African Parliament, Mar. 2, 2001, art. 20, *at* http://www.au2002.gov.za/docs/key_oau/papprot.htm [hereinafter PAP Protocol]. Twenty-one Member States have so far signed the Protocol while three countries have ratified it. *See* Dep't of Foreign Affairs, Republic of South Africa, *Transition from the OAU to the African Union, at* http://www.au2002.gov.za/docs/background/oau_to_au.html (last visited Aug. 11, 2002). The Protocol will enter into force after the deposit of the instruments of ratification by a simple majority of the member states. PAP Protocol, *supra*, art. 22.

135. AU ACT, *supra* note 23, art. 26; PAP Protocol, *supra* note 134, art. 20.

the Assembly — composed predominantly of political leaders — would objectively interpret or even overturn their own decisions.

The Draft Protocol, however, vests the AU Court with both contentious and advisory jurisdiction.

a. Contentious Jurisdiction and Procedure

The Draft Protocol covers not only the jurisdiction *rationae materiae*[136] but also *rationae personiae*. For example, the Court shall have jurisdiction in all legal disputes concerning the interpretation of a treaty; questions of international law; the existence of any act that would constitute a breach of an international obligation, if established; and the nature or extent of the reparation to be made for the breach of an international obligation.[137] This is without prejudice to the right of the AU Assembly to "confer on the Court power to assume jurisdiction over any dispute other than those referred to in [the Protocol]." This savings clause leaves the mandate of the court wide open to adjudicate any matter.[138]

As regards jurisdiction *rationae personiae,* the Draft Protocol provides that all Member States of the AU "are *ipso facto* parties to the Statute of the Court,"[139] though a non-member State may also access the Court "on conditions to be determined by the Assembly in each case."[140] The Draft Protocol, in line with "the changing structure of international law,"[141] gives the right of standing to a staff member of the AU. Thus, where a staff of the Union is adjudged by an internal administrative tribunal "to be in breach of his or her obligation not to seek or receive instructions from any government or from any government or from any other authority external to the Union," such a staff "shall have a right to appeal to the Court."[142]

There is a very close connection, in terms of the functions, between the AU Court and the AEC Court of Justice ("AEC

---

136. *See* Draft Protocol, *supra* note 113, art. 20(1)
137. *Id.* art. 20(1). *Cf.* ICJ Statute, *supra* note 53, art. 36.
138. *See* Peter, *supra* note 28, at 120.
139. Draft Protocol, *supra* note 113, art. 18(1).
140. *Id.* art. 18(2).
141. *See passim* WOLFGANG FRIEDMAN, THE CHANGING STRUCTURE OF INTERNATIONAL LAW (1964).
142. Draft Protocol, *supra* note 113, art. 18(3).

Court"), provided for in the AEC Treaty but not yet established. Indeed, the AEC Treaty provides certain detailed information on its proposed Court, which allows some analysis and comparison with the AU Court. Like the AU Act, the AEC Treaty establishes an AEC Court to interpret its provisions.[143] Again, like the AU Act, the AEC Treaty provides that the statutes, membership, procedure and other matters relating to the AEC Court shall be determined by the Assembly of the AEC in a protocol relating to the Court.[144]

The AEC Court has "a very limited mandate" and is "entrusted with three basic tasks."[145] First, the Court will ensure adherence to law by interpreting and applying the AEC Treaty.[146] Thus, failing an amicable settlement, parties to a "dispute regarding the interpretation of the application of the provisions of [the AEC] Treaty" may refer the mater to the Court.[147] Second, the Court will provide advisory opinions requested by either the Assembly of Heads of State and Government or the Council of Ministers (now the Executive Council).[148] Third, it will adjudicate disputes submitted to it pursuant to the AEC Treaty provisions. Thus, the Court shall entertain "actions brought by a Member State or the Assembly on grounds of the violation of the provisions of this Treaty, or of a decision or a regulation or on grounds of lack of competence or abuse of powers by an organ, an authority or a Member State . . . ."[149] The Assembly may also refer any dispute concerning the AEC Protocol on Regional Economic Communities ("REC") to the Court as a "last resort."[150]

---

143. *See* AEC Treaty, *supra* note 25, art. 18(1).

144. *Id.* art. 20.

145. Peter, *supra* note 28, at 119.

146. *See* AEC Treaty, *supra* note 25, art. 18(2).

147. *Id.* art. 87(1).

148. *Id.* art. 18(3)(b).

149. *Id.* art. 18(3)(a). *Cf.* TEU, *supra* note 133, art. 170 (providing that "[a] Member State which considers that another Member State has failed to fulfill an obligation under this Treaty may bring the matter before the Court of Justice"). The TEU, however, provides that a Member State must first take a matter to the Commission, before proceeding to the ECJ. *Id.*

150. *See* Protocol on the Relationship Between the African Economic Community and the Regional Economic Communities, Feb. 25, 1998, art. 30, *reprinted in* 10 AFR. J. INT'L & COMP. L. 157 (1998).

It remains to add that, in view of the apparent conflict between the AEC Treaty and the AU Act,[151] the AEC Court will be subsumed in the AU Court. This interpretation is fortified by the fact that the AU Act establishes the AU "in conformity with the ultimate objectives of the Charter of [the OAU] and the provisions of the Treaty Establishing the African Economic Community."[152] The AU Act did not abrogate the AEC Treaty but only abrogated the OAU Charter.[153] In fact, through its Sirte initiative of 2001 the AU intended to speed up the economic integration process that the AEC Treaty started.

Mutatis mutandis, Article 19 of the Draft Protocol reproduces the provisions of the AEC Treaty on the functions of the Court. However, unlike the AEC Treaty, the Draft Protocol is silent on amicable settlement of disputes by Member States. The AEC Treaty, on its part, encourages parties to seek amicable solutions before bringing their claims to the Court. This preference for settlement, as noted earlier, is a hallmark of traditional African jurisprudence.[154] However, like the AEC Treaty, the Draft Protocol provides that the AU Court shall "ensure the adherence to law in the interpretation and application of the Constitutive Act."[155] The phrase "the interpretation and application of" — which refers to "two distinct terms relating to two distinct operations"[156] — has been given a broad interpretation to cover any dispute between states concerning the responsibility of one

---

151. *See* AU ACT, *supra* note 23, art. 33(2) ("The provisions of this Act shall take precedence over and supersede any inconsistent or contrary provisions of the Treaty establishing the African Economic Community.").

152. Sirte Declaration, Org. Afr. Unity, Assembly of Heads of State, 4th Extraordinary Sess., ¶ 8(i), EAHG/Draft/Decl. (IV) Rev.1, *available at* http://www.au2002.gov.za/docs/key_oau/sirte.htm. *Cf.* AU ACT, *supra* note 23, pmbl., ¶ 6 (being "[c]onvinced of the need to accelerate the process of implementing the Treaty establishing the African Economic Community in order to promote the socio-economic development of Africa").

153. *See* AU ACT, *supra* note 23, art. 33(1).

154. *See* AEC Treaty, *supra* note 25, art. 87(1). *Cf.* SADC Treaty, *supra* note 15, art. 32 (providing that disputes arising from the interpretation and application of the SADC Treaty should be settled in a friendly manner. Only if an amicable attempt fails, should the dispute be referred to the SADC Tribunal.).

155. Draft Protocol, *supra* note 113, art. 19(1). *Cf.* AEC Treaty, *supra* note 25, art. 18(2).

156. SHABTAI ROSENNE, DEVELOPMENTS IN THE LAW OF TREATIES, 1945–1986, at 224 (1989) [hereinafter ROSENNE, DEVELOPMENTS IN THE LAW OF TREATIES].

of them for an alleged breach of an international obligation, whatever the origin of such an obligation.[157] The *Nicaragua Case* was the "first significant judicial pronouncement [of the ICJ] regarding the meaning of 'application.'"[158] In that case, the Court maintained that the appraisal of conduct in the light of the relevant principles of the treaty pertains to the application of the law rather than to its interpretation; and this must be undertaken in the context of the general evaluation of the facts which are established in relation to the applicable law.[159]

Finally, the AU Assembly is empowered to "confer on the Court power to assume jurisdiction over any dispute other than those referred to in [the Protocol]."[160] This implies that the Assembly may refer to the Court disputes between natural or legal persons. Indeed, as the European experience has indicated, natural and legal persons have proved to be effective guardians of the European Community legal order and have contributed significantly to the evolution of the EC law.[161] Similarly, the future AU Court should also be accessible to individuals. As a court for the African Union with all its ambitious goals, the AU Court must be able to protect the "state of law." It is, therefore, vitally important that individuals are able to appeal "directly to the Court against an act of one of the institutions of the Union that infringes [on] their basic rights."[162]

---

157. *See, e.g.,* Mavrommatis Palestine Concessions (Greece v. U.S.), 1924 P.C.I.J. (ser. A) No. 2, at 16, 29 (Aug. 30); Military and Paramilitary Activities (Nicar. v. U.S.), 1984 I.C.J. 392, ¶¶ 81, 83, at 427–28 (Nov. 26); Application of the Convention on the Prevention and Punishment of the Crime of Genocide (Bosn. & Herz. v. Yugoslavia), 1996 I.C.J. 595, ¶¶ 30–32, at 615–17 (July 11); Oil Platforms (Iran v. U.S.), 1996 I.C.J. 803, ¶ 51, at 820 (Dec. 12); Questions of Interpretation and Application of the 1971 Montreal Convention Arising from the Aerial Incident at Lockerbie (Libyan Arab Jamahiriya v. U.S.), 1998 I.C.J. 115, ¶¶ 23–24, at 123 (Feb. 27).

158. ROSENNE, DEVELOPMENTS IN THE LAW OF TREATIES, *supra* note 156, at 224.

159. *See* Nicaragua Case, *supra* note 6, ¶ 225, at 117.

160. Draft Protocol, *supra* note 113, art. 20(2). *Cf.* AEC Treaty, *supra* note 25, art. 18(4).

161. *See, e.g.,* Christopher Harding, *The Private Interest in Challenging Community Action*, 5 EUR. L. REV. 354, 357 (1980); Carol Harlow, *Towards a Theory of Access for the European Court of Justice*, 12 Y.B. EUR. L. 357 (1992).

162. *See, e.g.,* Leo Tindemans, L' Union Europeenne, Bulletin des Communites Europeennes (Supp. 1/76, 1976).

The Draft Protocol spells out the procedure to be followed in contentious cases; and it consists of two parts: written and oral.[163] Unlike most domestic legal systems, written pleadings submitted to international tribunals usually contain a very full statement both of the facts considered relevant by the party and the arguments as to the law. Documentary evidence is also usually annexed. It is not surprising, therefore, that the Draft Protocol provides that written proceedings "shall consist of communication to the parties and to the institutions of the Union whose decisions are in dispute, of applications, statements of the case, defenses and observations and of replies if any, as well as all papers and documents in support, or of certified copies."[164] The oral proceedings, on the other hand, "shall, if necessary, consist of hearing by the Court of witnesses, experts, agents, counsel and advocates."[165]

Except for proceedings in arbitration cases, which "are almost invariably conducted in private,"[166] oral proceedings of most courts or tribunals are heard in public. Thus, the Draft Protocol provides that hearings shall be in public, unless the Court decides otherwise or the parties demand that the public be not admitted.[167]

The Draft Protocol empowers the AU Court to indicate, "if it considers that circumstances so require, any provisional measures which ought to be taken to preserve the respective rights of the parties."[168] Notice of such measures must be given to the parties and to the Chairperson of the Commission.[169] Interim

---

163. Draft Protocol, *supra* note113, art. 25(1). *Cf.* ICJ Statute, *supra* note 53, art. 43(1).

164. Draft Protocol, *supra* note 113, art. 25(2). *Cf.* ICJ Statute, *supra* note 53, art. 43(2).

165. Draft Protocol, *supra* note 113, art. 25(5).

166. H. W. A. Thirlway, *Procedure of International Courts and Tribunals, in* III ENCYCLOPEDIA OF PUBLIC INTERNATIONAL LAW 1129 (Rudolf Bernhardt ed., 2000) (arguing, however, that there seems to be no reason whey arbitration cases should not be in public if the parties so wish, citing the 1977 *Beagle Channel Arbitration (Argentina v. Chile)*, where the tribunal held a public inaugural hearings).

167. Draft Protocol, *supra* note 113, art. 27. *Cf.* ICJ Statute, *supra* note 53, art. 46.

168. Draft Protocol, *supra* note 113, art. 23(1). *Cf.* ICJ Statute, *supra* note 53, art. 41.

169. Draft Protocol, *supra* note 113, art. 23(2).

measures are adjuncts of the judicial process and "reflect the perennial judicial concern for effective decision-making."[170] They may be mandatory in nature; they may be injunctive or restraining.[171] Either way, they rest on "the wide and universal recognition of the enjoining powers of courts as an inherent part of their jurisdiction."[172] They serve to prevent a party to a dispute from prejudicing the final outcome of the process *de facto* by an arbitrary act before a judgment has been reached, thereby rendering ineffective any judgment of a tribunal. Indeed, interim measures "are of the utmost importance in any judicial proceeding, because without this instrument, the final outcome, that is, the judgment, would lack any efficacy or such efficacy would be very limited, in addition to the serious or irreversible injury the parties might suffer."[173]

All decisions of the AU Court shall be by a simple majority; and, in the event of equality of votes, the President or presiding Judge shall have a casting vote.[174] However, separate or dissenting opinions are permitted.[175] Like that of the Human Rights Court and, indeed, the AEC Court, the judgment of the AU Court "shall be final and without appeal."[176] It shall, however, have no binding force "except between the parties and in respect of that particular case."[177] The implication of this provision, which restates Article 59 of the ICJ Statute, is that the doctrine of judicial precedent will have a narrower application in the legal system of the AU than it has in municipal (common) law. There is an exception though; decisions on the interpreta-

---

170. Peter Goldsworth, *Interim Measures of Protection in the International Court of Justice,* 68 A.J.I.L. 258, 258 (1974).

171. *See* United States Diplomatic and Consular Staff in Terhan Case, Provisional Measures, 1979 I.C.J. 7 (Dec. 15).

172. Separate Opinion of Judge Weeramantry, *Application of the Convention on the Prevention and Punishment of the Crime of Genocide, Provisional Measures (Bosnia and Herzegovina v. Yugoslavia) (Serbia and Montenegro)),* Order of Sept. 13, 1993 ICJ REP. 325, 379.

173. Héctor Fix-Zamudio, *The European and the Inter-American Courts of Human Rights: A Brief Comparison, in* PROTECTING HUMAN RIGHTS: THE EUROPEAN PERSPECTIVE 507, 519 (Paul Mahoney ed., 2000).

174. Draft Protocol, *supra* note 113, art. 35. *Cf.* ICJ Statute, *supra* note 53, art. 55.

175. Draft Protocol, *supra* note 113, art. 37.

176. *Id.* art. 38. *Cf.* Human Rights Protocol, *supra* note 19, 28(1); AEC Treaty, *supra* note 25, art. 87(2).

177. Draft Protocol, *supra* note 113, art. 39.

tion and application of the Constitutive Act shall be binding on Member States and organs of the AU.[178] The Draft Protocol provides that in the event of disputes as to the meaning or scope of a judgment, the Court shall construe it at the request of any party.[179] The jurisprudence of the ICJ shows that "[t]his is rarely done, since the principle is that there should be an end to litigation and that judgments should not be freely expected to be modified except for good cause and also for the purpose of putting its meaning or scope beyond all doubt."[180]

Like the ICJ and the Human Rights Court, the AU Court will have the power to revise its own judgment in light of new evidence. Such "new evidence," however, must be "of such nature as to be a decisive factor, which fact was, when the judgment was given, unknown to the Court and also to the party claiming revision [and] provided that such ignorance was not due to negligence."[181] The application for revision should be made within six months of the discovery of the new fact.[182] Before proceeding with revision, the Court shall make a judgment "expressly recording the existence of the new fact, recognizing that it has such a character as to lay the case open to revision, and declaring the revision admissible on this ground."[183] Furthermore, in admitting proceedings in revision, "[t]he Court may require prior compliance with the terms of the judgment."[184]

The Draft Protocol allows a Member State to apply for permission to intervene in a case before the AU Court should such a member "consider that it has an interest of a legal nature,

---

178. *See id.* art. 40. *Cf.* AEC Treaty, *supra* note 25, art. 19 (providing that the judgment of the AEC Court is binding on the AEC member states and organs).

179. *See id.* art. 41. *Cf.* ICJ Statute, *supra* note 53, art. 60.

180. Taslim Olawale Elias, United Nations Charter and the World Court 120 (1989) [hereinafter Elias, United Nations Charter and the World Court].

181. Draft Protocol, *supra* note 113, art. 42(1). *Cf.* ICJ Statute, *supra* note 53, art. 61; Human Rights Protocol, *supra* note 19, art. 28(3); Statute of the Court of Justice of the European Community, art. 40, 298 U.N.T.S. 147 (as amended by Council Decision 88/591, 1989 O.J. (C 215) 1) [hereinafter ECJ Statute]; Court of Justice, Rules of Procedure of the Court of Justice of the European Communities of 19 June 1991, art. 102, 1991 O.J. (L 176) 7 [hereinafter ECJ Rules of Procedure].

182. Draft Protocol, *supra* note 113, art. 42(4).

183. *Id.* art. 42(2).

184. *Id.* art. 42(2)

which may be affected by the decision in the case."[185] Generally, what is an interest of a legal nature is a matter of law and fact[186] that has to be decided after the abduction of proof that the alleged legal interest is truly involved.[187]

b. Advisory Jurisdiction and Procedure

The AU Court is fitted with advisory jurisdiction "on any legal question."[188] The category of legal persons entitled to request the advisory opinion of the Court is elastic. It includes the Assembly and such other organs and specialized agencies of the AU, if authorized by the Assembly to make such request "regarding interpretation of the Constitutive Act or any decision or regulation enacted under the Act.[189] These other "family" members include the Executive Council, the Pan-African Parliament, the ECOSOCC, the Commission, any of the Financial Institutions or any other organ of the Union.[190] As earlier noted, advisory opinions can only be sought on legal questions, whether "concrete or abstract."[191] However, it is no objection to the giving of such opinion "that the questions submitted to the Court for advice involve issues of fact, provided that the questions remain nonetheless *essentially* legal questions."[192] Furthermore, the questions put to the Court may involve identification of the factual and legal background; and the legal questions

---

185. *Id.* art. 43. *Cf.* ICJ Statute, *supra* note 53, art. 62.

186. For an explanation of the phrase "an interest of a legal nature," see the separate opinion of Judge Oda in the *Land, Island and Maritime Frontier Dispute (El Salvador v. Honduras),* Application to Intervene, Judgment, 1990 I.C.J. 92, 137 (Sept. 13), which was the first time that an intervention under Article 62 of the ICJ Statute was permitted.

187. *See, e.g.,* Libya-Malta Continental Shelf Case, 1985 I.C.J. 33 (June 3) (in which the ICJ, in 1984, refused the request by Italy to intervene in the maritime dispute because, according to the Court, Italy did not show any interest of a legal nature that should enable it to intervene in the dispute).

188. Draft Protocol, *supra* note 113, art. 46(1).

189. *Id.*

190. *Id.* arts. 19(2)(b), 46(1). *Cf.* ICJ Statute, *supra* note 53, art. 65(1); Human Rights Protocol, *supra* note 19, art. 4(1).

191. IVAN ANTHONY SHEARER, STARKE'S INTERNATIONAL LAW 460 (1994).

192. *Id.* at n.10 (citing Advisory Opinion on the Western Sahara, 1975 I.C.J. 12 (Oct. 16)).

"may not necessarily correspond precisely to the questions thus submitted to the Court."[193]

The procedure for advisory opinions is that a written request must be laid before the Court. Such request "shall contain an exact statement of the question upon which the opinion is required and shall be accompanied by all relevant documents likely to be of assistance to the Court."[194] The Registrar then notifies all Member States "that the Court shall be prepared to accept, within a time limit fixed by the President, written submission or to hear oral submissions relating to the question."[195] When all written and oral submissions have been made, the Court "shall deliver its advisory opinion in open court, notice having been given to the Member States and the Chairperson of the Commission."[196]

Undoubtedly, the advisory opinions of the AU Court, like those of the ICJ,[197] will, beside the immediate benefit to the advisee, provide guidance to domestic courts of AU States. It will also enable Member States to introduce necessary domestic reforms or to oppose legislation that would be in breach of the AU Act. Governments also usually "find it easier to give effect to advisory opinion than to comply with a contentious decision in a case they lost."[198] Furthermore, advisory opinions "can provide speedy judicial responses to questions it would take years to determine in contentious proceedings, while avoiding the friction and bitterness judgments in contentious cases are likely to generate in some countries."[199]

---

193. *Id.* (citing Advisory Opinion on the Interpretation of the Agreement of March 25, 1981 between the WHO and Egypt, 1980 I.C.J. 73 (Dec. 20)).

194. Draft Protocol, *supra* note 113, art. 46(2). *Cf.* ICJ Statute, *supra* note 53, art. 65(2).

195. Draft Protocol, *supra* note 113, art. 47. Note that the ICJ Statute requires the Registrar to notify not only "all states entitled to appear before the Court" but also international organizations considered by the Court to be able to furnish information on the subject. *See* ICJ Statute, *supra* note 53, art. 66.

196. Draft Protocol, *supra* note 113, art. 48. *Cf.* ICJ Statute, *supra* note 53, art. 67.

197. For an example of advisory opinions rendered by the ICJ, see *Legality of the Threat or Use of Nuclear Weapons,* 1996 I.C.J. 266 (July 8).

198. Buergenthal, *Beneficial Interaction, supra* note 99, at 131.

199. *Id.*

3. Sources of Law

Writers in international law usually distinguish between the formal sources and the material sources of law. The former are those legal procedures and methods of creation of rules of general application that are legally binding on the addressees. The material sources, on the other hand, provide evidence of the existence of rules, which, when proved, have the status of legally binding rules of general application.[200] The Draft Protocol lists the literary sources of the law that the AU Court "shall have regard to"[201] both in its contentious and advisory jurisdiction.[202] They include the AU Act and treaties expressly recognized by contesting states[203] — sources of mutual obligations of the parties. Another source is international custom, as evidence of a general practice accepted by law.[204] The ICJ describes customary international law as "the generalization of the practice of States."[205]

Other sources that the Draft Protocol enumerates are general principles of law recognized by African States and teachings of publicists.[206] These provisions represent evidences of the existence of consensus among African States concerning particular rules of practice. Significantly, they are reproductions of Article 38(1) of the ICJ Statute, itself "widely recognised as the most authoritative statement as to the sources of international law."[207] The list, however, is not exhaustive, as it omits other important contemporary processes of international lawmaking, such as soft laws. Soft laws "are significant in signaling the evolution and establishment of guidelines, which ultimately

---

200. *See* BROWNLIE, *supra* note 54, at 1.

201. *See* Draft Protocol, *supra* note 113, art. 21.

202. *See, e.g., id.* art. 49 (providing that "[I]n the exercise of its advisory jurisdiction, the Court shall be guided by the provisions of the present Statute which apply in contentious cases to the extent to which it recognizes them to be applicable").

203. *See id.* art. 21(a)–(b).

204. *See id.* art. 21(c).

205. Fisheries Case (United Kingdom v. Norway), 1951 I.C.J. 191 (Dec. 18) (Judge Read).

206. *See* Draft Protocol, *supra* note 113, art. 21(d)–(e).

207. MALCOLM N. SHAW, INTERNATIONAL LAW 55 (1997) (noting further that Article 38(1) "expresses the universal perception as to the enumeration of sources of international law").

may be converted into legally binding rules."[208]   As a compromise, there should be an exception, similar to Article 38(2) of the ICJ Statute, giving the Court power to decide a case *ex aequo et bono*, if the parties so agree.

IV. TWO COURTS OR ONE COURT?

This Part examines arguments for and against two or more supra-national judicial institutions in Africa. Assuming, without prejudice to later conclusions, that the multiplication of courts in a collective Africa is a desirable goal, what are the benefits of such an exercise? On the other hand, is there a cynical notion on the part of African leaders, even if remote, that such an exercise will undermine the authority of these courts and dilute their potential power. What are the interests — official and non-official — of the different African countries on these issues, especially in a continent where political, ideological and cultural considerations remain paramount? This part examines some of these issues.

Subparts A and B address two arguments supporting a two-court regime. The first argument maintains that if two courts could thrive in Europe, they can also succeed in Africa. The second argument contends that multiple courts would speed up the progressive development of international law in Africa through judicial decisions. Subpart C points out the funding problem challenging the two-court system. While this article makes every attempt possible to balance the debate, it does not remain neutral. The thesis of this paper is that Africa does not need two or more courts and that the AU should settle for a single court to interpret all African legal instruments and adjudicate conflicts arising therefrom. Having two courts in Africa will not only present financial difficulty, but will also unnecessarily duplicate efforts and even create potential inconsistency.

A. *Arguments Based on the European Experience*

Europe provides a classic example of successful regional experiments in terms of both economic integration and human rights protection. European success has inspired other regions that are grappling with the problems of integration in an age of

---

208. *Id.* at 98.

globalization and human rights protection at the regional level. For example, the ACHR and its two judicial institutions, the Inter-American Commission on Human Rights and the Inter-American Court of Human Rights, were largely structured along the lines of the European experiment.

Europe created the impetus for a permanent regional international court through its adoption of the Treaty of Paris establishing the European Coal and Steel Community ("ECSC").[209] This treaty, established, *inter alia*, an independent court, the Court of Justice, to interpret and enforce its provisions. On March 25, 1957, the Treaties of Rome were adopted to set up the European Economic Community ("EEC") and the European Atomic Energy Community ("EAEC" or "Euratom").[210] These treaties established a framework to give more freedom of action to the Community institutions.[211] The two new communities were also permitted to use the Court of Justice. The EU Treaty[212] has retained as an organ of the EU the Court of Justice, now known as the European Court of Justice ("ECJ").

The ECJ has operated in Europe alongside the European Court of Human Rights ("E.Ct.H.R."). In 1959, pursuant to the European Convention on Human Rights, the Council of Europe[213] set up the E.Ct.H.R. located in Strasbourg, France.[214]

---

209. *See* Treaty Establishing the European Coal and Steel Community, Apr. 18, 1951, 261 U.N.T.S. 140. The Treaty Establishing the European Coal and Steel Community, which entered into force on July 25, 1952, provided "for the control of the coal and steel industries of the six signatory states by a High Authority, [with] the necessary powers to carry out its mandate." PHILIP RAWORTH, INTRODUCTION TO THE LEGAL SYSTEM OF THE EUROPEAN UNION 2 (2001). This was the first "significant step along the road of European integration." *Id.*

210. *See* Treaty Establishing the European Economic Community, Mar. 25, 1957, 298 U.N.T.S. 11; Treaty Establishing the European Atomic Energy Community, Mar. 25, 1957, 298 U.N.T.S. 169. (These treaties entered into force on January 1, 1958).

211. *See* RAWORTH, *supra* note 138, at 3.

212. *See* TEU, *supra* note 133, art. 4.

213. The Council of Europe was established in 1949. *See* Statute of the Council of Europe, May 5, 1949, 87 U.N.T.S. 103. The Council's aim was, and remains, "to achieve a greater unity between its Members for the purpose of safeguarding and realising the ideals and principles which are their common heritage and facilitating their economic and social progress." *Id.* art. 1(a). The Council seeks to pursue this aim "through the organs of the Council by discussion of questions of common concern and by agreements and common action in economic, social, cultural, scientific, legal and administrative mat-

AFRICAN COURTS

The establishment of the E.Ct.H.R. was the first step towards a collective enforcement of human rights in Europe. The ECHR created, *inter alia,* a right of individual petition, i.e., a right of individuals and organizations to challenge their governments for human rights violations. Thus, individuals were able to take their cases to the European Commission of Human Rights (established in 1954) and then to the E.Ct.H.R. Until 1998, the Convention mandated individual litigants to pass through the Commission before getting to the Court. However, Protocol 11 to ECHR brought about fundamental changes in the system.[215] The reforms were aimed at resolving several of the system's weaknesses. First, the inability of individuals to petition the Court conflicted with the principle of "equality of arms." Second, the commission was faced with a growing number of applications[216] and with increasingly complex cases. In addition, the system could not function efficiently with thirty-four Contracting States, since it was established to work with ten or twelve Member Countries. Finally, there was the time consideration: by 1993, an average case took more than five years to move through the Convention organs.[217]

Consequently, the European Human Rights Commission was abolished on October 31, 1998 and the old, part-time Court was reorganized to become a permanent, full-time, Court, retaining its name as the E.Ct.H.R. There was, however, a transitional period of one year before the protocol entered into force in order to allow the Commission to dispose of cases that had been declared admissible.[218]

---

ters and in the maintenance and further realisation of human rights and fundamental freedoms." *Id.* art. 1(b).

214. *See* ECHR, *supra* note 80, art. 19(b).

215. *See* Protocol No. 11, *supra* note 94, art. 34.

216. In 1993, 2,087 cases were registered, as opposed to 404 in 1981. *See* Françoise Roth & Claudia Martín, *The European System for the Protection of Human Rights: A System in Motion, at* http://www.wcl.american.edu/hrbrief/v2i2/eurosystem.htm (last visited May 27, 2003).

217. *See id.*

218. On the European system and its processes, see, e.g., PHILIP LEACH, TAKING A CASE TO THE EUROPEAN COURT OF HUMAN RIGHTS 7 (2000); ALASTAIR MOWBRAY, CASES AND MATERIALS ON THE EUROPEAN CONVENTION ON HUMAN RIGHTS 778 (2001); D.J. HARRIS ET AL., LAW OF THE EUROPEAN CONVENTION ON HUMAN RIGHTS 648 (1995); Henry G. Schermers, *The Eleventh Protocol to the European Convention on Human Rights*, 19 EUR. L. REV. 367, 369 (1994); Ru-

Curiously, the European policy makers deem it desirable to introduce a human rights component into the existing EU structure, which is essentially economic in nature. In December 2000, the EU adopted a Human Rights Charter,[219] which, undoubtedly, raises issues of potential conflict with the E.Ct.H.R. Besides, although the Charter specifies that it is addressed to the institutions and bodies of the Union with due regard for the principle of subsidiarity,"[220] "it remains unclear what the relationship between subsidiarity and human rights will prove to be in the European Union."[221]

It is not clear which of these developments has influenced African countries in their current designs of African judicial institutions. What is clear is that Africa is currently embarking on economic and political integration. Thus, it appears natural for the AU to emulate the European experience of having a separate human rights court and a court of justice. A seemingly logical, but not necessarily correct, argument maintains that if the experiment has succeeded in Europe, it can also prosper in Africa. This is probably the reason why Africa's integration agenda is closely patterned after the European model. The argument also explains the continent's desire to have both a

---

dolf Bernhardt, *Reform of the Control Machinery under the European Convention on Human Rights: Protocol No. 11*, 89 AM. J. INT'L L. 145 (1995).

219. *See* Charter of Fundamental Rights of the European Union, 2000 O.J. (C 364) 1.

220. *Id.* art. 51. Subsidiarity, in the context of the ECHR, has been explained to mean "a distribution of powers between the supervisory machinery and the national authorities which has necessarily to be weighed in favour of the latter." Ryssdall, *supra* note 111, at 24. Subsidiarity, according to Ryssdall, reflects three basic features:

> First, the list of rights and freedoms is not exhaustive, so that the Convention States are free to provide better protection under their law or any other agreement (Article 60). Secondly, the Convention does not impose uniform rules; it lays down standards of conduct and leaves the choice of the means of implementation to the Contracting State. Finally, as the court and Commission have repeatedly stressed, the national authorities are in a better position than the supervisory bodies to strike the right balance between the sometimes conflicting interests of the Community and the protection of the fundamental rights of the individual.

Id. at 24–25.

221. Paolo G. Carozza, *Subsidiarity as a Structural Principle of International Human Rights Law*, 97 A.J.I.L. 38, 39 (2003).

Court of Justice and a Court of Human Rights, in addition to many other institutions. Indeed, converts are sometimes more zealous than those brought up in the faith. However, the issue of establishing an African supra-national judicial system is not so straightforward, and mere emulation of the European experiment may not work in Africa.

To start with, the historical experiences of the two continents are fundamentally different exactly where they are superficially similar. What motivates Africa's current integration endeavor differs from the European motivation. The architects of the European movement sought, by emphasizing common traditions and common interests, "to have the European nations work together rather than just living together or working against one another, as in the past."[222] The movement towards European unification started after World War II and was concentrated mainly in Western Europe.[223] These countries were motivated to unify because of the tragic and costly war, the fear of Nazi Germany, and the apprehension of communist expansion. In contrast, Africa's current movement has more to do with the challenges resulting from globalization than the euphoria of unity. The socio-economic origin of the AU emanated from the desire of African leaders to meet the present challenges of globalization and regional integration. Facing increasing globalization, the leaders saw the need to develop appropriate strategies. This search for an original solution for Africa led to the revision of the OAU's objectives, mandate and mode of functioning, and also caused re-orientation of the strategies addressing the globalization challenge. This search further explains the flood of binding and non-binding instruments that the continent has churned out very recently, including the New Partnership for Africa's Development ("NEPAD").[224]

---

222. Christian Kohler, *The Court of Justice of the European Communities and the European Court of Human Rights*, *in* SUPRANATIONAL AND CONSTITUTIONAL COURTS IN EUROPE: FUNCTIONS AND SOURCES 15, 18 (Igor I. Kavass ed., 1992).

223. *See* VISIONS OF EUROPEAN UNITY (Philomena Murray & Paul Rich eds., 1996) (discussing ideas of European unity, from the inter-war period to the present).

224. *See New Partnership for Africa's Development (NEPAD)* (Oct. 2001), *at* http://www.dfa.gov.za/events/nepad.pdf [hereinafter *NEPAD*]. NEPAD is:

In addition, the European political structure is different from that in Africa. In Europe, two courts had to be established to cater for two distinct bodies: one is the Council of Europe, which created the E.Ct.H.R., and the other is the European Union, which established the ECJ. Although all member states of the EU are members of the Council of Europe, the reverse is not the case. There are presently fifteen member states of the EU[225] while the Council of Europe has over forty member states, all of which are now signatories to the ECHR.[226] In contrast, Africa has always had one continental body, the OAU, which metamorphosed into the AU. The signatories to the Human Rights Protocol establishing the Human Rights Court are the same countries that signed the AU Act creating the AU Court. It is very likely that the same parties will adopt and ratify the proposed Protocol on the AU Court. Therefore, the dichotomy of courts' parental bodies does not exist in Africa.

There is still another reason why the European experiment cannot be transported to Africa wholesale. Georges Abi-Saab summarizes the reason in these thoughtful words:

> Every legal order has its own frontiers that separate it from other legal orders, because it has a different basis of legiti-

---

[A] pledge by African leaders, based on a common vision and a firm and shared conviction, that they have a pressing duty to eradicate poverty and to place their countries, both individually and collectively, on a path of sustainable economic growth and development, and, at the same time, to participate actively in the world economy and body politic.

Id. at ¶ 67. *See also generally* Nsongurua Udombana, *How Should We Then Live? Globalization and the New Partnership for Africa's Development,* 20 B.U. INT'L L.J. 293 (2002) (examining the phenomena of globalization and the challenges of the NEPAD and calling on African countries to consolidate democracy and sound economic management on the continent). The author, in a previous article, also called on the international community to respond positively to Africa's new initiative and for an equitable implementation of normative standards that govern the various aspects of globalization. *Id. See also* Nsongurua J. Udombana, *A Harmony or a Cacophony? The Music of Integration in the African Union Treaty and the New Partnership for Africa's Development,* 13 IND. INT'L & COMP. L. REV. 185 (2002).

225. These countries are Sweden, the United Kingdom, Denmark, Finland, Ireland, the Netherlands, Germany, Belgium, Luxembourg, France, Austria, Portugal, Spain, Italy, and Greece.

226. These include all countries of the former Western Europe and most countries of the former Eastern Europe.

macy and different mechanisms for creating, applying, and enforcing its rules. In other words, every legal order generates and specifies its rules in different ways, with different results, and these rules and procedures ultimately derive their legitimacy from the fact of belonging to this legal order. It constitutes a *unicum*: an entity held together by its own internal cohesive forces, while remaining separate and distinguishable from other legal orders.[227]

Africa must find its own rhythm and cohesive forces to build its institutions. The AU cannot transplant the European model of integration, including the paraphernalia of courts and other institutions, to Africa and expect it to flourish without carefully tailoring it to the specific needs of the region. Africa does not need multiple courts or institutions in order "to eradicate poverty and to place their countries . . . on a path of sustainable economic growth and development, and, at the same time, to participate actively in the world economy and body politic."[228] What Africa needs for sustainable development is a good and responsible government, which can be achieved with or without multiplication of institutions including courts. In the nectar and ambrosia of their sunny paradise, African leaders should recognize that the continent's past and present experiences, including unremitting conflicts, and future expectations do not support two supra-national courts, at least for now.

B. Arguments Based on the Development of International Law in Africa

Judicial decisions have long been recognized as a "subsidiary means for the determination of rules of law."[229] Although strictly speaking, judicial decisions are not formal sources of law, they are sometimes regarded as authoritative evidence of the state of law. A unanimous, or almost unanimous, decision has a role in the progressive development of the law; which is to say that a coherent body of jurisprudence will naturally have important consequences for the law.[230] Therefore, it seems logi-

---

227. Georges Abi-Saab, *Fragmentation or Unification: Some Concluding Remarks*, 31 N.Y.U. J. INT'L L. & POL. 919, 920 (1999).
228. *NEPAD, supra* note 224, ¶ 1.
229. I.C.J. Statute, *supra* note 52, art. 38(1)(d).
230. *See* BROWNLIE, *supra* note 54, at 2.

cal to argue that having more courts in the international arena is beneficial to the development of international law.[231] However, the proliferation of international courts and tribunals also has shortcomings. Particularly in a collective Africa, multiple courts might lead to conflicts in jurisdiction and confusion in the doctrinal development of international law. There is a danger that different institutions may give the same rule of law different interpretations in different cases. Charney states on the problem:

> Not only may a cacophony of views on the norms of international law undermine the perception that an international legal system exists, but if like cases are not treated alike, the very essence of a normative system of law will be lost. Should this develop, the legitimacy of international law as a whole will be placed at risk.[232]

The President of the ICJ has added his voice to these concerns:

> The proliferation of international courts gives rise to a serious risk of conflicting jurisprudence, as the same rule of law might be given different interpretations in different cases . . . . A dialogue among judicial bodies is crucial. The International Court of Justice, the principal judicial organ of the United Nations, stands ready to apply itself to this end if it receives the necessary resources.[233]

---

231. Even in the ordinary state of human affairs, it has been said that "[t]wo are better than one, [b]ecause they have a good reward for their labor. For if they fall, one will lift up his companion. But woe to him who is alone when he falls, [f]or he has no one to help him up." *Ecclesiastes* 4:9–10 (New King James).

232. Charney, *Impact of International Courts, supra* note 11, at 699. However, his research seem to show that the current system of various tribunals does not appear to disrupt the cohesion of international law, though he also admits that complete uniformity of decisions is impossible:

> [I]n those core areas of international law, the different international tribunals of the late twentieth century do share relatively coherent views on those doctrines of international law. Although differences exist, these tribunals are clearly engaged in the same dialectic. The fundamentals of this general international law remain the same regardless of which tribunal decides the case.

Id. at 699.

233. President of the ICJ Gilbert Guillaume, Statement to the U.N. General Assembly (Oct. 26, 2000), *available at* http://www.icj-cij.org/icjwww/ipresscom/

It is important to stress that opponents of court proliferation have legitimate concerns. There indeed have been incidents of conflicting interpretations of international law by different tribunals in the past. The *Nicaragua* Case decided by the ICJ in 1986[234] and the *Tadic* Case decided by the Appeals Chamber of the ICTY in 1997[235] provide an example. The issue before the Appeals Chamber of the ICTY in the *Tadic* case was whether the armed conflict in Bosnia and Herzegovina between the Bosnian Serbs of Republika Srpska and the central authorities of Bosnia and Herzegovina could be qualified as an international conflict after the Yugoslav National Army had withdrawn from the area. A related question was whether the armed forces of the Bosnian Serbs were to be regarded as armed forces of the Federal Republic of Yugoslavia or of Bosnia and Herzegovina. If they were regarded as the latter, then the conflict was an international one according to the Third Geneva Convention Relative to the Treatment of Prisoners of War of 1949 ("3GC").[236]

According to the Appeals Chamber, the 3GC requirement concerning the "belonging [of armed forces] to a Party to the conflict"[237] implicitly "refers to a test of control."[238] To examine the degree of control that defines whether armed forces belong to one or the other party, the Appeals Chamber referred to the concept of control defined by the ICJ in the *Nicaragua* Case. In *Nicaragua* the ICJ concluded that the control exercised by a state over armed forces acting in another state, in this case the Contras of Nicaragua, had to be an "effective control of the military or paramilitary operations in the course of which alleged

---

SPEECHES/iSpeechPresident_Guillaume_GA55_2001026.htm, *cited in* Oellers-Frahm, *supra* note 5, at 68; *cf.* ICJ Press Communique 99/46, Failure by Member States of the United Nations to Pay Their Dues Transgresses Principles of International Law, President Schwebel tells United Nations General Assembly (Oct. 26, 1999), *at* http://www.icj-cij.org/icjwww/ipresscom/ipress 1999/ipresscom9946_19991026.htm (statement of former President of the ICJ Judge Stephen M. Schwebel).

234. *See* Nicaragua Case, *supra* note 6.

235. *See* Tadic Case (Prosecutor v. Du [Ko Tadic]), 1999 I.C.T.Y. No. IT-94-1-A (July 15), *available at* http://www.un.org/icty/tadic/appeal/judgment/tad-aj990715e.pdf [hereinafter Tadic Case].

236. *See* Geneva Convention Relative to the Treatment of Prisoners of War; Aug. 12, 1949, 6 U.S.T. 3316, 75 U.N.T.S. 135.

237. *Id.* art. 4(2).

238. Tadic Case, *supra* note 235, ¶ 95.

violations were committed."[239] However, in the *Tadic* Case, the Appeals Chamber refused to share the findings of the ICJ. Instead, it went into an exhaustive discussion and a review of the ICJ findings, criticizing the ICJ decision as "not always following a straight line of reasoning" and as "at first sight somewhat unclear."[240] By so doing, the Appeals Chamber "by far overstepped its judicial function."[241] As Oellers-Frahm pointed out:

> Although it is not only legitimate but even desirable that a court or tribunal in finding its decisions gives regard to decisions of other courts and tribunals on comparable items, the scope of regard given to a decision of another court or tribunal cannot, however, result in a review of that decision but has to be restricted to examining how far that decision may serve as a guideline for the case in hand and whether the circumstances of the case allow its application.[242]

There have been similar conflicting interpretations of international human rights law between the ECJ and E.Ct.H.R.[243] It has even been asserted that many laymen and experts "are frequently confused" between the mandates of the two European courts. Thus,

> [I]ndividuals have been known to submit to the Court of Justice of the European Communities applications alleging violations of human rights, and national courts have even been known to request the European Court of Human Rights to give a preliminary ruling on the interpretation of European Community law. Mistakes of this kind can have far graver consequences for those concerned than the errors which are frequently made in addressing the application, most of which give Brussels as their destination — an eminently European

---

239. Nicaragua Case, *supra* note 6, ¶ 115, at 65.

240. Tadic Case, *supra* note 235, ¶¶ 108, 114.

241. Oellers-Frahm, *supra* note 5, at 79 (maintaining that the function of the Appeals Chamber was to review the judgments of the Trial Chambers of the I.C.T.Y. and I.C.T.R. and not the judgments of the ICJ or any other court or tribunal).

242. *Id.* at 79–80.

243. *See, e.g.,* Rick Lawson, *Confusion and Conflict? Diverging Interpretations of the European Convention on Human Rights in Strasbourg and Luxembourg, in* III THE DYNAMICS OF THE PROTECTION OF HUMAN RIGHTS IN EUROPE: ESSAYS IN HONOUR OF HENRY G. SCHERMERS 219 (1994).

city, but one in which neither of the two "European" courts have their seat.[244]

Therefore, confusion about the two courts still persists in Europe, notwithstanding its advanced communication and information technology, as well as other comparative advantages. This begs the question whether having two courts would not cause even greater confusion to ordinary Africans or even government officials.

International law should develop uniformly in the Africa continent and throughout the international legal community. For Africa, having two courts is likely to create more confusion than benefits. The proposed two courts will probably be given both contentious and advisory jurisdictions to interpret various legal instruments including human rights treaties; thus, there is a real danger that the two bodies might give conflicting interpretations to treaties invoked before them and thus create disparate legal norms. The problem could be compounded by the fact that neither court is envisaged to be superior to the other and, thus, neither can overrule decisions of the other. The resultant confusion would impede, rather than facilitate, the development of human rights jurisprudence in Africa.[245]

C. Arguments Based on Funding

Do African leaders have the political will and material wherewithal to operate two supra-national judicial institutions? Even if it is desirable to have two courts in the continent, can the continent afford them at the moment? These practical considerations must be taken into account in making the choice of having one court or two. Before looking at the financial strength of the AU, it is necessary to identify the basic needs of the proposed two courts. The following discussion concerns mainly with the proposed two judicial bodies, but it will also apply, *mutatis mutandis,* to many other organs expressly or impliedly created under the AU Act.

---

244. Kohler, *supra* note 222, at 17.

245. *See* Nsongurua J. Udombana, *The Institutional Structure of the African Union: A Legal Analysis,* 33 CAL. WEST. INT'L L.J. 69 (2002); Nsongurua J. Udombana, *Can the Leopard Change Its Spots? The African Union Treaty and Human Rights,* 17 AM. UNIV. INT'L L. REV. 1177 (2002).

To start with, each of the proposed courts will require a building to house the court rooms, the judges' chambers, and the offices for secretariats, including the Registrars. These offices must be equipped with furniture and other necessary supplies. Furthermore, in an age of information and technological revolution, the judges and the staff will need Internet-ready computers, telephones, fax machines, and other equipment. The AU will also have to provide accommodation for the judges and their support staff, particularly the senior ones. For judges who will serve on permanent basis, like the President of the African Human Rights Court,[246] as well as the Registrars,[247] permanent accommodations are envisaged. Other judges will possibly have to be accommodated in (potentially more expensive) hotels whenever their services are called for.

In addition to the Registry staff, different courts will also require legal secretaries, known as *attaché,* which have become indispensable to the modern adjudicatory systems.[248] Two *attaché* are currently serving the African Commission. To support the function of two courts more *attaché* will be needed. In this regard, the E.Ct.H.R. Legal Secretariat provides some guidance. In the Registry of the E.Ct.H.R., teams of lawyers are employed, whose functions are, *inter alia,* to administer the cases. In particular, they undertake preliminary research on cases, and draft essential procedural documents, case correspondence, and court decisions to be considered by Judge Rapporteur. Many of these lawyers have in-depth knowledge of the case law of both the European Commission and the E.Ct.H.R. They work closely with the judge or judges to whom they are attached. They also advise the practicing lawyers on case progress or even substantive law and court procedures.[249] The ECJ also has a similar pool of lawyers serving as legal secretariat. The proposed Afri-

---

246. *See, e.g.,* Human Rights Protocol, *supra* note 19, art. 21(2) ("The president shall perform judicial functions on a full-time basis and shall reside at the seat of the Court.").

247. *See id.* art. 24(2) ("The office and residence of the Registrar shall be at the place where the Court has its seat.").

248. The closest analogy to legal secretaries in the common law world is the law clerk of the American judicial system, where outstanding law graduates are usually invited to serve for a year or two as personal assistant to a senior judge.

249. *See* LEACH, *supra* note 218, at 20.

can courts will particularly need legal secretariats given that not all judges will have prior practical experience in international adjudication.

Another major resource the courts will require is a library and documentation center. The library must be stocked with rich legal materials dealing with both African and comparative law. It must also maintain a comprehensive collection of the laws of member states. In addition, there should be facilities for users, such as legal research and photocopying services, and separate similar facilities for the judges of the Courts. Furthermore, like any modern library, the African court library must be equipped with computers with Internet access. Competent librarians will need to be employed. They will also have to be trained in each of the principal legal systems and the courts' languages and regularly exposed to modern information systems. They will further be expected to provide the judges, lawyers, and the legal secretaries with background information on the legal problems presented before the courts.

Next, given the multi-lingual character they promote, the Courts will need teams of qualified linguists to translate court documents. Pleadings and other court processes will need to be translated into the working languages of the courts, which include English, French, Arabic, Portuguese and, maybe, African languages. The court decisions will have to be translated both for inclusion in the annual reports to the Assembly of the AU (as required, for example, by the Protocol to the African Charter[250]), as well as for publication. The court will need interpreters to provide simultaneous translations during oral proceedings and at other court meetings and conferences. Whether these translators and interpreters will serve as permanent staff of the courts or will be hired on an *ad hoc* basis, as is the case with the African Commission, there is no doubt that they will be required.

The foregoing identifies just some, not all, of what the African Courts will require to function properly. Sufficiently financing these needs will be a big problem. Indeed, many supranational

---

250. *See* Human Rights Protocol, *supra* note 19, art. 31 ("The Court shall submit to each regular session of the Assembly, a report on its work during the previous year. The report shall specify, in particular, the cases in which a State has not complied with the Court's judgement.").

institutions in Africa are suffering from chronic financial inca-
pacity and their leaders constantly receive less than adequate
resources; like bread in a besieged town, every man gets a little,
but no man gets a full meal. The problem is compounded by the
fact that African states have routinely defaulted in meeting
their financial obligations to the continental body. The AU, for
example, has inherited an empty treasury from the OAU and its
finances are predictably dry. Many uncompleted projects embarked upon by the OAU dot the continent. It is also unfortunate to note that the AU has no befitting building as its headquarters because the OAU failed to erect one. For thirty-nine
years, the OAU operated from a former prison that Emperor
Haile Selassie of Ethiopia donated to the body at its founding in
1963. The Secretariat of the AU is also located here. It seems
ironic that an organization that was set up to liberate Africa
and its peoples from the bitter herbs of colonialism has itself
been operating from a former prison! How will the AU manage
to provide the proposed two courts with resources when it itself
does not have a suitable headquarters?

For more than sixteen years after the inauguration of the African Commission — the existing quasi-judicial institution for
the implementation of the African Charter — it is yet to have a
permanent building. One is being constructed in a snail speed.
Meanwhile, the Commission still operates in a rented apartment in Bunjul, the Gambia. In contrast, the E.Ct.H.R. — not
to mention the European Council Secretariat — in Strasbourg
has "a striking building designed by Sir Richard Rodgers."[251]
Like beggars, many existing OAU/AU institutions constantly
carry their bowls to look for crumbs from the table of European
institutions in the form of grants. The Council of Ministers of
the OAU, now Executive Council of the AU, has repeatedly expressed "serious concern about the increasing arrears of contributions, thus undermining the capacity of the Secretariat to
carry out approved programmes and activities."[252] The AU Assembly at its First Ordinary Session in July 2002 at Durban,

---

251. Ryssdall, *supra* note 111, at 20 (noting also that the new building became necessary "because the former home of the Convention institutions was
in danger of collapsing under the weight of files").

252. *Decision on the Report of the Eighteenth Ordinary Session of the Committee on Contributors,* OAU Council of Ministers, 76th Ord. Sess., CM/Dec.
652,¶ 2 (June 28–July 6, 2002).

South Africa authorized the Interim Commission of the AU "to continue with the process of transferring the assets and liabilities of the OAU to the African Union."[253] The liabilities that the Interim Commission has assumed from the OAU include huge arrears of contributions totaling $54.53 million. This debt is owed to the AU by forty-five out of its fifty-four member countries.[254] This financial crisis of the AU does not bode well for the proposed two courts.

Although the AU was formally inaugurated in July 2002, many of its organs are not yet functional, largely due to the lack of funds. Only three organs appear to have been officially commissioned — the Assembly of the AU, the Executive Council, and the Commission. The other organs, including the Pan-African Parliament, the Court of Justice, the Permanent Representatives Council, the Specialized Technical Committees, the Economic, Social and Cultural Council, the Financial Institutions,[255] and the proposed Peace and Security Council[256] are yet to see the light of the day. Even the Commission, which serves as the secretarial arm of the AU, is presently designated as "the Interim Commission," while the Secretary-General has been designated as "the Interim Chairperson of the Commission and the Assistant Secretaries General shall be acting Commissioners."[257] This evidences that all is not well with the AU.

Africa must act cautiously in light of the AU's present reality. Establishing two courts seems overly ambitious given the serious financial challenges of the AU.[258]

---

253. *Decision on the Interim Period,* Assembly of the AU, First Ordinary Session, ASS/AU/Dec. 1(1), ¶ 2(ix) (July 2002).

254. For the list of defaulting countries, see Baffour Ankomah, *African Union in Danger of Being Stillborn,* NEW AFR. 16, 20 (2002).

255. *See,* AU ACT, *supra* note 23, art. 5 (listing of the main organs of the AU).

256. The Peace and Security Council was established pursuant to the Protocol Relating to the Establishment of the Peace and Security Council of the African Union, AU Assembly, 1st Ordinary Sess., July 9, 2002, *available at* http://www.au2002.gov.za/docs/summit_council/secprot.htm. This protocol establishes an operational structure "for the effective implementation of the decisions taken in the areas of conflict prevention, peace-making, peace support operations and intervention, as well as peace-building and post-conflict reconstruction." *Id.* at pmbl., ¶ 17.

257. Decision on Interim Period, *supra* note 183, ¶ 2(iv)–(v).

258. Jeremiah's question to the children of Israel several centuries ago is relevant to Africa's current situation: "If you have run with the footmen, and

V. RECOMMENDATIONS

It is significant that five years after the adoption of the Human Rights Protocol to establish an African Human Rights Court only a handful of states — six as at September 2002 — have ratified it. These states include Burkina Faso (December 31, 1998), Mali (October 5, 2000), Senegal (September 29, 1998), Gambia (June 30, 1999), Uganda (February 16, 2001), and South Africa (July 3, 2002).[259] A total of fifteen ratifications are needed for the Protocol to enter into force.[260] It appears that with the adoption of the AU Act, which provides for the establishment of an AU Court of Justice, African leaders do not know what to make of the Human Rights Court. They seem to have boxed themselves into a corner! Wittingly or unwittingly, they also appear to have crushed Africans' rising hope for the timely creation of a Human Rights Court to compliment the weak mandate of the African Commission and to effectively enforce the provisions of the African Charter and other relevant human rights instruments ratified by their governments.

But there is a way out of the dilemma. Actually, the road to the city and the road out of it are usually the same road; it depends on which direction one travels. As this Article has indicated, though multiplication of judicial institutions may in many other cases facilitate the development of international law, having more than one court in a collective Africa is not a sensible decision. Establishing two courts under the current climate of uncertainty would have regrettable consequences, like sending a man to the sea without preparing him for tempests. A realistic approach is for the AU to establish and strengthen one judicial institution, which may be, but not necessarily, the African Human Rights Court, before ever embarking on another. The jurisdiction of the Human Rights Court could be enlarged to cover the interpretation and application of the AU Act and allied instruments. There is an alternative approach, which this Article favors. It is this: The AU should establish the AU Court, not as an arm of the AU but as an

---

they have wearied you, [t]hen how can you contend with horses? And if in the land of peace, [i]n which you trusted, they have wearied you, [t]hen how will you do in the flooding of the Jordan?" *Jeremiah* 12:5 (New King James).

259. *See* AU Doc. CAB/LEG/66.5 (2002).

260. *See* Human Rights Protocol, *supra* note 19, art. 34(3).

autonomous institution capable of addressing the myriad of problems confronting the continent. The AU Court could have different chambers to deal with different major problems afflicting the continent. Thus, one chamber could be seized with matters of international economic law including economic integration, another with human rights issues, and still others with environment or international criminal law including terrorism, etc. Such divisions of labor would be justifiable because they would create specialization and efficiency.

The chamber system is not really new; it is practiced in the ICJ. The ICJ Statute provides that the Court may, from time to time, form one or more chambers composed of three or more judges as the Court may determine. Such chambers are authorized to deal with particular classes of cases; for example, laces and cases relating to transit and communications.[261] The Court also may, at any time, form a chamber to deal with a particular case, in which case the number of judges to constitute such a chamber will be determined by the Court with the approval of the parties.[262] The ICJ has, in practice, established special chambers to deal with particular cases. In July 1993, for example, the Court created a special Chamber to deal with environmental questions,[263] a subject that has become as topical as human rights.

Happily, the Draft Protocol is designed along the above suggestions. Taking inspiration from Article 26(1) of the ICJ Statute, the Draft Protocol creates "Special Chambers." It provides that "[t]he Court may from time to time form one or more chambers, composed of three or more Judges as the Court may determine, for dealing with particular categories of cases; for example violation of the Constitutive Act; human rights; disputes on budgetary matters; and commercial matters."[264] More significantly, it provides that the African Human Rights Court shall be constituted as a Chamber of the AU Court, upon entry into force of the Protocol to the African Charter or the adoption of the Draft Protocol, "whichever may be sooner."[265]

---

261. *See* ICJ Statute, *supra* note 53, art. 26(1).
262. *Id.* art. 26(2)&(3).
263. *See* SHAW, *supra* note 207, at 585.
264. Draft Protocol, *supra* note 113, art. 60(1).
265. *Id.* art. 60(2).

The Draft Protocol also allows for other category of chambers to be created annually "[w]ith a view to the speedy dispatch of business."[266] Such chambers, which shall be composed of five Judges, may, at the request of the parties, "hear and determine cases by summary procedure."[267] A judgment given by any of these chambers, including those to deal with particular category of cases, "shall be considered as rendered by the Court."[268] T. O. Elias questions a similar provision in Article 27 of the ICJ Statute.[269] According to this former President of the ICJ, Article 27:

> [H]as far-reaching implications for the jurisprudence of the Court, particularly when it is observed that there is no requirement of consultation between the court and the fraction of it constituting the chamber in question. There is no provision for the Court itself to have seen even the draft judgment of any chamber before it is rendered to the Court, nor is there any provision for the Court itself (that is, such other Members of it other than those of the chamber concerned) to have seen the draft or express an opinion.[270]

Elias believes that it is "highly desirable that the chamber should operate as no more than a committee of the whole of the Court, and mainly answerable to it for its judgment."[271]

Notwithstanding these reservations, it may be said that the chamber system is a welcome development in a collective Africa, in view of the arguments earlier advanced in this Article. Indeed, if States Parties to the AU Act agree on these provisions, then the goal of this Article would have been achieved. Besides, any fear that a single African court will not be able to interpret and apply all the existing and future legal instruments executed by the OAU/AU is unfounded. Compared to the relatively few multilateral treaties so far enacted by the OAU/AU,[272] some 260 bilateral or multilateral treaties provide

---

266. *Id.* art. 61.
267. *Id.*
268. *Id.* art. 62.
269. ELIAS, UNITED NATIONS CHARTER AND THE WORLD COURT, *supra* note 180, at 204.
270. *Id.*
271. *Id.*
272. The legally binding instruments adopted under the auspices of the OAU/AU include the Bamako Convention on the Ban of the Import into Africa and the Control of Transboundary Movement and Management of Hazardous

for the ICJ to have jurisdiction in the resolution of disputes arising out of their application or interpretation.[273] In addition, states regularly submit special disputes to the ICJ by way of special agreements.[274] The dispute caseload of the ICJ has also increased over the years. In the 1970s, the ICJ had only one or two cases on its docket at any one time; this number varied between 9 and 10 from 1990 to 1997. As of July 31, 2001, the number rose to 22.[275] The subject matters of these cases are also varied. The Court continues to decide classical disputes such as those between neighboring states seeking a determination of their land and maritime boundaries. Currently the ICJ is hearing such territorial dispute cases between Indonesia and Malaysia, and Nicaragua and Honduras. Other cases involve complaints of human rights violation made by states whose nationals suffered injuries in other states. Currently such cases involve Guinea and the Democratic Republic of Congo, and Liechtenstein and Germany.[276]

The ICJ has creatively managed this increasing responsibility by, *inter alia,* taking steps to simplify proceedings, "in particu-

---

Wastes within Africa, Jan. 29, 1991, 30 I.L.M. 773, *reprinted in* 1 AFR. Y.B. INT'L L. 268 (1993) (entered into force Apr. 22, 1998); and the AEC Treaty, *supra* note 25. Others are: the African Charter on the Rights and Welfare of the Child, July, 1990, OAU Doc. CAB/LEG/24.9/49, *reprinted in* 18 COMMONWEALTH L. BULL. 1112 (1999); OAU Convention Governing the Specific Aspects of Refugee Problems in Africa, Sept. 10, 1969, 1001 U.N.T.S. 45 (entered into force June 20, 1974); African Convention on the Conservation of Nature and Natural Resources, 1968, OAU Doc. CAB/LEG/24.1, *available at* http://sedac.ciesin.org/entri/texts/african.conv.conserva.1969.html (entered into force June 16, 1969); the African Charter, *supra* note 20; Human Rights Protocol, *supra* note 19, and the OAU Convention on the Prevention and Combating of Terrorism, AHG/Dec.132 (XXXV), *available at* http://www.fidh. org/intgouv/ua/rapport/1999/antiterroconvention (not yet in force).

273. *See* 2000–2001 I.C.J. ANN. REP., *supra* note 58, at 1.

274. *Id.* The ICJ may exercise jurisdiction over a dispute where the parties give consent *ad hoc* by special agreement (*compromis*). The special agreement, however, need not take a particular form; in fact, the ICJ has held that such consent *ad hoc* may arise where the plaintiff state has accepted the jurisdiction by a unilateral application followed by a separate act of consent by the other party, either by a communication to the Court or by taking part in the institution of proceedings. *See* Corfu Channel case (Prelim. Objections), 1948 I.C.J. 27–28 (Apr. 9); BROWNLIE, *supra* note 54, at 716–17.

275. 2000–2001 I.C.J. ANN. REP., *supra* note 58, at 2.

276. For these and other examples, see *id.*

lar as regards preliminary objections and counter-claims."[277]   In 1997, the ICJ took various measures "to rationalize the work of the Registry, to make greater use of information technology, to improve its own working methods and to secure greater collaboration from the parties in relation to its procedures."[278]   The ICJ's approach has shown that it is not the number of courts at the international level that matters but the quality of the court's output.   Size never determines usefulness.   The ICJ is small measured by numbers[279] but big in its commitment.   The ICJ's achievement is also made possible by the moral and financial support of its parent body, the UN. Similarly, the AU must be prepared to give such support to its own institutions, including the proposed court(s).

The moral from all of the above is that the human entity is endowed with the intelligence and vision to regulate its conduct and constantly recreate its existence.   It is worthwhile to stress once again that in November 1998 the Council of Europe jettisoned the former two-tier institutional structure for the enforcement of the ECHR in favor of a single court.   The E.Ct.H.R presently has four sections, and each section is broken into chambers.[280]   There is also a Grand Chamber, which determines the merit of cases relinquished to its jurisdiction by the other chambers under article 30 of the ECHR or where it accepts a request for a referral — in effect, a re-hearing — of a case following a judgment by a chamber.   The beauty of the European arrangement is that it "allows for a more fluid exercise of the adjudicatory powers of the European Court."[281]

From a pragmatic perspective, it is better to have one African court that is normatively and structurally strong than having two weak institutions that exist only on paper.   The AU should recognize that two African courts are simply not feasible.   It

---

277. 2000–2001 I.C.J. ANN. REP., *supra* note 58, at 6.

278. *Id.* at 5–6 (citing its earlier report to the General Assembly, in response to GA Res. 52/161 of Dec. 15, 1997). *See* Report of the ICJ, supra note _, Appendix I (during the period Aug. 1 to July 31 1998, the ICJ gave an account of these various measures).

279. The ICJ consists of 15 judges elected for a term of nine years by the UN General Assembly and the Security Council. One third of the Court is, however, renewed every three years. I.C.J. Statute, *supra* note 54, art. 13(1).

280. *See* Protocol 11, *supra* note 90, art. 1.

281. Fix-Zamudio, *supra* note 173, at 513.

should either urge its member states to ratify the Human Rights Protocol to the African Charter in order to bring the Human Rights Court on board or immediately adopt the Protocol on the AU Court and set the process of ratification in motion. It makes inordinately good sense that one court should give way for the other because a divided house cannot stand. In fact, there are already many sub-regional courts that could compliment and supplement the work of a single African judicial institution.

If the AU rejects the Protocol to the African Charter and opts for one court — the AU Court — then it must incorporate some critical provisions of the Human Rights Protocol into the new Protocol. The relevant provisions will include Articles 3 and 4 on jurisdiction, Article 5 on access to the Court (*locus standi*), excluding the unnecessary and irritating optional clause of Article 34(6),[282] and Article 10 on hearing and representation, particularly on legal aid. Article 17 on the independence of the Court and Article 18 on incompatibility must also be incorporated. In addition, Article 27 on findings and remedies, Article 28 on judgment and Article 30 on execution of judgments must also be included. It will also be necessary to define the relationship between the African Commission and the AU Court. The Commission could be effectively utilized as a filter mechanism for the Court, with respect to human rights matters. It could, for example, handle issues of admissibility, including provisional measures, while the AU Court addresses the merits. Overall, there will be a need to balance efficiency considerations with the due process requirements. Furthermore, African civil societies must be vigilant with the exercise of judicial power to assure compliance of human rights.

VI. CONCLUSION

Africa, undoubtedly, is in dire need of a court to develop international law, strengthen the rule of law and deal with inter-

---

282. The Draft Protocol, unfortunately, retains this provision, providing that the Court, in exercising its functions, "shall have jurisdiction to hear applications from individuals and non-governmental organizations of Member States in accordance with paragraph 3 of Article 5 and paragraph 6 of Article 34 of the Protocol on Human and Peoples' Rights." Draft Protocol, *supra* note 113, art. 60(3).

national legal crisis in the continent. This Article, however, argues for one continental judicial institution to fulfill these goals and has adduced some reasons for this position. Even assuming (which this Article constantly denies) that proliferation of judicial institutions is a good thing for a collective Africa, it is submitted that the timing is not ripe. Africa must learn to walk before it runs. Establishing many courts will obviously be great fun; but it should be remembered that there is a bill to pay for it. Indeed, unless the AU streamlines its current over-bloated operational structures, its current efforts at economic and political integration will be a waste of time. The present experiment is like trying to reconstruct a forest out of broken branches and withered leaves. That is not the path to sustainable development, the major goal of the AU enterprise.

The Article has shown the direction that the AU should move towards actualizing its objectives in the AU Act, in particular with regards to the establishment of a judicial institution to administer Africa's legal system. The ultimate decision whether to establish one court or two or multiple courts, of course, rests with the AU Assembly; and it is hoped that, when push comes to shove, the Assembly will make the right choice. However, whichever court the AU chooses to establish, it must act fast to end the anguished anticipation of Africans and the international community. Africans cannot afford the climate of uncertainty regarding what and which judicial institution should and will be created to serve their needs. "Hope differed makes the heart sick, but a longing fulfilled is a tree of life."[283]

---

283. *Proverbs 13:12* (NIV).

[22]

NOTE

THE NEW AFRICAN UNION:

WILL IT PROMOTE ENFORCEMENT OF THE DECISIONS OF THE AFRICAN COURT OF HUMAN AND PEOPLES' RIGHTS?

*Carolyn Scanlon Martorana**

I. Introduction

In July 2006, the first eleven judges of the African Court on Human and Peoples' Rights (African Court or Court) were sworn in during the Seventh Session of the Assembly of Heads of State and Government in Banjul, the Gambia.[1] Even more recently, the African Court found a home in Arusha, in Tanzania.[2] The African Court was established in 1998 pursuant to the Protocol to the African Charter on Human and Peoples' Rights on the Establishment of an African Court on Human and Peoples' Rights (Protocol) and, after achieving the required fifteen ratifications of African nations, entered into force on January 1, 2004.[3]

The Court's precursor was the African Commission on Human and Peoples' Rights (Commission), which was created pursuant to the African Charter on Human and Peoples' Rights (Charter) in

---

*   J.D. 2008, The George Washington University Law School; B.A. 2001, The College of William & Mary.

1.   Scott Lyons, *The African Court on Human and Peoples' Rights*, 10 ASIL Insights 24 (2006), *available at* http://www.asil.org/insights060919.cfm.

2.   Activity Report of the Court for 2006, www.africancourtcoalition.org/listDocuments.asp?page_id=75, ¶ 10, (last visited February 29, 2008). The Court presented its annual report to the Assembly of the African Union's Eight Ordinary Session, held January 29-30, 2007 in Addis Ababa, Ethiopia. The Assembly adopted the Court's Report during its Ninth Ordinary Council in Accra, Ghana. *See* Activity Report of the Court for 2006 (July 3, 2007) www.africancourtcoalition.org/listDocuments.asp?page_id=75 (last visited February 28, 2008).

3.   Lyons, *supra* note 1.

1981.[4] The Commission was formally inaugurated in 1987,[5] and since its inception, it has served as the sole forum for African countries to bring their grievances under the Charter.[6] The Charter sets forth the rights and duties of member states as well as individuals,[7] focusing upon the protection of human and peoples' rights on the African continent by establishing bodies for that purpose and passing human rights legislation by the respective member states.[8]

The Commission, which was created to promote human rights and ensure their protection in Africa,[9] has authority to interpret all provisions of the Charter.[10] The Assembly of Heads of State and Government of the Organisation of African Unity (Assembly)[11] choose the Commissioners. Often, the Commissioners also hold important government positions[12] despite the Charter's provision that they must serve in their personal capacities,[13] which could compromise their independence.[14] Another shortcoming of the Commission is its inability to issue binding orders.[15] Without these orders, the Commission merely pleads with nations to come into compliance with the Charter.[16] Due to the Commission's lack of independence and lack of power to enforce its determinations

---

4. African Commission on Human and Peoples' Rights - History, Information Sheet No. 1, http://www.achpr.org/english/_info/history_en.html [hereinafter History of ACHPR] (last visited February 2, 2008); African Charter on Human and Peoples' Rights, art. 30, http://www.achpr.org/english/_info/history_en.html [hereinafter Charter] (last visited February 2, 2008) (establishing the African Commission on Human and Peoples' Rights [hereinafter Commission]).

5. History of the ACHPR, *supra* note 4, at 3.

6. *See* Charter, *supra* note 4, art. 45(3) (mandating that one of the functions of the Commission shall be to "[i]nterpret all the provisions of the present Charter").

7. *See id.* ch. I (entitled "Human and Peoples' Rights); *see id.* ch. II (entitled "Duties").

8. *See id.* art. 1 (stating that members of the OAU "shall undertake to adopt legislative and other measures to give effect to [the rights included in the Charter]").

9. *Id.* art. 30.

10. *Id.* art. 45 (1)-(3).

11. *Id.* art. 33 (providing that the "members of the Commission shall be elected by secret ballot by the Assembly of Heads of State and Government").

12. *See* Nsongurua J. Udombana, *Toward the African Court on Human and Peoples' Rights: Better Late Than Never*, 3 YALE HUM. RTS. & DEV. L.J. 45, 71 (2000) (noting that two senior officials in The Congo served as Commissioners).

13. Charter, *supra* note 4, art. 31(2).

14. *Id.* (noting that human rights abuses occurred frequently in The Congo while two government officials served as Commissioners, and suggesting that the Commissioners were more likely to turn a blind eye towards complaints brought pursuant to the Charter).

15. *See* Charter, art. 52 (stating that after investigating and considering an allegation of a violation of the Charter, the Commission shall prepare a report of its findings and recommendations for the States involved as well as for the Assembly).

16. *See id.* art. 58 (stating that if the Assembly considers a report of the Commission to concern "a series of serious or massive" human rights abuses, it can request an "in-depth

under the Charter, the Organization of African Unity (OAU) eventually recognized the need for an independent judicial body with the authority to bind parties under the Charter.[17] Thus, the OAU conceived the Court to complement, but not replace, the Commission.[18]

The Protocol gives the African Court the power to order reparations for human rights offenses[19] committed in violation of the Charter or any other human rights instrument that the parties to a particular dispute have ratified.[20] When the African Court begins its work, the Council of Ministers, an organ of the OAU, will monitor execution of the Court's judgments,[21] and in cases of noncompliance with the Court's orders, the Court will identify recalcitrant states to the Assembly in its annual report.[22]

This Note will attempt to analyze the likelihood of compliance with the African Court's mandates once it begins hearing disputes, in light of African states' abandonment of the OAU for a new body, the African Union (AU).[23] The AU provides a new framework for relationships between African nations centered around a more pan-Africanist theme, which the OAU did not emphasize.[24] Part II provides background information about the AU, the Commission, and the Court. This Part also discusses the new institutions created by the AU, as well as those that were carried over from the OAU, particularly the Assembly and the Council of Ministers. Part II.B discusses the Commission and how the Charter contributed to its failure, and Part II.C identifies features of the Protocol that are significant departures from the Commission's regime.

---

study" of the case). No provision of the Charter explains what occurs after the Commission undertakes and "in-depth study" for the Assembly. *See id.*

17. *See* Frans Viljoen, *A Human Rights Court for Africa, and Africans*, 30 BROOK. J. INT'L L. 1, 6-7 (2004).

18. *See* Protocol to the African Charter on Human and Peoples' Rights on the Establishment of an African Court on Human and Peoples' Rights, pmbl., http://www.achpr.org/english/_info/court_en.html [hereinafter Protocol] (last visited February 2, 2008) (noting that the "attainment of the objectives of the [Charter] *requires* the establishment of [an African Court]") (emphasis added).

19. *Id.* art. 27.

20. *Id.* art. 3 (giving the African Court on Human and Peoples' Rights jurisdiction over disputes arising out of the Charter as well as "any other relevant Human Rights instrument ratified by the States concerned.).

21. *Id.* art. 29.

22. *Id.* art. 31.

23. *See* Constitutive Act of the African Union, pmbl., art. 2 [hereinafter Constitutive Act] (declaring that "[w]e, heads of State and Government of the Member States of the [OAU] . . . have agreed . . . [that] the African Union is hereby established").

24. *Id.* pmbl. (declaring that the new AU is determined to "build a partnership between governments").

Part III suggests that the Court, heralded as a much needed solution to the shortcomings of the Commission, may still face hurdles in enforcing its judgments if the benefits of membership to the AU do not provide enough incentive to ensure compliance. This Part will also discuss how, in cases where the offending party fails to comply with the Court's judgment, the matter will end up in the same hands as it would have in the days of the ineffective Commission: those of the Assembly.[25] Accordingly, this Part analyzes whether the AU and Protocol offer solutions sufficient to overcome the problems that existed under the old regime. As this Note will argue, the Court and the Commission should be in a partnership with the AU to promote compliance with the Court's orders. The language of the Constitutive Act of the AU, however, does not provide that the Court and the Commission will be organs of the AU, and thus the relationship between the AU and the Court and the Commission is ambiguous.[26] This Note proposes that the AU should seize the opportunity to refine the Charter, the Protocol, and its Constitutive Act to make compliance more likely. In this vein, Part IV concludes that the Court and the Commission should both be organs of the AU, and the AU should make adherence to the Charter and to the Court's orders prerequisites for membership in the AU.

The ratification of the Protocol itself is evidence of the member states' and Assembly's resolve to be bound by the Court's judgments in order to eradicate human rights abuses in Africa. On the other hand, they could be merely paying lip service to the international community.[27] Until the African Court opens its doors, one can only speculate.

---

25. *See* Protocol, *supra* note 18, art. 31 (providing that the Court shall submit to the Assembly "the cases in which a State has not complied with the Court's judgment").

26. *See* Constitutive Act, *supra* note 23, art. 5 (listing the organs of the Union; neither the Court nor the Commission is included).

27. *See* Nsongurua J. Udombana, *Can the Leopard Change Its Spots? The African Union Treaty and Human Rights*, 17 Am. U. Int'l L. Rev. 1177, 1198 (2002) (suggesting that "this rhetoric on democracy, good governance and human rights could be a mere cosmetic exercise by the OAU's Member States to impress Western donor countries and international financial institutions").

II. Discussion

A. *How the Organization of African Unity Became the African Union*

In May 2001, the AU replaced the OAU, which until then, had served as the unifying body on the African continent.[28] The OAU came into being in 1963[29] and initially set out to eradicate colonial rule by "safeguard[ing] and consolidate[ing] the hard-won independence as well as the sovereignty and territorial integrity of [African] states, and [by] fight[ing] against neo-colonialism in all its forms."[30] Thus, the OAU aimed to deal with the human rights abuses associated with colonialism, rather than the separate issue of human rights abuses committed by Africans against Africans.[31] The OAU successfully supported African nations in their fight to end colonialism, which culminated in the abolition of apartheid in South Africa in 1994.[32]

The OAU failed, however, to respond to serious conflicts between African nations.[33] This failure stemmed from the OAU's policy of non-interference, adopted in the spirit of anti-colonialism.[34] The OAU Charter enunciated principles by which the member states were to abide, including: sovereign equality among all states;[35] non-interference with the internal affairs of states;[36] and respect for the sovereignty and territorial integrity of states.[37] These principles made the OAU reluctant to become involved when duly-selected or coup governments committed human rights

---

28. *See* http://www.africa-union.org/Official_documents/Treaties_%20Conventions_ %20Protocols/offTreaties_Conventions_&_Protocols.htm item 1, 2 [hereinafter Chart] (listing Treaties, Conventions, Protocols, and Charters ratified by the Member States of the African Union and the Organization of African Unity, as well as the dates they were opened for signature and the dates on which each entered into force) (last visited February 28, 2008).

29. Charter of the Organization of African Unity [hereinafter OAU Charter] (stating that the Member States signed the Charter "in the City of Addis Ababa, Ethiopia, 25th day of May, 1963").

30. *Id.* pmbl.

31. Vincent O. Nmehielle, *The African Union and African Renaissance*, 7 Sing. J. Int'l & Comp. L. 412, 419 (2003).

32. *See* The OAU After Thirty Years 173 (Yassin El-Ayouty ed., Westport: Praeger Publishers) (1994).

33. Corinne A.A. Packer & Donald Rukare, *The New African Union and Its Constitutive Act*, 96 Am. J. Int'l L. 365, 366 (2002).

34. *Id.* at 367 (noting that "[e]xperts agreed that the OAU Charter needed revision the most, specifically with regard to the principles of sovereignty and noninterference" because since its inception, African leaders had "watched civil wars erupt and destroy states and their populations").

35. OAU Charter, *supra* note 29, art. III (1).

36. *Id.* art. III (2).

37. *Id.* art. III (3).

abuses within their own countries.[38] For example, in 1980 the president of Liberia was executed by firing squad during a military coup and other members of his regime were executed shortly thereafter.[39] The Council of Ministers of the OAU appealed to the coup leaders to exercise restraint, but affirmed the right of any member state to change its government in any way it sees fit.[40]

In fact, the OAU's original goals became moot as African nations gained independence from their colonial rulers[41] and the Assembly recognized the need for a new set of goals emphasizing unity among African nations.[42] Thus, the member states of the OAU signed the Constitutive Act of the African Union in 2001. Although the AU affirmed the principle of non-interference,[43] the Act notes the interdependence of states[44] and encourages international cooperation.[45] Moreover, the Act recognized the AU's right to intervene in the internal affairs of a member state in the case of grave circumstances such as war crimes, genocide, or crimes against humanity.[46] The AU's overall objectives are to harmonize the economic and political policies of all African nations in order to improve pan-African welfare and to provide Africans with a solid voice in international affairs.[47]

Thus, the AU is tailored more towards political and economic development of African nations than was the OAU.[48] To achieve its goals, the Constitutive Act envisioned several organs of the AU:

---

38.   Udombana, *supra* note 27, at 1209-10.

39.   *Id.* at 1212.

40.   Udombana, *supra* note 27, at 1212.

41.   *See* Nmehielle, *supra* note 31, at 420-21 (noting that the principle of non-interference "eventually weakened the [OAU's] resolve to challenge the squandering of the gains of Africa's hard won independence" and likening the OAU to a "toothless bulldog"); Nsongurua Udombana, *The Unfinished Business: Conflicts, the African Union, and the New Partnership for Africa's Development*, 35 GEO. WASH. INT'L L. REV. 55, 57 (2003) (quoting Mammo Muchie, who said "what the OAU was able to do, it has done. What was beyond it has to pass on to the African Union") (internal quotations omitted).

42.   Nmehielle, *supra* note 31, at 416-17 (pointing out that after the end of apartheid in South Africa, the Constitutive Act was the "culmination of a new feeling and consciousness in the African continent . . . which encapsulates the need for Africa to arise from oppression, neocolonial subjugation, lack of continental accountability, in order to enable the continent to reach its greatest potential").

43.   *See* Constitutive Act, *supra* note 23, art. 4(g).

44.   *Id.* art. 4(a).

45.   *Id.* art. 3(e).

46.   *Id.* art. 4(h).

47.   NATALIE STEINBERG, WORLD FEDERALIST MOVEMENT, BACKGROUND PAPER ON THE AFRICAN UNION 1 (2001), *available at* http://www.wfm.org/site/index.php/documents/526,.

48.   Elizabeth Justice, *The African Union: Building a Dream to Facilitate Trade, Development, and Debt Relief*, 12 CURRENTS: INT'L TRADE L.J. 127, 130 (Summer 2003).

the Assembly of the Union;[49] Executive Council;[50] Pan-African Parliament;[51] Court of Justice;[52] the Commission, also called the Secretariat;[53] the Permanent Representatives Committee;[54] Specialized Technical Committees;[55] the Economic, Social, and Cultural Committee;[56] and Financial Institutions.[57] This list demonstrates the breadth of the OAU's reformation and metamorphosis into the AU, but as many of these organs are beyond the scope of this Note, they will not be discussed further. Notably absent from the list is the Court and the African Commission of Human and Peoples' Rights, which were originally "established *within* the [OAU]."[58]

Interestingly, the African Court of Justice was established by the Constitutive Act,[59] but the Act states that the "statute, composition and functions of the Court of Justice shall be defined in a protocol relating thereto."[60] The AU has not yet adopted such a protocol,[61] and its Web page dedicated to the Court of Justice contains only a recitation of Article 18 of the Constitutive Act, with a link to the Protocol establishing the African Court of Human and Peoples'

---

49.   Constitutive Act, *supra* note 23, art. 5(a).

50.   *Id.* art. 5(b).

51.   *Id.* art. 5(c).

52.   *Id.* art. 5(d).

53.   *Id.* art. 5(e).

54.   *Id.* art. 5(f). The Permanent Representatives Committee is composed of permanent representatives to the Union, art. 21(1), and takes instruction from the Executive Council. *Id.* art. 21(2). This note will not discuss the functions of the Permanent Representatives Committee.

55.   *Id.* art. 5(g). The Specialized Technical Committees include: the Committee on Rural Economy and Agricultural Matters, art. 14(1)(a); the Committee on Monetary and Financial Affairs, art. 14(1)(b); the Committee on Trade, Customs and Immigration Matters, art. 14(1)(c); the Committee on Industry, Science and Technology, Energy, Natural Resources and Environment, art. 14(1)(d); The Committee on Transport, Communications and Tourism, art. 14(1)(e); the Committee on Health, Labour and Social Affairs, art. 14(1)(f); and the Committee on Education, Culture and Human Resources, art. 14 (1)(g). Every committee is responsible to the Executive Council. *Id.* art. 14(1). The Specialized Technical Committees will not be discussed in this Note.

56.   *Id.* art. 5(h). The Economic, Social and Cultural Council (ESCC) "shall be an advisory organ composed of different social and professional groups," art. 22(1), and its powers and functions "shall be determined by the Assembly." *Id.* art 22(2). The ESCC will not be discussed in this note.

57.   *Id.* art. 5(i). The Constitutive Act calls for the establishment of three financial institutions: the African Central Bank, art. 19(a); the African Monetary Fund, art. 19(b); and the African Investment Bank, art. 19(c).

58.   Charter, *supra* note 4, art. 30 (emphasis added).

59.   Constitutive Act, *supra* note 23, art. 18(1).

60.   *Id.* art. 18(2).

61.   Nsongurua Udombana, *An African Human Rights Court and an African Union Court: A Needful Duality or a Needless Duplication?*, 28 Brook. J. Int'l L. 811, 816-17 (2003).

Rights.[62] In 2005, the Executive Council recommended that the Assembly consider merging the two infant courts into one court named the African Court of Justice and Human Rights.[63] Although the Assembly endorsed the Council's recommendation, it has not adopted any document effectuating the merger as of March 2009.[64] Thus, it remains unclear whether the Court of Justice will ever be formed, and if it is formed, what its jurisdiction will be.[65]

The Constitutive Act carried over two institutions from the OAU: the Assembly and the Executive Council. These bodies are relevant to an evaluation of the effectiveness of the Court, and each will be discussed in turn.

1. The Assembly of the Union

According to the Constitutive Act, the Assembly of the Union "shall be composed of the Heads of States and Government or their accredited representatives,"[66] and "shall be the supreme organ of the Union."[67] The powers and functions of the Assembly include: determining the Union's common policies;[68] receiving and considering reports and recommendations from the organs of the Union;[69] considering requests for membership to the Union;[70] establishing any organ of the Union;[71] monitoring the implementation of the Union's policies and decisions and ensure compliance therewith;[72] adopting the budget of the Union;[73] and directing the Executive Council on conflict management and restoring peace.[74]

---

62. The African Court of Justice, http://www.africa-union.org/root/au/organs/Court_of_Justice_en.htm (last visited February 28, 2008).

63. Decision on the Merger of the African Court on Human and Peoples' Rights and the Court of Justice of the African Union, Ex.Cl/Dec.165 (VI), Sixth Ordinary Session of the Executive Council, January 24-28, 2005.

64. Decision on the Draft Single Instrument on the Merger of the African Court on Human and Peoples' Rights and the Court of Justice of the African Union, Assembly/AU/Dec/118 (VII), Seventh Ordinary Session of the Assembly of the African Union, July 2, 2006. The Decision asks for further recommendations on such a document, but no protocol has been drafted to date. *See* www.africa-union.org (last visited February 28, 2008).

65. Udombana, *supra* note 61, at 870.

66. Constitutive Act, supra note 23, art. 6(1).

67. *Id.* art. 6(2).

68. *Id.* art. 9(1)(a).

69. *Id.* art. 9(1)(b).

70. *Id.* art. 9(1)(c).

71. *Id.* art. 9(1)(d).

72. *Id.* art. 9(1)(e).

73. *Id.* art. 9(1)(f).

74. *Id.* art. 9(1)(g).

The Assembly of the AU is essentially the same as the Assembly of Heads of State and Government of the OAU, which likewise was the "supreme organ of the Organization."[75] Further confirming this connection, upon adoption of the Constitutive Act, the members of the OAU Assembly automatically became the members of the AU Assembly.[76] As the "supreme organ," the Assembly has ultimate oversight over much of the AU's work.[77]

2. The Executive Council

Under the OAU Charter, the Council of Ministers was composed of "Foreign Ministers or other Ministers as are designated by the Governments of Member States,"[78] and was "responsible to the Assembly of Heads of State and Government."[79] The Constitutive Act of the AU provides that the Executive Council "shall be composed of the Ministers of Foreign Affairs or other such Ministers or Authorities as are designated by the Governments of Member States."[80] Like the Council of Ministers, the Executive Council of the AU "shall be responsible to the Assembly.[81] Moreover, it has responsibilities similar to those of the Council of Ministers.[82] It "consider[s] issues that the Assembly refers to it and monitors the implementation of policies the Assembly formulates."[83] Though the Constitutive Act was signed after the Protocol, the Constitutive Act does not explicitly assign to the Executive Council the over-

---

75. OAU Charter, *supra* note 29, art. VIII.

76. Tiyanjana Maluwa, *The OAU/African Union and International Law: Mapping New Boundaries or Revising Old Terrain?*, 98 AM. SOC'Y INT'L L. PROC. 232, 235 (2004) ("[W]hile the name of the organization and the operational framework may have changed, the actors – the members – remain exactly the same.").

77. In addition to the powers and functions enumerated above, the Assembly oversees the Executive Council, Constitutive Act art. 13(2); can restructure the Specialized Technical Committees, *id.* art 14 (2); determine the functions and powers of the ESCC, *id.* art. 22 (2); and determines sanctions for noncompliance with payment of dues or decisions of the AU, *id.* art. 23(1)-(2).

78. OAU Charter, *supra* note 29, art. XII (1).

79. *Id.* art. XIII(1).

80. Constitutive Act, *supra* note 23, art. 10(1).

81. *Id.* art. 13(2).

82. *See* Nsongurua Udombana, *The Institutional Structure of the African Union: A Legal Analysis*, 33 CAL. W. INT'L L.J. 69, 94 (2002) ("[The Executive Council] is analogous to the composition of the Council of Ministers of the OAU . . ."); *see also* African Union, The Organs of the AU, http://www.africa-union.org/root/au/organs/Executive_Council_en. htm (stating that "'Executive Council' means the Executive *Council of Ministers* of the Union") (emphasis added) (last visited February 28, 2008).

83. Udombana, *supra* note 82, at 96.

sight of execution of decisions of the Court,[84] which was the responsibility of the Council of Ministers of the OAU.[85]

In addition to these organic institutions, the AU has initiated special programs such as the New Partnership for Africa's Development (NEPAD), a program that, among other things, proposes a way for member states to pay off major debts that hinder their growth.[86] NEPAD's primary objectives are to eradicate poverty, promote the integration of Africa in the global economy, and place African countries on the path to sustainable development.[87] Its long-term goal is for Africans to "extricate themselves and the continent from the malaise of underdevelopment and exclusion in a globalizing world."[88] NEPAD is a long-term debt-relief mechanism whereby African nations partner with industrialized nations, which will provide aid for infrastructure projects, education, and debt relief, as well as eased access for African goods in their markets.[89] In order to take advantage of these programs, African nations must agree to principles of good governance and self-policing.[90]

B. *The Failures of the African Commission of Human and Peoples' Rights*

The OAU created the Commission in 1981 "to promote human and peoples' rights and ensure their protection in Africa."[91] The Charter sets forth a broad array of human and peoples' rights that the Commission is to protect.[92] Individuals are entitled to, *inter alia*, the right to equal protection under the Charter,[93] the right to

---

84. Konstantinos D. Magliveras & Gino J Naldi, *The African Union – A New Dawn for Africa?*, 51 Int'l & Comp. L.Q. 415, 420-21 (2002) (pointing out that it is "noteworthy that the Council has such a focused role to play, while wider issues relating to Union objectives (e.g . . . protection of human rights . . .) have not been included in its terms of reference").

85. Protocol, *supra* note 18, art. 29(2).

86. *See* NEPAD Framework Document, art. 3 www.nepad.org/2005/files/documents/inbrief.pdf (last visited February 28, 2008) (noting that credit from other countries has led to a "debt deadlock which . . . hinders the growth of African countries").

87. *Id.* art. 67(1).

88. *Id.* art. 1.

89. Romilly Greenhill & Sasha Blackmore, New Economics Foundation, Relief Works: African Proposals for Debt Cancellation – And Why Debt Relief Works 3 (2002), *available at* http://www.jubileeresearch.org (last visited February 29, 2008).

90. Justice, *supra* note 48, 131.

91. Charter, *supra* note 4, art. 30

92. *See id.* part 1, ch. I (setting forth Human and Peoples' Rights); *id.* ch. II (setting forth the duties of individuals to others).

93. *Id.* art. 3.

life,[94] access to courts,[95] freedom of conscience,[96] the right to receive information,[97] freedom of assembly,[98] freedom of movement,[99] and the right to education.[100] In addition, all peoples are made equal under the law[101] and entitled to the right to exist,[102] the right to freely use their wealth and natural resources,[103] the right to economic, social, and cultural development,[104] the right to national peace and security,[105] and the right to a satisfactory environment.[106] Thus, if any of these rights is violated, *any* member state has a cause of action before the Commission.[107]

Despite the importance of these rights, the Commission has failed in its role as protector.[108] The characteristics of the Commission contributing to its inability to curb human rights abuses among member states are: 1) it wields no power to issue binding opinions or to grant remedies; 2) its proceedings are conducted in secret; and 3) it lacks the financial resources necessary to carry out its functions.[109] A discussion of each of these characteristics follows.

1. Enforcement

The most crippling aspect of the Commission is its lack of enforcement power.[110] Three major features of the Charter make enforcement unlikely. First, the Charter does not provide for an enforcement mechanism other than a report and an in-depth study

---

94. *Id.* art. 4.
95. *Id.* art. 7.
96. *Id.* art. 8.
97. *Id.* art. 9.
98. *Id.* art. 11.
99. *Id.* art. 12.
100. *Id.* art. 17.
101. *Id.* art. 19.
102. *Id.* art. 20.
103. *Id.* art. 21.
104. *Id.* art. 22.
105. *Id.* art. 23.
106. *Id.* art. 24.
107. *Id.* art. 47.
108. Vincent O. Orlu Nmehielle, *Towards an African Court of Human Rights: Structuring and the Court,* 6 Ann Surv. Int'l. & Comp. L. 27, 30-31 (2000).
109. *Id.* at 31.
110. Justice C. Nwobike, *The African Commission on Human and Peoples' Rights and the Demystification of Second and Third Generation Rights Under the African Charter: Social and Economic Rights Action Center (SERAC) and the Center for Economic and Social Rights (CESR) v. Nigeria,* 1 Afr. J. Legal Stud., 129, 145 (2005) ("The greatest institutional weakness of the African Commission is its inability to enforce its decisions against State parties.").

from the Commission to the Assembly.[111] Second, the members of the Assembly may have conflicts of interest that prevent them from actively seeking compliance with the Charter.[112] Finally, the Charter contains "claw-back clauses" that allow member states to limit the rights that the Charter guarantees by operation of their own domestic laws.[113]

The Charter simply does not create an enforcement mechanism.[114] A member state may complain to the Commission of suspected Charter violations by any other member state.[115] The Commission may consider a complaint, or "communication," only after all local remedies have been exhausted[116] and after the state concerned has been notified of the communication.[117] After obtaining all necessary information from the states parties and trying to reach an amicable solution, the Commission prepares a report to the states concerned and provides the report to the Assembly as well.[118] If after consideration by the Commission it appears that there has been a "serious or massive" violation of human or peoples' rights, the Commission may notify the Assembly.[119] The Assembly may then request that the Commission undertake an "in-depth study" of such cases, making factual findings and recommendations.[120] In cases of emergency, the Commission may notify the Chairman of the Assembly, rather than the entire Assembly, and the Chairman may request an in-depth study.[121]

But the Charter does not provide any enforcement mechanisms to implement the Commission's recommendations after the report is made to the states involved as provided for in Article 52 or after

---

111. *See* Charter, *supra* note 4, arts. 52, 58.

112. Arthur E. Anthony, *Beyond the Paper Tiger: The Challenge of a Human Rights Court in Africa*, 32 Tex. Int'l L.J., 511, 517 (1997) (pointing out that the Commission is controlled in large part by the Assembly, the members of which are often the targets of human rights claims, negates the independence of the Commissioners that is provided for in Articles 31 and 38 of the Charter).

113. Udombana, *supra* note 12, at 62 n.91 (2000) (citing Professor Rosalyn Higgins' coining of the phrase "claw-back clause," which means a limitation clause that "permits, in normal circumstances, breach of an obligation for a specified number of public reasons") (internal quotations omitted).

114. Nmehielle, *supra* note 108, at 34-35 ("In fact, the Charter does not offer significant remedies.").

115. Charter, *supra* note 4, art. 47.

116. *Id.* arts. 50, 52, 56(5).

117. *Id.* art. 57.

118. *Id.* art. 52.

119. *Id.* art. 58(1).

120. *Id.* art. 58(2).

121. *Id.* art. 58(3).

it conducts an in-depth study pursuant to Article 58.[122] Enforcement appears to be in the hands of the Assembly, but the Charter does not set forth guidelines describing how the Assembly must implement a solution to the problem reported in the communications either.[123] Thus "there is in fact no remedy within the Charter."[124]

In practice, the Assembly has never ordered an in-depth study,[125] and has been unable to prevent or curtail any human rights abuses that the Commission has called to its attention. For example, when the military regime of General Abacha detained members and leaders of the Ogoni tribe in Nigeria in the mid-1990s, the Assembly condemned the violation of human rights, urging the military government to respect the rights of minorities and take immediate steps to return Nigeria to democratic rule.[126] Nonetheless, the military government executed the detainees despite the Assembly's admonitions.[127] Another more publicized conflict, the Rwandan Genocide, also proceeded despite the deployment of human rights monitors to Rwanda by the Assembly.[128] Evidently, these African governments and regimes have not taken the Commission or the Assembly seriously enough to heed their exhortations, despite their being parties to the Charter.[129]

The Assembly's failure to successfully influence member states after referral of matters by the Commission may be due to unwillingness among members of the Assembly to crack down on other nations for abuses that they themselves may have committed or might commit.[130] This conflict of interest may make it less likely that the Assembly will speak out against a member state, lest the finger be pointed at them next.[131] For example, two senior govern-

---

122.   The Protocol is silent as to these matters. *See* Protocol, *supra* note 18.

123.   Nmehielle, *supra* note 108, at 36 (citing U.O. MOZURIKE, THE AFRICAN CHARTER ON HUMAN AND PEOPLES' RIGHTS, NIGERIAN INSTITUTE OF ADVANCED LEGAL STUDIES 25 (1992)).

124.   *Id.*

125.   *Id.* at 35.

126.   African Commission on Human and People's Rights Res.16(XVII)95: Resolution on Nigeria (1995) (hereinafter ACHPR), http://www.achpr.org/english/resolutions/resolution21_en.html (last visited Feb. 28, 2008).

127.   Yemi Akinseye-George, *New Trends in African Human Rights Law: Prospects of an African Court of Human Rights*, 10 U. MIAMI INT'L & COMP. L. REV. 159, 167 (2002).

128.   *See* ACHPR, *supra* note 126; Udombana, *supra* note 27, at 1224.

129.   Udombana, *supra* note 12, at 67-68.

130.   *See* Anthony, *supra* note 112, at 517.

131.   *See* Chidi Anselm Odinkalu, *The Individual Complaints Procedures of the African Commission on Human and Peoples' Rights: A Preliminary Assessment*, 8 TRANSNAT'L L. & CONTEMP. PROBS. 359, 365-66 (1998) (noting that "the process of nomination and election to the Commission minimizes the likelihood of the body being composed of persons who may be

ment officials from the Congo, a state rampant with human rights violations, served as Commissioners.[132] Because the Assembly is permitted to review communications before the Commission does, the Assembly has the discretion to determine the validity of complaints submitted under the Charter.[133] In this way, the Commission is made dependent upon the political control of the Assembly, which is composed of the member states whose actions the Commission is set up to consider.[134] Thus, a communication alleging a violation of the Charter by one of the Assembly members' own nations could be swept under the rug without much controversy.

Member states have also devised means of circumventing the force of the Charter by taking advantage of its "claw-back clauses."[135] Claw-back clauses are provisions in the Charter that permit member states to act in contravention of the Charter to the extent that such conduct is in accordance with that nation's own laws.[136] For example, Article 14 provides that individuals have the right to own property, subject to domestic laws that may encroach upon that right in the "general interest of the community."[137] Similarly, individuals have the right to receive information[138] and the right to express and disseminate their opinions, but only within the restrictions set forth by domestic law.[139] Thus, a member state effectively can deprive individuals of these rights by passing a national law limiting them.[140] Such actions are permitted by the plain language of the Charter. Therefore, neither the Commission nor the Assembly can condemn encroachments upon these rights if such encroachments are in accordance with a nation's laws.[141] In this way, the power of the Assembly and the Commission are limited, and the guarantee of human and peoples' rights is never absolute.[142] These claw-back clauses, lack of enforcement power, and

---

substantially or rigorously impervious to state pressure," because "[m]embers of the Commission are elected by the Assembly").

132. Udombana, *supra* note 12, at 71.

133. *See* Anthony, *supra* note 112, at 517.

134. Nmehielle, *supra* note 108, at 31.

135. Udombana *supra* note 12, at 62.

136. *See* Charter, *supra* note 4, arts. 6, 8, 9(2), 10(1), 11, 12(1), 12(3), 13, 14.

137. *Id.* art. 14.

138. *Id.* art. 9(1).

139. *Id.* art. 9(2).

140. J. Oloka-Onyango, *Human Rights and Sustainable Development in Contemporary Africa: A New Dawn, or Retreating Horizons?*, 6 Buff. Hum. Rts. L. Rev. 39, 55 (2000) (noting that in some cases, the law to which a right is subjected completely negates the right guaranteed by the Charter).

141. *Id.*

142. *Id.*

potential conflicts of interest among members of the Assembly therefore seriously reduce the degree to which the Commission can effectively curtail human rights abuses in Africa through its interpretations of the Charter.

2. Secrecy

The second feature of the Charter that hinders its successful implementation is the confidentiality of Commission proceedings.[143] Despite the provision for diplomatic immunity and non-liability for the Commissioners in Article 43, Article 59 provides that all measures taken within the provisions of the Charter shall remain confidential until the Assembly decides to publicize them.[144] Additionally, the reports of the Commission will only be published after the Assembly considers them.[145] Perhaps due to the conflicts of interest that members of the Assembly may have had, the Assembly did not readily authorize the publication of any report of the Commission until the inception of the AU.[146] This has diminished confidence in the Charter's effectiveness and, in turn, has reduced the number of appeals to the Commission for help.[147]

3. Resources

Lack of financial resources also has contributed to the Commission's lackluster performance.[148] The Commission is supposed to be financed with dues from member states of the AU, but most are delinquent in paying.[149] As a result, the Commission must rely on donations from abroad.[150]

---

143. *See* Charter, *supra* note 4, art. 59.

144. *Id.* at art. 59(1).

145. *Id.* at art. 59(3).

146. Nmehielle, *supra* note 108, at 31.

147. *Id.*

148. *See* Udombana, *supra* note 27, at 1250 (noting that "[t]he Commission is operating against the background or reiterated failure and incessant peril," because it "is suffering from chronic financial incapacities").

149. Nmehielle, *supra* note 108, at 59.

150. Udombana, *supra* note 12, at 72 (2000); *see also* Udombana, *An African Human Rights Court and an African Union Court: A Needful Duality or a Needless Duplication?*, 28 Brook. J. Int'l L. 811, 862 (2003) (stating that "many existing OAU/AU institutions constantly carry their bowls to look for crumbs from the table of European institutions in the form of grants").

Without adequate resources, the Commission cannot perform its promotion function, which the Charter mandates in Article 30.[151] This lack of resources also may be responsible for the Assembly's failure to order publication and dissemination of the Commission's reports and activities.[152] Thus, financial weakness also has contributed to the infrequent use of the Commission by member states who may have grievances under the Charter.[153]

In summary, the inability of the Commission and possible unwillingness of the Assembly to enforce decisions regarding Charter violations, coupled with the secrecy of the Commission's proceedings and lack of resources to conduct and promote the Commission's functions, led to the realization that the Commission is an insufficient solution to the myriad of human rights abuses in Africa.[154] A stronger, more independent body with enforcement power was needed if improvements were to be made and abuses curtailed.[155]

C. *The Features of the African Court of Human and Peoples' Rights Intended to Address the Commission's Failures*

On October 6, 1998, the OAU issued the Protocol to the African Charter of Human and Peoples' Rights on the Establishment of an African Court on Human and Peoples' Rights.[156] The Protocol appears to address the major failures of the Commission by arming the Court with the power to issue binding orders and remedies,[157] creating a judicial body with stringent rules intended to prevent conflicts of interest,[158] and providing that the Court's proceedings

---

151. Udombana, *supra* note 61, at 862 (noting that as of 2003, the Commission still did not have a permanent building; rather it was located in a rented apartment in The Gambia).

152. Viljoen, *supra* note 17, at 21-22.

153. *Id.* at 21.

154. *See* Nmehielle, *supra* note 31, at 423-26 (calling the adoption of the Protocol part of an African "renaissance" after repeated scholarly criticisms of the Commission's many weaknesses).

155. *See* Nmehielle, *supra* note 108, at 28 (arguing that, "for an effective African regional human rights protection and enforcement mechanism to exist, the African system must be made more effective and supplemented with a court of human rights").

156. *See* Chart, *supra* note 28, item 21.

157. Protocol, *supra* note 18, art. 28(2) (providing that the judgment of a majority of the Court shall be final); art. 27(1) (providing that if a violation of human rights is found, the court "shall make appropriate orders to remedy the violation, including the payment of fair compensation or reparation").

158. *See id.* art. 16 (providing that the judges shall take an oath of office, solemnly declaring that they will discharge their duties "impartially and faithfully"); art. 17(1) (providing that the independence of judges shall be "fully ensured in accordance with international law"); art. 17(2) (requiring recusal of a judge who has previously taken part in case, whether as agent or advocate for any party); art. 18 (providing that "[t]he position of judge

will be conducted publicly.[159] Thus, this enabling document theoretically provides a solution to many of the Commission's deficiencies.[160] The Court has not yet begun hearing cases, however, so it is uncertain whether it will have any more success in implementing its decisions than the Commission.

1. Effect of the Court's Orders

Because the absence of an enforcement provision in the Charter was arguably its greatest weakness,[161] the Protocol's provision for binding orders shows the greatest promise. The Protocol provides that if "the Court finds that there has been a violation of human or peoples' rights, it shall make appropriate orders to remedy the violation, including the payment of fair compensation or reparation."[162] The Court may do this even without first attempting to settle the matter amicably between the states parties as required of the Commission; rather, the Protocol grants the Court discretion in this respect.[163] The decisions of the Court must be read publicly, thereby giving notice to the states parties and to the world that a judgment has been made.[164] Moreover, the Protocol demands that states parties "shall undertake to comply with the judgment"[165] and do so within the time period set forth by the Court.[166] Finally, the Council of Ministers, on behalf of the Assembly, shall monitor the execution of the Court's orders.[167] This increased pressure to comply with the judgments may give member states more incentive to rectify human rights abuses.[168]

---

of the court is incompatible with any activity that might interfere with the independence or impartiality of such a judge or the demands of the office"); art. 22 (requiring recusal of any judge who is "a national of any State which is a party to a case submitted to the Court").

159. *Id.* art. 28(5)-(6) (requiring that the judgment of the court and the reasons therefore shall be given in open court).

160. *See* Nmehielle, *supra* note 108, at 60 (stating that by drafting the Protocol, "the stage has been set" to solve the problem of the Commission's ineffectiveness).

161. *See* Nwobike, *supra* note 110, at 25.

162. Protocol, *supra* note 18, art. 27(1).

163. *Id.* art. 9 (stating that "the Court *may* try to reach an amicable settlement in a case pending before it in accordance with the provisions of the Charter") (emphasis added).

164. *See id.* art. 28(5).

165. *Id.* art. 30.

166. *Id.*

167. *Id.* art. 29(2).

168. Udombana, *supra* note 12, at 111 (predicting that while the Protocol will not end human rights abuses overnight, it will strengthen the African system and provide an important deterrent to human rights abuses).

2. Greater Judicial Independence From the Assembly

The Protocol also provides several assurances that the judges of the Court will be neutral decision-makers. First, the Court itself decides which communications to consider.[169] This stands in contrast to the Charter in that the required communications previously had to be submitted to both the secretary general of the OAU *and* to the chairman of the Commission.[170] Second, the Protocol requires the recusal of any judge who: a) is a national of any state party to the case to be heard;[171] or b) has previously taken part in the case in any capacity.[172] Finally, the Court must establish its own rules of procedure setting forth a list of activities in which judges may not engage due to potential incompatibility with judicial duties.[173] One feature borrowed from the Charter, however, was the procedure for selecting judges, who, like selection of the Commissioners,[174] must be elected by the Assembly.[175] The judges' independent judgments as well as the Court's independence from the Assembly in deciding which cases to hear are potential solutions to the problems that paralyzed the Commission's effectiveness.

3. Publicity

The Protocol provides that the Court shall conduct its proceedings in public.[176] The Court must also explain the reasoning behind its judgments.[177] By reporting its activity openly, the Court is more likely to attract media attention as well as generate more interest and awareness.[178] Thus, the abused may be more likely to take their grievances to the Court if they know that the offending state will be publicly recognized and condemned.[179] Moreover, the fear of public condemnation will ideally deter future human rights

---

169. Protocol, *supra* note 18, art. 6(2).

170. Charter, *supra* note 4, arts. 47, 49.

171. Protocol, *supra* note 18, art. 22

172. *Id.* art. 17(2).

173. *Id.* art. 18.

174. Charter, *supra* note 4 art. 33.

175. *Compare* Protocol, *supra* note 18, art. 14(1) *with* Charter, *supra* note 4, art. 33.

176. *Id.* art. 10(1).

177. *Id.*

178. Yemi Akinseye-George, *New Trends in African Human Rights Law: Prospects of an African Court of Human Rights*, 10 U. Miami Int'l & Comp. L. Rev. 159, 172 (2002).

179. *See* Nmehielle, *supra* note 108, at 58 (noting that African states are more willing to publicly condemn human rights abuses due to the continent's desire "not to be left behind in the new world order of things, especially in the areas of human rights and democratization, which have increasingly become the basis of international relations").

abuses.[180] In this way, the Protocol demonstrates a recognition of and potential solution to the problems that the Commission's secrecy created. Furthermore, the Protocol's provisions safeguarding the independence of the Court's judges and the binding nature of its judgments hopefully will bode well for African citizens who could be affected by human rights abusers.

In summary, the AU and the Court demonstrate African nations' move toward global acceptance of Africa through rejecting human rights abuse.[181] Notwithstanding this ideological shift, the Assembly retains oversight of both the ultimate implementation of the Court's decisions and the economic programs that could benefit African nations. Therefore, it is uncertain whether the new ideology will manifest itself through adherence with the Charter and compliance with the Court's decisions.[182] This uncertainty arises from the Assembly's continuing role in addressing human rights, despite its failures under the OAU and the Commission. The next Part will attempt to analyze whether the new system will have increased success despite the retention of the Assembly's supervisory role.

III. ANALYSIS

One scholar has termed the creation of the Human Rights Court and the transition from the OAU to the AU an "African Renaissance" providing great hope that the failures of the old OAU are coming to an end.[183] Indeed, many scholars agree that the AU provides a stronger normative framework than the OAU.[184] Others point out, however, that "good initiatives do not implement themselves,"[185] and that there is doubt as to the "capacity of the [AU] to achieve any of those goals beyond what its predecessor, the [OAU],

---

180. Udombana, *supra* note 12, at 95 ("Public exposure and authoritative condemnation of human rights violations is an extremely effective tool in the promotion and protection of human rights.")

181. *See* Constitutive Act, *supra* note 23, pmbl. (stating that the AU is "Determined to take up the multifaceted challenges that confront our continent and peoples in the light of the social, economic and political changes taking place in the world").

182. *See* J. Oloka-Orjango, *Human Rights and Sustainable Development in Contemporary Africa: A New Dawn, or Retreating Horizons?*, 6 BUFF. HUM. RTS. L. REV. 39, 71-72 (noting that, in light of the Commission's utter failures, "the establishment of [the Court] is a development that can only be greeted with caution").

183. Nmehielle, *supra* note 31, at 414, 416-17.

184. *See e.g.*, Packer & Rukare, *supra* note 33, at 379 (noting that "the importance of the entry into force of the [Constitutive Act] establishing the new Union may lie mainly in its symbolism").

185. Nmehielle, *supra* note 31, at 415.

could achieve."[186] This Part will analyze the distinguishing features of the Court and the Commission as between the OAU and AU, as well as address whether these changes are sufficient to ensure compliance with the Court's orders. Assuming they are sufficient, the AU should make membership contingent on adherence to the Charter and compliance with Court decisions.

A. *Potential Effects of the Protocol's Characteristics on the Enforcement of Court Decisions*

1. The Court's Potential Shortcomings

Although the Court has power to issue binding judgments and the increased independence of the decision-making body and publication of its judgments are direct attempts to remedy the shortcomings of the Commission, several glitches still may exist.[187] In addition, some of the factors that prevented the success of the Commission, such as lack of resources and apathy on the part of the Assembly, continue to exist.[188] The effectiveness of the Court remains uncertain as the world awaits its inauguration. But the following problems are potential obstacles to its complete success.

First, the Court may face the same financial difficulties as the Commission.[189] A preliminary report on the financial implications of the Court already indicates that the Court will have inadequate resources to meet its needs.[190] Moreover, the Protocol calls for complementarity between the Court and Commission,[191] indicat-

---

186. Dejo Olowu, *Regional Integration, Development, and the African Union Agenda: Challenges, Gaps, and Opportunities*, 13 Transnat'l L. & Contemp. Probs. 211, 212 (2003).

187. *See* Nmehielle, *supra* note 108, at 58-59 (arguing that while the court could make a great difference in human rights enforcement, the Protocol "will need further refinement to realize its potential," including assurance of a stable infrastructure and recognition by African leaders of the effect of being branded an abuser of human rights).

188. *See* Oloka-Onyango, *supra* note 140, at 71-72 (noting that "[i]t is likely that the Court will be plagued by the very same problems that hampered the work of the Commission. Even if by some miraculous occurrence the infrastructural issues were to be tackled, the paramount issue of political will remains an outstanding one").

189. *See* Mashood A. Baderin, *Recent Developments in the African Regional Human Rights System*, 5 Hum. Rts. L. Rev. 117, 148-49 (2005) (advising that "[i]t is important to provide the Court with appropriate funding to avoid the financial predicament of the [Commission]").

190. Frans Viljoen, *A Human Rights Court for Africa, and Africans*, 30 Brook. J. Int'l L. 1, 64 (2004).

191. Protocol, *supra* note 18, art. 8 (2).

ing that the Court is *not a replacement* for the Commission. Thus, the Court is an added expense to an already insufficient budget.[192]

Second, the ability of the Court and Council of Ministers to actually effectuate the Court's judgments is questionable.[193] Although the Protocol provides more power to compel compliance with the Court's judgments than the Charter did for the Commission,[194] the consequences of continuing refusal to comply with a judgment are unclear.[195] The Protocol states that the Court shall submit an annual report to the Assembly identifying the states that have not complied with its decisions.[196] Therefore, an offending state may avoid its duty to comply by simply waiting out the Council of Ministers. If a state does this, then the matter is in the hands of the Assembly,[197] the same body that previously hampered the Commission's effectiveness. Thus, there must be some benefit in abiding by the Court's judgments that will provide incentives for states to obey.

2. The Protocol's Potential to Increase Compliance with the Charter

The Protocol has some features that might successfully address the Assembly's conflicts of interest. These include an added buffer between the Court and the Assembly that did not exist between the Assembly and the Commission,[198] as well as the provision that the Court's proceedings will be publicized.[199] First, the role of the Council of Ministers ensures that the Court's orders are carried out. Although the Assembly is the ultimate arbiter of compliance

---

192. *See* Udombana, *supra* note 27, at 1255 (recommending that the [AU] needs to "trim down its existing institutions," but instead it has created new ones "to add to those that are already moribund").

193. *See* Nmehielle, *supra* note, 108 at 58 (noting that while this enforcement mechanism is an improvement over the Charter's provisions, "the Council of Ministers is a political body that may sometimes allow political considerations to interfere with its supervisory role").

194. *Id.*

195. *Id.* (noting that it remains to be seen whether offending states will be concerned with the stigma of not complying with the order of a human rights tribunal).

196. Protocol, *supra* note 18, art. 31.

197. *Id.*

198. *See id.* art. 29 (inserting the Council of Ministers into the enforcement procedure by providing that the "Council of Ministers shall also be notified of the judgment and shall monitor its execution").

199. *See id.* art. 28(5) (providing that the judgment of the Court "shall be read in open court").

with the Court's orders when the Council's efforts fail,[200] the added scrutiny of this separate body could serve as a check on the Assembly's performance, making the Assembly less likely to turn a blind eye toward Charter violations.

In addition to inserting the Council of Ministers between the Court and Assembly, the Protocol requires the Court to submit fewer reports to the Assembly than the Charter requires of the Commission: The Protocol only commands the Court to report to the Assembly once per year.[201] In its report, the Court must specify "the cases in which a State has not complied with the Court's judgment."[202] In contrast, the Charter requires not only that the Commission submit a report of its activities to the Assembly after each ordinary session,[203] but also that the Commission submit a report of its findings in *every case* that did not reach an amicable solution.[204] In transmitting these reports, the Commission "may make to the [Assembly] such recommendations as it deems useful."[205] Thus, the Commission may advise the Assembly, but the Assembly is charged with seeking a resolution to the case. Finally, the proceedings and recommendation of the Commission must remain confidential, unless the Assembly decides otherwise.[206] Therefore, if the Assembly does not want to enforce the Charter in a particular case, it can simply refuse to declassify the Commission's reports.

The Protocol provision requiring publication of the Court's proceedings, orders, and reasons therefore precludes the Assembly from keeping the Court's activities secret.[207] In this way, the Assembly is not in fact the ultimate authority for ensuring compliance with the Court's orders. Rather, the international community will be aware that a judgment has been made and a remedy ordered.[208] Presumably, the world will likewise bear witness to a nation's compliance failures despite the Council of Ministers'

---

200. *See id.* art. 31 (providing that if a State does not comply with the judgment of the Court, the Court shall notify the Assembly).

201. *See* Protocol, *supra* note 18, art. 31 (stating that the Court shall provide the Assembly with a "report on its work during the previous year").

202. *Id.*

203. Charter, art. 54.

204. *Id.* art. 52.

205. *Id.* art. 53.

206. *Id.* art. 59(1)-(2).

207. *See* Protocol, *supra* note 18, art. 28(5)-(6).

'208. *See* Akinseye-George, *supra* note 127, at 172 (suggesting that because the Court will do its work openly, it will attract media attention and raise awareness about the human rights system in Africa).

efforts.[209] Finally, the international community, aware of the judgment and a state's noncompliance, can exert pressure on the Assembly not to resort to its old ways.[210]

B.   *The AU's Potential Ability to Ensure Compliance With Court Orders*

The OAU's transformation into the AU marks an ideological change from non-interference in sovereign affairs to cooperation and pan-Africanism,[211] with the intent of delivering the continent from poverty and marginalization from the international community. While the Constitutive Act and the mechanisms it created to achieve these goals are inspiring on paper, it remains to be seen whether the new AU will effectuate the ideological differences that distinguish it from the OAU.

The Constitutive Act of the AU envisioned several institutions and programs intended to promote economic growth in Africa that could compel African nations to comply with the Court's orders.[212] In particular, NEPAD's promise of sustainable development in the long-term could encourage African governments to comply with Court decisions and also promote the success of the Court as an institution through its debt-relief program.[213] In addition, the AU's relaxation of the OAU's staunch policy of non-interference is a step toward reducing human rights abuses in Africa.

The Assembly adopted the Constitutive Act of the AU at its Thirty-Sixth Ordinary Session on July 11, 2000.[214] By signing the Act, fifty-three nations[215] bore witness to the African nations' determination to "promote and protect human and peoples' rights in accordance with the African Charter on Human and Peoples' Rights and other relevant human rights instruments."[216] More-

---

209.   *See id.*

210.   *See* Udombana, *supra* note 27, at 1260 (noting that civil society must "pressurize the AU to ensure that human rights are given due consideration").

211.   *See* Constitutive Act, *supra* note 23, pmbl. (noting that while the OAU played an "invaluable role in the liberation of the continent," there is a "need to build a partnership between governments and all segments of civil society").

212.   *Id.* art. 22(1)-(2) (establishing the Economic, Social, and Cultural Council), art. 22(1)-(2) (establishing the Economic, Social, and Cultural Council); *see id.* art.19(a)-(c) (establishing three financial institutions: the African Central Bank, the African Monetary Fund, and the African Investment Bank).

213.   *See* Udombana, *supra* note 41, at 72 (noting that NEPAD's blueprint for sustainable development requires "political measures to address the political and social vulnerabilities of conflicts," and in order to manage conflict, efforts "must focus on strengthening existing regional . . . institutions").

214.   Constitutive Act, *supra* note 23.

215.   *Id.*

216.   *Id.* art. 3(h).

over, these nations agreed that the AU shall recognize the "right of the Union to intervene in a Member State pursuant to a decision of the Assembly in respect of grave circumstances, namely: war crimes, genocide and crimes against humanity."[217] Such provisions suggest that in forming the AU, the Assembly recognized that the policy of non-interference hindered achievement of the Commission's objectives. Despite this marked change in values, the same Assembly of the OAU that failed to enforce the Charter became the "supreme organ of the Union,"[218] just as it was the "supreme organ of the Organization."[219] Likewise, the Council of Ministers of the OAU continues under the Constitutive Act as the Executive Council.[220]

The Constitutive Act also states that the AU aims to "promote and protect human and peoples' rights in accordance with the African Charter on Human and Peoples' Rights,"[221] but does not name the Commission or the Court on its list of organic institutions.[222] Moreover, the Act does not place the responsibility of ensuring compliance with Court' orders with the Executive Council.[223] It also provides for the imposition of sanctions for both defaults in payment and noncompliance with the decisions of the Union,[224] and that "governments which shall come to power through unconstitutional means shall not be allowed to participate in the activities of the Union."[225] Finally, the Act provides for amendment and revision of its provisions.[226]

Thus, although the OAU transformed into the AU, the Assembly continues to be the ultimate enforcer of decisions made pursuant to the Charter, whether the initial decision was made by the Commission or the Court. This raises a question as to whether the statement of renewed ideals in the Act is enough to overcome the

---

217. *Id.* art. 4(h).

218. *See id.* art. 6(2).

219. OAU Charter, *supra* note 29, art. VIII.

220. *See* Constitutive Act, *supra* note 23, arts. 10-13 (describing the composition, procedures, and functions of the Executive Council).

221. *Id.* art. 3(h).

222. *See id.* art. 5 (listing the organs of the AU; neither the Court nor the Commission is included).

223. *See id.* arts. 10-13 (describing the Executive Council, its decisions, its procedures, and its functions).

224. *Id.* art. 23(1)-(2).

225. *Id.* art. 30.

226. *Id.* art. 32.

Assembly's demonstrated apathy concerning enforcement of the Commission's recommendations.[227]

As noted above, the Assembly has never ordered an in-depth study as provided in the Charter, even when presented with extra-judicial executions by a military coup and the Rwandan Genocide.[228] Nonetheless, requiring a member state to comply with an order of the Court seems a much more forceful act than merely looking into a situation more closely.[229] Thus, the conflicts of interest that made the Assembly unwilling to order these studies could likely limit its resolve to require an affirmative act on the part of a member state to comply with an order of the Court.

The Assembly's continuation as the ultimate enforcer of Court orders may dampen the Protocol's promise that the Court's decisions will be binding in practice.[230] The Protocol provides that, upon finding a human rights violation, the Court shall issue orders to remedy the violation,[231] that such orders shall be final,[232] and that the Council of Ministers shall monitor their execution.[233] Despite these safeguards, the Court must report a failure to comply with its orders to the Assembly in its annual report.[234] The Protocol does not describe how the Assembly is to respond to a report of noncompliance.[235] Similarly, it fails to provide the Court with any "authority to take effective enforcement action if its judgments are

---

227. *See* Nmehielle, *supra* note 31, at 446 (opining that "[w]ith the necessary political will and a strong AU, it is more likely than not that a new human rights era is in the offing" assuming that the AU can "battle the legacy of the [OAU] – the failure to adopt a proactive human rights stance that characterized the past 40 years of its existence").

228. *Id.* at 440-41.

229. *See* Anthony, *supra* note 112, at 518 (noting that the reluctance of the Assembly to order an in-depth study was due to an unwillingness to "undertake to embarrass a fellow Member State given that African heads of state have in the past 'comport[ed] themselves like a club or a trade union in their solidarity'") (*quoting* B. Obinna Okere, *The Protection of Human Rights in Africa and the African Charter on Human and Peoples' Rights: A Comparative Analysis with the European and American Systems*, 6 Hum. Rts. Q. 141, 159 (1984)).

230. *See* Udombana, *supra* note 27, at 1258-59 (commenting that "the AU Treaty is an old wine in a new wineskin; and the AU is a reincarnation of the OAU. . . . it is not likely to take human rights seriously – even though that is greatly desired – for the simply reason that a married woman does not recover her virginity by divorce").

231. Protocol, *supra* note 18, art. 27(1).

232. *Id.* art. 28(2).

233. *Id.* art. 29(2).

234. *Id.* art. 31.

235. *See id.* art. 31 (providing that the Court shall notify the Assembly of States that fail to comply with its judgments). Notwithstanding that provision, there are no provisions describing what the Assembly will do to rectify such noncompliance. *See id.*

not implemented."[236] Given the Assembly's lackluster performance in the past and the more forceful nature of a binding order, it is questionable whether the Assembly will become any more effective under the Protocol. As noted above, however, the Protocol's provisions for publicity and oversight by the Council of Ministers could discourage the Assembly from being complicit in violations of the Charter.

These two features invite pressure from the international community.[237] Indeed, due to the fact that the AU and its economic programs are still in their infancy, peer pressure could be a significant incentive to adhere to the Charter and the Court's orders, since "[t]he threat of being branded a violator of human rights can damage a nation's well-being and the personal prestige and monetary rewards of a corrupt or oppressive regime."[238] Recently, an inverse relationship between human rights violations and development aid has become apparent.[239] Thus, the more abuses committed and the continued defiance of court orders will make it less likely that impoverished African nations will receive aid from other countries.[240]

The AU's new initiatives, specifically NEPAD, may promote compliance with the Court's orders and facilitate the success of the Court as an institution.[241] NEPAD requires African leaders' pledge in promoting the principles of "peace, security, democracy, good governance, human rights, and sound economic management" because they are "conditions for sustainable development."[242] The promise of long-term financial self-sufficiency may promote adherence to the Charter today. Moreover, NEPAD's debt-relief program will enable African nations to put less money toward foreign debt and more toward their own people and the Court. In this

---

236. Curtis F.J. Doebbler, *A Complex Ambiguity: The Relationship Between the African Commission on Human and Peoples' Rights and the Other African Union Initiatives Affecting Respect for Human Rights*, 13 Transnat'l L. & Contemp. Probs. 7, 16 (2003).

237. *See* Udombana, *supra* note 12, at 104 (recommending that for the Court to be effective, pressure from civil society is needed for the Protocol's reforms to become a reality).

238. Jimmy Carter, *Essay: The Rule of Law and the State of Human Rights*, 4 Harv. Hum. Rts. J. 1, 8 (1991).

239. *Id.*

240. *See id.*

241. *See* Nmehielle, *supra* note 31, at 417, 445 (arguing that while one commentator does not believe that the AU will bring with it any meaningful advancement in the arena of human rights, he views the reincarnation of the OAU to the AU as an African "renaissance" and that the Constitutive Act and NEPAD promises a "new Africa").

242. NEPAD Framework Document, *supra* note 86, art. 71.

way, the Commission's chronic problem of underfunding can be alleviated.

NEPAD has been described as "the most dynamic instrument among the collection of development-oriented blueprints for African regional development."[243] By offering much-needed debt relief to African nations, they will be more capable of meeting their obligations not only to their own people, but also to the AU and the African human rights institutions.[244] Since participation in NEPAD is voluntary and predicated on good governance, its effects will improve Africa both intra- and inter-nationally.[245]

Assuming that NEPAD is a viable program, debt relief for African nations could resolve the financial deficiency of the Commission and the Court, but *only if* they are *both* organs of the AU and supported by it, financially as well as morally. To do this, the AU must amend its Constitutive Act to include the Human Rights Court as one of its organs and condition membership to the AU upon adherence to the Charter and compliance with Court decisions. Thus, nations that do not respect their obligations under the Charter and the Protocol could not benefit from the opportunities for development that the Constitutive Act and NEPAD have to offer.[246]

IV. CONCLUSION

The births of the AU and the Court are steps in the right direction for developing the African continent and protecting human rights. The Court still faces some of the challenges the Commission faced in enforcing the Charter in the days of the OAU.[247] These challenges include the resolve of the Assembly to assist the

---

243. Dejo Olowu, *Regional Integration, Development, and the African Union Agenda: Challenges, Gaps, and Opportunities*, 13 TRANSNAT'L L. & CONTEMP. PROBS. 211, 218 (2003).

244. *See* Justice, *supra* note 48, at 131 (pointing out that "most African governments still spend up to three times more on debt repayments than on health care and education combined").

245. *See id.* at 129 (noting that Denmark recently refused to assist developing countries that misused funds to support dictators, namely Robert Mugabe in Zimbabwe). Thus the principles of good governance that NEPAD espouses will attract aid from outside, and the debt relief will allow African countries to support educational health care programs. *Id.*

246. *See* Doebbler, *supra* note 236, at 31 (surmising that "NEPAD is a framework by which the international community can provide Africa with the resources to protect Africans' basic human rights, but only if it is used with due respect to the international human rights instruments and mechanisms that already exist").

247. *See* Baderin, *supra* note 189, at 148-49 (noting the importance of proper funding to avoid the financial problems faced by the Commission); *see also* Oloka-Onyango, *supra* note 140, at 71-72 (noting that the Court will likely experience the same problems as the Commission, most notably political will).

International Human Rights Institutions and Enforcement II   *619*

610   The Geo. Wash. Int'l L. Rev.   [Vol. 40

Court in enforcing its orders in human rights disputes and the likely meager resources on which the Court will have to operate.[248]

The Protocol, the Constitutive Act of the AU, and the AU's special program, NEPAD, offer potential solutions to these challenges. One solution lies in the Constitutive Act's ambiguity regarding the relationship of the Commission and the Court with the AU. Further, NEPAD provides a potential way to alleviate the financial difficulties that the Court is bound to face.[249]

The door is still open for clarification of the relationship between the AU, the Court, and the Commission. This clarification should ensure that the Court and the Commission are organs of the AU effectuated by an affirmative merger of the Court and the elusive Court of Justice. In turn, the Assembly should amend the Constitutive Act to condition membership upon respect for the values the Charter mandates. This sanction can be meaningful through the success of the NEPAD program, and may ultimately reduce human rights abuses in Africa.

---

248. *Id.*
249. *See* Justice, *supra* note 48.

[23]

THE ROLE OF SUB-REGIONAL COURTS IN THE AFRICAN HUMAN RIGHTS SYSTEM

Lucyline Nkatha Murungi and
Jacqui Gallinetti

1 Introduction

Regional integration in post-colonial Africa began in 1963, with the adoption of the Charter of the Organisation of African Unity (OAU). This regional initiative was followed by the formation of sub-regional economic communities, commonly referred to as Regional Economic Communities (RECs) such as the East Africa Community (1967), the Economic Community of West African States (1975) and the Southern Africa Development Coordinating Conference (SADCC, 1980). In general, the main objective of the co-operation was the pursuit of economic development of member states.[1] Save for a remote reference to the United Nations Declaration of Human Rights the purposes of the OAU did not include the promotion or protection of human rights. In addition, though the African Charter on Human and Peoples' Rights (African Charter) was adopted in 1981, promotion and protection of human rights only became an objective of the African Union (AU) in the year 2000 upon the adoption of the Constitutive Act of the African Union.[2]

Similarly, the founding documents of most RECs adopted before the African Charter, did not provide for protection or promotion of human rights whether as a goal or principle thereof. Currently however, promotion and protection of human rights and democracy is part of the fundamental principles or goals of most RECs. In effect, the RECs have introduced a new layer of supranational protection and promotion of human rights in Africa. Their courts now play an important role in the protection of human rights through the determination of human rights cases.

Whereas the entry of RECs as an avenue for protection of rights is generally favourably hailed (VILJOEN, 2007, p. 503), its novelty demands a consideration as

Notes to this text start on page 141.

to their appropriateness as fora for the protection of human rights. Particularly, there is need to establish the place of REC courts within the African human rights system (AHRS) and their relationship with the regional human rights institutions. There is also concern over their capacity to effectively exercise the new competence in light of the economic focus of their founding treaties. The potential impact of the proliferation of human rights courts on the unity of international human rights law in Africa and how best to deal with this reality is another outstanding issue for advocates for human rights in the region.

This article examines the significance of the role of the REC courts in the protection of human rights in Africa. In doing so some of the challenges facing their place in the African human rights system will be interrogated such as their suitability as *fora* to resolve human rights disputes and the implications of their integration into the larger regional framework.

2 Regional integration in Africa - historical background to the inclusion of a general human rights agenda

After the demise of colonial rule in Africa, mainly in the 1960s, the reality of the political and economic fragility of post-colonial African states became apparent. In response to this reality, African states were called upon to integrate politically and economically in order to achieve development and to undo the balkanization of Africa brought by colonialism (LOLETTE, 2005). This was to be done through the creation of larger markets and consolidation of the resources and potential of the poor economies (THOKO, 2004, p. 1). Though this agenda was not immediately achieved at the regional level, states began to come together in their respective sub-regions following a pattern of geographical proximity (ECONOMIC COMMISSION FOR AFRICA, 2006). Hence, most RECs are centred on geographical sub-regions (VILJOEN, 2007, p. 488). The 1996 OAU decision to divide Africa into 5 sub-regions along geographical lines seems to have endorsed this approach (AJULU, 2005, p. 19). In 1980 the OAU adopted the Lagos Plan of Action triggering a process that culminated in the adoption of the Treaty establishing the African Economic Community, commonly referred as the Abuja Treaty (KOUASSI, 2007; RUPPEL, 2009). While the Abuja process postdates the formation of some of the RECs, its influence on the place of human rights in their operations is evident from the framing of their documents which in some cases almost replicate its provisions (EAST AFRICAN COMMUNITY, 2007, art. 3(g), art. 6 (d)).

Pursuit of African economic integration through the African Economic Community (AEC) is a core project of the OAU/AU. Arguments that economic integration did not take centre stage in the transformation of the OAU into the AU (VILJOEN, 2007, p. 480) notwithstanding, the Constitutive Act of the AU recognises the need to coordinate and harmonize policies between the existing and future RECs for gradual attainment of the objectives of the Union (AFRICAN UNION, 2000, art. 3 (c, l)). This reaffirms the centrality of RECs to AU agenda and their role as economic building blocks within the AU. Alongside other factors (RUPPEL, 2009, p. 275),[3] the

LUCYLINE NKATHA MURUNGI AND JACQUI GALLINETTI

Abuja process can be regarded as the key driver behind both the formation of RECs across the continent,[4] and the inclusion of human rights in the agenda of the RECs.

There are other reasons for the integration of human rights into the mandate of RECs. First, the adoption of the African Charter has made human rights a common feature in interstate relations on the continent (EBOBRAH, 2009a, p. 80). The obligations of states emanating from the Charter and other human rights treaties to which African states are party, oblige them to reflect human rights protection in subsequent commitments such as those arising from REC treaties (THOKO, 2004, p. 112).[5] Second, human rights coupled with good governance create an appropriate investment climate that is critical to furthering economic development (RUPPEL, 2009, p. 279). The adoption of strong human rights values and institutions creates confidence for investors and trading partners and ensures effective participation of individuals.

Finally,

> *international human rights law emphasises the importance of human rights obligations in all areas of governance and development and requires governments and economic policy forums [such as RECs] to take into account human rights principles while formulating national, regional and international economic agendas.*

(OLOKA-ONYANGO; UDAGAMA, 1999, para. 47).

3 Evolution of human rights into the mandate of REC courts[6]

It is evident that in the recent past human rights have become a fundamental component of the task of RECs in Africa. This development can be regarded as a response to the regional agenda as set out in the African Charter and the Abuja Treaty. The mandate of REC courts has also now been extended to cover human rights. However, the approaches adopted by RECs in this regard are dissimilar and uncoordinated. Hence concerns persist as to their suitability as forums for promotion and protection of human rights, the delimitation of such role so as to remain legitimate yet sufficiently utilitarian within the existing frameworks of RECs, and the implications of these new actors on the human rights discourse in the continent.

RECs tend to have an institutional structure that includes a court which is the judicial or principal legal organ of the community to deal with controversies relating to the interpretation or application of the REC's law (RUPPEL, 2009, p. 282). As the organs vested with such responsibility, they have, as a result of the incorporation of human rights into the agenda of RECs, been required to adjudicate over cases, to interpret provisions of their treaties or to advise their principals on questions with implications for human rights. The treaties of most RECs have therefore gradually moved towards according REC courts competence to hear human rights cases (EBOBRAH, 2009a, p. 80).

The evolution of protection of human rights as an agenda of RECs and as part of the jurisdiction of their courts is unique to each one of them, and the approaches adopted in this regard are also different. Thus to trace these developments, it is necessary to look at some of these RECs and their courts in turn.

3.1 Economic Community of the West African States, (ECOWAS)

ECOWAS is a fifteen member group of West African states formed in 1975 to promote economic integration of member states.[7] This scope of co-operation expanded in tandem with the need to respond to issues in the member states which also created an entry point for human rights into the agenda of ECOWAS (EBOBRAH, 2008, p. 7). Its founding Treaty did not contain any references to human rights (EBOBRAH, 2008, p. 9). Gradually however, protocols adopted under the Treaty incorporated different rights in their scope, culminating in the 1991 ECOWAS Declaration of Political Principles which expressed, amongst others, a determination by member states to respect fundamental human rights as embodied in the African Charter.[8] In 1993 the Treaty of ECOWAS was amended to recognise promotion and protection of human and peoples' rights in accordance with the African Charter as a fundamental principle of ECOWAS.[9] The move towards rights consciousness was therefore a combination of necessity and changing international dynamics (NWOGU, 2007, p. 349).

The ECOWAS Community Court of Justice (ECOWAS Court) is the judicial arm (ECONOMIC COMMUNITY OF WEST AFRICAN STATES, 1993, art. 6 (1)(e)) and the principal legal organ (ECONOMIC COMMUNITY OF WEST AFRICAN STATES, 1991b) of ECOWAS. The Protocol to operationalize the ECOWAS Court was adopted in 1991 and amended in 2005 and 2006 respectively[10] to give the ECOWAS Court competence to determine cases of violation of human rights occurring in any of the member states (EBOBRAH, 2009a, p. 86). The ECOWAS Court has since admitted and determined several cases on human rights[11] and is the only of the courts highlighted in this article that has an express mandate over questions of human rights.

3.2 The Southern Africa Development Community, (SADC)

SADC is the Southern Africa sub-regional equivalent of ECOWAS with a current membership of 15 states.[12] The SADC framework of co-operation is based on *inter alia* a guarantee of human rights (SOUTHERN AFRICAN DEVELOPMENT COMMUNITY, 2001, art. 5 (a)(b) (c)(i)(j)(k)) which is also one of the principles of SADC (SOUTHERN AFRICAN DEVELOPMENT COMMUNITY, 2001, art. 4 (c)). The political institution building envisaged by SADC is said to promote economic development into a community based on human rights, democracy and the rule of law (THOKO, 2004, p. 110). However, despite the human rights centred conception of development within the Treaty and the centrality of human rights in its objectives, it is argued that human rights protection under the SADC Treaty has a secondary, almost cursory status (THOKO, 2004, p. 110), and that the promotion and protection of human rights is not the top priority of SADC (RUPPEL, 2009, p. 291).

The SADC Tribunal was established as one of the institutions of SADC (SOUTHERN AFRICAN DEVELOPMENT COMMUNITY, 2001, art. 9 (1), (g)) with the duty to ensure adherence to and proper interpretation of the Treaty and its subsidiary instruments, and to adjudicate disputes referred to it (SOUTHERN AFRICAN DEVELOPMENT COMMUNITY, 2001, art. 16 (1)). The Tribunal has jurisdiction over the interpretation and application of the Treaty, protocols and

LUCYLINE NKATHA MURUNGI AND JACQUI GALLINETTI

subsidiary instruments of SADC and on all matters arising from specific agreements between member states, whether within the community or amongst themselves (SOUTHERN AFRICAN DEVELOPMENT COMMUNITY, 2000, art. 14). However, the provision establishing its jurisdiction omits an express mention of jurisdiction over human rights and therefore it has been argued that the tribunal lacks a clear human rights mandate (EBOBRAH, 2009b, p. 20). Nevertheless, despite the arguments regarding the nature of its jurisdiction over human rights, the SADC Tribunal has thus far heard and determined matters relating to human rights.[13]

The tribunal has the potential to contribute significantly to a deeper harmonisation of law and jurisprudence and to better protection of human rights in SADC. This, however, depends on the commitment of member states and SADC institutions to the enforcement of the tribunal's judgments (RUPPEL, 2009, p. 301) and clarification of the court's jurisdiction over human rights.

3.3 The East Africa Community, (EAC)

Economic integration in post-colonial East Africa dates back to the East African Co-operation Treaty of 1967 concluded between Kenya, Uganda and Tanzania, which later collapsed (ADAR, 2008, p. 2; EAST AFRICAN COMMUNITY, 2007, para. 2 of the Preamble). The EAC was revived in 1999 through the signing of the Treaty Establishing the East Africa Community and its entry into force in 2000. The fundamental principles of the EAC include good governance which entails *amongst others the* recognition, protection and promotion of human and peoples' rights in accordance with the African Charter (EAST AFRICAN COMMUNITY, 2007, art. 6). This provision can be regarded as an entry point for human rights into the EAC. To the extent that the Treaty refers to respect for human rights as a component of good governance, makes reference to aspects of human rights, and even predicates the admission of new members of the community on their human rights record (EAST AFRICAN COMMUNITY, 2007, art. 3 (3)b) then it can be argued that it has incorporated human rights into the treaty (RUPPEL, 2009, p. 277).

The EAC Treaty establishes the East Africa Court of Justice (EACJ) as the judicial organ of the EAC (EAST AFRICAN COMMUNITY, 2007, art. 9) with the responsibility to ensure adherence to law in the interpretation, application of, and compliance with the Treaty (EAST AFRICAN COMMUNITY, 2007, art. 23). The EACJ is vested with an initial jurisdiction over the interpretation and application of the EAC Treaty (EAST AFRICAN COMMUNITY, 2007, art. 27 (1)) and other original, appellate, human rights or other jurisdiction at a subsequent date upon a determination by the Council of Ministers (EAST AFRICAN COMMUNITY, 2007, art. 27 (2)).

Article 27(2) of the EAC Treaty (EAST AFRICAN COMMUNITY, 2007) deals with the jurisdiction of the EACJ. In doing so, reference is made to both an initial as well as 'other jurisdiction as will be determined' by the Council. This indicates that the member states of the EAC intended to develop its jurisdiction in phases (OJIENDA, 2004, p. 95). As a result, the second set of areas of the EACJ's jurisdiction which fall to be determined at a future date (and which includes human rights) is beyond its current jurisdiction. Therefore, in the absence of the relevant determination and adoption of the necessary protocol, it is said that the EACJ does not yet have jurisdiction over human rights (PETER, 2008, p. 210; OJIENDA, 2004, p. 98; EBOBRAH, 2009b, p. 315).[14]

However, the inference of lack of mandate is contested. While some commentators interpret it to mean that the jurisdiction is lacking (RUPPEL, 2009, p. 306),[15] it is also argued that the provision is simply not clear (VILJOEN, 2007, p. 504). The latter view implies the existence of an implied mandate and is backed by several factors including extensive references to human rights under the EAC Treaty and the fact that the EACJ has thus far adjudicated over cases raising human rights questions.[16] Further, exercise of the jurisdiction articles 27(1), 31 and 32 of the EAC Treaty is likely to touch on human rights questions. In these circumstances, the response of the EACJ to issues arising in such instances is of essence in determining whether indeed it has a human rights mandate at all.

Ultimately, the need for a clear provision on the law applicable by the EACJ or for a Protocol as required by article 27(2) is underscored (PETER, 2008, p. 213). This is in view of the fact that the EAC Treaty does not clearly outline the law applicable by the EACJ save for the references made to the principles of the African Charter in the objectives of the EAC (EAST AFRICAN COMMUNITY, 2007, art. 6, 7).

4 Specific issues relating to the human rights mandate of the REC Courts

As highlighted above, the role of RECs in the protection and promotion of human rights in Africa is relatively new. The contribution of REC courts to the protection of rights in Africa notwithstanding, there are concerns in relation to their suitability in this regard and how this impacts on the discourse on human rights in the continent. These concerns are discussed below.

4.1 Relationship of REC courts with the AHRS

A human rights system consists of a set of norms and institutions accepted by states as binding (FREEMAN, 2002, p. 53). Assessed against such a system, the efforts of RECs with respect to human rights fall short of constituting independent human rights systems. This is because despite making extensive references to human rights, they lack corresponding institutions established specifically to deal with human rights. This is the basis of the argument that there are no sub-regional human rights systems existing in Africa but that they are simply sub-regional intergovernmental groupings with human rights as a concern within their mandate (VILJOEN, 2007 p. 10). This may ultimately change if RECs commit to developing the existing initiatives into fully fledged systems. The African Commission on Human and Peoples' Rights (African Commission) at a 2006 brainstorming meeting acknowledged that human rights do not fall under its mandate to the exclusion of the other organs of the AU (AFRICAN COMMISSION ON HUMAN AND PEOPLE'S RIGHTS, 2006, annex 2). This means that the other organs of the AU, including the AEC to which RECs attribute their role, are equally bound to integrate human rights into their mandates and function.

LUCYLINE NKATHA MURUNGI AND JACQUI GALLINETTI

The assertions that the AHRS does not include the role of RECs must be understood to refer to the AHRS as established in the formal documents and institutions of the AU. However, it is submitted that in view of the depth of integration of human rights into the economic and other agenda of the AU, it is difficult to understand human rights in Africa without recognising the role of RECs. It is further arguable that despite the absence of an express linkage between RECs and the AHRS, it is undeniable that RECs sit in a relationship with the AU.

Strengthening the existing RECs and establishing new ones where none exist are the first steps on the road towards the agenda of African economic integration pursued by the AEC.[17] Thus it is argued that RECs as part of the AEC have a duty to respect and promote human rights in their jurisdictions (RUPPEL, 2009, p. 281; AFRICAN UNION, 2000, art. 3 (c), (l)). By analogy, REC courts, to the extent that they preside over matters of human rights, can be deemed to be in an informal relationship with the African Court on Human and Peoples' Rights (African Court) and the African Commission.

A human rights system comprises of a set of norms and institutions accepted by states as binding (FREEMAN, 2002, p. 53). In the AHRS, these are contained in the African Charter and its protocols and the African Charter on the Rights and Welfare of the Child. These treaties establish the African Commission (ORGANISATION OF AFRICAN UNITY, 1986, art. 30), the African Court[18] and the Committee of Experts on the Rights and Welfare of the Child (The Committee)[19] respectively. These bodies promote and protect the rights established under the respective treaties.[20] There are, however, different opinions on the scope of the AHRS. Some scholars restrict it to the foregoing documents and institutions (BENEDEK, 2006, p. 46) while others extend it to include all documents adopted by the AU which relate to an element of human rights (HEYNS, 2004, p. 681).

In 2008, the AU adopted a protocol[21] to establish an African Court of Justice and Human Rights (ACJHR). The statute of the ACJHR is, as at the time of this work, not yet in force pending deposit of the 15th instrument of ratification (AFRICAN UNION, 2008b, art. 60). Once it is in force, the role currently vesting in the African Court will be overtaken by the human rights wing of the ACJHR.[22] Hence this article focuses on the African Court, as opposed to the ACJHR, as the only existing judicial enforcement mechanism of the AHRS.

Entry of RECs into the protection of human rights has led to a complex institutional framework in the region (CHIDI, 2003, p. 3). Creation of REC courts with a human rights competence means that the African Court no longer has a monopoly in the interpretation and enforcement of the African Charter. However, the African Charter does not contemplate the existence of other supra-national courts in Africa (such as REC courts) dealing with human rights. This is explained by the fact that the African Charter predates the entry of RECs in the field on human rights.

As discussed in section 2 above, RECs are the building blocks of the AEC that was established out of the Abuja process. As the AEC is a core project of the AU, a relationship can be said to exist between the AHRS and RECs as institutions established under the auspices of the AU. Hence it is arguably incorrect to treat the AEC and the RECs as distinct systems. It is therefore submitted that the literature and documents of the AHRS have long been overtaken by practice. Nevertheless, this article proceeds on the basis of the formal parameters of the AHRS as described earlier in this section.

4.2 Jurisdictional relationship between REC courts, the African Court and the African Commission

In the absence of any jurisprudence, this relationship may be inferred from the weight that would be accorded to the decisions of REC courts by the African Court and the African Commission. The primary avenue to determine this relationship is to consider the criterion for admissibility of matters before the African Court and Commission as set out in article 56 of the African Charter (VILJOEN, 2008, p. 78). The article raises two issues that could be relevant to the relationship between RECs and the AHRS. These relate to the exhaustion of local remedies and the principle of *res judicata*.

4.2.1 Exhaustion of local remedies

In this regard it is argued that there is no obligation on victims to go to the REC court before submitting their matter to the African Court or the African Commission. The requirement of exhaustion of local remedies is relevant to the relationship between an international/regional court and a state. It is founded on the principle that the national authorities should have an opportunity to remedy the breach within their own jurisdiction (VILJOEN, 2007, p. 336). Local remedies refer to 'the ordinary remedies of common law existing in jurisdictions and normally accessible to persons seeking justice' (AFRICAN COMMISSION ON HUMAN RIGHTS, 2004) as opposed to a supra-national court such as an REC court. Therefore, it is doubtful that the African Commission or African Court could decline to admit a matter on the basis that it has not been heard by the relevant REC court or even that this question might arise at all.

4.2.2 Matters settled by another court or tribunal

Article 56(7) of the African Charter (ORGANISATION OF AFRICAN UNITY, 1986) provides that the African Commission may not admit for consideration cases which have been settled by the states involved in accordance with the principles of the United Nations, the Charter of the OAU or the African Charter. This provision embodies the principle of *res judicata* to the extent that it excludes a matter which has been 'settled by the states' involved (VILJOEN, 2007 p. 340). It however does not preclude the consideration of matters that are before another judicial or quasi-judicial forum, and hence leaves an opening for judicial forum shopping. In the absence of a prohibition of concurrent proceedings on the basis of the principle of *lis pendens* in the 'other forum', it is possible for a litigant to institute concurrent proceedings before a REC court and the African Commission or Court (VILJOEN, 2007, p. 340).

LUCYLINE NKATHA MURUNGI AND JACQUI GALLINETTI

The concern that this raises is whether one whose cause has been heard and determined by a REC court can approach the African Commission or Court for redress in the same case. This depends on both the provisions of each REC regarding the finality of their decisions, and the approach of the African Court or Commission to such matters. However, it is submitted that to allow an unsuccessful litigant at the sub-regional level to pursue a remedy at the regional level would be tantamount to establishing the African Court as an appellate body, which it is not. Helfer makes a similar argument in respect of the European Court of Human Rights and the UN Human Rights Committee (HELFER, 1999, p. 285).[23]

The approaches adopted by different RECs on the relationship of their courts with the African Court vary.[24] For instance, article 38 of the EAC Treaty provides that a dispute referred to the EACJ cannot be settled by any other method other than that established under the Treaty. This implies finality of the decisions of the EACJ. The Protocol of the SADC tribunal on the other hand is explicit that the decisions of the SADC Tribunal are final and binding (SOUTHERN AFRICAN DEVELOPMENT COMMUNITY, 2000, art. 24 (3)). Difficulty arises where there is no finality clause because in that case it has to be determined whether REC courts are forums for dispute settlement in terms of the principles of the UN Charter, the OAU or the African Charter (VILJOEN, 2007, p. 339).

The Charter of the OAU encourages peaceful settlement of disputes through non-judicial means (ORGANISATION OF AFRICAN UNITY, 1963, art. 7 (4))[25] but this does not proscribe judicial means. The provision is not specific to human rights cases, but the recurrent theme is peaceful settlement. To the extent that international judicial settlement is considered a means for the peaceful settlement of disputes (ALFORD, 2000, p. 160), coupled with the presence of finality clauses in the REC treaties, there is potential that the decisions of the REC tribunals could completely oust the jurisdiction of the African Commission and the Court by virtue of article 56(7) of the African Charter.

4.3 Regional and sub-regional human rights mechanisms – the merits and de-merits

Whether or not the proliferation of REC courts may be deemed a blessing or a liability depends partly on its relative advantage or disadvantage over the existing regional mechanisms. There is a general underlying assumption that REC tribunals are favourable forums and an illustration of state commitment to the cause of human rights. But certain issues hold sway on the practical benefit of one relative to the other. These include but are not limited to accessibility, enforcement, the quality of jurisprudence, responsiveness to the peculiar needs of a region, potential for better standards of rights and the capacity to complement existing mechanisms.

First, it is argued that RECs (as opposed to regional mechanisms) are better suited to address sub-region specific issues. The small number of states constituting RECs allows them to address the issues with particular detail to its peculiar circumstances. Also, the notoriety of certain issues in a sub-region necessitates the development of jurisprudence on them in a manner that may

THE ROLE OF SUB-REGIONAL COURTS IN THE AFRICAN HUMAN RIGHTS SYSTEM

not have been considered at the regional level. In addition, the judges of a REC court are likely to have a better appreciation of the issues affecting a sub-region than those at the broader regional level.

Second, in as far as enforcement is concerned, the African Court has the capacity to make binding decisions[26] but it has not really presided over any matter yet.[27] The African Commission on the other hand, despite regularly deciding on human rights complaints submitted to it, does not render binding decisions. In these circumstances, it could be argued that the binding decisions (EAST AFRICAN COMMUNITY 2007, art. 35) of REC courts are the best alternative for enforcement of rights. However, the difficulty of enforcing the decisions of international courts arising from the consensual nature of international law equally affects REC courts. As with international courts, REC courts lack institutions with power to compel states to comply with its orders (EBOBRAH, 2009a, p. 96). For instance the government of Zimbabwe expressed its intention not to comply with the judgment of the SADC tribunal in the *Campbell* case (SOUTHERN AFRICAN DEVELOPMENT COMMUNITY TRIBUNAL, 2007; RUPPEL, 2009, p. 300). The only point of recourse for the SADC Tribunal in such circumstance is to refer the finding of non-compliance to the Summit of Heads of States or Governments (SOUTHERN AFRICAN DEVELOPMENT COMMUNITY, 2000, art. 32 (5)). Interestingly, an attempt has been made in recent times to enforce a decision of the SADC Tribunal against Zimbabwe in the South African national courts.[28] This is a seemingly novel approach to judicial enforcement of supra-national decisions and the outcome of the case will be instructive regarding the prospects of success of such endeavours.

The third issue for discussion relates to the accessibility of courts. Accessibility may be classified in two categories: physical accessibility and capacity to bring a matter before the forum. With respect to the former, the geographical proximity of REC courts to the victims of rights violations in some cases makes it easier for the victims to approach the court. In this way, the REC courts are more responsive to the needs of the victims. In practical terms, it means less travel cost and ease of litigation especially with respect to witness appearances (NWOGU, 2007, p. 354). While it is recognised that the Interim Rules of Procedure of the African Commission allow it to sit in the state of origin of the claim (AFRICAN UNION, 2008a, art. 30), in the practice of the African Commission however, matters are heard during its sessions which mostly take place in Banjul, the Gambia (VILJOEN, 2007, p. 313). Besides, hosting the sessions has financial implications for the host state thus it is not an attractive option. On this basis, REC courts are a more accessible forum for a victim of rights violations.

Regarding the right to be heard, most REC courts allow individuals direct access (VILJOEN, 2007, p. 507). This contrasts access to the African Court which is subject to the consent of the state concerned, effected by declaration accepting the competence of the Court in terms of article 34(6) of the Protocol on the African Court (AFRICAN UNION, 2004, art. 5(3)). As of December 2010, only four states had tendered such a declaration[29] to allow individual communications. Also, some of the REC treaties admit cases without the need for exhaustion of local remedies[30] thereby making it easy for individuals to access the court.

LUCYLINE NKATHA MURUNGI AND JACQUI GALLINETTI

Fourth, there is concern with respect to the capacity of the REC Courts to perform their protective functions regarding human rights effectively. RECs have demonstrated the intention to accord human rights a place in their agenda, but their capacity to achieve this goal is doubtful within the existing frameworks. Whereas there are extensive provisions on the duty of the REC member states to protect rights, it has been argued that there are no corresponding institutions to oversee the performance of these obligations or to drive the agenda of human rights in the REC (THOKO, 2004, p. 111).[31] There is the potential for human rights to become secondary to the economic interests in the day to day business of the REC (LAMIN, 2008, p. 233). This could mean that the REC courts are more focused on the other functions of the REC at the expense of the development of human rights jurisprudence.

Most of the REC courts have a combined jurisdiction, doubling as courts of justice and of human rights (RUPPEL, 2009, p. 307). This vast responsibility and a corresponding small number of judges appointed to the various courts raise questions as to whether these courts are sufficiently equipped to competently discharge their dual responsibilities. A further concern relates to the human rights competence of the judges of REC courts to determine human rights matters. Whereas the appointment of judges at the regional level of the AHRS emphasises their competence in respect of human rights (AFRICAN UNION, 2004, art. 11 (1), 2008b, art. 4), there is no corresponding emphasis on a human rights competence for the appointment of judges to the REC courts (EAST AFRICAN COMMUNITY, 2007, art. 24 (1)).

Despite the foregoing concerns, through litigation before REC courts and the harmonisation of legislation in the member states, there is growing jurisprudence on human rights in the respective sub-regions. In addition, the deliberations emanating from these forums are essential in enriching the human rights discourse in the sub-regions and hence empowering the citizens. Furthermore, the judicial emphasis on respect for human rights emanating from REC treaty obligations serves to create pressure on the member states to adhere to higher standards of rights.

Finally, most RECs in Africa recognise the African Charter as the minimum standard on human rights for the region, hence any attempts at the protection of rights within the RECs would have to build upon those contained in the African Charter (VILJOEN, 2007, p. 500). However, in view of the fact that there is not yet a human rights catalogue in any of the RECs considered in this article, this inference can be deemed speculative. On the other hand the evolution of rights into the agenda of the RECs may reveal disparate approaches to the incorporation of human rights into the mandate of REC courts. These differences would possibly translate into varying degrees of protection in each of the sub-regions. This in turn exposes the entire region to disparate standards and makes it difficult to reach a common African human rights standard. This places in question the competence of the RECs as building blocks to an effective regional human rights mechanism.

The foregoing factors would persist even after the establishment of the ACJHR (NWOGU, 2007, p. 354) and therefore, there is a strong case for the continued development of a human rights competence for REC courts and tribunals.

4.4 The proliferation of supranational human rights courts in Africa

The dramatic increase in the number of international judicial bodies represents what is referred to as the proliferation of international courts and tribunals (SHANY, 2003, p. 5). This phenomenon is neither unique to Africa nor specific to REC courts. Rather, it is global, attributable to both the nature of international law and the recent development in the field of international law (OELLERS-FRAHM, 2001, p. 71).[32] The ramifications of this phenomenon on the protection of human rights in Africa raise some issues for consideration.

Firstly, in the absence of properly coordinated judicial integration on the continent, it is argued that multiplicity of courts poses a threat to the unity of international human rights law in the region through the establishment of separate uncoordinated systems of international human rights standards and norms in different parts of Africa. This in turn creates the potential for varied interpretations of substantive and procedural human rights norms in the different sub-regions. Whereas it is highly probable that there will be disaggregated jurisprudence emerging from the different REC courts, it is submitted that the real problem is the lack of a systematically coordinated or defined relationship between the different REC courts rather than the issue of multiplicity of courts. Such structural organisation demands the existence of a normative or institutional hierarchy or system established under each relevant treaty.

As stipulated above, RECs do not form part of the AHRS *per se,* hence the threat of disintegration is very real. In addition, the varied approaches of REC courts towards the African Charter impacts on the unity of jurisprudence. For instance the use of the African Charter as a rights catalogue for a REC court as in the case of the ECOWAS Court coupled with a finality clause creates the possibility of variant interpretations of the same provision at regional and REC level. Currently only the EAC proposes a separate rights catalogue, and it may happen that the rights that will be contained therein may be similar in content to rights in the African Charter. Should this occur, there is the potential for the EACJ to decide a case on the same legal basis and reasoning as the African Court but derived from a different normative source and with no obligation to refer to either the African Commissiom or Court. Having said this, there is no guarantee that there would be a similar reasoning or outcome and likewise there is also a possibility that no conflict may arise.

Nevertheless, it is noted that it is difficult to point at an instance in practice where an REC court or the African Commission contradicted one another. On the contrary, REC courts have often referred to the jurisprudence of the African Commission with approval to aid their decisions.[33] This implies that there is an informal inter-fora respect and interaction. However, it would be important to have this relationship institutionalised to lessen the possibility of subjectivity.

Secondly the proliferation of courts could lead to the overlap of jurisdiction of various courts and the possibility of conflicting decisions on the same law. It is argued that the availability of several judicial forums that have concurrent jurisdiction creates an opportunity for human rights practitioners to pursue the

LUCYLINE NKATHA MURUNGI AND JACQUI GALLINETTI

most favourable option or to institute several proceedings in the various forums. In the current context, it would entail a choice between one REC court over another or a REC court[34] and the African Court or Commission. This type of forum shopping is generally regarded in a negative light due to its potential to undermine the authority of the courts, generate conflicting decisions and create possibilities for endless litigation (HELFER, 1999, p. 286-287).[35]

The concern regarding forum shopping can, in as far as human rights are concerned in Africa, be regarded as perceived rather than real. Certain other factors mitigate the potency of this threat such as the indigence of most victims of rights violations (HELFER, 1999, p. 287),[36] and geographical distance from the court. On the other hand, Helfer also argues that if well regulated, forum shopping can materially benefit international human rights law. For instance, forum shopping encourages jurists to dialogue on norms shared in the cross- cutting treaties thereby encouraging the development of jurisprudence. However, in view of the overlapping membership of African states in various RECs (RUPPEL, 2009, p. 283) and the possibility of conflicting decisions, it would be advisable to regulate the practice.[37]

5 The implications of the human rights mandate of the REC courts

This article identifies three critical issues that arise from the human rights mandate of the REC courts: their jurisdictional competence; the normative framework in which they operate, and their location within the structural framework of the AHRS. Each of these is discussed in more detail below.

5.1 Jurisdictional competence

Jurisdiction is a legal term referring to either a power or competence to exercise authority over a legally defined relationship between the subjects (EVANS; CAPPS; KONSTADINIDIS, 2003, p. xix). It creates a capacity to generate legal norms and to alter the position of those subject to such norms (ALEXY, 2002 p. 132). It also refers to the power of a court to determine a case before it in terms of an instrument either creating it or defining the jurisdiction (CHENG, 2006, p. 259). The terms competence and jurisdiction are so deeply intertwined that they are often used interchangeably (KOROMA, 2003, p. 189). But subtle distinctions can be made between the two, such as that while jurisdiction relates to a court's capacity to decide a concrete case with final and binding force, competence regards the propriety of the exercise of such jurisdiction (ROSENNE, 1997, p. 536). A tribunal is generally incompetent to act beyond its jurisdiction (CHENG, 2006, p. 259).

Various approaches have been adopted in defining the jurisdiction of REC courts with respect to human rights. Mainly, such competence is either expressly established by treaty or the specific intention of the state parties to the treaty is not clearly set out. However, despite seemingly clear distinctions between the approaches, the existence of jurisdiction is a matter of interpretation in each case especially where it is not expressly stated.

5.1.1 Express versus implied mandates

Of the three REC courts referred to in this article, the ECOWAS Court is said to have an express human rights mandate (EBOBRAH, 2009a, p. 80). With respect to the EACJ and the SADC Tribunal, the answer is not so obvious though the general inclination is that they have an implied mandate (RUPPEL, 2009, p. 307). It is reported that inclusion of a specific human rights mandate for the SADC Tribunalwas discussed and rejected, with a panel of experts mandated to draft a proposal for the tribunal preferring a general jurisdiction with respect to human rights (VILJOEN, 2007, p. 505). The absence of express provisions notwithstanding, both the EACJ and the SADC tribunal have decided cases that impact on human rights issues.[38]

While the two tribunals are often collectively said to lack express jurisdiction over human rights (EBOBRAH, 2009a, p. 80), a subtle but critical distinction must be made between their provisions regarding human rights. The Protocol on SADC Tribunal is silent on the human rights mandate of the tribunal.[39] The EAC Treaty on the other hand expressly excludes such jurisdiction until the adoption of a Protocol to expand the jurisdiction of the EACJ to human rights (EAST AFRICAN COMMUNITY, 2007, art. 27 (2)). In effect, while the silence of the SADC Protocol can be interpreted as indifference on the subject, legitimacy of the exercise of a human rights jurisdiction by the EACJ is even more precarious.

The exercise or assertion of jurisdiction rests on a quest for legitimacy to be found in the expression of state consent (KOROMA, 2003, p. 198). Legitimacy of the court's actions is circumscribed by the bounds of its authority. It affects the response of the parties to the decision rendered; if such decision is deemed to exceed the power of the court, it is unlikely to be enforced effectively. Absence of an express jurisdiction leaves it upon the court and the parties to delimit the scope of the courts authority. This opens an opportunity for subjectivity and conservativism that could injure genuine pursuit of redress.

In *Katabazi and 21 others v Secretary General of the East African Community and another* (EAST AFRICAN COURT OF JUSTICE, 2007), the applicants were part of a group of 21 charged with treason and misprision of treason. The application claimed *inter alia* a breach of articles 6, 7(2) and 8 (1) (c) of the EAC treaty relative to the fundamental principles of the EAC, the operational principles thereof and the general undertaking of the states to implement the EAC Treaty. Counsel for the applicants requested the EACJ to regard the matter as an application for determination of whether the conduct of the state of Uganda was in breach of a fundamental principle of the EAC. Counsel for the respondent on the other hand argued that the claims of the applicants related to a question of human rights over which the EACJ did not have jurisdiction by virtue of article 27(2) of the EAC Treaty.

In response to the question of its jurisdiction, the EACJ stated as follows

> *Does this Court have jurisdiction to deal with human rights issues? The quick answer is: No it does not have......It is very clear that jurisdiction with respect to human rights requires a determination of the Council and a conclusion of a Protocol to that effect.*

LUCYLINE NKATHA MURUNGI AND JACQUI GALLINETTI

> *Both of those steps have not been taken. It follows, therefore, that this Court may not adjudicate on disputes concerning violation of human rights per se.*

Yet it continued,

> *While the Court will not assume jurisdiction to adjudicate on human rights disputes, it will not abdicate from exercising its jurisdiction of interpretation under Article 27 (1) merely because the reference includes allegation of human rights violation.*
> (EAST AFRICAN COMMUNITY, 2007, art. 27 (1)). [40]

On this basis, the EACJ found that the principle of the rule of law, a fundamental principle of the community, had been breached.

    The decision of the court to deal with the matter in the face of an express exclusion of its jurisdiction over human rights is nothing short of extreme judicial activism, skewed towards a usurpation of legislative functions (EBOBRAH, 2009a, p. 82). Yet, if the court had determined otherwise, it would indeed have 'abdicated itself' from performing a duty with which it is vested in terms of the treaty; that to interpret a provision of the Treaty. Therein lies the dilemma of courts whose express mandate does not sufficiently cover the scope of its functions. The capacity of a court to address an issue is circumscribed by the scope of its mandate. Hence a clear articulation of the mandate of the EACJ is necessary to avoid this impasse.

    During the hearing of the main application in the *Campbell* case[41] the respondent contested the jurisdiction of the SADC Tribunal arguing that in the absence of a rights protocol, the tribunal had no jurisdiction over human rights. In response, the SADC Tribunal stated that stipulation of human rights, democracy and the rule of law as a principle of SADC sufficed to grant it jurisdiction over matters of human rights, democracy and rule of law. Though the mandate of SADC Tribunal is not expressly excluded as in the case of the EAC, it is clear that this omission gave an opportunity for contestation and is hence undesirable.

    In *Olajide v Nigeria* (ECONOMIC COMMUNITY OF WEST AFRICAN STATES, 2004) the ECOWAS Court declined to adjudicate over questions of human rights arguing that its protocol did not confer such jurisdiction. The matter arose prior to the 2005 amendment of the Protocol relating to the ECOWAS Court which vested the court with jurisdiction over human rights and allowed individual access to the court. The decision was taken despite the existence of 'sufficient human rights content in the constitutional and other legislative instruments of ECOWAS' (EBOBRAH, 2008, p. 17). It was argued that where the meaning of the treaty was clear, the court would apply it as such (ECONOMIC COMMUNITY OF WEST AFRICAN STATES, 2004, para. 53-54). The decision has been criticised as shying away from activism in that case since nothing in the Protocol prevented the admission of the matter (VILJOEN, 2007, p. 507). Thus, in light of this case, the benefit of an express mandate is clear.

    The foregoing cases illustrate three main issues underlying the exercise of an implied jurisdiction. First, the exercise of such jurisdiction can be interpreted as exceeding the authority of the court and therefore compromise the legitimacy of the decision. It also makes the scope of the power of the court elusive. Secondly, it creates an opening for litigious contestation of the courts authority thereby lengthening the

THE ROLE OF SUB-REGIONAL COURTS IN THE AFRICAN HUMAN RIGHTS SYSTEM

process unnecessarily which is undesirable for human rights litigation. Lastly, it accords discretion to the judicial officers to determine the court's competence. This introduces subjectivity and in the face of a conservative bench, the likelihood that such matters may not be admitted. This is for instance clear when the decisions of the EAC and the ECOWAS Court in *Katabazi* (EAST AFRICAN COURT OF JUSTICE, 2007) and *Olajide* (ECONOMIC COMMUNITY OF WEST AFRICAN STATES, 2004) are contrasted.

In light of the foregoing factors, it can be concluded that an implied mandate for human rights, whilst not absolutely barring exercise of jurisdiction, does not achieve optimum protection for rights and is inconsistent with the commitment of RECs to protection of human rights evident in their founding documents.

5.2 Normative framework

This refers to the body of law applied by REC courts in dispensing their obligations under their respective treaties and which defines the values and goals pursued by the REC and the primary rules that impose duties on actors to perform or abstain from actions (DIEHL; KU; ZAMORA, 2003, p. 51). The normative sources applied by REC courts in exercise of the human rights mandate vary from one REC to the next. For instance, the literal reading of article 21 of the SADC Protocol on the Tribunal implies sufficiency to direct the tribunal on what law to apply. With respect to human rights, however, the answer is not as obvious. The SADC treaty establishes an obligation for states to abide by the principle of human rights, democracy and the rule of law. But the normative source of such standards is not specified.

Similarly, article 27(2) of the EAC Treaty can be interpreted to mean that the law to be applied by the EACJ with respect to human rights will be defined in the Protocol that will expand the court's jurisdiction. However, the EAC Treaty establishes 'recognition, promotion and protection of human rights in accordance with the provisions of the African Charter as a fundamental principle of the EAC (EAST AFRICAN COMMUNITY, 2007, art. 6 (d)). Hence, a determination of whether a state party is in breach of the treaty would inevitably entail a determination of whether or not the conduct is a breach of the African Charter. That demands an enquiry into the substantive content of the rights. Nevertheless, it is submitted that this does not suffice to establish the African Charter as a normative source or standard of rights in the EAC.

5.2.1 The African Charter as a rights catalogue for REC courts

It has been suggested that in view of the wide recognition of the African Charter as a standard for rights in the RECs, it can be employed as the normative source of rights for REC courts as all the AU members are party to the African Charter (VILJOEN, 2007, p. 500). It is further argued that the development of 'distinct sub-regional human rights standards, such as the SADC Charter of Fundamental Social Rights, is likely to accentuate differences, [thereby] undermining the movement towards African unity and legal integration' (VILJOEN, 2007, p. 501). These arguments are founded on an assumption that the RECs recognize the African Charter as a standard for rights. Notably however, the SADC Treaty does not make any reference to the African

LUCYLINE NKATHA MURUNGI AND JACQUI GALLINETTI

Charter. But this does not mean that failure to refer to it implies disaccord with its provisions. Indeed, in the *Campbell* case, the SADC Tribunal referred to the African Charter extensively and even relied on the jurisprudence of the African Commission.

The interpretation and enforcement of the African Charter is a function of the African Commission and the African Court. The suggestion of its application by REC courts would create another forum for interpretation and enforcement. Recalling the absence of judicial hierarchy, the use of finality clauses with respect to the decisions of REC courts, the exclusion of REC courts from the formal structure of the AHRS and lack of judicial coordination in the region, the inevitable result of this suggestion is a replication of forums with a similar mandate and a real chance of conflicting decisions. It does not hold promise for addressing the threats to the unity of human rights law in the region.

The use of the African Charter as a rights catalogue blurs the normative hierarchy between the regional and sub-regional human rights instruments that underlies the intention of the eventual unification at the regional level. Such hierarchy is implicit in judicial order and is an invaluable asset for the AHRS. Thus the argument for the African Charter as a rights catalogue for the RECs is not as obviously advantageous as some authors contend.

In supporting his argument for the African Charter as a rights catalogue for RECs, Viljoen observes that separate cataloguing of human rights is likely to accentuate differences and undermine integration (VILJOEN, 2007, p. 500). However, it is submitted that the possibility of accentuating differences is adequately mitigated by the recognition of the African Charter and other international standards of human rights as a normative minimum. For instance the draft East African Bill of Rights (PETER, 2008, p. 336)[42] has extensive provisions covering both the rights established under the African Charter and beyond. If adopted, it would present better protection than the African Charter. In the case of SADC, there are differences of opinion on whether the SADC Charter of Fundamental Social Rights can be deemed as a rights catalogue for the SADC Tribunal (VILJOEN, 2007, p. 500; RUPPEL, 2009, p. 295-296).

5.3 Structural framework

The structural framework refers to the institutional organisation of the AHRS. A system is a purposeful arrangement of interrelated elements or components which cannot be adequately described and understood in isolation from one another (SHANY, 2003, p. 78). It has been established in the preceding sections that REC courts are not formally recognised as part of the AHRS. A concern arises regarding the relationship between the REC courts and the institutions established at the regional level, and how the AHRS institutional framework can be modified (if at all) to accommodate the role of REC courts.

Generally RECs do not constitute independent human rights systems (VILJOEN, 2007, p. 10). They are created for the pursuit of economic integration and the promotion and protection of human rights is barely incidental to that main purpose. Furthermore, they do not have institutions specifically tailored towards the performance of human rights functions. If RECs indeed fall short of independent human rights systems in Africa, then, in order for them to achieve the optimum protection of rights as envisaged in their respective documents they need either to fully develop their institutions to a fully fledged system or to align with a better co-ordinated and institutionally established system, namely the AHRS.

6 Conclusion

The significance of the role played by REC courts in the protection of human rights in the Africa today cannot be denied. It is a reflection of a renewed commitment by African states to the realisation of human rights in the region. It also points to the fact that the traditional human rights institutional framework in the region has long been overtaken by practice. The formal parameters of the AHRS do not adequately cater for the role of RECs in the field of human rights. This deprives the region of the benefits of the coordinated development of protective mechanisms that would create an optimum environment for the protection of rights. Though there are numerous problems associated with the emerging role of RECs in the protection of human rights, there is an equal wealth of benefits to be reaped from their work. The problems highlighted in this article render themselves to a solution through proper delimitation of the role of REC courts and restructuring of the system to take cognisance of the recent developments.

Whether or not the region stands to benefit from the role of these new players is almost entirely dependent on the willingness of states to revisit the AHRS and to align the operations of the RECs with the regional framework.

REFERENCES

Bibliography and Other Sources

ADAR, K. 2008. **Federalism and East Africa Community Integration Process:** The Role of the East African Legislative Assembly. Bordeaux-France: Paper prepared for presentation at CIGI/GARNET Conference on Mapping Integration and Regionalism in a Global World: The EU and Regional Governance outside EU.

AFRICAN COMMISSION ON HUMAN AND PEOPLE'S RIGHTS. 2006. **Report of the Brain Storming Meeting of the African Commission on Human and Peoples' Rights.** Banjul, The Gambia.

AJULU, R. (Ed.). 2005. **The making of a Region: Revival of the East Africa Community.** Midrand: Institute for Global Dialogue.

ALEXY, R. 2002. **Theory of Constitutional Rights.** Oxford: Oxford Press.

ALFORD, R. 2000. The proliferation of international courts and tribunals; international adjudication in ascendance. **American Society of International Law Proceedings,** v.94, p. 160-165.

BENEDEK, W. (Ed.). 2006. **Understanding human rights: manual on human rights education** Antwerpen: Intersentia.

LUCYLINE NKATHA MURUNGI AND JACQUI GALLINETTI

CHENG, B. 2006. **General Principles of Law as applied by International Courts and Tribunals**. Cambridge: Cambridge University Press.

CHIDI, A.O. 2003. **Complementary, competition, contradiction: the relationship between the African Court on Human and People's Rights and regional courts in East and Southern Africa. Gaborone-Botswana**: Paper presented to the conference of Eastern and Southern African States on the Protocol Establishing the African Court on Human and Peoples' Rights.

DIEHL, P.F.; KU, C. 2003. The dynamics of international law: the interaction of normative and operating systems. In: _____. (Ed.). **International Law**: Classic and Contemporary Readings. 2nd ed. Boulder: Lynne Rienner Publishers.

DIEHL, P.; KU, C.; ZAMORA D. 2003. The Dynamics of International Law: The Interaction of Normative and Operating Systems. **Cambridge University Press Journal**, v. 57, n. 1, p. 43-75.

EBOBRAH, S.T. 2008. **A critical analysis of the human rights mandate of ECOWAS Community Court of Justice**. Copenhagen: Danish Institute for Human Rights.

_____. 2009a. Litigating human rights before sub-regional courts in Africa: prospects and challenges. **African Journal of International and Comparative Law**, v.17, n.1, p. 79-101.

_____. 2009b. Human rights developments in sub-regional courts in Africa in 2008. **Africa Human Rights Law Journal**, v.9, n.1, p.312 - 335.

ECONOMIC COMMISSION FOR AFRICA. 2006. **Assessing Regional Integration in Africa II:** Rationalizing Regional Economic Communities. Addis Ababa: Economic Commission for Africa.

EVANS, M.; CAPPS, P.; KONSTADINIDIS, S. (Ed.). 2003. **Asserting jurisdiction:** international and European legal perspectives. Oxford: Hart Publishing.

EVANS, M.; MURRAY, R. (Ed.). 2008. **The African Charter on Human and Peoples' Rights**. 2nd ed. Cambridge: Cambridge University Press.

FREEMAN, M. 2002. **Human Rights: An Interdisciplinary Approach**. Cambridge: Cambridge University Press, Polity

HELFER, L. 1999. Forum Shopping for Human Rights. **University of Pennsylvania Law Review**, v. 148, n. 2, p. 285-400.

HEYNS, C. 2004. The African regional human rights system: The African Charter. _Pennsylvania State Law Review_, _v._ 108, n. 3, p. 679-702.

HEYNS, C.; KILLANDER, M. (Ed.). 2007. **Compendium of Key Human Rights Documents of the African Union**. 3rd ed. Pretoria: Pretoria University Law Press.

KOROMA, A. 2003. Asserting Jurisdiction by the International Court of Justice. In: EVANS, M.; CAPPS, P.; KONSTADINIDIS, S. (Ed.). **Asserting jurisdiction:** international and European legal perspectives. Oxford: Hart Publishing.

KOUASSI, R.N. 2007. The itinerary of the African integration process: an overview of the historic landmarks. **Africa Integration Review**, v. 1, n. 2, p. 1-23.

LAMIN, A.R. 2008. African sub-regional human rights courts: The ECOWAS Court of Justice, the SADC Tribunal and the EAC Court of Justice in comparative perspective. In: AKOKPARI, J.; ZIMBLER, D.S. (Ed.). **African Human Rights Architecture**. Johannesburg: Jacana Media.

LOLETTE, K. N. 2005. **Regional integration: concepts, advantages, disadvantages and lessons of experience.** Available at: <http://www.sarpn.org.za/documents/d0001249/P1416-RI-concepts_May2005.pdf>. Last accessed on: 5 Sept. 2009.

NWOGU, N. 2007. Regional integration as an instrument of human rights; re-conceptualizing ECOWAS. **Journal of Human Rights**, v. 6, n. 3, p. 345-360.

OELLERS-FRAHM, K. 2001. Multiplication of international courts and tribunals and conflicting jurisdiction – problems and possible solutions. In: FROWEIN, JOCHEN ABR. AND WOLFRUM, RÜDIGER (Ed.). **Max Planck Year Book of the United Nations Law.** The Hague: Kluwer Law International. v. 5. p. 67-104.

OJIENDA, T.O. 2004. Alice's adventures in wonderland: preliminary reflections on the jurisdiction of the East African Court of Justice. **East African Journal of Human Rights and Democracy**, v. 2, n. 2, p. 94.

OLOKA-ONYANGO, J.; UDAGAMA, D. 1999. **Human rights as the primary objective of international trade, investment and finance policy and practice.** United Nations: UN Doc.E/CN.4/Sub.2.

PETER, C.M. (Ed.). 2008. **The protectors: human rights commissions and accountability in East Africa.** Kampala: Fountain Publishers.

ROSENNE, S. 1997. **The law and practice of the International Court 1920 -1996.** The Hague: Martinus Nijhoff.

RUPPEL, O. 2009. Regional economic communities and human rights in East and Southern Africa. In: BÖSL, A.; DIESCHO, J. (Ed.). **Human Rights Law in Africa:** Legal perspectives on their Protection and Promotion. Windhoek: McMillan Education.

SA TO CHALLENGE Zim land ruling. 2010. **News24.com**, 2 Apr. 2010. Available at: <http://www.news24.com/SouthAfrica/News/SA-to-challenge-Zim-land-ruling-20100402>. Last accessed on: 23 June 2010.

SHANY, Y. 2003. **The competing jurisdiction of international courts and tribunals.** Oxford: Oxford University Press.

THOKO, K. 2004. SADC and human rights: fitting human rights into the trade matrix. **African Security Review**, v. 13, n. 1, p. 109-117.

VILJOEN, F. 2007. **International Human Rights Law in Africa.** Oxford: Oxford University Press.

_____. 2008. Communications under the African Charter: procedure and admissibility. In: EVANS, M.; MURRAY, R. (Ed.). **The African Charter on Human and Peoples' Rights.** 2nd ed. Cambridge: Cambridge University Press.

Jurisprudence

AFRICAN COMMISSION ON HUMAN AND PEOPLES' RIGHTS. 2000. Communication N.140/94 **Constitutional Rights Project and Others v Nigeria.** Africa Human Rights Law Reports 227

_____. 2004. Communication N.242/2001, **Interights and others v Mauritania** (2004) Africa Human Rights Law Report 87.

_____. 2006. Communication N. 245/2002 **Zimbabwe Human Rights NGO Forum v Zimbabwe.** Africa Human Rights Law Reports 128.

LUCYLINE NKATHA MURUNGI AND JACQUI GALLINETTI

AFRICAN COURT ON HUMAN AND PEOPLE'S RIGHTS. 2008. Application N. 001/2008. **Michelot Yogombaye v The Republic of Senegal.** Unreported

AFRICAN ECONOMIC COMMUNITY. 1991. **Treaty Establishing the African Economic Community.**

AFRICAN UNION. 2000. **Constitutive Act of the African Union.** 2000/2001.

_____. 2004. **Protocol to the African Charter on Human and Peoples' Rights on the Establishment of an African Court on Human and Peoples' Rights.**

_____. 2008a. **Interim Rules of Procedure of the African Commission on Human and Peoples' Rights.** Available at: <www.achpr.org/english/other/Interim Rules/Interim Rules of Procedure.pdf>. Last accessed on: Nov. 2010.

_____. 2008b. **Protocol on the Statute of the African Court of Justice and Human Rights.**

EAST AFRICA COURT OF JUSTICE. 2006. N. 1 of 2006. **Nyong'o and 10 others v The Attorney General of Kenya and others.**

_____. 2007. N. 1 of 2007. **Katabazi and 21 others v Secretary General of the EAC and another.**

EAST AFRICAN COMMUNITY. 2005. **Draft Protocol to Operationalize the Extended Jurisdiction of the East Africa Court of Justice.**

_____. 2007. Amended **Treaty for the Establishment of the East Africa Community.** 14 December 2006 and 20 August 2007.

_____. s.d. **Draft East African Bill of Rights.**

ECONOMIC COMMUNITY OF WEST AFRICAN STATES (ECOWAS). 1975. **Treaty of the Economic Community of West African States.**

_____. 1991a. **Declaration of Political Principles of the Economic Community of West African States.**

_____. 1991b. **Protocol on the Community Court of Justice** A/P.1/7/91

_____. 1993. **Economic Community of West African States Revised Treaty.**

_____. 2004. Court of Justice. Unreported Suit no. 2004/ECW/CCJ/04. **Afolabi Olajide v Federal Republic of Nigeria.**

_____. 2005a. **Supplementary Protocol** A/SP.1/01/05 Amending Protocol A/P.1/7/91 on the Community Court of Justice.

_____. 2005b. **Ugokwe v Nigeria and Others.**

_____. 2007a. **Kéiita and Another v Mali.**

_____. 2007b. **Essein v The Republic of the Gambia.** Africa Human Rights Law Reports 131.

_____. 2008a. **Manneh v The Gambia.** Africa Human Rights Law Journal 171.

_____. 2008b. **Karou v Niger.** African Human Rights Law Journal 182.

_____. 2009. Suit N. ECW/CCJ/APP/0808 **Registered Trustees of Socio-Economic Rights and Accountability Project (SERAP) v Federal Republic of Nigeria and Another.**

ORGANISATION OF AFRICAN UNITY. 1963. **Charter of the Organization of African Unity.**

_____. 1980. **Lagos Plan of Action for the Economic Development of Africa.**

_____. 1986. **African Charter on Human and Peoples' Rights.** 1981/1986.

_____. 1990. **African Charter on the Rights and Welfare of the Child.** 1990/1999.

SOUTH AFRICA. 2009. North Gauteng High Court Case No. 77881/2009. **Louis Karel Fick & Others v Government of the Republic of Zimbabwe (Unreported).**

SOUTHERN AFRICAN DEVELOPMENT COMMUNITY. 2000. **SADC Protocol on the Tribunal and Rule of Procedure Thereof.**

_____. 2001. **Amended Declaration and Treaty of the Southern African Development Community.**

_____. 2003. **Charter of Fundamental Social Rights in the Southern African Development Community.**

SOUTHERN AFRICAN DEVELOPMENT COMMUNITY TRIBUNAL (SADC Tribunal). 2007. Case Number. 2/2007. **Mike Campbell (PVT) Limited and another v The Republic of Zimbabwe.**

-_____. 2008. Case N. SADC (T) 07/2008. **Luke Muntandu Tembani v The Republic of Zimbabwe.**

SOUTHERN AFRICAN DEVELOPMENT CO-ORDINATING CONFERENCE. 1980. **Lusaka Declaration forming the Southern African Development Coordinating Conference.**

UNITED NATIONS. 1948. **Universal Declaration of Human Rights.**

_____. 1969. **Vienna Convention on the Law of Treaties.**

LIST OF ABBREVIATIONS

African Charter:	African Charter on Human and Peoples' Rights
African Commission:	African Commission on Human and Peoples' Rights
African Court:	African Court on Human and Peoples' Rights
ACJHR:	African Court of Justice and Human Rights
AEC:	African Economic Community
AHRS:	African Human Rights System
AU:	African Union
EAC:	East Africa Community
EACJ:	East Africa Court of Justice
ECOWAS:	Economic Community of the West African States
ECOWAS Court:	ECOWAS Community Court of Justice
OAU:	Organisation of African Unity
REC:	Regional Economic Community
REC Courts:	Regional Economic Community Courts
SADC:	Southern African development Community
SADC Tribunal:	Southern African Development Community Tribunal

LUCYLINE NKATHA MURUNGI AND JACQUI GALLINETTI

NOTES

1. See <http://www2.gtz.de/wbf/4tDx9kw63gma/RECs_Final_Report.pdf> or <http://www.kas.de/upload/auslandshomepages/namibia/Human_Rights_in_Africa/9_Ruppel.pdf> generally for an outline of the existing RECs in Africa and their corresponding memberships. Last accessed on: 6 Dec. 2010.

2. Articles 3(h) and 4(m) of the Constitutive Act of the AU (AFRICAN UNION, 2000) establish promotion, protection and respect of human rights as part of the objectives and principles of the AU. Nevertheless, it is noted that other documents adopted under the auspices of the OAU such as the Treaty Establishing the African Economic Community (1991) had already established human rights as a fundamental concern thereof. This suggests an incremental approach in the adoption of human rights as an agenda of the OAU. See chapter II article 3(g) and 5(1) of the AEC Treaty (AFRICAN ECONOMIC COMMUNITY, 1991).

3. Such as calls by the UN Economic Commission for Africa (UNECA) on African States to work towards a single economic union through the creational of sub-regional economies.

4. There are at least 14 RECs in Africa today, 8 of which are recognised by the African Union. See <www.africa-union.org> for a list of the recognised RECs.

5. Thoko argues that the obligations contained in the Universal Bill of Rights establish the civil, political, economic and social needs of people as rights which may not be curtailed in the pursuit of economic development. It is hence proposed that the Treaties of these RECs may not be interpreted in isolation of the other human rights obligations, but rather in a manner that furthers these objectives. This approach is derived and supported by the provisions of Article 31(3) (c) of the Vienna Convention on the Law of Treaties. In the context of RECs, one is bound to interpret their treaties in line with their obligations as obtaining under other human rights instruments.

6. The term 'courts' as used in this work refers to both courts and tribunals.

7. See generally <http://www.comm.ecowas.int/sec/index.php?id=about-a&lang-en>. See also paragraph 6 of the preamble to the 1975 ECOWAS Treaty (ECONOMIC COMMUNITY OF WEST AFRICAN STATES, 1975).

8. See para. 5 of the preamble and paras. 4, 5 and 6 of the substantive part of the Declaration (ECONOMIC COMMUNITY OF WEST AFRICAN STATES, 1991).

9. Article 4(g) of the 1993 Revised Treaty of ECOWAS (ECONOMIC COMMUNITY OF WEST AFRICAN STATES, 1993) which also refers to specific rights and obligations of member states as in article 56(2), 59 and 66(2) c.

10. By Supplementary Protocol A/SP.1/01/05 and A/SP.2/06/06.

11. These include Ugokwe v Nigeria and Others (ECONOMIC COMMUNITY OF WEST AFRICAN STATES, 2005b), *Kéiita and Another v Mali* (ECONOMIC COMMUNITY OF WEST AFRICAN STATES, 2007a), Essein v The Republic of Gambia (ECONOMIC COMMUNITY OF WEST AFRICAN STATES, 2007b) AHRLR 131, *Manneh v The Gambia* (ECONOMIC COMMUNITY OF WEST AFRICAN STATES, 2008a) AHRLR 171, *Karou v Niger* (ECONOMIC COMMUNITY OF WEST AFRICAN STATES, 2008b) AHRLR 182, *Registered Trustees of Socio-Economic Rights and Accountability Project (SERAP) v Federal Republic of Nigeria and Another* (ECONOMIC COMMUNITY OF WEST AFRICAN STATES, 2009).

12. See <http://www.sadc.int> on the member states of SADC.

13. *Mike Campbell (PVT) Limited and Another v The Republic of Zimbabwe* SADC (T) 2/2007 and in *Luke Muntandu Tembani v The Republic of Zimbabwe*, case number SADC (T) 07/2008 (SOUTHERN AFRICAN DEVELOPMENT COMMUNITY TRIBUNAL, 2008). In the Campbell case, the SADC Tribunal considered whether compulsory acquisition of private land owned by the applicants through an amendment of the Respondent's constitution was a violation of human rights obligations under the SADC Treaty. In the Tembani case, the SADC Tribunal was required to determine whether a provision of the Respondent's law which ousted the jurisdiction of courts in respect of the foreclosure of property charged to loan was a violation of human rights.

14. In 2005, the secretariat of the EAC developed a draft protocol for the expansion of the EACJ's jurisdiction to *inter alia* human rights as required in article 27(2). The process of consultation on the draft was scheduled to be completed by August 2006, and to date has not been finalised. This delay in adoption of the Protocol is attributable to several factors including unrealistic time framing of the schedule for adoption, limited consultation with stakeholders, and susceptibility of the process to political manipulation.

15. He argues that though the Treaty provides for broad protection with regard to human rights, the EACJ has no jurisdiction over human rights issues.

16. *Katabazi and 21 others v Secretary General of the EAC and another* (EAST AFRICAN COURT OF JUSTICE, 2007) and *Nyong'o and 10 others v The Attorney General of Kenya and others* (EAST AFRICA COURT OF JUSTICE, 2006).

17. Article 4(2) of the Treaty Establishing the African Economic Community (AFRICAN ECONOMIC COMMUNITY, 1991). See also article 3(g) of the same Treaty.

18. Article 1 of the Protocol on African Court (AFRICAN UNION, 2004).

THE ROLE OF SUB-REGIONAL COURTS IN THE AFRICAN HUMAN RIGHTS SYSTEM

19. Chapter 2 of the African Charter on the Rights and Welfare of the Child (ORGANISATION OF AFRICAN UNITY, 1990).

20. See articles 30 of the African Charter (ORGANISATION OF AFRICAN UNITY, 1986), 2 of the Court Protocol (AFRICAN UNION, 2004) and 32 of the African Charter on the Rights and Welfare of the Child (ORGANISATION OF AFRICAN UNITY, 1990).

21. Protocol on the Statute of the African Court of Justice and Human Rights (Statute of the ACJHR) adopted by the eleventh ordinary session of the AU Assembly, held in Sharm el-Sheikh, Egypt, 1st July 2008 (AFRICAN UNION, 2008b).

22. In terms of Article 16 of the Statute of the African Court of Justice and Human Rights, the ACJHR is to have two sections; a general affairs section composed of 8 judges and a human rights section composed of 8 judges. The general affairs section is to be competent to hear all cases submitted under article 28 of the Statute save for those concerning human and/or peoples' rights. The human rights section is to be competent to hear all cases relating to human and or peoples' rights.

23. An analogy can be drawn from his argument to the present relationship between the African Charter and the RECs.

24. Article 38 of the EAC treaty provides that a dispute referred to the EACJ cannot be settled by any other method other than that established under the Treaty. This can be read as establishing the finality of the decisions of the EACJ.

25. Its successor the Constitutive Act of the AU has similar provisions but leaves the definition of peaceful means to the AU Assembly.

26. See articles 30 and 46(2) of the African Charter (ORGANISATION OF AFRICAN UNITY, 1986) and the Statute of the ACJHR (AFRICAN UNION, 2008b) respectively.

27. Only the case of *Michelot Yogombaye v The Republic of Senegal* (AFRICAN COURT ON HUMAN AND PEOPLE'S RIGHTS, 2008), has been brought before the Court so far. However, the African Court dismissed this matter on the basis that the Respondent state, Senegal, had not accepted the jurisdiction of the African Court in terms of article 34(6) of the 1998 Protocol to the African Charter on African Court (AFRICAN UNION, 2004).

28. In *Louis Karel Fick & Others versus Government of the Republic of Zimbabwe* (SOUTH AFRICA, 2009) the North Gauteng High Court, Pretoria upheld the application by successful litigants before the SADC Tribunal to attach the non-diplomatic property owned by the Government of Zimbabwe in South Africa. However, the Court failed to provide substantive reasons for its order, save for stating it relied on the papers before it. As a consequence, the Government of South Africa is appealing the decision. The appeal is yet to be determined as at the date of this article (SA TO CHALLENGE..., 2010).

29. These are Burkina Faso, Mali, Malawi and Tanzania.

30. Article 10(d) of Supplementary Protocol A/ SP.1/01/05 Amending Protocol A/P.1/7/91 on the Community Court of Justice (ECONOMIC COMMUNITY OF WEST AFRICAN STATES, 2005a) on the requirements for admissibility of a matter before the ECOWAS Court.

31. Thoko argues in respect of SADC that the SADC Treaty does not create any institution with a specific mandate to deal with human rights despite having an unequivocal commitment to human rights.

32. He argues that international law is not a comprehensive body of laws consisting of a fixed body of rules applicable to all states with a central legislative organ. Rather, it is in permanent development with its actors and ambit of activity increasing considerably in the past few years.

33. In the *Campbell* case (SOUTHERN AFRICAN DEVELOPMENT COMMUNITY TRIBUNAL, 2007) for instance, the SADC Tribunal relied on the decision of the African Commission in *Constitutional Rights Project and Others v Nigeria* (AFRICAN COMMISSION ON HUMAN AND PEOPLES' RIGHTS, 2000) AHRLR 227 and in *Zimbabwe Human Rights NGO Forum v Zimbabwe* (AFRICAN COMMISSION ON HUMAN AND PEOPLES' RIGHTS, 2006) AHRLR128.

34. Countries that are members or party to more than one sub-region have a choice of REC courts to approach (which is the majority of most African countries).

35. He identifies three types of forum shopping based on the nature of choice available to the potential litigant: choice of tribunal, simultaneous petitioning and successive petitioning.

36. He argues that successive litigation is not costless.

37. Article 56(7) of the African Charter (ORGANISATION OF AFRICAN UNITY, 1986) which is material in this regard only prohibits admission of successive claims. This is insufficient to deal with the possibility of forum shopping.

38. See notes 16 and 13 above respectively.

39. Article 15 which provides for the jurisdiction of the SADC Tribunal neither provides for competence over human rights questions nor excludes such jurisdiction.

40. Article 27(1) of the Treaty relates to the jurisdiction of the EACJ to interpret and apply the EAC Treaty.

41. See note 13 above

42. The Draft East African Bill of Rights (PETER, 2008, Annexure II) developed by the National Human Rights Institutions in the East African region under the auspices of Kituo Cha Katiba. The draft, though not formally adopted by the EAC is intended to be a human rights code to guide the human rights jurisprudence and operations of the EACJ.

[24]

A NEW INTERNATIONAL HUMAN RIGHTS COURT FOR WEST AFRICA: THE ECOWAS COMMUNITY COURT OF JUSTICE

By Karen J. Alter, * *Laurence R. Helfer,*[†] *and Jacqueline R. McAllister*[‡]

The Community Court of Justice of the Economic Community of West African States (ECOWAS Court) is an increasingly active and bold adjudicator of human rights. Since acquiring jurisdiction over human rights complaints in 2005, the ECOWAS Court has issued numerous decisions condemning human rights violations by the member states of the Economic Community of West African States (Community).[1] Among this Court's path-breaking cases[2] are judgments against Niger for condoning modern forms of slavery and against Nigeria for impeding the right to free basic education for all children.[3] The ECOWAS Court also has broad access and standing rules that permit individuals and nongovernmental organizations (NGOs) to bypass national courts and file suits directly with the Court. Although the Court is generally careful in the proof that it requires of complainants and in the remedies that it demands of governments, it has not shied away from politically courageous decisions, such as rulings against

* Professor of Political Science and Law, Northwestern University, and Permanent Visiting Professor, iCourts: The Danish National Research Foundation's Center of Excellence for International Courts. Email: kalter@northwestern.edu. The authors thank Kristina Alayan, Ethan Blevins, and Abraham Smith for excellent research assistance. For comments on earlier drafts, we thank the participants in conferences and workshops held at the American Society of International Law Research Forum at UCLA Law School; the Cegla Center for Interdisciplinary Research at the University of Tel Aviv; Duke University School of Law; iCourts; the Hauser Colloquium at New York University Law School; the Program of African Studies, Northwestern University; the University of St. Gallen; and the University of Wisconsin Regional Colloquium on Globalization and Law.

† Of the Board of Editors. Email: helfer@law.duke.edu.

‡ Ph.D. candidate, Department of Political Science, Northwestern University. Email: j-mcallister@u.northwestern.edu.

1 Fifteen nations are currently members of ECOWAS: Benin, Burkina Faso, Cape Verde, Côte d'Ivoire, the Gambia, Ghana, Guinea, Guinea-Bissau, Liberia, Mali, Nigeria, Senegal, Sierra Leone, and Togo.

2 A list of all judgments and rulings of the ECOWAS Court, as well as copies of selected decisions, are available on the Court's website. ECOWAS Community Court of Justice, *List of Decided Cases from 2004 Till Date*, at http://www.courtecowas.org/site2012/index.php?option=com_content&view=article&id=157&Itemid=27. The first five years of judgments and rulings have been published in an official reporter, but it is not widely available. 2004–2009 COMMUNITY COURT OF JUSTICE, ECOWAS LAW REPORT (2011). Selected decisions, some in unofficial translation, are available on other online databases. *E.g.*, Centre for Human Rights, University of Pretoria, *African Human Rights Case Law Database*, at http://www1.chr.up.ac.za/index.php/browse-by-institution/ecowas-ccj.html; WorldCourts, *ECOWAS Community Court of Justice: Decisions*, at http://www.worldcourts.com/ecowasccj/eng/.

3 *E.g.*, Lydia Polgreen, *Court Rules Niger Failed by Allowing Girl's Slavery*, N.Y. TIMES, Oct. 28, 2008, at A6; *ECOWAS Court Orders Gambia to Pay Musa Saidykhan $200,000 in Landmark Case*, JOLLOFNEWS (Dec. 16, 2010), *at* http://www.jollofnews.com/human-rights/1629-ecowas-court-orders-gambia-to-pay-musa-saidykhan-200000-?in-landmark-case-; African Child Information Hub, *West Africa: ECOWAS Court Orders Nigeria to Provide Free Education for Every Child* (Dec. 2, 2010), *at* http://www.africanchildinfo.net/index.php?option=com_k2&view=item&id=5046%3Awest-africa-ecowas-court-orders-nigeria-to-provide-free-education-for-every-child&Itemid=67&lang=en#; Amnesty International, *Nigeria: Ground-Breaking Judgment Calls for Punishing Oil Companies over Pollution* (Dec. 17, 2012), *at* http://www.amnesty.org/en/news/nigeria-ground-breaking-judgment-calls-punishing-oil-companies-over-pollution-2012-12-17.

the Gambia for the torture of journalists and against Nigeria for failing to regulate multinational companies that have degraded the environment of the oil-rich Niger Delta.

Our primary goal in this article is to explain how an international tribunal, initially established to help build a common market, was redeployed as a human rights court. In particular, we ask why West African governments, which set up the ECOWAS Court in a way that has allowed persistent flouting of Community economic rules, later delegated to ECOWAS judges remarkably far-reaching human rights jurisdiction.

The ECOWAS Court's transformation is surprising in many ways. By all accounts, ECOWAS has made little progress toward its professed goal of regional economic integration. Trade flows among West African nations remain extremely low; tariffs, customs regulations, nontariff barriers, and roadblocks hinder cross-border economic transactions;[4] and member states have yet to challenge barriers to intraregional trade before the ECOWAS Court. If our story ended here, with a new international court struggling for relevance, few would be surprised. However, our story takes a sharp and unexpected turn in 2005 with an expansion of the Court's jurisdiction to include human rights complaints by private litigants.

When we began our study, we had low expectations for the ECOWAS Court. Human rights violations, destabilizing coups, and civil unrest are sadly commonplace in West Africa, and domestic legal institutions are generally weak.[5] We anticipated that national governments in such a region would resist giving an international court the power to review human rights claims from private litigants. And if officials did give the court such authority, we expected that they would put in place political checks to carefully control the judges and their decisions. What we found—based on a review of ECOWAS Court decisions and more than two dozen interviews with judges, Community officers, government officials, attorneys, and NGOs[6]—was quite different. The member states gave the ECOWAS Court a broad human rights jurisdiction, and they have eschewed opportunities to narrow the Court's authority.

The ECOWAS Court's repurposing and subsequent survival as an international human rights court have several unexpected dimensions. First, the Court did not claim human rights competence for itself via judicial lawmaking. Rather, it acquired this authority in response to a coordinated campaign in which bar associations, NGOs, and ECOWAS officials—in addition to ECOWAS Court judges themselves—mobilized to secure member states' consent to the transformation. Second, the Court has strikingly capacious jurisdiction and access rules, with no specified catalogue of human rights, with direct access for private litigants, and with no requirement to exhaust domestic remedies. These design features are especially curious because West African states have been reluctant to grant similar authority to the judicial institutions

---

[4] S. K. B. Asante, *Economic Community of West African States, in* THE OXFORD COMPANION TO POLITICS OF THE WORLD 233, 234 (Joël Krieger ed., 2d ed. 2001).

[5] *See, e.g.*, Emmanuel Kwesi Aning, *Investing in Peace and Security in Africa: The Case of ECOWAS, in* SECURITY AND DEVELOPMENT: INVESTING IN PEACE AND PROSPERITY 337, 351 (Robert Picciotto & Rachel Weaving eds., 2006); Eghosa E. Osaghae, *Human Rights and Transition Societies in West Africa, in* HUMAN RIGHTS AND SOCIETIES IN TRANSITION: CAUSES, CONSEQUENCES, RESPONSES 315, 315 (Shale Asher Horowitz & Albrecht Schnabel eds., 2004); ISSAKA K. SOUARÉ, CIVIL WARS AND COUPS D'ÉTAT IN WEST AFRICA: AN ATTEMPT TO UNDERSTAND THE ROOTS AND PRESCRIBE POSSIBLE SOLUTIONS 135 (2006).

[6] To preserve anonymity in accordance with the approval granted by our universities' institutional review boards, unless expressly requested by our sources, the names of our interviewees have been redacted. Each interview is identified here by date, location, and category, and by a unique identifying letter that is used in our records of all interviews.

of the African Charter on Human and Peoples' Rights[7] (African Charter).Third, when the ECOWAS Court's early rulings generated opposition from some governments, the member states eschewed opportunities to rein in the Court. Instead, they adopted institutional reforms that arguably strengthen the judges' independence and authority. Nevertheless, the Court faces an ongoing challenge of securing compliance with its judgments, a challenge that the judges are attempting to meet by tailoring the remedies that they award to successful applicants and by publicly pressuring governments to implement the Court's rulings.

Our study of the ECOWAS Court's transformation has two broader theoretical implications.[8] The first relates to how international institutions, including courts, evolve over time. Rationalist theories of cooperation generally conceive of international institutions as problem-solving devices to further states' functional goals. We contrast rationalist approaches that tether institutions to the states that created them to historical institutionalist accounts that expect institutions to evolve in response to political contestation and societal pressures. States nevertheless play an important part in our narrative, particularly through their decisions in the 1990s to authorize humanitarian intervention in West Africa and expand ECOWAS's regional security role. We argue that these decisions triggered a cascade of smaller reforms in the Community that, in the mid-2000s, created an opening for an alliance of civil society groups and supranational actors to mobilize in favor of court reform.

A second theoretical implication relates to the repurposing of international courts. The ECOWAS Court's shift into human rights is not unique. The European Court of Justice (ECJ) made an equivalent shift in the 1970s. More recently, courts associated with other subregional economic communities—most notably, the East African Court of Justice (EACJ) and the Tribunal of the Southern African Development Community (SADC Tribunal)—have made similar moves. In all three instances, however, the judges themselves asserted the authority to adjudicate human rights claims. In Africa, the political and legal consequences of these bold assertions of competence are still unfolding, but early evidence indicates that the EACJ and the SADC Tribunal have faced greater opposition from governments than has the ECOWAS Court.[9] We argue that the manner by which an international court acquires a human rights jurisdiction matters, for reasons we will elaborate.

The remainder of this article proceeds as follows. Part I reviews the founding of ECOWAS and the ECOWAS Court, and the expansion of the Community's role in regional security. We explain that member states added a tribunal to ECOWAS as part of a wider re-launch of regional integration in the early 1990s. Yet they also rejected a proposal to give private litigants access to the Court to facilitate enforcement of regional economic rules. As a result, the Court sat unused for several years.

---

[7] African (Banjul) Charter on Human and Peoples' Rights, June 27, 1981, 1520 UNTS 217, 21 ILM 58 (1982) [hereinafter African Charter].

[8] This theoretical account builds on our prior work. *See, e.g.,* KAREN J. ALTER, THE NEW TERRAIN OF INTERNATIONAL LAW: COURTS, POLITICS, RIGHTS (forthcoming 2014); Karen J. Alter & Laurence R. Helfer, *Nature or Nurture? Judicial Law-Making in the European Court of Justice and the Andean Tribunal of Justice*, 64 INT'L ORG. 563 (2010); Laurence R. Helfer & Anne-Marie Slaughter, *Toward a Theory of Effective Supranational Adjudication*, 107 YALE L.J. 273 (1997).

[9] *E.g.,* Solomon Tamarabrakemi Ebobrah, *Litigating Human Rights Before Sub-regional Courts in Africa*, 17 AFR. J. INT'L & COMP. L. 79 (2009); James Gathii, *The Under-appreciated Jurisprudence of Africa's Regional Trade Judiciaries*, 12 OR. REV. INT'L L. 245 (2010); Lucyline Nkatha Murungi & Jacqui Gallinetti, *The Role of Sub-regional Courts in the African Human Rights System*, 7 INT'L J. HUM. RTS. 119 (2010).

Part II begins by summarizing the dismissal of the ECOWAS Court's first case—a suit by a private trader challenging a border closure. The case served as the catalyst for a campaign by bar associations, NGOs, Community officials, and ECOWAS judges, which resulted in the 2005 Protocol that gives the Court broad human rights jurisdiction.[10] After summarizing the rationales and mobilization campaign behind the 2005 Protocol, we analyze three distinctive features of the restructured Court's design—direct access for private parties, the absence of ECOWAS-specific human rights standards, and non-exhaustion of domestic remedies.

In part III we evaluate the ECOWAS Court's track record as a human rights tribunal. We focus on three major challenges to the Court's authority—a controversial election decision that engendered criticism from the public and legal elites in Nigeria; a proposal by the Gambia to narrow the Court's jurisdiction in response to rulings declaring the government responsible for torture; and concerns relating to noncompliance with ECOWAS Court rulings. We explain how the Court has weathered these challenges by mobilizing supportive constituencies, adjusting the remedies it orders, and publicly cajoling governments to implement its decisions.

Part IV considers the theoretical implications of our analysis, contrasting rationalist international relations and historical institutionalist theories of institutional change. We explain how the strategy that advocates adopted—conflating the economic goals of ECOWAS with its human rights objectives—contributed to the ironic result that an international court established to promote regional integration now adjudicates cases involving high-profile human rights violations while remaining largely unavailable to traders and other economic actors in the region.

In part V, we conclude by assessing the implications of the ECOWAS Court's transformation for the survival prospects of Africa's other subregional courts and for broader debates about fragmentation and the coherent interpretation of international human rights law.

I. THE POLITICAL, LEGAL, AND INSTITUTIONAL FRAMEWORK OF ECOWAS AND ITS COMMUNITY COURT OF JUSTICE

This part discusses the motives for establishing an economic integration regime in West Africa and why the commitment of ECOWAS member states to this regime has remained shallow. We then explain how, in the 1990s, the Community became involved in regional security and good governance issues, which later created a political opening to transform the ECOWAS Court. We conclude by linking the creation of the Court to these developments and explaining the member states' rejection of a proposal to grant private litigants direct access to the Court.

The Founding of ECOWAS and the Barriers to Economic Integration in West Africa

Why were West African governments interested in economic integration? At the founding of ECOWAS in 1975, the Community's primary goals, as defined by the Treaty, were to promote cooperation and development in a wide array of issue areas, including commerce, agriculture, natural resources, monetary and financial policy, security, and social and cultural mat-

---

[10] Supplementary Protocol A/SP1/01/05 Amending the Preamble and Articles 1, 2, 9 and 30 of Protocol (A/P.1/7/91) Relating to the Community Court of Justice and Article 4 Paragraph 1 of the English Version of the Said Protocol, Jan. 19, 2005 [hereinafter 2005 Protocol], *at* http://www.courtecowas.org/site2012/pdf_files/supplementary_protocol.pdf.

ters.[11] The project included removing intraregional trade barriers, reflecting the conventional view that open markets attract foreign investment and encourage development. Member states understood from the project's inception, however, that integration of national markets would be only one of many ECOWAS objectives.[12]

The names given to ECOWAS institutions mimicked their European Community counterparts. In reality, however, the 1975 ECOWAS Treaty created a system of policymaking bodies that governments tightly controlled. The principal Community institutions included an Authority of Heads of State and Government (Authority), the highest ECOWAS decision-making body; a Council of Ministers, which served in an advisory capacity to the Authority; and an Executive Secretariat responsible for the day-to-day administration of ECOWAS policies. These bodies adopted initiatives that, on paper, committed governments to phase out quantitative and other restrictions on intraregional trade, create a customs union, establish a common commercial policy, and permit the free movement of goods and persons.[13]

In reality, the legal framework required to carry out these policies was lacking. The institutions created by the 1975 Treaty, unlike those of the European Community, "left national sovereignty intact."[14] The decisions of the Authority and the Council of Ministers were binding only on ECOWAS institutions. They had no legal force for member states, which had merely agreed to "make every effort to plan and direct their policies with a view to creating favourable conditions for the achievement of" the Community's aims.[15] In the absence of delegated supranational decision-making powers, ECOWAS policies were formulated using a standard tool of public international law—a series of protocols adopted unanimously that accorded each government discretion with respect to ratification and implementation, and that entered into force only after a majority of countries had ratified. This cumbersome and politicized decision-making process was a "slow and inadequate" mechanism for Community lawmaking.[16]

At a deeper level, there was also good reason to question the economic and political logic of a West African integration project. ECOWAS countries are geographically proximate, and instability in one nation can easily destabilize neighboring countries. But in other respects, the divisions among the member states were and remain profound. Regional infrastructure is woefully underdeveloped, which makes intraregional trade costly.[17] Francophone countries are deeply linked to France's economic and political system, whereas Nigeria and Ghana—the two

---

[11] Treaty of the Economic Community of West African States, May 28, 1975, 1010 UNTS 17, 14 ILM 1200.

[12] The economic theory motivating the creation of ECOWAS is discussed in KOFI OTENG KUFUOR, THE INSTITUTIONAL TRANSFORMATION OF THE ECONOMIC COMMUNITY OF WEST AFRICAN STATES 2–8 (2006).

[13] Charles D. Jebuni, *The Role of ECOWAS in Trade Liberalization, in* TRADE REFORM AND REGIONAL INTEGRATION IN AFRICA 489, 493 (Zubair Iqbal & Mohsin S. Khan eds., 1998).

[14] Committee of Eminent Persons for the Review of the ECOWAS Treaty, Final Report 16 (June 1992) [hereinafter *Final CEP Report*] (on file with authors).

[15] Treaty of the Economic Community of West African States, *supra* note 11, Art. 3.

[16] S. K. B. ASANTE, THE POLITICAL ECONOMY OF REGIONALISM IN AFRICA: A DECADE OF THE ECONOMIC COMMUNITY OF WEST AFRICAN STATES (ECOWAS) 70 (1986); *see also* MUHAMMED TAWFIQ LADAN, INTRODUCTION TO ECOWAS COMMUNITY LAW AND PRACTICE: INTEGRATION, MIGRATION, HUMAN RIGHTS, ACCESS TO JUSTICE, PEACE AND SECURITY 7 (2009) (explaining that "most often, Community texts adopted in the so-called areas of sovereignty were in the form of protocols, and there was considerable delay in their application owing to the slow pace of protocol ratification").

[17] Chukwuma Agu, *Obstacles to Regional Integration: The Human Factor Challenge to Trade Facilitation and Port Reforms in Nigeria*, 2 INT'L J. PRIVATE L. 445 (2009).

largest Anglophone economies—have different capabilities and economic goals.[18] The key trading partners for West African countries are outside of the region, and the little intraregional trade that occurs involves natural resources, agricultural products, and low-value-added consumption products such as rubber, plastics, and cosmetics.[19] Although some traders stand to benefit from easier access to regional markets, many local producers actively seek to avoid competition from firms in other ECOWAS countries.[20]

Building a common market in West Africa was nonetheless attractive for a different reason. The 1975 ECOWAS Treaty signaled to its poorer neighbors that Nigeria—the "big brother"[21] of West Africa, which then accounted for nearly 70 percent of the region's total GDP[22]—favored regional cooperation. ECOWAS helped Nigeria to consolidate its status as regional hegemon by indicating to neighboring countries that they would benefit from Nigeria's oil wealth and from access to its large and lucrative market.[23] For example, the Community's goal of promoting the free movement of workers could enable desperately poor West Africans to move to a country where jobs and resources were more plentiful.[24] Nigeria's financial backing was also important. In 1975, import and export taxes ranged from 15 to 50 percent of national revenues.[25] Governments envisioned that ECOWAS would replace these tax proceeds with a Fund for Cooperation, Compensation and Development. All member states were required to contribute to the fund, but in proportion to each country's gross domestic product and per capita income. Nigerian largesse thus provided the bulk of the Community revenue to replace domestic trade taxes.[26] It also provided extra funds to support the activities of Community institutions.[27]

Notwithstanding this planned reduction in trade taxes, ECOWAS did not endorse a free market philosophy. To the contrary, its policies reflected the then widely held view that industrialized countries preyed on the economic weaknesses of the developing world. The remedy for this dependency, according to this view, was to build local industrial capacity and an export

---

[18] *E.g.*, ASANTE, *supra* note 16, at 48; Julius Emeka Okolo, *The Development and Structure of ECOWAS*, *in* WEST AFRICAN REGIONAL COOPERATION AND DEVELOPMENT 19, 42 (Julius Emeka Okolo & Stephen Wright eds., 1990).

[19] Mary E. Burfisher & Margaret B. Missiaen, *Intraregional Trade in West Africa*, *in* WEST AFRICAN REGIONAL COOPERATION AND DEVELOPMENT, *supra* note 18, at 185–213; Phoebe Kornfeld, *ECOWAS, The First Decade: Towards Collective Self-Reliance, or Maintenance of the Status Quo?*, *in* WEST AFRICAN REGIONAL COOPERATION AND DEVELOPMENT, *supra* note 18, at 87, 91 (noting that intraregional trade averaged between 2.8 percent and 4.1 percent of the member states' total trade volume during the first ten years of ECOWAS). These trade volumes have remained stable since the 1970s. IBRAHIM A. GAMBARI, POLITICAL AND COMPARATIVE DIMENSIONS OF REGIONAL INTEGRATION: THE CASE OF ECOWAS 40–41 (1991).

[20] *E.g.*, Agu, *supra* note 17, at 455; Kofi Oteng Kufuor, *Sub-state Protectionism in Ghana*, 18 AFR. J. INT'L & COMP. L. 78, 80–81 (2010).

[21] *E.g.*, OLAYIWOLA ABEGUNRIN, AFRICA IN GLOBAL POLITICS IN THE TWENTY-FIRST CENTURY: A PAN-AFRICAN PERSPECTIVE 42 (2009) (explaining that "Nigeria has become the *big brother* (Super power) of West Africa").

[22] Okolo, *supra* note 18, at 42.

[23] GAMBARI, *supra* note 19, at 18; KUFUOR, *supra* note 12, at 22; Olatunde Ojo, *Nigeria and the Formation of ECOWAS*, 34 INT'L ORG. 571, 584 (1980).

[24] Julius Emeka Okolo, *Free Movement of Persons in ECOWAS and Nigeria's Expulsion of Illegal Aliens*, 40 WORLD TODAY 428, 431 (1984).

[25] GAMBARI, *supra* note 19, at 42; Okolo, *supra* note 18, at 49 n.43.

[26] Okolo, *supra* note 18, at 32 (explaining that Nigeria provided nearly one-third of the contributions to the Community fund).

[27] GAMBARI, *supra* note 19, at 58.

sector to replace reliance on foreign imports.[28] Nigeria, in particular, favored a region-wide effort to build indigenous industries.[29] The Francophone countries, however, were heavily dependent on investment from France, and foreign investors were primarily interested in gaining access to regional markets. Voting as a bloc, the Francophone members of ECOWAS prevented the adoption of Community rules of origin. Anglophone members reacted, in turn, by opposing free-trade rules that would have given French producers open access to their markets.[30] The net result of these intraregional tensions was a stalemate within ECOWAS and rampant noncompliance with Community rules.[31] Not surprisingly, assessments of the on-the-ground impact of the first phase of West African integration were overwhelmingly negative.[32]

The Rise of Regional Security, Good Governance, and Human Rights in ECOWAS

The 1980s was a period of economic turmoil and political conflict in West Africa. Early in the decade, the collapse of world oil prices and the mismanagement of oil revenues led Nigeria to focus on domestic priorities and deemphasize its commitment to ECOWAS.[33] A further low point followed in 1983 when Nigeria expelled hundreds of thousands of "illegal" workers from other member states. Mass expulsions had occurred before in West Africa. But the 1975 ECOWAS Treaty and its free-movement protocols professed a commitment to a different and more open migration policy.[34] Nigeria's expulsions increased employment opportunities for domestic workers and thus were politically popular at home. But they were widely viewed as flouting the spirit, if not the letter, of ECOWAS free-movement rules.[35]

The end of the Cold War had a significant impact on the Community. West African countries began to liberalize their economies as a condition of receiving loans from the World Bank, gaining access to European markets and, eventually, joining the World Trade Organization. These powerful external forces made the embrace of regional economic integration newly attractive.[36]

The revival and expansion of ECOWAS was embodied in a new agreement, the 1993 Treaty,[37] that replaced the 1975 founding charter. The 1993 Treaty recommitted West African governments to economic integration, setting timetables for establishing the customs and monetary unions, and further reducing barriers to intraregional trade. The member states also endorsed structural changes to achieve these goals. They authorized certain ECOWAS decisions

---

[28] ASANTE, *supra* note 16, at 42–43; GAMBARI, *supra* note 19, at 42–43; KUFUOR, *supra* note 12, at xii.

[29] KUFUOR, *supra* note 12, at 27.

[30] *Id.* at 26–29.

[31] GAMBARI, *supra* note 19, at 44; Jebuni, *supra* note 13, at 495.

[32] *E.g.*, KUFUOR, *supra* note 12, at 19–34; Jebuni, *supra* note 13, at 490–99.

[33] GAMBARI, *supra* note 19, at 47.

[34] *E.g.*, Protocol A/P.1/5/79 Relating to Free Movement of Persons, Residence and Establishment, Art. 2.1, May 29, 1979, *at* http://www.comm.ecowas.int/sec/index.php?id=protocole&lang=en; *see also* ASANTE, *supra* note 16, at 151 ("As far as ECOWAS is concerned, the movement of labor is part of the philosophy of its founders . . . .").

[35] Okolo, *supra* note 24, at 432–33; GAMBARI, *supra* note 19, at 47.

[36] KUFUOR, *supra* note 12, at 42–43.

[37] Revised Treaty of the Economic Community of West African States, July 24, 1993, 35 ILM 660 [hereinafter 1993 Treaty].

to be adopted by a vote of two-thirds of the member states, made those decisions expressly binding on the member states, created new ECOWAS institutions such as the Community Parliament,[38] and increased the power of existing bodies.[39]

Although the 1993 Treaty reads primarily as a recommitment to economic integration, in practice the second phase of ECOWAS came to be dominated by security, good governance, and human rights concerns. Early on, the Community had acquired a role in promoting regional security. A 1978 Protocol on Non-aggression[40] and a 1981 Protocol Relating to Mutual Assistance on Defense[41] provided the legal basis for these tasks. These initiatives were primarily aimed at deflecting foreign interventions, but they also established a Defense Council and Defense Commission that could more broadly supervise regional security initiatives.[42]

The Liberian civil war marked a turning point. Although there had been previous conflicts in the region, the civil war in that country led Anglophone member states to establish the Economic Community of West African States Monitoring Group (ECOMOG).[43] What began as a monitoring and mediation effort as part of the Protocol on Mutual Assistance and Defense became a full-fledged military intervention.[44] Most observers credited the intervention with preventing the spread of violence and restoring a semblance of stability in Liberia. But the intervention also generated credible and serious allegations of human rights abuses by ECOMOG forces.[45] Subsequent military missions to quell civil wars and armed conflicts in Sierra Leone in 1997, Guinea Bissau in 1999, and Côte d'Ivoire and Liberia in 2003 increased the political salience of security and humanitarian activities in ECOWAS and led to the adoption in 1999 of a Protocol Relating to the Mechanism for Conflict Prevention, Management, Resolution, Peace-Keeping and Security (1999 Conflict Prevention Protocol) that underscored the importance of protecting human rights and put regional intervention on a firmer legal footing.[46] These expansions of the Community's powers contributed to a growing mobilization around

---

[38] Protocol A/P.2/8/94 Relating to the Community Parliament, Aug. 6, 1994, *at* http://www.parl.ecowas.int/doc/protocols_eng.pdf.

[39] For an overview of the 1993 Treaty, see KUFUOR, *supra* note 12, at 35–68; Iwa Akinrinsola, *Legal and Institutional Requirements for West African Economic Integration*, 10 L. & BUS. REV. AM. 493, 504–08 (2004).

[40] Apr. 22, 1978, *in* COMPENDIUM OF ECOWAS PEACE & SECURITY DECISIONS 57 (Emmanuel Kwesi Aning, Emma Birikorang & Thomas Jaye eds., 2010), *at* http://www.kaiptc.org/getattachment/Media-Room/News/Compendium-of-ECOWAS-Peace-and-Security-Decisions/Compendium-of-ECOWAS-Peace-and-Security-Decisions.pdf.aspx.

[41] A/SP3/5/8l, May 29, 1981, *in* COMPENDIUM OF ECOWAS PEACE & SECURITY DECISIONS, *supra* note 40, at 61.

[42] *See* Peter Jenkins, *The Economic Community of West African States and the Regional Use of Force*, 32 DENV. J. INT'L L. & POL'Y 333, 335–36 (2008).

[43] JOHN M. KABIA, HUMANITARIAN INTERVENTION AND CONFLICT RESOLUTION IN WEST AFRICA 57–160 (2009); *see also* ADEKEYE ADEBAJO & ISMAIL O. D. RASHID, WEST AFRICA'S SECURITY CHALLENGES: BUILDING PEACE IN A TROUBLED REGION (2004).

[44] *See* Jenkins, *supra* note 42, at 342–44.

[45] *E.g.*, Peter Arthur, *ECOWAS and Regional Peacekeeping Integration in West Africa: Lessons for the Future*, 57 AFRICA TODAY 2, 16 (2010); KABIA, *supra* note 43, at 86–87.

[46] Protocol Relating to the Mechanism for Conflict Prevention, Management, Resolution, Peace-Keeping and Security, Art. 2, Dec. 10, 1999 (declaring as a "fundamental principles" the "protection of fundamental human rights and freedoms and the rules of international humanitarian laws"), *in* COMPENDIUM OF ECOWAS PEACE & SECURITY DECISIONS, *supra* note 40, at 61; *see also* Isaac Terwase Sampson, *The Responsibility to Protect and ECOWAS Mechanisms on Peace and Security: Assessing Their Convergence and Divergence on Intervention*, 16 J. CONFLICT & SECURITY L. 507, 515–18 (2011).

human rights in West Africa, and as we explain in part IV, opened the door for the transformation of the ECOWAS Court into an international human rights court.

As part of the 1993 overhaul, member states agreed to broaden public participation in ECOWAS by expanding access for civil society groups. National NGOs were precluded from participating in Community policymaking, but regional civil society groups could be accredited to observe public meetings, make presentations, and circulate documents.[47] These institutional reforms created an incentive for civil society groups to mobilize within ECOWAS and to create regional advocacy bodies. In 2001, NGOs formed the West African Human Rights Forum, an umbrella organization that gained accreditation from ECOWAS and attempted to influence Community policymaking.[48] These opportunities for regional mobilization provided an avenue in 2004 for human rights groups to contribute to proposals to expand the Court's jurisdiction. NGO access was also important five years later when the Gambian government, unhappy with Court's rulings against it, proposed curbing its newly acquired authority to hear human rights cases.

Another expansion of ECOWAS competence was an important precursor for the ECOWAS Court's transformation. In 2001, the member states adopted a Protocol on Democracy and Good Governance (2001 Good Governance Protocol) to deter military coups and unconstitutional changes of government.[49] The Protocol wove multiple references to human rights into the fabric of an ambitious regional effort to promote democracy, accountability, transparency, and the rule of law.[50] It also included a clause promising that the jurisdiction of the ECOWAS Court "shall be reviewed so as to give the Court the power to hear, inter-alia, cases relating to violations of human rights, after all attempts to resolve the matter at the national level have failed."[51] These developments gave human rights advocates a legal foothold when they later lobbied to give the Court a human rights jurisdiction.

The Decision to Create a Community Court of Justice for Interstate Disputes

We now situate the creation of the ECOWAS Court within these wider regional developments. ECOWAS's founders envisioned a tribunal to "ensure the observance of law and justice in the interpretation of the provisions of [the 1975] Treaty" and to "settl[e] such disputes as may be referred to it" by the member states.[52] But the tribunal was never created during the founding period for two reasons. The first relates to Nigeria's regional hegemony. ECOWAS

---

[47] Decision A/DEC.9/8/94 Establishing Regulations for the Grant to Non-governmental Organisations (NGOs) the Status of Observer Within the Institutions of the Community, Aug. 6, 1994, *discussed in* KUFUOR, *supra* note 12, at 49–50.

[48] Telephone interview with Human Rights Advocate B (Feb. 3, 2011).

[49] Protocol A/SP1/12/01 on Democracy and Good Governance Supplementary to the Protocol Relating to the Mechanism for Conflict Prevention, Management, Resolution, Peacekeeping and Security, Dec. 21, 2001 [hereinafter 2001 Good Governance Protocol], *at* http://www.comm.ecowas.int/sec/en/protocoles/Protocol %20on%20good-governance-and-democracy-rev-5EN.pdf. For a recent assessment, see Frederick Cowell, *The Impact of the ECOWAS Protocol on Good Governance and Democracy*, 19 AFR. J. INT'L AND COMP. L. 331 (2011).

[50] *See* Solomon T. Ebobrah, Legitimacy and Feasibility of Human Rights Realisation Through Regional Economic Communities in Africa: The Case of the Economic Community of West African States 100–02 (2009) (LLD dissertation, University of Pretoria), *at* http://upetd.up.ac.za/thesis/available/etd-02102010-085034/ unrestricted/00front.pdf.

[51] 2001 Good Governance Protocol, *supra* note 49, Art. 39.

[52] Treaty of the Economic Community of West African States, *supra* note 11, Arts. 11, 56.

institutions have always depended on the largesse of Nigerian oil revenues, and Nigeria was reluctant to embrace "an organ that could circumscribe its role as the regional hegemon."[53] The second relates to the weak legal underpinnings for a Community court. ECOWAS protocols did not have direct effect in national law,[54] and as noted above, most were rarely implemented. In an environment in which member states neither implemented nor complied with Community rules, a supranational tribunal would have been "largely redundant."[55]

The decision to create the ECOWAS Court was part of the broader recommitment to regional integration in the early 1990s.[56] As governments prepared to relaunch the Community, national interior ministers submitted to the member states a proposal to create a court. The ministers wanted a court to resolve disputes relating to key ECOWAS instruments and programs, including the Protocol on Free Movement of Persons, Residence and Establishment,[57] the Trade Liberalisation Scheme, the Agricultural Cooperation Programme, and the Protocol on Community Enterprises.[58] The renewed governmental support for a court in the early 1990s reflected a growing sense that deeper regional integration required a judicial body to resolve disputes and interpret legal rules.[59]

A 1991 Community protocol (1991 Protocol) created an international court to carry out these tasks.[60] The Protocol authorized the ECOWAS Court to adjudicate two types of cases relating to "the interpretation and application" of ECOWAS legal instruments: (1) "disputes referred . . . by Member States or the Authority, when such disputes arise between the Member States or between one or more Member States and the Institutions of the Community," and (2) proceedings instituted by a member state "on behalf of its nationals . . . against another Member State or Institution of the Community . . . after attempts to settle the dispute amicably have failed."[61]

The 1991 Protocol also included what, in retrospect, was a portentous decision: it established the ECOWAS Court as a permanent institution. At the time, member states were uncertain what kind of judicial body the Community needed. Officials in the ECOWAS Legal Affairs Directorate favored an ad hoc tribunal, which would be less costly and appropriate for the small number of interstate disputes capable of judicial resolution. Member states, however, were

---

[53] KUFUOR, *supra* note 12, at 44.

[54] Akinrinsola, *supra* note 39, at 503.

[55] *Id.* at 504.

[56] *Final CEP Report*, *supra* note 14, at 19–21; LADAN, *supra* note 16, at 2.

[57] *See supra* note 34.

[58] Protocol A/P1/11/84 Relating to Community Enterprises, Nov. 23, 1984; *see ECOWAS Ministers of Justice Meet in Lagos*, 2 CONTACT MAG., no. 3, 1990, at 15 (on file with authors) (reporting statements by ECOWAS Deputy Executive Secretary Adelino Queta).

[59] Akinrinsola, *supra* note 39, at 507–08; Kofi Oteng Kufuor, *Securing Compliance with the Judgements of the ECOWAS Court of Justice*, 8 AFR. J. INT'L & COMP. L. 1, 4 (1996).

[60] Protocol A/P.1/7/91 on the Community Court of Justice, Arts. 3(1), 4(1), July 6, 1991 [hereinafter 1991 Protocol], provided for a court comprising seven independent judges, each of whom served for a five-year term renewable once. The judges were appointed "by the Authority and selected from a list of persons nominated by Member States" who had qualifications similar to those associated with other international courts and tribunals. *Id.*, Art. 3(1), (4).

[61] *Id.*, Art. 9(2), (3). The 1991 Protocol also authorized the ECOWAS Court to issue advisory opinions concerning the Treaty "at the request of the Authority, Council, one or more Member States, or the Executive Secretary and any other institution of the Community." *Id.*, Art. 10(1).

more focused on expanding ECOWAS competences and creating new Community institutions. In this heady atmosphere of supranational expansion, "the Authority said, 'let's have a court.'"[62]

The 1991 Protocol did not, however, include another design feature favored by the supporters of supranational integration—a provision granting private litigants access to the Court. As part of a review process leading to the restructuring of ECOWAS in the 1993 Treaty, the Authority appointed a Committee of Eminent Persons, chaired by General Yakubu Gowon of Nigeria, to assess the shortcomings of the founding period. The committee's reports to the Authority stressed the "importance of [private actors and] interest groups in the integration process," both in the interests of democratic legitimacy and because "some of the Community decisions have to be implemented either directly or indirectly" by these actors.[63] The committee also endorsed granting individuals, firms, and interest groups access to the Court:

> Where, however, a Community citizen alleges a breach or denial of a right conferred on him by a Community legislation, a Treaty provision or a protocol, it should be possible for him to seek redress in the national Court or the Community Court of Justice. . . . This proposal would also require amendment to Article 9 of the [1991] Protocol . . . . Under the present provisions, nationals do not have a *locus standi* in the Court of Justice. Member States have to act on their behalf, and even so, only in cases relating to the interpretation and application of the provisions of the Treaty, "after attempts to settle the dispute amicably have failed."[64]

We do not know why the member states did not act on this proposal. Perhaps it was politically expedient not to deviate from a design template that the ECOWAS Authority had previously vetted and approved. Or perhaps the member states, especially Nigeria, did not actually want a tribunal with design features that would enhance the supranational aspects of ECOWAS or constrain their freedom of action.[65]

The delay in establishing the ECOWAS Court as a working court is consistent with the latter explanation. The 1991 Protocol did not enter into force until November 1996.[66] Even then, the Court existed only on paper. The situation changed in 1999 when Olusegun Obasanjo assumed the presidency of Nigeria. Obasanjo increased the country's international profile, in part by reviving its leadership of the Community.[67] With the region's economic powerhouse

---

[62] Interview with ECOWAS Legal Affairs Directorate A, in Abuja, Nigeria (Mar. 7, 2011).

[63] Committee of Eminent Persons for the Review of the ECOWAS Treaty, Draft Report 28, ECOWAS Doc. ECW/CEP/TREV/VI/2 (June 1992) [hereinafter Draft CEP Report] (on file with authors); *Final CEP Report*, *supra* note 14, at 23–24 (containing a similar statement).

[64] *Final CEP Report*, *supra* note 14, at 20–21; Draft CEP Report, *supra* note 63, at 20. Elsewhere, the final report suggests that the committee's recommendation was for private litigants to have direct access to the ECOWAS Court rather than access via national courts. *Final CEP Report*, *supra* note 14, at 8.

[65] Several scholars have argued that private access contributes to the effectiveness of international courts. *See, e.g.*, Robert O. Keohane, Andrew Moravcsik & Anne-Marie Slaughter, *Legalized Dispute Resolution: Interstate and Transnational*, 54 INT'L ORG. 457, 472–76 (2000); Helfer & Slaughter, *supra* note 8, at 287–90. Other scholars have applied this insight to subregional courts in Africa. *See, e.g.*, RICHARD FRIMPONG OPPONG, LEGAL ASPECTS OF ECONOMIC INTEGRATION IN AFRICA 119 (2011).

[66] The Protocol was provisionally effective from the date of its conclusion in 1991, but it did not enter into force "definitively" until it had been ratified by seven member states. 1991 Protocol, *supra* note 60, Art. 34.

[67] *E.g.*, JOHN ILIFFE, OBASANJO, NIGERIA AND THE WORLD 129, 217–24 (2011); J. Shola Omotola, *From Importer to Exporter: The Changing Role of Nigeria in Promoting Democratic Values in Africa*, *in* AFRICAN POLITICS: BEYOND THE THIRD WAVE OF DEMOCRATISATION 31, 39 (Joelien Pretorius ed., 2008).

once again favoring integration, ECOWAS institutions—including the Court—became a priority. In December 2000, the member states appointed the first seven judges, who were sworn into office on January 31, 2001. The judges picked Hansine Donli as the Court's president. Donli was a natural choice to lead the Court. As a Nigerian with a network of contacts in the country, it would be easier for her to arrange for the infrastructure and administrative support that the judges required.[68]

Among the Court's initial tasks was finding courtrooms and offices for the judges, the chief registrar, and their staffs.[69] The judges secured the construction of a new building in Abuja, paid for by Nigeria. They next began outreach efforts to attract cases.[70] According to Donli, member states were largely unaware of "the need to seek [the Court's] advice with respect [to] the different problems they will be facing, arising from interpretation of the Treaty and Protocols."[71] Notwithstanding these outreach efforts, however, the ECOWAS Court remained idle for nearly three years after opening its doors for business.

II. EXPANDING THE JURISDICTION AND ACCESS RULES OF THE ECOWAS COURT

The member states created the ECOWAS Court to adjudicate interstate economic disputes. But in the wake of the humanitarian interventions of the 1990s, and as human rights NGOs became more active in regional policymaking—an involvement made possible by the Community's new openness to civil society—the NGOs saw an opportunity to redeploy an existing institution to promote their objectives. They focused on a provision in the 2001 Good Governance Protocol that suggested that the not-yet-operational Court might one day hear "cases relating to violations of human rights, after all attempts to resolve the matter at the national level have failed."[72] In 2001, such a possibility seemed remote. In this part we explain how advocates transformed that vague promise into a reality.

The opportunity for change presented itself following the Court's first decision—*Afolabi v. Nigeria*—a case challenging blatant noncompliance with ECOWAS free-movement rules.[73] We first review the Court's dismissal of the case and then explain how ECOWAS judges, civil society groups, and ECOWAS officials lobbied the member states to expand the Court's jurisdiction. We then consider how these actors created an international human rights court with design features different from other human rights tribunals.

---

[68] Interview with judges at the headquarters of the ECOWAS Community Court of Justice, in Abuja, Nigeria (Mar. 11, 2011); Adelanwa Bamgboye, *Nigeria: Some Judges Are Strong Even at 80—Hansine Donli*, DAILY TRUST (Nigeria) (Sept. 28, 2010), *at* http://allafrica.com/stories/201009280476.html. Although the news archive at AllAfrica.com requires a subscription, each of the links to that archive leads to a web page with the first few sentences of the article, information about its publication, and a link to the full article. All sources cited from AllAfrica.com are also on file with authors.

[69] The ECOWAS Court was initially located in Lagos, Nigeria. It moved to its permanent headquarters in the capital of Abuja after Nigeria was designated in 2002 as the host country of the Court. Adewale Banjo, *The ECOWAS Court and the Politics of Access to Justice in West Africa*, 32 AFR. DEV. 69, 77 (2007).

[70] Interview with judges at the headquarters of the ECOWAS Community Court of Justice, *supra* note 68; *see also* Lillian Okenwa, *Law Personality: 'ECOWAS Court Jurisdiction Will Be Expanded,'* ALLAFRICA.COM (Sept. 21, 2004) (describing outreach efforts by ECOWAS judges), *at* http://allafrica.com/stories/200409210061.html.

[71] Banjo, *supra* note 69, at 77.

[72] 2001 Good Governance Protocol, *supra* note 49, Art. 39.

[73] Afolabi v. Nigeria, Case No. ECW/CCJ/APP/01/03, Judgment (Apr. 27, 2004), *reprinted in* 2004–2009 COMMUNITY COURT OF JUSTICE, ECOWAS LAW REPORT 1 (2011).

The Afolabi *Case: Justice Denied for Private Litigants*

Olajide Afolabi was a Nigerian trader who had entered into a contract to purchase goods in Benin. Afolabi could not complete the transaction because Nigeria unilaterally closed the border between the two countries. He filed suit with the ECOWAS Court, alleging that the border closure violated the right to free movement of persons and goods.[74]

Nigeria challenged the Court's jurisdiction and Afolabi's standing, arguing that the 1991 Protocol did not authorize private parties to litigate before the Court. Afolabi countered by invoking a Protocol provision stating that a "Member State *may*, on behalf of its nationals, institute proceedings against another member State."[75] He asserted that the word "may" permits states to raise such cases but does not preclude the Court from receiving complaints from individuals.[76] Afolabi also argued that when a private party sues his own country, that nation "cannot represent the party because the Member State cannot be both the plaintiff and the defender."[77] Finally, Afolabi invoked "the principles of equity"[78] in the 1991 Protocol to support an expansive interpretation of the Court's jurisdiction.[79]

The Court rejected each of these arguments and dismissed the suit. The judges acknowledged that Afolabi's complaint raised "a serious claim touching on free movement and free movement of goods,"[80] but they reasoned that an ECOWAS legal instrument must expressly grant the Court jurisdiction. Article 9 of the 1991 Protocol is "plain" and "unambiguous" on this issue: only states can institute proceedings on behalf of their nationals.[81] The Protocol must therefore be applied as written, even if the result—insulating states against suits by their own nationals alleging violations of ECOWAS rules—seems "repugnant," "absurd[]," or "harsh."[82]

The ECOWAS Court also rejected Afolabi's broad interpretation of the word "equity" in the 1991 Protocol, comparing it to a similar provision in the Treaty Establishing the European Community.[83] According to the Court, "activist[] judges" on the European Court of Justice had applied this provision to "define the role of the [European] court very broadly," "to extend its review on jurisdiction to cover bodies which were not listed in the Treaty," and "to fill in gaps in treaties."[84] The ECOWAS judges candidly declared that, because "some of the [ECJ's] decisions [have] attracted criticisms," "[w]e . . . do not want to tow on the same line."[85]

The *Afolabi* case was a paradigmatic illustration of the serious physical and legal barriers confronting the region's importers and exporters. Like the ECJ before it, the ECOWAS Court

---

[74] Afolabi invoked this right as guaranteed in the 1993 Treaty, *supra* note 37, Protocol A/P.1/5/79 (free movement), *supra* note 34, and the African Charter, *supra* note 7. *Id.*, para. 7.

[75] 1991 Protocol, *supra* note 60, Art. 9(3) (emphasis added).

[76] Afolabi v. Nigeria, Judgment, *supra* note 73, paras. 14, 23.

[77] *Id.*, para. 15.

[78] 1991 Protocol, *supra* note 60, Art. 9(1) ("The Court shall ensure the observance of law and of the principles of equity in the interpretation and application of the provisions of the Treaty.").

[79] Afolabi v. Nigeria, Judgment, *supra* note 73, para. 41.

[80] *Id.*, para. 55.

[81] *Id.*, paras. 59, 61.

[82] *Id.*, paras. 37, 54.

[83] Treaty Establishing the European Economic Community, Art. 164, Mar. 25, 1957, 298 UNTS 3 (requiring the ECJ to "ensure observance of law and justice in the interpretation and application of this Treaty").

[84] Afolabi v. Nigeria, Judgment, *supra* note 73, para. 56.

[85] *Id.*

could have adopted a purposive interpretation of Community economic rules to enable private traders to challenge those barriers. Instead, the judges responded with restraint. They strictly interpreted the 1991 Protocol and concluded that only ECOWAS member states could authorize the Court to review complaints from private actors.

The Coordinated Campaign by Nonstate Actors to Redesign the ECOWAS Court, and the Surprising Absence of Member State Opposition

The dismissal of the *Afolabi* suit exposed a basic flaw in the Court's architecture: governments had little incentive to challenge barriers to regional integration, and private traders had no judicial mechanism for doing so. Responding to this flaw, ECOWAS judges, NGOs, and Community officials launched a campaign to expand the Court's jurisdiction. The campaign succeeded, but the institutional reforms did not address the unsatisfactory outcome in *Afolabi*. Instead, the changes gave the ECOWAS Court a capacious human rights mandate. In this section, we describe the coordinated campaign by ECOWAS judges, NGOs, and Community officials to lobby for giving the Court jurisdiction over human rights cases. We also explore the surprising lack of member state opposition to the campaign. In part IV, we return to these events to explain why court reform omitted private litigant access in economic cases.

ECOWAS judges had long recognized the problems that the *Afolabi* case illustrated. As one judge explained in an interview: "Individuals started to come and asked us if they had access to the Court. They were surprised because ECOWAS has Protocols that affected them—such as free movement of people and goods—and they didn't understand how the Protocols were supposed to be effective." The judges were discussing how to address the situation when Afolabi filed his complaint in October 2003. The case's sympathetic facts "assisted us in making a proposal" to expand the Court's jurisdiction, relying on a clause in the 1991 Protocol that invites such proposals.[86]

In contrast to the narrow, formalist analysis of the *Afolabi* decision, the judges raised expansive policy arguments outside the courtroom to lobby for an overhaul of the 1991 Protocol. On the same day that the Court released the *Afolabi* judgment, it also issued a press release urging governments "to enable individuals to bring actions before the court as there are cases member states cannot bring on behalf of [their] nationals."[87] The Court also published a booklet that summarized the legal arguments of parties in *Afolabi* and the judgment dismissing the suit. The judges distributed the booklet widely to show that they had finally issued a decision and to highlight the flaws in the ECOWAS legal system.[88] During the next several months, in meetings with lawyers, civil society groups, and government officials, and in statements to the

[86] Interview with judges at the headquarters of the ECOWAS Community Court of Justice, *supra* note 68; 1991 Protocol, *supra* note 60, Art. 33(1) (providing that "the President of the Court may . . . submit proposals for amendments of this Protocol").

[87] Lillian Okenwa, *ECOWAS Court Not Open to Individual Litigants*, THIS DAY (Nigeria) (Apr. 28, 2004) (on file with authors); *see also ECOWAS Throws Out Suit Against Nigeria over Land Border Closure with Benin*, VANGUARD (Nigeria) (Apr. 28, 2004), 2004 WLNR 7109799.

[88] During interviews at the Federal Ministry of Trade and Commerce of Nigeria, March 8, 2011, in Abuja, Nigeria, we were shown the booklet and discussed how it had been distributed.

news media,[89] the judges continued to publicize the need to provide access for private litigants.[90]

Regional bar associations and human rights groups joined the judges' campaign. The focus on human rights issues in ECOWAS—which, as part I explained, began with the abuses linked to ECOMOG's humanitarian interventions—expanded during the ensuing decade as civil society groups capitalized on the shift to more democratic governments, the rebranding of ECOWAS as a "people-centered" institution, and the enhanced access rules for transnational NGOs.[91]

Shortly after the Court dismissed the *Afolabi* case, human rights groups seized the opportunity for court reform.[92] Leaders of the West African Bar Association met with ECOWAS judges and staff to press the case for "a Court that could address human rights issues."[93] With the judges' support, bar association attorneys consulted with other NGOs and ECOWAS officials to develop a proposal to revise the Court's jurisdiction. The key stakeholders met in Dakar, Senegal, in October 2004 at a consultative forum organized by the Open Society Initiative for West Africa.[94] The forum issued a declaration calling for the

[89] *E.g.*, Lillian Okenwa, *Broaden ECOWAS Court's Jurisdiction*, THIS DAY (Nigeria) (Sept. 2, 2004), *at* http://allafrica.com/stories/200409020666.html; Justice Aminata Malle Sanogo, Practice and Procedure in ECOWAS Court, paper presented at the 2007 Annual General Conference of the Nigerian Bar Association at Ilorin, Kwara State, Nigeria (Aug. 26–31, 2007), *quoted in* A. O. Enabulele, *Reflections on the ECOWAS Community Court Protocol and the Constitutions of Member States*, 12 INT'L COMMUNITY L. REV. 111, 117 (2010).

[90] The judges appear to have favored giving private litigants access to the Court in both economic and human rights cases:

> [T]he right of access to the Court is the keystone in the development of the Community law. The promotion and protection of human rights and fundamental freedoms of Community Citizens cannot be ensured, if right of direct access to the Community Court of Justice is not guaranteed. A cardinal objective of ECOWAS is the formation of an economic union and a common market. . . . [T]his scheme and the intended benefits cannot be realized, unless individuals, consumers, manufacturers and corporate bodies that are the prime movers in commercial transactions have direct access to the Court of Justice.

ECOWAS: Court Procedure and the Application of Protocols 10–12 (n.d.), *at* http://www.crin.org/docs/ecowas procedure.doc. Circumstantial evidence suggests that the Court prepared this document. Specifically, in press interviews ECOWAS judges echoed similar themes. *See, e.g.*, Lillian Okenwa, *ECOWAS Court: Individuals to Have Access*, THIS DAY (Nigeria) (Feb. 9, 2005), *at* http://allafrica.com/stories/200502090527.html. In part IV, we discuss why access for private litigants alleging violations of ECOWAS economic rules was dropped from the court reform agenda.

[91] Telephone interview with Human Rights Advocate A (Jan. 11, 2011); Telephone interview with Human Rights Advocate B, *supra* note 48; Interview with Human Rights Advocate F, in Abuja, Nigeria (Mar. 7, 2011); Interview with Human Rights Advocate H, in Abuja, Nigeria (Mar. 10, 2011). In 2002, Mohammed Ibn Chambas, ECOWAS's executive secretary from 2002 to 2006, committed to making the Community a "people-centered" institution and expanding access to civil society and the public. *Interview with Mohamed Ibn Chambas, Executive Secretary of ECOWAS*, UN INTEGRATED REGIONAL INFORMATION NETWORK (Mar. 12, 2002), *at* http://www.irinnews.org/report/30701/west-africa-irin-interview-with-mohamed-ibn-chambas-executive-secretary-of-ecowas.

[92] Interview with Human Rights Advocate C, in Abuja, Nigeria (Mar. 9, 2011); Telephone interview with Human Rights Advocate B, *supra* note 48.

[93] Interview with Human Rights Advocate C, *supra* note 92; *see also* Femi Falana, *The Community Court of Justice, ECOWAS and the Experiences of Other Regional Courts*, *in* COMPENDIUM OF THE INTERNATIONAL CONFERENCE ON "THE LAW IN THE PROCESS OF INTEGRATION IN WEST AFRICA," ABUJA, NIGERIA (NOV. 13–14, 2007) 143, 145 (after the *Afolabi* judgment, the "West African Bar Association collaborated with the Court in the campaign" to give private actors direct access to the ECOWAS Court "for the enforcement of their human rights").

[94] The Consultative Forum on Protecting the Rights of ECOWAS Citizens Through the ECOWAS Court of Justice was held in Dakar, Senegal on October 18–20, 2004. *See* http://aros.trustafrica.org/index.php/ECOWAS _Community_Court_of_Justice.

urgent adoption of a protocol to give individuals direct access to the Court in human rights cases.[95]

At this stage, officials in the ECOWAS Executive Secretariat became key players. The secretariat had long supported making ECOWAS more relevant to civil society and adding a human rights mandate to Community legal texts and institutions.[96] Its officials were also frustrated by the Court's budgetary needs. The Court is a permanent judicial body. But with no cases on its docket, the Court was, in the words of one official, a "huge body with nothing to do."[97] The secretariat wanted to give the judges and staff enough work to justify the large expenditure of Community resources.[98]

The secretariat's backing greatly increased the likelihood that the member states would approve the protocol advocated by ECOWAS judges and NGOs. We asked officials in the Legal Affairs Directorate how national political leaders viewed the court reform proposal. "They trusted us" was the response:

> When we draft [legal] texts, we consult a lot. We write memoranda that explain why we are making the proposal. We exchange views with the member states. Member states comment on the draft proposals before we convey any draft legislation. We incorporate all of this input before the actual meeting where the proposal is discussed.[99]

Notwithstanding the ECOWAS secretariat's support for the proposal, the absence of government opposition to giving the Court a human rights mandate is striking. We queried numerous stakeholders to probe for such opposition. They all responded that the proposal was approved without much controversy. By all appearances, that is accurate. We found no evidence that individual countries, or member states collectively, attempted to block, stall, or narrow the protocol. Nonetheless, civil society groups recognized that they needed to "mobilize" to secure the protocol's adoption—in particular, by soliciting the support of sympathetic governments.[100] They met with the president of Senegal (the only nation in West Africa never ruled by a military dictatorship), arguing that a human rights court was "especially needed for countries whose legal and judicial systems are weak."[101] The president agreed to support the protocol at the next meeting of the ECOWAS Authority. The NGOs also consulted officials from the justice and integration ministries in several countries, and conferred with the staff of the ECOWAS Legal Affairs Directorate, which was preparing the final draft of the protocol.[102]

Barely nine months after the dismissal of the *Afolabi* case, the coordinated court reform campaign reached a successful conclusion. On January 19, 2005, the member states adopted the

---

[95] *Id.*; Interview with Human Rights Advocate C, *supra* note 92; Nneoma Nwogu, *Regional Integration as an Instrument of Human Rights: Reconceptualizing ECOWAS*, 6 J. HUM. RTS. 345, 352 (2007).

[96] Nwogu, *supra* note 95, at 350.

[97] Interview with ECOWAS Legal Affairs Directorate A, *supra* note 62.

[98] *Id.*; Interview with ECOWAS Legal Affairs Directorate B, in Abuja, Nigeria (Mar. 7, 2011).

[99] Interview with ECOWAS Legal Affairs Directorate B, *supra* note 98.

[100] Interview with Human Rights Advocate C, *supra* note 92; Telephone interview with Human Rights Advocate B, *supra* note 48.

[101] Interview with Human Rights Advocate C, *supra* note 92.

[102] *Id.*

2005 Protocol by consensus and with immediate provisional effect.[103] The Protocol markedly expands the ECOWAS Court's authority, most notably by giving the Court a capacious human rights mandate.

The Distinctive Features of the ECOWAS Court's Human Rights Jurisdiction

The 2005 Protocol's most important clauses appear in two short sentences in articles redefining the ECOWAS Court's jurisdiction and access rules. Article 3 revises Article 9 of the 1991 Protocol and lists each ground of jurisdiction. The fourth paragraph states: "The Court has jurisdiction to determine case[s] of violation of human rights that occur in any Member State."[104] Article 4, which adds a new Article 10 to the 1991 Protocol, identifies the litigants who have access to the ECOWAS Court. It includes a subparagraph authorizing the Court to receive complaints from "individuals on application for relief for violation of their human rights."[105] On first impression, these simple provisions appear straightforward. In reality, they mask three design features that collectively gave the ECOWAS Court much broader authority than other human rights tribunals.

Direct access for private litigants. First, the ECOWAS Court is unusual for a new human rights court in granting direct access to private litigants. For the vast majority of cases in the African and American human rights systems (and in the European system prior to 1998), complainants must first submit their allegations to a quasi-judicial commission that screens complaints and issues nonbinding recommendations for those petitions that it deems admissible. Review by a court with the power to issue a legally binding judgment occurs only if a state has voluntarily accepted the court's jurisdiction and if the commission or the state refers the case for a judicial resolution.[106]

This tiered review structure—a commission to vet complaints, optional jurisdiction, and limiting the actors who can refer cases to a court—provides states with multiple layers of political protection. In the African Charter system, for example, private litigants have direct access to the African Court on Human and Peoples' Rights only if the respondent state has ratified the protocol establishing the Court and filed a separate optional declaration allowing private litigants to submit such complaints. To date, only seven of fifty-four African nations—four of them ECOWAS member states—have filed such declarations.[107]

The ECOWAS Court lacks any of these political buffers. ECOWAS judges have repeatedly affirmed that private litigants "have direct access to . . . the Court when their human rights are

---

[103] 2005 Protocol, *supra* note 10, Art. 11 (providing that the protocol "shall enter into force provisionally upon signature by the Heads of State and Government" and "shall definitively enter into force upon the ratification by at least nine (9) signatory States").

[104] *Id.*, Art. 3 (revising Art. 9(4) of the 1991 Protocol).

[105] *Id.*, Art. 4 (inserting Art. 10(d) into the 1991 Protocol). Article 10(d) also provides that applications alleging human rights violations may not be anonymous and many not be made while the same matter is pending before another international court.

[106] Thomas Buergenthal, *The Evolving International Human Rights System*, 100 AJIL 783, 791–801 (2006).

[107] Only twenty-six of fifty-four African Charter member states have ratified the African Court Protocol. Seven of these twenty-six states—Burkina Faso, Côte d'Ivoire, Ghana, Malawi, Mali, Rwanda, and Tanzania—have filed separate optional declarations giving private litigants direct access the Africa Court. *See* Côte d'Ivoire Deposits the Declaration Allowing Individuals Direct Access (July 31, 2013), *at* http://www.african-court.org/en/index.php/news/latest-news/426-the-republic-of-cote-d-ivoire-deposits-the-declaration-allowing-individuals-and-ngos-direct-access-to-the-african-court.

violated."[108] The judges have extended access not only to individuals—who are expressly mentioned in the 2005 Protocol—but to NGOs.[109] They have also rejected attempts by governments to circumvent the direct access provision, rebuffing arguments that human rights are matters essentially within a state's domestic jurisdiction, that ECOWAS treaties and protocols have no domestic effect, and that direct access for NGOs should be denied because litigants have no standing to challenge human rights violations before national courts.[110]

An indeterminate human rights jurisdiction. A second distinctive feature of the Court's design is that no ECOWAS legal instrument prescribes which human rights its judges can adjudicate. The primary role of the European, Inter-American, and African courts is to interpret and apply their respective regional human rights charters.[111] Their association with these instruments provides a sanctioned source of law and legal authority for their judges. By contrast, ECOWAS judges have no designated human rights charter to apply. By declining to designate a prescribed catalogue of rights, the 2005 Protocol avoided provoking political controversy over which rights the ECOWAS Court could review. The absence such of an enumerated list, however, also presented risks for the Court—namely, that its new human rights jurisdiction could be challenged as an overbroad delegation to interpret expansively this rapidly evolving area of international law. As we later explain, the Court is also open to the charge that it applies human rights instruments that are not legally binding.[112]

ECOWAS judges have viewed the lack of designated human rights norms as an "opportunity to define and delimit the scope and legal parameters of its human rights mandate in its own image."[113] The Court has underscored the primacy of the African human rights system, noting that all ECOWAS member states are parties to the African Charter, which is also referenced in

---

[108] Tidjani v. Nigeria, Case No. ECW/CCJ/APP/01/06, Judgment, para. 22 (July 28, 2007).

[109] *E.g.*, Socio-Economic Rights and Accountability Project v. Nigeria, Case No. ECW/CCJ/APP/08/09, Ruling, paras. 59–61 (Dec. 10, 2010) [hereinafter SERAP Niger Delta Ruling]; Socio-Economic Rights and Accountability Project v. Nigeria, Case No. ECW/CCJ/APP/08/08, Ruling, paras. 33–34 (Oct. 27, 2009), [hereinafter SERAP Basic Education Ruling]. By contrast, the Court has held that "no corporate body can bring a human rights case before this court as a plaintiff as an alleged victim of human rights abuse." Starcrest Investment Ltd. v. Nigeria, Case No. ECW/CCJ/APP/01/08, Judgment, para. 17 (July 8, 2011).

[110] *E.g.*, SERAP Basic Education Ruling, *supra* note 109, paras. 18–20; Saidykhan v. The Gambia, Case No. ECW/CCJ/APP/11/07, Ruling, para. 39 (June 30, 2009).

[111] Laurence R. Helfer, *Forum Shopping for Human Rights*, 148 U. PA. L. REV. 285, 301 (1999). For example, the contentious jurisdiction of the Inter-American Court of Human Rights "relates mainly to the application of the [American Convention on Human Rights], but has also been extended to a few other regional human rights treaties." Gerald L. Neuman, *Import, Export, and Regional Consent in the Inter-American Court of Human Rights*, 19 EUR. J. INT'L L. 101, 102 (2008). The Court's advisory jurisdiction is wider, extending to the interpretation of other human rights treaties ratified by Organization of American States member states. *Id.* at 102 & n.2. The jurisdiction of the African Court on Human and Peoples' Rights is broader still. It applies principally to the African Charter but also extends to "other relevant Human Rights instrument[s] ratified by the States concerned" (contentious jurisdiction) and "any other relevant human rights instruments" (advisory jurisdiction). Protocol to the African Charter on Human and Peoples' Rights on the Establishment of an African Court on Human and Peoples' Rights, Arts. 3, 4, June 10, 1998, OAU Doc. OAU/LEG/EXP/AFCHPR/PROT (III) (entered into force Jan. 25, 2004).

[112] *See* Ebobrah, *supra* note 9, at 93; Solomon T. Ebobrah, *Critical Issues in the Human Rights Mandate of the ECOWAS Court of Justice*, 54 J. AFR. L. 1, 3–7 (2010) [hereinafter Ebobrah, *Critical Issues*].

[113] Tony Anene-Maidoh, The Mandate of a Regional Court: Experiences from ECOWAS Court of Justice, paper presented at the Regional Colloquium on the SADC Tribunal, Johannesburg (Mar. 12–13, 2013) (statement by ECOWAS Court chief registrar).

the 1993 Treaty.[114] But ECOWAS judges also regularly apply the Universal Declaration of Human Rights and UN human rights conventions that member states have ratified,[115] including the International Covenant on Civil and Political Rights,[116] the International Covenant on Economic, Social and Cultural Rights,[117] and the UN Convention Against Torture.[118]

The ECOWAS Court also considers a broad array of other sources when interpreting human rights norms. The Court draws inspiration from the 1991 Protocol's directive to "apply, as necessary, the body of laws as contained in Article 38 of the Statute of the International Court of Justice,"[119] which, in turn, specifies that treaties, custom, and general principles of law, as well as national judicial decisions and the teachings of highly qualified publicists, are all sources of international law.[120] The Court has relied on this provision to consult a wide array of binding and hortatory international human rights instruments and national laws.[121] In *Hadijatou Mani Kouraou v. Niger*, for example, the judges cited a multiplicity of sources in reaffirming the peremptory norm against slavery, and they endorsed the definition of modern forms of slavery adopted by the International Criminal Tribunal for the Former Yugoslavia.[122]

No requirement to first exhaust domestic remedies. The ECOWAS Court's ability to hear human rights cases is aided by the absence of a requirement to exhaust local remedies. In all other regional and UN human rights petition systems, individuals must first seek relief in national courts, administrative agencies, or other domestic venues.[123] If a petitioner does not exhaust such remedies—or explain why they are unavailable, ineffective, or insufficient—the international tribunal will dismiss her complaint.[124]

---

[114] *E.g.*, Alade v. Nigeria, Case No. ECW/CCJ/APP/05/11, Judgment, para. 24 (June 11, 2012); Keita v. Mali, Case No. ECW/CCJ/APP/05/06, Judgment, para. 34 (Mar. 22, 2007).

[115] *E.g.*, Alade v. Nigeria, Judgment, *supra* note 114, para. 25 (asserting the authority to interpret "UN Conventions . . . acceded to by Member States of ECOWAS").

[116] Dec. 16, 1966, 999 UNTS 171.

[117] Dec. 16, 1966, 999 UNTS 3.

[118] Convention Against Torture and Other Cruel, Inhuman or Degrading Treatment or Punishment, Dec. 10, 1984, S. TREATY DOC. NO. 100-20 (1988), 1465 UNTS 113.

[119] 1991 Protocol, *supra* note 60, Art. 19.

[120] Statute of the International Court of Justice, Art. 38.

[121] *E.g.*, David v. Uwechue, Case No. ECW/CCJ/APP/04/09, Ruling, para. 41 (June 11, 2010) ("As an international court with jurisdiction over human rights violation[s,] the court cannot disregard the basic principles as well as the practice that guide the adjudication of the disputes on human rights at the international level.").

[122] Hadijatou Mani Koraou v. Niger, Case No. ECW/CCJ/APP/08/07, Judgment, paras. 74–75, 77 (Oct. 27, 2008), *unofficial translation available at* http://www.refworld.org/pdfid/496b41fa2.pdf.

[123] "The rule that local remedies must be exhausted before international proceedings may be instituted is a well-established rule of customary international law[.]" Interhandel (Switz. v. U.S.), 1959 ICJ REP. 6, 27 (Mar. 21). Some international agreements—most notably, bilateral investment treaties—intentionally omit an exhaustion requirement. *E.g.*, George K. Foster, *Striking a Balance Between Investor Protections and National Sovereignty: The Relevance of Local Remedies in Investment Treaty Arbitration*, 49 COLUM. J. TRANSNAT'L L. 201 (2011). For human rights treaties, however, exhaustion is ubiquitous. For example, the African Commission "can only deal with a matter submitted to it after making sure that all local remedies, if they exist, have been exhausted, unless it is obvious to the Commission that the procedure of achieving these remedies would be unduly prolonged." African Charter, *supra* note 7, Art. 50; *see also* Office of the United Nations High Commissioner for Human Rights, Human Rights Treaty Bodies—Individual Communications, Procedure for Complaints by Individuals Under the Human Rights Treaties, *at* http://www2.ohchr.org/english/bodies/petitions/individual.htm.

[124] According to the African Commission, "A remedy is considered *available* if the petitioner can pursue it without impediment; it is deemed *effective* if it offers a prospect of success, and it is found *sufficient* if it is capable of redressing the complaint." Dawda Jawara v. The Gambia, Comm. Nos. 147/95 & 149/96, para. 31, AFR. COMM'N ON HUM. & PEOPLES' RTS., 13 ANN. ACTIVITY REP., Annex V (1999–2000), *at* http://www.achpr.org/files/activity-reports/13/achpr26and27_actrep13_19992000_eng.pdf.

In the human rights context, an exhaustion requirement acts as a buffer between domestic and international legal systems. It "reinforces the subsidiary and complementary relationship of the international system to systems of internal protection,"[125] and reflects a belief that domestic institutions should have "a first shot" at addressing human rights complaints.[126] An exhaustion rule also reduces "forum shopping and unnecessary rivalry between municipal and international courts," as well as the risk of conflicting decisions.[127] Finally, it prevents international tribunals from being overburdened by a flood of human rights cases.[128]

Since granting the ECOWAS Court the authority to hear human rights cases, West African governments have repeatedly asserted that individuals must exhaust domestic remedies before petitioning the Court in Abuja. The judges have unwaveringly rebuffed these arguments, reasoning that the lack of an exhaustion rule is neither an inadvertent omission nor a flaw in the Court's human rights mandate, but a deliberately chosen element of its judicial architecture.[129] Just as the judges in the *Afolabi* case refused to imply jurisdiction over suits by private parties, they have also held that non-exhaustion "cannot be taken away by implication" but requires an express amendment of the 2005 Protocol.[130] Nor is the doctrine limited to situations where litigants have bypassed national proceedings. The ECOWAS Court has also decided cases that were pending before domestic courts,[131] leading commentators to warn of potential conflicts between ECOWAS and national judges.[132]

A Broad Authority for Human Rights Suits, but a Narrower Mandate for Economic Cases

Why did the member states agree to give the Court such expansive authority to adjudicate human rights suits? And why did they allow direct access for human rights complaints but not for suits alleging violations of ECOWAS economic rules?

In our interviews, stakeholders suggested several plausible explanations. First, states appear to have accepted that the judges, secretariat officials, and civil society groups were acting in good faith and within the scope of their delegated authority. Participants in the court reform campaign underscored that their actions were consistent with ECOWAS rules. Community legal texts expressly authorize the judges to propose changes to the 1991 Protocol. They also

---

[125] Nsongurna Udombana, *So Far, So Fair: The Local Remedies Rule in the Jurisprudence of the African Commission on Human and Peoples' Rights*, 97 AJIL 1, 9 (2003).

[126] Ebobrah, *supra* note 9, at 88.

[127] A. O. Enabulele, *Sailing Against the Tide: Exhaustion of Domestic Remedies and the ECOWAS Community Court of Justice*, 56 J. AFR. L. 268 (2012).

[128] Ebobrah, *supra* note 9, at 92.

[129] *E.g.*, Saidykhan v. The Gambia, Ruling, *supra* note 110, para. 43 (explaining that "the Supplementary Protocol is an example of legislating out of the rule of customary international law regarding the exhaustion of local remedies"); Hadijatou Mani Kouraou v. Niger, Judgment, *supra* note 122, para. 45 (rejecting the argument that the lack of an exhaustion requirement is "a gap that should be filled" by judicial interpretation). Although states are free to dispense with an exhaustion of local remedies requirement, they have almost never done so for international human rights courts and review bodies. *See supra* note 123.

[130] Saidykhan v. The Gambia, Ruling, *supra* note 110, para. 42.

[131] *E.g.*, Ayika v. Liberia, Case No. ECW/CCJ/APP/07/11, Ruling (Dec. 19, 2011); Hadijatou Mani Kouraou v. Niger, Judgment, *supra* note 122.

[132] Enabulele, *supra* note 127, at 293–94. The risk of conflict is mitigated by the ECOWAS Court's repeated assertion that it is not an appellate tribunal and will not generally review challenges to national court decisions. *See, e.g.*, Keita v. Mali, Judgment, *supra* note 114, para. 31; Alade v. Nigeria, Judgment, *supra* note 114, paras. 34–35.

empower NGOs to participate in discussions in ECOWAS forums. As for the Executive Secretariat, one of its key tasks is drafting protocols to ECOWAS legal instruments.

Second, all stakeholders supported giving the Court something to do. The frustration with idle judges was a direct, albeit unintended, artifact of the earlier decision to make the ECOWAS Court a full-time judicial body. The 2005 Protocol put cases on the Court's docket, and it gave member states a concrete way to fulfill their promise to make ECOWAS a more people-centered organization. Moreover, Community legal texts—in particular, the 2001 Good Governance Protocol—had clearly envisioned giving a human rights jurisdiction to the Court.

Third, human rights NGOs lobbied hard for a human rights jurisdiction and for the specific design features that we have highlighted. They argued that exhaustion would make it too difficult for West Africans to access the Court, especially since most countries "had weak judiciaries" and lacked "any functioning human rights apparatus."[133] They also highlighted frustrations with the African Commission on Human and Peoples' Rights' slow review of complaints and the spotty compliance with its nonbinding recommendations.[134] ECOWAS officials were receptive to the advocates' concerns. They also recognized that an exhaustion requirement would do little to remedy the lack of cases on the Court's docket.[135] As for the lack of enumerated human rights, governments apparently assumed that the references to the African Charter in the 1993 Treaty would lead the Court to view the Charter as the primary source of human rights norms in ECOWAS.[136]

Fourth, observers stressed that the 2005 Protocol—like other ECOWAS protocols—entered into force on a provisional basis.[137] Governments may therefore have believed that the Court's human rights jurisdiction would be relatively easy to undo if the Court later behaved in ways that encroached on national sovereignty. The same rationale may also explain the protocol's other design features. For example, ECOWAS officials characterized the absence of an exhaustion requirement as an "experiment" that could be revisited in the future.[138] As we explain below, however, despite the nominally provisional status of the 2005 Protocol, its acceptance as an ongoing feature of the Court became a political, if not a legal, fait accompli.

A final issue concerns the more circumscribed jurisdiction and access provisions for cases unrelated to human rights. The 2005 Protocol authorizes the ECOWAS Court to interpret all Community legal instruments and to determine the "failure by Member States to honor their obligations" under those instruments.[139] Only member states and ECOWAS officials,

---

[133] Interview with Human Rights Advocate C, *supra* note 92.

[134] Interview with Academic A, in Abuja, Nigeria, and by telephone (Feb.–Mar. 2011); *see also* FRANS VILJOEN, INTERNATIONAL HUMAN RIGHTS LAW IN AFRICA 297, 487 (2d ed. 2012) (reviewing the "major impediments to the[] effectiveness and impact" of the African Commission on Human Rights and describing the Commission's "weaknesses . . . in providing a credible and timely forum for . . . recourse" to victims).

[135] Interview with ECOWAS Legal Affairs Directorate B, *supra* note 98.

[136] Interview with Human Rights Advocate C, *supra* note 92.

[137] Interview with ECOWAS Legal Affairs Directorate A, *supra* note 62; Telephone interview with Human Rights Advocate A, *supra* note 91; Telephone interview with Human Rights Advocate B, *supra* note 48; Interview with ECOWAS Court Official C, in Abuja, Nigeria (Mar. 11, 2011).

[138] Interview with ECOWAS Legal Affairs Directorate A, *supra* note 62.

[139] 2005 Protocol, *supra* note 103, Art. 3 (revising Article 9(1)(a), (b) & (d) of the 1991 Protocol).

however, can file such suits; individuals cannot.[140] The Protocol does permit private actors to challenge actions or omissions of Community officials,[141] and it authorizes national judges to refer to the Court, either "on [their] own or at the request of any of the parties," questions concerning the interpretation of ECOWAS legal texts.[142] These reforms increase the Court's potential role in adjudicating challenges to noncompliance with ECOWAS economic rules. Despite the continuation of barriers to intraregional trade, however, no noncompliance suits have actually been filed by the secretariat or member states, and no national judges have referred cases to the Court.[143] Part IV returns to this issue, delving further into the puzzle of why the Court's adjudicatory role in economic disputes remains virtually nonexistent.

III. Challenges to the ECOWAS Court's Human Rights Authority

In its eight years of operation as a human rights court, the ECOWAS Court has survived several political controversies and challenges. The first challenge stemmed from the Court's intervention in a contested Nigerian election—which triggered protests from Nigerian politicians, judges, and lawyers. A second, more serious threat involved an effort by the Gambia to curtail the Court's jurisdiction in response to decisions finding that state responsible for the torture of journalists. As we explain, the ECOWAS Court emerged from these two events largely unscathed and arguably strengthened. The third challenge, which is ongoing, focuses on improving member state compliance with the Court's judgments.

A Controversial Intervention in a Nigerian Election Dispute and the Creation of the ECOWAS Judicial Council

When the ECOWAS Court began to hear cases under its new human rights jurisdiction, some national judges and attorneys expressed concern that the Court would become embroiled in domestic political disputes. These concerns came to a head in 2005—the first year of the Court's new mandate—when the Court's president issued a controversial ruling in an election imbroglio involving a seat in the Nigerian Federal House of Representatives.

Jerry Ugokwe had been declared the winner of the election by the Independent National Electoral Commission. A Nigerian Elections Tribunal reversed the commission, finding that Ugokwe was ineligible to run for the seat. The Nigerian Federal Appeals Court—the final court of review for all election disputes in Nigeria—upheld Ugokwe's disqualification.[144] Dissatisfied with this outcome, Ugokwe filed a complaint with the ECOWAS Court alleging a violation of his right to a fair hearing.[145] Ugokwe asked the Court to issue a special interim order to

---

[140] *Id.*, Art. 4 (inserting Article 10(a) & (b) into the 1991 Protocol).

[141] *Id.* (inserting Article 10(c) into the 1991 Protocol).

[142] *Id.* (inserting Article 10(f) into the 1991 Protocol).

[143] Anene-Maidoh, *supra* note 113, at 9–10 (stating that the "concept of Preliminary Ruling as practiced by the [ECJ] is yet to take root in the context of regional integration in Africa").

[144] Lillian Okenwa, *Election Petition: ECOWAS Court Stops Ugokwe's Successor*, THIS DAY (Nigeria) (June 2, 2005), *at* http://allafrica.com/stories/200506030463.html.

[145] Iheanacho Nwosu, *West Africa: I Am at ECOWAS Court to Get Fair Hearing—Hon. Ugokwe*, DAILY CHAMPION (Nigeria) (June 21, 2005), *at* http://allafrica.com/stories/200506210089.html.

prevent the Nigerian government from invalidating his election victory or from seating his opponent.[146] President Donli issued the interim order barring the legislature from swearing in Okeke while Ugokwe's complaint was pending.[147] Nigeria promptly sought to dismiss the suit for lack of jurisdiction, accusing Ugokwe of "forum shopping with courts."[148] President Donli responded by renewing the interim order prior to leaving for a recess.[149] These were audacious acts, but Donli publicly defended them as necessary, temporary measures to preserve the existence of a justiciable controversy until the judges could review Ugokwe's allegations.[150]

Notwithstanding concerns over the orders' validity, Nigerian officials complied with the Court's interim directive. The attorney general and minister of justice issued a request to the speaker of the House of Representatives "not to swear [Okeke] in until the case is fully settled by the [ECOWAS Court]."[151] The request created a political uproar that spilled onto the front pages of the country's newspapers. Politicians, judges, and lawyers focused on a provision of the Nigerian Constitution that designates election disputes as exclusively domestic matters.[152] They argued that this clause deprived the ECOWAS Court of jurisdiction to hear the election disputes.[153]

After returning from a month-long recess, the judges dramatically reversed course and dismissed the suit. They reasoned that "no provision, whether general or specific, gives the Court powers to adjudicate on electoral issues or matters arising thereof."[154] They also asserted that the ECOWAS Court "is not a Court of Appeal or a Court of cassation" over domestic courts. The judges thus declared themselves without authority to intervene "against the execution of the Judgment already made by the Federal Appeal Court of the Member State of Nigeria."[155] The judges did not explain the about-face from the preliminary order, but the categorical nature of the decision suggests that they wanted to send a clear message that they would not intervene in future election disputes.

The Court's dramatic change of position did little, however, to quell the underlying legal and political controversy. As one Community official observed, "national high courts were

[146] Specifically, Ugokwe requested a "special interim order" enjoining (1) the INEC from (a) invalidating Ugokwe's election or (b) "tak[ing] any steps" toward his replacement, and (2) the Federal National Assembly from relieving Ugokwe of his seat. Ugokwe v. Nigeria, Case No. ECW/CCJ/APP/02/05, Judgment, paras. 7, 14.2–.3 (Oct. 7, 2005), *reprinted in* 2004–09 COMMUNITY COURT OF JUSTICE, ECOWAS LAW REPORT 37 (2011).

[147] Okenwa, *supra* note 144.

[148] *FG Asks ECOWAS Court to Dismiss Ugokwe Suit*, VANGUARD (Nigeria) (June 17, 2005), *at* http://allafrica.com/stories/200506170727.html.

[149] Ise-Olu-Oluwa Ige, *ECOWAS Court Goes on Recess*, VANGUARD (Nigeria) (July 7, 2005), *at* http://allafrica.com/stories/200507070032.html.

[150] Okenwa, *supra* note 144.

[151] Ugokwe v. Nigeria, Judgment, *supra* note 146, para. 10.

[152] Constitution of the Federal Republic of Nigeria, Art. 246(3), 1999, *at* http://www.nigeria-law.org/ConstitutionOfTheFederalRepublicOfNigeria.htm#CourtOfAppeal.

[153] Ige, *supra* note 149; Okenwa, *supra* note 144. The individuals whom we interviewed repeated these arguments. Telephone interview with Academic A (Jan. 6, 2011); Interview with Human Rights Advocate C, *supra* note 92; Interview with ECOWAS Legal Affairs Directorate A, *supra* note 62; Interview with ECOWAS Legal Affairs Directorate B, *supra* note 98.

[154] Ugokwe v. Nigeria, Judgment, *supra* note 146, para. 19.

[155] *Id.*, paras. 32, 33.

760 THE AMERICAN JOURNAL OF INTERNATIONAL LAW [Vol. 107:737

upset that [ECOWAS] judges with less qualifications and experience than they had could issue rulings that would be final and binding on them."[156] The *Ugokwe* case exacerbated these anxieties by putting the ECOWAS Court in direct conflict with the Nigerian judiciary and political establishment.

The member states responded to these concerns by creating a new ECOWAS institution that appears to have enhanced the Court's independence and authority. In 2006, as part of a wider overhaul of the Community,[157] the member states created a Judicial Council[158] "to ensure that the Court is endowed with the best qualified and competent persons to contribute . . . to the establishment of Community laws capable of consolidating and accelerating the regional integration process."[159] The council comprises the chief justices from member states not then represented on the seven-member Court.[160]

The Judicial Council increases the influence of national judges in the selection process for the ECOWAS Court, and it creates misconduct review procedures that insulate judges from attempts by governments to remove them from office. ECOWAS judges are "statutory appointments"—high-level positions that rotate among the member states. West African governments collectively decide which country is next in line for a statutory appointment to the Court. The Legal Affairs Directorate then advertises for the position and collects submissions from eligible applicants. Applications that meet specified criteria are forwarded to the Judicial Council, which vets applications and interviews candidates. The council then selects three candidates and forwards their names, together with point-based rankings, to the ECOWAS Authority, which decides which candidate to appoint to the Court. For sitting judges, the Council is tasked with reviewing complaints alleging judicial bias and other forms of malfeasance, providing a layer of political insulation for ECOWAS judges against whom such charges are filed.[161]

Also included in the Judicial Council reforms was a revision of the tenure of ECOWAS judges—from a five-year term with the possibility of one reappointment to a single, nonrenewable four-year term.[162] Secretariat officials explained this reform as a way to bring judicial appointments to the Court in line with other statutory appointments in the Community. Although the shortening of terms may seem like a rebuke of the ECOWAS Court, no one we interviewed characterized the change in this way. Rather, they noted that shorter, nonrenew-

---

[156] Interview with ECOWAS Legal Affairs Directorate A, *supra* note 62; *see also* Donald Andoor, *Nigeria: Ugokwe Loses House Seat*, THIS DAY (Nigeria) (Sept. 22, 2005), *at* http://allafrica.com/stories/200509230288.html.

[157] ECOWAS NEWSLETTER, no. 1, Oct. 2006 (describing institutional changes), *at* http://www.ecowas.int/publications/en/newsletter/ECOWAS_NewsLetter_01-Eng.pdf.

[158] Decision A/Dec.2/06/06 Establishing the Judicial Council of the Community (adopted June 14, 2006) (on file with authors).

[159] ECOWAS NEWSLETTER, *supra* note 157, at 4.

[160] Decision A/Dec.2/06/06, *supra* note 158, Arts. 1, 2.

[161] Regulation C/Reg.23/12/07, Adopting the Rules of Procedure of the Community–Judicial Council, Art. 5, Dec. 14–15, 2007 (on file with authors). The dismissal of judges for politically unpopular rulings has been a significant concern in the East African Community legal system. James T. Gathii, *Mission Creep or a Search for Relevance: The East African Court of Justice's Human Rights Strategy*, 24 DUKE J. COMP. & INT'L L. (forthcoming 2014) (manuscript at 24–25) (on file with authors).

[162] This reform amends Article 4 of the 1991 Protocol. *See* ECOWAS NEWSLETTER, *supra* note 157, at 4.

able terms would increase the opportunity of all ECOWAS member states to appoint judges to the Court.[163]

The Judicial Council and tenure reforms have been favorably received by stakeholders. As one lawyer noted, "Now that the Judicial Council exists, the stature of the Court will be higher, which will improve the quality of judges [since] more qualified candidates will apply."[164] The process is still relatively new, however, and only one set of appointments has been made using the new procedures: in 2008, the ECOWAS Authority approved the slate of judges recommended by the council.[165] In addition, some concerns over judicial qualifications persist—in particular, the absence of a requirement that judges be well versed in international human rights law.[166]

The Gambia's Proposal to Restrict the ECOWAS Court's Human Rights Jurisdiction

The next political flashpoint for the ECOWAS Court concerned two decisions against the Gambia—both finding that state responsible for the disappearance and torture of journalists—that were widely viewed as legally sound, albeit politically audacious. Unable to challenge the judgments as poorly reasoned or as an improper interference with domestic authority, the Gambia launched a campaign in 2009 to narrow the Court's human rights jurisdiction.

The case of Chief Ebrima Manneh involved a reporter for the *Daily Observer* who disclosed information that appeared in a news article critical of the government.[167] Plainclothes intelligence agents arrested Manneh in July 2006. He disappeared until January 2007, when reports emerged that he was being detained at a local police station. Intelligence and police officials denied that he was in their custody.[168] In May 2007, the NGO Media Foundation for West Africa filed a complaint with the ECOWAS Court charging the Gambia with numerous human rights abuses, demanding Manneh's release, and requesting compensation for his injuries.[169] The Gambia refused to respond to the complaint and ignored multiple requests to appear or

---

[163] Interview with ECOWAS Legal Affairs Directorate A, *supra* note 62. Other studies have found that international judges who are ineligible for reappointment are more likely to rule against the governments that appointed them. Erik Voeten, *The Impartiality of International Judges: Evidence from the European Court of Human Rights*, 102 AM. POL. SCI. REV. 417, 427 (2008).

[164] Interview with Human Rights Advocate C, *supra* note 92.

[165] African Press Organization, *ECOWAS Council of Ministers Seeks Regional Infrastructural Development* (Nov. 30, 2008) (reporting results of a 2008 meeting of the ECOWAS Council of Ministers at which the "Council . . . endorsed the report of the ECOWAS Judicial Council on the appointment of three new judges" for the Court), *at* http://appablog.wordpress.com/2008/11/30/burkina-faso-ecowas-council-of-ministers-seeks-regional-infrastructural-development/; Interview with ECOWAS Legal Affairs Directorate B, *supra* note 98.

[166] Solomon T. Ebobrah, *A Critical Analysis of the Human Rights Mandate of the ECOWAS Community Court of Justice* 47 n.194 (2008) (noting statement by ECOWAS Court vice president that "the human rights competence of prospective appointees should be taken into consideration" even though such competence is not expressly stated as a criterion for appointment), *at* http://www.humanrights.dk/files/doc/forskning/Research%20partnership%20programme%20publications/S.Ebobrah.pdf.

[167] *IPI Calls on the Gambian Government to Cooperate with ECOWAS Legal Proceedings*, FREEDOM NEWSPAPER (Mar. 13, 2008), *at* http://www.freemedia.at/press-room/public-statements/press-releases/singleview/article/ipi-calls-on-the-gambian-government-to-cooperate-with-ecowas-legal-proceedings.html.

[168] Manneh v. The Gambia, Case No. ECW/CCJ/APP/04/07, Judgment, paras. 7–8 (June 5, 2008), *reprinted in* 2004–09 COMMUNITY COURT OF JUSTICE, ECOWAS LAW REPORT 181 (2011), *available at* http://www1.chr.up.ac.za/index.php/browse-by-institution/ecowas-ccj.html.

[169] *Id.*, para. 3.

file documents, delaying the proceedings.[170] In June 2008, the Court ruled for Manneh, ordering the Gambia to release him from "unlawful detention without any further delay," pay him U.S.$100,000 in damages, and bear the costs of the litigation.[171]

The Gambia ignored the judgment—a decision that received a great deal of unfavorable publicity from governments, international organizations, and NGOs.[172] For example, the International Press Institute publicly stated that the "Gambian media environment has long been hostile and dangerous, but the government's flagrant disregard for the ECOWAS legal proceedings represents a low point."[173] Likewise, the African Commission on Human Rights called on the Gambia "to immediately and fully comply" with the ECOWAS Court's judgment.[174]

The second case, concerning the detention and torture of Musa Saidykhan, was harder for the government to ignore, because the plaintiff was alive, exhibited clear evidence of torture, and pursued the case from the safety of another country.[175] After a coup attempt in 2006, the *Independent* newspaper published the names of individuals that the Gambian National Intelligence Agency had arrested. Shortly thereafter and without a warrant, soldiers and policemen arrested Saidykhan, the newspaper's editor.[176] Security agents took Saidykhan to a detention center, where he was held for twenty-two days and repeatedly tortured.[177] Intelligence officials eventually released Saidykhan, but they continued to monitor his movements and threatened his family, ultimately causing Saidykhan and his family to flee the country.[178]

In 2007, Saidykhan, supported by the Media Foundation for West Africa, filed a complaint with the ECOWAS Court seeking a declaration that his arrest and detention were illegal and that he had been tortured and denied a fair hearing.[179] This time, the Gambia participated in the proceedings. It asked the ECOWAS Court to dismiss the suit on the grounds that the Court lacked jurisdiction, that the Court's intervention was "an affront to [its] sovereignty," and that the suit should be heard by a national court.[180] In 2009, the Court issued an interim ruling rejecting these arguments.[181]

The Gambia's political attack on the ECOWAS Court occurred while the merits phase of *Saidykhan* was pending. Gambian officials noted that the government was "aggrieved" by the

---

[170] *Id.*, paras. 4, 28.

[171] *Id.*, para. 44.

[172] *E.g.*, *U.S. Senators Call for Release of Journalist*, FOROYAA NEWSPAPER (Serrekunda) (Apr. 28, 2009), at http://business.highbeam.com/437649/article-1G1-198772071/us-senators-call-release-journalist; *Durbin, Other Senators Press Commonwealth Nations on Case of Missing Journalist*, STATES NEWS SERVICE, Mar. 18, 2010 (on file with authors), *available at* http://www.highbeam.com/doc/1G1-221599405.html.

[173] International Press Institute, *IPI Calls on the Gambian Government to Cooperate with ECOWAS Legal Proceedings*, SENEGAMBIA NEWS (Mar. 13, 2008), *at* http://www.freemedia.at/archives/singleview/article/ipi-calls-on-the-gambian-government-to-cooperate-with-ecowas-legal-proceedings.html.

[174] Linda Akrasi Kotey, *Ghana: Akoto Ampaw, Two Others in Gambia*, GHANAIAN CHRONICLE (July 17, 2009), *at* http://allafrica.com/stories/200907171086.html.

[175] *ECOWAS Torture Case Against the Gambia Nears an End*, AFROL NEWS (Sept. 22, 2010), *at* http://www.afrol.com/articles/36623.

[176] Saidykhan v. The Gambia, Ruling, *supra* note 110, para. 4.

[177] *Id.*, para. 7.

[178] *Id.*, paras. 8–9.

[179] *Id.*, para. 2.

[180] *Id.*, para. 11.

[181] *Id.*, para. 37.

judgment in the *Manneh* case and had "set the political process in motion to take the matter to the next level and get the decision set aside."[182] In September 2009, the Gambia called for a Meeting of Government Experts to revise the 2005 Protocol and restrict the Court's authority.[183] Most importantly, the Gambia sought to limit the ECOWAS Court's human rights jurisdiction to treaties ratified by the respondent state and to require exhaustion of domestic remedies.[184]

On their face, these proposals seem uncontroversial. As noted above, other international human rights tribunals operate under similar limitations. According to a consortium of NGOs, however, the "Gambian government propose[d] these amendments so that the Court will be weakened in its capacity to deal effectively with tyrannical governments trampling on citizens' rights." In the NGOs' view, the proposal to require exhaustion of local remedies aimed to "depriv[e] citizens of free access" to an "independent judicial instrument that is not usually available in many countries" in a region "where the judiciary is an arm of the executive." And the attempt to limit the ECOWAS Court's jurisdiction to ratified human rights treaties was a ploy "to prevent the Court from adjudicating on the [*Saidykhan*] case against The Gambia"— "one of the rare African countries which has not ratified" the UN Convention Against Torture.[185]

The ECOWAS Commission (which, under the 2006 reorganization mentioned above, replaced the Executive Secretariat) responded to the Gambian proposals by invoking the procedures for public participation in ECOWAS decision making. The commission also invited West African lawyers to consider the proposed, multipart amendment.[186] Based on their input, the ECOWAS Committee of Legal Experts recommended against narrowing the Court's human rights jurisdiction. In October 2009, the Council of Justice Ministers unanimously endorsed the committee's recommendation—with the consequence that the proposals were implicitly rejected at a meeting of the Council of Foreign Ministers the following month.[187]

The Gambia's proposals provided a clear opportunity for ECOWAS member states to reconsider the 2005 Protocol. Their decision to reject the Gambian challenge is striking. In our interviews, officials offered different explanations for this decision. One source explained that governments did not want to reward the Gambia for its poor human rights record. These

---

[182] *Gambian Attorney-General Denies Holding Missing Journalist*, AGENCE FRANCE PRESSE, Apr. 7, 2009.

[183] *West Africa: Country Submits Proposals to Amend ECOWAS Protocol*, FOROYAA NEWSPAPER (Serrekunda) (Sept. 25, 2009), *at* http://allafrica.com/stories/200909250810.html; *see also* Nana Adu Ampofo, *Gambian Authorities Seek to Limit Reach of Regional Human Rights Court*, GLOBAL INSIGHT (Sept. 28, 2009) (on file with authors); Innocent Anaba, *SERAP, CHRDA Challenge Plans to Amend ECOWAS' Court Powers*, VANGUARD (Nigeria), June 26, 2008 (on file with authors).

[184] The Gambia also proposed that cases should be admissible for only twelve months after the exhaustion of domestic remedies, that applicants should not be anonymous, and that complaints submitted to the ECOWAS Court should be barred from later being filed with other international courts. The Gambia reiterated the need for a process to appeal all ECOWAS Court decisions. *West Africa: Country Submits Proposals to Amend ECOWAS Protocol*, *supra* note 183.

[185] *Four IFEX Members, Civil Society Groups Fear Gambia Proposal Will Prevent ECOWAS Court from Ruling in Saidykhan Case*, IFEX (Sept. 28, 2009), *at* http://www.ifex.org/west_africa/2009/09/28/ecowas_court_jurisdiction/.

[186] *Id.*; Interview with Human Rights Advocate C, *supra* note 92.

[187] *Justice Ministers Endorse Experts' Decision on ECOWAS Jurisdiction*, IFEX, (Oct. 14, 2009), *at* http://www.ifex.org/west_africa/2009/10/14/gambian_proposal_defeated/. One source told us that, while the justice ministers unanimously rejected the Gambia's proposals, the foreign ministers were split, with one-third supporting and two-thirds opposing the proposals. Telephone interview with Human Rights Advocate A, *supra* note 91.

governments recognized that Gambian officials were acting in a blatantly "self-interested way" by attempting to circumvent the Court's review of serious and widely known human rights abuses.[188] Also important were the mobilization efforts of human rights NGOs and attorneys, who made sure that the issues were well covered in the press. One interviewee even suggested that ECOWAS officials had a hand in opposing the Gambian proposals by leaking information to human rights lawyers.[189]

In December 2010, the ECOWAS Court issued a judgment holding the Gambia responsible for the illegal detention and torture of Saidykhan and ordering the state to pay him U.S.$200,000 in damages.[190] The Gambia has refused to comply, however, with either the *Saidykhan* or the *Manneh* judgments. In 2011, in addition to denying responsibility for Manneh's death,[191] the Gambia asked the Court to set aside both judgments, and attacked *Saidykhan* as a "miscarriage of justice since the court failed to properly appraise the evidence on record." The Media Foundation for West Africa opposed the application and reiterated its demands for compliance.[192] In 2012, the judges rejected the Gambia's arguments and reaffirmed the two judgments and remedial orders.[193]

Although the Gambia continues to resist the ECOWAS Court's authority, the defeat of its judicial reform campaign has had the opposite of its intended effect: it has bolstered the Court's legitimacy. As previously explained, the 2005 Protocol entered into force provisionally pending ratification by individual member states, a process that is still ongoing. In 2006, however, West African governments restructured ECOWAS rulemaking to increase its supranational character. The reforms authorize the Authority to adopt "supplementary acts." These legal instruments are equivalent to protocols but with one crucial difference—they are "binding on Member States and the institutions of the Community" without the need for country-by-country ratification.[194]

The effect of these reforms on previously adopted protocols is unclear. One attorney worried that the continuation of the 2005 Protocol's provisional status remains a potential "liability" for the ECOWAS Court.[195] Even if this interpretation is correct as a legal matter, those whom

---

[188] Interview with ECOWAS Legal Affairs Directorate A, *supra* note 62.

[189] Interviews with Human Rights Advocates B, *supra* note 48, C, *supra* note 92; Interview with ECOWAS Legal Affairs Directorate A, *supra* note 62; *see also Four IFEX Members, Civil Society Groups Fear Gambia Proposal Will Prevent ECOWAS Court from Ruling in Saidykhan Case, supra* note 185 (listing regional civil society groups that mobilized against the Gambia's proposals).

[190] Saidykhan v. The Gambia, Case No. ECW/CCJ/APP/11/07, Judgment, para. 47 (Dec. 16. 2010); *see also* Ousman Njie, *ECOWAS Court Awards Musa Saidykhan $200,000*, FOROYAA NEWSPAPER (Serrekunda) (Dec. 17, 2010), *at* http://www.foroyaa.gm/international-news/7445-gambia-news-archive.

[191] In 2011, the country's president suggested that Manneh had died but that "the government has nothing to do with" his death. *Critical Activists and Journalists Detained Under "Bogus Charges,"* IFEX (July 27, 2011), *at* http://www.ifex.org/the_gambia/2011/07/27/bogus_charges/.

[192] Media Foundation for West Africa, *Alerts and Updates 2011: ECOWAS Court Adjourns Hearing on Gambian Government Request for Review of Two Landmark Judgements* (Dec. 29, 2011), *at* http://www.mediafound.org/?p=3188.

[193] Saidykhan v. The Gambia, Case No. ECW/CCJ/APP/11/07, Application for Review (Feb. 7, 2012); *see Gambia: ECOWAS Court Rules in Favour of Musa Saidykhan*, FOROYAA NEWSPAPER (Serrekunda) (Feb. 11, 2012), *at* http://allafrica.com/stories/201202140302.html.

[194] ECOWAS NEWSLETTER, *supra* note 157, at 2.

[195] Telephone interview with Human Rights Advocate A, *supra* note 91.

we interviewed all agreed that the rejection of the Gambia's proposals made the Protocol's provisional status a non-issue politically.[196] Having survived this attempt to curb its jurisdiction, the Court's human rights authority now rests on a more solid foundation than when the member states first gave the Court that authority in 2005.

Strategies to Promote Compliance: Strict Proof Requirements, Limited Remedies, and Public Outreach

Since the expansion of its jurisdiction in 2005, the ECOWAS Court has issued nearly seventy merits judgments, the large majority of which concern human rights.[197] Many of these decisions are legally and politically consequential. In a well-publicized early case, ECOWAS judges found Niger liable for condoning a customary practice of female slavery.[198] More recently, the Court issued a pathbreaking judgment against Nigeria for failing to regulate multinational oil companies that polluted the Niger Delta.[199] Other high-profile decisions have barred the domestic prosecution of former Chadian president Hissein Habré as contrary to the non-retroactivity of criminal law;[200] ordered the restoration of funds embezzled from a program to provide free basic education to children;[201] granted NGOs standing to challenge violations of economic and social rights;[202] and awarded damages to individuals arbitrarily detained by police and security officials.[203]

These decisions grab headlines, and they significantly enhance the Court's salience and visibility across West Africa.[204] It is less clear, however, whether these decisions have improved respect for human rights in the region.[205] According to a 2013 paper by the Court's chief reg-

---

[196] Interview ECOWAS Legal Affairs Directorate A, *supra* note 62; Interview with Human Rights Advocate C, *supra* note 92; Interview with ECOWAS Court Official C, *supra* note 137.

[197] As of July 2013, the ECOWAS Court's decisions included seventeen rulings and sixty-seven judgments on the merits. Amie Sanneh, *West Africa: ECOWAS Court of Justice Brief the Press,* FOROYAA NEWSPAPER (Serrekunda) (July 26, 2013) (reporting statement of the ECOWAS Court chief registrar), *at* http://allafrica.com. proxy.lib.duke.edu/stories/201307291277.html. Solomon Ebobrah has provided the most detailed analysis of the ECOWAS Court's human rights jurisprudence. *See, e.g.*, Ebobrah, *Critical Issues, supra* note 112.

[198] Hadijatou Mani Kouraou v. Niger, Judgment, *supra* note 122.

[199] Socio-Economic Rights and Accountability Project v. Nigeria, Case No. ECW/CCJ/APP/08/09, Judgment (Dec. 14, 2012) [hereinafter SERAP Niger Delta Judgment].

[200] Habré v. Senegal, Case No. ECW/CCJ/APP/07/08, Judgment (Nov. 18, 2010).

[201] Socio-Economic Rights and Accountability Project v. Nigeria, Case No. ECW/CCJ/APP/08/08, Judgment (Nov. 30, 2010) [hereinafter SERAP Basic Education Judgment].

[202] SERAP Basic Education Ruling, *supra* note 109.

[203] *E.g.*, Alade v. Nigeria, Judgment, *supra* note 114; Tandja v. Niger, Case No. ECW/CCJ/APP/05/10, Judgment (Nov. 8, 2010).

[204] One indication of this salience is the increasing discussion of ECOWAS Court cases in the West African news media. A search for "ECOWAS Court" and "Community Court of Justice" on AllAfrica.com—a news aggregator Web service—yielded the following number of "hits" each year:

2001	2002	2003	2004	2005	2006	2007	2008	2009	2010	2011	2012
6	4	2	12	50	28	47	61	53	67	79	90

[205] Article 15(4) of the 1993 Treaty, *supra* note 37, provides that the ECOWAS Court's judgments "shall be binding on the Member States, the Institutions of the Community and on individuals and corporate bodies," and Article 19(2) of Protocol A/P.1/7/91 on the Community Court of Justice, *supra* note 61, makes the Court's decisions "final and immediately enforceable." As with other international courts, however, the ECOWAS Court does "not have the benefit of institutions with powers of coercion to enforce [its] judgments" and has to rely on "pressure generated

istrar, "not many decisions of the Court have been enforced."[206] Perhaps aware of the challenges of inducing governments to comply with its judgments, the Court has tempered the legal and political impact of its decisions by requiring applicants to provide persuasive proof that the relevant human rights norms are widely accepted and by limiting the remedies that it demands of governments.

Complainants have raised a wide array of legal issues before the ECOWAS Court. Some allegations relate to human rights only tangentially; others seek expansive interpretations of established rights; still others allege multiple violations but offer few supporting facts. The Court has responded to these diverse complaints by adopting fairly strict pleading and proof requirements. Applicants must "specify the particular human right which has been violated"[207] and provide evidence that is "sufficiently convincing and unequivocal."[208] ECOWAS judges have also rejected litigants' attempts to assert human rights claims against individuals, corporations, and subnational political bodies[209]—issues that have also been litigated in the United States.[210]

The judges' circumspection with regard to remedies is also noteworthy. In the modern forms of slavery case, for example, the Court ordered Niger to pay the equivalent of U.S.$20,000 to a woman who had been enslaved.[211] The government paid the damages within three months, and, while not formally required to do so, prosecuted her former master.[212] Yet the Court made compliance fairly easy for Niger by refusing the applicant's entreaties to find fault with the laws, practices, and customs that gave rise to the modern slavery violations in the first instance.[213]

Other high-profile decisions exhibit similar remedial caution. In the Nigerian education case, the ECOWAS Court declared that "every Nigerian child is entitled to free and compulsory basic education."[214] Yet it did not order the government to allocate whatever funds were required to educate all primary school age children. Instead, based on evidence that specific funds had been embezzled from the national education program, the Court ordered Nigeria to "take the necessary steps to provide the money to cover the shortfall" while the government pursued efforts "to recover the funds or prosecute the suspects."[215]

---

by the political arms of [the Community], the indulgence of national executives or the goodwill of national courts." Ebobrah, *supra* note 9, at 96.

[206] Anene-Maidoh, *supra* note 113, at 27.

[207] Keita v. Mali, Judgment, *supra* note 114, para. 33.

[208] Garba v. Benin, Case No. ECW/CCJ/APP/09/08, Judgment, para. 39 (Feb. 17, 2010). The Court recently reaffirmed this evidentiary standard and extended it to defenses raised by states. Alade v. Nigeria, Judgment, *supra* note 114, paras. 48–50.

[209] *See, e.g.*, David v. Uwechue, Ruling, *supra* note 121, para. 48 (individuals); Hassan v. Nigeria, Case No. ECW/CCJ/APP/03/10, Judgment, para. 41 (Mar. 15, 2012) (subnational political entities and their officials); SERAP Niger Delta Ruling, *supra* note 109, paras. 69–71 (corporations).

[210] *E.g.*, Kiobel v. Royal Dutch Petroleum Co., 133 S.Ct. 1659 (2013) (Alien Tort Statute does not apply to human rights violations by foreign corporations committed on the territory of another state); Mohamad v. Palestinian Authority, 132 S.Ct. 1702 (2012) (only individuals, not corporate entities, can be liable under the Torture Victim Protection Act); Samantar v. Yousuf, 560 U.S. 305 (2010) (foreign official sued for conduct undertaken in his official capacity is not a "foreign state" entitled to immunity from suit).

[211] Hadijatou Mani Koraou v. Niger, Judgment, *supra* note 122, para. 92.

[212] Helen Duffy, *Human Rights Cases in Sub-regional African Courts: Towards Justice for Victims or Just More Fragmentation, in* THE DIVERSIFICATION AND FRAGMENTATION OF INTERNATIONAL CRIMINAL LAW 163, 179–81 (Larissa van den Herik & Carsten Stahn eds., 2012).

[213] ALTER, *supra* note 8, at 264–66.

[214] SERAP Basic Education Judgment, *supra* note 201, para. 26.

[215] *Id.*, para. 28.

The judges took a different tack in a judgment touching the "third rail" of Nigerian politics—the activities of multinational oil companies in the Niger Delta. The Court declared that Nigeria was responsible for failing to regulate companies that had despoiled the area. It rejected a demand, however, for U.S.$1 billion in damages on the ground that the applicants had not identified particular victims and that awarding mass damages would be impractical "in terms of justice, morality and equity."[216] The judges instead ordered Nigeria to "take all measures" to restore the environment, prevent future damage, and hold the perpetrators accountable— without, however, specifying how the government was to achieve these goals.[217]

Strict proof requirements and limited remedies may be strategically wise choices for a young human rights court whose judgments have yet to elicit widespread compliance. A 2012 NGO report supports this conclusion. In addition to full compliance in the *Hadijatou Mani Koraou* slavery case against Niger, the report lists a few instances of partial compliance,[218] including the *Habré* decision against Senegal, the release of the former president of Niger from house arrest, and the payment of damages to members of the Togolese Parliament wrongfully removed from office.[219] Other judgments, including the high-profile decisions against Nigeria and the Gambia discussed above, have yet to garner even partial compliance.[220]

ECOWAS judges readily admit these compliance challenges. In 2012, the current ECOWAS Court president, Awa Nana Daboya, publicly "decried the attitude of the Nigerian government for not honoring any of" the ten merits judgments that the Court had issued against that country.[221] At the same time, the Court has praised those countries—including Nigeria—that have designated a public ministry to oversee the implementation of its judgments. And it has discussed ways to promote compliance in meetings with government officials and national judges.[222] Civil society groups have added their voices to these efforts, issuing public declarations demanding that states comply with ECOWAS Court decisions and urging Community officials to step up enforcement efforts.[223] A few political leaders have also expressed support

---

[216] SERAP Niger Delta Judgment, *supra* note 199, paras. 113–15.

[217] *Id.*, para. 121.

[218] Recent studies suggest that partial compliance is the norm for human rights tribunals. *See, e.g.*, Darren Hawkins and Wade Jacoby, *Partial Compliance: A Comparison of the European and Inter-American Court of Human Rights*, 6 J. INT'L L. & INT'L REL. 35, 56–83 (2010); Alexandra Huneeus, *Courts Resisting Courts: Lessons from the Inter-American Court's Struggle to Enforce Human Rights*, 44 CORNELL INT'L L.J. 493, 509–29 (2011).

[219] Horace Adjolohoun, *Status of Human Rights Judgments of the ECOWAS Court: Implications on Human Rights and Democracy in the Region* (Aug. 7, 2012) (on file with authors).

[220] *Id.*

[221] Eyo Charles, *West Africa: Nigeria Doesn't Respect Our Rulings—ECOWAS Court*, DAILY TRUST (Mar. 13, 2012), *at* http://allafrica.com/stories/201203130408.html.

[222] *E.g.*, Community Court of Justice, *ECOWAS, Summary of Activities for the Year 2011*, at 5 (2012), *available at* http://www.courtecowas.org/site2012/pdf_files/annual_reports/activities_report_2011.pdf; Press Release, Media Foundation for West Africa, MFWA Holds Forum on ECOWAS Court in Abuja (July 27, 2012), *at* http://www.mediafound.org/index.php?option=com_content&task=view&id=857.

[223] Bassey Udo, *West Africa: Human Rights Groups Want Mechanism to Enforce ECOWAS Court Decisions*, PREMIUM TIMES (Nigeria) (May 2, 2013), *at* http://allafrica.com/stories/201305020992.html; Media Foundation for West Africa *Abuja Declaration of the Regional Civil Society Forum on the Enforcement of Judgements of the ECOWAS Community Court of Justice* (July 30, 2012), *at* http://www.mediafound.org/en/?p=3073; Press Release, Media Foundation for West Africa, ECOWAS Commission Commits to Ensuring Member States Comply with Decisions of the Community Court of Justice (Nov. 15, 2012) (on file with authors).

for compliance in specific cases, even when the government as a whole remains noncommittal.[224]

Pressure for compliance also comes from outside ECOWAS. For example, the disappearance of Chief Ebrima Manneh, the applicant in the 2008 unlawful detention case discussed above, was raised in 2010 during the Universal Periodic Review of the Gambia before the UN Human Rights Council.[225] Recent human rights reports by the United States and the United Kingdom also highlight the Gambia's continued noncompliance with the ECOWAS Court's judgments.[226]

In sum, although the ECOWAS Court is still a young international tribunal with an uncertain future, the Court has survived two major challenges to the exercise its human rights authority, arguably emerging stronger for having weathered those travails. The judges are also aware of ongoing concerns about noncompliance and are responding both in their jurisprudence and in actions outside the courtroom. Finally, as we discuss below in our conclusion, the ECOWAS Court's status as a human rights court is far more settled than that of subregional community courts elsewhere in Africa.

IV. EXPLAINING INSTITUTIONAL CHANGE: THEORETICAL IMPLICATIONS OF THE ECOWAS COURT'S REDEPLOYMENT AS A HUMAN RIGHTS COURT

This part considers the theoretical implications of the ECOWAS Court's redeployment. The broad delegation of human rights authority to the ECOWAS Court is likely to elicit incredulity from those who expect African leaders to be jealous of their sovereignty and to tightly control the international institutions that they create. This expectation is reflected in rational functionalist international relations theory, which assumes that states delegate authority to international institutions only when doing so furthers narrowly conceived functional objectives. We agree that state interests and sovereignty matter, and that the creation of a far-reaching and domestically intrusive international human rights review mechanism in West Africa is surprising. We are not, however, surprised that an international institution created to achieve one objective evolved to take on very different functions or that such an institution developed in a way that constrains the discretion of governments.

In the subsections that follow, we contrast rational functionalist theories with historical institutionalist accounts, which recognize that institutions can evolve over time to become quite different from what the founders first envisioned. We then return to part I's discussion of how the humanitarian interventions of the 1990s reoriented regional politics and ECOWAS institutions in ways that opened a door for NGOs, Community officials, and judges to expand

---

[224] *E.g.*, Socio-Economic Rights and Accountability Project, *Senate President Wants Action on ECOWAS Right to Education Judgment* (n.d.) (stating that the head of the Nigerian Senate was the "first political leader to acknowledge the [SERAP Basic Education Judgment] and to take action towards its implementation"), *at* http://serap-nigeria.org/senate-president-wants-action-on-ecowas-right-to-education-judgment/.

[225] UN Human Rights Council, Report of the Working Group on the Universal Periodic Review: Gambia, UN Doc. A/HRC/14/6, at 4, 21 (Mar. 24, 2010), *at* http://daccess-dds-ny.un.org/doc/UNDOC/GEN/G10/125/20/PDF/G1012520.pdf?OpenElement.

[226] U.S. DEPARTMENT OF STATE, COUNTRY REPORTS ON HUMAN RIGHTS PRACTICES FOR 2012: THE GAMBIA, *at* http://www.state.gov/j/drl/rls/hrrpt/humanrightsreport/index.htm?year=2012&dlid=204123; FOREIGN AND COMMONWEALTH OFFICE, HUMAN RIGHTS AND DEMOCRACY 2012, *at* http://www.hrdreport.fco.gov.uk/.

the ECOWAS Court's mandate. Finally, we address the puzzle of how the court reform campaign—triggered by a desire to increase judicial enforcement of ECOWAS economic rules—ended up as a delegation of expansive human rights authority.

Mechanisms of Change in International Institutions

Toward the end of the twentieth century, the increasing number and influence of international institutions called into question the long-standing claim of realist scholars that states pursue their national interests above all else. Seeking to explain these developments, scholars spawned an extensive literature that merges rational choice institutional analysis, functional analysis, and realist assumptions about state behavior. This literature proceeds from the premise that international institutions and regimes are primarily either mechanisms for states to coordinate to achieve joint gains or vehicles for powerful nations to influence the behavior of weaker states.[227]

These rationalist approaches assume that the design of international institutions is shaped by functional goals, such as addressing the structural features of underlying cooperation problems while accommodating diverse state capabilities and interests.[228] These approaches also identify the mechanisms by which states control international institutions, including appointment processes, allocation of budgets, voting rules, political vetoes, and threats of noncompliance. Although state control remains incomplete, governments are expected to oppose activities that compromise important national interests.[229]

Rationalist scholars recognize that international institutions can change over time. In the case of global terrorism, for example, a fundamental shift in the nature of the cooperation problem resulted in modifications of institutional competences. Similarly, changes in membership, relative power, or state interests can lead to revisions of decision-making rules and other design features, such as occurred with the transformation from the General Agreement on Tariffs and Trade into the World Trade Organization. In these and other instances, however, the underlying assumption is that international institutions remain closely tethered to the interests of governments.

Historical institutionalist theory proceeds from different premises. The theory does not assume that the primary goal of the actors who populate institutions is to meet government demands. Instead, when elections, economic crises, exogenous shocks, or policy failures change state and societal preferences, institutions come under pressure to respond and evolve. Initial

---

[227] This literature began with a 1982 special issue of the journal *International Organization*, which was later republished as INTERNATIONAL REGIMES (Stephen Krasner ed., 1983). Similar assumptions underpin recent rationalist international law scholarship. *See, e.g.*, JACK L. GOLDSMITH & ERIC A. POSNER, THE LIMITS OF INTERNATIONAL LAW (2005); ANDREW T. GUZMAN, HOW INTERNATIONAL LAW WORKS: A RATIONAL CHOICE THEORY (2008).

[228] *E.g.*, Barbara Koremenos, Charles Lipson & Duncan Snidal, *The Rational Design of International Institutions*, 55 INT'L ORG. 761 (2001); Barbara Koremenos, *When, What, and Why Do States Choose to Delegate?*, 71 LAW & CONTEMP. PROBS. 153 (2008).

[229] DELEGATION AND AGENCY IN INTERNATIONAL ORGANIZATIONS (Darren Hawkins, David A. Lake, Daniel L. Nielson & Michael J. Tierney eds., 2006); *see also* Curtis A. Bradley & Judith G. Kelley, *The Concept of International Delegation*, 71 LAW & CONTEMP. PROBS. 1 (2008). For a criticism of this scholarship, see Karen J. Alter, *Agents or Trustees? International Courts in Their Political Context*, 14 EUR. J. INT'L REL. 33 (2008).

design choices and vested interests interact with shifts in the environment to produce path-dependent change.[230] These contestations and the adaptation that they engender are a normal part of politics.

Contemporary historical institutionalist work focuses in depth on the modalities of institutional evolution. Early studies emphasized inertia and suggested that major policy reorientations occur primarily during critical junctures—infrequent moments of political, social, or economic upheaval when an unusual opening of political space enables the overturning of entrenched ideas and approaches.[231] Recent scholarship focuses on incremental shifts that occur through political contestation and realignments of coalitions that support institutions. These more gradual changes can cumulate into transformations that are as large as, or larger than, the changes that occur during critical junctures.[232]

Two modalities of incremental change are especially relevant to the institutional transformations in ECOWAS. Change initially occurred via "layering"—the addition of rules, goals, or priorities that over time can become defining features of the institution.[233] We argue that the humanitarian interventions of the 1990s expanded the Community's mandate and created concomitantly greater constraints on state sovereignty due to expanding conceptions of regional security. These incremental shifts, in turn, created a permissive environment for non-state actors to convince states to give the ECOWAS Court a human rights jurisdiction. The addition of private litigant access in human rights cases led to the Court's "conversion" or "redeployment," a change that allowed new actors to redirect the institution toward new goals, functions, and purposes.[234]

Layering: From Economic Integration to Regional Security, Good Governance, and Human Rights

As we discussed in part I, although the founding goals of ECOWAS emphasized economic integration and development, West African governments also created a limited security role for the Community. The 1978 Protocol of Non-aggression pledged member states to refrain from threats or use of force and from "encouraging or condoning acts of subversion" in neighboring

---

[230] Wolfgang Streeck & Kathleen Thelen, *Introduction: Institutional Change in Advanced Political Economies, in* BEYOND CONTINUITY: INSTITUTIONAL CHANGE IN ADVANCED POLITICAL ECONOMIES 1, 7, 11 (Wolfgang Streeck & Kathleen Thelen eds., 2005). Historical institutionalist approaches have a growing, but less well known, foothold in international relations scholarship. *See, e.g.*, Orfeo Fioretos, *Historical Institutionalism in International Relations*, 65 INT'L ORG. 367 (2011); Laurence R. Helfer, *Understanding Change in International Organizations: Globalization and Innovation in the ILO*, 59 VAND. L. REV. 649, 666–69 (2006).

[231] For foundational studies that examine critical junctures, see PETER ALEXIS GOUREVITCH, POLITICS IN HARD TIMES: COMPARATIVE RESPONSES TO INTERNATIONAL ECONOMIC CRISES (1986); BARRINGTON MOORE, SOCIAL ORIGINS OF DICTATORSHIP AND DEMOCRACY: LORD AND PEASANT IN THE MAKING OF THE MODERN WORLD (1967); THEDA SKOCPOL, STATES AND SOCIAL REVOLUTION: A COMPARATIVE ANALYSIS OF FRANCE, RUSSIA AND CHINA (1979). For a recent discussion of how critical junctures contribute to institutional change, see Giovanni Capoccia & R. Daniel Kelemen, *The Study of Critical Junctures in Historical Institutionalism*, 59 WORLD POL. 341 (2007).

[232] *E.g.*, KATHLEEN THELEN, HOW INSTITUTIONS EVOLVE: THE POLITICAL ECONOMY OF SKILLS IN COMPARATIVE-HISTORICAL PERSPECTIVE (2004); Paul Pierson, *The Path to European Integration: A Historical Institutionalist Perspective*, 29 COMP. POL. STUD. 123 (1996).

[233] Streeck & Thelen, *supra* note 230, at 22–24.

[234] *Id.* at 26–29.

countries,[235] and the 1981 Protocol on Mutual Assistance and Defense promised a collective response to foreign aggression.[236] For more than a decade, these Protocols remained mostly ornamental symbols of the Community's postcolonial commitment to the sovereignty and territorial integrity of its member states.[237] In the early 1990s, however, Liberia's civil war spilled over into Sierra Leone, generating mass atrocities and refugee flows. In response, the member states, led by Nigeria, invoked the dormant security protocols to justify military intervention to quell the violence and prevent the spread of instability.

The humanitarian interventions of the 1990s were a watershed for ECOWAS in several respects. First, the interventions were a sharp break from the norm of noninterference in internal affairs.[238] The collective response to mass atrocities on the territory of one of their own, despite vociferous protestations by some francophone member states, revealed that African governments were willing to limit national sovereignty to achieve other Community goals. Political leaders initially identified these goals as the immediate need to restore peace and security in particular countries. Over time, however, the goals expanded to a broader conception of regional conflict prevention that included constitutional transitions of power, good governance, and human rights. Court reform advocates stressed that this expansion "reoriented thinking [in West Africa] about jurisdictional sovereignty."[239]

Second, the interventions exposed gaps in ECOWAS legal instruments that created opportunities for a wider overhaul of the Community. The member states' decision to put security issues on a firmer legal footing occurred at the same time as the high-level review of the integration project and the decision to create the ECOWAS Court. The Committee of Eminent Persons, convened in 1991 to assess the shortcomings of ECOWAS's founding period and propose institutional reforms, gave equal emphasis to security and economic issues. The committee defined security broadly as including "peace and stability" within states, and it highlighted that the "whirlwind of political reform sweeping through various parts of the world [has not] exempted West Africa, where demands for democratisation, based on political pluralism and respect for human rights, have multiplied in recent times."[240] Whereas the 1975 ECOWAS Treaty "d[id] not mention human rights and completely avoid[ed] any use of human rights language,"[241] following the Committee's recommendations the 1993 Revised Treaty identified the African Charter as a "fundamental principle" of ECOWAS.[242] These revisions created another facilitating condition for the member states' later decision to give the ECOWAS Court jurisdiction over human rights.

---

[235] *Supra* note 40, Arts. 1, 2.

[236] *Supra* note 41.

[237] These protocols reflected the then prevalent idea of a *Pax Africana*, wherein African leaders would manage their own internal affairs. COMFORT ERO, WAHEGURU PAL SINGH SIDHU & AUGUSTINE TOUREET (RAPPORTEURS), TOWARD A PAX WEST AFRICANA: BUILDING PEACE IN A TROUBLED SUB-REGION (2001), *available at* http://www.ipinst.org/media/pdf/publications/pdf_report_pax_w__africana.pdf.

[238] Comfort Ero, *ECOMOG: A Model for Africa*, *in* BUILDING STABILITY IN AFRICA: CHALLENGES FOR THE NEW MILLENNIUM 97 (Jakkie Cilliers & Annika Hildung-Norberg eds., 2000).

[239] *E.g.*, Telephone interview with Human Rights Advocate A, *supra* note 91.

[240] *Final CEP Report*, *supra* note 14, at 37; *see also* VILJOEN, *supra* note 134, at 482 ("as the winds of democracy swept authoritarianism and militarism from the continent in a post–Cold War world, . . . human rights became mainstreamed into all forms of subregional cooperation").

[241] Ebobrah, *Critical Issues*, *supra* note 112, at 3.

[242] 1993 Treaty, *supra* note 37, Art. 4(g).

Third, although the member states justified the interventions on humanitarian grounds, ECOMOG forces sadly added to the humanitarian tragedy. The "numerous reports of ECOMOG peacekeepers engag[ing] in looting, expropriation and theft" and accusations of "human-rights abuses, and sexual exploitation of women and children . . . bespoke of the lack of discipline and accountability of the armed forces of the countries involved, especially Nigeria."[243] The abuses and subsequent lack of accountability highlighted that the Community had "not done enough to incorporate human rights in its conflict resolution initiative[s]."[244] These events also triggered "a re-examination of the role of human rights in guaranteeing regional stability and security in ECOWAS,"[245] adding to the "demands for democratisation, based on political pluralism and respect for human rights" from civil society groups that now had input into Community decision making.[246]

Taken together, the layered-on addition of these broad security goals fundamentally shifted ECOWAS's normative orientation, a change exemplified by the 1999 Conflict Prevention Protocol and the 2001 Good Governance Protocol discussed in part II. This shift helps to explain why the arguments of court reform advocates resonated with government and Community officials, who saw advantages to fulfilling the pledge to give the ECOWAS Court "the power to hear . . . cases relating to violations of human rights,"[247] and to taking a concrete step toward creating a more "people-centered" Community.[248] Compared to authorizing collective military intervention in a member state, empowering the Court to adjudicate individual human rights violations was a relatively modest step.

Redeployment: Why Human Rights Have Eclipsed Economic Issues in the ECOWAS Court

The expansion of the ECOWAS Court's jurisdiction to include human rights did not supplant the Court's original mandate to interpret and apply Community economic rules. Seen from this perspective, the 2005 Protocol is an example of "layering"—the addition of a new goal or priority to an existing institution that also retains its original mandate. In practice, however, the ECOWAS Court functions primarily as an international human rights tribunal, and its docket is bereft of cases challenging violations of Community economic rules. The Court's transformation is thus more accurately viewed an example of "redeployment" or "conversion," a change that allows a new set of actors to fundamentally reorient an institution in a new direction.

The absence of a practical role for the Court in enforcing regional economic rules does not mean that member states have abandoned cooperation in that area. ECOWAS continues to advertise its one-sentence mission as "promot[ing] economic integration in all fields of economic activity,"[249] and the Community has made meaningful policy steps toward this goal. For example, the 2005 Protocol enhanced the Court's role in overseeing compliance with

---

[243] Arthur, *supra* note 45, at 16.

[244] KABIA, *supra* note 43, at 87.

[245] Chidi Anselm Odinkalu, *ECOWAS Court of Justice in the Protection of Human Rights, in* COMPENDIUM OF THE INTERNATIONAL CONFERENCE ON "THE LAW IN THE PROCESS OF INTEGRATION IN WEST AFRICA," *supra* note 93, at 185.

[246] KUFUOR, *supra* note 12, at 161; *see also id.,* at 49–50 (discussing NGO participation).

[247] 2001 Good Governance Protocol, *supra* note 49, Art. 39.

[248] *Interview with Mohamed Ibn Chambas, Executive Secretary of ECOWAS, supra* note 91.

[249] *ECOWAS in Brief* (n.d.), *at* http://www.comm.ecowas.int/sec/index.php?id=about_a&lang=en.

ECOWAS economic rules by permitting preliminary references from national courts and authorizing enforcement actions by the ECOWAS Commission.[250] In addition, since the 2006 overhaul of the Community, it can be argued persuasively that ECOWAS rules are now directly applicable in national legal orders, with the consequence that judges should, in theory, be able to apply those rules directly.

But significant barriers to enforcing economic rules persist. As a formal matter, although ECOWAS protocols are directly applicable, the member states have not created "legislative provisions that 'speak to' the relations between [Community and domestic] legal systems."[251] In addition, national judges and lawyers have little knowledge of how the ECOWAS legal system is designed to function. Without formal rules or habituated practices, national judges are disinclined to invalidate conflicting national laws or to refer cases to the ECOWAS Court.

Member states might have reduced these barriers had the 2005 Protocol given private traders direct access to the ECOWAS Court. The absence of such access from the 2005 reforms is one of the most puzzling aspects of the Court's transformation. It is especially so in the wake of the *Afolabi* case, which directly raised the issue of economic actors not having standing before the Court.[252]

Explaining why access for private traders vanished from the court reform campaign requires us to search for "dogs that did not bark," an inquiry that is necessarily no more than suggestive. Our research reveals two plausible explanations for this omission: no regionally organized constituency sought the vigorous enforcement of ECOWAS economic rules, and court reform advocates strategically conflated human rights and economic freedoms and then sacrificed direct access of one to achieve the other.

The first explanation is true but insufficient. Economic interest groups are present in West Africa, and they are aware of the many obstacles to intraregional trade. We interviewed the leadership of one of these groups, the National Association of Nigeria Traders (NANTs), whose officials are knowledgeable about the ECOWAS legal system.[253] They identified specific practices in Ghana and Nigeria that violate Community economic rules, including border closings and impediments to establishing a business, and they showed us letters of complaint filed with the ECOWAS Commission. To enhance their ability to challenge these violations, NANTs recently asked West African governments to allow private firms direct access to the Court.[254]

NANTs was not, however, part of the 2005 court reform campaign. One impediment to its inclusion was that the group is nationally organized, whereas ECOWAS rules only allow for participation by regional groups. But ECOWAS officials could have facilitated the mobilization of economic groups, or national traders with a presence in multiple countries could have organized regionally. Perhaps such groups did not see any benefit from using ECOWAS institutions to promote their objectives. But then one has to ask why they would not adopt a strategy that worked so well for human rights groups. Our answer is that West African

---

[250] See the sub-subsection in part II entitled "A broad authority for human rights suits, but a narrower mandate for economic cases" (explaining these provisions of the 2005 Protocol).

[251] Ebobrah, *Critical Issues, supra* note 112, at 15.

[252] See subsection in part II entitled "The *Afolabi* Case: Justice Denied for Private Litigants."

[253] The organization's website is at http://nants.org/.

[254] Crusoe Osagie, *West Africa: Traders Task ECOWAS on Regional Integration*, THIS DAY (Aug. 29, 2011), *at* http://allafrica.com/stories/201108300754.html.

774   THE AMERICAN JOURNAL OF INTERNATIONAL LAW   [Vol. 107:737

governments benefit from maintaining barriers to intraregional trade and that these benefits, at least in the current political and economic climate, outweigh the advantages of achieving a functioning common market. In the words of a recent NANTs newsletter, "Member States did not desire the Court to be an engine for realizing the economic integration objective."[255]

Although economic groups did not gain direct access to the Court in the 2005 reforms, human rights groups did, and they have since capitalized on this access by filing numerous suits against governments. To convert the Court to their objective, these groups argued that the Community's recently endorsed goal of protecting human rights and its long-standing plan to promote economic development were one and the same. Many West African scholars, NGOs, and litigants strategically conflate the goals of economic integration and the protection of human rights. For example, one such scholar, Nneoma Nwogu, points to provisions in the 1993 Treaty that embrace social values, including human rights, and argues that these values are fundamental to the Community's economic motivations.[256] Our interviews revealed a similar tendency to elide these objectives. A human rights attorney told us that ECOWAS was created in response to problems, such as Nigeria's expulsion of West Africans in the 1970s, that implicated both economic and human rights issues.[257] The applicant's lawyer in the *Afolabi* case also invoked both the African Charter's human right to freedom of movement and ECOWAS's free-movement obligations, seemingly drawing on the growing human rights zeitgeist to bolster Afolabi's legal claim.[258]

Court reform advocates may have genuinely believed that human rights encompass economic freedoms, but they also must have been aware that the two legal fields intersect only in part. It is more likely that advocates strategically conflated the two fields to suggest that giving the Court a human rights mandate would also further ECOWAS's primary objective of promoting regional integration. Governments and ECOWAS officials were seemingly happy to go along with this diversion.

The strategy worked. But as the NANTs newsletter explains, the ability to file human rights complaints with the ECOWAS Court does not help to challenge most economic violations, such as a Ghanaian law that privileges domestic traders and requires significant cash investments for foreigners to establish a business.[259] In reality, then, the decision to grant direct access only for human rights reflects a political choice to prioritize one set of Community goals over another. The ironic result is that, notwithstanding that the *Afolabi* suit triggered a major revision of the ECOWAS Court's protocol, litigants like Afolabi are still unable to challenge the many barriers to intraregional trade in West Africa.

Our principal theoretical claim is that international institutions, like their domestic counterparts, respond and adapt to changing norms and societal pressures. Even if rational func-

---

[255] *Sovereignty, Supra-nationality and Trade: The Case of ECOWAS Laws*, 2 ECOWAS VANGUARD, Feb. 2013, at 7, *available at* http://nants.org/wp-content/uploads/2013/03/Soveriegnty-Supranationality-and-Trade-The-Case-of-ECOWAS-Laws-ECO-VANGUARD-FEB-2013-English-Edition.pdf.

[256] Nwogu, *supra* note 95, at 348–49; *see also* OPPONG, *supra* note 65, at 148 (asserting that the "links between economic development and human rights are too obvious to merit discussing").

[257] Telephone interview with Human Rights Advocate B, *supra* note 48.

[258] Afolabi v. Nigeria, Judgment, *supra* note 73, para. 7.

[259] *Sovereignty, Supra-nationality and Trade*, *supra* note 255, at 7.

tionalist goals shape an international institution's initial design, those objectives do not control how the institution evolves over time. We have suggested that the ECOWAS Court's transformation is a result of the incremental layering on of new security roles for the Community together with civil society pressures to entrench respect for human rights. ECOWAS's contested involvement in humanitarian intervention brought human rights concerns into Community politics. Eager to prevent civil wars and violent unrest in the region, ECOWAS assumed a conflict prevention role and then expanded its activities to include promoting constitutional transitions, good governance, and human rights. These developments created a permissive environment for civil society groups and ECOWAS judges to lobby member states to give the Court a human rights jurisdiction, in part by arguing that doing so would also further economic integration. In practice, however, the choices made by government leaders, Community officials, and NGOs implicitly maintained the barriers to judicial enforcement of regional economic rules while facilitating a wave of human rights complaints by private litigants that completed the Court's redeployment.

V. CONCLUSION: HOW DEEP IS ECOWAS'S COMMITMENT TO PROTECTING HUMAN RIGHTS?

This article has examined the transformation of the ECOWAS Community Court of Justice into a new international human rights court for West Africa. Our study reveals that the ECOWAS Court belongs on any list of human rights tribunals. Most such lists are limited to judicial and quasi-judicial bodies linked to specific human rights treaties, such as the African Charter system and the African Commission and Court on Human and Peoples' Rights. Although the ECOWAS Court exercises jurisdiction over fewer states, it is at least as active in adjudicating human rights violations as are these two continent-wide institutions. The Court issues judgments quickly and provides legally binding remedies to victims who have direct access to the Court without exhausting local remedies. Moreover, as scholars such as Solomon Ebobrah have shown, ECOWAS judges have addressed many issues that have yet to come before the African Commission or Court and are making important contributions to regional human rights jurisprudence.[260]

In this last part, we briefly consider three issues relating to whether a redeployed international human rights court can survive in the rough and tumble world of African politics. The first issue concerns the sincerity of states' commitment to the ECOWAS Court's human rights jurisdiction. The second is whether the ECOWAS Court is likely to face a backlash similar to those that the East African Court of Justice and the Tribunal of the Southern African Development Community have experienced. Finally, we discuss whether the overlapping human rights competences between the subregional courts and the African Charter system will contribute to the fragmentation of international law in ways that undermine legal certainty and respect for human rights.

---

[260] *E.g.*, Solomon T. Ebobrah, *Human Rights Developments in African Sub-regional Economic Communities During 2009*, 10 AFR. HUM. RTS. J. 233 (2010); Solomon T. Ebobrah, *Human Rights Developments in African Sub-regional Economic Communities During 2010*, 11 AFR. HUM. RTS. J. 216 (2011); Ebobrah, *Critical Issues*, *supra* note 112.

Skeptics of the Court's expansion into human rights have suggested that the 2005 Protocol was an insincere commitment by ECOWAS member states.[261] They have intimated that West African leaders agreed to the Protocol not out of a desire to remedy human rights violations in the region but rather because they expected that the ECOWAS Court, whatever its powers on paper, would have little influence on national laws or practices.[262]

We found no evidence to support this claim. The 2005 Protocol's specific grant of "jurisdiction to determine cases of violation of human rights that occur in any member state" was drafted, vetted, and approved in the same manner as other ECOWAS legal instruments. If some government officials predicted that the Protocol would be ignored, they were misinformed or turned a blind eye to the plain language of the agreement.[263] States also declined to extend private litigant access to economic cases, a decision that suggests a careful choice about which types of suits private litigants would be permitted to file. It is noteworthy that states later rejected plausible proposals to curtail the Court's human rights authority and adopted reforms that strengthened the independence and quality of ECOWAS judges. Taken together, these actions suggest that West African governments want the Court to review human rights complaints.

As noted in the introduction, the ECOWAS Court's expansion into human rights is not unique. In the 1970s, the European Court of Justice made a similar shift, albeit for different reasons,[264] as did (more recently) the courts associated with two other subregional economic communities in Africa—the East African Court of Justice and the Tribunal of the Southern African Development Community. Unlike the situation of the ECOWAS Court, however, these expansions occurred via judicial lawmaking.[265] In Europe, member states later ratified the ECJ's jurisprudential advances, most recently when they adopted the Lisbon Treaty that made the EU Charter of Fundamental Rights legally binding.[266] The consequences of the bold judicial assertions of human rights competence by the EACJ and SADC Tribunal are still unfolding, but early evidence indicates that both courts have faced substantial opposition from governments.[267]

In response to an early controversial ruling involving appointments to the East African Legislative Assembly, member states amended the East African Community Treaty to divide the East African Court of Justice into two divisions (first instance and appellate), impose strict time

---

[261] *See, e.g.*, HEATHER SMITH-CANNOY, INSINCERE COMMITMENTS: HUMAN RIGHTS TREATIES, ABUSIVE STATES, AND CITIZEN ACTIVISM 9 (2012).

[262] A variant of this argument asserts that West African leaders adopted the 2005 Protocol to signal to international organizations, foreign donors, or domestic interest groups a seemingly real but, in fact, temporary or disingenuous commitment to human rights or to other goals desired by those actors. For a critique of the claim that human rights treaty ratifications are "costless signals," see Ryan Goodman and Derek Jinks, *Measuring the Effects of Human Rights Treaties*, 14 EUR. J. INT'L L. 171, 179 (2003).

[263] *See* BETH SIMMONS, MOBILIZING FOR HUMAN RIGHTS 78 (2009) (explaining that states often "underestimate the probability that they will be pressured to live up to their international treaty commitments in the years to come").

[264] *See, e.g.*, Gráinne de Búrca, *The Road Not Taken: The European Union as a Global Human Rights Actor*, 105 AJIL 649, 687 (2011).

[265] Laurence R. Helfer & Karen J. Alter, *Legitimacy and Lawmaking: A Tale of Three International Courts*, 14 THEORETICAL INQUIRIES IN L. 479, 492–93 (2013); *see also* Karen J. Alter & Laurence R. Helfer, *Nature or Nurture? Judicial Law-Making in the European Court of Justice and the Andean Tribunal of Justice*, 64 INT'L ORG. 563 (2010).

[266] De Búrca, *supra* note 264, at 670–73.

[267] See sources cited *supra* notes 9 and 260.

limits on filing complaints, and add new grounds for removing and suspending judges.[268] The Court later interpreted the Treaty as conferring a limited mandate to adjudicate human rights issues. Government officials have since repeatedly challenged the Court's jurisdiction over human rights suits.[269] In Southern Africa, the reaction has been more severe. Beginning in 2008, the SADC Tribunal upheld suits by white farmers challenging land seizures in Zimbabwe as violating the human rights and rule-of-law provisions in the SADC Treaty.[270] President Robert Mugabe responded to these decisions by mobilizing the SADC's highest political body to suspend the Tribunal pending the drafting of a new protocol that strips its jurisdiction over complaints from private litigants. These measures have ended, at least for the foreseeable future, the SADC Tribunal's ability to adjudicate human rights claims.[271]

The ECOWAS Court's experience is different in several respects. First, unlike their colleagues in eastern and southern Africa, ECOWAS judges do not need to finesse whether they have a human rights competence, because member states have expressly given the Court jurisdiction to review and remedy human rights violations. Second, West African governments conferred this jurisdiction on the Court for reasons internal to the Community—namely, ECOWAS's growing role in regional security and a desire to facilitate constitutional transitions and good governance. Third, the supranational status of ECOWAS is further advanced than the other two subregional integration projects. In 2006, ECOWAS member states made Community protocols directly applicable in national legal orders without the need for ratification and enhanced the supranational authority of ECOWAS institutions. By contrast, the SADC and, to a lesser extent, EAC remain predominantly interstate bodies whose secretariats are largely reactive to shifts in governments' commitments to community and integration. Fourth, the ECOWAS Court's human rights mandate enjoys the strong support of the ECOWAS Commission, whose officials can help assess the political landscape and redirect opposition to the Court in ways that address member states' concerns without compromising the judges' independence. Taken together, these differences explain why the ECOWAS Court's human rights mandate stands on politically and legally firmer footing than that of its subregional neighbors, and why the Court has survived unpopular judgments and a campaign to curtail its jurisdiction.

To be sure, the challenge of eliciting compliance with the ECOWAS Court's judgments remains formidable.[272] But this problem must be put in perspective. The European Court of Human Rights and the Inter-American Court of Human Rights took decades to establish their authority, whereas subregional tribunals in Africa are still in their infancy. ECOWAS judges have demonstrated political savvy as they navigate this fraught terrain. The judges have been circumspect in interpreting international law and in modulating the remedies that they award to successful applicants. Such strategies help to establish a politically safe space for the

---

[268] Henry Onoria, *Botched-Up Elections, Treaty Amendments and Judicial Independence in the East African Community*, 54 J. AFR. L. 74, 83 (2010).

[269] Gathii, *supra* note 161, manuscript at 24–27 (describing the backlash by governments following the *Nyong'o* election case). The precise relationship between the timing of the treaty amendments and their influence on the EACJ's human rights case law remains to be explored.

[270] Treaty of the South African Development Community, Aug. 17, 1992, 32 ILM 116 (1993), *at* http://www.sadc.int/documents-publications/sadc-treaty/.

[271] *E.g.*, Frederick Cowell, *The Death of the Southern African Development Community Tribunal's Human Rights Jurisdiction*, 13 HUM. RTS. L. REV. 153 (2013); Erika de Wet, *The Rise and Fall of the Tribunal of the Southern African Development Community: Implications for Dispute Settlement in Southern Africa*, 28 ICSID REV. 45 (2013).

[272] *See supra* notes 218–26 and accompanying text.

Court—a space in which it can condemn clear violations of human rights and pressure governments outside the courtroom to comply with its rulings.

Many government officials, human rights groups and lawyers anticipate that the member states will eventually specify which human rights treaties can be adjudicated by the ECOWAS Court, add an exhaustion of domestic remedies requirement, and create an appellate review mechanism. These revisions, if they do occur, should not be seen as rebukes of either the Court or its judges. Rather, such revisions are more likely to reflect a maturing legal system that is evolving in conjunction with fundamental reorientations of ECOWAS objectives.

A final issue concerns whether the multiplicity of human rights adjudicatory bodies is problematic insofar as it exacerbates the fragmentation of international law in Africa. Scholars who express concerns about fragmentation cite the lack of clarity from inconsistent legal rulings and the fear that governments may use that inconsistency to follow the most lenient interpretations of their human rights obligations.[273] The ECOWAS Court contributed to these fragmentation concerns in one high-profile case—a judgment against Senegal that it violated the rights of former Chadian President Hissein Habré by taking steps to prosecute him for torture and other international crimes.[274] The Court disallowed the prosecution, and in a later ICJ proceeding, Senegal argued that it had delayed prosecuting Habré due to its obligation to comply with the ECOWAS Court judgment.[275]

Although other examples may arise, the adjudication of human rights by the ECOWAS Court enhances, on balance, the clarity of international law and raises, not lowers, human rights protections in West Africa. For civil society groups, the ECOWAS Court and other subregional tribunals offer a way to minimize the "obstruction, haggling, [and] delay" that many observers associate with the continental human rights system.[276] For lawyers, subregional litigation provides a corrective to the limited avenues of legal recourse available to victims of rights abuses in Africa.[277] For judges on subregional courts, the adjudication of human rights provides an opportunity to expand their dockets, develop legal doctrine, and issue rulings that are relevant to stakeholders. If the courts' decisions also complement or extend the norms of the African Charter, so much the better.[278]

This conclusion has provided only a cursory overview of the many issues implicated by the burgeoning of international human rights litigation in Africa. The contemporaneous move

---

[273] *E.g.*, VILJOEN, *supra* note 134, at 437 (warning that the existence of multiple international venues for adjudicating human rights claims "may lead to divergence in jurisprudence and to forum shopping, where quasi-judicial and judicial institutions are compared and played off against one another").

[274] Habré v. Senegal, Judgment, *supra* note 200, paras. 58, 61.

[275] Questions Relating to the Obligation to Prosecute or Extradite (Belg. v. Sen.), 2012 ICJ REP. 1, para. 110 (July 20). The ICJ rejected Senegal's argument, holding that "Senegal's duty to comply with its obligations under the [UN] Convention [Against Torture] cannot be affected by the decision of the ECOWAS Court of Justice." *Id.*, para. 111. In fact, the ECOWAS Court had left open the option of trying Habré before an ad hoc or international tribunal. Habré v. Senegal, Judgment, *supra* note 200, paras. 58, 61. In 2012, Senegal and the African Union agreed to create a hybrid court within the Senegalese judicial system, known as the Extraordinary African Chambers, with jurisdiction over genocide, crimes against humanity, war crimes, and torture committed in Chad in the 1980s. Sangeeta Shah, *Questions Relating to the Obligation to Prosecute or Extradite* (Belgium v Senegal), 13 HUM. RTS. L. REV. 351, 363–66 (2013).

[276] KOFI OTENG KUFUOR, THE AFRICAN HUMAN RIGHTS SYSTEM: ORIGIN AND EVOLUTION 104 (2010); *see also* Solomon Ebobrah, *Litigating Human Rights Before Sub-regional Courts in Africa: Prospects and Challenges*, 17 AFR. J. INT'L & COMP L. 78, 87 (2009).

[277] Duffy, *supra* note 212, at 182–87.

[278] *See* KUFUOR, *supra* note 275, at 105; VILJOEN, *supra* note 134, at 453–55.

into human rights by three similarly situated subregional community courts, together with the increasing activity of the African Charter institutions, creates a natural experiment to examine the different ways that government officials, judges, and civil society groups mobilize and navigate the often fraught politics of human rights compliance. Our initial review of this experiment suggests that the manner in which international courts acquire jurisdiction over human rights is legally and politically consequential. The mode of acquisition affects issues such as the strategies of litigants, the interpretive methodologies of judges, the remedies awarded, and the responses of governments to the courts' exercise of their newly acquired authority.[279] The explicit delegation of human rights authority also provides international judges with a political buffer as they take on the challenging task of adjudicating state violations of human rights.

[279] *See* Joost Pauwelyn & Manfred Elsig, *The Politics of Treaty Interpretation: Variations and Explanations Across International Tribunals, in* INTERDISCIPLINARY PERSPECTIVES ON INTERNATIONAL LAW AND INTERNATIONAL RELATIONS: THE STATE OF THE ART 445 (Jeffrey L. Dunoff & Mark A. Pollack eds., 2013) (suggesting a connection between the institutional structure of international courts and the types of treaty interpretation adopted by their judges).

Part III
Interim Measures as a Means for Enforcing Human Rights

[25]

INTERIM MEASURES IN THE EUROPEAN CONVENTION SYSTEM OF PROTECTION OF HUMAN RIGHTS

LAURENCE BURGORGUE-LARSEN*

1. INTRODUCTION

Protecting the fundamental rights of individuals in cases of urgency.[1] This is the general issue that is raised by the study of "interim measures" in international human rights law. Such a simple assertion still requires one to assess the progress made in this field. The interim measure in international human rights law originally stems from a procedural mechanism in the national legal order – often referred to as "provisional measures"[2] – that has traditionally been used to ensure the equal rights of the parties in legal proceedings; in short, its aim is to protect the effectiveness of the judicial system.[3] Along the same lines, the functioning of this tool in the international legal order appears to mimic the functioning of provisional measures in the national legal order. For a long time, the object of the interim measure in public international law has logically[4] been to preserve the rights invoked by a party to a dispute, thereby

---

*   Laurence Burgorgue-Larsen is a Professor of Public Law at the Université Paris I Panthéon Sorbonne.

[1]   The notion of urgency is fairly ambiguous from a legal perspective as it depends on the judge's appreciation; it appears to be both an attribute of judicial authority and a reference to a standard, see. E. Jouannet, "Quelques observations sur la signification de la notion d'urgence", in H. Ruiz-Fabri and J-M. Sorel (eds.), *Le contentieux de l'urgence et l'urgence dans le contentieux devant les juridictions internationales, regards croisés* (Paris, Pedone 2001), p. 205.

[2]   The *Dictionnaire de Droit international public* drafted under the direction of J. Salmon (Bruxelles, Bruylant 2001) presents very similar definitions of interim measures and provisional measures and systematically cross-refers to both expressions (see p. 698, 701).

[3]   It is thought that the Italian "proceduralist" scholars were the ones that gave "autonomy" to "preservation" action, see A. Cançado Trindade, "Les mesures provisoires de protection dans la jurisprudence de la Cour interaméricaine des droits de l'homme", in G. Cohen-Jonathan and J-F. Flauss (eds.), *Mesures conservatoires et droits fondamentaux* (Bruxelles, Bruylant 2005), p. 146.

[4]   The reason lies in the stated roles of the "historical" international jurisdictions – the Permanent Court of International Justice and the International Court of Justice – which had no *prima facie* connection with the protection of fundamental rights.

Laurence Burgorgue-Larsen

maintaining the integrity of the decision on the merits of the case. In other words, the aim was to prevent both the object and the effectiveness of the decision from being denied so that the final outcome of the case was not prejudiced.[5]

The state of affairs changed substantially with the appearance of international courts for the protection of human rights, whose key role consists above all in protecting the rights of individuals. The emergence of international human rights litigation, alongside traditional litigation between States, has served not to modify but instead to add to the *purpose* of interim measures. The protection of the fundamental rights of individuals has been added to the objective of ensuring a fair and equal balance of the parties' rights in legal proceedings and preserving the integrity of decisions of international justice; in short, protecting the judicial function. Remarkably, in the context of protecting the fundamental rights of individuals, the International Court of Justice, stated of its own motion in the *Lagrand* case that interim measures had mandatory force, even though its rules did not refer to this in circumstances where the life of a man was at stake.[6] For a change, it was the International Court of Justice that paved the way for the European Court of Human Rights (the Court) to overturn its previous case law in the landmark case of *Mamatkulov*, notwithstanding partly dissenting opinions that were also well-reasoned.[7]

One may state that in today's international legal order, these two functions coexist regardless of the main role of the international court in question (i.e. whether it adjudicates on litigation between States or reviews State action towards individuals). In this context, it is interesting to evaluate more precisely the manner in which these two purposes coexist side by side within the European Convention system of

---

[5] The text of Article 41 of the Statute of the International Court of Justice illustrates this case in point: "1. The Court shall have the power to indicate, if it considers that circumstances so require, any provisional measures which ought to be taken to preserve the respective rights of either party. 2. Pending the final decision, notice of the measures suggested shall forthwith be given to the parties and to the Security Council." The case law has often confirmed this "traditional" goal of interim measures whose object was "preservation", see ICJ (Judgment) 27 June 1986, *Nicaragua v. United States*.

[6] ICJ (Judgment) 21 June 2001, *LaGrand (Germany v. United States)*, paras. 48–117.

[7] The reversal of the previous case-law took place in two stages: it was declared by a panel of 7 judges, then confirmed by the Grand Chamber: ECtHR (Judgment) 6 February 2003, Case No. 46827/99; 46951/99, *Mamatkulov and Abdurasulovic v. Turkey*; ECtHR, Grand Chamber (Judgment) 4 February 2005, Case No. 46827/99; 46951/99, *Mamatkulov and Askarov v. Turkey*. See G. Cohen-Jonathan, "Sur la force obligatoire des mesures provisoires. L'arrêt de la Grande Chambre européenne du 4 février 2005", *Revue Générale de Droit International Public* (2005), p. 421; P. Frumer, "Un arrêt définitif sur les mesures provisoires: la Cour européenne des droits de l'homme persiste et signe. Commentaire de l'arrêt *Mamatkulov et Askarov c. Turquie* du 4 février 2005", *Revue trimestrielle des droits de l'homme* (2005), p. 799–826; P. Tavernier, "Observations – Chronique de jurisprudence de la Cour européenne des droits de l'homme", *Journal du droit international* (2006), p. 1077–1079; H. Tigroudja, "La force obligatoire des mesures provisoires indiquée par la Cour européenne des droits de l'homme. Observations sous l'arrêt du 6 février 2003, *Mamatkulov c. Turquie*", *Revue Générale de Droit International Public* (2003), p. 601–632.

guaranteeing rights through the effectiveness of interim measures.[8] We will begin by assessing the basis of effectiveness of interim measures (2) then decipher their practical manifestations (3) and end with some conclusions (4).

2.   THE BASIS OF EFFECTIVENESS

The *Mamatkulov* case is particularly important in the field of the European Convention of Human Rights (the Convention) due to its specific "conventionary" context. Indeed, we know that, just as in the "universal" system, but unlike the American system, the Convention system of human rights protection does not have a legal base that expressly provides for interim measures to have binding force. Rule 39 of the Rules of the Court[9] (the Rules) appears somewhat circumspect in comparison to Article 63(1) of the American Convention of Human Rights.[10] In the absence of an express provision in the European Convention, the assertion of the binding force of interim measures leads back to the more general question of the source or the basis of the power of the judge.[11] It is relevant to analyse in turn both the Court's justification for determining its own competence (2.1), as well as its justification for declaring that interim measures have binding force (2.2).

2.1.   THE POWER OF THE JUDGE

In order to assess the importance of the Court's assertion of its power to order binding interim measures, it is useful to briefly recall the position of the law before this "change

---

[8]   Effectiveness means for these purposes: "having a mandatory nature, binding".

[9]   Rule 39 of the Rules of the Court: "1. The chamber or, where appropriate, its President may, at the request of a party or of any other person concerned, or of its own motion, indicate to the parties any interim measure which it considers should be adopted in the interests of the parties or of the proper conduct of the proceedings before it. 2. Notice of these measures shall be given to the Committee of Ministers. 3. The Chamber may request information from the parties on any matter connected with the implementation of any interim measure it has indicated."

[10]   Article 63(2) of the American Convention on Human Rights: "In cases of extreme gravity and urgency, and when necessary to avoid irreparable damage to persons, *the Court shall adopt such provisional measures* as it deems pertinent in matters it has under consideration. With respect to a case not yet submitted to the Court, it may act at the request of the Commission." This article must be read in conjunction with Article 25 of the Rules of Procedure of the Inter-American Court of Human Rights. (NB: emphasis added).

[11]   C. Grewe, "Réflexions sur la fonction de juger à partir de l'arrêt *Mamatkulov c. Turquie* rendu par la Cour européenne des droits de l'homme le 4 février 2005", in M.N. Shaw, K.P. Sommermann, B. Fassbender and P.M. Dupuy (eds.), *Common Values in International Law. Essays in Honour of Christian Tomuschat* (Kehl am Rhein, Engel Verlag 2006), p. 536.

Laurence Burgorgue-Larsen

of direction"[12] in the *Mamatkulov* case.[13] Whereas at first, the silence of the Convention was favoured (2.1.1.), the issue was nonetheless re-visited (2.1.2.) a few years later.

2.1.1. *The silence of the Convention as a favoured approach*

On the silence of the Convention, the European Commission of Human Rights (the Commission)[14] as well as the Court[15] determined they had the power to *propose* to the respondent State, interim measures that provisionally preserved the status quo. The practice of the Commission was to intervene, prior to ruling upon the admissibility of an application, in order to request the respondent State to suspend the execution of a disputed judicial decision if it would have irreversible effects.[16] The *Soering*[17] case brought the issue of interim measures to the fore in the realm of the Convention, as the case highlighted the dire consequences of the applicant's extradition to the United States where he could face the death penalty. The United Kingdom cooperated with the request by the Court not to extradite the applicant, despite breaching as a result its obligations under the extradition treaty signed with the United States government. The calls of the Commission and the Court for interim measures in these cases were only requests and were void of any legal effect with regards to both the admissibility of the application as well as the decision on the merits. Given the importance of compliance by States with the interim measures indicated by the Commission and the Court, some applicants did not hesitate to develop the argument that these measures

---

[12] We used this expression to make a critical assessment of the modalities of reversal of case law by the Court, see L. Burgorgue-Larsen, "De l'art de changer de Cap. Libres propos sur les "nouveaux" revirements de jurisprudence de la Cour européenne des droits de l'homme", *Libertés, Justice, Tolérance. Mélanges en hommage au Doyen Gérard Cohen-Jonathan* (Bruxelles, Bruylant 2004), p. 329–344.

[13] ECtHR, Grand Chamber (Judgment) 4 February 2005, Case No. 46827/99; 46951/99, *Mamatkulov and Askarov v. Turkey.*

[14] Rule 36 of its Rules of Procedure. It entered into force on 13 December 1973 and provided: "The Commission, or when it is not in session, the President may indicate to the parties any interim measure the adoption of which seems desirable in the interest of the parties or the proper conduct of the proceedings before it."

[15] Rule 39 of the Rules of Court.

[16] In para. 106 of the *Mamatkulov* case of 2005 (ECtHR, Grand Chamber (Judgment) 4 February 2005, Case No. 46827/99; 46951/99, *Mamatkulov and Askarov v. Turkey*), one discovers certain practical elements in relation to the practice of the Commission: "The Commission adopted that practice very early on, particularly in extradition and deportation cases, and the States concerned proved very cooperative (see, *inter alia*, ECommHR (Report) 26 September 1958, Case No. 176/56, *Greece v. UK*, unpublished; ECommHR (Report) 19 December 1969, Case No. 2396/65, *X v. Germany*, 13 *Yearbook of the European Convention on Human Rights* (1970); ECommHR (Report) 5 November 1969, Case Nos. 3321/67, 3322/67, 3323/67 and 3344/67, *Denmark, Norway, Sweden and the Netherlands v. Greece*, 12 *Yearbook of the European Convention on Human Rights* (1969); ECommHR (Report) 4 October 1976, Case No. 4448/70, *Denmark, Norway and Sweden v. Greece*, 6 *Decisions and Reports of the European Commission of Human Rights* (1970); and ECommHR (Decision) 13 December 1971, Case No. 5207/71, *E.R. v. Germany, Collection of Decisions* 39.

[17] ECommHR (Report) 19 January 1989, Case No. 14038/88, *Soering v. UK.*

Interim Measures in the European Convention System of Protection of Human Rights

were binding. In the *Cruz Varas* case, the applicants were able to argue successfully in favour of the binding nature of interim measures.[18] They made the point that while the Convention did not contain any specific rule with regards to the interim measures indicated by the Commission, it was necessary to attribute binding force to these measures so as to give full effect to the right to individual application guaranteed by Article 34 (ex Article 25(1)) ECHR. Whereas on the one hand the Commission concluded in this case – by 12 votes to 1 – that there had been a violation of the right to bring an application, on the other hand the Court distanced itself from this position because of the lack of an express legal basis.[19] The Court upheld its position in the *Conka* case, this time not in relation to the interim measures indicated by the Commission, but in respect of its own interim measures which had not been complied with by the respondent State.[20] The Court emphasised in these cases that it was not able (whether through the path of constructive interpretation or through the path of adoption of rules of procedure or both) to introduce new provisions to the Convention where the Convention itself is silent on the question.[21] Two years later, in 2003, the

---

18 ECtHR (Judgment) 20 March 1991, Case No. 15576/89, *Cruz Varas v. Sweden*. See G. Cohen-Jonathan, "De l'effet juridique des mesures provisoires dans certaines circonstances et de l'efficacité du droit de recours individuel. A propos de l'arrêt Cruz Varas", *Revue universelle des droits de l'Homme* (1991), p. 205; E. Garcia De Enterria, "De la légitimité des mesures provisoires prises par la Commission et la Cour européennes. L'affaire *Cruz Varas*," 11 *Revue trimestrielle des droits de l'homme* (1992), p. 251.

19 ECtHR (Judgment) 20 March 1991, Case No. 15576/89, *Cruz Varas v. Sweden*, para. 98: "In the absence of a provision in the Convention for interim measures an indication given under Rule 36 cannot be considered to give rise to a binding obligation on Contracting Parties"; para. 99: "It would strain the language of Article 25 [current article 34] to infer from the words 'undertake not to hinder in any way the effective exercise of this right' an obligation to comply with a Commission indication under Rule 36 [current Article 39 of the Rules]"; para. 102: "the power to order binding interim measures cannot be inferred from either Article 25 para. 1 (art. 25-1) *in fine* or from other sources." The only element that the Court accepted in this case (by ten votes to nine) was that failure to comply with an interim measure aggravated the breach of the requirements of Article 3 of the Convention. Michele De Salvia, legal counsel at the European Court of Human Rights, explains the profound reasons (to some extent coming from within the Court) that pushed the Court to "tip-toe". He comments that the reason for this method of dealing with the problem may possibly stem from the fact that the 'former' Court had no direct and immediate contact with applicants and neither therefore, with the reality of sometimes dramatic situations that needed to be dealt with through an approach that was both pragmatic and courageous. Also, it may be due to the fact that the Court thought it should refrain from ratifying a practice originating from the Commission, a body that did not have complete judicial competence and whose conclusions (opinions) were not binding. (NB: translated from the original version in French), M. De Salvia, "La pratique de la Cour européenne des droits de l'homme relative aux mesures provisoires", in G. Cohen-Jonathan and J-F. Flauss (eds.), *Mesures conservatoires et droits fondamentaux* (Bruxelles, Bruylant 2005), p. 178.

20 ECtHR (Decision) 13 March 2001, Case No. 51564/99, *Conka v. Belgium* and ECtHR (Judgment) 5 February 2002, Case. No. 51564/99, *Conka v. Belgium*. The much expected reversal of case law did not take place even though one might have thought that the reforms brought about by Protocol No. 11, in particular the mandatory nature of the right of individual application, were good grounds for a reversal of case law.

21 This is how the partly dissenting judges in the *Mamatkulov* case presented the legal position (para. 6 of their opinion).

Laurence Burgorgue-Larsen

Court changed direction, a change that was confirmed in a decision by the Grand Chamber in 2005. In doing so, the Court reassessed the limits it had expressed regarding its power to judge.

2.1.2. *The silence of the Convention revisited*

The change of direction is a masterstroke, as the silence of the Convention regarding the binding force of interim measures no longer constitutes an insurmountable barrier in 2005. It was completely revisited before being overridden.[22] Two types of arguments were put forward by the Court to justify its power to order binding interim measures. First, the Court pointed to "the special character of the Convention as a treaty for the collective enforcement of human rights and fundamental freedoms."[23] The Court highlighted one of the key differences that distinguishes the European Convention of Human Rights from classic international treaties,[24] namely that it goes beyond the principle of reciprocity towards the creation of "objective obligations." Following this justification pertaining to the *specificity* of the protection of human rights in international law, here in the form of the Convention as a treaty for the "collective enforcement", and as an "instrument of human rights protection,"[25] the Court reaped the benefits of its *teleological method of interpretation*.[26] The consequence is to give special importance, not only to the effectiveness of individual applications, but also to the general spirit of the Convention, an instrument designed to "maintain and promote the ideals and values of a democratic society". Thus the Court supported an objective interpretation of the Convention, which relied on the importance of the values that underpin it and that play a key role, namely that of determining the purpose and limits of the judge's action, just like in a number of national legal systems.[27] Hence one can see that the arguments for limiting the powers of the judge from the 1991 *Cruz Varas* case are set aside in 2005 and demoted to the rank of minor arguments. Judges Caflisch, Türmen and Kovler are the ones who disputed the power of the Court to fill the gap left by the Convention on interim measures,[28] and concluded that the Court

---

22 ECtHR, Grand Chamber (Judgment) 4 February 2005, Case No. 46827/99; 46951/99, *Mamatkulov and Askarov v. Turkey*, paras. 100–102.

23 Ibid., para. 100.

24 This is often highlighted by a number of internationalist legal scholars.

25 ECtHR, Grand Chamber (Judgment) 4 February 2005, Case No. 46827/99; 46951/99, *Mamatkulov and Askarov v. Turkey*, para. 111.

26 Ibid., para. 101.

27 Grewe, *supra*, n. 12, p. 539.

28 Para. 11 of the joint partly dissenting opinion of judges Caflisch, Türmen et Kovler under ECtHR, Grand Chamber (Judgment) 4 February 2005, Case No. 46827/99; 46951/99, *Mamatkulov and Askarov v. Turkey*: "neither Article 26 (d) of that Convention, empowering the Court to enact Rules of Procedure, nor Article 34, instituting the right of individual application, is sufficiently connected to the issue under consideration to fill a "gap" in the Convention by instituting binding interim

Interim Measures in the European Convention System of Protection of Human Rights

acted *ultra vires*.[29] With reference to a classic distinction, they deny the Court's power to exercise a legislative function instead of interpreting the law.[30] They therefore disputed the Court's use of its teleological method of interpretation[31] and put forward instead the other techniques of interpretation mentioned in Articles 31 and 32 of the Vienna Convention. The outcome they reached is obviously the opposite of the Court's solution. Furthermore, they considered that the text of the Convention (which is silent on interim measures), together with reference to the preparatory work in drawing up the Convention (which showed the failure to insert a provision dealing with interim measures), as well as the subsequent practice of the States (which did not demonstrate agreement on considering interim measures as binding), and finally the relevant rules of international law (that consist here of the constituting treaties setting up the international courts and tribunals which indicate interim measures but without any impact on the current Court), were all elements showing that the Court was not entitled to grant itself the power to consider interim measures as binding. Even recourse to the general rules of international law or the general principles recognised by the civilised nations was cast aside.[32]

---

measures *ex nihilo*, thereby imposing on the States Parties to the Convention an obligation without their consent. In other words, there is a big difference between a simple *interpretation* of a treaty and its *amendment*, or between the exercise of the judicial role and international legislation."

[29]   Para. 25 of the joint partly dissenting opinion of judges Caflisch, Türmen and Kovler ECtHR, Grand Chamber (Judgment) 4 February 2005, Case No. 46827/99; 46951/99, *Mamatkulov and Askarov v. Turkey*: "Our basic conclusion is, therefore, that the matter examined here is one of *legislation* rather than of *judicial action*. As neither the constitutive instrument of this Court nor general international law allows for holding that interim measures must be complied with by States, the Court cannot decide the contrary and, thereby, impose a new obligation on States Parties. To conclude that this Court is empowered, de *lege lata*, to issue binding provisional measures is *ultra vires*. Such a power may appear desirable; but it is up to the Contracting Parties to supply it."

[30]   Para. 12 of the joint partly dissenting opinion of the judges Caflish, Türmen et Kovler ECtHR, Grand Chamber (Judgment) 4 February 2005, Case No. 46827/99; 46951/99, *Mamatkulov and Askarov v. Turkey*.

[31]   Para 13 of the joint partly dissenting opinion of the judges Caflish, Türmen et Kovler ECtHR, Grand Chamber (Judgment) 4 February 2005, Case No. 46827/99; 46951/99, *Mamatkulov and Askarov v. Turkey*.

[32]   Paras. 22 and 23 of the joint partly dissenting opinion of the judges Caflish, Türmen et Kovler ECtHR, Grand Chamber (Judgment) 4 February 2005, Case No. 46827/99; 46951/99, *Mamatkulov and Askarov v. Turkey*: "There remains the question of whether the Court may, on the basis of a *rule of general international law* or a *general principle of law recognised by civilised nations*: (i) indicate provisional measures; and (ii) order such measures. If that were the case, the Court could justify the enactment of mandatory interim measures by such a rule or principle even in the absence of any enabling treaty provision. Regarding *general principles of law recognised by civilised nations*, there may well be a widespread rule on obligatory interim measures on the domestic level, based on the rule of compulsory jurisdiction applicable on that level. By contrast, as pointed out earlier (see paragraph 16 above), that rule does not prevail on the international level, which is why it cannot be applied as such on that level. In other words, the principle cannot be transposed to the business of international courts." (Para. 22); "There must, however, be a *customary rule* allowing international courts and tribunals, even in the absence of a treaty provision, to enact Rules of Procedure, a rule which may include the power to *formulate* interim measures. But that rule cannot be taken to include the power to *prescribe* such measures." (Para. 23).

Laurence Burgorgue-Larsen

Instead of adopting an approach that one might be quick to describe as "positivist", the Court preferred to embrace a specific approach (collective enforcement and objective protection of rights) as well as a humanist attitude to the Convention (based on the promotion of ideals and values). Having confirmed its *imperium*,[33] the Court was able to develop the second part of its argumentation without any difficulty, which enabled it to deal with the issue of the effects of interim measures.

2.2.   THE EFFECT OF INTERIM MEASURES

Although the *Mamatkoulov* case revealed a new approach concerning the effect of interim measures (2.2.1.), it was not entirely explicit and much was left " unsaid " which thus prevented one from ascertaining the exact effect of interim measures. We had to wait for the Court to deal with further cases for a clear approach to emerge on the binding force of interim measures (whatever the particularities of the cases brought before the Court) to replace the ambiguity of its early cases (2.2.2.).

2.2.1. An ambiguous effect

In relying on the general principles of international law and on the fact that "other international bodies have expressed a view on this subject since Cruz Varas and Others",[34] the Court created an unbreakable legal connection between the respect for interim measures and the effectiveness of the Convention's right to individual application. All of the Court's reasoning wavers between these two elements. First, the international context, characterised by the doctrine of convention committees (the Human Rights Committee of the United Nations and the United Nations Committee against Torture)[35] and associated with the jurisprudence of the international tribunals (that of the Inter-American Court of Human Rights and that of the International Court of Justice)[36] – is a further sign of the internationalisation of judicial dialogue.[37] The importance of the Convention's right to individual application is "now a key component of the machinery for protecting the rights and freedoms set forth in the Convention,"[38] especially since the transformation of the

---

[33]   The *imperium* consists in determining the dispute with binding force, having the necessary authority to confer efficiency and effectiveness upon judicial acts whereas *jurisdictio* is the mandate or the act of stating the law and determining the dispute by applying the law.

[34]   ECtHR (Judgment) 20 March 1991, Case No. 15576/89, *Cruz Varas v. Sweden*, para. 110.

[35]   Ibid., paras. 114–115.

[36]   Ibid., paras. 116–117.

[37]   L. Burgorgue-Larsen, "De l'internationalisation du dialogue des juges. Missive doctrinale à l'attention de Bruno Genevois", in X. (ed.), *Mélanges en hommage au Président Bruno Genevois, Le dialogue des juges* (Paris, Dalloz 2009), p. 95–130.

[38]   ECtHR (Judgment) 20 March 1991, Case No. 15576/89, *Cruz Varas v. Sweden*, para. 122.

system effected by Protocol No. 11.[39] In other words, on the one hand it takes into account[40] the international judicial environment and the resulting general principles of international law (in favour of what some call the *unity* of the judicial function);[41] thus stating that "whatever the legal system in question, the proper administration of justice requires that no irreparable action be taken while proceedings are pending."[42] On the other hand, it relies on the extraordinary specificity of the Convention's right to individual application (emphasising here the single nature of the European judicial system) which must not be obstructed in any way. The Convention's right to individual application was also brought to the fore when the Court noted "the importance of a suspensory application" consistent with the right to bring an effective legal claim as per Article 13 of the Convention which, as we know, has been given a new meaning by the Court since the *Kudla* case.[43] Effectiveness is thus a "multi-layered" concept as it concerns simultaneously the effectiveness of the Convention right to individual application as such (Article 34), i.e. the right to bring an international claim, as well as the right to an effective legal remedy in national law (Article 13). The comment made by Grewe in relation to this link is that we are witnessing a genuine interconnection linking national judges and European judges in order to build a substantial European constitutional order.[44]

On the basis of these different elements, the Court reversed its previous case law and – through an ingenious combination of Articles 1, 34 and 46 of the Convention – held that a State that did not comply with an interim measure ordered by the Court would be in breach of its obligations under these provisions of the Convention.[45] It held that such a failure to comply would "undermine the effectiveness of the right of individual application" given that it would neither enable the Court to "carry out an effective examination of the application" (Article 34) nor to "ensure that the protection

---

[39] ECtHR, Grand Chamber (Judgment) 4 February 2005, Case No. 46827/99; 46951/99, *Mamatkulov and Askarov* v. *Turkey*, para. 122: "Under the system in force until 1 November 1998, the Commission only had jurisdiction to hear individual applications if the Contracting Party issued a formal declaration recognising its competence, which it could do for a fixed period. The system of protection as it now operates has, in that regard, been modified by Protocol No. 11, *and the right of individual application is no longer dependent on a declaration by the Contracting States. Thus, individuals now enjoy at the international level a real right of action to assert the rights and freedoms to which they are directly entitled under the Convention.*" (NB: emphasis added).

[40] This "taking into account" is not always linear and the reader must take care not to distort the logic behind its argumentation but instead to reconstruct it so as not to distinguish the key message.

[41] C. Grewe, *supra* n. 12, p. 541.

[42] ECtHR (Judgment) 20 March 1991, Case No. 15576/89, *Cruz Varas* v. *Sweden*, para. 124.

[43] ECtHR, Grand Chamber (Judgment) 26 October 2000, Case No. 30210/96, *Kudla* v. *Poland*.

[44] C. Grewe, *supra* n. 12, p. 535: In French, this comment reads: l'on assiste à "une véritable interconnexion qui relie juges internes et juge européen dans l'édification concrète de l'ordre constitutionnel européen."

[45] ECtHR, Grand Chamber (Judgment) 4 February 2005, Case No. 46827/99; 46951/99, *Mamatkulov and Askarov* v. *Turkey*, para. 126: "The effects of the indication of an interim measure to a Contracting State – in this instance the respondent State – must be examined in the light of the obligations which are imposed on the Contracting States by Articles 1, 34 and 46 of the Convention."

Laurence Burgorgue-Larsen

afforded to the applicant by the Convention is effective" (the new object of interim measures) (Article 1). The legal argumentation might have concluded at this stage but the Court included in its argument the supervisory role of the Committee of Ministers in relation to the execution of final judgments, which might also be undermined in the event of a failure to comply with an interim measure. Paragraph 125 is key in that it clearly displays the traditional object of interim measures – shown in the European Convention system by the proper examination of an application and the effective monitoring of the execution of a final judgment pursuant to Articles 34 and 46 – as well as its more innovative object, to ensure the effective protection of the fundamental rights established by Article 1 of the Convention.

At this stage, the following comments must be made. Whereas, in the end, it is the protection of fundamental rights of individuals that constitutes the ultimate *rationale* of such jurisprudence,[46] the argument for the binding effect of interim measures is nonetheless based on the nature of Article 34, which was entirely reassessed on this occasion.[47] Above all, at no moment did the Court use the magic word "mandatory" to describe the effect of interim measures, though this was much hoped for by legal scholars and by human rights activists.[48] Equally, the wording of the decision in *Mamatkulov* is fairly ambiguous regarding whether the fulfilment by States of their obligation to comply with interim measures should be linked to the subsequent observation of obstacles to the effective exercise of the Convention right to individual application.[49] Fortunately, the subsequent case law gave clear and express answers to these different issues.

---

[46]   This idea had already previously motivated the European Commission of Human Rights. Michele De Salvia thus comments that the Commission established a precise legal base providing for the possibility of indicating interim measures because it felt the need to formally bring to the attention of the governments concerned the need to avoid executing specific measures that were the subject of the litigation. The principle being that, as far as possible, the applicant should not have to suffer a serious and irreparable damage precisely because of the execution of such measures, see De Salvia, *supra* n. 12, p. 177–178.

[47]   The drafting of para. 125 is significant because it relegates to the second stage (as shown by the wording "where appropriate") the "newer" object of interim measures, namely the protection of applicants' fundamental rights. Notably, it reads: "Likewise, under the Convention system, interim measures, as they have consistently been applied in practice (see paragraph 104 above), play a vital role in avoiding irreversible situations that would prevent the Court from properly examining the application and, where appropriate, securing to the applicant the practical and effective benefit of the Convention rights asserted. Accordingly, in these conditions a failure by a respondent State to comply with interim measures will undermine the effectiveness of the right of individual application guaranteed by Article 34 and the State's formal undertaking in Article 1 to protect the rights and freedoms set forth in the Convention."

[48]   Para. 128 is revealing in this regard: "A failure by a Contracting State to comply with interim measures is to be regarded as preventing the Court from effectively examining the applicant's complaint and as hindering the effective exercise of his or her right and, accordingly, as a violation of Article 34."

[49]   J-F Flauss, in assessing the impact of this reversal of case law, writes that a literal reading of the Court's justification in the *Mamatkulov* case, leads to the conclusion that failure to comply with interim measures is not unlawful *per se*; it only becomes unlawful when it hinders the effective

---

2.2.2. *An explicit effect*

The first use of the adjective "mandatory" took place in the *Aoulmi* decision taken against France in 2006[50] and removed any ambiguity regarding the obligation of States to comply with interim measures. However, in relation to the observation (be it subsequent or not) of obstacles to the effective exercise of the Convention's right to individual application, there remained the question of the specific circumstances of each case. The first cases that confirmed the reversal by *Mamatkulov* of the Court's previous case law – i.e. the *Shamayev* and *Aoulmi* cases – were not able to give a precise answer, given that the obstacles to the Convention's right to individual application had been duly shown.[51] The question therefore remained whether, in the event that the obstacles to the Convention's right to individual application were not effective in the long run, the failure by the respondent State to comply with the interim measures would nonetheless constitute a breach of Article 34. The *Olaechea Cahuas* case[52] – since confirmed by the *Mostafa* case[53] – brought an end to the questions raised by the analytical blind spots left by the Court's reversal of its jurisprudence.

The *Olaechea Cahuas* case thus allows the Court – even in the absence of an effective obstacle to the Convention's right to individual application – to conclude that there had been a breach of Article 34 of the Convention.[54] In order to reach this result,

---

exercise of the Convention right to individual application. In other words, the applicant must imperatively prove that failure to comply with interim measures constituted an obstacle to the exercise by him of his Convention right to individual application. If such a neutralising interpretation were shown to be well-founded in the future, the result would be that the contribution of the *Mamatkulov* case would be relegated to the rank of "safety valve": the breach of Article 34 would only be entertained once all other alleged breaches had been dismissed. (NB: translated from the original version in French) J-F. Flauss, "Discussion", in G. Cohen-Jonathan and J-F. Flauss (eds.), *Mesures conservatoires et droits fondamentaux* (Bruxelles, Bruylant 2005), p. 210.

50   ECtHR (Judgment) 17 January 2006, Case No. 50278/99, *Aoulmi v. France*, para. 111: "(…) even though *the binding nature of measures adopted under Rule 39* had not yet been expressly asserted at the time of the applicant's expulsion, Contracting States were nevertheless already required to comply with Article 34 and fulfil their ensuing obligations" (para. 111)." (NB: emphasis added).

51   ECtHR (Judgment) 12 April 2005, Case No. 36378/02, *Shamayev and Others v. Georgia and Russia*, para. 478: "The difficulties faced by Mr Shamayev, Mr Aziev, Mr Khadjiev and Mr Vissitov following their extradition to Russia were of such a nature that the effective exercise of their right under Article 34 of the Convention was seriously obstructed"; ECtHR (Judgment) 17 January 2006, Case No. 50278/99, *Aoulmi v. France*, paras. 93, 110: "Counsel for the applicant pointed out that he had not been able to make contact with his client since his removal to Algeria" (para. 93), which brought the Court to the conclusion that "the applicant has been hindered in the effective exercise of his right of individual application" (para. 110).

52   ECtHR (Judgment), 10 August 2006, Case No. 24668/03, *Olaechea Cahuas v. Spain*. See I. Moulier, "Observations – Chronique de jurisprudence de la Cour européenne des droits de l'homme", 2 *Journal de droit international* (2007), p. 783–785.

53   ECtHR (Judgment) 15 January 2008, Case No. 16348/05, *Mostafa and Others v. Turkey*.

54   ECtHR (Judgment), 10 August 2006, Case No. 24668/03, *Olaechea Cahuas v. Spain*, paras. 79–80: "It appears from the documents submitted by the parties in the instant case that after having been extradited in spite of the interim measures indicated by the Court, the applicant had been placed in a Peruvian prison then granted conditional release three months later, and that he had constantly

Laurence Burgorgue-Larsen

the Court linked in the strongest possible way Article 39 of the Rules of the Court to Article 34 of the Convention. Moreover it brought to the fore the ability of the Court, on the basis of its Rules, to assess whether there is a "risk of irreparable damage" to the applicant through any "acts or omissions" of the respondent State that might constitute an obstacle to the effective exercise of the Convention's right to individual application. This link between a regulatory rule and a Convention rule was the technique found by the Court to give the Convention its effectiveness or *"effet utile"*. It resulted, based on a "constructive interpretation", in "promoting a simple rule of procedure to the rank of a Convention rule."[55] The European judge took the opportunity to make some conceptual remarks on the nature and the objectives of interim measures: "a provisional measure is by its very own nature, provisional, (and…) its need is assessed at a given moment as a result of there being a risk that might obstruct the effective exercise of the Convention right to individual application guaranteed by Article 34 (…). The simple lack of compliance with an interim measure decided by the Court due to the existence of such a risk is *per se*, a serious obstacle, at that given moment, to the effective exercise of the Convention right to individual application."[56]

3. THE MANIFESTATIONS OF EFFECTIVENESS

The progress achieved in the context of the Convention is hugely significant. Whereas it was established by both practice and the case law of the Court that the filing of an application in Strasbourg did not suspend the execution of a national measure that appeared *a priori* contrary to the Convention,[57] the Commission took the opportunity to amend its rules of procedure to change the state of affairs (Rule 36). The Court followed suit on this procedural route (Rule 39) and ended up elevating a simple procedural recommendation to the status of a Convention rule (with its binding effects), thanks to the virtues of constructive interpretation (in *Mamatkulov* and subsequent cases). At this stage, it is important to analyse the specific treatment of urgency so as to assess the practice of the former Commission as well as the current Court. We will address the substantive aspects of effectiveness (i.e. the material scope of measures) (3.1.) as well as the procedural aspects (3.2.).

---

been in touch with his counsel in London. *It is therefore not possible to conclude that the applicant's right to an effective remedy was hindered in the same way as in the cases cited above. However, that fact, which became known after the decision to apply the interim measure had been taken, does not mean that the Government complied with their obligation not to hinder in any way the effective exercise of the right enshrined in Article 34."* (NB: emphasis added).

55   F. Sudre, *Droit européen et international des droits de l'homme* (Paris, PUF 2008, 9th ed.), p. 673.

56   ECtHR (Judgment), 10 August 2006, Case No. 24668/03, *Olaechea Cahuas v. Spain*, para. 81.

57   ECommHR (Decision) 18 April 1964, Case No. 2136/64, *X. v. Germany*, 7 Yearbook of the European Convention on Human Rights (1964), p. 298.

3.1.   THE MATERIAL MANIFESTATIONS

Whereas the indication of binding interim measures only affects a narrow pool of guaranteed rights (3.1.1.), it is relevant to ask the question whether the Court will develop its case law so as to expand the scope of the interim measures (3.1.2.).

3.1.1. *The material limits*

The requests for interim measures generally made by the applicants and submitted to the Court cover a broad range of rights guaranteed by the Convention.[58] Nevertheless, in practice, it can be shown that the quasi totality of interim measures indicated by the former Commission and the new Court concerned grievances based on breaches of Article 2 (the right to life) and Article 3 (the prohibition of torture and of inhuman or degrading treatment or punishment) of the Convention as well as Protocol n°6 (abolition of the death penalty)[59] concerning matters of expulsion and extradition. Indeed, these "serious cases" – which highlight the risk incurred by the applicant of being subject to, for example, ill-treatment in the event of effective implementation of a deportation measure – gave legitimacy to the Commission's initial approach. In the same vein, the Court has not departed from this philosophy and has applied Rule 39 "strictly."[60] In other words, the Court will only indicate interim measures (which very often consist in requesting the suspension of the execution of a national measure) only if there is a risk of creating an irreversible situation or an "irreparable damage" and if this risk is "imminent." The bulk of cases concerns situations of expulsion and extradition to third countries where the applicants risk being subjected to ill-treatment.[61] The *Jabari* case and the *D. and Others* case are good examples. Indeed the Court held that the corporal punishments provided for under Islamic criminal law –

---

[58]   C.A. Norgaard and H.C. Kruger, "Interim and conservatory Measures under the European System of Protection of Human Rights", in M. Nowak, D. Steurer and H. Tretter (eds.), *Progress in the Spirit of Human Rights, Festschrift für Felix Ermacora* (Engel Verlag, Kehl am Rhein 1988), p. 109–117.

[59]   Flauss, *supra* n. 49, p. 195; H.R. Garry, "When procedures involves Matters of life and death: Interim Measures and the European Convention on Human Rights", 7 *European Public Law* (2001), p. 415–417; Y. Haeck and C. Burbano Herrera, "Interim Measures in the case of the European Court of Human Rights", 21 *Netherlands Quarterly of Human Rights* (2003), p. 631–639.

[60]   ECtHR, Grand Chamber (Judgment) 4 February 2005, Case No. 46827/99; 46951/99, *Mamatkulov and Askarov v. Turkey*, para. 103.

[61]   The *Jabari v. Turkey* case (ECtHR (Judgment) 11 July 2000, Case No. 40035/98, *Jabari v. Turkey*, para. 38) refers to the classic *dictum* since the *Soering* case as follows: "It is well established in the case-law of the Court that expulsion by a Contracting State may give rise to an issue under Article 3, and hence engage the responsibility of that State under the Convention, where substantial grounds have been shown for believing that the person in question, if expelled, would face a real risk of being subjected to treatment contrary to Article 3 in the receiving country. In these circumstances, Article 3 implies the obligation not to expel the person in question to that country (ECtHR (Judgment) 7 July 1989, Case No. 14038/88, *Soering v. UK*, para. 90–91; ECtHR (Judgment) 20 March 1991, Case No. 15576/89, *Cruz Varas and Others v. Sweden* paras. 69–70; and ECommHR (Report) 15 November 1996, Case No. 22414/93, *Chahal v. UK*, paras. 73–74).

Laurence Burgorgue-Larsen

such as stoning and flogging – violated the dignity and the physical and psychological integrity of human beings.[62]

The question posed at this stage is whether the binding force of interim measures only applies to "absolute" rights to which there is no exception. In addition to the practice of the Court, the extract in paragraph 108 of the decision in *Mamatkulov* suggests this may be the case.[63] Should such a material limitation be confirmed – which currently appears to be the case given that the Court replicated word for word that extract in its judgment in *Mostafa* in 2008[64] – it would mark the existence of "two standards of protection." Flauss noted in this regard that interim judicial protection may be subject to less stringent requirements that those imposed on national courts in relation to the protection of rights guaranteed by the Convention.[65] Indeed, in the *Conka* case, the European judge was especially keen for the applicants to benefit from interim judicial protection that was genuinely effective at national level and going far beyond the simple scope of "core rights."[66]

Is this limitation likely to be overcome? This is a fairly tricky question. On the one hand, the current case law does not leave any scope for a possible evolution, whereas on the other hand, the practice of other international jurisdictions for the protection of human rights would suggest that this would not only be possible but that it would also be desirable.

3.1.2. The material extension?

The two cases that concerned *prima facie* rights other than "absolute rights" were in fact cases in which the right to life was at stake. The *Öcalan*[67] and *Evans*[68] cases show

---

62   ECtHR (Judgment) 11 July 2000, Case No. 40035/98, *Jabari* v. *Turkey*. This case was about an applicant who was liable to be stoned for adultery committed by her in Iran, where she risked being expelled to; ECtHR (Judgment) 22 June 2006, Case No. 24245/03, *D and Others* v. *Turkey*: flogging for "fornication", was considered inhuman punishment.

63   ECtHR, Grand Chamber (Judgment) 4 February 2005, Case No. 46827/99; 46951/99, *Mamatkulov and Askarov* v. *Turkey*, para. 108: "In cases such as the present one where there is plausibly asserted to be a risk of irreparable damage to the enjoyment by the applicant of *one of the core rights under the Convention*, the object of an interim measure is to maintain the *status quo* pending the Court's determination of the justification for the measure." (NB: emphasis added).

64   ECtHR (Judgment) 15 January 2008, Case No. 16348/05, *Mostafa and Others* v. *Turkey*, para. 37.

65   Flauss, *supra* n. 49, p. 210–211: "la protection juridictionnelle provisoire serait soumise à des exigences moins prégnantes que celles imposées au juridictions nationales relativement à la défense des droits garantis par la Convention de sauvegarde."

66   Article 13 of the Convention goes so far as to imply the existence of a remedy that would oppose the implementation of a measure of collective expulsion of foreign nationals prior to the assessment by the national authorities of its respect of the Convention (ECtHR (Judgment) 5 February 2002, Case. No. 51564/99, *Conka* v. *Belgium*, combination of Article 13 ECHR and Article 4 of Protocol No. 4).

67   ECtHR (Judgment) 12 March 2003, Case No. 46221/99, *Öcalan* v. *Turkey*; ECtHR, Grand Chamber (Judgment) 12 May 2005, Case No. 46221/99, *Öcalan* v. *Turkey*.

68   ECtHR (Judgment) 7 March 2006, Case No. 6339/05, *Evans* v. *UK*; ECtHR, Grand Chamber (Judgment) 10 April 2007, Case No. 6339/05, *Evans* v. *UK*.

---

that risks of "irreparable damage," which are likely to trigger interim measures, are not just limited to litigation concerning foreign nationals (who have subsequently moved outside a State's territory); nevertheless, these cases reveal in essence that the Court continues to apply a strict analysis on the use of Rule 39.

In relation to the first case, the applicant – known for his fierce defence of the Kurdish identity in Turkey, as leader of the PKK – complained about his arrest in Kenya by Turkish secret agents and of his transfer to Turkey where he was the subject of criminal proceedings for attempting to bring about the secession of part of the national territory, an offence for which the prosecution sought the death penalty. The Court applied Rule 39 of its Rules in order to protect the rights guaranteed by Article 6(1).[69] Nonetheless, the life of the applicant was ultimately at stake given that he had been condemned to death. Therefore, the specific circumstances of the case may explain why Rule 39 was applied in order to ensure the requirements of a fair trial. Above all, would not the use of Article 34 in situations where Article 6(1) is at stake, surely commit the Court, in some cases, "to grant extra-territorial effects" to the requirements of the right to a fair trial, which the Court has always refused to do in relation to this provision?[70] One must note here the significant difference between the treatment afforded by Article 6(1) and by Article 3. The Court has not hesitated to recognise the extra-territorial scope of Article 3 of the Convention, thereby projecting the values of a "democratic society" on third party States that are not signatories to the Convention. On this point, the Court does not play lightly with those values that it has decided to defend, nor does it accept that the "pluralism of cultures or of legal traditions" justifies "practices or rules that are incompatible with the fundamental values of a democratic society."[71]

In the *Evans* case, the question concerned the possible destruction of frozen embryos of a couple that had undergone treatment for *in vitro* fertilisation (IVF) a few years before, but the male partner had subsequently withdrawn his consent. In this case, the Court hid behind the lack of a European consensus in order not to bring the question of when life begins within the scope of Article 2 of the Convention;[72] it dealt

---

69 ECtHR (Decision) 14 December 2000, Case No. 46221/99, *Öcalan* v. *Turkey.* The Court requested the Turkish Government to "take interim measures within the meaning of Rule 39 of the Rules of Court, notably to ensure that the requirements of Article 6 in the proceedings against the applicant in the State Security Court were complied with and that the applicant was able to exercise his right to individual application to the Court through lawyers of his own choosing effectively."

70 This is the question posed by Flauss, *supra* n. 49, p. 196.

71 F. Sudre, "Le pluralisme saisi par le juge européen", in L. Fontaine (ed.), *Droit et pluralisme* (Bruxelles, Bruylant 2007), p. 272.

72 The Court re-iterated in the process the solution stemming from the *Vo* v. *France* case. The reading of paras. 54 and 56 of the judgment in *Evans* (Grand Chamber) clearly shows this in para. 54: "In its judgment of 7 March 2006, the Chamber recalled that in *Vo v. France* 53924/00, para. 82, the Grand Chamber had held that, in the absence of any European consensus on the scientific and legal definition of the beginning of life, *the issue of when the right to life begins comes within the margin of appreciation which the Court generally considers that States should enjoy in this sphere.* Under English law, as was made clear by the domestic courts in the present applicant's case, an embryo

---

Laurence Burgorgue-Larsen

with the case exclusively from the angle of Article 8 of the Convention. One might have thought that the seeds had been sown for a substantive extension of Rule 39 of the Rules. However, in reality, what was at the heart of the interim measures in this case was in fact the "potential life" of the frozen embryos. Indeed, when the President of the Chamber indicated to the British government that the Court was applying Rule, it did so "without prejudice to any decision of the Court as to the merits of the case." Indeed, it was "desirable in the interests of the proper conduct of the proceedings that the Government take appropriate measures to ensure that the embryos, the destruction of which formed the subject-matter of the applicant's complaints, were preserved until the Court had completed its examination of the case."[73]

Thus, one may observe that a material extension on the basis of an innovative shake-up of the European case law is not on the agenda. However, the fact that the binding force has been elevated to the rank of "general principle of international law" by the International Court of Justice and that the Inter-American Court of Human Rights does not in any way limit the application of interim measures to intangible rights[74] should encourage the Court to be less restrained. We dare not imagine that the overstretched capacity of the Court, which is suffocating under its caseload, could be the cause of such judicial restraint.

3.2. THE PROCEDURAL MANIFESTATIONS

Individuals and the State are face to face in a confrontation with much at stake each time a request for an interim measure is made. It is interesting to take a closer look at the respective role of these two players within the mechanism of Rule 39 of the Rules.

3.2.1. *The role of individuals in the procedure*

Individuals are at the source of the requested interim measures, but they may also be – exceptionally – the addressees of such measures.

Applicants that are subject to an expulsion order, or to extradition or to "refoulement" to a third country ask the Court, through their legal counsel, to indicate interim measures. Indeed, it remains very rare for the Court to act of its own motion

---

does not have independent rights or interests and cannot claim – or have claimed on its behalf – a right to life under Article 2. There had not, accordingly, been a violation of that provision;" and para. 56: "*The Grand Chamber*, for the reasons given by the Chamber, *finds that the embryos created by the applicant and J do not have a right to life within the meaning of Article 2, and that there has not, therefore, been a violation of that provision.*" (NB: emphasis added).

73 ECtHR, Grand Chamber (Judgment) 10 April 2007, Case No. 6339/05, *Evans v. UK*, para. 3.

74 L. Burgorgue-Larsen and A. Úbeda de Torres, *Les Grandes décisions de la Cour interaméricaine des droits de l'homme* (Bruxelles, Bruylant 2008), p. 211.

– to date only one case between States has illustrated such a scenario.[75] Nonetheless, one should not neglect the role of non-governmental organisations, which to some extent take on the role of informal counsel for the applicants by instigating requests for interim measures. Equally, by being able to intervene during the course of proceedings, through the mechanism of "third party intervention", i.e. acting in the capacity of *amicus curiae* – based on Article 36(2) of the Convention and Article 44(2) of the Rules – one suspects that their role in this field may become even more important and more visible.[76] It will be noted at this stage that observations were submitted by several organisations to the Court in the *Mamatkulov* case. Thus, the International Commission of Jurists as well as Human Rights Watch and Aire Centre were present as *amici curiae*.[77] The application of interim measures shows that a number of private entities, following the example of organisations for the protection of human rights, use this technique, which in addition to enriching the Convention procedure, often highlights specific issues for the Court's benefit.[78]

Exceptionally, individuals are sometimes the addressees of interim measures in addition to States. Therefore, an interim measure may be simultaneously addressed to the respondent State as well as to the applicant. In a case dealt with by the former Commission, Germany was recommended to suspend the extradition of the applicant to Turkey, while at the same time the applicant was requested not to take advantage of his liberation to escape and leave German territory.[79] In the same way, the Strasbourg institutions have on a number of occasions requested applicants not to commence or pursue a hunger strike that might endanger their lives.[80]

---

[75] See ECommHR (Report), 26 March 1970, Case No. 4448/67, *Denmark, Norway and Sweden v. Greece*, 13 *Yearbook of the European Convention on Human Rights* (1970), p. 110 and 126, quoted by Flauss, *supra* n. 49, p. 198, footnote 10.

[76] This point was admitted by the Court in ECtHR (Judgment) 6 May 2003, Case No. 26307/95, *Tahsin Acar v. Turkey*.

[77] ECtHR, Grand Chamber (Judgment) 4 February 2005, Case No. 46827/99; 46951/99, *Mamatkulov and Askarov v. Turkey*, para. 9.

[78] See the intervention by l'Association nationale d'assistance aux frontières pour les étrangers (National Association for Assisting Aliens at Borders) in ECtHR (Judgment) 26 April 2007, Case No. 25389/05, *Gebremedhin* [Gaberamadhien] v. *France*, para. 5. On the use of this technique of intervention in proceedings by the "barreaux" (the French bar), see P. Lambert, "La pratique de la tierce intervention devant la Cour européenne des droits de l'homme: l'expérience de l'intervention des barreaux," *Revue trimestrielle des droits de l'homme* (2006), p. 331. In general, on the role of NGOs at the judicial level, see J-F. Flauss, "Les organisations non gouvernementales devant les juridictions internationales compétentes dans le domaine de la protection des droits de l'homme", G. Cohen-Jonathan and J-F. Flauss (eds.), *Les Organisations non gouvernementales et le droit international des droits de l'homme* (Bruxelles, Bruylant 2005), p. 71–101.

[79] ECtHR (Decision) 3 May 1983, Case No. 10308/83, *Altun v. Federal Republic of Germany*, quoted by Flauss, *supra* n. 78, p. 197.

[80] ECtHR (Decision) 15 January 1993, Case No. 19796/92, *Vakalis v. Greece*; ECommHR (Decision) 14 September 1995, Case No. 26516/95, *Bhuyian v. Sweden*; ECommHR (Decision) 20 October 1997, Case No. 33977/96, *Ilijkov v. Bulgaria*.

Laurence Burgorgue-Larsen

3.2.2. *The role of States in the procedure*

Obviously, States are the principle addressees of interim measures. Until recently, such measures have arisen in cases brought by individual applicants. The events of summer 2008 gave the Court the opportunity to order such measures in the context of litigation between States, which created a new and dramatic precedent[81] in which Europe was once again the scene of huge violations of human rights.[82] Here, several kinds of questions arise. First of all, one must determine the manner in which the Court assesses the situation within States, whether these States are signatories to the Convention or third party States, in order to be properly informed and able to indicate interim measures affecting them. The next question is to see whether and how the States respond.

What are the criteria established by the Court to assess the risk of serious and irreparable damage? The assessment of the imminence of danger is carried out by the President of the Chamber or by the Chamber itself. It goes without saying that, as a general rule, both the Registrars of the Chambers as well as the Registrar of the Court, play a major role in the matter, as does the national judge whose opinion is sought. Two types of criteria are used to assess the risk of "irreparable damage". The first type concerns the *personal situation* of the applicant; the second type deals with the *general situation* of respect of human rights in the country concerned.

Therefore, when an applicant is subject to expulsion and has a history of political opposition and/or has already been imprisoned or tortured in the country of destination, the risk of "serious damage" is systematically presumed. The same presumption will apply when the foreign national has been granted the status of political refugee, either by the United Nations High Commission for Refugees,[83] or by

---

[81]   On 11 August 2008, Georgia, which had planned to file a complaint against the Russian Federation for breach of Articles 2 and 3 of the Convention and Article 1 of the first additional protocol, requested that the Court indicate interim measures on the basis of Rule 39 against Russia. Georgia asked the Court to call upon the "Russian Government to abstain from taking any measure that might threaten the life or health of the civilian populations and to enable the Georgian emergency services to take all necessary measures to provide assistance, through a humanitarian corridor, to the civilian and military casualties on the ground." The following day, on 12 August 2008, the Court considered that the situation carried a "real and continuous risk of serious breaches of the Convention" (in particular with regards to Articles 2 and 3) and its President asked both governments to inform it of all measures taken to ensure total compliance with the Convention.

[82]   This is a major challenge that the European Convention system will need to meet in the years to come. Is it equipped to do so? Nothing is less certain. In this context, the Court decided, in accordance with Article 41 of its Statute, to deal as a priority with seven claims against Georgia as a result of the hostilities instigated in South Ossetia, brought by inhabitants of South Ossetia and by a member of the Russian armed forces seconded to the corps for maintaining peace based in Tskhinvali. The press communication by the Registrar of the Court on 16 January 2009 clarifies that these instances are part of a group of 3,300 cases with a similar context that have been filed since August 2008.

[83]   See ECtHR (Judgment) 11 July 2000, Case No. 40035/98, *Jabari* v. *Turkey*, para. 41: "The Court for its part must give due weight to the UNHCR's conclusion on the applicant's claim in making its own assessment of the risk which the applicant would face if her deportation were to be implemented. It

a State other than the respondent State. Finally, as shown in the *Jabari* and *D. and Others* cases, the Court also pays attention to the nature of punishments inflicted, which although legal in the countries to which the foreign nationals are liable to be expelled, appear contrary to the values that underpin the Convention. In this respect, several legal scholars have asked the question as to whether the Court has put in place a "double standard" dependant on whether the foreign national is to be transferred to a third country or to a State that is a signatory to the Convention. Some consider that the Court's assessment is narrower when the transfer is towards a third country, namely because the applicant will not be able to avail himself/herself of the protection afforded by the Convention's right to individual application under Article 34 of the Convention.[84] Although some cases show that a high threshold of requirements applies when third countries are concerned, is it possible at the same time to infer with absolute scientific certainty that the general practice of the Court goes in this direction? Nothing is less certain when the Court has reported no comprehensive data in this regard[85] and since no scientific research has been undertaken that analysis.

With regards to the assessment of the general situation within the country of destination, the Court – which frequently repeats that it assesses the risks undergone "at the time when it is itself assessing the merits of the case"[86] – gives special importance to the public reports of non-governmental organisations just as it does in relation to the information that the latter transmit to the Court's registry on a case by case basis.[87] In this respect, the *N.A.* case is exemplary. It clearly establishes the Court's jurisprudence in a case concerning a Tamil threatened with expulsion to Sri-Lanka where he feared being subjected to inhuman treatment by the Sri-Lankan armed forces. The Court was successful in enforcing compliance by the United Kingdom

---

is to be observed in this connection that the UNHCR interviewed the applicant and had the opportunity to test the credibility of her fears and the veracity of her account of the criminal proceedings initiated against her in Iran by reason of her adultery".

[84] Haeck and Burbano Herrera, *supra* n. 59, p. 646; Flauss *supra* n. 78, p. 200.

[85] Michele De Salvia, former jurisconsult at the Court, has thus commented in relation to the statistical information available, that the percentage of requests made to the Court, and the circulation of decisions of acceptance or rejection, does not appear to have changed much compared with the practice of the Commission. According to him, there is no reliable data on this matter, due to lack of precise data collection, *supra* n. 12, p. 193.

[86] ECtHR (Judgment) 11 July 2000, Case No. 40035/98, *Jabari* v. *Turkey*, para. 41.

[87] ECtHR (Judgment) 8 April 2008, Case No. 21878/06, *Nnyanzi* v. *UK*, para.54: "In order to determine whether there is a risk of ill-treatment, the Court must examine the foreseeable consequences of sending the applicant to the receiving country, bearing in mind the general situation there and his personal circumstances (see *Vilvarajah and Others, para.* 108 *in fine*; and *Saadi*, cited above, *para.* 128–129). To that end, as regards the general situation in a particular country, the Court has often attached importance to the information contained in recent reports from independent international human-rights-protection associations such as Amnesty International, or governmental sources, including the US State Department (see, for example, *Chahal v. United Kingdom*, cited above, para. 99–100; *Müslim v. Turkey*, no. 53566/99, para. 67, 26 April 2005; *Said v. the Netherlands*, no. 2345/02, para. 54, 5 July 2005; and *Al-Moayad v. Germany* (dec.), no. 35865/03, para. 65–66, 20 February 2007)."

Laurence Burgorgue-Larsen

(with whom a divergence of opinion had arisen regarding the conditions of assessment of the general human rights situation in Sri Lanka[88]) with Rule 39 of the Rules in no less than 342 cases similar to this one. If in the future, when Protocol No. 14 has entered into force, the Commissioner for Human Rights will no doubt become a reliable and respected source of information.[89] On the basis of these different elements, the European judge takes into account the deficiencies affecting the functioning of justice, the racist or xenophobic behaviour towards minorities and, in some cases, the revealed "practices" of systematic torture and inhuman treatment.

4. CONCLUSIONS

The theme of interim measures will not fail to continue to gain importance in an international context marked by a high level of political, social and economic instability. The "Great Europe" has not been spared from dramatic and turbulent situations where shocking violations of Articles 2 and 3 of the Convention have taken place in certain countries.[90] Interim measures, now binding and taken seriously by States, generally contribute to the prevention of serious and irreparable damage affecting applicants.[91] However, will the case of the war between Russia and Georgia reveal their lack of effectiveness? More generally, is the Convention system capable of dealing with cases of massive human rights violations?

---

[88] On 25 June 2007, on the basis of Rule 39 of the Rules, the Court indicated to the United Kingdom that it should suspend the expulsion of *N.A.* until the examination of the case. In October 2007, given the increasing number of applications by Tamils in the same situation as the applicant, the Registrar of the Chamber dealing with the case warned the British Government's agent that interim measures had been indicated in 22 cases and requested that it suspend the execution of expulsion orders. The response was negative, as the United Kingdom considered that the situation in Sri Lanka did not justify a *systematic suspension* of *all* expulsions of Tamils invoking Article 3 of the Convention insofar as the real and serious risk was not widespread. The Court continued to apply Rule 39 in all the instances of Tamils threatened with expulsion to Sri-Lanka; thus the Court established its position on the current situation of Tamils in Sri Lanka and the influence of the general context of a country when assessing specific and individual situations.

[89] According to Article 36(3) ECHR (as amended by Protocol No. 14), the Commissioner for Human Rights will be able to make written observations and take part in the hearings in all cases before a Chamber or the Grand Chamber. It has been commented that if the President of the Court had the ability to invite the Commissioner to intervene in pending cases, the new rule would not be useless as it would reinforce the defence of the general interest, see J-F. Renucci, *Traité de droit européen des droits de l'homme* (Paris, LGDJ 2007), p. 853.

[90] The war in Chechnya is a tragic illustration of this. The Court issued between May and June 2008 no less than ten judgments where it unanimously observed the violation by Russia of Article 2, both material and substantial, due to the disappearance by force of men who had fought for the Chechen army.

[91] It is urgent that the Court put together precise data in order to determine the degree of implementation of interim measures by States and, where applicable, by applicants to whom such measures have also been addressed.

[26]

PART A: ARTICLES

LETTING STATES OFF THE HOOK? THE PARADOX OF THE LEGAL CONSEQUENCES FOLLOWING STATE NON-COMPLIANCE WITH PROVISIONAL MEASURES IN THE INTER-AMERICAN AND EUROPEAN HUMAN RIGHTS SYSTEMS

Clara Burbano Herrera and Yves Haeck*

Abstract

Anyone who proves that he or she is in a situation of danger and who is a potential victim of a violation of a right set forth in the American or the European Convention on Human Rights may be protected by interim measures. Interim measures in the human rights systems may be defined as an instrument, the purpose of which is to prevent irreparable harm to persons who are in a situation of extreme gravity and urgency, which a favourable final judgment would therefore not be able to undo. They result in protection offered by the State in compliance with the legally binding order of the Inter-American or European Court on Human Rights. While this legal figure is nowadays applied more and more frequently and in most cases the American and European countries have complied with the order of their respective Court of Human Rights, the question that this contribution would like to answer is what the legal consequences of incompliance are and whether the difference as to the legal basis of the interim measures in both human rights systems has influenced the legal effect that the respective Courts have given to non-compliance with the measures. After an overview of the case-law, it will be shown that in fact each regional system has given different legal consequences to

---

*   Clara Burbano Herrera is a Senior Research Fellow at the Human Rights Centre of Ghent University, Belgium, a Postdoctoral Fellow of the Research Foundation Flanders and a former Professor of Law at the Universidad de Los Andes, Bogotá, Colombia. Yves Haeck is an Associate Professor in Human Rights at the Netherlands Institute of Human Rights (SIM), Utrecht University, the Netherlands, and a Senior Research Fellow at the Human Rights Centre and the Department of Constitutional Law of Ghent University, Belgium. This article has been made possible through the award of the *Prince Bernhard Prize/Scholarship 2008* to the first mentioned author. The judgments and decisions of the European Court of Human Rights and the Inter-American Court of Human Rights can be consulted on www.echr.coe.int (HUDOC database) and www.corteidh.or.cr, respectively. All internet sites were last accessed on 1 July 2010.

the incompliance with its interim measures, but paradoxically, the effects are not directly related to the type of legal instrument in which the interim measures are contemplated. The issue is relevant because on the one hand interim measures are mostly adopted in dramatic contexts where the life and personal integrity of human beings are endangered and because a survey of the case-law shows that under the European system the cases of incompliance seem to be on the rise, and on the other hand, because it appears that under the Inter-American system there are many cases in which provisional measures have been issued which will be decided soon on the merits, and therefore during the examination of which it will be decided whether the member States have complied or not with the Inter-American Court's interim measures and what consequences incompliance entails.

1.   INTRODUCTION

Nowadays provisional measures or interim measures are a key instrument for the Inter-American and European Courts of Human Rights to prevent irreparable harm to persons who are in a situation of extreme gravity and urgency. The measures result in protection offered by the State in compliance with an order of the Inter-American or European Court, which may act at the request of a party or on their own motion.

To date, the beneficiaries of interim measures have been, among others, family members of alleged victims, witnesses, journalists, political candidates, human rights defenders, members of indigenous communities, prisoners who live in deplorable conditions, the seriously ill or those on hunger strikes, officials of the justice system, aliens under orders of deportation or extradition and those sentenced to capital punishment. In the vast majority of cases the provisional measures are taken to protect the right to life and/or the right to personal integrity of the above-mentioned persons and groups.

Although this legal figure is applied more frequently and in most cases the American and European countries have complied with the order of their respective regional court of human rights, the question arises of what happens on those occasions that the States refuse to comply?; or in other words: what are the legal consequences of non-abidance? The issue is important, not only because provisional measures are adopted in dramatic contexts where the life and personal integrity of human beings are endangered, but also because on the one hand, under the European system the cases of non-compliance seem to be on the rise, both with founding member States of the Council of Europe and thus old member States to the European Convention on Human Rights (ECHR) and countries that have recently ratified the European Convention, and on the other hand, because it appears that under the Inter-American System there are many cases in which provisional measures have been issued which will be decided soon on the merits.

Clara Burbano Herrera and Yves Haeck

To meet the objective, we will start by presenting the normative structure regulating the figure of the provisional measure. It will be demonstrated that both human rights systems start off from different points of departure; while in the Inter-American system the measures have a conventional nature, under the European system it only has a regulatory basis. Given this normative differentiation, it will be examined whether this distinction has influenced the legal effect that the respective courts have given to the non-compliance with provisional measures. After an overview of the case-law, we will show that in fact each regional system has given different legal consequences to the non-abidance to provisional measures, but paradoxically, the effects are not directly related to the type of instrument in which they are contemplated.

In this sense, the final question that arises is why the Inter-American Court does not consider the non-compliance with an order for provisional measures as a violation of the American Convention on Human Rights (ACHR), notwithstanding that the legal figure of provisional measures is expressly contemplated therein (Article 63(2) ACHR), while the Strasbourg Court, through a teleological interpretation and after a lengthy jurisprudential debate has concluded that its provisional measures are binding, and therefore that the failure of States to comply with a provisional measure leads to an almost automatic violation of the right to petition of the European Convention (Article 34 ECHR), although the figure of the provisional measure is not mentioned at all in the text of the Convention. This article attempts to answer this question, which in turn allows us in the form of a conclusion to give some indication of the challenges that lie ahead for both regional human rights courts to evolve towards giving better protection to the individual.

2. A REMINDER OF HOW THE PROVISIONAL MEASURES WERE CREATED AND THEIR LEGAL CHARACTER: EXPLICIT CONVENTIONAL BASIS *VERSUS* REGULATORY BASIS

2.1. INTER-AMERICAN SYSTEM: EXPLICIT CONVENTIONAL BASIS

Unlike under other systems, such as the universal and the European, where provisional measures are provided for in the Statute and/or Rules of Court (for example the International Court of Justice, the UN Human Rights Committee and the European Court of Human Rights, respectively), in the Inter-American system these measures are expressly contemplated in Article 63(2) of the American Convention on Human Rights, which states:

> In cases of extreme gravity and urgency, and when necessary to avoid irreparable damage to persons, the Court shall adopt such provisional measures as it deems pertinent in matters

it has under consideration. With respect to a case not yet submitted to the Court, it may act at the request of the Commission.[1]

Although the language employed in Article 63(2) is clear with respect to the compulsory nature of provisional measures, it is unfortunate that the Proceedings of the Specialised Inter-American Conference do not indicate whether there was any discussion on the scope and nature of provisional measures. These Proceedings contain the debate that took place on the draft American Convention on Human Rights presented by the Inter-American Council of Jurisconsults, which was responsible for up-dating and completing a draft, taking into account the earlier drafts of the pre-existing Inter-American Commission and drafts presented by Chile and Uruguay. The proceedings may thus be considered as the *travaux préparatoires* of the American Convention on Human Rights. It may be seen from the Proceedings that the Draft American Convention on the Protection of Human Rights did not provide for the figure of provisional measures in any of its provisions.[2] It was during the Sixth Meeting of the Second Commission of the Inter-American Conference on 19 November 1969, that the delegate of Costa Rica, José Luis Redondo Gómez, proposed that the Court would be able to act in grave situations and in emergency situations. The delegate held that this function was common in every tribunal in the world. He proposed that there be included a text that would state the following:

> The Court shall take the provisional measures that it deems pertinent in emergency situations and when there is sufficient cause that justifies it to protect the right that is claimed to be infringed.[3]

When the amendment was voted upon, it was rejected by one vote in favour, none against and 16 abstentions. Two days later, on 21 November, during the Third Plenary Session, once again the delegate of Costa Rica, this time José Francisco Chaverri, when Article 63 was being considered, proposed that a paragraph be added, which was nearly the same as that presented previously, with the following text:

> In cases of extreme gravity and urgency, and when necessary to avoid irreparable damage to persons, the Court shall adopt such provisional measures as it deems pertinent in matters

---

[1]   As it can be seen, the Court can also adopt provisional measures in relation with matters which are not (yet) under its consideration. To be able to adopt such measures, a request is necessary from the Inter-American Commission.

[2]   See *Conferencia Especializada Interamericana sobre Derechos Humanos* [Specialised Inter-American Conference on Human Rights], San José, Costa Rica, 7–22 November 1969, Actas y Documentos, OEA/Ser.K/XVI/1.2, pp. 13–35. A study on the *travaux préparatoires* of the American Convention compared to that of the European Convention may be found in Buergenthal, Th., 'The European and Inter-American Human Rights Courts: Beneficial Interaction', in: Mahoney, P., Matscher, F., Petzold H. and Wildhaber, L. (eds), *Protecting Human Rights: The European Perspective, Studies in memory of Rolv Ryssdal*, Carl Heymanns Verlag, Köln, 2000, pp. 123–133.

[3]   See *Conferencia Especializada Interamericana sobre Derechos Humanos, op.cit.* (note 2), p. 361.

Clara Burbano Herrera and Yves Haeck

it has under consideration. With respect to a case not yet submitted to the Court, it may act at the request of the Commission.[4]

According to the minutes of the Third Plenary Session (summary version) the proposal was considered and it was decided to incorporate a paragraph 1 in the text presented. The minutes say nothing about the arguments of the Costa Rican delegate nor as to whether there were comments by the delegates of the other States or the results of the voting. This was the text that was incorporated into the Convention.

Despite the apparent lack of discussion on the incorporation of provisional measures, there can be no doubt whatsoever about the compulsory nature of provisional measures since they are expressly provided for in the American Convention. The language, plus the location of Article 63(2) in Chapter VIII, Section 2 on 'Jurisdiction and Functions', permits to conclude that the clear intention of the drafters was to grant true binding force to the provisional measures and not be simple suggestions or indications.[5] While the Statute of the International Court of Justice and the Rules of the European Court of Human Rights use the word 'indicate',[6] it was preferred that the American Convention express that the Court 'shall adopt' such measures as it deems pertinent.[7]

2.2. EUROPEAN SYSTEM: REGULATORY BASIS

In the European System, a provision on interim measures (Article 35), inspired by Article 41 of the Statute of the International Court of Justice, was included by the

---

[4]   *Ibidem*, p. 457.

[5]   Nieto Navia, R., 'Las medidas provisionales en la Corte Interamericana de Derechos Humanos' [Provisional Measures in the Inter-American Court of Human Rights], in: Nieto Navia, R. (ed.), *La Corte y el Sistema Interamericano de Derechos Humanos* [The Inter-American Court and the Inter-American Human Rights System], Inter-American Court of Human Rights, San José, 1994, pp. 369–398, at p. 392; Cançado Trindade, A., *Medidas Provisionales. Prólogo del Presidente de la Corte Interamericana de Derechos Humanos al Tomo III de la Serie E.* [Provisional Measures. Prologue of the President of the Inter-American Court of Human Rights to Volume III of Series E], [Inter-American Court of Human Rights, San José], 2001, paras 13 and 21; Pasqualucci, J.M., *The Practice and Procedure of the Inter-American Court of Human Rights*, Cambridge University Press, Cambridge, 2003, p. 318; and Pasqualucci, Jo M., 'Provisional Measures in the Inter-American Human Rights System: An Innovative Development in International Law', *Vanderbilt Journal of Transnational Law*, Vol. 26, 1993–1994, pp. 803–863, at pp. 823, 824 and 849.

[6]   Article 73 of the Rules of the International Court of Justice (ICJ), Article 41 of the Statute of the ICJ and Article 39 of the European Court of Human Rights. On this matter it is important to point out that the verb 'indicate' used in the Statute of the ICJ generated a widespread doctrinal debate on the 'binding' character of the provisional measures leading to the development of an extensive jurisprudence on the subject. In its judgment in the *LaGrand* Case of 27 June 2001, the ICJ concluded that its provisional measures are binding.

[7]   Having been established in a treaty freely consented to and accepted by the States, they must be complied with in accordance with the principle of *pacta sunt servanda*, which obligates the States to comply in good faith with the provisions of the treaties to which they are parties. Article 26 Vienna Convention on the Law of Treaties of 23 May 1969.

International Juridical Section of the European Movement in the Draft Statute of the European Court, that was added to the Draft European Convention, which held:

a) The Court shall have the power to indicate, if it considers that circumstances so require, any provisional measures which ought to be taken to preserve the respective rights of either party.

b) Pending the final decision, notice of the measures suggested shall forthwith be given to the parties and to the European Human Rights Commission and to the Secretary-General.[8]

This draft provision, which was presented to the Committee of Ministers of the Council of Europe on 12 July 1949, was not withheld in the later European Convention. Unfortunately, the *travaux préparatoires* of the European Convention on Human Rights do not contain any discussion on the matter.[9] Some authors have stated that the silence was due to the fact that the system created by the Convention was not conceived to operate in the practical sense that it does today or, in other words, it was not foreseen that the system under the Convention would be developed with the speed and magnitude as has in fact occurred, especially given the events of the Second World War.[10]

Nonetheless, the need for interim measures became evident very early in the work of the European Commission. In fact, this supervisory organ, shortly after it was established, began to make informal requests to member States that they suspend implementation of the death penalty and deportations and extraditions while it was examining the applications. The first time occurred in 1957 in the first inter-State case that was presented under the system; only two years after the Commission began functioning. On this occasion, the British Government, at the request of Greece, was asked not to execute Nicholas Sampson, who had seized power following a *coup* on Cyprus, a British Crown Colony, and who had subsequently been captured by the British authorities and sentenced to death.[11]

---

8   Council of Europe, *Collected Edition of the 'Travaux Préparatoires' of the European Convention on Human Rights*, The Hague, Martinus Nijhoff, 1975–85, Vol. I, pp. 302–320.

9   Council of Europe, *Collected Edition of the 'Travaux Préparatoires' of the European Convention on Human Rights*, Martinus Nijhoff, The Hague, 1975–1985, Vol. I, xxiv and p. 314; and Buquicchio de Boer, M., 'Interim Measures by the European Commission of Human Rights', in: De Salvia, M. and Villiger, M.E. (eds), *The Birth of European Human Rights Law, Liber Amicorum Carl Aage Norgaard*, Nomos, Baden-Baden, 1998, pp. 229–236, at p. 229.

10   Vajic, N., 'Interim Measures and the Mamatkulov Judgment of the European Court of Human Rights', in: Kohen, M. (ed.), *Promoting Justice, Human Rights and Conflict Resolution through International Law. Liber Amicorum Lucius Caflisch*, Brill, Leiden, 2007, pp. 601–622, at p. 607; and Nörgaard, C.A. and Krüger, H.C., 'Interim and Conservatory Measures under the European System of Protection of Human Rights', in: Nowak, M., Steurer, D. and Tretter, H. (eds), *Progress in the spirit of Human Rights: Festschrift für Felix Ermacora*, Engel Verlag, Kehl am Rhein, 1988, pp. 109–117, at pp. 109–110.

11   Commission, *Greece* vs *the United Kingdom*, decision of 2 June 1956, Application No. 176/56. Greece presented two petitions against the United Kingdom on 7 May 1956. The Greek Government

Clara Burbano Herrera and Yves Haeck

In most of the cases, the States complied with the order of the Commission. Thus, between 1960 and 1970 there was a clear practice of respect for the measures, even though they were not included in any legal document. Given the absence in the European Convention of an express provision on interim measures, and the fact that the measures were taken a few times in practice, the Consultative Assembly of the Council of Europe recommended in 1971 to the Committee of Ministers that an additional Protocol to the Convention be drafted that would enable the supervisory organs under the European Convention to adopt interim measures in the appropriate cases.[12] The Committee of Ministers did not endorse the Recommendation, believing that it was not necessary in the light of the adequate informal system that had been developed, since in practice the States complied with the measures requested by the Commission.[13]

Given this climate of confidence, the Commission decided to include interim measures in the 1974 reform of its Rules of Procedure, which codified the practice of some years. Rule 36 of the Rules stated the following:

> The Commission or, where it is not in session, the President may indicate to the parties any interim measure the adoption of which seems desirable in the interest of the parties or the proper conduct of the proceedings before it.[14]

Given the refusal to include a provision of this type in a protocol, the Consultative Assembly opted in 1977 to recommend to the Committee of Ministers that it invite the member States not to extradite or deport someone to a non-State party to the Convention when the Commission or the Court was examining for example alleged violations of Article 3.[15] Consequently, the Committee of Ministers on 27 June

---

submitted that the derogation from the provisions of the Convention notified by the British Government and applied to Cyprus by virtue of Article 15 ECHR was irregular in form and, furthermore, that the conditions required by the Article were not present in this case. It also maintained that a series of emergency laws and regulations in force in Cyprus were incompatible with the provisions of the ECHR. It alleged, in particular, that the legislation providing for the imposition of whipping and various forms of collective punishment was an infringement of Article 3 ECHR which, under Article 15, the contracting parties may not depart from even in time of war or other public emergency. For its part, the British Government denied that it violated the ECHR, relying partly on the definition of the rights and freedoms recognised by the ECHR and partly on the existence in Cyprus of a 'public emergency threatening the life of the nation' within the meaning of the aforesaid Article 15. See *Yearbook of the European Convention on Human Rights*, Vol. 2, Martinus Nijhoff, The Hague, 1958–1959, p. 174.

[12]   Recommendation No. 623–1971, *Yearbook of the European Convention on Human Rights*, Vol. 14, Martinus Nijhoff, The Hague, 1971, pp. 68–71.

[13]   Garry, H., 'When Procedure Involves Matters of Life and Death: Interim Measures and the European Convention on Human Rights', *European Public Law*, Vol. 7, 2001, pp. 399–431, at p. 407.

[14]   This reform to the Rules of the Commission entered into force on 13 December 1974. See *Yearbook of the Convention on Human Rights*, Vol. 17, Martinus Nijhoff, The Hague, 1974, pp. 34 and 54.

[15]   Recommendation No. 817–1977 on certain aspects of the right to asylum, *Yearbook of the European Convention on Human Rights*, Vol. 20, Martinus Nijhoff, The Hague, pp. 82–85.

1980 decided to adopt a Recommendation to member States with regard to cases of extradition of persons from a member State to a non-member State to the European Convention. The Recommendation advises the member States 'to comply with any interim measures which the European Commission of Human Rights might indicate under Rule 36 of its Rules of Procedure, as for instance, a request to stay extradition proceedings pending a decision on the matter'.[16]

The experience of the European Court with regard to interim measures has been a little different than that of the European Commission, since, although the measures were provided for in 1959 in Rule 34 of its original Rules,[17] the Court did not deal with the matter until 30 years later in the *Soering* Case.[18] Rule 34 provided the following:

> *(Interim measures)*. 1. Before the constitution of a Chamber, the President of the Plenary Court may, at the request of a Party, the Commission, or any person concerned or *propio motu*, bring to the attention of the Parties any interim measure the adoption of which seems desirable. The Chamber, when constituted, or, if the Chamber is not on session, its President, shall have the same right. 2. Notice of these measures shall be immediately given to the Committee of the Ministers.[19]

Although the legal figure of the provisional measures was formally included in the Rules of the European Court before they were included in the Rules of Procedure of the European Commission, the Court only made use of its competence to issue provisional measures for the first time much later than the Commission. This was because, before the Commission was abolished under Protocol No. 11, interim measures were adopted at the beginning of the case, when the petition was presented to the Commission, which meant that the Court only dealt with the measures when the Commission or State(s) referred the case to the Court. Protocol No. 11 was then drafted and the entire protective system was restructured. The Committee of Ministers again missed an opportunity to introduce a provision on interim measures, even though various bodies such as the Commission,[20] Court, Committee on Migration,

---

16 Recommendation No. R (80) 9, *Yearbook of the European Convention on Human Rights*, Vol. 23, Martinus Nijhoff, The Hague, 1980, pp. 78–79.

17 The first Rules of the European Court of Human Rights established under the former Article 55 of the Convention were adopted on 18 September 1959. The Rules were completely amended on 24 November 1982 and again modified after the entry into force of Protocol No. 11. The current Rules can be found on: www.echr.coe.int/NR/rdonlyres/D1EB31A8–4194–436E-987E-5AC8864BE4F/0/ RulesOfCourt.pdf.

18 ECtHR, *Soering vs the United Kingdom*, judgment of 7 July 1989, Application No. 14038/88, para. 77. The Court extended the interim measures that the Commission had adopted.

19 See *Yearbook of the European Convention on Human Rights, op.cit.* (note 11), pp. 26–28.

20 Comments on Draft Protocol No. 11 to the European Convention on Human Rights to the Committee of Experts for the Improvement of Procedures for the Protection of Human Rights from the European Commission of Human Rights, Doc. DH-PR(94)2, 21 January 1994.

Clara Burbano Herrera and Yves Haeck

Refugees and Demography of the Parliamentary Assembly[21] and the Swiss delegation[22] recommended that interim measures be part of the European Convention.

As in 1949, interim measures were not mentioned in the *travaux préparatoires*. A report of the Commission of Experts states that the proposal was not taken up because it was not considered to be urgent and, therefore, could be dealt with on another occasion. It is possible that the lack of time and the search for consensus in more important matters of the reform were the main reason for this omission.[23] The Court, expressing its opinion on the draft Protocol, lamented that in the context of the radical change of the Convention's protection machinery, the opportunity had not been taken to fill at least one obvious gap, specifically the power to indicate interim measures. On this point, the Court referred to Article 63(2) of the American Convention.[24]

The context that we have just described on interim measures has resulted in a debate on their binding character since there is no express provision regarding them in the Convention but only in the Rules of the former Commission and the Rules of the Court. The controversy, therefore, has focused on determining whether non-compliance of the measures adopted by the Court under Rule 39 (previously Rule 36) is a violation of Article 34 (previously Article 25) of the Convention. In other words, the question that arises is whether the Court among its functions has a system of measures that are binding on the States parties to the European Convention or whether the measures are simple suggestions and whether the failure to comply would lead to some sort of international responsibility.

3. LEGAL EFFECTS OF NON-COMPLIANCE: AGGRAVATION OF THE VIOLATION OF A SUBSTANTIAL RIGHT VERSUS VIOLATION OF THE CONVENTION

3.1. INTER-AMERICAN SYSTEM: DISCOURSE *VERSUS* LEGAL EFFECT

Throughout its case-law, the Inter-American Court has maintained rhetorically that its interim measures are binding. However, when the Court was faced with a situation of incompliance, it only established the 'aggravation' of the substantial right that

---

21   Draft Report AS/PR(1997)2 rev., 19 February 1997.

22   Doc DH-PR(93)17 misc. 3 and Doc. DH-PR(93)20, 22 November 1993.

23   See Report of the Committee of Experts of the Meeting 33 DH-PR (12–16 October 1992), Doc. DH-PR (93)12, para. 42. See also Rudolf, B., 'Der Entwurf eines Zusatzprotokolls uber die Reform des Kontroll-mechanismus der Europäischen Menschensrechtskonvention' [The Draft of an Additional Protocol on the Reform of the Supervisory Mechanism of the European Convention on Human Rights], *Europäische Grundrechte Zeitschrift* [European Rights Journal], Vol. 21, 1994, pp. 53–58, at p. 54.

24   Opinion of the Court on Draft Protocol No. 11 to the European Convention on Human Rights, Doc. DH-PR (94)4, 31 January 1994, para. 9.

Letting States off the Hook?

was found to have been violated by the member State, thus avoiding declaring the procedural violation of the provision on provisional measures that is contemplated in the American Convention. This situation allows us to consider that the Court has simultaneously managed two discourses in connection with the legal figure of provisional measures: a theoretical discourse and another discourse in practice. At the theoretical level, the Court has elevated the provisional measures into a special category, which it has endowed with full legal authority, while at the practical level, it has taken away any legal effect from its provisional measures.

Indeed, in its case-law on provisional measures the Court has held that States must comply with everything ordered by way of provisional measure by the Court in its resolutions. In general the language used by the Court is sufficiently clear for States to take all necessary measures to comply and therefore to protect persons who find themselves in a situation of risk. The resolutions on provisional measures in its preambular paragraphs recall that States have ratified the American Convention and accepted the jurisdiction of the Inter-American Court. Its case-law shows that the Court has relied on Articles 1(1),[25] 2,[26] 33,[27] 62(1),[28] 63(2)[29] and 68(1)[30] of the American Convention to hold that its provisional measures are binding. The Court has also held that the obligation to comply with its decisions corresponds to a basic principle of the law of international responsibility, according to which States must fulfil their obligations under international treaties in good faith (*pacta sunt servanda*) and, in

---

[25]   Article 1(1) ACHR specifies the obligation of the State parties to respect the rights and freedoms recognised therein and to ensure to all persons subject to their jurisdiction the free and full exercise of those rights and freedoms. See IACtHR, *Caballero Delgado and Santana* vs *Colombia*, order of 7 December 1994, preambular para. 2; IACtHR, *Urso Branco Prison* vs *Brazil*, order of 29 August 2002, preambular para. 5; IACtHR, *Carlos Nieto Palma* vs *Venezuela*, order of 5 August 2008, preambular para.3.

[26]   According to Article 2 of the Convention, the State parties undertake to adopt the legislative or other measures as may be necessary to give effect to the rights or freedoms contemplated in the Convention. IACtHR, *Blake* vs *Guatemala*, order of 16 August 1995, preambular paras 1 and 3; IACtHR, *Ivcher Bronstein* vs *Peru*, order of 21 November 2000, preambular paras 1 and 5; and IACtHR, *Plan de Sánchez Massacre* vs *Guatemala*, order of the President of 30 July 2004, preambular paras 1 and 4.

[27]   Pursuant to Article 33 of the Convention, the State parties recognise the Court and the Commission as the competent organs to ensure the object and purpose of the Convention, that is, the protection of human rights, and in the case of the Court, its contentious jurisdiction when it has been accepted. See IACtHR, *Liliana Ortega* et al. vs *Venezuela*, order of 4 May 2004, preambular para. 2.

[28]   Pursuant to Article 62(1), the States declare that they recognise as binding, *ipso facto*, and not requiring special agreement, the jurisdiction of the Court on all matters relating to the interpretation or application of the American Convention. See IACtHR, *Carpio Nicolle* vs *Guatemala*, order of 4 June1995, preambular para. 1; IACtHR, *Mendoza Prisons* vs *Argentina*, order of 22 November 2004, preambular para. 1; and *Carlos Nieto Palma* vs *Venezuela*, *supra* note 26, preambular para. 1.

[29]   IACtHR, *Gutiérrez Soler* vs *Colombia*, order of 27 November 2007, preambular para. 2; and IACtHR, *Urso Branco Prison* vs *Brazil*, order of 2 May 2008, preambular para. 2.

[30]   According to Article 68(1) of the American Convention, the State parties undertake to comply with the judgment of the Court in any case to which they are parties. See IACtHR, *James* et al. vs *Trinidad and Tobago*, order of 16 August 2000, preambular para. 10; and IACtHR, *Lysias Fleury* vs *Haiti*, order of 2 December 2003, preambular para. 7.

Clara Burbano Herrera and Yves Haeck

conformity with Article 27 of the Vienna Convention on the Law of Treaties of 1969, they cannot for domestic reasons fail to assume their already established international responsibility.[31] The measures are, therefore, compulsory even in situations of internal armed conflict.[32]

Taking into account the aforementioned articles, the Court has held that compliance with provisional measures does not depend on the discretion or goodwill of States. Provisional measures are binding because they are explicitly set forth in the American Convention, and the States as parties to the Convention have the duty to comply with all the provisions in that treaty.[33] This is also true for those who maintain that the Court may only adopt provisional measures with respect to the States that have accepted its contentious jurisdiction,[34] because they consider that the measures are binding since the States have made an express declaration in which they recognise

---

[31]   *Lysias Fleury* vs *Haiti, supra* note 31, preambular para. 7; and IACtHR, *Luis Uzcátegui* vs *Venezuela*, order of 2 December 2003, preambular para. 14.

[32]   In the cases of the *Communities of the Jiguamiandó and of the Curbaradó* vs *Colombia* and the *Peace Community of San José de Apartadó* vs *Colombia*, the Court held that the State must guarantee the protection of the beneficiaries of the measures in the light of the provisions of the American Convention as well as the norms of international humanitarian law. The Court called upon Colombia to ensure that said norms were respected by all the actors of the armed conflict and urged it to guarantee the principle of distinction in international humanitarian law with respect to the members of the Peace Community, who were civilians not involved in the internal armed conflict. See IACtHR, *Peace Community of San José de Apartadó* vs *Colombia*, order of 17 November 2004, preambular para. 13; and IACtHR, *Communities of the Jiguamiandó and of the Curbaradó* vs *Colombia*, order of 15 March 2005, preambular paras 15 and 28.

[33]   See Articles 1(1) and 2 ACHR. See also Cançado Trindade, A., 'The Evolution of Provisional Measures of Protection under the Case Law of the Inter-American Court of Human Rights (1987–2002)', *Human Rights Law Journal*, Vol. 24, 2003, pp. 162–174, at pp. 163–164.

[34]   While there is no doubt that the Inter-American Commission may order precautionary measures with respect to any member State of the Organisation of Amercian States (OAS), whether or not it has ratified the American Convention, it is not so clear which States are subject to provisional measures ordered by the Court. One school (Faúndez Ledesma) holds that the Court may adopt measures with respect to those States that have ratified the American Convention, while another view (Buergenthal, Nieto Navia, Pasqualucci and Gros Espiell) holds that the Court may adopt them only with respect to States that, in addition to having ratified the American Convention, have accepted its contentious jurisdiction under Article 62 of the Convention. Here it is important to recall that the jurisdiction of the Inter-American Court does not operate *ipso iure*, and a State is not considered to have accepted its jurisdiction by merely ratifying the Convention. The principal difference between the two positions is that one starts with the idea that the adoption of provisional measures is part of the Court's general function of human rights protection as the organ of supervision of the Convention, while for the other the competence of the Court to adopt provisional measures arises from its contentious jurisdiction. See Faúndez Ledesma, H., *El Sistema Interamericano de Protección de los Derechos Humanos* [The Inter-American System of Human Rights], IIDH, San José, 3rd ed., 2004, pp. 519–529; Nieto Navia, *loc.cit.* (note 5), p. 385; Buergenthal, Th., 'The Inter-American Court of Human Rights', *American University Law Review*, Vol. 76, 1982, pp. 231–245, at p. 241; Buergenthal, Th., 'The Inter-American System for the Protection of Human Rights', in: Meron Th. (ed.), *Human Rights in International Law, Legal and Policy Issues*, Clarendon Press, Oxford, 1984, pp. 439–494, at pp. 465–466; Pasqualucci, *loc.cit.* (note 5), pp. 823–824; and Gros Espiell, H., *Estudios sobre Derechos Humanos II* [Studies on Human Rights], Civitas, Madrid, 1988, pp. 169–171.

Letting States off the Hook?

as binding the Court's jurisdiction in all cases concerning the interpretation and application of the Convention. The States are thus committed to comply with all the decisions of the Court, including, naturally, orders of provisional measures.[35]

So far, Trinidad and Tobago (in 2002) has been the only State that has intentionally disobeyed an order of interim measures, as has been established in a judgment on the merits.[36] In all the other cases the Court has explicitly decided not to pronounce itself on the incompliance by a State[37] or maintained the provisional measures, while rendering a judgment on the merits of the case without saying anything about (in) compliance,[38] and in a last kind of cases, there is no judgment on the merits yet.[39] In the aforementioned case, the State effectively implemented the death penalty against two beneficiaries, notwithstanding an interim measure ordered by the Inter-American Court to suspend the implementation. The respondent State argued in the case of the death of Anthony Briggs that, since the Inter-American Commission had decided to publish the reports mentioned in Articles 50[40] and 51[41] of the American

---

[35]   See Articles 62(1) and 68(1) ACHR.

[36]   In that regard, it is important to mention that the Court supervises the implementation of the provisional measures through the organisation of public hearings and the issuance of reports.

[37]   IACtHR, *Luisiana Ríos and Others* vs *Venezuela*, judgment of 28 January 2009, paras 57–59 and 125.

[38]   IACtHR, *Bámaca Velásquez* vs *Guatemala*, judgment of 25 November 2000, paras 65–70. The provisional measures are still in place in 2009. See IACtHR, *Bamaca Velasquez* vs *Guatemala*, order of 27 June 2009.

[39]   It was reported that beneficiaries were killed notwithstanding provisional measures in the cases of the *Peace Community of San Jose de Apartadó* vs *Colombia*, *Urso Branco Prison* vs *Brazil*, the *Communities of the Jiguamiandó and of the Curbaradó* vs *Colombia*, *Eloisa Barrios* et al. vs *Venezuela*, *Giraldo Cardona* vs *Colombia*. See *Peace Community of San José de Apartadó Case* vs *Colombia*, *supra* note 33, explanatory statements 10, 13(c), 21, order of 15 March 2005, explanatory statement 12, preambular para. 24, order of 2 February 2006, explanatory statement 12(b) (12 beneficiaries were killed), order of 6 February 2008, preambular para. 12 and 19; IACtHR, *Communities of the Jiguamiandó and of the Curbaradó* vs *Colombia*, order of 17 November 2004, explanatory statements 3(a), 6(d) and 7 (8 beneficiaries were killed) and order of 5 February 2008, preambular 7 and 11; IACtHR, *Eloisa Barrios* et al. vs *Venezuela*, order of 29 June 2005, explanatory statements 4, 6 and 8, preambular para. 13 (a 16 year old beneficiary had been shot eight times and as a result died a few days later); IACtHR, *Urso Branco Prison* vs *Brazil*, order of 7 July 2004, preambular para. 8 (where the Court expresses its great concern that, while the measures were still in effect, people had continued to die in the Urso Branco Prison, notwithstanding the fundamental purpose of the adoption of these measures to protect the life and personal integrity of all the inmates and those who were in the prison buildings) and order of 2 May 2008, preambular para. 10 and enacting part 3; and IACtHR, *Giraldo Cardona* vs *Colombia*, order of 30 September 1999, explanatory statement 4(c) (two beneficiaries were killed).

[40]   Article 50(1) ACHR. If a settlement is not reached, the Commission shall, within the time limit established by its Statute, draw up a report setting forth the facts and stating its conclusions on the merits of the case.

[41]   Article 51(1) ACHR. If, within a period of three months from the date of the transmittal of the report of the Commission to the States concerned, the matter has not either been settled or submitted by the Commission or by the State concerned to the Court and its jurisdiction accepted, the Commission may, by the vote of an absolute majority of its members, set forth its opinion and conclusions on the merits concerning the question submitted for its consideration.

Clara Burbano Herrera and Yves Haeck

Convention, there was no case anymore relating to that person before the Inter-American Commission, or capable of being submitted to the Inter-American Court. In this sense, this body had, according to the respondent State, lost all power to adopt interim measures. Thus, the order made after the publication of that Commission report was invalid because the Inter-American Court had no jurisdiction.

In the opinion of the Inter-American Court however, the State was bound by its interim measures, whether the case was sent to it or not, because the situation of extreme gravity and urgency provided the foundations necessary to maintain the measures to protect the rights of the petitioner. It also found that, although, following the publication of the reports on the matter, the proceedings before the Inter-American Commission had ended, the same could not be said with regard to the case of the Inter-American Court, because from the moment that the Court had received the request for interim measures, the case was under its jurisdiction. In this regard, the study of the case had not been completed under the Inter-American System. Once the Inter-American Commission requests interim measures to the Court, the only restriction in Article 63(2) to the jurisdiction of the Court is that the situation of extreme gravity and urgency should continue and that the measures are indeed necessary to avoid damage to the rights of persons.[42] Despite this ruling, the Court did not derive any legal effect from the failure to abide because no judgment was passed on the merits in relation to Anthony Briggs.

Regarding the other beneficiary (Joey Ramiah) who had been executed, the State pointed out that it had not received any order to adopt protective measures in favour of Joey Ramiah. Taking into account these circumstances, in its judgment on the merits in the case of *Hilaire, Constantine and Benjamin* et al. vs *Trinidad and Tobago* (2002), the Inter-American Court held the State internationally responsible. The Court considered in the judgment that his execution by Trinidad and Tobago was an arbitrary deprivation of the right to life that was 'aggravated' because the victim was protected by provisional measures that it had ordered, indicating that his execution should have been stayed pending the resolution of the case under the Inter-American Human Rights system.[43] Joey Ramiah had been found guilty of murder and sentenced to death under the obligatory death penalty act.[44] By order of 25 May 1999, the Court required Trinidad and Tobago to adopt whatever means were necessary to preserve his life so as not to frustrate consideration of the case in the Inter-American system. Notwithstanding the measure of protection expressly ordered by the Court, the State executed the beneficiary on 4 June 1999, thus applying the death penalty.[45]

---

[42]   IACtHR, *James, Briggs, Noel, Garcia and Bethel* vs *Trinidad and Tobago*, order of 25 September 1999, preambular para. 10 and order of 26 November 2000, preambular para. 10.

[43]   IACtHR, *Hilaire, Constantine and Benjamin* et al. vs *Trinidad and Tobago*, judgment of 21 June 2002, paras 33, 84 and 197–200.

[44]   *Ibidem*, paras 190–191, 196–200 and 216, Enacting Part 7. See also *Eloisa Barrios* et al. vs *Venezuela*, *supra* note 40, Separate Opinion of Judge Cançado Trindade, para. 8.

[45]   *Ibidem*, para. 216.

Intersentia

Letting States off the Hook?

The case of Trinidad and Tobago shows that at a practical level, the decision to give legal effect to a failure of a State to comply with a provisional measure is subject to the referral of the case to the Court and the establishment of a violation of a substantial right. That means that if an incompliance with Article 63(2) does not result in a violation of one of the material rights, the failure to comply would have no legal consequences, the disobeyance would go completely unpunished. In this case, most probably the Inter-American Court will mention in the expositive paragraphs of its judgment that interim measures were taken and not complied with by the State. It will further indicate 'in its discourse' that the measures are compulsory as they are provided in the American Convention, but it will at the same time refrain from mentioning them in the resolutive part.

In our opinion, the position taken by the Inter-American Court is contradictory because from a logical point of view it cannot be maintained simultaneously that a legal figure is mandatory but its failure to comply has no legal effects, or that it is compulsory but its legal consequences following incompliance depend upon the violation of another legal provision. That is nonetheless precisely what occurs with the provisional measures under the Inter-American system of Human Rights. One might argue that the Court does give legal effect to its provisional measures in case of non-compliance because the Court 'aggravates' the violation of a substantial right that has already been found violated. In a way that is true, however, we must not forget the total lack of legal effect when no violation of a substantial right has been established and, secondly, that in no case and under no circumstances the Court will hold a State in violation of Article 63(2) of the American Convention, which is the provision that expressly provides for provisional measures. The position taken by the Court may be criticised, not only because of the lack of legal rigor with regard to this concrete issue, but also because this position can be considered as a clear signal towards the States that the measures are simple suggestions or indications and not real orders that must be obeyed.

3.2. EUROPEAN SYSTEM: LONG JURISPRUDENTIAL DEBATE

The binding character of provisional measures ordered by the European supervisory organs has been controversial and uncertain throughout the 20th century. In the *Cruz Varas and Others* Case (1991),[46] the Swedish Government was informed by

---

[46] Commission, *Cruz Varas and Others* vs *Sweden*, report of 7 December 1989, Application No. 15576/89; and ECtHR, *Cruz Varas and Others* vs *Sweden*, judgment of 20 March 1991, Application No. 15576/89, paras 56–60. On this topic, see Cohen-Jonathan, G., 'De l'effet juridique des "mesures provisoires" dans certaines circonstances et de l'efficacité du droit de recours individuel: à propos de l'arrêt Cruz Varas de la Cour européenne des droits de l'homme' [From the legal effect of 'provisional measures' in some circumstances and the efficiency of the right of individual petition: on the Cruz Varas judgment of the European Court of Human Rights translation], *Revue Universelle des Droits de L'Homme* [Universal Review of Human Rightstranslation], Vol. 3, No. 6, 1991, pp. 205–209; García de Enterría, E., 'De la légitimité des mesures provisoires prises par la Commission et la Cour

Clara Burbano Herrera and Yves Haeck

telephone that the European Commission had indicated an interim measure to protect the applicants, a Chilean married couple and their young son who alleged that their deportation to Chile would expose them to imminent, serious and irreparable damage in the form of ill-treatment contrary to Article 3 ECHR, whereby Sweden was requested to stay the enforcement of the deportation to Chile until the Commission had had sufficient time to study the application in depth. The Swedes ignored the provisional measure and Mr Cruz Varas was deported to Chile, while his wife and their child went into hiding in Sweden.[47]

According to the European Commission, Sweden had thus decisively obstructed the individual right of petition, which constituted a violation of Article 25(1), *in fine* of the ECHR (now Article 34),[48] even if the examination on the merits of the case might not reveal any violation of Article 3 ECHR.[49] The European Court, however, rejected the reasoning of the Commission. The Court held that, although Article 25(1) ECHR imposes an obligation upon the States parties not to interfere with the right of the individual to present and pursue a complaint to the Commission, that right was procedural and must therefore be distinguished from the substantive rights of the European Convention. Nevertheless, according to the Court, it must be open to individuals to submit a complaint of alleged infringements of a procedural provision. But Article 25(1) read in conjunction with Rule 36(1) of the (former) Commission's Rules of Procedure or even in conjunction with Articles 1 and 19 of the Convention, did not, in the words of the Court, generate any legal obligations on the part of the States parties to comply with the interim measure indicated by the Commission, particularly because there is no specific provision in the European Convention empowering the Commission to order interim measures.[50]

The decision of the (new) European Court in the *Conka and Others* Case (2001) indicated that the Court had not changed its earlier position in the case of *Cruz Varas*

---

européenne des droits de l'homme. L'affaire Cruz Varas' [The Legitimacy of the Interim Measures Adopted by the European Commission and Court of Human Rights. The case of Cruz Varas], *Revue trimestrielle des droits de l'Homme*, [Quarterly Review of Human Rights], Vol. 11, 1992, pp. 251–280; and Oellers-Frahm, K., 'Zur Verbindlichkeit einstweiliger Anordnung der Europäischen Kommission für Menschenrechte/Anmerkung zum Urteil des EGMR im Fall Cruz Varas gegen Schweden' [On the Binding Force of an Interim Measure of the European Commission on Human Rights/Commentary on the Judgment of the ECommHR in the Cruz Varas Case Against Sweden], *Europäische Grundrechte Zeitschrift*, Vol. 18, 1991, pp. 197–199.

[47]   In the end, Cruz Varas was not ill-treated upon his arrival in Chile. He fled and sought refuge in Argentina. His wife and child were later given permission to stay in Sweden, in compliance with a second interim measure issued by the European Commission.

[48]   Article 34, *in fine* states: 'The High Contracting Parties undertake not to hinder in any way the effective exercise of this right.'

[49]   Commission, *Cruz Varas and Others* vs *Sweden, supra* note 47; and ECtHR, *Cruz Varas and Others* vs *Sweden, supra* note 47, para. 122.

[50]   ECtHR, *Cruz Varas and Others* vs *Sweden, supra* note 46 para. 99. See Ermacora, F., 'Problems about the Application of the European Convention on Human Rights in Asylum Cases', in: Lawson, R. and De Blois, M. (eds), *The Dynamics of the Protection of Human Rights in Europe. Essays in Honour of Henry G. Schermers*, Martinus Nijhoff, Dordrecht, 1994, Vol. III, pp. 155–164, at p. 161.

and Others.[51] In the *Conka* Case, the applicants, a number of Slovak Roma gypsies, were, after their application for asylum had been refused, rounded up by the Belgian police on a false pretext and, with a view to deportation, were transferred to a closed transit centre in the immediate vicinity of Brussels airport. On 4 October 1999, their lawyer submitted an application to the Court alleging a violation of Articles 3 ECHR (prohibition of torture), 8 ECHR (protection of family life) and 14 ECHR (prohibition of discrimination) as well as Article 4 of Protocol No. 4 (prohibition of collective deportation) and requested the Court to indicate an interim measure. On 5 October, the Belgian Government was notified of the request from the Vice-President of the Third Section of the Court to stay the deportation temporarily. Furthermore, although the application was confirmed by fax, the Belgian authorities decided not to comply with the interim measure indicated by the Court.[52]

In its decision on admissibility, the Court expressly referred to its judgment in the *Cruz Varas and Others* Case and labelled the Belgian action as 'hardly compatible with the will to collaborate in a loyal fashion with the European Court in cases which the state in question considers practicable and reasonable', and referred as such to the custom of the member States that had been established over the past decades to comply with the interim measures that had been indicated by the Commission.[53] Nonetheless, the Court refused to consider the request of the applicants to review its earlier position in the *Cruz Varas and Others* Case and to state that interim measures indicated under Rule 39 were legally binding. The Court repeated that the power to order interim measures could not be inferred from either Article 34, *in fine*, or from other sources. The refusal to comply with an interim measure, which was issued under Rule 39, could only be viewed as 'an aggravated breach' of Article 3 which could

---

51 ECtHR, *Conka and Others* vs *Belgium*, decision of 13 March 2001, Application No. 51564/99. On this case, see Carlier, J.-Y., 'La détention et l'expulsion collective des étrangers' [Detention and Collective Expulsion of Alienstranslation], *Revue trimestrielle des Droits de l'Homme*, Vol. 53, 2003, pp. 198–222; Skordas, A., 'Human Rights and Effective Migration Policies: An Uneasy Co-existence. The Conka Judgment of the European Court of Human Rights', in: Dias Urbano De Sousa, C. and De Bruycker, P. (eds), *The Emergence of a European Asylum Policy*, Bruylant, Brussels, 2004, pp. 297–327.

52 Haeck, Y. and Burbano Herrera, Cl., 'Interim Measures in the Case-Law of the European Court of Human Rights', *Netherlands Quarterly of Human Rights*, Vol. 21, No. 4, 2003, pp. 625–675, at p. 660, footnote 117. With regard to the whereabouts of the Minister of Justice and the Minister of Internal Affairs at the moment of the incoming telephone call from Strasbourg, see Belgian newspaper *De Standaard*, 17 February 2003, 'Binnenlandse Zaken wist van Europees voorbehoud' [Home Affairs knew about European reservation], www.standaard.be.

53 *Conka and Others* vs *Belgium, supra* note 51, with reference to Commission; Commission, *Cruz Varas and Others* vs *Sweden, supra* note 47; and ECtHR, *Cruz Varas and Others* vs *Sweden, supra* note 47, paras 100 and 103.

Clara Burbano Herrera and Yves Haeck

subsequently be laid down by the Court.[54] In short, the *Cruz Varas* case-law remained in full force.[55]

Some years later, in the *Mamatkulov and Askarov* Case (2003), the Court changes its point of view.[56] A Chamber of the Court (First Section) held for the first time (by six votes to one) that its interim measures under Rule 39 are compulsory or legally binding for the State to which they are addressed. If a State does not comply with an interim measure, this may, in view of the special nature of Article 3 ECHR (prohibition of torture), lead to a violation of the right of individual complaint (under Article 34 ECHR), as long as the contested act – *in casu* the extradition – has affected the core of the right of individual application.

In the aforementioned case, the applicants, two Uzbeks, who were members of an opposition party, were arrested at Istanbul airport under an international arrest warrant on suspicion of involvement in terrorist activities in their home country. The Uzbek authorities asked for their extradition. They stated, among others, that, if extradited to Uzbekistan, their lives would be at risk (Article 2 ECHR) and they would be in danger of being subjected to torture (Article 3 ECHR). The President of the First Section indicated to the Turkish Government that it was desirable in the interest of the parties and the proper conduct of the proceedings before the Court not to extradite the applicants to Uzbekistan until the Court had had an opportunity to examine further the applications. On 19 March 1999, the Turkish Government issued a decree for the applicants' extradition and handed information to the Court on the guarantees obtained by the Uzbek Government. Notwithstanding the decision of the Chamber, the applicants were extradited on 27 March.[57]

In its Chamber judgment, the European Court first stated that the European Convention was 'a living instrument that had to be interpreted in the light of the

---

[54] Commission, *Cruz Varas and Others* vs *Sweden, supra* note 46; and ECtHR, *Cruz Varas and Others* vs *Sweden, supra* note 46, paras 102–103.

[55] The aspect of the complaint that relates to the binding force of interim measures was declared inadmissible by the Court and therefore did not qualify to be re-examined under a possible request for a re-hearing (under Article 43(1) ECHR).

[56] ECtHR, *Mamatkulov and Abdurasulovic* vs *Turkey,* decision of 31 August 1999, Application Nos 46827/99 and 46951/99; ECtHR, *Mamatkulov and Abdurasulovic* vs *Turkey,* judgment of 6 February 2003, Application Nos 46827/99 and 46951/99; ECtHR, *Mamatkulov and Askarov* vs *Turkey,* judgment of 4 February 2005, Application Nos 46827/99 and 46951/99. See Brown, Ch., 'Strasbourg Follows Suit on Interim Measures', *Cambridge Law Journal,* Vol. 62, 2003, pp. 532–534; Oellers-Frahm, K., 'Verbindlichkeit einstweiliger Maßnahmen: Der EGMR vollzieht – endlich – die erforderliche Wende in seiner Rechtsprechung' [The ECtHR implements – at last – the required change in its case-law], *Europäische Grundrechte Zeitschrift* [European Journal of Human Rights], Vol. 30, 2003, pp. 689–693; Tigroudja, H., 'La force obligatoire des mesures provisoires indiquées par la Cour européenne des droits de l'homme. Observations sous l'arrêt du 6 février 2003, Mamatkulov c. Turquie', *Revue Générale du Droit International Public* [The binding force of provisional measures indicated by the European Court of Human Rights. Comments on Case 6 February 2003, Mamatkulov vs Turkey], Vol. 107, No. 3, 2003, pp. 601–632.

[57] *Mamatkulov and Abdurasulovic* vs *Turkey,* decision of 31 August 1999 and judgment of 6 February 2003, *supra* note 57; and *Mamatkulov and Askarov* vs *Turkey, supra* note 57, paras 1–5 and 25–36.

present-day conditions'. This was also valid with regard to procedural provisions such as Article 34 ECHR (right of individual application).[58] *In casu*, the applicants' representatives had not been able to contact the applicants, who had thus been deprived of the possibility of having further inquiries carried out to obtain evidence in support of their allegations.[59] The Court distinguished the current situation from its earlier case-law and pointed to the fact that it was not bound by that case-law, on the condition that there was a good motivation available.[60] Of crucial importance in the eyes of the Court, was that the European Convention had to be interpreted and applied in a way that made the guarantees effective and not theoretical or illusory. The interpretation of the scope of interim measures could not be seen apart from the proceedings to which they related or the decision on the merits they sought to safeguard.[61] Accordingly, by failing to comply with the interim measures indicated by the Court, Turkey had violated its obligations under Article 34 ECHR.[62] In its final judgment in the case of *Mamatkulov and (Abdurasulovic) Askarov vs Turkey* (2005),[63] the Grand Chamber of the European Court largely endorsed (with 13 votes against 4)[64] the first judgment passed by the Chamber.[65]

But the violation of Article 34 ECHR seemed by no means a mechanical or automatic consequence of the finding of the incompliance with the interim measure,

---

58   *Ibidem, Mamatkulov and Askarov vs Turkey, supra* note 57, para. 94.

59   *Ibidem*, para. 96.

60   *Ibidem*, paras 104–105.

61   *Ibidem*, para. 105.

62   *Ibidem*, paras 109–111.

63   *Idem.* See Docquir, P., 'Les mesures provisoires ordonnées par la Cour européenne des droits de l'Homme: un renforcement... provisoire!', *Journal du Juriste* [Journal of Jurists], 2003, Vol. 22, p. 10; Frumer, Ph., 'Un arrêt définitif sur les mesures provisoires: la Cour européenne des droits de l'homme persiste et signe. Commentaire de l'arrêt Mamatkulov et Askarov c. Turquie du 4 février 2005' [A final judgment on provisional measures: the European Court of Human Rights persists and signs. A Commentary on the Judgment of Mamatkulov and Askarov vs Turkey of 4 February 2005], *Revue trimestrielle des Droits de l'Homme*, Vol. 64, 2005, pp. 799–826; Krenc, F., 'L'arrêt Mamatkulov et Askarov c. Turquie du 4 février 2005: le caractère obligatoire des mesures provisoires indiquées para la Cour européenne des droits de l'homme' [The Judgment of Mamatkulov and Askarov vs Turkey of 4 February 2005], *Journal des Tribunaux* [Journal of the Tribunals], Vol. 124, No. 6190, 2005, p. 526; Mowbray, A., 'A New Strasbourg Approach to the Legal Consequences of Interim Measures', *Human Rights Law Review*, Vol. 5, No. 2, 2005, pp. 377–386; and Oellers-Frahm, K., 'Verbindlichkeit einstweiliger Anordnungen des EGMR – Epilog/Das Urteil der Großen Kammer im Fall Mamatkulov u.a. gegen Türkei' [Binding force of interim measures of the ECtHR – Epilogue / The Judgment of the Grand Chamber in the case of Mamatkulov and Others against Turkey], *Europäische Grundrechte Zeitschrift* [European Journal of Human Rights], Vol. 32, 2005, pp. 347–350.

64   Some judges considered that the Court was legislating in defiance of a clear intention of the member States. See Dissenting Opinion of Judges Caflisch, Turmen and Kovler in *Mamatkulov and Abdurasulovic vs Turkey*, decision of 31 August 1999 and judgment of 6 February 2003, *supra* note 57; and *Mamatkulov and Askarov vs Turkey, supra* note 57.

65   *Mamatkulov and Abdurasulovic vs Turkey*, decision of 31 August 1999 and judgment of 6 February 2003, *supra* note 57; and *Mamatkulov and Askarov vs Turkey, supra* note 57, para. 128.

Clara Burbano Herrera and Yves Haeck

as is shown by the European Court's case-law,[66] for the finding of a violation of Article 34 ECHR depends on the evaluation whether the non-compliance with the measure indicated has *in casu* encroached upon the core of the right of application.[67] Consequently, the Court has been deciding on this aspect on a case-by-case basis. In the *Öcalan* vs *Turkey* case (2003–2005)[68] for example, the Court had asked Turkey, among other, to take all necessary measures to protect the rights under Article 6 ECHR of the PKK-leader Abdullah Öcalan, who had been arrested in Kenya and brought before a Turkish court where he faced the death penalty, and inform the Court on the measures taken in that regard. This request for information was, however, set aside by the Turkish Government. In its judgment the Grand Chamber of the European Court confirmed its position on the binding force of provisional measures, but held that *in casu* there was no violation of the individual right of application (Article 34 ECHR). The Court ruled in this case that the non-compliance with an interim measure by a State should be regarded as preventing the Court from effectively examining the applicant's complaint and as hindering the effective exercise of his right, and as such is to be considered incompatible with Article 34 ECHR. In that regard, the Grand Chamber referred to its previous judgment in the case of *Mamatkulov and Askarov* vs *Turkey* (2005), but it nevertheless concluded that although regrettable, the Turkish Government's failure to supply the information requested by the Court earlier did not, in the special circumstances of the case, prevent the applicant from setting out his complaints about the criminal proceedings that had been brought against him. Consequently, he has not been obstructed in the exercise of his right of individual application.[69]

Earlier, a Chamber of the European Court (First Section) had already come to the same conclusion, that there has not been a violation of Article 34, while at the same time confirming the binding force of interim measures. The Court stated that, in the special circumstances of the case, the Government's refusal to provide the Court with the requested information did not amount to a violation. In fact, these complaints, which mainly concerned Article 6 ECHR (right to a fair trial), were examined by the Court, which subsequently found a violation with regard to those issues.[70] The

---

[66] For three examples where a violation of Article 34 has been found as a result of the non-compliance with an interim measure, see *Mamatkulov and Abdurasulovic* vs *Turkey*, decision of 31 August 1999 and judgment of 6 February 2003, *supra* note 57; and *Mamatkulov and Askarov* vs *Turkey*, *supra* note 57, para. 128; ECtHR, *Shamayev and 12 Others* vs *Russia and Georgia*, decision of 16 September 2003, Application No. 36378/02 and ECtHR, *Shamayev and 12 Others* vs *Russia and Georgia*, judgment of 12 April 2005, Application No. 36378/02, para. 479; and ECtHR, *Aoulmi* vs *France*, judgment of 17 January 2000, Application No. 50278/99, para. 112.

[67] Reference may be made to ECtHR, *Öcalan* vs *Turkey*, decision of 14 December 2000, Application No. 46221/99 and ECtHR, *Öcalan* vs *Turkey*, judgment of 12 May 2005, Application No. 46221/99, para. 201; and (foremost) *Shamayev and 12 Others* vs *Russia and Georgia*, decision of 16 September 2003 and judgment of 12 April 2005, para. 472, *supra* note 67.

[68] *Öcalan* vs *Turkey*, decision of 14 December 2000 and judgment of 12 May 20005, *supra* note 68.

[69] *Öcalan* vs *Turkey*, judgment of 12 May 2005, *supra* note 68, para. 201.

[70] *Ibidem*, para. 241.

juridical binding character of interim measures has explicitly been confirmed at the beginning of 2006 in a judgment in the *Aoulmi* Case,[71] where the Court for the first time explicitly used the term 'binding' (*obligatoire*) to refer to the legal force of interim measures.

The problem as to the possible lack of immediate legal consequences for a State unwilling to abide by an interim measure issued by the European Court, has seemingly been definitively resolved by the *Olaechea Cahuas* Case,[72] where the Spanish authorities did not comply with a interim measure concerning the staying of the extradition (on 7 August 2003) by Spain to Peru of a Peruvian national, Adolfo Olaechea Cahuas, an alleged member of *Sendero Luminoso* (the Shining Path) in Europe, who was sought in his home country for support to terrorist activities of the above-mentioned Maoist guerrilla group.

While in earlier cases (*Mamatkulov and Askarov, Shamayev, Aoulmi*), the petitioners' right of application after their extradition or deportation had been effectively hindered by the fact that all contact of the lawyers with their clients had come to a halt, the situation was not the same in the *Olaechea Cahuas* Case, as the applicant, once he was on Peruvian soil, had been released provisionally after three months on the condition that he would not leave Lima, his city of residence, during the judicial investigation.[73] Moreover, during the whole Peruvian procedure, the applicant had been in contact with his London-based lawyer. This prompted the Spanish authorities to conclude that there could not have been any kind of hindrance to the right of application.[74] However, the Court did not agree with this reasoning and acknowledged that non-compliance by a respondent State with whatever interim measure adopted by the Court would indeed lead to a violation of the European Convention, that is the right of application under Article 34, independently of the establishment *post facto* of the existence of a hindrance of the effective exercise of the right to individual application.

The State's decision as to whether it complies with the measure cannot be deferred pending the hypothetical confirmation of the existence of a risk of irreparable damage. Failure to comply with an interim measure because of the existence of a risk is in itself a serious hindrance, at that particular time, of the effective exercise of the right of individual application.[75] In the end, the Court applied the only logical juridical consequence resulting from the above-mentioned assessment of how one can arrive

---

71   *Aoulmi vs France, supra* note 67, para. 111. See Ziss, M., 'Du respect des articles 3 et 8 de la Convention au respect des mesures provisoires indiquées par la Cour de Strasbourg' [On the Respect for Articles 3 and 8 of the Convention to Respect for the Provisional Measures indicated by the Strasbourg Court], in: Tavernier, P. (ed.), *La France et la Cour européenne des droits de l'homme. La jurisprudence en 2006* [France and the European Court of Human Rights], Bruylant, Brussels, 2007, pp. 211–220.

72   ECtHR, *Olaechea Cahuas vs Spain*, judgment of 10 July 2006, Application No. 24668/03.

73   *Ibidem*, paras 7–17.

74   *Ibidem*, paras 76–79.

75   *Ibidem*, para. 81.

Clara Burbano Herrera and Yves Haeck

at a 'serious hindrance' of the effective exercise of the right of individual application, by holding that 'in failing to comply with the interim measures indicated under Rule 39 of its Rules of Court, Spain failed to honour its commitments under Article 34 of the Convention'.[76] The Chamber came to its conclusion unanimously, without any concurring or dissenting opinions.[77]

Nowadays, the European Court is developing its case-law in relation to the legal consequences for a State that has complied with an interim measure, but not immediately. The European Court in a number of recent judgments[78] seems to be particularly strict as to the timeliness of compliances and holds States that have not complied (almost) immediately with interim measures, fully responsible under Article 34 (right of individual application).

Arguments from the respondent State tending to escape its international responsibility and condemnation by indicating that they had not had the necessary time to put into place the measures that are necessary to avoid the damage[79] are being scrutinised by the Court with utmost strictness, as is illustrated in the *Paladi* Case[80] concerning compliance with an interim measure by the State only four days after the measure had been issued. In fact, on the evening of 10 November 2005, the Court had indicated an interim measure by fax to the Moldovan Government, stating that the applicant, who suffered from different diseases and had been committed to a specialised neurological health centre, should not be transferred from that centre to the prison hospital until the Court had had the opportunity to examine the case. On 11 November 2005, a Deputy Registrar of the Court tried unsuccessfully several times to contact by telephone the Government Agent's Office in Moldova. The applicant was transferred to the prison hospital on that same day. On 14 November, following requests by the applicant's lawyer and the Agent of the Government, the domestic court finally ordered the applicant to be transferred back to the neurological centre.[81]

In its Chamber judgment, the European Court considered that 'the failure of the domestic authorities to comply as a matter of urgency with the interim measure indicated by the Court in itself jeopardised the applicant's ability to pursue his application before the Court and was thus contrary to the requirements of Article 34 of

---

[76]   *Ibidem*, paras 82–83.

[77]   No request for a re-hearing was submitted by the applicant or the Spanish Government. Therefore, the judgment was final as from 11 December 2006 in accordance with Article 44(2) of the Convention. See Haeck, Y., Burbano Herrera, C. and Zwaak, L., 'Strasbourg Takes Away any Remaining Doubts and Broadens its Pan-European Protection: Non-Compliance with a Provisional Measure Automatically Leads to a Violation of the Right of Individual Application… or Doesn't it?', *European Constitutional Law Review*, Vol. 4, 2008, pp. 41–63, at pp. 50–51.

[78]   For example ECtHR, *Grori* vs *Albania*, judgment of 7 July 2009, Application No. 25336/04, paras 181–195.

[79]   *Olaechea Cahuas* vs *Spain*, *supra* note 73, para. 65.

[80]   ECtHR, *Paladi* vs *Moldova*, decision of 10 July 2007, Application No. 39806/05.

[81]   *Ibidem*, paras 45–50.

the Convention'.[82] Indeed, there were 'serious deficiencies at each stage of the process of complying with the interim measures, starting with the absence, in the Government Agent's Office, of officials to answer urgent calls from the Registry and continuing with the lack of action taken by that office between the morning of 11 November 2005 and the afternoon of 14 November 2005', coupled with 'the Centru District Court's failure to deal urgently with the issue when it was asked to do so on 11 November 2005 by the applicant's lawyer'. Finally, 'the refusal for six hours to admit the applicant to the Republican Neurological Centre (RNC) despite the Court's interim measures and the domestic court's decision is also a matter of concern'.[83] The Court noted that the applicant was in a serious condition, which, as appeared from the documents available at the relevant time, put his health at immediate and irremediable risk. That risk was the very reason for the Court's decision to indicate the interim measure. Fortunately, no adverse consequences to the applicant's life or health resulted from the delay in implementing that measure. The European Court consequently found that '[i]n the light of the very serious risk to which the applicant was exposed as a result of the delay in complying with the interim measure and notwithstanding the relatively short period of such delay', there had been a violation of Article 34 of the Convention.[84]

The Grand Chamber, whom the case was referred to by request of the respondent State, arrived at the same conclusion. However, on this occasion, the Grand Chamber, after a lengthy debate (resulting in a vote of 9 *versus* 8) presented a clearer and more developed view with regard to the underlying motives why a late compliance with a provisional measure violates Article 34 of the Convention. In that judgment, the Court began by indicating that its role was not to examine whether the decision of the Chamber to adopt interim measures was correct or not. At that stage of the proceedings, it was for the Government to demonstrate to the Court that the interim measures were complied with or, in an exceptional case, that there was an objective impediment which prevented compliance and that the Government took all reasonable steps to remove the impediment and to keep the Court informed about the situation.[85] That means that, as a general rule, a late incompliance with an interim measure will automatically result in a violation of the Convention, unless three conditions are cumulatively met: a) there were objective obstacles; b) the State took all reasonable steps to remove those obstacles; and c) the State kept the Court informed. Having completed the test, the Grand Chamber found that *in casu* none of the above-mentioned constitutive criteria for a situation to be deemed exceptional had been met and that therefore the State had violated Article 34 of the European Convention. Finally, the Grand Chamber held that the fact that, ultimately, the risk did not materialise and that information obtained subsequently suggests that the risk may have been exaggerated does not

---

[82] *Ibidem*, para. 99.

[83] *Ibidem*, para. 97.

[84] *Ibidem*, para. 100.

[85] ECtHR, *Paladi vs Moldova*, judgment of 10 March 2009, Application No. 39806/05, para. 92.

Clara Burbano Herrera and Yves Haeck

alter the fact that the attitude and lack of action on the part of the authorities were incompatible with their obligations under Article 34 ECHR. In this regard, the Court concluded that domestic authorities did not fulfil their obligation to comply with the interim measure at issue and that in the circumstances of the case there was nothing to absolve them from that obligation.[86]

4.   CONCLUSION: NEED TO CONSOLIDATE THE STRONG PROTECTIVE VISION (EUROPEAN SYSTEM) *VERSUS* NEED TO DEVELOP LEGAL ARGUMENTS (INTER-AMERICAN SYSTEM)

Although the legal figure of the interim measures has been included in the legal texts of both systems, the principal difference between them is that while in the Inter-American system it is included in its principal legal instrument, the American Convention on Human Rights (Article 63(2)), in the European System it can only be found in the Rules of Court (Article 39). This difference has resulted in a debate in the European system as to their binding character; some argue that the lack of this figure in the European Convention is a clear indication that the measures are not true orders that must be followed by the States parties, while others deduce the binding character from a teleological interpretation of the Convention.

Indeed, the case-law under the European System shows that there are two interpretations on this controversial topic: one favours State sovereignty and argues for the judicial restraint of the Court regarding its jurisdiction and the other, more progressive, argues for judicial activism and favours the effective protection of rights and tends to regard the European Convention from an evolutive, dynamic or teleological perspective. The first trend favours State discretion. The Convention's silence is frequently invoked as an argument to deny binding force to provisional measures. In addition, the language that provides for them in the legal texts states that their adoption would be 'desirable or advisable'. In this regard, some European Court judges and some legal doctrine, argue that, given the persistent refusal of member States to include a provision in the European Convention making interim measures binding, the departure of the Court in the *Mamatkulov and Askarov* Case from its own case-law is an illustration that the majority of the Court have been legislating in

---

[86]   *Ibidem,* paras 102–105. See also especially the Partly Dissenting Opinion of Judge Malinverni, joined by Costa, Jungwiert, Myjer, Sajó, Lazarova Trajkovska and Karakaş in *ibidem,* sub para. 3, who basically argue that a short delay in complying with an interim measure – in cases other than expulsion or extradition cases – may in some cases expose the applicant to a real risk and amount to hindrance to the effective exercise of Convention rights, but such delay does not automatically expose an applicant to an immediate or particularly severe risk to his life or health and therefore does not automatically lead to the establishment of a violation of Article 34 ECHR.

Letting States off the Hook?

defiance of a clear intention of these member States. The second trend, on the other hand, is more protective of the individual and, thus, understands that the reach of the legal obligations assumed by the States parties goes beyond the strict language of the European Convention.

The analysis of the case-law shows that while the former European Commission had originally held that the failure to comply with one of its interim measures amounted to a violation of the right to individual application under Article 34 (former Article 25) of the European Convention (*Cruz Varas*), the European Court on the contrary on two occasions (*Cruz Varas; Conka*) held that the power to order interim measures could not be inferred from either the obligation not to obstruct the right to individual application under Article 34 (the right being procedural rather than substantive), or from any other (international) source. A failure on the part of a respondent State to comply with an interim measure indicated by the European Court could only constitute an 'aggravated liability (or breach)', in case a substantial provision was *post facto* deemed to be violated, that is if, apart from the above-mentioned non-compliance, a violation of a material right were established, then the non-compliance with the interim measure would constitute a kind of reason or motive that would worsen, that is 'aggravate', the responsibility of the State for the violation of the substantial right concerned.

In subsequent cases, however, against Turkey (*Mamatkulov and Askarov; Öcalan*), Russia and Georgia (*Shamayev*), France (*Aoulmi*) and Spain (*Olaechea Cahuas*), the European Court has changed its view and has held that its interim measures are legally binding. Moreover, while at the outset non-compliance by a State with a interim measure 'could' lead to an autonomous finding of a violation of the right of individual application (*Mamatkulov and Askarov; Öcalan; Shamayev; Aoulmi*), it is now accepted that such non-compliance virtually 'automatically' leads to a finding of a violation of the right of individual application (*Olaechea Cahuas*). The latter is also true even if a State has complied with an interim measure, but not immediately (*Paladi*). The only way for a respondent State to escape its responsibility under Article 34 ECHR is if compliance was prevented by an objective impediment and the State manages to prove that it took all reasonable steps to remove the impediment and to keep the Court informed (*Paladi*).

It has taken the European Court around 15 years to issue a clear judgment on the legally binding character of an interim measure and its consequences in case of non-compliance by the State to whom it is directed. The recent case-law of the European Court can certainly be seen as truly historic as to the legal consequences of the binding force of provisional measures indicated (one may now safely say 'ordered') by the European Court. Respondent States that do not conform to a provisional measure issued by the Strasbourg Court, will find their inaction virtually automatically interpreted as a violation of the right of individual application under Article 34 of the European Convention, whatever the outcome of the assessment of the Court

Clara Burbano Herrera and Yves Haeck

regarding the materialisation of the violation of the substantive right(s) invoked by the applicant.

This is an interpretation that we share because, while it is true that the European Convention, unlike the American Convention, does not include a specific provision on the matter, it has to be understood that its interpretation and application in concrete cases should be in the direction of providing the Court with the necessary authority to ensure the effectiveness of the protection of the rights that it must safeguard. From our point of view, the binding character came not from this provision, but rather from the fact that its non-compliance could affect the entire system of protection and the rights specifically included in the European Convention. Although it is true that this figure was not included in the Convention, the silence on its exclusion in the *travaux préparatoires* cannot be interpreted as a clear intention to wrest from them their binding character because there was simply no discussion on the topic.

It is noteworthy that, although theoretically the case-law in the Inter-American system is consistent with the compulsory nature of the measures, the practical implication of their breach (in the only case in which there was non-compliance with the judgment on the merits) does not reasonably correspond to what should be concluded from the theoretical possibility. In fact, although the jurisprudence in the Inter-American system has consistently indicated that interim measures are binding, their non-compliance only results in aggravating the violation of a substantial right if there is a violation, but in no case the violation of the article that authorises them (Article 63(2) ACHR). From the standpoint of comparative law, this situation shows, on the one hand, that the case-law under the Inter-American system – which does not link incompliance with a provisional measure with a violation of a Convention provision – is at the first stage of the jurisprudence of the European system that was developed during the period 1950–2003 and, on the other hand, that today the legal effects of non-compliance are much less severe than today in the European system, where the compulsory nature of interim measures and the legal consequences in case of incompliance have been the result of an arduous jurisprudential debate. The current legal situation under the Inter-American system consequently seems unsound and illogical.

No doubt, many positive comments could be made about the work of the Inter-American Court of Human Rights with regard to its provisional measures. However, as regards the legal effect that the Court has granted them, they leave much to be desired. In its work, the Inter-American Court not only has not given full legal effect to the failure to comply with the measures, but it has also not offered sound legal arguments for reaching that decision. Thus, unlike the road travelled by the current and former supervisory organs under the European system, which, since they started to function, have only after strong and lengthy legal debate developed interesting opinions and judgments with regard to the legal force of provisional measures, none of this can be found in the Inter-American system.

Of course, one could argue that it is not easy to give legal effects to measures which must be taken in difficult cases, that is in situations where the borderline between compliance and incompliance is difficult to establish. This is, for example, the fact in matters relating to persons who are in serious danger inside a prison. In such cases, the State party may take various measures in order to protect the rights of detainees, such as reducing the prison population, improving the prison infrastructure, and so on. The problem remains that, despite these measures, serious violations continue to occur, since these measures alone are not sufficient to end the situation of extreme gravity. Indeed, fights between inmates continue to happen, resulting in many wounded and dead, and overcrowding and sanitary problems in prisons remain unresolved. The point is that such situations not only require the adoption of short-term actions, but also medium and long term actions, including for example, the adoption and implementation of a State policy that involves greater public spending in the prison system and changes to criminal policy. Therefore, actions of the various branches of government (executive, legislative, judiciary) are needed in order to bring the rights of prisoners in line with international minimum standards.

When taking a look at the case-law, one will agree that the one case in which – until now – the Inter-American Court has ruled on the merits, and in which a breach of an order for provisional measures has been established, was 'a relatively easy' case. It concerned a relatively easy case because there were no external factors that could affect the desired result and the compliance with the provisional measure issued did not require medium or long-term action on behalf of the respondent State. Indeed, only one action was required from the State to comply with the measure, that is the State had to suspend the implementation of the death penalty upon the beneficiaries, pending the examination of the complaint under the Inter-American system.

In this case, the State was asked to suspend the death penalty because the Court was presented with *prima facie* evidence from which it could be assumed that in the domestic judicial proceedings some rights and freedoms under the American Convention had been violated. Precisely the fact that it was a relatively easy case, where the deduction of the incompliance was rather simple, makes it difficult to understand the decision taken by the Inter-American Court. The Court held that the incompliance by the State implied an 'aggravation' of the violation of the substantive provision (Article 4 ACHR), but not the violation of the provision contemplating the legal figure of the interim measures (Article 63(2) ACHR). It is worth mentioning that if the Court had not even found a violation of Article 4 of the American Convention, it would not have given any type of effect whatsoever to the non-compliance with the provisional measure either.

In the context described above it is pertinent to question what motives could lie behind the decision and interpretation given by the Inter-American Court on the legal effects of its provisional measures. Why did the Court not find the State concerned in violation of Article 63(2) of the American Convention? In our view, three hypotheses could explain the decision by the Court.

Clara Burbano Herrera and Yves Haeck

Firstly, the decision of the Inter-American Court may be motivated by political reasons. Indeed, the members of the Court might not be thinking that much in terms of legal arguments, but more in terms of the real possibility that their orders for provisional measures are complied with, especially given the fact that they know from experience that the vast majority of cases are 'difficult cases'. In this hypothesis, the Court, being genuinely concerned about the possibility of giving real protection to rights through provisional measures, and taking into account that in many cases, the economic possibilities (as to prisons) and the social possibilities (as to armed conflict) of States to comply were scarce, or at least difficult to evaluate, therefore chose to refrain from initiating a judicial precedent under which a State would be declared internationally responsible and therefore condemned for the incompliance with a provisional measure. In addition, the Inter-American Court has avoided to create a doctrine or interpretation that would attract new cases in the future, as such a doctrine might indeed 'open the door' for applicants and non-governmental organisations (NGOs) to start systematically requesting the Court to find States in violation of Article 63(2) ACHR, thus forcing the Court to spend more time and human resources on these decisions, time which the Court might think preferable should be used to work and decide on the alleged violations of the more classical substantial rights and freedoms. However, the absence of a doctrine might also be the result of an internal political decision within the Court, given that the Court has developed a specific procedure around the figure of provisional measures. The Court has, for example, held public hearings, has enabled the beneficiaries to submit their comments directly, and in many cases has requested that the measures are implemented in common agreement between the State and the other party. In this context, the Court might fear that by declaring the States internationally responsible for violations of its provisional measures, such decisions could have an adverse effect on the behaviour of States with regard to the current procedure in place: States, rather than taking the Court's orders more seriously, might then decide not to report to the Court on the follow-up given to the order, might stop to attend the public hearings organised in that regard and, in general, might decide to give less or no importance to this figure, making it lose the power and impact it has gained in practice over the years.

Secondly, the reluctance of the Inter-American Court to hold that States have violated Article 63(2) of the American Convention may be due to the fact that the Inter-American Court considers this Article 63(2) to be a procedural provision – as the old European Court once did – and not a substantive right in itself, and therefore does not permit it to find States internationally responsible in case of non-compliance with the provision. Indeed, this idea leads us to think that perhaps the Inter-American Court has tried to follow the case-law of the European Court of Human Rights (until 2002), without noticing the significant existing differences in both human rights systems, especially in relation to the instrument that provides the provisional measures.

Finally, it may be that the Inter-American Court has not been aware of the situation. While the judges of the current Court have at no moment expressed an opinion on the issue, from a number of talks with members of the Secretariat of the Court, in combination with the wording and contents of the judgment discussed above (case of *Trinidad and Tobago*) and an exhaustive examination of the wording and analysis of the resolutions on provisional measures, we can deduce that the Court has not really been aware of the legal debate behind the failure of a State to comply with a provisional measure. This may be due to the fact that it has focused in its work on issues it considers more important, such as the decisions on the merits in contentious cases where traditional substantive rights such as the right to life or physical integrity have allegedly been violated.

Ultimately, in this whole scenario, the discourse seems to suggest that under the Inter-American system, the purpose of provisional measures is not so much to prevent the violation of the rights of persons in a situation of extreme gravity and urgency, because this would somehow suppose the need for the Inter-American Court to interfere with the often structural problems the vast majority of American States are currently facing, but rather to act or to be an instrument of political denunciation. Certainly for people who are in a situation of extreme gravity and urgency and for human rights organisations that are working actively in the field of human rights at the regional level in the Americas, the adoption of provisional measures and the possible ensuing international denunciation of States through the Inter-American Court in connection with their case, somehow represents a victory, but for the moment being, the doubt remains whether this is really the objective of these protective measures.

Whatever the reason, the need for the Inter-American Court to have an explicit and elaborate legal reflection on this point should be underlined, because the Court as a judicial organ under the Inter-American System is governed by the American Convention on Human Rights. It is primarily this document that is the benchmark or the key instrument dealing with the competence as to provisional measures and according to this document, provisional measures are compulsory. If, for the Inter-American Court, both the legal instrument contemplating the instrument of provisional measures and the language used in the conventional provisional are not sufficient to lead to a condemnation of a State, holding that State internationally responsible for incompliance of Article 63(2) ACHR, the Court should at least provide objective legal grounds to allow the parties in the case, the citizen in general and also the academic community, to understand that legal interpretation. As such, the problem with the issue of provisional measures under the Inter-American System is not only that no real legal effects arise from the failure to abide by a provisional measure, but also the absence of full and sound reasoning for such a conclusion. At this point it is worth indicating that it is extremely strange that Latin-American NGOs and even the other supervisory organ under the Inter-American system, that is the Inter-American Commission, the work of which can be characterised as serious and responsible, have not pronounced themselves in relation to this important legal issue. Indeed, the lack of legal discussion in this regard is surprising and striking, not only because it concerns a mechanism contemplated directly in the American Convention,

Clara Burbano Herrera and Yves Haeck

but also because every day provisional measures become more and more prominent in the international human rights systems, both at the regional and universal level.

It is important that the case-law of the Inter-American Court starts to grant the legal effects that may logically be concluded from the debate on the legal nature of provisional measures or to indicate the motives why it does not deduce legal effects to a protection mechanism that is explicitly contemplated in the American Convention. With respect to the European system, it is necessary that it continues to develop the interpretation of the European Convention and consolidates its case-law on provisional measures in some more Grand Chamber judgments (preferably supported by more judges than has been the case in its most recent Grand Chamber judgments), so that non-compliance of interim measures produces an almost automatic violation of Article 34 ECHR.

The absence of true legal effect given to provisional measures by the Inter-American Court and the lack of decisions that endorse its position on the legal consequences of non-compliance by States with provisional measures go against the very credibility of the institution because its decisions may begin to be perceived by individuals and other social actors as decisions that are simply theoretical (in the case of the Inter-American system) or are for the moment being still more or less isolated decisions rather than the collective work of a united Court (in the case of the European system).

[27]

Interim Relief Compared: Use of Interim Measures by the UN Human Rights Committee and the European Court of Human Rights

Helen Keller*/*Cedric Marti***

---

* Judge at the European Court of Human Rights, former member of the UN Human Rights Committee and Professor of Public International Law, European Law and Constitutional Law at the University of Zurich.

** Ph.D. candidate at the University of Zurich.

The authors are very grateful to Professor *Sir Nigel Rodley*, member of the UN Human Rights Committee, *Carmen Rueda* and *Anita Trimaylova* from the OHCHR, *Stephen Phillips* from the Registry of the ECtHR and former Vice-President and Judge at the ECtHR *Françoise Tulkens* for the invaluable information provided during the preparation of this contribution. Special thanks also go to *Corina Heri* for proofreading the article. The views and statements expressed in this article are strictly personal.

Abstract

The institution of interim measures is a powerful instrument to the human rights judiciary, and one of great practical significance. Interim measures safeguard the effectiveness of the human rights protection system by preventing particularly harmful violations that would not be reparable by a decision on the merits. This article undertakes a comprehensive comparison of the UN Human Rights Committee's and the European Court of Human Rights' use of interim measures. It argues that, while the practice of the Committee and the Court displays surprisingly strong similarities with respect to key issues, there exist some important procedural and substantive divergences which could arguably lead to forum shopping with respect to interim relief.

I. Introduction

The UN Human Rights Committee (hereinafter HRC) and the European Court of Human Rights (hereinafter ECtHR) are, as part of their (quasi-) judicial function and as is virtually every international adjudicator,[1] vested with the power to indicate interim measures.[2] The purpose of interim meas-

---

[1] *R. Wolfrum*, Interim (Provisional) Measures of Protection, in: R. Wolfrum (ed.), MPEPIL, 2006, online edition, margin number 1, available at <http://www.mpepil.com>. All links in this article were last accessed in May 2013.

[2] Rule 39 (1) of the Rules of Court of the ECtHR, amended by the Plenary Court on 14.1.13 and 6.2.2013, entered into force 1.5.2013; Rule 92 of the Rules of Procedure of the HRC, adopted at the Committee's 2852nd meeting during its 103rd session, CCPR/C/3/Rev.10,

ures in international adjudication is to preserve the equal rights of the parties pending the examination of a case in order to ensure the effectiveness and integrity of a final decision.[3] In the particular context of international human rights law, this usually means the protection of persons from "irreparable damage to the enjoyment"[4] of certain fundamental rights in situations of urgency.[5] The institution of interim measures offers the human rights judiciary a unique and powerful instrument for safeguarding the effectiveness of the protection it affords by preventing particularly harmful human rights violations that would not be reparable by a decision on the merits.[6] Not without reason, the power to issue interim measures has therefore been referred to as a procedural "weapon in the arsenal of the adjudicator".[7]

Despite the significance and practical relevance of interim measures in human rights adjudication, their use in practice has been fairly ambiguous. This holds true not only for the range of situations in which interim measures are applied, but also for the procedure through which they are requested, granted or denied. Said abstruseness stems from the fact that granting interim relief is largely discretionary and that adjudicators such as the Committee or the Court neither publish nor give reasons for a decision to apply or deny interim measures. Recently, the issue of interim measures has increasingly become the focus of attention. For the HRC's 107th session, *Sir Nigel Rodley* prepared a draft report on the Mandate of the Special Rapporteur on New Communications and Interim Measures;[8] similarly, at the

---

11.1.2012; interim measures are sometimes also termed "provisional measures" or "precautionary measures".

[3] *S. Rosenne*, Provisional Measures in International Law: The International Court of Justice and the International Tribunal for the Law of the Sea, 2005, 3 and 4; *C. Brown*, A Common Law of International Adjudication, 2007, 121; *W. A. Thirlway*, The Indication of Provisional Measures by the International Court of Justice, in: R. Bernhardt (ed.), Interim Measures Indicated by International Courts, 1994, 5 and 6; see also Article 41 of the Statute of the International Court of Justice (hereinafter ICJ), 26.6.1945, 33 U.N.T.S. 993, entered into force 24.10.1945.

[4] ECtHR, *Mamatkulov and Askarov v. Turkey* (GC), Appl. Nos. 46827/99 and 46951/99, 4.2.2005, ECHR 2005-I, § 108.

[5] *E. Rieter*, Preventing Irreparable Harm: Provisional Measures in International Human Rights Adjudication, 2010, 1088.

[6] ECtHR, *Savriddin Dzhurayev v. Russia*, Appl. No. 71386/10, 25.4.2013, § 212; *Mamatkulov and Askarov v. Turkey* (note 4), § 125.

[7] *J. M. Pasqualucci*, Interim Measures in International Human Rights: Evolution and Harmonization, Vand. J. Transnat'l L. 38 (2005), 3 et seq.; *S. Ghandhi*, The Human Rights Committee and Interim Measures of Relief, Canterbury L. Rev. 13 (2007), 203.

[8] Interview with *Sir Nigel Rodley*, member of the HRC and former Special Rapporteur on New Communications and Interim Measures (Geneva, 25.3.2013).

Council of Europe, the Steering Committee for Human Rights (CDDH) published a report on interim measures under Rule 39 of the Rules of Court.[9] These efforts to examine and review practice under both systems provides a timely opportunity to undertake a comprehensive comparison of the HRC's and the ECtHR's use of interim measures. On the basis of the co-author's personal experience as a Judge at the ECtHR and former member of the HRC, this article gives insight into the functioning and case-law of the two adjudicators with a view to identifying commonalities and differences in their approaches to interim protection.

Relying on the premise that the prospect of effective interim relief can under certain circumstances be a decisive factor for forum choice, such a comparison can provide applicants in a situation of urgency with a better understanding of how and before which adjudicator they can most effectively request interim measures in a given context.[10] It is discussed that both adjudicators primarily indicate interim measures with respect to risks for life and limb, but that outside this mutual field of application the HRC may occasionally grant interim measures in situations in which the Court would not, and vice versa. Moreover, this article reveals that, under the Committee, a practice of indicating so-called protection measures – a new category of measures unknown to the Court – emerged to accommodate risks which do not necessarily affect the object of the dispute but can arise out of the submission of a complaint. Regarding the ECtHR, on the other hand, since the Izmir Conference and the introduction of a new centralised unit within the Registry dealing with requests for interim measures, a clear intent to keep the number of cases in which interim measures are granted to a strict minimum can be observed.

---

[9] Council of Europe, Steering Committee for Human Rights (CDDH), Report on interim measures under Rule 39 of the Rules of Court, CDDH(2013)R77 Addendum III, 22.3.2013; Drafting Group C on the Reform of the Court (GT-GDR-C), Article 39 of the Rules of Court: Modalities of Application and Procedure, Information document by the Registry of the Court, GT-GDR-C(2012)009, 7.12.2012; the High Level Conference in Brighton recalling the Izmir Declaration "invited the Committee of Ministers to consider further the question of interim measures (...)" and "(...) propose any necessary action" (High Level Conference on the Future of the European Court of Human Rights, Brighton Declaration, 20.4.2012, para. 12 lit. e)).

[10] As to the Court's use of interim measures in the field of asylum and migration, two very useful reports were recently published; UNHCR, Toolkit on How to Request Interim Measures under Rule 39 of the Rules of the European Court of Human Rights for Persons in Need of International Protection, February 2012, available at <http://www.refworld.org>; European Council on Refugees and Exiles (ECRE)/ European Legal Network on Asylum (ELENA), Research on ECHR Rule 39 Interim Measures, April 2012, available at <www.ecre.org>.

The present comparison may, however, not only be of interest to applicants but may also help to increase the HRC's and the ECtHR's self-perception regarding their approaches in a field that has, until now, largely been shaped by informal practices and procedures. A look beyond their own systems can assist these bodies in scrutinising their current practice and developing criteria that could lead to a more consistent and transparent use of interim measures within and also between the two systems.

Part II of this article compares the procedures through which the HRC and the ECtHR grant, deny or revisit the indication of interim relief. Part III discusses the material, temporal and personal scope of interim protection as well as the legal effect of interim measures. Without claiming to be exhaustive, Part IV then exemplifies the typology of cases in which interim measures are usually granted followed by a digression on the special category of protection measures used by the Committee (Part V). Part VI turns to the issue of non-compliance. It discusses and compares the establishment of non-compliance as well as the legal and diplomatic consequences thereof as reflected in the current practice of the two adjudicators.

II. Procedural Issues

1. Authority to Indicate Interim Measures

The ECtHR and the HRC are entrusted with ensuring the observance of the commitments undertaken by states and to that effect have the competence to receive individual or interstate complaints about violations of the rights set forth in the ECHR (or its Optional Protocols) and the ICCPR, respectively.[11] In order to be able to assume this function, they are entitled to establish their own rules of procedure.[12] Both the Court and Committee adopted relatively broad rules wherein provision is made for the indication of interim measures. Rule 39 (1) of the Rules of Court states that

---

[11] Article 1 of the Optional Protocol to the International Covenant on Civil and Political Rights, 16.12.1966, 999 U.N.T.S. 302, ratified by 114 states (status May 2013), entered into force 23.3.1976; Article 41 of the International Covenant on Civil and Political Rights, 16.12.1966, 999 UNTS 171, 6 ILM 368 (1967), ratified by 167 states (status May 2013), entered into force 23.3.1976; Article 19 of the European Convention for the Protection of Human Rights and Fundamental Freedoms, 4.11.1950, 213 U.N.T.S. 222, E.T.S. 5, ratified by 47 states (status May 2013), entered into force 3.9.1953, as amended by Protocols Nos. 11 and 14, which entered into force 1.11.1998 and 1.6.2010, respectively.

[12] Article 39 (2) ICCPR; Article 25 (d) ECHR.

the Chamber or, where appropriate, its President may, at the request of a party or of any other person concerned, or of its own motion, indicate to the parties any interim measure which it considers should be adopted in the interests of the parties or of the proper conduct of the proceedings before it.

Rule 92 of the Rules of Procedure of the HRC similarly provides that

(t)he Committee may, prior to forwarding its views on the communication to the State party concerned, inform that State of its views as to whether interim measures may be desirable to avoid irreparable damage to the victim of the alleged violation (...).

Although it would certainly be desirable to also codify such an explicit legal basis for the adoption of interim measures at treaty level,[13] the lack thereof in the ECHR or the Optional Protocol to the ICCPR should, however, not lead to doubt regarding the Court's or Committee's authority to grant interim relief. Today, the institution of interim measures is widely accepted as being an inherent or implied power flowing from the very judicial function that an international court, tribunal or (quasi-)judicial organ was set up to perform.[14]

2. Requesting Interim Measures

While interim measures can, in principle, be requested by either of the parties to the proceedings,[15] recourse to the institution of interim measures in the field of human rights law has always been fairly one-sided. In almost all cases, it is the individual seeking redress for an alleged human rights violation before the relevant adjudicator who asks for interim relief. Before the ECtHR, it is usually the (potential) applicants in an individual application or their legal representatives who submit a request for interim measures; before the HRC, the authors of a communication or the alleged victims

---

[13] The attempt to give Convention status to Rule 39 has not been successful thus far, but is not off the table (CDDH Report, note 9, para. 7).

[14] One can thus argue that the provisions providing for the indication of interim measures are only declaratory in nature. *C. Brown* (note 3), 127 et seq.; *K. Oellers-Frahm*, Expanding the Competence to Issue Provisional Measures – Strengthening the International Judicial Function, GLJ 12 (2011), 1283; *R. St. J. Macdonald*, Interim Measures in International Law, With Special Reference to the European System for the Protection of Human Rights, ZaöRV 52 (1992), 726 et seq.; *D. McGoldrick*, The Human Rights Committee: Its Role in the Development of the International Covenant on Civil and Political Rights, 1991, 131 and 132.

[15] Rule 39 (1) of the Rules of Court.

usually request interim protection.[16] State parties, on the other hand, hardly ever make use of this possibility – an exception being interstate cases such as *Georgia v. Russia (II)*.[17]

The adjudicator may also indicate interim relief *proprio motu*,[18] although this is rarely the case in practice. Currently, the HRC does generally not afford interim relief on its own motion, and the ECtHR only applied Rule 39 *ex officio* in an interstate case in 1970[19] and more recently on two occasions to request that a lawyer be appointed for an applicant who was not represented before the Court.[20] Lastly, with respect to the ECtHR, a request for interim measures can also stem from "any other person".[21] So far, no practice has emerged in this category.

3. The Underlying Application

Based on the fact that the institution of interim measures is part of an adjudicator's judicial function to settle disputes it also follows that interim measures do not have autonomous character but must, in principle, relate to an individual or interstate complaint procedure.[22] The specific nexus required between the request for interim relief and the underlying application differs, however, under the ECHR and the ICCPR. Before the Committee, interim measures can only be requested in the context of a submitted communication, which was already registered by the Special Rapporteur.[23] Before the Court, in contrast, a request for interim measures may precede the actual lodging of an application as long as it discloses elements that suggest an arguable case under the Convention. In this case, the Court can apply

---

[16] For the sake of simplicity, the terms "applicant" and "application" are henceforth used whenever issues are discussed that relate to proceedings both before the ECtHR and the HRC.

[17] ECtHR, *Georgia v. Russia (II)* (dec.), Appl. No. 38263/08, 13.12.2011, § 5.

[18] Rule 39 (1) of the Rules of Court; HRC, General Comment No. 33, The Obligations of States Parties under the Optional Protocol to the International Covenant on Civil and Political Rights (advanced unedited version), CCPR/C/GC/33, 5.11.2008, para. 19.

[19] ECtHR, *Denmark, Norway and Sweden v. Greece* (dec.), Appl. No. 4448/67, 26.3.1970, Y.B. Eur. Conv. Hum. Rts. 13 (1970), 110.

[20] ECtHR, *X v. Croatia*, Appl. No. 11223/04, 17.7.2008, §§ 2 and 61; ECtHR, *Öcalan v. Turkey* (GC), Appl. No. 46221/99, 12.5.2005, ECHR 2005-IV, § 5.

[21] See Rule 39 (1) of the Rules of Court.

[22] When an applicant does not pursue his or her application, the interim measure is lifted; see, for example, ECtHR, *H.N. v. the United Kingdom* (dec.), Appl. No. 56676/10, 13.12.2011; G. J. Naldi, Interim Measures in the Human Rights Committee, ICLQ 53 (2004), 447.

[23] Interview with *Sir Nigel Rodley* (note 8).

Rule 39 under the presumption that an application may follow. In some cases, this more lenient approach has led to abuse. It is, for example, not uncommon for applicants whose removal was stayed under Rule 39 to disappear into hiding once interim measures are applied.[24]

The purpose of interim relief requires that the adjudicator be able to issue interim measures before deciding on the admissibility (or merits) of the case.[25] At the stage when a request for interim measures is examined, neither the time nor the necessary information is available to analyse the underlying application in depth.[26] For this reason, the granting or refusal of interim measures remains without prejudice to any decision as to the admissibility or the merits of the case.[27] At the same time, however, the Committee and the Court – the latter where an application has already been lodged – do assess *prima facie* whether the underlying application meets the basic admissibility criteria and has a reasonable likelihood of success on the merits before considering applying interim measures.[28]

Under the ECHR, a decision to apply Rule 39 leads to a prioritisation in the processing of the application and is usually combined with a decision to communicate the case to the Government. A refusal to apply Rule 39, on the other hand, is often coupled with a decision on inadmissibility.[29]

---

[24] See, for example, ECtHR, *J.Z. v. France and R.Z. v. France* (dec.), Appl. Nos. 43341/09 and 43342/09, 11.12.2012 or ECtHR, *Kaderi and Others v. Switzerland* (dec.), Appl. No. 29919/12, 18.6.2013, §§ 16 and 17.

[25] ECtHR, *M.S.S. v. Belgium and Greece* (GC), Appl. No. 30696/09, 21.1.2011, § 355: "At this stage, when an interim measure is indicated, it is not for the Court to analyse the case in depth – and indeed it will often not have all the information it would need in order to do so (...)."

[26] The government has usually not yet submitted any observations on the case at that point.

[27] See, for example, ECtHR, *Evans v. the United Kingdom* (GC), Appl. No. 6339/05, 10.4.2007, ECHR 2007-I, § 5.

[28] See the approach of the Committee against Torture, which applies also to the HRC (CAT, Annual Report, 45th [1.-19.11.2010] and 46th session [9.5.-3.6.2011], A/66/44, paras. 91 et seq.).

[29] CDDH Report (note 9), para. 14; this practice serves to ensure that applications in which interim measures are indicated are dealt with speedily; Rule 41 of the Rules of Court.

4. Requirements Surrounding a Request for Interim Relief

Thus far, only the Court has, in its Practice Direction, codified some formal and substantive requirements as to requests for interim measures.[30] Research undertaken by the authors, however, shows that similar requirements also apply to requests before the HRC.

Firstly, what can be described as formal conditions require that a request be made in writing, that it indicates in some way that it concerns interim relief (expressly or in substance)[31] and that it be submitted in good time, so as to allow the adjudicator to intervene effectively. In "good time" means as soon as possible – with respect to deportation cases before the ECtHR, submission must come at least one working day before the removal, the date of which must be indicated in the request. Further "where the final domestic decision is imminent and there is a risk of immediate enforcement (…) applicants and their representatives should submit the request for interim measures without waiting for that decision, indicating clearly the date on which it will be taken and that the request is subject to the final domestic decision being negative".[32]

Secondly, a request for interim measures must meet the threshold of gravity and urgency applied by both the HRC and the ECtHR. Therefore, the requesting person must demonstrate that he or she faces an imminent risk of irreparable harm if the interim measure is not applied.[33] Although there is no formal obligation to exhaust domestic remedies in the context of interim relief, with respect to removal cases, the threshold of imminence requires an applicant under both the ICCPR and the ECHR to make use of domestic avenues capable of suspending a removal (remedies with suspensive effect) before applying for interim measures at international level.[34]

Finally, it rests upon the applicant to substantiate his request. As a request for interim measures is usually submitted at the very outset of the proceedings and in a situation of urgency, the standard of proof it has to

---

[30] Practice Direction, Requests for interim measures issued by the President of the Court in accordance with Rule 32 of the Rules of Court on 5.3.2003 and amended on 16.10.2009 and on 7.7.2011, available at <http://www.echr.coe.int>.

[31] Before the ECtHR, requests are to be made by facsimile or letter and should be marked with "Rule 39 – Urgent" (Practice Direction, note 30), 2.

[32] Practice Direction (note 30), 1 and 2.

[33] Practice Direction (note 30), 1 and 2; see below III. 1., 339 et seq.

[34] This requirement has to be distinguished from the formal obligation to exhaust domestic remedies with respect to the underlying application, although both often overlap in practice; Practice Direction (note 30), 1; see *mutatis mutandi* CAT, Annual Report (note 28), para. 91.

meet is lower than what is required for the underlying application at the stages of admissibility or merits of the case.[35] In abstract terms, a request for interim measures must make plausible the existence of an imminent risk of irreversible harm. In this context, both the HRC and the ECtHR seem to rely on the plausibility and credibility of the applicant's assertions.[36] In order to meet this level of proof, a request must include relevant supporting documents such as, for example, domestic court decisions,[37] medical reports, or specific country information compiled by NGOs or UN bodies such as the UNHCR or the OHCHR.[38]

The burden of proof resting on the applicant does not, however, hinder the adjudicator from seeking information *proprio motu*. In removal cases, for example, the ECtHR can double-check or complete the applicants' submission by using its own or other relevant databases.[39] Furthermore, sometimes, in cases where the substantiation of an alleged risk is particularly difficult, for example when a prisoner complains about inadequate medical treatment, the Rapporteur, the Registry, or even the Court's President have requested further information from the government concerned.[40] The HRC, on the other hand, cannot solicit information from the State party prior to the registration of a communication.

---

[35] *C. Burbano Herrera/Y. Haeck*, Staying the Return of Aliens from Europe through Interim Measures: The Case-law of the European Commission and the European Court of Human Rights, European Journal of Migration and Law 13 (2011), 33; these authors consider very *prima facie* evidence sufficient; *E. Rieter* (note 5), 874, refers to *prima prima facie* evidence.

[36] *M.S.S. v. Belgium and Greece* (note 25), § 40: "On 2 July 2009, having regard to the growing insecurity in Afghanistan, the *plausibility* of the applicant's story concerning the risks he had faced and would still face if he were sent back to that country and the lack of any reaction on the part of the Greek authorities, the Court decided to apply Rule 39 and indicate to the Greek Government, in the parties' interest and that of the smooth conduct of the proceedings, not to have the applicant deported pending the outcome of the proceedings before the Court" (emphasis added); *Mamatkulov and Askarov v. Turkey* (note 4), § 108; *H. R. Garry*, When Procedure Becomes a Matter of Life or Death: Interim Measures and the European Court of Human Rights, European Public Law 7 (2001), 410.

[37] Practice Direction (note 30), 1, according to which "(a) mere reference to submissions in other documents or domestic proceedings is not sufficient".

[38] *H. R. Garry* (note 36), 411.

[39] ECtHR, *Hilal v. the United Kingdom*, Appl. No. 45276/99, 6.3.2001, § 60: "In determining whether it has been shown that the applicant runs a real risk, if deported to Tanzania, of suffering treatment proscribed by Article 3, the Court will assess the issue in the light of all the material placed before it, or, if necessary, material obtained *proprio motu* (…)."

[40] Rule 54 para. 2 (a) of the Rules of Court; ECtHR, *M.S.S. v. Belgium and Greece* (note 25), § 39: "The Greek authorities were given until 29 June 2009 to provide this information, it being specified that: 'Should you not reply to our letter within the deadline, the Court will seriously consider applying Rule 39 against Greece.'"

5. Examination of the Request and Decision-Making

In practice, both systems have delegated the competence to issue interim measures within the adjudicator and have developed a streamlined procedure to process and examine incoming request individually and in a prompt and efficient manner.

Under the ECHR, requests are subject to a first triage by the Registry's case lawyers.[41] They identify requests that either fall short of meeting the threshold of a real risk of irreversible harm (requests outside the scope of Rule 39 *stricto sensu*), are incomplete (not substantiated) or were sent too late. Even though it is not an absolute rule, and exceptions can be made in particularly serious cases, these requests are usually directly rejected as belonging to the category of those "outside the scope of Rule 39".[42] For all other requests, a checklist is prepared that is first subject to a centralised quality control by the Registry's Rule 39 unit and then submitted for decision to one of three Section Vice-Presidents, who constitute the decision centre for the application of Rule 39.[43] This new centralised procedure was put into place in 2011 as a response to the influx of requests[44] and after the Contracting Parties expressed their expectations during that Izmir Conference of "a significant reduction in the number of interim measures granted by the Court (...)".[45]

While the centralised procedure "aims at ensuring better consistency and increasing the legibility of decisions taken by the Court in the matter"[46] it is particularly striking that, since its establishment, a person's prospect of benefitting from interim measures has declined considerably: during the year 2010, for example, roughly 40 % of all decisions taken under Rule 39

---

[41] Information document by the Registry (note 9), para. 7.

[42] Information document by the Registry (note 9), para. 9. Thus, a request that fails to comply with the requirements set out in the Practice Direction risks not being examined by the competent Vice-President. "It must be emphasised that failure to comply with the conditions set out in the Practice Direction may lead to such cases not being accepted for examination by the Court." (Statement on requests for interim measures issued by the President of the Court on 11.2.2011, available at <http://www.echr.coe.int>).

[43] Information document by the Registry (note 9), para. 3; Rule 39 (1) of the Rules of Court; the Vice-President usually consults with the rapporteur judge (the national judge) concerned, who also receives a copy of the checklist.

[44] Between 2006 and 2010 the number of requests for interim measures increased by 4,000 %. At the time, the Court's President voiced his concern about "the alarming rise in the number of requests for interim measures and its implications for an already overburdened Court" (Statement on requests for interim measures, note 42).

[45] High level Conference on the Future of the European Court of Human Rights, Izmir Declaration, 27.4.2011, Follow-up Plan (Implementation), para. 4.

[46] Information document by the Registry (note 9), para. 3.

resulted in the use of interim measures. This number has dropped to only 5 % in 2012.[47]

Under the HRC, the Committee member appointed Special Rapporteur on New Communications and Interim Measures applies Rule 92 upon the recommendation of the Committee's Secretariat.[48] Usually, all requests are submitted to the Special Rapporteur for decision. In addition, a practice has emerged in the Committee that leads to a certain easing or shifting of the burden of proof. In cases of doubt as to the imminence, credibility or irreparability of the alleged harm, it can indicate so-called "provisional" interim measures. If "provisional" interim measures are applied, the Special Rapporteur explicitly informs the State party that his decision can be revised in light of further information provided by the State party.[49]

By far the largest category of requests for interim measures in practice concerns the staying of removals/deportations allegedly contrary to the *non-refoulment* principle. The examination of such requests is particularly delicate because it requires the adjudicative body to evaluate, usually in a very short period of time, the applicant's hypothetical situation in the receiving state.[50] The report prepared by the Registry of the Court provides an idea of the elements taken into consideration by the ECtHR when exam-

---

[47] See official statistics published by the Court on Rule 39 requests granted and refused in 2008, 2009 and 2010, 2011 and 2012 by responding state, available at <http://www.echr.coe.int>. The statistic relates to the total number of decisions taken by the Court under Rule 39. It does not provide any information as to the number of requests submitted to the Court (CDDH Report, note 9, para. 10).

[48] The HRC lacks resources and technical means to collect statistical data on the number of requests for interim relief submitted. Its annual reports, however, provide some information as to the Committee's use of interim measures. Over the last three reporting periods, from 1.8.2009 to 30.3.2012, for instance, the Special Rapporteur issued a total of 42 decisions calling for interim measures with respect to a total of 256 registered cases; from 1.8.2011 to 30.3.2012 the Special Rapporteur issued 10 requests for interim measures (HRC, Annual Report, A/67/40 [Vol. I], para. 128); from 1.8.2010 to 31.7.2011 and from 1.8.2009 to 31.7.2010 the Special Rapporteur issued 16 requests respectively (HRC, Annual Reports, A/66/40 [Vol. I] and A/65/40 [Vol. I], paras. 10).

[49] Interview with *Sir Nigel Rodley* (note 8).

[50] In general, both the ECtHR and the HRC attach more importance to the personal situation of the applicant than to the general situation in the receiving state. Hence, the systematic application of interim measures with a view to halting deportations to a particular country remains the exception. Under the ECHR, Somalis facing deportation to Mogadishu have benefitted from the systematic application of Rule 39. In 2010, a similar practice was temporarily applied with respect to removals to Iraq (*F. Tulkens*, La procédure d'urgence devant la Cour européenne des droits de l'homme, Colloque L'Europe et les droits de l'homme, Conseil National des Barreaux / Délégation des Barreaux de France, Bruxelles, 1.4.2011, 30 and 31, available at <www.dbfbruxelles.eu>). Sometimes Rule 39 was applied in a quasi-systematic manner pending the adoption of a lead judgment by the Court; see, for example, ECtHR, *NA. v. the United Kingdom*, Appl. No. 25904/07, 17.7.2008, § 21.

ining a request for interim measures in this field. These include the general situation in the destination country, the existence of a personal risk for the applicant established by a substantiated account, the seriousness of the damage alleged in the case of return, the elements of proof provided and their *prima facie* authenticity (arrest/search warrant, medical certificates etc.), the relevant case-law of the Court (judgments and decisions, but also precedents relating to Rule 39) and the reasoning behind the decisions of national authorities and courts.[51] As to the last element, the Registry also emphasised that the Court attaches particular importance to the conclusions reached by national bodies. As the ECtHR considers national courts to be better placed to evaluate evidence presented before them, a "detailed and precise reasoning of national courts constitutes a solid base allowing the Court to be assured that the examination of the risks alleged by the applicant has been in conformity with the requirements of the Convention, and consequently to conclude by the possible rejection of the request for interim measures".[52] Thus, in certain situations, the principle of subsidiarity may lead the adjudicator to exercise particular restraint when examining a request for interim relief.[53]

Under both the ECHR and the ICCPR, the decision to grant or deny interim relief is communicated to the parties only, usually without disclosing the reasons for which interim relief was ordered or denied.[54]

6. Re-Examination and Challenging of Interim Measures

The adjudicator may revisit its initial decision to issue interim measures in the course of the proceedings and reassess whether the application of a specific interim measure is still justified and should be prolonged or even adapted to new circumstances, or alternatively whether the measures should be lifted. The adjudicator can do so of its own motion, but most often, such re-examination is performed on request of the State party concerned. Even though the decision to afford interim protection can, formally, not be appealed, both the HRC and the ECtHR allow the challenging of an interim

---

[51] Information document by the Registry (note 9), para. 28.

[52] Information document by the Registry (note 9), para. 29.

[53] The principle of subsidiarity also has bearing in the context of interim relief. As concerns the ECtHR, this was explicitly expressed during the Izmir Conference, where it was recalled that the Court is not an immigration appeals tribunal or a court of fourth instance and that interim protection must be granted in accordance with the principle of subsidiarity (Izmir Declaration, note 45, Follow-up Plan, A. para. 3).

[54] CDDH Report (note 9), para. 33.

measure[55] and thereby alleviate, to a certain extent, the fact that the State party is normally not consulted during the initial examination. Under the ECHR, a state "(...) which considers that it is in possession of materials capable of convincing the Court to annul the interim measure (...)"[56] can ask for the lifting of the measure at any time.[57] The same possibility exists before the HRC, particularly but not only when it indicates "provisional" interim measures.[58]

7. Transparency

The lack of transparency with which the human rights judiciary handles interim relief has raised some criticism among legal scholars, first and foremost regarding decision-making. *Rieter* for example has argued that adjudicators should publish and give reasons for their decisions on interim measures for grants and refusals alike. This would render their practice more consistent, coherent and thereby also more predictable and persuasive vis-à-vis states.[59] Recent developments show that these concerns have been heard – at least to a certain extent. Under the Convention system, the Committee of Experts on the Reform of the Court recently discussed whether the Court could give reasoning for its grants of interim measures "(...) to better understand what amounts to irreparable harm, to address necessary issues at the domestic level (i. e. the need for a more thorough examination of risk by domestic courts) and to enable States to more appropriately challenge the imposition of interim measures".[60] The Registry of the Court, however, took the position that, for practical reasons, motivating decisions could only

---

[55] For an example regarding the ECtHR in which an interim measure was lifted upon request of the Government, see *Shamayev and Others v. Georgia and Russia*, Appl. No. 36378/02, 12.4.2005, ECHR 2005-III, §§ 20 and 21; in *Paladi v. Moldova* (GC), Appl. No. 39806/05, 10.3.2009, the ECtHR held in § 90: "(...) while a State which considers that it is in possession of materials capable of convincing the Court to annul the interim measure should inform the Court accordingly (...)"; for an example from the HRC, in which an interim measure was extended and adapted, see *Liliana Assenova Naidenova et al. v. Bulgaria*, Communication No. 2073/2011, 30.10.2012, para. 10.

[56] *Paladi v. Moldova* (note 55), § 90.

[57] Information document by the Registry (note 9), para. 21.

[58] HRC, *Jouni E. Länsman et al. v. Finland*, Communication No. 671/1995, 30.10.1996, para. 4.1.; see also *S. Ghandhi* (note 7), 215.

[59] *E. Rieter* (note 5), 1083 et seq.; see also, for example, *Y. Haeck/C. Burbano Herrera/L. Zwaak*, Non-compliance with a Provisional Measure Automatically Leads To a Violation of the Right of Individual Application ... or Doesn't It?, EuConst 4 (2008), 57 et seq.

[60] CDDH Report (note 9), para. 33.

be envisaged in exceptional circumstances and on an *ad hoc* basis.[61] A compromise favoured by the CDDH could consist in publishing a summary of the reasons for which interim relief was granted or denied over a given period.[62] The Special Rapporteur on New Communications and Interim Measures recently suggested such an approach also for the HRC.[63]

III. Scope of Interim Protection

1. Threshold for Interim Protection

a) Gravity

In line with the case-law of the ICJ,[64] the HRC and the ECtHR rely on the criterion of "irreparable harm" to decide whether the indication of interim measures is justified in a given case. While the HRC has codified, in Rule 92 of the Rules of Procedure, that interim measures are only meant to "avoid *irreparable damage* to the victim of the alleged violation" (emphasis added), the ECtHR has held in its case-law that in practice it "applies Rule 39 only if there is a *risk of irreparable damage*" (emphasis added).[65] What – exactly – constitutes irreparable damage, however, is determined on a case-by-case basis by both the HRC and the ECtHR.[66] The closest that the case-law of the two adjudicators has come to a general definition of irreparability was in *Charles E. Stewart v. Canada*, in which the HRC held:

> The essential criterion is indeed the irreversibility of the consequences, in the sense of the inability of the author to secure his rights, should there later be a

---

[61] Information document by the Registry (note 9), para. 31.

[62] CDDH Report (note 9), para. 44.

[63] Interview with *Sir Nigel Rodley* (note 8). The fact that the issue of interim measures is currently examined by the adjudicators or related expert bodies can by itself contribute its part on rendering practices and procedures more transparent.

[64] ICJ, *Fisheries Jurisdiction (United Kingdom of Great Britain and Northern Ireland v. Iceland)*, Interim Protection, Order of 17.8.1972, I.C.J. Reports 1972, 16, § 21.

[65] *Mamatkulov and Askarov v. Turkey* (note 4), §§ 104 and also § 103 and 108: "(…) The grounds on which Rule 39 may be applied are not set out in the Rules of Court but have been determined by the Court through its case-law. (…) As far as the applicant is concerned, the result that he or she wishes to achieve through the application is the preservation of the asserted Convention right before irreparable damage is done to it."

[66] HRC, *Charles E. Stewart v. Canada*, Communication No. 538/1993, 1.11.1996, para. 7.7: "(…) what may constitute *irreparable damage* to the victim within the meaning of rule 86 [now rule 92] cannot be determined generally" (emphasis added). *Mamatkulov and Askarov v. Turkey* (note 4), § 103.

finding of a violation of the Covenant on the merits. The Committee may decide, in any given case, not to issue a request under rule 86 [now rule 92] where it believes that compensation would be an adequate remedy.[67]

Compared to the extensive catalogue of guarantees the observance of which the ECtHR and the HRC are tasked with monitoring, the risk of a violation of only a very limited number of rights has been considered "irreparable" in practice so far.[68] The Court has repeatedly held that interim measures are only applied in limited spheres;[69] most recently, it has even stated that it "(...) issues them, as a matter of principle, in truly exceptional cases".[70] Typically, interim measures are granted in cases that involve asserted violations of the right to life (Article 2 ECHR, Article 6 ICCPR) and the right not to be subjected to torture or inhuman treatment (Article 3 ECHR, Article 7 ICCPR).[71] Irreparable harm is therefore first and foremost understood as physical harm to life and limb.[72] Aside from this "common core",[73] a certain expansion of the interpretation of irreparability can be observed. Accordingly, alleged violations of the right to respect for private and family life (Article 8 ECHR, Article 17 ICCPR) have occasionally also led the HRC and the ECtHR to grant interim relief.[74] In very exceptional cases, the HRC has even issued interim measures to prevent potential violations of the freedom of thought, conscience and religion (Article 18), the freedom of expression (Article 19 ICCPR) or the rights of indigenous peoples (Article 27 ICCPR).[75] On its part, the ECtHR may exceptionally apply interim measures to prevent allegedly flagrant violations of the right to a fair trial (Article 6 ECHR) or the right to liberty and security (Article 5 ECHR) but also with respect the right of individual petition (Article 34 ECHR) or the right to property (Article 1 Protocol 1).[76]

---

[67] *Charles E. Stewart v. Canada* (note 66), para. 7.7.

[68] *Mamatkulov and Askarov v. Turkey* (note 4), § 104; for an overview see ECtHR, Press Unit, Factsheet – Interim measures, January 2013, available at <http://www.echr.coe.int>.

[69] *Mamatkulov and Askarov v. Turkey* (note 4), § 104.

[70] *Savriddin Dzhurayev v. Russia* (note 6), § 213.

[71] *Mamatkulov and Askarov v. Turkey* (note 4), § 104.

[72] *Savriddin Dzhurayev v. Russia* (note 6), § 213.

[73] *E. Rieter* (note 5), 1089.

[74] *Mamatkulov and Askarov v. Turkey* (note 4), § 104.

[75] Interview with *Sir Nigel Rodley* (note 8).

[76] Information document by the Registry (note 9), para. 26.

b) Temporal Urgency

The alleged risk of harm must not only be of certain gravity, but must also be imminent. Interim measures are only applied where the temporal proximity of the risk requires urgent action on the part of the adjudicator. The assessment of whether a risk is imminent will, again, depend on the nature and circumstances of a given case. In the context of deportations, "imminent" means that the deportation is about to take place or the person concerned can be removed without any further decisions being taken. This is regularly the case where a removal date is already scheduled or a person is subject to an enforceable removal order. On the other hand, both the Court and the HRC do not consider a risk as imminent where domestic avenues capable of suspending removal are available.[77] In general, whenever it is still possible for the applicant to obtain what he seeks by his request for interim relief also at domestic level, a risk is likely not to be regarded imminent.

Länsman et al. v. Finland (I) is one of the only instances in which one of the adjudicators, the HRC in this particular case, explicitly discussed the requirement of imminence in its views on the merits. The authors of the communication, a group of indigenous people, feared that the quarrying of stone could cause irreparable damage to their rights under Article 27 of the Covenant. The HRC agreed with the Government's position and refused to apply interim measures. Because only limited test quarrying in a specific area had been carried out at the time, the indication of interim protection would have been premature.[78]

2. Addressees and Beneficiaries

Addressees of an interim measure are almost exclusively states. The ECtHR usually directs its orders under Rule 39 towards the Government of the responding state, while the HRC addresses its interim measures to the State party concerned. On few occasions only, the ECtHR has asked an applicant who was on hunger strike in prison to end the strike while his case

---

[77] For the requirement to exhaust domestic remedies with suspensive effect, see above II. 4., 333.

[78] HRC, *Länsman et al. v. Finland (I)*, Communication No. 511/1992, 14.10.1993, paras. 4.3 and 6.3.

was under consideration by the Court. This remains a rare category of cases in which applicants have been the addressees of interim measures.[79]

Inversely, the applicants or alleged victims of a violation are the beneficiaries of interim measures. Exceptionally and unlike under the ECHR, individuals in the immediate environment of the author or alleged victim have also benefitted from interim relief before the Committee. In *Gunaratna v. Sri Lanka*, for example, the Special Rapporteur asked "the State party, under Rule 92 of its rules of procedure, to afford the author *and his family* protection against further intimidations and threats" (emphasis added).[80] An unspecified circle of beneficiaries, potentially including all individuals under the jurisdiction of the State parties, was protected in *Georgia v. Russia (II)*, where the Court called "upon both the High Contracting Parties concerned to honour their commitments under the Convention, particularly in respect of Articles 2 and 3 of the Convention".[81]

3. Duration of Protection

Theoretically, interim measures are only necessary as long as the imminent risk of irreparable harm, which led to the adoption of the measure in the first place, persists. As, however, a periodical re-assessment of a given risk is not practicable, interim measures are normally adopted for the duration of the proceedings.[82] This is usually the case where an interim measure is indicated "until further notice" (ECtHR)[83] or while the case is "under examination" (HRC)[84]. In some instances, the ECtHR applied Rule 39 for a specified period, mostly to allow it to gather further evidence.[85] Since incomplete requests are now increasingly dismissed under the centralised processing system, interim measures with a time limit will probably be indicated less often in future. The so-called provisional interim measures developed by the Committee are not adopted for a specified duration, but remain

---

[79] See, for example, EComm, *Bhuyian v. Sweden* (dec.), Appl. No. 26516/95, 14.9.1995; in a recent case the Court refused to apply Rule 39 (ECtHR, *Rappaz v. Switzerland* [dec.], Appl. No. 73175/10, 26.3.2013).

[80] HRC, *Gunaratna v. Sri Lanka*, Communication No. 1432/2005, 17.3.2009, para. 1.2.

[81] *Georgia v. Russia (II)* (note 17), § 5.

[82] CDDH Report (note 9), para. 34.

[83] CDDH Report (note 9), para. 34.

[84] See, for example, HRC, *Lyubov Kovaleva and Tatyana Kozyar v. Belarus*, Communication No. 2120/2011, 29.10.2012, para. 1.2.

[85] See, for example, ECtHR, *F.H. v. Sweden*, Appl. No. 32621/06, 20.1.2009, §§ 40 and 44.

in force during the consideration of the communication if not challenged and lifted.

Where the application of a particular measure is re-assessed, the adjudicator may decide to lift an interim measure if it considers that the imminent risk of irreparable harm never existed or does not exist anymore. Alternatively, if it finds that a risk persists, an interim measure can be maintained or extended.[86] An interim measure is usually lifted when an applicant does not pursue his application, the judgment or decision becomes final (ECtHR), or the Committee has rendered its views, respectively.[87]

4. Nature of Protection

The content and nature of an interim measure varies from case to case and depends on the characteristics of the risk of irreparable harm the realisation of which it is designed to prevent. Mostly, an interim measure consists of a simple request to the state to abstain from a particular action, such as not to deport, evict or execute a person. Less often, the HRC and the ECtHR require states to take positive action. The degree of specificity of such positive measures may, however, vary considerably. For example, in the context of the protection of detainees, both the HRC and ECtHR have issued rather specific measures requiring a state to, *inter alia*, provide adequate medical treatment, transfer a detainee to a specialised medical institution or grant him access to a lawyer.[88] In other situations, more general measures were adopted, such as the call upon the State parties "to honour their commitments under the Convention, particularly in respect of Articles 2 and 3 of the Convention",[89] "to avoid any action that might cause irreparable harm to the alleged victim"[90] or to "take all necessary measures in order to guarantee the applicants' personal security".[91]

---

[86] See above II. 6., 337, in particular note 55.
[87] See note 22.
[88] See below IV. 3., 353.
[89] *Georgia v. Russia (II)* (note 17), § 5.
[90] HRC, *Katombe L. Tshishimbi v. Zaire*, Communication No. 542/1993, 25.3.1996, para. 4.1.
[91] ECtHR, *R.R. and Others v. Hungary*, Appl. No. 19400/11, 4.12.2012, § 4.

5. The Legal Effect of the Protection

The effectiveness of interim protection depends on the legal force the indicated measure is capable of producing. Both the HRC and the ECtHR acknowledged this when they, relying on an evolving interpretation of the relevant provisions, endowed their interim measures with obligatory character. Although neither the HRC's nor the Court's constitutive document or rules of procedure contain provisions on the effect of interim measures, and the issue has long been the subject of controversy, both adjudicators used their case-law to establish a state obligation to abide by a request for interim measures.[92]

In *Dante Piandong et al. v. The Philippines,* the Committee held that a failure to implement an interim measure is incompatible with the obligation of a state under the Optional Protocol to cooperate in good faith with the Committee and abstain from any action that could frustrate the consideration or examination of a communication or render its views nugatory or futile.[93] It held that "(...) interim measures pursuant to rule 86 of the Committee's rules adopted in conformity with article 39 of the Covenant, are essential to the Committee's role under the Protocol" and that "(f)louting of the Rule, especially by irreversible measures such as the execution of the alleged victim or his/her deportation from the country, undermines the protection of Covenant rights through the Optional Protocol".[94]

In addition to the obligation to cooperate in good faith flowing from the Optional Protocol, the Committee also inferred a duty to respect interim measures from the Covenant itself. In its Concluding Observations with respect to the second periodic report submitted by Uzbekistan, the Com-

---

[92] It should be noted here that it was the Committee against Torture that established, as the first international adjudicator to do so, an obligation to respect interim measures (CAT, *Cecilia Rosana Nunez Chipana v. Venezuela*, Communication No. 110/1998, 10.11.1998). The HRC followed in 2000 and, in the same year, the IACtHR was the first international court to state that its provisional measures were mandatory. In its *LaGrand* judgment in 2001, the ICJ similarly held that its provisional measures, as indicated under Article 41 of the ICJ Statute, are binding on the parties. In 2005, it was then up to the ECtHR to reconsider its previous case law, in which it had until then denied the obligatory character of interim measures. Thus, in *Mamatkulov and Askarov v. Turkey* (note 4), the Grand Chamber ruled that interim measures would be obligatory also under the Convention system from that point on (*K. Oellers-Frahm* [note 14], 1280 et seq.). See also *J. M. Pasqualucci* (note 7), 20 et seq. who refers to an inter-system harmonisation of the legal effect of interim measures in international human rights law.

[93] HRC, *Dante Piandong et al. v. The Philippines*, Communication No. 869/1999, 19.10.2000, paras. 5.1, 5.2 and 5.4; General Comment No. 33 (note 18), para. 19.

[94] *Dante Piandong et al. v. The Philippines* (note 93), para. 5.4.

mittee stated that "a disregard of the Committee's requests for interim measures constitutes a grave breach of the State party's obligations *under the Covenant* and the Optional Protocol (...)" (emphasis added)[95] and in General Comment No. 31 [80] it specified that the right to an effective remedy set forth in Article 2 (3) ICCPR may require State parties to provide for and implement provisional or interim measures.[96] Thus, even though the HRC has never used the term "binding" – a decision probably due to its sensitivity to the fact that, unlike the ECtHR's judgments, the Committee's views on the merits are not considered to be legally binding under international law[97] – it has implicitly endowed its interim measures with obligatory character in so far as it considers incompliance as a separate or autonomous breach of the Optional Protocol and the Covenant.[98] While the majority of States seems to have accepted this approach, a few openly contest the Committee's practice. Only recently, for instance, Belarus argued, that a request for interim protection is "beyond the mandate of the Committee and (...) not binding in terms of its international legal obligations".[99] A similar argument was relied upon by the Canadian Government in *Ahani v. Canada*, in which the Government argued "(...) that neither the Covenant nor the Optional Protocol provide for interim measures requests and (...) that such requests are recommendatory, rather than binding".[100]

The origin of the Court's current approach to the effect of interim measures is to be found in the impactful Grand Chamber judgment of 2005 in *Mamatkulov and Askarov v. Turkey* and is very much based on the HRC's

---

[95] The HRC further held that "(t)he State party should adhere to *its obligations under the Covenant* and the Optional Protocol, in accordance with the principle of *pacta sunt servanda* (...)" (emphasis added) (HRC, Concluding Observations with respect to Uzbekistan, CCPR/CO/83/UZB, 31.3.2005, para. 6). The second paragraph was later reproduced with respect to Canada (HRC, Concluding Observations with respect to Canada, CCPR/C/CAN/CO/5, 28.10.2005, para. 7).

[96] HRC, General Comment No. 31 (80), Nature of the General Legal Obligation Imposed on States Parties to the Covenant, CCPR/C/21/Rev.1/Add.13, 29.3.2004, para. 19: "The Committee further takes the view that the right to an effective remedy may in certain circumstances require States Parties to provide for and implement provisional or interim measures to avoid continuing violations and to endeavor to repair at the earliest possible opportunity any harm that may have been caused by such violations." See also *S. Ghandhi* (note 7), 216.

[97] *C. Tomuschat*, Human Rights: Between Idealism and Realism, 2nd ed. 2008, 220.

[98] *G. J. Naldi* (note 22), 449: "Although the Committee did not explicitly hold that requests for interim measures are legally binding as such on States the end result, for all practical purposes, is essentially the same." See also *J. Harrington*, Punting Terrorists, Assassins and Other Undesirables: Canada, the Human Rights Committee and Requests for Interim Measures of Protection, McGill L. J. 48 (2003), 67 et seq.

[99] *Lyubov Kovaleva and Tatyana Kozyar v. Belarus* (note 84), para. 6.3.

[100] HRC, *Ahani v. Canada*, Communication No. 1051/2002, 29 March 2004, para. 5.3; for a detailed discussion of the case see the article of *J. Harrington* (note 98).

practice of finding an autonomous violation of the Optional Protocol.[101] After recalling that interim measures "play a vital role in avoiding irreversible situations that would prevent the Court from properly examining the application and, where appropriate, securing to the applicant the practical and effective benefit of the Convention rights asserted" the Court held in *Mamatkulov and Askarov v. Turkey* that "a failure by a Contracting State to comply with interim measures is to be regarded as preventing the Court from effectively examining the applicant's complaint and as hindering the effective exercise of his or her right of [individual petition] and, accordingly, as a violation of Article 34".[102] More generally, the Court stated that "the effects of the indication of an interim measure to a Contracting State (...) must be examined in the light of the obligations which are imposed on the Contracting States by Articles 1 (...) and 46 of the Convention".[103] By virtue of the latter, a State party has to abide by the final judgment of the Court in any case to which it is party. On the basis of this reasoning, the Court explicitly stated in its subsequent practice that its interim measures have binding force on states.[104] The Contracting Parties have confirmed this position in the Follow-up Plan to the Izmir Declaration, in which they reiterated the requirement to comply with interim measures.[105]

IV. Typology of Cases

1. Executions

Probably the most obvious manifestation of "irreparable" damage or harm is where the applicant is executed before the international adjudicative

---

[101] *Mamatkulov and Askarov v. Turkey* (note 4), § 42. Among other international cases, the ECtHR referred to the HRC's views in *Dante Piandong et al. v. The Philippines*. For a detailed discussion of the case, see, for example, A. Mowbray, A New Strasbourg Approach to the Legal Consequences of Interim Measures, HRLR 5 (2005), 377 et seq.; L. Burgorgue-Larsen, Interim Measures in the European System of Human Rights, Inter-American and European Human Rights Journal/Revista Interamericana y Europea de Derechos Humanos, 2 (2009), 99 et seq.; or H. Jorem, Protecting Human Rights in Cases of Urgency: Interim Measures and the Right of Individual Application under Article 34 ECHR, Nordic Journal of Human Rights 4 (2012), 404 et seq.

[102] *Mamatkulov and Askarov v. Turkey* (note 4), §§ 125 and 128.

[103] *Mamatkulov and Askarov v. Turkey* (note 4), § 126.

[104] ECtHR, *Aoulmi v. France*, Appl. No. 50278/99, 17.1.2006, ECHR 2006-I, § 111; *Savriddin Dzhurayev v. Russia* (note 6), § 213.

[105] Izmir Declaration (note 45), Follow-up Plan, A. para. 3; see also CDDH Report (note 9), para. 2.

body can determine whether his or her execution contravenes human rights guarantees. Accordingly, interim measures have served the purpose of requesting governments to suspend the execution of an applicant on death row. As the death penalty has been either abolished or is no longer applied among member states of the Council of Europe,[106] the Strasbourg organs have only made three such requests.[107] Before the HRC, on the other hand, halting executions has long been the main field of application of interim measures.[108] The case of *Lyubov Kovaleva and Tatyana Kozyar v. Belarus* is a recent example. *Mr. Kovaleva* was sentenced to death by the Belarusian authorities after he had been found responsible for the Minsk bombing of 2011. He petitioned the Committee, complaining, *inter alia*, that he would be arbitrarily deprived of his life (Article 6 ICCPR) as the criminal proceedings brought against him had allegedly violated several of his fair trial rights under Article 14 of the Covenant. He also claimed that he had been subjected to ill-treatment during his interrogation "with the purpose to secure a confession of guilt" from him.[109] The Special Rapporteur on New Communications and Interim Measures granted the petitioner's request for interim relief and asked Belarus not to execute *Mr. Kovaleva* while his case was under consideration by the Committee.[110]

2. Deportations

a) General Remarks

Today, interim measures are mainly used in *refoulement* cases where it seems plausible that the applicant runs a "real and personal risk"[111] of being deprived of his or her life or subjected to treatment contrary to the prohibi-

---

[106] Article 1 Protocol No. 13 to the Convention for the Protection of Human Rights and Fundamental Freedoms, concerning the abolition of the death penalty in all circumstances, 3.5.2002, E.T.S. 187, ratified by 43 states (status May 2013), entered into force 1.7.2003.

[107] See, for example, *Öcalan v. Turkey* (note 20), § 5.

[108] HRC, Annual Report, 103rd (17.10.-4.11.2011) and 104th session (12.-30.3.2012), A/67/40 (Vol. I), para. 155.

[109] *Lyubov Kovaleva and Tatyana Kozyar v. Belarus* (note 84), paras. 3.2 and 3.8.

[110] *Lyubov Kovaleva and Tatyana Kozyar v. Belarus* (note 84), para. 1.2; however, Belarus did not comply with the interim measure, see below VI. 2. a), 364.

[111] See, *inter alia*, *A.A. and Others v. Sweden*, Appl. No. 14499/09, 28.6.2012, § 67; for the general principles of the Court's case-law in this field see, for example, ECtHR, *Saadi v. Italy* (GC), Appl. No. 37201/06, 28.2.2008, §§ 124-133 or ECtHR, *Salah Sheekh v. the Netherlands*, Appl. No. 1948/04, 11.1.2007, §§ 135-137.

tion of torture or inhuman treatment in the receiving state.[112] In a few cases, interim measures were also indicated to stay deportations or removals allegedly contrary to the right to family life, the right to a fair trial or the right to liberty and security.

b) Risk of Being Subjected to the Death Penalty in the Receiving State

Both the HRC and the ECtHR have afforded interim protection to an applicant with a view to halting his or her deportation to a country where he or she could be subjected to the death penalty. As mentioned above, unlike under the ICCPR, the *espace juridique* of the Council of Europe is a *de facto* death penalty free zone.[113] An extradition or expulsion by a Contracting party of person to a country where he or she runs the risk of being subjected to the death penalty violates not only Article 2 ECHR (right to life) and Article 3 ECHR (prohibition of torture and inhuman or degrading treatment) but is also contrary to Article 1 of Protocol 13 (abolition of the death penalty).[114] In a recent case, the ECtHR ordered the Albanian Government not to extradite an applicant to the US, where he had been charged with several criminal offences, one of which allowed – in case of a conviction by the US courts – for the application of the death penalty.[115] In *Al-Saadoon and Mufdhi v. the United Kingdom*, Rule 39 was applied to request the Government of the United Kingdom not to remove or transfer two Iraqis from the custody of the British army, *inter alia* because of their fear that they would be sentenced to death by the Iraqi authorities.[116]

Under the ICCPR, the extradition of a petitioner to a State that practises capital punishment may interfere with Articles 6 (2) and 7. The former states that "(i)n countries which have not abolished the death penalty, sentence of death may be imposed only for the most serious crimes in accordance with the law in force at the time of the commission of the crime and not contrary to the provisions of the present Covenant and to the Convention on the Prevention and Punishment of the Crime of Genocide".[117] In

---

[112] For a comprehensive overview of the Court's use of interim measures in this field, see C. *Burbano Herrera/Y. Haeck* (note 35).

[113] See note 106.

[114] ECtHR, *Al-Saadoon and Mufdhi v. the United Kingdom*, Appl. No. 61498/08, 2.3.2010, § 137.

[115] ECtHR, *Rrapo v. Albania*, Appl. No. 58555/10, 25.9.2012, §§ 31 and 32.

[116] *Al-Saadoon and Mufdhi v. the United Kingdom* (note 114), § 4.

[117] The article further reads "(t)his penalty can only be carried out pursuant to a final judgement rendered by a competent court".

Maksudov et al. v. Kyrgyzstan for example, the HRC asked Kyrgyzstan not to remove four Uzbek nationals to their home country, where they feared the imposition of the death penalty in a manner inconsistent with the requirements of Articles 6 (2) and 7 of the Covenant.[118]

c) Other Risks for Life and Limb in the Receiving State

Besides the possibility of being subjected to the death penalty, other alleged risks for life and limb in the receiving state have triggered the application of interim relief. In most cases, the asserted risk originates from public authorities; however, it may also stem from private actors or even parties to an armed conflict. Similarly, the reasons for which an applicant is allegedly exposed to such risk may vary. Often, an applicant claims to be prosecuted for political reasons. In *F.H. v. Sweden,* for example, the expulsion of a former officer in *Saddam Hussein's* regime to his home country was stayed in light of his claims that he faced execution (not only by death penalty but also through extra-judicial killing), torture and imprisonment if returned.[119] In other cases, it was the applicants' ethnic background or religious beliefs that would allegedly put them at risk vis-à-vis the receiving states' authorities. Thus, in the case of *Abdulkhakov v. Russia*, the ECtHR asked for the halting of the extradition of an applicant of Muslim belief to Uzbekistan, where he was wanted for belonging to "an extremist organisation of a religious, separatist or fundamentalist nature" and several criminal offences related thereto. The applicant claimed that he risked being ill-treated if returned to Uzbekistan.[120] The ECtHR applied Rule 39 despite the fact that Russia had received assurances from the Deputy Prosecutor General of Uzbekistan "that the applicant would not be subjected to torture, violence or other forms of inhuman or degrading treatment and that the rights of the defence would be respected (…) and (…) that the Uzbek authorities had no intention of persecuting the applicant for political motives or on account of his race or religious beliefs".[121]

Other risks raised under Articles 2 or 3 of the Convention that led to the application of Rule 39 include, *inter alia*, the risk of being sentenced to life

---

[118] HRC, *Maksudov et al. v. Kyrgyzstan*, Communication Nos. 1461, 1462, 1476 and 1477/2006, 16.7.2008, para. 1.2.

[119] *F.H. v. Sweden* (note 85), § 4.

[120] ECtHR, *Abdulkhakov v. Russia*, Appl. No. 14743/11, 2.10.2012, §§ 18 and 3.

[121] *Abdulkhakov v. Russia* (note 120), §§ 23 and 4.

imprisonment without the possibility of parole,[122] of ill-treatment related to the sexual orientation of the applicant,[123] of being prosecuted for adultery,[124] of female genital mutilation,[125] of sexual exploitation,[126] or of family vengeance[127].[128]

Although there is a general presumption that every Contracting State honours its obligations under the ECHR,[129] the ECtHR has also halted removals between states of the Council of Europe. In *Shamayev and Others v. Georgia and Russia*[130] and in *Gasayev v. Spain*,[131] for example, the Court requested the suspension of the extraditions of Chechens to Russia, where they were wanted for alleged terrorist activities. More recent applications of Rule 39 concerned mostly transfers of asylum seekers under the Dublin II Regulation to the country of first entry, such as Greece, Malta or Italy. Applicants whose transfer to Greece was stayed claimed that inhuman and degrading detention conditions in Greek holding centres and the deficiencies in the state's asylum procedure (risk of indirect *refoulement*) would expose them to the risk of a violation of Articles 2 and 3 ECHR.[132] With respect to transfers to Malta and Italy, particularly vulnerable people who feared the inhumane living conditions of asylum seekers and refugees have benefitted from a request to stay their Dublin transfer for the duration of the proceedings before the Court.[133]

Under the ICCPR, several cases in this category concern the removal of persons to Sri Lanka, *inter alia* by Canada. In *Pillai et al. v. Canada*, for example, the HRC stopped the repatriation of an asylum-seeking family.[134]

---

[122] ECtHR, *Babar Ahmad and Others v. the United Kingdom*, Appl. Nos. 24027/07, 11949/08, 36742/08, 66911/09 and 67354/09, 10.4.2012.

[123] ECtHR, *K.N. v. France and 5 other applications* (dec.), Appl. No. 47129/09, 19.6.2012.

[124] ECtHR, *Jabari v. Turkey*, Appl. No. 40035/98, 11.7.2000, ECHR 2000-VIII.

[125] ECtHR, *Abraham Lunguli v. Sweden* (dec.), Appl. No. 33692/02, 1.7.2003.

[126] ECtHR, *M. v. the United Kingdom* (dec.), Appl. No. 16081/08, 1.12.2009. The applicant in this case also invoked Article 4 of the ECHR (prohibition of slavery and forced labour).

[127] ECtHR, *H.N. v. the Netherlands*, Appl. No. 20651/11 (case pending at the time of writing).

[128] Factsheet - Interim measures (note 68).

[129] *M.S.S. v. Belgium and Greece* (note 25), § 32.

[130] *Shamayev and Others v. Georgia and Russia* (note 55), § 6.

[131] ECtHR, *Gasayev v. Spain* (dec.), Appl. No 48514/06, 17.2.2009.

[132] See, for example, ECtHR, *Shakor and 48 other applications v. Finland* (dec.), Appl. No. 10941/10, 28.6.2011.

[133] With respect to Italy, see, for example, ECtHR, *M.S.M. and Others v. Denmark* (dec.), Appl. No. 25404/12, 27.11.2012; with respect to Malta, see, for example, ECtHR, *F.S. and Others v. Finland*, Appl. No. 57264/09, 13.12.2011.

[134] HRC, *Pillai et al. v. Canada*, Communication No. 1763/2008, 25.3.2011, para. 1.2.

The family left Sri Lanka for Canada in 2003 after the spouses were allegedly arrested and tortured twice by police forces that suspected them of supporting the Tamil Tigers. When the Canadian authorities rejected their refugee claim, they petitioned the Committee, alleging that they would again risk torture and ill-treatment if returned.[135] On the basis of similar claims, the Special Rapporteur requested, in *Warsame v. Canada*, the suspension of the removal of a Somali to his home country. The request was upheld although the Canadian Government asked that the interim measure be lifted, arguing that the petitioner posed a danger to public security and failed to present a *prima facie* case.[136] In *Israil v. Kazakhstan*, the State was asked not to extradite a Chinese national of Uighur origin pending the Committee's consideration of the case. The petitioner, who provided a radio station with information on the alleged killing of Uighurs by the police, feared torture and the death penalty upon return to China.[137]

d) Health Risks

Occasionally, the ECtHR has also granted interim measures in cases where applicants claimed that their state of health would render removal contrary to Articles 2 and/or 3 ECHR. In *Ahmed v. Sweden*, the ECtHR halted the deportation of an applicant who "complained that his expulsion to either Somalia or Kenya would amount to a violation of Article 3 of the Convention since the specific medical treatment and medicines required by his HIV infection were not available in these countries".[138] Rule 39 was, however, also applied in cases where the risk lay in the effects of the deportation itself. Thus, in *Einhorn v. France*, the extradition of a suicidal applicant was stayed. The measure was lifted after the Government submitted a medical certificate demonstrating that the applicant's medical condition allowed for the transfer.[139]

---

[135] *Pillai et al. v. Canada* (note 134), para. 3.1.

[136] HRC, *Warsame v. Canada*, Communication No. 1959/2010, 21.7.2011, paras. 1.2 and 6.1.

[137] HRC, *Israil v. Kazakhstan*, Communication No. 2024/2011, 31.10.2011, paras. 1.2, 2.1 and 3.1; other examples by the HRC are *Mahmoud Walid Nakrash and Liu Qifen v. Sweden*, Communication No. 1540/2007, 30.10.2008; *Kaur v. Canada*, Communication No. 1455/2006, 30.10.2008.

[138] See, for example, ECtHR, *Ahmed v. Sweden*, Appl. No. 9886/05, 22.2.2007, §§ 20 and 4.

[139] ECtHR, *Einhorn v. France* (dec.), Appl. No. 71555/01, 16.10.2001, §§ 9 and 10.

e)   Risks of a Flagrant Breach of Fair Trial Rights and Indefinite Arbitrary Detention

In *Othman (Abu Qatada) v. the United Kingdom* the ECtHR stayed an expulsion on the basis of an application alleging not only a violation of Articles 2 and 3, but also of Articles 6 (right to a fair trial) and 5 (right to liberty and security) of the ECHR.[140] The case concerned a Jordanian applicant who was convicted *in absentia* "of conspiracy to carry out bombings in Jordan, which resulted in (...) attacks on the American School and the Jerusalem Hotel in Amman in 1998".[141] Having fled Jordan, the applicant was granted refugee status in the UK until the Secretary of State decided to remove him on the basis of a memorandum of understanding (MOU) with Jordan. The applicant feared that, if he were to be removed to Jordan, he would be retried and run a real risk of being tortured for the purpose of obtaining a confession (alleged violation of Articles 3 and 6 ECHR). Under Article 5 ECHR, he further complained that he would be at a risk of being held for up to 50 days in *incommunicado* detention. On the merits, while the Court did not consider that there was a risk of ill-treatment for the applicant, it did find, for the first time, that the extradition of the applicant would violate Article 6 ECHR. According to the Court, the fact that evidence obtained by the torture of third persons could be admitted at the applicant's retrial amounted to a risk of a flagrant denial of justice, rendering an extradition to Jordan contrary to the Convention.[142] Further, the Court held that, while a risk of a grave breach of the rights enshrined in Article 5 in the receiving state may also, in principle, as under Article 6, forbid the expulsion or extradition of a person, the alleged risk of *incommunicado* detention put forward by the applicant did not have the gravity required.[143] It seems possible that, in future, an Article 5 or Article 6 claim alone may trigger an intervention by the ECtHR under Rule 39. However, the threshold to be reached is high: an applicant will have to demonstrate that he or she is at risk of a flagrant denial of justice for Article 6 claims or of indefinite arbitrary detention for Article 5 claims.[144]

---

[140] ECtHR, *Othman (Abu Qatada) v. the United Kingdom*, Appl. No. 8139/09, 17.1.2012, §§ 3 and 4.

[141] *Othman (Abu Qatada) v. the United Kingdom* (note 140), § 10.

[142] *Othman (Abu Qatada) v. the United Kingdom* (note 140), §§ 269-286.

[143] *Othman (Abu Qatada) v. the United Kingdom* (note 140), §§ 231-235.

[144] Information document by the Registry (note 9), para. 26.

f) Risks for a Child's Well-Being

Under the ECHR, an alleged violation of the right to respect for private and family life (Article 8 ECHR) has also exceptionally led to the adoption of interim measures, mostly for the purpose of preventing the separation of parents from children or vice versa where the child's well-being was in danger.[145] In *B. v. Belgium*, interim measures were ordered to suspend the Hague Convention return of a girl to her allegedly violent father in the US.[146] Similarly, in *Neulinger and Shuruk v. Switzerland*, the ECtHR requested Switzerland not to enforce the return of *Noam Shuruk* to Israel, where he would have risked suffering harm from his unstable father (alleged violation of Article 8, taken separately and in conjunction with Articles 3 and 9 of the Convention).[147] The Court has also applied Rule 39 to halt the expulsion or extradition of a parent in cases in which the child was not to be removed. It does not, however, grant interim measures where the family can be expected to accompany the expelled parent or child if no risk of harm for the child is shown or in cases that do not involve a child at all.

3. Detention

Interim measures have served the purpose of protecting detainees from risks arising out of their situation in detention. Both the ECtHR and the HRC have indicated interim measures to ensure a detainee's access to adequate medical care and legal assistance during detention.

In the case of *Yakovenko v. Ukraine,* for instance, the applicant, relying on Article 3 ECHR, complained about a lack of medical assistance during his detention in a Ukrainian prison. He was infected with HIV and suffered from tuberculosis but, despite his poor health, had never been hospitalised. Under Rule 39, the President of the Chamber requested that the Government "ensure that the applicant was transferred immediately to a hospital or other medical institution where he could receive the appropriate treatment for his medical condition".[148]

---

[145] In some cases, the risk for the child may also raise an issue under Article 2 or 3 ECHR.

[146] ECtHR, *B. v. Belgium*, Appl. No. 4320/11, 10.7.2012, § 35.

[147] ECtHR, *Neulinger and Shuruk v. Switzerland*, Appl. No. 41615/07, 6.7.2010, §§ 5 and 3.

[148] ECtHR, *Yakovenko v. Ukraine*, Appl. No. 15825/06, 25.10.2007, § 3; see also ECtHR, *Tymoshenko v. Ukraine*, Appl. No. 49872/11, 30.4.2013, § 122; for a similar recent case, in which the interim measure was not complied with and the applicant died in detention, see ECtHR, *Salakhov and Islyamova v. Ukraine*, Appl. No. 28005/08, 14.3.2013.

It appears from its case-law, however, that the ECtHR only applies Rule 39 where the applicant has a life-threatening condition, is in serious pain or suffers great psychological distress. Untenable detention conditions in general, which might admittedly be contrary to Article 3 but do not pose a specific and grave risk for the health of the applicant, have not led the Court to apply Rule 39. In *Lorsé and Others v. the Netherlands,* an applicant claiming that the maximum security detention regime to which he was subjected constituted inhuman or degrading treatment asked the Court to order his transfer to another prison under Rule 39. Although the ECtHR found, on the merits, that "the combination of routine strip-searching with the other stringent security measures (...) amounted to inhuman or degrading treatment in violation of Article 3 of the Convention", it did not grant the applicant's request for interim measures.[149]

An interesting application of Rule 39 can be found in *Aleksanyan v. Russia*, a case which also concerned a HIV-positive detainee. In complement to requesting the applicant's transfer to a specialised medical institution, the Court asked the Government to form a medical commission, composed on a bipartisan basis, to diagnose the applicant's health problems, suggest treatment and decide whether the applicant's medical conditions could be adequately treated in the medical facility of the detention centre.[150] In its judgment on the merits, the Court explained that, by requesting the establishment of a mixed commission, "it sought to obtain more detailed information about the applicant's state of health and the medical facilities existing in the remand prison, which would allow it to corroborate or rebut the parties' conflicting accounts".[151] Though, whilst the indicated measure aims to assure the proper establishment of the facts of the case, it may also have helped the applicant to substantiate his claim and thereby to protect the Convention rights he had asserted (Articles 2 and 3 ECHR).

Umarova v. Uzbekistan is a recent example in which the HRC used interim measures to protect a person in detention and ensure adequate access to medical treatment. The author of the communication claimed that her husband was arbitrarily detained, tortured and ill-treated. She addressed the Committee with a request for interim measures, submitting that her husband's health had severely deteriorated during his detention. In a rather broad manner the Special Rapporteur requested the State party to adopt all necessary measures to protect *Mr. Umarova's* life, safety and personal integrity, in particular by providing him with the necessary and appropriate

---

[149] ECtHR, *Lorsé and Others v. the Netherlands*, Appl. No. 52750/99, 4.2.2003, § 74.

[150] ECtHR, *Aleksanyan v. Russia*, Appl. No. 46468/06, 22.12.2008, §§ 80 and 76.

[151] *Aleksanyan v. Russia* (note 150), § 231.

medical care and by abstaining from administering any drugs detrimental to his mental or physical health, so as to avoid irreparable harm to him, while the case was under consideration of the Committee.[152]

Furthermore, interim measures have been applied to ensure that detained applicants had access to a lawyer. In the case of *Shtukaturov v. Russia,* the applicant alleged "that by depriving him of his legal capacity without his participation and knowledge the domestic courts had breached his rights under Articles 6 and 8 of the Convention". In addition, he put forward that his detention in a psychiatric hospital would infringe upon Articles 3 and 5 of the Convention.[153] In its judgment on the merits, the Court reproduced – in unprecedented detail – the order for interim measures it had indicated in the case:

> (T)he respondent Government was directed to organise, by appropriate means, a meeting between the applicant and his lawyer. That meeting could take place in the presence of the personnel of the hospital where the applicant was detained, but outside their hearing. The lawyer was to be provided with the necessary time and facilities to consult with the applicant and help him in preparing the application before the European Court. The Russian Government was also requested not to prevent the lawyer from having such a meeting with his client at regular intervals in future. The lawyer, in turn, was obliged to be cooperative and comply with reasonable requirements of the hospital regulations.[154]

The HRC has issued similar requests. In the above-mentioned case of *Umarova v. Uzbekistan,* the Special Rapporteur, in complement to ordering interim relief with respect to the victim's state of health, asked the State party to allow *Mr. Umarova* to see his lawyer.[155]

4. Safety and Physical Integrity in General

Both adjudicators have also intervened outside the context of detention pending the proceedings when an applicant's safety, security or life has allegedly been in danger. In *Bitiyeva and X. v. Russia,* the ECtHR granted interim relief to a woman who claimed that she was being threatened and harassed by the military and law-enforcement bodies in Chechnya. She

---

[152] HRC, *Umarova v. Uzbekistan,* Communication No. 1449/2006, 19.10.2010, paras. 5.1 and 5.2.

[153] ECtHR, *Shtukaturov v. Russia,* Appl. No. 44009/05, 27.3.2008, § 3.

[154] *Shtukaturov v. Russia* (note 153), § 33.

[155] *Umarova v. Uzbekistan* (note 152), para. 5.2.

seized the Court under Articles 2, 3, 13 and 34 of the Convention after her mother, a political figure and the second applicant in the case, had been killed by a group of uniformed gunmen. She submitted that she had felt intimidated ever since and stated that the police was looking for her and had questioned her aunt about the proceedings in Strasbourg. In addition, she claimed that, after the killing of her mother, her brother had been detained and ill-treated by military forces. Acting under Rule 39 the Court "requested the Russian Government to take all measures to ensure that there was no hindrance in any way of the effective exercise of the second applicant's right of individual petition as provided by Article 34 of the Convention".[156] While the indicated measures referred explicitly to the protection of the effective right of individual petition under Article 34 ECHR, given the context of the case, one can also argue that it aimed at guaranteeing the applicant's general safety and security, thereby protecting her rights under Articles 2 or 3 of the Convention. A request similarly broad as the one in *Bitiyeva and X. v. Russia* was recently made in *R.R. and Others v. Hungary*. The case concerned an applicant who agreed to collaborate in a case against a drug trafficking mafia, of which he was once an active member. After he and his family were removed from a witness protection programme that should have shielded them from acts of vengeance, the Court requested the Hungarian government to take all necessary measures in order to guarantee the applicants' personal security pending the Court's examination of the case.[157]

Another, although peculiar, example of this category of interim measures can be found the recent interstate case of *Georgia v. Russia (II)*, in which the Court applied Rule 39 in the context of an armed conflict. Following the outbreak of hostilities in August 2008, Georgia requested the application of Rule 39 against Russia. The President of the Court himself "decided to apply Rule 39 of the Rules, calling upon both the High Contracting Parties concerned to honour their commitments under the Convention, particularly in respect of Articles 2 and 3 of the Convention".[158]

An example of the Committee's use of interim measures to protect a petitioner's safety, security or life can be found in *Katombe L. Tshishimbi v. Zaire*, for instance, where the alleged victim of an enforced disappearance benefitted from an interim measure. *Mr. Tshishimbi*, a military advisor to the oppositional Government of the time, had allegedly been abducted and was being ill-treated in the headquarters of the National Intelligence Ser-

---

[156] ECtHR, *Bitiyeva and X v. Russia*, Appl. Nos. 57953/00 and 37392/03, 21.6.2007, § 63.
[157] *R.R. and Others v. Hungary* (note 91), § 4.
[158] *Georgia v. Russia (II)* (note 17), § 5.

vice. The Special Rapporteur requested the State "to avoid any action that might cause irreparable harm to the alleged victim".[159] In *Gunaratna v. Sri Lanka*, a more recent case, the HRC granted interim protection to the petitioner and his family. *Mr. Gunaratna*, who was allegedly tortured by police forces, claimed to have received several death threats after he took legal action against his ill-treatment. The Special Rapporteur asked "the State party, under Rule 92 of its rules of procedure, to afford the author and his family protection against further intimidations and threats. The State party was also requested to provide the Committee, at its earliest convenience, with its comments on the author's allegations that he and his family have been denied such protection."[160]

5. Evictions

More recently, the HRC and the ECtHR have indicated interim measures to prevent evictions from being carried out. In *Yordanova and Others v. Bulgaria*, an illegal Roma settlement was about to be destroyed and its members to be forcibly removed. The ECtHR "indicated to the Government of Bulgaria, under Rule 39 of the Rules of Court, that the applicants should not be evicted from their houses (...) pending receipt by the Court of detailed information about any arrangements made by the authorities to secure housing for the children, elderly, handicapped or otherwise vulnerable individuals to be evicted". After the Court had received information that "two local social homes could provide five rooms each and that several elderly persons could be housed in a third home" and "that none of the applicants was willing to be separated from the community and housed under such conditions, not least because it was impossible, according to them, to earn a living outside the community", the Court "decided (...) to lift the interim measures, specifying that the decision was taken on the assumption that the Court and the applicants would be given sufficient notice of any change in the authorities' position for consideration to be given to a further measure under Rule 39 of the Rules of Court".[161]

The above-cited passages suggest that the ECtHR only applies interim measures if the eviction is likely to be conducted in a manner that would raise an Article 3 issue of extreme hardship, most notably vis-à-vis vulner-

---

[159] *Katombe L. Tshishimbi v. Zaire* (note 90), paras. 4.1 and 2.1-2.5.

[160] *Gunaratna v. Sri Lanka* (note 80), paras. 1.2 and 2.1-3.2, in particular para. 2.4.

[161] ECtHR, *Yordanova and Others v. Bulgaria* (dec.), Appl. No. 25446/06, 14.9.2010, A. para. 4.

able people.[162] In its case-law concerning forced evictions, the Court has, in multiple cases, not only found a violation of Article 3, but also of Articles 8 and 1 of Protocol 1.[163]

Only recently, a very similar case has come before the HRC and led to the first use of interim measures by the Special Rapporteur for the purpose of suspending an eviction. The case concerned the eviction order against a Roma community in Bulgaria whose housing had been *de facto* recognised by the public authorities. Acting under Rule 92, the Special Rapporteur on New Communications "requested the State party not to evict *Liliana Assenova Naidenova* and the other authors, and not to demolish their dwellings while their communication was under consideration by the Committee".[164] At a later stage, this request was reiterated and "the State party was requested to re-establish water supply to the community", which had been cut off in the meanwhile. The Special Rapporteur "was informed that, while the authors have not been forcibly evicted, cutting off the water supply to the Dobri Jeliazkov community could be considered as indirect means of achieving eviction".[165] On the merits, the HRC found that, if enforced, the eviction order would amount to an unlawful and arbitrary interference with the victims' homes (Article 17 ICCPR) as long as no satisfactory replacement housing was available and they risked becoming homeless. Thus, with respect to evictions and unlike the ECtHR, the HRC seems to apply interim measures also in cases in which the applicant has not claimed a risk of ill-treatment.

6. Protection of Indigenous Peoples

The HRC has, in several cases, adopted interim measures to protect the rights of indigenous peoples and the environment in which they live. As early as 1990, in *Lubicon Lake Band v. Canada,* interim relief was afforded to a group of indigenous people whose land was expropriated by the Canadian Government for the exploration of oil and gas. The author of the complaint alleged a violation of the right to self-determination and the right of

---

[162] In *A.M.B. and Others v. Spain,* Appl. No. 77842/12 (case pending at the time of writing), the Court halted the expulsion of a mother and her children from their residence. The applicants seized the Court under Article 3 and 8 ECHR.

[163] Protocol to the Convention for the Protection of Human Rights and Fundamental Freedoms, adopted 20.3.1952, E.T.S. 9, ratified by 45 states (status May 2013), entered into force 18.5.1954.

[164] *Liliana Assenova Naidenova et al. v. Bulgaria* (note 55), para. 1.2.

[165] *Liliana Assenova Naidenova et al. v. Bulgaria* (note 55), para. 10.

the members of the Lubicon Lake Band to dispose freely of their natural wealth and resources, as granted in Articles 1 and 27 ICCPR.[166] "In view of the seriousness of the author's allegations that the Lubicon Lake Band was at the verge of extinction", the HRC requested the State party "to avoid irreparable damage to [the author of the communication] and other members of the Lubicon Lake Band".[167] In another case involving an alleged violation of Article 27 ICCPR, the HRC even went a step further and adopted interim measures aiming at the protection of the environment itself. In *Länsman (Jouni E.) et al. v. Finland,* in which the logging of an area used by the Sami people for reindeer-breeding was at issue, the HRC requested Finland "to refrain from adopting measures which would cause irreparable harm to the environment which the authors claim is vital to their culture and livelihood".[168]

7. Miscellaneous Cases

Exceptionally, other situations not falling into one of the above categories have led to the application of interim measures. In *Hak-Chul Shin v. Republic of Korea,* the HRC asked the State party not to destroy a painting that, according to its author, was protected by the freedom of expression under Article 19 (2) of the Covenant.[169] The ECtHR, on the other hand, has, in multiple cases, indicated the preservation of embryos and foetuses that were the subject of an Article 8 claim (right to respect for private and family life)[170] and in *Guidi v. Italy*[171] it issued interim measures to order the Italian Goverment to expedite the payment of a so-called Pinto compensation. It also applied Rule 39 to request that a lawyer be appointed for an applicant who was not represented,[172] and – very exceptionally – in a death penalty case "to ensure that the requirements of Article 6 were complied with".[173]

---

[166] HRC, *Lubicon Lake Band v. Canada,* Communication No. 167/1984, 26.3.1990, para. 2.1.

[167] *Lubicon Lake Band v. Canada* (note 166), para. 29.3.

[168] *Jouni E. Länsman et al. v. Finland* (note 58), para. 4.1.

[169] HRC, *Hak-Chul Shin v. Republic of Korea,* Communication No. 926/2000, 16.3.2004, paras. 1.2 and 3.1.

[170] For a recent case, see ECtHR, *Knecht v. Romania,* Appl. No. 10048/10, 2.10.2012, §§ 4 and 18; see also *Evans v. the United Kingdom* (note 27), § 5.

[171] ECtHR, *Guidi v. Italy,* Appl. No. 18177/10 (case pending at the time of writing).

[172] See note 20.

[173] *Öcalan v. Turkey* (note 20), § 5.

8. Outside the Scope of Application

By implication, cases that do not fall within the above-proposed typology will, according to current practice, most likely not give rise to the application of interim measures by the Court or the Committee. Under the ECHR, this is particularly the case for requests regarding property and financial matters, such as a request to prevent bankruptcy or the destruction of property (Article 1 Protocol 1 claims).[174] The same goes for requests related to the right to respect for private and family life outside the context of removals. Furthermore, both the HRC and the ECtHR regularly refuse to indicate interim measures to order a person's release from detention allegedly contrary to Articles 5 ECHR and 9 ICCPR respectively, or to prevent potential violations of fair trial rights (Articles 6 ECHR and 14 ICCPR claims).

V. The Special Category of Protection Measures Before the HRC

In its use of interim measures under Rule 92, the Committee has developed a distinct category of measures, so-called protection measures. The proposal for a definition of these measures put forward by *Sir Nigel Rodley* reads as follows:

> Protection measures are to be distinguished from interim measures in that their purpose is not to prevent irreparable damage affecting the object of the communication itself, but simply to protect those who might suffer adverse consequences for having submitted the communication, or to call the State party's attention to their aggravating situation linked to the alleged violations of their rights.[175]

The Committee currently applies protection measures without mentioning them in its Views and despite the fact that it lacks a legal basis for doing so. For this reason, it is difficult at this point to grasp, in detail, the threshold required for the application of such measures or their use in practice. Similarly, the requirements on a request for protection measures have yet to be clearly delineated.

---

[174]	*F. Tulkens* (note 50), 33.
[175]	Interview with *Sir Nigel Rodley* (note 8).

In a series of disappearance complaints against Algeria, *Grioua v. Algeria*,[176] *Boucherf v. Algeria*[177] and *Kimouche v. Algeria*,[178] the HRC asked the State party not to invoke the provisions of a draft amnesty law against individuals who had submitted or might submit communications to the Committee.[179] In each of the cases, counsel for the victims had argued that the draft law would put "(…) at risk those persons who were still missing, and (…) deprive victims of an effective remedy".[180] These remain the only cases to date in which the HRC indicated a measure without referring to Rule 92 or the term "interim". One can therefore assume that the HRC applied protection measures in these particular cases. In *Alzery v. Sweden*, although the Committee explicitly based the measure it indicated on Rule 92, the protection afforded did not relate to the object of the complaint. Accordingly, it could represent another example of the indication of a protection measure. *Mr. Alzery*, an Egyptian national, entered Sweden in 1999 as he was allegedly persecuted in Egypt for his opposition to the government. In 2002, the Swedish authorities expelled him and handed him over to Egyptian military security at Cairo airport. Subsequently, he was held in different prisons, where he was allegedly tortured and ill-treated. In 2005, he lodged a complaint with the HRC, claiming, *inter alia*, that Sweden – by expelling him to Egypt – had violated the Covenant. During his detention in Egypt, the Swedish Embassy approached *Mr. Alzery* on several occasions and inquired about different issues of his complaint, which, according to his counsel, put him at great risk vis-à-vis the Egyptian authorities.[181] The Special Rapporteur "in the light of counsel's comments on the State party's submissions (…) and of the material before the Committee related to the author's situation, requested, pursuant to Rule 92 of its Rules of Procedure, that the State party take necessary measures to ensure that the author was not exposed to a foreseeable risk of substantial personal harm as a result of any act of the State party in respect of the author".[182]

In practice "interim" and "protection" measures may overlap and can be difficult to distinguish: the alleged victim, for example, might benefit from an interim measure preventing irreparable harm to his or her person or claim, whereas protection measures could be indicated for the alleged victim's family or legal counsel.

---

[176] HRC, *Grioua v. Algeria*, Communication No. 1327/2004, 10.7.2007.
[177] HRC, *Kimouche v. Algeria*, Communication No. 1328/2004, 10.7.2007.
[178] HRC, *Boucherf v. Algeria*, Communication No. 1196/2003, 30.3.2006.
[179] See, for example, *Kimouche v. Algeria* (note 177), paras. 1.3 and 9.
[180] *Kimouche v. Algeria* (note 177), para. 1.2.
[181] HRC, *Alzery v. Sweden*, Communication No. 1416/2005, 25.10.2006, para. 6.2.
[182] *Alzery v. Sweden* (note 181), para. 2.3.

VI. Non-Compliance With Interim Measures

1. Establishing Non-Compliance

As *Louis Henkin* might say, most states implement most of the requests for interim measures most of the time.[183] Nonetheless, in both of the systems considered, there have been some significant exceptions to this rule. In practice, it is usually the applicant who brings the alleged non-compliance to the attention of the adjudicator. It is then up to the latter to ultimately decide, at the stage of the merits of a case,[184] whether an interim measure was complied with or not. Yet, both the HRC and the ECtHR can already express their views on the issue of compliance at an earlier stage of the proceedings: first, the adjudicator may reiterate an interim measure which was not yet – but could still be – implemented, and second, in cases where non-compliance has already resulted in the exposure of the applicant to a risk of irreparable harm, the adjudicator can decide to deplore it by way of a *note verbale* to the government concerned.[185]

As most cases of interim measures take the form of requests for a specific abstention, establishing non-compliance is a relatively simple task and a factual rather than a legal question that is often undisputed by the parties (e. g., a determination of whether the applicant was executed or extradited). However, if an interim measure requires positive action or is formulated in a very general manner, establishing (non-)compliance can be more complicated. While not much is known about the HRC's approach in such situations, the ECtHR held in *Paladi v. Moldova,* with reference to the ICJ's judgment in *LaGrand (Germany v. United States of America)*,[186] that "(t)he point of departure for verifying whether the respondent State has complied with the measure is the formulation of the interim measure itself (...)" and that the Court must examine "whether the respondent State complied with the letter and the spirit of the interim measure indicated to it".[187]

In *Makharadze and Sikharulidze v. Georgia*, for example, the Court had to interpret a positive interim measure that required the applicant be placed

---

[183] For the Court see ECRE/ELENA Report (note 10), 17 and 18.

[184] *Paladi v. Moldova* (note 55), § 90: "It is for the Court to verify compliance with the interim measure (...)."

[185] See below, VI. 2. b), 368 et seq.

[186] ICJ, *LaGrande Case (Germany v. United States of America)*, Judgment of 27.6.2001, I.C.J. Reports 2001, 466, §§ 111-115.

[187] *Paladi v. Moldova* (note 55), § 91.

"in a specialised medical establishment capable of dispensing appropriate anti-tuberculosis treatment":

> (…) the major qualifying element of the measure was for a medical establishment in question, whether in the civil or penitentiary sector, to be specialised in treatment of tuberculosis. Consequently, a legitimate question arises as to whether the new prison hospital could have represented, at the material time, such a specialised medical unit (…). However, the response is negative, since, as was already established above, that hospital did not possess either the necessary laboratory equipment or the second-line anti-tuberculosis drugs, and, most importantly, its medical staff did not possess, at the material time, the necessary skills for the management of complex treatment of multi-drug resistant forms of tuberculosis. All those serious deficiencies of the prison hospital were or should have been known to the respondent Government, as the qualified medical experts had denounced on several occasions the adequacy of the treatment dispensed to the applicant in the penitentiary sector, noting his rapid decline and equally recommending his transfer to a hospital specialised in tuberculosis treatment (…).[188]

In *Abdulkhakov v. Russia*, relying on the spirit rather than the letter of the measure, the Court held that the transfer of an applicant to Tajikistan amounted to a failure to comply with the interim measure that was, by nature of its wording, supposed to prevent the applicant's removal to Uzbekistan.[189]

In another case, *Savriddin Dzhurayev v. Russia*, where the Court also requested the Russian Government to suspend an extradition to Tajikistan, the applicant was forcibly removed by way of a special operation in which State agents were found to have been involved. The Government argued that it complied with the indicated measure as the applicant's "(…) transfer to Tajikistan had not taken place through the extradition procedure, which had been immediately stayed following the Court's (…)" request. Rejecting this overly literal interpretation of the measure, the Court held in reference to *Paladi v. Moldova* that it "must have regard not only to the letter but also to the spirit of the interim measure indicated (…) and indeed, to its

---

[188] ECtHR, *Makharadze and Sikharulidze v. Georgia*, Appl. No. 35254/07, 22.11.2011, §§ 35 and 101.

[189] *Abdulkhakov v. Russia* (note 120), §§ 4 and 227: "The Court considers that in certain circumstances a transfer of an applicant against his will to a country other than the country in which he allegedly faces a risk of ill-treatment may amount to a failure to comply with such an interim measure. If it were otherwise, the Contracting States would be able to transfer an applicant to a third country which is not party to the Convention, from where they might be further removed to their country of origin, thereby circumventing the interim measure applied by the Court and depriving the applicant of effective Convention protection."

very purpose". In the case at hand, the purpose of the measure was "to prevent the applicant's exposure to a real risk of ill-treatment in the hands of the Tajik authorities. (...) By using another domestic procedure for the applicant's removal to the country of destination or, even more alarming, by allowing him to be arbitrarily removed to that country in a manifestly unlawful manner (...) the State frustrated the purpose of the interim measure (...)" and consequently acted in disrespect thereof.[190]

2. Consequences of Non-Compliance

a) Autonomous Treaty Violation

If the HRC considers a State party to have failed to comply with an interim measure, it is its established practice to find, at the stage of the merits, a breach of the Optional Protocol "apart from any other violation of the Covenant charged to a State party in a communication".[191] The Committee reiterated this principle in the above-mentioned case of *Lyubov Kovaleva and Tatyana Kozyar v. Belarus*, a particularly severe case of state failure to abide by interim measures. On 13.5.2012, the Belarusian authorities executed *Mr. Kovaleva* notwithstanding the HRC's repeated request to refrain from doing so. Referencing the relevant passages from its views in *Dante Piandong et al. v. The Philippines*, the Committee held that "(h)aving been notified of the communication and the Committee's request for interim measures, the State party breached its obligations under the Protocol by executing the alleged victim before the Committee concluded its consideration of the communication".[192]

Other countries have, in the recent past, similarly disregarded requests for interim relief. Strikingly many of these are central Asian states. In *Shukurova v. Tajikistan* and *Tolipkhuzhaev v. Uzbekistan*, petitioners were executed even though the Committee had requested the suspension of their executions,[193] and in *Israil v. Kazakhstan* and *Maksudov et al. v. Kyr-*

---

[190] *Savriddin Dzhurayev v. Russia* (note 6), §§ 215-217.

[191] *Dante Piandong et al. v. The Philippines* (note 93), para. 5.2; see, *inter alia*, HRC, *Saidova v. Tajikistan*, Communication No. 964/2001, 8.7.2004, paras. 4.1-4.4; HRC, *Shukurova v. Tajikistan*, Communication No. 1044/2002, 17.3.2006, paras. 6.1-6.3; HRC, *Tolipkhuzhaev v. Uzbekistan*, Communication No. 1280/2004, 22.7.2009, paras. 6.1-6.4.

[192] *Lyubov Kovaleva and Tatyana Kozyar v. Belarus* (note 84), para. 9.4.

[193] *Shukurova v. Tajikistan* (note 191); *Tolipkhuzhaev v. Uzbekistan* (note 191).

gyzstan, the State parties extradited the applicants in defiance of the HRC's grant of interim relief.[194]

While the Committee found a breach of the Optional Protocol in all of these cases, three observations can be made. Firstly, it is interesting to note that the Committee never specified which exact article(s) of the Protocol a State party has contravened by not complying with an interim measure. Rather, it has limited itself to referring to the state's general obligation to cooperate in good faith. Secondly, although it considers a failure to implement interim measures to also contravene the Covenant, more precisely Article 2 (3) thereof,[195] this consideration never found its way into the Committee's case-law. And thirdly, according to the Committee's practice, non-compliance can never be justified, but instead always entails a breach of the Optional Protocol. Hence, the Committee has, in its case-law, never addressed the different reasons put forward by a State party for disregarding a measure.[196]

Under the ECHR, a failure by a Contracting State to comply with interim measures usually amounts to a separate violation of the right of individual application guaranteed by Article 34 *in fine* of the ECHR. After *Mamatkulov and Askarov v. Turkey,* some doubts remained as to whether non-compliance must lead to an actual hindrance of the effective exercise of the right of individual application in order for the Court to find a violation of Article 34 ECHR.[197] In its subsequent case-law, the Court clarified that any disrespect for a Rule 39 request is in itself to be seen as such a violation, regardless of whether the applicant experienced any difficulties pursuing his application with the Court.[198] This is reflected in the Court's current for-

---

[194] *Israil v. Kazakhstan* (note 137); *Maksudov et al. v. Kyrgyzstan* (note 118).

[195] See above III. 5., 344.

[196] The only exception being *Dante Piandong et al. v. The Philippines* (note 93), para. 5.3.

[197] These doubts stemmed from the following statement of the Court: "(...) In the present case, because of the extradition of the applicants to Uzbekistan, the level of protection which the Court was able to afford the rights which they were asserting under Articles 2 and 3 of the Convention was irreversibly reduced. (...) In the present case, the applicants were extradited and thus, by reason of their having lost contact with their lawyers, denied an opportunity to have further inquiries made in order for evidence in support of their allegations under Article 3 of the Convention to be obtained" (*Mamatkulov and Askarov v. Turkey* [note 4], § 108).

[198] ECtHR, *Olaechea Cahuas v. Spain*, Appl. No. 24668/03, 10.8.2006, ECHR 2006-X, §§ 75-83, particularly § 81 *in fine*: "Failure to comply with an interim measure indicated by the Court because of the existence of a risk is in itself alone a serious hindrance, at that particular time, of the effective exercise of the right of individual application." See also *Paladi v. Moldova* (note 55), § 89: "For the same reasons, the fact that the damage which an interim measure was designed to prevent subsequently turns out not to have occurred despite a State's failure to act in full compliance with the interim measure is equally irrelevant for the assessment of whether this State has fulfilled its obligations under Article 34." For a detailed discus-

mula, which was first applied in *Paladi v. Moldova* and stipulates that "(…) Article 34 will be breached if the authorities of a Contracting State fail to take all steps which could reasonably have been taken in order to comply with the measure indicated by the Court".[199]

In the same judgment, the Court also introduced an exception to this rule. In cases in which there was an "objective impediment which prevented compliance" with the interim measure and as long as the Government took "all reasonable steps to remove the impediment" and kept the Court "informed about the situation", a State would not be held accountable under Article 34 ECHR.[200] The Court construes this exception very narrowly and has only allowed States to thus discharge their responsibility under Article 34 in a very few cases. Examples include cases in which an interim measure was indicated only very shortly before the litigious act was to be carried out, making it impossible for the Court to determine whether the authorities could have reacted in due time. Thus, in *M.B. and Others v. Turkey*, for instance, the Court held that "(h)aving regard to the short time which elapsed between the receipt of the fax message by the Government and the deportation of the applicants, the Court considers that it has not been established that the Government had failed to demonstrate the necessary diligence in complying with the measure indicated by the Court".[201] Another constellation in which non-compliance might not necessarily amount to a violation of Article 34 ECHR is that where an applicant consented to the litigious act that is to be prevented by the interim measure.[202] This could be inferred from *Rajaratnam Sivanathan v. United Kingdom*, where the Court struck a complaint off the list after the applicant had wished to pursue his deportation although the Court requested the latter to be stayed under Rule 39.[203]

---

sion of *Olaechea Cahuas v. Spain*, see Y. Haeck/C. Burbano Herrera/L. Zwaak (note 59), 41 et seq.

[199] *Paladi v. Moldova* (note 55), § 88; for a recent case, see *Rrapo v. Albania* (note 115), § 82, or *Al-Saadoon and Mufdhi v. the United Kingdom* (note 114), § 161.

[200] *Paladi v. Moldova* (note 55), § 92.

[201] ECtHR, *M.B. and Others v. Turkey*, Appl. No. 36009/08, 15.6.2010, § 48; another example is ECtHR, *Muminov v. Russia*, Appl. No. 42502/06, 11.12.2008, § 137.

[202] See Y. Haeck/C. Burbano Herrera/L. Zwaak, Strasbourg's Interim Measures Under Fire: Does the Rising Number of State Incompliances with Interim Measures Pose a Threat to the European Court of Human Rights?, European Yearbook on Human Rights 11 (2011), 393 et seq.

[203] ECtHR, *Rajaratnam Sivanathan v. United Kingdom* (dec.), Appl. No. 38108/07, 3.2.2009: "The Court notes that the Government are unable to provide a copy of the document signed by the applicant but accepts that such a document was signed. It further accepts that the applicant's return to Sri Lanka was entirely voluntary and that he gave written informed consent to that effect. The Court also recognises that new procedures have been im-

No objective impediment is posed, however, by conflicting international obligations stemming, for example, from extradition treaties[204] or domestic law, which cannot be relied upon for not implementing the measure ordered.[205] This is illustrated by the above-mentioned case of *Rrapo v. Albania*, in which the Albanian authorities extradited *Mr. Rrapo* to the US even though he benefitted from an interim measure issued by the Court.

Similarly, the argument that the competent authorities were not aware of the indication of interim relief, although the Government was informed of the application of Rule 39 in due time, has so far failed to justify non-compliance with Article 34 of the Convention.[206] Further, in *Makharadze and Sikharulidze v. Georgia*, the Court rejected the Government's claim that a waiting list constituted an objective impediment to the transfer of the applicant "to an establishment specialised in tuberculosis treatment". The Court noted that "the only possible objective impediment to the fulfilment of the measure in question could have been the absence of such a specialised establishment in Georgia at the material time".[207]

In *D.B. v. Turkey*, the Turkish authorities initially prevented an applicant in detention from meeting with a lawyer because the latter did not submit a power of attorney proving that he was the applicant's representative. The

---

plemented by the Government which ensure that in all future cases of voluntary departure the appropriate documentation will be available. Finally, the Court observes that the applicant has not communicated with the Court since his removal and, prior to his removal, he did not provide any address in Sri Lanka or in the United Kingdom at which he could be contacted. It therefore considers that, in these circumstances, the applicant may be regarded as no longer wishing to pursue his application, within the meaning of Article 37 § 1 (a) of the Convention. Furthermore, in accordance with Article 37 § 1 in fine, the Court finds no special circumstances regarding respect for human rights as defined in the Convention and its Protocols which require the continued examination of the case. Accordingly, it is appropriate to discontinue the application of Article 29 § 3, lift the interim measure indicated under Rule 39 of the Rules of Court and strike the case out of the list."

[204] *Al-Saadoon and Mufdhi v. the United Kingdom* (note 114), § 162; *Rrapo v. Albania* (note 115), § 86.

[205] *Rrapo v. Albania* (note 115), § 87: "...(N)either the existing state of national law expounded by the Government, notably the alleged legal vacuum concerning the continuation of detention beyond the time-limit provided for in Article 499 of the CCP, nor deficiencies in the national judicial system and the difficulties encountered by the authorities in seeking to achieve their legislative and regulatory objectives, can be relied upon to the applicant's detriment, in the absence of a final domestic court judgment authorising his extradition, or avoid or negate the respondent State's obligations under the Convention(...)."

[206] See, for example, ECtHR, *Zokhidov v. Russia*, Appl. No. 67286/10, 5.2.2013, § 196: "Accordingly, it was for those State bodies, including the Russian GPO and the Office of the Representative of the Russian Federation at the European Court of Human Rights, to ensure that the information on the Court's application of the interim measure was brought to the attention of all authorities involved."

[207] *Makharadze and Sikharulidze v. Georgia* (note 188), § 102.

Court dismissed what it described as "administrative obtuseness", considering that it applied Rule 39 precisely to enable a lawyer to meet with the applicant "with a view to obtaining a power of attorney and information concerning the alleged risks that the applicant would face in Iran".[208]

In *Aleksanyan v. Russia*, the Russian Government failed, for over two months, to transfer the detained applicant to a specialised medical institution as requested by the Court under Rule 39. The Court rejected the Government's argument "that the delay in the implementation of this measure was fully imputable to the applicant himself, who refused to be subjected to specific analysis and treatment".[209]

Finally, if non-abidance with an interim measure amounts to a violation of Article 34, the Court may, in addition to finding a violation of the Convention, afford just satisfaction to the applicant for any pecuniary and non-pecuniary damage suffered.[210] Hence, in *Mamatkulov and Askarov v. Turkey,* the Court awarded each applicant EUR 5,000 for the non-pecuniary damage caused by Turkey's failure to comply with the interim measures and thereby with its obligations under Article 34.[211]

b) A Diplomatic Way of Addressing Non-Compliance

Apart from by finding an autonomous treaty violation, non-compliance has also been reproved by non-legal means. The ECtHR's judgment in *Rrapo v. Albania,* for example, discloses the content of a letter sent by the Registrar of the Court to the Albanian Government on the same day that the latter had confirmed to the Court that it had disregarded the interim measure indicated by the Court.

> The President of the Court ... has instructed me to express on his behalf his profound regret at the decision taken by your authorities to extradite *Mr. Almir Rrapo* to the United States of America in flagrant disrespect of the Court's interim measure adopted under Rule 39 of the Rules of Court.[212]

---

[208] ECtHR, *D.B. v. Turkey*, Appl. No. 33526/08, 13.7.2010, § 67.

[209] *Aleksanyan v. Russia* (note 150), § 223 and § 230: "The Government did not suggest that the measure indicated under Rule 39 was practically unfeasible; on the contrary, the applicant's subsequent transfer to Hospital no. 60 shows that this measure was relatively easy to implement. In the circumstances, the Court considers that the non-implementation of the measure is fully attributable to the authorities' reluctance to cooperate with the Court."

[210] Article 41 ECHR.

[211] *Mamatkulov and Askarov v. Turkey* (note 4), § 134.

[212] *Rrapo v. Albania* (note 115), § 38.

In addition to asking for further information as to the reasons why the interim measure was not complied with, the Registrar also noted:

> As an indication of the seriousness with which he views this turn of events, the President has asked that the Chairman of the Committee of Ministers, the President of the Parliamentary Assembly, the Commissioner for Human Rights and the Secretary General of the Council of Europe be informed immediately.[213]

Sending such a letter seems to have become standard procedure in removal cases before the ECtHR where there has been non-compliance with the interim measures indicated. This practice certainly serves to gather more information for a possible judgment on the merits, in which the Court must determine whether the state can be held accountable under Article 34 ECHR for its failure to implement the interim measure. Moreover, the message of regret conveyed and the fact that other bodies of the Council of Europe are informed, which puts the issue of non-compliance on their agenda,[214] can create useful diplomatic pressure for the purpose of strengthening future observance of such measures. This is particularly important in cases which are declared inadmissible or struck out at a later stage. In these instances, non-compliance with an interim measure would otherwise not be reproved at all.

The HRC has also deplored non-compliance by way of a diplomatic note from the Committee Chairperson to the Government concerned, and has requested additional information from the State party. In *Sholam Weiss v. Austria,* for example, the Chairperson asked the Government for "an explanation of how it intended to secure compliance with such requests in the future".[215] Belarus's repeated failure to suspend the execution of death row inmates has even led the Committee to issue press releases during the course of its sessions informing the public about the State party's breach of the Optional Protocol and expressing its dismay and indignation.[216]

---

[213] *Rrapo v. Albania* (note 115).

[214] See, for example, Council of Europe, Parliamentary Assembly Resolution 1788 (2011), Preventing harm to refugees and migrants in extradition and expulsion cases: Rule 39 indications by the European Court of Human Rights, 26.1.2011; see also Rule 39 (2) of the Rules of Court: Where it is considered appropriate, immediate notice of the measure adopted in a particular case may be given to the Committee of Ministers. In the context of its task to supervise the execution of judgments of the Court according to Article 46 (2) ECHR, the Committee of Ministers has also dealt with the issue of non-abidance with interim measures (Council of Europe, Committee of Ministers, Interim Resolution CM/ResDH(2010)83, Execution of the judgments of the European Court of Human Rights, *Ben Khemais against Italy*, 3.6.2010).

[215] HRC, *Sholam Weiss v. Austria*, Communication No. 1086/2002, 3.4.2003, para. 5.1.

[216] HRC, Annual Report, 100th (11.-29.10.2010), 101st (14.3.-1.4.2011) and 102nd session (11.-29.7.2011), A/66/40 (Vol. I), para. 50/51.

VII. Conclusion and Outlook

This comprehensive comparison has shown that, with respect to key issues, the HRC's and the ECtHR's use of interim measures displays surprisingly strong similarities. However, closer analysis also reveals the existence of some important divergences, an awareness of which can be important for applicant and adjudicator alike.

Broad statutory provisions allowed the ECtHR and the HRC to develop a flexible and pragmatic procedure to take into account the urgency with which and the very early stage of the proceedings in which interim relief is decided upon. While, under both systems considered, an applicant requesting interim relief must in principle make plausible that he faces an imminent risk of irreversible harm, the Committee has adopted a more lenient approach by indicating provisional interim measures in cases of doubt as to the imminence, credibility or irreparability of the alleged harm.

The ECtHR has partly codified some formal and substantive requirements that a request for interim measures is expected to meet in order to be properly examined and potentially successful. Although research has shown that these requirements also largely hold true before the HRC, there is currently no information document available on the matter. Because knowledge of the requirements that must be met by a request for interim relief is crucial for applicants, it is suggested that the HRC publishes a document similar to the Court's Practice Direction.

As to transparency in general, it is to be welcomed that, with respect to the Committee and the Court, suggestions have been put forward to provide more information on the adjudicators' reasons for granting or refusing interim measures in particular cases. It remains to be seen, however, if and in what form these suggestions can be put into practice.

The most striking difference between the Committee's and the Court's uses of interim measures lies in the scope of application of their respective measures. Although both adjudicators grant interim relief primarily to protect applicants from risks for life and limb, they also do so in other situations. It is the use of interim measures beyond this mutual field of application that is not identical for the Committee and the Court. In the context of deportations, the ECtHR has adopted a more inclusive approach and can indicate – based on its broader understanding of the *non-refoulement* principle – interim measures to prevent potential violations of Articles 5, 6 or 8 ECHR. Outside of the *refoulement* context, however, it is the Committee that uses interim measures in a broader way, as is illustrated by recent examples of its jurisprudence concerning eviction, the protection of the environment, indigenous peoples or the freedom of expression. In addition, the Committee has developed a practice of indicating a new category of measures, thereby further broadening the scope of possible protection pending the consideration of a communication. Even though the Committee has yet to define the precise contours of these protection measures and is certainly well advised to create an explicit legal basis for their use, this development must be welcomed.

The Committee's willingness to broaden the scope of interim relief can be explained by virtue of the greater leeway enjoyed by the Special Rapporteur for New Communications and Interim Measures. At the Court, on the other hand, it seems that the current situation is not favourable to such an expansion of interim protection. On the contrary: the influx of requests for interim measures to the already overburdened ECtHR has alerted Court and Contracting parties alike and one observes that, since the establishment of the centralised procedure, a stricter threshold for granting interim relief is being applied.

While arguments can be made in favour as well as against an expansion of the use of interim measures, the eviction case of *Liliana Assenova Naidenova et al. v. Bulgaria* demonstrates that divergences in practice between the Committee and the Court may result in increased forum shopping with respect to interim relief.[217] Consequently, applicants who could take their claims to either Geneva or Strasbourg may envisage petitioning the Committee rather than the Court if they seek protection in a situation not involving risks for life and limb and outside the *refoulement* context. However, it must also be borne in mind that the Court will not consider an application that has already been submitted to the Committee.[218] Thus, an applicant must decide at the very outset of the litigation whether the more auspicious prospects of interim relief before the Committee outweigh the possibility of obtaining a legally binding judgment and eventually being awarded just satisfaction in Strasbourg.

The Court and the Committee have both established an obligation for states to abide by a request for interim measures. The reluctance of the Committee to refer to its interim measures as legally binding in the way that the Court does is arguably linked to the non-binding nature of its Views on

---

[217] In *Sholam Weiss v. Austria* (note 215), paras. 2.9, 2.11 and 1.2, an applicant who was refused interim relief before the ECtHR withdrew his application from the Court and petitioned the HRC, which subsequently requested the staying of his extradition, see also *J. F. Flauss*, Discussion, in: G. Cohen-Jonathan/J.-F. Flauss (eds.), Mesures conservatoires et droits fondamentaux, 2005, 212 et seq.

[218] Article 35 (2) (b) ECHR.

the merits. In order to reinforce and consolidate the authority of interim measures, it is suggested to codify, if possible at treaty level, the binding effect of interim measures. Codification of their binding nature could foster compliance with interim measures, which is key for the effectiveness of interim relief and ultimately also for the protection system as a whole.

Part IV
A Universal Judicial Enforcement of Human Rights?

[28]

Human Rights Law Review 7:1 © The Author [2007]. Published by Oxford University Press.
All rights reserved. For Permissions, please email: journals.permissions@oxfordjournals.org
doi:10.1093/hrlr/ngl026   Advance Access published on 27 January 2007

The Need for a World Court of Human Rights

Manfred Nowak*

1. Relationship between the Human Rights Council and the World Court

On 15 March 2006, the General Assembly of the United Nations finally decided to replace the present Commission on Human Rights with a new body at a higher level, the Human Rights Council.[1] One of the main new features of the Council will be the universal periodic review of the human rights performance of all States, based on 'reliable and objective information [. . .] in a manner which ensures universality of coverage and equal treatment with respect to all States'.[2] As one of the explicit purposes of this reform of the UN human rights system was to depoliticise the Commission, it is evident that the so-called 'peer review' cannot be meant to be an assessment of the human rights situation in States by other States. This would not only duplicate the work of treaty bodies and special procedures,[3] it would also mean a major step backwards.

The universal periodic review must, therefore, be understood as a follow-up mechanism similar to the one practised in the Council of Europe in relation to the European Convention on Human Rights (ECHR). There the assessment of the actual human rights situation is entrusted to the permanent and fully

*Director of the Ludwig Boltzmann Institute of Human Rights at the University of Vienna and United Nations Special Rapporteur on Torture. This paper was presented at an Expert Meeting on 'The United Nations Human Rights Council: Facing the Challenges', Madrid, 7 April 2006. (manfred.nowak@univie.ac.at).

1   GA Res. 60/251, 15 March 2006, A/RES/60/251. This resolution was adopted by a vote of 170 in favour, four against (Israel, Marshall Islands, Palau and United States), with three abstentions (Belarus, Iran and Venezuela).
2   Para. 5(e), GA Res. 60/251, ibid.
3   Para. 5, GA Res. 60/251, ibid., explicitly states that 'such a mechanism shall complement and not duplicate the work of treaty bodies'.

independent European Court of Human Rights which renders binding judgments on individual and inter-State complaints[4] and the Committee of
Ministers of the Council of Europe, its highest political body, whose role is to
supervise the execution of the Court's judgments. The United Nations lacks a
similar division of labour between expert and political bodies, which is one of
the main reasons for the inefficiency and the high level of politicisation of the
UN human rights system. While the Commission on Human Rights based its
assessment of country situations to some extent on the reports and recommendations of special rapporteurs and other experts of the Commission, the treaty
monitoring bodies were left alone in supervising the implementation of their
non-binding decisions on individual complaints as well as their concluding
observations and recommendations relating to the State reporting and inquiry
procedures. The creation of the Human Rights Council as the main political
human rights body of the United Nations with a stronger mandate demands a
stronger counter-part among the independent expert bodies in order to develop
a functioning division of labour between political and expert bodies.

2. Overcoming the Legacy of the Cold War

The treaty body system of the United Nations is a product of the Cold War, which
only allowed for the lowest common denominator between the East, West and
South. Western countries had introduced a strong division between civil and
political rights on the one hand, and economic, social and cultural rights on
the other, and permitted a complaint system only with respect to the former
category. Socialist countries promoted the indivisibility and interdependence of
all human rights, but considered at the same time any efficient system of international human rights monitoring, above all individual complaints mechanisms, as an undue interference with their internal affairs. The newly
independent States of the South seemed to be only interested in a few selected
human rights problems, such as the fight against racism, apartheid and
colonialism and the collective rights of peoples to self-determination and
development. The only mandatory monitoring system on which the United
Nations could, therefore, agree when adopting the two International Covenants
in 1966 and the other core treaties was a fairly weak State reporting system
which was supplemented by an equally weak and optional inter-State
and individual communication system before quasi-judicial expert bodies lacking the competence to hand down any binding decisions.

   In contrast to the United Nations, the Council of Europe and the
Organization of American States had already during the Cold War established

---

4   Article 46(2), European Convention on Human Rights 1950 (as amended by Protocols 3, 5, 8
    and 11) (ECHR), ETS No. 5.

fully independent human rights courts with the power to render final and binding judgments on both individual and inter-State complaints.[5] In addition, the Organization of African Unity (now the African Union) decided in 1998 to establish an African Court on Human and Peoples' Rights.[6] In other words, all three world regions where a regional organisation for the protection of human rights exists decided to entrust the decision on human rights complaints to a regional human rights court. Only the Asian region lacks a human rights court, but this has to do with the general lack of a regional organisation and human rights system. In view of this broad consensus on the need for human rights complaints to be decided by an independent court, the often cited argument that the creation of a World Court of Human Rights was politically far too controversial for States does not seem to be very convincing.

The practice of individual and inter-State communications before the UN treaty bodies is indeed not very encouraging. Despite the fact that Article 11 of the Convention on the Elimination of Racial Discrimination 1966 (CERD)[7] even provides for a mandatory inter-State communication procedure which had entered into force already in 1970, not one of the 169 States Parties to CERD has so far availed itself of this opportunity *vis à vis* any of the other States Parties where systematic racial discrimination and ethnic cleansing had even led to genocide. The same holds true for the optional inter-State communications procedures under the International Covenant on Civil and Political Rights 1966 (CCPR)[8] and the Convention Against Torture and Other Cruel, Inhuman or Degrading Treatment or Punishment 1984 (CAT).[9] While the full-time European Court of Human Rights presently decides by a binding judgment on some 1000 individual complaints per year (in relation to 46 States Parties to the ECHR), all UN treaty bodies competent to deal with individual communications together (the Human Rights Committee, the Racial Discrimination Committee, the Committee against Torture and recently also the Committee on the Elimination of Discrimination against Women) have handed down only little more than 500 non-binding decisions on the merits ('final views') within almost 30 years in relation to more than 100 States Parties![10] Although the

---

5   The European Court of Human Rights was established in 1959 pursuant to Section IV, ECHR, but the full division of labour between a single and permanent Court and the Committee of Ministers as a political body entrusted only with the supervision of the execution of the Court's judgments was only achieved with the entry into force of the Protocol 11 to the ECHR on 1 November 1998. The Inter-American Court of Human Rights was established in 1979 by the American Convention on Human Rights 1969 (ACHR), OAS No. 36.

6   Protocol to the African Charter of Human and Peoples' Rights on the Establishment of an African Court on Human and Peoples' Rights 1998, 6 IHRR 891 (1999). The Protocol entered into force on 1 January 2004. The judges have been elected, but the Court has not yet begun hearing cases.

7   660 UNTS 196.

8   999 UNTS 171.

9   1465 UNTS 85.

10   Nowak, *Introduction to the International Human Rights Regime* (Leiden: Martinus Nijhoff, 2003) at 100.

254   *HRLR* **7** (2007), 251–259

Human Rights Committee has done its utmost to interpret its powers under the first Optional Protocol to the CCPR 1966[11] in a broad manner and renders highly professional quasi-judicial decisions on the merits, this procedure seems to be very little known in the world, and/or the billions of human beings in all regions of the world entitled to lodge complaints with the UN treaty bodies have little confidence in this procedure. The Petitions Team in the Office of the UN High Commissioner for Human Rights in Geneva is a small and grossly understaffed unit which cannot be compared to the Registry of the European Court of Human Rights in Strasbourg. No political body in the United Nations feels responsible to supervise the implementation of the treaty bodies' decisions by States Parties which has led to the absurd situation that the treaty bodies themselves have developed their own follow-up procedures. No wonder that many States Parties simply ignore the decisions of the treaty bodies, and even Western States increasingly argue that they are not bound by the decisions of the Human Rights Committee.[12]

The very notion of human rights implies that rights-holders must have some possibility to hold duty bearers accountable for not living up to their legally binding human rights obligations. This basic insight has found legal expression in the right to an effective remedy against violations of human rights, as laid down in Article 2(3) of the CCPR. This right to an effective remedy and reparation has been further developed by the so-called van Boven/Bassiouni Guidelines on the Right to a Remedy and Reparation, which were adopted by the General Assembly on 16 December 2005.[13] By far the most effective method to implement the right to an effective remedy on the international level is to allow direct access of the rights holders to a fully independent international human rights court with the power to render binding judgments and to grant adequate reparation to the victims of human rights violations.

The establishment of the Human Rights Council seems to be the right moment to start seriously thinking about the creation of a World Court of Human Rights as its independent counter-part!

---

11   999 UNTS 171.

12   See the cases of *Perterer v Austria* (1015/01), CCPR/C/81/D/1015/2001 (2004), as to which see E.U. Network of Independent Experts on Fundamental Rights, Report on the Situation of Fundamental Rights in Austria in 2004, submitted to the Network by Manfred Nowak and Alexander Lubich, 3 January 2005, CDR-CDF/AT/2004, available at: http://cridho.cpdr.-ucl.ac.be, at 82–4; and *Derksen and Bakker v the Netherlands* (976/01), CCPR/C/80/D/976/2001 (2004), as to which see Nowak, 'Diskriminatie van buiten echt geboren wezen onder de anw Nederland botst met VN-Mensenrechtencomité', (2005) 30 *NJCM Bulletin* 186 (text in English) 186.

13   Basic Principles and Guidelines on the Right to a Remedy and Reparation for Gross Violations of International Human Rights Law and Serious Violations of International Humanitarian Law, GA Res. 60/147, 16 December 2005, A/RES/60/147; 13 IHRR 907 (2006).

3. Smooth Introduction of the Court Without Any Treaty Amendments

While the creation of a unified treaty monitoring body as presently proposed by the UN High Commissioner for Human Rights[14] will require the cumbersome process of amending all UN core treaties with the exception of the Covenant on Economic, Social and Cultural Rights 1966 (CESCR),[15] the establishment of a World Court of Human Rights could be achieved smoothly without any treaty amendments and without abolishing the present treaty bodies.[16] Similar to the International Criminal Court, the Court would be based on a new treaty, the Statute of the World Court of Human Rights. It would enter into force after a sufficient number of States, as provided for in its Statute, had ratified the Statute. States would not only be free to decide whether or not to ratify the Statute and thereby to accept the binding jurisdiction of the Court, they would also be free to decide on the rights which they wish to subject to the Court's jurisdiction. At the time of ratification, they should indicate the treaties which the Court may apply in cases brought against them, but they would of course be free to add new treaties later. If a State Party, for example, preferred at the beginning only to subject civil and political rights to the binding jurisdiction of the Court, it could indicate at the time of ratification that only the CCPR rights should be adjudicated upon, and should at the same time withdraw from the first Optional Protocol to the CCPR in accordance with Article 12 of that treaty. Having been satisfied with the professionalism of the World Court, the State might at any later stage also entrust the Court to decide on complaints based on CERD, the CAT or the Convention on the Elimination of Discrimination Against Women 1979 (CEDAW),[17] and at the same time withdraw its optional declarations under Article 14 of CERD, Article 22 of CAT and/or Article 10(2) of the Optional Protocol to CEDAW 1999.[18] In addition, it might also recognise the binding jurisdiction of the Court in relation to treaties which presently do not provide for any complaints mechanisms (such as CESCR and the Convention on the Rights of the Child 1989[19]), or which do not even provide for a special treaty monitoring body (such as the Genocide Convention,[20] the Geneva Refugee Convention[21] and most other early UN human rights treaties[22]).

14   Concept Paper on the High Commissioner's Proposal for a Unified Standing Treaty Body, HRI/MC/2006/2, 22 March 2006.
15   993 UNTS 3.
16   See also Scheinin, 'Towards a World Human Rights Court' [on file with author].
17   1249 UNTS 13.
18   7 IHRR 294 (2000).
19   1577 UNTS 3.
20   Convention on the Prevention and Punishment of the Crime of Genocide 1948, 78 UNTS 277.
21   Convention Relating to the Status of Refugees 1951, 189 UNTS 137.
22   Such as the Convention on the Political Rights of Women 1953, 193 UNTS 135; and the Convention Relating to the Status of Stateless Persons 1954, 360 UNTS 117.

256   *HRLR* **7** (2007), 251–259

This smooth introduction of the World Court into the present system of UN treaty monitoring would first lead to a parallel system of dealing with complaints. While the Court would only be competent to decide on complaints in relation to States Parties to the Statute and in respect of those treaties for which its binding jurisdiction was recognised, the Human Rights Committee and the other treaty bodies would continue to render non-binding decisions in relation to other States. But gradually the World Court would take over from the treaty bodies the jurisdiction to decide on individual and inter-State complaints as well as to initiate inquiry procedures, as presently foreseen in Article 20 of the CAT and Article 8 of the Optional Protocol to CEDAW. But the treaty bodies would continue to exercise their main function of examining State reports unless they were replaced by a unified treaty body for this purpose.[23]

4. Ratification by Non-State Actors

In addition to States Parties, the Statute of the World Court of Human Rights might also provide for the possibility of non-State actors to become parties. This would constitute a welcome opportunity to solve the difficult problem of holding at least some types of non-State actors accountable in relation to international human rights law. One may think, first of all, of *inter-governmental organisations*, such as the United Nations and its specialised agencies; the European Union; the World Bank and other financial institutions, the World Trade Organisation; and the North Atlantic Treaty Organisation (NATO). The United Nations, for example, does exercise jurisdiction in the context of interim administrations, such as those established in relation to Kosovo[24] and East Timor,[25] which may lead to human rights violations by military, police and other components. Similarly, NATO forces involved in peace-keeping, peace-building or peace-enforcement missions might be held accountable for possible violations of international human rights standards. The same holds true for any other inter-governmental organisation willing to ratify the Statute of the World Court.

Secondly, *transnational corporations* which adopt voluntary codes of conduct with references to human rights standards in the framework of their corporate social responsibilities (CSR) and which become members of the Global Compact of the United Nations[26] might be invited and encouraged to accept the binding jurisdiction of the World Court in relation to selected human rights in the sphere of their respective influence, such as the prohibition of forced or child labour;

---

23   Concept Paper, supra n. 14.
24   United Nations Interim Administration Mission in Kosovo (UNMIK), established by SC Res. 1244, 10 June 1999, S/RES/1999/1244.
25   United Nations Transitional Administration in East Timor (UNTAET), established by SC Res. 1272, 22 October 1999, S/RES/1999/1272, replaced by United Nations Mission of Support in East Timor, established by SC Res. 1410, 17 May 2002, S/RES/2002/1410.
26   Information on the Global Compact initiative can be found at: www.unglobalcompact.org.

the right to form and join trade unions; the right to collective bargaining; and the prohibition of discrimination. The World Court would not only be in a position to decide in a binding judgment whether or not a business corporation subject to its jurisdiction has violated any human right of an employee, a client or any other person affected, but it might also provide proper reparation to the victim concerned. In principle, any non-State actor might be interested, for various reasons including upholding ethical standards, marketing, corporate identity or a genuine interest in strengthening human rights, to recognise the jurisdiction of the World Court of Human Rights.

5. Providing Victims of Human Rights Violations with a Right to Reparation

As stated above, the right of victims of human rights violations to an effective remedy and reparation is a genuine element of human rights. Nevertheless, current human rights complaints mechanisms usually do not provide for adequate reparation.[27] For example, the most sophisticated individual complaints mechanism before the European Court of Human Rights lacks the possibility to provide for proper reparation. The 'just satisfaction' which the European Court may afford to the injured party in accordance with Article 41 of the ECHR is restricted to monetary compensation and often only consists of compensation for legal expenses. The van Boven/Bassiouni Guidelines on the Right to Remedy and Reparation go, however, far beyond monetary compensation for material and immaterial damages and include, for example, measures of restitution (restitution of property, release of detainees), rehabilitation (legal, psychological, medical and social measures), satisfaction (truth commissions, criminal prosecution of perpetrators) and guarantees of non-repetition (amendments of laws, abolition of certain institutions).

In a case of arbitrary detention, for example, the victim usually is much more interested in his or her immediate release than in monetary compensation. Even the European Court of Human Rights lacks, however, the power to order the State concerned to immediately release the victim. Often, the victim will have to go through a new set of domestic procedures to achieve his or her

---

27   One exception to this general rule is the remedies that have been ordered by the Inter-American Court. For example, in *Plan de Sánchez Massacre v Guatemala (Merits)* IACtHR Series C 105 (2004); 13 IHRR 986 (2006), the Inter-American Court ordered the State to hold a ceremony to publicly honour the memory of persons slaughtered in the massacre; to contribute to the maintenance and improvement of the chapel where people pay tribute to the victims of the massacre; to provide a health centre with trained health personnel; to translate the American Convention and the judgment into the Maya Achí language and publish relevant sections of the judgment on the merits in both Spanish and Maya Achí. See, generally, Shelton, *Remedies in International Human Rights Law,* 2nd edn (Oxford: Oxford University Press, 2005) at 285–9 and Annex.

release, and the Committee of Ministers of the Council of Europe often closes the case on the basis of mere promises of the State Party and verification of the payment of monetary compensation. In the case of a victim of torture, no adequate restitution measure seems possible. But compensation might also not be the proper means of providing reparation to the victim. The victim might be in need of long-term medical and psychological rehabilitation measures in a proper centre for the rehabilitation of torture victims. The World Court might order the State concerned or the relevant non-State actor to provide adequate rehabilitation measures and to pay for all the costs involved, which might go far beyond the compensation for immaterial damages presently awarded to torture victims. In addition, the Court might order a proper investigation into gross and systematic human rights violations, such as summary executions, systematic torture and enforced disappearances with the aim of bringing the perpetrators to justice, as the Human Rights Chamber for Bosnia and Herzegovina has done in the well-known case relating to the Srebrenica massacres.[28]

In such cases it might take many years until full reparation was afforded to the victims of gross human rights violations. The World Court might first decide to order binding interim measures to prevent further violations and damages to the victims and only at a later stage decide on the reparations which the victim is entitled to. Some of the measures, such as amending laws or institutions or providing full rehabilitation to the victim may need several years to be fully implemented. During all those years, the supervision of the execution of the judgment of the World Court of Human Rights would need to be kept on the agenda of the Human Rights Council as part of its universal periodic review mechanism.

6. Conclusions

The few examples cited in this short overview illustrate the need for the creation of a World Court of Human Rights and the potential of such an institution. It would provide a major contribution to ensuring the right of victims of human rights violations to an effective remedy and to an adequate reparation for the

---

28   See decision of the Human Rights Chamber for Bosnia and Herzegovina in *Ferida Selimović et al. v the Republika Srpska ('Srebrenica cases')* Case nos. CH/01/8365 *et al.*, 7 March 2003; 14 IHRR 250 (2007). The Chamber ordered the Republika Srpska to provide the victims with the following remedies and reparations: 'to release all information. . .with respect to the fate and whereabouts of the missing. . .to immediately release any such missing person. . .to conduct a full, meaningful, thorough, and detailed investigation. . ., to publish the text of this entire decision. . ., to make a lump sum contribution to the to the Foundation of the Srebrenica-Potočari Memorial and Cemetery'. See also Nowak, 'Reparation by the Human Rights Chamber for Bosnia-Herzegovina', in Humanitarian Law Centre (ed.), *Strategy for Transitional Justice in the former Yugoslavia* (Belgrade: Humanitarian Law Centre, 2005) 280.

harms suffered. It would also offer the opportunity to address a number of unsolved contemporary human rights problems, such as the accountability of non-State actors. The creation of the World Court can be achieved in a smooth manner without any treaty amendment and without abolishing the present treaty monitoring bodies. It is a purely voluntary measure as States would decide freely whether or not to ratify the Statute of the Court and for which rights they were willing to recognise the binding jurisdiction of the Court. Finally, the Court should become the major counter-part of the Human Rights Council within the treaty system, and by supervising the execution of the binding judgments of the Court, the universal periodic review mechanism of the Human Rights Council would fulfil a meaningful and important function based on a strict division of labour between the two major future political and expert bodies of the United Nations in the field of human rights.

[29]

ANNIVERSARY OF THE UNIVERSAL
DECLARATION OF HUMAN RIGHTS

Swiss Initiative to Commemorate the 60th Anniversary of the UDHR

Protecting Dignity: An Agenda for Human Rights

RESEARCH PROJECT ON A WORLD HUMAN RIGHTS COURT:

"Towards a World Court of Human Rights"

by Martin Scheinin, European University Institute, Florence, Italy

JUNE 2009

The year 2008 marked the 60th Anniversary of the Universal Declaration of Human Rights. To commemorate this occasion, and in order to make a meaningful contribution to the protection of human rights, the Swiss Government decided to launch "An Agenda for Human Rights". The initiative aims to explore new ways of giving human rights the weight and place they deserve in the 21st century. It is designed as an evolving and intellectually independent process.

The text *Protecting Dignity: An Agenda for Human Rights* was authored by a Panel of Eminent Persons, co-chaired by Mary Robinson and Paulo Pinheiro. This *Agenda* and the Swiss Initiative are designed to achieve two objectives: firstly, to set out some of the main contemporary challenges on the enjoyment of human rights, and secondly, to encourage research and discussion on a number of separate topics linked to the *Agenda*. These include: Human Dignity – Prevention – Detention – Migration – Statelessness – Climate Change and Human Rights – the Right to Health – and A World Human Rights Court.

The project is sponsored and financed by the Swiss Federal Department of Foreign Affairs. The Ministry of Foreign Affairs of Norway and the Ministry of Foreign Affairs of Austria have actively supported the project. The Geneva Academy of International Humanitarian Law and Human Rights is responsible for the coordination and organisation of the Initiative.

Towards a World Court of Human Rights

Research report within the framework of the Swiss Initiative to commemorate the 60th anniversary of the Universal Declaration of Human Rights

by Professor Martin Scheinin (European University Institute)

"One future step which seems to us essential in addressing many of these issues is the establishment of a fully independent World Court of Human Rights. Such a court, which should complement rather than duplicate existing regional courts, could make a wide range of actors more accountable for human rights violations."

Protecting Dignity: An Agenda for Human Rights

Swiss Initiative to commemorate the 60th anniversary of the Universal Declaration of Human Rights

Martin Scheinin, Towards a World Court of Human Rights 2

LIST OF CONTENTS

Martin Scheinin, Towards a World Court of Human Rights   3

Martin Scheinin, Towards a World Court of Human Rights 4

FOREWORD

It is rare that the beginning of a long exercise of thinking, studying and writing can be afterwards identified with precision as to the time, place and participants. But in this case things are very clear. In September 2000 we had the constituent meeting of the Association of Human Rights Institute in Iceland. After the meeting, we traveled back to the Eurasian continent with my Austrian colleague and good friend, professor Manfred Nowak. We spent the whole flight and afterwards an hour or two more at Copenhagen airport by discussing the feasibility and modalities of a future World Court of Human Rights.

The idea has haunted me ever since. Quite soon I wrote a research project proposal on the topic but never published it, aiming at a real book. I gave a number of lectures and kept talking about the idea with colleagues, even late at night after dinner.

It is wonderful that the Swiss initiative to commemorate the sixtieth anniversary of the Universal Declaration of Human Rights now made me put on paper my thoughts in the form of a Draft Statute and accompanying explanations. What is even more intriguing is that Manfred Nowak is working on a parallel project, drafting his own version of the Statute. Over the years channels of communication have remained open between us but we did not exchange drafts.

Two important sources of inspiration that preceded September 2000 need to be mentioned. From January 1997 I served for eight years as a member of the Human Rights Committee, the treaty body under the International Covenant on Civil and Political Rights. My view that this body is the closest we now have, to a future World Court of Human Rights, has served as a major intellectual beacon for the evolution of my project. And by being a member, rather than a commentator, of that body, I got a sense of what it means to serve on the Bridge of a big ship. It is one thing to paint a nice picture of a four-masted sailing ship, and another to steer it through a narrow passage.

During my first year on the Committee, I started my academic sabbatical at the University of Toronto. There, professor Craig Scott was always eager to hear and comment my reflections on the work and role of the Committee, and of human rights law more generally. One day, I don't remember which one, he came with the slogan 'From Consent to Constitution' as an overall assessment where the world was moving, with human rights law more and more achieving the status of a global constitution, a set of norms that bind all states irrespective of their will. The project about the World Court is very much about that trend.

This report presented to the Swiss Initiative is not the end station of the project. In a year or two, there will also be an academic monograph which gives more room for the evolution so far in the process "from consent to constitution", and where the sources are properly documented. I save for that later occasion my thanks to academic environments, academic funders and research assistants.

In Geneva/Florence, 30 April 2009

Martin Scheinin

Martin Scheinin, Towards a World Court of Human Rights   5

ABSTRACT

In the report, a proposal is made to establish a World Court of Human Rights. To that end, the report includes an elaborate Draft Statute of the Court. The proposal responds to several contemporary challenges in the international protection of human rights and comes with one coherent solution that addresses those challenges.

The proposed Statute would not include new substantive human rights norms. Instead, the jurisdiction of the World Court would be based on the existing normative catalogue of human rights treaties, interpreted on the basis of the principle of interdependence and indivisibility of all human rights and drawing inspiration from customary international law and general principles of law.

Primarily, the Court would exercise legally binding jurisdiction in respect of states that have ratified its Statute. In so doing, it would have the powers to issue binding orders on interim measures of protection, to determine the permissibility of reservations to human rights treaties and not to apply impermissible reservations, and to make concrete and binding orders on the remedies to be provided to a victim of a human rights violations. The Human Rights Council, as the main intergovernmental United Nations body dealing with human rights issues, would be mandated to oversee the effective implementation of the judgments by the Court.

All these proposals are radical, but they have their basis in the evolution of human rights law until now. The revolutionary proposals are elsewhere, and only they make the proposed Statute worthy of the name World Court of Human Rights, rather than just an international court.

Under the proposed Statute, the Court would exercise jurisdiction beyond the circle of States Parties to the Statute, hence responding to the challenges posed by the emergence and evolution of transnational actors that for their capacity to affect the enjoyment of human rights are comparable to states but that so far have not been accountable under existing human rights treaty regimes.

Entities other than states would be able to accept the legally binding jurisdiction of the Court. Technically, they would not be States Parties to the Statute. But cases could be brought against them, and they would be subject to the legally binding jurisdiction of the Court, including in the issue of remedies. Intergovernmental organizations, transnational corporations, international non-governmental organizations, organized opposition movements exercising a degree of factual control over a territory and autonomous communities within one or more states would be the types of entities that could accept the jurisdiction of the Court.

For states that have not yet ratified the Statute, and for entities that have not yet accepted the general jurisdiction of the Court, there would be a possibility of accepting the Court's legally binding ad hoc jurisdiction in respect of a specific complaint.

Martin Scheinin, Towards a World Court of Human Rights 6

Finally, the Court could receive complaints also in respect of states and entities that do not accept its legally binding jurisdiction. However, the Court could consider such complaints only upon a request by the United Nations High Commissioner for Human Rights. Instead of a legally binding judgment, it would in such cases issue an Opinion representing its interpretation of the issues of international human rights law raised by the complaint.

I. TWENTY-TWO QUESTIONS AND TWENTY-TWO ANSWERS ABOUT THE PROPOSAL

1. Why is a World Court of Human Rights needed?

The proposal made in this report, of the establishment of a World Court of Human Rights, is a response to many of the most important challenges of the 21st century.

Although the 20th century was a breakthrough for the novel idea of the international protection of human rights, the realization of that idea remains far from complete. The adoption of the Universal Declaration of Human Rights in 1948 by the United Nations General Assembly was a milestone that has been followed up by the gradual elaboration of a web of legally binding human rights treaties. In the first decade of the 21st century, that piecemeal work is still continuing but in general terms one can assess that the promises made in the Universal Declaration have materialized in the form of human rights treaties.

On some other fronts the achievements are more meager. The central idea of human rights law, protecting the individual against States, including and even primarily his or her own State, has not systematically permeated the framework of public international law. International law is still primarily law between nations, i.e. law created by States and for States. For instance, consent by a State is still a precondition for legally binding human rights treaty obligations. True, the evolution in the understanding of customary international law, and within it the category of peremptory norms (*jus cogens*), renders the requirement of consent less absolute. Nevertheless, there are various ways in which States may try to resist their commitment to human rights by denying their consent, including by not ratifying a treaty, by entering extensive reservations or by not accepting optional monitoring mechanisms, such as a procedure for individual complaints under a specific human rights treaty. At times of emergency, States may also derogate from some of their otherwise legally binding human rights obligations.

Even where States have given their consent to be bound by a human rights treaty, there are failures in compliance. Under United Nations human rights treaties periodic reporting by States and the consideration of these reports by independent expert bodies (the treaty bodies) is the only mandatory monitoring mechanism. Many States are seriously in delay in submitting their periodic reports. And even where the reporting does occur, or a State has accepted optional procedures of individual complaint, there are all too many cases of non-compliance with the findings by the treaty bodies. This is largely because such findings have no legally binding authority of their own. Instead, their authority is derived from the powers of the treaty body to interpret the treaty in question, including as to whether the State violated the treaty and is under an obligation to provide an effective remedy. Findings by treaty bodies are authoritative and persuasive but strictly speaking not legally binding. Some States take the liberty of refusing their implementation on such grounds, ignoring the fact that the treaty provisions subject to the interpretive function of the treaty body are legally binding.

Martin Scheinin, Towards a World Court of Human Rights   8

Non-enforcement is a major failure of the United Nations human rights treaty system. The treaty bodies themselves are usually left with the task of overseeing the implementation of their own findings. This situation is in stark contrast with the unconditional binding force of judicial decisions in national jurisdictions, or with the role of intergovernmental organs in the non-selective supervision of the implementation of rulings by regional human rights courts, such as the European Court of Human Rights within the Council of Europe framework.

A further shortcoming of the current status of human rights law within the broader framework of public international law is the exclusive focus of human rights treaties and their monitoring mechanisms upon States as the duty-bearers. This no longer corresponds to the realities of our globalized world where other actors besides States, such as international financial institutions and other intergovernmental organizations, transnational corporations and other non-state actors enjoy increasing powers that affect the lives of individuals irrespective of national borders, and therefore possess also the capacity to affect or even deny the enjoyment of human rights by people.

2. How does the proposal respond to these challenges?

The proposal includes the creation of a World Court of Human Rights. Instead of an 'international court', an expression that would reflect the consent-based and inter-state oriented nature of human rights law so far, the notion of a World Court signals the capacity of the proposal to respond to contemporary challenges in our globalized world. The Court would exercise jurisdiction not only in respect of States but also in respect of a wide range of other actors, jointly referred to as 'Entities' in the Draft Statute. They would include intergovernmental organizations, transnational corporations, and other non-state actors.

Consent - in the form of ratification of the Statute by a State, or the general acceptance of the Court's jurisdiction by an Entity - would not be an absolute limit to the Court's jurisdiction. All types of duty-bearers would have the possibility also to accept the Court's jurisdiction in respect of a single case (ad hoc). What is more important is that complains against States and Entities could be submitted even in the absence of such ad hoc acceptance. However, the Court could entertain these complaints in the absence of a consent only on the basis of a request from the United Nations High Commissioner for Human Rights. In such cases not based on consent by the respondent, the Court would issue authoritative Opinions instead of legally binding Judgments.

The Court would have the power to determine the permissibility of reservations entered by States to human rights treaties, and to declare a case admissible even when its subject matter would be covered by an impermissible reservation.

The Judgments by the Court, as well as its orders for interim measures of protection, would be binding as a matter of international law. The United Nations Human Rights Council would be entrusted with a task to supervise the implementation of the Court's findings.

Martin Scheinin, Towards a World Court of Human Rights   9

3. In what ways does the proposal build upon achievements so far?

Although the overall proposal made in this report is radical, it has its foundation in the gradual evolution of human rights law towards a 'global constitution', i.e. a framework of norms that are considered legally binding beyond the explicit consent by states, and even beyond the circle of states. These piecemeal developments that have paved the way for the major leap of the creation of a World Court of Human Rights can be demonstrated with reference to the stages of evolution in the functioning and role of the Human Rights Committee, the treaty body monitoring compliance with the International Covenant on Civil and Political Rights (ICCPR). The Human Rights Committee can be seen as the closest that already exists, compared to a future World Court of Human Rights. The small steps listed below jointly represent a paradigm shift that already has occurred. Although the Human Rights Committee is referred to as a platform where that shift is particularly systematic, the same trends are in fact visible also in the operation of other treaty bodies which have adopted identical or similar solutions to many of the contemporary challenges facing the role of human rights law in an evolving world order. Within some regional systems of human rights protection, the trend has been even stronger, e.g. through the recognition of a regional human rights treaty as an instrument of constitutional significance across borders within the whole region.

Here, the broad trend 'from consent to constitution', from a state-centred world order to a new global order with focus on the individual endowed with rights, is demonstrated through a chronology of a number of separate small steps:

(a) In 1966, the United Nations General Assembly adopts the International Covenant on Civil and Political Rights, after a process of 18 years of drafting and negotiation since the adoption of the Universal Declaration of Human Rights in 1948. The texts of these treaties include many concessions to conservative states, such as the absence of legally binding powers for the Human Rights Committee, the separation of the procedure for individual complaints (called 'communications') from the Covenant itself to an Optional Protocol, and the ambiguous reference to the outcome of such cases as 'Final Views' by the Human Rights Committee, rather than judgments or decisions.

(b) In 1976 both the ICCPR and its Optional Protocol enter into force after a sufficient number of ratifications by States. Consequently, the Human Rights Committee is elected to monitor State compliance with the treaty, through the examination of periodic reports by states and through the consideration of complaints by individuals against states. By the standards of the time, the latter step is nothing short of radical.

(c) In its early years 1977-1982, the Human Rights Committee is confronted with a wave of individual cases from Uruguay, where a military coup has resulted in gross violations of human rights, including torture, disappearances and arbitrary detention. Despite of the Cold War that in many respects paralyses it, the Committee utilizes the Optional Protocol to develop a firm quasi-judicial approach to individual complaints. It establishes violations of the ICCPR by Uruguay in a long line of cases. In so doing, it refuses to follow a deferential attitude to the arguments or interests of a state but focuses on the human rights of the individual. Perhaps most importantly, the Committee adopts a position that article 2, paragraph 3, of the ICCPR entails a right to an effective remedy in any case where the Committee has established a violation of the Covenant. That right translates into a legally binding state obligation to provide for an effective remedy. The Committee's practice transforms its Final Views to authoritative interpretations of the legal obligations of the state, rather than being mere 'recommendations'. In its Final Views on the very first Uruguayan case submitted to it (*William Torres Ramirez v. Uruguay, Communication No. 4/1977*), the Committee concluded:

> The Committee, accordingly, is of the view that the State party is under an obligation to provide the victim with effective remedies, including compensation, for the violations which he has suffered and to take steps to ensure that similar violations do not occur in the future.

(d) During the years of the Cold War the Human Rights Committee is very cautious in its consideration of periodic reports by states. Instead of making collective findings on a state's compliance with the ICCPR, the Committee ends its consideration of a report with a round of individual remarks by its members. The shift comes only after the fall of the Berlin Wall in 1989 and after the outbreak of violence in then Yugoslavia. In its March 1992 session, the Committee finally adopts country-specific Concluding Observations on Algeria, Belgium, Colombia and Yugoslavia, identifying areas of concern but also 'widespread human rights violations'. Since, 1992, the practice of adopting Concluding Observations has been systematic and has resulted in a follow-up mechanism by the Committee itself.

(e) The next important step comes very soon, and is also triggered by the tragic events in former Yugoslavia. In its October-November session of 1992 the Human Rights Committee considers urgent special reports by the new or emerging entities Bosnia-Herzegovina, Croatia and Federal Republic of Yugoslavia (Serbia and Montenegro). Confronted with the challenge of the dissolution of two federal states that had been parties to the ICCPR - Yugoslavia and the Soviet Union - the Committee develops its position of human rights devolving with territory and the Covenant therefore being applicable in respect of any new sovereign entity that emerges from within a territory that formerly belonged to a State Party to the Covenant. This position is subsequently developed to its logical completion in 1997 when North Korea announces its denunciation of the ICCPR. In its General Comment No. 26, the Human Rights Committee concludes that as human rights belong to the population of a country, the Covenant cannot be denounced by a State that already was a party:

> 2. That the parties to the Covenant did not admit the possibility of denunciation ... was not a mere oversight on their part... It can therefore be concluded that the drafters of the Covenant deliberately intended to exclude the possibility of denunciation. The same conclusion applies to the Second Optional Protocol in the drafting of which a denunciation clause was deliberately omitted.

3. Furthermore, it is clear that the Covenant is not the type of treaty which, by its nature, implies a right of denunciation. Together with the simultaneously prepared and adopted International Covenant on Economic, Social and Cultural Rights, the Covenant codifies in treaty form the universal human rights enshrined in the Universal Declaration of Human Rights, the three instruments together often being referred to as the "International Bill of Human Rights". As such, the Covenant does not have a temporary character typical of treaties where a right of denunciation is deemed to be admitted, notwithstanding the absence of a specific provision to that effect.

4. The rights enshrined in the Covenant belong to the people living in the territory of the State party. The Human Rights Committee has consistently taken the view, as evidenced by its long-standing practice, that once the people are accorded the protection of the rights under the Covenant, such protection devolves with territory and continues to belong to them, notwithstanding change in government of the State party, including dismemberment in more than one State or State succession or any subsequent action of the State party designed to divest them of the rights guaranteed by the Covenant.

5. The Committee is therefore firmly of the view that international law does not permit a State which has ratified or acceded or succeeded to the Covenant to denounce it or withdraw from it.

(f) Meanwhile, in 1994, the Human Rights Committee adopts its General Comment No. 24 on reservations to the ICCPR and its two Optional Protocols. This general comment represents a shift from a state-centred view on public international law to the application of human rights law as a 'global constitution' that is legally binding for states even beyond their explicit consent. According to the Committee, it has the power, when exercising its functions of considering state party reports and individual complaints, to determine that a reservation is incompatible with the object and purpose of the Covenant and therefore impermissible. The normal consequence of such determination will be that the reservation is severable, i.e. the state is considered a party to the Covenant but without the benefit of the reservation. The paradigm shift represented in the move 'from consent to constitution' is clearly visible in some passages of the general comment:

8. ... Although treaties that are mere exchanges of obligations between States allow them to reserve inter se application of rules of general international law, it is otherwise in human rights treaties, which are for the benefit of persons within their jurisdiction...

17. ..., it is the Vienna Convention on the Law of Treaties that provides the definition of reservations and also the application of the object and purpose test in the absence of other specific provisions. But the Committee believes that its provisions on the

Martin Scheinin, Towards a World Court of Human Rights   12

role of State objections in relation to reservations are inappropriate to address the problem of reservations to human rights treaties. Such treaties, and the Covenant specifically, are not a web of inter-State exchanges of mutual obligations. They concern the endowment of individuals with rights. The principle of inter-State reciprocity has no place, save perhaps in the limited context of reservations to declarations on the Committee's competence under article 41. And because the operation of the classic rules on reservations is so inadequate for the Covenant, States have often not seen any legal interest in or need to object to reservations. The absence of protest by States cannot imply that a reservation is either compatible or incompatible with the object and purpose of the Covenant...

18. It necessarily falls to the Committee to determine whether a specific reservation is compatible with the object and purpose of the Covenant. This is in part because, as indicated above, it is an inappropriate task for States parties in relation to human rights treaties, and in part because it is a task that the Committee cannot avoid in the performance of its functions... Because of the special character of a human rights treaty, the compatibility of a reservation with the object and purpose of the Covenant must be established objectively, by reference to legal principles, and the Committee is particularly well placed to perform this task. The normal consequence of an unacceptable reservation is not that the Covenant will not be in effect at all for a reserving party. Rather, such a reservation will generally be severable, in the sense that the Covenant will be operative for the reserving party without benefit of the reservation.

(g) The ceding over of the territories of Hong Kong and Macau from two States Parties to the Covenant, respectively the United Kingdom and Portugal, to the People's Democratic Republic of China which is not a party to the ICCPR, poses a new challenge to the Committee's application of the principle of continuity of obligations that are owed to the population once protected by the Covenant. In the benefit of the population, the Committee extends the continuity doctrine beyond States Parties, by attributing corresponding obligations both to the regional authorities and the central authorities of China. In its Concluding Observations on Hong Kong, it states, inter alia:

In 1995 (before the transition):

7. The Committee urges the United Kingdom of Great Britain and Northern Ireland (Hong Kong) Government to take all necessary steps to ensure effective and continued application of the provisions of the Covenant in the territory of Hong Kong in accordance with the Joint Declaration and the Basic Law.

8. The Committee reminds the United Kingdom of Great Britain and Northern Ireland Government of its continuing responsibility to ensure to the people of Hong Kong the rights protected by the

Martin Scheinin, Towards a World Court of Human Rights   13

> Covenant and to carry out its obligations under the Covenant including in particular article 40; in that regard, it requests the Government of the United Kingdom to report on the human rights situation in the territory of Hong Kong up to 30 June 1997.

In 1999 (after the transition):

> 230. The Committee expresses its appreciation to the delegation from HKSAR for the information it provided and for its willingness to submit further information in writing. It further welcomes the recognition given by the delegation to the contribution made by NGOs to the consideration of the HKSAR report.

> 231. The Committee thanks the Government of China for its willingness to participate in the reporting procedure under article 40 of the Covenant by submitting the report prepared by the HKSAR authorities and by introducing the HKSAR delegation to the Committee. The Committee affirms its earlier pronouncements on the continuity of the reporting obligations in relation to Hong Kong.

> 259. The Committee sets the date for the submission of the next periodic report at 31 October 2003. That report should be prepared in accordance with the Committee's revised guidelines and should give particular attention to the issues raised by the Committee in these concluding observations. The Committee urges that the text of these concluding observations be made available to the public as well as to the legislative and administrative authorities. It requests that the next periodic report be widely disseminated among the public, including civil society and non-governmental organizations operating in HKSAR.

(h) In its Final Views in the case of *Vladimir Petrovich Laptsevich v. Belarus* (Communication No. 780/1997), adopted in March 2000, the Committee continues on the path opened in the early Uruguayan cases by quantifying the amount of compensation to be paid by the respondent state. Instead of deciding on a fixed amount of money, however, the Committee gives a formula for the calculation of the compensation, including adjusting it to the inflation rate. This 'Laptsevich formula' has been applied in some subsequent cases as well, albeit not systematically.

(i) In July 2001, the Human Rights Committee adopts its General Comment No. 29 on states of emergency. This document represents a shift away from the traditional view that a situation of emergency triggers the sovereign right of a state to 'suspend' the application of a human rights treaty. Instead, the Committee emphasizes that the Covenant remains applicable during any type of emergency, including armed conflict, and that the power of the state to derogate from some of its provisions merely constitutes a specific form of restrictions on human rights, restrictions that must always be compatible with the other international obligations of the same state, necessary and proportionate.

Martin Scheinin, Towards a World Court of Human Rights   14

(j) In 2002 the Human Rights Committee starts to tackle the problem of non-compliance with the obligation of periodic reporting. It moves to scheduling for consideration countries that have for a long time failed to submit a report. The new mechanism is aimed at encouraging the submission of overdue reports but the Committee is determined also to consider the human rights situation of the country even in the absence of a report. This has been done several times since 2002.

(k) In March 2004 the Human Rights Committee adopts its General Comment No. 31 on the nature of obligations of states under the Covenant. This document codifies the Committee's earlier approach of addressing conduct by non-state actors that affects the enjoyment of Covenant rights, albeit through the available monitoring mechanisms that are geared towards States Parties.

> 8. The article 2, paragraph 1, obligations are binding on States [Parties] and do not, as such, have direct horizontal effect as a matter of international law. The Covenant cannot be viewed as a substitute for domestic criminal or civil law. However the positive obligations on States Parties to ensure Covenant rights will only be fully discharged if individuals are protected by the State, not just against violations of Covenant rights by its agents, but also against acts committed by private persons or entities that would impair the enjoyment of Covenant rights in so far as they are amenable to application between private persons or entities. There may be circumstances in which a failure to ensure Covenant rights as required by article 2 would give rise to violations by States Parties of those rights, as a result of States Parties' permitting or failing to take appropriate measures or to exercise due diligence to prevent, punish, investigate or redress the harm caused by such acts by private persons or entities. States are reminded of the interrelationship between the positive obligations imposed under article 2 and the need to provide effective remedies in the event of breach under article 2, paragraph 3. The Covenant itself envisages in some articles certain areas where there are positive obligations on States Parties to address the activities of private persons or entities. For example, the privacy-related guarantees of article 17 must be protected by law. It is also implicit in article 7 that States Parties have to take positive measures to ensure that private persons or entities do not inflict torture or cruel, inhuman or degrading treatment or punishment on others within their power. In fields affecting basic aspects of ordinary life such as work or housing, individuals are to be protected from discrimination within the meaning of article 26.

As earlier case law upon which this doctrinal statement is based, reference can be made to the cases of *Delgado Paez v. Colombia* (Communication No. 195/1985; threats and violence from the side of private parties) *Bernard Ominayak, Chief of the Lubicon Lake Band v. Canada* (Communication No. 167/1984; exploitation of natural resources by corporations), *Ilmari Länsman et*

Martin Scheinin, Towards a World Court of Human Rights   15

al. v. Finland (Communication No. 511/1992; same issue), and *Cabal and Pasini v. Australia* (Communication No. 1020/2001; private prisons).

(l) The placing of Kosovo, through Security Council Resolution No. 1244 (1999), under international administration, poses a further challenge in the issue of continuity of obligations. When dealing in 2004 with a report by Serbia and Montenegro, the Committee takes the view that it is the United Nations that is now bound by the ICCPR to the benefit of the population of Kosovo and that is to submit a periodic report:

> 3. The State party explained its inability to report on the discharge of its own responsibilities with regard to the human rights situation in Kosovo, and suggested that, owing to the fact that civil authority is exercised in Kosovo by the United Nations Interim Administration Mission in Kosovo (UNMIK), the Committee may invite UNMIK to submit to it a supplementary report on the human rights situation in Kosovo. The Committee notes that, in accordance with Security Council resolution 1244 (1999), Kosovo currently remains a part of Serbia and Montenegro as successor State to the Federal Republic of Yugoslavia, albeit under interim international administration, and the protection and promotion of human rights is one of the main responsibilities of the international civil presence (para. 11 (j) of the resolution). It also notes the existence of provisional institutions of self-government in Kosovo that are bound by the Covenant by virtue of article 3.2 (c) of UNMIK Regulation No. 2001/9 on a Constitutional Framework for Provisional Self-Government in Kosovo. The Committee considers that the Covenant continues to remain applicable in Kosovo. It welcomes the offer made by the State party to facilitate the consideration of the situation of human rights in Kosovo and encourages UNMIK, in cooperation with the Provisional Institutions of Self-Government (PISG), to provide, without prejudice to the legal status of Kosovo, a report on the situation of human rights in Kosovo since June 1999.

Such a report is indeed submitted by UNMIK and considered by the Committee in 2006, creating a precedent for holding intergovernmental organizations, and not only states, to account for their compliance, or non-compliance with the Covenant.

The chronological account of developments over a period of 40 years presented above is by no means exhaustive. Nevertheless, it demonstrates a pattern of moving 'from consent to constitution' in the application of human rights law. All these developments have paved the way for the creation of a World Court of Human Rights.

4. Is it not enough that we already have the International Court of Justice and the International Criminal Court?

The creation by the United Nations Security Council of two international criminal tribunals (for former Yugoslavia and Rwanda) and ultimately the determination

Martin Scheinin, Towards a World Court of Human Rights   16

of States to establish a standing International Criminal Court (ICC) were major revolutions in international law in the 1990s. Subject to the fairly complicated conditions for the exercise of the ICC's jurisdiction, individuals - including soldiers, civilians or political leaders - can now be held to account, prosecuted and tried, convicted and sentenced, directly at the level of international law, for the gravest international crimes. The jurisdiction of the ICC is (for the time being) restricted to three categories of core crimes, i.e. genocide, war crimes and crimes against humanity. The ICC does not directly address the question whether there was a human rights violation, or order remedies for such violations. But of course grave international crimes will invariably entail violations of the human rights of the victims of those crimes. Prosecuting and punishing, through the means of criminal law, the individuals who perpetrated those crimes will constitute an important element also in remedying the human rights violation. Still, the overlap with human rights adjudication is only partial. The possibility of individual criminal responsibility does not eliminate the need for mechanisms of accountability for attributing the action to a state or other entity for the assessment whether it is to be held responsible for a human rights violation, which usually is broader in scope, both in substantive and personal coverage, than the international crime committed within the broader context.

Therefore, the establishment of the ICC, or the advances within the broader framework of international criminal law, have not done away with the need for a World Court of Human Rights.

The International Court of Justice, in turn, has legally binding jurisdiction only in respect of states, only when seized by states, and only in respect of rights and obligations of states vis-a-vis each other. The individual and her human rights are not in focus. It is true that the procedure for advisory opinions by the ICJ opens a broader room for actors and issues, so that (primarily) the United Nations General Assembly can ask for an advisory opinion in any issue of international law. Some of the advisory opinions have, in fact, addressed human rights issues, such as an advisory opinion on the legality of the use of nuclear weapons, and another on the lawfulness of the Israeli separation barrier (or Wall) built within the occupied Palestinian territory.

Even so, the ICJ is primarily a court for disputes between states, and only in that role it has legally binding jurisdiction. It cannot decide, even upon the initiative of a state, a case against an international organisation, a transnational corporation or some other entity. And individuals have no power to initiate the advisory opinion procedure.

Therefore, the proposal made in this report is the establishment of a totally new institution, the World Court of Human Rights.

However, it should me mentioned that also another option was considered. Most human rights treaties include a clause according to which a dispute concerning the application or interpretation of the treaty can be submitted to the ICJ. Even in the case of treaties that do not include such a clause, the same outcome results from the ICJ Statute and the power of states to take any dispute related to international law - including an issue of interpretation under a human rights treaty - to the ICJ. Also the advisory opinion procedure could be utilized by the

General Assembly to submit selected legal issues of controversy under existing human rights treaties to the ICJ.

These features of the architecture of the ICJ explain why the other model considered in the writing of this report was the operation of the ICJ as an "appeal court" above the United Nations human rights treaty bodies. For instance, if the Human Rights Committee decides a case against Australia concerning its immigration detention practices and Australia does not like the decision, Australia or some other state could seek the determination of the disputed legal issue by a higher authority, the ICJ. This could take place under the legally binding (contentious) jurisdiction in the form of a dispute between Australia and another state (let's say, Norway). Alternatively, when the General Assembly considers the annual report by the Human Rights Committee, Australia could propose that the Assembly requests from the ICJ an advisory opinion on the proper interpretation of article 9 of the International Covenant on Civil and Political Rights.

This model might work in practice. In the short term it would relativize the authority of the human rights treaty bodies by subjecting them to review by a higher judicial authority. But in the long run it would strengthen the human rights system as a whole, because there would be a heavier counterpart to the unilateral exercise of sovereignty by states which today may just ignore the findings by the Human Rights Committee or exceptionally, as Australia did in respect of the Final Views by the Committee in the case of *A. v. Australia* (Communication No. 560/1993), openly contest them without resorting to any higher legal authority than their own Foreign Ministry lawyers.

There are two reasons why the model of transforming the ICJ into a human rights appeal instance above the treaty bodies is not proposed in this report. Firstly, states and the General Assembly have had 40 years to utilize this option if they thought it is a good idea. And they haven't. Secondly, this model does not reflect the idea of the human being, her rights and her empowerment, as the centerpiece of the international law of the 21st century. States and only states, either directly as states or as participants in the General Assembly, could transform the ICJ into a human rights court. This represents a contradiction in terms.

Again, the conclusion is that a World Court of Human Rights is needed. The proposal made in this report concerning its creation has benefited from the experiences of the ICJ and the ICC. In fact, the Rome Statute for the International Criminal Court, a highly advanced result of most skillful drafting and most intensive negotiation, has been the single most important source of inspiration in the drafting of the Statute proposed here.

5. What will be the relationship between the World Court and the United Nations High Commissioner for Human Rights?

The High Commissioner for Human Rights will remain as the leader of the United Nations human rights program, supported by the Office of the High Commissioner. The Court will have its own secretariat, the Registry. The two institutions will be linked through a new function of the High Commissioner, namely her or his power to seek an Opinion from the Court, in respect of any human rights complaint and any state or other entity as respondent, provided that the Court will not have legally binding jurisdiction in the matter. This procedure for Opinions complements the binding jurisdiction of the Court and makes it literally into a World Court, i.e. a court that when the need arises can provide an authoritative legal opinion on an alleged human rights violation anywhere in the world and committed by whomsoever.

The High Commissioner is best placed to trigger the Opinions function of the Court. She is independent from states and of the political organs of the United Nations. She is a recognized professional with experience, expertise and judgment. She is supported by staff capable of assisting her in the formulation of a request for an Opinion.

The Court will have discretion to accept or not to accept the High Commissioner's request for an Opinion.

6. Who will be able to seize the Court?

The power of the High Commissioner for Human Rights to request an Opinion from the Court will be only one of the channels through which the Court can be seized and invited to deal with an alleged human rights violation. This channel will be a complement to the more direct and regular methods of bringing a case before the Court.

Complaints by individuals, or groups of individuals, will be the main channel for taking cases before the Court. Such complaints can be submitted by persons claiming to be a victim of a human rights violation by the respondent which can be a State or an Entity. (For the notion of Entity, see the following answer.)

Also States can initiate cases, by alleging that another State, or an Entity, has committed a human rights violation.

7. Who will be subject to the Court's jurisdiction?

The Statute of the World Court of Human Rights will be an international treaty, drafted, adopted and ratified by States. Hence, ratifying States will be the primary category subject to the jurisdiction of the Court. In line with the traditional rules of public international law, no State will become party to the Statute and subject to the Court's general jurisdiction, without its explicit consent.

However, there are three proposals that extend the jurisdiction of the Court beyond this core area that reflects traditional rules of public international law.

Firstly, while only States may become parties to the Statute as an international treaty, a whole range of other actors besides States will be able to accept, through their own free decision, the legally binding jurisdiction of the Court. This proposal transforms the Court from a traditional international court into a transnational court, or to a World Court of Human Rights as its name indicates.

As listed in article 6 of the Statute, the various actors that, besides States and jointly called 'Entities' in the Draft Statute, could accept the jurisdiction of the Court, are the following:

a) International organizations constituted through a treaty between States, or between States and international organizations;

b) Transnational corporations, i.e. business corporations that conduct a considerable part of the production or service operations in a country or in countries other than the home State of the corporation as a legal person;

c) International non-governmental organizations, i.e. associations or other types of legal persons that are not operating for economic profit and conduct a considerable part of their activities in a country or in countries other than the home State of the organization as a legal person;

d) Organized opposition movements exercising a degree of factual control of a territory, to the effect that they carry out some of the functions that normally are taken care of by the State or other public authorities; and

e) Autonomous communities within a State or within a group of States and exercising a degree of public power on the basis of the customary law of the group in question or official delegation of powers by the State or States.

Of these categories of Entities, the last one is subject to a requirement that the territorial state(s) must give its consent to the declaration by an autonomous community to accept the jurisdiction of the Court (article 59, paragraph 4).

A second extension of the Court's jurisdiction is provided for by article 9 which allows both States that are not parties to the Statute, and Entities that have not generally accepted the jurisdiction of the Court, to accept that jurisdiction on an ad hoc basis in respect of a particular case (complaint) submitted to the Court. This model of ad hoc acceptance of jurisdiction is also applicable when a State or Entity has accepted the jurisdiction of the Court but excluded a particular human rights treaty, and now a complaint is submitted in respect of an issue not governed by the existing acceptance of jurisdiction.

All forms of exercise of jurisdiction described so far result in a legally binding judgment of the Court. In contrast, the third extension of the Court's jurisdiction, also applicable both in respect of States and Entities, results in an Opinion by the Court. The legal nature of such opinions is similar to the present Final Views by the Human Rights Committee or other United Nations human rights treaty bodies. While lacking legally binding force they represent the interpretation of international law by an expert body entrusted by States with such a function and hence carrying considerable weight. As the Court will be a fully judicial institution, it is expected that its Opinions will in fact be acknowledged as authoritative and definitive, even if lacking legally binding force. The Court will proceed to the issuing of an Opinion only through three preceding steps: (a) the receipt of a complaint in respect of a State or Entity that has not accepted the general jurisdiction of the Court, (b) the refusal of the State or Entity to accept the ad hoc jurisdiction of the Court in the case, (c) a request by the United

Martin Scheinin, Towards a World Court of Human Rights 20

Nations High Commissioner for Human Rights that the Court will issue an Opinion. Even then, the Court will exercise discretion whether to grant the High Commissioner's request.

8. Does it make sense to apply the Law of State Responsibility in respect of non-state actors?

In 2001 the International Law Commission of the United Nations concluded its work on codifying the international law of state responsibility. Since then, the Articles on State Responsibility have been mildly endorsed by the General Assembly and the question of possible formalization of their status remains pending.

Traditionally, the law of state responsibility has been seen as one of the bastions of the state-centred approach to international law. The law of state responsibility is constituted by the secondary norms that apply when one state has committed an internationally wrongful act and another state - 'the injured state' - seeks to hold that other state to account for its wrongful conduct. This may take place primarily through unilateral counter-measures by the injured state. The law of state responsibility does not leave much space for other actors besides states, such as independent monitoring bodies, individuals or other third parties.

Despite these shortcomings in its point of departure, the law of state responsibility has evolved into highly technical and precise rules concerning the attribution of wrongful conduct to a state. In this area the achievements of the law of state responsibility overshadow the rather modest developments in the field of human rights law related to the nature of state obligations and concepts such as 'jurisdiction' or 'extraterritorial scope'. For this reason international courts and tribunals, as well as human rights treaty bodies, increasingly refer to the law of state responsibility in attributing allegedly wrongful conduct to a respondent state.

According to article 5, paragraph 2, of the proposed Draft Statute, the World Court shall determine whether an act or omission is attributable to a State or Entity for the purposes of establishing whether it committed a human rights violation. In so doing, the Court shall be guided by the principles of the international law of state responsibility which it shall apply also in respect of Entities subject to its jurisdiction, 'as if the act or omission attributed to an Entity was attributable to a State'. This provision demonstrates how the rules of the international law of state responsibility will be applied for the purpose of making non-state actors accountable for conduct that results in the denial of the enjoyment of human rights by individuals or groups of individuals. The Court can be expected to refer directly to the Articles on State Responsibility when addressing such issues. In particular, the provisions of Chapter II on attribution, Chapter IV on shared or joint responsibility of more than one duty-bearer, and Chapter V on circumstances precluding wrongfulness will be instructive for the Court in extending the application of substantive human rights norms to Entities subject to its jurisdiction.

9. Why is international humanitarian law not included in the jurisdiction of the Court?

Martin Scheinin, Towards a World Court of Human Rights   21

There is considerable overlap between the substantive norms of human rights
law and international humanitarian law, codified into the 1949 Geneva
Conventions and their two Protocols of 1977 but also reflecting norms of
customary international law. As the rapid progress in the field of international
criminal law in the 1990s and thereafter constitute a qualitative leap in the
implementation and enforcement of international humanitarian law, and as
human rights law remains applicable also in times of armed conflict, the
proposal restricts itself to creating a World Court for human rights law. The
Court would exercise jurisdiction also in times of emergency or armed conflict. It
would need to address the question to what extent the exigencies of a situation
of armed conflict provide proper justification for a State derogating from some of
its human rights obligations. Further, in cases related to alleged human rights
violations in the course of an armed conflict, the Court would take into account
the norms of international humanitarian law in the interpretation of human
rights law, particularly in issues where the norms of humanitarian law are more
specific than the rules enshrined in human rights treaties. Such an approach of
harmonizing interpretation is reflected in article 5, paragraph 3, of the Draft
Charter, according to which the Court shall seek inspiration from customary
international law when exercising its jurisdiction.

*10. Why is the Refugee Convention included in the material jurisdiction of the
Court?*

The 1951 Convention on the Status of Refugees and its Protocol of 1967 are part
and parcel of the normative code of international human rights law. They fulfill
the promise made in article 14 of the Universal Declaration of Human Rights.
Largely because of the urgency of the refugee issue in the post World War Two
situation, this particular child in the family of human rights treaties was born
prematurely. Hence, it lacks proper mechanisms of international monitoring,
such as the establishment of an international treaty body composed of
independent experts. Only later on have the creation of such a body, and
gradually also of a procedure for individual complaints, become standard
elements of United Nations human rights treaties.

In our world of today, the need to upgrade the monitoring of the Refugee
Convention is more burning than ever before. The number of refugees, the
massive dimension of flows of other persons seeking to migrate, the diversity of
the situations, and the complexity of measures taken by states to cut, curtail,
manage or facilitate migration and asylum-seeking result in a massive need for
legal analysis, assessment and response.

While other options to create proper monitoring mechanisms under the Refugee
Convention regime may need to be discussed, this proposal includes the idea of
individuals and states obtaining the possibility to submit complaints of violations
of the Refugee Convention to the World Court of Human Rights.

11. What about remedies, and their enforcement?

The judgments by the Court, which will be legally binding, will also include an
order for the remedies the victims of the human rights violation are entitled to.
Under the terms of article 47 of the Draft Statute, the Court will, in a Judgment

Martin Scheinin, Towards a World Court of Human Rights 22

that establishes a human rights violation, make an order directly against the respondent specifying appropriate reparations to, or in respect of, victims, including restitution, compensation and rehabilitation. Similarly, in an Opinion the Court may issue a recommendation to the respondent specifying appropriate reparations to, or in respect of, victims, including restitution, compensation and rehabilitation

Where appropriate, the Court may in its judgment or opinion order that the award for reparations be made through the Trust Fund provided for in article 35 of the Draft Statute.

Proposed article 48 will address one of the main shortcomings of the current United Nations human rights system. It will establish an intergovernmental mechanism for the implementation of the judgments and opinions by the Court by entrusting the Human Rights Council with the function of supervising such implementation. For this purpose, the Human Rights Council may appoint subsidiary bodies. The proposal draws inspiration from the monitoring of the European Convention of Human Rights where the unconditional and nonselective duty of the main political body of Council of Europe, the Committee of Ministers, is to supervise the implementation of the judgments by the European Court of Human Rights.

12. Will the Court be able to intervene in ongoing or imminent human rights violations?

The proposed Statute includes a clause on the power of the World Court to issue legally binding orders on interim measures of protection. They can be addressed to any state or entity in relation to which the Court exercises jurisdiction. This proposal builds upon the practice of the International Court of Justice, regional human rights treaties and the United Nations treaty bodies. The exercise of this power will be in the hands of the three-person Presidency of the Court, a solution that signals the exceptional nature of such an order. As soon as the case is assigned to a Chamber of the Court, the Chamber will also decide on interim measures. The institution will be applicable only in cases where an individual or a group of individuals faces a real risk of death or other grave and irreversible consequence. (Article 16.)

13. Will it take several years for the Court to decide a case?

The experience of the ad hoc criminal tribunals and the International Criminal Court has been surprising and troubling, in that the duration of the proceedings is often very long. This will not be the case at the World Court of Human Rights. It is not a criminal court and need not engage in the painful task of collecting, hearing and assessing hard evidence beyond any reasonable doubt. That task is difficult even for a domestic court sitting in the same village where the crime was committed, not to speak of the additional difficulties an international court sitting thousands of kilometers away will confront.

The task of the World Court of Human Rights is very different. It will conduct oral hearings and guarantee a day in court both for the complainant and for the respondent, be it a State or Entity. But the hearings are more about legal

Martin Scheinin, Towards a World Court of Human Rights   23

arguments, counter-arguments and conclusions, than about actual evidence. To the extent hard evidence is needed for assessing whether there was a human rights violation, this will usually be collected and submitted by the parties well in advance of the hearing.

It can reasonably be expected that the Court will seek to decide every case within one year from submission. It will secure equal treatment of the parties, their chance to be heard, and their real possibility to comment each others' submissions. But it will not tolerate delaying tactics by any of the parties involved.

14. Who will be the Judges of the Court?

The World Court will be composed of 18 full-time judges, serving a non-renewable nine-year term. According to article 17, paragraph 2, of the Draft Statute, the judges shall be chosen from among persons of high moral character, impartiality and integrity who possess the qualifications required in their respective countries for appointment to the highest judicial offices. As every State wishing to nominate a candidate would be obliged to nominate one male and one female candidate (article 18), it is expected that the gender balance within the Court will be better than amongst the judges of many other international courts or tribunals.

Pursuant to article 19, paragraph 4, States shall, in the selection of judges take into account the need, within the membership of the Court, for the representation of the principal legal systems of the world, equitable geographical representation, expertise on specific issues, including, but not limited to, rights of women, rights of the child, rights of persons with disabilities, and rights of members of minorities and indigenous peoples, and a fair representation of female and male judges. However, similarly to the rules on elections for United Nations human rights treaty bodies this provision is addressed to individual States for the consideration of casting their own votes, and no actual quotas are proposed for any of the diverse factors mentioned in article 19.

15. Is it not an impossible task to amend all existing human rights treaties, through cumbersome procedures, to pave the way for a World Court?

The proposed Statute of the World Court of Human Rights is a new international treaty and does not require amending any existing treaties. Both the substance and the monitoring mechanisms under existing treaties will remain intact. However, the proposed Statute does include a provision according to which an instrument of ratification of or accession to the Statute by a state shall be understood as a notification of its withdrawal from those individual complaint procedures that the same state has accepted under existing United Nations human rights treaties and now subjects to the jurisdiction of the Court (Article 61, paragraph 2).

16. What will happen to United Nations human rights treaty bodies?

Through the solution explained under the previous question the proposal avoids the duplication of procedures and launches a gradual process where the quasi-judicial function of treaty bodies to deal with individual complaints is replaced by the Court's fully judicial function. The pace of this process will depend on how quickly and how extensively states accept the jurisdiction of the Court. The treaty bodies, however, will continue to exercise their other functions, including the handling of individual complaints in respect of states that have not yet accepted the jurisdiction of the Court. Gradually, the limited resources of the treaty bodies will be directed to the consideration of periodic reports by states and to the issuing of general comments. In preparing their general comments the treaty bodies will, of course, need to take into account the emerging case law by the Court.

In the course of preparing this proposal on the establishment of a World Court of Human Rights also another option for upgrading the United Nations human rights treaty monitoring system was considered. While the more ambitious plan of establishing a World Court was ultimately chosen, also the other option needs to be presented here. This is particularly because it not only represents an alternative to the World Court project but could also be pursued parallel to the establishment of the Court, in order to improve the operation of the treaty bodies and their monitoring functions.

This other option makes use of the name of the treaty monitoring body under the International Covenant on Civil and Political Rights as the 'Human Rights Committee' and the absence of a treaty body in the text of the sister Covenant, the International Covenant on Economic, Social and Cultural Rights. Originally, the ICESCR was to be monitored by an intergovernmental body, the Economic and Social Council of the United Nations. Only some ten years after the entry into force of the Covenant, ECOSOC by way of a resolution established an independent expert body, the Committee on Economic, Social and Cultural Rights (CESCR) to consider periodic state reports under the ICESCR. These features open a window for a merger of the two Covenant bodies, simply through a decision by ECOSOC to entrust the Human Rights Committee to monitor states' compliance with the ICESCR. Such a reform of a merger of the two Covenant bodies would mean a boost to the principle of interdependence and indivisibility of all human rights and result in the creation of a true Human Rights Committee. Naturally, the composition of the merged Committee would need to reflect the need for expertise on both Covenants. To this end it would be natural that several members of the CESCR would run as candidates and be elected to the Human Rights Committee.

Subsequent to this merger of the two Covenant bodies, better integration of the work by other treaty bodies into the overall framework of human rights treaty monitoring would be achieved through the election of some of their members to the new Human Rights Committee, or, conversely, through the election of some Human Rights Committee members to serve simultaneously on the more specialized committees. The specialized treaty bodies would thereafter operate as 'satellite' bodies of the new Human Rights Committee.

The treaty body reform as outlined here would have many advantages. It would result in the professionalization of treaty body membership and the better integration of the work of all treaty bodies with each others. Moving towards better coordination of state reporting to the various treaty bodies would be greatly enhanced, inter alia through joint reporting guidelines or, where appropriate, even joint reports.

The partly merged and partly integrated new treaty body structure could very well be coupled with the creation of a fully judicial World Court of Human Rights. While the consideration of complaints through a judicial procedure would gradually shift from the treaty bodies to the World Court, the former would in an integrated manner continue to consider State Party reports, to elaborate separate or joint general comments under the respective human rights treaties, and to exercise the other functions of the treaty bodies.

The creation of a World Court of Human Rights is not dependent on a reform of the United Nations human rights treaty body system. But the two processes should be seen as mutually supportive.

17. Why would States ratify the Statute of the Court?

There are at least four reasons why States should ratify the Statute. Firstly, many States wish to demonstrate their unwavering commitment to human rights, and elevating the global protection of human rights to a qualitatively new level by establishing the Court will be an important way to demonstrate that commitment.

Secondly, many States wish to see more consistency in the application of human rights law. Bringing all United Nations human rights treaties within the jurisdiction of a single human rights court that will simultaneously apply all treaties accepted by the State in question, and in so doing, where necessary, resolve any tensions between the various human rights treaties, will greatly enhance the coherence and consistency in the application of human rights treaties.

Thirdly, this will improve foreseeability and legal certainty, as the World Court will be a fully judicial institution with highly qualified full-time judges.

And fourthly, States should welcome the initiative of expanding the binding force of human rights norms beyond States only, to cover also international organizations, transnational corporations and other Entities subject to the jurisdiction of the Court.

18. Why would international organizations accept the jurisdiction of the Court?

Within international organizations, including among their chief officials, staff and governmental representatives serving on their decision-making bodies, there is growing uncertainty about the proper place of human rights norms in the operation of intergovernmental organizations. These organizations, their organs and operations, are subject to increasing criticism as to their lack of commitment to or compliance with human rights norms. International financial institutions and the United Nations Security Council, for instance, are receiving their part of the criticism. There are increasing calls for subjecting international organizations to some sort of judicial, or at least independent, review as to their compliance with human rights. Domestic courts and regional human rights

Martin Scheinin, Towards a World Court of Human Rights   26

courts, in turn, may hold individual States to account for their action within international organizations, or for the implementation of decisions by international organizations, at least as long as there is no regime of equivalent protection of human rights in respect of the acts of the organization itself.

A much discussed issue is the practice of the United Nations Security Council to list individuals as Taliban, Al-Qaida, or 'associated' terrorists under Security Council Resolution No. 1267 (1999). This listing is done with reference to the Security Council's powers under Chapter VII of the United Nations Charter, resulting in a legal obligation for all Member States to subject the listed individuals to sanctions such as a travel ban and the freezing of all assets. As this obligation is generally seen as an obligation under the UN Charter, it is said to enjoy, under Article 103 of the Charter, primacy in respect of the same states' human rights obligations. Growing hesitation by states to grant such primacy in the absence of any international or domestic judicial review, and repeated calls for the Security Council itself to introduce fair and clear procedures to its listing and delisting of terrorists, have resulted in piecemeal reforms of the listing regime, most recently the adoption of Security Council Resolution No. 1822 (2008). Despite the reforms, the listing of individuals remains a diplomatic, rather than judicial, procedure and delisting takes place only by consensus. In the case of *Sayadi and Vinck v. Belgium* (Communication No. 1472/2006) the Human Rights Committee already established that the listing of two individuals constituted a violation of the International Covenant on Civil and Political Rights, attributable to Belgium because of its role as initiator of the listing by the Security Council.

If the United Nations were to accept the jurisdiction of the World Court of Human Rights as an Entity under article 5 of the Draft Statute, the Court could exercise jurisdiction in respect of the listing of individuals as terrorists under Resolution 1267 (1999), or the refusal by the Security Council to delist persons. However, when accepting the Court's jurisdiction the United Nations could specify what remedies need to be exhausted before seizing the Court. If the Security Council were to develop a mechanism of independent expert review as a part of its listing and delisting procedures, this could constitute a remedy that needs to be exhausted. Perhaps more importantly, it can also be expected that when addressing the complaint after the exhaustion of those remedies, the World Court would pay due attention to the procedure and outcome of such an independent review before assessing the case on the merits. If it were to found that the Security Council's internal mechanisms of independent review in fact provided for an equivalent level of human rights protection, the Court might very well exercise deference and decide that the listing, or refusal to delist, in the particular case did not constitute a human rights violation.

Irrespective of such considerations, it is of fundamental importance that the acceptance by the United Nations of the jurisdiction of the World Court would in principle open a prospect for judicial review over Security Council decisions. Such review would be limited in the sense that it would only relate to the question whether the human rights of one or more individuals were violated by the Security Council. Nevertheless, the finding of a violation and the order of a remedy would be legally binding upon the United Nations. While such a prospect may appear as radical, an easy solution for the Security Council would be to defer from making such decisions that directly affect the enjoyment of human rights by individuals. In fact, there is wide agreement that the role, composition and procedures of the Security Council are not appropriate for making decisions that have such far-reaching consequences for specific individuals.

By accepting the jurisdiction of the Court, international organizations will subject themselves to highly qualified and fully independent judicial review. In so doing, they will under article 8, paragraph 4, of the Statute be able to identify internal procedures of redress that need to be exhausted before seizing the Court. It is expected that this proposed architecture will be well received within many an international organization.

19. Why would corporations accept the jurisdiction of the Court?

Analogous considerations apply in respect of transnational business corporations. They, too, are under criticism for being insensitive to human rights. At the same time they have no say in the formulation of human rights treaties and no way of subjecting themselves to professional and external human rights review.

Similarly to international organizations, also transnational corporations will be able, when accepting the jurisdiction of the Court, to identify mechanisms of redress that need to be exhausted before taking a case to the World Court. This arrangement will enable corporations to take a proactive approach by designing their own mechanisms for human rights accountability but nevertheless also demonstrating to the world their commitment to external and independent judicial review of the outcome.

It is expected that article 8, paragraph 3 of the Draft Statute will be of particular relevance to business corporations. The provision allows that an Entity accepting the jurisdiction of the Court may extend that jurisdiction through the inclusion of human rights instruments that do not take the form of an international treaty. If work progresses on normative instruments specifically drafted for the purpose of addressing human rights responsibilities of business corporations, it is expected that many of them will acknowledge the jurisdiction of the Court to base its decisions on such instruments. One candidate for such acceptance by corporations is the document entitled 'Norms on the responsibilities of transnational corporations and other business enterprises with regard to human rights', adopted by the former Sub-Commission on the promotion and protection of human rights in 2003.

Finally, the creation of the World Court and the inclusion of the possibility of business corporations accepting the jurisdiction of the Court under article 8, will greatly enhance the possibilities of consumer, labour, environmental and human rights organizations to campaign for corporations to accept the jurisdiction of the Court. Once certain key businesses accept the Court's jurisdiction, such acceptance will become a competitive advantage for any corporation. An assessment of competitive business advantage will be a driving force for corporations gradually accepting the jurisdiction of the Court.

20. Why are 'autonomous communities' within nation States included among Entities that can accept the jurisdiction of the Court?

Indeed, the list of article 6 of the Draft Statute, of Entities that in addition to States may accept the jurisdiction of the Court, includes also autonomous communities within a State, or within a group of States. Such communities may be regional, ethnic, linguistic or religious in nature. They may include, for instance, indigenous peoples with their own legal traditions. The reference in the said provision to groups present in a group of States, is particularly relevant for indigenous or minority groups who reside in an area divided by an international border but nevertheless wish to perceive of themselves as one community. According to the proposed provision, it is a precondition for a community being able to accept the jurisdiction of the Court that it exercises a degree of public power on the basis of the customary law of the group in question, or official delegation of powers by the State or States. The Saami people inhabiting the northernmost parts of Finland, Norway and Sweden would be an illustrative example of a cross-border community exercising a degree of public powers.

The inclusion of autonomous communities within the range of Entities that may accept the jurisdiction of the Court, would enable international adjudication by highly qualified independent judges as to whether a group violates the human rights of its members. Such concerns may be among the chief obstacles for States delegating or recognizing the exercise of powers by autonomous groups. The proposal would at the same time secure accountability for human rights violations and avoid giving the final say to the organs of the State. It is expected that in many cases relevant groups would, in agreement with the nation State in question, designate courts of the State as remedies that need to be exhausted before taking a case to the World Court. Nevertheless, the ultimate jurisdiction of the Court would serve as an important counterbalance and help in avoiding a power monopoly of the State in the delicate balance between the rights of the individual, the powers of the group and the powers of the State.

21. What will happen to regional human rights courts?

In preparing the Draft Statute, two options were on the drawing board. In the first option, regional human rights courts would belong to the remedies that need to be exhausted before taking a case to the World Court. The World Court would, in a sense, become a court of appeals in respect of the regional human rights systems. This would have the benefits of reducing the potential case load of the World Court and of implementing the principle of subsidiarity in the meaning that complainants would be obliged to try to reach a remedy on the regional level first, taking their case to the global level only if that effort fails.

Despite these advantages, however, a different model was chosen. Article 13, paragraph 1 (d), of the Draft Statute includes among the admissibility conditions before the World Court that the same matter is not pending before any other human rights complaints body and has not been finally decided by a regional human rights court with legally binding jurisdiction. Hence, the initiation of a case before the African Court of Human and Peoples' Rights, the European Court of Human Rights or the Inter-American Court of Human Rights will automatically and indefinitely close the access to the World Court in the same matter. In line with the jurisprudence under existing human rights treaties, 'same matter' refers to a case where both the legal issues and the parties are the same.

The advantages of the proposed model are that it respects the integrity of regional human rights courts by not subjecting them to an appeal court on the global level, and that it avoids adding a new layer to the delays that often characterize regional human rights systems with a heavy workload.

What is of course lost in the proposed model is the role of the World Court to secure overall coherence into the application of human rights across the world and irrespective of regional particularities. Human rights are, and should remain, universal in nature. It is realistic to expect that a satisfactory and gradually close to perfect degree of coherence will be possible to reach through close interaction between the World Court and regional human rights courts. This interaction may take many forms but real-time exchange of jurisprudence and regular colloquia both on judicial and on registry level will be key elements to success. It is submitted that in the long run the outcome for the coherence and universality of human rights law will be better through the proposed model of interaction between parallel 'pillars' of human rights protection, than what hierarchical subordination of regional human rights courts to the World Court as a higher instance would deliver.

22. How will the plan evolve from here?

This report was prepared as part of the Swiss Initiative to commemorate the 60th anniversary of the Universal Human Rights and written in the course of five months. However, the research behind the particular design proposed here dates much further back and will continue beyond the current report that represents one important phase of the overall project.

The backbone of the proposal for a World Court of Human Rights is the Draft Statute annexed already to this report. It will also be included in the next phase of the project, to be published as an academic book that will also more thoroughly explain the legal developments paving the way for the creation of the Court and provide detailed commentary of the provisions of the Draft Statute.

Martin Scheinin, Towards a World Court of Human Rights 30

II. STATUTE OF THE WORLD COURT OF HUMAN RIGHTS (DRAFT)

Preamble

The States Parties to this Statute,

Faithful to the goals and principles of the Universal Declaration of Human Rights adopted by the United Nations General Assembly on 10 December 1948 and the aspiration to make the universal protection of human rights subject to judicial oversight on the international level,

Deploring that human rights violations are ongoing in many parts of the world and affect every day the lives of hundreds of millions of children, women and men,

Determined to put an end to the lack of international enforcement of human rights and thus to contribute to the prevention of such violations,

Reaffirming the purposes and principles of the Charter of the United Nations,

Determined to these ends and for the sake of present and future generations, to establish an independent permanent World Court of Human Rights in relationship with the United Nations system, with jurisdiction over human rights violations committed by States and other actors,

Inviting in that spirit all States and other public and private actors that due to their position or powers are capable of violating human rights, to accept the jurisdiction of the World Court of Human Rights,

Emphasizing that the World Court of Human Rights established under this Statute shall be complementary to national courts, regional human rights courts and existing international courts and tribunals,

Resolved to guarantee lasting respect for human rights and their international enforcement,

Have agreed as follows:

Part I. Establishment of the Court

Article 1. The Court

A World Court of Human Rights ('the Court') is hereby established. It shall be a permanent institution and shall have the power to exercise its jurisdiction over States and Entities for violations of human rights. The jurisdiction and functioning of the Court shall be governed by the provisions of this Statute.

Article 2. Relationship of the Court with the United Nations

The Court shall be brought into a relationship with the United Nations through an agreement to be approved by the Assembly of States Parties to this Statute and thereafter concluded by the President of the Court on its behalf.

Article 3. Seat of the Court

1. The seat of the Court shall be established in Geneva in Switzerland ('the host State').

2. The Court shall enter into a headquarters agreement with the host State, to be approved by the Assembly of States Parties and thereafter concluded by the President of the Court on its behalf.

3. The Court may sit elsewhere, whenever it considers it desirable.

Article 4. Legal status and powers of the Court

1. The Court shall have international legal personality. It shall also have such legal capacity as may be necessary for the exercise of its functions and the fulfilment of its purposes.

2. The Court may exercise its functions and powers, as provided for in this Statute, on the territory of any State Party and, by special arrangement, on the territory of any other State.

Part II. Jurisdiction, Admissibility and Applicable Law

Article 5. General clause on the jurisdiction of the Court

1. The Court shall have jurisdiction in respect of human rights violations committed by any State or by any other Entity referred to in article 6 pursuant to the provisions of this Part II.

2. In exercising its jurisdiction, the Court shall determine whether an act or omission is attributable to a State or Entity for the purposes of establishing whether it committed a human rights violation. In so doing, the Court shall be guided by the principles of the international law of state responsibility which it shall apply also in respect of Entities subject to its jurisdiction, as if the act or omission attributed to an Entity was attributable to a State. The Court shall determine the wrongfulness of an act or omission by a State or Entity through the interpretation of international human rights law.

3. In exercising its jurisdiction, the Court shall be guided by the principle of the interdependence and indivisibility of all human rights and shall seek inspiration from customary international law and general principles of law.

Article 6. Entities

The reference to 'Entity' in article 5 and elsewhere in this Statute includes the following types of legal persons that may under the provisions of this Part II come under the jurisdiction of the Court:

Martin Scheinin, Towards a World Court of Human Rights   32

a) International organizations constituted through a treaty between States, or between States and international organizations;

b) Transnational corporations, i.e. business corporations that conduct a considerable part of the production or service operations in a country or in countries other than the home State of the corporation as a legal person;

c) International non-governmental organizations, i.e. associations or other types of legal persons that are not operating for economic profit and conduct a considerable part of their activities in a country or in countries other than the home State of the organization as a legal person;

d) Organized opposition movements exercising a degree of factual control over a territory, to the effect that they carry out some of the functions that normally are taken care of by the State or other public authorities; and

e) Autonomous communities within a State or within a group of States and exercising a degree of public power on the basis of the customary law of the group in question or official delegation of powers by the State or States.

Article 7. Judgments in respect of States Parties

1. The Court shall issue judgments in respect of States Parties. These judgments shall be legally binding.

2. Unless otherwise specified in the instrument of ratification or accession by the State Party, or any subsequent notification modifying it, the material jurisdiction of the Court shall extend to determining violations of the following human rights treaties, provided the State Party is a party to the treaty in question:

a) The Convention on the Prevention and Punishment of the Crime of Genocide of 9 December 1948;

b) The Convention relating to the Status of Refugees of 28 July 1951 and the Protocol relating to the Status of Refugees of 16 December 1966;

c) The International Convention on the Elimination of All Forms of Racial Discrimination of 21 December 1965;

d) The International Covenant on Economic, Social and Cultural Rights of 16 December 1966;

e) The International Covenant on Civil and Political Rights of 16 December 1966 and its Second Optional Protocol to the International Covenant on Civil and Political Rights, aiming at the abolition of the death penalty, of 15 December 1989;

f) The Convention on the Elimination of All Forms of Discrimination against Women of 18 December 1979;

g) The Convention against Torture and Other Cruel, Inhuman or Degrading Treatment or Punishment of 10 December 1984;

Martin Scheinin, Towards a World Court of Human Rights 33

h) The Convention on the Rights of the Child of 20 November 1989 and its two Optional protocols on the involvement of children in armed conflict and on the sale of children, child prostitution and child pornography, both of 25 May 2000;

i) The International Convention on the Protection of the Rights of All Migrant Workers and Members of Their Families of 18 December 1990;

j) The Convention on the Rights of Persons with Disabilities of 13 December 2006; and

k) The International Convention for the Protection of All Persons from Enforced Disappearance of 20 December 2006.

3. The specifications and modifications referred to in paragraph 2 may extend the jurisdiction of the Court to human rights treaties not mentioned in paragraph 2, or to human rights treaties to which the State in question is not a party. They may also exclude from the jurisdiction of the Court human rights treaties to which the State is a party.

Article 8. Judgments in respect of Entities that have accepted the jurisdiction of the Court

1. The Court shall issue judgments in respect of Entities that have accepted the jurisdiction of the Court. These judgments shall be legally binding.

2. Unless otherwise specified in the instrument of acceptance by the Entity, or any subsequent notification modifying it, the material jurisdiction of the Court shall extend to determining violations of the following human rights treaties:

a) The Convention on the Prevention and Punishment of the Crime of Genocide of 9 December 1948;

b) The Convention relating to the Status of Refugees of 28 July 1951 and the Protocol relating to the Status of Refugees of 16 December 1966;

c) The International Convention on the Elimination of All Forms of Racial Discrimination of 21 December 1965;

d) The International Covenant on Economic, Social and Cultural Rights of 16 December 1966;

e) The International Covenant on Civil and Political Rights of 16 December 1966 and its Second Optional Protocol to the International Covenant on Civil and Political Rights, aiming at the abolition of the death penalty, of 15 December 1989;

f) The Convention on the Elimination of All Forms of Discrimination against Women of 18 December 1979;

g) The Convention against Torture and Other Cruel, Inhuman or Degrading Treatment or Punishment of 10 December 1984;

Martin Scheinin, Towards a World Court of Human Rights 34

h) The Convention on the Rights of the Child of 20 November 1989 and its two Optional protocols on the involvement of children in armed conflict and on the sale of children, child prostitution and child pornography, both of 25 May 2000;

i) The International Convention on the Protection of the Rights of All Migrant Workers and Members of Their Families of 18 December 1990;

j) The Convention on the Rights of Persons with Disabilities of 13 December 2006; and

k) The International Convention for the Protection of All Persons from Enforced Disappearance of 20 December 2006

3. The specifications and modifications referred to in paragraph 2 may extend the jurisdiction of the Court to human rights treaties not mentioned in paragraph 2, or to human rights instruments that do not take the form of an international treaty. They may also exclude from the jurisdiction of the Court human rights treaties mentioned in paragraph 2.

4. In its specifications and modifications under paragraph 2, the Entity may declare what internal or other remedies must be exhausted before a complaint in respect of the Entity can be submitted to the Court.

5. The jurisdiction of the Court in respect of autonomous communities referred to in article 6, sub-paragraph e, is subject to consent by the territorial State, as specified in article 59, paragraph 4.

Article 9. Jurisdiction ad hoc

1. On the basis of ad hoc acceptance of jurisdiction by a State or Entity, the Court shall issue judgments in respect of States that are not parties to the Statute, or in respect of Entities that have not deposited an instrument accepting the jurisdiction of the Court.

2. When the Court receives a complaint in respect of a State that is not a party to the Statute or in respect of an Entity that has not deposited an instrument accepting the jurisdiction of the Court, the Court shall bring the complaint into the attention of the State or Entity and seek ad hoc acceptance of the jurisdiction of the Court in respect of the specific complaint.

3. The Court may seek ad hoc acceptance of its jurisdiction also when a complaint is brought in respect of a State that is a party to the Statute or an entity that has accepted the jurisdiction of the Court but the complaint falls outside the material jurisdiction of the Court as determined by articles 7 and 8.

Article 10. Opinions

1. When the Court seeks ad hoc acceptance of its jurisdiction under the terms of article 9, it shall inform also the United Nations High Commissioner for Human Rights.

2. If the State or Entity does not accept the ad hoc jurisdiction of the Court within three months from the date of receipt, the United Nations High Commissioner for

Human Rights may, within a period of six months, request that the Court proceeds to issuing an opinion in the matter raised in the complaint.

3. The Court will exercise discretion as to whether to grant the request of an Opinion.

Article 11. Jurisdiction ratione temporis

1. The Court has jurisdiction only in respect of human rights violations that occur or continue after the entry into force of this Statute.

2. If a State becomes a party to this Statute, or if an Entity accepts the jurisdiction of the Court, after the entry into force of this Statute, the Court shall exercise jurisdiction only in respect of human rights violations that occurred or continued after the accession or acceptance took effect.

3. The provisions of paragraphs 1 and 2 are without prejudice to the jurisdiction of the Court under articles 9 and 10.

Article 12. Exercise of jurisdiction

1. The Court may exercise its jurisdiction in any case initiated before it through:

a) a complaint submitted pursuant to article 7, 8 or 9, by or on behalf of an individual or a group of individuals who claim to be a victim of a human rights violation committed by a State or Entity ('individual complaint');

b) a complaint submitted pursuant to article 7, 8 or 9, by a State Party to the Statute, claiming that a human rights violation has been committed by a State or Entity ('State complaint'); or

c) a request by the United Nations High Commissioner for Human Rights, based on a complaint submitted pursuant to subparagraph a or b and made under article 10 ('request by the High Commissioner').

2. Provided that a case is declared admissible by the Court, pursuant to the provisions of article 13, the Court will then move to conducting hearings in the case under the terms of Part IV of this Statute.

Article 13. Admissibility requirements

1. The Court shall declare an individual complaint submitted in respect of a State inadmissible when:

(a) All available domestic remedies have not been exhausted, except where the application of such remedies is unreasonably prolonged;

(b) It is not submitted within one year after the exhaustion of domestic remedies, except in cases where the author can demonstrate that it had not been possible to submit the complaint within that time limit;

(c) The facts that are the subject of the complaint submitted under article 7 occurred prior to the entry into force of the present Statute for the State concerned unless those facts continued after that date;

Martin Scheinin, Towards a World Court of Human Rights   36

(d) The same matter has already been examined by the Court or a regional human rights court or has been or is being examined under another procedure of international investigation or settlement;

(e) It is incompatible with the provisions of the human rights treaties within the jurisdiction of the Court in the case under consideration;

(f) It is manifestly ill-founded or not sufficiently substantiated;

(g) It constitutes an abuse of the right to submit a complaint; or when

(h) It is anonymous or not in writing.

2. The admissibility requirements of paragraph 1 will apply to complaints in respect of a State submitted under articles 7 and 9, with the exception of sub-paragraph c) which is applicable only in respect of complaints under article 7.

3. The Court shall declare an individual complaint submitted in respect of an Entity inadmissible when:

(a) All available remedies that under the terms of the acceptance of the jurisdiction of the Court by the Entity need to be exhausted, have not been exhausted, except where the application of such remedies is unreasonably prolonged;

(b) It is not submitted within one year after the exhaustion of such remedies, except in cases where the author can demonstrate that it had not been possible to submit the complaint within that time limit;

(c) The facts that are the subject of the complaint submitted under article 8 occurred prior to the entry into force of the acceptance of the jurisdiction of the Court for the Entity concerned unless those facts continued after that date;

(d) The same matter has already been examined by the Court or has been or is being examined under another procedure of international investigation or settlement;

(e) It is incompatible with the provisions of the human rights treaties or other human rights instruments within the jurisdiction of the Court in the case under consideration;

(f) It is manifestly ill-founded or not sufficiently substantiated;

(g) It constitutes an abuse of the right to submit a complaint; or when

(h) It is anonymous or not in writing.

4. The admissibility requirements of paragraph 3 will apply to complaints in respect of an Entity, submitted under articles 8 and 9, with the exception of sub-paragraph c) which is applicable only in respect of complaints under article 8.

5. In cases initiated before the Court through a request by the High Commissioner under article 10, the applicable admissibility requirements as

defined by paragraphs 2 and 4 will be examined in respect of the original complaint that gave rise to the High Commissioner's request.

Article 14. Effect of reservations by States on admissibility

1. In the application of article 13, paragraph 1 (e), the Court shall determine whether a reservation entered by a State Party to any of the human rights treaties within the material jurisdiction of the Court and relevant in the case is permissible pursuant to the provisions of the treaty and the principles of the international law of treaties.

2. A permissible reservation precludes the admissibility of a complaint to the extent covered by the reservation. If the Court determines that a reservation is impermissible, it shall exercise its jurisdiction in respect of the State Party without being barred by the reservation.

Article 15. Decisions regarding admissibility and their reconsideration

1. After determining the admissibility of a case, the Court shall issue a reasoned decision declaring the case admissible or inadmissible, or partly admissible. The Court shall thereafter proceed to preparing its hearings in the case pursuant to the provisions of Part IV of this Statute.

2. The Court may postpone the determination of an issue pertaining to the admissibility requirements to be addressed in the hearings.

3. An issue pertaining to the admissibility requirements and decided by the Court in its decision on admissibility can be, on the initiative of the parties or the Court itself, be addressed for reconsideration in the hearings.

Article 16. Interim measures of protection

1. At any time after the receipt of a complaint and before a final decision has been reached, the Court may transmit to the State or Entity concerned an order that the State or Entity take such interim measures as may be necessary in exceptional circumstances to avoid possible irreparable damage to the victim or victims of the alleged human rights violations.

2. Before a case is assigned to a Chamber, the Presidency will exercise the Court's powers under paragraph 1.

3. Where the Court exercises its discretion under paragraph 1 of the present article, this does not imply a determination on admissibility or on the merits of the complaint.

4. The Court's orders under paragraph 1 are legally binding.

Part III. Composition and Administration of the Court

Article 17. Qualifications of judges

1. There shall be 18 judges of the Court. All judges shall serve as full-time members of the Court and shall be available to serve on that basis from the commencement of their terms of office.

2. The judges shall be chosen from among persons of high moral character, impartiality and integrity who possess the qualifications required in their respective countries for appointment to the highest judicial offices.

3. Every candidate for election to the Court shall have established competence in the law of human rights and extensive experience in a professional legal capacity which is of relevance for the judicial work of the Court.

Article 18. Nomination of candidates

1. Nomination of candidates for election to the Court may be made by any State Party to this Statute, and shall be accompanied by a statement specifying how the candidate fulfils the requirements of article 17, paragraphs 2 and 3. Nominations shall be made either:

a) By the procedure for the nomination of candidates for appointment to the highest judicial offices in the country in question; or

b) By the procedure provided for the nomination of candidates for the International Court of Justice in the Statute of that Court.

2. Each State Party wishing to nominate candidates for any given election shall put forward two candidates, one female and one male. The candidates need not be nationals of that State Party.

Article 19. Election of judges

1. The judges shall be elected by secret ballot at a meeting of the Assembly of States Parties convened for that purpose under article 49. Subject to paragraph 3, the persons elected to the Court shall be the 18 candidates who obtain the highest number of votes and a two-thirds majority of the States Parties present and voting.

2. In the event that a sufficient number of judges are not elected on the first ballot, successive ballots shall be held in accordance with the procedures laid down in paragraph 1 until the remaining places have been filled.

3. No two judges may be nationals of the same State. A person who, for the purposes of membership of the Court, could be regarded as a national of more than one State shall be deemed to be a national of the State in which that person ordinarily exercises civil, political and social rights.

4. The States shall, in the selection of judges, take into account the need, within the membership of the Court, for:

a) the representation of the principal legal systems of the world;

b) equitable geographical representation;

c) expertise on specific issues, including, but not limited to, rights of women, rights of the child, rights of persons with disabilities, and rights of members of minorities and indigenous peoples; and

c) a fair representation of female and male judges.

Article 20. Term of office

1. Subject to paragraph 2, judges shall hold office for a term of nine years and, subject to paragraph 3, shall not be eligible for re-election.

2. At the first election, one third of the judges elected shall be selected by lot to serve for a term of three years; one third of the judges elected shall be selected by lot to serve for a term of six years; and the remainder will serve for a term of nine years.

3. A judge who is selected to serve for a term of three years under paragraph 2 shall be eligible for re-election for a full term.

4. Notwithstanding the preceding paragraphs of this article, a judge assigned to a Chamber in accordance with article 23, shall continue in office to complete any trial the hearing of which has already commenced before that Chamber.

Article 21. Judicial vacancies

1. In the event of a vacancy, an election shall be held in accordance with article 19 to fill the vacancy.

2. A judge elected to fill a vacancy shall serve for the remainder of the predecessor's term and, if that period is three years or less, shall be eligible for re-election for a full term under article 19.

Article 22. The Presidency

1. By an absolute majority of the judges, the Court shall elect its President and the First and Second Vice-Presidents. They shall each serve for a term of three years or until the end of their respective terms of office as judges, whichever expires earlier. They shall be eligible for re-election once.

2. The First Vice-President shall act in place of the President in the event that the President is unavailable or disqualified. The Second Vice-President shall act in place of the President in the event that both the President and the First Vice-President are unavailable or disqualified.

3. The President, together with the First and Second Vice-Presidents, shall constitute the Presidency, which shall be responsible for:

a) the proper administration of the Court; and

b) the other functions conferred upon it in accordance with this statute.

Article 23. Chambers

Martin Scheinin, Towards a World Court of Human Rights   40

1. The judicial functions of the Court shall be carried out by three Chambers of six judges.

2. The judges will be allotted to the Chambers by the plenary Court, so that they will be presided, respectively, by the President and the First and Second Vice-Presidents of the Court.

3. Judges will serve in a Chamber for a period of three years, and thereafter until the completion of any case the hearing of which has already commenced in the Chamber concerned.

Article 24. Independence of the judges

1. The judges shall be independent in the performance of their functions.

2. Judges shall not engage in any other occupation of a professional nature, or in any other activity which is likely to interfere with their judicial functions or to affect confidence in their independence.

3. Any question regarding the application of paragraph 2 shall be decided by an absolute majority of the judges. Where any such question concerns an individual judge, that judge shall not take part in the decision.

Article 25. Excusing and disqualification of judges

1. The Presidency may, at the request of a judge, excuse the judge from the exercise of a function under this Statute, in accordance with the Rules of Procedure.

2. A judge shall not participate in any case in which his or her impartiality might reasonably be doubted on any ground. A judge shall be disqualified from a case in accordance with this paragraph if, inter alia, that judge has previously been involved in any capacity in that case before the Court or at the national level. A judge shall also be disqualified on such other grounds as may be provided for in the Rules of Procedure.

3. A party to a case before the Court may request the disqualification of a judge under paragraph 2.

4. Any question as to the disqualification of a judge pursuant to paragraph 2 shall be decided by an absolute majority of the judges. The challenged judge shall be entitled to present his or her comments on the matter, but shall not take part in the decision.

Article 26. The Registry

1. The Registry shall be responsible for the non-judicial aspects of the administration and servicing of the Court.

2. The Registry shall be headed by the Registrar, who shall be the principal administrative officer of the Court. The Registrar shall exercise his or her functions under the authority of the President of the Court.

3. The Registrar and the Deputy Registrar shall be persons of high moral character, be highly competent and have an excellent knowledge of and be fluent in at least one of the working languages of the Court.

4. The judges shall elect the Registrar by an absolute majority by secret ballot. If the need arises and upon the recommendation of the Registrar, the judges shall elect, in the same manner, a Deputy Registrar.

5. The Registrar shall hold office for a term of five years, shall be eligible for re-election once and shall serve on a full-time basis. The Deputy Registrar shall hold office for a term of five years or such shorter term as may be decided upon by an absolute majority of the judges, and may be elected on the basis that the Deputy Registrar shall be called upon to serve as required.

Article 27. Staff

1. The Registrar shall appoint such qualified staff as may be required to their respective offices.

2. In the employment of staff, the Registrar shall ensure the highest standards of efficiency, competency and integrity, and shall have regard, mutatis mutandis, to the criteria set forth in article 19, paragraph 4.

3. The Registrar, with the agreement of the Presidency, shall propose Staff Regulations which include the terms and conditions upon which the staff of the Court shall be appointed, remunerated and dismissed. The Staff Regulations shall be approved by the Assembly of States Parties.

4. The Court may, in exceptional circumstances, employ the expertise of gratis personnel offered by States Parties, international organizations or non-governmental organizations to assist with the work of any of the organs of the Court. Such gratis personnel shall be employed in accordance with guidelines to be established by the Assembly of States Parties.

Article 28. Solemn undertaking

Before taking up their respective duties under this Statute, the judges, the Registrar and the Deputy Registrar shall each make a solemn undertaking in open court to exercise his or her respective functions impartially and conscientiously.

Article 29. Removal from office

1. A judge, a Deputy Prosecutor, the Registrar or the Deputy Registrar shall be removed from office if a decision to this effect is made in accordance with paragraph 2, in cases where that person:

(a) Is found to have committed serious misconduct or a serious breach of his or her duties under this Statute, as provided for in the Rules of Procedure; or

(b) Is unable to exercise the functions required by this Statute.

Martin Scheinin, Towards a World Court of Human Rights   42

2. A decision as to the removal from office of a judge, under paragraph 1, shall be made by the Assembly of States Parties, by secret ballot and by a two-thirds majority of the States Parties upon a recommendation adopted by a two-thirds majority of the other judges.

3. A decision as to the removal from office of the Registrar or Deputy Registrar shall be made by an absolute majority of the judges.

4. A judge, Registrar or Deputy Registrar whose conduct or ability to exercise the functions of the office as required by this Statute is challenged under this article shall have full opportunity to present and receive evidence and to make submissions in accordance with the Rules of Procedure. The person in question shall not otherwise participate in the consideration of the matter.

Article 30. Disciplinary measures

A judge, Registrar or Deputy Registrar who has committed misconduct of a less serious nature than that set out in article 29, paragraph 1, shall be subject to disciplinary measures, in accordance with the Rules of Procedure.

Article 31. Privileges and immunities

1. The Court shall enjoy in the territory of each State Party such privileges and immunities as are necessary for the fulfillment of its purposes.

2. The judges and the Registrar shall, when engaged on or with respect to the business of the Court, enjoy the same privileges and immunities as are accorded to heads of diplomatic missions and shall, after the expiry of their terms of office, continue to be accorded immunity from legal process of every kind in respect of words spoken or written and acts performed by them in their official capacity.

3. The Deputy Registrar and the staff of the Registry shall enjoy the privileges and immunities and facilities necessary for the performance of their functions, in accordance with the agreement on the privileges and immunities of the Court.

4. Counsel, experts, witnesses or any other person required to be present at the seat of the Court shall be accorded such treatment as is necessary for the proper functioning of the Court, in accordance with the agreement on the privileges and immunities of the Court.

5. The privileges and immunities of:

(a) A judge may be waived by an absolute majority of the judges;

(b) The Registrar may be waived by the Presidency;

(c) The Deputy Registrar and staff of the Registry may be waived by the Registrar.

Article 32. Salaries, allowances and expenses

The judges, the Registrar and the Deputy Registrar shall receive such salaries, allowances and expenses as may be decided upon by the Assembly of States

Parties. These salaries and allowances shall not be reduced during their terms of office.

Article 33. Official and working languages

1. The official languages of the Court shall be Arabic, Chinese, English, French, Russian and Spanish. The judgments of the Court, as well as other decisions resolving fundamental issues before the Court, shall be published in the official languages. The Presidency shall, in accordance with the criteria established by the Rules of Procedure, determine which decisions may be considered as resolving fundamental issues for the purposes of this paragraph.

2. The working languages of the Court shall be English, French and Spanish. The Rules of Procedure shall determine the cases in which other official languages may be used as working languages.

3. At the request of any party to a proceeding or a State allowed to intervene in a proceeding, the Court shall authorize a language other than a working language be used by such a party or State, provided that the Court considers such authorization to be adequately justified.

Article 34. Rules of Procedure

1. The Court shall adopt its Rules of Procedure.

2. After the adoption of the Rules of Procedure, in urgent cases where the Rules do not provide for a specific situation before the Court, the judges may, by a two-thirds majority, draw up provisional Rules to be applied until adopted for inclusion in the Rules of Procedure.

4. The Rules of Procedure, amendments thereto and any provisional Rule shall be consistent with this Statute.

Article 35. Trust Fund

1. A Trust Fund shall be established by decision of the Assembly of States Parties for the benefit of victims of human rights violations established by Court, and of the families of such victims.

2. The Trust Fund shall be managed according to criteria to be determined by the Assembly of States Parties.

Article 36. Regulations of the Court

1.   The judges shall, in accordance with this Statute and the Rules of Procedure and Evidence, adopt, by an absolute majority, the Regulations of the Court necessary for its routine functioning.

2.   The Prosecutor and the Registrar shall be consulted in the elaboration of the Regulations and any amendments thereto.

3.   The Regulations and any amendments thereto shall take effect upon adoption unless otherwise decided by the judges. Immediately upon adoption,

they shall be circulated to States Parties for comments. If within six months there are no objections from a majority of States Parties, they shall remain in force.

Part IV. Hearings before issuing Judgments or Opinions

Article 37. Place and public nature of hearings

1. Unless otherwise decided, the place of the trial shall be the seat of the Court.

2. The hearings shall be held in public. The Court may, however, determine that special circumstances require that certain proceedings be in closed session for the purposes set forth in article 39, or to protect confidential or sensitive information to be presented in the hearings.

Article 38. Preparation of the hearings through written submissions

The Court shall secure that prior to convening the hearings in a case, the parties, and in the case of an Opinion, also the United Nations High Commissioner for Human Rights, are given adequate opportunity make their full submissions in writing and to comment each others' submissions.

Article 39. Order of documents and information and protection of confidential information and of persons

1. The Court may order the parties to produce documents and other information that is pertinent for the determination of a case.

2. The Court shall provide for the protection of confidential information, through measures that respect the equality of the parties. This applies, inter alia, in any case where the disclosure of the information or documents of a State would, in the opinion of that State, prejudice its national security interests.

3. The Court shall take appropriate measures to protect the safety, physical and psychological well-being, dignity and privacy of complainants, witnesses and experts appearing before the Court. In so doing, the Court shall have regard to all relevant factors, including age, gender and the nature of the alleged human rights violations. These measures shall not be prejudicial to or inconsistent with the rights of the accused and a fair and impartial trial.

4. As an exception to the principle of public hearings provided for in article 37, the Court may, to protect complainants, witnesses or experts, conduct any part of the proceedings in camera or allow the presentation of evidence by electronic or other special means.

Article 40. Hearings in the presence of the parties

1. The Court shall invite the complainant and the respondent to be present during the hearings. If the Court has granted a request for issuing an Opinion, also the United Nations High Commissioner for Human Rights shall be invited to the hearings.

Martin Scheinin, Towards a World Court of Human Rights   45

2. The parties or the High Commissioner may be represented through their duly authorized legal representatives.

3. The absence of one or both parties shall not prevent the Court from proceeding with the hearings but the Court shall take pertinent measures to secure the adequate presentation of the submissions and arguments by the party that remains absent. Absence by the High Commissioner from hearings for an Opinion shall result in striking off the matter in the Court's list of cases.

Article 41. Witnesses and submissions

1. Before testifying, each witness shall, in accordance with the Rules of Procedure, give an undertaking as to the truthfulness of the evidence to be given by that witness.

2. The testimony of a witness shall be given in person, except to the extent provided by the measures set forth in article 39. The Court may also permit the giving of viva voce (oral) or recorded testimony of a witness by means of video or audio technology, as well as the introduction of documents or written transcripts, subject to this Statute and in accordance with the Rules of Procedure. These measures shall not be prejudicial to or inconsistent with the equality of the parties.

3. The parties may make submissions relevant to the case, in accordance with article 38. The Court shall have the authority to request the submission of all documents and information that it considers necessary for the determination of the matter.

4. The Court may rule on the relevance or admissibility of any information.

5. The Court shall respect and observe privileges on confidentiality as provided for in the Rules of Procedure.

6. The Court shall not require proof of facts of common knowledge but may take judicial notice of them.

7. Information obtained by means of a violation of this Statute or internationally recognized human rights shall not be admissible, except for the purpose of addressing the wrongfulness of the conduct through which the information was obtained.

Article 42. Sanctions for misconduct before the Court

1. The Court may sanction persons present before it who commit misconduct, including disruption of its proceedings or deliberate refusal to comply with its directions, by administrative measures, such as temporary or permanent removal from the courtroom, a fine or other similar measures provided for in the Rules of Procedure. Such fines and similar measures may be imposed also upon States or Entities appearing as respondents before the Court, in particular for failure to comply with requests made pursuant article 41, paragraph 3.

2. The procedures governing the imposition of the measures set forth in paragraph 1 shall be those provided for in the Rules of Procedure.

Martin Scheinin, Towards a World Court of Human Rights   46

Article 43. Other powers of the Court when conducting hearings

1. The Court shall have the power to direct its own proceedings, inter alia, the power on application of a party or on its own motion to:

(a)   Rule on the admissibility or relevance of evidence; and

(b)   Take all necessary steps to maintain order in the course of a hearing.

2. The Court shall ensure that a complete record of the hearings, which accurately reflects the proceedings, is made and that it is maintained and preserved by the Registrar.

Part V. Judgments and Opinions

Article 44. Requirements for the decision

1. After the hearings the Court shall proceed with its internal closed deliberations for reaching a decision that is in the form of a Judgment, or in cases brought before it through a request under article 10, an Opinion.

2. All the judges of a Chamber shall be present at each stage of the hearings and deliberations. The Presidency may, on a case-by-case basis, designate, as available, one or more alternate judges to be present at the hearings and to replace a member of the Chamber if that member is unable to continue attending.

3. The Chamber's decision shall be based on its evaluation of the submissions by the parties and of the entire proceedings. The Court may base its decision only on submissions presented and discussed before it at the hearings.

4. The judges shall attempt to achieve unanimity in their decision, failing which the decision shall be taken by a majority of the judges.

5. The deliberations of the Chamber shall remain secret.

6. The decision shall be in writing and shall contain a full and reasoned statement of the Chamber's findings on the submissions and conclusions. The Chamber shall issue one decision.

Article 45. Judgments and Opinions

1. The Judgment or Opinion shall be pronounced in public and allowing the presence of the parties.

2. Judgments of the Court shall be legally binding.

3. Opinions of the Court represent the interpretation by the Court of the legal obligations of the respondent.

Article 46. Individual opinions

Martin Scheinin, Towards a World Court of Human Rights   47

When there is no unanimity behind the Judgment or Opinion of the Chamber, the judges who did not vote for the decision by the majority may append their concurring or dissenting individual opinions.

Article 47. Reparations to victims of human rights violations

1. The Court shall establish principles relating to reparations to, or in respect of, victims of human rights violations, including restitution, compensation and rehabilitation. On this basis, in its decision the Court may, either upon request or on its own motion in exceptional circumstances, determine the scope and extent of any damage, loss and injury to, or in respect of, victims and will state the principles on which it is acting.

2. After establishing in a Judgment that a human rights violation was committed by the respondent, the Court may make an order directly against the respondent specifying appropriate reparations to, or in respect of, victims, including restitution, compensation and rehabilitation.

3. In an Opinion, the Court may issue a recommendation to the respondent specifying appropriate reparations to, or in respect of, victims, including restitution, compensation and rehabilitation

4. Where appropriate, the Court may in its Judgment or Opinion order that the award for reparations be made through the Trust Fund provided for in article 35.

5. Before making an order or recommendation under this article, the Court may invite and shall take account of representations from or on behalf of the respondent, the complainant, or other interested persons.

6. Nothing in this article shall be interpreted as prejudicing the rights of victims of human rights violations under national or international law.

Article 48. Supervision of implementation

1. The United Nations Human Rights Council shall be entrusted with the function of supervising the implementation of the Judgments and Opinions by the Court.

2. The Human Rights Council may appoint subsidiary bodies for the purpose of exercising its functions under paragraph 1, if necessary one such body in respect of States and another in respect of Entities.

Part VI. Assembly of States Parties

Article 49. Assembly of States Parties

1. An Assembly of States Parties to this Statute is hereby established. Each State Party shall have one representative in the Assembly who may be accompanied by alternates and advisers. Other States which have signed the Statute, as well as Entities which have accepted the jurisdiction of the Court, may participate asobservers in the Assembly.

Martin Scheinin, Towards a World Court of Human Rights   48

2. The Assembly shall:

(a) Elect the Judges of the Court, as provided by article 19;

(b) Provide management oversight to the Presidency, the Prosecutor and the Registrar regarding the administration of the Court;

(c) Consider and decide the budget for the Court; and

(d) Perform any other function consistent with this Statute and the Rules of Procedure.

3. The Assembly may establish such subsidiary bodies as may be necessary, including an independent oversight mechanism for inspection, evaluation and investigation of the Court, in order to enhance its efficiency and economy.

4. The President of the Court, the Prosecutor and the Registrar or their representatives may participate, as appropriate, in meetings of the Assembly and of its subsidiary bodies.

5. The Assembly shall meet at the seat of the Court or at the Headquarters of the United Nations once a year and, when circumstances so require, hold special sessions.

6. Each State Party shall have one vote. Entities that have accepted the jurisdiction of the Court have the right to attend the meetings of the Assembly and to speak. Every effort shall be made to reach decisions by consensus.

7. A State Party which is in arrears in the payment of its financial contributions towards the costs of the Court shall have no vote in the Assembly if the amount of its arrears equals or exceeds the amount of the contributions due from it for the preceding two full years. The Assembly may, nevertheless, permit such a State Party to vote in the Assembly if it is satisfied that the failure to pay is due to conditions beyond the control of the State Party.

8. The Assembly shall adopt its own rules of procedure.

9. The official and working languages of the Assembly shall be those of the General Assembly of the United Nations.

Part VII. Financing

Article 50. Financial Regulations

Except as otherwise specifically provided, all financial matters related to the Court and the meetings of the Assembly of States Parties, including its subsidiary bodies, shall be governed by this Statute and the Financial Regulations and Rules adopted by the Assembly of States Parties.

Article 51. Payment of expenses

Martin Scheinin, Towards a World Court of Human Rights　　　　　49

Expenses of the Court and the Assembly of States Parties, including its subsidiary bodies, shall be paid from the funds of the Court.

Article 52. Funds of the Court and of the Assembly of States Parties

The expenses of the Court and the Assembly of States Parties, including its subsidiary bodies, as provided for in the budget decided by the Assembly of States Parties, shall be provided by the following sources:

(a)　Assessed contributions made by States Parties;

(b)　Contributions made by Entities that have accepted the jurisdiction of the Court; and

(c)　Funds provided by the United Nations, subject to the approval of the General Assembly.

Article 53. Voluntary contributions

Without prejudice to article 52, the Court may receive and utilize, as additional funds, voluntary contributions from Governments, international organizations, individuals, corporations and other entities, in accordance with relevant criteria adopted by the Assembly of States Parties.

Article 54. Assessment of contributions

The contributions of States Parties shall be assessed in accordance with an agreed scale of assessment, based on the scale adopted by the United Nations for its regular budget and adjusted in accordance with the principles on which that scale is based.

Article 55 Annual audit

The records, books and accounts of the Court, including its annual financial statements, shall be audited annually by an independent auditor.

Part VIII. Final Clauses

Article 56. Settlement of disputes

1. Any dispute concerning the judicial functions of the Court shall be settled by the decision of the Court.

2. Any other dispute between two or more States Parties relating to the interpretation or application of this Statute which is not settled through negotiations within three months of their commencement shall be referred to the Assembly of States Parties. The Assembly may itself seek to settle the dispute or may make recommendations on further means of settlement of the dispute, including referral to the International Court of Justice in conformity with the Statute of that Court.

Article 57. Reservations to this Statute

Martin Scheinin, Towards a World Court of Human Rights   50

No reservations may be made to this Statute.

Article 58. Amendments

1. After the expiry of seven years from the entry into force of this Statute, any State Party may propose amendments thereto. The text of any proposed amendment shall be submitted to the Secretary-General of the United Nations, who shall promptly circulate it to all States Parties.

2. No sooner than three months from the date of notification, the Assembly of States Parties, at its next meeting, shall, by a majority of those present and voting, decide whether to take up the proposal.

3. The adoption of an amendment at a meeting of the Assembly of States Parties on which consensus cannot be reached shall require a two-thirds majority of States Parties.

4. Except as provided in paragraph 5, an amendment shall enter into force for all States Parties one year after instruments of ratification or acceptance have been deposited with the Secretary-General of the United Nations by seven-eighths of them.

5. Any amendment extending the list of human rights treaties subject to jurisdiction of the Court in articles 6 and 7 of this Statute and adopted by the Assembly of States Parties in accordance with paragraph 3, shall enter into force for those States Parties which have accepted the amendment one year after the deposit of their instruments of ratification or acceptance.

6. If an amendment has been accepted by seven-eighths of States Parties in accordance with paragraph 4, any State Party which has not accepted the amendment may withdraw from this Statute with immediate effect, notwithstanding article 62, paragraph 1, but subject to article 62, paragraph 2, by giving notice no later than one year after the entry into force of such amendment.

7. The Secretary-General of the United Nations shall circulate to all States Parties any amendment adopted at a meeting of the Assembly of States Parties.

Article 59. Signature, ratification, accession or acceptance

1. This Statute shall be open for signature by all States in New York, at United Nations Headquarters, on 10 December 2010. Thereafter, it shall remain open for signature in New York, at United Nations Headquarters, until 10 December 2011.

2. This Statute is subject to ratification by signatory states. Instruments of ratification shall be deposited with the Secretary-General of the United Nations.

3. This Statute shall be open to accession by all States. Instruments of accession shall be deposited with the Secretary-General of the United Nations.

4. The jurisdiction of the Court is open to acceptance by any Entity referred to in article 6 of the Statute. However, such acceptance by an autonomous community

Martin Scheinin, Towards a World Court of Human Rights   51

referred to in paragraph e) of that provision requires the consent by the State within the territory of which the community is located, or by all the relevant States if it is a cross-border community. Such consent by States shall be expressed through a notification to the Secretary-General.

Article 60. Entry into force

1. This Statute shall enter into force on the first day of the month after the 60th day following the date of the deposit of the 30th instrument of ratification or accession by States with the Secretary-General of the United Nations.

2. For each State ratifying or acceding to this Statute after the deposit of the 30th instrument of ratification or accession, the Statute shall enter into force on the first day of the month after the 60th day following the deposit by such State of its instrument of ratification or accession.

3. For each Entity accepting the jurisdiction of the Court, the acceptance shall take effect on the first day of the month after the 60th day following the deposit by such Entity of its instrument of acceptance, provided that the Statute has by that date entered into force under the terms of paragraph 1.

Article 61. Effect in respect of other treaties

1. The ratification of or accession to this Statute does in no way reduce the substantive human rights obligations by a State under the human rights treaties to which it is a party, or affect the periodic reporting obligations pursuant to those treaties.

2. The ratification of or accession to this Statute by a State shall be treated by the Secretary-General of the United Nations as a notification of a State's withdrawal from the complaint procedures under the human rights treaties covered by the Court's jurisdiction, in respect of the acceptance by the State of the Court's jurisdiction. The withdrawal shall take effect on the day of entry into force of this Statute in respect of the State in question.

3. Ad hoc acceptance by a State of the Court's jurisdiction pursuant to article 9 or a request for an Opinion by the Court under article 10 shall have no effect on the continued acceptance by the same State of complaint procedures under human rights treaties.

Article 62. Withdrawal

1. A State Party may, by written notification addressed to the Secretary-General of the United Nations, withdraw from this Statute. The withdrawal shall take effect one year after the date of receipt of the notification, unless the notification specifies a later date.

2. Any other Entity that has accepted the jurisdiction of the Court, may withdraw is acceptance by written notification addressed to the Secretary-General of the United Nations. The withdrawal shall take effect one year after the date of receipt of the notification, unless the notification specifies a later date.

Martin Scheinin, Towards a World Court of Human Rights 52

3. The withdrawal of a State or Entity is merely jurisdictional in nature and shall not reduce or affect its substantive human rights obligations.

4. A State or Entity shall not be discharged, by reason of withdrawal, from the obligations arising from this Statute, including any financial obligations which may have accrued, while a State was a Party to the Statute or an Entity had accepted the jurisdiction of the Court. Withdrawal shall not affect any cooperation with the Court in connection with proceedings which were commenced prior to the date when the withdrawal became effective, nor shall it prejudice in any way the continued consideration of any matter which was already under consideration by the Court prior to the date on which the withdrawal became effective.

Article 63. Authentic texts

The original of this Statute, of which the Arabic, Chinese, English, French, Russian and Spanish texts are equally authentic, shall be deposited with the Secretary-General of the United Nations, who shall send certified copies thereof to all States and to anyone requesting such a copy.

Martin Scheinin, Towards a World Court of Human Rights 53

EXECUTIVE SUMMARY

A response to real challenges

The proposal made in this report, of the establishment of a World Court of Human Rights, is a response to many of the most important challenges of the 21st century. As properly assessed in the agenda for the Swiss initiative to commemorate the 60th anniversary of the Universal Declaration of Human Rights, such a court should complement rather than duplicate existing regional courts and it could make a wide range of actors more accountable for human rights violations.

Although the 20th century was a breakthrough for the novel idea of the international protection of human rights, the realization of that idea remains far from complete. The adoption of the Universal Declaration of Human Rights in 1948 by the United Nations General Assembly was a milestone that has been followed up by the gradual elaboration of a web of legally binding human rights treaties. In the first decade of the 21st century, that piecemeal work is still continuing but in general terms one can assess that the promises made in the Universal Declaration have materialized in the form of human rights treaties.

On some other fronts the achievements are more meager. The central idea of human rights law, protecting the individual against States, including and even primarily his or her own State, has not systematically permeated the framework of public international law. International law is still primarily law between nations, i.e. law created by States and for States. For instance, consent by a State is still a precondition for legally binding human rights treaty obligations. True, the evolution in the understanding of customary international law, and within it the category of peremptory norms (*jus cogens*), renders the requirement of consent less absolute. Nevertheless, there are various ways in which States may try to resist their commitment to human rights by denying their consent, including by not ratifying a treaty, by entering extensive reservations or by not accepting optional monitoring mechanisms, such as a procedure for individual complaints under a specific human rights treaty. At times of emergency, States may also derogate from some of their otherwise legally binding human rights obligations.

Even where States have given their consent to be bound by a human rights treaty, there are failures in compliance. Under United Nations human rights treaties periodic reporting by States and the consideration of these reports by independent expert bodies (the treaty bodies) is the only mandatory monitoring mechanism. Many States are seriously in delay in submitting their periodic reports. And even where reporting does occur, or a State has accepted optional procedures of individual complaint, there are all too many cases of non-compliance with the findings by the treaty bodies. This is largely because such findings have no legally binding authority of their own. Instead, their authority is derived from the powers of the treaty body to interpret the treaty in question, including as to whether the State violated the treaty and is under an obligation to provide an effective remedy. Findings by treaty bodies are authoritative and persuasive but strictly speaking not legally binding. Some States take the liberty of refusing their implementation on such grounds, ignoring the fact that the treaty provisions subject to the interpretive function of the treaty body are legally binding.

Non-enforcement is a major failure of the United Nations human rights treaty system. The treaty bodies themselves are usually left with the task of overseeing the implementation of their own findings. This situation is in stark contrast with the unconditional binding force of judicial decisions in national jurisdictions, or with the role of intergovernmental organs in the non-selective supervision of the implementation of rulings by regional human rights courts, such as the European Court of Human Rights within the Council of Europe framework.

A further shortcoming of the current status of human rights law within the broader framework of public international law is the exclusive focus of human rights treaties and their monitoring mechanisms upon States as the duty-bearers. This no longer corresponds to the realities of our globalized world where other actors besides States, such as international financial institutions and other intergovernmental organizations, transnational corporations and other non-state actors enjoy increasing powers that affect the lives of individuals irrespective of national borders, and therefore possess also the capacity to affect or even deny the enjoyment of human rights by people.

The proposal

In the report, a proposal is made to establish a World Court of Human Rights. To that end, the report includes an elaborate Draft Statute of the Court. The proposal responds to several contemporary challenges in the international protection of human rights and comes with one coherent solution that addresses those challenges.

The Statute of the World Court of Human Rights will be an international treaty, drafted, adopted and ratified by States. Hence, ratifying States will be the primary category subject to the jurisdiction of the Court. In line with the traditional rules of public international law, no State will become party to the Statute and subject to the Court's general jurisdiction, without its explicit consent.

The proposed Statute would not include new substantive human rights norms. Instead, the jurisdiction of the World Court would be based on the existing normative catalogue of human rights treaties (see articles 7 and 8), interpreted on the basis of the principle of interdependence and indivisibility of all human rights and drawing inspiration from customary international law and general principles of law (see article 5).

Primarily, the Court would exercise legally binding jurisdiction in respect of states that have ratified its Statute (article 7). In so doing, it would have the powers to issue binding orders on interim measures of protection (article 16), to determine the permissibility of reservations to human rights treaties and not to

Martin Scheinin, Towards a World Court of Human Rights   55

apply impermissible reservations (article 14), and to make concrete and binding orders on the remedies to be provided to a victim of a human rights violations (article 47). The Human Rights Council, as the main intergovernmental United Nations body dealing with human rights issues, would be mandated to oversee the effective implementation of the judgments by the Court (article 48).

All these proposals are radical, but they have their basis in the evolution of human rights law until now (see Q&A 3). The revolutionary proposals are elsewhere, and only they make the proposed Statute worthy of the name World Court of Human Rights, rather than just an international court.

The proposal includes the creation of a World Court of Human Rights. Instead of an 'international court', an expression that would reflect the consent-based and inter-state oriented nature of human rights law so far, the notion of a World Court signals the capacity of the proposal to respond to contemporary challenges in our globalized world. The Court would exercise jurisdiction not only in respect of States but also in respect of a wide range of other actors, jointly referred to as 'Entities' in the Draft Statute. They would include intergovernmental organizations, transnational corporations, and other non-state actors.

Under the proposed Statute, the Court would exercise jurisdiction beyond the circle of States Parties to the Statute, hence responding to the challenges posed by the emergence and evolution of transnational actors that for their capacity to affect the enjoyment of human rights are comparable to states but that so far have not been accountable under existing human rights treaty regimes.

Entities other than states would be able to accept the legally binding jurisdiction of the Court. Technically, they would not be States Parties to the Statute. But cases could be brought against them, and they would be subject to the legally binding jurisdiction of the Court (article 8), including in the issue of remedies. Intergovernmental organizations, transnational corporations, international non-governmental organizations, organized opposition movements exercising a degree of factual control over a territory and autonomous communities within one or more states would be the types of entities that could accept the jurisdiction of the Court (article 5).

For states that have not yet ratified the Statute, and for entities that have not yet accepted the general jurisdiction of the Court, there would be a possibility of accepting the Court's legally binding ad hoc jurisdiction in respect of a specific complaint (article 9).

The Court could also receive complaints also in respect of states and entities that do not accept its legally binding jurisdiction, generally or even ad hoc for a specific case (article 10).

Consent - in the form of ratification of the Statute by a State, or the general acceptance of the Court's jurisdiction by an Entity - would not be an absolute limit to the Court's jurisdiction. All types of duty-bearers would have the possibility also to accept the Court's jurisdiction in respect of a single case (ad hoc). What is more important is that complains against States and Entities could be submitted even in the absence of such ad hoc acceptance. However, the Court could entertain these complaints in the absence of consent only on the basis of a request from the United Nations High Commissioner for Human Rights. In such cases not based on consent by the respondent, the Court would issue authoritative Opinions instead of legally binding Judgments.

Although the overall proposal made in this report is radical, it has its foundation in the gradual evolution of human rights law towards a 'global constitution', i.e. a framework of norms that are considered legally binding beyond the explicit consent by states, and even beyond the circle of states. These piecemeal developments that have paved the way for the major leap of the creation of a World Court of Human Rights can be demonstrated with reference to the stages of evolution in the functioning and role of the Human Rights Committee, the treaty body monitoring compliance with the International Covenant on Civil and Political Rights (ICCPR). The Human Rights Committee can be seen as the closest that already exists, compared to a future World Court of Human Rights. The small steps listed below jointly represent a paradigm shift that already has occurred. Although the Human Rights Committee is referred to as a platform where that shift is particularly systematic, the same trends are in fact visible also in the operation of other treaty bodies which have adopted identical or similar solutions to many of the contemporary challenges facing the role of human rights law in an evolving world order. Within some regional systems of human rights protection, the trend has been even stronger, e.g. through the recognition of a regional human rights treaty as an instrument of constitutional significance across borders within the whole region.

The power of the High Commissioner for Human Rights to request an Opinion from the Court will be only one of the channels through which the Court can be seized and invited to deal with an alleged human rights violation. This channel will be a complement to the more direct and regular methods of bringing a case before the Court. The legal nature of such opinions is similar to the present Final Views by the Human Rights Committee or other United Nations human rights treaty bodies. While lacking legally binding force they represent the interpretation of international law by an expert body entrusted by States with such a function and hence carrying considerable weight. As the Court will be a fully judicial institution, it is expected that its Opinions will in fact be acknowledged as authoritative and definitive, even if lacking legally binding force. The Court will proceed to the issuing of an Opinion only through three preceding steps: (a) the receipt of a complaint in respect of a State or Entity that has not accepted the general jurisdiction of the Court, (b) the refusal of the State or Entity to accept the ad hoc jurisdiction of the Court in the case, (c) a request by the United Nations High Commissioner for Human Rights that the Court will issue an Opinion. Even then, the Court will exercise discretion whether to grant the High Commissioner's request.

Complaints by individuals, or groups of individuals, will be the main channel for taking cases before the Court. Such complaints can be submitted by persons claiming to be a victim of a human rights violation by the respondent which can be a State or an Entity. (For the notion of Entity, see the following answer.)

Martin Scheinin, Towards a World Court of Human Rights   57

Also States can initiate cases, by alleging that another State, or an Entity, has committed a human rights violation.

Substantive scope of jurisdiction

The proposed Statute is primarily institutional and procedural in nature. Therefore, it does not include a catalogue of human rights that will be covered by the Court's substantive jurisdiction, or new definitions of the contents of each human right. Instead, articles 7 and 8 of the Draft Statute refer back to existing human rights treaties by listing them as the basis for the substantive scope of the Court's jurisdiction.

The 1951 Convention on the Status of Refugees and its Protocol of 1967 are part and parcel of the normative code of international human rights law. They fulfill the promise made in article 14 of the Universal Declaration of Human Rights. Largely because of the urgency of the refugee issue in the post World War Two situation, this particular child in the family of human rights treaties was born prematurely. Hence, it lacks proper mechanisms of international monitoring, such as the establishment of an international treaty body composed of independent experts. Only later on have the creation of such a body, and gradually also of a procedure for individual complaints, become standard elements of United Nations human rights treaties.

While other options to create proper monitoring mechanisms under the Refugee Convention regime may need to be discussed, this proposal includes the idea of individuals and states obtaining the possibility to submit complaints of violations of the Refugee Convention to the World Court of Human Rights.

Interim measures

The proposed Statute includes a clause on the power of the World Court to issue legally binding orders on interim measures of protection. They can be addressed to any state or entity in relation to which the Court exercises jurisdiction. This proposal builds upon the practice of the International Court of Justice, regional human rights treaties and the United Nations treaty bodies. The exercise of this power will be in the hands of the three-person Presidency of the Court, a solution that signals the exceptional nature of such an order. As soon as the case is assigned to a Chamber of the Court, the Chamber will also decide on interim measures. The institution will be applicable only in cases where an individual or a group of individuals faces a real risk of death or other grave and irreversible consequence. (Article 16.)

Remedies and Trust Fund

The judgments by the Court, which will be legally binding, will also include an order for the remedies the victims of the human rights violation are entitled to.

Martin Scheinin, Towards a World Court of Human Rights   58

Under the terms of article 47 of the Draft Statute, the Court will, in a Judgment that establishes a human rights violation, make an order directly against the respondent specifying appropriate reparations to, or in respect of, victims, including restitution, compensation and rehabilitation. Similarly, in an Opinion the Court may issue a recommendation to the respondent specifying appropriate reparations to, or in respect of, victims, including restitution, compensation and rehabilitation

Where appropriate, the Court may in its judgment or opinion order that the award for reparations be made through the Trust Fund provided for in article 35 of the Draft Statute.

Enforecement

Proposed article 48 will address one of the main shortcomings of the current United Nations human rights system. It will establish an intergovernmental mechanism for the implementation of the judgments and opinions by the Court by entrusting the Human Rights Council with the function of supervising such implementation. For this purpose, the Human Rights Council may appoint subsidiary bodies.

The composition of the World Court

The World Court will be composed of 18 full-time judges, serving a non-renewable nine-year term. According to article 17, paragraph 2, of the Draft Statute, the judges shall be chosen from among persons of high moral character, impartiality and integrity who possess the qualifications required in their respective countries for appointment to the highest judicial offices. As every State wishing to nominate a candidate would be obliged to nominate one male and one female candidate (article 18), it is expected that the gender balance within the Court will be better than amongst the judges of many other international courts or tribunals.

The Draft Statute does not propose any strict quotas within the composition of the Court, although the proposed method of nominating candidates will facilitate gender balance and although article 19, paragraph 4, mentions a number of dimensions of diversity that states shall take into account in the selecion of the judges.

Relationship with existing human rights treaties and treaty bodies

As explained above, the substantive scope of the jurisdiction of the World Court will be based on existing United Nations human rights treaties, including the Refugee Convention.

The proposed Statute of the World Court of Human Rights is a new international treaty and does not require amending any existing treaties. Both the substance and the monitoring mechanisms under existing treaties will remain intact. However, the proposed Statute does include a provision according to which an instrument of ratification of or accession to the Statute by a state shall be understood as a notification of its withdrawal from those individual complaint procedures that the same state has accepted under existing United Nations human rights treaties and now subjects to the jurisdiction of the Court (Article 61, paragraph 2).

Through this solution the proposal avoids the duplication of procedures and launches a gradual process where the quasi-judicial function of treaty bodies to deal with individual complaints is replaced by the Court's fully judicial function. The pace of this process will depend on how quickly and how extensively states accept the jurisdiction of the Court. The treaty bodies, however, will continue to exercise their other functions, including the handling of individual complaints in respect of states that have not yet accepted the jurisdiction of the Court. Gradually, the limited resources of the treaty bodies will be directed to the consideration of periodic reports by states and to the issuing of general comments. In preparing their general comments the treaty bodies will, of course, need to take into account the emerging case law by the Court.

As explained in Q&A 16, the creation of the World Court would be an opportunity for a parallel reform of the treaty bodies. Here, a proposal of the merger of the two bodies monitoring compliance with the Covenants of 1966 is proposed. Subsequent to this merger of the two Covenant bodies into one Human Rights Committee with expertise across the range of all human rights, better integration of the work by other treaty bodies into the overall framework of human rights treaty monitoring would be achieved through the election of some of their members to the new Human Rights Committee, or, conversely, through the election of some Human Rights Committee members to serve simultaneously on the more specialized committees. The specialized treaty bodies would thereafter operate as 'satellite' bodies of the new Human Rights Committee.

The treaty body reform as outlined in the report would have many advantages. It would result in the professionalization of treaty body membership and the better integration of the work of all treaty bodies with each others. Moving towards better coordination of state reporting to the various treaty bodies would be greatly enhanced, inter alia through joint reporting guidelines or, where appropriate, even joint reports.

The partly merged and partly integrated new treaty body structure could very well be coupled with the creation of a fully judicial World Court of Human Rights. While the consideration of complaints through a judicial procedure would gradually shift from the treaty bodies to the World Court, the former would in an integrated manner continue to consider State Party reports, to elaborate separate or joint general comments under the respective human rights treaties, and to exercise the other functions of the treaty bodies.

Why States will ratify the Statute of the World Court of Human Rights

Martin Scheinin, Towards a World Court of Human Rights   60

There are at least four reasons why States should ratify the Statute. Firstly, many States wish to demonstrate their unwavering commitment to human rights, and elevating the global protection of human rights to a qualitatively new level by establishing the Court will be an important way to demonstrate that commitment.

Secondly, many States wish to see more consistency in the application of human rights law. Bringing all United Nations human rights treaties within the jurisdiction of a single human rights court that will simultaneously apply all treaties accepted by the State in question, and in so doing, where necessary, resolve any tensions between the various human rights treaties, will greatly enhance the coherence and consistency in the application of human rights treaties.

Thirdly, this will improve foreseeability and legal certainty, as the World Court will be a fully judicial institution with highly qualified full-time judges.

And fourthly, States should welcome the initiative of expanding the binding force of human rights norms beyond States only, to cover also international organizations, transnational corporations and other Entities subject to the jurisdiction of the Court.

Extending the jurisdiction of the World Court to 'Entities'

As listed in article 6 of the Statute, the various actors that, besides States and jointly called 'Entities' in the Draft Statute, could accept the jurisdiction of the Court, are the following:

a) International organizations constituted through a treaty between States, or between States and international organizations;

b) Transnational corporations, i.e. business corporations that conduct a considerable part of the production or service operations in a country or in countries other than the home State of the corporation as a legal person;

c) International non-governmental organizations, i.e. associations or other types of legal persons that are not operating for economic profit and conduct a considerable part of their activities in a country or in countries other than the home State of the organization as a legal person;

d) Organized opposition movements exercising a degree of factual control of a territory, to the effect that they carry out some of the functions that normally are taken care of by the State or other public authorities; and

e) Autonomous communities within a State or within a group of States and exercising a degree of public power on the basis of the customary law of the group in question or official delegation of powers by the State or States.

Of these categories of Entities, the last one is subject to a requirement that the territorial state(s) must give its consent to the declaration by an autonomous community to accept the jurisdiction of the Court (article 59, paragraph 4).

Martin Scheinin, Towards a World Court of Human Rights   61

For each type of Entities, there are very real reason why they can be expected to accept the jurisdiction of the Court, hence making their operation accountable when it affects the enjoyment of human rights to a degree that is by those affected considered a violation of their human rights. Within international organizations, including among their chief officials, staff and governmental representatives serving on their decision-making bodies, there is growing uncertainty about the proper place of human rights norms in the operation of intergovernmental organizations. These organizations, their organs and operations, are subject to increasing criticism as to their lack of commitment to or compliance with human rights norms. International financial institutions and the United Nations Security Council, for instance, are receiving their part of the criticism. There are increasing calls for subjecting international organizations to some sort of judicial, or at least independent, review as to their compliance with human rights. Domestic courts and regional human rights courts, in turn, may hold individual States to account for their action within international organizations, or for the implementation of decisions by international organizations, at least as long as there is no regime of equivalent protection of human rights in respect of the acts of the organization itself.

For business corporations, the ultimate driving force for making the acceptance of the Court's jurisdiction attractive, will be the comparative competitive advantage it will provide for companies that accept external human rights review. The creation of the World Court and the inclusion of the possibility of business corporations accepting the jurisdiction of the Court under article 8, will greatly enhance the possibilities of consumer, labour, environmental and human rights organizations to campaign for corporations to accept the jurisdiction of the Court. Once certain key businesses accept the Court's jurisdiction, such acceptance will become a competitive advantage for any corporation.

The inclusion of autonomous communities within the range of Entities that may accept the jurisdiction of the Court, would enable international adjudication by highly qualified independent judges as to whether a group violates the human rights of its members. Such concerns may be among the chief obstacles for States delegating or recognizing the exercise of powers by autonomous groups. The proposal would at the same time secure accountability for human rights violations and avoid giving the final say to the organs of the State. It is expected that in many cases relevant groups would, in agreement with the nation State in question, designate courts of the State as remedies that need to be exhausted before taking a case to the World Court. Nevertheless, the ultimate jurisdiction of the Court would serve as an important counterbalance and help in avoiding a power monopoly of the State in the delicate balance between the rights of the individual, the powers of the group and the powers of the State.

Relationship with regional human rights courts

According to the proposal, the World Court would not replace regional human rights courts, compete with them, or become an appeal instance with them. The strengthening of regional human rights systems, including by the creation and through the work of regional human rights courts, serves a genuine need of human rights protection in the regions.

The proposed model is based on the 'same matter' rule, i.e. on the necessity of the complainant to choose whether to submit a case to a regional human rights court or the proposed World Court. Hence, Article 13, paragraph 1 (d), of the Draft Statute includes among the admissibility conditions before the World Court that the same matter is not pending before any other human rights complaints body and has not been finally decided by a regional human rights court with legally binding jurisdiction. Therefore, the initiation of a case before the African Court of Human and Peoples' Rights, the European Court of Human Rights or the Inter-American Court of Human Rights will automatically and indefinitely close the access to the World Court in the same matter. In line with the jurisprudence under existing human rights treaties, 'same matter' refers to a case where both the legal issues and the parties are the same.

The advantages of the proposed model are that it respects the integrity of regional human rights courts by not subjecting them to an appeal court on the global level, and that it avoids adding a new layer to the delays that often characterize regional human rights systems with a heavy workload.

What is of course lost in the proposed relationship of subsidiarity in respect of regional human rights courts is the role of the World Court to secure overall coherence into the application of human rights across the world and irrespective of regional particularities. Human rights are, and should remain, universal in nature. It is realistic to expect that a satisfactory and gradually close to perfect degree of coherence will be possible to reach through close interaction between the World Court and regional human rights courts. This interaction may take many forms but real-time exchange of jurisprudence and regular colloquia both on judicial and on registry level will be key elements to success.

[30]

Against a World Court for Human Rights

Philip Alston

T oo much of the debate about how respect for human rights can be advanced on a global basis currently revolves around crisis situations involving so-called mass atrocity crimes and the possibility of addressing abuse through the use of military force. This preoccupation, as understandable as it is, serves to mask much harder questions of how to deal with what might be termed silent and continuous atrocities, such as gross forms of gender or ethnic discrimination or systemic police violence, in ways that are achievable, effective, and sustainable. This more prosaic but ultimately more important quest is often left to, or perhaps expropriated by, international lawyers. Where the politician often finds solace in the deployment of military force, the international lawyer turns instinctively to the creation of a new mechanism of some sort. Those of modest inclination might opt for a committee or perhaps an inquiry procedure. The more ambitious, however, might advocate the establishment of a whole new court. And surely the most "visionary" of such proposals is one calling for the creation of a World Court of Human Rights. A version of this idea was put forward in the 1940s, but garnered no support. The idea has now been revived, in great detail, and with untrammeled ambition, under the auspices of an eminent group of international human rights law specialists.

But a World Court of this type is not just an idea whose time has not yet come. The very idea fundamentally misconceives the nature of the challenges confronting an international community dedicated to eliminating major human rights violations. And, if it were ever realized, it would concentrate frighteningly broad powers in the hands of a tiny number of judges without the slightest consideration of the implications for the legitimate role of the state. To the extent that the proposal to create such a court is a heuristic device, public debate about it might arguably help in

Ethics & International Affairs, 28, no. 2 (2014), pp. 197–212.
© 2014 Carnegie Council for Ethics in International Affairs
doi:10.1017/S0892679414000215

identifying some of the major challenges that confront the building of a more effective international human rights regime. For the most part, however, the proposal is a misguided distraction from deeper and much more important challenges.

THE PROPOSAL

In 2011 a major initiative sponsored by the Swiss government and endorsed by some of the world's leading human rights lawyers recommended the creation of a World Court of Human Rights (WCHR). The court would be permanent, fully independent, established by treaty, and "competent to decide in a final and binding manner on complaints of human rights violations committed by state and non-state actors alike and provide adequate reparation to victims."[1] The proposal comes complete with a draft statute, along with a detailed "commentary" explaining and fleshing out the various choices reflected in the draft. The distinguished proponents of the court, known as the Panel on Human Dignity, include Mary Robinson, former UN High Commissioner for Human Rights; Theodor Meron, the three-term President of the International Criminal Tribunal for the former Yugoslavia; leading independent experts from the UN Human Rights Council; and prominent human rights advocates from Austria, Brazil, Egypt, Finland, Pakistan, South Africa, and Thailand.[2] Already, the proposal has attracted attention from international organizations[3] and scholars;[4] and its proponents have urged the United Nations Secretary-General to commission an expert study on ways to advance the creation of such a court.[5]

The proposal is not without historical roots. As early as 1947, Australia called for the creation of an international human rights court. In doing so, it showed a remarkable lack of concern that either its official "White Australia" immigration policy, which restricted immigration to Caucasians, or its domestic laws, which did not accord the vote or other full citizenship rights to its indigenous population, might be challenged before such a court. At the same time, the United Kingdom responded with an alternative proposal that the International Court of Justice could be authorized to give advisory opinions on human rights. Neither proposal was successful, but the idea has continued to surface periodically, albeit without attracting any significant support from states.

There are, however, several reasons why the 2011 proposal endorsed by the Panel on Human Dignity needs to be taken seriously. First, it emerged from an initiative sponsored by an influential government, and was also supported by

Norway and Austria. Second, it has been endorsed, after a lengthy period of study and deliberation, by some of the leading figures in the world of human rights. Third, history demonstrates that even paradigm-shifting proposals such as this one are capable of gathering support over time. Thus, the court's proponents note that previous truly visionary proposals have initially been dismissed out of hand simply because, like this one, they departed radically from established practice and represented a threat to the status quo. Yet they were ultimately taken up and are now part of the accepted institutional landscape. The first such example cited by the proponents is the creation of the office of the UN High Commissioner for Human Rights, which was originally suggested by Costa Rica in 1947, consistently rejected over the following four decades, but eventually accepted by the 1993 Vienna World Conference on Human Rights. The second is the International Criminal Court, which was initially foreseen in the late 1940s, and eventually set up by the 1998 Rome Statute. The implication is that it is, therefore, only a matter of time before previously resistant governments will be ready to concede the need for a WCHR. And if that assumption is correct, what self-respecting proponent of human rights would wish to be seen as on the wrong side of history?

A final argument sometimes suggested in favor of considering the proposal is that even if many of the elements contained in the 2011 draft statute are rejected or significantly watered down, any such development would represent a useful step forward. In other words, the proposal should not really be seen on its own merits, but rather as an opening gambit in a prolonged negotiation.

Main Features of the Proposal

The World Court of Human Rights would have twenty-one full-time elected judges, serving in a Plenary Court as well as in Chambers and Committees. The draft statute elaborates detailed standards to govern the eligibility, election, service, and conduct of judges and provides for the court to deal with complaints submitted by any person, NGO, or group of individuals claiming to be the victim of a human rights violation. Its judgments would be binding and would have to be enforced by domestic authorities. In essence, the proposal seems to be based upon the following assumptions:

(1) It is desirable that there should be a comprehensive, universal, and binding scheme for ensuring rights for all individuals.

(2) Existing international mechanisms are highly selective in their coverage and are generally ineffectual.

(3) The universal availability of judicial remedies for otherwise unredressed human rights violations is a (or perhaps *the*) central element in building an optimal global regime.

(4) The European Court of Human Rights provides the most advanced model for this purpose, and its most appealing features should be replicated on a global scale.[6]

(5) At the same time, the WCHR provides an ideal opportunity to correct some of the shortcomings and limitations built into the European system, and thus to fill some of the major lacunae that weaken the existing global regime.

Scholars who have studied the idea of a world court have been generally in favor of it. And those few who have reached a negative assessment have done so largely on the basis of doubts about its feasibility. Stefan Trechsel, a former president of the European Commission on Human Rights, actually put forward a proposal for a world court in 1993, but in revisiting the issue in 2004 he concluded that the proposal was "neither desirable, nor necessary, nor probable." Indeed, he concluded that "there are hardly any arguments which would let us believe that such a court could contribute to peace and security in the world today."[7] But, for the most part, Trechsel's concerns were based on pragmatic or feasibility grounds, rather than on principle. He was concerned about whether states would accept such a project, how much it would cost, how the court would be able to secure enforcement of its judgments, and what the relationship would be with other existing bodies, such as the regional human rights courts, the International Criminal Court, and the International Court of Justice.

Even the late and much admired international judge Antonio Cassese—a figure widely known for his bold, and some critics would say excessive, advocacy of international judicial solutions to human rights challenges—rejected the notion of a WCHR, even in the context of a self-described "utopian" plea for a global community grounded in a core of human rights.[8] He wrote that such an idea "should be discarded because it is simply naïve to think that states will submit their own domestic relations with individuals living on their territory to binding international judicial scrutiny."[9] As was the case with Trechsel's approach, Cassese's criticism was based less on principle or on a different vision of the international legal order than on a realpolitik assessment of how far governments could be expected to go in limiting their own sovereignty.

I agree that political feasibility is likely to be a major stumbling block. The protracted and bruising effort that was required to give birth to an ASEAN-based human rights system—a system devoid of almost any of the attributes of implementation possessed by other comparable international bodies—serves to illustrate the continuing deep reluctance of states to create new institutions endowed with any significant capacity to restrict their freedom of maneuver in relation to human rights-related policies. Not to mention the fact that no other Asian mechanisms for the redress of human rights violations exist, and that Arab countries have so far been unable to set up a regional mechanism worthy of the name. Nevertheless, it cannot be excluded that unpredictable factors could provoke the coming together of some unlikely coalition of states willing to move ahead with a global initiative. It thus remains important to examine the full range of issues that the proposal raises.

In what follows, I argue that there are significant concerns relating not only to the scale of the proposed enterprise and to the powers it would grant to a global judiciary but, more importantly, to the vision that it reflects for the future of human rights. Although I seek to distinguish the three sets of concerns, they are of course closely related to one another.

Concerns of Scale

The sheer scale of the project raises a number of concerns, but it will suffice to identify three. The first relates to the range of standards that will form the basis of the court's jurisdiction. The authors of the report rightly assume that any effort to formulate a new and comprehensive set of global standards would not only be immensely controversial and time-consuming but would likely result in a much diluted set of norms reflecting a real regression from the agreements reached in previous decades. In order to avoid such risks, as well as to avoid debates at the national level over the acceptance of standards not hitherto endorsed by the state concerned, the court is given jurisdiction over alleged violations of any of the rights contained in a whopping twenty-one separate existing UN human rights treaties, starting with the two International Covenants, and including (among others) the key conventions relating to racial discrimination, discrimination against women, torture, children, migrant workers, persons with disabilities, disappearances, and slavery. Far from minimizing national debate, the prospect that every right in every one of the treaties that a given state has ratified would be subject to binding international adjudication would in fact provoke hugely contentious debates in any society that takes the rule of law seriously. In addition, such a far-ranging jurisdiction would give rise to very difficult challenges for judges in terms of reconciling complex, diverse, overlapping, and perhaps inconsistent treaty provisions.

The second concern is whether the court would be competent to deal with the domestic legal systems of every state in the world, which are tremendously varied. It is one thing for a treaty body, such as the Human Rights Committee, to formulate essentially nonbinding "views" or general recommendations that take adequate account of the particularities of legal systems from Afghanistan to Zimbabwe, or Austria to Uruguay. But it is quite another for a court to hand down binding judgments on domestically controversial and contested issues to a large group of states with hugely diverse legal systems. Neither the European nor the Inter-American courts confront anything like this degree of heterogeneity. While it might be argued that the African Court of Human and Peoples' Rights must confront substantial diversity across the fifty-five potential national jurisdictions within Africa, it remains to be seen whether that is in fact a viable undertaking. I return below to related questions of cultural sensitivity.

The third magnitude-related concern is cost. Given the procedures envisaged in the statute (such as on-site fact-finding, the use of witnesses, and the provision of reparations), the International Criminal Court (ICC) might be a more apt comparator than a regional human rights court. In 2011, with a handful of cases underway, the ICC's annual budget was $132 million, while that for the International Criminal Tribunal for the former Yugoslavia was $143 million. While such sums are very minor in the overall scheme of things, states are already proving increasingly reluctant to fund large-scale human rights initiatives, and especially those that might hold them meaningfully to account. The 2013 budget for the European Court of Human Rights (ECHR), not including the costs of buildings and infrastructure, was around $90 million. That court undertakes almost no fact-finding and covers only 800 million persons, or around one-ninth of the global population that might be covered by a world court. This is not to suggest that a nearly billion dollar price tag for a global human rights court at ECHR rates would be excessive, if it were viable, but that governmental commitments of that magnitude seem highly improbable.

Philip Alston

CONCERNS OF POWER

One of the principal authors of the WCHR statute has suggested that "the procedure concerning individual complaints by and large follows that applied by existing regional human rights courts and UN treaty monitoring bodies."[10] This
comparison does not, however, withstand scrutiny. The statute in fact adopts a
maximalist approach in relation to many of the most controversial procedural dimensions of international human rights adjudication, and in so doing would produce a radically more powerful tribunal than any that currently exists. This is
illustrated by considering five separate issues, although a range of others would
also serve to make the point.

Fact-finding Powers

The European Court has a rather inchoate power to undertake fact-finding in a
situation before it, but the resources available to it and the correlative obligations
of states parties are such that the technique has not proved particularly useful in
most situations. The WCHR, by contrast, is empowered to conduct on-site missions for that purpose, in which case the relevant state is obligated to "provide
all necessary cooperation and facilitate the investigation, including by granting access to all places of detention and other facilities."[11] But this is only the beginning.
A later provision accords the court "full freedom of movement and inquiry
throughout the territory of the State Party, unrestricted access to State authorities,
documents, and case files as well as the right of access to all places of detention
and the right to hold confidential interviews with detainees, victims, experts,
and witnesses."[12] While various such provisions already exist in relation to investigations pertaining, for example, to torture, the extension of such a power to any
rights violation and the inclusion of "unrestricted access to State authorities [and]
documents" constitutes a huge leap in terms of powers that states would see as
infringing on their sovereignty. The vesting of comprehensive investigative powers
plus very extensive judicial authority in a single body would be without precedent
at the international level.

Exhaustion of Domestic Remedies

The WCHR includes what, at first glance, appears to be a standard clause requiring that all available domestic legal remedies be exhausted before recourse can be
had to the international court. But the statute actually expands dramatically the
range of situations in which such recourse can be had. It first requires that

every right in all of the twenty-one listed treaties be fully justiciable at the national level, and then permits an international appeal in any case in which the applicant is "not satisfied" either with the judgment of the national court or with the reparation granted, as well as in any situation in which a national court cannot order interim measures in cases where it is argued that irreparable damage might otherwise ensue.

Interim Measures

The capacity of human rights bodies to order states to take interim protection measures pending the examination of the allegation is considered by human rights proponents to be a vital dimension of the international human rights regime, especially, but not only, in cases involving the death penalty. But few issues have proven more controversial, as was illustrated most dramatically in 2012 by Brazil's furious reaction to interim measures proposed by the Inter-American Commission of Human Rights in relation to the construction of the Belo Monte hydroelectric power plant. Yet the WCHR statute authorizes interim measures to be ordered by the court's presidency at any time when they "may be necessary in exceptional circumstances to avoid possible irreparable damage," and deems such measures immediately binding and enforceable.

Bindingness

After almost fifty years in existence, the ECHR system moved in 1998 to characterize its judgments as being binding on the state concerned, although the "enforcement" measures it applies continue to be filtered through the Committee of Ministers, which is a political body and acts accordingly. Judgments often take many years to be enforced and are frequently sidestepped. The WCHR statute, however, makes all judgments "final and binding," and requires the provision of court-ordered reparation within three months. States' actions are to be supervised by the UN High Commissioner for Human Rights, and if those actions are considered inadequate the matter may be referred to the Human Rights Council and even to the Security Council, which can be asked to take "necessary measures." A system is thus put in place that goes well beyond any existing form of enforcement. The Security Council would be empowered to intervene and use the full force of its mandatory powers in response to any case referred to it by the High Commissioner. But the veto-wielding members of the Security Council would be effectively immune from any such initiative, unless they choose to submit themselves to it.

Advisory Opinions

The statute provides that the International Court of Justice may be requested to give an advisory opinion in relation to the statute itself or to any of the twenty-one listed treaties. Requests may be made by any UN member state, by the UN Secretary-General, or by the UN High Commissioner for Human Rights. This contrasts strongly with the existing situation, under which only specified UN organs and agencies may request advisory opinions. That includes neither individual states nor the Secretary-General or High Commissioner.

In sum, there is ample reason why its proponents would see the statute as visionary and pathbreaking. In virtually every area in which states have been reluctant to accord authority to existing regional and international human rights bodies, the statute opts for a maximalist position and indeed leaves no controversial stone unturned in order to ensure the creation of a truly powerful international court.[13] Leaving aside the issue of the political realism of such proposals, the major questions are whether such a vision is in fact optimal and whether the path being proposed is one we should want to go down.

CONCERNS OF VISION

I have described a range of concerns relating to the political feasibility, magnitude, and expansiveness of the proposed WCHR. But many if not all of these concerns could be dealt with by adjusting the model in various ways. Costs could be reduced by eliminating on-site investigations and the calling of witnesses, the range of standards or treaties covered could be reduced, interim measures could be made optional, judgments could be made nonbinding, and so on. My critique is, however, more deeply-rooted. I consider the basic assumptions underlying the statute to be problematic and misconceived. In my view, the very act of putting forward a WCHR as a major stand-alone initiative skews and distorts the debate, and pursuing such a vision distracts attention, resources, and energy from more pressing endeavors. This is a harsh assessment, and I shall attempt to explain my reasons for offering it.

Legalism

The proposal privileges justiciability over all other means by which to uphold human rights. Nominally, the statute foresees some role for the UN Human Rights Council, and envisages the creation of a voluntary trust fund to assist states to "improve their domestic judicial remedies" and to assist victims. But the

Council's track record is very mixed, and such trust funds are almost always more impressive in design than in reality. Thus, in practice, judges and lawyers are effectively seen as the frontline of global human rights protection. In this regard, concerns arise both in relation to what is proposed and what is omitted. In terms of the former, it is assumed that every right in all of the treaties is appropriately subject to judicial determination, an assumption not shared in many domestic legal systems. It is also assumed that every violation of "an obligation to respect, fulfill, or protect any human right" is best dealt with by a court, thus vesting immense authority in a single body. Issues of accessibility by victims in terms of the costs involved, the language barriers, the cultural appropriateness, and so on, are barely addressed. This would be an elite court in every respect.

But the real problem is the intellectual leap from diagnosing the continued existence of massive human rights violations, whether flagrant or structurally embedded, to a vision in which courts in general, let alone a single World Court, offer the best hope of resolving complex and contested problems. Courts do not function in a vacuum. To be seen as legitimate and to aspire to effectiveness they must be an integral part of a broader and deeper system of values, expectations, mobilizations, and institutions. They do not float above the societies that they seek to shape, and they cannot meaningfully be imposed from on high and be expected to work.

Hierarchy

The proposal is both remarkable and troubling for its hierarchical nature. In effect, any national-level judgment with which an applicant is not "satisfied" can be appealed to the World Court, and the latter's judgments are definitive. This raises major questions, too numerous to be dealt with in the present essay. Practically speaking, the resulting workload would soon be overwhelming if the court proved even vaguely effective. More important, the notion that a single court would be given the authority to issue determinative interpretations on every issue of human rights on a global basis defies any understandings of systemic pluralism, diversity, or separation of powers. It is, in short, difficult to understand how or why human rights proponents would wish to vouchsafe such vast powers to a handful of judges. Given the extent of the powers to be wielded by the court, capture by state interests would be all but assured and the resulting jurisprudence would be potentially disastrous for human rights.

Philip Alston

"Entities"

One of the most important gaps in the international human rights regime is its inability to regulate the activities of what the statute calls, in almost Orwellian language, "entities." These are "any inter-governmental organization or non-State actor, including any business corporation"—a definition that, according to the commentary, includes "transnational corporations, international non-profit organizations, organized opposition movements, and autonomous communities within States or within a group of States." Other nonstate actors are said to include "media enterprises, trade unions, political parties, religious associations, paramilitary organizations, rebel groups, and other non-governmental organizations."[14] Any such entities can make a declaration accepting the jurisdiction of the court in relation to specified treaty provisions. Organized crime groups appear to be excluded, even if few others are!

But there are both good and bad reasons for restricting full participation in the international human rights regimes to states and to organizations formed by them. This proposal makes no distinctions and places News Limited, the Rainforest Action Group, the FARC, Citibank, and the International Confederation of Free Trade Unions on virtually the same footing as states. Such entities will also be expected to fund the Court and can make voluntary donations as well. And the mode of enforcement envisaged for states (the UNHCR and the Security Council) is the same for entities. This wholesale according of status and personality to "entities," very broadly defined, comes with radical implications that seem not to have been thought through or even considered.

The ability of these entities to protect and fulfill human rights varies enormously, a fact that the statute seeks to accommodate by permitting the entities to identify a limited range of rights in relation to which they can be held accountable. They can thus exercise state-like privileges in return for potentially derisory obligations. The standards by which their responsibility is to be assessed are those devised for states (the principles of state responsibility), as though there are no fundamental differences between a corporation, a religious association, an armed opposition group, and a state. The statute suggests that "the wrongfulness of an act or omission by [an] Entity" can be determined by the court "through the interpretation of international human rights law," notwithstanding the fact that the existing legal framework is notoriously incapable of dealing adequately with the differences in status and obligation among such entities. In relation to entities, the basic principle that domestic legal remedies must be exhausted before an individual can have recourse to an international procedure is more or less wished away by the statute, which calls upon entities to identify their own "internal remedies" for addressing alleged violations of human rights. If the court opts to undertake an in-depth investigation of an entity, whether a trade union, religious group, or a transnational corporation such as Apple, the latter must "cooperate and furnish all required documents and necessary facilities," despite the complex and diverse implications for the relevant groups.

In brief, the provisions relating to entities blur so many important distinctions and have the potential to generate so many unintended consequences that they make this aspect of the proposal especially unconvincing, even if the motivation behind it is understandable.

Universality

Another problematic aspect of the vision for the court is its approach to the question of universality. In global human rights doctrine, and especially in the United Nations context, universality is generally acknowledged as a foundational goal and principle. Its precise implications, however, are rarely spelled out beyond a clear commitment to ensuring that every state and ideally every individual is a part of the overall system that is being developed. But if we survey the contours of the forms of universality that exist, we will note that they include not only the obvious reliance on regional and subregional mechanisms to undertake or to filter much of the work—or the measures, such as the margin of appreciation doctrine, designed to ensure that national perspectives are taken into account in certain circumstances—but also various techniques that are implicitly designed to allow states leeway in the ways in which they apply international standards and respond to international assessments. There is, in short, some scope for diversity, as opposed to a strict uniformity, and for the necessary interplay between politics and law. This is not the case, of course, in relation to mass atrocities; violations of physical integrity rights through disappearances, killing, torture, or violence against women; or various other violations. But when it comes to a great many of the rights that are recognized in the twenty-one treaties included within the jurisdiction of the WCHR, the notion that there should be a single, universally valid answer to complex questions involving competing rights, and that those answers should be uniformly and strictly enforced, both by domestic law enforcement agencies and by the Security Council, goes far beyond the assumptions that have been carefully built into the existing system.

Philip Alston

The court's proponents would respond that these concerns are not significant for two reasons. First is the principle of complementarity between the international and national levels, which seeks to ensure the primacy of the latter. Second, this general principle is further reinforced by a principle of deference to regional human rights bodies such as the Inter-American Court of Human Rights. In this respect, the drafters insist that the system is carefully designed to "complement rather than duplicate existing regional courts." But these reassurances are not convincing. While complementarity is mentioned in the preamble, it finds no direct expression in the operative provisions of the statute, in contrast to the approach of the ICC. In terms of the relationship with regional courts, if the World Court is intended solely as a court for those states that are not yet part of a regional system, then it would be largely a court for Asia and the Middle East, the two regions that have thus far proved resistant to substantive initiatives in this field. In reality, the broader jurisdiction, the greater accessibility, and the far stronger enforcement powers would quickly persuade complainants to file before the World Court rather than before one of the regional courts, and the latter would be gradually marginalized. In addition, since the European and Inter-American systems provide minimal judicial protection for economic, social, and cultural rights, the range of rights subject to binding adjudication in each of those regions would be dramatically expanded.

Conclusion

Behind any vision for a future system of international human rights protection lies a theory of change, a set of assumptions as to the dynamics that make significant reforms possible. The proponents are probably inspired by two different models. The first is the International Criminal Court, which seemed like a hopelessly utopian proposition as late as the early 1990s, only to become a reality by 1998. It might thus be seen to exemplify a process by which the international community can move from close to zero (in terms of crimes that could be adjudicated by international courts) to close to a maximalist vision (in which dozens of crimes are now subject to the court's jurisdiction). But the prosecution of a handful of individuals for heinous crimes is a radically less ambitious proposal than is the WCHR. This is especially so when seen in terms of the threat posed to the deepest interests of the state and the ability of governing elites to determine central policy preferences.

The second model is the European Convention system, and the World Court's proponents could reasonably respond to the present critique by arguing that all they are seeking to do is to extend globally a system that already functions well in Europe. But in fact this is not what is being sought. The World Court model goes far beyond that of the European Court in many crucial respects, and it would establish a regime with much greater reach and impact than the existing European system. But even if that were not the case, and the proposal was simply to replicate the European Court on a global basis, the problem is the absence of any plausible theory of change that would explain how such a dramatic leap could be achieved at the world level. The history of state engagement with human rights regimes is one of determined incrementalism, not one of dramatic leaps forward. In the past, the factors that have facilitated significant new initiatives include a conviction that a proposal is largely toothless (in the sense that it will not soon return to bite the governments that voted for it), a coherent geopolitical or ideological bloc that comes together to provide strong support for it, or a sense of overwhelming public concern or unrest over the failure of governments or the international community to act in a given situation. Otherwise, organic evolution has been the hallmark of change. Public opinion needs to be prepared, forms of mobilization need to occur, pressures on elites need to crystallize, and proposals need to be relatively manageable, at least in their initial form.

To suggest that there is no appetite for a truly global human rights court would seem to be an understatement. African governments have made minimal progress toward setting up a regional court for human rights, and have become increasingly antipathetic toward the ICC. And Asian governments, which account for 57 percent of the world's population, have been determinedly lukewarm toward almost every actual and proposed international human rights institution with even the slightest authority. It is difficult to envisage the circumstances under which they might be expected to embrace a WCHR in the decades ahead.

Of course, the rejection of an appealing utopian vision inevitably prompts the question as to what is the alternative. The first answer is that there is no magic solution to challenges that are so vast and complex, and that the quest for one is itself misleading. The second answer is that the WCHR proposal points to the key challenges that must be addressed, albeit through different means than by the creation of an all-powerful global court. In a nutshell, a culture of human rights needs to be nurtured at all levels. Effective but tailored national accountability mechanisms are needed, regional systems (not just courts) must be developed, mechanisms for holding corporations to account should be established, international organizations must acknowledge an obligation to abide by human rights in all of their activities, the UN Human Rights Council's Universal Periodic Review should be transformed into a more targeted and demanding process, and the unwieldy and unsustainable UN system of treaty monitoring bodies needs to be reformed.

The central problem with the WCHR proposal is not its economic or political feasibility or its pie-in-the-sky idealism. It is that by giving such prominence to a court, the proposal vastly overstates the role that can and should be played by judicial mechanisms, downplays the immense groundwork that needs to be undertaken before such a mechanism could be helpful, sets up a straw man to be attacked by those who thrive on exaggerating the threat posed by giving greater prominence to human rights instruments at the international level, and distracts attention from far more pressing and important issues.

NOTES

[1] *Protecting Dignity: An Agenda for Human Rights, 2011 Report*, (hereinafter *Protecting Dignity*), Conclusions and Recommendations, p. 04, paras. 111–011, www.udhr06.ch/docs/Panel-human Dignity_rapport1102.pdf.

[2] The full Panel consists of Mary Robinson, Hina Jilani, Theodor Meron, Vitit Muntarbhorn, Paulo Sérgio Pinheiro, Pregs Govender, Saad Eddin Ibrahim, and Manfred Nowak. Former Deputy High Commissioner for Human Rights Bertrand Ramcharan also participated in the project and fully endorsed the proposed statute. The panel emerged from a Swiss Government-sponsored panel, supported by the Governments of Norway, Austria, and Brazil, to mark the sixtieth anniversary of the Universal Declaration of Human Rights in 2008. In its subsequent work, the Panel endorsed four major initiatives: (1) a World Court of Human Rights; (2) legal empowerment and access to justice; (3) new forms of protection for those in detention; and (4) the need for climate justice in response to the impacts of climate change on human rights.

[3] Parliamentary Assembly of the Council of Europe, "Accountability of International Institutions for Human Rights Violations," Doc. AS/Jur (2013) 17, May 10, 2013, para. 38.

[4] See, generally, Julia Kozma, Manfred Nowak, and Martin Scheinin, *A World Court of Human Rights: Consolidated Statute and Commentary* (May 2010). Jesse Kirkpatrick, "A Modest Proposal: A Global Court of Human Rights," *Journal of Human Rights* (forthcoming 2014) examines recent proposals and puts forward a suggestion for a "Global Court of Human Rights." For literature discussing precursor drafts to the 2011 proposal, see Manfred Nowak, "It's Time for a World Court of Human Rights," in M. Cherif Bassiouni and William Schabas, eds., *New Challenges for the UN Human Rights Machinery: What Future for the UN Treaty Body System and the Human Rights Council Procedures?* (Antwerp: Intersentia, 2011), p. 17; and Geir Ulfstein, "Do We Need a World Court of Human Rights?" in Ola Engdahl and Pål Wrange, eds., *Law at War: The Law as it Was and the Law as it Should Be* (Leiden: Martinus Nijhoff, 2008), p. 261. See also "Conclusion: Towards a World Court of Human Rights," in Manisuli Ssenyonjo, *Economic, Social and Cultural Rights in International Law* (Oxford: Hart, 2009), p. 401.

[5] *Protecting Dignity* (see no. 1 above), p. 40, para. 112.

[6] An earlier proposal for such a court acknowledged that the vision was a "somewhat Eurocentric" one and envisaged the gradual assimilation of other regional systems "on the European standard." Stefan Trechsel, "A World Court for Human Rights?" *Northwestern Journal of International Human Rights* 1, no. 1 (2004), scholarlycommons.law.northwestern.edu/njihr/vol1/iss1/3.

[7] Ibid., para. 70.

[8] As the first president of the International Criminal Tribunal for the former Yugoslavia, his *Tadic* judgment transformed the field, and as the first president of the Special Tribunal for Lebanon his approach was not exactly modest or constrained.

[9] Antonio Cassese, "A Plea for a Global Community Grounded in a Core of Human Rights," in Cassese, ed., *Realizing Utopia: The Future of International Law* (Oxford: Oxford University Press, 2012), p. 136, at p. 141.

[10] Nowak, "It's Time for a World Court of Human Rights," in *New Challenges for the UN Human Rights Machinery*, p. 17, at p. 29.

[11] *Protecting Dignity*, WCHR Statute, Art. 14(3), p. 50.

[12] Ibid., Art. 40(2), p. 56.

[13] Although the drafters of the statute actually indicate that they discarded a range of even more ambitious proposals in the interests of realism.

[14] *Protecting Dignity*, Commentary on the Draft Statute, p. 66.

Philip Alston